FEDERAL TRANSFER TAXES

CODE AND REGULATIONS

(SELECTED INCOME TAX PROVISIONS)

2026 Edition

KEVIN M. YAMAMOTO
Professor of Law
South Texas College of Law Houston

FOUNDATION PRESS

860 Blue Gentian Road, Suite 350
Eagan, MN 55121
1-877-888-1330

Published in the United States of America

ISBN: 979-8-31770-446-9

Preface

This code book is designed for use by law students in courses in federal estate and gift taxation, wealth transfer taxation, income taxation of trusts and estates, estate planning, or similar topics. It is not designed for professional use. It is specifically tailored to be used along with the various law casebooks in the areas of Subchapter J, federal transfer taxation, and estate planning.

The core Code provisions in this book are the estate, gift, and generation-skipping transfer tax Code provisions, the special valuation rules, and Subchapter J of the income tax. Each core Code provision is followed by nearly all of the final, temporary, and proposed regulations. Users are cautioned that since many of the final regulations have not been updated for a long time, some are omitted either because they are so out of date that their inclusion would be more confusing than helpful, or they are seldom used in teaching the subject matter. Additionally, proposed regulations that are more than ten years old are generally omitted. The regulations are set forth in double-column type; proposed regulations' titles are in italics. The treasury decision (TD) dates are included for all regulations. Although § 7805(e) provides that any temporary regulation must also be issued as a proposed regulation, this book does not repeat the proposed counterpart of a temporary regulation. This book also contains other related income tax and procedure and administration Code provisions, but, with the exception of § 7520 (Valuation Tables) and § 7872 (Treatment of Loans with Below-market Interest Rates), omits most of the regulations to these provisions.

Several of the tables in Subchapter J are deleted from the book and can be accessed on the internet. The appropriate web address is given in replacement of the table. Please contact the editor if you believe any of the omitted tables should be reinstated in later editions.

The materials in this code book are current through November 23, 2025 and include the changes made by P.L. 119–21 (commonly known as "The One Big Beautiful Bill Act." Any major changes made after the above date and before the next publication date will be available at the book's web page at *westacademic.com*.

EDITOR
KEVIN M. YAMAMOTO
PROFESSOR OF LAW
SOUTH TEXAS COLLEGE OF LAW HOUSTON

Summary of Contents

Table of Contents

Subpart F. Miscellaneous

Part II. Income in Respect of Decedents

Subchapter B. Estates of Nonresidents Not Citizens

Subchapter B. Transfers

Federal Generation-Skipping Tax

Subtitle B. Estate and Gift Taxes

Chapter 13. Tax On Certain Generation-Skipping Transfers

Subchapter A. Tax Imposed

Subchapter B. Generation-Skipping Transfers

Subchapter C. Taxable Amount

Subchapter D. GST Exemption

Subchapter E. Applicable Rate; Inclusion Ratio

Subchapter F. Other Definitions and Special Rules

Chapter 79. Definitions

Chapter 80. General Rules

Subchapter A. Application of Internal Revenue Laws

Subchapter C. Provisions Affecting More than One Subtitle

Appendix. Priority of Claims; Personal Liability of Executor

FEDERAL TRANSFER TAXES

CODE AND REGULATIONS

(SELECTED INCOME TAX PROVISIONS)

2026 Edition

Income Tax

Code and Regulations
Selected and Edited

SUBTITLE A. INCOME TAXES

Chapter 1. Normal Taxes and Surtaxes

Subchapter A. Determination of Tax Liability

Part I. Tax on Individuals

§ 1. Tax Imposed

* * *

(e) Estates and Trusts. There is hereby imposed on the taxable income of—

(1) every estate, and

(2) every trust,

taxable under this subsection a tax determined in accordance with the following table:

If taxable income is:	*The tax is:*
Not over $1,500	15% of taxable income.
Over $1,500 but not over $3,500	$225, plus 28% of the excess over $1,500.
Over $3,500 but not over $5,500	$785, plus 31% of the excess over $3,500.
Over $5,500 but not over $7,500	$1,405 plus 36% of the excess over $5,500.
Over $7,500	$2,125, plus 39.6% of the excess over $7,500.

(f) Phaseout of marriage penalty in 15-percent bracket; Adjustments to Tax Tables So That Inflation Will Not Result in Tax Increases.

(1) In general. Not later than December 15 of 1993, and each subsequent calendar year, the Secretary shall prescribe tables which shall apply in lieu of the tables contained in subsection[ ] . . . (e) with respect to taxable years beginning in the succeeding calendar year.

(2) Method of prescribing tables. The table which under paragraph (1) is to apply in lieu of the table contained in subsection[ ] . . . (e) . . . shall be prescribed—

(A) except as provided in paragraph (8), by increasing the minimum and maximum dollar amounts for each rate bracket for which a tax is imposed under such table by the cost-of-living adjustment for such calendar year,

(B) by not changing the rate applicable to any rate bracket as adjusted under subparagraph (A), and

(C) by adjusting the amounts setting forth the tax to the extent necessary to reflect the adjustments in the rate brackets.

* * *

(h) Maximum capital gains rate.

(1) In general. If a taxpayer has a net capital gain for any taxable year, the tax imposed by this section for such taxable year shall not exceed the sum of—

(A) a tax computed at the rates and in the same manner as if this subsection had not been enacted on the greater of—

(i) taxable income reduced by the net capital gain; or

(ii) the lesser of—

(I) the amount of taxable income taxed at a rate below 25 percent; or

(II) taxable income reduced by the adjusted net capital gain;

(B) 0 percent of so much of the adjusted net capital gain (or, if less, taxable income) as does not exceed the excess (if any) of—

(i) the amount of taxable income which would (without regard to this paragraph) be taxed at a rate below 25 percent, over

(ii) the taxable income reduced by the adjusted net capital gain;

(C) 15 percent of the lesser of—

(i) so much of the adjusted net capital gain (or, if less, taxable income) as exceeds the amount on which a tax is determined under subparagraph (B), or

(ii) the excess of—

(I) the amount of taxable income which would (without regard to this paragraph) be taxed at a rate below 39.6 percent, over

(II) the sum of the amounts on which a tax is determined under subparagraphs (A) and (B),

(D) 20 percent of the adjusted net capital gain (or, if less, taxable income) in excess of the sum of the amounts on which tax is determined under subparagraphs (B) and (C),

(E) 25 percent of the excess (if any) of—

(i) the unrecaptured section 1250 gain (or, if less, the net capital gain (determined without regard to paragraph (11))), over

(ii) the excess (if any) of—

(I) the sum of the amount on which tax is determined under subparagraph (A) plus the net capital gain, over

(II) taxable income; and

(F) 28 percent of the amount of taxable income in excess of the sum of the amounts on which tax is determined under the preceding subparagraphs of this paragraph.

(2) Net capital gain taken into account as investment income. For purposes of this subsection, the net capital gain for any taxable year shall be reduced (but not below zero) by the amount which the taxpayer takes into account as investment income under section 163(d)(4)(B)(iii).

(3) Adjusted net capital gain. For purposes of this subsection, the term "adjusted net capital gain" means net capital gain reduced (but not below zero) by the sum of—

(A) net capital gain (determined without regard to paragraph (11)) reduced (but not below zero) by the sum of—

(i) unrecaptured section 1250 gain; and

(ii) 28-percent rate gain, plus

(B) qualified dividend income (as defined in paragraph (11)).

(4) 28-percent rate gain. For purposes of this subsection, the term "28-percent rate gain" means the excess (if any) of—

(A) the sum of—

(i) collectibles gain; and

(ii) section 1202 gain, over

(B) the sum of—

(i) collectibles loss;

(ii) the net short-term capital loss; and

(iii) the amount of long-term capital loss carried under section 1212(b)(1)(B) to the taxable year.

(5) Collectibles gain and loss. For purposes of this subsection.

(A) In general. The terms "collectibles gain" and "collectibles loss" mean gain or loss (respectively) from the sale or exchange of a collectible (as defined in section 408(m) without regard to paragraph (3) thereof) which is a capital asset held for more than 1 year but only to the extent such gain is taken into account in computing gross income and such loss is taken into account in computing taxable income.

(B) Partnerships, etc. For purposes of subparagraph (A), any gain from the sale of an interest in a partnership, S corporation, or trust which is attributable to unrealized appreciation in the value of collectibles shall be treated as gain from the sale or exchange of a collectible. Rules similar to the rules of section 751 shall apply for purposes of the preceding sentence.

(6) Unrecaptured section 1250 gain. For purposes of this subsection.

(A) In general. The term "unrecaptured section 1250 gain" means the excess (if any) of—

(i) the amount of long-term capital gain (not otherwise treated as ordinary income) which would be treated as ordinary income if section 1250(b)(1) included all depreciation and the applicable percentage under section 1250(a) were 100 percent, over

(ii) the excess (if any) of—

(I) the amount described in paragraph (4)(B); over

(II) the amount described in paragraph (4)(A).

(B) Limitation with respect to section 1231 property. The amount described in subparagraph (A)(i) from sales, exchanges, and conversions described in section 1231(a)(3)(A) for any taxable year shall not exceed the net section 1231 gain (as defined in section 1231(c)(3)) for such year.

(7) Section 1202 gain. For purposes of this subsection, the term "section 1202 gain" means the excess of

(A) the gain which would be excluded from gross income under section 1202 but for the percentage limitation in section 1202(a), over

(B) the gain excluded from gross income under section 1202.

(8) Coordination with recapture of net ordinary losses under section 1231.—If any amount is treated as ordinary income under section 1231(c), such amount shall be allocated among the separate categories of net section 1231 gain (as defined in section 1231(c)(3)) in such manner as the Secretary may by forms or regulations prescribe.

(9) Regulations. The Secretary may prescribe such regulations as are appropriate (including regulations requiring reporting) to apply this subsection in the case of sales and exchanges by pass-thru entities and of interests in such entities.

(10) Pass-thru entity defined. For purposes of this subsection, the term "pass-thru entity" means—

(A) a regulated investment company;

(B) a real estate investment trust;

(C) an S corporation;

(D) a partnership;

(E) an estate or trust;

(F) a common trust fund; and

(G) a qualified electing fund (as defined in section 1295).

(11) Dividends taxed as net capital gain.—

(A) In general.—For purposes of this subsection, the term "net capital gain" means net capital gain (determined without regard to this paragraph) increased by qualified dividend income.

(B) Qualified dividend income.—For purposes of this paragraph—

(i) In general.—The term "qualified dividend income" means dividends received during the taxable year from—

(I) domestic corporations, and

(II) qualified foreign corporations.

(ii) Certain dividends excluded.—Such term shall not include—

(I) any dividend from a corporation which for the taxable year of the corporation in which the distribution is made, or the preceding taxable year, is a corporation exempt from tax under section 501 or 521,

(II) any amount allowed as a deduction under section 591 (relating to deduction for dividends paid by mutual savings banks, etc.), and

(III) any dividend described in section 404(k).

* * *

(4) Adjustment of tables. The Secretary shall adjust the tables prescribed under subsection (f) to carry out this subsection.

* * *

(j) Modifications for taxable years beginning after 2017.

(1) In general. In the case of a taxable year beginning after December 31, 2017

(A) subsection (i) shall not apply, and

(B) this section (other than subsection (i)) shall be applied as provided in paragraphs (2) through (6).

(2) Rate tables.

* * *

(E) Estates and trusts. The following table shall be applied in lieu of the table contained in subsection (e):

If taxable income is:	The tax is:
Not over $2,550	10% of taxable income.
Over $2,550 but not over $9,150	$255, plus 24% of the excess over $2,550.
Over $9,150 but not over $12,500	$1,839, plus 35% of the excess over $9,150.
Over $12,500	$3,011.50, plus 37% of the excess over $12,500.

* * *

(5) Application of current income tax brackets to capital gains brackets.

(A) In general. Section 1(h)(1) shall be applied

(i) by substituting "below the maximum zero rate amount" for "which would (without regard to this paragraph) be taxed at a rate below 25 percent" in subparagraph (B)(i), and

(ii) by substituting "below the maximum 15-percent rate amount" for "which would (without regard to this paragraph) be taxed at a rate below 39.6 percent" in subparagraph (C)(ii)(I).

(B) Maximum amounts defined. For purposes of applying section 1(h) with the modifications described in subparagraph (A)

(i) Maximum zero rate amount. The maximum zero rate amount shall be

(I) in the case of a joint return or surviving spouse, $77,200,

(II) in the case of an individual who is a head of household (as defined in section 2(b)), $51,700,

(III) in the case of any other individual (other than an estate or trust), an amount equal to ½ of the amount in effect for the taxable year under subclause (I), and

(IV) in the case of an estate or trust, $2,600.

(ii) Maximum 15-percent rate amount. The maximum 15-percent rate amount shall be

(I) in the case of a joint return or surviving spouse, $479,000 (½ such amount in the case of a married individual filing a separate return),

(II) in the case of an individual who is the head of a household (as defined in section 2(b)), $452,400,

(III) in the case of any other individual (other than an estate or trust), $425,800, and

(IV) in the case of an estate or trust, $12,700.

* * *

Regulations

§ 1.1–1 Income tax on individuals.

* * *

(c) Who is a citizen. Every person born or naturalized in the United States and subject to its jurisdiction is a citizen. For other rules governing the acquisition of citizenship, see chapters 1 and 2 of title III of the Immigration and Nationality Act (8 U.S.C. 1401–1459). For rules governing loss of citizenship, see sections 349 to 357, inclusive, of such Act (8 U.S.C. 1481–1489), Schneider v. Rusk, (1964) 377 U.S. 163, and Rev. Rul. 70–506, C.B. 1970–2, 1. For rules pertaining to persons who are nationals but not citizens at birth, e.g., a person born in American Samoa, see section 308 of such Act (8 U.S.C. 1408). For special rules applicable to certain expatriates who have lost citizenship with a principal purpose of avoiding certain taxes, see section 877. A foreigner who has filed his declaration of intention of becoming a citizen but who has not yet been admitted to citizenship by a final order of a naturalization court is an alien.

* * *

[T.D. 6500, 25 FR 11402, Nov. 26, 1960, as amended by T.D. 7117, 36 FR 9396, May 25, 1971; T.D. 7332, 39 FR 44216, Dec. 23, 1974; T.D. 9391, 73 FR 19358, April 9, 2008]

§ 1.1(h)–1 Capital gains look-through rule for sales or exchanges of interests in a partnership, S corporation, or trust.

(a) In general. When an interest in a partnership held for more than one year is sold or exchanged, the transferor may recognize ordinary income (e.g., under section 751(a)), collectibles gain, section 1250 capital gain, and residual long-term capital gain or loss. When stock in an S corporation held for more than one year is sold or exchanged, the transferor may recognize ordinary income (e.g., under sections 304, 306, 341, 1254), collectibles gain, and residual long-term capital gain or loss. When an interest in a trust held for more than one year is sold or exchanged, a transferor who is not treated as the owner of the portion of the trust attributable to the interest sold or exchanged (sections 673 through 679) (a non-grantor transferor) may recognize collectibles gain and residual long-term capital gain or loss.

(b) Look-through capital gain. (1) *In general.* Look-through capital gain is the share of collectibles gain allocable to an interest in a partnership, S corporation, or trust, plus the share of section 1250 capital gain allocable to an interest in a partnership, determined under paragraphs (b)(2) and (3) of this section.

(2) *Collectibles gains.* (i) *Definition.* For purposes of this section, collectibles gain shall be treated as gain from the sale or exchange of a collectible (as defined in section 408(m) without regard to section 408(m)(3)) that is a capital asset held for more than 1 year.

(ii) *Share of collectibles gain allocable to an interest in a partnership, S corporation, or a trust.* When an interest in a partnership, S corporation, or trust held for more than one year is sold or exchanged in a transaction in which all realized gain is recognized, the transferor shall recognize as collectibles gain the amount of net gain (but not net loss) that would be allocated to that partner (taking into account any remedial allocation under § 1.704–3(d)), shareholder, or beneficiary (to the extent attributable to the portion of the partnership interest, S corporation stock, or trust interest transferred that was held for more than one year) if the partnership, S corporation, or trust transferred all of its collectibles for cash equal to the fair market value of the assets in a fully taxable transaction immediately before the transfer of the interest in the partnership, S corporation, or trust. If less than all of the realized gain is recognized upon the sale or exchange of an interest in a partnership, S corporation, or trust, the same methodology shall apply to determine the collectibles gain recognized by the transferor, except that the partnership, S corporation, or trust shall be treated as transferring only a proportionate amount of each of its collectibles determined as a fraction that is the amount of gain recognized in the sale or exchange over the amount of gain realized in the sale or exchange. With respect to the transfer of an interest in a trust, this paragraph (b)(2) applies only to transfers by non-grantor transferors (as defined in paragraph (a) of this section). This paragraph (b)(2) does not apply to a transaction that is treated, for Federal income tax purposes, as a redemption of an interest in a partnership, S corporation, or trust.

(c) Residual long-term capital gain or loss. The amount of residual long-term capital gain or loss recognized by a partner, shareholder of an S corporation, or beneficiary of a trust on account of the sale or exchange of an interest in a partnership, S corporation, or trust shall equal the amount of long-term capital gain or loss that the partner would recognize under section 741, that the shareholder would recognize upon the sale or exchange of stock of an S corporation, or that the beneficiary would recognize upon the sale or exchange of an interest in a trust (pre-look-through long-term capital gain or loss) minus the amount of look-through capital gain determined under paragraph (b) of this section.

(d) Special rule for tiered entities. In determining whether a partnership, S corporation, or trust has gain from collectibles, such partnership, S corporation, or trust shall be treated as owning its proportionate share of the collectibles of any partnership, S corporation, or trust in which it owns an interest either directly or indirectly through a chain of such entities. In determining whether a partnership has section 1250 capital gain, such partnership shall be treated as owning its proportionate share of the section 1250 property of any partnership in which it owns an interest, either directly or indirectly through a chain of partnerships.

(e) Notification requirements. Reporting rules similar to those that apply to the partners and the partnership under section 751(a) shall apply in the case of sales or exchanges of interests in a partnership, S corporation, or trust that cause holders of such interests to recognize collectibles gain and in the case of sales or exchanges of interests in a partnership that cause holders of such interests to recognize section 1250 capital gain. See § 1.751–1(a)(3).

* * *

[T.D. 8902, 65 FR 57096, Sept. 21, 2000]

Subchapter B. Computation of Taxable Income

Part I. Definition of Gross Income, Adjusted Gross Income, Taxable Income, Etc.

Part II. Items Specifically Included in Gross Income

Part III. Items Specifically Excluded from Gross Income

Part VI. Itemized Deductions for Individuals and Corporations

Part VII. Additional Itemized Deductions for Individuals

Part IX. Items Not Deductible

Part I. Definition of Gross Income, Adjusted Gross Income, Taxable Income, Etc.

§ 61. Gross Income Defined

(a) General Definition. Except as otherwise provided in this subtitle, gross income means all income from whatever source derived, including (but not limited to) the following items:

(1) Compensation for services, including fees, commissions, fringe benefits, and similar items;

(2) Gross income derived from business;

(3) Gains derived from dealings in property;

(4) Interest;

(5) Rents;

(6) Royalties;

(7) Dividends;

(8) Annuities;

(9) Income from life insurance and endowment contracts;

(10) Pensions;

(11) Income from discharge of indebtedness;

(12) Distributive share of partnership gross income;

(13) Income in respect of a decedent; and

(14) Income from an interest in an estate or trust.

(b) Cross references. For items specifically included in gross income, see part II (sec. 71 and following). For items specifically excluded from gross income, see part III (sec. 101 and following).

§ 63. Taxable Income Defined

(a) In general. Except as provided in subsection (b), for purposes of this subtitle, the term "taxable income" means gross income minus the deductions allowed by this chapter (other than the standard deduction).

(b) Individuals who do not itemize their deductions. In the case of an individual who does not elect to itemize his deductions for the taxable year, for purposes of this subtitle, the term "taxable income" means adjusted gross income, minus

(1) the standard deduction,

(2) the deduction for personal exemptions provided in section 151,

(3) any deduction provided in section 199A, and

(4) the deduction provided in section 170(p).

* * *

§ 67. 2-Percent Floor on Miscellaneous Itemized Deductions

(a) General rule. In the case of an individual, the miscellaneous itemized deductions for any taxable year shall be allowed only to the extent that the aggregate of such deductions exceeds 2 percent of adjusted gross income.

(b) Miscellaneous itemized deductions. For purposes of this section, the term "miscellaneous itemized deductions" means the itemized deductions other than—

(1) the deduction under section 163 (relating to interest),

(2) the deduction under section 164 (relating to taxes),

(3) the deduction under section 165(a) for casualty or theft losses described in paragraph (2) or (3) of section 165(c) or for losses described in section 165(d),

(4) the deductions under section 170 (relating to charitable, etc., contributions and gifts) and section 642(c) (relating to deduction for amounts paid or permanently set aside for a charitable purpose),

(5) the deduction under section 213 (relating to medical, dental, etc., expenses),

(6) any deduction allowable for impairment-related work expenses,

(7) the deduction under section 691(c) (relating to deduction for estate tax in case of income in respect of the decedent),

(8) any deduction allowable in connection with personal property used in a short sale,

(9) the deduction under section 1341 (relating to computation of tax where taxpayer restores substantial amount held under claim of right),

(10) the deduction under section 72(b)(3) (relating to deduction where annuity payments cease before investment recovered),

(11) the deduction under section 171 (relating to deduction for amortizable bond premium), and

(12) the deduction under section 216 (relating to deductions in connection with cooperative housing corporations).

* * *

(c) Disallowance of indirect deduction through pass-thru entity.

(1) In general. The Secretary shall prescribe regulations which prohibit the indirect deduction through pass-thru entities of amounts which are not allowable as a deduction if paid or incurred directly by an individual and which contain such reporting requirements as may be necessary to carry out the purposes of this subsection.

* * *

(3) Treatment of certain other entities. Paragraph (1) shall not apply—

(A) with respect to cooperatives and real estate investment trusts, and

(B) except as provided in regulations, with respect to estates and trusts.

* * *

(e) Determination of adjusted gross income in case of estates and trusts. For purposes of this section, the adjusted gross income of an estate or trust shall be computed in the same manner as in the case of an individual, except that—

(1) the deductions for costs which are paid or incurred in connection with the administration of the estate or trust and which would not have been incurred if the property were not held in such trust or estate, and

(2) the deductions allowable under sections 642(b), 651, and 661, shall be treated as allowable in arriving at adjusted gross income. Under regulations, appropriate adjustments shall be made in the application of part I of subchapter J of this chapter to take into account the provisions of this section.

* * *

(h) Suspension for taxable years beginning after 2017. Notwithstanding subsection (a), no miscellaneous itemized deduction shall be allowed for any taxable year beginning after December 31, 2017, and before January 1, 2026.

Regulations

§ 1.67–4 Costs paid or incurred by estates or non-grantor trusts.

(a) Deductions (1) *Section 67(e) deductions* (i) *In general.* An estate or trust (including the S portion of an electing small business trust) not described in § 1.67–2T(g)(1)(i) (a non-grantor trust) must compute its adjusted gross income in the same manner as an individual, except that the following deductions (section 67(e) deductions) are allowed in arriving at adjusted gross income:

(A) Costs that are paid or incurred in connection with the administration of the estate or trust that would not have been incurred if the property were not held in such estate or trust; and

(B) Deductions allowable under section 642(b) (relating to the personal exemption) and sections 651 and 661 (relating to distributions).

(ii) *Not disallowed under section 67(g).* Section 67(e) deductions are not itemized deductions under section 63(d) and are not miscellaneous itemized deductions under section 67(b). Therefore, section 67(e) deductions are not disallowed under section 67(g).

(2) *Deductions subject to 2-percent floor.* A cost is not a section 67(e) deduction and thus is subject to both the 2-percent floor in section 67(a) and section 67(g) to the extent that it is included in the definition of miscellaneous itemized deductions under section 67(b), is incurred by an estate or non-grantor trust (including the S portion of an electing small business trust), and commonly or customarily would be incurred by a hypothetical individual holding the same property.

(b) "Commonly" or "Customarily" Incurred (1) *In general.* In analyzing a cost to determine whether it commonly or customarily would be incurred by a hypothetical individual owning the same property, it is the type of product or service rendered to the estate or non-grantor trust in exchange for the cost, rather than the description of the cost of that product or service, that is determinative. In addition to the types of costs described as commonly or customarily incurred by individuals in paragraphs (b)(2), (3), (4), and (5) of this section, costs that are incurred commonly or customarily by individuals also include, for example, costs incurred in defense of a claim against the estate, the decedent, or the non-grantor trust that are unrelated to the existence, validity, or administration of the estate or trust.

(2) *Ownership costs.* Ownership costs are costs that are chargeable to or incurred by an owner of property simply by reason of being the owner of the property. Thus, for purposes of section 67(e), ownership costs are commonly or customarily incurred by a hypothetical individual owner of such property. Such ownership costs include, but are not limited to, partnership costs deemed to be passed through to and reportable by a partner if these costs are defined as miscellaneous itemized deductions pursuant to section 67(b), condominium fees, insurance premiums, maintenance and lawn services, and automobile registration and insurance costs. Other expenses incurred merely by reason of the ownership of property may be fully deductible under other provisions of the Code, such as sections 62(a)(4), 162, or 164(a), which would not be miscellaneous itemized deductions subject to section 67(e).

(3) *Tax preparation fees.* Costs relating to all estate and generation-skipping transfer tax returns, fiduciary income tax returns, and the decedent's final individual income tax returns are not subject to the 2-percent floor. The costs of preparing all other tax returns (for example, gift tax returns) are costs commonly and customarily incurred by individuals and thus are subject to the 2-percent floor.

(4) *Investment advisory fees.* Fees for investment advice (including any related services that would be provided to any individual investor as part of an investment advisory fee) are incurred commonly or customarily by a hypothetical individual investor and therefore are subject to the 2-percent floor. However, certain incremental costs of investment advice beyond the amount that normally would be charged to an individual investor are not subject to the 2-percent floor. For this purpose, such an incremental cost is a special, additional charge that is added solely because the investment advice is rendered to a trust or estate rather than to an individual or attributable to an unusual investment objective or the need for a specialized balancing of the interests of various parties (beyond the usual balancing of the varying interests of current beneficiaries and remaindermen) such that a reasonable comparison with individual investors would be improper. The portion of the investment advisory fees not subject to the 2-percent floor by reason of the preceding sentence is limited to the amount of those fees, if any, that exceeds the fees normally charged to an individual investor.

(5) *Appraisal fees.* Appraisal fees incurred by an estate or a non-grantor trust to determine the fair market value of assets as of the decedent's date of death (or the alternate valuation date), to determine value for purposes of making distributions, or as otherwise required to properly prepare the estate's or trust's tax returns, or a generation-skipping transfer tax return, are not incurred commonly or customarily by an individual and thus are not subject to the 2-percent floor. The cost of appraisals for other purposes (for example, insurance) is commonly or customarily incurred by individuals and is subject to the 2-percent floor.

(6) *Certain Fiduciary Expenses.* Certain other fiduciary expenses are not commonly or customarily incurred by individuals, and thus are not subject to the 2-percent floor. Such expenses include without limitation the following: Probate court fees and costs; fiduciary bond premiums; legal publication costs of notices to creditors or heirs; the cost of certified copies of the decedent's death certificate; and costs related to fiduciary accounts.

(c) Bundled fees (1) *In general.* If an estate or a non-grantor trust pays a single fee, commission, or other expense (such as a fiduciary's commission, attorney's fee, or accountant's fee) for both costs that are subject to the 2-percent floor and costs (in more than a de minimis amount) that are not, then, except to the extent provided otherwise by guidance published in the Internal Revenue Bulletin, the single fee, commission, or other expense (bundled fee) must be allocated, for purposes of computing the adjusted gross income of the estate or non-grantor trust in compliance with section 67(e), between the costs that are subject to the 2-percent floor and those that are not.

(2) *Exception.* If a bundled fee is not computed on an hourly basis, only the portion of that fee that is attributable to investment advice is subject to the 2-percent floor; the remaining portion is not subject to that floor.

(3) *Expenses Not Subject to Allocation.* Out-of-pocket expenses billed to the estate or non-grantor trust are treated as separate from the bundled fee. In

addition, payments made from the bundled fee to third parties that would have been subject to the 2-percent floor if they had been paid directly by the estate or non-grantor trust are subject to the 2-percent floor, as are any fees or expenses separately assessed by the fiduciary or other payee of the bundled fee (in addition to the usual or basic bundled fee) for services rendered to the estate or non-grantor trust that are commonly or customarily incurred by an individual.

(4) *Reasonable Method.* Any reasonable method may be used to allocate a bundled fee between those costs that are subject to the 2-percent floor and those costs that are not, including without limitation the allocation of a portion of a fiduciary commission that is a bundled fee to investment advice. Facts that may be considered in determining whether an allocation is reasonable include, but are not limited to, the percentage of the value of the corpus subject to investment advice, whether a third party advisor would have charged a comparable fee for similar advisory services, and the amount of the fiduciary's attention to the trust or estate that is devoted to investment advice as compared to dealings with beneficiaries and distribution decisions and other fiduciary functions. The reasonable method standard does not apply to determine the portion of the bundled fee attributable to payments made to third parties for expenses subject to the 2-percent floor or to any other separately assessed expense commonly or customarily incurred by an individual, because those payments and expenses are readily identifiable without any discretion on the part of the fiduciary or return preparer.

(d) Applicability date. This section applies to taxable years beginning after December 31, 2014. Paragraph (a) of this section applies to taxable years beginning after October 19, 2020. Taxpayers may choose to apply paragraph (a) of this section to taxable years beginning after December 31, 2017, and on or before October 19, 2020.

[T.D. 9664, 79 FR 26619, May 9, 2014; 79 FR 41636, July 17, 2014; T.D. 9918, 85 FR 66224, Oct. 19, 2020]

Part II. Items Specifically Included in Gross Income

§ 72. Annuities; Certain Proceeds of Endowment and Life Insurance Contracts

§ 72. Annuities; Certain Proceeds of Endowment and Life Insurance Contracts

(a) General rules for annuities.

(1) Income inclusion. Except as otherwise provided in this chapter, gross income includes any amount received as an annuity (whether for a period certain or during one or more lives) under an annuity, endowment, or life insurance contract.

(2) Partial annuitization. If any amount is received as an annuity for a period of 10 years or more or during one or more lives under any portion of an annuity, endowment, or life insurance contract—

(A) such portion shall be treated as a separate contract for purposes of this section,

(B) for purposes of applying subsections (b), (c), and (e), the investment in the contract shall be allocated pro rata between each portion of the contract from which amounts are received as an annuity and the portion of the contract from which amounts are not received as an annuity, and

(C) a separate annuity starting date under subsection (c)(4) shall be determined with respect to each portion of the contract from which amounts are received as an annuity.

(b) Exclusion ratio.

(1) In general. Gross income does not include that part of any amount received as an annuity under an annuity, endowment, or life insurance contract which bears the same ratio to such amount as the investment in the contract (as of the annuity starting date) bears to the expected return under the contract (as of such date).

(2) Exclusion limited to investment. The portion of any amount received as an annuity which is excluded from gross income under paragraph (1) shall not exceed the unrecovered investment in the contract immediately before the receipt of such amount.

(3) Deduction where annuity payments cease before entire investment recovered.

(A) In general. If—

(i) after the annuity starting date, payments as an annuity under the contract cease by reason of the death of an annuitant, and

(ii) as of the date of such cessation, there is unrecovered investment in the contract,

the amount of such unrecovered investment (in excess of any amount specified in subsection (e)(5) which was not included in gross income) shall be allowed as a deduction to the annuitant for his last taxable year.

(B) Payments to other persons. In the case of any contract which provides for payments meeting the requirements of subparagraphs (B) and (C) of subsection (c)(2), the deduction under subparagraph (A) shall be allowed to the person entitled to such payments for the taxable year in which such payments are received.

(C) Net operating loss deductions provided. For purposes of section 172, a deduction allowed under this paragraph shall be treated as if it were attributable to a trade or business of the taxpayer.

* * *

Regulations

§ 1.72–4 Exclusion ratio.

(a) General rule. (1)(i) To determine the proportionate part of the total amount received each year as an annuity which is excludable from the gross income of a recipient in the taxable year of receipt * * *, an exclusion ratio is to be determined for each contract. In general, this ratio is determined by dividing the investment in the contract as found under § 1.72–6 by the expected return under such contract as found under § 1.72–5. Where a single consideration is given for a particular contract which provides for two or more annuity elements, an exclusion ratio shall be determined for the contract as a whole by dividing the investment in such contract by the aggregate of the expected returns under all the annuity elements provided thereunder. * * *

(ii) The exclusion ratio for the particular contract is then applied to the total amount received as an annuity during the taxable year by each recipient. * * * Any excess of the total amount received as an annuity during the taxable year over the amount determined by the application of the exclusion ratio to such total amount shall be included in the gross income of the recipient for the taxable year of receipt.

(2) The principles of subparagraph (1) may be illustrated by the following example:

Example. Taxpayer A purchased an annuity contract providing for payments of $100 per month for a consideration of $12,650. Assuming that the expected return under this contract is $16,000 the exclusion ratio to be used by A is $12,650/16,000; or 79.1 percent (79.06 rounded to the nearest tenth). If 12 such monthly payments are received by A during his taxable year, the total amount he may exclude from his gross income in such year is $949.20 ($1,200 * 79.1 percent). The balance of $250.80 ($1,200 less $949.20) is the amount to be included in gross income. If A instead received only five such payments during the year, he should exclude $395.50 (500 * 79.1 percent) of the total amounts received.

* * *

[T.D. 6500, 25 FR 11402, Nov. 26, 1960, as amended by T.D. 7043, 35 FR 8477, June 2, 1970; T.D. 7352, 40 FR 16663, April 14, 1975; T.D. 8115, 51 FR 45691, Dec. 19, 1986; 52 FR 10223, March 31, 1987]

§ 1.72–5 Expected return.

(a) Expected return for but one life. (1) If a contract to which section 72 applies provides that one annuitant is to receive a fixed monthly income for life, the expected return is determined by multiplying the total of the annuity payments to be received annually by the multiple shown in Table I or V (whichever is applicable) of § 1.72–9 under the age (as of the annuity starting date) and, if applicable, sex of the measuring life (usually the annuitant's). Thus, where a male purchases a contract before July 1, 1986, providing for an immediate annuity of $100 per month for his life and, as of the annuity starting date (in this case the date of purchase), the annuitant's age at his nearest birthday is 66, the expected return is computed as follows:

Monthly payment of $100 * 12 months equals annual payment of	$1,200
Multiple shown in Table I, male, age 66	14.4
Expected return (1,200 * 14.4)	17,280

If, however, the taxpayer had purchased the contract after June 30, 1986, the expected return would be $23,040, determined by multiplying 19.2 (multiple shown in Table V, age 66) by $1,200.

* * *

[T.D. 6500, 25 FR 11402, Nov. 26, 1960; T.D. 8115, 51 FR 45694, Dec. 19, 1986]

§ 1.72–6 Investment in the contract.

(a) General rule. (1) For the purpose of computing the "investment in the contract", it is first necessary to determine the "aggregate amount of premiums or other consideration paid" for such contract. See section 72(c)(1). This determination is made as of the later of the annuity starting date of the contract or the date on which an amount is first received thereunder as an annuity. The amount so found is then reduced by the sum of the following amounts in order to find the investment in the contract:

(i) The total amount of any return of premiums or dividends received (including unrepaid loans or dividends applied against the principal or interest on such loans) on or before the date on which the foregoing determination is made, and

(ii) The total of any other amounts received with respect to the contract on or before such date which were excludable from the gross income of the recipient under the income tax law applicable at the time of receipt. * * *

* * *

[T.D. 6500, 25 FR 11402, Nov. 26, 1960, as amended by T.D. 6676, 28 FR 10134, Sept. 17, 1963; T.D. 7311, 39 FR 11880, April 1, 1974; T.D. 8115, 51 FR 45700, Dec. 19, 1986; 52 FR 10223, March 31, 1987]

Part III. Items Specifically Excluded from Gross Income

§ 101. Certain Death Benefits

(a) Proceeds of life insurance contracts payable by reason of death.

(1) General rule. Except as otherwise provided in paragraphs (2) and (3), subsection (d), subsection (f), and subsection (j), gross income does not include amounts received (whether in a single sum or otherwise) under a life insurance contract, if such amounts are paid by reason of the death of the insured.

(2) Transfer for valuable consideration. In the case of a transfer for a valuable consideration, by assignment or otherwise, of a life insurance contract or any interest therein, the amount excluded from gross income by paragraph (1) shall not exceed an amount equal to the sum of the actual value of such consideration and the premiums and other amounts subsequently paid by the transferee. The preceding sentence shall not apply in the case of such a transfer

(A) if such contract or interest therein has a basis for determining gain or loss in the hands of a transferee determined in whole or in part by reference to such basis of such contract or interest therein in the hands of the transferor, or

(B) if such transfer is to the insured, to a partner of the insured, to a partnership in which the insured is a partner, or to a corporation in which the insured is a shareholder or officer.

The term "other amounts" in the first sentence of this paragraph includes interest paid or accrued by the transferee on indebtedness with respect to such contract or any interest therein if such interest paid or accrued is not allowable as a deduction by reason of section 264(a)(4).

(3) Exception to valuable consideration rules for commercial transfers.

(A) In general. The second sentence of paragraph (2) shall not apply in the case of a transfer of a life insurance contract, or any interest therein, which is a reportable policy sale.

(B) Reportable policy sale. For purposes of this paragraph, the term "reportable policy sale" means the acquisition of an interest in a life insurance contract, directly or indirectly, if the acquirer has no substantial family, business, or financial relationship with the insured apart from the acquirer's interest in such life insurance contract. For purposes of the preceding sentence, the term "indirectly" applies to the acquisition of an interest in a partnership, trust, or other entity that holds an interest in the life insurance contract.

(b) [Repealed.]

(c) Interest. If any amount excluded from gross income by subsection (a) is held under an agreement to pay interest thereon, the interest payments shall be included in gross income.

(d) Payment of life insurance proceeds at a date later than death.

(1) General rule. The amounts held by an insurer with respect to any beneficiary shall be prorated (in accordance with such regulations as may be prescribed by the Secretary) over the period or periods with respect to which such payments are to be made. There shall be excluded from the gross income of such beneficiary in the taxable year received any amount determined by such proration. Gross income includes, to the extent not excluded by the preceding sentence, amounts received under agreements to which this subsection applies.

(2) Amount held by an insurer. An amount held by an insurer with respect to any beneficiary shall mean an amount to which subsection (a) applies which is—

(A) held by any insurer under an agreement provided for in the life insurance contract, whether as an option or otherwise, to pay such amount on a date or dates later than the death of the insured, and

(B) equal to the value of such agreement to such beneficiary

(i) as of the date of death of the insured (as if any option exercised under the life insurance contract were exercised at such time), and

(ii) as discounted on the basis of the interest rate used by the insurer in calculating payments under the agreement and mortality tables prescribed by the Secretary.

(3) Application of subsection. This subsection shall not apply to any amount to which subsection (c) is applicable.

* * *

(g) Treatment of certain accelerated death benefits.

(1) In general. For purposes of this section, the following amounts shall be treated as an amount paid by reason of the death of an insured:

(A) Any amount received under a life insurance contract on the life of an insured who is a terminally ill individual.

(B) Any amount received under a life insurance contract on the life of an insured who is a chronically ill individual.

(2) Treatment of viatical settlements.

(A) In general. If any portion of the death benefit under a life insurance contract on the life of an insured described in paragraph (1) is sold or assigned to a viatical settlement provider, the amount paid for the sale or assignment of such portion shall be treated as an amount paid under the life insurance contract by reason of the death of such insured.

(B) Viatical settlement provider.

(i) In general. The term "viatical settlement provider" means any person regularly engaged in the trade or business of purchasing, or taking assignments of, life insurance contracts on the lives of insureds described in paragraph (1) if—

(I) such person is licensed for such purposes (with respect to insureds described in the same subparagraph of paragraph (1) as the insured) in the State in which the insured resides, or

(II) in the case of an insured who resides in a State not requiring the licensing of such persons for such purposes with respect to such insured, such person meets the requirements of clause (ii) or (iii), whichever applies to such insured.

(ii) Terminally ill insureds. A person meets the requirements of this clause with respect to an insured who is a terminally ill individual if such person—

(I) meets the requirements of sections 8 and 9 of the Viatical Settlements Model Act of the National Association of Insurance Commissioners, and

(II) meets the requirements of the Model Regulations of the National Association of Insurance Commissioners (relating to standards for evaluation of reasonable payments) in determining amounts paid by such person in connection with such purchases or assignments.

(iii) Chronically ill insureds. A person meets the requirements of this clause with respect to an insured who is a chronically ill individual if such person—

(I) meets requirements similar to the requirements referred to in clause (ii)(I), and

(II) meets the standards (if any) of the National Association of Insurance Commissioners for evaluating the reasonableness of amounts paid by such person in connection with such purchases or assignments with respect to chronically ill individuals.

(3) Special rules for chronically ill insureds. In the case of an insured who is a chronically ill individual—

(A) In general. Paragraphs (1) and (2) shall not apply to any payment received for any period unless—

(i) such payment is for costs incurred by the payee (not compensated for by insurance or otherwise) for qualified long-term care services provided for the insured for such period, and

(ii) the terms of the contract giving rise to such payment satisfy—

(I) the requirements of section 7702B(b)(1)(B), and

(II) the requirements (if any) applicable under subparagraph (B). For purposes of the preceding sentence, the rule of section 7702B(b)(2)(B) shall apply.

(B) Other requirements. The requirements applicable under this subparagraph are—

(i) those requirements of section 7702B(g) and section 4980C which the Secretary specifies as applying to such a purchase, assignment, or other arrangement,

(ii) standards adopted by the National Association of Insurance Commissioners which specifically apply to chronically ill individuals (and, if such standards are adopted, the analogous requirements specified under clause (i) shall cease to apply), and

(iii) standards adopted by the State in which the policyholder resides (and if such standards are adopted, the analogous requirements specified under clause (i) and (subject to section 4980C(f)) standards under clause (ii), shall cease to apply).

(C) Per diem payments. A payment shall not fail to be described in subparagraph (A) by reason of being made on a per diem or other periodic basis without regard to the expenses incurred during the period to which the payment relates.

(D) Limitation on exclusion for periodic payments. For limitation on amount of periodic payments which are treated as described in paragraph (1), see section 7702B(d).

(4) Definitions. For purposes of this subsection—

(A) Terminally ill individual. The term "terminally ill individual" means an individual who has been certified by a physician as having an illness or physical condition which can reasonably be expected to result in death in 24 months or less after the date of the certification.

(B) Chronically ill individual. The term "chronically ill individual" has the meaning given such term by section 7702B(c)(2); except that such term shall not include a terminally ill individual.

(C) Qualified long-term care services. The term "qualified long-term care services" has the meaning given such term by section 7702B(c).

(D) Physician. The term "physician" has the meaning given to such term by section 1861(r)(1) of the Social Security Act (42 U.S.C. 1395x(r)(1)).

(5) Exception for business-related policies. This subsection shall not apply in the case of any amount paid to any taxpayer other than the insured if such taxpayer has an insurable interest with respect to the life of the insured by reason of the insured being a director, officer, or employee of the taxpayer or by reason of the insured being financially interested in any trade or business carried on by the taxpayer.

* * *

Regulation

§ 1.101–1 Exclusion from gross income of proceeds of life insurance contracts payable by reason of death.

(a)(1) *In general.* Section 101(a)(1) states the general rule that the proceeds of life insurance policies, if paid by reason of the death of the insured, are excluded from the gross income of the recipient. Death benefit payments having the characteristics of life insurance proceeds payable by reason of death under contracts, such as workmen's compensation insurance contracts, endowment contracts, or accident and health insurance contracts, issued on or before December 31, 1984, are covered by this provision. The exclusion from gross income allowed by section 101(a) applies whether payment is made to the estate of the insured or to any beneficiary (individual, corporation, or partnership) and whether it is made directly or in trust. The extent to which this exclusion applies in cases where life insurance policies have been transferred for a valuable consideration is stated in section 101(a)(2) and in paragraph (b) of this section. In cases where the proceeds of a life insurance policy, payable by reason of the death of the insured, are paid other than in a single sum at the time of such death, the amounts to be excluded from gross income may be affected by the provisions of section 101(c) (relating to amounts held under agreements to pay interest) or section 101(d) (relating to amounts payable at a date later than death).

See §§ 1.101–3 and 1.101–4. However, neither section 101(c) nor section 101(d) applies to a single sum payment which does not exceed the amount payable at the time of death even though such amount is actually paid at a date later than death. If the life insurance contract is an employer-owned life insurance contract within the definition of section 101(j)(3), the amount to be excluded from gross income may be affected by the provisions of section 101(j).

(2) *Cross references.* For rules governing the taxability of insurance proceeds constituting benefits payable on the death of an employee

(i) Under pension, profit-sharing, or stock bonus plans described in section 401(a) and exempt from tax under section 501(a), or under annuity plans described in section 403(a), see section 72(m)(3) and paragraph (c) of § 1.72–16;

(ii) Under annuity contracts to which § 1.403(b)–3 applies, see § 1.403(b)–7; or

(iii) Under eligible State deferred compensation plans described in section 457(b), see paragraph (c) of § 1.457–1.

For the definition of a life insurance company, see section 801.

(b) Transfers of life insurance policies. (1) *Transfer of an interest in a life insurance contract for valuable consideration* (i) *In general.* In the case of a transfer of an interest in a life insurance contract for valuable consideration, including a reportable policy sale for valuable consideration, the amount of the proceeds attributable to the interest that is excludable from gross income under section 101(a)(1) is limited under section 101(a)(2) to the sum of the actual value of the consideration for the transfer paid by the transferee and the premiums and other amounts subsequently paid by the transferee with respect to the interest. For exceptions to this general rule for certain transfers for valuable consideration that are not reportable policy sales, see paragraph (b)(1)(ii) of this section. The application of section 101(d), (f) or (j), which is not addressed in paragraph (b) of this section, may further limit the amount of the proceeds excludable from gross income.

(ii) *Exceptions* (A) *Exception for carryover basis transfers.* The limitation described in paragraph (b)(1)(i) of this section does not apply to the transfer of an interest in a life insurance contract for valuable consideration if each of the following requirements are satisfied. First, the transfer is not a reportable policy sale. Second, the basis of the interest, for the purpose of determining gain or loss with respect to the transferee, is determinable in whole or in part by reference to the basis of the interest in the hands of the transferor (see section 101(a)(2)(A)). Third, paragraph (b)(1)(ii)(B) of this section does not apply. In the case of a transfer described in this paragraph (b)(1)(ii)(A), the amount of the proceeds attributable to the interest that is excludable from gross income under section 101(a)(1) is limited to the sum of the amount that would have been excludable by the transferor if the transfer had not occurred and the premiums and other amounts subsequently paid by the transferee with respect to the interest. The preceding sentence applies without regard to whether the interest previously has been transferred and the nature of any prior transfer of the interest.

(B) *Exception for transfers to certain persons* (1) *In general.* The limitation described in paragraph (b)(1)(i) of this section does not apply to the transfer of an interest in a life insurance contract for valuable consideration if both of the following requirements are satisfied. First, the transfer is not a reportable policy sale and the interest was not previously transferred for valuable consideration in a reportable policy sale. Second, the interest is transferred to the insured, a partner of the insured, a partnership in which the insured is a partner, or a corporation in which the insured is a shareholder or officer (see section 101(a)(2)(B)).

(2) *Transfers to certain persons subsequent to a reportable policy sale.* Except as provided in paragraph (b)(1)(ii)(B)(3) of this section, if a transfer of an interest in a life insurance contract would be described in paragraph (b)(1)(ii)(B)(1) of this section, but for the fact that the interest previously was transferred for valuable consideration in a reportable policy sale (whether in the immediately preceding transfer or an earlier transfer), then the amount of the proceeds attributable to the interest that is excludable from gross income under section 101(a)(1) is limited to the sum of

(i) The higher of the amount that would have been excludable by the transferor if the transfer had not occurred or the actual value of the consideration for the transfer paid by the transferee; and

(ii) The premiums and other amounts subsequently paid by the transferee with respect to the interest.

(3) *Transfers to the insured subsequent to a reportable policy sale* (i) Except as provided in paragraph (b)(1)(ii)(B)(3)(ii) of this section, to the extent that an interest (or portion of an interest) in a life insurance contract that was transferred for valuable consideration in a reportable policy sale subsequently is transferred to the insured for valuable consideration, the limitations described in paragraph (b)(1)(i) of this section and paragraph (b)(1)(ii)(B)(2) of this section do not apply. To the extent that fair market value is not paid by the insured for the transferred interest, the transfer of the portion of the interest with a value in excess of the consideration paid will be treated as a gift under the bargain sale rule in paragraph (b)(2)(iii) of this section.

(ii) This paragraph (b)(1)(ii)(B)(3)(ii) applies with respect to an interest described in paragraph (b)(1)(ii)(B)(3)(i) of this section (or portion of such an interest) that subsequently is transferred by the insured to any other person. If all subsequent transfers of the interest (or portion of the interest) are gratuitous transfers that are not reportable policy sales, the amount of the proceeds excluded from gross income is determined under paragraph (b)(2)(i) of this section, taking into account the application of paragraph (b)(1)(ii)(B)(3)(i) of this section to the insured's acquisition of the interest. If any subsequent transfer of the interest (or portion of the interest) is for valuable consideration or is a reportable policy sale, the amount of the policy proceeds excludable from gross income is determined in accordance with paragraph (b) of this section; if the amount that would have been excludable from gross income by the insured following the transaction described in paragraph (b)(1)(ii)(B)(3)(i) of this section if no subsequent transfer had occurred is relevant, that amount is determined under paragraph (b)(1)(ii)(B)(2) of this section. Paragraph (g)(8) (Example 8) of this section and paragraph (g)(9) (Example 9) of this section illustrate the application of this paragraph (b)(1)(ii)(B)(3)(ii).

(2) *Other transfers* (i) *Gratuitous transfer of an interest in a life insurance contract.* To the extent that a transfer of an interest in a life insurance contract is gratuitous, including a reportable policy sale that is not for valuable consideration, the amount of the proceeds attributable to the interest that is excludable from gross income under section 101(a)(1) is limited to the sum of the amount of the proceeds attributable to the gratuitously transferred interest that would have been excludable by the transferor if the transfer had not occurred and the premiums and other amounts subsequently paid by the transferee with respect to the interest. However, if an interest in a life insurance contract is transferred gratuitously to the insured, and that interest has not previously been transferred for value in a reportable policy sale, the entire amount of the proceeds attributable to the interest transferred to the insured is excludable from gross income.

(ii) *Partial transfers.* When only part of an interest in a life insurance contract is transferred, the transferor's exclusion is ratably apportioned between or among the several parts. If multiple parts of an interest are transferred, the transfer of each part is treated as a separate transaction, with each transaction subject to the rule under paragraph (b) of this section that is applicable to the type of transfer involved.

(iii) *Bargain sales.* When the transfer of an interest in a life insurance contract is in part a transfer for valuable consideration and in part a gratuitous transfer, the transfer of each part is treated as a separate transaction for purposes of determining the amount of the proceeds attributable to the interest that is excludable from gross income under section 101(a)(1). Each separate transaction is subject to the rule under paragraph (b) of this section that is applicable to the type of transfer involved.

(3) *Determination of amounts paid by the transferee.* For purposes of paragraphs (b)(1) and (2) of this section, in determining the amounts, if any, of consideration paid by the transferee for the transfer of an interest in a life insurance contract and premiums and other amounts subsequently paid by the transferee with respect to that interest, the amounts paid by the transferee are reduced, but not below zero, by amounts received by the transferee under the life insurance contract that are not received as an annuity, to the extent excludable from gross income under section 72(e).

(c) Reportable policy sale (1) *In general.* Except as provided in paragraph (c)(2) of this section, a reportable policy sale for purposes of this section and section 6050Y is any direct or indirect acquisition of an interest in a life insurance contract if the acquirer has, at the time of the acquisition, no substantial family, business, or financial relationship with the insured apart from the acquirer's interest in the life insurance contract.

(2) *Exceptions.* None of the following transactions is a reportable policy sale:

(i) A transfer of an interest in a life insurance contract between entities with the same beneficial owners, if the ownership interest of each beneficial owner in the transferor entity does not vary by more than a 20 percent ownership interest from that beneficial owner's ownership interest in the transferee entity. In a series of transfers, the prior sentence is applied by comparing the beneficial owners' ownership interest in the first transferor entity and the last transferee entity. For purposes of this paragraph (c)(2)(i), each beneficial owner of a trust is deemed to have an ownership interest determined by the broadest possible exercise of a trustee's discretion in that beneficial owner's favor. Paragraph (g)(13) (Example 13) of this section provides an illustration of the application of this paragraph (c)(2)(i).

(ii) A transfer between corporations that are members of an affiliated group (as defined in section 1504(a)) that files a consolidated U.S. income tax return for the taxable year in which the transfer occurs.

(iii) The indirect acquisition of an interest in a life insurance contract by a person if

(A) A partnership, trust, or other entity in which an ownership interest is being acquired directly or indirectly holds the interest in the life insurance contract and acquired that interest before January 1, 2019, or acquired that interest in a reportable policy sale reported in compliance with section 6050Y(a) and § 1.6050Y–2; or

(B) Immediately before the acquisition, no more than 50 percent of the gross value of the assets (as determined under paragraph (f)(4) of this section) of the partnership, trust, or other entity that directly or indirectly holds the interest in the life insurance contract, and in which an ownership interest is being directly acquired, consists of life insurance contracts, provided that, after the acquisition, with respect to that partnership, trust, or other entity, the person indirectly acquiring the interest in the life insurance contract and his or her family members own, in the aggregate

(1) With respect to an S corporation, stock possessing 5 percent or less of the total combined voting power of all classes of stock entitled to vote and 5 percent or less of the total value of shares of all classes of stock of the S corporation;

(2) With respect to a trust or decedent's estate, 5 percent or less of the corpus and 5 percent or less of the annual income (taking into account, for the purpose of determining any person's ownership interest, the maximum amount of income and corpus that could be distributed to or held for the benefit of that person); or

(3) With respect to a partnership or other entity that is not a corporation or a trust, 5 percent or less of the capital interest and 5 percent or less of the profits interest.

(iv) The acquisition of a life insurance contract by an insurance company that issues a life insurance contract in an exchange pursuant to section 1035.

(v) The acquisition of a life insurance contract by a policyholder in an exchange pursuant to section 1035, if the policyholder has a substantial family, business, or financial relationship with the insured, apart from its interest in the life insurance contract, at the time of the exchange.

(d) Substantial relationship (1) *Substantial family relationship.* For purposes of this section, a substantial family relationship means the relationship between an individual and any family member of that individual as defined in paragraph (f)(3) of this section. In addition, a substantial family relationship exists between an individual and his or her former spouse with regard to the transfer of an interest in a life insurance contract to (or in trust for the benefit of) that former spouse incident to divorce.

(2) *Substantial business relationship.* For purposes of this section, a substantial business relationship between the insured and the acquirer exists in each of the following situations:

(i) The insured is a key person (as defined in section 264) of, or materially participates (within the meaning of section 469) in, an active trade or business as an owner, employee, or contractor, and at least 80 percent of that trade or business is owned (directly or indirectly, through one or more partnerships, trusts, or other entities) by the acquirer or the beneficial owners of the acquirer.

(ii) The acquirer acquires an active trade or business and acquires the interest in the life insurance contract either as part of that acquisition or from a person owning significant property leased to the acquired trade or business or life insurance policies held to facilitate the succession of the ownership of the business if

(A) The insured

(*1*) Is an employee within the meaning of section 101(j)(5)(A) of the acquired trade or business immediately preceding the acquisition (for purposes of this paragraph (d)(2)(ii)(A)(*1*), however, the reference in section 101(j)(5)(A) to highly compensated employee within the meaning of section 414(q) does not include a former employee); or

(*2*) Was a director, highly compensated employee, or highly compensated individual within the meaning of section 101(j)(2)(A)(ii) of the acquired trade or business, and the acquirer, immediately after the acquisition, has ongoing financial obligations to the insured with respect to the insured's employment by the trade or business (for example, the life insurance contract is maintained by the acquirer to fund current or future retirement, pension, or survivorship obligations based on the insured's relationship with the entity or to fund a buy-out of the insured's interest in the acquired trade or business); and

(B) The acquirer either carries on the acquired trade or business or uses a significant portion of the acquired business assets in an active trade or business that does not include investing in interests in life insurance contracts.

(3) *Substantial financial relationship.* For purposes of this section, a substantial financial relationship between the insured and the acquirer exists in each of the following situations:

(i) The acquirer (directly or indirectly, through one or more partnerships, trusts, or other entities of which it is a beneficial owner) has, or the beneficial owners of the acquirer have, a common investment (other than the interest in the life insurance contract) with the insured and a buy-out of the insured's interest in the common investment by the co-investor(s) after the insured's death is reasonably foreseeable.

(ii) The acquirer maintains the life insurance contract on the life of the insured to provide funds to purchase assets of or to satisfy liabilities of the insured or the insured's estate, heirs, legatees, or other successors in interest, or to satisfy other liabilities arising upon or by reason of the death of the insured.

(iii) The acquirer is an organization described in sections 170(c), 2055(a), and 2522(a) that previously received from the insured either financial support in a substantial amount or significant volunteer support or that meets other requirements prescribed in guidance published in the Internal Revenue Bulletin (see § 601.601(d)(2) of this chapter) for establishing that a substantial financial relationship exists between the insured and the organization.

(4) *Special rules.* Paragraphs (d)(4)(i), (ii), and (iii) of this section apply for purposes of determining whether a substantial relationship (whether family, business, or financial) exists under paragraph (d)(1), (2), or (3) of this section, respectively.

(i) *Indirect acquisitions.* The acquirer of an interest in a life insurance contract in an indirect acquisition is deemed to have a substantial business or financial relationship with the insured if the direct holder of the interest in the life insurance contract has a substantial business or financial relationship with the insured immediately before and after the date the acquirer acquires its interest.

(ii) *Acquisitions by certain persons.* The sole fact that an acquirer is a partner of the insured, a partnership in which the insured is a partner, or a corporation in which the insured is a shareholder or officer, is not sufficient to establish a substantial business or financial relationship with the insured. In addition, an acquirer need not be a partner of the insured, a partnership in which the insured is a partner, or a corporation in which the insured is a shareholder or officer to have a substantial business or financial relationship with the insured.

(iii) *Acquisitions by those with differing types of substantial relationships.* A substantial family, business, or financial relationship exists between the insured and a partnership, trust, or other entity if each beneficial owner of that partnership, trust, or other entity has a substantial family, business, or financial relationship with the insured. For example, a substantial family, business, or financial relationship exists between the insured and a trust if each trust beneficiary is a family member of the insured or an organization described in paragraph (d)(3)(iii) of this section.

(e) Interest in a life insurance contract (1) *Definition.* For purposes of this section and section 6050Y, the term interest in a life insurance contract means the interest held by any person that has taken title to or possession of the life insurance contract (also referred to as a life insurance policy), in whole or part, for state law purposes, including any person that has taken title or possession as nominee for another person, and the interest held by any person that has an enforceable right to receive all or a part of the proceeds of a life insurance contract or to any other economic benefits of the policy as described in § 20.2042–1(c)(2) of this chapter, such as the enforceable right to designate a contract beneficiary. Any person named as the owner in the life insurance contract generally is the owner (or an owner) of the contract and holds an interest in the contract.

(2) *Transfer of an interest in a life insurance contract.* For purposes of this section and section 6050Y, the term transfer of an interest in a life insurance contract means the transfer of any interest in the life insurance contract, including any transfer of title to, possession of, or legal or beneficial ownership of the life insurance contract itself. The creation of an enforceable right to receive all or a part of the proceeds of a life insurance contract constitutes the transfer of an interest in the life insurance contract. The following events are not a transfer of an interest in a life insurance contract: The revocable designation of a beneficiary of the policy proceeds (until the designation becomes irrevocable other than by reason of the death of the insured); the pledging or assignment of a policy as collateral security; and the issuance of a life insurance contract to a policyholder, other than the issuance of a policy in an exchange pursuant to section 1035.

(3) *Acquisition of an interest in a life insurance contract.* For purposes of this section and section 6050Y, the acquisition of an interest in a life insurance contract may be direct or indirect.

(i) *Direct acquisition of an interest in a life insurance contract.* For purposes of this section and section 6050Y, the transfer of an interest in a life insurance contract results in the direct acquisition of the interest by the transferee (acquirer).

(ii) *Indirect acquisition of an interest in a life insurance contract.* For purposes of this section and section 6050Y, an indirect acquisition of an interest in a life insurance contract occurs when a person (acquirer) becomes a beneficial owner of a partnership, trust, or other entity that holds (whether directly or indirectly) the interest (whether legal or beneficial) in the life insurance contract. For purposes of this paragraph (e)(3)(ii), the term other entity does not include a C corporation, unless more than 50 percent of the gross value of the assets of the C corporation consists of life insurance contracts (as determined under paragraph (f)(4) of this section) immediately before the indirect acquisition.

(f) Definitions. The following definitions apply for purposes of this section:

(1) *Beneficial owner.* A beneficial owner of a partnership, trust, or other entity is an individual or C corporation with an ownership interest in that entity. The interest may be held directly or indirectly, through one or more other partnerships, trusts, or other entities. For instance, an individual that directly owns an interest in a partnership (P1), which directly owns an interest in another partnership (P2), is an indirect beneficial owner of P2 and any assets or other entities owned by P2 directly or indirectly. For purposes of this paragraph (f)(1), the beneficial owners of a trust include those who may receive current distributions of trust income or corpus and those who could receive distributions if the trust were to terminate currently.

(2) *C corporation.* The term C corporation has the meaning given to it in section 1361(a)(2).

(3) *Family member.* With respect to any individual, the term family member refers to any person described in paragraphs (f)(3)(i) through (vi) of this section. For purposes of this paragraph (f)(3), full effect is given to a legal adoption, and a step-child is deemed to be a descendant. The family members of an individual include:

(i) The individual;

(ii) The individual's spouse or a person with whom the individual is in a registered domestic partnership, civil union, or other similar relationship established under state law;

(iii) Any parent, grandparent, or great-grandparent of the individual or of the person described in paragraph (f)(3)(ii) of this section and any spouse of such parent, grandparent, or great-grandparent, or person with whom the parent, grandparent, or great-grandparent is in a registered domestic partnership, civil union, or other similar relationship established under state law;

(iv) Any lineal descendant of the individual or of any person described in paragraph (f)(3)(ii) or (iii) of this section;

(v) Any spouse of a lineal descendant described in paragraph (f)(3)(iv) of this section and any person with whom such a lineal descendant is in a registered domestic partnership, civil union, or other similar relationship established under state law; and

(vi) Any lineal descendant of a person described in paragraph (f)(3)(v) of this section.

(4) *Gross value of assets* (i) *Determination of gross value of assets.* Except as provided in paragraph (f)(4)(ii) or (iii) of this section, for purposes of paragraphs (c)(2)(iii)(B) and (e)(3)(ii) of this section, the term gross value of assets means, with respect to any entity, the fair market value of the entity's assets, including assets beneficially owned by the entity under paragraph (f)(1) of this section as a beneficial owner of a partnership, trust, or other entity.

(ii) *Determination of gross value of assets of publicly traded entity.* For purposes of determining the gross value of assets of an entity that is publicly traded, if the entity's annual Form 10-K filed with the United States Securities and Exchange Commission (or equivalent annual filing if the entity is publicly traded in a non-U.S. jurisdiction) for the period immediately preceding a person's acquisition of an ownership interest in the entity does not contain information demonstrating that more than 50 percent of the gross value of the entity's assets consists of life insurance contracts, that person may assume that no more than 50 percent of the gross value of the entity's assets consists of life insurance contracts, unless that person has actual knowledge or reason to know that more than 50 percent of the gross value of the entity's assets consists of life insurance contracts.

(iii) *Safe harbor definition of gross value of assets.* An entity may choose to determine the gross value of all the entity's assets for purposes of this section using the following alternative definition of gross value of assets:

(A) In the case of assets that are life insurance policies or annuity or endowment contracts that have cash values, the cash surrender value as defined in section 7702(f)(2)(A); and

(B) In the case of assets not described in paragraph (f)(4)(iii)(A) of this section, the adjusted bases (within the meaning of section 1016) of such assets.

(5) *Transfer for valuable consideration.* A transfer for valuable consideration means any transfer of an interest in a life insurance contract for cash or other consideration reducible to a money value.

(g) Examples. The application of this section is illustrated by the following examples. Each example assumes that the transferee did not receive any amounts under the life insurance contract other than the amounts described in the examples. With the exception of paragraph (g)(7) (Example 7) of this section, the bargain sale rules set forth in paragraph (b)(2)(iii) of this section do not apply in the examples because the consideration paid for the policy transferred is fair market value:

(1) *Example 1.* A is the initial policyholder of a $100,000 insurance policy on A's life. A sells the policy to B, A's child, for $6,000, its fair market value. B is not a partner in a partnership in which A is a partner. B receives the proceeds of $100,000 upon the death of A. Because the transfer to B was for valuable consideration, and none of the exceptions in paragraph (b)(1)(ii) of this section applies, the amount of the proceeds B may exclude from B's gross income under this section is limited under paragraph (b)(1)(i) of this section to $6,000 plus any premiums and other amounts paid by B with respect to the policy subsequent to the transfer.

(2) *Example 2.* The facts are the same as in Example 1 in paragraph (g)(1) of this section except that, before A's death, B gratuitously transfers the policy back to A. A's estate receives the proceeds of $100,000 on A's death. Because the transfer from B to A is a gratuitous transfer to the insured, and the preceding transfer from A to B was not a reportable policy sale, the amount of the proceeds A's estate may exclude from gross income under this section is not limited by paragraph (b)(2)(i) of this section.

(3) *Example 3.* The facts are the same as in Example 1 in paragraph (g)(1) of this section except that, before A's death, B sells the policy back to A for its fair market value. A's estate receives the proceeds of $100,000 on A's death. The transfer from A to B is not a reportable policy sale because the acquirer B has a substantial family relationship with the insured, A. The transfer from B to A also is not a reportable policy sale because the acquirer A has a substantial family relationship with the insured, A. Accordingly, paragraph (b)(1)(ii)(B)(1) of this section applies to the transfer to A, and the amount of the proceeds A's estate may exclude from gross income is not limited by paragraph (b) of this section.

(4) *Example 4.* A is the initial policyholder of a $100,000 insurance policy on A's life. A transfers the policy for $6,000, its fair market value, to an individual, C, who does not have a substantial family, business, or financial relationship with A. The transfer from A to C is a reportable policy sale. C receives the proceeds of $100,000 on A's death. The amount of the proceeds C may exclude from C's gross income under this section is limited under paragraph (b)(1)(i) of this section to $6,000 plus any premiums and other amounts paid by C with respect to the policy subsequent to the transfer.

(5) *Example 5.* The facts are the same as in Example 4 in paragraph (g)(4) of this section, except that before A's death, C transfers the policy to D, a partner of A who co-owns real property with A, for $8,000, the policy's fair market value. D receives the proceeds of $100,000 on A's death. The transfer from C to D is not a reportable policy sale because the acquirer D has a substantial financial relationship with the insured, A. However, because that transfer follows a reportable policy sale (the transfer from A to C), the amount of the proceeds that D may exclude from gross income under this section is limited by paragraph (b)(1)(ii)(B)(2) of this section to the sum of

(i) The higher of the amount C could have excluded had the transfer to D not occurred ($6,000 plus any premiums and other amounts paid by C with respect to the policy subsequent to the transfer to C, as described in Example 4 in paragraph (g)(4) of this section) or the actual value of the consideration for that transfer paid by D ($8,000); and

(ii) Any premiums and other amounts paid by D with respect to the policy subsequent to the transfer to D.

(6) *Example 6.* The facts are the same as in Example 4 in paragraph (g)(4) of this section, except that before A's death, C transfers the policy back to A for $8,000, its fair market value. A's estate receives the proceeds of $100,000 on A's death. The transfer from C to A is not a reportable policy sale because the acquirer A has a substantial family relationship with the insured, A. Although the transfer follows a reportable policy sale (the initial transfer from A to C), A's estate may exclude all of the policy proceeds from gross income because paragraph (b)(1)(ii)(B)(3)(i) of this section applies and, therefore, the amount of the proceeds that A may exclude from gross income is not limited by paragraph (b)(1)(i) of this section or (b)(1)(ii)(B)(2) of this section.

(7) *Example 7.* The facts are the same as in Example 6 in paragraph (g)(6) of this section, except that C transfers the policy back to A for $4,000, rather than its fair market value of $8,000. A's estate receives the proceeds of $100,000 on A's death. Because A did not pay fair market value for the policy, the transfer is bifurcated and treated as a bargain sale under paragraph (b)(2)(iii) of this section. A therefore is treated as having purchased 50% of the policy interest for valuable consideration equal to fair market value and as having received 50% of the policy interest in a gratuitous transfer. The transfer from C to A is not a reportable policy sale because the acquirer, A, has a substantial family relationship with the insured, A, but the transfer from C to A follows a reportable policy sale (the transfer from A to C).

(i) *Treatment of policy interest purchased by A.* A's estate may exclude from income all of the policy proceeds related to the 50% policy interest transferred for valuable consideration ($50,000) because, under paragraph (b)(1)(ii)(B)(3)(i) of this section, the amount of the proceeds that may be excluded from gross income is not limited by paragraph (b)(1)(i) of this section or (b)(1)(ii)(B)(2) of this section.

(ii) *Treatment of policy interest gratuitously transferred to A.* The amount of the policy proceeds related to the 50% policy interest transferred gratuitously that A's estate may exclude from income is limited under paragraph (b)(2)(i) of this section to the sum of the amount C could have excluded with respect to 50% of the policy had the transfer back to A not occurred (that is, 50% of the $6,000 that C paid A for the policy, plus 50% of any premiums and other amounts paid by C with respect to the policy subsequent to the transfer to C), plus 50% of any premiums and other amounts paid by A with respect to the policy subsequent to the transfer to A.

(8) *Example 8.* The facts are the same as in Example 6 in paragraph (g)(6) of this section, except that, before A's death, A gratuitously transfers 50% of the policy interest to B, A's child, and sells 50% of the policy interest for its fair market value to an individual, E, who does not have a substantial family, business, or financial relationship with A. B and E each receive $50,000 of the proceeds on A's death. Paragraph (b)(1)(ii)(B)(3)(ii) of this section applies to determine the amount of the proceeds that B and E may exclude from gross income because the policy interests transferred to B and E were first transferred for valuable consideration in a reportable policy sale (the transfer by A to C) and then transferred to the insured, A, for fair market value.

(i) *Treatment of policy interest transferred to B.* With respect to the portion of the policy interest transferred to B, because the transfer to B was the only transfer subsequent to the transfer to A and the transfer to B was gratuitous and not a reportable policy sale, under paragraph (b)(1)(ii)(B)(3)(ii) of this section, the amount of the policy proceeds excludable from gross income by B is determined under paragraph (b)(2)(i) of this section, taking into account the application of paragraph (b)(1)(ii)(B)(3)(i) of this section to A's acquisition of the interest. Under paragraph (b)(2)(i) of this section, the amount of the proceeds B may exclude is limited to the sum of the amount A could have excluded had the transfer to B not occurred, and any premiums and other amounts paid by B with respect to the policy subsequent to the transfer to B. As described in Example 6 in paragraph (g)(6) of this section, under paragraph (b)(1)(ii)(B)(3)(i) of this section, the amount of the proceeds that A may exclude from gross income is not limited by paragraph (b)(1)(i) of this section or (b)(1)(ii)(B)(2) of this section. Accordingly, the amount of the proceeds that B may exclude from gross income is not limited by paragraph (b) of this section.

(ii) *Treatment of policy interest transferred to E.* With respect to the portion of the policy interest transferred to E, because the transfer to E was not gratuitous and was a reportable policy sale, under paragraph (b)(1)(ii)(B)(3)(ii) of this section, the amount of the policy proceeds excludable from gross income by E is determined in accordance with paragraph (b) of this section. Accordingly, because the transfer to E was for valuable consideration, the amount excludable from gross income by E is limited by paragraph (b)(1)(i) of this section unless an exception in paragraph (b)(1)(ii) of this section applies. Because the transfer from A to E is a reportable policy sale, none of the exceptions in paragraph (b)(1)(ii) of this section apply. Therefore, the amount of the proceeds E may exclude from gross income under this section is limited by paragraph (b)(1)(i) of this section to the sum of the consideration paid by E and the premiums and other amounts paid by E with respect to the policy subsequent to the transfer to E.

(9) *Example 9.* The facts are the same as in Example 8 in paragraph (g)(8) of this section, except that, before A's death, B transfers B's policy interest to Partnership F, whose partners are A and other family members of A, in exchange for a partnership interest in Partnership F. Partnership F receives $50,000 of the proceeds on A's death. With respect to the policy interest transferred to Partnership F, paragraph (b)(1)(ii)(B)(3)(ii) of this section applies to determine the amount of the proceeds that Partnership F may exclude from gross income for the reasons described in Example 8 in paragraph (g)(8) of this section.

(i) *Treatment of policy interest transferred to Partnership F.* The transfer to Partnership F was not a reportable policy sale. However, because the transfer to Partnership F was not gratuitous, the amount of the policy proceeds excludable from gross income by Partnership F is determined in accordance with paragraph (b) of this section as if the amount that would have been excludable from gross income by A following the transfer to A, if no subsequent transfer had occurred, was determined under paragraph (b)(1)(ii)(B)(2) of this section. Because B's transfer to Partnership F was a transfer for valuable consideration to a partnership in which the insured is a partner that was preceded by a reportable policy sale (the transfer to C), the amount of the proceeds Partnership F may exclude from gross income under this section is limited under paragraph (b)(1)(ii)(B)(2) of this section to the higher of the amount that would have been excludable by B if the transfer to Partnership F had not occurred or the actual value of the consideration for the policy paid by Partnership F, plus any premiums and other amounts paid by Partnership F with respect to the policy subsequent to the transfer to Partnership F.

(ii) *Amount that B could have excluded.* Because the transfer from A to B was a gratuitous transfer, the amount of the proceeds B could have excluded from gross income under this section if the transfer to Partnership F had not occurred is limited under paragraph (b)(2)(i) of this section to the sum of the amount A could have excluded had the transfer to B not occurred, and any premiums and other amounts paid by B with respect to the policy subsequent to the transfer to B.

(iii) *Amount that A could have excluded.* As described in paragraph (g)(9)(i) of this section, the amount of the proceeds A could have excluded under this section if the transfer to B had not occurred must be determined under paragraph (b)(1)(ii)(B)(2) of this section in accordance with paragraph (b)(1)(ii)(B)(3)(ii) of this section. Under paragraph (b)(1)(ii)(B)(2) of this section, the amount that would have been excludable by A is limited to the higher of the amount that would have been excludable by C if the transfer to A had not occurred ($6,000 plus premiums and other amounts subsequently paid by C) or the actual value of the consideration for the policy paid by A ($8,000), plus any premiums and other amounts paid by A with respect to the policy subsequent to the transfer to A.

(10) *Example 10.* A is the initial policyholder of a $100,000 insurance policy on A's life. A contributes the policy to Corporation X in exchange for stock. Corporation X's basis in the policy is determinable in whole or in part by reference to A's basis in the policy. Corporation X conducts an active trade or business that it wholly owns, and A materially participates in that active trade or business as an employee of Corporation X. Corporation X receives the proceeds of $100,000 on A's death. A's contribution of the policy to Corporation X is not a reportable policy sale because Corporation X has a substantial business relationship with A under paragraph (d)(2)(i) of this section. Although Corporation X's basis in the policy is determinable in whole or in part by reference to A's basis in the policy, paragraph (b)(1)(ii)(A) of this section does not apply because the insured, A, is a shareholder of Corporation X and the other requirements under paragraph (b)(1)(ii)(B) of this section are satisfied. Accordingly, paragraph (b)(1)(ii)(B) of this section applies, and paragraph (b)(1)(ii)(A) of this section is inapplicable. Under paragraph (b)(1)(ii)(B)(1) of this section, Corporation X's exclusion is not limited by paragraph (b) of this section.

(11) *Example 11.* The facts are the same as in Example 10 in paragraph (g)(10) of this section, except that Corporation X transfers its active trade or business and the policy on A's life to Corporation Y in a tax-free reorganization at a time when A is still employed by Corporation X, but is no longer a shareholder of Corporation X. Corporation Y's basis in the policy is determinable in whole or in part by reference to Corporation X's basis in the policy, and Corporation Y carries on the trade or business acquired from Corporation X. Corporation Y receives the proceeds of $100,000 on A's death. The transfer from Corporation X to Corporation Y is not a reportable policy sale because Corporation Y has a substantial business relationship with A under paragraph (d)(2)(ii) of this section. The amount of the proceeds that Corporation Y may exclude from gross income is limited under paragraph (b)(1)(ii)(A) of this section to the sum of the amount that would have been excludable by Corporation X had the transfer to Corporation Y not occurred, plus any premiums and other amounts paid by Corporation Y with respect to the policy subsequent to the transfer. Accordingly, because Corporation X's exclusion is not limited by paragraph (b) of this section, as described in Example 10 in paragraph (g)(10) of this section, Corporation Y's exclusion is not limited by paragraph (b) of this section.

(12) *Example 12.* A is the initial policyholder of a $100,000 insurance policy on A's life. A contributes the policy to a C corporation, Corporation W, in exchange for stock. After the acquisition, A owns less than 20% of the outstanding stock of Corporation W and owns stock possessing less than 20% of the total combined voting power of all stock of Corporation W and is therefore not a key person with respect to Corporation W under section 264(e)(3). Corporation W's basis in the policy is determinable in whole or in part by reference to A's basis in the policy. However, no substantial family, business, or financial relationship exists between A and Corporation W, so A's contribution of the policy to Corporation W is a reportable

policy sale. Corporation W receives the proceeds of $100,000 on A's death. Under paragraph (b)(1)(i) of this section, the amount of the proceeds Corporation W may exclude from gross income is limited to the actual value of the stock exchanged for the policy, plus any premiums and other amounts paid by Corporation W with respect to the policy subsequent to the transfer. The exceptions in paragraph (b)(1)(ii) of this section do not apply because the transfer to Corporation W is a reportable policy sale.

(13) *Example 13.* Partnership X and Partnership Y are owned by individuals A, B, and C. A holds 40% of the capital and profits interest of Partnership X and 20% of the capital and profits interest of Partnership Y. B holds 35% of the capital and profits interest of Partnership X and 40% of the capital and profits interest of Partnership Y. C holds 25% of the capital and profits interest of Partnership X and 40% of the capital and profits interest of Partnership Y. Partnership X is the initial policyholder of a $100,000 insurance policy on the life of A. Partnership Y purchases the policy from Partnership X. Under paragraph (c)(2)(i) of this section, this transfer is not a reportable policy sale because the ownership interest of each beneficial owner in Partnership X does not vary from that owner's interest in Partnership Y by more than a 20% ownership interest. A's ownership varies by a 20% interest, B's ownership varies by a 5% interest, and C's ownership varies by a 15% interest.

(14) *Example 14.* Partnership X conducts an active trade or business and is the initial policyholder of a $100,000 insurance policy on the life of its full-time employee, A. A materially participates in Partnership X's active trade or business in A's capacity as an employee. Individual B acquires a 10% profits interest in Partnership X in exchange for a cash payment of $1,000,000. Under paragraphs (d)(1) through (3) of this section, B does not have a substantial family, business, or financial relationship with A. Under paragraph (d)(4)(i) of this section, however, B is deemed to have a substantial business relationship with A because, under paragraph (d)(2)(i) of this section, Partnership X (the direct policyholder) has a substantial business relationship with A. Accordingly, although the acquisition of the 10% partnership interest by B is an indirect acquisition of a 10% interest in the insurance policy covering A's life, the acquisition is not a reportable policy sale.

(15) *Example 15.* The facts are the same as in Example 14 in paragraph (g)(14) of this section, except that A is no longer an employee of Partnership X, and Partnership X has no substantial family, business, or financial relationship with A, when B acquires the profits interest in Partnership X. Also, B acquires only a 5% profits interest in exchange for a cash payment of $500,000. Partnership X does not own an interest in any other life insurance policies, and the gross value of its assets is $10 million. Although neither Partnership X nor B has a substantial family, business, or financial relationship with A at the time of B's indirect acquisition of an interest in the policy covering A's life, because B's profits interest in Partnership X does not exceed 5%, and because no more than 50% of Partnership X's asset value consists of life insurance contracts, the exception in paragraph (c)(2)(iii)(B) of this section applies, and B's indirect acquisition of an interest in the policy covering A's life is not a reportable policy sale.

(16) *Example 16.* A is the initial policyholder of a $100,000 insurance policy on A's life. A sells the policy for its fair market value. As a result of the sale, Bank X holds legal title to the life insurance contract as the nominee of Partnership B, and Partnership B has the enforceable right to designate the contract beneficiary. Under paragraphs (d)(1) through (4) of this section, neither Bank X nor Partnership B has a substantial family, business, or financial relationship with the insured, A, at the time of the sale. Accordingly, the transfer of legal title to the policy to Bank X is a reportable policy sale under paragraph (c)(1) of this section, unless an exception set forth in paragraph (c)(2) of this section applies. The same is true of the transfer of the economic benefits of the policy to Partnership B. At a later date, Partnership B sells its economic interest in the policy to Partnership C for fair market value. Bank X continues to hold legal title to the life insurance contract, but now holds it as Partnership C's nominee. Partnership C has no substantial family, business, or financial relationship with the insured, A, under paragraphs (d)(1) through (4) of this section at the time of the transfer. Accordingly, Partnership C's acquisition of the economic interest in the policy from Partnership B is a reportable policy sale under paragraph (c)(1) of this section, unless an exception set forth in paragraph (c)(2) of this section applies.

[T.D. 6500, 25 FR 11402, Nov. 26, 1960, as amended by T.D. 6783, 29 FR 18356, Dec. 24, 1964; T.D. 7836, 47 FR 42337, Sept. 27, 1982; T.D. 9340, 72 FR 41159, July 26, 2007; T.D. 9879, 84 FR 58478, Oct. 31, 2019; 84 FR 68043, Dec. 13, 2019]

§ 102. Gifts and Inheritances

(a) General rule. Gross income does not include the value of property acquired by gift, bequest, devise, or inheritance.

(b) Income. Subsection (a) shall not exclude from gross income—

(1) the income from any property referred to in subsection (a); or

(2) where the gift, bequest, devise, or inheritance is of income from property, the amount of such income.

Where, under the terms of the gift, bequest, devise, or inheritance, the payment, crediting, or distribution thereof is to be made at intervals, then, to the extent that it is paid or credited or to be distributed out of income from property, it shall be treated for purposes of paragraph (2) as a gift, bequest, devise, or inheritance of income from property. Any amount included in the gross income of a beneficiary under subchapter J shall be treated for purposes of paragraph (2) as a gift, bequest, devise, or inheritance of income from property.

(c) Employee gifts.

(1) In general. Subsection (a) shall not exclude from gross income any amount transferred by or for an employer to, or for the benefit of, an employee.

(2) Cross references. For provisions excluding certain employee achievement awards from gross income, see section 74(c).

For provisions excluding certain de minimis fringes from gross income, see section 132(e).

Regulation

§ 1.102–1 Gifts and inheritances.

(a) General rule. Property received as a gift, or received under a will or under statutes of descent and distribution, is not includible in gross income, although the income from such property is includible in gross income. An amount of principal paid under a marriage settlement is a gift. However, see section 71 and the regulations thereunder for rules relating to alimony or allowances paid upon divorce or separation. Section 102 does not apply to prizes and awards (see section 74 and § 1.74–1) nor to scholarships and fellowship grants (see section 117 and the regulations thereunder).

(b) Income from gifts and inheritances. The income from any property received as a gift, or under a will or statute of descent and distribution shall not be excluded from gross income under paragraph (a) of this section.

(c) Gifts and inheritances of income. If the gift, bequest, devise, or inheritance is of income from property, it shall not be excluded from gross income under paragraph (a) of this section. Section 102 provides a special rule for the treatment of certain gifts, bequests, devises, or inheritances which by their terms are to be paid, credited, or distributed at intervals. Except as provided in section 663(a)(1) and paragraph (d) of this section, to the extent any such gift, bequest, devise, or inheritance is paid, credited, or to be distributed out of income from property, it shall be considered a gift, bequest, devise, or inheritance of income from property. Section 102 provides the same treatment for amounts of income from property which is paid, credited, or to be distributed under a gift or bequest whether the gift or bequest is in terms of a right to payments at intervals (regardless of income) or is in terms of a right to income. To the extent the amounts in either case are paid, credited, or to be distributed at intervals out of income, they are not to be excluded under section 102 from the taxpayer's gross income.

(d) Effect of subchapter J. Any amount required to be included in the gross income of a beneficiary under sections 652, 662, or 668 shall be treated for purposes of this section as a gift, bequest, devise, or inheritance of income from property. On the other hand, any amount excluded from the gross income of a beneficiary under section 663(a)(1) shall be treated for purposes of this section as property acquired by gift, bequest, devise, or inheritance.

(e) Income taxed to grantor or assignor. Section 102 is not intended to tax a donee upon the same income which is taxed to the grantor of a trust or assignor of income under section 61 or sections 671 through 677, inclusive.

[T.D. 6500, 25 FR 11402, Nov. 26, 1960]

§ 121. Exclusion of Gain from Sale of Principal Residence

(a) Exclusion. Gross income shall not include gain from the sale or exchange of property if, during the 5-year period ending on the date of the sale or exchange, such property has been owned and used by the taxpayer as the taxpayer's principal residence for periods aggregating 2 years or more.

(b) Limitations.

(1) In general. The amount of gain excluded from gross income under subsection (a) with respect to any sale or exchange shall not exceed $250,000.

(2) Special rules for joint returns. In the case of a husband and wife who make a joint return for the taxable year of the sale or exchange of the property—

(A) $500,000 limitation for certain joint returns. Paragraph (1) shall be applied by substituting "$500,000" for "$250,000" if—

(i) either spouse meets the ownership requirements of subsection (a) with respect to such property;

(ii) both spouses meet the use requirements of subsection (a) with respect to such property; and

(iii) neither spouse is ineligible for the benefits of subsection (a) with respect to such property by reason of paragraph (3).

* * *

(3) Application to only 1 sale or exchange every 2 years. Subsection (a) shall not apply to any sale or exchange by the taxpayer if, during the 2-year period ending on the date of such sale or exchange, there was any other sale or exchange by the taxpayer to which subsection (a) applied.

* * *

(4) Special rule for certain sales by surviving spouses. In the case of a sale or exchange of property by an unmarried individual whose spouse is deceased on the date of such sale, paragraph (1) shall be applied by substituting "$500,000" for "$250,000" if such sale occurs not later than 2 years after the date of death of such spouse and the requirements of paragraph (2)(A) were met immediately before such date of death.

* * *

(d) Special rules.

* * *

(2) Property of deceased spouse. For purposes of this section, in the case of an unmarried individual whose spouse is deceased on the date of the sale or exchange of property, the period such unmarried individual owned and used such property shall include the period such deceased spouse owned and used such property before death.

* * *

(7) Determination of use during periods of out-of-residence care.—In the case of a taxpayer who

(A) becomes physically or mentally incapable of selfcare, and

(B) owns property and uses such property as the taxpayer's principal residence during the 5-year period described in subsection (a) for periods aggregating at least 1 year, then the taxpayer shall be treated as using such property as the taxpayer's principal residence during any time during such 5-year period in which the taxpayer owns the property and resides in any facility (including a nursing home) licensed by a State or political subdivision to care for an individual in the taxpayer's condition.

(8) Sales of remainder interests. For purposes of this section—

(A) In general. At the election of the taxpayer, this section shall not fail to apply to the sale or exchange of an interest in a principal residence by reason of such interest being a remainder interest in such residence, but this section shall not apply to any other interest in such residence which is sold or exchanged separately.

(B) Exception for sales to related parties. Subparagraph (A) shall not apply to any sale to, or exchange with, any person who bears a relationship to the taxpayer which is described in section 267(b) or 707(b).

* * *

(e) Denial of exclusion for expatriates. This section shall not apply to any sale or exchange by an individual if the treatment provided by section 877(a)(1) applies to such individual.

(f) Election to have section not apply. This section shall not apply to any sale or exchange with respect to which the taxpayer elects not to have this section apply.

* * *

Part VI. Itemized Deductions for Individuals and Corporations

§ 162. Trade or Business Expenses

(a) In general. There shall be allowed as a deduction all the ordinary and necessary expenses paid or incurred during the taxable year in carrying on any trade or business, including—

(1) a reasonable allowance for salaries or other compensation for personal services actually rendered;

(2) traveling expenses (including amounts expended for meals and lodging other than amounts which are lavish or extravagant under the circumstances) while away from home in the pursuit of a trade or business; and

(3) rentals or other payments required to be made as a condition to the continued use or possession, for purposes of the trade or business, of property to which the taxpayer has not taken or is not taking title or in which he has no equity.

For purposes of the preceding sentence, the place of residence of a Member of Congress (including any Delegate and Resident Commissioner) within the State, congressional district, or possession which he represents in Congress shall be considered his home, but amounts expended by such Members within each taxable year for living expenses shall not be deductible for income tax purposes. For purposes of paragraph (2), the taxpayer shall not be treated as being temporarily away from home during any period of employment if such period exceeds 1 year. The preceding sentence shall not apply to any Federal employee during any period for which such employee is certified by the Attorney General (or the designee thereof) as traveling on behalf of the United States in temporary duty status to investigate or prosecute, or provide support services for the investigation or prosecution of, a Federal crime.

* * *

§ 163. Interest

(a) General rule. There shall be allowed as a deduction all interest paid or accrued within the taxable year on indebtedness.

* * *

(k) Section 6166 interest. No deduction shall be allowed under this section for any interest payable under section 6601 on any unpaid portion of the tax imposed by section 2001 for the period during which an extension of time for payment of such tax is in effect under section 6166.

* * *

§ 165. Losses

(a) General rule. There shall be allowed as a deduction any loss sustained during the taxable year and not compensated for by insurance or otherwise.

(b) Amount of deduction. For purposes of subsection (a), the basis for determining the amount of the deduction for any loss shall be the adjusted basis provided in section 1011 for determining the loss from the sale or other disposition of property.

* * *

§ 167. Depreciation

(a) General rule. There shall be allowed as a depreciation deduction a reasonable allowance for the exhaustion, wear and tear (including a reasonable allowance for obsolescence)

(1) of property used in the trade or business, or

(2) of property held for the production of income.

(b) Cross Reference.

For determination of depreciation deduction in case of property to which section 168 applies, see section 168.

(c) Basis for depreciation.

(1) In general. The basis on which exhaustion, wear and tear, and obsolescence are to be allowed in respect of any property shall be the adjusted basis provided in section 1011, for the purpose of determining the gain on the sale or other disposition of such property.

* * *

(d) Life tenants and beneficiaries of trusts and estates. In the case of property held by one person for life with remainder to another person, the deduction shall be computed as if the life tenant were the absolute owner of the property and shall be allowed to the life tenant. In the case of property held in trust, the allowable deduction shall be apportioned between the income beneficiaries and the trustee in accordance with the pertinent provisions of the instrument creating the trust, or, in the absence of such provisions, on the basis of the trust income allocable to each. In the case of an estate, the allowable deduction shall be apportioned between the estate and the heirs, legatees, and devisees on the basis of the income of the estate allocable to each.

* * *

Regulation

§ 1.167(h)–1 Life tenants and beneficiaries of trusts and estates.

(a) Life tenants. In the case of property held by one person for life with remainder to another person, the deduction for depreciation shall be computed as if the life tenant were the absolute owner of the property so that he will be entitled to the deduction during his life, and thereafter the deduction, if any, shall be allowed to the remainderman.

(b) Trusts. If property is held in trust, the allowable deduction is to be apportioned between the income beneficiaries and the trustee on the basis of the trust income allocable to each, unless the governing instrument (or local law) requires or permits the trustee to maintain a reserve for depreciation in any amount. In the latter case, the deduction is first allocated to the trustee to the extent that income is set aside for a depreciation reserve, and any part of the deduction in excess of the income set aside for the reserve shall be apportioned between the income beneficiaries and the trustee on the basis of the trust income (in excess of the income set aside for the reserve) allocable to each. For example:

(1) If under the trust instrument or local law the income of a trust computed without regard to depreciation is to be distributed to a named beneficiary, the beneficiary is entitled to the deduction to the exclusion of the trustee.

(2) If under the trust instrument or local law the income of a trust is to be distributed to a named beneficiary, but the trustee is directed to maintain a reserve for depreciation in any amount, the deduction is allowed to the trustee (except to the extent that income set aside for the reserve is less than the allowable deduction). The same result would follow if the trustee sets aside income for a depreciation reserve pursuant to discretionary authority to do so in the governing instrument.

No effect shall be given to any allocation of the depreciation deduction which gives any beneficiary or the trustee a share of such deduction greater than his pro rata share of the trust income, irrespective of any provisions in the trust instrument except as otherwise provided in this paragraph when the trust instrument or local law requires or permits the trustee to maintain a reserve for depreciation.

(c) Estates. In the case of an estate the allowable deduction shall be apportioned between the estate and the heirs, legatees, and devisees on the basis of income of the estate which is allocable to each.

[T.D. 6500, 25 FR 11402, Nov. 26, 1960. Redesignated by T.D. 6712, 29 FR 3653, March 24, 1964]

§ 170. Charitable, Etc., Contributions and Gifts

(a) Allowance of deduction.

(1) General rule. There shall be allowed as a deduction any charitable contribution (as defined in subsection (c)) payment of which is made within the taxable year. A charitable contribution shall be allowable as a deduction only if verified under regulations prescribed by the Secretary.

* * *

(3) Future interests in tangible personal property. For purposes of this section, payment of a charitable contribution which consists of a future interest in tangible personal property shall be treated as made only when all intervening interests in, and rights to the actual possession or enjoyment of, the property have expired or are held by persons other than the taxpayer or those standing in a relationship to the taxpayer described in section 267(b) or 707(b). For purposes of the preceding sentence, a fixture which is intended to be severed from the real property shall be treated as tangible personal property.

(b) Percentage limitations.

(1) Individuals. In the case of an individual, the deduction provided in subsection (a) shall be limited as provided in the succeeding subparagraphs.

(A) General rule. Any charitable contribution to—

(i) a church or a convention or association of churches,

(ii) an educational organization which normally maintains a regular faculty and curriculum and normally has a regularly enrolled body of pupils or students in attendance at the place where its educational activities are regularly carried on,

(iii) an organization the principal purpose or functions of which are the providing of medical or hospital care or medical education or medical research, if the organization is a hospital, or if the organization is a medical research organization directly engaged in the continuous active conduct of medical research in conjunction with a hospital, and during the calendar year in which the contribution is made such organization is committed to spend such contributions for such research before January 1 of the fifth calendar year which begins after the date such contribution is made,

(iv) an organization which normally receives a substantial part of its support (exclusive of income received in the exercise or performance by such organization of its charitable, educational, or other purpose or function constituting the basis for its exemption under section 501(a)) from the United States or any State or political subdivision thereof or from direct or indirect contributions from the general public, and which is organized and operated exclusively to receive, hold, invest, and administer property and to make expenditures to or for the benefit of a college or university which is an organization referred to in clause (ii) of this subparagraph and which is an agency or instrumentality of a State or political subdivision thereof, or which is owned or operated by a State or political subdivision thereof or by an agency or instrumentality of one or more States or political subdivisions,

(v) a governmental unit referred to in subsection (c)(1),

(vi) an organization referred to in subsection (c)(2) which normally receives a substantial part of its support (exclusive of income received in the exercise or performance by such organization of its charitable, educational, or other purpose or function constituting the basis for its exemption under section 501(a)) from a governmental unit referred to in subsection (c)(1) or from direct or indirect contributions from the general public,

(vii) a private foundation described in subparagraph (F), or

(viii) an organization described in section 509(a)(2) or (3), or

(ix) an agricultural research organization directly engaged in the continuous active conduct of agricultural research (as defined in section 1404 of the National Agricultural Research, Extension, and Teaching Policy Act of 1977) in conjunction with a land grant college or university (as defined in such section) or a non-land grant college of agriculture (as defined in such section), and during the calendar year in which the contribution is made such organization is committed to spend such contribution for such research before January 1 of the fifth calendar year which begins after the date such contribution is made, or

(x) an organization described in section 501(c)(19) that is a federally chartered corporation,

shall be allowed to the extent that the aggregate of such contributions does not exceed 50 percent of the taxpayer's contribution base for the taxable year.

(B) Other contributions. Any charitable contribution other than a charitable contribution to which subparagraph (A) or (G) applies shall be allowed to the extent that the aggregate of such contributions does not exceed the lesser of—

(i) 30 percent of the taxpayer's contribution base for the taxable year, or

(ii) the excess of 50 percent of the taxpayer's contribution base for the taxable year over—

(I) the amount of charitable contributions allowable under subparagraph (A) (determined without regard to subparagraph (C)) and subparagraph (G), reduced by

(II) so much of the contributions taken into account under subparagraph (G) as does not exceed 10 percent of the taxpayer's contribution base.

If the aggregate of such contributions exceeds the limitation of the preceding sentence, such excess shall be treated (in a manner consistent with the rules of subsection (d)(1)) as a charitable contribution (to which subparagraph (A) or (G) does not apply) in each of the 5 succeeding taxable years in order of time.

(C) Special limitation with respect to contributions described in subparagraph (A) of certain capital gain property.

(i) In the case of charitable contributions described in subparagraph (A) of capital gain property to which subsection (e)(1)(B) does not apply, the total amount of contributions of such property which may be taken into account under subsection (a) for any taxable year shall not exceed 30 percent of the taxpayer's contribution base for such year. For purposes of this subsection, contributions of capital gain property to which this subparagraph applies shall be taken into account after all other charitable contributions (other than charitable contributions to which subparagraph (D) applies).

(ii) If charitable contributions described in subparagraph (A) of capital gain property to which clause (i) applies exceeds 30 percent of the taxpayer's contribution base for any taxable year, such excess shall be treated, in a manner consistent with the rules of subsection (d)(1), as a charitable contribution of capital gain property to which clause (i) applies in each of the 5 succeeding taxable years in order of time.

(iii) At the election of the taxpayer (made at such time and in such manner as the Secretary prescribes by regulations), subsection (e)(1) shall apply to all contributions of capital gain property (to which subsection (e)(1)(B) does not otherwise apply) made by the taxpayer during the taxable year. If such an election is made, clauses (i) and (ii) shall not apply to contributions of capital gain property made during the taxable year, and, in applying subsection (d)(1) for such taxable year with respect to contributions of capital gain property made in any prior contribution year for which an election was not made under this clause, such contributions shall be reduced as if subsection (e)(1) had applied to such contributions in the year in which made.

(iv) For purposes of this paragraph, the term "capital gain property" means, with respect to any contribution, any capital asset the sale of which at its fair market value at the time of the contribution would have resulted in gain which would have been long-term capital gain. For purposes of the preceding sentence, any property which is property used in the trade or business (as defined in section 1231(b)) shall be treated as a capital asset.

(D) Special limitation with respect to contributions of capital gain property to organizations not described in subparagraph (A).

(i) In general. In the case of charitable contributions (other than charitable contributions to which subparagraph (A) applies) of capital gain property, the total amount of such contributions of such property taken into account under subsection (a) for any taxable year shall not exceed the lesser of—

(I) 20 percent of the taxpayer's contribution base for the taxable year, or

(II) the excess of 30 percent of the taxpayer's contribution base for the taxable year over the amount of the contributions of capital gain property to which subparagraph (C) applies.

For purposes of this subsection, contributions of capital gain property to which this subparagraph applies shall be taken into account after all other charitable contributions.

(ii) Carryover. If the aggregate amount of contributions described in clause (i) exceeds the limitation of clause (i), such excess shall be treated (in a manner consistent with the rules of subsection (d)(1)) as a charitable contribution of capital gain property to which clause (i) applies in each of the 5 succeeding taxable years in order of time.

(E) Contributions of qualified conservation contributions.

(i) In general. Any qualified conservation contribution (as defined in subsection (h)(1)) shall be allowed to the extent the aggregate of such contributions does not exceed the excess of 50 percent of the taxpayer's contribution base over the amount of all other charitable contributions allowable under this paragraph.

(ii) Carryover. If the aggregate amount of contributions described in clause (i) exceeds the limitation of clause (i), such excess shall be treated (in a manner consistent with the rules of subsection (d)(1)) as a charitable contribution to which clause (i) applies in each of the 15 succeeding years in order of time.

(iii) Coordination with other subparagraphs. For purposes of applying this subsection and subsection (d)(1), contributions described in clause (i) shall not be treated as described in subparagraph (A), (B), (C), or (D) and such subparagraphs shall apply without regard to such contributions.

(iv) Special rule for contribution of property used in agriculture or livestock production.

(I) In general. If the individual is a qualified farmer or rancher for the taxable year for which the contribution is made, clause (i) shall be applied by substituting "100 percent" for "50 percent".

(II) Exception. Subclause (I) shall not apply to any contribution of property made after the date of the enactment of this subparagraph which is used in agriculture or livestock production (or available for such production) unless such contribution is subject to a restriction that such property remain available for such production. This subparagraph shall be applied separately with respect to property to which subclause (I) does not apply by reason of the preceding sentence prior to its application to property to which subclause (I) does apply.

(v) Definition. For purposes of clause (iv), the term "qualified farmer or rancher" means a taxpayer whose gross income from the trade or business of farming (within the meaning of section 2032A(e)(5)) is greater than 50 percent of the taxpayer's gross income for the taxable year.

* * *

(F) Certain private foundations. The private foundations referred to in subparagraph (A)(vii) and subsection (e)(1)(B) are—

(i) a private operating foundation (as defined in section 4942(j)(3)),

(ii) any other private foundation (as defined in section 509(a)) which, not later than the 15th day of the third month after the close of the foundation's taxable year in which contributions are received, makes qualifying distributions (as defined in section 4942(g), without regard to paragraph (3) thereof), which are treated, after the application of section 4942(g)(3), as distributions out of corpus (in accordance with section 4942(h)) in an amount equal to 100 percent of such contributions, and with respect to which the taxpayer obtains adequate records or other sufficient evidence from the foundation showing that the foundation made such qualifying distributions, and

(iii) a private foundation all of the contributions to which are pooled in a common fund and which would be described in section 509(a)(3) but for the right of any substantial contributor (hereafter in this clause called "donor") or his spouse to designate annually the recipients, from among organizations described in paragraph (1) of section 509(a), of the income attributable to the donor's contribution to the fund and to direct (by deed or by will) the payment, to an organization described in such paragraph (1), of the corpus in the common fund attributable to the donor's contribution; but this clause shall apply only if all of the income of the common fund is required to be (and is) distributed to one or more organizations described in such paragraph (1) not later than the 15th day of the third month after the close of the taxable year in which the income is realized by the fund and only if all of the corpus attributable to any donor's contribution to the fund is required to be (and is) distributed to one or more of such organizations not later than one year after his death or after the death of his surviving spouse if she has the right to designate the recipients of such corpus.

(G) Increased limitation for cash contributions.

(i) In general. For taxable years beginning after December 31, 2017, any contribution of cash to an organization described in subparagraph (A) shall be allowed as a deduction under subsection (a) to the extent that the aggregate of such contributions does not exceed the excess of—

(I) 60 percent of the taxpayer's contribution base for the taxable year, over

(II) the aggregate amount of contributions taken into account under subparagraph (A) for such taxable year.

(ii) Carryover. If the aggregate amount of contributions described in clause (i) exceeds the applicable limitation under clause (i) for any taxable year described in such clause, such excess shall be treated (in a manner consistent with the rules of subsection (d)(1)) as a charitable contribution to which clause (i) applies in each of the 5 succeeding years in order of time.

(iii) Coordination with subparagraph (A).

(I) In general. Contributions taken into account under this subparagraph shall not be taken into account under subparagraph (A).

(II) Limitation reduction. For each taxable year described in clause (i), and each taxable year to which any contribution under this subparagraph is carried over under clause (ii), subparagraph (A) shall be applied by reducing (but not below zero) the contribution limitation allowed for the taxable year under such subparagraph by the aggregate contributions allowed under this subparagraph for such taxable year.

(H) Contribution base defined. For purposes of this section, the term "contribution base" means adjusted gross income (computed without regard to any net operating loss carryback to the taxable year under section 172).

(I) 0.5-percent floor. Any charitable contribution otherwise allowable (without regard to this subparagraph) as a deduction under this section shall be allowed only to the extent that the aggregate of such contributions exceeds 0.5 percent of the taxpayer's contribution base for the taxable year. The preceding sentence shall be applied—

(i) first, by taking into account charitable contributions to which subparagraph (D) applies to the extent thereof,

(ii) second, by taking into account charitable contributions to which subparagraph (C) applies to the extent thereof,

(iii) third, by taking into account charitable contributions to which subparagraph (B) applies to the extent thereof,

(iv) fourth, by taking into account charitable contributions to which subparagraph (E) applies to the extent thereof,

(v) fifth, by taking into account charitable contributions to which subparagraph (A) applies to the extent thereof, and

(vi) sixth, by taking into account charitable contributions to which subparagraph (G) applies to the extent thereof.

* * *

(c) Charitable contribution defined. For purposes of this section, the term "charitable contribution" means a contribution or gift to or for the use of—

(1) A State, a possession of the United States, or any political subdivision of any of the foregoing, or the United States or the District of Columbia, but only if the contribution or gift is made for exclusively public purposes.

(2) A corporation, trust, or community chest, fund, or foundation—

(A) created or organized in the United States or in any possession thereof, or under the law of the United States, any State, the District of Columbia, or any possession of the United States;

(B) organized and operated exclusively for religious, charitable, scientific, literary, or educational purposes, or to foster national or international amateur sports competition (but only if no part of its activities involve the provision of athletic facilities or equipment), or for the prevention of cruelty to children or animals;

(C) no part of the net earnings of which inures to the benefit of any private shareholder or individual; and

(D) which is not disqualified for tax exemption under section 501(c)(3) by reason of attempting to influence legislation, and which does not participate in, or intervene in (including the publishing or distributing of statements), any political campaign on behalf of (or in opposition to) any candidate for public office.

A contribution or gift by a corporation to a trust, chest, fund, or foundation shall be deductible by reason of this paragraph only if it is to be used within the United States or any of its possessions exclusively for purposes specified in subparagraph (B). Rules similar to the rules of section 501(j) shall apply for purposes of this paragraph.

(3) A post or organization of war veterans, or an auxiliary unit or society of, or trust or foundation for, any such post or organization—

(A) organized in the United States or any of its possessions, and

(B) no part of the net earnings of which inures to the benefit of any private shareholder or individual.

(4) In the case of a contribution or gift by an individual, a domestic fraternal society, order, or association, operating under the lodge system, but only if such contribution or gift is to be used exclusively for religious, charitable, scientific, literary, or educational purposes, or for the prevention of cruelty to children or animals.

(5) A cemetery company owned and operated exclusively for the benefit of its members, or any corporation chartered solely for burial purposes as a cemetery corporation and not permitted by its charter to engage in any business not necessarily incident to that purpose, if such company or corporation is not operated for profit and no part of the net earnings of such company or corporation inures to the benefit of any private shareholder or individual.

(6) An organization described in section 501(c)(19) that is a federally chartered corporation.

For purposes of this section, the term "charitable contribution" also means an amount treated under subsection (g) as paid for the use of an organization described in paragraph (2), (3), or (4).

(d) Carryovers of excess contributions.

(1) Individuals.

(A) In general. In the case of an individual, if the amount of charitable contributions described in subsection (b)(1)(A) payment of which is made within a taxable year (hereinafter in this paragraph referred to as the "contribution year") exceeds 50 percent of the taxpayer's contribution base for such year, such excess shall be treated as a charitable contribution described in subsection (b)(1)(A) paid in each of the 5 succeeding taxable years in order of time, but, with respect to any such succeeding taxable year, only to the extent of the lesser of the two following amounts:

(i) the amount by which 50 percent of the taxpayer's contribution base for such succeeding taxable year exceeds the sum of the charitable contributions described in subsection (b)(1)(A) payment of which is made by the taxpayer within such succeeding taxable year (determined without regard to this subparagraph) and the charitable contributions described in subsection (b)(1)(A) payment of which was made in taxable years before the contribution year which are treated under this subparagraph as having been paid in such succeeding taxable year; or

(ii) in the case of the first succeeding taxable year, the amount of such excess, and in the case of the second, third, fourth, or fifth succeeding taxable year, the portion of such excess not treated under this subparagraph as a charitable contribution described in subsection (b)(1)(A) paid in any taxable year intervening between the contribution year and such succeeding taxable year.

(B) Special rule for net operating loss carryovers. In applying subparagraph (A), the excess determined under subparagraph (A) for the contribution year shall be reduced to the extent that such excess reduces taxable income (as computed for purposes of the second sentence of section 172(b)(2)) and increases the net operating loss deduction for a taxable year succeeding the contribution year.

* * *

(e) Certain contributions of ordinary income and capital gain property.

(1) General rule. The amount of any charitable contribution of property otherwise taken into account under this section shall be reduced by the sum of—

(A) the amount of gain which would not have been long-term capital gain (determined without regard to section 1221(b)(3)) if the property contributed had been sold by the taxpayer at its fair market value (determined at the time of such contribution), and

(B) in the case of a charitable contribution—

(i) of tangible personal property—

(I) if the use by the donee is unrelated to the purpose or function constituting the basis for its exemption under section 501 (or, in the case of a governmental unit, to any purpose or function described in subsection (c)), or

(II) which is applicable property (as defined in paragraph (7)(C), but without regard to clause (ii) thereof) which is sold, exchanged, or otherwise disposed of by the donee before the last day of the taxable year in which the contribution was made and with respect to which the donee has not made a certification in accordance with paragraph (7)(D),

(ii) to or for the use of a private foundation (as defined in section 509(a)), other than a private foundation described in subsection (b)(1)(F),

(iii) of any patent, copyright (other than a copyright described in section 1221(a)(3) or 1231(b)(1)(C)), trademark, trade name, trade secret, know-how, software (other than software described in section 197(e)(3)(A)(i)), or similar property, or applications or registrations of such property, or

(iv) of any taxidermy property which is contributed by the person who prepared, stuffed, or mounted the property or by any person who paid or incurred the cost of such preparation, stuffing, or mounting,

the amount of gain which would have been long-term capital gain if the property contributed had been sold by the taxpayer at its fair market value (determined at the time of such contribution).

For purposes of applying this paragraph (other than in the case of gain to which section 617(d)(1), 1245(a), 1250(a), 1252(a), or 1254(a) applies), property which is property used in the trade or business (as defined in section 1231(b)) shall be treated as a capital asset. For purposes of applying this paragraph in the case of a charitable contribution of stock in an S corporation, rules similar to the rules of section 751 shall apply in determining whether gain on such stock would have been long-term capital gain if such stock were sold by the taxpayer.

(2) Allocation of basis. For purposes of paragraph (1), in the case of a charitable contribution of less than the taxpayer's entire interest in the property contributed, the taxpayer's adjusted basis in such property shall be allocated between the interest contributed and any interest not contributed in accordance with regulations prescribed by the Secretary.

* * *

(5) Special rule for contributions of stock for which market quotations are readily available.

(A) In general. Subparagraph (B)(ii) of paragraph (1) shall not apply to any contribution of qualified appreciated stock.

(B) Qualified appreciated stock. Except as provided in subparagraph (C), for purposes of this paragraph, the term "qualified appreciated stock" means any stock of a corporation—

(i) for which (as of the date of the contribution) market quotations are readily available on an established securities market, and

(ii) which is capital gain property (as defined in subsection (b)(1)(C)(iv)).

(C) Donor may not contribute more than 10 percent of stock of corporation.

(i) In general. In the case of any donor, the term "qualified appreciated stock" shall not include any stock of a corporation contributed by the donor in a contribution to which paragraph (1)(B)(ii) applies (determined without regard to this paragraph) to the extent that the amount of the stock so contributed (when increased by the aggregate amount of all prior such contributions by the donor of stock in such corporation) exceeds 10 percent (in value) of all of the outstanding stock of such corporation.

(ii) Special rule. For purposes of clause (i), an individual shall be treated as making all contributions made by any member of his family (as defined in section 267(c)(4)).

* * *

(7) Recapture of deduction on certain dispositions of exempt use property.

(A) In general. In the case of an applicable disposition of applicable property, there shall be included in the income of the donor of such property for the taxable year of such donor in which the applicable disposition occurs an amount equal to the excess (if any) of—

(i) the amount of the deduction allowed to the donor under this section with respect to such property, over

(ii) the donor's basis in such property at the time such property was contributed.

(B) Applicable disposition. For purposes of this paragraph, the term "applicable disposition" means any sale, exchange, or other disposition by the donee of applicable property—

(i) after the last day of the taxable year of the donor in which such property was contributed, and

(ii) before the last day of the 3-year period beginning on the date of the contribution of such property,

unless the donee makes a certification in accordance with subparagraph (D).

(C) Applicable property. For purposes of this paragraph, the term "applicable property" means charitable deduction property (as defined in section 6050L(a)(2)(A))—

(i) which is tangible personal property the use of which is identified by the donee as related to the purpose or function constituting the basis of the donee's exemption under section 501, and

(ii) for which a deduction in excess of the donor's basis is allowed.

(D) Certification. A certification meets the requirements of this subparagraph if it is a written statement which is signed under penalty of perjury by an officer of the donee organization and—

(i) which—

(I) certifies that the use of the property by the donee was substantial and related to the purpose or function constituting the basis for the donee's exemption under section 501, and

(II) describes how the property was used and how such use furthered such purpose or function, or

(ii) which—

(I) states the intended use of the property by the donee at the time of the contribution, and

(II) certifies that such intended use has become impossible or infeasible to implement.

(f) Disallowance of deduction in certain cases and special rules.

(1) In general. No deduction shall be allowed under this section for a contribution to or for the use of an organization or trust described in section 508(d) or 4948(c)(4) subject to the conditions specified in such sections.

(2) Contributions of property placed in trust.

(A) Remainder interest. In the case of property transferred in trust, no deduction shall be allowed under this section for the value of a contribution of a remainder interest unless the trust is a charitable remainder annuity trust or a charitable remainder unitrust (described in section 664), or a pooled income fund (described in section 642(c)(5)).

(B) Income interests, etc. No deduction shall be allowed under this section for the value of any interest in property (other than a remainder interest) transferred in trust unless the interest is in the form of a guaranteed annuity or the trust instrument specifies that the interest is a fixed percentage distributed yearly of the fair market value of the trust property (to be determined yearly) and the grantor is treated as the owner of such interest for purposes of applying section 671. If the donor ceases to be treated as the owner of such an interest for purposes of applying section 671, at the time the donor ceases to be so treated, the donor shall for purposes of this chapter be considered as having received an amount of income equal to the amount of any deduction he received under this section for the contribution reduced by the discounted value of all amounts of income earned by the trust and taxable to him before the time at which he ceases to be treated as the owner of the interest. Such amounts of income shall be discounted to the date of the contribution. The Secretary shall prescribe such regulations as may be necessary to carry out the purposes of this subparagraph.

(C) Denial of deduction in case of payments by certain trusts. In any case in which a deduction is allowed under this section for the value of an interest in property described in subparagraph (B), transferred in trust, no deduction shall be allowed under this section to the grantor or any other person for the amount of any contribution made by the trust with respect to such interest.

(D) Exception. This paragraph shall not apply in a case in which the value of all interests in property transferred in trust are deductible under subsection (a).

(3) Denial of deduction in case of certain contributions of partial interests in property.

(A) In general. In the case of a contribution (not made by a transfer in trust) of an interest in property which consists of less than the taxpayer's entire interest in such property, a deduction shall be allowed under this section only to the extent that the value of the interest contributed would be allowable as a deduction under this section if such interest had been transferred in trust. For purposes of this subparagraph, a contribution by a taxpayer of the right to use property shall be treated as a contribution of less than the taxpayer's entire interest in such property.

(B) Exceptions. Subparagraph (A) shall not apply to—

(i) a contribution of a remainder interest in a personal residence or farm,

(ii) a contribution of an undivided portion of the taxpayer's entire interest in property, and

(iii) a qualified conservation contribution.

(4) Valuation of remainder interest in real property. For purposes of this section, in determining the value of a remainder interest in real property, depreciation (computed on the straight line method) and depletion of such property shall be taken into account, and such value shall be discounted at a rate of 6 percent per annum, except that the Secretary may prescribe a different rate.

(5) Reduction for certain interest. If, in connection with any charitable contribution, a liability is assumed by the recipient or by any other person, or if a charitable contribution is of property which is subject to a liability, then, to the extent necessary to avoid the duplication of amounts, the amount taken into account for purposes of this section as the amount of the charitable contribution—

(A) shall be reduced for interest (i) which has been paid (or is to be paid) by the taxpayer, (ii) which is attributable to the liability, and (iii) which is attributable to any period after the making of the contribution, and

(B) in the case of a bond, shall be further reduced for interest (i) which has been paid (or is to be paid) by the taxpayer on indebtedness incurred or continued to purchase or carry such bond, and (ii) which is attributable to any period before the making of the contribution.

The reduction pursuant to subparagraph (B) shall not exceed the interest (including interest equivalent) on the bond which is attributable to any period before the making of the contribution and which is not (under the taxpayer's method of accounting) includible in the gross income of the taxpayer for any taxable year. For purposes of this paragraph, the term "bond" means any bond, debenture, note, or certificate or other evidence of indebtedness.

* * *

(7) Reformations to comply with paragraph (2).

(A) In general. A deduction shall be allowed under subsection (a) in respect of any qualified reformation (within the meaning of section 2055(e)(3)(B)).

(B) Rules similar to section 2055(e)(3) to apply. For purposes of this paragraph, rules similar to the rules of section 2055(e)(3) shall apply.

* * *

(10) Split-dollar life insurance, annuity, and endowment contracts.

(A) In general. Nothing in this section or in section 545(b)(2), 642(c), 2055, 2106(a)(2), or 2522 shall be construed to allow a deduction, and no deduction shall be allowed, for any transfer to or for the use of an organization described in subsection (c) if in connection with such transfer—

(i) the organization directly or indirectly pays, or has previously paid, any premium on any personal benefit contract with respect to the transferor, or

(ii) there is an understanding or expectation that any person will directly or indirectly pay any premium on any personal benefit contract with respect to the transferor.

(B) Personal benefit contract. For purposes of subparagraph (A), the term "personal benefit contract" means, with respect to the transferor, any life insurance, annuity, or endowment contract if any direct or indirect beneficiary under such contract is the transferor, any member of the transferor's family, or any other person (other than an organization described in subsection (c)) designated by the transferor.

(C) Application to charitable remainder trusts. In the case of a transfer to a trust referred to in subparagraph (E), references in subparagraphs (A) and (F) to an organization described in subsection (c) shall be treated as a reference to such trust.

(D) Exception for certain annuity contracts. If, in connection with a transfer to or for the use of an organization described in subsection (c), such organization incurs an obligation to pay a charitable gift annuity (as defined in section 501(m)) and such organization purchases any annuity contract to fund such obligation, persons receiving payments under the charitable gift annuity shall not be treated for purposes of subparagraph (B) as indirect beneficiaries under such contract if—

(i) such organization possesses all of the incidents of ownership under such contract,

(ii) such organization is entitled to all the payments under such contract, and

(iii) the timing and amount of payments under such contract are substantially the same as the timing and amount of payments to each such person under such obligation (as such obligation is in effect at the time of such transfer).

(E) Exception for certain contracts held by charitable remainder trusts. A person shall not be treated for purposes of subparagraph (B) as an indirect beneficiary under any life insurance, annuity, or endowment contract held by a charitable remainder annuity trust or a charitable remainder unitrust (as defined in section 664(d)) solely by reason of being entitled to any payment referred to in paragraph (1)(A) or (2)(A) of section 664(d) if—

(i) such trust possesses all of the incidents of ownership under such contract, and

(ii) such trust is entitled to all the payments under such contract.

(F) Excise tax on premiums paid.

(i) In general. There is hereby imposed on any organization described in subsection (c) an excise tax equal to the premiums paid by such organization on any life insurance, annuity, or endowment contract if the payment of premiums on such contract is in connection with a transfer for which a deduction is not allowable under subparagraph (A), determined without regard to when such transfer is made.

(ii) Payments by other persons. For purposes of clause (i), payments made by any other person pursuant to an understanding or expectation referred to in subparagraph (A) shall be treated as made by the organization.

(iii) Reporting. Any organization on which tax is imposed by clause (i) with respect to any premium shall file an annual return which includes—

(I) the amount of such premiums paid during the year and the name and TIN of each beneficiary under the contract to which the premium relates, and

(II) such other information as the Secretary may require.

The penalties applicable to returns required under section 6033 shall apply to returns required under this clause. Returns required under this clause shall be furnished at such time and in such manner as the Secretary shall by forms or regulations require.

(iv) Certain rules to apply. The tax imposed by this subparagraph shall be treated as imposed by chapter 42 for purposes of this title other than subchapter B of chapter 42.

(G) Special rule where State requires specification of charitable gift annuitant in contract. In the case of an obligation to pay a charitable gift annuity referred to in subparagraph (D) which is entered into under the laws of a State which requires, in order for the charitable gift annuity to be exempt from insurance regulation by such State, that each beneficiary under the charitable gift annuity be named as a beneficiary under an annuity contract issued by an insurance company authorized to transact business in such State, the requirements of clauses (i) and (ii) of subparagraph (D) shall be treated as met if—

(i) such State law requirement was in effect on February 8, 1999,

(ii) each such beneficiary under the charitable gift annuity is a bona fide resident of such State at the time the obligation to pay a charitable gift annuity is entered into, and

(iii) the only persons entitled to payments under such contract are persons entitled to payments as beneficiaries under such obligation on the date such obligation is entered into.

(H) Member of family. For purposes of this paragraph, an individual's family consists of the individual's grandparents, the grandparents of such individual's spouse, the lineal descendants of such grandparents, and any spouse of such a lineal descendant.

(I) Regulations. The Secretary shall prescribe such regulations as may be necessary or appropriate to carry out the purposes of this paragraph, including regulations to prevent the avoidance of such purposes.

(11) Qualified appraisal and other documentation for certain contributions.

(A) In general.

(i) Denial of deduction. In the case of an individual, partnership, or corporation, no deduction shall be allowed under subsection (a) for any contribution of property for which a deduction of more than $500 is claimed unless such person meets the requirements of subparagraphs (B), (C), and (D), as the case may be, with respect to such contribution.

(ii) Exceptions.

(I) Readily valued property. Subparagraphs (C) and (D) shall not apply to cash, property described in subsection (e)(1)(B)(iii) or section 1221(a)(1), publicly traded securities (as defined in section 6050L(a)(2)(B)), and any qualified vehicle described in paragraph (12)(A)(ii) for which an acknowledgement under paragraph (12)(B)(iii) is provided.

(II) Reasonable cause. Clause (i) shall not apply if it is shown that the failure to meet such requirements is due to reasonable cause and not to willful neglect.

(B) Property description for contributions of more than $500. In the case of contributions of property for which a deduction of more than $500 is claimed, the requirements of this subparagraph are met if the individual, partnership or corporation includes with the return for the taxable year in which the contribution is made a description of such property and such other information as the Secretary may require. The requirements of this subparagraph shall not apply to a C corporation which is not a personal service corporation or a closely held C corporation.

(C) Qualified appraisal for contributions of more than $5,000. In the case of contributions of property for which a deduction of more than $5,000 is claimed, the requirements of this subparagraph are met if the individual, partnership, or corporation obtains a qualified appraisal of such property and attaches to the return for the taxable year in which such contribution is made such information regarding such property and such appraisal as the Secretary may require.

(D) Substantiation for contributions of more than $500,000. In the case of contributions of property for which a deduction of more than $500,000 is claimed, the requirements of this subparagraph are met if the individual, partnership, or corporation attaches to the return for the taxable year a qualified appraisal of such property.

(E) Qualified appraisal and appraiser. For purposes of this paragraph—

(i) Qualified appraisal. The term "qualified appraisal" means, with respect to any property, an appraisal of such property which—

(I) is treated for purposes of this paragraph as a qualified appraisal under regulations or other guidance prescribed by the Secretary, and

(II) is conducted by a qualified appraiser in accordance with generally accepted appraisal standards and any regulations or other guidance prescribed under subclause (I).

(ii) Qualified appraiser. Except as provided in clause (iii), the term "qualified appraiser" means an individual who—

(I) has earned an appraisal designation from a recognized professional appraiser organization or has otherwise met minimum education and experience requirements set forth in regulations prescribed by the Secretary,

(II) regularly performs appraisals for which the individual receives compensation, and

(III) meets such other requirements as may be prescribed by the Secretary in regulations or other guidance.

(iii) Specific appraisals. An individual shall not be treated as a qualified appraiser with respect to any specific appraisal unless—

(I) the individual demonstrates verifiable education and experience in valuing the type of property subject to the appraisal, and

(II) the individual has not been prohibited from practicing before the Internal Revenue Service by the Secretary under section 330(c) of title 31, United States Code, at any time during the 3-year period ending on the date of the appraisal.

(F) Aggregation of similar items of property. For purposes of determining thresholds under this paragraph, property and all similar items of property donated to 1 or more donees shall be treated as 1 property.

(G) Special rule for pass-thru entities. In the case of a partnership or S corporation, this paragraph shall be applied at the entity level, except that the deduction shall be denied at the partner or shareholder level.

(H) Regulations. The Secretary may prescribe such regulations as may be necessary or appropriate to carry out the purposes of this paragraph, including regulations that may provide that some or all of the requirements of this paragraph do not apply in appropriate cases.

* * *

(17) Recordkeeping. No deduction shall be allowed under subsection (a) for any contribution of a cash, check, or other monetary gift unless the donor maintains as a record of such contribution a bank record or a written communication from the donee showing the name of the donee organization, the date of the contribution, and the amount of the contribution.

(18) Contributions to donor advised funds. A deduction otherwise allowed under subsection (a) for any contribution to a donor advised fund (as defined in section 4966(d)(2)) shall only be allowed if—

(A) the sponsoring organization (as defined in section 4966(d)(1)) with respect to such donor advised fund is not—

(i) described in paragraph (3), (4), or (5) of subsection (c), or

(ii) a type III supporting organization (as defined in section 4943(f)(5)(A)) which is not a functionally integrated type III supporting organization (as defined in section 4943(f)(5)(B)), and

(B) the taxpayer obtains a contemporaneous written acknowledgment (determined under rules similar to the rules of paragraph (8)(C)) from the sponsoring organization (as so defined) of such donor advised fund that such organization has exclusive legal control over the assets contributed.

* * *

(h) Qualified conservation contribution.

(1) In general. For purposes of subsection (f)(3)(B)(iii), the term "qualified conservation contribution" means a contribution—

(A) of a qualified real property interest,

(B) to a qualified organization,

(C) exclusively for conservation purposes.

(2) Qualified real property interest. For purposes of this subsection, the term "qualified real property interest" means any of the following interests in real property:

(A) the entire interest of the donor other than a qualified mineral interest,

(B) a remainder interest, and

(C) a restriction (granted in perpetuity) on the use which may be made of the real property.

(3) Qualified organization. For purposes of paragraph (1), the term "qualified organization" means an organization which—

(A) is described in clause (v) or (vi) of subsection (b)(1)(A), or

(B) is described in section 501(c)(3) and—

(i) meets the requirements of section 509(a)(2), or

(ii) meets the requirements of section 509(a)(3) and is controlled by an organization described in subparagraph (A) or in clause (i) of this subparagraph.

(4) Conservation purpose defined.

(A) In general. For purposes of this subsection, the term "conservation purpose" means—

(i) the preservation of land areas for outdoor recreation by, or the education of, the general public,

(ii) the protection of a relatively natural habitat of fish, wildlife, or plants, or similar ecosystem,

(iii) the preservation of open space (including farmland and forest land) where such preservation is—

(I) for the scenic enjoyment of the general public, or

(II) pursuant to a clearly delineated Federal, State, or local governmental conservation policy, and will yield a significant public benefit, or

(iv) the preservation of an historically important land area or a certified historic structure.

(B) Special rules with respect to buildings in registered historic districts. In the case of any contribution of a qualified real property interest which is a restriction with respect to the exterior of a building described in subparagraph (C)(ii), such contribution shall not be considered to be exclusively for conservation purposes unless—

(i) such interest—

(I) includes a restriction which preserves the entire exterior of the building (including the front, sides, rear, and height of the building), and

(II) prohibits any change in the exterior of the building which is inconsistent with the historical character of such exterior,

(ii) the donor and donee enter into a written agreement certifying, under penalty of perjury, that the donee—

(I) is a qualified organization (as defined in paragraph (3)) with a purpose of environmental protection, land conservation, open space preservation, or historic preservation, and

(II) has the resources to manage and enforce the restriction and a commitment to do so, and

(iii) in the case of any contribution made in a taxable year beginning after the date of the enactment of this subparagraph, the taxpayer includes with the taxpayer's return for the taxable year of the contribution—

(I) a qualified appraisal (within the meaning of subsection (f)(11)(E)) of the qualified property interest,

(II) photographs of the entire exterior of the building, and

(III) a description of all restrictions on the development of the building.

(C) Certified historic structure. For purposes of subparagraph (A)(iv), the term "certified historic structure" means—

(i) any building, structure, or land area which is listed in the National Register, or

(ii) any building which is located in a registered historic district (as defined in section 47(c)(3)(B)) and is certified by the Secretary of the Interior to the Secretary as being of historic significance to the district.

A building, structure, or land area satisfies the preceding sentence if it satisfies such sentence either at the time of the transfer or on the due date (including extensions) for filing the transferor's return under this chapter for the taxable year in which the transfer is made.

(5) Exclusively for conservation purposes. For purposes of this subsection—

(A) Conservation purpose must be protected. A contribution shall not be treated as exclusively for conservation purposes unless the conservation purpose is protected in perpetuity.

(B) No surface mining permitted.

(i) In general. Except as provided in clause (ii), in the case of a contribution of any interest where there is a retention of a qualified mineral interest, subparagraph (A) shall not be treated as met if at any time there may be extraction or removal of minerals by any surface mining method.

(ii) Special rule. With respect to any contribution of property in which the ownership of the surface estate and mineral interests has been and remains separated, subparagraph (A) shall be treated as met if the probability of surface mining occurring on such property is so remote as to be negligible.

(6) Qualified mineral interest. For purposes of this subsection, the term "qualified mineral interest" means—

(A) subsurface oil, gas, or other minerals, and

(B) the right to access to such minerals.

* * *

(*o*) Special rules for fractional gifts.

(1) Denial of deduction in certain cases.

(A) In general. No deduction shall be allowed for a contribution of an undivided portion of a taxpayer's entire interest in tangible personal property unless all interests in the property are held immediately before such contribution by—

(i) the taxpayer, or

(ii) the taxpayer and the donee.

(B) Exceptions. The Secretary may, by regulation, provide for exceptions to subparagraph (A) in cases where all persons who hold an interest in the property make proportional contributions of an undivided portion of the entire interest held by such persons.

(2) Valuation of subsequent gifts. In the case of any additional contribution, the fair market value of such contribution shall be determined by using the lesser of—

(A) the fair market value of the property at the time of the initial fractional contribution, or

(B) the fair market value of the property at the time of the additional contribution.

(3) Recapture of deduction in certain cases; addition to tax.

(A) Recapture. The Secretary shall provide for the recapture of the amount of any deduction allowed under this section (plus interest) with respect to any contribution of an undivided portion of a taxpayer's entire interest in tangible personal property—

(i) in any case in which the donor does not contribute all of the remaining interests in such property to the donee (or, if such donee is no longer in existence, to any person described in section 170(c)) on or before the earlier of—

(I) the date that is 10 years after the date of the initial fractional contribution, or

(II) the date of the death of the donor, and

(ii) in any case in which the donee has not, during the period beginning on the date of the initial fractional contribution and ending on the date described in clause (i)—

(I) had substantial physical possession of the property, and

(II) used the property in a use which is related to a purpose or function constituting the basis for the organizations' exemption under section 501.

(B) Addition to tax. The tax imposed under this chapter for any taxable year for which there is a recapture under subparagraph (A) shall be increased by 10 percent of the amount so recaptured.

(4) Definitions. For purposes of this subsection—

(A) Additional contribution. The term "additional contribution" means any charitable contribution by the taxpayer of any interest in property with respect to which the taxpayer has previously made an initial fractional contribution.

(B) Initial fractional contribution. The term "initial fractional contribution" means, with respect to any taxpayer, the first charitable contribution of an undivided portion of the taxpayer's entire interest in any tangible personal property.

(p) Special rule for taxpayers who do not elect to itemize deductions. In the case of any taxable year, if the individual does not elect to itemize deductions for such taxable year, the deduction under this section shall be equal to the deduction, not in excess of $1,000 ($2,000 in the case of a joint return), which would be determined under this section if the only charitable contributions taken into account in determining such deduction were contributions made in cash during such taxable year (determined without regard to subsections (b)(1)(G)(ii), (b)(1)(I) , and (d)(1)) to an organization described in section 170(b)(1)(A) and not—

(1) to an organization described in section 509(a)(3), or

(2) for the establishment of a new, or maintenance of an existing, donor advised fund (as defined in section 4966(d)(2)).

(q) Other cross references.

* * *

(2) For charitable contributions of estates and trusts, see section 642(c).

* * *

Part VII. Additional Itemized Deductions for Individuals

§ 212. Expenses for Production of Income

In the case of an individual, there shall be allowed as a deduction all the ordinary and necessary expenses paid or incurred during the taxable year—

(1) for the production or collection of income;

(2) for the management, conservation, or maintenance of property held for the production of income; or

(3) in connection with the determination, collection, or refund of any tax.

§ 213. Medical, Dental, Etc., Expenses

(a) Allowance of deduction. There shall be allowed as a deduction the expenses paid during the taxable year, not compensated for by insurance or otherwise, for medical care of the taxpayer, his spouse, or a dependent (as defined in section 152, determined without regard to subsections (b)(1), (b)(2), and (d)(1)(B) thereof), to the extent that such expenses exceed 7.5 percent of adjusted gross income.

* * *

(c) Special rule for decedents.

(1) Treatment of expenses paid after death.—For purposes of subsection (a), expenses for the medical care of the taxpayer which are paid out of his estate during the 1-year period beginning with the day after the date of his death shall be treated as paid by the taxpayer at the time incurred.

(2) Limitation.—Paragraph (1) shall not apply if the amount paid is allowable under section 2053 as a deduction in computing the taxable estate of the decedent, but this paragraph shall not apply if (within the time and in the manner and form prescribed by the Secretary) there is filed—

(A) a statement that such amount has not been allowed as a deduction under section 2053, and

(B) a waiver of the right to have such amount allowed at any time as a deduction under section 2053.

* * *

Part IX. Items Not Deductible

§ 267. Losses, Expenses, and Interest with Respect to Transactions Between Related Taxpayers

(a) In general.

(1) Deduction for losses disallowed. No deduction shall be allowed in respect of any loss from the sale or exchange of property, directly or indirectly, between persons specified in any of the paragraphs of subsection (b). The preceding sentence shall not apply to any loss of the distributing corporation (or the distributee) in the case of a distribution in complete liquidation.

* * *

(b) Relationships. The persons referred to in subsection (a) are:

* * *

(4) A grantor and a fiduciary of any trust;

(5) A fiduciary of a trust and a fiduciary of another trust, if the same person is a grantor of both trusts;

(6) A fiduciary of a trust and a beneficiary of such trust;

(7) A fiduciary of a trust and a beneficiary of another trust, if the same person is a grantor of both trusts;

(8) A fiduciary of a trust and a corporation more than 50 percent in value of the outstanding stock of which is owned, directly or indirectly, by or for the trust or by or for a person who is a grantor of the trust;

* * *

(13) Except in the case of a sale or exchange in satisfaction of a pecuniary bequest, an executor of an estate and a beneficiary of such estate.

(c) Constructive ownership of stock. For purposes of determining, in applying subsection (b), the ownership of stock—

(1) Stock owned, directly or indirectly, by or for a corporation, partnership, estate, or trust shall be considered as being owned proportionately by or for its shareholders, partners, or beneficiaries;

(2) An individual shall be considered as owning the stock owned, directly or indirectly, by or for his family;

* * *

(4) The family of an individual shall include only his brothers and sisters (whether by the whole or half blood), spouse, ancestors, and lineal descendants; and

(5) Stock constructively owned by a person by reason of the application of paragraph (1) shall, for the purpose of applying paragraph (1), (2), or (3), be treated as actually owned by such person, but stock constructively owned by an individual by reason of the application of paragraph (2) or (3) shall not be treated as owned by him for the purpose of again applying either of such paragraphs in order to make another the constructive owner of such stock.

(d) Amount of Gain Where Loss Previously Disallowed.

(1) In General. If—

(A) in the case of a sale or exchange of property to the taxpayer a loss sustained by the transferor is not allowable to the transferor as a deduction by reason of subsection (a)(1), and

(B) the taxpayer sells or otherwise disposes of such property (or of other property the basis of which in the taxpayer's hands is determined directly or indirectly by reference to such property) at a gain, then such gain shall be recognized only to the extent that it exceeds so much of such loss as is properly allocable to the property sold or otherwise disposed of by the taxpayer.

(2) Exception for Wash Sales. Paragraph (1) shall not apply if the loss sustained by the transferor is not allowable to the transferor as a deduction by reason of section 1091 (relating to wash sales).

(3) Exception for Transfers from Tax Indifferent Parties. Paragraph (1) shall not apply to the extent any loss sustained by the transferor (if allowed) would not be taken into account in determining a tax imposed under section 1 or 11 or a tax computed as provided by either of such sections.

* * *

(g) Coordination with section 1041. Subsection (a)(1) shall not apply to any transfer described in section 1041(a) (relating to transfers of property between spouses or incident to divorce).

Regulation

§ 1.267(a)–1 Deductions disallowed.

* * *

(c) Scope of section. Section 267(a) requires that deductions for losses or unpaid expenses or interest described therein be disallowed even though the transaction in which such losses, expenses, or interest were incurred was a bona fide transaction. However, section 267 is not exclusive. No deduction for losses or unpaid expenses or interest arising in a transaction which is not bona fide will be allowed even though section 267 does not apply to the transaction.

[T.D. 6500, 25 FR 11402, Nov. 26, 1960]

§ 273. Holders of Life or Terminable Interest

Amounts paid under the laws of a State, the District of Columbia, a possession of the United States, or a foreign country as income to the holder of a life or terminable interest acquired by gift, bequest, or inheritance shall not be reduced or diminished by any deduction for shrinkage (by whatever name called) in the value of such interest due to the lapse of time.

Regulation

§ 1.273–1 Life or terminable interests.

(a) In general. Amounts paid as income to the holder of a life or a terminable interest acquired by gift, bequest, or inheritance shall not be subject to any deduction for shrinkage (whether called by depreciation or any other name) in the value of such interest due to the lapse of time. In other words, the holder of such an interest so acquired may not set up the value of the expected future payments as corpus or principal and claim deduction for shrinkage or exhaustion thereof due to the passage of time. For the treatment generally of distributions to beneficiaries of an estate or trust, see Subparts A, B, C, and D (section 641 and following), Subchapter J, Chapter 1 of the Code, and the regulations thereunder. For basis of property acquired from a decedent and by gifts and transfers in trust, see sections 1014, 1015, and 1022, and the regulations thereunder.

(b) Effective/applicability date. The provisions in this section are applicable for taxable years beginning on or after September 16, 1958. The provisions of this section relating to section 1022 are effective on and after January 19, 2017.

[T.D. 6500, 25 FR 11402, Nov. 26, 1960; T.D. 9811, 82 FR 6237, Jan. 19, 2017]

Subchapter C. Corporate Distributions and Adjustments

Part I. Distributions by Corporations

Subpart A. Effects on Recipients

§ 303. Distributions in Redemption of Stock to Pay Death Taxes

(a) In general. A distribution of property to a shareholder by a corporation in redemption of part or all of the stock of such corporation which (for Federal estate tax purposes) is included in determining the gross estate of a decedent, to the extent that the amount of such distribution does not exceed the sum of—

(1) the estate, inheritance, legacy, and succession taxes (including any interest collected as a part of such taxes) imposed because of such decedent's death, and

(2) the amount of funeral and administration expenses allowable as deductions to the estate under section 2053 (or under section 2106 in the case of the estate of a decedent nonresident, not a citizen of the United States),

shall be treated as a distribution in full payment in exchange for the stock so redeemed.

(b) Limitations on application of subsection (a).

(1) Period for distribution. Subsection (a) shall apply only to amounts distributed after the death of the decedent and—

(A) within the period of limitations provided in section 6501(a) for the assessment of the Federal estate tax (determined without the application of any provision other than section 6501(a)), or within 90 days after the expiration of such period,

(B) if a petition for redetermination of a deficiency in such estate tax has been filed with the Tax Court within the time prescribed in section 6213, at any time before the expiration of 60 days after the decision of the Tax Court becomes final, or

(C) if an election has been made under section 6166 and if the time prescribed by this subparagraph expires at a later date than the time prescribed by subparagraph (B) of this paragraph, within the time determined under section 6166 for the payment of the installments.

(2) Relationship of stock to decedent's estate.

(A) In general. Subsection (a) shall apply to a distribution by a corporation only if the value (for Federal estate tax purposes) of all of the stock of such corporation which is included in determining the value of the decedent's gross estate exceeds 35 percent of the excess of—

(i) the value of the gross estate of such decedent, over

(ii) the sum of the amounts allowable as a deduction under section 2053 or 2054.

(B) Special rule for stock in 2 or more corporations. For purposes of subparagraph (A), stock of 2 or more corporations, with respect to each of which there is included in determining the value of the decedent's gross estate 20 percent or more in value of the outstanding stock, shall be treated as the stock of a single corporation. For purposes of the 20-percent requirement of the preceding sentence, stock which, at the decedent's death, represents the surviving spouse's interest in property held by the decedent and the surviving spouse as community property or as joint tenants, tenants by the entirety, or tenants in common shall be treated as having been included in determining the value of the decedent's gross estate.

(3) Relationship of shareholder to estate tax. Subsection (a) shall apply to a distribution by a corporation only to the extent that the interest of the shareholder is reduced directly (or through a binding obligation to contribute) by any payment of an amount described in paragraph (1) or (2) of subsection (a).

(4) Additional requirements for distributions made more than 4 years after decedent's death. In the case of amounts distributed more than 4 years after the date of the decedent's death, subsection (a) shall apply to a distribution by a corporation only to the extent of the lesser of—

(A) the aggregate of the amounts referred to in paragraph (1) or (2) of subsection (a) which remained unpaid immediately before the distribution, or

(B) the aggregate of the amounts referred to in paragraph (1) or (2) of subsection (a) which are paid during the 1-year period beginning on the date of such distribution.

(c) Stock with substituted basis. If—

(1) a shareholder owns stock of a corporation (referred to in this subsection as "new stock") the basis of which is determined by reference to the basis of stock of a corporation (referred to in this subsection as "old stock"),

(2) the old stock was included (for Federal estate tax purposes) in determining the gross estate of a decedent, and

(3) subsection (a) would apply to a distribution of property to such shareholder in redemption of the old stock,

then, subject to the limitations specified in subsection (b), subsection (a) shall apply in respect of a distribution in redemption of the new stock.

(d) Special rules for generation-skipping transfers. Where stock in a corporation is the subject of a generation-skipping transfer (within the meaning of section 2611(a)) occurring at the same time as and as a result of the death of an individual—

(1) the stock shall be deemed to be included in the gross estate of such individual;

(2) taxes of the kind referred to in subsection (a)(1) which are imposed because of the generation-skipping transfer shall be treated as imposed because of such individual's death (and for this purpose the tax imposed by section 2601 shall be treated as an estate tax);

(3) the period of distribution shall be measured from the date of the generation-skipping transfer; and

(4) the relationship of stock to the decedent's estate shall be measured with reference solely to the amount of the generation-skipping transfer.

Subpart C. Definitions; Constructive Ownership of Stock

§ 318. Constructive Ownership of Stock

(a) General rule. For purposes of those provisions of this subchapter to which the rules contained in this section are expressly made applicable—

(1) Members of family.

(A) In general. An individual shall be considered as owning the stock owned, directly or indirectly, by or for—

(i) his spouse (other than a spouse who is legally separated from the individual under a decree of divorce or separate maintenance), and

(ii) his children, grandchildren, and parents.

(B) Effect of adoption. For purposes of subparagraph (A)(ii), a legally adopted child of an individual shall be treated as a child of such individual by blood.

(2) Attribution from partnerships, estates, trusts, and corporations.

(A) From partnerships and estates. Stock owned, directly or indirectly, by or for a partnership or estate shall be considered as owned proportionately by its partners or beneficiaries.

(B) From trusts.

(i) Stock owned, directly or indirectly, by or for a trust (other than an employees' trust described in section 401(a) which is exempt from tax under section 501(a)) shall be considered as owned by its beneficiaries in proportion to the actuarial interest of such beneficiaries in such trust.

(ii) Stock owned, directly or indirectly, by or for any portion of a trust of which a person is considered the owner under subpart E of part I of subchapter J (relating to grantors and others treated as substantial owners) shall be considered as owned by such person.

(C) From corporations. If 50 percent or more in value of the stock in a corporation is owned, directly or indirectly, by or for any person, such person shall be considered as owning the stock owned, directly or indirectly, by or for such corporation, in that proportion which the value of the stock which such person so owns bears to the value of all the stock in such corporation.

(3) Attribution to partnerships, estates, trusts, and corporations.

(A) To partnerships and estates. Stock owned, directly or indirectly, by or for a partner or a beneficiary of an estate shall be considered as owned by the partnership or estate.

(B) To trusts.

(i) Stock owned, directly or indirectly, by or for a beneficiary of a trust (other than an employees' trust described in section 401(a) which is exempt from tax under section 501(a)) shall be considered as owned by the trust, unless such beneficiary's interest in the trust is a remote contingent interest. For purposes of this clause, a contingent interest of a beneficiary in a trust shall be considered remote if, under the maximum exercise of discretion by the trustee in favor of such beneficiary, the value of such interest, computed actuarially, is 5 percent or less of the value of the trust property.

(ii) Stock owned, directly or indirectly, by or for a person who is considered the owner of any portion of a trust under subpart E of part I of subchapter J (relating to grantors and others treated as substantial owners) shall be considered as owned by the trust.

(C) To corporations. If 50 percent or more in value of the stock in a corporation is owned, directly or indirectly, by or for any person, such corporation shall be considered as owning the stock owned, directly or indirectly, by or for such person.

(4) Options. If any person has an option to acquire stock, such stock shall be considered as owned by such person. For purposes of this paragraph, an option to acquire such an option, and each one of a series of such options, shall be considered as an option to acquire such stock.

(5) Operating rules.

(A) In general. Except as provided in subparagraphs (B) and (C), stock constructively owned by a person by reason of the application of paragraph (1), (2), (3), or (4), shall, for purposes of applying paragraphs (1), (2), (3), and (4), be considered as actually owned by such person.

(B) Members of family. Stock constructively owned by an individual by reason of the application of paragraph (1) shall not be considered as owned by him for purposes of again applying paragraph (1) in order to make another the constructive owner of such stock.

(C) Partnerships, estates, trusts, and corporations. Stock constructively owned by a partnership, estate, trust, or corporation by reason of the application of paragraph (3) shall not be considered as owned by it for purposes of applying paragraph (2) in order to make another the constructive owner of such stock.

(D) Option rule in lieu of family rule.—For purposes of this paragraph, if stock may be considered as owned by an individual under paragraph (1) or (4), it shall be considered as owned by him under paragraph (4).

* * *

Subchapter E. Accounting Periods and Methods of Accounting

Part I. Accounting Periods

§ 443. Returns for a Period of Less than 12 Months

(a) Returns for short period. A return for a period of less than 12 months (referred to in this section as "short period") shall be made under any of the following circumstances:

* * *

(2) Taxpayer not in existence for entire taxable year. When the taxpayer is in existence during only part of what would otherwise be his taxable year.

* * *

(c) Adjustment in deduction for personal exemption. In the case of a taxpayer other than a corporation, if a return is made for a short period by reason of subsection (a)(1) and if the tax is not computed under subsection (b)(2), then the exemptions allowed as a deduction under section 151 (and any deduction in lieu thereof) shall be reduced to amounts which bear the same ratio to the full exemptions as the number of months in the short period bears to 12.

Subchapter F. Exempt Organizations

Part VIII. Certain Savings Entities

§ 529. Qualified Tuition Programs

(a) General rule. A qualified tuition program shall be exempt from taxation under this subtitle. Notwithstanding the preceding sentence, such program shall be subject to the taxes imposed by section 511 (relating to imposition of tax on unrelated business income of charitable organizations).

* * *

(c) Tax treatment of designated beneficiaries and contributors

* * *

(2) Gift tax treatment of contributions. For purposes of chapters 12 and 13—

(A) In general. Any contribution to a qualified tuition program on behalf of any designated beneficiary—

(i) shall be treated as a completed gift to such beneficiary which is not a future interest in property, and

(ii) shall not be treated as a qualified transfer under section 2503(e).

(B) Treatment of excess contributions. If the aggregate amount of contributions described in subparagraph (A) during the calendar year by a donor exceeds the limitation for such year under section 2503(b), such aggregate amount shall, at the election of the donor, be taken into account for purposes of such section ratably over the 5-year period beginning with such calendar year.

* * *

(4) Estate tax treatment.

(A) In general. No amount shall be includible in the gross estate of any individual for purposes of chapter 11 by reason of an interest in a qualified tuition program.

(B) Amounts includible in estate of designated beneficiary in certain cases. Subparagraph (A) shall not apply to amounts distributed on account of the death of a beneficiary.

(C) Amounts includible in estate of donor making excess contributions. In the case of a donor who makes the election described in paragraph (2)(B) and who dies before the close of the 5-year period referred to in such paragraph, notwithstanding subparagraph (A), the gross estate of the donor shall include the portion of such contributions properly allocable to periods after the date of death of the donor.

(5) Other gift tax rules. For purposes of chapters 12 and 13—

(A) Treatment of distributions. Except as provided in subparagraph (B), in no event shall a distribution from a qualified tuition program be treated as a taxable gift.

(B) Treatment of designation of new beneficiary. The taxes imposed by chapters 12 and 13 shall apply to a transfer by reason of a change in the designated beneficiary under the program (or a rollover to the account of a new beneficiary) unless the new beneficiary is—

(i) assigned to the same generation as (or a higher generation than) the old beneficiary (determined in accordance with section 2651), and

(ii) a member of the family of the old beneficiary.

(6) Additional tax. The tax imposed by section 530(d)(4) shall apply to any payment or distribution from a qualified tuition program in the same manner as such tax applies to a payment or distribution from a Coverdell education savings account. This paragraph shall not apply to any payment or distribution in any taxable year beginning before January 1, 2004, which is includible in gross income but used for qualified higher education expenses of the designated beneficiary.

* * *

(e) Other definitions and special rules. For purposes of this section—

(1) Designated beneficiary. The term "designated beneficiary" means—

(A) the individual designated at the commencement of participation in the qualified tuition program as the beneficiary of amounts paid (or to be paid) to the program,

(B) in the case of a change in beneficiaries described in subsection (c)(3)(C), the individual who is the new beneficiary, and

(C) in the case of an interest in a qualified tuition program purchased by a State or local government (or agency or instrumentality thereof) or an organization described in section 501(c)(3) and exempt from taxation under section 501(a) as part of a scholarship program operated by such government or organization, the individual receiving such interest as a scholarship.

(2) Member of family. The term "member of the family" means, with respect to any designated beneficiary—

(A) the spouse of such beneficiary;

(B) an individual who bears a relationship to such beneficiary which is described in subparagraphs (A) through (G) of section 152(d)(2);

(C) the spouse of any individual described in subparagraph (B); and

(D) any first cousin of such beneficiary.

(3) Qualified higher education expenses.

(A) In general. The term "qualified higher education expenses" means

(i) tuition, fees, books, supplies, and equipment required for the enrollment or attendance of a designated beneficiary at an eligible educational institution,

(ii) expenses for special needs services in the case of a special needs beneficiary which are incurred in connection with such enrollment or attendance, and

(iii) expenses for the purchase of computer or peripheral equipment (as defined in section 168(i)(2)(B)), computer software (as defined in section 197(e)(3)(B)), or Internet access and related services, if such equipment, software, or services are to be used primarily by the beneficiary during any of the years the beneficiary is enrolled at an eligible educational institution.

Clause (iii) shall not include expenses for computer software designed for sports, games, or hobbies unless the software is predominantly educational in nature. The amount of cash distributions from all qualified tuition programs described in subsection (b)(1)(A)(ii) with respect to a beneficiary during any taxable year shall, in the aggregate, include not more than $20,000 in expenses described in subsection (c)(7) incurred during the taxable year.

(B) Room and board included for students who are at least half-time.

(i) In general. In the case of an individual who is an eligible student (as defined in section 25A(b)(3)) for any academic period, such term shall also include reasonable costs for such period (as determined under the qualified tuition program) incurred by the designated beneficiary for room and board while attending such institution. For purposes of subsection (b)(6), a designated beneficiary shall be treated as meeting the requirements of this clause.

(ii) Limitation. The amount treated as qualified higher education expenses by reason of clause (i) shall not exceed—

(I) the allowance (applicable to the student) for room and board included in the cost of attendance (as defined in section 472 of the Higher Education Act of 1965 (20 U.S.C. 1087ll), as in effect on the date of the enactment of the Economic Growth and Tax Relief Reconciliation Act of 2001) as determined by the eligible educational institution for such period, or

(II) if greater, the actual invoice amount the student residing in housing owned or operated by the eligible educational institution is charged by such institution for room and board costs for such period.

* * *

(4) Application of section 514. An interest in a qualified tuition program shall not be treated as debt for purposes of section 514.

(5) Eligible educational institution. The term "eligible educational institution" means an institution—

(A) which is described in section 481 of the Higher Education Act of 1965 (20 U.S.C. 1088), as in effect on the date of the enactment of this paragraph, and

(B) which is eligible to participate in a program under title IV of such Act.

* * *

(g) Regulations. Notwithstanding any other provision of this section, the Secretary shall prescribe such regulations as may be necessary or appropriate to carry out the purposes of this section and to prevent abuse of such purposes, including regulations under chapters 11, 12, and 13 of this title.

Regulation

Proposed § 1.529–5 (REG–106177–97, Aug. 24, 1998) Estate, gift, and generation-skipping transfer tax rules relating to qualified State tuition programs.

* * *

(b) Gift and generation-skipping transfer tax treatment of contributions after August 5, 1997. (1) *In general.* A contribution on behalf of a designated beneficiary to a QSTP (or to a program that meets the transitional rule requirements under § 1.529–6(b)) after August 5, 1997, is a completed gift of a present interest in property under section 2503(b) from the person making the contribution to the designated beneficiary. As such, the contribution is eligible for the annual gift tax exclusion provided under section 2503(b). The portion of a contribution excludible from taxable gifts under section 2503(b) also satisfies the requirements of section 2642(c)(2) and, therefore, is also excludible for purposes of the generation-skipping transfer tax imposed under section 2601. A contribution to a QSTP after August 5, 1997, is not treated as a qualified transfer within the meaning of section 2503(e).

(2) *Contributions that exceed the annual exclusion amount.* (i) Under section 529(c)(2)(B) a donor may elect to take certain contributions to a QSTP into account ratably over a five year period in determining the amount of gifts made during the calendar year. The provision is applicable only with respect to contributions not in excess of five times the section 2503(b) exclusion amount available in the calendar year of the contribution. Any excess may not be taken into account ratably and is treated as a taxable gift in the calendar year of the contribution.

(ii) The election under section 529(c)(2)(B) may be made by a donor and his or her spouse with respect to a gift considered to be made one-half by each spouse under section 2513.

(iii) The election is made on Form 709, Federal Gift Tax Return, for the calendar year in which the contribution is made.

(iv) If in any year after the first year of the five year period described in section 529(c)(2)(B), the amount excludible under section 2503(b) is increased as provided in section 2503(b)(2), the donor may make an additional contribution in any one or more of the four remaining years up to the difference between the exclusion amount as increased and the original exclusion amount for the year or years in which the original contribution was made.

(v) *Example.* The application of this paragraph (b)(2) is illustrated by the following example:

Example. In Year 1, when the annual exclusion under section 2503(b) is $10,000, P makes a contribution of $60,000 to a QSTP for the benefit of P's child, C. P elects under section 529(c)(2)(B) to account for the gift ratably over a five year period beginning with the calendar year of contribution. P is treated as making an excludible gift of $10,000 in each of Years 1 through 5 and a taxable gift of $10,000 in Year 1. In Year 3, when the annual exclusion is increased to $12,000, P makes an additional contribution for the benefit of C in the amount of $8,000. P is treated as making an excludible gift of $2,000 under section 2503(b); the remaining $6,000 is a taxable gift in Year 3.

(3) *Change of designated beneficiary or rollover.* (i) A transfer which occurs by reason of a change in the designated beneficiary, or a rollover of credits or account balances from the account of one beneficiary to the account of another beneficiary, is not a taxable gift and is not subject to the generation-skipping transfer tax if the new beneficiary is a member of the family of the old beneficiary, as defined in § 1.529–1(c), and is assigned to the same generation as the old beneficiary, as defined in section 2651.

(ii) A transfer which occurs by reason of a change in the designated beneficiary, or a rollover of credits or account balances from the account of one beneficiary to the account of another beneficiary, will be treated as a taxable gift by the old beneficiary to the new beneficiary if the new beneficiary is assigned to a lower generation than the old beneficiary, as defined in section 2651, regardless of whether the new beneficiary is a member of the family of the old beneficiary. The transfer will be subject to the generation-skipping transfer tax if the new beneficiary is assigned to a generation which is two or more levels lower than the generation assignment of the old beneficiary. The five year averaging rule described in paragraph (b)(2) of this section may be applied to the transfer.

(iii) *Example.* The application of this paragraph (b)(3) is illustrated by the following example:

Example. In Year 1, P makes a contribution to a QSTP on behalf of P's child, C. In Year 4, P directs that a distribution from the account for the benefit of C be made to an account for the benefit of P's grandchild, G. The rollover distribution is treated as a taxable gift by C to G, because, under section 2651, G is assigned to a generation below the generation assignment of C.

* * *

(d) Estate tax treatment for estates of decedents dying after June 8, 1997. (1) *In general.* Except as provided in paragraph (d)(2) of this section, the gross estate of a decedent dying after June 8, 1997, does not include the value of any interest in a QSTP which is attributable to contributions made by the decedent to such program on behalf of any designated beneficiary.

(2) *Excess contributions.* In the case of a decedent who made the election under section 529(c)(2)(B) and paragraph (b)(3)(i) of this section who dies before the close of the five year period, that portion of the contribution allocable to calendar years beginning after the date of death of the decedent is includible in the decedent's gross estate.

(3) *Designated beneficiary decedents.* The gross estate of a designated beneficiary of a QSTP includes the value of any interest in the QSTP.

§ 529A. Qualified ABLE Programs

(a) General rule. A qualified ABLE program shall be exempt from taxation under this subtitle. Notwithstanding the preceding sentence, such program shall be subject to the taxes imposed by section 511 (relating to imposition of tax on unrelated business income of charitable organizations).

* * *

(c) Tax treatment.

* * *

(2) Gift tax rules. For purposes of chapters 12 and 13—

(A) Contributions. Any contribution to a qualified ABLE program on behalf of any designated beneficiary—

(i) shall be treated as a completed gift to such designated beneficiary which is not a future interest in property, and

(ii) shall not be treated as a qualified transfer under section 2503(e).

(B) Treatment of distributions. In no event shall a distribution from an ABLE account to such account's designated beneficiary be treated as a taxable gift.

(C) Treatment of Transfer to New Designated Beneficiary. The taxes imposed by chapters 12 and 13 shall not apply to a transfer by reason of a change in the designated beneficiary under subsection (c)(1)(C).

(3) Additional tax for distributions not used for disability expenses.

(A) In general. The tax imposed by this chapter [26 USCS § 1 et seq.] for any taxable year on any taxpayer who receives a distribution from a qualified ABLE program which is includible in gross income shall be increased by 10 percent of the amount which is so includible.

(B) Exception. Subparagraph (A) shall not apply if the payment or distribution is made to a beneficiary (or to the estate of the designated beneficiary) on or after the death of the designated beneficiary.

* * *

(e) Other definitions and special rules. For purposes of this section—

* * *

(3) Designated beneficiary. The term "designated beneficiary" in connection with an ABLE account established under a qualified ABLE program means the eligible individual who established an ABLE account and is the owner of such account.

* * *

(g) Regulations. The Secretary shall prescribe such regulations or other guidance as the Secretary determines necessary or appropriate to carry out the purposes of this section, including regulations—

* * *

(6) under chapters 11, 12, and 13 of this title [26 USCS §§ 2001 et seq., 2501 et seq. and 2601 et seq.], and

* * *

Regulation

Proposed § 1.529A–4 (REG–102837–15, July 6, 2015) Gift, estate, and generation-skipping transfer taxes.

(a) Contributions. (1) *In general.* Each contribution by a person to an ABLE account other than by the designated beneficiary of that account is treated as a completed gift to the designated beneficiary of the account for gift tax purposes. Under the applicable gift tax rules, a contribution from a corporation, partnership, trust, estate, or other entity is treated as a gift by the shareholders, partners, or other beneficial owners in proportion to their respective ownership interests in the entity. See § 25.2511–1(c) and (h). A gift into an ABLE account is not treated as either a gift of a future interest in property, or a qualified transfer under section 2503(e). To the extent a contributor's gifts to the designated beneficiary, including gifts paid into the designated beneficiary's ABLE account, do not exceed the annual limit in section 2503(b), the contribution is not subject to gift tax. This provision, however, does not change any other provision applicable to the transfer. For example, a contribution by the employer of the designated beneficiary's parent continues to constitute earned income to the parent and then a gift by the parent to the designated beneficiary.

(2) *Generation-skipping transfer (GST) tax*. To the extent the contribution into an ABLE account is a nontaxable gift for gift tax purposes, the inclusion ratio for purposes of the GST tax will be zero pursuant to section 2642(c)(1).

(3) *Designated beneficiary as contributor*. A designated beneficiary may make a contribution to fund his or her own ABLE account. That contribution is not a gift. However, in the event of any change of designated beneficiary, the portion of the then fair market value of the ABLE account attributable to that contribution and any earnings attributable to that contribution will constitute a gift by the designated beneficiary to the successor designated beneficiary, and the usual gift and GST tax rules will apply.

(b) Distributions. No distribution from an ABLE account to or for the benefit of the designated beneficiary is treated as a taxable gift to that designated beneficiary.

(c) Change of designated beneficiary. Neither gift tax nor generation-skipping transfer tax applies to a change of designated beneficiary if the successor designated beneficiary is both an eligible individual and a member of the family (as described in § 1.529A–1(b)(13)) of the designated beneficiary. The previous sentence does not apply to any other change of designated beneficiary.

(d) Transfer tax on death of designated beneficiary. Upon the death of the designated beneficiary, the designated beneficiary's ABLE account is includible in his or her gross estate for estate tax purposes under section 2031. The payment of outstanding qualified disability expenses and the payment of certain claims made by a State under its Medicaid plan may be deductible for estate tax purposes if the requirements of section 2053 are satisfied.

(e) Effective/applicability date. This section applies to taxable years beginning after December 31, 2014.

Subchapter J. Estates, Trusts, Beneficiaries, and Decedents

Part I. Estates, Trusts, and Beneficiaries

Subpart A. General Rules for Taxation of Estates and Trusts

§ 641. Imposition of Tax

(a) Application of tax. The tax imposed by section 1(e) shall apply to the taxable income of estates or of any kind of property held in trust, including—

(1) income accumulated in trust for the benefit of unborn or unascertained persons or persons with contingent interests, and income accumulated or held for future distribution under the terms of the will or trust;

(2) income which is to be distributed currently by the fiduciary to the beneficiaries, and income collected by a guardian of an infant which is to be held or distributed as the court may direct;

(3) income received by estates of deceased persons during the period of administration or settlement of the estate; and

(4) income which, in the discretion of the fiduciary, may be either distributed to the beneficiaries or accumulated.

(b) Computation and payment. The taxable income of an estate or trust shall be computed in the same manner as in the case of an individual, except as otherwise provided in this part. The tax shall be computed on such taxable income and shall be paid by the fiduciary. For purposes of this subsection, a foreign trust or foreign estate shall be treated as a nonresident alien individual who is not present in the United States at any time.

(c) Special rules for taxation of electing small business trusts.

(1) In general. For purposes of this chapter—

(A) the portion of any electing small business trust which consists of stock in 1 or more S corporations shall be treated as a separate trust, and

(B) the amount of the tax imposed by this chapter on such separate trust shall be determined with the modifications of paragraph (2).

(2) Modifications. For purposes of paragraph (1), the modifications of this paragraph are the following:

(A) Except as provided in section 1(h), the amount of the tax imposed by section 1(e) shall be determined by using the highest rate of tax set forth in section 1(e).

(B) The exemption amount under section 55(d) shall be zero.

(C) The only items of income, loss, deduction, or credit to be taken into account are the following:

(i) The items required to be taken into account under section 1366.

(ii) Any gain or loss from the disposition of stock in an S corporation.

(iii) To the extent provided in regulations, State or local income taxes or administrative expenses to the extent allocable to items described in clauses (i) and (ii).

(iv) Any interest expense paid or accrued on indebtedness incurred to acquire stock in an S corporation.

No deduction or credit shall be allowed for any amount not described in this paragraph, and no item described in this paragraph shall be apportioned to any beneficiary.

(D) No amount shall be allowed under paragraph (1) or (2) of section 1211(b).

(E)

(i) Section 642(c) shall not apply.

(ii) For purposes of section 170(b)(1)(G), adjusted gross income shall be computed in the same manner as in the case of an individual, except that the deductions for costs which are paid or incurred in connection with the administration of the trust and which would not have been incurred if the property were not held in such trust shall be treated as allowable in arriving at adjusted gross income.

(3) Treatment of remainder of trust and distributions. For purposes of determining—

(A) the amount of the tax imposed by this chapter on the portion of any electing small business trust not treated as a separate trust under paragraph (1), and

(B) the distributable net income of the entire trust, the items referred to in paragraph (2)(C) shall be excluded. Except as provided in the preceding sentence, this subsection shall not affect the taxation of any distribution from the trust.

(4) Treatment of unused deductions where termination of separate trust. If a portion of an electing small business trust ceases to be treated as a separate trust under paragraph (1), any carryover or excess deduction of the separate trust which is referred to in section 642(h) shall be taken into account by the entire trust.

(5) Electing small business trust. For purposes of this subsection, the term "electing small business trust" has the meaning given such term by section 1361(e)(1).

Regulations

§ 1.641(a)–0 Scope of subchapter J.

(a) In general. Subchapter J (sections 641 and following), Chapter 1 of the Code, deals with the taxation of income of estates and trusts and their beneficiaries, and of income in respect of decedents. Part I of Subchapter J contains general rules for taxation of estates and trusts (Subpart A), specific rules relating to trusts which distribute current income only (Subpart B), estates and trusts which may accumulate income or which distribute corpus (Subpart C), treatment of excess distributions by trusts (Subpart D), grantors and other persons treated as substantial owners (Subpart E), and miscellaneous provisions relating to limitations on charitable deductions, income of an estate or trust in case of divorce, and taxable years to which the provisions of Subchapter J are applicable (Subpart F). Part I has no application to any organization which is not to be classified for tax purposes as a trust under the classification rules of §§ 301.7701–2, 301.7701–3, and 301.7701–4 of this chapter (Regulations on Procedure and Administration). Part II of Subchapter J relates to the treatment of income in respect of decedents. However, the provisions of Subchapter J do not apply to employee trusts subject to Subchapters D and F, Chapter 1 of the Code, and common trust funds subject to Subchapter H, Chapter 1 of the Code.

(b) Scope of Subparts A, B, C, and D. Subparts A, B, C, and D (section 641 and following), Part I, Subchapter J, Chapter 1 of the Code, relate to the taxation of estates and trusts and their beneficiaries. These subparts have no application to any portion of the corpus or income of a trust which is to be regarded, within the meaning of the Code, as that of the grantor or others treated as its substantial owners. See Subpart E (section 671 and following), Part I, Subchapter J, Chapter 1 of the Code, and the regulations thereunder for rules for the treatment of any portion of a trust where the grantor (or another person) is treated as the substantial owner. So-called alimony trusts are treated under Subparts A, B, C, and D, except to the extent otherwise provided in section 71 or section 682. These subparts have no application to beneficiaries of nonexempt employees' trusts. See section 402(b) and the regulations thereunder.

(c) Multiple trusts. Multiple trusts that have:

(1) No substantially independent purposes (such as independent dispositive purposes),

(2) The same grantor and substantially the same beneficiary, and

(3) The avoidance or mitigation of (i) the progressive rates of tax (including mitigation as a result of deferral of tax) or (ii) the minimum tax for tax preferences imposed by section 56 as their principal purpose, shall be consolidated and treated as one trust for the purposes of Subchapter J.

[T.D. 6500, 25 FR 11814, Nov. 26, 1960, as amended by T.D. 6989, 34 FR 731, Jan. 17, 1969; T.D. 7204, 37 FR 17158, Aug. 25, 1972]

§ 1.641(a)–1 Imposition of tax; application of tax.

For taxable years beginning after December 31, 1970, section 641 prescribes that the taxes imposed by section 1(d), as amended by the Tax Reform Act of 1969, shall apply to the income of estates or of any kind of property held in trust. For taxable years ending before January 1, 1971, section 641 prescribes that the taxes imposed upon individuals by chapter 1 of the Code apply to the income of estates or of any kind of property held in trust. The rates of tax, the statutory provisions respecting gross income, and, with certain exceptions, the deductions and credits allowed to individuals apply also to estates and trusts.

[T.D. 6500, 25 FR 11814, Nov. 26, 1960, as amended by T.D. 7117, 36 FR 9421, May 25, 1971]

§ 1.641(a)–2 Gross income of estates and trusts.

The gross income of an estate or trust is determined in the same manner as that of an individual. Thus, the gross income of an estate or trust consists of all items of gross income received during the taxable year, including:

(a) Income accumulated in trust for the benefit of unborn or unascertained persons or persons with contingent interests;

(b) Income accumulated or held for future distribution under the terms of the will or trust;

(c) Income which is to be distributed currently by the fiduciary to the beneficiaries, and income collected by a guardian of an infant which is to be held or distributed as the court may direct;

(d) Income received by estates of deceased persons during the period of administration or settlement of the estate; and

(e) Income which, in the discretion of the fiduciary, may be either distributed to the beneficiaries or accumulated. The several classes of income enumerated in this section do not exclude others which also may come within the general purposes of section 641.

[T.D. 6500, 25 FR 11814, Nov. 26, 1960]

§ 1.641(b)–1 Computation and payment of tax; deductions and credits of estates and trusts.

Generally, the deductions and credits allowed to individuals are also allowed to estates and trusts. However, there are special rules for the computation of certain deductions and for the allocation between the estate or trust and the beneficiaries of certain credits and deductions. See section 642 and the regulations thereunder. In addition, an estate or trust is allowed to deduct, in computing its taxable income, the deductions provided by sections 651 and 661 and regulations thereunder, relating to distributions to beneficiaries.

[T.D. 6500, 25 FR 11814, Nov. 26, 1960]

§ 1.641(b)–2 Filing of returns and payment of the tax.

(a) The fiduciary is required to make and file the return and pay the tax on the taxable income of an estate or of a trust. Liability for the payment of the tax on the taxable income of an estate attaches to the person of the executor or administrator up to and after his discharge if, prior to distribution and discharge, he had notice of his tax obligations or failed to exercise due diligence in ascertaining whether or not such obligations existed. For the extent of such liability, see section 3467 of the Revised Statutes, as amended by section 518 of the Revenue Act of 1934 (31 U.S.C. 192).* Liability for the tax also follows the assets of the estate distributed to heirs, devisees, legatees, and distributees, who may be required to discharge the amount of the tax due and unpaid to the extent of the distributive shares received by them. See section 6901. The same considerations apply to trusts.

(b) The estate of an infant, incompetent, or other person under a disability, or, in general, of an individual or corporation in receivership or a corporation in bankruptcy is not a taxable entity separate from the person for whom the fiduciary is acting, in that respect differing from the estate of a deceased person or of a trust. See section 6012(b)(2) and (3) for provisions relating to the obligation of the fiduciary with respect to returns of such persons.

[T.D. 6500, 25 FR 11814, Nov. 26, 1960, as amended by T.D. 6580, 26 FR 11486, Dec. 5, 1961]

§ 1.641(b)–3 Termination of estates and trusts.

(a) The income of an estate of a deceased person is that which is received by the estate during the period of administration or settlement. The period of administration or settlement is the period actually required by the administrator or executor to perform the ordi-

* 31 U.S.C. § 192 has been revised and relocated. For the current version, see the Appendix. *Ed.*

nary duties of administration, such as the collection of assets and the payment of debts, taxes, legacies, and bequests, whether the period required is longer or shorter than the period specified under the applicable local law for the settlement of estates. For example, where an executor who is also named as trustee under a will fails to obtain his discharge as executor, the period of administration continues only until the duties of administration are complete and he actually assumes his duties as trustee, whether or not pursuant to a court order. However, the period of administration of an estate cannot be unduly prolonged. If the administration of an estate is unreasonably prolonged, the estate is considered terminated for Federal income tax purposes after the expiration of a reasonable period for the performance by the executor of all the duties of administration. Further, an estate will be considered as terminated when all the assets have been distributed except for a reasonable amount which is set aside in good faith for the payment of unascertained or contingent liabilities and expenses (not including a claim by a beneficiary in the capacity of beneficiary). Notwithstanding the above, if the estate has joined in making a valid election under section 645 to treat a qualified revocable trust, as defined under section 645(b)(1), as part of the estate, the estate shall not terminate under this paragraph prior to the termination of the section 645 election period. See section 645 and the regulations thereunder for rules regarding the termination of the section 645 election period.

(b) Generally, the determination of whether a trust has terminated depends upon whether the property held in trust has been distributed to the persons entitled to succeed to the property upon termination of the trust rather than upon the technicality of whether or not the trustee has rendered his final accounting. A trust does not automatically terminate upon the happening of the event by which the duration of the trust is measured. A reasonable time is permitted after such event for the trustee to perform the duties necessary to complete the administration of the trust. Thus, if under the terms of the governing instrument, the trust is to terminate upon the death of the life beneficiary and the corpus is to be distributed to the remainderman, the trust continues after the death of the life beneficiary for a period reasonably necessary to a proper winding up of the affairs of the trust. However, the winding up of a trust cannot be unduly postponed and if the distribution of the trust corpus is unreasonably delayed, the trust is considered terminated for Federal income tax purposes after the expiration of a reasonable period for the trustee to complete the administration of the trust. Further, a trust will be considered as terminated when all the assets have been distributed except for a reasonable amount which is set aside in good faith for the payment of unascertained or contingent liabilities and expenses (not including a claim by a beneficiary in the capacity of beneficiary).

(c)(1) Except as provided in subparagraph (2) of this paragraph, during the period between the occurrence of an event which causes a trust to terminate and the time when the trust is considered as terminated under this section, whether or not the income and the excess of capital gains over capital losses of the trust are to be considered as amounts required to be distributed currently to the ultimate distributee for the year in which they are received depends upon the principles stated in § 1.651(a)–2. See § 1.663–1 et seq. for application of the separate share rule.

(2)(i) Except in cases to which the last sentence of this subdivision applies, for taxable years of a trust ending before September 1, 1957, subparagraph (1) of this paragraph shall not apply and the rule of subdivision (ii) of this subparagraph shall apply unless the trustee elects to have subparagraph (1) of this paragraph apply. Such election shall be made by the trustee in a statement filed on or before April 15, 1959, with the district director with whom such trust's return for any such taxable year was filed. The election provided by this subdivision shall not be available if the treatment given the income and the excess of capital gains over capital losses for taxable years for which returns have been filed was consistent with the provisions of subparagraph (1) of this paragraph.

(ii) The rule referred to in subdivision (i) of this subparagraph is as follows: During the period between the occurrence of an event which causes a trust to terminate and the time when a trust is considered as terminated under this section, the income and the excess of capital gains over capital losses of the trust are in general considered as amounts required to be distributed for the year in which they are received. For example, a trust instrument provides for the payment of income to A during her life, and upon her death for the payment of the corpus to B. The trust reports on the basis of the calendar year. A dies on November 1,

1955, but no distribution is made to B until January 15, 1956. The income of the trust and the excess of capital gains over capital losses for the entire year 1955, to the extent not paid, credited, or required to be distributed to A or A's estate, are treated under sections 661 and 662 as amounts required to be distributed to B for the year 1955.

(d) If a trust or the administration or settlement of an estate is considered terminated under this section for Federal income tax purposes (as for instance, because administration has been unduly prolonged), the gross income, deductions, and credits of the estate or trust are, subsequent to the termination, considered the gross income, deductions, and credits of the person or persons succeeding to the property of the estate or trust.

[T.D. 6500, 25 FR 11814, Nov. 26, 1960; T.D. 9032, 67 FR 78376, Dec. 24, 2002]

§ 1.641(c)–0 Table of contents. [*Omitted. Ed.*]

[T.D. 8994, 67 FR 34394, May 14, 2002]

§ 1.641(c)–1 Electing small business trust. [*Omitted. Ed.*]

[T.D. 8994, 67 FR 34395, May 14, 2002; T.D. 9868, 84 FR 28215, June 18, 2019]

§ 642. Special Rules for Credits and Deductions

(a) Foreign tax credit allowed. An estate or trust shall be allowed the credit against tax for taxes imposed by foreign countries and possessions of the United States, to the extent allowed by section 901, only in respect of so much of the taxes described in such section as is not properly allocable under such section to the beneficiaries.

(b) Deduction for personal exemption.

(1) Estates. An estate shall be allowed a deduction of $600.

(2) Trusts.

(A) In general. Except as otherwise provided in this paragraph, a trust shall be allowed a deduction of $100.

(B) Trusts distributing income currently. A trust which, under its governing instrument, is required to distribute all of its income currently shall be allowed a deduction of $300.

(C) Disability trusts.

(i) In general. A qualified disability trust shall be allowed a deduction equal to the exemption amount under section 151(d), determined—

(I) by treating such trust as an individual described in section 68(b)(1)(C), and

(II) by applying section 67(e) (without the reference to section 642(b)) for purposes of determining the adjusted gross income of the trust.

(ii) Qualified disability trust. For purposes of clause (i), the term "qualified disability trust" means any trust if—

(I) such trust is a disability trust described in subsection (c)(2)(B)(iv) of section 1917 of the Social Security Act (42 U.S.C. 1396p), and

(II) all of the beneficiaries of the trust as of the close of the taxable year are determined by the Commissioner of Social Security to have been disabled (within the meaning of section 1614(a)(3) of the Social Security Act, 42 U.S.C. 1382c(a)(3)) for some portion of such year.

(iii) Years when personal exemption amount is zero.

(I) In general. In the case of any taxable year in which the exemption amount under section 151(d) is zero, clause (i) shall be applied by substituting "$4,150" for "the exemption amount under section 151(d)".

(II) Inflation adjustment. In the case of any taxable year beginning in a calendar year after 2018, the $4,150 amount in subparagraph (A) shall be increased in the same manner as provided in section 6334(d)(4)(C).

A trust shall not fail to meet the requirements of subclause (II) merely because the corpus of the trust may revert to a person who is not so disabled after the trust ceases to have any beneficiary who is so disabled.

(3) Deductions in lieu of personal exemption. The deductions allowed by this subsection shall be in lieu of the deductions allowed under section 151 (relating to deduction for personal exemption).

(c) Deduction for amounts paid or permanently set aside for a charitable purpose.

(1) General rule. In the case of an estate or trust (other than a trust meeting the specifications of subpart B), there shall be allowed as a deduction in computing its taxable income (in lieu of the deduction allowed by section 170(a), relating to deduction for charitable, etc., contributions and gifts) any amount of the gross income, without limitation, which pursuant to the terms of the governing instrument is, during the taxable year, paid for a purpose specified in section 170(c) (determined without regard to section 170(c)(2)(A)). If a charitable contribution is paid after the close of such taxable year and on or before the last day of the year following the close of such taxable year, then the trustee or administrator may elect to treat such contribution as paid during such taxable year. The election shall be made at such time and in such manner as the Secretary prescribes by regulations.

(2) Amounts permanently set aside. In the case of an estate, and in the case of a trust (other than a trust meeting the specifications of subpart B) required by the terms of its governing instrument to set aside amounts which was—

(A) created on or before October 9, 1969, if—

(i) an irrevocable remainder interest is transferred to or for the use of an organization described in section 170(c), or

(ii) the grantor is at all times after October 9, 1969, under a mental disability to change the terms of the trust; or

(B) established by a will executed on or before October 9, 1969, if—

(i) the testator dies before October 9, 1972, without having republished the will after October 9, 1969, by codicil or otherwise,

(ii) the testator at no time after October 9, 1969, had the right to change the portions of the will which pertain to the trust, or

(iii) the will is not republished by codicil or otherwise before October 9, 1972, and the testator is on such date and at all times thereafter under a mental disability to republish the will by codicil or otherwise,

there shall also be allowed as a deduction in computing its taxable income any amount of the gross income, without limitation, which pursuant to the terms of the governing instrument is, during the taxable year, permanently set aside for a purpose specified in section 170(c), or is to be used exclusively for religious, charitable, scientific, literary, or educational purposes, or for the prevention of cruelty to children or animals, or for the establishment, acquisition, maintenance, or operation of a public cemetery not operated for profit. In the case of a trust, the preceding sentence shall apply only to gross income earned with respect to amounts transferred to the trust before October 9, 1969, or transferred under a will to which subparagraph (B) applies.

(3) Pooled income funds. In the case of a pooled income fund (as defined in paragraph (5)), there shall also be allowed as a deduction in computing its taxable income any amount of the gross income attributable to gain from the sale of a capital asset held for more than 1 year, without limitation, which pursuant to the terms of the governing instrument is, during the taxable year, permanently set aside for a purpose specified in section 170(c).

(4) Adjustments. To the extent that the amount otherwise allowable as a deduction under this subsection consists of gain described in section 1202(a), proper adjustment shall be made for any exclusion allowable to the estate or trust under section 1202. In the case of a trust, the deduction allowed by this subsection shall be subject to section 681 (relating to unrelated business income).

(5) Definition of pooled income fund. For purposes of paragraph (3), a pooled income fund is a trust—

(A) to which each donor transfers property, contributing an irrevocable remainder interest in such property to or for the use of an organization described in section 170(b)(1)(A) (other than in clauses (vii) or (viii)), and retaining an income interest for the life of one or more beneficiaries (living at the time of such transfer),

(B) in which the property transferred by each donor is commingled with property transferred by other donors who have made or make similar transfers,

(C) which cannot have investments in securities which are exempt from the taxes imposed by this subtitle,

(D) which includes only amounts received from transfers which meet the requirements of this paragraph,

(E) which is maintained by the organization to which the remainder interest is contributed and of which no donor or beneficiary of an income interest is a trustee, and

(F) from which each beneficiary of an income interest receives income, for each year for which he is entitled to receive the income interest referred to in subparagraph (A), determined by the rate of return earned by the trust for such year.

For purposes of determining the amount of any charitable contribution allowable by reason of a transfer of property to a pooled fund, the value of the income interest shall be determined on the basis of the highest rate of return earned by the fund for any of the 3 taxable years immediately preceding the taxable year of the fund in which the transfer is made. In the case of funds in existence less than 3 taxable years preceding the taxable year of the fund in which a transfer is made, the rate of return shall be deemed to be 6 percent per annum, except that the Secretary may prescribe a different rate of return.

(6) Taxable private foundations. In the case of a private foundation which is not exempt from taxation under section 501(a) for the taxable year, the provisions of this subsection shall not apply and the provisions of section 170 shall apply.

(d) Net operating loss deduction. The benefit of the deduction for net operating losses provided by section 172 shall be allowed to estates and trusts under regulations prescribed by the Secretary.

(e) Deduction for depreciation and depletion. An estate or trust shall be allowed the deduction for depreciation and depletion only to the extent not allowable to beneficiaries under sections 167(d) and 611(b).

(f) Amortization deductions. The benefit of the deductions for amortization provided by sections 169 and 197 shall be allowed to estates and trusts in the same manner as in the case of an individual. The allowable deduction shall be apportioned between the income beneficiaries and the fiduciary under regulations prescribed by the Secretary.

(g) Disallowance of double deductions. Amounts allowable under section 2053 or 2054 as a deduction in computing the taxable estate of a decedent shall not be allowed as a deduction (or as an offset against the sales price of property in determining gain or loss) in computing the taxable income of the estate or of any other person, unless there is filed, within the time and in the manner and form prescribed by the Secretary, a statement that the amounts have not been allowed as deductions under section 2053 or 2054 and a waiver of the right to have such amounts allowed at any time as deductions under section 2053 or 2054. Rules similar to the rules of the preceding sentence shall apply to amounts which may be taken into account under section 2621(a)(2) or 2622(b). This subsection shall not apply with respect to deductions allowed under part II (relating to income in respect of decedents).

(h) Unused loss carryovers and excess deductions on termination available to beneficiaries. If on the termination of an estate or trust, the estate or trust has—

(1) a net operating loss carryover under section 172 or a capital loss carryover under section 1212, or

(2) for the last taxable year of the estate or trust deductions (other than the deductions allowed under subsections (b) or (c)) in excess of gross income for such year, then such carryover or such excess shall be allowed as a deduction, in accordance with regulations prescribed by the Secretary, to the beneficiaries succeeding to the property of the estate or trust.

(i) Certain distributions by cemetery perpetual care funds. In the case of a cemetery perpetual care fund which—

(1) was created pursuant to local law by a taxable cemetery corporation for the care and maintenance of cemetery property, and

(2) is treated for the taxable year as a trust for purposes of this subchapter,

any amount distributed by such fund for the care and maintenance of gravesites which have been purchased from the cemetery corporation before the beginning of the taxable year of the trust and with respect to which there is an obligation to furnish care and maintenance shall be considered to be a distribution solely for purposes of sections 651 and 661, but only to the extent that the aggregate amount so distributed during the taxable year does not exceed $5 multiplied by the aggregate number of such gravesites.

Regulations

§ 1.642(a)(1)–1 Partially tax-exempt interest.

An estate or trust is allowed the credit against tax for partially tax-exempt interest provided by section 35 only to the extent that the credit does not relate to interest properly allocable to a beneficiary under section 652 or 662 and the regulations thereunder. A beneficiary of an estate or trust is allowed the credit against tax for partially tax-exempt interest provided by section 35 only to the extent that the credit relates to interest properly allocable to him under section 652 or 662 and the regulations thereunder. If an estate or trust holds partially tax-exempt bonds and elects under section 171 to treat the premium on the bonds as amortizable, the credit allowable under section 35, with respect to the bond interest (whether allowable to the estate or trust or to the beneficiary), is reduced under section 171(a)(3) by reducing the shares of the interest allocable, respectively, to the estate or trust and its beneficiary by the portion of the amortization deduction attributable to the shares.

[T.D. 6500, 25 FR 11814, Nov. 26, 1960]

§ 1.642(a)(2)–1 Foreign taxes.

An estate or trust is allowed the credit against tax for taxes imposed by foreign countries and possessions of the United States to the extent allowed by section 901 only for so much of those taxes as are not properly allocable under that section to the beneficiaries. See section 901(b)(4). For purposes of section 901(b)(4), the term “beneficiaries” includes charitable beneficiaries.

[T.D. 6500, 25 FR 11814, Nov. 26, 1960]

§ 1.642(a)(3)–1 Dividends received by an estate or trust.

An estate or trust is allowed a credit against the tax for dividends received on or before December 31, 1964 (see section 34), only for so much of the dividends as are not properly allocable to any beneficiary under section 652 or 662. Section 642(a)(3), and this section do not apply to amounts received as dividends after December 31, 1964. For treatment of the credit in the hands of the beneficiary see § 1.652(b)–1.

[T.D. 6500, 25 FR 11814, Nov. 26, 1960, as amended by T.D. 6777, 29 FR 17808, Dec. 16, 1964]

§ 1.642(a)(3)–2 Time of receipt of dividends by beneficiary.

In general, dividends are deemed received by a beneficiary in the taxable year in which they are includible in his gross income under section 652 or 662. For example, a simple trust, reporting on the basis of a fiscal year ending October 30, receives quarterly dividends on November 3, 1954, and February 3, May 3, and August 3, 1955. These dividends are all allocable to beneficiary A, reporting on a calendar year basis, under section 652 and are deemed received by A in 1955. See section 652(c). Accordingly, A may take all these dividends into account in determining his credit for dividends received under section 34 and his dividends exclusion under section 116. However, solely for purposes of determining whether dividends deemed received by individuals from trusts or estates qualify under the time limitations of section 34(a) or section 116(a), section 642(a)(3) provides that the time of receipt of the dividends by the trust or estate is also considered the time of receipt by the beneficiary. For example, a simple trust reporting on the basis of a fiscal year ending October 30 receives quarterly dividends on December 3, 1953, and March 3, June 3, and September 3, 1954. These dividends are all allocable to beneficiary A, reporting on the calendar year basis, under section 652 and are includible in his income for 1954. However, for purposes of section 34(a) or section 116(a), these dividends are deemed received by A on the same dates that the trust received them. Accordingly, A may take into account in determining the credit under section 34 only those dividends received by the trust on September 3, 1954, since the dividend received credit is not allowed under section 34 for dividends received before August 1, 1954 (or after December 31, 1964). Section 642(a)(3) and this section do not apply to amounts received by an estate or trust as dividends after December 31, 1964. However, the rules in this section relating to time of receipt of dividends by a beneficiary are applicable to dividends received by an state or trust prior to January 1, 1965, and accordingly, such dividends are deemed to be received by the beneficiary (even though received after December 31, 1964) on the same dates that the estate or trust received them for purposes of determining the credit under section 34 or the exclusion under section 116.

[T.D. 6500, 25 FR 11814, Nov. 26, 1960, as amended by T.D. 6777, 29 FR 17808, Dec. 16, 1964]

§ 1.642(a)(3)–3 Cross reference.

See § 1.683–2(c) for examples relating to the treatment of dividends received by an estate or trust during a fiscal year beginning in 1953 and ending in 1954.

[T.D. 6500, 25 FR 11814, Nov. 26, 1960]

§ 1.642(b)–1 Deduction for personal exemption.

In lieu of the deduction for personal exemptions provided by section 151:

(a) An estate is allowed a deduction of $600,

(b) A trust which, under its governing instrument, is required to distribute currently all of its income for the taxable year is allowed a deduction of $300, and

(c) All other trusts are allowed a deduction of $100.

A trust which, under its governing instrument, is required to distribute all of its income currently is allowed a deduction of $300, even though it also distributes amounts other than income in the taxable year and even though it may be required to make distributions which would qualify for the charitable contributions deduction under section 642(c) (and therefore does not qualify as a "simple trust" under sections 651–652). A trust for the payment of an annuity is allowed a deduction of $300 in a taxable year in which the amount of the annuity required to be paid equals or exceeds all the income of the trust for the taxable year. For the meaning of the term "income required to be distributed currently", see § 1.651(a)–2.

[T.D. 6500, 25 FR 11814, Nov. 26, 1960]

§ 1.642(c)–0 Effective dates.

The provisions of section 642(c) (other than section 642(c)(5)) and of §§ 1.642(c)–1 through 1.642(c)–4 apply to amounts paid, permanently set aside, or to be used for a charitable purpose in taxable years beginning after December 31, 1969. The provisions of section 642(c)(5) and of §§ 1.642(c)–5 through 1.642(c)–7 apply to transfers in trust made after July 31, 1969. For provisions relating to amounts paid, permanently set aside, or to be used for a charitable purpose in taxable years beginning before January 1, 1970, see 26 CFR 1.642(c)–1 through 1.642(c)–4 (Rev. as of Jan. 1, 1971).

[T.D. 7357, 40 FR 23739, June 2, 1975]

§ 1.642(c)–1 Unlimited deduction for amounts paid for a charitable purpose.

(a) In general. (1) Any part of the gross income of an estate, or trust which, pursuant to the terms of the governing instrument is paid (or treated under paragraph (b) of this section as paid) during the taxable year for a purpose specified in section 170(c) shall be allowed as a deduction to such estate or trust in lieu of the limited charitable contributions deduction authorized by section 170(a). In applying this paragraph without reference to paragraph (b) of this section, a deduction shall be allowed for an amount paid during the taxable year in respect of gross income received in a previous taxable year, but only if no deduction was allowed for any previous taxable year to the estate or trust, or in the case of a section 645 election, to a related estate, as defined under § 1.645–1(b), for the amount so paid.

(2) In determining whether an amount is paid for a purpose specified in section 170(c)(2) the provisions of section 170(c)(2)(A) shall not be taken into account. Thus, an amount paid to a corporation, trust, or community chest, fund, or foundation otherwise described in section 170(c)(2) shall be considered paid for a purpose specified in section 170(c) even though the corporation, trust, or community chest, fund, or foundation is not created or organized in the United States, any State, the District of Columbia, or any possession of the United States.

(3) See section 642(c)(6) and § 1.642(c)–4 for disallowance of a deduction under this section to a trust which is, or is treated under section 4947(a)(1) as though it were a private foundation (as defined in section 509(a) and the regulations thereunder) and not exempt from taxation under section 501(a).

(b) Election to treat contributions as paid in preceding taxable year. (1) *In general.* For purposes of determining the deduction allowed under paragraph (a) of this section, the fiduciary (as defined in section 7701(a)(6)) of an estate or trust may elect under section 642(c)(1) to treat as paid during the taxable year (whether or not such year begins before January 1, 1970) any amount of gross income received during such taxable year or any preceding taxable year which is otherwise deductible under such paragraph and which is paid after the close of such taxable year but on or before the last day of the next succeeding taxable year of the estate or trust. The preceding sentence applies only in the case of payments actually made in a taxable year which is a taxable year beginning after December 31, 1969. No election shall be made, however, in respect of any amount which was deducted for any previous taxable year or which is deducted for the taxable year in which such amount is paid.

(2) *Time for making election.* The election under subparagraph (1) of this paragraph shall be made not later than the time, including extensions thereof, prescribed by law for filing the income tax return for the succeeding taxable year. Such election shall, except as provided in subparagraph (4) of this paragraph, become irrevocable after the last day prescribed for making it. Having made the election for any taxable year, the fiduciary may, within the time prescribed for making it, revoke the election without the consent of the Commissioner.

(3) *Manner of making the election.* The election shall be made by filing with the income tax return (or an amended return) for the taxable year in which the contribution is treated as paid a statement which:

(i) States the name and address of the fiduciary,

(ii) Identifies the estate or trust for which the fiduciary is acting,

(iii) Indicates that the fiduciary is making an election under section 642(c)(1) in respect of contributions treated as paid during such taxable year,

(iv) Gives the name and address of each organization to which any such contribution is paid, and

(v) States the amount of each contribution and date of actual payment or, if applicable, the total amount of contributions paid to each organization during the succeeding taxable year, to be treated as paid in the preceding taxable year.

(4) *Revocation of certain elections with consent.* An application to revoke with the consent of the Commissioner any election made on or before June 8, 1970, must be in writing and must be filed not later than September 2, 1975.

No consent will be granted to revoke an election for any taxable year for which the assessment of a deficiency is prevented by the operation of any law or rule of law. If consent to revoke the election is granted, the fiduciary must attach a copy of the consent to the return (or amended return) for each taxable year affected by the revocation. The application must be addressed to the Commissioner of Internal Revenue, Washington, D.C. 20224, and must indicate:

(i) The name and address of the fiduciary and the estate or trust for which he was acting,

(ii) The taxable year for which the election was made,

(iii) The office of the district director, or the service center, where the return (or amended return) for the year of election was filed, and

(iv) The reason for revoking the election.

[T.D. 6500, 25 FR 11814, Nov. 26, 1960, as amended by T.D. 7357, 40 FR 23739, June 2, 1975; 40 FR 24361, June 6, 1975; T.D. 9032, 67 FR 78376, Dec. 24, 2002]

Proposed § 1.642(c)–1 (LR–83–87, May 5, 1988) Unlimited deduction for amounts paid for charitable purpose.

(a) In general. (1) Any part of the gross income of an estate or trust which, pursuant to the terms of the governing instrument, is paid (or treated under paragraph (b) of this section as paid) during the taxable year for a purpose specified in section 170(c) shall be allowed as a deduction to such estate or trust in lieu of the limited charitable contributions deduction authorized by section 170(a) (provided that the recordkeeping and return requirements for charitable contribution deductions contained in § 1.170A–13 are satisfied).

§ 1.642(c)–2 Unlimited deduction for amounts permanently set aside for a charitable purpose.

(a) Estates. Any part of the gross income of an estate which pursuant to the terms of the will:

(1) Is permanently set aside during the taxable year for a purpose specified in section 170(c), or

(2) Is to be used (within or without the United States or any of its possessions) exclusively for religious, charitable, scientific, literary, or educational purposes, or for the prevention of cruelty to children or animals, or for the establishment, acquisition, maintenance, or operation of a public cemetery not operated for profit, shall be allowed as a deduction to the estate in lieu of the limited charitable contributions deduction authorized by section 170(a).

* * *

(c) Pooled income funds. Any part of the gross income of a pooled income fund to which § 1.642(c)–5 applies for the taxable year that is attributable to net long-term capital gain (as defined in section 1222(7)) which, pursuant to the terms of the governing instrument, is permanently set aside during the taxable year for a purpose specified in section 170(c) shall be allowed as a deduction to the fund in lieu of the limited charitable contributions deduction authorized by section 170(a). No amount of net long-term capital gain shall be considered permanently set aside for charitable purposes if, under the terms of the fund's governing instrument and applicable local law, the trustee has the power, whether or not exercised, to satisfy the income beneficiaries' right to income by the payment of either: an amount equal to a fixed percentage of the fair market value of the fund's assets (whether determined annually or averaged on a multiple year basis); or any amount that takes into account unrealized appreciation in the value of the fund's assets. In addition, no amount of net long-term capital gain shall be considered permanently set aside for charitable purposes to the extent the trustee distributes proceeds from the sale or exchange of the fund's assets as income within the meaning of § 1.642(c)–5(a)(5)(i). No deduction shall be allowed under this paragraph for any portion of the gross income of such fund which is (1) attributable to income other than net long-term capital gain (2) earned with respect to amounts transferred to such fund before August 1, 1969. However, see paragraph (b) of this section for a deduction (subject to the limitations of such paragraph) for amounts permanently set aside by a pooled income fund which meets the requirements of that paragraph. The principles of paragraph (b) or (2) of this section with respect to investment, reinvestment, and separate accounting shall apply under this paragraph in the case of amounts transferred to the fund after July 31, 1969.

(d) Disallowance of deduction for certain amounts not deemed to be permanently set aside for charitable purposes. No amount will be considered to be permanently set aside, or to be used, for a purpose described in paragraph (a) or (b)(1) of this section unless under the terms of the governing instrument and the circumstances of the particular case the possibility that the amount set aside, or to be used, will not be devoted to such purpose or use is so remote as to be negligible. Thus, for example, where there is possibility of the invasion of the corpus of a charitable remainder trust, as defined in § 1.664–1(a)(1)(ii), in order to make payment of the annuity amount or unitrust amount, no deduction will be allowed under paragraph (a) of this section in respect of any amount set aside by an estate for distribution to such a charitable remainder trust.

(e) Effective dates. Generally, the second sentence of paragraph (c) of this section, concerning the loss of any charitable deduction for long-term capital gains if the fund's income may be determined by a fixed percentage of the fair market value of the fund's assets or by any amount that takes into account unrealized appreciation in the value of the fund's assets, applies for taxable years beginning after January 2, 2004. In a state whose statute permits income to be determined by reference to a fixed percentage of, or the unrealized appreciation in, the value of the fund's assets, net long-term capital gain of a pooled income fund may be considered to be permanently set aside for charitable purposes if the fund's governing instrument is amended or reformed to eliminate the possibility of determining income in such a manner and if income has not been determined in this manner. For this purpose, a judicial proceeding to reform the fund's governing instrument must be commenced, or a nonjudicial reformation that is valid under state law must be completed, by the date that is nine months after the later of January 2, 2004 or the effective date of the state statute authorizing determination of income in such a manner.

For treatment of distributions by an estate to a charitable remainder trust, see paragraph (a)(5)(iii) of § 1.664–1.

[T.D. 6500, 25 FR 11814, Nov. 26, 1960, as amended by T.D. 7357, 40 FR 23740, June 2, 1975; 40 FR 24361, June 6, 1975; T.D. 9102, 69 FR 17, Jan. 2, 2004]

§ 1.642(c)–3 Adjustments and other special rules for determining unlimited charitable contributions deduction.

(a) Income in respect of a decedent. For purposes of §§ 1.642(c)–1 and 1.642(c)–2, an amount received by an estate or trust which is includible in its gross income under section 691(a)(1) as income in respect of a decedent shall be included in the gross income of the estate or trust.

(b) Determination of amounts deductible under section 642(c) and the character of such amounts. (1) *Reduction of charitable contributions deduction by amounts not included in gross income.* If an estate, pooled income fund, or other trust pays, permanently sets aside, or uses any amount of its income for a purpose specified in section 642(c)(1), (2) or (3) and that amount includes any items of estate or trust income not entering into the gross income of the estate or trust, the deduction allowable under § 1.642(c)–1 or § 1.642(c)–2 is limited to the gross income so paid, permanently set aside, or used. In the case of a pooled income fund for which a deduction is allowable under paragraph (c) of § 1.642(c)–2 for amounts permanently set aside, only the gross income of the fund which is attributable to net long-term capital gain (as defined in section 1222(7)) shall be taken into account.

(2) *Determination of the character of an amount deductible under section 642(c).* In determining whether the amounts of income so paid, permanently set aside, or used for a purpose specified in section 642(c)(1), (2), or (3) include particular items of income of an estate or trust, whether or not included in gross income, a provision in the governing instrument or in local law that specifically provides the source out of which amounts are to be paid, permanently set aside, or used for such a purpose controls for Federal tax purposes to the extent such provision has economic effect independent of income tax consequences. § 1.652(b)–2(b). In the absence of such specific provisions in the governing instrument or in local law, the amount to which section 642(c) applies is deemed to consist of the same proportion of each class of the items of income of the estate or trust as the total of each class bears to the total of all classes. § 1.643(a)–5(b) for the method of determining the allocable portion of exempt income and foreign income. This paragraph (b)(2) is illustrated by the following examples:

Example (1). A charitable lead annuity trust has the calendar year as its taxable year, and is to pay an annuity of $10,000 annually to an organization described in section 170(c). A provision in the trust governing instrument provides that the $10,000 annuity should be deemed to come first from ordinary income, second from short-term capital gain, third from fifty percent of the unrelated business taxable income, fourth from long-term capital gain, fifth from the balance of unrelated business taxable income, sixth from tax-exempt income, and seventh from principal. This provision in the governing instrument does not have economic effect independent of income tax consequences, because the amount to be paid to the charity is not dependent upon the type of income from which it is to be paid. Accordingly, the amount to which section 642(c) applies is deemed to consist of the same proportion of each class of the items of income of the trust as the total of each class bears to the total of all classes.

Example (2). A trust instrument provides that 100 percent of the trust's ordinary income must be distributed currently to an organization described in section 170(c) and that all remaining items of income must be distributed currently to B, a noncharitable beneficiary. This income ordering provision has economic effect independent of income tax consequences because the amount to be paid to the charitable organization each year is dependent upon the amount of ordinary income the trust earns within that taxable year. Accordingly, for purposes of section 642(c), the full amount distributed to charity is deemed to consist of ordinary income.

(3) *Other examples*. For examples showing the determination of the character of an amount deductible under § 1.642(c)–1 or § 1.642(c)–2, see examples 1 and 2 in § 1.662(b)–2 and paragraph (e) of the example in § 1.662(c)–4.

(4) For the purpose of this paragraph, the provision of section 116 are not to be taken into account.

(c) Capital gains included in charitable contribution. Where any amount of the income paid, permanently set aside, or used for a purpose specified in section 642(c)(1), (2), or (3), is attributable to net long-term capital gain (as defined in section 1222(7)), the amount of the deduction otherwise allowable under § 1.642(c)–1 or § 1.642(c)–2, must be adjusted for any deduction provided in section 1202 of 50 percent of the excess, if any, of the net long-term capital gain over the net short-term capital loss. For determination of the extent to which the contribution to which § 1.642(c)–1 or § 1.642(c)–2 applies is deemed to consist of net long-term capital gains, see paragraph (b) of this section. The application of this paragraph may be illustrated by the following examples:

Example (1). Under the terms of the trust instrument, the income of a trust described in § 1.642(c)–2(b)(3)(i) is currently distributable to A during his life and capital gains are allocable to corpus. No provision is made in the trust instrument for the invasion of corpus for the benefit of A. Upon A's death the corpus of the trust is to be distributed to M University, an organization described in section 501(c)(3) which is exempt from taxation under section 501(a). During the taxable year ending December 31, 1970, the trust has long-term capital gains of $100,000 from property transferred to it on or before October 9, 1969, which are permanently set aside for charitable purposes. The trust includes $100,000 in gross income but is allowed a deduction of $50,000 under section 1202 for the long-term capital gains and a charitable contributions deduction of $50,000 under section 642(c)(2) ($100,000 permanently set aside for charitable purposes less $50,000 allowed as a deduction under section 1202 with respect to such $100,000).

Example (2). Under the terms of the will, $200,000 of the income (including $100,000 capital gains) for the taxable year 1972 of an estate is distributed, one-quarter to each of two individual beneficiaries and one-half to N University, an organization described in section 501(c)(3) which is exempt from taxation under section 501(a). During 1972 the estate has ordinary income of $200,000, long-term capital gains of $100,000, and no capital losses. It is assumed that for 1972 the estate has no other items of income or any deductions other than those discussed herein. The entire capital gains of $100,000 are included in the gross income of the estate for 1972, and N University receives $100,000 from the estate in such year. However, the amount allowable to the estate under section 642(c)(1) is subject to appropriate adjustment for the deduction allowable under section 1202. In view of the distributions of $25,000 of capital gains to each of the individual beneficiaries, the deduction allowable to the estate under section 1202 is limited by such section to $25,000 [($100,000 capital gains less $50,000 capital gains includible in income of individual beneficiaries under section 662) x 50%]. Since the whole of this $25,000 deduction under section 1202 is attributable to the distribution of $50,000 of capital gains to N University, the deduction allowable to the estate in 1972 under section 642(c)(1) is $75,000 [$100,000 (distributed to N) less $25,000 (proper adjustment for section 1202 deduction)].

Example (3). Under the terms of the trust instrument, 30 percent of the gross income (exclusive of capital gains) of a trust described in § 1.642(c)–2(b)(3)

(i) is currently distributed to B, the sole income beneficiary. Net capital gains (capital gain net income for taxable years beginning after December 31, 1976) and undistributed ordinary income are allocable to corpus. No provision is made in the trust instrument for the invasion of corpus for the benefit of B. Upon B's death the remainder of the trust is to be distributed to M Church. During the taxable year 1972, the trust has ordinary income of $100,000, long-term capital gains of $15,000, short-term capital gains of $1,000, long-term capital losses of $5,000, and short-term capital losses of $2,500. It is assumed that the trust has no other items of income or any deductions other than those discussed herein. All the ordinary income and capital gains and losses are attributable to amounts transferred to the trust before October 9, 1969. The trust includes in gross income for 1972 the total amount of $116,000 [$100,000 (ordinary income)+$16,000 (total capital gains determined without regard to capital losses)]. Pursuant to the terms of the governing instrument the trust distributes to B in 1972 the amount of $30,000 ($100,000 x 30%). The balance of $78,500 [($116,000 less $7,500 capital losses) - $30,000 distribution] is available for the set-aside for charitable purposes. In determining taxable income for 1972 the capital losses of $7,500 ($5,000 + $2,500) are allowable in full under section 1211(b)(1). The net capital gain (capital gain net income for taxable years beginning after December 31, 1976) of $8,500 ($16,000 less $7,500) is the excess of the net long-term capital gain of $10,000 ($15,000 less $5,000) over the net short-term capital loss of $1,500 ($2,500 less $1,000). The deduction under section 1202 is $4,250 ($8,500 x 50%), all of which is attributable to the set-aside for charitable purposes. Accordingly, for 1972 the deduction allowable to the trust under section 642(c)(2) is $74,250 [$78,500 (set-aside for M) less $4,250 (proper adjustment for section 1202 deduction)].

Example (4). During the taxable year a pooled income fund, as defined in § 1.642(c)–5, has in addition to ordinary income long-term capital gains of $150,000, short-term capital gains of $15,000, long-term capital losses of $100,000, and short-term capital losses of $10,000. Under the Declaration of Trust and pursuant to State law net long-term capital gain is allocable to corpus and net short-term capital gain is to be distributed to the income beneficiaries of the fund. All thc capital gains and losses are attributable to amounts transferred to the fund after July 31, 1969. In view of the distribution of the net short-term capital gain of $5,000 ($15,000 less $10,000) to the income beneficiaries, the deduction allowed to the fund under section 1202 is limited by such section to $25,000 [($150,000 (long-term capital gains) less $100,000 (long-term capital losses) * 50%]. Since the whole of this deduction under section 1202 is attributable to the set-aside for charitable purposes, the deduction of $50,000 ($150,000 less $100,000) otherwise allowable under section 642(c)(3) is subject to appropriate adjustment under section 642(c)(4) for the deduction allowable under section 1202. Accordingly, the amount of the set-aside deduction is $25,000 [$50,000 (set-aside for public charity) less $25,000 (proper adjustment for section 1202 deduction)].

Example (5). The facts are the same as in example (4) except that under the Declaration of Trust and pursuant to State law all the net capital gain (capital gain net income for taxable years beginning after December 31, 1976) for the taxable year is allocable to corpus of the fund. The fund would thus include in gross income total capital gains of $165,000 ($150,000+$15,000). In determining taxable income for the taxable year the capital losses of $110,000 ($100,000+$10,000) are allowable in full under section 1211(b)(1). The net capital gain of $55,000 ($165,000 less $110,000) is available for the set-aside for charitable purposes under section 642(c)(3) only in the amount of the net long-term capital gain of $50,000 ($150,000 long-term gains less $100,000 long-term losses). The deduction under section 1202 is $25,000 ($50,000 x 50%), all of which is attributable to the set-aside for charitable purposes. Accordingly, the deduction allowable to the fund under section 642(c)(3) is $25,000 [$50,000 (set-aside for public charity) less $25,000 (proper adjustment for section 1202 deduction)]. The $5,000 balance of net capital gain (capital gain net income for taxable years beginning after December 31, 1976) is taken into account in determining taxable income of the pooled income fund for the taxable year.

(d) Disallowance of deduction for amounts allocable to unrelated business income. In the case of a trust, the deduction otherwise allowable under § 1.642(c)–1 or § 1.642(c)–2 is disallowed to the extent of amounts allocable to the trust's unrelated business income. See section 681(a) and the regulations thereunder.

(e) Disallowance of deduction in certain cases. For disallowance of certain deductions otherwise allowable under section 642(c)(1), (2), or (3), see sections 508(d) and 4948(c)(4).

(f) Information returns. For rules applicable to the annual information return that must be filed by trusts claiming a deduction under section 642(c) for the taxable year, see section 6034 and the regulations thereunder.

(g) Payments resulting in state or local tax benefits. (1) *In general.* If the trust or decedent's estate makes a payment of gross income for a purpose specified in section 170(c), and the trust or decedent's estate receives or expects to receive a state or local tax benefit in consideration for such payment, § 1.170A–1(h)(3) applies in determining the charitable contribution deduction under section 642(c).

(2) *Effective/applicability date.* Paragraph (g)(1) of this section applies to payments of gross income after August 27, 2018.

[T.D. 6500, 25 FR 11814, Nov. 26, 1960, as amended by T.D. 7357, 40 FR 23741, June 2, 1975; 40 FR 24361, June 6, 1975; T.D. 7728, 45 FR 72650, Nov. 3, 1980; T.D. 9582, 77 FR 22484, April 16, 2012; T.D. 9864, 84 FR 27530, June 13, 2019]

§ 1.642(c)–4 Nonexempt private foundations.

In the case of a trust which is, or is treated under section 4947(a)(1) as though it were, a private foundation (as defined in section 509(a) and the regulations thereunder) that is not exempt from taxation under section 501(a) for the taxable year, a deduction for amounts paid or permanently set aside, or used for a purpose specified in section 642(c)(1), or (2) shall not be allowed under § 1.642(c)–1 or § 1.642(c)–2, but such trust shall, subject to the provisions applicable to individuals, be allowed a deduction under section 170 for charitable contributions paid during the taxable year. Section 642(c)(6) and this section do not apply to a trust described in section 4947(a)(1) unless such trust fails to meet the requirements of section 508(e). However, if on October 9, 1969, or at any time thereafter, a trust is recognized as being exempt from taxation under section 501(a) as an organization described in section 501(c)(3), if at such time such trust is a private foundation, and if at any time thereafter such trust is determined not to be exempt from taxation under section 501(a) as an organization described in section 501(c)(3), section 642(c)(6) and this section will apply to such trust. See § 1.509(b)–1(b).

[T.D. 6500, 25 FR 11814, Nov. 26, 1960, as amended by T.D. 7357, 40 FR 23742, June 2, 1975; 40 FR 24362, June 6, 1975]

§ 1.642(c)–5 Definition of pooled income fund.

(a) In general. (1) *Application of provisions.* Section 642(c)(5) prescribes certain rules for the valuation of contributions involving transfers to certain funds described in that section as pooled income funds. This section sets forth the requirements for qualifying as a pooled income fund and provides for the manner of allocating the income of the fund to the beneficiaries. Section 1.642(c)–6 provides for the valuation of a remainder interest in property transferred to a pooled income fund. § 1.642(c)–7 provides transitional rules under which certain funds may be amended so as to qualify as pooled income funds in respect to transfers of property occurring after July 31, 1969.

(2) *Tax status of fund and its beneficiaries.* Notwithstanding any other provision of this chapter, a fund which meets the requirements of a pooled income fund, as defined in section 642(c)(5) and paragraph (b) of this section, shall not be treated as an association within the meaning of section 7701(a)(3). Such a fund, which need not be a trust under local law, and its beneficiaries shall be taxable under Part I, Subchapter J, Chapter 1 of the Code, but the provisions of Subpart E (relating to grantors and others treated as substantial owners) of such part shall not apply to such fund.

(3) *Recognition of gain or loss on transfer to fund.* No gain or loss shall be recognized to the donor on the transfer of property to a pooled income fund. In such case, the fund's basis and holding period with respect to property transferred to the fund by a donor shall be determined as provided in sections 1015(b) and 1223(2). If, however, a donor transfers property to a pooled income fund and, in addition to creating or retaining a life income interest therein, receives property from the fund, or transfers property to the fund which is subject to an indebtedness, this subparagraph shall not apply to the gain realized by reason of (i) the receipt of such property or (ii) the amount of such indebtedness, whether or not assumed by the pooled income fund, which is required to be treated as an amount realized on the transfer. For applicability

of the bargain sale rules, see section 1011(b) and the regulations thereunder.

(4) *Charitable contributions deduction.* A charitable contributions deduction for the value of the remainder interest, as determined under § 1.642(c)–6, may be allowed under section 170, 2055, 2106, or 2522, where there is a transfer of property to a pooled income fund. For a special rule relating to the reduction of the amount of a charitable contribution of certain ordinary income property or capital gain property, see section 170(e)(1)(A) or (B)(i) and the regulations thereunder.

(5) *Definitions.* For purposes of this section, §§ 1.642(c)–6, and 1.642(c)–7:

(i) The term income has the same meaning as it does under section 643(b) and the regulations thereunder, except that income generally may not include any long-term capital gains. However, in conformance with the applicable state statute, income may be defined as or satisfied by a unitrust amount, or pursuant to a trustee's power to adjust between income and principal to fulfill the trustee's duty of impartiality, if the state statute both provides for a reasonable apportionment between the income and remainder beneficiaries of the total return of the trust and meets the requirements of § 1.643(b)–1. In exercising a power to adjust, the trustee must allocate to principal, not to income, the proceeds from the sale or exchange of any assets contributed to the fund by any donor or purchased by the fund at least to the extent of the fair market value of those assets on the date of their contribution to the fund or of the purchase price of those assets purchased by the fund. This definition of income applies for taxable years beginning after January 2, 2004.

(ii) The term "donor" includes a decedent who makes a testamentary transfer of property to a pooled income fund.

(iii) The term "governing instrument" means either the governing plan under which the pooled income fund is established and administered or the instrument of transfer, as the context requires.

(iv) The term "public charity" means an organization described in clause (i) to (vi) of section 170(b)(1)(A). If an organization is described in clause (i) to (vi) of section 170(b)(1)(A) and is also described in clause (viii) of such section, it shall be treated as a public charity.

(v) The term "fair market value", when used with respect to property, means its value in excess of the indebtedness or charges against such property.

(vi) The term "determination date" means each day within the taxable year of a pooled income fund on which a valuation is made of the property in the fund. The property in the fund shall be valued on the first day of the taxable year of the fund and on at least 3 other days within the taxable year. The period between any two consecutive determination dates within the taxable year shall not be greater than 3 calendar months. In the case of a taxable year of less than 12 months, the property in the fund shall be valued on the first day of such taxable year and on such other days within such year as occur at successive intervals of no greater than 3 calendar months. Where a valuation date falls on a Saturday, Sunday, or legal holiday (as defined in section 7503 and the regulations thereunder), the valuation may be made on either the next preceding day which is not a Saturday, Sunday, or legal holiday or the next succeeding day which is not a Saturday, Sunday, or legal holiday, so long as the next such preceding day or next such succeeding day is consistently used where the valuation date falls on a Saturday, Sunday, or legal holiday.

(6) *Cross references.* (i) See section 4947(a)(2) and section 4947(b)(3)(B) for the application to pooled income funds of the provisions relating to private foundations and section 508(e) for rules relating to provisions required in the governing instrument prohibiting certain activities specified in section 4947(a)(2).

(ii) For rules for postponing the time for deduction of a charitable contribution of a future interest in tangible personal property, see section 170(a)(3) and the regulations thereunder.

(b) Requirements for qualification as a pooled income fund. A pooled income fund to which this section applies must satisfy all of the following requirements:

(1) *Contribution of remainder interest to charity.* Each donor must transfer property to the fund and contribute an irrevocable remainder interest in such property to or for the use of a public charity, retaining for himself, or creating for another beneficiary or beneficiaries, a life income interest in the transferred property. A contingent remainder interest shall not be

treated as an irrevocable remainder interest for purposes of this subparagraph.

(2) *Creation of life income interest.* Each donor must retain for himself for life an income interest in the property transferred to such fund, or create an income interest in such property for the life of one or more beneficiaries, each of whom must be living at the time of the transfer of the property to the fund by the donor. The term "one or more beneficiaries" includes those members of a named class who are alive and can be ascertained at the time of the transfer of the property to the fund. In the event more than one beneficiary of the income interest is designated, such beneficiaries may enjoy their shares of income concurrently, consecutively, or both concurrently and consecutively. The donor may retain the power exercisable only by will to revoke or terminate the income interest of any designated beneficiary other than the public charity. The governing instrument must specify at the time of the transfer the particular beneficiary or beneficiaries to whom the income is payable and the share of income distributable to each person so specified. The public charity to or for the use of which the remainder interest is contributed may also be designated as one of the beneficiaries of an income interest. The donor need not retain or create a life interest in all the income from the property transferred to the fund provided any income not payable under the terms of the governing instrument to an income beneficiary is contributed to, and within the taxable year in which it is received is paid to, the same public charity to or for the use of which the remainder interest is contributed. No charitable contributions deduction shall be allowed to the donor for the value of such income interest of the public charity or for the amount of any such income paid to such organization.

(3) *Commingling of property required.* The property transferred to the fund by each donor must be commingled with, and invested or reinvested with, other property transferred to the fund by other donors satisfying the requirements of subparagraphs (1) and (2) of this paragraph. The governing instrument of the pooled income fund must contain a provision requiring compliance with the preceding sentence. The public charity to or for the use of which the remainder interest is contributed may maintain more than one pooled income fund, provided that each such fund is maintained by the organization and is not a device to permit a group of donors to create a fund which may be subject to their manipulation. The fund must not include property transferred under arrangements other than those specified in section 642(c)(5) and this paragraph. However, a fund shall not be disqualified as a pooled income fund under this paragraph because any portion of its properties is invested or reinvested jointly with other properties, not a part of the pooled income fund, which are held by, or for the use of, the public charity which maintains the fund, as for example, with securities in the general endowment fund of the public charity to or for the use of which the remainder interest is contributed. Where such joint investment or reinvestment of properties occurs, records must be maintained which sufficiently identify the portion of the total fund which is owned by the pooled income fund and the income earned by, and attributable to, such portion. Such a joint investment or reinvestment of properties shall not be treated as an association or partnership for purposes of the Code. A bank which serves as trustee of more than one pooled income fund may maintain a common trust fund to which section 584 applies for the collective investment and reinvestment of moneys of such funds.

(4) *Prohibition against exempt securities.* The property transferred to the fund by any donor must not include any securities, the income from which is exempt from tax under subtitle A of the Code, and the fund must not invest in such securities. The governing instrument of the fund must contain specific prohibitions against accepting or investing in such securities.

(5) *Maintenance by charitable organization required.* The fund must be maintained by the same public charity to or for the use of which the irrevocable remainder interest is contributed. The requirement of maintenance will be satisfied where the public charity exercises control directly or indirectly over the fund. For example, this requirement of control shall ordinarily be met when the public charity has the power to remove the trustee or trustees of the fund and designate a new trustee or trustees. A national organization which carries out its purposes through local organizations, chapters, or auxiliary bodies with which it has an identity of aims and purposes may maintain a pooled income fund (otherwise satisfying the requirements of this paragraph) in which one or more local organizations, chapters, or auxiliary bodies which are public charities have been named as recipients of the remain-

der interests. For example, a national church body may maintain a pooled income fund where donors have transferred property to such fund and contributed an irrevocable remainder interest therein to or for the use of various local churches or educational institutions of such body. The fact that such local organizations or chapters have been separately incorporated from the national organization is immaterial.

(6) *Prohibition against donor or beneficiary serving as trustee.* The fund must not have, and the governing instrument must prohibit the fund from having, as a trustee a donor to the fund or a beneficiary (other than the public charity to or for the use of which the remainder interest is contributed) of an income interest in any property transferred to such fund. Thus, if a donor or beneficiary (other than such public charity) directly or indirectly has general responsibilities with respect to the fund which are ordinarily exercised by a trustee, such fund does not meet the requirements of section 642(c)(5) and this paragraph. The fact that a donor of property to the fund, or a beneficiary of the fund, is a trustee, officer, director, or other official of the public charity to or for the use of which the remainder interest is contributed ordinarily will not prevent the fund from meeting the requirements of section 642(c)(5) and this paragraph.

(7) *Income of beneficiary to be based on rate of return of fund.* Each beneficiary entitled to income of any taxable year of the fund must receive such income in an amount determined by the rate of return earned by the fund for such taxable year with respect to his income interest, computed as provided in paragraph (c) of this section. The governing instrument of the fund shall direct the trustee to distribute income currently or within the first 65 days following the close of the taxable year in which the income is earned. Any such payment made after the close of the taxable year shall be treated as paid on the last day of the taxable year. A statement shall be attached to the return of the pooled income fund indicating the date and amount of such payments after the close of the taxable year. Subject to the provisions of Part I, Subchapter J, Chapter 1 of the Code, the beneficiary shall include in his gross income all amounts properly paid, credited, or required to be distributed to the beneficiary during the taxable year or years of the fund ending within or with his taxable year. The governing instrument shall provide that the income interest of any designated beneficiary shall either terminate with the last regular payment which was made before the death of the beneficiary or be prorated to the date of his death.

(8) *Termination of life income interest.* Upon the termination of the income interest retained or created by any donor, the trustee shall sever from the fund an amount equal to the value of the remainder interest in the property upon which the income interest is based. The value of the remainder interest for such purpose may be either (i) its value as of the determination date next succeeding the termination of the income interest or (ii) its value as of the date on which the last regular payment was made before the death of the beneficiary if the income interest is terminated on such payment date. The amount so severed from the fund must either be paid to, or retained for the use of, the designated public charity, as provided in the governing instrument. However, see subparagraph (3) of this paragraph for rules relating to commingling of property.

(c) Allocation of income to beneficiary. (1) *In general.* Every income interest retained or created in property transferred to a pooled income fund shall be assigned a proportionate share of the annual income earned by the fund, such share, or unit of participation, being based on the fair market value of such property on the date of transfer, as provided in this paragraph.

(2) *Units of participation.* (i) *Unit plan.* (a) On each transfer of property by a donor to a pooled income fund, one or more units of participation in the fund shall be assigned to the beneficiary or beneficiaries of the income interest retained or created in such property, the number of units of participation being equal to the number obtained by dividing the fair market value of the property by the fair market value of a unit in the fund at the time of the transfer.

(b) The fair market value of a unit in the fund at the time of the transfer shall be determined by dividing the fair market value of all property in the fund at such time by the number of units then in the fund. The initial fair market value of a unit in a pooled income fund shall be the fair market value of the property transferred to the fund divided by the number of units assigned to the income interest in that property. The value of each unit of participation will fluctuate with each new transfer of property to the fund in relation to the appreciation or depreciation in the fair market value of the property in the fund, but all units in the fund will always have equal value.

(c) The share of income allocated to each unit of participation shall be determined by dividing the income of the fund for the taxable year by the outstanding number of units in the fund at the end of such year, except that, consistently with paragraph (b)(7) of this section, income shall be allocated to units outstanding during only part of such year by taking into consideration the period of time such units are outstanding. For this purpose the actual income of such part of the taxable year, or a prorated portion of the annual income, may be used, after making such adjustments as are reasonably necessary to reflect fluctuations during the year in the fair market value of the property in the fund.

(ii) *Other plans*. The governing instrument of the fund may provide any other reasonable method not described in subdivision (i) of this subparagraph for assigning units of participation in the fund and allocating income to such units which reaches a result reasonably consistent with the provisions of such subdivision.

(iii) *Transfers between determination dates*. For purposes of subdivisions (i) and (ii) of this subparagraph, if a transfer of property to the fund by a donor occurs on other than a determination date, the number of units of participation assigned to the income interest in such property may be determined by using the fair market value of the property in the fund on the determination date immediately preceding the date of transfer (determined without regard to the property so transferred), subject, however, to appropriate adjustments on the next succeeding determination date. Such adjustments may be made by any reasonable method, including the use of a method whereby the fair market value of the property in the fund at the time of the transfer is deemed to be the average of the fair market values of the property in the fund on the determination dates immediately preceding and succeeding the date of transfer. For purposes of determining such average any property transferred to the fund between such preceding and succeeding dates, or on such succeeding date, shall be excluded. The application of this subdivision may be illustrated by the following example:

Example. The determination dates of a pooled income fund are the first day of each calendar month. On April 1, 1971, the fair market value of the property in the fund is $100,000, at which time 1,000 units of participation are outstanding with a value of $100 each. On April 15, 1971, B transfers property with a fair market value of $50,000 to the fund, retaining for himself for life an income interest in such property. No other property is transferred to the fund after April 1, 1971. On May 1, 1971, the fair market value of the property in the fund, including the property transferred by B, is $160,000. The average of the fair market values of the property in the fund (excluding the property transferred by B) on April 1 and May 1, 1971, is $105,000 ($100,000+[$160,000-$50,000]/2). Accordingly, the fair market value of a unit of participation in the fund on April 15, 1971, at the time of B's transfer may be deemed to be $105 ($105,000/1,000 units), and B is assigned 476.19 units of participation in the fund ($50,000/$105).

(3) *Special rule for partial allocation of income to charity*. Notwithstanding subparagraph (2) of this paragraph, the governing instrument may provide that a unit of participation is entitled to share in the income of the fund in a lesser amount than would otherwise be determined under such subparagraph, provided that the income otherwise allocable to the unit under such subparagraph is paid within the taxable year in which it is received to the public charity to or for the use of which the remainder interest is contributed under the governing instrument.

(4) *Illustrations*. The application of this paragraph may be illustrated by the following examples:

Example (1). On July 1, 1970, A and B transfer separate properties with a fair market value of $20,000 and $10,000, respectively, to a newly created pooled income fund which is maintained by Y University and uses as its taxable year the fiscal year ending June 30. A and B each retain in themselves for life an income interest in such property, the remainder interest being contributed to Y University. The pooled income fund assigns an initial value of $100 to each unit of participation in the fund, and under the governing instruments A receives 200 units, and B receives 100 units, in the fund. On October 1, 1970, which is a determination date, C transfers property to the fund with a fair market value of $12,000, retaining in himself for life an income interest in such property and contributing the remainder interest to Y University. The fair market value of the property in the fund at the time of C's transfer is $36,000. The fair market value of A's and B's units at the time of such transfer is $120 each

($36,000/300). By reason of his transfer of property C is assigned 100 units of participation in the fund ($12,000/$120).

Example (2). Assume that the pooled income fund in example (1) earns $2,600 for its taxable year ending June 30, 1971, and there are no further contributions of property to the fund in such year. Further assume $300 is earned in the first quarter ending September 30, 1970. Therefore, the fund earns $1 per unit for the first quarter ($300 divided by 300 units outstanding) and $5.75 per unit for the remainder of the taxable year ([$2,600-$300] divided by 400 units out-standing). If the fund distributes its income for the year based on its actual earnings per quarter, the income must be distributed as follows:

Beneficiary	***Share of income***
A	$1,350 ([200 * $1] + [200 * 5.75]).
B	675 ([100 * $1] + [100 * 5.75]).
C	$575 (100 * $5.75).

Example (3). (a) On July 1, 1970, A and B transfer separate properties with a fair market value of $10,000 and $20,000, respectively, to a newly created pooled income fund which is maintained by X University and uses as its taxable year the fiscal year ending June 30. A and B each retain in themselves an income interest for life in such property, the remainder interest being contributed to X University. The governing instrument provides that each unit of participation in the fund shall have a value of not more than its initial fair market value; the instrument also provides that the income allocable to appreciation in the fair market value of such unit (to the extent in excess of its initial fair market value) at the end of each quarter of the fiscal year is to be distributed currently to X University. On October 1, 1970, which is a determination date, C contributes to the fund property with a fair market value of $60,000 and retains in himself an income interest for life in such property, the remainder interest being contributed to X University. The initial fair market value of the units assigned to A, B, and C is $100. A, B, and C's units of participation are as follows:

Beneficiary	***Units of participation***
A	100 ($10,000 divided by 100).
B	200 ($20,000 divided by 100).
C	100 ($10,000 divided by 100).

(b) The fair market value of the property in the fund at the time of C's contribution is $40,000. Assuming the fair market value of the property in the fund is $100,000 on December 31, 1970, and that the income of the fund for the second quarter ending December 31, 1970, is $2,000, the income is shared by the income beneficiaries and X University as follows:

Beneficiary	***Allocation of income***
A, B, and C	90% ($90,000 divided by $100,000).
X University	10% ($10,000 divided by $100,000).

(c) For the quarter ending December 31, 1970, each unit of participation is allocated $2 (90 percent * $2,000 divided by 900) of the income earned for that quarter. A, B, C, and X University share in the income as follows:

Beneficiary	***Share of income***
A	$200 (100 * $2).
B	$400 (200 * $2).
C	$1,200 (600 * $2).
X University	$200 (10% * $2,000).

[T.D. 7105, 36 FR 6477, Apr. 6, 1971; 36 FR 7004, Apr. 13, 1971, as amended by T.D. 7125, 36 FR 11032, June 8, 1971; T.D. 7357, 40 FR 23742, June 2, 1975; T.D. 7633, 44 FR 57925, Oct. 9, 1979; T.D. 9102, 69 FR 18, Jan. 2, 2004]

§ 1.642(c)–6 Valuation of a remainder interest in property transferred to a pooled income fund.

(a) In general. (1) For purposes of sections 170, 2055, 2106, and 2522, the fair market value of a remainder interest in property transferred to a pooled income fund is its present value determined under paragraph (d) of this section.

(2) The present value of a remainder interest at the time of the transfer of property to the pooled income fund is determined by computing the present value (at the time of the transfer) of the life income interest and subtracting that value from the fair market value of the transferred property on the valuation date. The fact that the income beneficiary may not receive the last income payment, as provided in paragraph (b)(7) of § 1.642(c)–5, is not taken into account for purposes of determining the value of the life income interest. For purposes of this section, the valuation date is the date on which property is transferred to the fund by the do-

nor except that, for purposes of section 2055 or 2106, it is the alternate valuation date, if elected, under the provisions and limitations set forth in section 2032 and the regulations thereunder.

(3) Any claim for a deduction on any return for the value of the remainder interest in property transferred to a pooled income fund must be supported by a statement attached to the return showing the computation of the present value of the interest.

(b) Actuarial computations by the Internal Revenue Service. The regulations in this and in related sections provide tables of actuarial factors and examples that illustrate the use of the tables in determining the value of remainder interests in property. Section 1.7520–1(c)(2) refers to government publications that provide additional tables of factors and examples of computations for more complex situations. If the computation requires the use of a factor that is not provided in this section, the Commissioner may supply the factor upon a request for a ruling. A request for a ruling must be accompanied by a recitation of the facts including the pooled income fund's highest yearly rate of return for the 3 taxable years immediately preceding the date of transfer, the date of birth of each measuring life, and copies of the relevant documents. A request for a ruling must comply with the instructions for requesting a ruling published periodically in the Internal Revenue Bulletin (see §§ 601.201 and 601.601(d)(2)(ii)(b) of this chapter) and include payment of the required user fee. If the Commissioner furnishes the factor, a copy of the letter supplying the factor should be attached to the tax return in which the deduction is claimed. If the Commissioner does not furnish the factor, the taxpayer must furnish a factor computed in accordance with the principles set forth in this section.

(c) Computation of pooled income fund's yearly rate of return. (1) For purposes of determining the present value of the life income interest, the yearly rate of return earned by a pooled income fund for a taxable year is the percentage obtained by dividing the amount of income earned by the pooled income fund for the taxable year by an amount equal to—

(i) The average fair market value of the property in such fund for that taxable year; less

(ii) The corrective term adjustment.

(2) The average fair market value of the property in a pooled income fund for a taxable year shall be the sum of the amounts of the fair market value of all property held by the pooled income fund on each determination date, as defined in paragraph (a)(5)(vi) of § 1.642(c)–5, of such taxable year divided by the number of determination dates in such taxable year. For such purposes the fair market value of property held by the fund shall be determined without including any income earned by the fund.

(3)(i) The corrective term adjustment shall be the sum of the products obtained by multiplying each income payment made by the pooled income fund within its taxable year by the percentage set forth in column (2) of the following table opposite the period within such year, set forth in column (1), which includes the date on which that payment is made:

Table

(1) *Payment Period*	*(2)* *Percentage of Payment*
Last week of 4th quarter	0
Balance of 4th quarter	25
Last week of 3d quarter	25
Balance of 3d quarter	50
Last week of 2d quarter	50
Balance of 2d quarter	75
Last week of 1st quarter	75
Balance of 1st quarter	100

(ii) If the taxable year of the fund consists of less than 12 months, the corrective term adjustment shall be the sum of the products obtained by multiplying each income payment made by the pooled income fund within such taxable year by the percentage obtained by subtracting from 1 a fraction the numerator of which is the number of days from the first day of such taxable year to the date of such income payment and the denominator of which is 365.

(4) A pooled income fund's method of calculating its yearly rate of return must be supported by a full statement attached to the income tax return of the pooled income fund for each taxable year.

(5) The application of this paragraph may be illustrated by the following examples:

Example (1). (a) The pooled income fund maintained by W University has established determination dates on the first day of each calendar quarter. The pooled income fund is on a calendar-year basis. The pooled income fund earned $5,000 of income during 1971. The fair market value of its property (determined without including any income earned by the fund), and the income paid out, on the first day of each calendar quarter in 1971 are as follows:

Date	***Fair Market Value of Property***	***Income Payment***
Jan. 1	$100,000	$ 1,200
Apr. 1	105,000	1,200
July 1	95,000	1,200
Oct. 1	100,000	1,400
	400,000	5,000

(b) The average fair market value of the property in the fund for 1971 is $100,000 ($400,000, divided by 4).

(c) The corrective term adjustment for 1971 is $3,050, determined by applying the percentages obtained in column (2) of the table in subparagraph (3) of this paragraph:

Multiplication:	***Product***
100% * $1,200	$1,200
75% * $1,200	900
50% * $1,200	600
25% * $1,400	350
Sum of products	3,050

(d) The pooled income fund's yearly rate of return for 1971 is 5.157 percent, determined as follows:

$$\frac{\$5{,}000}{\$100{,}000 - \$3{,}050} = 0.05157$$

Example (2). (a) The pooled income fund maintained by X University has established determination dates on the first day of each calendar quarter. The pooled income fund is on a calendar-year basis. The pooled income fund earned $5,000 of income during 1971 and paid out $3,000 on December 15, 1971, and $2,000 on January 15, 1972, the last amount being treated under paragraph (b)(7) of § 1.642(c)–5 as paid on December 31, 1971. The fair market value of its property (determined without including any income earned by the fund) on the determination dates in 1971 and the income paid out during 1971 are as follows:

Date	***FMV of Property***	***Income Payment***
Jan. 1	$125,000	....
Apr. 1	125,000	....
July 1	75,000	....
Oct. 1	75,000	....
Dec. 15	....	$3,000
Dec. 31	....	2,000
	400,000	5,000

(b) The average fair market value of the property in the fund for 1971 is $100,000 ($400,000 divided by 4).

(c) The corrective term adjustment for 1971 is $750, determined by applying the percentages obtained in column (2) of the table in subparagraph (3) of this paragraph:

Multiplication:	***Product***
0% * $2,000	$0
25% * $3,000	$750
Sum of products	$750

(d) The pooled income fund's yearly rate of return for 1971 is 5.038 percent, determined as follows:

$$\frac{\$5{,}000}{\$100{,}000 - \$750} = 0.05038$$

(d) Valuation. The present value of the remainder interest in property transferred to a pooled income fund on or after June 1, 2023, is determined under paragraph (e) of this section. The present value of the remainder interest in property transferred to a pooled income fund for which the valuation date is before June 1, 2023, is determined (subject to paragraph (e)(2) of this section) under the following sections:

Valuation Dates		*Applicable Regulations*
After	*Before*	
—	01-01-52	§ 1.642(c)–6A(a)
12-31-51	01-01-71	§ 1.642(c)–6A(b)
12-31-70	12-01-83	§ 1.642(c)–6A(c)
11-30-83	05-01-89	§ 1.642(c)–6A(d)
04-30-89	05-01-99	§ 1.642(c)–6A(e)
04-30-99	05-01-09	§ 1.642(c)–6A(f)
04-30-09	06-01-23	§ 1.642(c)–6A(g)

(e) Present value of the remainder interest in the case of transfers to pooled income funds for which the valuation date is on or after June 1, 2023 (1) *In general.* In the case of transfers to pooled income funds for which the valuation date is on or after June 1, 2023, the present value of a remainder interest is determined under this section. See, however, § 1.7520–3(b) (relating to exceptions to the use of prescribed tables under certain circumstances). The present value of a remainder interest that is dependent on the termination of the life of one individual is computed by using the formula in § 20.2031–7(d)(2)(ii)(B) of this chapter to derive a remainder factor from the appropriate mortality table to at least five decimal places. For the convenience of taxpayers, actuarial factors have been computed by the IRS and appear in Table S. Table S currently is available, at no charge, electronically via the IRS website at *https://www.irs.gov/retirement-plans/actuarial-tables* (or a corresponding URL as may be updated from time to time). Table S is referenced and explained by IRS Publication 1457, Actuarial Valuations Version 4A, which will be available within a reasonable time after June 1, 2023. For purposes of the computations under this section, the age of an individual is the age at the individual's nearest birthday.

(2) *Transitional rule for valuation of transfers to pooled income funds.* For purposes of section 170, 2055, 2106, 2522, or 2624, in the case of transfers to a pooled income fund for which the valuation date is after April 30, 2019, and on or before June 1, 2023, the present value of the remainder interest under this section is determined by using the section 7520 interest rate for the month in which the valuation date occurs (see §§ 1.7520–1(b) and 1.7520–2(a)(2)) and the appropriate actuarial factors derived from the selected mortality table, either Table 2010CM in § 20.2031–7(d)(7)(ii) of this chapter or Table 2000CM in § 20.2031–7A(g)(4) of this chapter, at the option of the donor or the decedent's executor, as the case may be. If any previously filed income tax return is amended to use the actuarial factors based on Table 2010CM, the amended return must state at the top "AMENDED PURSUANT TO TD 9974." If any previously filed gift or estate tax return is supplemented to use the actuarial factors based on Table 2010CM, the supplemental return must state at the top "SUPPLEMENTED PURSUANT TO TD 9974." For the convenience of taxpayers, actuarial factors based on Table 2010CM appear in the current version of Table S, and actuarial factors based on Table 2000CM appear in the previous version of Table S. Both versions of Table S currently are available, at no charge, electronically via the IRS website at *https://www.irs.gov/retirement-plans/actuarial-tables* (or a corresponding URL as may be updated from time to time). The donor or decedent's executor must consistently use the same mortality basis with respect to each interest (income, remainder, partial, etc.) in the same property, and with respect to all transfers occurring on the same valuation date. For example, gift and income tax charitable deductions with respect to the same transfer must be determined based on factors with the same mortality basis, and all assets includible in the gross estate and/or estate tax deductions claimed must be valued based on factors with the same mortality basis.

(3) *Present value of a remainder interest.* The present value of a remainder interest in property transferred to a pooled income fund is computed on the basis of

(i) Life contingencies determined from the values of lx that are set forth in Table 2010CM in § 20.2031–7(d)(7)(ii) of this chapter (see § 20.2031–7A of this chapter for certain prior periods); and

(ii) Discount at a rate of interest, compounded annually, equal to the highest yearly rate of return of the pooled income fund for the three taxable years immediately preceding its taxable year in which the transfer of property to the fund is made. For purposes of this paragraph (e), the yearly rate of return of a pooled income fund is determined as provided in paragraph (c) of this section unless the highest rate of return is deemed to be the rate described in paragraph (e)(4) of this section for funds in existence less than 3 taxable years. For purposes of this paragraph (e)(3)(ii), the first taxable year of a pooled income fund is considered a taxable year even though the taxable year consists of less than 12 months. However, appropriate adjustments must be made to annualize the rate of return earned by the fund for that period. Where it appears from the facts and circumstances that the highest yearly rate of return of the fund for the three taxable years immediately preceding the taxable year in which the transfer of property is made has been purposely manipulated to be substantially less than the rate of return that otherwise would be reasonably anticipated with the purpose of obtaining an excessive charitable deduction, that rate of return may not be used. In that case, the highest yearly rate of return of the fund is determined by treating the fund as a pooled income fund that has been in existence for less than three preceding taxable years.

(4) *Pooled income funds in existence less than three taxable years.* If a pooled income fund has been in existence less than three taxable years immediately preceding the taxable year in which the transfer is made to the fund and the transfer to the fund is made on or after May 1, 1989, the highest rate of return is deemed to be the interest rate (rounded to the nearest two-tenths of one percent) that is one percent less than the highest annual average of the monthly section 7520 rates for the three calendar years immediately preceding the calendar year in which the transfer to the pooled income fund is made. The deemed rate of return for transfers to new pooled income funds is recomputed each calendar year using the monthly section 7520 rates for the three year period immediately preceding the calendar year in which each transfer to the fund is made until the fund has been in existence for three taxable years and can compute its highest rate of return for the three taxable years immediately preceding the taxable year in which the transfer of property to the fund is made in accordance with the rules set forth in the first sentence of paragraph (e)(3)(ii) of this section.

(5) *Computation of value of remainder interest* (i) Factor. The factor that is used in determining the present value of a remainder interest that is dependent on the termination of the life of one individual is the factor obtained through use of the formula in § 20.2031–7(d)(2)(ii)(B) of this chapter to derive a remainder factor from the appropriate mortality table to at least five decimal places. For the convenience of taxpayers, actuarial factors have been computed by the IRS and appear in Table S. Table S currently is available, at no charge, electronically via the IRS website at *https://www.irs.gov/retirement-plans/actuarial-tables.* Table S is referenced and explained in IRS Publication 1457, Actuarial Valuations Version 4A, which will be available within a reasonable time after June 1, 2023. In using the section of Table S for the interest rate equal to the appropriate yearly rate of return, the appropriate remainder factor is opposite the number that corresponds to the age of the individual upon whose life the value of the remainder interest is based (See § 1.642(c)–6A for certain prior periods). The tables referenced by IRS Publication 1457, Actuarial Valuations Version 4A, include factors for yearly rates of return from 0.2 to 20 percent, inclusive, in increments of two-tenths of one percent. For other situations, see paragraph (b) of this section. If the yearly rate of return is a percentage that is between the yearly rates of return for which factors are provided by Table S, an exact method of obtaining the applicable factors (such as through software using the actual rate of return and the actuarial formulas provided in § 20.2031–7(d)(2)(ii)(B) of this chapter) or a linear interpolation must be used, provided whichever method used is applied consistently in valuing all interests in the same property. The applicable remainder factors derived by an exact method or by interpolation must be expressed to at least five decimal places. The present value of the remainder interest is determined by multiplying the fair market value of the property on the valuation date by the appropriate remainder factor.

(ii) Sample factors from actuarial Table S. For purposes of the example in paragraph (e)(5)(iii) of this section, the following factors from Table S will be used:

Factors from Table S—Based on Table 2010CM			
Interest at 5.4 Percent			
Age	Annuity	Life Estate	Remainder
55	13.2515	0.71558	0.28442
Interest at 5.6 Percent			
Age	Annuity	Life Estate	Remainder
55	12.9710	0.72637	0.27363

(iii) *Example of interpolation.* After June 1, 2023, A, whose age is 54 years and 8 months, transfers $100,000 to a pooled income fund, and retains a life income interest in the property. The highest yearly rate of return earned by the fund for its 3 preceding taxable years is 5.43 percent. In Table S, the remainder factor opposite 55 years under 5.4 percent is 0.28442 and under 5.6 percent is 0.27363. The present value of the remainder interest is $28,280, computed as illustrated in Figure 1 to this paragraph (e)(5)(iii).

Figure 1 to Paragraph (e)(5)(iii) Illustration of Interpolation Method

A.	Remainder Factor at 5.4 percent for age 55	0.28442
B.	Less: Remainder Factor at 5.6 percent for age 55	- 0.27363
C.	Difference: A - B	0.01079

D. Interpolation Adjustment:

$$\frac{5.43\% - 5.40\%}{5.60\% - 5.40\%} = \frac{z}{0.01079}$$

E.

$$\frac{5.43\% - 5.40\%}{5.60\% - 5.40\%} \cdot 0.01079 = z = 0.00162$$

F.	Remainder Factor at 5.4 percent for age 55	0.28442
G.	Less: Interpolation Adjustment z	- 0.00162
H.	Interpolated Factor: F - G	0.28280
I.	Amount Transferred	$ 100,000
J.	Present Value of Remainder Interest: H x I	$ 28,280

(6) *Actuarial tables.* In the case of transfers for which the valuation date is on or after June 1, 2023, the present value of a remainder interest dependent on the termination of one life in the case of a transfer to a pooled income fund is determined by using the formula in § 20.2031–7(d)(2)(ii)(B) of this chapter to derive a remainder factor from the appropriate mortality table to at least five decimal places. For the convenience of taxpayers, actuarial factors have been computed by the IRS and appear in Table S. Table S currently is available, at no charge, electronically via the IRS website at *https://www.irs.gov/retirement-plans/actuarial-tables.* Table S is referenced and explained in IRS Publication 1457, Actuarial Valuations Version 4A, which will be available within a reasonable time after June 1, 2023.

(f) Applicability date. This section applies on and after June 1, 2023.

[T.D. 7105, 36 FR 6480, April 6, 1971, as amended by 36 FR 9512, May 26, 1971; 36 FR 12290, June 30, 1971; T.D. 7955, 49 FR 19976, May 11, 1984; T.D. 8540, 59 FR 30102, 30105, June 10, 1994; T.D. 8819, 64 FR 23190, April 30, 1999; T.D. 8886, 65 FR 36910, June 12, 2000; T.D. 9448, 74 FR 21440, May 7, 2009;

T.D. 9540, 76 FR 49572, Aug. 10, 2011; T.D. 9974, 88 FR 37429, June 7, 2023]

§ 1.642(c)–6A Valuation of charitable remainder interests for which the valuation date is before June 1, 2023.

(a) Valuation of charitable remainder interests for which the valuation date is before January 1, 1952. [*Omitted. Ed.*]

(b) Valuation of charitable remainder interests for which the valuation date is after December 31, 1951, and before January 1, 1971. [*Omitted. Ed.*]

(c) Present value of remainder interest in the case of transfers to pooled income funds for which the valuation date is after December 31, 1970, and before December 1, 1983. [*Omitted. Ed.*]

(d) Present value of remainder interest dependent on the termination of one life in the case of transfers to pooled income funds made after November 30, 1983, for which the valuation date is before May 1, 1989. [*Omitted. Ed.*]

(e) Present value of the remainder interest in the case of transfers to pooled income funds for which the valuation date is after April 30, 1989, and before May 1, 1999. [*Omitted. Ed.*]

(f) Present value of the remainder interest in the case of transfers to pooled income funds for which the valuation date is after April 30, 1999, and before May 1, 2009. [*Omitted. Ed.*]

(g) Present value of the remainder interest in the case of transfers to pooled income funds for which the valuation date is on or after May 1, 2009, and before June 1, 2023.

(1) *In general.* In the case of transfers to pooled income funds for which the valuation date is on or after May 1, 2009, and before June 1, 2023, the present value of a remainder interest is determined under this section. See, however, § 1.7520–3(b) (relating to exceptions to the use of prescribed tables under certain circumstances). The present value of a remainder interest that is dependent on the termination of the life of one individual is computed by the use of Table S in paragraph (g)(6) of this section. For purposes of the computations under this section, the age of an individual is the age at the individual's nearest birthday.

(2) *Transitional rules for valuation of transfers to pooled income funds.* (i) For purposes of section 2055, 2106, or 2624, if on May 1, 2009, the decedent was under a mental disability so that the disposition of the property could not be changed, and the decedent died on or after May 1, 2009, but before June 2, 2023, without having regained the ability to dispose of the decedent's property, or if the decedent died within 90 days of the date that the decedent first regained that ability on or after May 1, 2009, but before June 2, 2023, the present value of a remainder interest is determined as if the valuation date with respect to the decedent's gross estate is either before May 1, 2009, or after April 30, 2009, at the option of the decedent's executor.

(ii) For purposes of section 170, 2055, 2106, 2522, or 2624, in the case of transfers to a pooled income fund for which the valuation date is on or after May 1, 2009, and before July 1, 2009, the present value of the remainder interest under this section is determined by using the section 7520 interest rate for the month in which the valuation date occurs (see §§ 1.7520–1(b) and 1.7520–2(a)(2)) and the appropriate actuarial tables under either paragraph (f)(6) or (g)(6) of this section, at the option of the donor or the decedent's executor, as the case may be.

(iii) For purposes of paragraphs (g)(2)(i) and (ii) of this section, where the donor or decedent's executor is given the option to use the appropriate actuarial tables under either paragraph (f)(6) or (g)(6) of this section, the donor or decedent's executor must consistently use the same mortality basis with respect to each interest (income, remainder, partial, etc.) in the same property, and with respect to all transfers occurring on the same valuation date. For example, gift and income tax charitable deductions with respect to the same transfer must be determined based on factors with the same mortality basis, and all assets includible in the gross estate and/or estate tax deductions claimed must be valued based on factors with the same mortality basis.

(iv) In the case of transfers to a pooled income fund for which the valuation date is after April 30, 2019, and before June 1, 2023, the present value of the remainder interest under this section is determined under § 1.642(c)–6(e)(2).

(3) *Present value of a remainder interest.* The present value of a remainder interest in property transferred to a pooled income fund is computed on the basis of

(i) Life contingencies determined from the values of lx that are set forth in Table 2000CM [*Tables are omitted from current version of this Code book. Ed.*] in § 20.2031–7A(g)(4) of this chapter; and

(ii) Discount at a rate of interest, compounded annually, equal to the highest yearly rate of return of the pooled income fund for the three taxable years immediately preceding its taxable year in which the transfer of property to the fund is made. The provisions of § 1.642(c)–6(c) apply for determining the yearly rate of return. However, where the taxable year is less than 12 months, the provisions of § 1.642(c)–6(e)(3)(ii) apply for the determining the yearly rate of return.

(4) *Pooled income funds in existence less than three taxable years*. The provisions of § 1.642(c)–6(e)(4) apply for determining the highest yearly rate of return when the pooled income fund has been in existence less than three taxable years.

(5) *Computation of value of remainder interest*. The factor that is used in determining the present value of a remainder interest that is dependent on the termination of the life of one individual is the factor from Table S in paragraph (g)(6) of this section under the appropriate yearly rate of return opposite the number that corresponds to the age of the individual upon whose life the value of the remainder interest is based. Table S in paragraph (g)(6) of this section includes factors for yearly rates of return from 0.2 to 14 percent, inclusive, in increments of two-tenths of one percent. Actuarial factors that do not appear in paragraph (g)(6) of this section may be computed directly by using the formula in § 20.2031–7(d)(2)(ii)(B) of this chapter to derive a remainder factor from the appropriate mortality table to at least five decimal places. For the convenience of taxpayers, actuarial factors have been computed by the IRS and appear in Table S that is referenced and explained by IRS Publication 1457, Actuarial Valuations Version 3A (2009). The table is available at no charge, electronically via the IRS website at *https://www.irs.gov/retirement-plans/actuarial-tables* (or a corresponding URL as may be updated from time to time). For other situations, see § 1.642(c)–6(b). If the yearly rate of return is a percentage that is between the yearly rates of return for which factors are provided by Table S, an exact method of obtaining the applicable factors (such as through software using the actual rate of return and actuarial formulas provided in § 20.2031–7(d)(2)(ii)(B) of this chapter) or a linear interpolation must be used, provided whichever method used is applied consistently in valuing all interests in the same property. The present value of the remainder interest is determined by multiplying the fair market value of the property on the valuation date by the appropriate remainder factor. For an example of a computation of the present value of a remainder interest requiring a linear interpolation adjustment, see § 1.642(c)–6(e)(5).

(6) *Actuarial tables*. In the case of transfers for which the valuation date is on or after May 1, 2009, and before June 1, 2023, and without regard to the headings in the tables in this paragraph (g)(6) that do not contain this termination date for the applicability of the tables, the present value of a remainder interest dependent on the termination of one life in the case of a transfer to a pooled income fund is determined by using the following tables:

[*Tables are omitted from current version of this Code book. Ed.*]

(7) *Applicability dates*. Paragraphs (g)(1) through (6) of this section apply on and after May 1, 2009, and before June 1, 2023.

[T.D. 8540, 59 FR 30105, 30116, June 10, 1994; T.D. 8819, 64 FR 23190, 23199, 23228, April 30, 1999; 64 FR 33196, June 22, 1999; T.D. 8886, 65 FR 36943, June 12, 2000; T.D. 9448, 74 FR 21440, 21464, May 7, 2009; T.D. 9540, 76 FR 49612, Aug. 10, 2011; T.D. 9974, 88 FR 37429, 37432, June 7, 2023]

§ 1.642(c)–7 Transitional rules with respect to pooled income funds. [*Omitted. Ed.*]

[T.D. 7105, 36 FR 6486, April 6, 1971, as amended by T.D. 7125, 36 FR 11032, June 8, 1971; T.D. 8540, 59 FR 30102, June 10, 1994]

§ 1.642(d)–1 Net operating loss deduction.

The net operating loss deduction allowed by section 172 is available to estates and trusts generally, with the following exceptions and limitations:

(a) In computing gross income and deductions for the purposes of section 172, a trust shall exclude that portion of the income and deductions attributable to the grantor or another person under sections 671 through 678 (relating to grantors and others treated as substantial owners).

(b) An estate or trust shall not, for the purposes of section 172, avail itself of the deductions allowed by section 642(c) (relating to charitable contributions deductions) and sections 651 and 661 (relating to deductions for distributions).

[T.D. 6500, 25 FR 11814, Nov. 26, 1960]

§ 1.642(e)–1 Depreciation and depletion.

An estate or trust is allowed the deductions for depreciation and depletion, but only to the extent the deductions are not apportioned to beneficiaries under sections 167(h) and 611(b). For purposes of sections 167(h) and 611(b), the term "beneficiaries" includes charitable beneficiaries. See the regulations under those sections.

[T.D. 6500, 25 FR 11814, Nov. 26, 1960, as amended by T.D. 6712, 29 FR 3655, March 24, 1964]

§ 1.642(f)–1 Amortization deductions.

An estate or trust is allowed amortization deductions with respect to an emergency facility as defined in section 168(d), with respect to a certified pollution control facility as defined in section 169(d), with respect to qualified railroad rolling stock as defined in section 184(d), with respect to certified coal mine safety equipment as defined in section 187(d), with respect to on-the-job training and child-care facilities as defined in section 188(b), and with respect to certain rehabilitations of certified historic structures as defined in section 191, in the same manner and to the same extent as in the case of an individual. However, the principles governing the apportionment of the deductions for depreciation and depletion between fiduciaries and the beneficiaries of an estate or trust (see sections 167(h) and 611(b) and the regulations thereunder) shall be applicable with respect to such amortization deductions.

[T.D. 6500, 25 FR 11814, Nov. 26, 1960, as amended by T.D. 6712, 29 FR 3655, Mar. 24, 1964; T.D. 7116, 36 FR 9017, May 18, 1971; T.D. 7599, 44 FR 14552, Mar. 13, 1979; T.D. 7700, 45 FR 38055, June 6, 1980]

§ 1.642(g)–1 Disallowance of double deductions; in general.

Amounts allowable under section 2053(a)(2) (relating to administration expenses) or under section 2054 (relating to losses during administration) as deductions in computing the taxable estate of a decedent are not allowed as deductions in computing the taxable income of the estate unless there is filed a statement, in duplicate, to the effect that the items have not been allowed as deductions from the gross estate of the decedent under section 2053 or 2054 and that all rights to have such items allowed at any time as deductions under section 2053 or 2054 are waived. The statement should be filed with the return for the year for which the items are claimed as deductions or with the district director for the internal revenue district in which the return was filed, for association with the return. The statement may be filed at any time before the expiration of the statutory period of limitation applicable to the taxable year for which the deduction is sought. Allowance of a deduction in computing an estate's taxable income is not precluded by claiming a deduction in the estate tax return, so long as the estate tax deduction is not finally allowed and the statement is filed. However, after a statement is filed under section 642(g) with respect to a particular item or portion of an item, the item cannot thereafter be allowed as a deduction for estate tax purposes since the waiver operates as a relinquishment of the right to have the deduction allowed at any time under section 2053 or 2054.

[T.D. 6500, 25 FR 11814, Nov. 26, 1960]

§ 1.642(g)–2 Deductions included.

It is not required that the total deductions, or the total amount of any deduction, to which section 642(g) is applicable be treated in the same way. One deduction or portion of a deduction may be allowed for income tax purposes if the appropriate statement is filed, while another deduction or portion is allowed for estate tax purposes. Section 642(g) has no application to deductions for taxes, interest, business expenses, and other items accrued at the date of a decedent's death so that they are allowable as a deduction under section 2053(a)(3) for estate tax purposes as claims against the estate, and are also allowable under section 691(b) as deductions in respect of a decedent for income tax purposes. However, section 642(g) is applicable to deductions for interest, business expenses, and other items not accrued at the date of the decedent's death so that they are allowable as deductions for estate tax purposes only as administration expenses under section 2053(a)(2). Although deductible under section 2053(a)(3) in determining the value of the taxable estate of a decedent, medical, dental, etc., expenses of a decedent which are paid by the estate of the decedent are not deductible in computing the taxable income of the estate. See section 213(d) and the regulations thereunder for rules relating to the deductibility of such expenses in computing the taxable income of the decedent.

[T.D. 6500, 25 FR 11814, Nov. 26, 1960]

§ 1.642(h)–1 Unused loss carryovers on termination of an estate or trust.

(a) If, on the final termination of an estate or trust, a net operating loss carryover under section 172 or a capital loss carryover under section 1212 would be allowable to the estate or trust in a taxable year subsequent to the taxable year of termination but for the termination, the carryover or carryovers are allowed under section 642(h)(1) to the beneficiaries succeeding to the property of the estate or trust. See § 1.641(b)–3 for the determination of when an estate or trust terminates.

(b) The net operating loss carryover and the capital loss carryover are the same in the hands of a beneficiary as in the estate or trust, except that the capital loss carryover in the hands of a beneficiary which is a corporation is a short-term loss irrespective of whether it would have been a long-term or short-term capital loss in the hands of the estate or trust. The net operating loss carryover and the capital loss carryover are taken into account in computing taxable income, adjusted gross income, and the tax imposed by section 56 (relating to the minimum tax for tax preferences). The first taxable year of the beneficiary to which the loss shall be carried over is the taxable year of the beneficiary in which or with which the estate or trust terminates. However, for purposes of determining the number of years to which a net operating loss, or a capital loss under paragraph (a) of § 1.1212–1, may be carried over by a beneficiary, the last taxable year of the estate or trust (whether or not a short taxable year) and the first taxable year of the beneficiary to which a loss is carried over each constitute a taxable year, and, in the case of a beneficiary of an estate or trust that is a corporation, capital losses carried over by the estate or trust to any taxable year of the estate or trust beginning after December 31, 1963, shall be treated as if they were incurred in the last taxable year of the estate or trust (whether or not a short taxable year). For the treatment of the net operating loss carryover when the last taxable year of the estate or trust is the last taxable year to which such loss can be carried over, see § 1.642(h)–2.

(c) The application of this section may be illustrated by the following examples:

Example (1). A trust distributes all of its assets to A, the sole remainderman, and terminates on December 31, 1954, when it has a capital loss carryover of $10,000 attributable to transactions during the taxable year 1952. A, who reports on the calendar year basis, otherwise has ordinary income of $10,000 and capital gains of $4,000 for the taxable year 1954. A would offset his capital gains of $4,000 against the capital loss of the trust and, in addition, deduct under section 1211(b) $1,000 on his return for the taxable year 1954. The balance of the capital loss carryover of $5,000 may be carried over only to the years 1955 and 1956, in accordance with paragraph (a) of § 1.1212–1 and the rules of this section.

Example (2). A trust distributes all of its assets, one-half to A, an individual, and one-half to X, a corporation, who are the sole remaindermen, and terminates on December 31, 1966, when it has a short-term capital loss carryover of $20,000 attributable to short-term transactions during the taxable years 1964, 1965, and 1966, and a long-term capital loss carryover of $12,000 attributable to long-term transactions during such years. A, who reports on the calendar year basis, otherwise has ordinary income of $15,000, short-term capital gains of $4,000 and long-term capital gains of $6,000, for the taxable year 1966. A would offset his short-term capital gains of $4,000 against his share of the short-term capital loss carryover of the trust, $10,000 (one-half of $20,000), and, in addition deduct under section 1211(b) $1,000 (treated as a short-term gain for purposes of computing capital loss carryovers) on his return for the taxable year 1966. A would also offset his long-term capital gains of $6,000 against his share of the long-term capital loss carryover of the trust, $6,000 (one-half of $12,000). The balance of A's share of the short-term capital loss carryover, $5,000, may be carried over as a short-term capital loss carryover to the succeeding taxable year and treated as a short-term capital loss incurred in such succeeding taxable year in accordance with paragraph (b) of § 1.1212–1. X, which also reports on the calendar year basis, otherwise has capital gains of $4,000 for the taxable year 1966. X would offset its capital gains of $4,000 against its share of the capital loss carryovers of the trust, $16,000 (the sum of one-half of each the short-term carryover and the long-term carryover of the trust), on its return for the taxable year 1966. The balance of X's share, $12,000, may be carried over as a short-term capital loss only to the years 1967, 1968, 1969, and 1970, in accordance with paragraph (a) of § 1.1212–1 and the rules of this section.

[T.D.6500, 25 FR 11814, Nov. 26, 1960, as amended by T.D. 6828, 30 FR 7805, June 17, 1965; T.D. 7564, 43 FR 40495, Sept. 12, 1978]

§ 1.642(h)–2 Excess deductions on termination of an estate or trust.

(a) Excess deductions (1) *In general.* If, on the termination of an estate or trust, the estate or trust has for its last taxable year deductions (other than the deductions allowed under section 642(b) (relating to the personal exemption) or section 642(c) (relating to charitable contributions)) in excess of gross income, the excess deductions as determined under paragraph (b) of this section are allowed under section 642(h)(2) as items of deduction to the beneficiaries succeeding to the property of the estate or trust.

(2) *Treatment by beneficiary.* A beneficiary may claim all or part of the amount of the deductions provided for in paragraph (a) of this section, as determined after application of paragraph (b) of this section, before, after, or together with the same character of deductions separately allowable to the beneficiary under the Internal Revenue Code for the beneficiary's taxable year during which the estate or trust terminated as provided in paragraph (c) of this section.

(b) Character and amount of excess deductions (1) *Character.* The character and amount of the excess deductions on termination of an estate or trust will be determined as provided in this paragraph (b). Each deduction comprising the excess deductions under section 642(h)(2) retains, in the hands of the beneficiary, its character (specifically, as allowable in arriving at adjusted gross income, as a non-miscellaneous itemized deduction, or as a miscellaneous itemized deduction) while in the estate or trust. An item of deduction succeeded to by a beneficiary remains subject to any additional applicable limitation under the Internal Revenue Code and must be separately stated if it could be so limited, as provided in the instructions to Form 1041, U.S. Income Tax Return for Estates and Trusts, and the Schedule K-1 (Form 1041), Beneficiary's Share of Income, Deductions, Credit, etc., or successor forms.

(2) *Amount.* The amount of the excess deductions in the final year is determined as follows:

(i) Each deduction directly attributable to a class of income is allocated in accordance with the provisions in § 1.652(b)–3(a);

(ii) To the extent of any remaining income after application of paragraph (b)(2)(i) of this section, deductions are allocated in accordance with the provisions in § 1.652(b)–3(b) and (d); and

(iii) Deductions remaining after the application of paragraph (b)(2)(i) and (ii) of this section comprise the excess deductions on termination of the estate or trust. These deductions are allocated to the beneficiaries succeeding to the property of the estate of or trust in accordance with § 1.642(h)–4.

(c) Year of termination (1) *In general.* The deductions provided for in paragraph (a) of this section are allowable only in the taxable year of the beneficiary in which or with which the estate or trust terminates, whether the year of termination of the estate or trust is of normal duration or is a short taxable year.

(2) *Example.* Assume that a trust distributes all its assets to B and terminates on December 31, Year X. As of that date, it has excess deductions of $18,000, all characterized as allowable in arriving at adjusted gross income under section 67(e). B, who reports on the calendar year basis, could claim the $18,000 as a deduction allowable in arriving at B's adjusted gross income for Year X. However, if the deduction (when added to other allowable deductions that B claims for the year) exceeds B's gross income, the excess may not be carried over to any year subsequent to Year X.

(d) Net operating loss carryovers. A deduction based upon a net operating loss carryover will never be allowed to beneficiaries under both paragraphs (1) and (2) of section 642(h). Accordingly, a net operating loss deduction which is allowable to beneficiaries succeeding to the property of the estate or trust under the provisions of paragraph (1) of section 642(h) cannot also be considered a deduction for purposes of paragraph (2) of section 642(h) and paragraph (a) of this section. However, if the last taxable year of the estate or trust is the last year in which a deduction on account of a net operating loss may be taken, the deduction, to the extent not absorbed in that taxable year by the estate or trust, is considered an "excess deduction" under section 642(h)(2) and paragraph (a) of this section.

(e) Items included in net operating loss or capital loss carryovers. Any item of income or deduction, or any part thereof, which is taken into account in determining the net operating loss or capital loss carryover of the estate or trust for its last taxable year shall not be taken into account again in determining excess deductions on termination of the trust or estate within the meaning of section 642(h)(2) and paragraph (a) of this section (see example in § 1.642(h)–5).

(f) Applicability date. Paragraphs (a) through (c) of this section apply to taxable years beginning after October 19, 2020. The rules applicable to taxable years beginning on or before October 19, 2020 are contained in § 1.642(h)–2 as in effect prior to October 19, 2020 (see 26 CFR part 1 revised as of April 1, 2020). Taxpayers may choose to apply paragraphs (a) through (c) of this section to taxable years beginning after December 31, 2017, and on or before October 19, 2020.

[T.D. 6500, 25 FR 11814, Nov. 26, 1960, as amended by T.D. 7564, 43 FR 40495, Sept. 12, 1978; T.D. 9918, 85 FR 66224, Oct. 19, 2020]

§ 1.642(h)–3 Meaning of "beneficiaries succeeding to the property of the estate or trust".

(a) The phrase "beneficiaries succeeding to the property of the estate or trust" means those beneficiaries upon termination of the estate or trust who bear the burden of any loss for which a carryover is allowed, or of any excess of deductions over gross income for which a deduction is allowed, under section 642(h).

(b) With reference to an intestate estate, the phrase means the heirs and next of kin to whom the estate is distributed, or if the estate is insolvent, to whom it would have been distributed if it had not been insolvent. If a decedent's spouse is entitled to a specified dollar amount of property before any distribution to other heirs and next of kin, and if the estate is less than that amount, the spouse is the beneficiary succeeding to the property of the estate or trust to the extent of the deficiency in amount.

(c) In the case of a testate estate, the phrase normally means the residuary beneficiaries (including a residuary trust), and not specific legatees or devisees, pecuniary legatees, or other nonresiduary beneficiaries. However, the phrase does not include the recipient of a specific sum of money even though it is payable out of the residue, except to the extent that it is not payable in full. On the other hand, the phrase includes a beneficiary (including a trust) who is not strictly a residuary beneficiary but whose devise or bequest is determined by the value of the decedent's estate as reduced by the loss or deductions in question. Thus the phrase includes:

(1) A beneficiary of a fraction of a decedent's net estate after payment of debts, expenses, etc.;

(2) A nonresiduary legatee or devisee, to the extent of any deficiency in his legacy or devise resulting from the insufficiency of the estate to satisfy it in full;

(3) A surviving spouse receiving a fractional share of an estate in fee under a statutory right of election, to the extent that the loss or deductions are taken into account in determining the share. However, the phrase does not include a recipient of dower or curtesy, or any income beneficiary of the estate or trust from which the loss or excess deduction is carried over.

(d) The principles discussed in paragraph (c) of this section are equally applicable to trust beneficiaries. A remainderman who receives all or a fractional share of the property of a trust as a result of the final termination of the trust is a beneficiary succeeding to the property of the trust. For example, if property is transferred to pay the income to A for life and then to pay $10,000 to B and distribute the balance of the trust corpus to C, C and not B is considered to be the succeeding beneficiary except to the extent that the trust corpus is insufficient to pay B $10,000.

[T.D. 6500, 25 FR 11814, Nov. 26, 1960]

§ 1.642(h)–4 Allocation.

The carryovers and excess deductions to which section 642(h) applies are allocated among the beneficiaries succeeding to the property of an estate or trust (see § 1.642(h)–3) proportionately according to the share of each in the burden of the loss or deductions. A person who qualified as a beneficiary succeeding to the property of an estate or trust with respect to one amount and does not qualify with respect to another amount is a beneficiary succeeding to the property of the estate or trust as to the amount with respect to which he qualifies. The application of this section may be illustrated by the following example:

Example. A decedent's will leaves $100,000 to A, and the residue of his estate equally to B and C. His estate is sufficient to pay only $90,000 to A, and nothing to B and C. There is an excess of deductions over gross income for the last taxable year of the estate or trust of $5,000, and a capital loss carryover of $15,000, to both of which section 642(h) applies. A is a beneficiary succeeding to the property of the estate to the extent of $10,000, and since the total of the excess of deductions and the loss carryover is $20,000, A is entitled to the benefit of one half of each item, and the remaining half is divided equally between B and C.

[T.D. 6500, 25 FR 11814, Nov. 26, 1960]

§ 1.642(h)–5 Examples.

Paragraphs (a) and (b) of this section (*Examples 1 and 2*) illustrate the application of section 642(h).

(a) Example 1: Computations under section 642(h) when an estate has a net operating loss (1) *Facts.* On January 31, 2020, A dies leaving a will that provides for the distribution of all of A's estate equally to B and an existing trust for C. The period of administration of the estate terminates on December 31, 2020, at which time all the property of the estate is distributed to B and the trust. For tax purposes, B and the trust report income on a calendar year basis. During the period of administration, the estate has the following items of income and deductions:

Income:

Taxable interest	$2,500	
Business income	3,000	
Total income		5,500

Deductions:

Business expenses (including administrative expense allocable to business income)	5,000	
Administrative expenses not allocable to business income that would not have been incurred if property had not been held in a trust or estate (section 67(e) deductions)	9,800	
Total deductions		14,800

(2) *Computation of net operating loss.* (i) The amount of the net operating loss carryover is computed as follows:

Gross income		$5,500
Total deductions	14,800	
Less adjustment under section 172(d)(4) (allowable non-business expenses ($9,800) limited to non-business income ($2,500))	7,300	
Deductions as adjusted		7,500
Net operating loss		2,000

(ii) Under section 642(h)(1), B and the trust are each allocated $1,000 of the $2,000 unused net operating loss carryover of the terminated estate in 2020, with the allowance of any net operating loss carryover to B and the trust determined under section 172. Neither B nor the trust can carry back any of the net operating loss of A's estate made available to them under section 642(h)(1). See § 1.642(h)–1(b).

(3) *Section 642(h)(2) excess deductions.* The $7,300 of non-business deductions not taken into account in determining the net operating loss of the estate are excess deductions on termination of the estate under section 642(h)(2). Under § 1.642(h)–2(b)(1), such deductions retain their character as section 67(e) deductions. Under § 1.642(h)–4, B and the trust each are allocated $3,650 of excess deductions based on B's and the trust's respective shares of the burden of each cost.

(4) *Consequences for C.* The net operating loss carryover and excess deductions are not allowable directly to C, the trust beneficiary. To the extent the distributable net income of the trust is reduced by the net operating loss carryover and excess deductions, however, C may receive an indirect benefit from the carryover and excess deductions.

(b) Example 2: Computations under section 642(h)(2) (1) *Facts.* D dies in 2019 leaving an estate of which the residuary legatees are E (75%) and F (25%). The estate's income and deductions in its final year are as follows:

Income:

Dividends	$3,000
Taxable Interest	500
Rent	2,000
Capital Gain	1,000

Total Income		6,500
Deductions:		
Section 62(a)(4) deductions:		
Rental real estate expenses	2,000	
Section 67(e) deductions:		
Probate fees	1,500	
Estate tax preparation fees	8,000	
Legal fees	2,500	
Total Section 67(e) deductions	12,000	
Non-miscellaneous itemized deductions:		
Personal property taxes	3,500	
Total deductions		17,500

(2) *Determination of character.* Pursuant to § 1.642(h)–2(b)(2), the character and amount of the excess deductions is determined by allocating the deductions among the estate's items of income as provided under § 1.652(b)–3. Under § 1.652(b)–3(a), the $2,000 of rental real estate expenses is allocated to the $2,000 of rental income. In the exercise of the executor's discretion pursuant to § 1.652(b)–3(b), D's executor allocates $3,500 of personal property taxes and $1,000 of section 67(e) deductions to the remaining income. As a result, the excess deductions on termination of the estate are $11,000, all consisting of section 67(e) deductions.

(3) *Allocations among beneficiaries.* Pursuant to § 1.642(h)–4, the excess deductions are allocated in accordance with E's (75 percent) and F's (25 percent) interests in the residuary estate. E's share of the excess deductions is $8,250, all consisting of section 67(e) deductions. F's share of the excess deductions is $2,750, also all consisting of section 67(e) deductions.

(4) *Separate statement.* If the executor instead allocated $4,500 of section 67(e) deductions to the remaining income of the estate, the excess deductions on termination of the estate would be $11,000, consisting of $7,500 of section 67(e) deductions and $3,500 of personal property taxes. The non-miscellaneous itemized deduction for personal property taxes may be subject to limitation on the returns of both B and C's trust under section 164(b)(6)(B) and would have to be separately stated as provided in § 1.642(h)–2(b)(1).

(c) Applicability date. This section is applicable to taxable years beginning after October 19, 2020. Taxpayers may choose to apply this section to taxable years beginning after December 31, 2017, and on or before October 19, 2020.

[T.D. 6500, 25 FR 11814, Nov. 26, 1960, as amended by T.D. 6828, 30 FR 7806, June 17, 1965; T.D. 9918, 85 FR 66225, Oct. 19, 2020]

§ 1.642(i)–1 Certain distributions by cemetery perpetual care funds. [*Omitted. Ed.*]

[T.D. 7651, 44 FR 61596, Oct. 26, 1979]

§ 1.642(i)–2 Definitions. [*Omitted. Ed.*]

[T.D. 7651, 44 FR 61596, Oct. 26, 1979]

§ 643. Definitions Applicable to Subparts A, B, C, and D

(a) Distributable net income. For purposes of this part, the term "distributable net income" means, with respect to any taxable year, the taxable income of the estate or trust computed with the following modifications—

(1) Deduction for distributions. No deduction shall be taken under sections 651 and 661 (relating to additional deductions).

(2) Deduction for personal exemption. No deduction shall be taken under section 642(b) (relating to deduction for personal exemptions).

(3) Capital gains and losses. Gains from the sale or exchange of capital assets shall be excluded to the extent that such gains are allocated to corpus and are not (A) paid, credited, or required to be distributed to any beneficiary during the taxable year, or (B) paid, permanently set aside, or to be used for the purposes specified in section 642(c). Losses from the sale or exchange of capital assets shall be excluded, except to the extent such losses are taken into account in determining the amount of gains from the sale or exchange of capital assets which are paid, credited, or required to be distributed to any beneficiary during the taxable year. The exclusion under section 1202 shall not be taken into account.

(4) Extraordinary dividends and taxable stock dividends. For purposes only of subpart B (relating to trusts which distribute current income only), there shall be excluded those items of gross income constituting extraordinary dividends or taxable stock dividends which the fiduciary, acting in good faith, does not pay or credit to any beneficiary by reason of his determination that such dividends are allocable to corpus under the terms of the governing instrument and applicable local law.

(5) Tax-exempt interest. There shall be included any tax-exempt interest to which section 103 applies, reduced by any amounts which would be deductible in respect of disbursements allocable to such interest but for the provisions of section 265 (relating to disallowance of certain deductions).

(6) Income of foreign trust. In the case of a foreign trust—

(A) There shall be included the amounts of gross income from sources without the United States, reduced by any amounts which would be deductible in respect of disbursements allocable to such income but for the provisions of section 265(a)(1) (relating to disallowance of certain deductions).

(B) Gross income from sources within the United States shall be determined without regard to section 894 (relating to income exempt under treaty).

(C) Paragraph (3) shall not apply to a foreign trust. In the case of such a trust, there shall be included gains from the sale or exchange of capital assets, reduced by losses from such sales or exchanges to the extent such losses do not exceed gains from such sales or exchanges.

(D) [Repealed.]

(7) Abusive transactions. The Secretary shall prescribe such regulations as may be necessary or appropriate to carry out the purposes of this part, including regulations to prevent avoidance of such purposes.

If the estate or trust is allowed a deduction under section 642(c), the amount of the modifications specified in paragraphs (5) and (6) shall be reduced to the extent that the amount of income which is paid, permanently set aside, or to be used for the purposes specified in section 642(c) is deemed to consist of items specified in those paragraphs. For this purpose, such amount shall (in the absence of specific provisions in the governing instrument) be deemed to consist of the same proportion of each class of items of income of the estate or trust as the total of each class bears to the total of all classes.

(b) Income. For purposes of this subpart and subparts B, C, and D, the term "income", when not preceded by the words "taxable", "distributable net", "undistributed net", or "gross", means the amount of income of the estate or trust for the taxable year determined under the terms of the governing instrument and applicable local law. Items of gross income constituting extraordinary dividends or taxable stock dividends which the fiduciary, acting in good faith, determines to be allocable to corpus under the terms of the governing instrument and applicable local law shall not be considered income.

(c) Beneficiary. For purposes of this part, the term "beneficiary" includes heir, legatee, devisee.

(d) Coordination with back-up withholding. Except to the extent otherwise provided in regulations, this subchapter shall be applied with respect to payments subject to withholding under section 3406—

(1) by allocating between the estate or trust and its beneficiaries any credit allowable under section 31(c) (on the basis of their respective shares of any such payment taken into account under this subchapter),

(2) by treating each beneficiary to whom such credit is allocated as if an amount equal to such credit has been paid to him by the estate or trust, and

(3) by allowing the estate or trust a deduction in an amount equal to the credit so allocated to beneficiaries.

(e) Treatment of property distributed in kind.

(1) Basis of beneficiary. The basis of any property received by a beneficiary in a distribution from an estate or trust shall be—

(A) the adjusted basis of such property in the hands of the estate or trust immediately before the distribution, adjusted for

(B) any gain or loss recognized to the estate or trust on the distribution.

(2) Amount of distribution. In the case of any distribution of property (other than cash), the amount taken into account under sections 661(a)(2) and 662(a)(2) shall be the lesser of—

(A) the basis of such property in the hands of the beneficiary (as determined under paragraph (1)), or

(B) the fair market value of such property.

(3) Election to recognize gain.

(A) In general. In the case of any distribution of property (other than cash) to which an election under this paragraph applies—

(i) paragraph (2) shall not apply,

(ii) gain or loss shall be recognized by the estate or trust in the same manner as if such property had been sold to the distributee at its fair market value, and

(iii) the amount taken into account under sections 661(a)(2) and 662(a)(2) shall be the fair market value of such property.

(B) Election. Any election under this paragraph shall apply to all distributions made by the estate or trust during a taxable year and shall be made on the return of such estate or trust for such taxable year.

Any such election, once made, may be revoked only with the consent of the Secretary.

(4) Exception for distributions described in section 663(a). This subsection shall not apply to any distribution described in section 663(a).

(f) Treatment of multiple trusts. For purposes of this subchapter, under regulations prescribed by the Secretary, 2 or more trusts shall be treated as 1 trust if—

(1) such trusts have substantially the same grantor or grantors and substantially the same primary beneficiary or beneficiaries, and

(2) a principal purpose of such trusts is the avoidance of the tax imposed by this chapter.

For purposes of the preceding sentence, a husband and wife shall be treated as 1 person.

(g) Certain payments of estimated tax treated as paid by beneficiary.

(1) In general. In the case of a trust—

(A) the trustee may elect to treat any portion of a payment of estimated tax made by such trust for any taxable year of the trust as a payment made by a beneficiary of such trust,

(B) any amount so treated shall be treated as paid or credited to the beneficiary on the last day of such taxable year, and

(C) for purposes of subtitle F, the amount so treated—

(i) shall not be treated as a payment of estimated tax made by the trust, but

(ii) shall be treated as a payment of estimated tax made by such beneficiary on January 15 following the taxable year.

(2) Time for making election. An election under paragraph (1) shall be made on or before the 65th day after the close of the taxable year of the trust and in such manner as the Secretary may prescribe.

(3) Extension to last year of estate. In the case of a taxable year reasonably expected to be the last taxable year of an estate—

(A) any reference in this subsection to a trust shall be treated as including a reference to an estate, and

(B) the fiduciary of the estate shall be treated as the trustee.

(h) Distributions by certain foreign trusts through nominees. For purposes of this part, any amount paid to a United States person which is derived directly or indirectly from a foreign trust of which the payor is not the grantor shall be deemed in the year of payment to have been directly paid by the foreign trust to such United States person.

(i) Loans from foreign trusts. For purposes of subparts B, C, and D—

(1) General rule. Except as provided in regulations, if a foreign trust makes a loan of cash or marketable securities directly or indirectly to—

(A) any grantor or beneficiary of such trust who is a United States person, or

(B) any United States person not described in subparagraph (A) who is related to such grantor or beneficiary, the amount of such loan shall be treated as a distribution by such trust to such grantor or beneficiary (as the case may be).

(2) Definitions and special rules. For purposes of this subsection—

(A) Cash. The term "cash" includes foreign currencies and cash equivalents.

(B) Related person.

(i) In general. A person is related to another person if the relationship between such persons would result in a disallowance of losses under section 267 or 707(b). In applying section 267 for purposes of the preceding sentence, section 267(c)(4) shall be applied as if the family of an individual includes the spouses of the members of the family.

(ii) Allocation. If any person described in paragraph (1)(B) is related to more than one person, the grantor or beneficiary to whom the treatment under this subsection applies shall be determined under regulations prescribed by the Secretary.

(C) Exclusion of tax-exempts. The term "United States person" does not include any entity exempt from tax under this chapter.

(D) Trust not treated as simple trust. Any trust which is treated under this subsection as making a distribution shall be treated as not described in section 651.

(3) Subsequent transactions regarding loan principal. If any loan is taken into account under paragraph (1), any subsequent transaction between the trust and the original borrower regarding the principal of the loan (by way of complete or partial repayment, satisfaction, cancellation, discharge, or otherwise) shall be disregarded for purposes of this title.

Regulations

§ 1.643(a)–0 Distributable net income; deduction for distributions; in general.

The term "distributable net income" has no application except in the taxation of estates and trusts and their beneficiaries. It limits the deductions allowable to estates and trusts for amounts paid, credited, or required to be distributed to beneficiaries and is used to determine how much of an amount paid, credited, or required to be distributed to a beneficiary will be includible in his gross income. It is also used to determine the character of distributions to the beneficiaries. Distributable net income means for any taxable year, the taxable income (as defined in section 63) of the estate or trust, computed with the modifications set forth in §§ 1.643(a)–1 through 1.643(a)–7.

[T.D. 6500, 25 FR 11814, Nov. 26, 1960]

§ 1.643(a)–1 Deduction for distributions.

The deduction allowable to a trust under section 651 and to an estate or trust under section 661 for amounts paid, credited, or required to be distributed to beneficiaries is not allowed in the computation of distributable net income.

[T.D. 6500, 25 FR 11814, Nov. 26, 1960]

§ 1.643(a)–2 Deduction for personal exemption.

The deduction for personal exemption under section 642(b) is not allowed in the computation of distributable net income.

[T.D. 6500, 25 FR 11814, Nov. 26, 1960]

§ 1.643(a)–3 Capital gains and losses.

(a) In general. Except as provided in § 1.643(a)–6 and paragraph (b) of this section, gains from the sale or exchange of capital assets are ordinarily excluded from distributable net income and are not ordinarily considered as paid, credited, or required to be distributed to any beneficiary.

(b) Capital gains included in distributable net income. Gains from the sale or exchange of capital assets are included in distributable net income to the extent they are, pursuant to the terms of the governing instrument and applicable local law, or pursuant to a reasonable and impartial exercise of discretion by the fiduciary (in accordance with a power granted to the fiduciary by applicable local law or by the governing instrument if not prohibited by applicable local law)—

(1) Allocated to income (but if income under the state statute is defined as, or consists of, a unitrust amount, a discretionary power to allocate gains to income must also be exercised consistently and the amount so allocated may not be greater than the excess of the unitrust amount over the amount of distributable net income determined without regard to this subparagraph § 1.643(a)–3(b));

(2) Allocated to corpus but treated consistently by the fiduciary on the trust's books, records, and tax returns as part of a distribution to a beneficiary; or

(3) Allocated to corpus but actually distributed to the beneficiary or utilized by the fiduciary in determining the amount that is distributed or required to be distributed to a beneficiary.

(c) Charitable contributions included in distributable net income. If capital gains are paid, permanently set aside, or to be used for the purposes specified in section 642(c), so that a charitable deduction is allowed under that section in respect of the gains, they must be included in the computation of distributable net income.

(d) Capital losses. Losses from the sale or exchange of capital assets shall first be netted at the trust level against any gains from the sale or exchange of capital assets, except for a capital gain that is utilized under paragraph (b)(3) of this section in determining the amount that is distributed or required to be distributed to a particular beneficiary. See § 1.642(h)–1 with respect to capital loss carryovers in the year of final termination of an estate or trust.

(e) Examples. The following examples illustrate the rules of this section:

Example (1). Under the terms of Trust's governing instrument, all income is to be paid to A for life. Trustee is given discretionary powers to invade principal for A's benefit and to deem discretionary distributions to be made from capital gains realized during the year. During Trust's first taxable year, Trust has $5,000 of dividend income and $10,000 of capital gain from the sale of securities. Pursuant to the terms of the governing instrument and applicable local law, Trustee allocates the $10,000 capital gain to principal. During the year, Trustee distributes to A $5,000, representing A's right to trust income. In addition, Trustee distributes to A $12,000, pursuant to the discretionary power to distribute principal. Trustee does not exercise the discretionary power to deem the discretionary distributions of principal as being paid from capital gains realized during the year. Therefore, the capital gains realized during the year are not included in distributable net income and the $10,000 of capital gain is taxed to the trust. In future years, Trustee must treat all discretionary distributions as not being made from any realized capital gains.

Example (2). The facts are the same as in Example 1, except that Trustee intends to follow a regular practice of treating discretionary distributions of principal as being paid first from any net capital gains realized by Trust during the year. Trustee evidences this treatment by including the $10,000 capital gain in distributable net income on Trust's federal income tax return so that it is taxed to A. This treatment of the capital gains is a reasonable exercise of Trustee's discretion. In future years Trustee must treat all discretionary distributions as being made first from any realized capital gains.

Example (3). The facts are the same as in Example 1, except that Trustee intends to follow a regular practice of treating discretionary distributions of principal as being paid from any net capital gains realized by Trust during the year from the sale of certain specified assets or a particular class of investments. This treatment of capital gains is a reasonable exercise of Trustee's discretion.

Example (4). The facts are the same as in Example 1, except that pursuant to the terms of the governing instrument (in a provision not prohibited by applicable local law), capital gains realized by Trust are allocated to income. Because the capital gains are allocated to income pursuant to the terms of the governing instrument, the $10,000 capital gain is included in Trust's distributable net income for the taxable year.

Example (5). The facts are the same as in Example 1, except that Trustee decides that discretionary distributions will be made only to the extent Trust has realized capital gains during the year and thus the discretionary distribution to A is $10,000, rather than $12,000. Because Trustee will use the amount of any realized capital gain to determine the amount of the discretionary distribution to the beneficiary, the $10,000 capital gain is included in Trust's distributable net income for the taxable year.

Example (6). Trust's assets consist of Blackacre and other property. Under the terms of Trust's governing instrument, Trustee is directed to hold Blackacre for ten years and then sell it and distribute all the sales proceeds to A. Because Trustee uses the amount of the sales proceeds that includes any realized capital gain to determine the amount required to be distributed to A, any capital gain realized from the sale of Blackacre is included in Trust's distributable net income for the taxable year.

Example (7). Under the terms of Trust's governing instrument, all income is to be paid to A during the Trust's term. When A reaches 35, Trust is to terminate and all the principal is to be distributed to A. Because all the assets of the trust, including all capital gains, will be actually distributed to the beneficiary at the termination of Trust, all capital gains realized in the year of termination are included in distributable net income. See § 1.641(b)–3 for the determination of the year of final termination and the taxability of capital gains realized after the terminating event and before final distribution.

Example (8). The facts are the same as Example 7, except Trustee is directed to pay B $10,000 before distributing the remainder of Trust assets to A. Because the distribution to B is a gift of a specific sum of money within the meaning of section 663(a)(1), none of Trust's distributable net income that includes all of the capital gains realized during the year of termination is allocated to B's distribution.

Example (9). The facts are the same as Example 7, except Trustee is directed to distribute one-half of the principal to A when A reaches 35 and the balance to A when A reaches 45. Trust assets consist entirely of stock in corporation M with a fair market value of $1,000,000 and an adjusted basis of $300,000. When A reaches 35, Trustee sells one-half of the stock and distributes the sales proceeds to A. All the sales proceeds, including all the capital gain attributable to that sale, are actually distributed to A and therefore all the capital gain is included in distributable net income.

Example (10). The facts are the same as Example 9, except when A reaches 35, Trustee sells all the stock and distributes one-half of the sales proceeds to A. If authorized by the governing instrument and applicable state statute, Trustee may determine to what extent the capital gain is distributed to A. The $500,000 distribution to A may be treated as including a minimum of $200,000 of capital gain (and all of the principal amount of $300,000) and a maximum of $500,000 of the capital gain (with no principal). Trustee evidences the treatment by including the appropriate amount of capital gain in distributable net income on Trust's federal income tax return. If Trustee is not authorized by the governing instrument and applicable state statutes to determine to what extent the capital gain is distributed to A, one-half of the capital gain attributable to the sale is included in distributable net income.

Example (11). The applicable state statute provides that a trustee may make an election to pay an income beneficiary an amount equal to four percent of the fair market value of the trust assets, as determined at the beginning of each taxable year, in full satisfaction of that beneficiary's right to income. State statute also provides that this unitrust amount shall be considered paid first from ordinary and tax-exempt income, then from net short-term capital gain, then from net long-term capital gain, and finally from return of principal. Trust's governing instrument provides that A is to receive each year income as defined under state statute. Trustee makes the unitrust election under state statute. At the beginning of the taxable year, Trust assets are valued at $500,000. During the year, Trust receives $5,000 of dividend income and realizes $80,000 of net long-term gain from the sale of capital assets. Trustee distributes to A $20,000 (4% of $500,000) in satisfaction of A's right to income. Net long-term capital gain in the amount of $15,000 is allocated to income pursuant to the ordering rule of the state statute and is included in distributable net income for the taxable year.

Example (12). The facts are the same as in Example 11, except that neither state statute nor Trust's governing instrument has an ordering rule for the character of the unitrust amount, but leaves such a decision to the discretion of Trustee. Trustee intends to follow a regular practice of treating principal, other than capital gain, as distributed to the beneficiary to the extent that the unitrust amount exceeds Trust's ordinary and tax-exempt income. Trustee evidences this treatment by not including any capital gains in distributable net income on Trust's Federal income tax return so that the entire $80,000 capital gain is taxed to Trust. This treatment of the capital gains is a reasonable exercise of Trustee's discretion. In future years Trustee must consistently follow this treatment of not allocating realized capital gains to income.

Example (13). The facts are the same as in Example 11, except that neither state statutes nor Trust's governing instrument has an ordering rule for the character of the unitrust amount, but leaves such a decision to the discretion of Trustee. Trustee intends to follow a regular practice of treating net capital gains as distributed to the beneficiary to the extent the unitrust amount exceeds Trust's ordinary and tax-exempt income. Trustee evidences this treatment by including $15,000 of the capital gain in distributable net income on Trust's Federal income tax return. This treatment of the capital gains is a reasonable exercise of Trustee's discretion. In future years Trustee must consistently treat realized capital gain, if any, as distributed to the beneficiary to the extent that the unitrust amount exceeds ordinary and tax-exempt income.

Example (14). Trustee is a corporate fiduciary that administers numerous trusts. State statutes provide that a trustee may make an election to distribute to an income beneficiary an amount equal to four percent of the annual fair market value of the trust assets in full satisfaction of that beneficiary's right to income. Neither state statutes nor the governing instruments of any of the trusts administered by Trustee has an ordering rule for the character of the unitrust amount, but leaves such a decision to the discretion of Trustee. With respect to some trusts, Trustee intends to follow a regular practice of treating principal, other than capital gain, as distributed to the beneficiary to the extent that the unitrust amount exceeds the trust's ordinary and tax-exempt income. Trustee will evidence this treatment by not including any capital gains in distributable net income on the Federal income tax returns for those trusts. With respect to other trusts, Trustee intends to follow a regular practice of treating any net capital gains as distributed to the beneficiary to the extent the unitrust amount exceeds the trust's ordinary and tax-exempt income. Trustee will evidence this treatment by including net capital gains in distributable net income on the Federal income tax returns filed for these trusts. Trustee's decision with respect to each trust is a reasonable exercise of Trustee's discretion and, in future years, Trustee must treat the capital gains realized by each trust consistently with the treatment by that trust in prior years.

(f) Effective date. This section applies for taxable years of trusts and estates ending after January 2, 2004.

[T.D. 6500, 25 FR 11814, Nov. 26, 1960, as amended by T.D. 6989, 34 FR 731, Jan. 17, 1969; T.D. 7357, 40 FR 23742, June 2, 1975; T.D. 9102, 69 FR 18, Jan. 2, 2004]

§ 1.643(a)–4 Extraordinary dividends and taxable stock dividends.

In the case solely of a trust which qualifies under Subpart B (section 651 and following) as a "simple trust," there are excluded from distributable net income extraordinary dividends (whether paid in cash or in kind) or taxable stock dividends which are not distributed or credited to a beneficiary because the fiduciary in good faith determines that under the terms of the governing instrument and applicable local law such dividends are allocable to corpus. See section 665(e), paragraph (b) of § 1.665(e)–1, and paragraph (b) of § 1.665(e)–1A for the treatment of such dividends upon subsequent distribution.

[T.D. 6500, 25 FR 11814, Nov. 26, 1960, as amended by T.D. 6989, 34 FR 741, Jan. 17, 1969; T.D. 7204, 37 FR 17134, Aug. 25, 1972]

§ 1.643(a)–5 Tax-exempt interest.

(a) There is included in distributable net income any tax-exempt interest excluded from gross income under section 103, reduced by disbursements allocable to such interest which would have been deductible under section 212 but for the provisions of section 265 (relating to disallowance of deductions allocable to tax-exempt income).

(b) If the estate or trust is allowed a charitable contributions deduction under section 642(c), the amounts specified in paragraph (a) of this section and § 1.643(a)–6 are reduced by the portion deemed to be included in income paid, permanently set aside, or to be used for the purposes specified in section 642(c). If the governing instrument or local law specifically provides as to the source out of which amounts are paid, permanently set aside, or to be used for such charitable purposes, the specific provision controls for Federal tax purposes to the extent such provision has economic effect independent of income tax consequences. See § 1.652(b)–2(b). In the absence of such specific provisions in the governing instrument or local law, an amount to which section 642(c) applies is deemed to consist of the same proportion of each class of the items of income of the estate or trust as the total of each class bears to the total of all classes. For illustrations showing the determination of the character of an amount deductible under section 642(c), see Examples 1 and 2 of § 1.662(b)–2 and § 1.662(c)–4(e).

[T.D. 6500, 25 FR 11814, Nov. 26, 1960; T.D. 9582, 77 FR 22485, April 16, 2012]

§ 1.643(a)–6 Income of foreign trust. [*Omitted. Ed.*]

[T.D. 6500, 25 FR 11814, Nov. 26, 1960, as amended by T.D. 6989, 34 FR 731, Jan. 17, 1969; T.D. 7728, 45 FR 72650, Nov. 3, 1980]

§ 1.643(a)–7 Dividends.

Dividends excluded from gross income under section 116 (relating to partial exclusion of dividends received) are included in distributable net income. For this purpose, adjustments similar to those required by § 1.643(a)–5 with respect to expenses allocable to tax-exempt income and to income included in amounts paid or set aside for charitable purposes are not made. See the regulations under section 642(c).

[T.D. 6500, 25 FR 11814, Nov. 26, 1960, as amended by T.D. 7357, 40 FR 23742, June 2, 1975]

§ 1.643(a)–8 Certain distributions by charitable remainder trusts.

(a) Purpose and scope. This section is intended to prevent the avoidance of the purposes of the charitable remainder trust rules regarding the characterizations of distributions from those trusts in the hands of the recipients and should be interpreted in a manner consistent with this purpose. This section applies to all charitable remainder trusts described in section 664 and the beneficiaries of such trusts.

(b) Deemed sale by trust. (1) For purposes of section 664(b), a charitable remainder trust shall be treated as having sold, in the year in which a distribution of an annuity or unitrust amount is made from the trust, a pro rata portion of the trust assets to the extent that the distribution of the annuity or unitrust amount would (but for the application of this paragraph (b)) be characterized in the hands of the recipient as being from the category described in section 664(b)(4) and exceeds the amount of the previously undistributed

(i) Cash contributed to the trust (with respect to which a deduction was allowable under section 170, 2055, 2106, or 2522); plus

(ii) Basis in any contributed property (with respect to which a deduction was allowable under section 170, 2055, 2106, or 2522) that was sold by the trust.

(2) Any transaction that has the purpose or effect of circumventing the rules in this paragraph (b) shall be disregarded.

(3) For purposes of paragraph (b)(1) of this section, trust assets do not include cash or assets purchased with the proceeds of a trust borrowing, forward sale, or similar transaction.

(4) Proper adjustment shall be made to any gain or loss subsequently realized for gain or loss taken into account under paragraph (b)(1) of this section.

(c) Examples. The following examples illustrate the rules of paragraph (b) of this section:

Example (1). Deemed sale by trust. Donor contributes stock having a fair market value of $2 million to a charitable remainder unitrust with a unitrust amount of 50 percent of the net fair market value of the trust assets and a two-year term. The stock has a total adjusted basis of $400,000. In Year 1, the trust receives dividend income of $20,000. As of the valuation date, the trust's assets have a net fair market value of $2,020,000 ($2 million in stock, plus $20,000 in cash). To obtain additional cash to pay the unitrust amount to the noncharitable beneficiary, the trustee borrows $990,000 against the value of the stock. The trust then distributes $1,010,000 to the beneficiary before the end of Year 1. Under section 664(b)(1), $20,000 of the distribution is characterized in the hands of the beneficiary as dividend income. The rest of the distribution, $990,000, is attributable to an amount received by the trust that did not represent either cash contributed to the trust or a return of basis in any contributed asset sold by the trust during Year 1. Under paragraph (b)(3) of this section, the stock is a trust asset because it was not purchased with the proceeds of the borrowing. Therefore, in Year 1, under paragraph (b)(1) of this section, the trust is treated as having sold $990,000 of stock and as having realized $792,000 of capital gain (the trust's basis in the shares deemed sold is $198,000). Thus, in the hands of the beneficiary, $792,000 of the distribution is characterized as capital gain under section 664(b)(2) and $198,000 is characterized as a tax-free return of corpus under section 664(b)(4). No part of the $990,000 loan is treated as acquisition indebtedness under section 514(c) because the entire loan has been recharacterized as a deemed sale.

Example (2). Adjustment to trust's basis in assets deemed sold. The facts are the same as in Example 1. During Year 2, the trust sells the stock for $2,100,000. The trustee uses a portion of the proceeds of the sale to repay the outstanding loan, plus accrued interest. Under paragraph (b)(4) of this section, the trust's adjusted basis in the stock is $1,192,000 ($400,000 plus the $792,000 of gain recognized in Year 1). Therefore, the trust recognizes capital gain (as described in section 664(b)(2)) in Year 2 of $908,000.

Example (3). Distribution of cash contributions. Upon the death of D, the proceeds of a life insurance policy on D's life are payable to T, a charitable remainder annuity trust. The terms of the trust provide that, for a period of three years commencing upon D's death, the trust shall pay an annuity amount equal to $x annually to A, the child of D. After the expiration of such three-year period, the remainder interest in the trust is to be transferred to charity Z. In Year 1, the trust receives payment of the life insurance proceeds and pays the appropriate pro rata portion of the $x annuity to A from the insurance proceeds. During Year 1, the trust has no income. Because the entire distribution is attributable to a cash contribution (the insurance proceeds) to the trust for which a charitable deduction was allowable under section 2055 with respect to the present value of the remainder interest passing to charity, the trust will not be treated as selling a pro rata portion of the trust assets under paragraph (b)(1) of this section. Thus, the distribution is characterized in A's hands as a tax-free return of corpus under section 664(b)(4).

(d) Effective date. This section is applicable to distributions made by a charitable remainder trust after October 18, 1999.

[T.D. 8926, 66 FR 1037, Jan. 5, 2001]

§ 1.643(b)–1 Definition of income.

For purposes of subparts A through D, part I, subchapter J, chapter 1 of the Internal Revenue Code, "income," when not preceded by the words "taxable," "distributable net," "undistributed net," or "gross," means the amount of income of an estate or trust for the taxable year determined under the terms of the governing instrument and applicable local law. Trust provisions that depart fundamentally from traditional principles of income and principal will generally not be recognized. For example, if a trust instrument directs that all the trust income shall be paid to the income beneficiary but defines ordinary dividends and interest as principal, the trust will not be considered one that under its governing instrument is required to distribute all its income currently for purposes of section 642(b) (relating to the personal exemption) and section 651 (relating to simple trusts). Thus, items such as dividends, interest, and rents are generally allocated to income and proceeds from the sale or exchange of trust assets are generally allocated to principal. However, an allocation of amounts between income and principal pursuant to applicable local law will be respected if local law provides for a reasonable apportionment between the income and remainder beneficiaries of the total return of the trust for the year, including ordinary and tax-exempt income, capital gains, and appreciation. For example, a state statute providing that income is a unitrust amount of no less than 3% and no more than 5% of the fair market value of the trust assets, whether determined annually or averaged on a multiple year basis, is a reasonable apportionment of the total return of the trust. Similarly, a state statute that permits the trustee to make adjustments between income and principal to fulfill the trustee's duty of impartiality between the income and remainder beneficiaries is generally a reasonable apportionment of the total return of the trust. Generally, these adjustments are permitted by state statutes when the trustee invests and manages the trust assets under the state's prudent investor standard, the trust describes the amount that may or must be distributed to a beneficiary by referring to the trust's income, and the trustee after applying the state statutory rules regarding the allocation of receipts and disbursements to income and principal, is unable to administer the trust impartially. Allocations pursuant to methods prescribed by such state statutes for apportioning the total return of a trust between income and principal will be respected regardless of whether the trust provides that the income must be distributed to one or more beneficiaries or may be accumulated in whole or in part, and regardless of which alternate permitted method is actually used, provided the trust complies with all requirements of the state statute for switching methods. A switch between methods of determining trust income authorized by state statute will not constitute a recognition event for purposes of section 1001 and will not result in a taxable gift from the trust's grantor or any of the trust's beneficiaries. A switch to a method not specifically authorized by state statute, but valid under state law (including a switch via judicial decision or a binding non-judicial settlement) may constitute a recognition event to the trust or its beneficiaries for purposes of section 1001 and may result in taxable gifts from the trust's grantor and beneficiaries, based on the relevant facts and circumstances. In addition, an allocation to income of all or a part of the gains from the sale or exchange of trust assets will generally be respected if the allocation is made either pursuant to the terms of the governing instrument and applicable local law, or pursuant to a reasonable and impartial exercise of a discretionary power granted to the fiduciary by applicable local law or by the governing instrument, if not prohibited by applicable local law. This section is effective for taxable years of trusts and estates ending after January 2, 2004.

[T.D. 6500, 25 FR 11814, Nov. 26, 1960; T.D. 9102, 69 FR 19, Jan. 2, 2004]

§ 1.643(b)–2 Dividends allocated to corpus.

Extraordinary dividends or taxable stock dividends which the fiduciary, acting in good faith, determines to be allocable to corpus under the terms of the governing instrument and applicable local law are not considered "income" for purposes of Subpart A, B, C, or D, Part I, Subchapter J, Chapter 1 of the Code. See section 643(a)(4), § 1.643(a)–4, § 1.643(d)–2, section 665(e), paragraph (b) of § 1.665(e)–1, and paragraph (b) of § 1.665(e)–1A for the treatment of such items in the computation of distributable net income.

[T.D. 6500, 25 FR 11814, Nov. 26, 1960, as amended by T.D. 6989, 34 FR 741, Jan. 17, 1969; T.D. 7204, 37 FR 17134, Aug. 25, 1972]

§ 1.643(c)–1 Definition of "beneficiary".

An heir, legatee, or devisee (including an estate or trust) is a beneficiary. A trust created under a decedent's will is a beneficiary of the decedent's estate. The following persons are treated as beneficiaries:

(a) Any person with respect to an amount used to discharge or satisfy that person's legal obligation as that term is used in § 1.662(a)–4.

(b) The grantor of a trust with respect to an amount applied or distributed for the support of a dependent under the circumstances specified in section 677(b) out of corpus or out of other than income for the taxable year of the trust.

(c) The trustee or cotrustee of a trust with respect to an amount applied or distributed for the support of a dependent under the circumstances specified in section 678(c) out of corpus or out of other than income for the taxable year of the trust.

[T.D. 6500, 25 FR 11814, Nov. 26, 1960]

§ 1.643(d)–1 Definition of "foreign trust created by a United States person." [*Omitted. Ed.*]

[T.D. 6989, 34 FR 732, Jan. 17, 1969; T.D. 9849, 84 FR 9235, March 14, 2019]

§ 1.643(d)–2 Illustration of the provisions of section 643.

(a) The provisions of section 643 may be illustrated by the following example:

Example. (1) Under the terms of the trust instrument, the income of a trust is required to be currently distributed to W during her life. Capital gains are allocable to corpus and all expenses are charges against corpus. During the taxable year the trust has the following items of income and expenses:

Dividends from domestic corporations	$30,000
Extraordinary dividends allocated to corpus by the trustee in good faith	20,000
Taxable interest	10,000
Tax-exempt interest	10,000
Long-term capital gains	10,000
Trustee's commissions and miscellaneous expenses allocable to corpus	5,000

(2) The "income" of the trust determined under section 643(b) which is currently distributable to W is $50,000, consisting of dividends of $30,000, taxable interest of $10,000, and tax-exempt interest of $10,000. The trustee's commissions and miscellaneous expenses allocable to tax-exempt interest amount to $1,000 (10,000/50,000 * $5,000).

(3) The "distributable net income" determined under section 643(a) amounts to $45,000, computed as follows:

Dividends from domestic corporations		$30,000
Taxable interest		10,000
Nontaxable interest		$10,000
Less: Expenses allocable thereto	[1,000]	9,000
Total		49,000
Less: Expenses ($5,000 less $1,000 allocable to tax-exempt interest)		[4,000]
Distributable net income		45,000

In determining the distributable net income of $45,000, the taxable income of the trust is computed with the following modifications: No deductions are allowed for distributions to W and for personal exemption of the trust (section 643(a)(1) and (2)); capital gains allocable to corpus are excluded and the deduction allowable under section 1202 is not taken into account (section 643(a)(3)): the extraordinary dividends allocated to corpus by the trustee in good faith are excluded (sections 643(a)(4)); and the tax-exempt interest (as adjusted for expenses) and the dividend exclusion of $50 are included (section 643(a)(5) and (7)).

(b) See paragraph (c) of the example in § 1.661(c)–2 for the computation of distributable net income where there is a charitable contributions deduction.

[T.D. 6500, 25 FR 11814, Nov. 26, 1960. Redesignated by T.D. 6989, 34 FR 732, Jan. 1, 1969]

§ 1.643(f)–1 Treatment of multiple trusts.

(a) General rule. For purposes of subchapter J of chapter 1 of subtitle A of Title 26 of the United States Code, two or more trusts will be aggregated and treated as a single trust if such trusts have substantially the same grantor or grantors and substantially the same primary beneficiary or beneficiaries, and if a principal purpose for establishing one or more of such trusts or for contributing additional cash or other property to such trusts is the avoidance of Federal income tax. For purposes of applying this rule, spouses will be treated as one person.

(b) Applicability date. The provisions of this section apply to taxable years ending after August 16, 2018.

[T.D. 9847, 84 FR 3014, Feb. 8, 2019]

§ 1.643(h)–1 Distributions by certain foreign trusts through intermediaries. [*Omitted. Ed.*]

[T.D. 8831, 64 FR 43272, Aug. 10, 1999; T.D. 8890, 65 FR 41332, July 5, 2000]

Proposed § 1.643(i)–1 (REG–124850–08, May 8, 2024) Loans from and use of trust property of foreign nongrantor trusts. [*Omitted. Ed.*]

Proposed § 1.643(i)–2 (REG–124850–08, May 8, 2024) Exceptions. [*Omitted. Ed.*]

Proposed § 1.643(i)–3 (REG–124850–08, May 8, 2024) Consequences of section 643(i) distribution. [*Omitted. Ed.*]

Proposed § 1.643(i)–4 (REG–124850–08, May 8, 2024) Examples. [*Omitted. Ed.*]

Proposed § 1.643(i)–5 (REG–124850–08, May 8, 2024) Applicability date. [*Omitted. Ed.*]

§ 644. Taxable Year of Trusts

(a) In general. For purposes of this subtitle, the taxable year of any trust shall be the calendar year.

(b) Exception for trusts exempt from tax and charitable trusts. Subsection (a) shall not apply to a trust exempt from taxation under section 501(a) or to a trust described in section 4947(a)(1).

§ 645. Certain Revocable Trusts Treated as Part of Estate

(a) General rule. For purposes of this subtitle, if both the executor (if any) of an estate and the trustee of a qualified revocable trust elect the treatment provided in this section, such trust shall be treated and taxed as part of such estate (and not as a separate trust) for all taxable years of the estate ending after the date of the decedent's death and before the applicable date.

(b) Definitions. For purposes of subsection (a)—

(1) Qualified revocable trust. The term "qualified revocable trust" means any trust (or portion thereof) which was treated under section 676 as owned by the decedent of the estate referred to in subsection (a) by reason of a power in the grantor (determined without regard to section 672(e)).

(2) Applicable date. The term "applicable date" means—

(A) if no return of tax imposed by chapter 11 is required to be filed, the date which is 2 years after the date of the decedent's death, and

(B) if such a return is required to be filed, the date which is 6 months after the date of the final determination of the liability for tax imposed by chapter 11.

(c) Election. The election under subsection (a) shall be made not later than the time prescribed for filing the return of tax imposed by this chapter for the first taxable year of the estate (determined with regard to extensions) and, once made, shall be irrevocable.

Regulation

§ 1.645–1 Election by certain revocable trusts to be treated as part of estate.

(a) In general. If an election is filed for a qualified revocable trust, as defined in paragraph (b)(1) of this section, in accordance with the rules set forth in paragraph (c) of this section, the qualified revocable trust is treated and taxed for purposes of subtitle A of the Internal Revenue Code as part of its related estate, as defined in paragraph (b)(5) of this section (and not as a separate trust) during the election period, as defined in paragraph (b)(6) of this section. Rules regarding the use of taxpayer identification numbers (TINs) and the filing of a Form 1041, "U.S. Income Tax Return for Estates and Trusts," for a qualified revocable trust are in paragraph (d) of this section. Rules regarding the tax treatment of an electing trust and related estate and the general filing requirements for the combined entity during the election period are in paragraph (e)(2) of this section. Rules regarding the tax treatment of an electing trust and its filing requirements during the election period if no executor, as defined in paragraph (b)(4) of this section, is appointed for a related estate are in paragraph (e)(3) of this section. Rules for determining the duration of the section 645 election period are in paragraph (f) of this section. Rules regarding the tax effects of the termination of the election are in paragraph (h) of this section. Rules regarding the tax consequences of the appointment of an executor after a trustee has made a section 645 election believing that an executor would not be appointed for a related estate are in paragraph (g) of this section.

(b) Definitions. For purposes of this section:

(1) *Qualified revocable trust.* A qualified revocable trust (QRT) is any trust (or portion thereof) that on the date of death of the decedent was treated as owned by the decedent under section 676 by reason of a power held by the decedent (determined without regard to section 672(e)). A trust that was treated as owned by the decedent under section 676 by reason of a power that was exercisable by the decedent only with the approval or consent of a nonadverse party or with the

approval or consent of the decedent's spouse is a QRT. A trust that was treated as owned by the decedent under section 676 solely by reason of a power held by a nonadverse party or by reason of a power held by the decedent's spouse is not a QRT.

(2) *Electing trust.* An electing trust is a QRT for which a valid section 645 election has been made. Once a section 645 election has been made for the trust, the trust shall be treated as an electing trust throughout the entire election period.

(3) *Decedent.* The decedent is the individual who was treated as the owner of the QRT under section 676 on the date of that individual's death.

(4) *Executor.* An executor is an executor, personal representative, or administrator that has obtained letters of appointment to administer the decedent's estate through formal or informal appointment procedures. Solely for purposes of this paragraph (b)(4), an executor does not include a person that has actual or constructive possession of property of the decedent unless that person is also appointed or qualified as an executor, administrator, or personal representative of the decedent's estate. If more than one jurisdiction has appointed an executor, the executor appointed in the domiciliary or primary proceeding is the executor of the related estate for purposes of this paragraph (b)(4).

(5) *Related estate.* A related estate is the estate of the decedent who was treated as the owner of the QRT on the date of the decedent's death.

(6) *Election period.* The election period is the period of time during which an electing trust is treated and taxed as part of its related estate. The rules for determining the duration of the election period are in paragraph (f) of this section.

(c) The election. (1) *Filing the election if there is an executor.* (i) *Time and manner for filing the election.* If there is an executor of the related estate, the trustees of each QRT joining in the election and the executor of the related estate make an election under section 645 and this section to treat each QRT joining in the election as part of the related estate for purposes of subtitle A of the Internal Revenue Code by filing a form provided by the IRS for making the election (election form) properly completed and signed under penalties of perjury, or in any other manner prescribed after December 24, 2002 by forms provided by the Internal Revenue Service (IRS), or by other published guidance for making the election. For the election to be valid, the election form must be filed not later than the time prescribed under section 6072 for filing the Form 1041 for the first taxable year of the related estate (regardless of whether there is sufficient income to require the filing of that return). If an extension is granted for the filing of the Form 1041 for the first taxable year of the related estate, the election form will be timely filed if it is filed by the time prescribed for filing the Form 1041 including the extension granted with respect to the Form 1041.

(ii) *Conditions to election.* In addition to providing the information required by the election form, as a condition to a valid section 645 election, the trustee of each QRT joining in the election and the executor of the related estate agree, by signing the election form under penalties of perjury, that:

(A) With respect to a trustee—

(*1*) The trustee agrees to the election;

(*2*) The trustee is responsible for timely providing the executor of the related estate with all the trust information necessary to permit the executor to file a complete, accurate, and timely Form 1041 for the combined electing trust(s) and related estate for each taxable year during the election period;

(*3*) The trustee of each QRT joining the election and the executor of the related estate have agreed to allocate the tax burden of the combined electing trust(s) and related estate for each taxable year during the election period in a manner that reasonably reflects the tax obligations of each electing trust and the related estate; and

(*4*) The trustee is responsible for insuring that the electing trust's share of the tax obligations of the combined electing trust(s) and related estate is timely paid to the Secretary.

(B) With respect to the executor—

(*1*) The executor agrees to the election;

(*2*) The executor is responsible for filing a complete, accurate, and timely Form 1041 for the combined electing trust(s) and related estate for each taxable year during the election period;

(*3*) The executor and the trustee of each QRT joining in the election have agreed to allocate the tax burden of the combined electing trust(s) and related estate for each taxable year during the election period in a manner that reasonably reflects the tax obligations of each electing trust and the related estate;

(4) The executor is responsible for insuring that the related estate's share of the tax obligations of the combined electing trust(s) and related estate is timely paid to the Secretary.

(2) *Filing the election if there is no executor*—(i) *Time and manner for filing the election.* If there is no executor for a related estate, an election to treat one or more QRTs of the decedent as an estate for purposes of subtitle A of the Internal Revenue Code is made by the trustees of each QRT joining in the election, by filing a properly completed election form, or in any other manner prescribed after December 24, 2002 by forms provided by the IRS, or by other published guidance for making the election. For the election to be valid, the election form must be filed not later than the time prescribed under section 6072 for filing the Form 1041 for the first taxable year of the trust, taking into account the trustee's election to treat the trust as an estate under section 645 (regardless of whether there is sufficient income to require the filing of that return). If an extension is granted for the filing of the Form 1041 for the first taxable year of the electing trust, the election form will be timely filed if it is filed by the time prescribed for filing the Form 1041 including the extension granted with respect to the filing of the Form 1041.

(ii) *Conditions to election.* In addition to providing the information required by the election form, as a condition to a valid section 645 election, the trustee of each QRT joining in the election agrees, by signing the election form under penalties of perjury, that—

(A) The trustee agrees to the election;

(B) If there is more than one QRT joining in the election, the trustees of each QRT joining in the election have appointed one trustee to be responsible for filing the Form 1041 for the combined electing trusts for each taxable year during the election period (filing trustee) and the filing trustee has agreed to accept that responsibility;

(C) If there is more than one QRT, the trustees of each QRT joining in the election have agreed to allocate the tax liability of the combined electing trusts for each taxable year during the election period in a manner that reasonably reflects the tax obligations of each electing trust;

(D) The trustee agrees to:

(*1*) Timely file a Form 1041 for the electing trust(s) for each taxable year during the election period; or

(*2*) If there is more than one QRT and the trustee is not the filing trustee, timely provide the filing trustee with all of the electing trust's information necessary to permit the filing trustee to file a complete, accurate, and timely Form 1041 for the combined electing trusts for each taxable year during the election period;

(*3*) Insure that the electing trust's share of the tax burden is timely paid to the Secretary;

(E) There is no executor and, to the knowledge and belief of the trustee, one will not be appointed; and

(F) If an executor is appointed after the filing of the election form and the executor agrees to the section 645 election, the trustee will complete and file a revised election form with the executor.

(3) *Election for more than one QRT.* If there is more than one QRT, the election may be made for some or all of the QRTs. If there is no executor, one trustee must be appointed by the trustees of the electing trusts to file Forms 1041 for the combined electing trusts filing as an estate during the election period.

(d) TIN and filing requirements for a QRT. (1) *Obtaining a TIN.* Regardless of whether there is an executor for a related estate and regardless of whether a section 645 election will be made for the QRT, a TIN must be obtained for the QRT following the death of the decedent. See § 301.6109–1(a)(3) of this chapter. The trustee must furnish this TIN to the payors of the QRT. See § 301.6109–1(a)(5) of this chapter for the definition of payor.

(2) *Filing a Form 1041 for a QRT.* (i) *Option not to file a Form 1041 for a QRT for which a section 645 election will be made.* If a section 645 election will be made for a QRT, the executor of the related estate, if any, and the trustee of the QRT may treat the QRT as an electing trust from the decedent's date of death until the due date for the section 645 election. Accordingly, the trustee of the QRT is not required to file a Form 1041 for the QRT for the short taxable year beginning with the decedent's date of death and ending December 31 of that year. However, if a QRT is treated as an

electing trust under this paragraph from the decedent's date of death until the due date for the section 645 election but a valid section 645 election is not made for the QRT, the QRT will be subject to penalties and interest for failing to timely file a Form 1041 and pay the tax due thereon.

(ii) *Requirement to file a Form 1041 for a QRT if paragraph (d)(2)(i) of this section does not apply.* (A) *Requirement to file Form 1041.* If the trustee of the QRT and the executor of the related estate, if any, do not treat the QRT as an electing trust as provided under paragraph (d)(2)(i) of this section, or if the trustee of the electing trust and the executor, if any, are uncertain whether a section 645 election will be made for a QRT, the trustee of the QRT must file a Form 1041 for the short taxable year beginning with the decedent's death and ending December 31 of that year (unless the QRT is not required to file a Form 1041 under section 6012 for this period).

(B) *Requirement to amend Form 1041 if a section 645 election is made.* (1) *If there is an executor.* If there is an executor and a valid section 645 election is made for a QRT after a Form 1041 has been filed for the QRT as a trust (see paragraph (d)(2)(ii)(A) of this section), the trustee must amend the Form 1041. The QRT's items of income, deduction, and credit must be excluded from the amended Form 1041 filed under this paragraph and must be included on the Form 1041 filed for the first taxable year of the combined electing trust and related estate under paragraph (e)(2)(ii)(A) of this section.

(2) *If there is no executor.* If there is no executor and a valid section 645 election is made for a QRT after a Form 1041 has been filed for the QRT as a trust (see paragraph (d)(2)(ii)(A) of this section) for the short taxable year beginning with the decedent's death and ending December 31 of that year, the trustee must file an amended return for the QRT. The amended return must be filed consistent with paragraph (e)(3) of this section and must be filed by the due date of the Form 1041 for the QRT, taking into account the trustee's election under section 645.

(e) Tax treatment and general filing requirements of electing trust and related estate during the election period. (1) *Effect of election.* The section 645 election once made is irrevocable.

(2) *If there is an executor.* (i) *Tax treatment of the combined electing trust and related estate.* If there is an executor, the electing trust is treated, during the election period, as part of the related estate for all purposes of subtitle A of the Internal Revenue Code. Thus, for example, the electing trust is treated as part of the related estate for purposes of the set-aside deduction under section 642(c)(2), the subchapter S shareholder requirements of section 1361(b)(1), and the special offset for rental real estate activities in section 469(i)(4).

(ii) *Filing requirements.* (A) *Filing the Form 1041 for the combined electing trust and related estate during the election period.* If there is an executor, the executor files a single income tax return annually (assuming a return is required under section 6012) under the name and TIN of the related estate for the combined electing trust and the related estate. Information regarding the name and TIN of each electing trust must be provided on the Form 1041 as required by the instructions to that form. The period of limitations provided in section 6501 for assessments with respect to an electing trust and the related estate starts with the filing of the return required under this paragraph. Except as required under the separate share rules of section 663(c), for purposes of filing the Form 1041 under this paragraph and computing the tax, the items of income, deduction, and credit of the electing trust and related estate are combined. One personal exemption in the amount of $600 is permitted under section 642(b), and the tax is computed under section 1(e), taking into account section 1(h), for the combined taxable income.

(B) *Filing a Form 1041 for the electing trust is not required.* Except for any final Form 1041 required to be filed under paragraph (h)(2)(i)(B) of this section, if there is an executor, the trustee of the electing trust does not file a Form 1041 for the electing trust during the election period. Although the trustee is not required to file a Form 1041 for the electing trust, the trustee of the electing trust must timely provide the executor of the related estate with all the trust information necessary to permit the executor to file a complete, accurate and timely Form 1041 for the combined electing trust and related estate. The trustee must also insure that the electing trust's share of the tax obligations of the combined electing trust and related estate is timely paid to the Secretary. In certain situations, the trustee of a QRT may be required to file a Form 1041 for the QRT's short taxable year beginning with the date of the decedent's death and ending December 31 of that year. See paragraph (d)(2) of this section.

(iii) *Application of the separate share rules.* (A) *Distributions to beneficiaries (other than to a share (or shares) of the combined electing trust and related estate).* Under the separate share rules of section 663(c), the electing trust and related estate are treated as separate shares for purposes of computing distributable net income (DNI) and applying the distribution provisions of sections 661 and 662. Further, the electing trust share or the related estate share may each contain two or more shares. Thus, if during the taxable year, a distribution is made by the electing trust or the related estate, the DNI of the share making the distribution must be determined and the distribution provisions of sections 661 and 662 must be applied using the separately determined DNI applicable to the distributing share.

(B) *Adjustments to the DNI of the separate shares for distributions between shares to which sections 661 and 662 would apply.* A distribution from one share to another share to which sections 661 and 662 would apply if made to a beneficiary other than another share of the combined electing trust and related estate affects the computation of the DNI of the share making the distribution and the share receiving the distribution. The share making the distribution reduces its DNI by the amount of the distribution deduction that it would be entitled to under section 661 (determined without regard to section 661(c)), had the distribution been made to another beneficiary, and, solely for purposes of calculating DNI, the share receiving the distribution increases its gross income by the same amount. The distribution has the same character in the hands of the recipient share as in the hands of the distributing share. The following example illustrates the provisions of this paragraph (e)(2)(iii)(B):

Example. (i) A's will provides that, after the payment of debts, expenses, and taxes, the residue of A's estate is to be distributed to Trust, an electing trust. The sole beneficiary of Trust is C. The estate share has $15,000 of gross income, $5,000 of deductions, and $10,000 of taxable income and DNI for the taxable year based on the assets held in A's estate. During the taxable year, A's estate distributes $15,000 to Trust. The distribution reduces the DNI of the estate share by $10,000.

(ii) For the same taxable year, the trust share has $25,000 of gross income and $5,000 of deductions. None of the modifications provided for under section 643(a) apply. In calculating the DNI for the trust share, the gross income of the trust share is increased by $10,000, the amount of the reduction in the DNI of the estate share as a result of the distribution to Trust. Thus, solely for purposes of calculating DNI, the trust share has gross income of $35,000, and taxable income of $30,000. Therefore, the trust share has $30,000 of DNI for the taxable year.

(iii) During the same taxable year, Trust distributes $35,000 to C. The distribution deduction reported on the Form 1041 filed for A's estate and Trust is $30,000. As a result of the distribution by Trust to C, C must include $30,000 in gross income for the taxable year. The gross income reported on the Form 1041 filed for A's estate and Trust is $40,000.

(iv) *Application of the governing instrument requirement of section 642(c).* A deduction is allowed in computing the taxable income of the combined electing trust and related estate to the extent permitted under section 642(c) for—

(A) Any amount of the gross income of the related estate that is paid or set aside during the taxable year pursuant to the terms of the governing instrument of the related estate for a purpose specified in section 170(c); and

(B) Any amount of gross income of the electing trust that is paid or set aside during the taxable year pursuant to the terms of the governing instrument of the electing trust for a purpose specified in section 170(c).

(3) *If there is no executor*—(i) *Tax treatment of the electing trust.* If there is no executor, the trustee treats the electing trust, during the election period, as an estate for all purposes of subtitle A of the Internal Revenue Code. Thus, for example, an electing trust is treated as an estate for purposes of the set-aside deduction under section 642(c)(2), the subchapter S shareholder requirements of section 1361(b)(1), and the special offset for rental real estate activities under section 469(i)(4). The trustee may also adopt a taxable year other than a calendar year.

(ii) *Filing the Form 1041 for the electing trust.* If there is no executor, the trustee of the electing trust must, during the election period, file a Form 1041, under the TIN obtained by the trustee under § 301.6109–1(a)(3) of this chapter upon the death of the decedent, treating the trust as an estate. If there is more than one electing trust, the Form 1041 must be filed by the filing trustee (see paragraph (c)(2)(ii)(B) of this section) under the name and TIN of the electing trust of the filing trustee. Information regarding the names and TINs of the other electing trusts must be provided on the Form 1041 as required by the instructions to that form. Any return filed in accordance with this paragraph shall be treated as a return filed for the electing trust (or trusts, if there is more than one electing trust) and not as a return filed for any subsequently discovered related estate. Accordingly, the period of limitations provided in section 6501 for assessments with respect to a subsequently discovered related estate does not start until a return is filed with respect to the related estate. See paragraph (g) of this section.

(4) *Application of the section 6654(l)(2) to the electing trust.* Each electing trust and related estate (if any) is treated as a separate taxpayer for all purposes of subtitle F of the Internal Revenue Code, including, without limitation, the application of section 6654. The provisions of section 6654(*l*)(2)(A) relating to the two year exception to an estate's obligation to make estimated tax payments, however, will apply to each electing trust for which a section 645 election has been made.

(f) Duration of election period. (1) *In general.* The election period begins on the date of the decedent's death and terminates on the earlier of the day on which both the electing trust and related estate, if any, have distributed all of their assets, or the day before the applicable date. The election does not apply to successor trusts (trusts that are distributees under the trust instrument).

(2) *Definition of applicable date.* (i) *Applicable date if no Form 706 "United States Estate (and Generation Skipping Transfer) Tax Return" is required to be filed.* If a Form 706 is not required to be filed as a result of the decedent's death, the applicable date is the day which is 2 years after the date of the decedent's death.

(ii) *Applicable date if a Form 706 is required to be filed.* If a Form 706 is required to be filed as a result of the decedent's death, the applicable date is the later of the day that is 2 years after the date of the decedent's death, or the day that is 6 months after the date of final determination of liability for estate tax. Solely for purposes of determining the applicable date under section 645, the date of final determination of liability is the earliest of the following—

(A) The date that is six months after the issuance by the Internal Revenue Service of an estate tax closing letter, unless a claim for refund with respect to the estate tax is filed within twelve months after the issuance of the letter;

(B) The date of a final disposition of a claim for refund, as defined in paragraph (f)(2)(iii) of this section, that resolves the liability for the estate tax, unless suit is instituted within six months after a final disposition of the claim;

(C) The date of execution of a settlement agreement with the Internal Revenue Service that determines the liability for the estate tax;

(D) The date of issuance of a decision, judgment, decree, or other order by a court of competent jurisdiction resolving the liability for the estate tax unless a notice of appeal or a petition for certiorari is filed within 90 days after the issuance of a decision, judgment, decree, or other order of a court; or

(E) The date of expiration of the period of limitations for assessment of the estate tax provided in section 6501.

(iii) *Definition of final disposition of claim for refund.* For purposes of paragraph (f)(2)(ii)(B) of this section, a claim for refund shall be deemed finally disposed of by the Secretary when all items have been either allowed or disallowed. If a waiver of notification with respect to disallowance is filed with respect to a claim for refund prior to disallowance of the claim, the claim for refund will be treated as disallowed on the date the waiver is filed.

(iv) *Examples.* The application of this paragraph (f)(2) is illustrated by the following examples:

Example (1). A died on October 20, 2002. The executor of A's estate and the trustee of Trust, an electing trust, made a section 645 election. A Form 706 is not required to be filed as a result of A's death. The applicable date is October 20, 2004, the day that is two years after A's date of death. The last day of the election period is October 19, 2004. Beginning October 20, 2004, Trust will no longer be treated and taxed as part of A's estate.

Example (2). Assume the same facts as Example 1, except that a Form 706 is required to be filed as the result of A's death. The Internal Revenue Service issues an estate tax closing letter accepting the Form 706 as filed on March 15, 2005. The estate does not file a claim for refund by March 15, 2006, the day that is twelve months after the date of issuance of the estate tax closing letter. The date of final determination of liability is September 15, 2005, and the applicable date is March 15, 2006. The last day of the election period is March 14, 2006. Beginning March 15, 2006, Trust will no longer be treated and taxed as part of A's estate.

Example (3). Assume the same facts as Example 1, except that a Form 706 is required to be filed as the result of A's death. The Form 706 is audited, and a notice of deficiency authorized under section 6212 is mailed to the executor of A's estate as a result of the audit. The executor files a petition in Tax Court. The Tax Court issues a decision resolving the liability for estate tax on December 14, 2005, and neither party appeals within 90 days after the issuance of the decision. The date of final determination of liability is December 14, 2005. The applicable date is June 14, 2006, the day that is six months after the date of final determination of liability. The last day of the election period is June 13, 2006. Beginning June 14, 2006, Trust will no longer be treated and taxed as part of A's estate.

(g) Executor appointed after the section 645 election is made. (1) *Effect on the election.* If an executor for the related estate is not appointed until after the trustee has made a valid section 645 election, the executor must agree to the trustee's election, and the IRS must be notified of that agreement by the filing of a revised election form (completed as required by the instructions to that form) within 90 days of the appointment of the executor, for the election period to continue past the date of appointment of the executor. If the executor does not agree to the election or a revised election form is not timely filed as required by this paragraph, the election period terminates the day before the appointment of the executor. If the IRS issues other guidance after December 24, 2002 for notifying the IRS of the executor's agreement to the election, the IRS must be notified in the manner provided in that guidance for the election period to continue.

(2) *Continuation of election period.* (i) *Correction of returns filed before executor appointed.* If the election period continues under paragraph (g)(1) of this section, the executor of the related estate and the trustee of each electing trust must file amended Forms 1041 to correct the Forms 1041 filed by the trustee before the executor was appointed. The amended Forms 1041 must be filed under the name and TIN of the electing trust and must reflect the items of income, deduction, and credit of the related estate and the electing trust. The name and TIN of the related estate must be provided on the amended Forms 1041 as required in the instructions to that Form. The amended return for the taxable year ending immediately before the executor was appointed must indicate that this Form 1041 is a final return. If the period of limitations for making assessments has expired with respect to the electing trust for any of the Forms 1041 filed by the trustee, the executor must file Forms 1041 for any items of income, deduction, and credit of the related estate that cannot be properly included on amended forms for the electing trust. The personal exemption under section 642(b) is not permitted to be taken on these Forms 1041 filed by the executor.

(ii) *Returns filed after the appointment of the executor.* All returns filed by the combined electing trust and related estate after the appointment of the executor are to be filed under the name and TIN of the related estate in accordance with paragraph (e)(2) of this section. Regardless of the change in the name and TIN under which the Forms 1041 for the combined electing trust and related estate are filed, the combined electing trust and related estate will be treated as the same entity before and after the executor is appointed.

(3) *Termination of the election period.* If the election period terminates under paragraph (g)(1) of this section, the executor must file Forms 1041 under the name and TIN of the estate for all taxable years of the related estate ending after the death of the decedent. The trustee of the electing trust is not required to amend any returns filed for the electing trust during the election period. Following termination of the election period, the trustee of the electing trust must obtain a new TIN. See § 301.6109–1(a)(4) of this chapter.

(h) Treatment of an electing trust and related estate following termination of the election. (1) *The share (or shares) comprising the electing trust is deemed to be distributed upon termination of the election period.* On the close of the last day of the election period, the combined electing trust and related estate, if there is an executor, or the electing trust, if there is no executor, is deemed to distribute the share (or shares, as determined under section 663(c)) comprising the electing trust to a new trust in a distribution to which sections 661 and 662 apply. All items of income, including net capital gains, that are attributable to the share (or shares) comprising the electing trust are included in the calculation of the distributable net income of the electing trust and treated as distributed by the combined electing trust and related estate, if there is an executor, or by the electing trust, if there is no executor, to the new trust. The combined electing trust and related estate, if there is an executor, or the electing trust, if there is no executor, is entitled to a distribution deduction to the extent permitted under section 661 in the taxable year in which the election period terminates as a result of the deemed distribution. The new trust shall include the amount of the deemed distribution in gross income to the extent required under section 662.

(2) *Filing of the Form 1041 upon the termination of the section 645 election.* (i) *If there is an executor. (A) Filing the Form 1041 for the year of termination.* If there is an executor, the Form 1041 filed under the name and TIN of the related estate for the taxable year in which the election terminates includes—

(*1*) The items of income, deduction, and credit of the electing trust attributable to the period beginning with the first day of the taxable year of the combined electing trust and related estate and ending with the last day of the election period;

(*2*) The items of income, deduction, and credit, if any, of the related estate for the entire taxable year; and

(*3*) A deduction for the deemed distribution of the share (or shares) comprising the electing trust to the new trust as provided for under paragraph (h)(1) of this section.

(B) *Requirement to file a final Form 1041 under the name and TIN of the electing trust.* If the electing trust terminates during the election period, the trustee of the electing trust must file a Form 1041 under the name and TIN of the electing trust and indicate that the return is a final return to notify the IRS that the electing trust is no longer in existence. The items of income, deduction, and credit of the trust are not reported on this final Form 1041 but on the appropriate Form 1041 filed for the combined electing trust and related estate.

(ii) *If there is no executor.* If there is no executor, the taxable year of the electing trust closes on the last day of the election period. A Form 1041 is filed in the manner prescribed under paragraph (e)(3)(ii) of this section reporting the items of income, deduction, and credit of the electing trust for the short period ending with the last day of the election period. The Form 1041 filed under this paragraph includes a distribution deduction for the deemed distribution provided for under paragraph (h)(1) of this section. The Form 1041 must indicate that it is a final return.

(3) *Use of TINs following termination of the election.* (i) *If there is an executor.* Upon termination of the section 645 election, a former electing trust may need to obtain a new TIN. See § 301.6109–1(a)(4) of this chapter. If the related estate continues after the termination of the election period, the related estate must continue to use the TIN assigned to the estate during the election period.

(ii) *If there is no executor.* If there is no executor, the former electing trust must obtain a new TIN if the trust will continue after the termination of the election period. See § 301.6109–1(a)(4) of this chapter.

(4) *Taxable year of estate and trust upon termination of the election.* (i) *Estate.* Upon termination of the section 645 election period, the taxable year of the estate is the same taxable year used during the election period.

(ii) *Trust.* Upon termination of the section 645 election, the taxable year of the new trust is the calendar year. See section 644.

(i) Reserved.

(j) Effective date. Paragraphs (a), (b), (c), (d), (f), and (g) of this section apply to trusts and estates of decedents dying on or after December 24, 2002. Paragraphs (e) and (h) of this section apply to taxable years ending on or after December 24, 2002.

[T.D. 9032, 67 FR 78377, Dec. 24, 2002]

§ 646. Tax Treatment of Electing Alaska Native Settlement Trusts [*Omitted. Ed.*]

Subpart B. Trusts Which Distribute Current Income Only

§ 651. Deduction for Trusts Distributing Current Income Only

(a) Deduction. In the case of any trust the terms of which—

(1) provide that all of its income is required to be distributed currently, and

(2) do not provide that any amounts are to be paid, permanently set aside, or used for the purposes specified in section 642(c) (relating to deduction for charitable, etc., purposes),

there shall be allowed as a deduction in computing the taxable income of the trust the amount of the income for the taxable year which is required to be distributed currently. This section shall not apply in any taxable year in which the trust distributes amounts other than amounts of income described in paragraph (1).

(b) Limitation on deduction. If the amount of income required to be distributed currently exceeds the distributable net income of the trust for the taxable year, the deduction shall be limited to the amount of the distributable net income. For this purpose, the computation of distributable net income shall not include items of income which are not included in the gross income of the trust and the deductions allocable thereto.

Regulations

§ 1.651(a)–1 Simple trusts; deduction for distributions; in general.

Section 651 is applicable only to a trust the governing instruments of which:

(a) Requires that the trust distribute all of its income currently for the taxable year, and

(b) Does not provide that any amounts may be paid, permanently set aside, or used in the taxable year for the charitable, etc., purposes specified in section 642(c), and does not make any distribution other than of current income. A trust to which section 651 applies is referred to in this part as a "simple" trust. Trusts subject to section 661 are referred to as "complex" trusts. A trust may be a simple trust for one year and a complex trust for another year. It should be noted that under section 651 a trust qualifies as a simple trust in a taxable year in which it is required to distribute all its income currently and makes no other distributions, whether or not distributions of current income are in fact made. On the other hand a trust is not a complex trust by reason of distributions of amounts other than income unless such distributions are in fact made during the taxable year, whether or not they are required in that year.

[T.D. 6500, 25 FR 11814, Nov. 26, 1960]

§ 1.651(a)–2 Income required to be distributed currently.

(a) The determination of whether trust income is required to be distributed currently depends upon the terms of the trust instrument and the applicable local law. For this purpose, if the trust instrument provides that the trustee in determining the distributable income shall first retain a reserve for depreciation or otherwise make due allowance for keeping the trust corpus intact by retaining a reasonable amount of the current income for that purpose, the retention of current income for that purpose will not disqualify the trust from being a "simple" trust. The fiduciary must be under a duty to distribute the income currently even if, as a matter of practical necessity, the income is not distributed until after the close of the trust's taxable year. For example: Under the terms of the trust instrument, all of the income is currently distributable to A. The trust reports on the calendar year basis and as a matter of practical necessity makes distribution to A of each quarter's income on the fifteenth day of the month following the close of the quarter. The distribution made by the trust on January 15, 1955, of the income for the fourth quarter of 1954 does not disqualify the trust from treatment in 1955 under section 651, since the income is required to be distributed currently. However, if the terms of a trust require that none of the income be distributed until after the year of its receipt by the trust, the income of the trust is not required to be distributed currently and the trust is not a simple trust. For definition of the term "income" see section 643(b) and § 1.643(b)–1.

(b) It is immaterial, for purposes of determining whether all the income is required to be distributed currently, that the amount of income allocated to a particular beneficiary is not specified in the instrument. For example, if the fiduciary is required to distribute all the income currently, but has discretion to "sprinkle" the income among a class of beneficiaries, or among named beneficiaries, in such amount as he may see fit, all the income is required to be distributed currently, even though the amount distributable to a particular beneficiary is unknown until the fiduciary has exercised his discretion.

(c) If in one taxable year of a trust its income for that year is required or permitted to be accumulated, and in another taxable year its income for the year is required to be distributed currently (and no other amounts are distributed), the trust is a simple trust for the latter year. For example, a trust under which income may be accumulated until a beneficiary is 21 years old, and thereafter must be distributed currently, is a simple trust for taxable years beginning after the beneficiary reaches the age of 21 years in which no other amounts are distributed.

(d) If a trust distributes property in kind as part of its requirement to distribute currently all the income as defined under section 643(b) and the applicable regulations, the trust shall be treated as having sold the property for its fair market value on the date of distribution. If no amount in excess of the amount of income as defined under section 643(b) and the applicable regulations is distributed by the trust during the year, the trust will qualify for treatment under section 651 even though property in kind was distributed as part of a distribution of all such income. This paragraph (d) applies for taxable years of trusts ending after January 2, 2004.

[T.D. 6500, 25 FR 11814, Nov. 26, 1960; T.D. 9102, 69 FR 20, Jan. 2, 2004]

§ 1.651(a)–3 Distribution of amounts other than income.

(a) A trust does not qualify for treatment under section 651 for any taxable year in which it actually distributes corpus. For example, a trust which is required to distribute all of its income currently would not qualify as a simple trust under section 651 in the year of its termination since in that year actual distributions of corpus would be made.

(b) A trust, otherwise qualifying under section 651, which may make a distribution of corpus in the discretion of the trustee, or which is required under the terms of its governing instrument to make a distribution of corpus upon the happening of a specified event, will be disqualified for treatment under section 651 only for the taxable year in which an actual distribution of corpus is made. For example: Under the terms of a trust, which is required to distribute all of its income currently, half of the corpus is to be distributed to beneficiary A when he becomes 30 years of age. The trust reports on the calendar year basis. On December 28, 1954, A becomes 30 years of age and the trustee distributes half of the corpus of the trust to him on January 3, 1955. The trust will be disqualified for treatment under section 651 only for the taxable year 1955, the year in which an actual distribution of corpus is made.

(c) See section 661 and the regulations thereunder for the treatment of trusts which distribute corpus or claim the charitable contributions deduction provided by section 642(c).

[T.D. 6500, 25 FR 11814, Nov. 26, 1960]

§ 1.651(a)–4 Charitable purposes.

A trust is not considered to be a trust which may pay, permanently set aside, or use any amount for charitable, etc., purposes for any taxable year for which it is not allowed a charitable, etc., deduction under section 642(c). Therefore, a trust with a remainder to a charitable organization is not disqualified for treatment as a simple trust if either (a) the remainder is subject to a contingency, so that no deduction would be allowed for capital gains or other amounts added to corpus as amounts permanently set aside for a charitable, etc., purpose under section 642 (c), or (b) the trust receives no capital gains or other income added to corpus for the taxable year for which such a deduction would be allowed.

[T.D. 6500, 25 FR 11814, Nov. 26, 1960]

§ 1.651(a)–5 Estates.

Subpart B has no application to an estate.

[T.D. 6500, 25 FR 11814, Nov. 26, 1960]

§ 1.651(b)–1 Deduction for distributions to beneficiaries.

In computing its taxable income, a simple trust is allowed a deduction for the amount of income which is required under the terms of the trust instrument to be distributed currently to beneficiaries. If the amount of income required to be distributed currently exceeds the distributable net income, the deduction allowable to the trust is limited to the amount of the distributable net income. For this purpose the amount of income required to be distributed currently, or distributable net income, whichever is applicable, does not include items of trust income (adjusted for deductions allocable thereto) which are not included in the gross income of the trust. For determination of the character of the income required to be distributed currently, see § 1.652(b)–2. Accordingly, for the purposes of determining the deduction allowable to the trust under section 651, distributable net income is computed without the modifications specified in paragraphs (5), (6), and (7) of section 643(a), relating to tax-exempt interest, foreign income, and excluded dividends. For example: Assume that the distributable net income of a trust as computed under section 643(a) amounts to $99,000 but includes nontaxable income of $9,000. Then distributable net income for the purpose of determining the deduction allowable under section 651 is $90,000 ($99,000 less $9,000 nontaxable income).

[T.D. 6500, 25 FR 11814, Nov. 26, 1960]

§ 652. Inclusion of Amounts in Gross Income of Beneficiaries of Trusts Distributing Current Income Only

(a) Inclusion. Subject to subsection (b), the amount of income for the taxable year required to be distributed currently by a trust described in section 651 shall be included in the gross income of the beneficiaries to whom the income is required to be distributed, whether distributed or not. If such amount exceeds the distributable net income, there shall be included in the gross income of each beneficiary an amount which bears the same ratio to distributable net income as the amount of income required to be distributed to such beneficiary bears to the amount of income required to be distributed to all beneficiaries.

(b) Character of amounts. The amounts specified in subsection (a) shall have the same character in the hands of the beneficiary as in the hands of the trust. For this purpose, the amounts shall be treated as consisting of the same proportion of each class of items entering into the computation of distributable net income of the trust as the total of each class bears to the total distributable net income of the trust, unless the terms of the trust specifically allocate different classes of income to different beneficiaries. In the application of the preceding sentence, the items of deduction entering into the computation of distributable net income shall be allocated among the items of distributable net income in accordance with regulations prescribed by the Secretary.

(c) Different taxable years. If the taxable year of a beneficiary is different from that of the trust, the amount which the beneficiary is required to include in gross income in accordance with the provisions of this section shall be based upon the amount of income of the trust for any taxable year or years of the trust ending within or with his taxable year.

Regulations

§ 1.652(a)–1 Simple trusts; inclusion of amounts in income of beneficiaries.

Subject to the rules in §§ 1.652(a)–2 and 1.652(b)–1, a beneficiary of a simple trust includes in his gross income for the taxable year the amounts of income required to be distributed to him for such year, whether or not distributed. Thus, the income of a simple trust is includible in the beneficiary's gross income for the taxable year in which the income is required to be distributed currently even though, as a matter of practical necessity, the income is not distributed until after the close of the taxable year of the trust. See § 1.642(a)(3)–2 with respect to time of receipt of dividends. See § 1.652(c)–1 for treatment of amounts required to be distributed where a beneficiary and the trust have different taxable years. The term "income required to be distributed currently" includes income required to be distributed currently which is in fact used to discharge or satisfy any person's legal obligation as that term is used in § 1.662(a)–4.

[T.D. 6500, 25 FR 11814, Nov. 26, 1960]

§ 1.652(a)–2 Distributions in excess of distributable net income.

If the amount of income required to be distributed currently to beneficiaries exceeds the distributable net income of the trust (as defined in section 643(a)), each beneficiary includes in his gross income an amount equivalent to his proportionate share of such distributable net income. Thus, if beneficiary A is to receive two-thirds of the trust income and B is to receive one-third, and the income required to be distributed currently is $99,000, A will receive $66,000 and B, $33,000. However, if the distributable net income, as determined under section 643(a) is only $90,000, A will include two-thirds ($60,000) of that sum in his gross income, and B will include one-third ($30,000) in his gross income. See §§ 1.652(b)–1 and 1.652(b)–2, however, for amounts which are not includible in the gross income of a beneficiary because of their tax-exempt character.

[T.D. 6500, 25 FR 11814, Nov. 26, 1960]

§ 1.652(b)–1 Character of amounts.

In determining the gross income of a beneficiary, the amounts includible under § 1.652(a)–1 have the same character in the hands of the beneficiary as in the hands of the trust. For example, to the extent that the amounts specified in § 1.652(a)–1 consist of income exempt from tax under section 103, such amounts are not included in the beneficiary's gross income. Similarly, dividends distributed to a beneficiary retain their original character in the beneficiary's hands for purposes of determining the availability to the beneficiary of the dividends received credit under section 34 (for dividends received on or before December 31, 1964) and the dividend exclusion under section 116. Also, to the extent that the amounts specified in § 1.652(a)–1 consist of "earned income" in the hands of the trust under the provisions of section 1348 such amount shall be treated under section 1348 as "earned income" in the hands of the beneficiary. Similarly, to the extent such amounts consist of an amount received as a part of a lump sum distribution from a qualified plan and to which the provisions of section 72(n) would apply in the hands of the trust, such amount shall be treated as subject to such section in the hands of the beneficiary except where such amount is deemed under section 666(a) to have been distributed in a preceding taxable year of the trust and the partial tax described in section 668(a)(2) is determined under section 668(b)(1)(B). The tax treatment of amounts determined under § 1.652(a)–1 depends upon the beneficiary's status with respect to them not upon the status of the trust. Thus, if a beneficiary is deemed to have received foreign income of a foreign trust, the includibility of such income in his gross income depends upon his taxable status with respect to that income.

[T.D. 6500, 25 FR 11814, Nov. 26, 1960, as amended by T.D. 6777, 29 FR 17809, Dec. 16, 1964; T.D. 7204, 37 FR 17134, Aug. 25, 1972]

§ 1.652(b)–2 Allocation of income items.

(a) The amounts specified in § 1.652(a)–1 which are required to be included in the gross income of a beneficiary are treated as consisting of the same proportion of each class of items entering into distributable net income of the trust (as defined in section 643(a)) as the total of each class bears to such distributable net income, unless the terms of the trust specifically allocate different classes of income to different beneficiaries, or unless local law requires such an allocation. For example: Assume that under the terms of the governing instrument, beneficiary A is to receive currently one-half of the trust income and beneficiaries B and C are each to receive currently one-quarter, and the distributable net income of the trust (after allocation of expenses) consists of dividends of $10,000, taxable interest of $10,000, and tax-exempt interest of $4,000. A will be deemed to have received $5,000 of dividends, $5,000 of taxable interest, and $2,000 of tax-exempt interest; B and C will each be deemed to have received $2,500 of dividends, $2,500 of taxable interest, and $1,000 of tax-exempt interest. However, if the terms of the trust specifically allocate different classes of income to different beneficiaries, entirely or in part, or if local law requires such an allocation, each beneficiary will be deemed to have received those items of income specifically allocated to him.

(b) The terms of the trust are considered specifically to allocate different classes of income to different beneficiaries only to the extent that the allocation is required in the trust instrument, and only to the extent that it has an economic effect independent of the income tax consequences of the allocation. For example:

(1) Allocation pursuant to a provision in a trust instrument granting the trustee discretion to allocate different classes of income to different beneficiaries is not a specific allocation by the terms of the trust.

(2) Allocation pursuant to a provision directing the trustee to pay all of one income to A, or $10,000 out of the income to A, and the balance of the income to B, but directing the trustee first to allocate a specific class of income to A's share (to the extent there is income of that class and to the extent it does not exceed A's share) is not a specific allocation by the terms of the trust.

(3) Allocation pursuant to a provision directing the trustee to pay half the class of income (whatever it may be) to A, and the balance of the income to B, is a specific allocation by the terms of the trust.

[T.D. 6500, 25 FR 11814, Nov. 26, 1960]

§ 1.652(b)–3 Allocation of deductions.

Items of deduction of a trust that enter into the computation of distributable net income are to be allocated among the items of income in accordance with the following principles:

(a) All deductible items directly attributable to one class of income (except dividends excluded under section 116) are allocated thereto. For example, repairs to, taxes on, and other expenses directly attributable to the maintenance of rental property or the collection of rental income are allocated to rental income. See § 1.642(e)–1 for treatment of depreciation of rental property. Similarly, all expenditures directly attributable to a business carried on by a trust are allocated to the income from such business. If the deductions directly attributable to a particular class of income exceed that income, the excess is applied against other classes of income in the manner provided in paragraph (d) of this section.

(b) The deductions which are not directly attributable to a specific class of income may be allocated to any item of income (including capital gains) included in computing distributable net income, but a portion must be allocated to nontaxable income (except dividends excluded under section 116) pursuant to section 265 and the regulations thereunder. For example, if the income of a trust is $30,000 (after direct expenses), consisting equally of $10,000 of dividends, tax-exempt interest, and rents, and income commissions amount to $3,000, one-third ($1,000) of such commissions should be allocated to tax-exempt interest, but the balance of $2,000 may be allocated to the rents or dividends in such proportions as the trustee may elect. The fact that the governing instrument or applicable local law treats certain items of deduction as attributable to corpus or to income not included in distributable net income does not affect allocation under this paragraph. For instance, if in the example set forth in this paragraph the trust also had capital gains which are allocable to corpus under the terms of the trust instrument, no part of the deductions would be allocable thereto since the capital gains are excluded from the computation of distributable net income under section 643(a)(3).

(c) Examples of expenses which are considered as not directly attributable to a specific class of income are trustee's commissions, the rental of safe deposit boxes, and State income and personal property taxes.

(d) To the extent that any items of deduction which are directly attributable to a class of income exceed that class of income, they may be allocated to any other class of income (including capital gains) included in distributable net income in the manner provided in paragraph (b) of this section, except that any excess deductions attributable to tax-exempt income (other than dividends excluded under section 116) may not be offset against any other class of income. See section 265 and the regulations thereunder. Thus, if the trust has rents, taxable interest, dividends, and tax-exempt interest, and the deductions directly attributable to the rents exceed the rental income, the excess may be allocated to the taxable interest or dividends in such proportions as the fiduciary may elect. However, if the excess deductions are attributable to the tax-exempt interest, they may not be allocated to either the rents, taxable interest, or dividends.

[T.D. 6500, 25 FR 11814, Nov. 26, 1960]

§ 1.652(c)–1 Different taxable years.

If a beneficiary has a different taxable year (as defined in section 441 or 442) from the taxable year of the trust, the amount he is required to include in gross income in accordance with section 652(a) and (b) is based on the income of the trust for any taxable year or years ending with or within his taxable year. This rule applies to taxable years of normal duration as well as to so-called short taxable years. Income of the trust for its taxable year or years is determined in accordance with its method of accounting and without regard to that of the beneficiary.

[T.D. 6500, 25 FR 11814, Nov. 26, 1960]

§ 1.652(c)–2 Death of individual beneficiaries.

If income is required to be distributed currently to a beneficiary, by a trust for a taxable year which does not end with or within the last taxable year of a beneficiary (because of the beneficiary's death), the extent to which the income is included in the gross income of the beneficiary for his last taxable year or in the gross income of his estate is determined by the computations under section 652 for the taxable year of the trust in which his last taxable year ends. Thus, the distributable net income of the taxable year of the trust determines the extent to which the income required to be distributed currently to the beneficiary is included in his gross income for his last taxable year or in the gross income of his estate. (Section 652(c) does not apply to such amounts.) The gross income for the last taxable year of a beneficiary on the cash basis includes only income actually distributed to the beneficiary before his death. Income required to be distributed, but in fact distributed to his estate, is included in the gross income of the estate as income in respect of a decedent under section 691. See paragraph (e) of § 1.663(c)–3 with respect to separate share treatment for the periods before and after the decedent's death. If the trust does not qualify as a simple trust for the taxable year of the trust in which the last taxable year of the beneficiary ends, see section 662(c) and § 1.662(c)–2.

[T.D. 6500, 25 FR 11814, Nov. 26, 1960]

§ 1.652(c)–3 Termination of existence of other beneficiaries.

If the existence of a beneficiary which is not an individual terminates, the amount to be included under section 652(a) in its gross income for its last taxable year is computed with reference to §§ 1.652(c)–1 and 1.652(c)–2 as if the beneficiary were a deceased individual, except that income required to be distributed prior to the termination but actually distributed to the beneficiary's successor in interest is included in the beneficiary's income for its last taxable year.

[T.D. 6500, 25 FR 11814, Nov. 26, 1960]

§ 1.652(c)–4 Illustration of the provisions of sections 651 and 652.

The rules applicable to a trust required to distribute all of its income currently to its beneficiaries may be illustrated by the following example:

Example. (a) Under the terms of a simple trust all of the income is to be distributed equally to beneficiaries A and B and capital gains are to be allocated to corpus. The trust and both beneficiaries file returns on the calendar year basis. No provision is made in the governing instrument with respect to depreciation. During the taxable year 1955, the trust had the following items of income and expense:

Rents	$25,000
Dividends of domestic corporations	50,000
Tax-exempt interest on municipal bonds	25,000
Long-term capital gains	15,000
Taxes and expenses directly attributable to rents	5,000
Trustee's commissions allocable to income account	2,600
Trustee's commissions allocable to principal account	1,300
Depreciation	5,000

(b) The income of the trust for fiduciary accounting purposes is $92,400, computed as follows:

Rents		$25,000
Dividends		50,000
Tax-exempt interest		25,000
Total		100,000
Deductions:		
Expenses directly attributable to rental income	$5,000	
Trustee's commissions allocable to income account	2,600	7,600
Income computed under section 643(b)		92,400

One-half ($46,200) of the income of $92,400 is currently distributable to each beneficiary.

(c) The distributable net income of the trust computed under section 643(a) is $91,100, determined as follows (cents are disregarded in the computation):

Rents		$25,000
Dividends		50,000
Tax-exempt interest	$25,000	
Less: Expenses allocable thereto (25,000/100,000 * $3,900)	975	
		24,025
Total		99,025
Deductions:		
Expenses directly attributable to rental income	$ 5,000	
Trustee's commissions ($3,900 less $975 allocable to tax-exempt interest)	2,925	
		7,925
Distributable net income		91,100

In computing the distributable net income of $91,100, the taxable income of the trust was computed with the following modifications: No deductions were allowed for distributions to the beneficiaries and for personal exemption of the trust (section 643(a)(1) and (2)); capital gains were excluded and no deduction under section 1202 (relating to the 50-percent deduction for long-term capital gains) was taken into account (section 643(a)(3)); the tax-exempt interest (as adjusted for expenses) and the dividend exclusion of $50 were included (section 643(a)(5) and (7)). Since all of the income of the trust is required to be currently distributed, no deduction is allowable for depreciation in the absence of specific provisions in the governing instrument providing for the keeping of the trust corpus intact. See section 167(h) and the regulations thereunder.

(d) The deduction allowable to the trust under section 651(a) for distributions to the beneficiaries is $67,025, computed as follows:

Distributable net income computed under section 643(a) (see paragraph (c))		$91,100
Less:		
Tax-exempt interest as adjusted	$24,025	
Dividend exclusion	50	24,075
Distributable net income as determined under section 651(b)		67,025

Since the amount of the income ($92,400) required to be distributed currently by the trust exceeds the distributable net income ($67,025) as computed under section 651(b), the deduction allowable under section 651(a) is limited to the distributable net income of $67,025.

(e) The taxable income of the trust is $7,200 computed as follows:

Rents		$25,000
Dividends ($50,000 less $50 exclusion)		49,950
Long-term capital gains		15,000
Gross income		89,950
Deductions:		
Rental expenses	$ 5,000	
Trustee's commissions	2,925	
Capital gain deduction	7,500	
Distributions to beneficiaries	67,025	
Personal exemption	300	82,750
Taxable income		7,200

The trust is not allowed a deduction for the portion ($975) of the trustee's commissions allocable to tax-exempt interest in computing its taxable income.

(f) In determining the character of the amounts includible in the gross income of A and B, it is assumed that the trustee elects to allocate to rents the expenses not directly attributable to a specific item of income other than the portion ($975) of such expenses allocated to tax-exempt interest. The allocation of expenses among the items of income is shown below:

	Rents	*Dividends*	*Tax-Exempt Interest*	*Total*
Income for trust accounting purposes	$25,000	$50,000	$25,000	$100,000
Less: Rental Expenses	5,000			5,000
Trustee's commissions	2,925		975	3,900
Total Deductions	7,925	0	975	8,900
Character of amounts in the hands of the beneficiaries	17,075	50,000	24,025	91,100*

*Distributable net income

Inasmuch as the income of the trust is to be distributed equally to A and B, each is deemed to have received one-half of each item of income; that is, rents of $8,537.50, dividends of $25,000, and tax-exempt interest of $12,012.50. The dividends of $25,000 allocated to each beneficiary are to be aggregated with his other dividends (if any) for purposes of the dividend exclusion provided by section 116 and the dividend received credit allowed under section 34. Also, each beneficiary is allowed a deduction of $2,500 for depreciation of rental property attributable to the portion (one-half) of the income of the trust distributed to him.

[T.D. 6500, 25 FR 11814, Nov. 26, 1960, as amended by T.D. 6712, 29 FR 3655, March 24, 1964]

Subpart C. Estates and Trusts Which May Accumulate Income or Which Distribute Corpus

§ 661. Deduction for Estates and Trusts Accumulating Income or Distributing Corpus

(a) Deduction. In any taxable year there shall be allowed as a deduction in computing the taxable income of an estate or trust (other than a trust to which subpart B applies), the sum of—

(1) any amount of income for such taxable year required to be distributed currently (including any amount required to be distributed which may be paid out of income or corpus to the extent such amount is paid out of income for such taxable year); and

(2) any other amounts properly paid or credited or required to be distributed for such taxable year; but such deduction shall not exceed the distributable net income of the estate or trust.

(b) Character of amounts distributed. The amount determined under subsection (a) shall be treated as consisting of the same proportion of each class of items entering into the computation of distributable net income of the estate or trust as the total of each class bears to the total distributable net income of the estate or trust in the absence of the allocation of different classes of income under the specific terms of the governing instrument. In the application of the preceding sentence, the items of deduction entering into the computation of distributable net income (including the deduction allowed under section 642(c)) shall be allocated among the items of distributable net income in accordance with regulations prescribed by the Secretary.

(c) Limitation on deduction. No deduction shall be allowed under subsection (a) in respect of any portion of the amount allowed as a deduction under that subsection (without regard to this subsection) which is treated under subsection (b) as consisting of any item of distributable net income which is not included in the gross income of the estate or trust.

Regulations

§ 1.661(a)–1 Estates and trusts accumulating income or distributing corpus; general.

Subpart C, Part I, Subchapter J, Chapter 1 of the Code, is applicable to all decedents' estates and their beneficiaries, and to trusts and their beneficiaries other than trusts subject to the provisions of Subpart B of such Part I (relating to trusts which distribute current income only, or "simple" trusts). A trust which is required to distribute amounts other than income during the taxable year may be subject to Subpart B, and not Subpart C, in the absence of an actual distribution of amounts other than income during the taxable year. See §§ 1.651(a)–1 and 1.651(a)–3. A trust to which Subpart C is applicable is referred to as a "complex" trust in this part. Section 661 has no application to amounts excluded under section 663(a).

[T.D. 6500, 25 FR 11814, Nov. 26, 1960]

§ 1.661(a)–2 Deduction for distributions to beneficiaries.

(a) In computing the taxable income of an estate or trust there is allowed under section 661(a) as a deduction for distributions to beneficiaries the sum of:

(1) The amount of income for the taxable year which is required to be distributed currently, and

(2) Any other amounts properly paid or credited or required to be distributed for such taxable year.

However, the total amount deductible under section 661(a) cannot exceed the distributable net income as computed under section 643(a) and as modified by section 661(c). See § 1.661(c)–1.

(b) The term "income required to be distributed currently" includes any amount required to be distributed which may be paid out of income or corpus (such as an annuity), to the extent it is paid out of income for the taxable year. See § 1.651(a)–2 which sets forth additional rules which are applicable in determining whether income of an estate or trust is required to be distributed currently.

(c) The term "any other amounts properly paid, credited, or required to be distributed" includes all amounts properly paid, credited, or required to be distributed by an estate or trust during the taxable year other than income required to be distributed currently. Thus, the term includes the payment of an annuity to the extent it is not paid out of income for the taxable year, and a distribution of property in kind (see paragraph (f) of this section). However, see section 663(a) and regulations thereunder for distributions which are not included. Where the income of an estate or trust may be accumulated or distributed in the discretion of the fiduciary, or where the fiduciary has a power to distribute corpus to a beneficiary, any such discretionary distribution would qualify under section 661(a)(2). The term also includes an amount applied or distributed for the support of a dependent of a grantor or of a trustee or cotrustee under the circumstances described in section 677(b) or section 678(c) out of corpus or out of other than income for the taxable year.

(d) The terms "income required to be distributed currently" and "any other amounts properly paid or credited or required to be distributed" also include any amount used to discharge or satisfy any person's legal obligation as that term is used in § 1.662(a)–4.

(e) The terms "income required to be distributed currently" and "any other amounts properly paid or credited or required to be distributed" include amounts paid, or required to be paid, during the taxable year pursuant to a court order or decree or under local law, by a decedent's estate as an allowance or award for the support of the decedent's widow or other dependent for a limited period during the administration of the estate. The term "any other amounts properly paid or credited or required to be distributed" does not include the value of any interest in real estate owned by a decedent, title to which under local law passes directly from the decedent to his heirs or devisees.

(f) Gain or loss is realized by the trust or estate (or the other beneficiaries) by reason of a distribution of property in kind if the distribution is in satisfaction of a right to receive a distribution of a specific dollar amount, of specific property other than that distributed, or of income as defined under section 643(b) and the applicable regulations, if income is required to be distributed currently. In addition, gain or loss is realized if the trustee or executor makes the election to recognize gain or loss under section 643(e). This paragraph applies for taxable years of trusts and estates ending after January 2, 2004.

[T.D. 6500, 25 FR 11814, Nov. 26, 1960; 25 FR 14021, Dec. 31, 1960, as amended by T.D. 7287, 38 FR 26912, Sept. 27, 1973; T.D. 9102, 69 FR 20, Jan. 2, 2004]

§ 1.661(b)–1 Character of amounts distributed; in general.

In the absence of specific provisions in the governing instrument for the allocation of different classes of income, or unless local law requires such an allocation, the amount deductible for distributions to beneficiaries under section 661(a) is treated as consisting of the same proportion of each class of items entering into the computation of distributable net income as the total of each class bears to the total distributable net income. For example, if a trust has distributable net income of $20,000, consisting of $10,000 each of taxable interest and royalties and distributes $10,000 to beneficiary A, the deduction of $10,000 allowable under section 661(a) is deemed to consist of $5,000 each of taxable interest and royalties, unless the trust instrument specifically provides for the distribution or accumulation of different classes of income or unless local law requires such an allocation. See also § 1.661(c)–1.

[T.D. 6500, 25 FR 11814, Nov. 26, 1960]

§ 1.661(b)–2 Character of amounts distributed when charitable contributions are made.

In the application of the rule stated in § 1.661(b)–1, the items of deduction which enter into the computation of distributable net income are allocated among the items of income which enter into the computation of distributable net income in accordance with the rules set forth in § 1.652(b)–3, except that, in the absence of specific provisions in the governing instrument, or unless local law requires a different apportionment, amounts paid, permanently set aside, or to be used for the charitable, etc., purposes specified in section 642(c) are first ratably apportioned among each class of items of income entering into the computation of the distributable net income of the estate or trust, in accordance with the rules set out in paragraph (b) of § 1.643(a)–5.

[T.D. 6500, 25 FR 11814, Nov. 26, 1960]

§ 1.661(c)–1 Limitation on deduction.

An estate or trust is not allowed a deduction under section 661(a) for any amount which is treated under section 661(b) as consisting of any item of distributable net income which is not included in the gross income of the estate or trust. For example, if in 1962, a trust, which reports on the calendar year basis, has distributable net income of $20,000, which is deemed to consist of $10,000 of dividends and $10,000 of tax-exempt interest, and distributes $10,000 to beneficiary A, the deduction allowable under section 661(a) (computed without regard to section 661(c)) would amount to $10,000 consisting of $5,000 of dividends and $5,000 of tax-exempt interest. The deduction actually allowable under section 661(a) as limited by section 661(c) is $4,975, since no deduction is allowable for the $5,000 of tax-exempt interest and the $25 deemed distributed out of the $50 of dividends excluded under section 116, items of distributable net income which are not included in the gross income of the estate or trust.

[T.D. 6500, 25 FR 11814, Nov. 26, 1960, as amended by T.D. 6777, 29 FR 17809, Dec. 16, 1964]

§ 1.661(c)–2 Illustration of the provisions of section 661.

The provisions of section 661 may be illustrated by the following example:

Example. (a) Under the terms of a trust, which reports on the calendar year basis, $10,000 a year is required to be paid out of income to a designated charity. The balance of the income may, in the trustee's discretion, be accumulated or distributed to beneficiary A. Expenses are allocable against income and the trust instrument requires a reserve for depreciation. During the taxable year 1955 the trustee contributes $10,000 to charity and in his discretion distributes $15,000 of income to A. The trust has the following items of income and expense for the taxable year 1955:

Dividends	$10,000
Partially tax-exempt interest	10,000
Fully tax-exempt interest	10,000
Rents	20,000
Rental expenses	2,000

Depreciation of rental property		3,000
Trustee's commissions		5,000

(b) The income of the trust for fiduciary accounting purposes is $40,000, computed as follows:

Dividends		$10,000
Partially tax-exempt interest		10,000
Fully tax-exempt interest		10,000
Rents		20,000
Total		50,000
Less:		
Rental expenses	$2,000	
Depreciation	3,000	
Trustee's commissions	5,000	10,000
Income as computed under section 643(b)		40,000

(c) The distributable net income of the trust as computed under section 643(a) is $30,000, determined as follows:

Rents		$20,000
Dividends		10,000
Partially tax-exempt interest		10,000
Fully tax-exempt interest		$10,000
Less:		
Expenses allocable thereto (10,000/50,000 x $5,000)	[$1,000]	
Charitable contributions allocable thereto (10,000/50,000 x $10,000)	[2,000]	7,000
Total		47,000
Deductions:		
Rental expenses	2,000	
Depreciation of rental property	3,000	
Trustee's commissions ($5,000 less $1,000 allocated to tax-exempt interest)	4,000	
Charitable contributions ($10,000 less $2,000 allocated to tax-exempt interest)	8,000	17,000
Distributable net income (§ 643(a))	30,000	

(d) The character of the amounts distributed under section 661(a), determined in accordance with the rules prescribed in §§ 1.661(b)–1 and 1.661(b)–2 is shown by the following table (for the purpose of this allocation, it is assumed that the trustee elected to allocate the trustee's commissions to rental income except for the amount required to be allocated to tax-exempt interest):

	Rental Income	*Taxable Dividends*	*Excluded Dividends*	*Partially tax-exempt interest*	*Tax-exempt interest*	*Total*
Trust income	$20,000	$9,950	$50	$10,000	$10,000	$50,000
Less:						
Charitable contributions	4,000	2,000		2,000	2,000	10,000
Rental expenses	2,000					2,000
Depreciation	3,000					3,000
Trustee's commissions	4,000				1,000	5,000
Total deductions	13,000	2,000	0	2,000	3,000	20,000
Distributable net income	7,000	7,950	50	8,000	7,000	30,000
Amounts deemed distributed under section 661(a) before applying the limitation of section 661(c)	3,500	3,975	25	4,000	3,500	15,000

In the absence of specific provisions in the trust instrument for the allocation of different classes of income, the charitable contribution is deemed to consist of a pro rata portion of the gross amount of each items of income of the trust (except dividends excluded under section 116) and the trust is deemed to have distributed to A a pro rata portion (one-half) of each item of income included in distributable net income.

(e) The taxable income of the trust is $11,375 computed as follows:

Rental income		$20,000
Dividends ($10,000 less $50 exclusion)		9,950
Partially tax-exempt interest		10,000
Gross income		39,950
Deductions:		
Rental expenses	$ 2,000	
Depreciation of rental property	3,000	
Trustee's commissions	4,000	
Charitable contributions	8,000	
Distributions to A	11,475	
Personal exemption	100	28,575
Taxable income		11,375

In computing the taxable income of the trust no deduction is allowable for the portions of the charitable contributions deduction ($2,000) and trustee's commissions ($1,000) which are treated under section 661(b) as attributable to the tax-exempt interest excludable from gross income. Also, of the dividends of $4,000 deemed to have been distributed to A under section 661(a), $25 25/150ths of $50) is deemed to have been distributed from the excluded dividends and is not an allowable deduction to the trust. Accordingly, the deduction allowable under section 661 is deemed to be composed of $3,500 rental income, $3,975 of dividends, and $4,000 partially tax-exempt interest. No deduction is allowable for the portion of tax-exempt interest or for the portion of the excluded dividends deemed to have been distributed to the beneficiary.

(f) The trust is entitled to the credit allowed by section 34 with respect to dividends of $5,975 ($9,950 less $3,975 distributed to A) included in gross income. Also, the trust is allowed the credit provided by section 35 with respect to partially tax-exempt interest of $6,000 ($10,000 less $4,000 deemed distributed to A) included in gross income.

(g) Dividends of $4,000 allocable to A are to be aggregated with his other dividends (if any) for purposes of the dividend exclusion under section 116 and the dividend received credit under section 84.

[T.D. 6500, 25 FR 11814, Nov. 26, 1960]

§ 662. Inclusion of Amounts in Gross Income of Beneficiaries of Estates and Trusts Accumulating Income or Distributing Corpus

(a) Inclusion. Subject to subsection (b), there shall be included in the gross income of a beneficiary to whom an amount specified in section 661(a) is paid, credited, or required to be distributed (by an estate or trust described in section 661), the sum of the following amounts:

(1) Amounts required to be distributed currently. The amount of income for the taxable year required to be distributed currently to such beneficiary, whether distributed or not. If the amount of income required to be distributed currently to all beneficiaries exceeds the distributable net income (computed without the deduction allowed by section 642(c), relating to deduction for charitable, etc., purposes) of the estate or trust, then, in lieu of the amount provided in the preceding sentence, there shall be included in the gross income of the beneficiary an amount which bears the same ratio to distributable net income (as so computed) as the amount of income required to be distributed currently to such beneficiary bears to the amount required to be distributed currently to all beneficiaries. For purposes of this section, the phrase "the amount of income for the taxable year required to be distributed currently" includes any amount required to be paid out of income or corpus to the extent such amount is paid out of income for such taxable year.

(2) Other amounts distributed. All other amounts properly paid, credited, or required to be distributed to such beneficiary for the taxable year. If the sum of—

(A) the amount of income for the taxable year required to be distributed currently to all beneficiaries, and

(B) all other amounts properly paid, credited, or required to be distributed to all beneficiaries exceeds the distributable net income of the estate or trust, then, in lieu of the amount provided in the preceding sentence, there shall be included in the gross income of the beneficiary an amount which bears the same ratio to distributable net income (reduced by the amounts specified in (A)) as the other amounts properly paid, credited or required to be distributed to the beneficiary bear to the other amounts properly paid, credited, or required to be distributed to all beneficiaries.

(b) Character of amounts. The amounts determined under subsection (a) shall have the same character in the hands of the beneficiary as in the hands of the estate or trust. For this purpose, the amounts shall be treated as consisting of the same proportion of each class of items entering into the computation of distributable net income as the total of each class bears to the total distributable net income of the estate or trust unless the terms of the governing instrument specifically allocate different classes of income to different beneficiaries. In the application of the preceding sentence, the items of deduction entering into the computation of distributable net income (including the deduction allowed under section 642(c)) shall be allocated among the items of distributable net income in accordance with regulations prescribed by the Secretary. In the application of this subsection to the amount determined under paragraph (1) of subsection (a), distributable net income shall be computed without regard to any portion of the deduction under section 642(c) which is not attributable to income of the taxable year.

(c) Different taxable years. If the taxable year of a beneficiary is different from that of the estate or trust, the amount to be included in the gross income of the beneficiary shall be based on the distributable net income of the estate or trust and the amounts properly paid, credited, or required to be distributed to the beneficiary during any taxable year or years of the estate or trust ending within or with his taxable year.

Regulations

§ 1.662(a)–1 Inclusion of amounts in gross income of beneficiaries of estates and complex trusts; general.

There is included in the gross income of a beneficiary of an estate or complex trust the sum of:

(1) Amounts of income required to be distributed currently to him, and

(2) All other amounts properly paid, credited, or required to be distributed to him by the estate or trust. The preceding sentence is subject to the rules contained in § 1.662(a)–2 (relating to currently distributable income), § 1.662(a)–3 (relating to other amounts distributed), and §§ 1.662(b)–1 and 1.662(b)–2 (relating to character of amounts). Section 662 has no application to amounts excluded under section 663(a).

[T.D. 6500, 25 FR 11814, Nov. 26, 1960]

§ 1.662(a)–2 Currently distributable income.

(a) There is first included in the gross income of each beneficiary under section 662(a)(1) the amount of income for the taxable year of the estate or trust required to be distributed currently to him, subject to the provisions of paragraph (b) of this section. Such amount is included in the beneficiary's gross income whether or not it is actually distributed.

(b) If the amount of income required to be distributed currently to all beneficiaries exceeds the distributable net income (as defined in section 643(a) but computed without taking into account the payment, crediting, or setting aside of an amount for which a charitable contributions deduction is allowable under section 642(c)) of the estate or trust, then there is included in the gross income of each beneficiary an amount which bears the same ratio to distributable net income (as so computed) as the amount of income required to be distributed currently to the beneficiary bears to the amount required to be distributed currently to all beneficiaries.

(c) The phrase "the amount of income for the taxable year required to be distributed currently" includes any amount required to be paid out of income or corpus to the extent the amount is satisfied out of income for the taxable year. Thus, an annuity required to be paid in all events (either out of income or corpus) would qualify as income required to be distributed currently to the extent there is income (as defined in section 643(b)) not paid, credited, or required to be distributed to other beneficiaries for the taxable year. If an annuity or a portion of an annuity is deemed under this paragraph to be income required to be distributed currently, it is treated in all respects in the same manner as an amount of income actually required to be distributed currently. The phrase "the amount of income for the taxable year required to be distributed currently" also includes any amount required to be paid during the taxable year in all events (either out of income or corpus) pursuant to a court order or decree or under local law, by a decedent's estate as an allowance or award for the support of the decedent's widow or other dependent for a limited period during the administration of the estate to the extent there is income (as defined in section 643(b)) of the estate for the taxable year not paid, credited, or required to be distributed to other beneficiaries.

(d) If an annuity is paid, credited, or required to be distributed tax free, that is, under a provision whereby the executor or trustee will pay the income tax of the annuitant resulting from the receipt of the annuity, the payment of or for the tax by the executor or trustee will be treated as income paid, credited, or required to be distributed currently to the extent it is made out of income.

(e) The application of the rules stated in this section may be illustrated by the following examples:

Example (1). (1) Assume that under the terms of the trust instrument $5,000 is to be paid to X charity out of income each year; that $20,000 of income is currently distributable to A; and that an annuity of $12,000 is to be paid to B out of income or corpus. All expenses are charges against income and capital gains are allocable to corpus. During the taxable year the trust had income of $30,000 (after the payment of expenses) derived from taxable interest and made the payments to X charity and distributions to A and B as required by the governing instrument.

(2) The amounts treated as distributed currently under section 662(a)(1) total $25,000 ($20,000 to A and $5,000 to B). Since the charitable contribution is out of income the amount of income available for B's annuity is only $5,000. The distributable net income of the trust computed under section 643(a) without taking into consideration the charitable contributions deduction of $5,000 as provided by section 661(a)(1), is $30,000. Since the amounts treated as distributed currently of $25,000 do not exceed the distributable net income (as modified) of $30,000, A is required to include $20,000 in his gross income and B is required to include $5,000 in his gross income under section 662(a)(1).

Example (2). Assume the same facts as in paragraph (1) of example (1), except that the trust has, in addition, $10,000 of administration expenses, commissions, etc., chargeable to corpus. The amounts treated as distributed currently under section 662(a)(1) total $25,000 ($20,000 to A and $5,000 to B), since trust income under section 643(b) remains the same as in example (1). Distributable net income of the trust computed under section 643(a) but without taking into account the charitable contributions deduction of $5,000 as provided by section 662(a)(1) is only $20,000. Since the amounts treated as distributed currently of $25,000 exceed the distributable net income (as so computed) of $20,000, A is required to include $16,000 (20,000/25,000 of $20,000) in his gross income and B is required to include $4,000 (5,000/25,000 of $20,000) in his gross income under section 662(a)(1). Because A and B are beneficiaries of amounts of income required to be distributed currently, they do not benefit from the reduction of distributable net income by the charitable contributions deduction.

[T.D. 6500, 25 FR 11814, Nov. 26, 1960; 25 FR 14021, Dec. 31, 1960, as amended by T.D. 7287, 38 FR 26912, Sept. 27, 1973]

§ 1.662(a)–3 Other amounts distributed.

(a) There is included in the gross income of a beneficiary under section 662(a)(2) any amount properly paid, credited, or required to be distributed to the beneficiary for the taxable year, other than (1) income required to be distributed currently, as determined under § 1.662(a)–2, (2) amounts excluded under section 663(a) and the regulations thereunder, and (3) amounts in excess of distributable net income (see paragraph (c) of this section). An amount which is credited or required to be distributed is included in the gross income of a beneficiary whether or not it is actually distributed.

(b) Some of the payments to be included under paragraph (a) of this section are: (1) A distribution made to a beneficiary in the discretion of the fiduciary; (2) a distribution required by the terms of the governing instrument upon the happening of a specified event; (3) an annuity which is required to be paid in all events but which is payable only out of corpus; (4)

a distribution of property in kind (see paragraph (f) of § 1.661(a)–2); (5) an amount applied or distributed for the support of a dependent of a grantor or a trustee or cotrustee under the circumstances specified in section 677(b) or section 678(c) out of corpus or out of other than income for the taxable year; and (6) an amount required to be paid during the taxable year pursuant to a court order or decree or under local law, by a decedent's estate as an allowance or award for the support of the decedent's widow or other dependent for a limited period during the administration of the estate which is payable only out of corpus of the estate under the order or decree or local law.

(c) If the sum of the amounts of income required to be distributed currently (as determined under § 1.662(a)–2) and other amounts properly paid, credited, or required to be distributed (as determined under paragraph (a) of this section) exceeds distributable net income (as defined in section 643(a)), then such other amounts properly paid, credited, or required to be distributed are included in gross income of the beneficiary but only to the extent of the excess of such distributable net income over the amounts of income required to be distributed currently. If the other amounts are paid, credited, or required to be distributed to more than one beneficiary, each beneficiary includes in gross income his proportionate share of the amount includible in gross income pursuant to the preceding sentence. The proportionate share is an amount which bears the same ratio to distributable net income (reduced by amounts of income required to be distributed currently) as the other amounts (as determined under paragraphs (a) and (d) of this section) distributed to the beneficiary bear to the other amounts distributed to all beneficiaries. For treatment of excess distributions by trusts, see sections 665 to 668, inclusive, and the regulations thereunder.

(d) The application of the rules stated in this section may be illustrated by the following example:

Example. The terms of a trust require the distribution annually of $10,000 of income to A. If any income remains, it may be accumulated or distributed to B, C, and D in amounts in the trustee's discretion. He may also invade corpus for the benefit of A, B, C, or D. In the taxable year, the trust has $20,000 of income after the deduction of all expenses. Distributable net income is $20,000. The trustee distributes $10,000 of income to A. Of the remaining $10,000 of income, he distributes $3,000 each to B, C, and D, and also distributes an additional $5,000 to A. A includes $10,000 in income under section 662(a)(1). The "other amounts distributed" amount of $14,000, includible in the income of the recipients to the extent of $10,000, distributable net income less the income currently distributable to A. A will include an additional $3,571 (5,000/14,000 * $10,000) in income under this section, and B, C, and D will each include $2,143 (3,000/14,000 x $10,000).

[T.D. 6500, 25 FR 11814, Nov. 26, 1960; 25 FR 14021, Dec. 31, 1960, as amended by T.D. 7287, 38 FR 26913, Sept. 27, 1973]

§ 1.662(a)–4 Amounts used in discharge of a legal obligation.

Any amount which, pursuant to the terms of a will or trust instrument, is used in full or partial discharge or satisfaction of a legal obligation of any person is included in the gross income of such person under section 662(a)(1) or (2), whichever is applicable, as though directly distributed to him as a beneficiary, except in cases to which section 71 (relating to alimony payments) or section 682 (relating to income of a trust in case of divorce, etc.) applies. The term "legal obligation" includes a legal obligation to support another person if, and only if, the obligation is not affected by the adequacy of the dependent's own resources. For example, a parent has a "legal obligation" within the meaning of the preceding sentence to support his minor child if under local law property or income from property owned by the child cannot be used for his support so long as his parent is able to support him. On the other hand, if under local law a mother may use the resources of a child for the child's support in lieu of supporting him herself, no obligation of support exists within the meaning of this paragraph, whether or not income is actually used for support. Similarly, since under local law a child ordinarily is obligated to support his parent only if the parent's earnings and resources are insufficient for the purpose, no obligation exists whether or not the parent's earnings and resources are sufficient. In any event the amount of trust income which is included in the gross income of a person obligated to support a dependent is limited by the extent of his legal obligation under local law. In the case of a parent's obligation to support his child, to the extent that the parent's legal obligation of support, including education, is determined under local law by the family's station in life and by the means of the parent, it is to be determined without consideration of the trust income in question.

[T.D. 6500, 25 FR 11814, Nov. 26, 1960]

§ 1.662(b)–1 Character of amounts; when no charitable contributions are made.

In determining the amount includible in the gross income of a beneficiary, the amounts which are determined under section 662(a) and §§ 1.662(a)–1 through 1.662(a)–4 shall have the same character in the hands of the beneficiary as in the hands of the estate or trust. The amounts are treated as consisting of the same proportion of each class of items entering into the computation of distributable net income as the total of each class bears to the total distributable net income of the estate or trust unless the terms of the governing instrument specifically allocate different classes of income to different beneficiaries, or unless local law requires such an allocation. For this purpose, the principles contained in § 1.652(b)–1 shall apply.

[T.D. 6500, 25 FR 11814, Nov. 26, 1960]

§ 1.662(b)–2 Character of amounts; when charitable contributions are made.

When a charitable contribution is made, the principles contained in §§ 1.652(b)–1 and 1.662(b)–1 generally apply. However, before the allocation of other deductions among the items of distributable net income, the charitable contributions deduction allowed under section 642(c) is (in the absence of specific allocation under the terms of the governing instrument or the requirement under local law of a different allocation) allocated among the classes of income entering into the computation of estate or trust income in accordance with the rules set forth in paragraph (b) of § 1.643(a)–5. In the application of the preceding sentence, for the purpose of allocating items of income and deductions to beneficiaries to whom income is required to be distributed currently, the amount of the charitable contributions deduction is disregarded to the extent that it exceeds the income of the trust for the taxable year reduced by amounts for the taxable year required to be distributed currently. The application of this section may be illustrated by the following examples (of which example (1) is illustrative of the preceding sentence):

Example (1). (a) A trust instrument provides that $30,000 of its income must be distributed currently to A, and the balance may either be distributed to B, distributed to a designated charity, or accumulated. Accumulated income may be distributed to B and to the charity. The trust for its taxable year has $40,000 of taxable interest and $10,000 of tax-exempt income, with no expenses. The trustee distributed $30,000 to A, $50,000 to charity X, and $10,000 to B.

(b) Distributable net income for the purpose of determining the character of the distribution to A is $30,000 (the charitable contributions deduction, for this purpose, being taken into account only to the extent of $20,000, the difference between the income of the trust for the taxable year, $50,000, and the amount required to be distributed currently, $30,000).

(c) The charitable contributions deduction taken into account, $20,000, is allocated proportionately to the items of income of the trust, $16,000 to taxable interest and $4,000 to tax-exempt income.

(d) Under section 662(a)(1), the amount of income required to be distributed currently to A is $30,000, which consists of the balance of these items, $24,000 of taxable interest and $6,000 of tax-exempt income.

(e) In determining the amount to be included in the gross income of B under section 662 for the taxable year, however, the entire charitable contributions deduction is taken into account, with the result that there is no distributable net income and therefore no amount to be included in gross income.

(f) See subpart D (section 665 and following), part I, subchapter J, chapter 1 of the Code for application of the throwback provisions to the distribution made to B.

Example (2). The net income of a trust is payable to A for life, with the remainder to a charitable organization. Under the terms of the trust instrument and local law capital gains are added to corpus. During the taxable year the trust receives dividends of $10,000 and realized a long-term capital gain of $10,000, for which a long-term capital gain deduction of $5,000 is allowed under section 1202. Since under the trust instrument and local law the capital gains are allocated to the charitable organization, and since the capital gain deduction is directly attributable to the capital gain, the charitable contributions deduction and the capital gain deduction are both allocable to the capital gain, and dividends in the amount of $10,000 are allocable to A.

[T.D. 6500, 25 FR 11814, Nov. 26, 1960]

§ 1.662(c)–1 Different taxable years.

If a beneficiary has a different taxable year (as defined in section 441 or 442) from the taxable year of an estate or trust, the amount he is required to include in gross income in accordance with section 662(a) and (b) is based upon the distributable net income of the estate or trust and the amounts properly paid, credited, or required to be distributed to the beneficiary for any taxable year or years of the estate or trust ending with or within his taxable year. This rule applies as to so-called short taxable years as well as taxable years of normal duration. Income of an estate or trust for its taxable year or years is determined in accordance with its method of accounting and without regard to that of the beneficiary.

[T.D. 6500, 25 FR 11814, Nov. 26, 1960]

§ 1.662(c)–2 Death of individual beneficiary.

If an amount specified in section 662(a)(1) or (2) is paid, credited, or required to be distributed by an estate or trust for a taxable year which does not end with or within the last taxable year of a beneficiary (because of the beneficiary's death), the extent to which the amount is included in the gross income of the beneficiary for his last taxable year or in the gross income of his estate is determined by the computations under section 662 for the taxable year of the estate or trust in which his last taxable year ends. Thus, the distributable net income and the amounts paid, credited, or required to be distributed for the taxable year of the estate or trust, determine the extent to which the amounts paid, credited, or required to be distributed to the beneficiary are included in his gross income for his last taxable year or in the gross income of his estate. (Section 662(c) does not apply to such amounts.) The gross income for the last taxable year of a beneficiary on the cash basis includes only income actually distributed to the beneficiary before his death. Income required to be distributed, but in fact distributed to his estate, is included in the gross income of the estate as income in respect of a decedent under section 691. See paragraph (e) of § 1.663(c)–3 with respect to separate share treatment for the periods before and after the death of a trust's beneficiary

[T.D. 6500, 25 FR 11814, Nov. 26, 1960]

§ 1.662(c)–3 Termination of existence of other beneficiaries.

If the existence of a beneficiary which is not an individual terminates, the amount to be included under section 662(a) in its gross income for the last taxable year is computed with reference to §§ 1.662(c)–1 and 1.662(c)–2 as if the beneficiary were a deceased individual, except that income required to be distributed prior to the termination but actually distributed to the beneficiary's successor in interest is included in the beneficiary's income for its last taxable year.

[T.D. 6500, 25 FR 11814, Nov. 26, 1960]

§ 1.662(c)–4 Illustration of the provisions of sections 661 and 662.

The provisions of sections 661 and 662 may be illustrated in general by the following example:

Example. (a) Under the terms of a testamentary trust one-half of the trust income is to be distributed currently to W, the decedent's wife, for her life. The remaining trust income may, in the trustee's discretion, either be paid to D, the grantor's daughter, paid to designated charities, or accumulated. The trust is to terminate at the death of W and the principal will then be payable to D. No provision is made in the trust instrument with respect to depreciation of rental property. Capital gains are allocable to the principal account under the applicable local law. The trust and both beneficiaries file returns on the calendar year basis. The records of the fiduciary show the following items of income and deduction for the taxable year 1955:

Rents	$50,000
Dividends of domestic corporations	50,000
Tax-exempt interest	20,000
Partially tax-exempt interest	10,000
Capital gains (long term)	20,000
Depreciation of rental property	10,000
Expenses attributable to rental income	15,400
Trustee's commissions allocable to income account	2,800
Trustee's commissions allocable to principal account	1,100

(b) The income for trust accounting purposes is $111,800, and the trustee distributes one-half ($55,900) to W and in his discretion makes a contribution of one-quarter ($27,950) to charity X and distributes the remaining one-quarter ($27,950) to D. The total of the distributions to beneficiaries is $83,850, consisting of (1) income required to be distributed currently to W of $55,900 and (2) other amounts properly paid or credited to D of $27,950. The income for trust accounting purposes of $111,800 is determined as follows:

Rents		$ 50,000
Dividends of domestic corporations		$ 50,000
Tax-exempt interest		20,000
Partially tax-exempt interest		10,000
Total		130,000
Less: Rental Expenses	$15,400	
Trustee's commissions allocable to income account	2,800	18,200
Income as computed under section 643(b)	111,800	

(c) The distributable net income of the trust as computed under section 643(a) is $82,750, determined as follows:

Rents			$50,000
Dividends			50,000
Partially tax-exempt interest			10,000
Tax-exempt interest			$20,000
Less: Trustee's commissions allocable thereto (20,000/130,000 of $3,900)	$ 600		
Charitable contributions allocable thereto (20,000/130,000 of $27,950	4,300	4,900	15,100
Total			125,100
Deductions:			
Rental expenses			15,400
Trustee's commissions ($3,900 less $600 allocated to tax-exempt interest)			3,300
Charitable deduction ($27,950 less $4,300 attributable to tax-exempt interest)		23,650	42,350
Distributable net income			82,750

In computing the distributable net income of $82,750, the taxable income of the trust was computed with the following modifications: No deductions were allowed for distributions to beneficiaries and for personal exemption of the trust (section 643(a)(1) and (2)); capital gains were excluded and no deduction under section 1202 (relating to the 50 percent deduction for long-term capital gains) was taken into account (section 643(a)(3)); and the tax-exempt interest (as adjusted for expenses and charitable contributions) and the dividend exclusion of $50 were included (section 643(a)(5) and (7)).

(d) Inasmuch as the distributable net income of $82,750 as determined under section 643(a) is less than the sum of the amounts distributed to W and D of $83,850, the deduction allowable to the trust under section 661(a) is such distributable net income as modified under section 661(c) to exclude therefrom the items of income not included in the gross income of the trust, as follows:

Distributable net income		$82,750
Less: Tax-exempt interest (as adjusted for expenses and the charitable contributions)	$15,100	
Dividend exclusion allowable under [§] 116	50	15,150
Deduction allowable under section 661(a)		67,600

(e) For the purpose of determining the character of the amounts deductible under section 642(c) and section 661(a), the trustee elected to offset the trustee's commissions (other than the portion required to be allocated to tax-exempt interest) against the rental income. The following table shows the determination of the character of the amounts deemed distributed to beneficiaries and contributed to charity.

	Rents	*Taxable Dividends*	*Excluded Dividends*	*Tax-exempt interest*	*Partially tax-exempt interest*	*Total*
Trust income	$50,000	$49,950	$50	$20,000	$10,000	$130,000
Less:						
Charitable contribution	$10,750	$10,750		$4,300	$2,150	$27,950
Rental expenses	$15,400					$15,400
Trustee's commissions	3,300			600		3,900
Total deductions	29,450	10,750	0	4,900	2,150	47,250
Amounts distributed to beneficiaries	20,550	39,200	50	15,100	7,850	82,750

The character of the charitable contribution is determined by multiplying the total charitable contribution ($27,950) by a fraction consisting of each item of trust income, respectively, over the total trust income, except that no part of the dividends excluded from gross income are deemed included in the charitable contribution. For example, the charitable contribution is deemed to consist of rents of $10,750 (50,000/130,000 x $27,950).

(f) The taxable income of the trust is $9,900 determined as follows:

Rental income		$50,000
Dividends ($50,000 less $50 exclusion)		49,950
Partially tax-exempt interest		10,000
Capital gains		20,000
Gross income		129,950
Deductions:		
Rental expenses	15,400	
Trustee's commissions		3,300
Charitable contributions		23,650
Capital gain deductions		10,000
Distributions to beneficiaries		67,600
Personal exemption	100	120,050
Taxable income		9,900

(g) In computing the amount includible in W's gross income under section 662(a)(1), the $55,900 distribution to her is deemed to be composed of the following proportions of the items of income deemed to have been distributed to the beneficiaries by the trust (see paragraph (e) of this example):

Rents (20,550/82,750 * $55,900)	$13,882
Dividends (39,250/82,750 * $55,900)	26,515
Partially tax-exempt interest (7,850/82,750 * $55,900)	5,303
Tax-exempt interest (15,100/82,750 * $55,900)	10,200
Total	55,900

Accordingly, W will exclude $10,200 of tax-exempt interest from gross income and will receive the credits and exclusion for dividends received and for partially tax-exempt interest provided in sections 34, 116, and 35, respectively, with respect to the dividends and partially tax-exempt interest deemed to have been distributed to her, her share of the dividends being aggregated with other dividends received by her for purposes of the dividend credit and exclusion. In addition, she may deduct a share of the depreciation deduction proportionate to the trust income allocable to her; that is, one-half of the total depreciation deduction, or $5,000.

(h) Inasmuch as the sum of the amount of income required to be distributed currently to W ($55,900) and the other amounts properly paid, credited, or required to be distributed to D ($27,950) exceeds the distributable net income ($82,750) of the trust as determined under section 643(a), D is deemed to have received $26,850 ($82,750 less $55,900) for income tax purposes. The character of the amounts deemed distributed to her is determined as follows:

Rents (20,550/82,750 * $26,850)	$6,668
Dividends (39,250/82,750 * $26,850)	12,735
Partially tax-exempt interest (7,850/82,750 * $26,850)	2,547
Tax-exempt interest (15,100/82,750 * $26,850)	4,900
Total	26,850

Accordingly, D will exclude $4,900 of tax-exempt interest from gross income and will receive the credits and exclusion for dividends received and for partially tax-exempt interest provided in sections 34, 116, and 35, respectively, with respect to the dividends and partially tax-exempt interest deemed to have been distributed to her, her share of the dividends being aggregated with other dividends received by her for purposes of the dividend credit and exclusion. In addition, she may deduct a share of the depreciation deduction proportionate to the trust income allocable to her; that is, one-fourth of the total depreciation deduction, or $2,500.

(i) [Reserved]

(j) The remaining $2,500 of the depreciation deduction is allocated to the amount distributed to charity X and is hence nondeductible by the trust, W, or D. (See § 1.642(e)–1.)

[T.D. 6500, 25 FR 11814, Nov. 26, 1960]

§ 663. Special Rules Applicable to Sections 661 and 662

(a) Exclusions. There shall not be included as amounts falling within section 661(a) or 662(a)—

(1) Gifts, bequests, etc. Any amount which, under the terms of the governing instrument, is properly paid or credited as a gift or bequest of a specific sum of money or of specific property and which is paid or credited all at once or in not more than 3 installments. For this purpose an amount which can be paid or credited only from the income of the estate or trust shall not be considered as a gift or bequest of a specific sum of money.

(2) Charitable, etc., distributions. Any amount paid or permanently set aside or otherwise qualifying for the deduction provided in section 642(c) (computed without regard to sections 508(d), 681, and 4948(c)(4)).

(3) Denial of double deduction. Any amount paid, credited, or distributed in the taxable year, if section 651 or section 661 applied to such amount for a preceding taxable year of an estate or trust because credited or required to be distributed in such preceding taxable year.

(b) Distributions in first sixty-five days of taxable year.

(1) General rule. If within the first 65 days of any taxable year of an estate or a trust, an amount is properly paid or credited, such amount shall be considered paid or credited on the last day of the preceding taxable year.

(2) Limitation. Paragraph (1) shall apply with respect to any taxable year of an estate or a trust only if the executor of such estate or the fiduciary of such trust (as the case may be) elects, in such manner and at such time as the Secretary prescribes by regulations, to have paragraph (1) apply for such taxable year.

(c) Separate shares treated as separate estates or trusts. For the sole purpose of determining the amount of distributable net income in the application of sections 661 and 662, in the case of a single trust having more than one beneficiary, substantially separate and independent shares of different beneficiaries in the trust shall be treated as separate trusts. Rules similar to the rules of the preceding provisions of this subsection shall apply to treat substantially separate and independent shares of different beneficiaries in an estate having more than 1 beneficiary as separate estates. The existence of such substantially separate and independent shares and the manner of treatment as separate trusts or estates, including the application of subpart D, shall be determined in accordance with regulations prescribed by the Secretary.

Regulations

§ 1.663(a)–1 Special rules applicable to sections 661 and 662; exclusions; gifts, bequests, etc.

(a) In general. A gift or bequest of a specific sum of money or of specific property, which is required by the specific terms of the will or trust instrument and is properly paid or credited to a beneficiary, is not allowed as a deduction to an estate or trust under section 661 and is not included in the gross income of a beneficiary under section 662, unless under the terms of the will or trust instrument the gift or bequest is to be paid or credited to the recipient in more than three installments. Thus, in order for a gift or bequest to be excludable from the gross income of the recipient, (1) it must qualify as a gift or bequest of a specific sum of money or of specific property (see paragraph (b) of this section), and (2) the terms of the governing instrument must not provide for its payment in more than three installments (see paragraph (c) of this section). The date when the estate came into existence or the date when the trust was created is immaterial.

(b) Definition of a gift or bequest of a specific sum of money or of specific property. (1) In order to qualify as a gift or bequest of a specific sum of money or of specific property under section 663(a), the amount of money or the identity of the specific property must be ascertainable under the terms of a testator's will as of the date of his death, or under the terms of an inter vivos trust instrument as of the date of the inception of the trust. For example, bequests to a decedent's son of the decedent's interest in a partnership and to his daughter of a sum of money equal to the value of the partnership interest are bequests of specific property and of a specific sum of money, respectively. On the other hand, a bequest to the decedent's spouse of money or property, to be selected by the decedent's executor, equal in value to a fraction of the decedent's "adjusted gross estate" is neither a bequest of a specific sum of money or of specific property. The identity of the property and the amount of money specified in the preceding sentence are dependent both on the exercise of the executor's discretion and on the payment of administration expenses and other charges, neither of which are facts existing on the date of the decedent's death. It is immaterial that the value of the bequest is determinable after the decedent's death before the bequest is satisfied (so that gain or loss may be realized by the estate in the transfer of property in satisfaction of it).

(2) The following amounts are not considered as gifts or bequests of a sum of money or of specific property within the meaning of this paragraph:

(i) An amount which can be paid or credited only from the income of an estate or trust, whether from the income for the year of payment or crediting, or from the income accumulated from a prior year;

(ii) An annuity, or periodic gifts of specific property in lieu of or having the effect of an annuity;

(iii) A residuary estate or the corpus of a trust; or

(iv) A gift or bequest paid in a lump sum or in not more than three installments, if the gift or bequest is required to be paid in more than three installments under the terms of the governing instrument.

(3) The provisions of subparagraphs (1) and (2) of this paragraph may be illustrated by the following examples, in which it is assumed that the gift or bequest is not required to be made in more than three installments (see paragraph (c)):

Example (1). Under the terms of a will, a legacy of $5,000 was left to A, 1,000 shares of X company stock was left to W, and the balance of the estate was to be divided equally between W and B. No provision was made in the will for the disposition of income of the estate during the period of administration. The estate had income of $25,000 during the taxable year 1954, which was accumulated and added to corpus for estate accounting purposes. During the taxable year, the executor paid the legacy of $5,000 in a lump sum to A, transferred the X company stock to W, and made no other distributions to beneficiaries. The distributions to A and W qualify for the exclusion under section 663(a)(1).

Example (2). Under the terms of a will, the testator's estate was to be distributed to A. No provision was made in the will for the distribution of the estate's income during the period of administration. The estate had income of $50,000 for the taxable year. The estate distributed to A stock with a basis of $40,000 and with a fair market value of $40,000 on the date of distribution. No other distributions were made during the year. The distribution does not qualify for the exclusion under section 663(a)(1), because it is not a specific gift to A required by the terms of the will. Accordingly, the fair market value of the property ($40,000) represents a distribution within the meaning of sections 661(a) and 662(a) (see § 1.661(a)–2(c)).

Example (3). Under the terms of a trust instrument, trust income is to be accumulated for a period of 10 years. During the eleventh year, the trustee is to distribute $10,000 to B, payable from income or corpus, and $10,000 to C, payable out of accumulated income. The trustee is to distribute the balance of the accumulated income to A. Thereafter, A is to receive all the current income until the trust terminates. Only the distribution to B would qualify for the exclusion under section 663(a)(1).

(4) A gift or bequest of a specific sum of money or of specific property is not disqualified under this paragraph solely because its payment is subject to a condition. For example, provision for a payment by a trust to beneficiary A of $10,000 when he reaches age 25, and $10,000 when he reaches age 30, with payment over to B of any amount not paid to A because of his death, is a gift to A of a specific sum of money payable in two installments, within the meaning of this paragraph, even though the exact amount payable to A cannot be ascertained with certainty under the terms of the trust instrument.

(c) Installment payments. (1) In determining whether a gift or bequest of a specific sum of money or of specific property, as defined in paragraph (b) of this section, is required to be paid or credited to a particular beneficiary in more than three installments:

(i) Gifts or bequests of articles for personal use (such as personal and household effects, automobiles, and the like) are disregarded.

(ii) Specifically devised real property, the title to which passes directly from the decedent to the devisee under local law, is not taken into account, since it would not constitute an amount paid, credited, or required to be distributed under section 661 (see paragraph (e) of § 1.661(a)–2).

(iii) All gifts and bequests under a decedent's will (which are not disregarded pursuant to subdivisions (i) and (ii) of this subparagraph) for which no time of payment or crediting is specified, and which are to be paid or credited in the ordinary course of administration of the decedent's estate, are considered as required to be paid or credited in a single installment.

(iv) All gifts and bequests (which are not disregarded pursuant to subdivisions (i) and (ii) of this subparagraph) payable at any one specified time under the terms of the governing instrument are taken into account as a single installment.

For purposes of determining the number of installments paid or credited to a particular beneficiary, a decedent's estate and a testamentary trust shall each be treated as a separate entity.

(2) The application of the rules stated in subparagraph (1) of this paragraph may be illustrated by the following examples:

Example (1). (i) Under the terms of a decedent's will, $10,000 in cash, household furniture, a watch, an automobile, 100 shares of X company stock, 1,000 bushels of grain, 500 head of cattle, and a farm (title to which passed directly to A under local law) are bequeathed or devised outright to A. The will also provides for the creation of a trust for the benefit of A, under the terms of which there are required to be distributed to A, $10,000 in cash and 100 shares of Y company stock when he reaches 25 years of age, $25,000 in cash and 200 shares of Y company stock when he reaches 30 years of age, and $50,000 in cash and 300 shares of Y company stock when he reaches 35 years of age.

(ii) The furniture, watch, automobile, and the farm are excluded in determining whether any gift or bequest is required to be paid or credited to A in more than three installments. These items qualify for the exclusion under section 663(a)(1) regardless of the treatment of the other items of property bequeathed to A.

(iii) The $10,000 in cash, the shares of X company stock, the grain, the cattle and the assets required to create the trust, to be paid or credited by the estate to A and the trust are considered as required to be paid or credited in a single installment to each, regardless of the manner of payment or distribution by the executor, since no time of payment or crediting is specified in the will. The $10,000 in cash and shares of Y company stock required to be distributed by the trust to A when he is 25 years old are considered as required to be paid or distributed as one installment under the trust. Likewise, the distributions to be made by the trust to

A when he is 30 and 35 years old are each considered as one installment under the trust. Since the total number of installments to be made by the estate does not exceed three, all of the items of money and property distributed by the estate qualify for the exclusion under section 663(a)(1). Similarly, the three distributions by the trust qualify.

Example (2). Assume the same facts as in example (1), except that another distribution of a specified sum of money is required to be made by the trust to A when he becomes 40 years old. This distribution would also qualify as an installment, thus making four installments in all under the trust. None of the gifts to A under the trust would qualify for the exclusion under section 663(a)(1). The situation as to the estate, however, would not be changed.

Example (3). A trust instrument provides that A and B are each to receive $75,000 in installments of $25,000, to be paid in alternate years. The trustee distributes $25,000 to A in 1954, 1956, and 1958, and to B in 1955, 1957, and 1959. The gifts to A and B qualify for exclusion under section 663(a)(1), although a total of six payments is made. The gifts of $75,000 to each beneficiary are to be separately treated.

[T.D. 6500, 25 FR 11814, Nov. 26, 1960; T.D. 8849, 64 FR 72543, Dec. 28, 1999]

§ 1.663(a)–2 Charitable, etc., distributions.

Any amount paid, permanently set aside, or to be used for the charitable, etc., purposes specified in section 642(c) and which is allowable as a deduction under that section is not allowed as a deduction to an estate or trust under section 661 or treated as an amount distributed for purposes of determining the amounts includible in gross income of beneficiaries under section 662. Amounts paid, permanently set aside, or to be used for charitable, etc., purposes are deductible by estates or trusts only as provided in section 642(c). For purposes of this section, the deduction provided in section 642(c) is computed without regard to the provisions of section 508(d), section 681, or section 4948(c)(4) (concerning unrelated business income and private foundations).

[T.D. 6500, 25 FR 11814, Nov. 26, 1960, as amended by T.D. 7428, 41 FR 34627, Aug. 16, 1976]

§ 1.663(a)–3 Denial of double deduction.

No amount deemed to have been distributed to a beneficiary in a preceding year under section 651 or 661 is included in amounts falling within section 661(a) or 662(a). For example, assume that all of the income of a trust is required to be distributed currently to beneficiary A and both the trust and A report on the calendar year basis. For administrative convenience, the trustee distributes in January and February 1956 a portion of the income of the trust required to be distributed in 1955. The portion of the income for 1955 which was distributed by the trust in 1956 may not be claimed as a deduction by the trust for 1956 since it is deductible by the trust and includible in A's gross income for the taxable year 1955.

[T.D. 6500, 25 FR 11814, Nov. 26, 1960]

§ 1.663(b)–1 Distributions in first 65 days of taxable year; scope.

(a) Taxable years beginning after December 31, 1968. (1) *General rule.* With respect to taxable years beginning after December 31, 1968, the fiduciary of a trust may elect under section 663(b) to treat any amount or portion thereof that is properly paid or credited to a beneficiary within the first 65 days following the close of the taxable year as an amount that was properly paid or credited on the last day of such taxable year.

(2) *Effect of election.* (i) An election is effective only with respect to the taxable year for which the election is made. In the case of distributions made after May 8, 1972, the amount to which the election applies shall not exceed—

(a) The amount of income of the trust (as defined in § 1.643(b)–1) for the taxable year for which the election is made, or

(b) The amount of distributable net income of the trust (as defined in §§ 1.643(a)–1 through 1.643(a)–7) for such taxable year, if greater, reduced by any amounts paid, credited, or required to be distributed in such taxable year other than those amounts considered paid or credited in a preceding taxable year by reason of section 663(b) and this section. An election shall be made for each taxable year for which the treatment is desired. The application of this paragraph may be illustrated by the following example:

Example. X Trust, a calendar year trust, has $1,000 of income (as defined in § 1.643(b)–1) and $800 of distributable net income (as defined in §§ 1.643(a)–1 through 1.643(a)–7) in 1972. The trust properly pays $550 to A, a beneficiary, on January 15, 1972, which the trustee elects to treat under section 663(b) as paid on December 31, 1971. The trust also properly pays to A $600 on July 19, 1972, and $450 on January 17, 1973. For 1972, the maximum amount that may be elected under this subdivision to be treated as properly paid or credited on the last day of 1972 is $400 ($1,000-$600). The $550 paid on January 15, 1972, does not reduce the maximum amount to which the election may apply, because that amount is treated as properly paid on December 31, 1971.

(ii) If an election is made with respect to a taxable year of a trust, this section shall apply only to those amounts which are properly paid or credited within the first 65 days following such year and which are so designated by the fiduciary in his election. Any amount considered under section 663(b) as having been distributed in the preceding taxable year shall be so treated for all purposes. For example, in determining the beneficiary's tax liability, such amount shall be considered as having been received by the beneficiary in his taxable year in which or with which the last day of the preceding taxable year of the trust ends.

* * *

[T.D. 6500, 25 FR 11814, Nov. 26, 1960, as amended by T.D. 7204, 37 FR 17135, Aug. 25, 1972]

§ 1.663(b)–2 Election.

(a) Manner and time of election; irrevocability. (1) *When return is required to be filed.* If a trust return is required to be filed for the taxable year of the trust for which the election is made, the election shall be made in the appropriate place on such return. The election under this subparagraph shall be made not later than the time prescribed by law for filing such return (including extensions thereof). Such election shall become irrevocable after the last day prescribed for making it.

(2) *When no return is required to be filed.* If no return is required to be filed for the taxable year of the trust for which the election is made, the election shall be made in a statement filed with the internal revenue office with which a return by such trust would be filed if such trust were required to file a return for such taxable year. See section 6091 and the regulations thereunder for place for filing returns. The election under this subparagraph shall be made not later than the time prescribed by law for filing a return if such trust were required to file a return for such taxable year. Such election shall become irrevocable after the last day prescribed for making it.

(b) Elections under prior law. Elections made pursuant to section 663(b) prior to its amendment by section 331(b) of the Tax Reform Act of 1969 (83 Stat. 598), which, under prior law, were irrevocable for the taxable year for which the election was made and all subsequent years, are not effective for taxable years beginning after December 31, 1968. In the case of a trust for which an election was made under prior law, the fiduciary shall make the election for each taxable year beginning after December 31, 1968, for which the treatment provided by section 663(b) is desired.

[T.D. 6500, 25 FR 11814, Nov. 26, 1960, as amended by T.D. 7204, 37 FR 17135, Aug. 25, 1972]

§ 1.663(c)–1 Separate shares treated as separate trusts or as separate estates; in general.

(a) If a single trust (or estate) has more than one beneficiary, and if different beneficiaries have substantially separate and independent shares, their shares are treated as separate trusts (or estates) for the sole purpose of determining the amount of distributable net income allocable to the respective beneficiaries under sections 661 and 662. Application of this rule will be significant in, for example, situations in which income is accumulated for beneficiary A but a distribution is made to beneficiary B of both income and corpus in an amount exceeding the share of income that would be distributable to B had there been separate trusts (or estates). In the absence of a separate share rule B would be taxed on income which is accumulated for A. The division of distributable net income into separate shares will limit the tax liability of B. Section 663(c) does not affect the principles of applicable law in situations in which a single trust instrument creates not one but several separate trusts, as opposed to separate shares in the same trust within the meaning of this section.

(b) The separate share rule does not permit the treatment of separate shares as separate trusts (or estates) for any purpose other than the application of distributable net income. It does not, for instance, permit the treatment of separate shares as separate trusts (or estates) for purposes of:

(1) The filing of returns and payment of tax,

(2) The deduction of personal exemption under section 642(b), and

(3) The allowance to beneficiaries succeeding to the trust (or estate) property of excess deductions and unused net operating loss and capital loss carryovers on termination of the trust (or estate) under section 642(h).

(c) The separate share rule may be applicable even though separate and independent accounts are not maintained and are not required to be maintained for each share on the books of account of the trust (or estate), and even though no physical segregation of assets is made or required.

(d) Separate share treatment is not elective. Thus, if a trust (or estate) is properly treated as having separate and independent shares, such treatment must prevail in all taxable years of the trust (or estate) unless an event occurs as a result of which the terms of the trust (or estate) instrument and the requirements of proper administration require different treatment.

[T.D. 6500, 25 FR 11814, Nov. 26, 1960; T.D. 8849, 64 FR 72543, Dec. 28, 1999]

§ 1.663(c)–2 Rules of administration.

(a) When separate shares come into existence. A separate share comes into existence upon the earliest moment that a fiduciary may reasonably determine, based upon the known facts, that a separate economic interest exists.

(b) Computation of distributable net income for each separate share. (1) *General rule.* The amount of distributable net income for any share under section 663(c) is computed as if each share constituted a separate trust or estate. Accordingly, each separate share shall calculate its distributable net income based upon its portion of gross income that is includible in distributable net income and its portion of any applicable deductions or losses.

(2) *Section 643(b) income.* This paragraph (b)(2) governs the allocation of the portion of gross income includible in distributable net income that is income within the meaning of section 643(b). Such gross income is allocated among the separate shares in accordance with the amount of income that each share is entitled to under the terms of the governing instrument or applicable local law.

(3) *Income in respect of a decedent.* This paragraph (b)(3) governs the allocation of the portion of gross income includible in distributable net income that is income in respect of a decedent within the meaning of section 691(a) and is not income within the meaning of section 643(b). Such gross income is allocated among the separate shares that could potentially be funded with these amounts irrespective of whether the share is entitled to receive any income under the terms of the governing instrument or applicable local law. The amount of such gross income allocated to each share is based on the relative value of each share that could potentially be funded with such amounts.

(4) *Gross income not attributable to cash.* This paragraph (b)(4) governs the allocation of the portion of gross income includible in distributable net income that is not attributable to cash received by the estate or trust (for example, original issue discount, a distributive share of partnership tax items, and the pro rata share of an S corporation's tax items). Such gross income is allocated among the separate shares in the same proportion as section 643(b) income from the same source would be allocated under the terms of the governing instrument or applicable local law.

(5) *Deductions and losses.* Any deduction or any loss which is applicable solely to one separate share of the trust or estate is not available to any other share of the same trust or estate.

(c) Computations and valuations. For purposes of calculating distributable net income for each separate share, the fiduciary must use a reasonable and equitable method to make the allocations, calculations, and valuations required by paragraph (b) of this section.

[T.D. 6500, 25 FR 11814, Nov. 26, 1960; T.D. 8849, 64 FR 72543, Dec. 28, 1999]

§ 1.663(c)–3 Applicability of separate share rule to certain trusts.

(a) The applicability of the separate share rule provided by section 663(c) to trusts other than qualified revocable trusts within the meaning of section 645(b)(1) will generally depend upon whether distributions of the trust are to be made in substantially the same manner as if separate trusts had been created. Thus, if an instrument directs a trustee to divide the testator's residuary estate into separate shares (which under applicable law do not constitute separate trusts) for each of the testator's children and the trustee is given discretion, with respect to each share, to distribute or accumulate income or to distribute principal or accumulated income, or to do both, separate shares will exist under section 663(c). In determining whether separate shares exist, it is immaterial whether the principal and any accumulated income of each share is ultimately distributable to the beneficiary of such share, to his descendants, to his appointees under a general or special power of appointment, or to any other beneficiaries (including a charitable organization) designated to receive his share of the trust and accumulated income upon termination of the beneficiary's interest in the share. Thus, a separate share may exist if the instrument provides that upon the death of the beneficiary of the share, the share will be added to the shares of the other beneficiaries of the trust.

(b) Separate share treatment will not be applied to a trust or portion of a trust subject to a power to: (1) Distribute, apportion, or accumulate income, or (2) distribute corpus to or for one or more beneficiaries within a group or class of beneficiaries, unless payment of income, accumulated income, or corpus of a share of one beneficiary cannot affect the proportionate share of income, accumulated income, or corpus of any shares of the other beneficiaries, or unless substantially proper adjustment must thereafter be made (under the governing instrument) so that substantially separate and independent shares exist.

(c) A share may be considered as separate even though more than one beneficiary has an interest in it. For example, two beneficiaries may have equal, disproportionate, or indeterminate interests in one share which is separate and independent from another share in which one or more beneficiaries have an interest. Likewise, the same person may be a beneficiary of more than one separate share.

(d) Separate share treatment may be given to a trust or portion of a trust otherwise qualifying under this section if the trust or portion of a trust is subject to a power to pay out to a beneficiary of a share (of such trust or portion) an amount of corpus in excess of his proportionate share of the corpus of the trust if the possibility of exercise of the power is remote. For example, if the trust is subject to a power to invade the entire corpus for the health, education, support, or maintenance of A, separate share treatment is applied if exercise of the power requires consideration of A's other income which is so substantial as to make the possibility of exercise of the power remote. If instead it appears that A and B have separate shares in a trust, subject to a power to invade the entire corpus for the comfort, pleasure, desire, or happiness of A, separate share treatment shall not be applied.

(e) For taxable years ending before December 31, 1978, the separate share rule may also be applicable to successive interests in point of time, as for instance in the case of a trust providing for a life estate to A and a second life estate or outright remainder to B. In such a case, in the taxable year of a trust in which a beneficiary dies items of income and deduction properly allocable under trust accounting principles to the period before a beneficiary's death are attributed to one share, and those allocable to the period after the beneficiary's death are attributed to the other share. Separate share treatment is not available to a succeeding interest, however, with respect to distributions which would otherwise be deemed distributed in a taxable year of the earlier interest under the throwback provisions of Subpart D (section 665 and following), Part I, Subchapter J, Chapter 1 of the Code. The application of this paragraph may be illustrated by the following example:

Example. A trust instrument directs that the income of a trust is to be paid to A for her life. After her death income may be distributed to B or accumulated. A dies on June 1, 1956. The trust keeps its books on the basis of the calendar year. The trust instrument permits invasions of corpus for the benefit of A and B, and an invasion of corpus was in fact made for A's benefit in 1956. In determining the distributable net income of the trust for the purpose of determining the amounts includible in A's income, income and deductions properly allocable to the period before A's death are treated as income and deductions of a separate share; and for that purpose no account is taken of income and deductions allocable to the period after A's death.

[T.D. 6500, 25 FR 11814, Nov. 26, 1960; 25 FR 14021, Dec. 31, 1960, as amended by T.D. 7633, 44 FR 57926, Oct. 9, 1979; T.D. 8849, 64 FR 72543, Dec. 28, 1999]

§ 1.663(c)–4 Applicability of separate share rule to estates and qualified revocable trusts.

(a) General rule. The applicability of the separate share rule provided by section 663(c) to estates and qualified revocable trusts within the meaning of section 645(b)(1) will generally depend upon whether the governing instrument and applicable local law create separate economic interests in one beneficiary or class of beneficiaries of such estate or trust. Ordinarily, a separate share exists if the economic interests of the beneficiary or class of beneficiaries neither affect nor are affected by the economic interests accruing to another beneficiary or class of beneficiaries. Separate shares include, for example, the income on bequeathed property if the recipient of the specific bequest is entitled to such income and a surviving spouse's elective share that under local law is entitled to income and appreciation or depreciation. Furthermore, a qualified revocable trust for which an election is made under section 645 is always a separate share of the estate and may itself contain two or more separate shares. Conversely, a gift or bequest of a specific sum of money or of property as defined in section 663(a)(1) is not a separate share.

(b) Special rule for certain types of beneficial interests. Notwithstanding the provisions of paragraph (a) of this section, a surviving spouse's elective share that under local law is determined as of the date of the decedent's death and is not entitled to income or any appreciation or depreciation is a separate share. Similarly, notwithstanding the provisions of paragraph (a) of this section, a pecuniary formula bequest that, under the terms of the governing instrument or applicable local law, is not entitled to income or to share in appreciation or depreciation constitutes a separate share if the governing instrument does not provide that it is to be paid or credited in more than three installments.

(c) Shares with multiple beneficiaries and beneficiaries of multiple shares. A share may be considered as separate even though more than one beneficiary has an interest in it. For example, two beneficiaries may have equal, disproportionate, or indeterminate interests in one share which is economically separate and independent from another share in which one or more beneficiaries have an interest. Moreover, the same person may be a beneficiary of more than one separate share.

[T.D. 8849, 64 FR 72544, Dec. 28, 1999]

§ 1.663(c)–5 Examples.

Section 663(c) may be illustrated by the following examples:

Example (1). (i) A single trust was created in 1940 for the benefit of A, B, and C, who were aged 6, 4, and 2, respectively. Under the terms of the instrument, the trust income is required to be divided into three equal shares. Each beneficiary's share of the income is to be accumulated until he becomes 21 years of age. When a beneficiary reaches the age of 21, his share of the income may thereafter be either accumulated or distributed to him in the discretion of the trustee. The trustee also has discretion to invade corpus for the benefit of any beneficiary to the extent of his share of the trust estate, and the trust instrument requires that the beneficiary's right to future income and corpus will be proportionately reduced. When each beneficiary reaches 35 years of age, his share of the trust estate shall be paid over to him. The interest in the trust estate of any beneficiary dying without issue and before he has attained the age of 35 is to be equally divided between the other beneficiaries of the trust. All expenses of the trust are allocable to income under the terms of the trust instrument.

(ii) No distributions of income or corpus were made by the trustee prior to 1955, although A became 21 years of age on June 30, 1954. During the taxable year of 1955, the trust has income from royalties of $20,000 and expenses of $5,000. The trustee in his discretion distributes $12,000 to A. Both A and the trust report on the calendar year basis.

(iii) The trust qualifies for the separate share treatment under section 663(c) and the distributable net income must be divided into three parts for the purpose of determining the amount deductible by the trust under section 661 and the amount includible in A's gross income under section 662.

(iv) The distributable net income of each share of the trust is $5,000 ($6,667 less $1,667). Since the amount ($12,000) distributed to A during 1955 exceeds the distributable net income of $5,000 allocated to his share, the trust is deemed to have distributed to him $5,000 of 1955 income and $7,000 of amounts other than 1955 income. Accordingly, the trust is allowed a deduction of $5,000 under section 661. The taxable income of the trust for 1955 is $9,900, computed as follows:

Royalties		$20,000
Deductions:		
Expenses	$5,000	
Distribution to A	5,000	
Personal exemption	100	10,100
Taxable income		9,900

(v) In accordance with section 662, A must include in his gross income for 1955 an amount equal to the portion ($5,000) of the distributable net income of the trust allocated to his share. Also, the excess distribution of $7,000 made by the trust is subject to the throwback provisions of Subpart D (section 665 and following), Part I, Subchapter J, Chapter 1 of the Code, and the regulations thereunder.

Example (2). (i) *Facts*. Testator, who dies in 2000, is survived by a spouse and two children. Testator's will contains a fractional formula bequest dividing the residuary estate between the surviving spouse and a trust for the benefit of the children. Under the fractional formula, the marital bequest constitutes 60% of the estate and the children's trust constitutes 40% of the estate. During the year, the executor makes a partial proportionate distribution of $1,000,0000, ($600,000 to the surviving spouse and $400,000 to the children's trust) and makes no other distributions. The estate receives dividend income of $20,000, and pays expenses of $8,000 that are deductible on the estate's federal income tax return.

(ii) *Conclusion*. The fractional formula bequests to the surviving spouse and to the children's trust are separate shares. Because Testator's will provides for fractional formula residuary bequests, the income and any appreciation in the value of the estate assets are proportionately allocated between the marital share and the trust's share. Therefore, in determining the distributable net income of each share, the income and expenses must be allocated 60% to the marital share and 40% to the trust's share. The distributable net income is $7,200 (60% of income less 60% of expenses) for the marital share and $4,800 (40% of income less 40% of expenses) for the trust's share. Because the amount distributed in partial satisfaction of each bequest exceeds the distributable net income of each share, the estate's distribution deduction under section 661 is limited to the sum of the distributable net income for both shares. The estate is allowed a distribution deduction of $12,000 ($7,200 for the marital share and $4,800 for the trust's share). As a result, the estate has zero taxable income ($20,000 income less $8,000 expenses and $12,000 distribution deduction). Under section 662, the surviving spouse and the trust must include in gross income $7,200 and $4,800, respectively.

Example (3). The facts are the same as in Example 2, except that in 2000 the executor makes the payment to partially fund the children's trust but makes no payment to the surviving spouse. The fiduciary must use a reasonable and equitable method to allocate income and expenses to the trust's share. Therefore, depending on when the distribution is made to the trust, it may no longer be reasonable or equitable to determine the distributable net income for the trust's share by allocating to it 40% of the estate's income and expenses for the year. The computation of the distributable net income for the trust's share should take into consideration that after the partial distribution the relative size of the trust's separate share is reduced and the relative size of the spouse's separate share is increased.

Example (4). (i) *Facts*. Testator, who dies in 2000, is survived by a spouse and one child. Testator's will provides for a pecuniary formula bequest to be paid in not more than three installments to a trust for the benefit of the child in the amount needed to reduce the estate taxes to zero and a bequest of the residuary to the surviving spouse. The will provides that the bequest to the child's trust is not entitled to any of the estate's income and does not participate in appreciation or depreciation in estate assets. During the 2000 taxable year, the estate receives dividend income of $200,000 and pays expenses of $15,000 that are deductible on the estate's federal income tax return. The executor partially funds the child's trust by distributing to it securities that have an adjusted basis to the estate of $350,000 and a fair market value of $380,000 on the date of distribution. As a result of this distribution, the estate realizes long-term capital gain of $30,000.

(ii) *Conclusion*. The estate has two separate shares consisting of a formula pecuniary bequest to the child's trust and a residuary bequest to the surviving spouse. Because, under the terms of the will, no estate income is allocated to the bequest to the child's trust, the distributable net income for that trust's share is zero. Therefore, with respect to the $380,000 distribution to the child's trust, the estate is allowed no deduction under section 661, and no amount is included in the trust's gross income under section 662. Because no distributions were made to the spouse, there is no need to compute the distributable net income allocable to the marital share. The taxable income of the estate for the 2000 taxable year is $214,400 ($200,000 (dividend income) plus $30,000 (capital gain) minus $15,000 (expenses) and minus $600 (personal exemption)).

Example (5). The facts are the same as in Example 4, except that during 2000 the estate reports on its federal income tax return a pro rata share of an S corporation's tax items and a distributive share of a partnership's tax items allocated on Form K-1s to the estate by the S corporation and by the partnership, respectively. Because, under the terms of the will, no estate income from the S corporation or the partnership would be allocated to the pecuniary bequest to child's trust, none of the tax items attributable to the S corporation stock or the partnership interest is allocated to the trust's separate share. Therefore, with respect to the $380,000 distribution to the trust, the estate is allowed no deduction under section 661, and no amount is included in the trust's gross income under section 662.

Example (6). The facts are the same as in Example 4, except that during 2000 the estate receives a distribution of $900,000 from the decedent's individual retirement account that is included in the estate's gross income as income in respect of a decedent under section 691(a). The entire $900,000 is allocated to corpus under applicable local law. Both the separate share for the child's trust and the separate share for the surviving spouse may potentially be funded with the proceeds from the individual retirement account. Therefore, a portion of the $900,000 gross income must be allocated to the trust's separate share. The amount allocated to the trust's share must be based upon the relative values of the two separate shares using a reasonable and equitable method. The estate is entitled to a deduction under section 661 for the portion of the $900,000 properly allocated to the trust's separate share, and the trust must include this amount in income under section 662.

Example (7). (i) *Facts*. Testator, who dies in 2000, is survived by a spouse and three adult children. Testator's will divides the residue of the estate equally among the three children. The surviving spouse files an election under the applicable state's elective share statute. Under this statute, a surviving spouse is entitled to one-third of the decedent's estate after the payment of debts and expenses. The statute also provides that the surviving spouse is not entitled to any of the estate's income and does not participate in appreciation or depreciation of the estate's assets. However, under the statute, the surviving spouse is entitled to interest on the elective share from the date of the court order directing the payment until the executor actually makes payment. During the estate's 2001 taxable year, the estate distributes to the surviving spouse $5,000,000 in partial satisfaction of the elective share and pays $200,000 of interest on the delayed payment of the elective share. During that year, the estate receives dividend income of $3,000,000 and pays expenses of $60,000 that are deductible on the estate's federal income tax return.

(ii) *Conclusion*. The estate has four separate shares consisting of the surviving spouse's elective share and each of the three children's residuary bequests. Because the surviving spouse is not entitled to any estate income under state law, none of the estate's gross income is allocated to the spouse's separate share for purposes of determining that share's distributable net income. Therefore, with respect to the $5,000,000 distribution, the estate is allowed no deduction under section 661, and no amount is included in the spouse's gross income under section 662. The $200,000 of interest paid to the spouse must be included in the spouse's gross income under section 61. Because no distributions were made to any other beneficiaries during the year, there is no need to compute the distributable net income of the other three separate shares. Thus, the taxable income of the estate for the 2000 taxable year is $2,939,400 ($3,000,000 (dividend income) minus $60,000 (expenses) and $600 (personal exemption)). The estate's $200,000 interest payment is a nondeductible personal interest expense described in section 163(h).

Example (8). The will of Testator, who dies in 2000, directs the executor to distribute the X stock and all dividends therefrom to child A and the residue of the estate to child B. The estate has two separate shares consisting of the income on the X stock bequeathed to A and the residue of the estate bequeathed to B. The bequest of the X stock meets the definition of section 663(a)(1) and therefore is not a separate share. If any distributions, other than shares of the X stock, are made during the year to either A or B, then for purposes of determining the distributable net income for the separate shares, gross income attributable to dividends on the X stock must be allocated to A's separate share and any other income must be allocated to B's separate share.

Example (9). The will of Testator, who dies in 2000, directs the executor to divide the residue of the estate equally between Testator's two children, A and B. The will directs the executor to fund A's share first with the proceeds of Testator's individual retirement account. The date of death value of the estate after the payment of debts, expenses, and estate taxes is $9,000,000. During 2000, the $900,000 balance in Testator's individual retirement account is distributed to the estate. The entire $900,000 is allocated to corpus under applicable local law. This amount is income in respect of a decedent within the meaning of section 691(a). The estate has two separate shares, one for the benefit of A and one for the benefit of B. If any distributions are made to either A or B during the year, then, for purposes of determining the distributable net income for each separate share, the $900,000 of income in respect of a decedent must be allocated to A's share.

Example (10). The facts are the same as in Example 9, except that the will directs the executor to fund A's share first with X stock valued at $3,000,000, rather than with the proceeds of the individual retirement account. The estate has two separate shares, one for the benefit of A and one for the benefit of B. If any distributions are made to either A or B during the year, then, for purposes of determining the distributable net income for each separate share, the $900,000 of gross income attributable to the proceeds from the individual retirement account must be allocated between the two shares to the extent that they could potentially be funded with those proceeds. The maximum amount of A's share that could potentially be funded with the income in respect of decedent is $1,500,000 ($4,500,000 value of share less $3,000,000 to be funded with stock) and the maximum amount of B's share that could potentially be funded with income in respect of decedent is $4,500,000. Based upon the relative values of these amounts, the gross income attributable to the proceeds of the individual retirement account is allocated $225,000 (or one-fourth) to A's share and $675,000 (or three-fourths) to B's share.

Example (11). The will of Testator, who dies in 2000, provides that after the payment of specific bequests of money, the residue of the estate is to be divided equally among the Testator's three children, A, B, and C. The will also provides that during the period of administration one-half of the income from the residue is to be paid to a designated charitable organization. After the specific bequests of money are paid, the estate initially has three equal separate shares. One share is for the benefit of the charitable organization and A, another share is for the benefit of the charitable organization and B, and the last share is for the benefit of the charitable organization and C. During the period of administration, payments of income to the charitable organization are deductible by the estate to the extent provided in section 642(c) and are not subject to the distribution provisions of sections 661 and 662.

[T.D. 6500, 25 FR 11814, Nov. 26, 1960; T.D. 8849, 64 FR 72543, 72544, Dec. 28, 1999; 65 FR 16317, March 28, 2000]

§ 1.663(c)–6 Effective dates.

Sections 1.663(c)–1 through 1.663(c)–5 are applicable for estates and qualified revocable trusts within the meaning of section 645(b)(1) with respect to decedents who die after December 28, 1999. However, for estates and qualified revocable trusts with respect to decedents who died after the date that section 1307 of the Tax Reform Act of 1997 became effective but before December 28, 1999, the IRS will accept any reasonable interpretation of the separate share provisions, including those provisions provided in 1999–11 I.R.B. 41 (see § 601.601(d)(2)(ii)(b) of this chapter). For trusts other than qualified revocable trusts, § 1.663(c)–2 is applicable for taxable years of such trusts beginning after December 28, 1999.

[T.D. 8849, 64 FR 72545, Dec. 28, 1999; 65 FR 16317, March 28, 2000]

§ 664. Charitable Remainder Trusts

(a) General rule. Notwithstanding any other provision of this subchapter, the provisions of this section shall, in accordance with regulations prescribed by the Secretary, apply in the case of a charitable remainder annuity trust and a charitable remainder unitrust.

(b) Character of distributions. Amounts distributed by a charitable remainder annuity trust or by a charitable remainder unitrust shall be considered as having the following characteristics in the hands of a beneficiary to whom is paid the annuity described in subsection (d)(1)(A) or the payment described in subsection (d)(2)(A):

(1) First, as amounts of income (other than gains, and amounts treated as gains, from the sale or other disposition of capital assets) includible in gross income to the extent of such income of the trust for the year and such undistributed income of the trust for prior years;

(2) Second, as a capital gain to the extent of the capital gain of the trust for the year and the undistributed capital gain of the trust for prior years;

(3) Third, as other income to the extent of such income of the trust for the year and such undistributed income of the trust for prior years; and

(4) Fourth, as a distribution of trust corpus.

For purposes of this section, the trust shall determine the amount of its undistributed capital gain on a cumulative net basis.

(c) Taxation of trusts.

(1) Income tax. A charitable remainder annuity trust and a charitable remainder unitrust shall, for any taxable year, not be subject to any tax imposed by this subtitle.

(2) Excise tax.

(A) In general. In the case of a charitable remainder annuity trust or a charitable remainder unitrust which has unrelated business taxable income (within the meaning of section 512, determined as if part III of subchapter F applied to such trust) for a taxable year, there is hereby imposed on such trust or unitrust an excise tax equal to the amount of such unrelated business taxable income.

(B) Certain rules to apply. The tax imposed by subparagraph (A) shall be treated as imposed by chapter 42 for purposes of this title other than subchapter E of chapter 42.

(C) Tax court proceedings. For purposes of this paragraph, the references in section 6212(c)(1) to section 4940 shall be deemed to include references to this paragraph.

(d) Definitions.

(1) Charitable remainder annuity trust. For purposes of this section, a charitable remainder annuity trust is a trust—

(A) from which a sum certain (which is not less than 5 percent nor more than 50 percent of the initial net fair market value of all property placed in trust) is to be paid, not less often than annually, to one or more persons (at least one of which is not an organization described in section 170(c) and, in the case of individuals, only to an individual who is living at the time of the creation of the trust) for a term of years (not in excess of 20 years) or for the life or lives of such individual or individuals,

(B) from which no amount other than the payments described in subparagraph (A) and other than qualified gratuitous transfers described in subparagraph (C) may be paid to or for the use of any person other than an organization described in section 170(c),

(C) following the termination of the payments described in subparagraph (A), the remainder interest in the trust is to be transferred to, or for the use of, an organization described in section 170(c) or is to be retained by the trust for such a use or, to the extent the remainder interest is in qualified employer securities (as defined in subsection (g)(4)), all or part of such securities are to be transferred to an employee stock ownership plan (as defined in section 4975(e)(7)) in a qualified gratuitous transfer (as defined by subsection (g)), and

(D) the value (determined under section 7520) of such remainder interest is at least 10 percent of the initial net fair market value of all property placed in the trust.

(2) Charitable remainder unitrust. For purposes of this section, a charitable remainder unitrust is a trust—

(A) from which a fixed percentage (which is not less than 5 percent nor more than 50 percent) of the net fair market value of its assets, valued annually, is to be paid, not less often than annually, to one or more persons (at least one of which is not an organization described in section 170(c) and, in the case of individuals, only to an individual who is living at the time of the creation of the trust) for a term of years (not in excess of 20 years) or for the life or lives of such individual or individuals,

(B) from which no amount other than the payments described in subparagraph (A) and other than qualified gratuitous transfers described in subparagraph (c) may be paid to or for the use of any person other than an organization described in section 170(c),

(C) following the termination of the payments described in subparagraph (A), the remainder interest in the trust is to be transferred to, or for the use of, an organization described in section 170(c) or is to be retained by the trust for such a use or, to the extent the remainder interest is in qualified employer securities (as defined in subsection (g)(4)), all or part of such securities are to be transferred to an employee stock ownership plan (as defined in section 4975(e)(7)) in a qualified gratuitous transfer (as defined by subsection (g)), and

(D) with respect to each contribution of property to the trust, the value (determined under section 7520) of such remainder interest in such property is at least 10 percent of the net fair market value of such property as of the date such property is contributed to the trust.

(3) Exception. Notwithstanding the provisions of paragraphs (2)(A) and (B), the trust instrument may provide that the trustee shall pay the income beneficiary for any year—

(A) the amount of the trust income, if such amount is less than the amount required to be distributed under paragraph (2)(A), and

(B) any amount of the trust income which is in excess of the amount required to be distributed under paragraph (2)(A), to the extent that (by reason of subparagraph (A)) the aggregate of the amounts paid in prior years was less than the aggregate of such required amounts.

(4) Severance of certain additional contributions. If—

(A) any contribution is made to a trust which before the contribution is a charitable remainder unitrust, and

(B) such contribution would (but for this paragraph) result in such trust ceasing to be a charitable unitrust by reason of paragraph (2)(D), such contribution shall be treated as a transfer to a separate trust under regulations prescribed by the Secretary.

(e) Valuation of Interests. For purposes of determining the amount of any charitable contribution, the remainder interest of a charitable remainder annuity trust or charitable remainder unitrust shall be computed on the basis that an amount equal to 5 percent of the net fair market value of its assets (or a greater amount, if required under the terms of the trust instrument) is to be distributed each year. In the case of the early termination of a trust which is a charitable remainder unitrust by reason of subsection (d)(3), the valuation of interests in such trust for purposes of this section shall be made under rules similar to the rules of the preceding sentence.

(f) Certain contingencies permitted.

(1) General rule. If a trust would, but for a qualified contingency, meet the requirements of paragraph (1)(A) or (2)(A) of subsection (d), such trust shall be treated as meeting such requirements.

(2) Value determined without regard to qualified contingency. For purposes of determining the amount of any charitable contribution (or the actuarial value of any interest), a qualified contingency shall not be taken into account.

(3) Qualified contingency. For purposes of this subsection, the term "qualified contingency" means any provision of a trust which provides that, upon the happening of a contingency, the payments described in paragraph (1)(A) or (2)(A) of subsection (d) (as the case may be) will terminate not later than such payments would otherwise terminate under the trust.

(g) Qualified gratuitous transfer of qualified employer securities.

(1) In general. For purposes of this section, the term "qualified gratuitous transfer" means a transfer of qualified employer securities to an employee stock ownership plan (as defined in section 4975(e)(7)) but only to the extent that—

(A) the securities transferred previously passed from a decedent dying before January 1, 1999, to a trust described in paragraph (1) or (2) of subsection (d),

(B) no deduction under section 404 is allowable with respect to such transfer,

(C) such plan contains the provisions required by paragraph (3),

(D) such plan treats such securities as being attributable to employer contributions but without regard to the limitations otherwise applicable to such contributions under section 404, and

(E) the employer whose employees are covered by the plan described in this paragraph files with the Secretary a verified written statement consenting to the application of sections 4978 and 4979A with respect to such employer.

(2) Exception. The term "qualified gratuitous transfer" shall not include a transfer of qualified employer securities to an employee stock ownership plan unless—

(A) such plan was in existence on August 1, 1996,

(B) at the time of the transfer, the decedent and members of the decedent's family (within the meaning of section 2032A(e)(2)) own (directly or through the application of section 318(a)) no more than 10 percent of the value of the stock of the corporation referred to in paragraph (4), and

(C) immediately after the transfer, such plan owns (after the application of section 318(a)(4)) at least 60 percent of the value of the outstanding stock of the corporation.

(3) Plan requirements. A plan contains the provisions required by this paragraph if such plan provides that—

(A) the qualified employer securities so transferred are allocated to plan participants in a manner consistent with section 401(a)(4),

(B) plan participants are entitled to direct the plan as to the manner in which such securities which are entitled to vote and are allocated to the account of such participant are to be voted,

(C) an independent trustee votes the securities so transferred which are not allocated to plan participants,

(D) each participant who is entitled to a distribution from the plan has the rights described in subparagraphs (A) and (B) of section 409(h)(1),

(E) such securities are held in a suspense account under the plan to be allocated each year, up to the applicable limitation under paragraph (7) (determined on the basis of fair market value of securities when allocated to participants), after first allocating all other annual additions for the limitation year, up to the limitation under section 415(c), and

(F) on termination of the plan, all securities so transferred which are not allocated to plan participants as of such termination are to be transferred to, or for the use of, an organization described in section 170(c).

For purposes of the preceding sentence, the term "independent trustee" means any trustee who is not a member of the family (within the meaning of section 2032A(e)(2)) of the decedent or a 5-percent shareholder. A plan shall not fail to be treated as meeting the requirements of section 401(a) by reason of meeting the requirements of this subsection.

(4) Qualified employer securities. For purposes of this section, the term "qualified employer securities" means employer securities (as defined in section 409(*l*)) which are issued by a domestic corporation—

(A) which has no outstanding stock which is readily tradable on an established securities market, and

(B) which has only 1 class of stock.

(5) Treatment of securities allocated by employee stock ownership plan to persons related to decedent or 5-percent shareholders.

(A) In general. If any portion of the assets of the plan attributable to securities acquired by the plan in a qualified gratuitous transfer are allocated to the account of—

(i) any person who is related to the decedent (within the meaning of section 267(b)) or a member of the decedent's family (within the meaning of section 2032A(e)(2)), or

(ii) any person who, at the time of such allocation or at any time during the 1-year period ending on the date of the acquisition of qualified employer securities by the plan, is a 5-percent shareholder of the employer maintaining the plan, the plan shall be treated as having distributed (at the time of such allocation) to such person or shareholder the amount so allocated.

(B) 5-percent shareholder. For purposes of subparagraph (A), the term "5-percent shareholder" means any person who owns (directly or through the application of section 318(a)) more than 5 percent of the outstanding stock of the corporation which issued such qualified employer securities or of any corporation which is a member of the same controlled group of corporations (within the meaning of section 409(*l*)(4)) as such corporation. For purposes of the preceding sentence, section 318(a) shall be applied without regard to the exception in paragraph (2)(B)(i) thereof.

(C) Cross reference. For excise tax on allocations described in subparagraph (A), see section 4979A.

(6) Tax on failure to transfer unallocated securities to charity on termination of plan. If the requirements of paragraph (3)(F) are not met with respect to any securities, there is hereby imposed a tax on the employer maintaining the plan in an amount equal to the sum of—

(A) the amount of the increase in the tax which would be imposed by chapter 11 if such securities were not transferred as described in paragraph (1), and

(B) interest on such amount at the underpayment rate under section 6621 (and compounded daily) from the due date for filing the return of the tax imposed by chapter 11.

(7) Applicable limitation.

(A) In general. For purposes of paragraph (3)(E), the applicable limitation under this paragraph with respect to a participant is an amount equal to the lesser of—

(i) $30,000, or

(ii) 25 percent of the participant's compensation (as defined in section 415(c)(3)).

(B) Cost-of-living adjustment. The Secretary shall adjust annually the $30,000 amount under subparagraph (A)(i) at the same time and in the same manner as under section 415(d), except that the base period shall be the calendar quarter beginning October 1, 1993, and any increase under this subparagraph which is not a multiple of $5,000 shall be rounded to the next lowest multiple of $5,000.

Regulations

§ 1.664–1 Charitable remainder trusts.

(a) In general. (1) *Introduction.* (i) *General description of a charitable remainder trust.* Generally, a charitable remainder trust is a trust which provides for a specified distribution, at least annually, to one or more beneficiaries, at least one of which is not a charity, for life or for a term of years, with an irrevocable remainder interest to be held for the benefit of, or paid over to, charity. The specified distribution to be paid at least annually must be a sum certain which is not less than 5 percent of the initial net fair market value of all property placed in trust (in the case of a charitable remainder annuity trust) or a fixed percentage which is not less than 5 percent of the net fair market value of the trust assets, valued annually (in the case of a charitable remainder unitrust). A trust created after July 31, 1969, which is a charitable remainder trust, is exempt from all of the taxes imposed by subtitle A of the Code for any taxable year of the trust, except for a taxable year beginning before January 1, 2007, in which it has unrelated business taxable income. For taxable years beginning after December 31, 2006, an excise tax, treated as imposed by chapter 42, is imposed on charitable remainder trusts that have unrelated business taxable income. See paragraph (c) of this section.

(ii) *Scope.* This section provides definitions, general rules governing the creation and administration of a charitable remainder trust, and rules governing the taxation of the trust and its beneficiaries. For the application of certain foundation rules to charitable remainder trusts, see paragraph (b) of this section. If the trust has unrelated business taxable income, see paragraph (c) of this section. For the treatment of distributions to recipients, see paragraph (d) of this section. For the treatment of distributions to charity, see paragraph (e) of this section. For the time limitations for amendment of governing instruments, see paragraph (f) of this section. For transitional rules under which particular requirements are inapplicable to certain trusts, see paragraph (g) of this section. Section 1.664–2 provides rules relating solely to a charitable remainder annuity trust. Section 1.664–3 provides rules relating solely to a charitable remainder unitrust. Section 1.664–4 provides rules governing the calculation of the fair market value of the remainder interest in a charitable remainder unitrust. For rules relating to the filing of returns for a charitable remainder trust, see paragraph (a)(6) of § 1.6012–3 and section 6034 and the regulations thereunder.

(iii) *Definitions.* As used in this section and §§ 1.664–2, 1.664–3, and 1.664–4:

(a) *Charitable remainder trust.* The term "charitable remainder trust" means a trust with respect to which a deduction is allowable under section 170, 2055, 2106, or 2522 and which meets the description of a charitable remainder annuity trust (as described in § 1.664–2) or a charitable remainder unitrust (as described in § 1.664–3).

(b) *Annuity amount.* The term "annuity amount" means the amount described in paragraph (a)(1) of § 1.664–2 which is payable, at least annually, to the beneficiary of a charitable remainder annuity trust.

(c) *Unitrust amount.* The term "unitrust amount" means the amount described in paragraph (a)(1) of § 1.664–3 which is payable, at least annually, to the beneficiary of a charitable remainder unitrust.

(d) *Recipient.* The term "recipient" means the beneficiary who receives the possession or beneficial enjoyment of the annuity amount or unitrust amount.

(e) *Governing instrument.* The term "governing instrument" has the same meaning as in section 508(e) and the regulations thereunder.

(2) *Requirement that the trust must be either a charitable remainder annuity trust or a charitable remainder unitrust.* A trust is a charitable remainder trust only if it is either a charitable remainder annuity trust

in every respect or a charitable remainder unitrust in every respect. For example, a trust which provides for the payment each year to a noncharitable beneficiary of the greater of a sum certain or a fixed percentage of the annual value of the trust assets is not a charitable remainder trust inasmuch as the trust is neither a charitable remainder annuity trust (for the reason that the payment for the year may be a fixed percentage of the annual value of the trust assets which is not a "sum certain") nor a charitable remainder unitrust (for the reason that the payment for the year may be a sum certain which is not a "fixed percentage" of the annual value of the trust assets).

(3) *Restrictions on investments.* A trust is not a charitable remainder trust if the provisions of the trust include a provision which restricts the trustee from investing the trust assets in a manner which could result in the annual realization of a reasonable amount of income or gain from the sale or disposition of trust assets. In the case of transactions with, or for the benefit of, a disqualified person, see section 4941(d) and the regulations thereunder for rules relating to the definition of self-dealing.

(4) *Requirement that trust must meet definition of and function exclusively as a charitable remainder trust from its creation.* In order for a trust to be a charitable remainder trust, it must meet the definition of and function exclusively as a charitable remainder trust from the creation of the trust. Solely for the purposes of section 664 and the regulations thereunder, the trust will be deemed to be created at the earliest time that neither the grantor nor any other person is treated as the owner of the entire trust under Subpart E, Part 1, Subchapter J, Chapter 1, Subtitle A of the Code (relating to grantors and others treated as substantial owners), but in no event prior to the time property is first transferred to the trust. For purposes of the preceding sentence, neither the grantor nor his spouse shall be treated as the owner of the trust under such subpart E merely because the grantor or his spouse is named as a recipient. See examples 1 through 3 of subparagraph (6) of this paragraph for illustrations of the foregoing rule.

(5) *Rules applicable to testamentary transfers*—(i) *Deferral of annuity or unitrust amount.* Notwithstanding subparagraph (4) of this paragraph and §§ 1.664–2 and 1.664–3, for purposes of sections 2055 and 2106 a charitable remainder trust shall be deemed created at the date of death of the decedent (even though the trust is not funded until the end of a reasonable period of administration or settlement) if the obligation to pay the annuity or unitrust amount with respect to the property passing in trust at the death of the decedent begins as of the date of death of the decedent, even though the requirement to pay such amount is deferred in accordance with the rules provided in this subparagraph. If permitted by applicable local law or authorized by the provisions of the governing instrument, the requirement to pay such amount may be deferred until the end of the taxable year of the trust in which occurs the complete funding of the trust. Within a reasonable period after such time, the trust must pay (in the case of an underpayment) or must receive from the recipient (in the case of an overpayment) the difference between—

(a) Any annuity or unitrust amounts actually paid, plus interest on such amounts computed at the rate of interest specified in paragraph (a)(5)(iv) of this section, compounded annually, and

(b) The annuity or unitrust amounts payable, plus interest on such amounts computed at the rate of interest specified in paragraph (a)(5)(iv) of this section, compounded annually.

The amounts payable shall be retroactively determined by using the taxable year, valuation method, and valuation dates which are ultimately adopted by the charitable remainder trust. See subdivision (ii) of this subparagraph for rules relating to retroactive determination of the amount payable under a charitable remainder unitrust. See paragraph (d)(4) of this section for rules relating to the year of inclusion in the case of an underpayment to a recipient and the allowance of a deduction in the case of an overpayment to a recipient.

(ii) For purposes of retroactively determining the amount under subdivision (i)(b) of this subparagraph, the governing instrument of a charitable remainder unitrust may provide that the amount described in subdivision (i)(b) of this subparagraph with respect to property passing in trust at the death of the decedent for the period which begins on the date of death of the decedent and ends on the earlier of the date of death of the last recipient or the end of the taxable year of the trust in which occurs the complete funding of the trust shall be computed by multiplying—

(a) The sum of (1) the value, on the earlier of the date of death of the last recipient or the last day in such taxable year, of the property held in trust which is attributable to property passing to the trust at the death of the decedent, (2) any distributions in respect of unitrust amounts made by the trust or estate before such date, and (3) interest on such distributions computed at the rate of interest specified in paragraph (a)(5)(iv) of this section, compounded annually, from the date of distribution to such date by—

(b)(1) In the case of transfers made after November 30, 1983, for which the valuation date is before May 1, 1989, a factor equal to 1.000000 less the factor under the appropriate adjusted payout rate in Table D in § 1.664–4A(e)(6) opposite the number of years in column 1 between the date of death of the decedent and the date of the earlier of the death of the last recipient or the last day of such taxable year.

(2) In the case of transfers for which the valuation date is after April 30, 1989, a factor equal to 1.000000 less the factor under the appropriate adjusted payout rate in Table D in § 1.664–4(e)(6) opposite the number of years in column 1 between the date of death of the decedent and the date of the earlier of the death of the last recipient or the last day of such taxable year. The appropriate adjusted payout rate is determined by using the appropriate Table F contained in § 1.664–4(e)(6) for the section 7520 rate for the month of the valuation date.

(3) If the number of years between the date of death and the date of the earlier of the death of the last recipient or the last day of such taxable year is between periods for which factors are provided, a linear interpolation must be made.

(iii) *Treatment of distributions*. The treatment of a distribution to a charitable remainder trust, or to a recipient in respect of an annuity or unitrust amount, paid, credited, or required to be distributed by an estate, or by a trust which is not a charitable remainder trust, shall be governed by the rules of subchapter J, chapter 1, subtitle A of the Code other than section 664. In the case of a charitable remainder trust which is partially or fully funded during the period of administration of an estate or settlement of a trust (which is not a charitable remainder trust), the treatment of any amount paid, credited, or required to be distributed by the charitable remainder trust shall be governed by the rules of section 664.

(iv) *Rate of interest*. The following rates of interest shall apply for purposes of paragraphs (a)(5)(i) through (ii) of this section:

(a) The section 7520 rate for the month in which the valuation date with respect to the transfer is (or one of the prior two months if elected under § 1.7520–2(b)) after April 30, 1989;

(b) 10 percent for instruments executed or amended (other than in the case of a reformation under section 2055(e)(3)) on or after August 9, 1984, and before May 1, 1989, and not subsequently amended;

(c) 6 percent or 10 percent for instruments executed or amended (other than in the case of a reformation under section 2055(e)(3)) after October 24, 1983, and before August 9, 1984; and

(d) 6 percent for instruments executed before October 25, 1983, and not subsequently amended (other than in the case of a reformation under section 2055(e)(3)).

(6) *Examples*. The application of the rules in paragraphs (a)(4) and (a)(5) of this section require the use of actuarial factors contained in §§ 1.664–4(e) and 1.664–4A and may be illustrated by use of the following examples:

Example (1). On September 19, 1971, H transfers property to a trust over which he retains an inter vivos power of revocation. The trust is to pay W 5 percent of the value of the trust assets, valued annually, for her life, remainder to charity. The trust would satisfy all of the requirements of section 664 if it were irrevocable. For purposes of section 664, the trust is not deemed created in 1971 because H is treated as the owner of the entire trust under subpart E. On May 26, 1975, H predeceases W at which time the trust becomes irrevocable. For purposes of section 664, the trust is deemed created on May 26, 1975, because that is the earliest date on which H is not treated as the owner of the entire trust under subpart E. The trust becomes a charitable remainder trust on May 26, 1975, because it meets the definition of a charitable remainder trust from its creation.

Example (2). The facts are the same as in example (1), except that H retains the inter vivos power to revoke only one-half of the trust. For purposes of section 664, the trust is deemed created on September 19, 1971, because on that date the grantor is not treated as the owner of the entire trust under subpart E. Consequently, a charitable deduction is not allowable either at the creation of the trust or at H's death because the trust does not meet the definition of a charitable remainder trust from the date of its creation. The trust does not meet the definition of a charitable remainder trust from the date of its creation because the trust is subject to a partial power to revoke on such date.

Example (3). The facts are the same as in example (1), except that the residue of H's estate is to be paid to the trust and the trust is required to pay H's debts. The trust is not a charitable remainder trust at H's death because it does not function exclusively as a charitable remainder trust from the date of its creation which, in this case, is the date it becomes irrevocable.

Example (4). (i) In 1971, H transfers property to Trust A over which he retains an inter vivos power of revocation. Trust A, which is not a charitable remainder trust, is to provide income or corpus to W until the death of H. Upon H's death the trust is required by its governing instrument to pay the debts and administration expenses of H's estate, and then to terminate and distribute all of the remaining assets to a separate Trust B which meets the definition of a charitable remainder annuity trust.

(ii) Trust B will be charitable remainder trust from the date of its funding because it will function exclusively as a charitable remainder trust from its creation. For purposes of section 2055, Trust B will be deemed created at H's death if the obligation to pay the annuity amount begins on the date of H's death. For purposes of section 664, Trust B becomes a charitable remainder trust as soon as it is partially or completely funded. Consequently, unless Trust B has unrelated business taxable income, the income of the trust is exempt from all taxes imposed by subtitle A of the Code, and any distributions by the trust, even before it is completely funded, are governed by the rules of section 664. Any distributions made by Trust A, including distributions to a recipient in respect of annuity amounts, are governed by the rules of subchapter J, chapter 1, subtitle A of the Code other than section 664.

Example (5). In 1973, H dies testate leaving the net residue of his estate (after payment by the estate of all debts and administration expenses) to a trust which meets the definition of a charitable remainder unitrust. For purposes of section 2055, the trust is deemed created at H's death if the requirement to pay the unitrust amount begins on H's death and is a charitable remainder trust even though the estate is obligated to pay debts and administration expenses.

For purposes of section 664, the trust becomes a charitable remainder trust as soon as it is partially or completely funded. Consequently, unless the trust has unrelated business taxable income, the income of the trust is exempt from all taxes imposed by subtitle A of the Code, and any distributions by the trust, even before it is completely funded, are governed by the rules of section 664. Any distributions made by H's estate, including distributions to a recipient in respect of unitrust amounts, are governed by the rules of subchapter J, chapter 1, subtitle A of the Code other than section 664.

Example (6). (i) On January 1, 1974, H dies testate leaving the residue of his estate to a charitable remainder unitrust. The governing instrument provides that, beginning at H's death, the trustee is to make annual payments to W, on December 31 of each year of 5 percent of the net fair market value of the trust assets, valued as of December 31 of each year, for W's life and to pay the remainder to charity at the death of W. The governing instrument also provides that the actual payment of the unitrust amount need not be made until the end of the taxable year of the trust in which occurs the complete funding of the trust. The governing instrument also provides that the amount payable with respect to the period between the date of death and the end of such taxable year shall be computed under the special method provided in subparagraph (5)(ii) of this paragraph. The governing instrument provides that, within a reasonable period after the end of the taxable year of the trust in which occurs the complete funding of the trust, the trustee shall pay (in the case of an underpayment) or shall receive from the recipient (in the case of an overpayment) the difference between the unitrust amounts paid (plus interest at 6 percentage compounded annually) and the amount computed under the special method. The trust is completely funded on September 20, 1976. No amounts were paid before June 30, 1977. The trust adopts a fiscal year of July 1 to June 30. The net fair market value of the trust assets on June 30, 1977, is $100,000.

(ii) Because no amounts were paid prior to the end of the taxable year in which the trust was completely funded, the amount payable at the end of such taxable year is equal to the net fair market value of the trust assets on the last day of such taxable year (June 30, 1977) multiplied by a factor equal to 1.0 minus the factor in Table D corresponding to the number of years in the period between the date of death and the end of such taxable year. The adjusted payout rate (determined under § 1.664–4A(c) is 5 percent. Because the last day of the taxable year in which the trust is completely funded is June 30, 1977, there are 3 181/365 years in such period. Because there is no factor given in Table D for such a period, a linear interpolation must be made:

1.0 minus 0.814506 (factor at 5 percent for 4 years)	0.185494
1.0 minus 0.857375 (factor at 5 percent for 3 years)	0.142625
Difference	042869

$$\frac{181}{365} = \frac{X}{.042869}$$

$$X = 0.021258$$

1.0 minus 0.857375 (factor at 5 percent for 3 years)	0.142625
Plus: X	0.021258
Interpolated factor	0.163883

Thus, the amount payable for the period from January 1, 1974, to June 30, 1977, is $16,388.30 ($100,000 * 0.163883). Thereafter, the trust assets must be valued on December 31 of each year and 5 percent of such value paid annually to W for her life.

(7) *Valuation of unmarketable assets*—(i) *In general*. If unmarketable assets are transferred to or held by a trust, the trust will not be a trust with respect to which a deduction is available under section 170, 2055, 2106, or 2522, or will be treated as failing to function exclusively as a charitable remainder trust unless, whenever the trust is required to value such assets, the valuation is—

(a) Performed exclusively by an independent trustee; or

(b) Determined by a current qualified appraisal from a qualified appraiser, as those terms are defined in—

(1) Section 1.170A–13(c)(3) and 1.170A–13(c)(5), respectively, for appraisals prepared for returns or submissions filed on or before August 17, 2006;

(2) Section 3 of Notice 2006–96, 2006–2 CB 902, for appraisals prepared for returns or submissions filed after August 17, 2006, if the donations are made before January 1, 2019; or

(3) Section 1.170A–17(a) and 1.170A–17(b), respectively, for appraisals prepared for returns or submissions for donations made on or after January 1, 2019.

(ii) *Unmarketable assets*. Unmarketable assets are assets that are not cash, cash equivalents, or other assets that can be readily sold or exchanged for cash or cash equivalents. For example, unmarketable assets include real property, closely-held stock, and an unregistered security for which there is no available exemption permitting public sale.

(iii) *Independent trustee*. An independent trustee is a person who is not the grantor of the trust, a noncharitable beneficiary, or a related or subordinate party to the grantor, the grantor's spouse, or a noncharitable beneficiary (within the meaning of section 672(c) and the applicable regulations).

(b) Application of certain foundation rules to charitable remainder trusts. See section 4947(a)(2) and section 4947(b)(3)(B) and the regulations thereunder for the application to charitable remainder trusts of certain provisions relating to private foundations. See section 508(e) for rules relating to required provisions in governing instruments prohibiting certain activities specified in section 4947(a)(2).

(c) Excise tax on charitable remainder trusts. (1) *In general.* For each taxable year beginning after December 31, 2006, in which a charitable remainder annuity trust or a charitable remainder unitrust has any unrelated business taxable income, an excise tax is imposed on that trust in an amount equal to the amount of such unrelated business taxable income. For this purpose, unrelated business taxable income is as defined in section 512, determined as if part III, subchapter F, chapter 1, subtitle A of the Internal Revenue Code applied to such trust. Such excise tax is treated as imposed by chapter 42 (other than subchapter E) and is reported and payable in accordance with the appropriate forms and instructions. Such excise tax shall be allocated to corpus and, therefore, is not deductible in determining taxable income distributed to a beneficiary. (See paragraph (d)(2) of this section.) The charitable remainder trust income that is unrelated business taxable income constitutes income of the trust for purposes of determining the character of the distribution made to the beneficiary. Income of the charitable remainder trust is allocated among the charitable remainder trust income categories in paragraph (d)(1) of this section without regard to whether any part of that income constitutes unrelated business taxable income under section 512.

(2) *Examples.* The application of the rules in this paragraph (c) may be illustrated by the following examples:

Example (1). For 2007, a charitable remainder annuity trust with a taxable year beginning on January 1, 2007, has $60,000 of ordinary income, including $10,000 of gross income from a partnership that constitutes unrelated business taxable income to the trust. The trust has no deductions that are directly connected with that income. For that same year, the trust has administration expenses (deductible in computing taxable income) of $16,000, resulting in net ordinary income of $44,000. The amount of unrelated business taxable income is computed by taking gross income from an unrelated trade or business and deducting expenses directly connected with carrying on the trade or business, both computed with modifications under section 512(b). Section 512(b)(12) provides a specific deduction of $1,000 in computing the amount of unrelated business taxable income. Under the facts presented in this example, there are no other modifications under section 512(b). The trust, therefore, has unrelated business taxable income of $9,000 ($10,000 minus the $1,000 deduction under section 512(b)(12)). Undistributed ordinary income from prior years is $12,000 and undistributed capital gains from prior years are $50,000. Under the terms of the trust agreement, the trust is required to pay an annuity of $100,000 for year 2007 to the noncharitable beneficiary. Because the trust has unrelated business taxable income of $9,000, the excise tax imposed under section 664(c) is equal to the amount of such unrelated business taxable income, $9,000. The character of the $100,000 distribution to the noncharitable beneficiary is as follows: $56,000 of ordinary income ($44,000 from current year plus $12,000 from prior years), and $44,000 of capital gains. The $9,000 excise tax is allocated to corpus, and does not reduce the amount in any of the categories of income under paragraph (d)(1) of this section. At the beginning of year 2008, the amount of undistributed capital gains is $6,000, and there is no undistributed ordinary income.

Example (2). During 2007, a charitable remainder annuity trust with a taxable year beginning on January 1, 2007, sells real estate generating gain of $40,000. Because the trust had obtained a loan to finance part of the purchase price of the asset, some of the income from the sale is treated as debt-financed income under section 514 and thus constitutes unrelated business taxable income under section 512. The unrelated debt-financed income computed under section 514 is $30,000. Assuming the trust receives no other income in 2007, the trust will have unrelated business taxable income under section 512 of $29,000 ($30,000 minus the $1,000 deduction under section 512(b)(12)). Except for section 512(b)(12), no other exceptions or modifications under sections 512–514 apply when calculating unrelated business taxable income based on the facts presented in this example. Because the trust has unrelated business taxable income of $29,000, the excise tax imposed under section 664(c) is equal to the amount of such unrelated business taxable income, $29,000. The $29,000 excise tax is allocated to corpus, and does not reduce the amount in any of the categories of income under paragraph (d)(1) of this section. Regardless of how the trust's income might be treated under sections 511–514, the entire $40,000 is capital gain for purposes of section 664 and is allocated accordingly to and within the second of the categories of income under paragraph (d)(1) of this section.

(3) *Effective/applicability date.* This paragraph (c) is applicable for taxable years beginning after December 31, 2006. The rules that apply with respect to taxable years beginning before January 1, 2007, are contained in § 1.664–1(c) as in effect prior to June 24, 2008. (See 26 CFR part 1, § 1.664–1(c)(1) revised as of April 1, 2007).

(d) Treatment of annual distributions to recipients. (1) *Character of distributions.* (i) *Assignment of income to categories and classes at the trust level.* *(a)* A trust's income, including income includible in gross income and other income, is assigned to one of three categories in the year in which it is required to be taken into account by the trust. These categories are—

(1) Gross income, other than gains and amounts treated as gains from the sale or other disposition of capital assets (referred to as the ordinary income category);

(2) Gains and amounts treated as gains from the sale or other disposition of capital assets (referred to as the capital gains category); and

(3) Other income (including income excluded under part III, subchapter B, chapter 1, subtitle A of the Internal Revenue Code).

(b) Items within the ordinary income and capital gains categories are assigned to different classes based on the Federal income tax rate applicable to each type of income in that category in the year the items are required to be taken into account by the trust. For example, for a trust with a taxable year ending December 31, 2004, the ordinary income category may include a class of qualified dividend income as defined in section 1(h)(11) and a class of all other ordinary income, and the capital gains category may include separate classes for short-term and long-term capital gains and losses, such as a short-term capital gain class, a 28-percent long-term capital gain class (gains and losses from collectibles and section 1202 gains), an unrecaptured section 1250 long-term capital gain class (long-term gains not treated as ordinary income that would be treated as ordinary income if section 1250(b)(1) included all depreciation), a qualified 5-year long-term capital gain class as defined in section 1(h)(9) prior to amendment by the Jobs and Growth Tax Relief Reconciliation Act of 2003 (JGTRRA), Public Law 108–27 (117 Stat. 752), and an all other long-term capital gain class. After items are assigned to a class, the tax rates may change so that items in two or more classes would be taxed at the same rate if distributed to the recipient during a particular year. If the changes to the tax rates are permanent, the undistributed items in those classes are combined into one class. If, however, the changes to the tax rates are only temporary (for example, the new rate for one class will sunset in a future year), the classes are kept separate.

(ii) *Order of distributions. (a)* The categories and classes of income (determined under paragraph (d)(1)(i) of this section) are used to determine the character of an annuity or unitrust distribution from the trust in the hands of the recipient irrespective of whether the trust is exempt from taxation under section 664(c) for the year of the distribution. The determination of the character of amounts distributed or deemed distributed at any time during the taxable year of the trust shall be made as of the end of that taxable year. The tax rate or rates to be used in computing the recipient's tax on the distribution shall be the tax rates that are applicable, in the year in which the distribution is required to be made, to the classes of income deemed to make up that distribution, and not the tax rates that are applicable to those classes of income in the year the income is received by the trust. The character of the distribution in the hands of the annuity or unitrust recipient is determined by treating the distribution as being made from each category in the following order:

(1) First, from ordinary income to the extent of the sum of the trust's ordinary income for the taxable year and its undistributed ordinary income for prior years.

(2) Second, from capital gain to the extent of the trust's capital gains determined under paragraph (d)(1)(iv) of this section.

(3) Third, from other income to the extent of the sum of the trust's other income for the taxable year and its undistributed other income for prior years.

(4) Finally, from trust corpus (with corpus defined for this purpose as the net fair market value of the trust assets less the total undistributed income (but not loss) in paragraphs (d)(1)(i)(a)(1) through (3) of this section).

(b) If the trust has different classes of income in the ordinary income category, the distribution from that category is treated as being made from each class, in turn, until exhaustion of the class, beginning with the class subject to the highest Federal income tax rate and ending with the class subject to the lowest Federal income tax rate. If the trust has different classes of net gain in the capital gains category, the distribution from that category is treated as being made first from the short-term capital gain class and then from each class of long-term capital gain, in turn, until exhaustion of the class, beginning with the class subject to the highest Federal income tax rate and ending with the class subject to the lowest rate. If two or more classes within the same category are subject to the same current tax rate, but at least one of those classes will be subject to a different tax rate in a future year (for example, if the current rate sunsets), the order of that class in relation to other classes in the category with the same

current tax rate is determined based on the future rate or rates applicable to those classes. Within each category, if there is more than one type of income in a class, amounts treated as distributed from that class are to be treated as consisting of the same proportion of each type of income as the total of the current and undistributed income of that type bears to the total of the current and undistributed income of all types of income included in that class. For example, if rental income and interest income are subject to the same current and future Federal income tax rate and, therefore, are in the same class, a distribution from that class will be treated as consisting of a proportional amount of rental income and interest income.

(iii) *Treatment of losses at the trust level. (a) Ordinary income category.* A net ordinary loss for the current year is first used to reduce undistributed ordinary income for prior years that is assigned to the same class as the loss. Any excess loss is then used to reduce the current and undistributed ordinary income from other classes, in turn, beginning with the class subject to the highest Federal income tax rate and ending with the class subject to the lowest Federal income tax rate. If any of the loss exists after all the current and undistributed ordinary income from all classes has been offset, the excess is carried forward indefinitely to reduce ordinary income for future years and retains its class assignment. For purposes of this section, the amount of current income and prior years' undistributed income shall be computed without regard to the deduction for net operating losses provided by section 172 or 642(d).

(b) Other income category. A net loss in the other income category for the current year is used to reduce undistributed income in this category for prior years and any excess is carried forward indefinitely to reduce other income for future years.

(iv) *Netting of capital gains and losses at the trust level.* Capital gains of the trust are determined on a cumulative net basis under the rules of this paragraph (d)(1) without regard to the provisions of section 1212. For each taxable year, current and undistributed gains and losses within each class are netted to determine the net gain or loss for that class, and the classes of capital gains and losses are then netted against each other in the following order. First, a net loss from a class of long-term capital gain and loss (beginning with the class subject to the highest Federal income tax rate and ending with the class subject to the lowest rate) is used to offset net gain from each other class of long-term capital gain and loss, in turn, until exhaustion of the class, beginning with the class subject to the highest Federal income tax rate and ending with the class subject to the lowest rate. Second, either—

(a) A net loss from all the classes of long-term capital gain and loss (beginning with the class subject to the highest Federal income tax rate and ending with the class subject to the lowest rate) is used to offset any net gain from the class of short-term capital gain and loss; or

(b) A net loss from the class of short-term capital gain and loss is used to offset any net gain from each class of long-term capital gain and loss, in turn, until exhaustion of the class, beginning with the class subject to the highest Federal income tax rate and ending with the class subject to the lowest Federal income tax rate.

(v) *Carry forward of net capital gain or loss by the trust.* If, at the end of a taxable year, a trust has, after the application of paragraph (d)(1)(iv) of this section, any net loss or any net gain that is not treated as distributed under paragraph (d)(1)(ii)(a)(2) of this section, the net gain or loss is carried over to succeeding taxable years and retains its character in succeeding taxable years as gain or loss from its particular class.

(vi) *Special transitional rules.* To be eligible to be included in the class of qualified dividend income, dividends must meet the definition of section 1(h)(11) and must be received by the trust after December 31, 2002. Long-term capital gain or loss properly taken into account by the trust before January 1, 1997, is included in the class of all other long-term capital gains and losses. Long-term capital gain or loss properly taken into account by the trust on or after January 1, 1997, and before May 7, 1997, if not treated as distributed in 1997, is included in the class of all other long-term capital gains and losses. Long-term capital gain or loss (other than 28-percent gain (gains and losses from collectibles and section 1202 gains), unrecaptured section 1250 gain (long-term gains not treated as ordinary income that would be treated as ordinary income if section 1250(b)(1) included all depreciation), and qualified 5-year gain as defined in section 1(h)(9) prior to amendment by JGTRRA), properly taken into account by the trust before January 1, 2003, and distributed during 2003 is treated as if it were properly taken into account by the trust after May 5, 2003. Long-term capital gain or loss (other than 28-percent gain, unrecaptured section 1250 gain, and qualified 5-year gain), properly taken into account by the trust on or after January 1, 2003, and before May 6, 2003, if not treated as distributed during 2003, is included in the class of all other long-term capital gain. Qualified 5-year gain properly taken into account by the trust after December 31, 2000, and before May 6, 2003, if not treated as distributed by the trust in 2003 or a prior year, must be maintained in a separate class within the capital gains category until distributed. Qualified 5-year gain properly taken into account by the trust before January 1, 2003, and deemed distributed during 2003 is subject to the same current tax rate as deemed distributions from the class of all other long-term capital gain realized by the trust after May 5, 2003. Qualified 5-year gain properly taken into account by the trust on or after January 1, 2003, and before May 6, 2003, if treated as distributed by the trust in 2003, is subject to the tax rate in effect prior to the amendment of section 1(h)(9) by JGTRRA.

(vii) *Application of section 643(a)(7).* For application of the anti-abuse rule of section 643(a)(7) to distributions from charitable remainder trusts, see § 1.643(a)–8.

(viii) *Examples.* The following examples illustrate the rules in this paragraph (d)(1):

Example (1). (i) X, a charitable remainder annuity trust described in section 664(d)(1), is created on January 1, 2003. The annual annuity amount is $100. X's income for the 2003 tax year is as follows:

Interest income	$80
Qualified dividend income	50
Capital gains and losses	0
Tax-exempt income	0

(ii) In 2003, the year this income is received by the trust, qualified dividend income is subject to a different rate of Federal income tax than interest income and is, therefore, a separate class of income in the ordinary income category. The annuity amount is deemed to be distributed from the classes within the ordinary income category, beginning with the class subject to the highest Federal income tax rate and ending with the class subject to the lowest rate. Because during 2003 qualified dividend income is taxed at a lower rate than interest income, the interest income is deemed distributed prior to the qualified dividend income. Therefore, in the hands of the recipient, the 2003 annuity amount has the following characteristics:

Interest income	$80
Qualified dividend income	20

(iii) The remaining $30 of qualified dividend income that is not treated as distributed to the recipient in 2003 is carried forward to 2004 as undistributed qualified dividend income.

Example (2). (i) The facts are the same as in Example 1, and at the end of 2004, X has the following classes of income:

Interest income class	$5
Qualified dividend income class ($10 from 2004 and $30 carried forward from 2003)	40
Net short-term capital gain class	15
Net long-term capital loss in 28% class	[325]
Net long-term capital gain in unrecaptured section 1250 gain class	175
Net long-term capital gain in all other long-term capital gain class	350

(ii) In 2004, gain in the unrecaptured section 1250 gain class is subject to a 25-percent Federal income tax rate, and gain in the all other long-term capital gain class is subject to a lower rate. The net long-term capital loss in the 28-percent gain class is used to offset the net capital gains in the other classes of long-term capital gain and loss, beginning with the class subject to the highest Federal income tax rate and ending with the class subject to the lowest rate. The $325 net loss in the 28-percent gain class reduces the $175 net gain in the unrecaptured section 1250 gain class to $0.

The remaining $150 loss from the 28-percent gain class reduces the $350 gain in the all other long-term capital gain class to $200. As in Example 1, qualified dividend income is taxed at a lower rate than interest income during 2004. The annuity amount is deemed to be distributed from all the classes in the ordinary income category and then from the classes in the capital gains category, beginning with the class subject to the highest Federal income tax rate and ending with the class subject to the lowest rate. In the hands of the recipient, the 2004 annuity amount has the following characteristics:

Interest income	$ 5
Qualified dividend income	40
Net short-term capital gain	15
Net long-term capital gain in all other long-term capital gain class	40

(iii) The remaining $160 gain in the all other long-term capital gain class that is not treated as distributed to the recipient in 2004 is carried forward to 2005 as gain in that same class.

Example (3). (i) The facts are the same as in Examples 1 and 2, and at the end of 2005, X has the following classes of income:

Interest income class	$ 5
Qualified dividend income	20
Net loss in short-term capital gain class	[50]
Net long-term capital gain in 28% gain class	10
Net long-term capital gain in unrecaptured section 1250 gain class	135
Net long-term capital gain in all other long-term capital gain class (carried forward from 2004)	160

(ii) There are no long-term capital losses to net against the long-term capital gains. Thus, the net short-term capital loss is used to offset the net capital gains in the classes of long-term capital gain and loss, in turn, until exhaustion of the class, beginning with the class subject to the highest Federal income tax rate and ending with the class subject to the lowest rate. The $50 net short-term loss reduces the $10 net gain in the 28-percent gain class to $0. The remaining $40 net loss reduces the $135 net gain in the unrecaptured section 1250 gain class to $95. As in Examples 1 and 2, during 2005, qualified dividend income is taxed at a lower rate than interest income; gain in the unrecaptured section 1250 gain class is taxed at 25 percent; and gain in the all other long-term capital gain class is taxed at a rate lower than 25 percent. The annuity amount is deemed to be distributed from all the classes in the ordinary income category and then from the classes in the capital gains category, beginning with the class subject to the highest Federal income tax rate and ending with the class subject to the lowest rate. Therefore, in the hands of the recipient, the 2005 annuity amount has the following characteristics:

Interest income	$ 5
Qualified dividend income	20
Unrecaptured section 1250 gain	75

(iii) The remaining $20 gain in the unrecaptured section 1250 gain class and the $160 gain in the all other long-term capital gain class that are not treated as distributed to the recipient in 2005 are carried forward to 2006 as gains in their respective classes.

Example (4). (i) The facts are the same as in Examples 1, 2 and 3, and at the end of 2006, X has the following classes of income:

Interest income class	$ 95
Qualified dividend income class	10
Net loss in short-term capital gain class	[20]
Net long-term capital loss in 28% gain class	[350]
Net long-term capital gain in unrecaptured section 1250 gain class (carried forward from 2005)	20
Net long-term capital gain in all other long-term capital gain class (carried forward from 2005)	160

(ii) A net long-term capital loss in one class is used to offset the net capital gains in the other classes of long-term capital gain and loss, in turn, until exhaustion of the class, beginning with the class subject to the highest Federal income tax rate and ending with the class subject to the lowest rate. The $350 net loss in the 28-percent gain class reduces the $20 net gain in the unrecaptured section 1250 gain class to $0. The remaining $330 net loss reduces the $160 net gain in the all other long-term capital gain class to $0. As in Examples 1, 2 and 3, during 2006, qualified dividend income is taxed at a lower rate than interest income. The annuity amount is deemed to be distributed from all the classes in the ordinary income category and then from the classes in the capital gains category, beginning with the class subject to the highest Federal income tax rate and ending with the class subject to the lowest rate. In the hands of the recipient, the 2006 annuity amount has the following characteristics:

Interest income	$95
Qualified dividend income	5

(iii) The remaining $5 of qualified dividend income that is not treated as distributed to the recipient in 2006 is carried forward to 2007 as qualified dividend income. The $20 net loss in the short-term capital gain class and the $170 net loss in the 28-percent gain class are carried forward to 2007 as net losses in their respective classes.

Example (5). (i) X, a charitable remainder annuity trust described in section 664(d)(1), is created on January 1, 2002. The annual annuity amount is $100. Except for qualified 5-year gain of $200 realized before May 6, 2003, but not distributed, X has no other gains or losses carried over from former years. X's income for the 2007 tax year is as follows:

Interest income class	$10
Net gain in short-term capital gain class	5
Net long-term capital gain in 28% gain class	5
Net long-term capital gain in unrecaptured § 1250 gain class	10
Net long-term capital gain in all other long-term capital gain class	10

(ii) The annuity amount is deemed to be distributed from all the classes in the ordinary income category and then from the classes in the capital gains category, beginning with the class subject to the highest Federal income tax rate and ending with the class subject to the lowest rate. In 2007, gains distributed to a recipient from both the qualified 5-year gain class and the all other long-term capital gains class are taxed at a 15/5 percent tax rate. Since after December 31, 2008, gains distributed from the qualified 5-year gain class will be taxed at a lower rate than gains distributed from the other classes of long-term capital gain and loss, distributions from the qualified 5-year gain class are made after distributions from the other classes of long-term capital gain and loss. In the hands of the recipient, the 2007 annuity amount has the following characteristics:

Interest income	$10
Short-term capital gain	5
28-percent gain	5
Unrecaptured section 1250 gain	10
All other long-term capital gain	10
Qualified 5-year gain (taxed as all other long-term capital gain)	60

(iii) The remaining $140 of qualified 5-year gain that is not treated as distributed to the recipient in 2007 is carried forward to 2008 as qualified 5-year gain.

(iv) *Effective dates.* The rules in this paragraph (d)(1) that require long-term capital gains to be distributed in the following order: first, 28-percent gain (gains and losses from collectibles and section 1202 gains); second, unrecaptured section 1250 gain (long-term gains not treated as ordinary income that would be treated as ordinary income if section 1250(b)(1) included all depreciation); and then, all other long-term capital gains are applicable for taxable years ending on or after December 31, 1998. The rules in this paragraph (d)(1) that provide for the netting of capital gains and losses are applicable for taxable years ending on or after December 31, 1998. The rule in the second sentence of paragraph (d)(1)(vi) of this section is applicable for taxable years ending on or after December 31, 1998. The rule in the third sentence of paragraph (d)(1)(vi) of this section is applicable for distributions made in taxable years ending on or after December 31, 1998. All other provisions of this paragraph (d)(1) are applicable for taxable years ending after November 20, 2003.

(2) *Allocation of deductions*. Items of deduction of the trust for a taxable year of the trust which are deductible in determining taxable income (other than the deductions permitted by sections 642(b), 642(c), 661, and 1202) which are directly attributable to one or more classes of items within a category of income (determined under paragraph (d)(1)(i)(a) of this section) or to corpus shall be allocated to such classes of items or to corpus. All other allowable deductions for such taxable year which are not directly attributable to one or more classes of items within a category of income or to corpus (other than the deductions permitted by sections 642(b), 642(c), 661, and 1202) shall be allocated among the classes of items within the category (excluding classes of items with net losses) on the basis of the gross income of such classes for such taxable year reduced by the deductions allocated thereto under the first sentence of this subparagraph, but in no event shall the amount of expenses allocated to any class of items exceed such income of such class for the taxable year. Items of deduction which are not allocable un-

der the above two sentences (other than the deductions permitted by sections 642(b), 642(c), 661, and 1202) may be allocated in any manner. All taxes imposed by chapter 42 of the Code (including without limitation taxes treated under section 664(c)(2) as imposed by chapter 42) and, for taxable years beginning prior to January 1, 2007, all taxes imposed by subtitle A of the Code for which the trust is liable because it has unrelated business taxable income, shall be allocated to corpus. Any expense which is not deductible in determining taxable income and which is not allocable to any class of items described in paragraph (d)(1)(i)(a)(3) of this section shall be allocated to corpus. The deductions allowable to a trust under sections 642(b), 642(c), 661, and 1202 are not allowed in determining the amount or character of any class of items within a category of income described in paragraph (d)(1)(i)(a) of this section or to corpus.

(3) *Allocation of income among recipients.* If there are two or more recipients, each will be treated as receiving his pro rata portion of the categories of income and corpus. The application of this rule may be illustrated by the following example:

Example. X transfers $40,000 to a charitable remainder annuity trust which is to pay $3,000 per year to X and $2,000 per year to Y for a term of 5 years. During the first taxable year the trust has $3,000 of ordinary income, $500 of capital gain, and $500 of tax-exempt income after allocation of all expenses. X is treated as receiving ordinary income of $1,800 ($3,000/$5,000*$3,000), capital gain of $300 ($3,000/$5,000*$500), tax exempt income of $300 ($3,000/$5,000*$500), and corpus of $600 ($3,000/$5,000*[$5,000-$4,000]). Y is treated as receiving ordinary income of $1,200 ($2,000/$5,000*$3,000), capital gain of $200 ($2,000/$5,000*$500), tax exempt income of $200 ($2,000/$5,000*$500), and corpus of $400 ($2,000/$5,000*[$5,000-$4,000]).

(4) *Year of inclusion.* (i) *General rule.* To the extent required by this paragraph, the annuity or unitrust amount is includible in the recipient's gross income for the taxable year in which the annuity or unitrust amount is required to be distributed even though the annuity or unitrust amount is not distributed until after the close of the taxable year of the trust. If a recipient has a different taxable year (as defined in section 441 or 442) from the taxable year of the trust, the amount he is required to include in gross income to the extent required by this paragraph shall be included in his taxable year in which or with which ends the taxable year of the trust in which such amount is required to be distributed.

(ii) *Payments resulting from incorrect valuations.* Notwithstanding subdivision (i) of this subparagraph, any payments which are made or required to be distributed by a charitable remainder trust pursuant to paragraph (a)(5) of this section, under paragraph (f)(3) of this section because of an amendment to the governing instrument, or under paragraphs (a)(1) of §§ 1.664–2 and 1.664–3 because of an incorrect valuation, shall, to the extent required by this paragraph, be included in the gross income of the recipient in his taxable year in which or with which ends the taxable year of the trust in which the amount is paid, credited, or required to be distributed. For rules relating to required adjustments of underpayments and overpayments of the annuity or unitrust amounts in respect of payments made prior to the amendment of a governing instrument, see paragraph (f)(3) of this section. There is allowable to a recipient a deduction from gross income for any amounts repaid to the trust because of an overpayment during the reasonable period of administration or settlement or until the trust is fully funded, because of an amendment, or because of an incorrect valuation, to the extent such amounts were included in his gross income. See section 1341 and the regulations thereunder for rules relating to the computation of tax where a taxpayer restores substantial amounts held under a claim of right.

(iii) *Rules applicable to year of recipient's death.* If the taxable year of the trust does not end with or within the last taxable year of the recipient because of the recipient's death, the extent to which the annuity or unitrust amount required to be distributed to him is included in the gross income of the recipient for his last taxable year, or in the gross income of his estate, is determined by making the computations required under this paragraph for the taxable year of the trust in which his last taxable year ends. (The last sentence of subdivision (i) of this subparagraph does not apply to such amounts.) The gross income for the last taxable year of a recipient on the cash basis includes (to the extent required by this paragraph) amounts actually distributed to the recipient before his death. Amounts required to be distributed which are distributed to his estate, are included (to the extent required by this paragraph) in the gross income of the estate as income in respect of a decedent under section 691.

(5) *Distributions in kind.* The annuity or unitrust amount may be paid in cash or in other property. In the case of a distribution made in other property, the amount paid, credited, or required to be distributed shall be considered as an amount realized by the trust from the sale or other disposition of property. The basis of the property in the hands of the recipient is its fair market value at the time it was paid, credited, or required to be distributed. The application of these rules may be illustrated by the following example:

Example. On January 1, 1971, X creates a charitable remainder annuity trust, whose taxable year is the calendar year, under which X is to receive $5,000 per year. During 1971, the trust receives $500 of ordinary income. On December 31, 1971, the trust distributed cash of $500 and a capital asset of the trust having a fair market value of $4,500 and a basis of $2,200. The trust is deemed to have realized a capital gain of $2,300. X treats the distribution of $5,000 as being ordinary income of $500, capital gain of $2,300 and trust corpus of $2,200. The basis of the distributed property is $4,500 in the hands of X.

(e) Other distributions. (1) *Character of distributions.* An amount distributed by the trust to an organization described in section 170(c) other than the annuity or unitrust amount shall be considered as a distribution of corpus and of those categories of income specified in paragraph (d)(1)(i)(a) of this section in an order inverse to that prescribed in such paragraph. The character of such amount shall be determined as of the end of the taxable year of the trust in which the distribution is made after the character of the annuity or unitrust amount has been determined.

(2) *Distributions in kind.* In the case of a distribution of an amount to which subparagraph (1) of this paragraph applies, no gain or loss is realized by the trust by reason of a distribution in kind unless such distribution is in satisfaction of a right to receive a distribution of a specific dollar amount or in specific property other than that distributed.

(f) Effective date. (1) *General rule.* The provisions of this section are effective with respect to transfers in trust made after July 31, 1969. Any trust created (within the meaning of applicable local law) prior to August 1, 1969, is not a charitable remainder trust even if it otherwise satisfies the definition of a charitable remainder trust. The provisions of paragraph § 1.664–1(a)(7)(i)(b) apply as provided in that paragraph.

(2) *Transfers to pre-1970 trusts.* Property transferred to a trust created (within the meaning of applicable local law) before August 1, 1969, whose governing instrument provides that an organization described in section 170(c) receives an irrevocable remainder interest in such trust, shall, for purposes of subparagraphs (1) and (3) of this paragraph, be deemed transferred to a trust created on the date of such transfer provided that the transfer occurs after July 31, 1969, and prior to October 18, 1971, and the transferred property and any undistributed income therefrom is severed and placed in a separate trust before December 31, 1972, or if later, on or before the 30th day after the date on which any judicial proceedings begun before December 31, 1972, which are required to sever such property, become final.

(3) *Amendment of post-1969 trusts.* A trust created (within the meaning of applicable local law) subsequent to July 31, 1969, and prior to December 31, 1972, which is not a charitable remainder trust at the date of its creation, may be treated as a charitable remainder trust from the date it would be deemed created under § 1.664–1(a)(4) and (5)(i) for all purposes: Provided, That all the following requirements are met:

(i) At the time of the creation of the trust, the governing instrument provides that an organization described in section 170(c) receives an irrevocable remainder interest in such trust.

(ii) The governing instrument of the trust is amended so that the trust will meet the definition of a charitable remainder trust and, if applicable, will meet the requirement of paragraph (a)(5)(i) of this section that obligation to make payment of the annuity or unitrust amount with respect to property passing at death begin as of the date of death, before December 31, 1972, or if later, on or before the 30th day after the date on which any judicial proceedings which are begun before December 31, 1972, and which are required to amend its governing instrument, become final. In the case of a trust created (within the meaning of applicable local law) subsequent to July 31, 1969, and prior to December 31, 1972, the provisions of section 508(d)(2)(A) shall not apply if the governing instrument of the trust is amended so as to comply with the requirements of section 508(e) before December 31, 1972, or if later, on or before the 30th day after the date on which any judicial proceedings which are begun before December 31, 1972, and which are required to amend its governing instrument, become final. Notwithstanding the provisions of paragraphs (a)(3) and (a)(4) of §§ 1.664–2 and 1.664–3, the governing instrument may grant to the trustee a power to amend the governing instrument for the sole purpose of complying with the requirements of this section and § 1.664–2 or § 1.664–3: Provided, that at the creation of the trust, the governing instrument (a) provides for the payment of a unitrust amount described in § 1.664–3(a)(1)(i) or an annuity which meets the requirements of paragraph (a)(2) of § 1.664–2 or § 1.664–3, (b) designates the recipients of the trust and the period for which the amount described in (a) of this subdivision (ii) is to be paid, and (c) provides that an organization described in section 170(c) receives an irrevocable remainder interest in such trust. The mere granting of such a power is not sufficient to meet the requirements of this subparagraph that the governing instrument be amended in the manner and within the time limitations of this subparagraph.

(iii) (a) Where the amount of the distributions which would have been made by the trust to a recipient if the amended provisions of such trust had been in effect from the time of creation of such trust exceeds the amount of the distributions made by the trust prior to its amendment, the trust pays an amount equal to such excess to the recipient.

(b) Where the amount of distributions made to the recipient prior to the amendment of the trust exceeds the amount of the distributions which would have been made by such trust if the amended provisions of such trust had been in effect from the time of creation of such trust, such excess is repaid to the trust by the recipient.

See paragraph (d)(4) of this section for rules relating to the year of inclusion in the case of an underpayment to a recipient and the allowance of a deduction in the case of an overpayment to a recipient. A deduction for a transfer to a charitable remainder trust shall not be allowed until the requirements of this paragraph are met and then only if the deduction is claimed on a timely filed return (including extensions) or on a claim for refund filed within the period of limitations prescribed by section 6511(a).

(4) *Valuation of unmarketable assets.* The rules contained in paragraph (a)(7) of this section are applicable for trusts created on or after December 10, 1998. A trust in existence as of December 10, 1998 whose governing instrument requires that an independent trustee value the trust's unmarketable assets may be amended or reformed to permit a valuation method that satisfies the requirements of paragraph (a)(7) of this section for taxable years beginning on or after December 10, 1998.

(g) Transitional effective date. Notwithstanding any other provision of this section, § 1.664–2 or § 1.664–3, the requirement of paragraph (a)(5)(i) of this section that interest accrue on overpayments and underpayments, the requirement of paragraph (a)(5)(ii) of this section that the unitrust amount accruing under the formula provided therein cease with the death of the last recipient, and the requirement that the governing instrument of the trust contain the provisions specified in paragraph (a)(1)(iv) of § 1.664–2 (relating to computation of the annuity amount in certain circumstances), paragraph (a)(1)(v) of § 1.664–3 (relating to computation of the unitrust amount in certain circumstances), paragraphs (b) of §§ 1.664–2 and 1.664–3 (relating to additional contributions), and paragraph (a)(1)(iii) of § 1.664–3 (relating to incorrect valuations), paragraphs (a)(6)(iv) of §§ 1.664–2 and 1.664–3 (relating to alternative remaindermen) shall not apply to:

(1) A will executed on or before December 31, 1972, if:

(i) The testator dies before December 31, 1975, without having republished the will after December 31, 1972, by codicil or otherwise,

(ii) The testator at no time after December 31, 1972, had the right to change the provisions of the will which pertain to the trust, or

(iii) The will is not republished by codicil or otherwise before December 31, 1975, and the testator is on such date and at all times thereafter under a mental disability to republish the will by codicil or otherwise, or

(2) A trust executed on or before December 31, 1972, if:

(i) The grantor dies before December 31, 1975, without having amended the trust after December 31, 1972,

(ii) The trust is irrevocable on December 31, 1972, or

(iii) The trust is not amended before December 31, 1975, and the grantor is on such date and at all times thereafter under a mental disability to change the terms of the trust.

[T.D. 7202, 37 FR 16913, Aug. 23, 1972; 37 FR 28288, Dec. 22, 1972; T.D. 7955, 49 FR 19983, May 11, 1984; T.D. 8540, 59 FR 30102, 30116, June 10, 1994; T.D. 8791, 63 FR 68191, Dec. 10, 1998; T.D. 8819, 64 FR 23228, 23229, April 30, 1999; T.D. 8886, 65 FR 36943, June 12, 2000; T.D. 8926, 66 FR 1037, Jan. 5, 2001; T.D. 9190, 70 FR 12795, March 16, 2005; T.D. 9403, 73 FR 35584, June 24, 2008; T.D. 9448, 74 FR 21518, May 7, 2009; T.D. 9540, 76 FR 49612, Aug. 10, 2011; T.D. 9836, July 27, 2018]

§ 1.664–2 Charitable remainder annuity trust.

(a) Description. A charitable remainder annuity trust is a trust which complies with the applicable provisions of § 1.664–1 and meets all of the following requirements:

(1) *Required payment of annuity amount.* (i) *Payment of sum certain at least annually.* The governing instrument provides that the trust will pay a sum certain not less often than annually to a person or persons described in paragraph (a)(3) of this section for each taxable year of the period specified in paragraph (a)(5) of this section.

(a) *General rule applicable to all trusts.* A trust will not be deemed to have engaged in an act of self-dealing (within the meaning of section 4941), to have unrelated debt-financed income (within the meaning of section 514), to have received an additional contribution (within the meaning of paragraph (b) of this section), or to have failed to function exclusively as a charitable remainder trust (within the meaning of § 1.664–1(a)(4)) merely because the annuity amount is paid after the close of the taxable year if such payment is made within a reasonable time after the close of such taxable year and the entire annuity amount in the hands of the recipient is characterized only as income from the categories described in section 664(b)(1), (2), or (3), except to the extent it is characterized as corpus described in section 664(b)(4) because—

(1) The trust pays the annuity amount by distributing property (other than cash) that it owned at the close of the taxable year to pay the annuity amount, and the trustee elects to treat any income generated by the distribution as occurring on the last day of the taxable year in which the annuity amount is due;

(2) The trust pays the annuity amount by distributing cash that was contributed to the trust (with respect to which a deduction was allowable under section 170, 2055, 2106, or 2522); or

(3) The trust pays the annuity amount by distributing cash received as a return of basis in any asset that was contributed to the trust (with respect to which a deduction was allowable under section 170, 2055, 2106, or 2522), and that is sold by the trust during the year for which the annuity amount is due.

(b) *Special rule for trusts created before December 10, 1998.* In addition to the circumstances described in paragraph (a)(1)(i)(a) of this section, a trust created before December 10, 1998 will not be deemed to have engaged in an act of self-dealing (within the meaning of section 4941), to have unrelated debt-financed income (within the meaning of section 514), to have received an additional contribution (within the meaning of paragraph (b) of this section), or to have failed to function exclusively as a charitable remainder trust (within the meaning of § 1.664–1(a)(4)) merely because the annuity amount is paid after the close of the taxable year if such payment is made within a reasonable time after the close of such taxable year and the sum certain to be paid each year as the annuity amount is 15 percent or less of the initial net fair market value of the property irrevocably passing in trust as determined for federal tax purposes.

(c) *Reasonable time.* For this paragraph (a)(1)(i), a reasonable time will not ordinarily extend beyond the date by which the trustee is required to file Form 5227, "Split-Interest Trust Information Return," (including extensions) for the taxable year.

(d) *Example.* The following example illustrates the rules in paragraph (a)(1)(i)(a) of this section:

Example. X is a charitable remainder annuity trust described in section 664(d)(1) that was created after December 10, 1998. The prorated annuity amount payable from X for Year 1 is $100. The trustee does not pay the annuity amount to the recipient by the close of Year 1. At the end of Year 1, X has only $95 in the ordinary income category under section 664(b)(1) and no income in the capital gain or tax-exempt income categories under section 664(b)(2) or (3), respectively. By April 15 of Year 2, in addition to $95 in cash, the trustee distributes to the recipient of the annuity a capital asset with a $5 fair market value and a $2 adjusted basis to pay the $100 annuity amount due for Year 1. The trust owned the asset at the end of Year 1. Under § 1.664–1(d)(5), the distribution is treated as a sale by X, resulting in X recognizing a $3 capital gain. The trustee elects to treat the capital gain as occurring on the last day of Year 1. Under § 1.664–1(d)(1), the character of the annuity amount for Year 1 in the recipient's hands is $95 of ordinary income, $3 of capital gain income, and $2 of trust corpus. For Year 1, X satisfied paragraph (a)(1)(i)(a) of this section.

(e) *Effective date.* This paragraph (a)(1)(i) is applicable for taxable years ending after April 18, 1997. However, paragraphs (a)(1)(i)(a)(2) and (3) of this section apply only to distributions made on or after January 5, 2001.

(ii) *Definition of sum certain.* A sum certain is a stated dollar amount which is the same either as to each recipient or as to the total amount payable for each year of such period. For example, a provision for an amount which is the same every year to A until his death and concurrently an amount which is the same every year to B until his death, with the amount to each recipient to terminate at his death, would satisfy the above rule. Similarly, provisions for an amount to A and B for their joint lives and then to the survivor would satisfy the above rule. In the case of a distribution to an organization described in section 170(c) at the death of a recipient or the expiration of a term of years, the governing instrument may provide for a reduction of the stated amount payable after such a distribution: Provided, That:

(a) The reduced amount payable is the same either as to each recipient or as to the total amount payable for each year of the balance of such period, and

(b) The requirements of subparagraph (2)(ii) of this paragraph are met.

(iii) *Sum certain stated as a fraction or percentage.* The stated dollar amount may be expressed as a fraction or a percentage of the initial net fair market value of the property irrevocably passing in trust as finally determined for Federal tax purposes. If the stated dollar amount is so expressed and such market value is incorrectly determined by the fiduciary, the requirement of this subparagraph will be satisfied if the governing instrument provides that in such event the trust shall pay to the recipient (in the case of an undervaluation) or be repaid by the recipient (in the case of an overvaluation) an amount equal to the difference between the amount which the trust should have paid the recipient if the correct value were used and the amount which the trust actually paid the recipient. Such payments or repayments must be made within a reasonable period after the final determination of such value. Any payment due to a recipient by reason of such incorrect valuation shall be considered to be a payment required to be distributed at the time of such final determination for purposes of paragraph (d)(4)(ii) of § 1.664–1. See paragraph (d)(4) of § 1.664–1 for rules relating to the year of inclusion of such payments and the allowance of a deduction for such repayments. See paragraph (b) of this section for rules relating to future contributions. For rules relating to required adjustments for underpayments or overpayments of the amount described in this paragraph in respect of payments made during a reasonable period of administration, see paragraph (a)(5) of § 1.664–1. The application of the rule permitting the stated dollar amount to be expressed as a fraction or a percentage of the initial net fair market value of the property irrevocably passing in trust as finally determined for Federal tax purposes may be illustrated by the following example:

Example. The will of X provides for the transfer of one-half of his residuary estate to a charitable remainder annuity trust which is required to pay to W for life an annuity equal to 5 percent of the initial net fair market value of the interest passing in trust as finally determined for Federal tax purposes. The annuity is to be paid on December 31 of each year computed from the date of X's death. The will also provides that if such initial net fair market value is incorrectly determined, the trust shall pay to W, in the case of an undervaluation, or be repaid by W, in the case of an overvaluation, an amount equal to the difference between the amount which the trust should have paid if the correct value were used and the amount which the trust actually paid. X dies on March 1, 1971. The executor files an estate tax return showing the value of the residuary estate as $250,000 before reduction for taxes and expenses of $50,000. The executor paid to W $4,192 ([$250,000 - $50,000] * ½ * 5 percent * 306/365) on December 31, 1971. On January 1, 1972, the executor transfers one-half of the residue of the estate to the trust. The trust adopts the calendar year as its taxable year. The value of the residuary estate is finally determined for Federal tax purposes to be $240,000 ($290,000-$50,000). Accordingly, the amount which the executor should have paid to W is $5,030 ([$290,000 - $50,000] * ½ * 5 percent * 306/365). Consequently, an additional amount of $838 ($5,030 - $4,192) must be paid to W within a reasonable period after the final determination of value for Federal tax purposes.

(iv) *Computation of annuity amount in certain circumstances.* (a) *Short taxable years.* The governing instrument provides that, in the case of a taxable year which is for a period of less than 12 months other than the taxable year in which occurs the end of the period specified in subparagraph (5) of this paragraph, the annuity amount determined under subdivision (i) of this subparagraph shall be the amount otherwise determined under that subdivision multiplied by a fraction the numerator of which is the number of days in the taxable year of the trust and the denominator of which is 365 (366 if February 29 is a day included in the numerator).

(b) *Last taxable year of period.* The governing instrument provides that, in the case of the taxable year in which occurs the end of the period specified in subparagraph (5) of this paragraph, the annuity amount which must be distributed under subdivision (i) of this subparagraph shall be the amount otherwise determined under that subdivision multiplied by a fraction the numerator of which is the number of days in the period beginning on the first day of such taxable year and ending on the last day of the period specified in subparagraph (5) of this paragraph and the denominator of which is 365 (366 if February 29 is a day included in the numerator). See subparagraph (5) of this paragraph for a special rule allowing termination of payment of the annuity amount with the regular payment next preceding the termination of the period specified therein.

(2) *Minimum annuity amount.* (i) *General rule.* The total amount payable under subparagraph (1) of this paragraph is not less than 5 percent of the initial net fair market value of the property placed in trust as finally determined for Federal tax purposes.

(ii) *Reduction of annuity amount in certain cases.* A trust will not fail to meet the requirements of this subparagraph by reason of the fact that it provides for a reduction of the stated amount payable upon the death of a recipient or the expiration of a term of years provided that:

(a) A distribution is made to an organization described in section 170(c) at the death of such recipient or the expiration of such term of years, and

(b) The total amounts payable each year under subparagraph (1) of this paragraph after such distribution are not less than a stated dollar amount which bears the same ratio to 5 percent of the initial net fair market value of the trust assets as the net fair market value of the trust assets immediately after such distribution bears to the net fair market value of the trust assets immediately before such distribution.

(iii) *Rule applicable to inter vivos trust which does not provide for payment of minimum annuity amount.* In the case where the grantor of an inter vivos trust underestimates in good faith the initial net fair market value of the property placed in trust as finally determined for Federal tax purposes and specifies a fixed dollar amount for the annuity which is less than 5 percent of the initial net fair market value of the property placed in trust as finally determined for Federal tax purposes, the trust will be deemed to have met the 5 percent requirement if the grantor or his representative consents, by appropriate agreement with the District Director, to accept an amount equal to 20 times the annuity as the fair market value of the property placed in trust for purposes of determining the appropriate charitable contributions deduction.

(3) *Permissible recipients.* (i) *General rule.* The amount described in subparagraph (1) of this paragraph is payable to or for the use of a named person or persons, at least one of which is not an organization described in section 170(c). If the amount described in subparagraph (1) of this paragraph is to be paid to an individual or individuals, all such individuals must be living at the time of the creation of the trust. A named person or persons may include members of a named class provided that, in the case of a class which includes any individual, all such individuals must be alive and ascertainable at the time of the creation of the trust unless the period for which the annuity amount is to be paid to such class consists solely of a term of

years. For example, in the case of a testamentary trust, the testator's will may provide that an amount shall be paid to his children living at his death.

(ii) *Power to alter amount paid to recipients.* A trust is not a charitable remainder annuity trust if any person has the power to alter the amount to be paid to any named person other than an organization described in section 170(c) if such power would cause any person to be treated as the owner of the trust, or any portion thereof, if Subpart E, Part 1, Subchapter J, Chapter 1, Subtitle A of the Code were applicable to such trust. See paragraph (a)(4) of this section for a rule permitting the retention by a grantor of a testamentary power to revoke or terminate the interest of any recipient other than an organization described in section 170(c). For example, the governing instrument may not grant the trustee the power to allocate the annuity among members of a class unless such power falls within one of the exceptions to section 674(a).

(4) *Other payments.* No amount other than the amount described in subparagraph (1) of this paragraph may be paid to or for the use of any person other than an organization described in section 170(c). An amount is not paid to or for the use of any person other than an organization described in section 170(c) if the amount is transferred for full and adequate consideration. The trust may not be subject to a power to invade, alter, amend, or revoke for the beneficial use of a person other than an organization described in section 170(c). Notwithstanding the preceding sentence, the grantor may retain the power exercisable only by will to revoke or terminate the interest of any recipient other than an organization described in section 170(c). The governing instrument may provide that any amount other than the amount described in subparagraph (1) of this paragraph shall be paid (or may be paid in the discretion of the trustee) to an organization described in section 170(c) provided that in the case of distributions in kind, the adjusted basis of the property distributed is fairly representative of the adjusted basis of the property available for payment on the date of payment. For example, the governing instrument may provide that a portion of the trust assets may be distributed currently, or upon the death of one or more recipients, to an organization described in section 170(c).

(5) *Period of payment of annuity amount.* (i) *General rules.* The period for which an amount described in subparagraph (1) of this paragraph is payable begins with the first year of the charitable remainder trust and continues either for the life or lives of a named individual or individuals or for a term of years not to exceed 20 years. Only an individual or an organization described in section 170(c) may receive an amount for the life of an individual. If an individual receives an amount for life, it must be solely for his life. Payment of the amount described in subparagraph (1) of this paragraph may terminate with the regular payment next preceding the termination of the period described in this subparagraph. The fact that the recipient may not receive such last payment shall not be taken into account for purposes of determining the present value of the remainder interest. In the case of an amount payable for a term of years, the length of the term of years shall be ascertainable with certainty at the time of the creation of the trust, except that the term may be terminated by the death of the recipient or by the grantor's exercise by will of a retained power to revoke or terminate the interest of any recipient other than an organization described in section 170(c). In any event, the period may not extend beyond either the life or lives of a named individual or individuals or a term of years not to exceed 20 years. For example, the governing instrument may not provide for the payment of an annuity amount to A for his life and then to B for a term of years because it is possible for the period to last longer than either the lives of recipients in being at the creation of the trust or a term of years not to exceed 20 years. On the other hand, the governing instrument may provide for the payment of an annuity amount to A for his life and then to B for his life or a term of years (not to exceed 20 years), whichever is shorter (but not longer), if both A and B are in being at the creation of the trust because it is not possible for the period to last longer than the lives of recipients in being at the creation of the trust.

(ii) *Relationship to 5 percent requirement.* The 5 percent requirement provided in subparagraph (2) of this paragraph must be met until the termination of all of the payments described in subparagraph (1) of this paragraph. For example, the following provisions would satisfy the above rules:

(a) An amount equal to at least 5 percent of the initial net fair market value of the property placed in trust to A and B for their joint lives and then to the survivor for his life;

(b) An amount equal to at least 5 percent of the initial net fair market value of the property placed in trust to A for life or for a term of years not longer than 20 years, whichever is longer (or shorter);

(c) An amount equal to at least 5 percent of the initial net fair market value of the property placed in trust to A for a term of years not longer than 20 years and then to B for life (provided B was living at the date of creation of the trust);

(d) An amount to A for his life and concurrently an amount to B for his life (the amount to each recipient to terminate at his death) if the amount given to each individual is not less than 5 percent of the initial net fair market value of the property placed in trust; or

(e) An amount to A for his life and concurrently an equal amount to B for his life, and at the death of the first to die, the trust to distribute one-half of the then value of its assets to an organization described in section 170(c), if the total of the amounts given to A and B is not less than 5 percent of the initial net fair market value of the property placed in trust.

(6) *Permissible remaindermen*—(i) *General rule.* At the end of the period specified in subparagraph (5) of this paragraph the entire corpus of the trust is required to be irrevocably transferred, in whole or in part, to or for the use of one or more organizations described in section 170(c) or retained, in whole or in part, for such use.

(ii) *Treatment of trust.* If all of the trust corpus is to be retained for such use, the taxable year of the trust shall terminate at the end of the period specified in subparagraph (5) of this paragraph and the trust shall cease to be treated as a charitable remainder trust for all purposes. If all or any portion of the trust corpus is to be transferred to or for the use of such organization or organizations, the trustee shall have a reasonable time after the period specified in subparagraph (5) of this paragraph to complete the settlement of the trust. During such time, the trust shall continue to be treated as a charitable remainder trust for all purposes, such as sections 664, 4947(a)(2), and 4947(b)(3)(B). Upon the expiration of such period, the taxable year of the trust shall terminate and the trust shall cease to be treated as a charitable remainder trust for all purposes. If the trust continues in existence, it will be subject to the provisions of section 4947(a)(1) unless the trust is exempt from taxation under section 501(a). For purposes of determining whether the trust is exempt under section 501(a) as an organization described in section 501(c)(3), the trust shall be deemed to have been created at the time it ceases to be treated as a charitable remainder trust.

(iii) *Concurrent or successive remaindermen.* Where interests in the corpus of the trust are given to more than one organization described in section 170(c) such interests may be enjoyed by them either concurrently or successively.

(iv) *Alternative remaindermen.* The governing instrument shall provide that if an organization to or for the use of which the trust corpus is to be transferred or for the use of which the trust corpus is to be retained is not an organization described in section 170(c) at the time any amount is to be irrevocably transferred to or for the use of such organization, such amount shall be transferred to or for the use of one or more alternative organizations which are described in section 170(c) at such time or retained for such use. Such alternative organization or organizations may be selected in any manner provided by the terms of the governing instrument.

(b) Additional contributions. A trust is not a charitable remainder annuity trust unless its governing instrument provides that no additional contributions may be made to the charitable remainder annuity trust after the initial contribution. For purposes of this section, all property passing to a charitable remainder annuity trust by reason of death of the grantor shall be considered one contribution.

(c) Calculation of the fair market value of the remainder interest of a charitable remainder annuity trust. For purposes of sections 170, 2055, 2106, and 2522, the fair market value of the remainder interest of a charitable remainder annuity trust (as described in this section) is the net fair market value (as of the appropriate valuation date) of the property placed in trust less the present value of the annuity. For purposes of this section, valuation date means, in general, the date on which the property is transferred to the trust by the donor regardless of when the trust is created. In the case of transfers to a charitable remainder annuity trust for which the valuation date is after April 30, 1999, if an election is made under section 7520 and § 1.7520–2(b) to compute the present value of the charitable interest by using the interest rate component for either of the 2 months preceding the month in which the transfer is made, the month so elected is the valuation date for purposes of determining the interest rate and mortality tables. For purposes of section 2055 or 2106, the valuation date is the date of death unless the alternate valuation date is elected in accordance with section 2032 in which event, and within the limitations set forth in section 2032 and the regulations in this part under section 2032, the valuation date is the alternate valuation date. If the decedent's estate elects the alternate valuation date under section 2032 and also elects, under section 7520 and § 1.7520–2(b), to use the interest rate component for one of the 2 months preceding the alternate valuation date, the month so elected is the valuation date for purposes of determining the interest rate and mortality tables. The present value of an annuity is computed under § 20.2031–7(d) of this chapter for transfers for which the valuation date is on or after June 1, 2023, or under § 20.2031–7A(a) through (g) of this chapter, whichever is applicable, for transfers for which the valuation date is before June 1, 2023. See, however, §§ 20.2031–7(d)(3) and 25.2512–5(d)(3) (transition rules) and 1.7520–3(b) (relating to exceptions to the use of prescribed tables under certain circumstances).

(d) Deduction for transfers to a charitable remainder annuity trust. For rules relating to a deduction for transfers to a charitable remainder annuity trust, see sections 170, 2055, 2106, or 2522 and the regulations thereunder. Any claim for deduction on any return for the value of a remainder interest in a charitable remainder annuity trust must be supported by a full statement attached to the return showing the computation of the present value of such interest. The deduction allowed by section 170 is limited to the fair market value of the remainder interest of a charitable remainder annuity trust regardless of whether an organization described in section 170(c) also receives a portion of the annuity. For a special rule relating to the reduction of the amount of a charitable contribution deduction with respect to a contribution of certain ordinary income property or capital gain property, see sections 170(e)(1)(A) or 170(e)(1)(B)(i) and the regulations thereunder. For rules for postponing the time for deduction of a charitable contribution of a future interest in tangible personal property, see section 170(a)(3) and the regulations thereunder.

(e) Applicability date. Paragraph (c) of this section applies on and after June 1, 2023.

[T.D. 7202, 37 FR 16918, Aug. 23, 1972, as amended by T.D. 7955, 49 FR 19983, May 11, 1984; T.D. 8540, 59 FR 30116, June 10, 1994; T.D. 8791, 63 FR 68191, Dec. 10, 1998; T.D. 8819, 64 FR 23229, April 30, 1999; 65 FR 12471, March 9, 2000; T.D. 8926, 66 FR 1037, Jan. 5, 2001; T.D. 9448, 74 FR 21464, May 7, 2009; T.D. 9540, 76 FR 49595, Aug. 10, 2011; T.D. 9974, 88 FR 37433, June 7, 2023]

§ 1.664–3 Charitable remainder unitrust.

(a) Description. A charitable remainder unitrust is a trust which complies with the applicable provisions of § 1.664–1 and meets all of the following requirements:

(1) *Required payment of unitrust amount.* (i) *Payment of fixed percentage at least annually.* (a) *General rule.* The governing instrument provides that the trust will pay not less often than annually a fixed percentage of the net fair market value of the trust assets determined annually to a person or persons described in paragraph (a)(3) of this section for each taxable year of the period specified in paragraph (a)(5) of this section. This paragraph (a)(1)(i)(a) is applicable for taxable years ending after April 18, 1997.

(b) *Income exception.* Instead of the amount described in (a) of this subdivision (i), the governing instrument may provide that the trust shall pay for any year either the amount described in (1) or the total of the amounts described in (1) and (2) of this subdivision (b).

(1) The amount of trust income for a taxable year to the extent that such amount is not more than the amount required to be distributed under paragraph (a)(1)(i)(a) of this section.

(2) An amount of trust income for a taxable year that is in excess of the amount required to be distributed under paragraph (a)(1)(i)(a) of this section for such year to the extent that (by reason of paragraph (a)(1)(i)(b)(1) of this section) the aggregate of the amounts paid in prior years was less than the aggregate of such required amounts.

(3) For purposes of this paragraph (a)(1)(i)(b), trust income generally means income as defined under section 643(b) and the applicable regulations. However, trust income may not be determined by reference to

a fixed percentage of the annual fair market value of the trust property, notwithstanding any contrary provision in applicable state law. Proceeds from the sale or exchange of any assets contributed to the trust by the donor must be allocated to principal and not to trust income at least to the extent of the fair market value of those assets on the date of their contribution to the trust. Proceeds from the sale or exchange of any assets purchased by the trust must be allocated to principal and not to trust income at least to the extent of the trust's purchase price of those assets. Except as provided in the two preceding sentences, proceeds from the sale or exchange of any assets contributed to the trust by the donor or purchased by the trust may be allocated to income, pursuant to the terms of the governing instrument, if not prohibited by applicable local law. A discretionary power to make this allocation may be granted to the trustee under the terms of the governing instrument but only to the extent that the state statute permits the trustee to make adjustments between income and principal to treat beneficiaries impartially.

(4) The rules in paragraph (a)(1)(i)(b)(1) and (2) of this section are applicable for taxable years ending after April 18, 1997. The rule in the first sentence of paragraph (a)(1)(i)(b)(3) is applicable for taxable years ending after April 18, 1997. The rules in the second, fourth, and fifth sentences of paragraph (a)(1)(i)(b)(3) are applicable for taxable years ending after January 2, 2004. The rule in the third sentence of paragraph (a)(1)(i)(b)(3) is applicable for sales or exchanges that occur after April 18, 1997. The rule in the sixth sentence of paragraph (a)(1)(i)(b)(3) is applicable for trusts created after January 2, 2004.

(c) *Combination of methods*. Instead of the amount described in paragraph (a)(1)(i)(a) or (b) of this section, the governing instrument may provide that the trust will pay not less often than annually the amount described in paragraph (a)(1)(i)(b) of this section for an initial period and then pay the amount described in paragraph (a)(1)(i)(a) of this section (calculated using the same fixed percentage) for the remaining years of the trust only if the governing instrument provides that—

(1) The change from the method prescribed in paragraph (a)(1)(i)(b) to the method prescribed in paragraph (a)(1)(i)(a) is triggered on a specific date or by a single event whose occurrence is not discretionary with, or within the control of, the trustees or any other persons;

(2) The change from the method prescribed in paragraph (a)(1)(i)(b) of this section to the method prescribed in paragraph (a)(1)(i)(a) of this section occurs at the beginning of the taxable year that immediately follows the taxable year during which the date or event specified under paragraph (a)(1)(i)(c)(1) of this section occurs; and

(3) Following the trust's conversion to the method described in paragraph (a)(1)(i)(a) of this section, the trust will pay at least annually to the permissible recipients the amount described only in paragraph (a)(1)(i)(a) of this section and not any amount described in paragraph (a)(1)(i) (b) of this section.

(d) *Triggering event*. For purposes of paragraph (a)(1)(i)(c)(1) of this section, a triggering event based on the sale of unmarketable assets as defined in § 1.664–1(a)(7)(ii), or the marriage, divorce, death, or birth of a child with respect to any individual will not be considered discretionary with, or within the control of, the trustees or any other persons.

(e) *Examples*. The following examples illustrate the rules in paragraph (a)(1)(i)(c) of this section. For each example, assume that the governing instrument of charitable remainder unitrust Y provides that Y will initially pay not less often than annually the amount described in paragraph (a)(1)(i)(b) of this section and then pay the amount described in paragraph (a)(1)(i)(a) of this section (calculated using the same fixed percentage) for the remaining years of the trust and that the requirements of paragraphs (a)(1)(i)(c)(2) and (3) of this section are satisfied. The examples are as follows:

Example (1). Y is funded with the donor's former personal residence. The governing instrument of Y provides for the change in method for computing the annual unitrust amount as of the first day of the year following the year in which the trust sells the residence. Y provides for a combination of methods that satisfies paragraph (a)(1)(i)(c) of this section.

Example (2). Y is funded with cash and an unregistered security for which there is no available exemption permitting public sale under the Securities and Exchange Commission rules. The governing instrument of Y provides that the change in method for computing the annual unitrust amount is triggered on the earlier of the date when the stock is sold or at the time the restrictions on its public sale lapse or are otherwise lifted. Y provides for a combination of methods that satisfies paragraph (a)(1)(i)(c) of this section.

Example (3). Y is funded with cash and with a security that may be publicly traded under the Securities and Exchange Commission rules. The governing instrument of Y provides that the change in method for computing the annual unitrust amount is triggered when the stock is sold. Y does not provide for a combination of methods that satisfies the requirements of paragraph (a)(1)(i)(c) of this section because the sale of the publicly-traded stock is within the discretion of the trustee.

Example (4). S establishes Y for her granddaughter, G, when G is 10 years old. The governing instrument of Y provides for the change in method for computing the annual unitrust amount as of the first day of the year following the year in which G turns 18 years old. Y provides for a combination of methods that satisfies paragraph (a)(1)(i)(c) of this section.

Example (5). The governing instrument of Y provides for the change in method for computing the annual unitrust amount as of the first day of the year following the year in which the donor is married. Y provides for a combination of methods that satisfies paragraph (a)(1)(i)(c) of this section.

Example (6). The governing instrument of Y provides that if the donor divorces, the change in method for computing the annual unitrust amount will occur as of the first day of the year following the year of the divorce. Y provides for a combination of methods that satisfies paragraph (a)(1)(i)(c) of this section.

Example (7). The governing instrument of Y provides for the change in method for computing the annual unitrust amount as of the first day of the year following the year in which the noncharitable beneficiary's first child is born. Y provides for a combination of methods that satisfies paragraph (a)(1)(i)(c) of this section.

Example (8). The governing instrument of Y provides for the change in method for computing the annual unitrust amount as of the first day of the year following the year in which the noncharitable beneficiary's father dies. Y provides for a combination of methods that satisfies paragraph (a)(1)(i)(c) of this section.

Example (9). The governing instrument of Y provides for the change in method for computing the annual unitrust amount as of the first day of the year following the year in which the noncharitable beneficiary's financial advisor determines that the beneficiary should begin receiving payments under the second prescribed payment method. Because the change in methods for paying the unitrust amount is triggered by an event that is within a person's control, Y does not provide for a combination of methods that satisfies paragraph (a)(1)(i)(c) of this section.

Example (10). The governing instrument of Y provides for the change in method for computing the annual unitrust amount as of the first day of the year following the year in which the noncharitable beneficiary submits a request to the trustee that the trust convert to the second prescribed payment method. Because the change in methods for paying the unitrust amount is triggered by an event that is within a person's control, Y does not provide for a combination of methods that satisfies paragraph (a)(1)(i)(c) of this section.

(f) *Effective date*. (1) *General rule*. Paragraphs (a)(1)(i)(c), (d), and (e) of this section are applicable for charitable remainder trusts created on or after December 10, 1998.

(2) *General rule regarding reformations of combination of method unitrusts*. If a trust is created on or after December 10, 1998 and contains a provision allowing a change in calculating the unitrust amount that does not comply with the provisions of paragraph (a)(1)(i)(c) of this section, the trust will qualify as a charitable remainder unitrust only if it is amended or reformed to use the initial method for computing the unitrust amount throughout the term of the trust, or is reformed in accordance with paragraph (a)(1)(i)(f)(3) of this section. If a trust was created before December 10, 1998 and contains a provision allowing a change in calculating the unitrust amount that does not comply with the provisions of paragraph (a)(1)(i)(c) of this section, the trust may be reformed to use the initial method for computing the unitrust amount throughout the term of the trust without causing the trust to fail to function exclusively as a charitable remainder unitrust under § 1.664–1(a)(4), or may be reformed in accordance with paragraph (a)(1)(i)(f)(3) of this sec-

tion. Except as provided in paragraph (a)(1)(i)(f)(3) of this section, a qualified charitable remainder unitrust will not continue to qualify as a charitable remainder unitrust if it is amended or reformed to add a provision allowing a change in the method for calculating the unitrust amount.

(3) *Special rule for reformations of trusts that begin by June 8, 1999.* Notwithstanding paragraph (a)(1)(i)(f)(2) of this section, if a trust either provides for payment of the unitrust amount under a combination of methods that is not permitted under paragraph (a)(1)(i)(c) of this section, or provides for payment of the unitrust amount under only the method prescribed in paragraph (a)(1)(i)(b) of this section, then the trust may be reformed to allow for a combination of methods permitted under paragraph (a)(1)(i)(c) of this section without causing the trust to fail to function exclusively as a charitable remainder unitrust under § 1.664–1(a)(4) or to engage in an act of self-dealing under section 4941 if the trustee begins legal proceedings to reform by June 8, 1999. The triggering event under the reformed governing instrument may not occur in a year prior to the year in which the court issues the order reforming the trust, except for situations in which the governing instrument prior to reformation already provided for payment of the unitrust amount under a combination of methods that is not permitted under paragraph (a)(1)(i)(c) of this section and the triggering event occurred prior to the reformation.

(g) *Payment under general rule for fixed percentage trusts.* When the unitrust amount is computed under paragraph (a)(1)(i)(a) of this section, a trust will not be deemed to have engaged in an act of self-dealing (within the meaning of section 4941), to have unrelated debt-financed income (within the meaning of section 514), to have received an additional contribution (within the meaning of paragraph (b) of this section), or to have failed to function exclusively as a charitable remainder trust (within the meaning of § 1.664–1(a)(4)) merely because the unitrust amount is paid after the close of the taxable year if such payment is made within a reasonable time after the close of such taxable year and the entire unitrust amount in the hands of the recipient is characterized only as income from the categories described in section 664(b)(1), (2), or (3), except to the extent it is characterized as corpus described in section 664(b)(4) because—

(1) The trust pays the unitrust amount by distributing property (other than cash) that it owned at the close of the taxable year, and the trustee elects to treat any income generated by the distribution as occurring on the last day of the taxable year in which the unitrust amount is due;

(2) The trust pays the unitrust amount by distributing cash that was contributed to the trust (with respect to which a deduction was allowable under section 170, 2055, 2106, or 2522); or

(3) The trust pays the unitrust amount by distributing cash received as a return of basis in any asset that was contributed to the trust (with respect to which a deduction was allowable under section 170, 2055, 2106, or 2522), and that is sold by the trust during the year for which the unitrust amount is due.

(h) *Special rule for fixed percentage trusts created before December 10, 1998.* When the unitrust amount is computed under paragraph (a)(1)(i)(a) of this section, a trust created before December 10, 1998 will not be deemed to have engaged in an act of self-dealing (within the meaning of section 4941), to have unrelated debt-financed income (within the meaning of section 514), to have received an additional contribution (within the meaning of paragraph (b) of this section), or to have failed to function exclusively as a charitable remainder trust (within the meaning of § 1.664–1(a)(4)) merely because the unitrust amount is paid after the close of the taxable year if such payment is made within a reasonable time after the close of such taxable year and the fixed percentage to be paid each year as the unitrust amount is 15 percent or less of the net fair market value of the trust assets as determined under paragraph (a)(1)(iv) of this section.

(i) *Example.* The following example illustrates the rules in paragraph (a)(1)(i)(g) of this section:

Example. X is a charitable remainder unitrust that calculates the unitrust amount under paragraph (a)(1)(i)(a) of this section. X was created after December 10, 1998. The prorated unitrust amount payable from X for Year 1 is $100. The trustee does not pay the unitrust amount to the recipient by the end of the Year 1. At the end of Year 1, X has only $95 in the ordinary income category under section 664(b)(1) and no income in the capital gain or tax-exempt income categories under section 664(b)(2) or (3), respectively. By April 15 of Year 2, in addition to $95 in cash, the trustee distributes to the unitrust recipient a capital asset with a $5 fair market value and a $2 adjusted basis to pay the $100 unitrust amount due for Year 1. The trust owned the asset at the end of Year 1. Under § 1.664–1(d)(5), the distribution is treated as a sale by X, resulting in X recognizing a $3 capital gain. The trustee elects to treat the capital gain as occurring on the last day of Year 1. Under § 1.664–1(d)(1), the character of the unitrust amount for Year 1 in the recipient's hands is $95 of ordinary income, $3 of capital gain income, and $2 of trust corpus. For Year 1, X satisfied paragraph (a)(1)(i)(g) of this section.

(j) *Payment under income exception.* When the unitrust amount is computed under paragraph (a)(1)(i)(b) of this section, a trust will not be deemed to have engaged in an act of self-dealing (within the meaning of section 4941), to have unrelated debt-financed income (within the meaning of section 514), to have received an additional contribution (within the meaning of paragraph (b) of this section), or to have failed to function exclusively as a charitable remainder trust (within the meaning of § 1.664–1(a)(4)) merely because payment of the unitrust amount is made after the close of the taxable year if such payment is made within a reasonable time after the close of such taxable year.

(k) *Reasonable time.* For paragraphs (a)(1)(i)(g), (h), and (j) of this section, a reasonable time will not ordinarily extend beyond the date by which the trustee is required to file Form 5227, "Split-Interest Trust Information Return," (including extensions) for the taxable year.

(*l*) *Effective date.* Paragraphs (a)(1)(i) (g), (h), (i), (j), and (k) of this section are applicable for taxable years ending after April 18, 1997. Paragraphs (a)(1)(i)(g)(2) and (3) apply only to distributions made on or after January 5, 2001.

(ii) *Definition of fixed percentage.* The fixed percentage may be expressed either as a fraction or as a percentage and must be payable each year in the period specified in subparagraph (5) of this paragraph. A percentage is fixed if the percentage is the same either as to each recipient or as to the total percentage payable each year of such period. For example, provision for a fixed percentage which is the same every year to A until his death and concurrently a fixed percentage which is the same every year to B until his death, the fixed percentage to each recipient to terminate at his death, would satisfy the rule. Similarly, provision for a fixed percentage to A and B for their joint lives and then to the survivor would satisfy the rule. In the case of a distribution to an organization described in section 170(c) at the death of a recipient or the expiration of a term of years, the governing instrument may provide for a reduction of the fixed percentage payable after such distribution Provided That:

(a) The reduced fixed percentage is the same either as to each recipient or as to the total amount payable for each year of the balance of such period, and

(b) The requirements of subparagraph (2)(ii) of this paragraph are met.

(iii) *Rules applicable to incorrect valuations.* The governing instrument provides that in the case where the net fair market value of the trust assets is incorrectly determined by the fiduciary, the trust shall pay to the recipient (in the case of an undervaluation) or be repaid by the recipient (in the case of an overvaluation) an amount equal to the difference between the amount which the trust should have paid the recipient if the correct value were used and the amount which the trust actually paid the recipient. Such payments or repayments must be made within a reasonable period after the final determination of such value. Any payment due to a recipient by reason of such incorrect valuation shall be considered to be a payment required to be distributed at the time of such final determination for purposes of paragraph (d)(4)(ii) of § 1.664–1. See paragraph (d)(4) of § 1.664–1 for rules relating to the year of inclusion of such payments and the allowance of a deduction for such repayments. See paragraph (b) of this section for rules relating to additional contributions.

(iv) *Rules applicable to valuation.* In computing the net fair market value of the trust assets there shall be taken into account all assets and liabilities without regard to whether particular items are taken into account in determining the income of the trust. The net fair market value of the trust assets may be determined on any one date during the taxable year of the trust, or by taking the average of valuations made on more than one date during the taxable year of the trust, so long as the same valuation date or dates and valuation methods are used each year. If the governing instrument does not specify the valuation date or dates, the trustee must select such date or dates and indicate the selection on the first return on Form 5227, "Split-Interest Trust Information Return," that the trust must file. The amount described in subdivision (i)(a) of this subparagraph which must be paid each year must be based upon the valuation for such year.

(v) *Computation of unitrust amount in certain circumstances.* (a) *Short taxable years.* The governing instrument provides that, in the case of a taxable year which is for a period of less than 12 months other than the taxable year in which occurs the end of the period specified in subparagraph (5) of this paragraph:

(1) The amount determined under subdivision (i)(a) of this subparagraph shall be the amount otherwise determined under that subdivision multiplied by a fraction the numerator of which is the number of days in the taxable year of the trust and the denominator of which is 365 (366 if February 29 is a day included in the numerator),

(2) The amount determined under subdivision (i)(b) of this subparagraph shall be computed by using the amount determined under subdivision (a)(1) of this subdivision (v), and

(3) If no valuation date occurs before the end of the taxable year of the trust, the trust assets shall be valued as of the last day of the taxable year of the trust.

(b) *Last taxable year of period.* (1) The governing instrument provides that, in the case of the taxable year in which occurs the end of the period specified in subparagraph (5) of this paragraph:

(i) The unitrust amount which must be distributed under subdivision (i)(a) of this subparagraph shall be the amount otherwise determined under that subdivision multiplied by a fraction the numerator of which is the number of days in the period beginning on the first day of such taxable year and ending on the last day of the period specified in subparagraph (5) of this paragraph and the denominator of which is 365 (366 if February 29 is a day included in the numerator),

(ii) The amount determined under subdivision (i)(b) of this subparagraph shall be computed by using the amount determined under (b)(1)(i) of this subdivision (v), and

(iii) If no valuation date occurs before the end of such period, the trust assets shall be valued as of the last day of such period.

(2) See subparagraph (5) of this paragraph for a special rule allowing termination of payment of the unitrust amount with the regular payment next preceding the termination of the period specified therein.

(2) *Minimum unitrust amount*—(i) *General rule.* The fixed percentage described in subparagraph (1)(i) of this paragraph with respect to all beneficiaries taken together is not less than 5 percent.

(ii) *Reduction of unitrust amount in certain cases.* A trust will not fail to meet the requirements of this subparagraph by reason of the fact that it provides for a reduction of the fixed percentage payable upon the death of a recipient or the expiration of a term of years Provided That:

(a) A distribution is made to an organization described in section 170(c) at the death of such recipient or the expiration of such term of years, and

(b) The total of the percentage payable under subparagraph (1) of this paragraph after such distribution is not less than 5 percent.

(3) *Permissible recipients.* (i) *General rule.* The amount described in subparagraph (1) of this paragraph is payable to or for the use of a named person or persons, at least one of which is not an organization described in section 170(c). If the amount described in subparagraph (1) of this paragraph is to be paid to an individual or individuals, all such individuals must be living at the time of creation of the trust. A named person or persons may include members of a named class except in the case of a class which includes any individual, all such individuals must be alive and ascertainable at the time of the creation of the trust unless the period for which the unitrust amount is to be paid to such class consists solely of a term of years. For example, in the case of a testamentary trust, the testator's will may provide that the required amount shall be paid to his children living at his death.

(ii) *Power to alter amount paid to recipients.* A trust is not a charitable remainder unitrust if any person has the power to alter the amount to be paid to any named person other than an organization described in section 170(c) if such power would cause any person to be treated as the owner of the trust, or any portion thereof, if Subpart E, Part 1, Subchapter J, Chapter 1, Subtitle A of the Code were applicable to such trust. See paragraph (a)(4) of this section for a rule permitting the retention by a grantor of a testamentary power to revoke or terminate the interest of any recipient other than an organization described in section 170(c). For example, the governing instrument may not grant the trustee the power to allocate the fixed percentage among members of a class unless such power falls within one of the exceptions to section 674(a).

(4) *Other payments*. No amount other than the amount described in subparagraph (1) of this paragraph may be paid to or for the use of any person other than an organization described in section 170(c). An amount is not paid to or for the use of any person other than an organization described in section 170(c) if the amount is transferred for full and adequate consideration. The trust may not be subject to a power to invade, alter, amend, or revoke for the beneficial use of a person other than an organization described in section 170(c). Notwithstanding the preceding sentence, the grantor may retain the power exercisable only by will to revoke or terminate the interest of any recipient other than an organization described in section 170(c). The governing instrument may provide that any amount other than the amount described in subparagraph (1) of this paragraph shall be paid (or may be paid in the discretion of the trustee) to an organization described in section 170(c) provided that, in the case of distributions in kind, the adjusted basis of the property distributed is fairly representative of the adjusted basis of the property available for payment on the date of payment. For example, the governing instrument may provide that a portion of the trust assets may be distributed currently, or upon the death of one or more recipients, to an organization described in section 170(c).

(5) *Period of payment of unitrust amount*. (i) *General rules*. The period for which an amount described in subparagraph (1) of this paragraph is payable begins with the first year of the charitable remainder trust and continues either for the life or lives of a named individual or individuals or for a term of years not to exceed 20 years. Only an individual or an organization described in section 170(c) may receive an amount for the life of an individual. If an individual receives an amount for life, it must be solely for his life. Payment of the amount described in subparagraph (1) of this paragraph may terminate with the regular payment next preceding the termination of the period described in this subparagraph. The fact that the recipient may not receive such last payment shall not be taken into account for purposes of determining the present value of the remainder interest. In the case of an amount payable for a term of years, the length of the term of years shall be ascertainable with certainty at the time of the creation of the trust, except that the term may be terminated by the death of the recipient or by the grantor's exercise by will of a retained power to revoke or terminate the interest of any recipient other than an organization described in section 170(c). In any event, the period may not extend beyond either the life or lives of a named individual or individuals or a term of years not to exceed 20 years. For example, the governing instrument may not provide for the payment of a unitrust amount to A for his life and then to B for a term of years because it is possible for the period to last longer than either the lives of recipients in being at the creation of the trust or a term of years not to exceed 20 years. On the other hand, the governing instrument may provide for the payment of a unitrust amount to A for his life and then to B for his life or a term of years (not to exceed 20 years), whichever is shorter (but not longer), if both A and B are in being at the creation of the trust because it is not possible for the period to last longer than the lives of recipients in being at the creation of the trust.

(ii) *Relationship to 5 percent requirement*. The 5 percent requirement provided in subparagraph (2) of this paragraph must be met until the termination of all of the payments described in subparagraph (1) of this paragraph. For example, the following provisions would satisfy the above rules:

(a) A fixed percentage of at least 5 percent to A and B for their joint lives and then to the survivor for his life;

(b) A fixed percentage of at least 5 percent to A for life or for a term of years not longer than 20 years, whichever is longer (or shorter);

(c) A fixed percentage of at least 5 percent to A for life or for a term of years not longer than 20 years and then to B for life (provided B was living at the creation of the trust);

(d) A fixed percentage to A for his life and concurrently a fixed percentage to B for his life (the percentage to each recipient to terminate at his death) if the percentage given to each individual is not less than 5 percent;

(e) A fixed percentage to A for his life and concurrently an equal percentage to B for his life, and at the death of the first to die, the trust to distribute one-half of the then value of its assets to an organization described in section 170(c) if the total of the percentages is not less than 5 percent for the entire period described in this subparagraph.

(6) *Permissible remaindermen.* (i) *General rule.* At the end of the period specified in subparagraph (5) of this paragraph, the entire corpus of the trust is required to be irrevocably transferred, in whole or in part, to or for the use of one or more organizations described in section 170(c) or retained, in whole or in part, for such use.

(ii) *Treatment of trust.* If all of the trust corpus is to be retained for such use, the taxable year of the trust shall terminate at the end of the period specified in subparagraph (5) of this paragraph and the trust shall cease to be treated as a charitable remainder trust for all purposes. If all or any portion of the trust corpus is to be transferred to or for the use of such organization or organizations, the trustee shall have a reasonable time after the period specified in subparagraph (5) of this paragraph to complete the settlement of the trust. During such time, the trust shall continue to be treated as a charitable remainder trust for all purposes, such as section 664, 4947(a)(2), and 4947(b)(3)(B). Upon the expiration of such period, the taxable year of the trust shall terminate and the trust shall cease to be treated as a charitable remainder trust for all purposes. If the trust continues in existence, it will be subject to the provisions of section 4947(a)(1) unless the trust is exempt from taxation under section 501(a). For purposes of determining whether the trust is exempt under section 501(a) as an organization described in section 501(c)(3), the trust shall be deemed to have been created at the time it ceases to be treated as a charitable remainder trust.

(iii) *Concurrent or successive remaindermen.* Where interests in the corpus of the trust are given to more than one organization described in section 170(c) such interests may be enjoyed by them either concurrently or successively.

(iv) *Alternative remaindermen.* The governing instrument shall provide that if an organization to or for the use of which the trust corpus is to be transferred or for the use of which the trust corpus is to be retained is not an organization described in section 170(c) at the time any amount is to be irrevocably transferred to or for the use of such organization, such amount shall be transferred to or for the use of or retained for the use of one or more alternative organizations which are described in section 170(c) at such time. Such alternative organization or organizations may be selected in any manner provided by the terms of the governing instrument.

(b) Additional contributions. A trust is not a charitable remainder annuity trust unless its governing instrument either prohibits additional contributions to the trust after the initial contribution or provides that for the taxable year of the trust in which the additional contribution is made:

(1) Where no valuation date occurs after the time of the contribution and during the taxable year in which the contribution is made, the additional property shall be valued as of the time of contribution; and

(2) The amount described in paragraph (a)(1)(i)(a) of this section shall be computed by multiplying the fixed percentage by the sum of (i) the net fair market value of the trust assets (excluding the value of the additional property and any earned income from and any appreciation on such property after its contribution), and (ii) that proportion of the value of the additional property (that was excluded under subdivision (i) of this paragraph), which the number of days in the period which begins with the date of contribution and ends with the earlier of the last day of such taxable year or the last day of the period described in paragraph (a)(5) of this section bears to the number of days in the period which begins with the first day of such taxable year and ends with the earlier of the last day of such taxable year or the last day of the period described in paragraph (a)(5) of this section.

For purposes of this section, all property passing to a charitable remainder unitrust by reason of death of the grantor shall be considered one contribution. The application of the preceding rules may be illustrated by the following examples:

Example (1). On March 2, 1971, X makes an additional contribution of property to a charitable remainder unitrust. The taxable year of the trust is the calendar year and the regular valuation date is January 1 of each year. For purposes of computing the required payout with respect to the additional contribution for the year of contribution, the additional contribution is valued on March 2, 1971, the time of contribution. The property had a value on that date of $5,000. Income from such property in the amount of $250 was received on December 31, 1971. The required payout with respect to the additional contribution for the year of contribution is $208 (5 percent x $5,000 x 305/365). The income earned after the date of the contribution and after the regular valuation date does not enter into the computation.

Example (2). On July 1, 1971, X makes an additional contribution of $10,000 to a charitable remainder unitrust. The taxable year of the trust is the calendar year and the regular valuation date is December 31 of each year. The fixed percentage is 5 percent. Between July 1, 1971, and December 31, 1971, the additional property appreciates in value to $12,500 and earns $500 of income. Because the regular valuation date for the year of contribution occurs after the date of the additional contribution, the additional contribution including income earned by it is valued on the regular valuation date. Thus, the required payout with respect to the additional contribution is $325.87 (5 percent x [$12,500+$500] x 183/365).

(c) Calculation of the fair market value of the remainder interest of a charitable remainder unitrust. See § 1.664–4 for rules relating to the calculation of the fair market value of the remainder interest of a charitable remainder unitrust.

(d) Deduction for transfers to a charitable remainder unitrust. For rules relating to a deduction for transfers to a charitable remainder unitrust, see sections 170, 2055, 2106, or 2522 and the regulations thereunder. The deduction allowed by section 170 for transfers to charity is limited to the fair market value of the remainder interest of a charitable remainder unitrusts regardless of whether an organization described in section 170(c) also receives a portion of the amount described in § 1.664–3(a)(1). For a special rule relating to the reduction of the amount of a charitable contribution deduction with respect to a contribution of certain ordinary income property or capital gain property, see section 170(e)(1)(A) or (B)(i) and the regulations thereunder. For rules for postponing the time for deduction of a charitable contribution of a future interest in tangible personal property, see section 170(a)(3) and the regulations thereunder.

[T.D. 7202, 37 FR 16920, Aug. 23, 1972; T.D. 8791, 63 FR 68192, Dec. 10, 1998; T.D. 8926, 66 FR 1038, Jan. 5, 2001; T.D. 9102, 69 FR 20, Jan. 2, 2004]

§ 1.664–4 Calculation of the fair market value of the remainder interest in a charitable remainder unitrust.

(a) Rules for determining present value. For purposes of sections 170, 2055, 2106, and 2522, the fair market value of a remainder interest in a charitable remainder unitrust (as described in § 1.664–3) is its present value determined under paragraph (d) of this section. The present value determined under this section shall be computed on the basis of—

(1) Life contingencies determined as to each life involved, from the values of lx set forth in Table 2010CM in § 20.2031–7(d)(7)(ii) of this chapter in the case of transfers for which the valuation date is on or after June 1, 2023; or from Table 2000CM contained in § 20.2031–7A(g)(4) of this chapter in the case of transfers for which the valuation date is on or after May 1, 2009, and before June 1, 2023. See § 20.2031–7A(a) through (f) of this chapter, whichever is applicable, for transfers for which the valuation date is before May 1, 2009;

(2) *Interest at the section 7520 rate in the case of transfers for which the valuation date is after April 30, 1989, or 10 percent in the case of transfers to charitable remainder unitrusts made after November 30, 1983, for which the valuation date is before May 1, 1989*. See § 20.2031–7A (a) through (c) of this chapter, whichever is applicable, for transfers for which the valuation date is before December 1, 1983; and

(3) *The assumption that the amount described in § 1.664–3(a)(1)(i)(a) is distributed in accordance with the payout sequence described in the governing instrument*. If the governing instrument does not prescribe when the distribution is made during the period for which the payment is made, for purposes of this section, the distribution is considered payable on the first day of the period for which the payment is made.

(b) Actuarial computations by the Internal Revenue Service. The regulations in this and in related sections provide tables of actuarial factors and examples that illustrate the use of the tables in determining the value of remainder interests in property. Section 1.7520–1(c)(2) refers to government publications that provide additional tables of factors and examples of computations for more complex situations. If the computation requires the use of a factor that is not provided in this section, the Commissioner may supply the factor upon a request for a ruling. A request for a ruling must be accompanied by a recitation of the facts including the date of birth of each measuring life, and copies of the relevant documents. A request for a ruling must comply with the instructions for requesting a ruling published periodically in the Internal Revenue Bulletin (See § 601.601(d)(2)(ii)(b) of this chapter) and include payment of the required user fee. If the Commissioner furnishes the factor, a copy of the letter supplying the factor should be attached to the tax return in which the deduction is claimed. If the Commissioner does not furnish the factor, the taxpayer must furnish a factor computed in accordance with the principles set forth in this section.

(c) Statement supporting deduction required. Any claim for a deduction on any return for the value of a remainder interest in a charitable remainder unitrust must be supported by a full statement attached to the return showing the computation of the present value of such interest.

(d) Valuation. The fair market value of a remainder interest in a charitable remainder unitrust (as described in § 1.664–3) for transfers for which the valuation date is on or after June 1, 2023, is its present value determined under paragraph (e) of this section. The fair market value of a remainder interest in a charitable remainder unitrust (as described in § 1.664–3) for transfers for which the valuation date is before June 1, 2023, is its present value determined under the following sections:

Valuation Dates		*Applicable Regulations*
After	*Before*	
—	01-01-52	§ 1.642(c)–6A(a)
12-31-51	01-01-71	§ 1.642(c)–6A(b)
12-31-70	12-01-83	§ 1.642(c)–6A(c)
11-30-83	05-01-89	§ 1.642(c)–6A(d)
04-30-89	05-01-99	§ 1.642(c)–6A(e)
04-30-99	05-01-09	§ 1.642(c)–6A(f)
04-30-09	06-01-23	§ 1.642(c)–6A(g)

(e) Valuation of charitable remainder unitrusts having certain payout sequences for transfers for which the valuation date is on or after June 1, 2023

(1) *In general.* Except as otherwise provided in paragraph (e)(2) of this section, in the case of transfers for which the valuation date is on or after June 1, 2023, the present value of a remainder interest is determined under paragraphs (e)(3) through (7) of this section, provided that, in a short taxable year, the trustee must prorate the unitrust amount as provided in § 1.664–3(a)(1)(v). See, however, § 1.7520–3(b) (relating to exceptions to the use of the prescribed tables under certain circumstances).

(2) *Transitional rule for valuation of charitable remainder unitrusts.* For purposes of section 170, 2055, 2106, 2522, or 2624, in the case of transfers to a charitable remainder unitrust for which the valuation date is after April 30, 2019, and on or before June 1, 2023, the present value of a remainder interest based on one or more measuring lives is determined under this section by using the section 7520 interest rate for the month in which the valuation date occurs (see §§ 1.7520–1(b) and 1.7520–2(a)(2)) and the appropriate actuarial factors derived from the selected mortality table, either Table 2010CM in § 20.2031–7(d)(7)(ii) of this chapter or Table 2000CM in § 20.2031–7A(g)(4) of this chapter, at the option of the donor or the decedent's executor, as the case may be. If any previously filed income tax return is amended to use the actuarial factors based on Table 2010CM, the amended return must state at the top "AMENDED PURSUANT TO TD 9974." If any previously filed gift or estate tax return is supplemented to use the actuarial factors based on Table 2010CM, the supplemental return must state at the top "SUPPLEMENTED PURSUANT TO TD 9974." For the convenience of taxpayers, actuarial factors based on Table 2010CM appear in the current version of Table U(1), and actuarial factors based on Table 2000CM appear in the previous version of Table U(1). Both versions of Table U(1) currently are available, at no charge, electronically via the IRS website at *https://www.irs.gov/retirement-plans/actuarial-tables* (or a corresponding URL as may be updated from time to time). The donor or decedent's executor must consistently use the same mortality basis with respect to each interest (income, remainder, partial, etc.) in the same property, and with respect to all transfers occurring on the same valuation date. For example, gift and income tax charitable deductions with respect to the same transfer must be determined based on factors with the same mortality basis, and all assets includible

in the gross estate and/or estate tax deductions claimed must be valued based on factors with the same mortality basis.

(3) *Adjusted payout rate*. For transfers for which the valuation date is after April 30, 1989, the adjusted payout rate is determined by using the appropriate Table F in paragraph (e)(6) of this section, for the section 7520 interest rate applicable to the transfer. If the interest rate is between 4.2 and 14 percent, see paragraph (e)(6) of this section. If the interest rate is below 4.2 percent or greater than 14 percent, see paragraph (b) of this section. The adjusted payout rate is determined by multiplying the fixed percentage described in § 1.664–3(a)(1)(i)(a) by the factor describing the payout sequence of the trust and the number of months by which the valuation date for the first full taxable year of the trust precedes the first payout date for such taxable year. If the governing instrument does not prescribe when the distribution or distributions shall be made during the taxable year of the trust, see paragraph (a) of this section. In the case of a trust having a payout sequence for which no figures have been provided by the appropriate table, and in the case of a trust that determines the fair market value of the trust assets by taking the average of valuations on more than one date during the taxable year, see paragraph (b) of this section.

(4) *Period is a term of years*. If the period described in § 1.664–3(a)(5) is a term of years, the factor that is used in determining the present value of the remainder interest for transfers for which the valuation date is after November 30, 1983, is the factor under the appropriate adjusted payout rate in Table D of paragraph (e)(6) of this section corresponding to the number of years in the term. If the adjusted payout rate is an amount that is between adjusted payout rates for which factors are provided in Table D, a linear interpolation must be made. The present value of the remainder interest is determined by multiplying the net fair market value (as of the appropriate valuation date) of the property placed in trust by the factor determined under this paragraph. For purposes of this section, the valuation date is, in the case of an inter vivos transfer, the date on which the property is transferred to the trust by the donor. However, if an election is made under section 7520 and § 1.7520–2(b) to compute the present value of the charitable interest by use of the interest rate component for either of the 2 months preceding the month in which the date of transfer falls, the month so elected is the valuation date for purposes of determining the interest rate and mortality tables. In the case of a testamentary transfer under section 2055, 2106, or 2624, the valuation date is the date of death, unless the alternate valuation date is elected under section 2032, in which event, and within the limitations set forth in section 2032 and the regulations thereunder, the valuation date is the alternate valuation date. If the decedent's estate elects the alternate valuation date under section 2032 and also elects, under section 7520 and § 1.7520–2(b), to use the interest rate component for one of the 2 months preceding the alternate valuation date, the month so elected is the valuation date for purposes of determining the interest rate and mortality tables. The application of this paragraph (e)(4) may be illustrated by the following example:

Example. D transfers $100,000 to a charitable remainder unitrust on January 1. The trust instrument requires that the trust pay 8 percent of the fair market value of the trust assets as of January 1st for a term of 12 years to D in quarterly payments (March 31, June 30, September 30, and December 31). The section 7520 rate for January (the month that the transfer occurred) is 9.6 percent. Under Table F(9.6) in paragraph (e)(6) of this section, the appropriate adjustment factor is .944628 for quarterly payments payable at the end of each quarter. The adjusted payout rate is 7.557 (8% * .944628). Based on the remainder factors in Table D in paragraph (e)(6) of this section, the present value of the remainder interest is $38,950.30, computed as follows:

Factor at 7.4 percent for 12 years	0.397495
Factor at 7.6 percent for 12 years	0.387314
Difference	0.010181

Interpolation adjustment:

$$\frac{7.55\% - 7.4\%}{0.2\%} = \frac{x}{0.010181}$$

$$x = 0.007992$$

Factor at 7.4 percent for 12 years	0.397495
Less: Interpolation adjustment	0.007992
Interpolated factor	0.389503
Present value of remainder interest: ($ 100,000 * .389503)	$38,950.30

(5) *Period is the life of one individual* (i) *Factor*. If the period described in § 1.664–3(a)(5) is the life of one individual, the factor that is used in determining the present value of the remainder interest for transfers for which the valuation date is on or after June 1, 2023, is the factor obtained through the use of the formula in Figure 1 to this paragraph (e)(5)(i) to at least five decimal places. The prescribed mortality table is Table 2010CM as set forth in § 20.2031–7(d)(7)(ii) of this chapter, or for periods before June 1, 2023, the appropriate table found in § 20.2031–7A of this chapter. Table 2010CM is referenced by IRS Publication 1458, Actuarial Values Version 4B. The mortality tables prescribed for periods before June 1, 2023, are referenced by prior versions of IRS Publication 1458. Alternatively, the remainder factors have been determined for the convenience of taxpayers and appear in Table U(1) under the appropriate adjusted payout rate. Table U(1) currently is available, at no charge, electronically via the IRS website at *https://www.irs.gov/retirement-plans/actuarial-tables* (or a corresponding URL as may be updated from time to time). Table U(1) is referenced and explained by IRS Publication 1458, Actuarial Valuations Version 4B, which will be available within a reasonable time after June 1, 2023. For purposes of the computations described in this paragraph (e)(5), the age of an individual is the age of that individual at the individual's nearest birthday. If the adjusted payout rate is an amount that is between adjusted payout rates for which factors are provided in the appropriate table, an exact method of obtaining the applicable remainder factors (such as through software using the actual adjusted payout rate and the actuarial formula in this paragraph (e)(5)) or a linear interpolation must be used, provided whichever method used is applied consistently in valuing all interests in the same property. The applicable remainder factors derived by an exact method or by interpolation must be expressed to at least five decimal places. The present value of the remainder interest is determined by multiplying the net fair market value (as of the valuation date as determined in § 1.664–4(e)(4)) of the property placed in trust by the factor determined under this paragraph (e)(5). If the adjusted payout rate is from 0.2 to 20.0 percent, inclusive, taxpayers may see the actuarial tables referenced and explained by IRS Publication 1458, Actuarial Valuations Version 4B. Alternatively, the Commissioner may supply a factor upon a request for a ruling. See paragraph (b) of this section.

Figure 1 to paragraph (e)(5)(i) – Formula for determining unitrust remainder factors

$$\left(1+\frac{i}{2}\right)\sum_{t=0}^{\infty} v^{t+1}\left({}_{t+1}q_x - {}_{t}q_x\right)$$

where:

r = the adjusted payout rate;

v = 1 - r;

i = r / (1 – r)

$${}_{t}q_x = 1 - \frac{l_{x+t}}{l_x} \;;$$

x = the age of the measuring life (determined as age at nearest birthday); and

l_x = the number associated with age x as set forth in the prescribed mortality table, representing the number of persons alive at age x.

(ii) *Sample factors from actuarial Table U(1)*. For purposes of the example in paragraph (e)(5)(iii) of this section, the following factors from Table U(1) and Table F(3.2) (see paragraph (e)(6)(ii) of this section) will be used:

Factors from Table U(1)—Based on Table 2010CM			
Adjusted Payout Rate			
Age	4.8%	5.0%	5.2%
77	0.61491	0.60343	0.59223
Factors from Table F(3.2)			
Factors for Computing Adjusted Payout Rates for Unitrusts			
Interest at 3.2 Percent			
# of Months from Annual Valuation to First Payout		Adjustment Factors for Payments at End of Period	
At Least	But Less Than	Annual	Semiannual
6	7	0.984374	0.976683

(iii) *Example of interpolation.* After June 1, 2023, A, whose age is 76 years and 11 months, transfers $100,000 to a charitable remainder unitrust on January 1st. The trust instrument requires that the trust pay to A semiannually (on June 30 and December 31) 5 percent of the fair market value of the trust assets as of January 1st during A's life. The section 7520 rate for January is 3.2 percent. Under Table F(3.2), the appropriate adjustment factor is 0.976683 for semiannual payments payable at the end of the semiannual period. The adjusted payout rate is 4.883% (5% x 0.976683). Based on interpolating between the remainder factors in Table U(1), the present value of the remainder interest is $61,015, computed as illustrated in Figure 2 to this paragraph (e)(5)(iii).

Figure 2 to paragraph (e)(5)(iii) – Illustration of unitrust interpolation method

A.	Table U(1) Factor at 4.8 percent for age 77	0.61491
B.	Less: Table U(1) Factor at 5.0 percent for age 77	- 0.60343
C.	Difference: A - B	0.01148

D. Interpolation Adjustment:

$$\frac{4.883\% - 4.80\%}{5.0\% - 4.80\%} = \frac{z}{0.01148}$$

E.

$$\frac{4.883\% - 4.80\%}{5.0\% - 4.80\%} \cdot 0.01148 = z = 0.00476$$

F.	Table U(1) Factor at 4.8 percent for age 77	0.61491
G.	Less: Interpolation Adjustment z	- 0.00476
H.	Interpolated Factor: F - G	0.61015
I.	Amount Transferred	$ 100,000
J.	Present Value of Remainder Interest: H x I	$ 61,015

(6) *Actuarial Table D and Tables F(0.2) through F(20.0) for transfers for which the valuation date is on or after May 1, 1989* (i) *Remainder factors for charitable remainder unitrusts.* For transfers for which the valuation date is on or after May 1, 1989, the present value of a charitable remainder unitrust interest that is dependent upon a term of years is determined by using the formula in Figure 3 to this paragraph (e)(6)(i) and calculating the final result to at least six decimal places. For the convenience of taxpayers, actuarial factors have been computed by the IRS and appear in Table D. Table D can be found on the IRS website at *https://*

www.irs.gov/retirement-plans/actuarial-tables (or a corresponding URL as may be updated from time to time). Table D is referenced and explained in IRS Publication 1458, Actuarial Valuations Version 4B, which will be available within a reasonable time after June 1, 2023. The remainder factors from Table D also can be found in paragraph (e)(6)(iii) of this section, but only for adjusted payout rates from 4.2 to 14 percent, inclusive. For transfers for which the valuation date is on or after June 1, 2023, where the present value of a charitable remainder unitrust interest is dependent on the termination of a life interest, see paragraph (e)(5) of this section. See, however, § 1.7520–3(b) (relating to exceptions to the use of prescribed tables under certain circumstances).

Figure 3 to Paragraph (e)(6)(i)—Formula for Determining Term Certain Unitrust Remainder Factors

$(1 - r)^n$

where:

n = the term in years or fractions of a year, and

r = the adjusted payout rate

(ii) *Unitrust payout rate adjustment factors*. For transfers for which the valuation date is on or after May 1, 1989, the unitrust payout rate adjustment factors are determined by using the formula in Figure 4 to this paragraph (e)(6)(ii) and calculating the final result to at least six decimal places. For the convenience of taxpayers, actuarial factors have been computed by the IRS, for interest rates from 0.2 to 20 percent, inclusive, and appear in Tables F(0.2) through F(20.0). Tables F(0.2) through F(20.0) can be found on the IRS website at *https://www.irs.gov/retirement-plans/actuarial-tables* (or a corresponding URL as may be updated from time to time). Tables F(0.2) through F(20.0) are referenced and explained in IRS Publication 1458, Actuarial Valuations Version 4B, which will be available within a reasonable time after June 1, 2023. The factors from Table F also can be found in paragraph (e)(6)(iii) of this section, but only for interest rates from 4.2 to 14 percent, inclusive.

Figure 4 to paragraph (e)(6)(ii) – Formula for determining unitrust payout rate adjustment factors

$$\frac{(1+i)^{(1/p)} \cdot i \cdot v^{(d/12)}}{p\,(1+i)[(1+i)^{(1/p)} - 1]}$$

where:

p = the number of payments per year;

i = the applicable interest rate under section 7520 of the Internal Revenue Code;

v = 1 / (1 + i) ; and

d = the number of months between the annual valuation date and the regular first payout date of a standard full year of the trust.

(iii) Table D and Tables F(4.2) through F(14.0). The unitrust remainder factors from Table D, for interest rates from 4.2 to 14 percent, inclusive, and the unitrust payout factors from Tables F(4.2) through F(14.0) are as follows:

[*Tables D and F omitted. Ed.* Tables D and F can be found in "*Publication 1458: Unitrust Factors*" at *http://www.irs.gov/Retirement-Plans/Actuarial-Tables*].

(7) *Actuarial Table U(1) for transfers for which the valuation date is on or after June 1, 2023*. The present value of a remainder interest in a charitable remainder unitrust that is dependent on the termination of a life interest is determined by using the section 7520 rate, Tables F(0.2) through (20.0) (see paragraph (e)(6)(ii) of this section), and the formula in paragraph (e)(5)(i) of this section to derive a remainder factor from the appropriate mortality table to at least five decimal places. For the convenience of taxpayers, actuarial

factors have been computed by the IRS and appear in Table U(1). For transfers for which the valuation date is on or after June 1, 2023, the actuarial tables are currently available, at no charge, electronically via the IRS website at *https://www.irs.gov/retirement-plans/actuarial-tables*. These actuarial tables are referenced and explained by IRS Publication 1458, Actuarial Valuations Version 4B (2023). This publication will be available within a reasonable time after June 1, 2023. See, however, § 1.7520–3(b) (relating to exceptions to the use of prescribed tables under certain circumstances).

(f) Applicability date. This section applies on and after June 1, 2023.

[T.D. 7202, 37 FR 16922, Aug. 23, 1972; 38 FR 12918, May 17, 1973; 38 FR 14370, June 1, 1973; T.D. 7955, 49 FR 19983, May 11, 1984; T.D. 8540, 59 FR 30102, 30117, June 10, 1994; T.D. 8819, 64 FR 23200, April 30, 1999; T.D. 8886, 65 FR 36919, 36943, June 12, 2000; T.D. 9448, 74 FR 21465, May 7, 2009; T.D. 9540, 76 FR 49595, 49612, Aug. 10, 2011; T.D. 9974, 88 FR 37433, June 7, 2023]

§ 1.664–4A Valuation of charitable remainder interests for which the valuation date is before June 1, 2023.

(a) Valuation of charitable remainder interests for which the valuation date is before January 1, 1952. [*Omitted. Ed.*]

(b) Valuation of charitable remainder interests for which the valuation date is after December 31, 1951, and before January 1, 1971. [*Omitted. Ed.*]

(c) Valuation of charitable remainder unitrusts having certain payout sequences for transfers for which the valuation date is after December 31, 1970, and before December 1, 1983. [*Omitted. Ed.*]

(d) Valuation of charitable remainder unitrusts having certain payout sequences for transfers for which the valuation date is after November 30, 1983, and before May 1, 1989. [*Omitted. Ed.*]

(e) Valuation of charitable remainder unitrusts having certain payout sequences for transfers for which the valuation date is after April 30, 1989, and before May 1, 1999. [*Omitted. Ed.*]

(f) Valuation of charitable remainder unitrusts having certain payout sequences for transfers for which the valuation date is after April 30, 1999, and before May 1, 2009. [*Omitted. Ed.*]

(g) Valuation of charitable remainder unitrusts having certain payout sequences for transfers for which the valuation date is on or after May 1, 2009, and before June 1, 2023 (1) *In general.* Except as otherwise provided in paragraph (g)(2) of this section, in the case of transfers for which the valuation date is on or after May 1, 2009, and before June 1, 2023, the present value of a remainder interest is determined under paragraphs (g)(3) through (6) of this section, provided that the amount of the payout as of any payout date during any taxable year of the trust is not larger than the amount that the trust could distribute on such date under § 1.664–3(a)(1)(v) if the taxable year of the trust were to end on such date. See, however, § 1.7520–3(b) (relating to exceptions to the use of the prescribed tables under certain circumstances).

(2) *Transitional rules for valuation of charitable remainder unitrusts.* (i) For purposes of section 2055, 2106, or 2624, if on May 1, 2009, the decedent was under a mental disability so that the disposition of the property could not be changed, and the decedent died on or after May 1, 2009, but before June 2, 2023, without having regained the ability to dispose of the decedent's property, or if the decedent died within 90 days of the date that the decedent first regained that ability on or after May 1, 2009, but before June 2, 2023, the present value of a remainder interest under this section is determined as if the valuation date with respect to the decedent's gross estate is either before May 1, 2009, or after April 30, 2009, at the option of the decedent's executor.

(ii) For purposes of section 170, 2055, 2106, 2522, or 2624, in the case of transfers to a charitable remainder unitrust for which the valuation date is on or after May 1, 2009, and before July 1, 2009, the present value of a remainder interest based on one or more measuring lives is determined under this section by using the section 7520 interest rate for the month in which the valuation date occurs (see §§ 1.7520–1(b) and 1.7520–2(a)(2)) and the appropriate actuarial tables under either paragraph (f)(6) or (g)(6) of this section, at the option of the donor or the decedent's executor, as the case may be.

(iii) For purposes of paragraphs (g)(2)(i) and (ii) of this section, where the donor or decedent's executor is given the option to use the appropriate actuarial tables under either paragraph (f)(6) or (g)(6) of this section, the donor or decedent's executor must consistently use the same mortality basis with respect to each interest (income, remainder, partial, etc.) in the same property, and with respect to all transfers occurring on the same valuation date. For example, gift and income tax charitable deductions with respect to the same transfer must be determined based on factors with the same mortality basis, and all assets includible in the gross estate and/or estate tax deductions claimed must be valued based on factors with the same mortality basis.

(iv) In the case of transfers to a charitable remainder unitrust for which the valuation date is after April 30, 2019, and before June 1, 2023, the present value of the remainder interest under this section is determined under § 1.664(c)–4(e)(2).

(3) *Adjusted payout rate.* The adjusted payout rate is determined by applying the formula in § 1.664–4(e)(6)(ii) for the section 7520 interest rate applicable to the transfer to derive a factor and calculating the final result to at least six decimal places. For the convenience of taxpayers, actuarial factors have been computed by the IRS, for interest rates from 0.2 to 20 percent, inclusive, and appear in Tables F(0.2) through F(20.0). Tables F(0.2) through F(20.0) can be found on the IRS website at *https://www.irs.gov/retirement-plans/actuarial-tables* (or a corresponding URL as may be updated from time to time). Tables F(0.2) through F(20.0) are referenced and explained in IRS Publication 1458, Actuarial Valuations Version 3B. The payout adjustment factors from Table F can also be found in § 1.664–4(e)(6)(iii), but only for interest rates from 4.2 to 14 percent, inclusive. Alternatively, the Commissioner may supply a factor upon a request for a ruling. See § 1.664–4(b). See § 1.664–4(e) for rules applicable in determining the adjusted payout rate.

(4) *Period is a term of years.* If the period described in § 1.664–3(a)(5) is a term of years, the factor that is used in determining the present value of the remainder interest is determined by applying the formula in § 1.664–4(e)(6)(i) under the appropriate adjusted payout rate corresponding to the number of years in the term and calculating the final result to at least six decimal places. For the convenience of taxpayers, actuarial factors have been computed by the IRS and appear in Table D. Table D can be found on the IRS website at *https://www.irs.gov/retirement-plans/actuarial-tables* (or a corresponding URL as may be updated from time to time). Table D is referenced and explained in IRS Publication 1458, Actuarial Valuations Version 3B. The remainder factors from Table D also can be found in § 1.664–4(e)(6)(iii), but only for adjusted payout rates from 4.2 to 14 percent, inclusive. If the adjusted payout rate is a percentage that is between the adjusted payout rate for which factors are provided by Table D, an exact method of obtaining the applicable remainder factors (such as through software using the actual rate of return and the actuarial formula provided in § 1.664–4(e)(6)(i)) or a linear interpolation must be used, provided whichever method used is applied consistently in valuing all interests in the same property. The applicable remainder factors derived by an exact method or by interpolation must be expressed to at least six decimal places. The present value of the remainder interest is determined by multiplying the net fair market value (as of the appropriate valuation date) of the property placed in trust by the factor determined under this paragraph (g)(4). Generally, for purposes of this section, the valuation date is, in the case of an inter vivos transfer, the date on which the property is transferred to the trust by the donor, and, in the case of a testamentary transfer under section 2055, 2106, or 2624, the valuation date is the date of death. See § 1.664–4(e)(4) for additional rules regarding the valuation date, and for an example that illustrates the application of this paragraph (g)(4).

(5) *Period is the life of one individual.* If the period described in § 1.664–3(a)(5) is the life of one individual, the factor that is used in determining the present value of the remainder interest for transfers for which the valuation date is on or after May 1, 2009, and before June 1, 2023, may be computed directly by using the formula in § 1.664–4(e)(5)(i) to derive a remainder factor from the appropriate mortality table and calculating the final result to at least five decimal places. For the convenience of taxpayers, actuarial factors have been computed by the IRS and appear in Table U(1). Table U(1) can be found on the IRS website at *https://www.irs.gov/retirement-plans/actuarial-tables* (or a corresponding URL as may be updated from time to time). Table U(1) is referenced and explained in IRS Publication 1458, Actuarial Valuations Version 3B. The remainder factors from Table U(1) also can be found in paragraph (g)(6) of this section, but only

for adjusted payout rates from 4.2 to 14 percent, inclusive. For purposes of the computations described in this paragraph (g)(5), the age of an individual is the age of that individual at the individual's nearest birthday. If the adjusted payout rate is a percentage that is between the adjusted payout rate for which factors are provided by Table U(1), an exact method of obtaining the applicable factors (such as through software using the actual rate of return and the actuarial formula provided in § 1.664–4(e)(5)(i)) or a linear interpolation must be used, provided whichever method used is applied consistently in valuing all interests in the same property. The applicable remainder factors derived by an exact method or by interpolation must be expressed to at least five decimal places. The rules provided in § 1.664–4(e)(5) apply for determining the present value of the remainder interest. See § 1.664–4(e)(5) for an example illustrating the application of this paragraph (g)(5) (using current actuarial tables).

(6) *Actuarial Table U(1) for transfers for which the valuation date is on or after May 1, 2009, and before June 1, 2023.* For transfers for which the valuation date is on or after May 1, 2009, and before June 1, 2023, and without regard to the headings in the tables in this paragraph (g)(6) that do not contain this termination date for the applicability of the tables, the present value of a charitable remainder unitrust interest that is dependent on the termination of a life interest is determined by using the section 7520 rate, Table U(1) in this paragraph (g)(6), and Tables F(4.2) through F(14.0) in § 1.664–4(e)(6)(iii). See, however, § 1.7520–3(b) (relating to exceptions to the use of prescribed tables under certain circumstances). Actuarial factors that do not appear in the following tables may be computed directly by using the formula in § 1.664–4(e)(5)(i) to derive remainder factors from the appropriate mortality table and calculating the result to at least five decimal places. For the convenience of taxpayers, actuarial factors have been computed by the IRS and appear in Table U(1) that is referenced and explained by IRS Publication 1458, Actuarial Valuations Version 3B (2009). The table is available at no charge, electronically via the IRS website at *https://www.irs.gov/retirement-plans/actuarial-tables* (or a corresponding URL as may be updated from time to time).

[*"Table U(1) Unitrust Single Life Remainder Factors Based on Life Table 2000CM Applicable On or After May 1, 2009" is omitted. Ed.*]

(7) *Applicability dates.* Paragraphs (g)(1) through (6) of this section apply on and after May 1, 2009, and before June 1, 2023.

[T.D. 8540, 59 FR 30116, 30117, 30148, June 10, 1994; T.D. 8819, 64 FR 23199, 23209, April 30, 1999; T.D. 8886, 65 FR 36943, June 12, 2000; T.D. 9448, 74 FR 21465, 21482, May 7, 2009; T.D. 9540, 76 FR 49612, Aug. 10, 2011; T.D. 9974, 88 FR 37433, 37436, June 7, 2023]

Subpart D. Treatment of Excess Distributions by Trusts

§ 665. Definitions Applicable to Subpart D

(a) Undistributed net income. For purposes of this subpart, the term "undistributed net income" for any taxable year means the amount by which the distributable net income of the trust for such taxable year exceeds the sum of—

(1) the amounts for such taxable year specified in paragraphs (1) and (2) of section 661(a), and

(2) the amount of taxes imposed on the trust attributable to such distributable net income.

(b) Accumulation distribution. For purposes of this subpart, except as provided in subsection (c), the term "accumulation distribution" means, for any taxable year of the trust, the amount by which—

(1) the amounts specified in paragraph (2) of section 661(a) for such taxable year, exceed

(2) distributable net income for such year reduced (but not below zero) by the amounts specified in paragraph (1) of section 661(a).

For purposes of section 667 (other than subsection (c) thereof, relating to multiple trusts), the amounts specified in paragraph (2) of section 661(a) shall not include amounts properly paid, credited, or required to be distributed to a beneficiary from a trust (other than a foreign trust) as income accumulated before the birth of such beneficiary or before such beneficiary attains the age of 21. If the amounts properly paid, credited, or required to be distributed by the trust for the taxable year do not exceed the income of the trust for such year, there shall be no accumulation distribution for such year.

(c) Exception for accumulation distributions from certain domestic trusts. For purposes of this subpart—

(1) In general. In the case of a qualified trust, any distribution in any taxable year beginning after the date of the enactment of this subsection shall be computed without regard to any undistributed net income.

(2) Qualified trust. For purposes of this subsection, the term "qualified trust" means any trust other than—

(A) a foreign trust (or, except as provided in regulations, a domestic trust which at any time was a foreign trust), or

(B) a trust created before March 1, 1984, unless it is established that the trust would not be aggregated with other trusts under section 643(f) if such section applied to such trust.

(d) Taxes imposed on the trust. For purposes of this subpart—

(1) In general. The term "taxes imposed on the trust" means the amount of the taxes which are imposed for any taxable year of the trust under this chapter (without regard to this subpart or part IV of subchapter A) and which, under regulations prescribed by the Secretary, are properly allocable to the undistributed portions of distributable net income and gains in excess of losses from sales or exchanges of capital assets.) The amount determined in the preceding sentence shall be reduced by any amount of such taxes deemed distributed under section 666(b) and (c) to any beneficiary.

(2) Foreign trusts. In the case of any foreign trust, the term "taxes imposed on the trust" includes the amount, reduced as provided in the last sentence of paragraph (1), of any income, war profits, and excess profits taxes imposed by any foreign country or possession of the United States on such foreign trust which, as determined under paragraph (1), are so properly allocable.) Under rules or regulations prescribed by the Secretary, in the case of any foreign trust of which the settlor or another person would be treated as owner of any portion of the trust under subpart E but for section 672(f), the term "taxes imposed on the trust" includes the allocable amount of any income, war profits, and excess profits taxes imposed by any foreign country or possession of the United States on the settlor or such other person in respect of trust income.

(e) Preceding taxable year. For purposes of this subpart—

(1) In the case of a foreign trust created by a United States person, the term "preceding taxable year" does not include any taxable year of the trust to which this part does not apply.

(2) In the case of a preceding taxable year with respect to which a trust qualified, without regard to this subpart, under the provisions of subpart B, for purposes of the application of this subpart to such trust for such taxable year, such trust shall, in accordance with regulations prescribed by the Secretary, be treated as a trust to which subpart C applies.

Regulations

§ 1.665(a)–0A Excess distributions by trusts; scope of subpart D.

(a) In general. (1) Subpart D (section 665 and following), part I, subchapter J, chapter 1 of the Code as amended by the Tax Reform Act of 1969, is designed to tax the beneficiary of a trust that accumulates, rather than distributes, all or part of its income currently (i.e., an accumulation trust), in most cases, as if the income had been currently distributed to the beneficiary instead of accumulated by the trusts.) Accordingly, subpart D provides special rules for the treatment of amounts paid, credited, or required to be distributed by a complex trust (one that is subject to subpart C (section 661 and following) of such part I) in any year in excess of "distributable net income" (as defined in section 643(a)) for that year.) Such an excess distribution is an "accumulation distribution" (as defined in section 665(b)). The special rules of subpart D are generally inapplicable to amounts paid, credited, or required to be distributed by a trust in a taxable year in which it qualifies as a simple trust (one that is subject to subpart B (section 651 and following) of such part I). However, see § 1.665(e)–1A(b) for rules relating to the treatment of a simple trust as a complex trust.

(2) An accumulation distribution is deemed to consist of, first, "undistributed net income" (as defined in section 665(a)) of the trust from preceding taxable years, and, after all the undistributed net income for all preceding taxable years has been deemed distributed, "undistributed capital gain" (as defined in section 665(f)) of the trust for all preceding taxable years commencing with the first year such amounts were accumulated.) An accumulation distribution of undistributed capital gain is a "capital gain distribution" (as defined in section 665(g)). To the extent an accumulation distribution exceeds the "undistributed net income" and "undistributed capital gain" so determined, it is deemed to consist of corpus.

(3) The accumulation distribution is "thrown back" to the earliest "preceding taxable year" of the trust, which, in the case of distributions made for a taxable year beginning after December 31, 1973, from a trust (other than a foreign trust created by a U.S. person), is any taxable year beginning after December 31, 1968. Special transitional rules apply for distributions made in taxable years beginning before January 1, 1974. In the case of a foreign trust created by a U.S. person, a "preceding taxable year" is any year of the trust to which the Code applies.

(4) A distribution of undistributed net income (included in an accumulation distribution) and a capital gain distribution will be included in the income of the beneficiary in the year they are actually paid, credited, or required to be distributed to him.) The tax on the distribution will be approximately the amount of tax the beneficiary would have paid with respect to the distribution had the income and capital gain been distributed to the beneficiary in the year earned by the trust.) An additional amount equal to the "taxes imposed on the trust" for the preceding year is also deemed distributed.) To prevent double taxation, however, the beneficiary receives a credit for such taxes.

(b) Effective dates. All regulations sections under subpart D (sections 665 through 669) which have an "A" suffix (such as § 1.665(a)A and § 1.666(b)–1A) are applicable to taxable years beginning on or after January 1, 1969, and all references therein to sections 665 through 669 are references to such sections as amended by the Tax Reform Act of 1969. Sections without the "A" suffix (such as § 1.666(b)–1) are applicable only to taxable years beginning before January 1, 1969, and all references therein to sections 665 through 669 are references to such sections before amendment by the Tax Reform Act of 1969.

(c) Examples. Where examples contained in the regulations under subpart D refer to tax rates for years after 1968, such tax rates are not necessarily the actual rates for such years, but are only used for example purposes.

(d) Applicability to estates. Subpart D does not apply to any estate.

[T.D. 7204, 37 FR 17135, Aug. 25, 1972]

§ 1.665(a)–1A Undistributed net income.

(a) Domestic trusts. The term "undistributed net income", in the case of a trust (other than a foreign trust created by a U.S. person) means, for any taxable year beginning after December 31, 1968, the distributable net income of the trust for that year (as determined under section 643(a)), less:

(1) The amount of income required to be distributed currently and any other amounts properly paid or

credited or required to be distributed to beneficiaries in the taxable year as specified in section 661(a), and

(2) The amount of taxes imposed on the trust attributable to such distributable net income, as defined in § 1.665(d)–1A. The application of the rule in this paragraph to a taxable year of a trust in which income is accumulated may be illustrated by the following example:

Example. Under the terms of the trust, $10,000 of income is required to be distributed currently to A and the trustee has discretion to make additional distributions to A. During the taxable year 1971 the trust had distributable net income of $30,100 derived from royalties and the trustee made distributions of $20,000 to A. The taxable income of the trust is $10,000 on which a tax of $2,190 is paid.) The undistributed net income of the trust for the taxable year 1971 is $7,910, computed as follows:

Distributable net income		$30,100
Less:		
Income currently distributable to A	$10,000	
Other amounts distributed to A	10,000	
Taxes imposed on the trust attributable to the undistributed net income (see § 1.665(d)–1A)	2,190	
Total		22,190
Undistributed net income		7,910

(b) Foreign trusts. The undistributed net income of a foreign trust created by a U.S. person for any taxable year is the distributable net income of such trust (see § 1.643(a)–6 and the examples set forth in paragraph (b) thereof), less:

(1) The amount of income required to be distributed currently and any other amounts properly paid or credited or required to be distributed to beneficiaries in the taxable year as specified in section 661(a), and

(2) The amount of taxes imposed on such trust by chapter 1 of the Internal Revenue Code, which are attributable to items of income which are required to be included in such distributable net income.

For purposes of subparagraph (2) of this paragraph, the amount of taxes imposed on the trust for any taxable year by chapter 1 of the Internal Revenue Code is the amount of taxes imposed pursuant to section 871 (relating to tax on nonresident alien individuals) which is properly allocable to the undistributed portion of the distributable net income.) See § 1.665(d)–1A. The amount of taxes imposed pursuant to section 871 is the difference between the total tax imposed pursuant to that section on the foreign trust created by a U.S. person for the year and the amount which would have been imposed on such trust had all the distributable net income, as determined under section 643(a), been distributed. The application of the rule in this paragraph may be illustrated by the following examples:

Example (1). A trust was created in 1952 under the laws of Country X by the transfer to a trustee in Country X of property by a U.S. person.) The entire trust constitutes a foreign trust created by a U.S. person.) The governing instrument of the trust provides that $7,000 of income is required to be distributed currently to a U.S. beneficiary and gives the trustee discretion to make additional distributions to the beneficiary.) During the taxable year 1973 the trust had income of $10,000 from dividends of a U.S. corporation (on which Federal income taxes of $3,000 were imposed pursuant to section 871 and withheld under section 1441, resulting in the receipt by the trust of cash in the amount of $7,000), $20,000 in capital gains from the sale of stock of a Country Y corporation and $30,000 from dividends of a Country X corporation, none of the gross income of which was derived from sources within the United States.) No income taxes were required to be paid to Country X or Country Y in 1973. The trustee did not file a U.S. income tax return for the taxable year 1973. The distributable net income of the trust before distributions to the beneficiary for 1973 is $60,000 ($57,000 of which is cash). During 1973 the trustee made distributions to the U.S. beneficiary equaling one-half of the trust's distributable net income.) Thus, the U.S. beneficiary is treated as having had distributed to him $5,000 (composed of $3,500 as a cash distribution and $1,500 as the tax imposed pursuant to section 871 and withheld under section 1441), representing one-half of the income from U.S. sources; $10,000 in cash, representing one-half of the capital gains from the sale of stock of the Country Y corporation; and $15,000 in cash, representing one-half of the income from Country X sources for a total of $30,000. The undistributed net income of the trust at the close of taxable year 1973 is $28,500 computed as follows:

Distributable net income		$60,000
Less:		
(1) Amounts distributed to the beneficiary: Income currently distributed to the beneficiary	$7,000	
Other amounts distributed to the beneficiary	21,500	
Taxes under sec. 871 deemed distributed to the beneficiary	1,500	
Total amounts distributed to the beneficiary	30,000	
(2) Amount of taxes imposed on the trust under chapter 1 of the Code attributable to the undistributed net income (See § 1.665(d)–1A) $3,000 less $1,500)	$1,500	
Total		$31,500
Undistributed net income		28,500

Example (2). The facts are the same as in example (1) except that property has been transferred to the trust by a person other than a U.S. person, and during 1973 the foreign trust created by a U.S. person was 60 percent of the entire foreign trust.) The trustee paid no income taxes to Country X or Country Y in 1973.

(1) The undistributed net income of the portion of the entire trust which is a foreign trust created by a U.S. person for 1973 is $17,100, computed as follows:

Distributable net income (60% of each item of gross income of entire trust):		
60% of $10,000 U.S. dividends		$6,000
60% of $20,000 Country X capital gains		12,000
60% of $30,000 Country X dividends		18,000
Total		36,000
Less:		
(i) Amounts distributed to the beneficiary— Income currently distributed to the beneficiary (60% of $7,000)	$4,200	
Other amounts distributed to the beneficiary (60% of $21,500)	12,900	
Taxes under sec. 871 deemed distributed to the beneficiary (60% of $1,500)	900	
Total amounts distributed to the beneficiary	18,000	
(ii) Amount of taxes imposed on the trust under chapter 1 of the Code attributable to the undistributed net income (see § 1.665(d)–1A) (60% of $1,500)	900	
Total		18,900
Undistributed net income		17,100

(2) The undistributed net income of the portion of the entire trust which is not a foreign trust created by a U.S. person for 1973 is $11,400, computed as follows:

Distributable net income (40% of each item of gross income of entire trust)		
40% of $10,000 U.S. dividends	$4,000	
40% of $20,000 Country X capital gains	8,000	
40% of $30,000 Country X dividends	12,000	
Total	24,000	
Less:		
(i) Amounts distributed to the beneficiary Income currently distributed to the beneficiary (40% of $7,000)	$2,800	

Other amounts distributed to the beneficiary (40% of $21,500)	8,600	
Taxes under sec. 871 deemed distributed to the beneficiary (40% of $1,500)	600	
Total amounts distributed to the beneficiary	12,000	
(ii) Amount of taxes imposed on the trust under chapter 1 of the Code attributable to the undistributed net income (See § 1.665(d)–1A) (40% of $1,500)	600	
Total		12,600
Undistributed net income		11,400

(c) Effect of prior distributions. The undistributed net income for any year to which an accumulation distribution for a later year may be thrown back will be reduced by accumulation distributions in intervening years that are required to be thrown back to such year.) For example, if a trust has undistributed net income for 1975, and an accumulation distribution is made in 1980, there must be taken into account the effect on undistributed net income for 1975 of any accumulation distribution made in 1976, 1977, 1978, or 1979. However, undistributed net income for any year will not be reduced by any distributions in any intervening years that are excluded under section 663(a)(1), relating to gifts, bequests, etc.) See paragraph (d) of § 1.666(a)–1A for an illustration of the reduction of undistributed net income for any year by a subsequent accumulation distribution.

(d) Distributions made in taxable years beginning before January 1, 1974. For special rules relating to accumulation distributions of undistributed net income made in taxable years of the trust beginning before January 1, 1974, see § 1.665(b)–2A.

[T.D. 7204, 37 FR 17136, Aug. 25, 1972]

§ 1.665(b)–1A Accumulation distributions.

(a) In general. (1) For any taxable year of a trust the term "accumulation distribution" means an amount by which the amounts properly paid, credited, or required to be distributed within the meaning of section 661(a)(2) (i.e., all amounts properly paid, credited, or required to be distributed to the beneficiary other than income required to be distributed currently within the meaning of section 661(a)(1)) for that year exceed the distributable net income (determined under section 643(a)) of the trust, reduced (but not below zero) by the amount of income required to be distributed currently.) To the extent provided in section 663(b) and the regulations thereunder, distributions made within the first 65 days following a taxable year may be treated as having been distributed on the last day of such taxable year.

(2) An accumulation distribution also includes, for a taxable year of the trust, any amount to which section 661(a)(2) and the preceding paragraph are inapplicable and which is paid, credited, or required to be distributed during the taxable year of the trust by reason of the exercise of a power to appoint, distribute, consume, or withdraw corpus of the trust or income of the trust accumulated in a preceding taxable year. No accumulation distribution is deemed to be made solely because the grantor or any other person is treated as owner of a portion of the trust by reason of an unexercised power to appoint, distribute, consume, or withdraw corpus or accumulated income of the trust.) Nor will an accumulation distribution be deemed to have been made by reason of the exercise of a power that may affect only taxable income previously attributed to the holders of such power under subpart E (section 671 and following). See example 4 of paragraph (d) of this section for an example of an accumulation distribution occurring as a result of the exercise of a power of withdrawal.

(3) Although amounts properly paid or credited under section 661(a) do not exceed the income of the trust during the taxable year, an accumulation distribution may result if the amounts properly paid or credited under section 661(a)(2) exceed distributable net income reduced (but not below zero) by the amount required to be distributed currently under section 661(a)(1). This may occur, for example, when expenses, interest, taxes, or other items allocable to corpus are taken into account in determining taxable income and hence causing distributable net income to be less than the trust's income.

(b) Payments that are accumulation distributions. The following are some instances in which an accumulation distribution may arise:

(1) *One trust to another.* A distribution from one trust to another trust is generally an accumulation distribution.) See § 1.643(c)–1. This general rule will apply regardless of whether the distribution is to an existing trust or to a newly created trust and regardless of whether the trust to which the distribution is made was created by the same person who created the trust from which the distribution is made or a different person.) However, a distribution made from one trust to a second trust will be deemed an accumulation distribution by the first trust to an ultimate beneficiary of the second trust if the primary purpose of the distribution to the second trust is to avoid the capital gain distribution provisions (see section 669 and the regulations thereunder). An amount passing from one separate share of a trust to another separate share of the same trust is not an accumulation distribution.) See § 1.665(g)–2A. For rules relating to the computation of the beneficiary's tax under section 668 by reason of an accumulation distribution from the second trust, see paragraphs (b)(1) and (c)(1)(i) of § 1.668(b)–1A and paragraphs (b)(1) and (c)(1)(i) of § 1.669(b)–1A.

(2) *Income accumulated during minority.* A distribution of income accumulated during the minority of the beneficiary is generally an accumulation distribution.) For example, if a trust accumulates income until the beneficiary's 21st birthday, and then distributes the income to the beneficiary, such a distribution is an accumulation distribution.) However, see § 1.665(b)–2A for rules governing income accumulated in taxable years beginning before January 1, 1969.

(3) *Amounts paid for support.* To the extent that amounts forming all or part of an accumulation distribution are applied or distributed for the support of a dependent under the circumstances specified in section 677(b) or section 678(c) or are used to discharge or satisfy any person's legal obligation as that term is used in § 1.662(a)–4, such amounts will be considered as having been distributed directly to the person whose obligation is being satisfied.

(c) Payments that are not accumulation distributions. (1) *Gifts, bequests, etc., described in section 663(a)(1).* A gift or bequest of a specific sum of money or of specific property described in section 663(a)(1) is not an accumulation distribution.

(2) *Charitable payments.* Any amount paid, permanently set aside, or used for the purposes specified in section 642(c) is not an accumulation distribution, even though no charitable deduction is allowed under such section with respect to such payment.

(3) *Income required to be distributed currently.* No accumulation distribution will arise by reason of a payment of income required to be distributed currently even though such income exceeds the distributable net income of the trust because the payment is an amount specified in section 661(a)(1).

(d) Examples. The provisions of this section may be illustrated by the following examples:

Example (1). A trustee properly makes a distribution to a beneficiary of $20,000 during the taxable year 1976, of which $10,000 is income required to be distributed currently to the beneficiary.) The distributable net income of the trust is $15,000. There is an accumulation distribution of $5,000 computed as follows:

Total distribution	$20,000
Less: Income required to be distributed currently (section 661(a)(1))	10,000
Other amounts distributed (section 661(a)(2))	10,000
Distributable net income	$15,000
Less: Income required to be distributed currently	10,000
Balance of distributable net income	5,000
Accumulation distribution	5,000

Example (2). Under the terms of the trust instrument, an annuity of $15,000 is required to be paid to A out of income each year and the trustee may in his discretion make distributions out of income or corpus to B. During the taxable year the trust had income of $18,000, as defined in section 643(b), and expenses allocable to corpus of $5,000. Distributable net income amounted to $13,000. The trustee distributed $15,000 of income to A and, in the exercise of his discretion, paid $5,000 to B. There is an accumulation distribution of $5,000 computed as follows:

Total distribution	$20,000
Less: Income required to be distributed currently to A (section 661(a)(1))	15,000
Other amounts distributed (section 661(a)(2))	5,000
Distributable net income	$13,000
Less: Income required to be distributed currently to A	15,000
Balance of distributable net income	0
Accumulation distribution to B	5,000

Example (3). Under the terms of a trust instrument, the trustee may either accumulate the trust income or make distributions to A and B. The trustee may also invade corpus for the benefit of A and B. During the taxable year, the trust had income as defined in section 643(b) of $22,000 and expenses of $5,000 allocable to corpus. Distributable net income amounts to $17,000. The trustee distributed $10,000 each to A and B during the taxable year. There is an accumulation distribution of $3,000 computed as follows:

Total distribution	$ 20,000
Less: Income required to be distributed currently	0
Other amounts distributed (section 661(a)(2))	20,000
Distributable net income	$17,000
Less: Income required to be distributed currently	0
Balance of distributable net income	17,000
Accumulation distribution	3,000

Example (4). A dies in 1974 and bequeaths one-half the residue of his estate in trust. His widow, W, is given a power, exercisable solely by her, to require the trustee to pay her each year of the trust $5,000 from corpus. W's right to exercise such power was exercisable at any time during the year but was not cumulative, so that, upon her failure to exercise it before the end of any taxable year of the trust, her right as to that year lapsed. The trust's taxable year is the calendar year. During the calendar years 1975 and 1976, W did not exercise her right and it lapsed as to those years. In the calendar years 1977 and 1978, in which years the trust had no distributable net income, she exercised her right and withdrew $4,000 in 1977 and $5,000 in 1978. No accumulation distribution was made by the trust in the calendar years 1975 and 1976. An accumulation distribution of $4,000 was made in 1977 and an accumulation distribution of $5,000 was made in 1978. The accumulation distribution for the years 1977 and 1978 is not reduced by any amount of income of the trust attributable to her under section 678 by reason of her power of withdrawal.

[T.D. 7204, 37 FR 17137, Aug. 25, 1972]

§ 1.665(b)–2A Special rules for accumulation distributions made in taxable years beginning before January 1, 1974. [*Omitted. Ed.*]

[T.D. 7204, 37 FR 17138, Aug. 25, 1972]

§ 1.665(c)–1A Special rule applicable to distributions by certain foreign trusts.

(a) In general. Except as provided in paragraph (b) of this section, for purposes of section 665 any amount paid to a U.S. person which is from a payor who is not a U.S. person and which is derived directly or indirectly from a foreign trust created by a U.S. person shall be deemed in the year of payment to the U.S. person to have been directly paid to the U.S. person by the trust. For example, if a nonresident alien receives a distribution from a foreign trust created by a U.S. person and then pays the amount of the distribution over to a U.S. person, the payment of such amount to the U.S. person represents an accumulation distribution to the U.S. person from the trust to the extent that the amount received would have been an accumulation distribution had the trust paid the amount directly to the U.S. person in the year in which the payment was received by the U.S. person. This section also applies in a case where a nonresident alien receives indirectly an accumulation distribution from a foreign trust created by a U.S. person and then pays it over to a U.S. person. An example of such a transaction is one where the foreign trust created by a U.S. person makes the distribution to an intervening foreign trust created by either a U.S. person or a person other than a U.S. person and the intervening trust distributes the amount received to a nonresident alien who in turn pays it over to a U.S. person. Under these circumstances, it is deemed that the payment received by the U.S. person was received directly from a foreign trust created by a U.S. person.

(b) Limitation. In the case of a distribution to a beneficiary who is a U.S. person, paragraph (a) of this section does not apply if the distribution is received by such beneficiary under circumstances indicating lack of intent on the part of the parties to circumvent the purposes for which section 7 of the Revenue Act of 1962 (76 Stat. 985) was enacted.

[T.D. 7204, 37 FR 17139 Aug. 25, 1972]

§ 1.665(d)–1A Taxes imposed on the trust.

(a) In general. (1) For purposes of subpart D, the term "taxes imposed on the trust" means the amount of Federal income taxes properly imposed for any taxable year on the trust that are attributable to the undistributed portions of distributable net income and gains in excess of losses from the sales or exchanges of capital assets. Except as provided in paragraph (c)(2) of this section, the minimum tax for tax preferences imposed by section 56 is not a tax attributable to the undistributed portions of distributable net income and gains in excess of losses from the sales or exchanges of capital assets. See section 56 and the regulations thereunder.

(2) In the case of a trust that has received an accumulation distribution from another trust, the term "taxes imposed on the trust" also includes the amount of taxes deemed distributed under §§ 1.666(b)–1A, 1.666(c)–1A, 1.669(d)–1A, and 1.669(e)–1A (whichever are applicable) as a result of such accumulation distribution, to the extent that they were taken into account under paragraphs (b)(2) or (c)(1)(vi) of § 1.668(b)–1A and (b)(2) or (c)(1)(vi) of § 1.669(b)–1A in computing the partial tax on such accumulation distribution. For example, assume that trust A, a calendar year trust, makes an accumulation distribution in 1975 to trust B, also on the calendar year basis, in connection with which $500 of taxes are deemed under § 1.666(b)–1A to be distributed to trust B. The partial tax on the accumulation distribution is computed under paragraph (b) of § 1.668(b)–1A (the exact method) to be $600 and all of the $500 is used under paragraph (b)(2) of § 1.668(b)–1A to reduce the partial tax to $100. The taxes imposed on trust B for 1975 will, in addition to the $100 partial tax, also include the $500 used to reduce the partial tax.

(b) Taxes imposed on the trust attributable to undistributed net income. (1) For the purpose of subpart D, the term "taxes imposed on the trust attributable to the undistributed net income" means the amount of Federal income taxes for the taxable year properly allocable to the undistributed portion of the distributable net income for such taxable year. This amount is (i) an amount that bears the same relationship to the total taxes of the trust for the year (other than the minimum tax for tax preferences imposed by section 56), computed after the allowance of credits under section 642(a), as (a) the taxable income of the trust, other than the capital gains not included in distributable net income less their share of section 1202 deduction, bears to (b) the total taxable income of the trust for such year or, (ii) if the alternative tax computation under section 1201(b) is used and there are no net short-term gains, an amount equal to such total taxes less the amount of the alternative tax imposed on the trust and attributable to the capital gain. Thus, for the purposes of subpart D, in determining the amount of taxes imposed on the trust attributable to the undistributed net income, that portion of the taxes paid by the trust attributable to capital gain allocable to corpus is excluded. The rule stated in this subparagraph may be illustrated by the following example, which assumes that the alternative tax computation is not used:

Example. (1) Under the terms of a trust, which reports on the calendar year basis, the income may be accumulated or distributed to A in the discretion of the trustee and capital gains are allocable to corpus. During the taxable year 1974, the trust had income of $20,000 from royalties, long-term capital gains of $10,000, and expenses of $2,000. The trustee in his discretion made a distribution of $10,000 to A. The taxes imposed on the trust for such year attributable to the undistributed net income are $2,319, determined as shown below.

(2) The distributable net income of the trust computed under section 643(a) is $18,000 (royalties of $20,000 less expenses of $2,000). The total taxes paid by the trust are $3,787, computed as follows:

Royalties	$20,000
Capital gain allocable to corpus	10,000
Gross income	30,000
Deductions:	
Expenses	$ 2,000
Distributions to A	10,000
Capital gain deduction	5,000

Personal exemption	100
	17,100
Taxable income	12,900
Total income taxes	3,787

(3) Taxable income other than capital gains less the section 1202 deduction is $7,900 ($12,900-($10,000-$5,000)). Therefore, the amount of taxes imposed on the trust attributable to the undistributed net income is $2,319, computed as follows:

$3,787 (total taxes) * $7,900 (taxable income other than capital gains not included in d.n.i. less the § 1202 deduction) divided by $12,900 (taxable income) $2,319

(2) If in any taxable year an accumulation distribution of undistributed net income is made by the trust which results in a throwback to a prior year, the taxes of the prior year imposed on the trust attributable to any remaining undistributed net income of such prior year are the taxes prescribed in subparagraph (1) of this paragraph reduced by the taxes of the prior year deemed distributed under section 666(b) or (c). The provisions of this subparagraph may be illustrated by the following example:

Example. Assume the same facts as in the example in subparagraph (1) of this paragraph. In 1975 the trust makes an accumulation distribution, of which an amount of undistributed net income is deemed distributed in 1974. Taxes imposed on the trust (in the amount of $1,000) attributable to the undistributed net income are therefore deemed distributed in such year. Consequently, the taxes imposed on the trust subsequent to the 1975 distribution attributable to the remaining undistributed net income are $1,319 ($2,319 less $1,000).

(c) Taxes imposed on the trust attributable to undistributed capital gain. (1) *Regular tax.* For the purpose of subpart D the term "taxes imposed on the trust attributable to undistributed capital gain" means the amount of Federal income taxes for the taxable year properly attributable to that portion of the excess of capital gains over capital losses of the trust that is allocable to corpus for such taxable year. Such amount is the total of—

(i) The amount computed under subparagraph (2) of this paragraph (the minimum tax), plus

(ii) The amount that bears the same relationship to the total taxes of the trust for the year (other than the minimum tax), computed after the allowance of credits under section 642(a), as (a) the excess of capital gains over capital losses for such year that are not included in distributable net income, computed after its share of the deduction under section 1202 (relating to the deduction for capital gains) has been taken into account, bears to the greater of (b) the total taxable income of the trust for such year, or (c) the amount of capital gains computed under (a) of this subdivision.

However, if the alternative tax computation under section 1201(b) is used and there are no net short-term gains, the amount is the amount of the alternative tax imposed on the trust and attributable to the capital gain. The application of this subparagraph may be illustrated by the following example, which assumes that the alternative tax computation is not used:

Example. Assume the same facts as in the example in paragraph (b)(1). The capital gains not included in d.n.i. are $10,000, and the deduction under section 1202 is $5,000. The amount of taxes imposed on the trust attributable to undistributed capital gain is $1,468, computed as follows:

$3,787 (total taxes) * $5,000 (capital gains not included in d.n.i. less section 1202 deductions) divided by $12,900 (taxable income) $1,468

(2) *Minimum tax.* The term "taxes imposed on the trust attributable to the undistributed capital gain" also includes the minimum tax for tax preferences imposed on the trust by section 56 with respect to the undistributed capital gain. The amount of such minimum tax so included bears the same relation to the total amount of minimum tax imposed on the trust by section 56 for the taxable year as one-half the net capital gain (net section 1201 gain for taxable years beginning before January 1, 1977) (as defined in section 1222(11)) from such taxable year bears to the sum of the items of tax preference of the trust for such taxable year which are apportioned to the trust in accordance with § 1.58–3(a)(1).

(3) *Reduction for prior distribution.* If in any taxable year a capital gain distribution is made by the trust which results in a throwback to a prior year, the taxes of the prior year imposed on the trust attributable to any remaining undistributed capital gain of the prior

year are the taxes prescribed in subparagraph (1) of this paragraph reduced by the taxes of the prior year deemed distributed under section 669(d) or (e). The provisions of this subparagraph may be illustrated by the following example:

Example. Assume the same facts as in the example in subparagraph (1) of this paragraph. In 1976, the trust makes a capital gain distribution, of which an amount of undistributed capital gain is deemed distributed in 1974. Taxes imposed on the trust (in the amount of $500) attributable to the undistributed capital gain are therefore deemed distributed in such year. Consequently, the taxes imposed on the trust attributable to the remaining undistributed capital gain are $968 ($1,468 less $500).

[T.D. 7204, 37 FR 17139, Aug. 25, 1972, as amended by T.D. 7728, 45 FR 72650, Nov. 3, 1980]

§ 1.665(e)–1A Preceding taxable year.

(a) Definition. (1) *Domestic trusts.* (i) *In general.* For purposes of subpart D, in the case of a trust other than a foreign trust created by a U.S. person, the term "preceding taxable year" serves to identify and limit the taxable years of a trust to which an accumulation distribution consisting of undistributed net income or undistributed capital gain may be allocated (or "thrown back") under sections 666(a) and 669(a). An accumulation distribution consisting of undistributed net income or undistributed capital gain may not be allocated or "thrown back" to a taxable year of a trust if such year is not a "preceding taxable year."

(ii) *Accumulation distributions.* In the case of an accumulation distribution consisting of undistributed net income made in a taxable year beginning before January 1, 1974, any taxable year of the trust that precedes by more than 5 years the taxable year of the trust in which such accumulation distribution was made is not a "preceding taxable year." Thus, for a domestic trust on a calendar year basis, calendar year 1967 is not a "preceding taxable year" with respect to an accumulation distribution made in calendar year 1973, whereas calendar year 1968 is a "preceding taxable year." In the case of an accumulation distribution made during a taxable year beginning after December 31, 1973, any taxable year of the trust that begins before January 1, 1969, is not a "preceding taxable year." Thus, for a domestic trust on a calendar year basis, calendar year 1968 is not a "preceding taxable year" with respect to an accumulation distribution made in calendar year 1975, whereas calendar year 1969 is a "preceding taxable year."

(iii) *Capital gain distributions.* In the case of an accumulation distribution that is a capital gain distribution, any taxable year of the trust that (a) begins before January 1, 1969, or (b) is prior to the first year in which income is accumulated, whichever occurs later, is not a "preceding taxable year." Thus, for the purpose of capital gain distributions and section 669, only taxable years beginning after December 31, 1968, can be "preceding taxable years." See § 1.688(a)–1A(c).

(2) *Foreign trusts created by U.S. persons.* For purposes of Subpart D, in the case of a foreign trust created by a U.S. person, the term "preceding taxable year" does not include any taxable year to which Part I of Subchapter J does not apply. See section 683 and regulations thereunder. Accordingly, the provisions of Subpart D may not, in the case of a foreign trust created by a U.S. person, be applied to any taxable year which begins before 1954 or ends before August 17, 1954. For example, if a foreign trust created by a U.S. person (reporting on the calendar year basis) makes a distribution during the calendar year 1970 of income accumulated during prior years, the earliest year of the trust to which the accumulation distribution may be allocated under such Subpart D is 1954, but it may not be allocated to 1953 and prior years, since the Internal Revenue Code of 1939 applies to those years.

(b) Simple trusts. A taxable year of a trust during which the trust was a simple trust (that is, was subject to Subpart B) for the entire year shall not be considered a "preceding taxable year" unless during such year the trust received "outside income" or unless the trustee did not distribute all of the income of the trust that was required to be distributed currently for such year. In such event, undistributed net income for such year shall not exceed the greater of the "outside income" or income not distributed during such year. For purposes of this paragraph, the term "outside income" means amounts that are included in distributable net income of the trust for the year but that are not "income" of the trust as that term is defined in § 1.643(b)–1. Some examples of "outside income" are:

(1) Income taxable to the trust under section 691;

(2) Unrealized accounts receivable that were assigned to the trust; and

(3) Distributions from another trust that include distributable net income or undistributed net income of such other trust.

The term "outside income," however, does not include amounts received as distributions from an estate, other than income specified in (1) and (2), for which the estate was allowed a deduction under section 661(a). The application of this paragraph may be illustrated by the following examples:

Example (1). By his will D creates a trust for his widow W. The terms of the trust require that the income be distributed currently (i.e., it is a simple trust), and authorize the trustee to make discretionary payments of corpus to W. Upon W's death the trust corpus is to be distributed to D's then living issue. The executor of D's will makes a $10,000 distribution of corpus to the trust that carries out estate income consisting of dividends and interest to the trust under section 662(a)(2). The trust reports this income as its only income on its income tax return for its taxable year in which ends the taxable year of the estate in which the $10,000 distribution was made, and pays a tax thereon of $2,106. Thus, the trust has undistributed net income of $7,894 ($10,000-$2,106). Several years later the trustee makes a discretionary corpus payment of $15,000 to W. This payment is an accumulation distribution under section 665(b). However, since the trust had no "outside income" in the year of the estate distribution, such year is not a preceding taxable year. Thus, W is not treated as receiving undistributed net income of $7,894 and taxes thereon of $2,106 for the purpose of including the same in her gross income under section 668. The result would be the same if the invasion power were not exercised and the accumulation distribution occurred as a result of the distribution of the corpus to D's issue upon the death of W.

Example (2). Trust A, a simple trust on the calendar year basis, received in 1972 extraordinary dividends or taxable stock dividends that the trustee in good faith allocated to corpus, but that are determined in 1974 to have been currently distributable to the beneficiary. See section 643(a)(4) and § 1.643(a)–4. Trust A would qualify for treatment under Subpart C for 1974, the year of distribution of the extraordinary dividends or taxable stock dividends, because the distribution is not out of income of the current taxable year and is treated as another amount properly paid or credited or required to be distributed for such taxable year within the meaning of section 661(a)(2). Also, the distribution in 1974 qualifies as an accumulation distribution for the purposes of Subpart D. For purposes only of such Subpart D, trust A would be treated as subject to the provisions of such Subpart C for 1972, the preceding taxable year in which the extraordinary or taxable stock dividends were received, and, in computing undistributed net income for 1972, the extraordinary or taxable stock dividends would be included in distributable net income under section 643(a). The rule stated in the preceding sentence would also apply if the distribution in 1974 was made out of corpus without regard to a determination that the extraordinary dividends or taxable stock dividends in question were currently distributable to the beneficiary.

[T.D. 7204, 37 FR 17141, Aug. 25, 1972]

§ 1.665(g)–2A Application of separate share rule.

(a) In general. If the separate share rule of section 663(c) is applicable for any taxable year of a trust, Subpart D is applied as if each share were a separate trust except as provided in paragraph (c) of this section and in § 1.668(a)–1A(c). Thus, the amounts of an "accumulation distribution", "undistributed net income", "undistributed capital gain", and "capital gain distribution" are computed separately for each share.

(b) Allocation of taxes—Undistributed net income. The "taxes imposed on the trust attributable to the undistributed net income" are allocated as follows:

(1) There is first allocated to each separate share that portion of the "taxes imposed on the trust attributable to the undistributed net income" (as defined in § 1.665(d)–1A(b)), computed before the allowance of any credits under section 642(a), that bears the same relation to the total of such taxes that the distributable net income of the separate share bears to the distributable net income of the trust, adjusted for this purpose as follows:

(i) There is excluded from distributable net income of the trust and of each separate share any tax-exempt interest, foreign income of a foreign trust, and excluded dividends, to the extent such amounts are included in distributable net income pursuant to section 643(a) (5), (6), and (7); and

(ii) The distributable net income of the trust is reduced by any deductions allowable under section 661 for amounts paid, credited, or required to be distributed during the taxable year, and the distributable net income of each separate share is reduced by any such deduction allocable to that share.

(2) The taxes so determined for each separate share are then reduced by that portion of the credits against tax allowable to the trust under section 642(a) in computing the "taxes imposed on the trust" that bears the same relation to the total of such credits that the items of distributable net income allocable to the separate share with respect to which the credit is allowed bear to the total of such items of the trust.

(c) Allocation of taxes—Undistributed capital gain. The "taxes imposed on the trust attributable to undistributed capital gain" are allocated as follows:

(1) There is first allocated to each separate share that portion of the "taxes imposed on the trust attributable to undistributed capital gain" (as defined in § 1.665(d)–1A(c)), computed before the allowance of any credits under section 642(a), that bears the same relation to the total of such taxes that the undistributed capital gain (prior to the deduction of taxes under section 665(c)(2)) of the separate share bears to the total such undistributed capital gain of the trust.

(2) The taxes so determined for each separate share are then reduced by that portion of the credits against tax allowable to the trust under section 642(a) in computing the "taxes imposed on the trust" that bears the same relation to the total of such credits that the capital gain allocable to the separate share with respect to which the credit is allowed bear to the total of such capital gain of the trust.

(d) Termination of a separate share. (1) If upon termination of a separate share, an amount is properly paid, credited, or required to be distributed by the trust under section 661(a)(2) to a beneficiary from such share, an accumulation distribution will be deemed to have been made to the extent of such amount. In determining the distributable net income of such share, only those items of income and deduction for the taxable year of the trust in which such share terminates, properly allocable to such share, shall be taken into consideration.

(2) No accumulation distribution will be deemed to have been made upon the termination of a separate share to the extent that the property constituting such share, or a portion thereof, continues to be held as a part of the same trust. The undistributed net income, undistributed capital gain, and the taxes imposed on the trust attributable to such items, if any, for all preceding taxable years (reduced by any amounts deemed distributed under sections 666(a) and 669(a) by reason of any accumulation distribution of undistributed net income or undistributed capital gain in prior years or the current taxable year), which were allocable to the terminating share, shall be treated as being applicable to the trust itself. However, no adjustment will be made to the amounts deemed distributed under sections 666 and 669 by reason of an accumulation distribution of undistributed net income or undistributed capital gain from the surviving share or shares made in years prior to the year in which the terminating share was added to such surviving share or shares.

(3) The provisions of this paragraph may be illustrated by the following example:

Example. A trust was established under the will of X for the benefit of his wife and upon her death the property was to continue in the same trust for his two sons, Y and Z. The separate share rule is applicable to this trust. The trustee had discretion to pay or accumulate the income to the wife, and after her death was to pay each son's share to him after he attained the age of 25. When the wife died, Y was 23 and Z was 28.

(1) Upon the death of X's widow, there is no accumulation distribution. The entire trust is split into two equal shares, and therefore the undistributed net income and the undistributed capital gain of the trust are split into two shares.

(2) The distribution to Z of his share after his mother's death is an accumulation distribution of his separate share of one-half of the undistributed net income and undistributed capital gain.

[T.D. 7204, 37 FR 17142, Aug. 25, 1972]

§ 666. Accumulation Distribution Allocated to Preceding Years

(a) Amount allocated. In the case of a trust which is subject to subpart C, the amount of the accumulation distribution of such trust for a taxable year shall be deemed to be an amount within the meaning of paragraph (2) of section 661(a) distributed on the last day of each of the preceding taxable years, commencing with the earliest of such years, to the extent that such amount exceeds the total of any undistributed net income for all earlier preceding taxable years. The amount deemed to be distributed in any such preceding taxable year under the preceding sentence shall not exceed the undistributed net income for such preceding taxable year. For purposes of this subsection, undistributed net income for each of such preceding taxable years shall be computed without regard to such accumulation distribution and without regard to any accumulation distribution determined for any succeeding taxable year.

(b) Total taxes deemed distributed. If any portion of an accumulation distribution for any taxable year is deemed under subsection (a) to be an amount within the meaning of paragraph (2) of section 661(a) distributed on the last day of any preceding taxable year, and such portion of such distribution is not less than the undistributed net income for such preceding taxable year, the trust shall be deemed to have distributed on the last day of such preceding taxable year an additional amount within the meaning of paragraph (2) of section 661(a). Such additional amount shall be equal to the taxes (other than the tax imposed by section 55) imposed on the trust for such preceding taxable year attributable to the undistributed net income. For purposes of this subsection, the undistributed net income and the taxes imposed on the trust for such preceding taxable year attributable to such undistributed net income shall be computed without regard to such accumulation distribution and without regard to any accumulation distribution determined for any succeeding taxable year.

(c) Pro rata portion of taxes deemed distributed. If any portion of an accumulation distribution for any taxable year is deemed under subsection (a) to be an amount within the meaning of paragraph (2) of section 661(a) distributed on the last day of any preceding taxable year and such portion of the accumulation distribution is less than the undistributed net income for such preceding taxable year, the trust shall be deemed to have distributed on the last day of such preceding taxable year an additional amount within the meaning of paragraph (2) of section 661(a). Such additional amount shall be equal to the taxes (other than the tax imposed by section 55) imposed on the trust for such taxable year attributable to the undistributed net income multiplied by the ratio of the portion of the accumulation distribution to the undistributed net income of the trust for such year. For purposes of this subsection, the undistributed net income and the taxes imposed on the trust for such preceding taxable year attributable to such undistributed net income shall be computed without regard to the accumulation distribution and without regard to any accumulation distribution determined for any succeeding taxable year.

(d) Rule when information is not available. If adequate records are not available to determine the proper application of this subpart to an amount distributed by a trust, such amount shall be deemed to be an accumulation distribution consisting of undistributed net income earned during the earliest preceding taxable year of the trust in which it can be established that the trust was in existence.

(e) Denial of refund to trusts and beneficiaries. No refund or credit shall be allowed to a trust or a beneficiary of such trust for any preceding taxable year by reason of a distribution deemed to have been made by such trust in such year under this section.

Regulations

§ 1.666(a)–1A Amount allocated.

(a) In general. In the case of a trust that is subject to subpart C of part I of subchapter J of chapter 1 of the Code (relating to estates and trusts that may accumulate income or that distribute corpus), section 666(a) prescribes rules for determining the taxable years from which an accumulation distribution will be deemed to have been made and the extent to which the accumulation distribution is considered to consist of undistributed net income. In general, an accumulation distribution made in taxable years beginning after December 31, 1969, is deemed to have been made first from the earliest preceding taxable year of the trust for which there is undistributed net income. An accumulation distribution made in a taxable year beginning before January 1, 1970, is deemed to have been made first from the most recent preceding taxable year of the trust for which there is undistributed net income. See § 1.665(e)–1A for the definition of "preceding taxable year."

(b) Distributions by domestic trusts. (1) *Taxable years beginning after December 31, 1973.* An accumulation distribution made by a trust (other than a foreign trust created by a U.S. person) in any taxable year beginning after December 31, 1973, is allocated to the preceding taxable years of the trust (defined in § 1.665(e)–1A(a)(1)(ii) as those beginning after December 31, 1968) according to the amount of undistributed net income of the trust for such years. For this purpose, an accumulation distribution is first to be allocated to the earliest such preceding taxable year in which there is undistributed net income and shall then be allocated, beginning with the next earliest, to any remaining preceding taxable years of the trust. The portion of the accumulation distribution allocated to the earliest preceding taxable year is the amount of the undistributed net income for that preceding taxable year. The portion of the accumulation distribution allocated to any preceding taxable year subsequent to the earliest such preceding taxable year is the excess of the accumulation distribution over the aggregate of the undistributed net income for all earlier preceding taxable years. See paragraph (d) of this section for adjustments to undistributed net income for prior distributions. The provisions of this subparagraph may be illustrated by the following example:

Example. In 1977, a domestic trust reporting on the calendar year basis makes an accumulation distribution of $33,000. Therefore, years before 1969 are ignored. In 1969, the trust had $6,000 of undistributed net income; in 1970, $4,000; in 1971, none; in 1972, $7,000; in 1973, $5,000; in 1974, $8,000; in 1975, $6,000; and $4,000 in 1976. The accumulation distribution is deemed distributed $6,000 in 1969, $4,000 in 1970, none in 1971, $7,000 in 1972, $5,000 in 1973, $8,000 in 1974, and $3,000 in 1975.

[T.D. 7204, 37 FR 17143, Aug. 25, 1972]

§ 1.666(b)–1A Total taxes deemed distributed.

(a) If an accumulation distribution is deemed under § 1.666(a)–1A to be distributed on the last day of a preceding taxable year and the amount is not less than the undistributed net income for such preceding taxable year, then an additional amount equal to the "taxes imposed on the trust attributable to the undistributed net income" (as defined in § 1.665(d)–1A(b)) for such preceding taxable year is also deemed distributed under section 661(a)(2). For example, a trust has undistributed net income of $8,000 for the taxable year 1974. The taxes imposed on the trust attributable to the undistributed net income are $3,032. During the taxable year 1977, an accumulation distribution of $8,000 is made to the beneficiary, which is deemed under § 1.666(a)–1A to have been distributed on the last day of 1974. The 1977 accumulation distribution is not less than the 1974 undistributed net income. Accordingly, the taxes of $3,032 imposed on the trust attributable to the undistributed net income for 1974 are also deemed to have been distributed on the last day of 1974. Thus, a total of $11,032 will be deemed to have been distributed on the last day of 1974.

(b) For the purpose of paragraph (a) of this section, the undistributed net income of any preceding taxable year and the taxes imposed on the trust for such preceding taxable year attributable to such undistributed net income are computed after taking into account any accumulation distributions of taxable years intervening between such preceding taxable year and the taxable year. See paragraph (d) of § 1.666(a)–1A.

[T.D. 7204, 37 FR 17145, Aug. 25, 1972]

§ 1.666(c)–1A Pro rata portion of taxes deemed distributed.

(a) If an accumulation distribution is deemed under § 1.666(a)–1A to be distributed on the last day of a preceding taxable year and the amount is less than the undistributed net income for such preceding taxable year, then an additional amount is also deemed distributed under section 661(a)(2). The additional amount is equal to the "taxes imposed on the trust attributable to the undistributed net income" (as defined in § 1.665(a)–1A(b)) for such preceding taxable year, multiplied by a fraction, the numerator of which is the amount of the accumulation distribution allocated to such preceding taxable year and the denominator of which is the undistributed net income for such preceding taxable year. See paragraph (b) of example (1) and paragraphs (c) and (f) of example (2) in § 1.666(c)–2A for illustrations of this paragraph.

(b) For the purpose of paragraph (a) of this section, the undistributed net income of any preceding taxable year and the taxes imposed on the trust for such preceding taxable year attributable to such undistributed net income are computed after taking into account any accumulation distributions of any taxable years intervening between such preceding taxable year and the taxable year. See paragraph (d) of § 1.666(a)–1A and paragraph (c) of example (1) and paragraphs (e) and (h) of example (2) in § 1.666(c)–2A.

[T.D. 7204, 37 FR 17145, Aug. 25, 1972]

§ 1.666(c)–2A Illustration of the provisions of section 666(a), (b), and (c).

The application of the provisions of §§ 1.666(a)–1A, 1.666(b)–1A, and 1.666(c)–1A may be illustrated by the following examples:

Example (1). (a) A trust created on January 1, 1974, makes accumulation distributions as follows:

1979	$7,000
1980	26,000

For 1974 through 1978, the undistributed portion of distributable net income, taxes imposed on the trust attributable to the undistributed net income, and undistributed net income are as follows:

Year	*Undistributed portion of distributable net income*	*Taxes imposed on the trust attributable to the undistributed net income*	*Undistributed net income*
1974	$12,000	$3,400	$8,700
1975	16,100	5,200	10,900
1976	6,100	1,360	4,640
1977	None	None	None
1978	10,100	2,640	7,460

The trust has no undistributed capital gain.

(b) Since the entire amount of the accumulation distribution for 1979 ($7,000) is less than the undistributed net income for 1974 ($8,700), an additional amount of $2,736 (7,000/8,700 * $3,400) is deemed distributed under section 666(c).

(c) In allocating the accumulation distribution for 1980, the amount of undistributed net income for 1974 will reflect the accumulation distribution for 1979. The undistributed net income for 1974 will then be $1,700 and the taxes imposed on the trust for 1974 will be $664, determined as follows:

Undistributed net income as of the close of 1974	$8,700
Less: Accumulation distribution (1979)	7,000
Balance (undistributed net income as of the close of 1979)	1,700
Taxes imposed on the trust attributable to the undistributed net income as of the close of 1979 (1,700/8,700 * $3,400)	664

(d) The accumulation distribution of $26,000 for 1980 is deemed to have been made on the last day of the preceding taxable years of the trust to the extent of $24,800, the total of the undistributed net income for such years, as shown in the tabulation below. In addition, $9,864, the total taxes imposed on the trust attributable to the undistributed net income for such years is also deemed to have been distributed on the last day of such years, as shown below:

Year	*Undistributed net income*	*Taxes imposed on the trust*
1974	$1,700	$664
1975	10,900	5,200
1976	4,740	1,360
1977	None	None
1978	7,460	2,640
1979	None	None

Example (2). (a) Under the terms of a trust instrument, the trustee has discretion to accumulate or distribute the income to X and to invade corpus for the benefit of X. The entire income of the trust is from royalties. Both X and the trust report on the calendar year basis. All of the income for 1974 was accumulated. The distributable net income of the trust for the taxable year 1974 is $20,100 and the income taxes paid by the trust for 1974 attributable to the undistributed net income are $7,260. All of the income for 1975 and 1976 was distributed and in addition the trustee made accumulation distributions within the meaning of section 665(b) of $5,420 for each year.

(b) The undistributed net income of the trust determined under section 665(a) as of the close of 1974, is $12,840, computed as follows:

Distributable net income	$20,100
Less: Taxes imposed on the trust attributable to the undistributed net income	7,260
Undistributed net income as of the close of 1974	12,840

(c) The accumulation distribution of $5,420 made during the taxable year 1975 is deemed under section 666(a) to have been made on December 31, 1974. Since this accumulation distribution is less than the 1974 undistributed net income of $12,840, a portion of the taxes imposed on the trust for 1974 is also deemed under section 666(c) to have been distributed on December 31, 1974. The total amount deemed to have been distributed to X on December 31, 1974 is $8,484, computed as follows:

Accumulation distribution	$5,420
Taxes deemed distributed (5,420/12,840 * $7,260)	3,064
Total	8,484

(d) After the application of the provisions of subpart D to the accumulation distribution of 1975, the undistributed net income of the trust for 1974 is $7,420, computed as follows:

Undistributed net income as of the close of 1974	$12,840
Less: 1975 accumulation distribution deemed distributed on December 31, 1974 (paragraph (c) of this example)	5,420
Undistributed net income for 1974 as of the close of 1975	7,420

(e) The taxes imposed on the trust attributable to the undistributed net income for the taxable year 1974, as adjusted to give effect to the 1975 accumulation distribution, amount to $4,196, computed as follows:

Taxes imposed on the trust attributable to undistributed net income as of the close of 1974	$7,260
Less: Taxes deemed distributed in 1974	3,064
Taxes attributable to the undistributed net income determined as of the close of 1975	4,196

(f) The accumulation distribution of $5,420 made during the taxable year 1976 is, under section 666(a), deemed a distribution to X on December 31, 1974, within the meaning of section 661(a)(2). Since the accumulation distribution is less than the 1974 adjusted undistributed net income of $7,420, the trust is deemed under section 666(c) also to have distributed on December 31, 1974, a portion of the taxes imposed on the trust for 1974. The total amount deemed to be distributed on December 31, 1974, with respect to the accumulation distribution made in 1976, is $8,484, computed as follows:

Accumulation distribution	$5,420
Taxes deemed distributed (5,420/7,420 * $4,196)	3,064
Total	8,484

(g) After the application of the provisions of subpart D to the accumulation distribution of 1976, the undistributed net income of the trust for 1974 is $2,000, computed as follows:

Undistributed net income for 1974 as of the close of 1975	$7,420
Less: 1976 accumulation distribution deemed distributed on December 31, 1974 (paragraph (f) of this example)	5,420
Undistributed net income for 1974 as of the close of 1976	2,000

(h) The taxes imposed on the trust attributable to the undistributed net income of the trust for the taxable year 1974, determined as of the close of the taxable year 1976, amount to $1,132 ($4,196 less $3,064).

[T.D. 7204, 37 FR 17145, Aug. 25, 1972]

§ 1.666(d)–1A Information required from trusts.

(a) Adequate records required. For all taxable years of a trust, the trustee must retain copies of the trust's income tax return as well as information pertaining to any adjustments in the tax shown as due on the return. The trustee shall also keep the records of the trust required to be retained by section 6001 and the regulations thereunder for each taxable year as to which the period of limitations on assessment of tax under section 6501 has not expired. If the trustee fails to produce such copies and records, and such failure is due to circumstances beyond the reasonable control of the trustee or any predecessor trustee, the trustee may reconstruct the amount of corpus, accumulated income, etc., from competent sources (including, to the extent permissible, Internal Revenue Service records). To the extent that an accurate reconstruction can be made for a taxable year, the requirements of this paragraph shall be deemed satisfied for such year.

(b) Rule when information is not available—(1) *Accumulation distributions.* If adequate records (as required by paragraph (a) of this section) are not available to determine the proper application of subpart D to an accumulation distribution made in a taxable year by a trust, such accumulation distribution shall be deemed to consist of undistributed net income earned during the earliest preceding taxable year (as defined in § 1.665(e)–1A) of the trust in which it can be established that the trust was in existence. If adequate records are available for some years, but not for others, the accumulation distribution shall be allocated first to the earliest preceding taxable year of the trust for which there are adequate records and then to each subsequent preceding taxable year for which there are adequate records. To the extent that the distribution is not allocated in such manner to years for which adequate records are available, it will be deemed distributed on the last day of the earliest preceding taxable year of the trust in which it is established that the trust was in existence and for which the trust has no records. The provisions of this subparagraph may be illustrated by the following example

Example. A trust makes a distribution in 1975 of $100,000. The trustee has adequate records for 1973, 1974, and 1975. The records show that the trust is on the calendar year basis, had distributable net income in 1975 of $20,000, and undistributed net income in 1974 of $15,000, and in 1973 of $16,000. The trustee has no other records of the trust except for a copy of the trust instrument showing that the trust was established on January 1, 1965. He establishes that the loss of the records was due to circumstances beyond his control. Since the distribution is made in 1975, the earliest "preceding taxable year", as defined in § 1.665(e)–1A, is 1969. Since $80,000 of the distribution is an accumulation distribution, and $31,000 thereof is allocated to 1974 and 1973, $49,000 is deemed to have been distributed on the last day of 1969.

(2) *Taxes.* (i) If an amount is deemed under this paragraph to be undistributed net income allocated to a preceding taxable year for which adequate records are not available, there shall be deemed to be "taxes imposed on the trust" for such preceding taxable year an amount equal to the taxes that the trust would have paid if the deemed undistributed net income were the amount remaining when the taxes were subtracted from taxable income of the trust for such year. For example, assume that an accumulation distribution in 1975 of $100,000 is deemed to be undistributed net income from 1971, and that the taxable income required to produce $100,000 after taxes in 1971 would be $284,966. Therefore the amount deemed to be "taxes imposed on the trust" for such preceding taxable year is $184,966.

(ii) The credit allowed by section 667(b) shall not be allowed for any amount deemed under this subparagraph to be "taxes imposed on the trust."

[T.D. 7204, 37 FR 17146, Aug. 25, 1972]

§ 667. Treatment of Amounts Deemed Distributed by Trust in Preceding Years

(a) General rule. The total of the amounts which are treated under section 666 as having been distributed by a trust in a preceding taxable year shall be included in the income of a beneficiary of the trust when paid, credited, or required to be distributed to the extent that such total would have been included in the income of such beneficiary under section 662(a)(2) (and, with respect to any tax-exempt interest to which section 103 applies, under section 662(b)) if such total had been paid to such beneficiary on the last day of such preceding taxable year. The tax imposed by this subtitle on a beneficiary for a taxable year in which any such amount is included in his income shall be determined only as provided in this section and shall consist of the sum of—

(1) a partial tax computed on the taxable income reduced by an amount equal to the total of such amounts, at the rate and in the manner as if this section had not been enacted,

(2) a partial tax determined as provided in subsection (b) of this section, and

(3) in the case of a foreign trust, the interest charge determined as provided in section 668.

(b) Tax on distribution.

(1) In general. The partial tax imposed by subsection (a)(2) shall be determined—

(A) by determining the number of preceding taxable years of the trust on the last day of which an amount is deemed under section 666(a) to have been distributed,

(B) by taking from the 5 taxable years immediately preceding the year of the accumulation distribution the 1 taxable year for which the beneficiary's taxable income was the highest and the 1 taxable year for which his taxable income was the lowest,

(C) by adding to the beneficiary's taxable income for each of the 3 taxable years remaining after the application of subparagraph (B) an amount determined by dividing the amount deemed distributed under section 666 and required to be included in income under subsection (a) by the number of preceding taxable years determined under subparagraph (A), and

(D) by determining the average increase in tax for the 3 taxable years referred to in subparagraph (C) resulting from the application of such subparagraph.

The partial tax imposed by subsection (a)(2) shall be the excess (if any) of the average increase in tax determined under subparagraph (D), multiplied by the number of preceding taxable years determined under subparagraph (A), over the amount of taxes (other than the amount of taxes described in section 665(d)(2)) deemed distributed to the beneficiary under sections 666(b) and (c).

(2) Treatment of loss years. For purposes of paragraph (1), the taxable income of the beneficiary for any taxable year shall be deemed to be not less than zero.

(3) Certain preceding taxable years not taken into account. For purposes of paragraph (1), if the amount of the undistributed net income deemed distributed in any preceding taxable year of the trust is less than 25 percent of the amount of the accumulation distribution divided by the number of preceding taxable years to which the accumulation distribution is allocated under section 666(a), the number of preceding taxable years of the trust with respect to which an amount is deemed distributed to a beneficiary under section 666(a) shall be determined without regard to such year.

(4) Effect of other accumulation distributions. In computing the partial tax under paragraph (1) for any beneficiary, the income of such beneficiary for each of his prior taxable years shall include amounts previously deemed distributed to such beneficiary in such year under section 666 as a result of prior accumulation distributions (whether from the same or another trust).

(5) Multiple distributions in the same taxable year. In the case of accumulation distributions made from more than one trust which are includible in the income of a beneficiary in the same taxable year, the distributions shall be deemed to have been made consecutively in whichever order the beneficiary shall determine.

(6) Adjustment in partial tax for estate and generation-skipping transfer taxes attributable to partial tax.

(A) In general. The partial tax shall be reduced by an amount which is equal to the pre-death portion of the partial tax multiplied by a fraction—

(i) the numerator of which is that portion of the tax imposed by chapter 11 or 13, as the case may be, which is attributable (on a proportionate basis) to amounts included in the accumulation distribution, and

(ii) the denominator of which is the amount of the accumulation distribution which is subject to the tax imposed by chapter 11 or 13, as the case may be.

(B) Partial tax determined without regard to this paragraph. For purposes of this paragraph, the term "partial tax" means the partial tax imposed by subsection (a)(2) determined under this subsection without regard to this paragraph.

(C) Pre-death portion. For purposes of this paragraph, the pre-death portion of the partial tax shall be an amount which bears the same ratio to the partial tax as the portion of the accumulation distribution which is attributable to the period before the date of the death of the decedent or the date of the generation-skipping transfer bears to the total accumulation distribution.

(c) Special rule for multiple trusts.

(1) In general. If, in the same prior taxable year of the beneficiary in which any part of the accumulation distribution from a trust (hereinafter in this paragraph referred to as "third trust") is deemed under section 666(a) to have been distributed to such beneficiary, some part of prior distributions by each of 2 or more other trusts is deemed under section 666(a) to have been distributed to such beneficiary, then subsections (b) and (c) of section 666 shall not apply with respect to such part of the accumulation distribution from such third trust.

(2) Accumulation distributions from trust not taken into account unless they equal or exceed $1,000. For purposes of paragraph (1), an accumulation distribution from a trust to a beneficiary shall be taken into account only if such distribution, when added to any prior accumulation distributions from such trust which are deemed under section 666(a) to have been distributed to such beneficiary for the same prior taxable year of the beneficiary, equals or exceeds $1,000.

(d) Special rules for foreign trust.

(1) Foreign tax deemed paid by beneficiary.

(A) In general. In determining the increase in tax under subsection (b)(1)(D) for any computation year, the taxes described in section 665(d)(2) which are deemed distributed under section 666(b) or (c) and added under subsection (b)(1)(C) to the taxable income of the beneficiary for any computation year shall, except as provided in subparagraphs (B) and (C), be treated as a credit against the increase in tax for such computation year under subsection (b)(1)(D).

(B) Deduction in lieu of credit. If the beneficiary did not choose the benefits of subpart A of part III of subchapter N with respect to the computation year, the beneficiary may in lieu of treating the amounts described in subparagraph (A) (without regard to subparagraph (C)) as a credit may treat such amounts as a deduction in computing the beneficiary's taxable income under subsection (b)(1)(C) for the computation year.

(C) Limitation on credit; retention of character.

(i) Limitation on credit. For purposes of determining under subparagraph (A) the amount treated as a credit for any computation year, the limitations under subpart A of part III of subchapter N shall be applied separately with respect to amounts added under subsection (b)(1)(C) to the taxable income of the beneficiary for such computation year. For purposes of computing the increase in tax under subsection (b)(1)(D) for any computation year for which the beneficiary did not choose the benefits of subpart A of part III of subchapter N, the beneficiary shall be treated as having chosen such benefits for such computation year.

(ii) Retention of character. The items of income, deduction, and credit of the Trust shall retain their character (subject to the application of section 904(f)(5)) to the extent necessary to apply this paragraph.

(D) Computation year. For purposes of this paragraph, the term "computation year" means any of the three taxable years remaining after application of subsection (b)(1)(B).

(e) Retention of character of amounts distributed from accumulation trust to nonresident aliens and foreign corporations. In the case of a distribution from a trust to a nonresident alien individual or to a foreign corporation, the first sentence of subsection (a) shall be applied as if the reference to the determination of character under section 662(b) applied to all amounts instead of just to tax-exempt interest.

Regulations

§ 1.667(b)–1A Authorization of credit to beneficiary for taxes imposed on the trust.

(a) Determination of credit. (1) *In general.* Section 667(b) allows under certain circumstances a credit (without interest) against the tax imposed by subtitle A of the Code on the beneficiary for the taxable year in which the accumulation distribution is required to be included in income under section 668(a). In the case of an accumulation distribution consisting only of undistributed net income, the amount of such credit is the total of the taxes deemed distributed to such beneficiary under section 666(b) and (c) as a result of such accumulation distribution for preceding taxable years of the trust on the last day of which such beneficiary was in being, less the amount of such taxes for such preceding taxable years taken into account in reducing the amount of partial tax determined under § 1.668(b)–1A. In the case of an accumulation distribution consisting only of undistributed capital gain, the amount of such credit is the total of the taxes deemed distributed as a result of the accumulation distribution to such beneficiary under section 669(d) and (e) for preceding taxable years of the trust on the last day of which such beneficiary was in being, less the amount of such taxes for such preceding taxable years taken into account in reducing the amount of partial tax determined under § 1.669(b)–1A. In the case of an accumulation distribution consisting of both undistributed net income and undistributed capital gain, a credit will not be available unless the total taxes deemed distributed to the beneficiary for all preceding taxable years as a result of the accumulation distribution exceeds the beneficiary's partial tax determined under §§ 1.668(b)–1A and 1.669(b)–1A without reference to the taxes deemed distributed. A credit is not allowed for any taxes deemed distributed as a result of an accumulation distribution to a beneficiary by reason of sections 666(b) and (c) or sections 669(d) and (e) for a preceding taxable year of the trust before the beneficiary was born or created. However, if as a result of an accumulation distribution the total taxes deemed distributed under sections 668(a)(2) and 668(a)(3) in preceding taxable years before the beneficiary was born or created exceed the partial taxes attributable to amounts deemed distributed in such years, such excess may be used to offset any liability for partial taxes attributable to amounts deemed distributed as a result of the same accumulation distribution in preceding taxable years after the beneficiary was born or created.

(2) *Exact method.* In the case of the tax computed under the exact method provided in §§ 1.668(b)–1A(b) and 1.669(b)–1A(b), the credit allowed by this section is computed as follows:

(i) Compute the total taxes deemed distributed under §§ 1.666(b)–1A and 1.666(c)–1A or §§ 1.669(d)–1A and 1.669(e)–1A, whichever are appropriate, for the preceding taxable years of the trust on the last day of which the beneficiary was in being.

(ii) Compute the total of the amounts of tax determined under § 1.668(b)–1A(b)(1) or § 1.669(b)–1A(b)(1), whichever is appropriate, for the prior taxable years of the beneficiary in which he was in being.

If the amount determined under subdivision (i) of this subparagraph does not exceed the amount determined under subdivision (ii) of this subparagraph, no credit is allowable. If the amount determined under subdivision (i) of this subparagraph exceeds the amount determined under subdivision (ii) of this subparagraph, the credit allowable is the lesser of the amount of such excess or the amount of taxes deemed distributed to the beneficiary for all preceding taxable years to the extent that such taxes are not used in § 1.668(b)–1A(b)(2) or § 1.669(b)–1A(b)(2) in determining the beneficiary's partial tax under section 668(a)(2) or 668(a)(3). The application of this subparagraph may be illustrated by the following example:

Example. An accumulation distribution made in 1975 is deemed distribution in 1973 and 1974, years in which the beneficiary was in being. The taxes deemed distributed in such years are $4,000 and $2,000, respectively, totaling $6,000. The amounts of tax computed under § 1.668(b)–1A(b)(1) attributable to the amounts thrown back are $3,000 and $2,000, respectively, totaling $5,000. The credit allowable under this subparagraph is therefore $1,000 ($6,000 less $5,000).

(3) *Short-cut method.* In the case of the tax computed under the short-cut method provided in § 1.668(b)–1A(c) or 1.669(b)–1A(c), the credit allowed by this section is computed as follows:

(i) Compute the total taxes deemed distributed in all preceding taxable years of the trust under §§ 1.666(b)–1A and 1.666(c)–1A or §§ 1.669(d)–1A and 1.669(e)–1A, whichever are appropriate.

(ii) Compute the beneficiary's partial tax determined under either § 1.668(b)–1A(c)(1)(v) or § 1.669(b)–1A(c)(1)(v), whichever is appropriate.

If the amount determined under subdivision (i) of this subparagraph does not exceed the amount determined under subdivision (ii) of this subparagraph, no credit is allowable. If the amount determined under subdivision (i) of this subparagraph exceeds the amount determined under subdivision (ii) of this subparagraph,

(iii) Compute the total taxes deemed distributed under §§ 1.666(b)–1A and 1.666(c)–1A or §§ 1.669(d)–1A and 1.669(e)–1A, which are appropriate, for the preceding taxable years of the trust on the last day of which the beneficiary was in being.

(iv) Multiply the amount by which subdivision (i) of this subparagraph exceeds subdivision (ii) of this subparagraph by a fraction, the numerator of which is the amount determined under subdivision (iii) of this subparagraph and the denominator of which is the amount determined under subdivision (i) of this subparagraph. The result is the allowable credit. The application of this subparagraph may be illustrated by the following example:

Example. An accumulation distribution that consists only of undistributed net income is made in 1975. The taxes deemed distributed in the preceding years under §§ 1.666(b)–1A and 1.666(c)–1A are $15,000. The amount determined under § 1.668(b)–1A(c)(1)(v) is $12,000. The beneficiary was in being on the last day of all but one preceding taxable year in which the accumulation distribution was deemed made, and the taxes deemed distributed in those years was $10,000. Therefore, the excess of the subdivision (i) amount over the subdivision (ii) amount is $3,000, and is multiplied by 10,000/15,000, resulting in an answer of $2,000, which is the credit allowable when computed under the short-cut method.

(b) Year of credit. The credit to which a beneficiary is entitled under this section is allowed for the taxable year in which the accumulation distribution (to which the credit relates) is required to be included in the income of the beneficiary under section 668(a). Any excess over the total tax liability of the beneficiary for such year is treated as an overpayment of tax by the beneficiary. See section 6401(b) and the regulations thereunder.

[T.D. 7204, 37 FR 17147, Aug. 25, 1972]

§ 668. Interest Charge on Accumulation Distributions from Foreign Trusts

(a) General rule. For purposes of the tax determined under section 667(a)—

(1) Interest determined using underpayment rates. The interest charge determined under this section with respect to any distribution is the amount of interest which would be determined on the partial tax computed under section 667(b) for the period described in paragraph (2) using the rates and the method under section 6621 applicable to underpayments of tax.

(2) Period. For purposes of paragraph (1), the period described in this paragraph is the period which begins on the date which is the applicable number of years before the date of the distribution and which ends on the date of the distribution.

(3) Applicable number of years. For purposes of paragraph (2)—

(A) In general. The applicable number of years with respect to a distribution is the number determined by dividing—

(i) the sum of the products described in subparagraph (B) with respect to each undistributed income year, by

(ii) the aggregate undistributed net income.

The quotient determined under the preceding sentence shall be rounded under procedures prescribed by the Secretary.

(B) Product described. For purposes of subparagraph (A), the product described in this subparagraph with respect to any undistributed income year is the product of—

(i) the undistributed net income for such year, and

(ii) the sum of the number of taxable years between such year and the taxable year of the distribution (counting in each case the undistributed income year but not counting the taxable year of the distribution).

(4) Undistributed income year. For purposes of this subsection, the term "undistributed income year" means any prior taxable year of the trust for which there is undistributed net income, other than a taxable year during all of which the beneficiary receiving the distribution was not a citizen or resident of the United States.

(5) Determination of undistributed net income. Notwithstanding section 666, for purposes of this subsection, an accumulation distribution from the trust shall be treated as reducing proportionately the undistributed net income for undistributed income years.

(6) Periods before 1996. Interest for the portion of the period described in paragraph (2) which occurs before January 1, 1996, shall be determined—

(A) by using an interest rate of 6 percent, and

(B) without compounding until January 1, 1996.

(b) Limitation. The total amount of the interest charge shall not, when added to the total partial tax computed under section 667(b), exceed the amount of the accumulation distribution (other than the amount of tax deemed distributed by section 666(b) or (c)) in respect of which such partial tax was determined.

(c) Interest charge not deductible. The interest charge determined under this section shall not be allowed as a deduction for purposes of any tax imposed by this title.

Subpart E. Grantors and Others Treated as Substantial Owners

§ 671. Trust Income, Deductions, and Credits Attributable to Grantors and Others as Substantial Owners

Where it is specified in this subpart that the grantor or another person shall be treated as the owner of any portion of a trust, there shall then be included in computing the taxable income and credits of the grantor or the other person those items of income, deductions, and credits against tax of the trust which are attributable to that portion of the trust to the extent that such items would be taken into account under this chapter in computing taxable income or credits against the tax of an individual. Any remaining portion of the trust shall be subject to subparts A through D. No items of a trust shall be included in computing the taxable income and credits of the grantor or of any other person solely on the grounds of his dominion and control over the trust under section 61 (relating to definition of gross income) or any other provision of this title, except as specified in this subpart.

Regulations

§ 1.671–1 Grantors and others treated as substantial owners; scope.

(a) Subpart E (section 671 and following), part I, subchapter J, Chapter 1 of the Code, contains provisions taxing income of a trust to the grantor or another person under certain circumstances even though he is not treated as a beneficiary under Subparts A through D (section 641 and following) of such Part I. Sections 671 and 672 contain general provisions relating to the entire subpart. Sections 673 through 677 define the circumstances under which income of a trust is taxed to a grantor. These circumstances are in general as follows:

(1) If the grantor has retained a reversionary interest in the trust, within specified time limits (section 673);

(2) If the grantor or a nonadverse party has certain powers over the beneficial interests under the trust (section 674);

(3) If certain administrative powers over the trust exist under which the grantor can or does benefit (section 675);

(4) If the grantor or a nonadverse party has a power to revoke the trust or return the corpus to the grantor (section 676); or

(5) If the grantor or a nonadverse party has the power to distribute income to or for the benefit of the grantor or the grantor's spouse (section 677).

Under section 678, income of a trust is taxed to a person other than the grantor to the extent that he has the sole power to vest corpus or income in himself.

(b) Sections 671 through 677 do not apply if the income of a trust is taxable to a grantor's spouse under section 71 or 682 (relating respectively to alimony and separate maintenance payments, and the income of an estate or trust in the case of divorce, etc.).

(c) Except as provided in such Subpart E, income of a trust is not included in computing the taxable income and credits of a grantor or another person solely on the grounds of his dominion and control over the trust. However, the provisions of subpart E do not apply in situations involving an assignment of future income, whether or not the assignment is to a trust. Thus, for example, a person who assigns his right to future income under an employment contract may be taxed on that income even though the assignment is to a trust over which the assignor has retained none of the controls specified in sections 671 through 677. Similarly, a bondholder who assigns his right to interest may be taxed on interest payments even though the assignment is to an uncontrolled trust. Nor are the rules as to family partnerships affected by the provisions of subpart E, even though a partnership interest is held in trust. Likewise, these sections have no application in determining the right of a grantor to deductions for payments to a trust under a transfer and leaseback arrangement. In addition, the limitation of the last sentence of section 671 does not prevent any person from being taxed on the income of a trust when it is used to discharge his legal obligation. See § 1.662(a)–4. He is then treated as a beneficiary under subparts A through D or treated as an owner under section 677 because the income is distributed for his benefit, and not because of his dominion or control over the trust.

(d) The provisions of subpart E are not applicable with respect to a pooled income fund as defined in paragraph (5) of section 642(c) and the regulations thereunder, a charitable remainder annuity trust as defined in paragraph (1) of section 664(d) and the regulations thereunder, or a charitable remainder unitrust as defined in paragraph (2) of section 664(d) and the regulations thereunder.

(e) For the effective date of subpart E see section 683 and the regulations thereunder.

(f) For rules relating to the treatment of liabilities resulting on the sale or other disposition of encumbered trust property due to a renunciation of powers by the grantor or other owner, see § 1.1001–2.

[T.D. 6500, 25 FR 11814, Nov. 26, 1960, as amended by T.D. 7148, 36 FR 20749, Oct. 29, 1971; T.D. 7741, 45 FR 81745, Dec. 12, 1980]

§ 1.671–2 Applicable principles.

(a) Under section 671 a grantor or another person includes in computing his taxable income and credits those items of income, deduction, and credit against tax which are attributable to or included in any portion of a trust of which he is treated as the owner. Sections 673 through 678 set forth the rules for determining when the grantor or another person is treated as the owner of any portion of a trust. The rules for determining the items of income, deduction, and credit against tax that are attributable to or included in a portion of the trust are set forth in § 1.671–3.

(b) Since the principle underlying subpart E (section 671 and following), part I, subchapter J, chapter 1 of the Code, is in general that income of a trust over which the grantor or another person has retained substantial dominion or control should be taxed to the grantor or other person rather than to the trust which receives the income or to the beneficiary to whom the income may be distributed, it is ordinarily immaterial whether the income involved constitutes income or corpus for trust accounting purposes. Accordingly, when it is stated in the regulations under subpart E that "income" is attributed to the grantor or another person, the reference, unless specifically limited, is to income determined for tax purposes and not to income for trust accounting purposes. When it is intended to emphasize that income for trust accounting purposes (determined in accordance with the provisions set forth in § 1.643(b)–1 is meant, the phrase "ordinary income" is used.

(c) An item of income, deduction, or credit included in computing the taxable income and credits of a grantor or another person under section 671 is treated as if it had been received or paid directly by the grantor or other person (whether or not an individual). For example, a charitable contribution made by a trust which is attributed to the grantor (an individual) under sections 671 through 677 will be aggregated with his other charitable contributions to determine their deductibility under the limitations of section 170(b)(1). Likewise, dividends received by a trust from sources in a particular foreign country which are attributed to a grantor or another person under subpart E will be aggregated with his other income from sources within that country to determine whether the taxpayer is subject to the limitations of section 904 with respect to credit for the tax paid to that country.

(d) Items of income, deduction, and credit not attributed to or included in any portion of a trust of which the grantor or another person is treated as the owner under subpart E are subject to the provisions of subparts A through D (section 641 and following), of such part I.

(e)(1) For purposes of part I of subchapter J, chapter 1 of the Internal Revenue Code, a grantor includes any person to the extent such person either creates a trust, or directly or indirectly makes a gratuitous transfer (within the meaning of paragraph (e)(2) of this section) of property to a trust. For purposes of this section, the term property includes cash. If a person creates or funds a trust on behalf of another person, both persons are treated as grantors of the trust. (See section 6048 for reporting requirements that apply to grantors of foreign trusts.) However, a person who creates a trust but makes no gratuitous transfers to the trust is not treated as an owner of any portion of the trust under sections 671 through 677 or 679. Also, a person who funds a trust with an amount that is directly reimbursed to such person within a reasonable period of time and who makes no other transfers to the trust that constitute gratuitous transfers is not treated as an owner of any portion of the trust under sections 671 through 677 or 679. See also § 1.672(f)–5(a).

(2)(i) A gratuitous transfer is any transfer other than a transfer for fair market value. A transfer of property to a trust may be considered a gratuitous transfer without regard to whether the transfer is treated as a gift for gift tax purposes.

(ii) For purposes of this paragraph (e), a transfer is for fair market value only to the extent of the value of property received from the trust, services rendered by the trust, or the right to use property of the trust. For example, rents, royalties, interest, and compensation paid to a trust are transfers for fair market value only to the extent that the payments reflect an arm's length price for the use of the property of, or for the services rendered by, the trust. For purposes of this determination, an interest in the trust is not property received from the trust. In addition, a person will not be treated as making a transfer for fair market value merely because the transferor recognizes gain on the transaction. See, for example, section 684 regarding the recognition of gain on certain transfers to foreign trusts.

(iii) For purposes of this paragraph (e), a gratuitous transfer does not include a distribution to a trust with respect to an interest held by such trust in either a trust described in paragraph (e)(3) of this section or an entity other than a trust. For example, a distribution to a trust by a corporation with respect to its stock described in section 301 is not a gratuitous transfer.

(3) A grantor includes any person who acquires an interest in a trust from a grantor of the trust if the interest acquired is an interest in certain investment trusts described in § 301.7701–4(c) of this chapter, liquidating trusts described in § 301.7701–4(d) of this chapter, or environmental remediation trusts described in § 301.7701–4(e) of this chapter.

(4) If a gratuitous transfer is made by a partnership or corporation to a trust and is for a business purpose of the partnership or corporation, the partnership or corporation will generally be treated as the grantor of the trust. For example, if a partnership makes a gratuitous transfer to a trust in order to secure a legal obligation of the partnership to a third party unrelated to the partnership, the partnership will be treated as the grantor of the trust. However, if a partnership or a corporation makes a gratuitous transfer to a trust that is not for a business purpose of the partnership or corporation but is for the personal purposes of one or more of the partners or shareholders, the gratuitous transfer will be treated as a constructive distribution to such partners or shareholders under federal tax principles and the partners or the shareholders will be treated as the grantors of the trust. For example, if a partnership makes a gratuitous transfer to a trust that is for the benefit of a child of a partner, the gratuitous transfer will be treated as a distribution to the partner under section 731 and a subsequent gratuitous transfer by the partner to the trust.

(5) If a trust makes a gratuitous transfer of property to another trust, the grantor of the transferor trust generally will be treated as the grantor of the transferee trust. However, if a person with a general power of appointment over the transferor trust exercises that power in favor of another trust, then such person will be treated as the grantor of the transferee trust, even if the grantor of the transferor trust is treated as the owner of the transferor trust under subpart E of part I, subchapter J, chapter 1 of the Internal Revenue Code.

(6) The following examples illustrate the rules of this paragraph (e). Unless otherwise indicated, all trusts are domestic trusts and all other persons are United States persons.

The examples are as follows:

Example (1). A creates and funds a trust, T, for the benefit of her children. B subsequently makes a gratuitous transfer to T. Under paragraph (e)(1) of this section, both A and B are grantors of T.

Example (2). A makes an investment in a fixed investment trust, T, that is classified as a trust under § 301.7701–4(c)(1) of this chapter. A is a grantor of T. B subsequently acquires A's entire interest in T. Under paragraph (e)(3) of this section, B is a grantor of T with respect to such interest.

Example (3). A, an attorney, creates a foreign trust, FT, on behalf of A's client, B, and transfers $100 to FT out of A's funds. A is reimbursed by B for the $100 transferred to FT. The trust instrument states that the trustee has discretion to distribute the income or corpus of FT to B, and B's children. Both A and B are treated as grantors of FT under paragraph (e)(1) of this section. In addition, B is treated as the owner of the entire trust under section 677. Because A is reimbursed for the $100 transferred to FT on behalf of B, A is not treated as transferring any property to FT. Therefore, A is not an owner of any portion of FT under sections 671 through 677 regardless of whether A retained any power over or interest in FT described in sections 673 through 677. Furthermore, A is not treated as an owner of any portion of FT under section 679. Both A and B are responsible parties for purposes of the requirements in section 6048.

Example (4). A creates and funds a trust, T. A does not retain any power or interest in T that would cause A to be treated as an owner of any portion of the trust under sections 671 through 677. B holds an unrestricted power, exercisable solely by B, to withdraw certain amounts contributed to the trust before the end of the calendar year and to vest those amounts in B. B is treated as an owner of the portion of T that is subject to the withdrawal power under section 678(a)(1). However, B is not a grantor of T under paragraph (e)(1) of this section because B neither created T nor made a gratuitous transfer to T.

Example (5). A transfers cash to a trust, T, through a broker, in exchange for units in T. The units in T are not property for purposes of determining whether A has received fair market value under paragraph (e)(2)(ii) of this section. Therefore, A has made a gratuitous transfer to T, and, under paragraph (e)(1) of this section, A is a grantor of T.

Example (6). A borrows cash from T, a trust. A has not made any gratuitous transfers to T. Arm's length interest payments by A to T will not be treated as gratuitous transfers under paragraph (e)(2)(ii) of this section. Therefore, under paragraph (e)(1) of this section, A is not a grantor of T with respect to the interest payments.

Example (7). A, B's brother, creates a trust, T, for B's benefit and transfers $50,000 to T. The trustee invests the $50,000 in stock of Company X. C, B's uncle, purportedly sells property with a fair market value of $1,000,000 to T in exchange for the stock when it has appreciated to a fair market value of $100,000. Under paragraph (e)(2)(ii) of this section, the $900,000 excess value is a gratuitous transfer by C. Therefore, under paragraph (e)(1) of this section, A is a grantor with respect to the portion of the trust valued at $100,000, and C is a grantor of T with respect to the portion of the trust valued at $900,000. In addition, A or C or both will be treated as the owners of the respective portions of the trust of which each person is a grantor if A or C or both retain powers over or interests in such portions under sections 673 through 677.

Example (8). G creates and funds a trust, T1, for the benefit of G's children and grandchildren. After G's death, under authority granted to the trustees in the trust instrument, the trustees of T1 transfer a portion of the assets of T1 to another trust, T2, and retain a power to revoke T2 and revest the assets of T2 in T1. Under paragraphs (e)(1) and (5) of this section, G is the grantor of T1 and T2. In addition, because the trustees of T1 have retained a power to revest the assets of T2 in T1, T1 is treated as the owner of T2 under section 678(a).

Example (9). G creates and funds a trust, T1, for the benefit of B. G retains a power to revest the assets of T1 in G within the meaning of section 676. Under the trust agreement, B is given a general power of appointment over the assets of T1. B exercises the general power of appointment with respect to one-half of the corpus of T1 in favor of a trust, T2, that is for the benefit of C, B's child. Under paragraph (e)(1) of this section, G is the grantor of T1, and under paragraphs (e)(1) and (5) of this section, B is the grantor of T2.

(7) The rules of this section are applicable to any transfer to a trust, or transfer of an interest in a trust, on or after August 10, 1999.

[T.D. 6500, 25 FR 11814, Nov. 26, 1960; T.D. 8831, 64 FR 43274, Aug. 10, 1999; T.D. 8890, 65 FR 41332, July 5, 2000]

§ 1.671–3 Attribution or inclusion of income, deductions, and credits against tax.

(a) When a grantor or another person is treated under subpart E (section 671 and following) as the owner of any portion of a trust, there are included in computing his tax liability those items of income, deduction, and credit against tax attributable to or included in that portion. For example:

(1) If a grantor or another person is treated as the owner of an entire trust (corpus as well as ordinary income), he takes into account in computing his income tax liability all items of income, deduction, and credit (including capital gains and losses) to which he would have been entitled had the trust not been in existence during the period he is treated as owner.

(2) If the portion treated as owned consists of specific trust property and its income, all items directly related to that property are attributable to the portion. Items directly related to trust property not included in the portion treated as owned by the grantor or other person are governed by the provisions of subparts A through D (section 641 and following), part I, subchapter J, chapter 1 of the Code. Items that relate both to the portion treated as owned by the grantor and to the balance of the trust must be apportioned in a manner that is reasonable in the light of all the circumstances of each case, including the terms of the

governing instrument, local law, and the practice of the trustee if it is reasonable and consistent.

(3) If the portion of a trust treated as owned by a grantor or another person consists of an undivided fractional interest in the trust, or of an interest represented by a dollar amount, a pro rata share of each item of income, deduction, and credit is normally allocated to the portion. Thus, where the portion owned consists of an interest in or a right to an amount of corpus only, a fraction of each item (including items allocated to corpus, such as capital gains) is attributed to the portion. The numerator of this fraction is the amount which is subject to the control of the grantor or other person and the denominator is normally the fair market value of the trust corpus at the beginning of the taxable year in question. The share not treated as owned by the grantor or other person is governed by the provisions of subparts A through D. See the last three sentences of paragraph (c) of this section for the principles applicable if the portion treated as owned consists of an interest in part of the ordinary income in contrast to an interest in corpus alone.

(b) If a grantor or another person is treated as the owner of a portion of a trust, that portion may or may not include both ordinary income and other income allocable to corpus. For example—

(1) Only ordinary income is included by reason of an interest in or a power over ordinary income alone. Thus, if a grantor is treated under section 673 as an owner by reason of a reversionary interest in ordinary income only, items of income allocable to corpus will not be included in the portion he is treated as owning. Similarly, if a grantor or another person is treated under sections 674–678 as an owner of a portion by reason of a power over ordinary income only, items of income allocable to corpus are not included in that portion. (See paragraph (c) of this section to determine the treatment of deductions and credits when only ordinary income is included in the portion.)

(2) Only income allocable to corpus is included by reason of an interest in or a power over corpus alone, if satisfaction of the interest or an exercise of the power will not result in an interest in or the exercise of a power over ordinary income which would itself cause that income to be included. For example, if a grantor has a reversionary interest in a trust which is not such as to require that he be treated as an owner under section 673, he may nevertheless be treated as an owner under section 677(a)(2) since any income allocable to corpus is accumulated for future distribution to him, but items of income included in determining ordinary income are not included in the portion he is treated as owning. Similarly, he may have a power over corpus which is such that he is treated as an owner under section 674 or 676(a), but ordinary income will not be included in the portion he owns, if his power can only affect income received after a period of time such that he would not be treated as an owner of the income if the power were a reversionary interest. (See paragraph (c) of this section to determine the treatment of deductions and credits when only income allocated to corpus is included in the portion.)

(3) Both ordinary income and other income allocable to corpus are included by reason of an interest in or a power over both ordinary income and corpus, or an interest in or a power over corpus alone which does not come within the provisions of subparagraph (2) of this paragraph. For example, if a grantor is treated under section 673 as the owner of a portion of a trust by reason of a reversionary interest in corpus, both ordinary income and other income allocable to corpus are included in the portion. Further, a grantor includes both ordinary income and other income allocable to corpus in the portion he is treated as owning if he is treated under section 674 or 676 as an owner because of a power over corpus which can affect income received within a period such that he would be treated as an owner under section 673 if the power were a reversionary interest. Similarly, a grantor or another person includes both ordinary income and other income allocable to corpus in the portion he is treated as owning if he is treated as an owner under section 675 or 678 because of a power over corpus.

(c) If only income allocable to corpus is included in computing a grantor's tax liability, he will take into account in that computation only those items of income, deductions, and credit which would not be included under subparts A through D in the computation of the tax liability of the current income beneficiaries if all distributable net income had actually been distributed to those beneficiaries. On the other hand, if the grantor or another person is treated as an owner solely because of his interest in or power over ordinary income alone, he will take into account in computing his tax liability those items which would be included in computing the tax liability of a current income beneficiary, including expenses allocable to corpus which enter into the computation of distributable net income. If the grantor or other person is treated as an owner because of his power over or right to a dollar amount of ordinary income, he will first take into account a portion of those items of income and expense entering into the computation of ordinary income under the trust instrument or local law sufficient to produce income of the dollar amount required. There will then be attributable to him a pro rata portion of other items entering into the computation of distributable net income under subparts A through D, such as expenses allocable to corpus, and a pro rata portion of credits of the trust. For examples of computations under this paragraph, see paragraph (g) of § 1.677(a)–1.

[T.D. 6500, 25 FR 11814, Nov. 26, 1960, as amended by T.D. 6989, 34 FR 742, Jan. 17, 1969]

§ 1.671–4 Method of reporting.

(a) Portion of trust treated as owned by the grantor or another person. Except as otherwise provided in paragraph (b) of this section and § 1.671–5, items of income, deduction, and credit attributable to any portion of a trust that, under the provisions of subpart E (section 671 and following), part I, subchapter J, chapter 1 of the Internal Revenue Code, is treated as owned by the grantor or another person, are not reported by the trust on Form 1041, "U.S. Income Tax Return for Estates and Trusts," but are shown on a separate statement to be attached to that form. Section 1.671–5 provides special reporting rules for widely held fixed investment trusts. Section 301.7701–4(e)(2) of this chapter provides guidance regarding the application of the reporting rules in this paragraph (a) to an environmental remediation trust.

(b) A trust all of which is treated as owned by one or more grantors or other persons. (1) *In general.* In the case of a trust all of which is treated as owned by one or more grantors or other persons, and which is not described in paragraph (b)(6) or (7) of this section, the trustee may, but is not required to, report by one of the methods described in this paragraph (b) rather than by the method described in paragraph (a) of this section. A trustee may not report, however, pursuant to paragraph (b)(2)(i)(A) of this section unless the grantor or other person treated as the owner of the trust provides to the trustee a complete Form W-9 or acceptable substitute Form W-9 signed under penalties of perjury. See section 3406 and the regulations thereunder for the information to include on, and the manner of executing, the Form W-9, depending upon the type of reportable payments made.

(2) *A trust all of which is treated as owned by one grantor or by one other person*—(i) *In general.* In the case of a trust all of which is treated as owned by one grantor or one other person, the trustee reporting under this paragraph (b) must either—

(A) Furnish the name and taxpayer identification number (TIN) of the grantor or other person treated as the owner of the trust, and the address of the trust, to all payors during the taxable year, and comply with the additional requirements described in paragraph (b)(2)(ii) of this section; or

(B) Furnish the name, TIN, and address of the trust to all payors during the taxable year, and comply with the additional requirements described in paragraph (b)(2)(iii) of this section.

(ii) *Additional obligations of the trustee when name and TIN of the grantor or other person treated as the owner of the trust and the address of the trust are furnished to payors.* (A) Unless the grantor or other person treated as the owner of the trust is the trustee or a co-trustee of the trust, the trustee must furnish the grantor or other person treated as the owner of the trust with a statement that—

(*1*) Shows all items of income, deduction, and credit of the trust for the taxable year;

(*2*) Identifies the payor of each item of income;

(*3*) Provides the grantor or other person treated as the owner of the trust with the information necessary to take the items into account in computing the grantor's or other person's taxable income; and

(*4*) Informs the grantor or other person treated as the owner of the trust that the items of income, deduction and credit and other information shown on the statement must be included in computing the taxable income and credits of the grantor or other person on the income tax return of the grantor or other person.

(B) The trustee is not required to file any type of return with the Internal Revenue Service.

(iii) *Additional obligations of the trustee when name, TIN, and address of the trust are furnished to payors.* (A) *Obligation to file Forms 1099.* The trustee must file with the Internal Revenue Service the appropriate Forms 1099, reporting the income or gross proceeds paid to the trust during the taxable year, and showing the trust as the payor and the grantor or other person treated as the owner of the trust as the payee. The trustee has the same obligations for filing the appropriate Forms 1099 as would a payor making reportable payments, except that the trustee must report each type of income in the aggregate, and each item of gross proceeds separately. See paragraph (b)(5) of this section regarding the amounts required to be included on any Forms 1099 filed by the trustee.

(B) *Obligation to furnish statement.* (1) Unless the grantor or other person treated as the owner of the trust is the trustee or a co-trustee of the trust, the trustee must also furnish to the grantor or other person treated as the owner of the trust a statement that—

(i) Shows all items of income, deduction, and credit of the trust for the taxable year;

(ii) Provides the grantor or other person treated as the owner of the trust with the information necessary to take the items into account in computing the grantor's or other person's taxable income; and

(iii) Informs the grantor or other person treated as the owner of the trust that the items of income, deduction and credit and other information shown on the statement must be included in computing the taxable income and credits of the grantor or other person on the income tax return of the grantor or other person.

(2) By furnishing the statement, the trustee satisfies the obligation to furnish statements to recipients with respect to the Forms 1099 filed by the trustee.

(iv) *Examples.* The following examples illustrate the provisions of this paragraph (b)(2):

Example (1). G, a United States citizen, creates an irrevocable trust which provides that the ordinary income is to be payable to him for life and that on his death the corpus shall be distributed to B, an unrelated person. Except for the right to receive income, G retains no right or power which would cause him to be treated as an owner under sections 671 through 679. Under the applicable local law, capital gains must be added to corpus. Since G has a right to receive income, he is treated as an owner of a portion of the trust under section 677. The tax consequences of any items of capital gain of the trust are governed by the provisions of subparts A, B, C, and D (section 641 and following), part I, subchapter J, chapter 1 of the Internal Revenue Code. Because not all of the trust is treated as owned by the grantor or another person, the trustee may not report by the methods described in paragraph (b)(2) of this section.

Example (2). (i) (A) On January 2, 1996, G, a United States citizen, creates a trust all of which is treated as owned by G. The trustee of the trust is T. During the 1996 taxable year the trust has the following items of income and gross proceeds:

Interest	$2,500
Dividends	3,205
Proceeds from sale of B stock	2,000

(B) The trust has no items of deduction or credit.

(ii) (A) The payors of the interest paid to the trust are X ($2,000), Y ($300), and Z ($200). The payors of the dividends paid to the trust are A ($3,200), and D ($5). The payor of the gross proceeds paid to the trust is D, a brokerage firm, which held the B stock as the nominee for the trust. The B stock was purchased by T for $1,500 on January 3, 1996, and sold by T on November 29, 1996. T chooses to report pursuant to paragraph (b)(2)(i)(B) of this section, and therefore furnishes the name, TIN, and address of the trust to X, Y, Z, A, and D. X, Y, and Z each furnish T with a Form 1099-INT showing the trust as the payee. A furnishes T with a Form 1099-DIV showing the trust as the payee. D does not furnish T with a Form 1099-DIV because D paid a dividend of less than $10 to T. D furnishes T with a Form 1099-B showing the trust as the payee.

(B) On or before February 28, 1997, T files a Form 1099-INT with the Internal Revenue Service on which T reports interest attributable to G, as the owner of the trust, of $2,500; a Form 1099-DIV on which T reports dividends attributable to G, as the owner of the trust, of $3,205; and a Form 1099-B on which T reports gross proceeds from the sale of B stock attributable to G, as the owner of the trust, of $2,000. On or before April 15, 1997, T furnishes a statement to G which lists the following items of income and information necessary for G to take the items into account in computing G's taxable income:

Interest	$2,500
Dividends	3,205
Gain from sale of B stock	500

Information regarding sale of B stock:

Proceeds	$2,000
Basis	1,500
Date acquired	1/03/96
Date sold	11/29/96

(C) T informs G that any items of income, deduction and credit and other information shown on the statement must be included in computing the taxable income and credits of the grantor or other person on the income tax return of the grantor or other person.

(D) T has complied with T's obligations under this section.

(iii)(A) Same facts as paragraphs (i) and (ii) of this Example 2, except that G contributed the B stock to the trust on January 2, 1996. On or before April 15, 1997, T furnishes a statement to G which lists the following items of income and information necessary for G to take the items into account in computing G's taxable income:

Interest	$2,500
Dividends	3,205

Information regarding sale of B stock:

Proceeds	$2,000
Date sold	11/29/96

(B) T informs G that any items of income, deduction and credit and other information shown on the statement must be included in computing the taxable income and credits of the grantor or other person on the income tax return of the grantor or other person.

(C) T has complied with T's obligations under this section.

Example (3). On January 2, 1996, G, a United States citizen, creates a trust all of which is treated as owned by G. The trustee of the trust is T. The only asset of the trust is an interest in C, a common trust fund under section 584(a). T chooses to report pursuant to paragraph (b)(2)(i)(B) of this section and therefore furnishes the name, TIN, and address of the trust to C. C files a Form 1065 and a Schedule K-1 (Partner's Share of Income, Credits, Deductions, etc.) showing the name, TIN, and address of the trust with the Internal Revenue Service and furnishes a copy to T. Because the trust did not receive any amounts described in paragraph (b)(5) of this section, T does not file any type of return with the Internal Revenue Service. On or before April 15, 1997, T furnishes G with a statement that shows all items of income, deduction, and credit of the trust for the 1996 taxable year. In addition, T informs G that any items of income, deduction and credit and other information shown on the statement must be included in computing the taxable income and credits of the grantor or other person on the income tax return of the grantor or other person. T has complied with T's obligations under this section.

(3) *A trust all of which is treated as owned by two or more grantors or other persons.* (i) *In general.* In the case of a trust all of which is treated as owned by two or more grantors or other persons, the trustee must furnish the name, TIN, and address of the trust to all payors for the taxable year, and comply with the additional requirements described in paragraph (b)(3)(ii) of this section.

(ii) *Additional obligations of trustee.* (A) *Obligation to file Forms 1099.* The trustee must file with the Internal Revenue Service the appropriate Forms 1099, reporting the items of income paid to the trust by all payors during the taxable year attributable to the portion of the trust treated as owned by each grantor or other person, and showing the trust as the payor and each grantor or other person treated as an owner of the trust as the payee. The trustee has the same obligations for filing the appropriate Forms 1099 as would a payor making reportable payments, except that the trustee must report each type of income in the aggregate, and each item of gross proceeds separately. See paragraph (b)(5) of this section regarding the amounts required to be included on any Forms 1099 filed by the trustee.

(B) *Obligation to furnish statement.* (1) The trustee must also furnish to each grantor or other person treated as an owner of the trust a statement that—

(i) Shows all items of income, deduction, and credit of the trust for the taxable year attributable to the portion of the trust treated as owned by the grantor or other person;

(ii) Provides the grantor or other person treated as an owner of the trust with the information necessary to take the items into account in computing the grantor's or other person's taxable income; and

(iii) Informs the grantor or other person treated as the owner of the trust that the items of income, deduction and credit and other information shown on the statement must be included in computing the taxable income and credits of the grantor or other person on the income tax return of the grantor or other person.

(2) Except for the requirements pursuant to section 3406 and the regulations thereunder, by furnishing the statement, the trustee satisfies the obligation to furnish statements to recipients with respect to the Forms 1099 filed by the trustee.

(4) *Persons treated as payors.* (i) *In general.* For purposes of this section, the term payor means any person who is required by any provision of the Internal Revenue Code and the regulations thereunder to make any type of information return (including Form 1099 or Schedule K-1) with respect to the trust for the taxable year, including persons who make payments to the trust or who collect (or otherwise act as middlemen with respect to) payments on behalf of the trust.

(ii) *Application to brokers and customers.* For purposes of this section, a broker, within the meaning of section 6045, is considered a payor. A customer, within the meaning of section 6045, is considered a payee.

(5) *Amounts required to be included on Forms 1099 filed by the trustee.* (i) *In general.* The amounts that must be included on any Forms 1099 required to be filed by the trustee pursuant to this section do not include any amounts that are reportable by the payor on an information return other than Form 1099. For example, in the case of a trust which owns an interest in a partnership, the trust's distributive share of the income and gain of the partnership is not includible on any Forms 1099 filed by the trustee pursuant to this section because the distributive share is reportable by the partnership on Schedule K-1.

(ii) *Example.* The following example illustrates the provisions of this paragraph (b)(5):

Example. (i)(A) On January 2, 1996, G, a United States citizen, creates a trust all of which is treated as owned by G. The trustee of the trust is T. The assets of the trust during the 1996 taxable year are shares of stock in X, an S corporation, a limited partnership interest in P, shares of stock in M, and shares of stock in N. T chooses to report pursuant to paragraph (b)(2)(i)(B) of this section and therefore furnishes the name, TIN, and address of the trust to X, P, M, and N. M furnishes T with a Form 1099-DIV showing the trust as the payee. N does not furnish T with a Form 1099-DIV because N paid a dividend of less than $10 to T. X and P furnish T with Schedule K-1 (Shareholder's Share of Income, Credits, Deductions, etc.) and Schedule K-1 (Partner's Share of Income, Credits, Deductions, etc.), respectively, showing the trust's name, TIN, and address.

(B) For the 1996 taxable year the trust has the following items of income and deduction:

Dividends paid by M	$12
Dividends paid by N	6
Administrative expense	$20

Items reported by X on Schedule K-1 attributable to trust's shares of stock in X:

Interest	$20
Dividends	35

Items reported by P on Schedule K-1 attributable to trust's limited partnership interest in P:

Ordinary income	$300

(ii)(A) On or before February 28, 1997, T files with the Internal Revenue Service a Form 1099-DIV on which T reports dividends attributable to G as the owner of the trust in the amount of $18. T does not file any other returns.

(B) T has complied with T's obligation under paragraph (b)(2)(iii)(A) of this section to file the appropriate Forms 1099.

(6) *Trusts that cannot report under this paragraph (b).* The following trusts cannot use the methods of reporting described in this paragraph (b)—

(i) A common trust fund as defined in section 584(a);

(ii) A trust that has its situs or any of its assets located outside the United States;

(iii) A trust that is a qualified subchapter S trust as defined in section 1361(d)(3);

(iv) A trust all of which is treated as owned by one grantor or one other person whose taxable year is a fiscal year;

(v) A trust all of which is treated as owned by one grantor or one other person who is not a United States person; or

(vi) A trust all of which is treated as owned by two or more grantors or other persons, one of whom is not a United States person.

(7) *Grantors or other persons who are treated as owners of the trust and are exempt recipients for information reporting purposes.* (i) *Trust treated as owned by one grantor or one other person.* The trustee of a trust all of which is treated as owned by one grantor or one other person may not report pursuant to this paragraph (b) if the grantor or other person is an exempt recipient for information reporting purposes.

(ii) *Trust treated as owned by two or more grantors or other persons.* The trustee of a trust, all of which is treated as owned by two or more grantors or other persons, may not report pursuant to this paragraph (b) if one or more grantors or other persons treated as owners are exempt recipients for information reporting purposes unless—

(A) At least one grantor or one other person who is treated as an owner of the trust is a person who is not an exempt recipient for information reporting purposes; and

(B) The trustee reports without regard to whether any of the grantors or other persons treated as owners of the trust are exempt recipients for information reporting purposes.

(8) *Husband and wife who make a single return jointly.* A trust all of which is treated as owned by a husband and wife who make a single return jointly of income taxes for the taxable year under section 6013 is considered to be owned by one grantor for purposes of this paragraph (b).

(c) Due date for Forms 1099 required to be filed by trustee. The due date for any Forms 1099 required to be filed with the Internal Revenue Service by a trustee pursuant to this section is the due date otherwise in effect for filing Forms 1099.

(d) Due date and other requirements with respect to statement required to be furnished by trustee. (1) *In general.* The due date for the statement required to be furnished by a trustee to the grantor or other person treated as an owner of the trust pursuant to this section is the date specified by section 6034A(a). The trustee must maintain in its records a copy of the statement furnished to the grantor or other person treated as an owner of the trust for a period of three years from the due date for furnishing such statement specified in this paragraph (d).

(2) *Statement for the taxable year ending with the death of the grantor or other person treated as the owner of the trust.* If a trust ceases to be treated as owned by the grantor, or other person, by reason of the death of that grantor or other person (decedent), the due date for the statement required to be furnished for the taxable year ending with the death of the decedent shall be the date specified by section 6034A(a) as though the decedent had lived throughout the decedent's last taxable year. See paragraph (h) of this section for special reporting rules for a trust or portion of the trust that ceases to be treated as owned by the grantor or other person by reason of the death of the grantor or other person.

(e) Backup withholding requirements. (1) *Trustee reporting under paragraph (b)(2)(i)(A) of this section.* In order for the trustee to be able to report pursuant to paragraph (b)(2)(i)(A) of this section and to furnish to all payors the name and TIN of the grantor or other person treated as the owner of the trust, the grantor or other person must provide a complete Form W-9 to the trustee in the manner provided in paragraph (b)(1) of this section, and the trustee must give the name and TIN shown on that Form W-9 to all payors. In addition, if the Form W-9 indicates that the grantor or other person is subject to backup withholding, the trustee must notify all payors of reportable interest and dividend payments of the requirement to backup withhold. If the Form W-9 indicates that the grantor or other person is not subject to backup withholding, the trustee does not have to notify the payors that backup withholding is not required. The trustee should not give the Form W-9, or a copy thereof, to a payor because the Form W-9 contains the address of the grantor or other person and paragraph (b)(2)(i)(A) of this section requires the trustee to furnish the address of the trust to all payors and not the address of the grantor or other person. The trustee acts as the agent of the grantor or other person for purposes of furnishing to the payors the information required by this paragraph (e)(1). Thus, a payor may rely on the name and TIN provided to the payor by the trustee, and, if given, on the trustee's statement that the grantor is subject to backup withholding.

(2) *Other backup withholding requirements.* Whether a trustee is treated as a payor for purposes of

backup withholding is determined pursuant to section 3406 and the regulations thereunder.

(f) Penalties for failure to file a correct Form 1099 or furnish a correct statement. A trustee who fails to file a correct Form 1099 or to furnish a correct statement to a grantor or other person treated as an owner of the trust as required by paragraph (b) of this section is subject to the penalties provided by sections 6721 and 6722 and the regulations thereunder.

(g) Changing reporting methods. (1) *Changing from reporting by filing Form 1041 to a method described in paragraph (b) of this section.* If the trustee has filed a Form 1041 for any taxable year ending before January 1, 1996 (and has not filed a final Form 1041 pursuant to § 1.671–4(b)(3) (as contained in the 26 CFR part 1 edition revised as of April 1, 1995)), or files a Form 1041 for any taxable year thereafter, the trustee must file a final Form 1041 for the taxable year which ends after January 1, 1995, and which immediately precedes the first taxable year for which the trustee reports pursuant to paragraph (b) of this section, on the front of which form the trustee must write: "Pursuant to § 1.671–4(g), this is the final Form 1041 for this grantor trust.".

(2) *Changing from reporting by a method described in paragraph (b) of this section to the filing of a Form 1041.* The trustee of a trust who reported pursuant to paragraph (b) of this section for a taxable year may report pursuant to paragraph (a) of this section for subsequent taxable years. If the trustee reported pursuant to paragraph (b)(2)(i)(A) of this section, and therefore furnished the name and TIN of the grantor to all payors, the trustee must furnish the name, TIN, and address of the trust to all payors for such subsequent taxable years. If the trustee reported pursuant to paragraph (b)(2)(i)(B) or (b)(3)(i) of this section, and therefore furnished the name and TIN of the trust to all payors, the trustee must indicate on each Form 1096 (Annual Summary and Transmittal of U.S. Information Returns) that it files (or appropriately on magnetic media) for the final taxable year for which the trustee so reports that it is the final return of the trust.

(3) *Changing between methods described in paragraph (b) of this section.* (i) *Changing from furnishing the TIN of the grantor to furnishing the TIN of the trust.* The trustee of a trust who reported pursuant to paragraph (b)(2)(i)(A) of this section for a taxable year, and therefore furnished the name and TIN of the grantor to all payors, may report pursuant to paragraph (b)(2)(i)(B) of this section, and furnish the name and TIN of the trust to all payors, for subsequent taxable years.

(ii) *Changing from furnishing the TIN of the trust to furnishing the TIN of the grantor.* The trustee of a trust who reported pursuant to paragraph (b)(2)(i)(B) of this section for a taxable year, and therefore furnished the name and TIN of the trust to all payors, may report pursuant to paragraph (b)(2)(i)(A) of this section, and furnish the name and TIN of the grantor to all payors, for subsequent taxable years. The trustee, however, must indicate on each Form 1096 (Annual Summary and Transmittal of U.S. Information Returns) that it files (or appropriately on magnetic media) for the final taxable year for which the trustee reports pursuant to paragraph (b)(2)(i)(B) of this section that it is the final return of the trust.

(4) *Example.* The following example illustrates the provisions of paragraph (g) of this section:

Example. (i) On January 3, 1994, G, a United States citizen, creates a trust all of which is treated as owned by G. The trustee of the trust is T. On or before April 17, 1995, T files with the Internal Revenue Service a Form 1041 with an attached statement for the 1994 taxable year showing the items of income, deduction, and credit of the trust. On or before April 15, 1996, T files with the Internal Revenue Service a Form 1041 with an attached statement for the 1995 taxable year showing the items of income, deduction, and credit of the trust. On the Form 1041, T states that "pursuant to § 1.671–4(g), this is the final Form 1041 for this grantor trust." T may report pursuant to paragraph (b) of this section for the 1996 taxable year.

(ii) T reports pursuant to paragraph (b)(2)(i)(B) of this section, and therefore furnishes the name, TIN, and address of the trust to all payors, for the 1996 and 1997 taxable years. T chooses to report pursuant to paragraph (a) of this section for the 1998 taxable year. On each Form 1096 (Annual Summary and Transmittal of U.S. Information Returns) which T files for the 1997 taxable year (or appropriately on magnetic media), T indicates that it is the trust's final return. On or before April 15, 1999, T files with the Internal Revenue Service a Form 1041 with an attached statement showing the items of income, deduction, and credit of the trust. On the Form 1041, T uses the same TIN which T used on the Forms 1041 and Forms 1099 it filed for previous taxable years. T has complied with T's obligations under paragraph (g)(2) of this section.

(h) Reporting rules for a trust, or portion of a trust, that ceases to be treated as owned by a grantor or other person by reason of the death of the grantor or other person—

(1) *Definition of decedent.* For purposes of this paragraph (h), the decedent is the grantor or other person treated as the owner of the trust, or portion of the trust, under subpart E, part I, subchapter J, chapter 1 of the Internal Revenue Code on the date of death of that person.

(2) *In general.* The provisions of this section apply to a trust, or portion of a trust, treated as owned by a decedent for the taxable year that ends with the decedent's death. Following the death of the decedent, the trust or portion of a trust that ceases to be treated as owned by the decedent, by reason of the death of the decedent, may no longer report under this section. A trust, all of which was treated as owned by the decedent, must obtain a new TIN upon the death of the decedent, if the trust will continue after the death of the decedent. See § 301.6109–1(a)(3)(i) of this chapter for rules regarding obtaining a TIN upon the death of the decedent.

(3) *Special rules.* (i) *Trusts reporting pursuant to paragraph (a) of this section for the taxable year ending with the decedent's death.* The due date for the filing of a return pursuant to paragraph (a) of this section for the taxable year ending with the decedent's death shall be the due date provided for under § 1.6072–1(a)(2). The return filed under this paragraph for a trust all of which was treated as owned by the decedent must indicate that it is a final return.

(ii) *Trust reporting pursuant to paragraph (b)(2)(B) of this section for the taxable year of the decedent's death.* A trust that reports pursuant to paragraph (b)(2)(B) of this section for the taxable year ending with the decedent's death must indicate on each Form 1096 "Annual Summary and Transmittal of the U.S. Information Returns" that it files (or appropriately on magnetic media) for the taxable year ending with the death of the decedent that it is the final return of the trust.

(iii) *Trust reporting under paragraph (b)(3) of this section.* If a trust has been reporting under paragraph (b)(3) of this section, the trustee may not report under that paragraph if any portion of the trust has a short taxable year by reason of the death of the decedent and the portion treated as owned by the decedent does not terminate on the death of the decedent.

(i) Effective date and transition rule. (1) *Effective date.* The trustee of a trust any portion of which is treated as owned by one or more grantors or other persons must report pursuant to paragraphs (a), (b), (c), (d)(1), (e), (f), and (g) of this section for taxable years beginning on or after January 1, 1996.

(2) *Transition rule.* For taxable years beginning prior to January 1, 1996, the Internal Revenue Service will not challenge the manner of reporting of—

(i) A trustee of a trust all of which is treated as owned by one or more grantors or other persons who did not report in accordance with § 1.671–4(a) (as contained in the 26 CFR part 1 edition revised as of April 1, 1995) as in effect for taxable years beginning prior to January 1, 1996, but did report in a manner substantially similar to one of the reporting methods described in paragraph (b) of this section; or

(ii) A trustee of two or more trusts all of which are treated as owned by one or more grantors or other persons who filed a single Form 1041 for all of the trusts, rather than a separate Form 1041 for each trust, provided that the items of income, deduction, and credit of each trust were shown on a statement attached to the single Form 1041.

(3) *Effective date for paragraphs (d)(2) and (h) of this section.* Paragraphs (d)(2) and (h) of this section apply for taxable years ending on or after December 24, 2002.

(j) Cross-reference. For rules relating to employer identification numbers, and to the obligation of a payor of income or proceeds to the trust to furnish to the payee a statement to recipient, see § 301.6109–1(a)(2) of this chapter.

[T.D. 6500, 25 FR 11814, Nov. 26, 1960; T.D. 7796, 46 FR 57481, Nov. 24, 1981; T.D. 8633, 60 FR 66087, Dec. 21, 1995; T.D. 8668, 61 FR 19191, May 1, 1996; T.D. 9032, 67 FR 78381, Dec. 24, 2002; T.D. 9241, 71 FR 4009, Jan. 24, 2006]

§ 1.671–5 Reporting for widely held fixed investment trusts. [*Omitted. Ed.*]

[T.D. 9241, 71 FR 4009, Jan. 24, 2006; T.D. 9279, 71 FR 43971, Aug. 3, 2006; T.D. 9308, 71 FR 78356, Dec. 29, 2006]

§ 672. Definitions and Rules

(a) Adverse party. For purposes of this subpart, the term "adverse party" means any person having a substantial beneficial interest in the trust which would be adversely affected by the exercise or nonexercise of the power which he possesses respecting the trust. A person having a general power of appointment over the trust property shall be deemed to have a beneficial interest in the trust.

(b) Nonadverse party. For purposes of this subpart, the term "nonadverse party" means any person who is not an adverse party.

(c) Related or subordinate party. For purposes of this subpart, the term "related or subordinate party" means any nonadverse party who is—

(1) the grantor's spouse if living with the grantor;

(2) any one of the following: The grantor's father, mother, issue, brother or sister; an employee of the grantor; a corporation or any employee of a corporation in which the stock holdings of the grantor and the trust are significant from the viewpoint of voting control; a subordinate employee of a corporation in which the grantor is an executive.

For purposes of subsection (f) and sections 674 and 675, a related or subordinate party shall be presumed to be subservient to the grantor in respect of the exercise or nonexercise of the powers conferred on him unless such party is shown not to be subservient by a preponderance of the evidence.

(d) Rule where power is subject to condition precedent. A person shall be considered to have a power described in this subpart even though the exercise of the power is subject to a precedent giving of notice or takes effect only on the expiration of a certain period after the exercise of the power.

(e) Grantor treated as holding any power or interest of grantor's spouse.

(1) In general. For purposes of this subpart, a grantor shall be treated as holding any power or interest held by—

(A) any individual who was the spouse of the grantor at the time of the creation of such power or interest, or

(B) any individual who became the spouse of the grantor after the creation of such power or interest, but only with respect to periods after such individual became the spouse of the grantor.

(2) Marital status. For purposes of paragraph (1)(A), an individual legally separated from his spouse under a decree of divorce or of separate maintenance shall not be considered as married.

(f) Subpart not to result in foreign ownership.

(1) In general. Notwithstanding any other provision of this subpart, this subpart shall apply only to the extent such application results in an amount (if any) being currently taken into account (directly or through 1 or more entities) under this chapter in computing the income of a citizen or resident of the United States or a domestic corporation.

(2) Exceptions.

(A) Certain revocable and irrevocable trusts. Paragraph (1) shall not apply to any portion of a trust if—

(i) the power to revest absolutely in the grantor title to the trust property to which such portion is attributable is exercisable solely by the grantor without the approval or consent of any other person or with the consent of a related or subordinate party who is subservient to the grantor, or

(ii) the only amounts distributable from such portion (whether income or corpus) during the lifetime of the grantor are amounts distributable to the grantor or the spouse of the grantor.

(B) Compensatory trusts. Except as provided in regulations, paragraph (1) shall not apply to any portion of a trust distributions from which are taxable as compensation for services rendered.

(3) Special rule. Except as otherwise provided in regulations prescribed by the Secretary—

(A) a controlled foreign corporation (as defined in section 957) shall be treated as a domestic corporation for purposes of paragraph (1), and

(B) paragraph (1) shall not apply for purposes of applying section 1297.

(4) Recharacterization of purported gifts. In the case of any transfer directly or indirectly from a partnership or foreign corporation which the transferee treats as a gift or bequest, the Secretary may recharacterize such transfer in such circumstances as the Secretary determines to be appropriate to prevent the avoidance of the purposes of this subsection.

(5) Special rule where grantor is foreign person. If—

(A) but for this subsection, a foreign person would be treated as the owner of any portion of a trust, and

(B) such trust has a beneficiary who is a United States person, such beneficiary shall be treated as the grantor of such portion to the extent such beneficiary has made (directly or indirectly) transfers of property (other than in a sale for full and adequate consideration) to such foreign person. For purposes of the preceding sentence, any gift shall not be taken into account to the extent such gift would be excluded from taxable gifts under section 2503(b).

(6) Regulations. The Secretary shall prescribe such regulations as may be necessary or appropriate to carry out the purposes of this subsection, including regulations providing that paragraph (1) shall not apply in appropriate cases.

Regulations

§ 1.672(a)–1 Definition of adverse party.

(a) Under section 672(a) an adverse party is defined as any person having a substantial beneficial interest in a trust which would be adversely affected by the exercise or nonexercise of a power which he possesses respecting the trust. A trustee is not an adverse party merely because of his interest as trustee. A person having a general power of appointment over the trust property is deemed to have a beneficial interest in the trust. An interest is a substantial interest if its value in relation to the total value of the property subject to the power is not insignificant.

(b) Ordinarily, a beneficiary will be an adverse party, but if his right to share in the income or corpus of a trust is limited to only a part, he may be an adverse party only as to that part. Thus, if A, B, C, and D are equal income beneficiaries of a trust and the grantor can revoke with A's consent, the grantor is treated as the owner of a portion which represents three-fourths of the trust; and items of income, deduction, and credit attributable to that portion are included in determining the tax of the grantor.

(c) The interest of an ordinary income beneficiary of a trust may or may not be adverse with respect to the exercise of a power over corpus. Thus, if the income of a trust is payable to A for life, with a power (which is not a general power of appointment) in A to appoint the corpus to the grantor either during his life or by will, A's interest is adverse to the return of the corpus to the grantor during A's life, but is not adverse to a return of the corpus after A's death. In other words, A's interest is adverse as to ordinary income but is not adverse as to income allocable to corpus. Therefore, assuming no other relevant facts exist, the grantor would not be taxable on the ordinary income of the trust under section 674, 676, or 677, but would be taxable under section 677 on income allocable to corpus (such as capital gains), since it may in the discretion of a nonadverse party be accumulated for future distribution to the grantor. Similarly, the interest of a contingent income beneficiary is adverse to a return of corpus to the grantor before the termination of his interest but not to a return of corpus after the termination of his interest.

(d) The interest of a remainderman is adverse to the exercise of any power over the corpus of a trust, but not to the exercise of a power over any income interest preceding his remainder. For example, if the grantor creates a trust which provides for income to be distributed to A for 10 years and then for the corpus to go to X if he is then living, a power exercisable by X to revest corpus in the grantor is a power exercisable by an adverse party; however, a power exercisable by X to distribute part or all of the ordinary income to the grantor may be a power exercisable by a nonadverse party (which would cause the ordinary income to be taxed to the grantor).

[T.D. 6500, 25 FR 11814, Nov. 26, 1960]

§ 1.672(b)–1 Nonadverse party.

A "nonadverse party" is any person who is not an adverse party.

[T.D. 6500, 25 FR 11814, Nov. 26, 1960]

§ 1.672(c)–1 Related or subordinate party.

Section 672(c) defines the term "related or subordinate party". The term, as used in sections 674(c) and 675(3), means any nonadverse party who is the grantor's spouse if living with the grantor; the grantor's father, mother, issue, brother or sister; an employee of the grantor; a corporation or any employee of a corporation in which the stock holdings of the grantor and the trust are significant from the viewpoint of voting control; or a subordinate employee of a corporation in which the grantor is an executive. For purposes of sections 674(c) and 675(3), these persons are presumed to be subservient to the grantor in respect of the exercise or nonexercise of the powers conferred on them unless shown not to be subservient by a preponderance of the evidence.

[T.D. 6500, 25 FR 11814, Nov. 26, 1960]

§ 1.672(d)–1 Power subject to condition precedent.

Section 672(d) provides that a person is considered to have a power described in subpart E (section 671 and following), part I, subchapter J, chapter 1 of the Code, even though the exercise of the power is subject to a precedent giving of notice or takes effect only after the expiration of a certain period of time. However, although a person may be considered to have such a power, the grantor will nevertheless not be treated as an owner by reason of the power if its exercise can only affect beneficial enjoyment of income received after the expiration of a period of time such that, if the power were a reversionary interest, he would not be treated as an owner under section 673. See sections 674(b)(2), 676(b), and the last sentence of section 677(a). Thus, for example, if a grantor creates a trust for the benefit of his son and retains a power to revoke which takes effect only after the expiration of 2 years from the date of exercise, he is treated as an owner from the inception of the trust. However, if the grantor retains a power to revoke, exercisable at any time, which can only affect the beneficial enjoyment of the ordinary income of a trust received after the expiration of 10 years commencing with the date of the transfer in trust, or after the death of the income beneficiary, the power does not cause him to be treated as an owner with respect to ordinary income during the first 10 years of the trust or during the income beneficiary's life, as the case may be. See section 676(b).

[T.D. 6500, 25 FR 11814, Nov. 26, 1960]

§ 1.672(f)–1 Foreign persons not treated as owners.

(a) General rule. (1) *Application of the general rule.* Section 672(f)(1) provides that subpart E of part I, subchapter J, chapter 1 of the Internal Revenue Code (the grantor trust rules) shall apply only to the extent such application results in an amount (if any) being currently taken into account (directly or through one or more entities) in computing the income of a citizen or resident of the United States or a domestic corporation. Accordingly, the grantor trust rules apply to the extent that any portion of the trust, upon application of the grantor trust rules without regard to section 672(f), is treated as owned by a United States citizen or resident or domestic corporation. The grantor trust rules do not apply to any portion of the trust to the extent that, upon application of the grantor trust rules without regard to section 672(f), that portion is treated as owned by a person other than a United States citizen or resident or domestic corporation, unless the person is described in § 1.672(f)–2(a) (relating to certain foreign corporations treated as domestic corporations), or one of the exceptions set forth in § 1.672(f)–3 is met, (relating to: trusts where the grantor can revest trust assets; trusts where the only amounts distributable are to the grantor or the grantor's spouse; and compensatory trusts). Section 672(f) applies to domestic and foreign trusts. Any portion of the trust that is not treated as owned by a grantor or another person is subject to the rules of subparts A through D (section 641 and following), part I, subchapter J, chapter 1 of the Internal Revenue Code.

(2) *Determination of portion based on application of the grantor trust rules.* The determination of the portion of a trust treated as owned by the grantor or other person is to be made based on the terms of the trust and the application of the grantor trust rules and section 671 and the regulations thereunder.

(b) Example. The following example illustrates the rules of this section:

Example. (i) A, a nonresident alien, funds an irrevocable domestic trust, DT, for the benefit of his son, B, who is a United States citizen, with stock of Corporation X. A's brother, C, who also is a United States citizen, contributes stock of Corporation Y to the trust for the benefit of B. A has a reversionary interest within the meaning of section 673 in the X stock that would cause A to be treated as the owner of the X stock upon application of the grantor trust rules without regard to section 672(f). C has a reversionary interest within the meaning of section 673 in the Y stock that would cause C to be treated as the owner of the Y stock upon application of the grantor trust rules without regard to section 672(f). The trustee has discretion to accumulate or currently distribute income of DT to B.

(ii) Because A is a nonresident alien, application of the grantor trust rules without regard to section 672(f) would not result in the portion of the trust consisting of the X stock being treated as owned by a United States citizen or resident. None of the exceptions in § 1.672(f)–3 applies because A cannot revest the X stock in A, amounts may be distributed during A's lifetime to B, who is neither a grantor nor a spouse of a grantor, and the trust is not a compensatory trust. Therefore, pursuant to paragraph (a)(1) of this section, A is not treated as an owner under subpart E of part I, subchapter J, chapter 1 of the Internal Revenue Code, of the portion of the trust consisting of the X stock. Any distributions from such portion of the trust are subject to the rules of subparts A through D (641 and following), part I, subchapter J, chapter 1 of the Internal Revenue Code.

(iii) Because C is a United States citizen, paragraph (a)(1) of this section does not prevent C from being treated under section 673 as the owner of the portion of the trust consisting of the Y stock.

(c) Effective date. The rules of this section are applicable to taxable years of a trust beginning after August 10, 1999.

[T.D. 8831, 64 FR 43275, Aug. 10, 1999]

§ 1.672(f)–2 Certain foreign corporations.

(a) Application of general rule in this section. Subject to the provisions of paragraph (b) of this section, if the owner of any portion of a trust upon application of the grantor trust rules without regard to section 672(f) is a controlled foreign corporation or a passive foreign investment company (as defined in section 1297), the corporation is treated as a domestic corporation for purposes of applying the rules of § 1.672(f)–1. For purposes of this section, a controlled foreign corporation has the meaning provided in section 957, determined without applying section 318(a)(3)(A), (B), and (C) so as to consider a United States person as owning stock which is owned by a person who is not a United States person.

(b) Gratuitous transfers to United States persons (1) *Transfer from trust to which corporation made a gratuitous transfer.* If a trust (or portion of a trust) to which a controlled foreign corporation, passive foreign investment company, or foreign personal holding company has made a gratuitous transfer (within the meaning of § 1.671–2(e)(2)), makes a gratuitous transfer to a United States person, the controlled foreign corporation, passive foreign investment company, or foreign personal holding company, as the case may be, is treated as a foreign corporation for purposes of § 1.672(f)–4(c), relating to gratuitous transfers from trusts (or portions of trusts) to which a partnership or foreign corporation has made a gratuitous transfer.

(2) *Transfer from trust over which corporation has a section 678 power.* If a trust (or portion of a trust) that a controlled foreign corporation, passive foreign

investment company, or foreign personal holding company is treated as owning under section 678 makes a gratuitous transfer to a United States person, the controlled foreign corporation, passive foreign investment company, or foreign personal holding company, as the case may be, is treated as a foreign corporation that had made a gratuitous transfer to the trust (or portion of a trust) and the rules of § 1.672(f)–4(c) apply.

(c) Special rules for passive foreign investment companies (1) *Application of section 1297*. For purposes of determining whether a foreign corporation is a passive foreign investment company as defined in section 1297, the grantor trust rules apply as if section 672(f) had not come into effect.

(2) *References to renumbered Internal Revenue Code section*. For taxable years of shareholders beginning on or before December 31, 1997, and taxable years of passive foreign investment companies ending with or within such taxable years of the shareholders, all references in this § 1.672(f)–2 to section 1297 are deemed to be references to section 1296.

(d) Examples. The following examples illustrate the rules of this section. In each example, FT is an irrevocable foreign trust, and CFC is a controlled foreign corporation. The examples are as follows:

Example 1. Application of general rule. CFC creates and funds FT. CFC is the grantor of FT within the meaning of § 1.671–2(e). CFC has a reversionary interest in FT within the meaning of section 673 that would cause CFC to be treated as the owner of FT upon application of the grantor trust rules without regard to section 672(f). Under paragraph (a) of this section, CFC is treated as a domestic corporation for purposes of applying the general rule of § 1.672(f)–1. Thus, § 1.672(f)–1 does not prevent CFC from being treated as the owner of FT under section 673.

Example 2. Distribution from trust to which CFC made gratuitous transfer. A, a nonresident alien, owns 40 percent of the stock of CFC. A's brother B, a resident alien, owns the other 60 percent of the stock of CFC. CFC makes a gratuitous transfer to FT. FT makes a gratuitous transfer to A's daughter, C, who is a resident alien. Under paragraph (b)(1) of this section, CFC will be treated as a foreign corporation for purposes of § 1.672(f)–4(c). For further guidance, see § 1.672(f)–4(g) Example 2 through Example 4.

(e) Applicability dates. Except as provided in this paragraph (e), the rules of this section apply to taxable years of shareholders of controlled foreign corporations and passive foreign investment companies beginning after August 10, 1999, and taxable years of controlled foreign corporations and passive foreign investment companies ending with or within such taxable years of the shareholders. The provisions in paragraph (a) of this section relating to the controlled foreign corporations taken into account for purposes of this section apply to taxable years of foreign corporations ending on or after October 1, 2019, and taxable years of United States shareholders in which or with which such taxable years of foreign corporations end. For taxable years of foreign corporations ending before October 1, 2019, and taxable years of United States shareholders in which or with which such taxable years of foreign corporations end, a taxpayer may apply such provisions to the last taxable year of a foreign corporation beginning before January 1, 2018, and each subsequent taxable year of the foreign corporation, and to taxable years of United States shareholders in which or with which such taxable years of the foreign corporation end, provided that the taxpayer and United States persons that are related (within the meaning of section 267 or 707) to the taxpayer consistently apply such provisions with respect to all foreign corporations. For taxable years of foreign corporations ending before October 1, 2019, and taxable years of United States shareholders in which or with which such taxable years of foreign corporations end, where the taxpayer does not apply the provisions of paragraph (a) of this section relating to controlled foreign corporations, see paragraph (a) of this section as in effect and contained in 26 CFR part 1, as revised April 1, 2020.

[T.D. 8831, 64 FR 43276, Aug. 10, 1999; T.D. 8890, 65 FR 41334, July 5, 2000; T.D. 9908, 85 FR 59433, Sept. 22, 2020]

§ 1.672(f)–3 Exceptions to general rule.

(a) Certain revocable trusts. (1) *In general.* Subject to the provisions of paragraph (a)(2) of this section, the general rule of § 1.672(f)–1 does not apply to any portion of a trust for a taxable year of the trust if the power to revest absolutely in the grantor title to such portion is exercisable solely by the grantor (or, in the event of the grantor's incapacity, by a guardian or other person who has unrestricted authority to exercise such power on the grantor's behalf) without the approval or consent of any other person. If the grantor can exercise such power only with the approval of a related or subordinate party who is subservient to the grantor, such power is treated as exercisable solely by the grantor. For the definition of grantor, see § 1.671–2(e). For the definition of related or subordinate party, see § 1.672(c)–1. For purposes of this paragraph (a), a related or subordinate party is subservient to the grantor unless the presumption in the last sentence of § 1.672(c)–1 is rebutted by a preponderance of the evidence. A trust (or portion of a trust) that fails to qualify for the exception provided by this paragraph (a) for a particular taxable year of the trust will be subject to the general rule of § 1.672(f)–1 for that taxable year and all subsequent taxable years of the trust.

(2) *183-day rule.* For purposes of paragraph (a)(1) of this section, the grantor is treated as having a power to revest for a taxable year of the trust only if the grantor has such power for a total of 183 or more days during the taxable year of the trust. If the first or last taxable year of the trust (including the year of the grantor's death) is less than 183 days, the grantor is treated as having a power to revest for purposes of paragraph (a)(1) of this section if the grantor has such power for each day of the first or last taxable year, as the case may be.

(3) *Grandfather rule for certain revocable trusts in existence on September 19, 1995.* Subject to the rules of paragraph (d) of this section (relating to separate accounting for gratuitous transfers to the trust after September 19, 1995), the general rule of § 1.672(f)–1 does not apply to any portion of a trust that was treated as owned by the grantor under section 676 on September 19, 1995, as long as the trust would continue to be so treated thereafter. However, the preceding sentence does not apply to any portion of the trust attributable to gratuitous transfers to the trust after September 19, 1995.

(4) *Examples.* The following examples illustrate the rules of this paragraph (a):

Example (1). Grantor is owner. FP1, a foreign person, creates and funds a revocable trust, T, for the benefit of FP1's children, who are resident aliens. The trustee is a foreign bank, FB, that is owned and controlled by FP1 and FP2, who is FP1's brother. The power to revoke T and revest absolutely in FP1 title to the trust property is exercisable by FP1, but only with the approval or consent of FB. The trust instrument contains no standard that FB must apply in determining whether to approve or consent to the revocation of T. There are no facts that would suggest that FB is not subservient to FP1. Therefore, the exception in paragraph (a)(1) of this section is applicable.

Example (2). Death of grantor. Assume the same facts as in Example 1, except that FP1 dies. After FP1's death, FP2 has the power to withdraw the assets of T, but only with the approval of FB. There are no facts that would suggest that FB is not subservient to FP2. However, the exception in paragraph (a)(1) of this section is no longer applicable, because FP2 is not a grantor of T within the meaning of § 1.671–2(e).

Example (3). Trustee is not related or subordinate party. Assume the same facts as in Example 1, except that neither FP1 nor any member of FP1's family has any substantial ownership interest or other connection with FB. FP1 can remove and replace FB at any time for any reason. Although FP1 can replace FB with a related or subordinate party if FB refuses to approve or consent to FP1's decision to revest the trust property in himself, FB is not a related or subordinate party. Therefore, the exception in paragraph (a)(1) of this section is not applicable.

Example (4). Unrelated trustee will consent to revocation. FP, a foreign person, creates and funds an irrevocable trust, T. The trustee is a foreign bank, FB, that is not a related or subordinate party within the meaning of § 1.672(c)–1. FB has the discretion to distribute trust income or corpus to beneficiaries of T, including FP. Even if FB would in fact distribute all the trust property to FP if requested to do so by FP, the exception in paragraph (a)(1) of this section is not applicable, because FP does not have the power to revoke T.

(b) Certain trusts that can distribute only to the grantor or the spouse of the grantor. (1) *In general.* The general rule of § 1.672(f)–1 does not apply to any trust (or portion of a trust) if at all times during the lifetime of the grantor the only amounts distributable (whether income or corpus) from such trust (or portion thereof) are amounts distributable to the grantor or the spouse of the grantor. For purposes of this paragraph (b), payments of amounts that are not gratuitous transfers (within the meaning of § 1.671–2(e)(2)) are not amounts distributable. For the definition of grantor, see § 1.671–2(e).

(2) *Amounts distributable in discharge of legal obligations.* (i) *In general.* A trust (or portion of a trust) does not fail to satisfy paragraph (b)(1) of this section solely because amounts are distributable from the trust (or portion thereof) in discharge of a legal obligation of the grantor or the spouse of the grantor. Subject to the provisions of paragraph (b)(2)(ii) of this section, an obligation is considered a legal obligation for purposes of this paragraph (b)(2)(i) if it is enforceable under the local law of the jurisdiction in which the grantor (or the spouse of the grantor) resides.

(ii) *Related parties*—(A) *In general.* Except as provided in paragraph (b)(2)(ii)(B) of this section, an obligation to a person who is a related person for purposes of § 1.643(h)–1(e) (other than an individual who is legally separated from the grantor under a decree of divorce or of separate maintenance) is not a legal obligation for purposes of paragraph (b)(2)(i) of this section unless it was contracted bona fide and for adequate and full consideration in money or money's worth (see § 20.2043–1 of this chapter).

(B) *Exceptions*—(*1*) *Amounts distributable in support of certain individuals.* Paragraph (b)(2)(ii)(A) of this section does not apply with respect to amounts that are distributable from the trust (or portion thereof) to support an individual who—

(i) Would be treated as a dependent of the grantor or the spouse of the grantor under section 152(a)(1) through (9), without regard to the requirement that over half of the individual's support be received from the grantor or the spouse of the grantor; and

(ii) Is either permanently and totally disabled (within the meaning of section 22(e)(3)), or less than 19 years old.

(*2*) *Certain potential support obligations.* The fact that amounts might become distributable from a trust (or portion of a trust) in discharge of a potential obligation under local law to support an individual other than an individual described in paragraph (b)(2)(ii)(B)(*1*) of this section is disregarded if such potential obligation is not reasonably expected to arise under the facts and circumstances.

(3) *Reinsurance trusts.* [Reserved]

(3) *Grandfather rule for certain section 677 trusts in existence on September 19, 1995.* Subject to the rules of paragraph (d) of this section (relating to separate accounting for gratuitous transfers to the trust after September 19, 1995), the general rule of § 1.672(f)–1 does not apply to any portion of a trust that was treated as owned by the grantor under section 677 (other than section 677(a)(3)) on September 19, 1995, as long as the trust would continue to be so treated thereafter. However, the preceding sentence does not apply to any portion of the trust attributable to gratuitous transfers to the trust after September 19, 1995.

(4) *Examples.* The following examples illustrate the rules of this paragraph (b):

Example (1). Amounts distributable only to grantor or grantor's spouse. H and his wife, W, are both nonresident aliens. H is 70 years old, and W is 65. H and W have a 30-year-old child, C, a resident alien. There is no reasonable expectation that H or W will ever have an obligation under local law to support C or any other individual. H creates and funds an irrevocable trust, FT, using only his separate property. H is the grantor of FT within the meaning of § 1.671–2(e). Under the terms of FT, the only amounts distributable (whether income or corpus) from FT as long as either H or W is alive are amounts distributable to H or W. Upon the death of both H and W, C may receive distributions from FT. During H's lifetime, the exception in paragraph (b)(1) of this section is applicable.

Example (2). Effect of grantor's death. Assume the same facts as in Example 1. H predeceases W. Assume that W would be treated as owning FT under section 678 if the grantor trust rules were applied without regard to section 672(f). The exception in paragraph (b)(1) of this section is no longer applicable, because W is not a grantor of FT within the meaning of § 1.671–2(e).

Example (3). Amounts temporarily distributable to person other than grantor or grantor's spouse. Assume the same facts as in Example 1, except that C (age 30) is a law student at the time FT is created and the trust instrument provides that, as long as C is in law school, amounts may be distributed from FT to pay C's expenses. Thereafter, the only amounts distributable from FT as long as either H or W is alive will be amounts distributable to H or W. Even assuming there is an enforceable obligation under local law for H and W to support C while he is in school, distributions from FT in payment of C's expenses cannot qualify as distributions in discharge of a legal obligation under paragraph (b)(2) of this section, because C is neither permanently and totally disabled nor less than 19 years old. The exception in paragraph (b)(1) of this section is not applicable. After C graduates from law school, the exception in paragraph (b)(1) still will not be applicable, because amounts were distributable to C during the lifetime of H.

Example (4). Fixed investment trust. FC, a foreign corporation, invests in a domestic fixed investment trust, DT, that is classified as a trust under § 301.7701–4(c)(1) of this chapter. Under the terms of DT, the only amounts that are distributable from FC's portion of DT are amounts distributable to FC. The exception in paragraph (b)(1) of this section is applicable to FC's portion of DT.

Example (5). Reinsurance trust. A domestic insurance company, DI, reinsures a portion of its business with an unrelated foreign insurance company, FI. To satisfy state regulatory requirements, FI places the premiums in an irrevocable domestic trust, DT. The trust funds are held by a United States bank and may be used only to pay claims arising out of the reinsurance policies, which are legally enforceable under the local law of the jurisdiction in which FI resides. On the termination of DT, any assets remaining will revert to FI. Because the only amounts that are distributable from DT are distributable either to FI or in discharge of FI's legal obligations within the meaning of paragraph (b)(2)(i) of this section, the exception in paragraph (b)(1) of this section is applicable.

Example (6). Trust that provides security for loan. FC, a foreign corporation, borrows money from B, an unrelated bank, to finance the purchase of an airplane. FC creates a foreign trust, FT, to hold the airplane as security for the loan from B. The only amounts that are distributable from FT while the loan is outstanding are amounts distributable to B in the event that FC defaults on its loan from B. When FC repays the loan, the trust assets will revert to FC. The loan is a legal obligation of FC within the meaning of paragraph (b)(2)(i) of this section, because it is enforceable under the local law of the country in which FC is incorporated. Paragraph (b)(2)(ii) of this section is not applicable, because B is not a related person for purposes of § 1.643(h)–1(e). The exception in paragraph (b)(1) of this section is applicable.

(c) Compensatory trusts—(1) *In general.* The general rule of § 1.672(f)–1 does not apply to any portion of—

(i) A nonexempt employees' trust described in section 402(b), including a trust created on behalf of a self-employed individual;

(ii) A trust, including a trust created on behalf of a self-employed individual, that would be a nonexempt employees' trust described in section 402(b) but for the fact that the trust's assets are not set aside from the claims of creditors of the actual or deemed transferor within the meaning of § 1.83–3(e); and

(iii) Any additional category of trust that the Commissioner may designate in revenue procedures, notices, or other guidance published in the Internal Revenue Bulletin (see § 601.601(d)(2) of this chapter).

(2) *Exceptions.* The Commissioner may, in revenue rulings, notices, or other guidance published in the Internal Revenue Bulletin (see § 601.601(d)(2) of this chapter), designate categories of compensatory trusts to which the general rule of paragraph (c)(1) of this section does not apply.

(d) Separate accounting for gratuitous transfers to grandfathered trusts after September 19, 1995. If a trust that was treated as owned by the grantor under section 676 or 677 (other than section 677(a)(3)) on September 19, 1995, contains both amounts held in the trust on September 19, 1995, and amounts that were gratuitously transferred to the trust after September 19, 1995, paragraphs (a)(3) and (b)(3) of this section apply only if the amounts that were gratuitously transferred to the trust after September 19, 1995, are treated as a separate portion of the trust that is accounted for under the rules of § 1.671–3(a)(2). If the amounts that were gratuitously transferred to the trust after September 19, 1995 are not so accounted for, the general rule of § 1.672(f)–1 applies to the entire trust. If such amounts are so accounted for, and without regard to whether there is physical separation of the assets, the general rule of § 1.672(f)–1 does not apply to the portion of the trust that is attributable to amounts that were held in the trust on September 19, 1995.

(e) Effective date. The rules of this section are generally applicable to taxable years of a trust beginning after August 10, 1999. The initial separate accounting required by paragraph (d) of this section must be prepared by the due date (including extensions) for the tax return of the trust for the first taxable year of the trust beginning after August 10, 1999.

[T.D. 8831, 64 FR 43276, Aug. 10, 1999; T.D. 8890, 65 FR 41334, July 5, 2000]

§ 1.672(f)–4 Recharacterization of purported gifts.

(a) In general. (1) *Purported gifts from partnerships.* Except as provided in paragraphs (b), (e), and (f) of this section, and without regard to the existence of any trust, if a United States person (United States donee) directly or indirectly receives a purported gift or bequest (as defined in paragraph (d) of this section) from a partnership, the purported gift or bequest must be included in the United States donee's gross income as ordinary income.

(2) *Purported gifts from foreign corporations.* Except as provided in paragraphs (b), (e), and (f) of this section, and without regard to the existence of any trust, if a United States donee directly or indirectly receives a purported gift or bequest (as defined in paragraph (d) of this section) from any foreign corporation, the purported gift or bequest must be included in the United States donee's gross income as if it were a distribution from the foreign corporation. If the foreign corporation is a passive foreign investment company (within the meaning of section 1297), the rules of section 1291 apply. For purposes of section 1012, the United States donee is not treated as having basis in the stock of the foreign corporation. However, for purposes of section 1223, the United States donee is treated as having a holding period in the stock of the foreign corporation on the date of the deemed distribution equal to the weighted average of the holding periods of the actual interest holders (other than any interest holders who treat the portion of the purported gift attributable to their interest in the foreign corporation in the manner described in paragraph (b)(1) of this section). For purposes of section 902, a United States donee that is a domestic corporation is not treated as owning any voting stock of the foreign corporation.

(b) Exceptions. (1) *Partner or shareholder treats transfer as distribution and gift.* Paragraph (a) of this section does not apply to the extent the United States donee can demonstrate to the satisfaction of the Commissioner that either—

(i) A United States citizen or resident alien individual who directly or indirectly holds an interest in the partnership or foreign corporation treated and reported the purported gift or bequest for United States tax purposes as a distribution to such individual and a subsequent gift or bequest to the United States donee; or

(ii) A nonresident alien individual who directly or indirectly holds an interest in the partnership or foreign corporation treated and reported the purported gift or bequest for purposes of the tax laws of the nonresident alien individual's country of residence as a distribution to such individual and a subsequent gift or bequest to the United States donee, and the United States donee timely complied with the reporting requirements of section 6039F, if applicable.

(2) *All beneficial owners of domestic partnership are United States citizens or residents or domestic corporations.* Paragraph (a)(1) of this section does not apply to a purported gift or bequest from a domestic partnership if the United States donee can demonstrate to the satisfaction of the Commissioner that all beneficial owners (within the meaning of § 1.1441–1(c)(6)) of the partnership are United States citizens or residents or domestic corporations.

(3) *Contribution to capital of corporate United States donee.* Paragraph (a) of this section does not apply to the extent a United States donee that is a corporation can establish that the purported gift or bequest was treated for United States tax purposes as a contribution to the capital of the United States donee to which section 118 applies.

(4) *Charitable transfers.* Paragraph (a) of this section does not apply if either—

(i) The United States donee is described in section 170(c); or

(ii) The transferor has received a ruling or determination letter, which has been neither revoked nor modified, from the Internal Revenue Service recognizing its exempt status under section 501(c)(3), and the transferor made the transfer pursuant to an exempt purpose for which the transferor was created or organized. For purposes of the preceding sentence, a ruling or determination letter recognizing exemption may not be relied upon if there is a material change, inconsistent with exemption, in the character, the purpose, or the method of operation of the organization.

(c) Certain transfers from trusts to which a partnership or foreign corporation has made a gratuitous transfer. (1) *Generally treated as distribution from partnership or foreign corporation.* Except as provided in paragraphs (c)(2) and (3) of this section, if a United States donee receives a gratuitous transfer (within the meaning of § 1.671–2(e)(2)) from a trust (or portion of a trust) to which a partnership or foreign corporation has made a gratuitous transfer, the United States donee must treat the transfer as a purported gift or bequest from the partnership or foreign corporation that is subject to the rules of paragraph (a) of this section (including the exceptions in paragraphs (b) and (f) of this section). This paragraph (c) applies without regard to who is treated as the grantor of the trust (or portion thereof) under § 1.671–2(e)(4).

(2) *Alternative rule.* Except as provided in paragraph (c)(3) of this section, if the United States tax computed under the rules of paragraphs (a) and (c)(1) of this section does not exceed the United States tax that would be due if the United States donee treated the transfer as a distribution from the trust (or portion thereof), paragraph (c)(1) of this section does not apply and the United States donee must treat the transfer as a distribution from the trust (or portion thereof) that is subject to the rules of subparts A through D (section 641 and following), part I, subchapter J, chapter 1 of the Internal Revenue Code. For purposes of paragraph (f) of this section, the transfer is treated as a purported gift or bequest from the partnership or foreign corporation that made the gratuitous transfer to the trust (or portion thereof).

(3) *Exception.* Neither paragraph (c)(1) of this section nor paragraph (c)(2) of this section applies to the extent the United States donee can demonstrate to the satisfaction of the Commissioner that the transfer represents an amount that is, or has been, taken into account for United States tax purposes by a United States citizen or resident or a domestic corporation. A transfer will be deemed to be made first out of amounts that have not been taken into account for United States tax purposes by a United States citizen or resident or a domestic corporation, unless the United States donee can demonstrate to the satisfaction of the Commissioner that another ordering rule is more appropriate.

(d) Definition of purported gift or bequest. (1) *In general.* Subject to the provisions of paragraphs (d)(2) and (3) of this section, a purported gift or bequest for purposes of this section is any transfer of property by a partnership or foreign corporation other than a transfer for fair market value (within the meaning of § 1.671–2(e)(2)(ii)) to a person who is not a partner in the partnership or a shareholder of the foreign corporation (or to a person who is a partner in the partnership or a shareholder of a foreign corporation, if the amount transferred is inconsistent with the partner's interest in the partnership or the shareholder's interest in the corporation, as the case may be). For purposes of this section, the term property includes cash.

(2) *Transfers for less than fair market value*—(i) *Excess treated as purported gift or bequest.* Except as provided in paragraph (d)(2)(ii) of this section, if a transfer described in paragraph (d)(1) of this section is for less than fair market value, the excess of the fair market value of the property transferred over the value of the property received, services rendered, or the right to use property is treated as a purported gift or bequest.

(ii) *Exception for transfers to unrelated parties.* No portion of a transfer described in paragraph (d)(1) of this section will be treated as a purported gift or bequest for purposes of this section if the United States donee can demonstrate to the satisfaction of the Commissioner that the United States donee is not related to a partner or shareholder of the transferor within the meaning of § 1.643(h)–1(e) or does not have another relationship with a partner or shareholder of the transferor that establishes a reasonable basis for concluding that the transferor would make a gratuitous transfer to the United States donee.

(e) Prohibition against affirmative use of recharacterization by taxpayers. A taxpayer may not use the rules of this section if a principal purpose for using such rules is the avoidance of any tax imposed by the Internal Revenue Code. Thus, with respect to such taxpayer, the Commissioner may depart from the rules of this section and recharacterize (for all purposes of the Internal Revenue Code) the transfer in accordance with its form or its economic substance.

(f) Transfers not in excess of $10,000. This section does not apply if, during the taxable year of the United States donee, the aggregate amount of purported gifts or bequests that is transferred to such United States donee directly or indirectly from all partnerships or foreign corporations that are related (within the meaning of section 643(i)) does not exceed $10,000. The aggregate amount must include gifts or bequests from persons that the United States donee knows or has reason to know are related to the partnership or foreign corporation (within the meaning of section 643(i)).

(g) Examples. The following examples illustrate the rules of this section. In each example, the amount that is transferred exceeds $10,000. The examples are as follows:

Example (1). Distribution from foreign corporation. FC is a foreign corporation that is wholly owned by A, a nonresident alien who is resident in Country C. FC makes a gratuitous transfer of property directly to A's daughter, B, who is a resident alien. Under paragraph (a)(2) of this section, B generally must treat the transfer as a dividend from FC to the extent of FC's earnings and profits and as an amount received in excess of basis thereafter. If FC is a passive foreign investment company, B must treat the amount received as a distribution under section 1291. B will be treated as having the same holding period as A. However, under paragraph (b)(1)(ii) of this section, if B can establish to the satisfaction of the Commissioner that, for purposes of the tax laws of Country C, A treated (and reported, if applicable) the transfer as a distribution to himself and a subsequent gift to B, B may treat the transfer as a gift (provided B timely complied with the reporting requirements of section 6039F, if applicable).

Example (2). Distribution of corpus from trust to which foreign corporation made gratuitous transfer. FC is a foreign corporation that is wholly owned by A, a nonresident alien who is resident in Country C. FC makes a gratuitous transfer to a foreign trust, FT, that has no other assets. FT immediately makes a gratuitous transfer in the same amount to A's daughter, B, who is a resident alien. Under paragraph (c)(1) of this section, B must treat the transfer as a transfer from FC that is subject to the rules of paragraph (a)(2) of this section. Under paragraph (a)(2) of this section, B must treat the transfer as a dividend from FC unless she can establish to the satisfaction of the Commissioner that, for purposes of the tax laws of Country C, A treated (and reported, if applicable) the transfer as a distribution to himself and a subsequent gift to B and that B timely complied with the reporting requirements of section 6039F, if applicable. The alternative rule in paragraph (c)(2) of this section would not apply as long as the United States tax computed under the rules of paragraph (a)(2) of this section is equal to or greater than the United States tax that would be due if the transfer were treated as a distribution from FT.

Example (3). Accumulation distribution from trust to which foreign corporation made gratuitous transfer. FC is a foreign corporation that is wholly owned by A, a nonresident alien. FC is not a passive foreign investment company (as defined in section 1297). FC makes a gratuitous transfer of 100X to a foreign trust, FT, on January 1, 2001. FT has no other assets on January 1, 2001. Several years later, FT makes a gratuitous transfer of 1000X to A's daughter, B, who is a United States resident. Assume that the section 668 interest charge on accumulation distributions will apply if the transfer is treated as a distribution from FT. Under the alternative rule of paragraph (c)(2) of this section, B must treat the transfer as an accumulation distribution from FT, because the resulting United States tax liability is greater than the United States tax that would be due if the transfer were treated as a transfer from FC that is subject to the rules of paragraph (a) of this section.

Example (4). Transfer from trust that is treated as owned by United States citizen. Assume the same facts as in Example 3, except that A is a United States citizen. Assume that A treats and reports the transfer to FT as a constructive distribution to himself, followed by a gratuitous transfer to FT, and that A is properly treated as the grantor of FT within the meaning of § 1.671–2(e). A is treated as the owner of FT under section 679 and, as required by section 671 and the regulations thereunder, A includes all of FT's items of income, deductions, and credit in computing his taxable income and credits. Neither paragraph (c)(1) nor paragraph (c)(2) of this section is applicable, because the exception in paragraph (c)(3) of this section applies.

Example (5). Transfer for less than fair market value. FC is a foreign corporation that is wholly owned by A, a nonresident alien. On January 15, 2001, FC transfers property directly to A's daughter, B, a resident alien, in exchange for 90X. The Commissioner later determines that the fair market value of the property at the time of the transfer was 100X. Under paragraph (d)(2)(i) of this section, 10X will be treated as a purported gift to B on January 15, 2001.

(h) Effective date. The rules of this section are generally applicable to any transfer after August 10, 1999, by a partnership or foreign corporation, or by a trust to which a partnership or foreign corporation makes a gratuitous transfer after August 10, 1999.

[T.D. 8831, 64 FR 43278, Aug. 10, 1999; T.D. 8890, 65 FR 41334, July 5, 2000]

§ 1.672(f)–5 Special rules.

(a) Transfers by certain beneficiaries to foreign grantor. (1) *In general.* If, but for section 672(f)(5), a foreign person would be treated as the owner of any portion of a trust, any United States beneficiary of the trust is treated as the grantor of a portion of the trust to the extent the United States beneficiary directly or indirectly made transfers of property to such foreign person (without regard to whether the United States beneficiary was a United States beneficiary at the time of any transfer) in excess of transfers to the United States beneficiary from the foreign person. The rule of this paragraph (a) does not apply to the extent the United States beneficiary can demonstrate to the satisfaction of the Commissioner that the transfer by the United States beneficiary to the foreign person was wholly unrelated to any transaction involving the trust. For purposes of this paragraph (a), the term property includes cash, and a transfer of property does not include a transfer that is not a gratuitous transfer (within the meaning of § 1.671–2(e)(2)). In addition, a gift is not taken into account to the extent such gift would not be characterized as a taxable gift under section 2503(b). For a definition of United States beneficiary, see section 679.

(2) *Examples.* The following examples illustrate the rules of this section:

Example (1). A, a nonresident alien, contributes property to FC, a foreign corporation that is wholly owned by A. FC creates a foreign trust, FT, for the benefit of A and A's children. FT is revocable by FC without the approval or consent of any other person. FC funds FT with the property received from A. A and A's family move to the United States. Under paragraph (a)(1) of this section, A is treated as a grantor of FT. (A may also be treated as an owner of FT under section 679(a)(4).)

Example (2). B, a United States citizen, makes a gratuitous transfer of $1 million to B's uncle, C, a nonresident alien. C creates a foreign trust, FT, for the benefit of B and B's children. FT is revocable by C without the approval or consent of any other person. C funds FT with the property received from B. Under paragraph (a)(1) of this section, B is treated as a grantor of FT. (B also would be treated as an owner of FT as a result of section 679.)

(b) Entity characterization. Entities generally are characterized under United States tax principles for purposes of §§ 1.672(f)–1 through 1.672(f)–5. See §§ 301.7701–1 through 301.7701–4 of this chapter. However, solely for purposes of § 1.672(f)–4, a transferor that is a wholly owned business entity is treated as a corporation, separate from its single owner.

(c) Effective date. The rules in paragraph (a) of this section are applicable to transfers to trusts on or after August 10, 1999. The rules in paragraph (b) of this section are applicable August 10, 1999.

[T.D. 8831, 64 FR 43280, Aug. 10, 1999; T.D. 8890, 65 FR 41334, July 5, 2000]

§ 673. Reversionary Interests

(a) General rule. The grantor shall be treated as the owner of any portion of a trust in which he has a reversionary interest in either the corpus or the income therefrom, if, as of the inception of that portion of the trust, the value of such interest exceeds 5 percent of the value of such portion.

(b) Reversionary interest taking effect at death of minor lineal descendant beneficiary. In the case of any beneficiary who—

(1) is a lineal descendant of the grantor, and

(2) holds all of the present interests in any portion of a trust,

the grantor shall not be treated under subsection (a) as the owner of such portion solely by reason of a reversionary interest in such portion which takes effect upon the death of such beneficiary before such beneficiary attains age 21.

(c) Special rule for determining value of reversionary interest. For purposes of subsection (a), the value of the grantor's reversionary interest shall be determined by assuming the maximum exercise of discretion in favor of the grantor.

(d) Postponement of date specified for reacquisition. Any postponement of the date specified for the reacquisition of possession or enjoyment of the reversionary interest shall be treated as a new transfer in trust commencing with the date on which the postponement is effective and terminating with the date prescribed by the postponement. However, income for any period shall not be included in the income of the grantor by reason of the preceding sentence if such income would not be so includible in the absence of such postponement.

Regulations

§ 1.673(a)–1 Reversionary interests; income payable to beneficiaries other than certain charitable organizations; general rule.

(a) Under section 673(a), a grantor, in general, is treated as the owner of any portion of a trust in which he has a reversionary interest in either the corpus or income if, as of the inception of that portion of the trust, the grantor's interest will or may reasonably be expected to take effect in possession or enjoyment within 10 years commencing with the date of transfer of that portion of the trust. However, the following types of reversionary interests are excepted from the general rule of the preceding sentence:

(1) A reversionary interest after the death of the income beneficiary of a trust (see paragraph (b) of this section); and

(2) Except in the case of transfers in trust made after April 22, 1969, a reversionary interest in a charitable trust meeting the requirements of section 673(b) (see § 1.673(b)–1).

Even though the duration of the trust may be such that the grantor is not treated as its owner under section 673, and therefore is not taxed on the ordinary income, he may nevertheless be treated as an owner under section 677(a)(2) if he has a reversionary interest in the corpus. In the latter case, items of income, deduction, and credit allocable to corpus, such as capital gains and losses, will be included in the portion he owns. See § 1.671–3 and the regulations under section 677. See § 1.673(d)–1 with respect to a postponement of the date specified for reacquisition of a reversionary interest.

(b) Section 673(c) provides that a grantor is not treated as the owner of any portion of a trust by reason of section 673 if his reversionary interest in the portion is not to take effect in possession or enjoyment until the death of the person or persons to whom the income of the portion is regardless of the life expectancies of the income beneficiaries. If his reversionary interest is to take effect on or after the death of an income beneficiary or upon the expiration of a specific term of years, whichever is earlier, the grantor is treated as the owner if the specific term of years is less than 10 years (but not if the term is 10 years or longer).

(c) Where the grantor's reversionary interest in a portion of a trust is to take effect in possession or enjoyment by reason of some event other than the expiration of a specific term of years or the death of the income beneficiary, the grantor is treated as the owner of the portion if the event may reasonably be expected to occur within 10 years from the date of transfer of that portion, but he is not treated as the owner under section 673 if the event may not reasonably be expected to occur within 10 years from that date. For example, if the reversionary interest in any portion of a trust is to take effect on or after the death of the grantor (or any person other than the person to whom the income is payable) the grantor is treated under section 673 as the owner of the portion if the life expectancy of the grantor (or other person) is less than 10 years on the date of transfer of the portion, but not if the life expectancy is 10 years or longer. If the reversionary interest in any portion is to take effect on or after the death of the grantor (or any person other than the person to whom the income is payable) or upon the expiration of a specific term of years, whichever is earlier, the grantor is treated as the owner of the portion if on the date of transfer of the portion either the life expectancy of the grantor (or other person) or the specific term is less than 10 years; however, if both the life expectancy and the specific term are 10 years or longer the grantor is not treated as the owner of the portion under section 673. Similarly, if the grantor has a reversionary interest in any portion which will take effect at the death of the income beneficiary or the grantor, whichever is earlier, the grantor is not treated as an owner of the portion unless his life expectancy is less than 10 years.

(d) It is immaterial that a reversionary interest in corpus or income is subject to a contingency if the reversionary interest may, taking the contingency into consideration, reasonably be expected to take effect in possession or enjoyment within 10 years. For example, the grantor is taxable where the trust income is to be paid to the grantor's son for 3 years, and the corpus is then to be returned to the grantor if he survives that period, or to be paid to the grantor's son if he is already deceased.

(e) See section 671 and §§ 1.671–2 and 1.671–3 for rules for treatment of items of income, deduction, and credit when a person is treated as the owner of all or only a portion of a trust.

[T.D. 6500, 25 FR 11814, Nov. 26, 1960, as amended by T.D. 7357, 40 FR 23742, June 2, 1975]

§ 1.673(b)–1 Income payable to charitable beneficiaries (before amendment by Tax Reform Act of 1969). [*Omitted. Ed.*]

[T.D. 6500, 25 FR 11814, Nov. 26, 1960, as amended by T.D. 6605, 27 FR 8097, Aug. 15, 1962; T.D. 7357, 40 FR 23743, June 2, 1975]

§ 1.673(c)–1 Reversionary interest after income beneficiary's death.

The subject matter of section 673(c) is covered in paragraph (b) of § 1.673(a)–1.

[T.D. 6500, 25 FR 11814, Nov. 26, 1960]

§ 1.673(d)–1 Postponement of date specified for reacquisition.

Any postponement of the date specified for the reacquisition of possession or enjoyment of any reversionary interest is considered a new transfer in trust commencing with the date on which the postponement is effected and terminating with the date prescribed by the postponement. However, the grantor will not be treated as the owner of any portion of a trust for any taxable year by reason of the foregoing sentence if he would not be so treated in the absence of any postponement. The rules contained in this section may be illustrated by the following example:

Example. G places property in trust for the benefit of his son B. Upon the expiration of 12 years or the earlier death of B the property is to be paid over to G or his estate. After the expiration of 9 years G extends the term of the trust for an additional 2 years. G is considered to have made a new transfer in trust for a term of 5 years (the remaining 3 years of the original transfer plus the 2-year extension). However, he is not treated as the owner of the trust under section 673 for the first 3 years of the new term because he would not be so treated if the term of the trust had not been extended. G is treated as the owner of the trust, however, for the remaining 2 years.

[T.D. 6500, 25 FR 11814, Nov. 26, 1960]

§ 674. Power to Control Beneficial Enjoyment

(a) General rule. The grantor shall be treated as the owner of any portion of a trust in respect of which the beneficial enjoyment of the corpus or the income therefrom is subject to a power of disposition, exercisable by the grantor or a nonadverse party, or both, without the approval or consent of any adverse party.

(b) Exceptions for certain powers. Subsection (a) shall not apply to the following powers regardless of by whom held:

(1) Power to apply income to support of a dependent. A power described in section 677(b) to the extent that the grantor would not be subject to tax under that section.

(2) Power affecting beneficial enjoyment only after occurrence of event. A power, the exercise of which can only affect the beneficial enjoyment of the income for a period commencing after the occurrence of an event such that a grantor would not be treated as the owner under section 673 if the power were a reversionary interest; but the grantor may be treated as the owner after the occurrence of the event unless the power is relinquished.

(3) Power exercisable only by will. A power exercisable only by will, other than a power in the grantor to appoint by will the income of the trust where the income is accumulated for such disposition by the grantor or may be so accumulated in the discretion of the grantor or a nonadverse party, or both, without the approval or consent of any adverse party.

(4) Power to allocate among charitable beneficiaries. A power to determine the beneficial enjoyment of the corpus or the income therefrom if the corpus or income is irrevocably payable for a purpose specified in section 170(c) (relating to definition of charitable contributions) or to an employee stock ownership plan (as defined in section 4975(e)(7)) in a qualified gratuitous transfer (as defined in section 664(g)(1)).

(5) Power to distribute corpus. A power to distribute corpus either—

(A) to or for a beneficiary or beneficiaries or to or for a class of beneficiaries (whether or not income beneficiaries) provided that the power is limited by a reasonably definite standard which is set forth in the trust instrument; or

(B) to or for any current income beneficiary, provided that the distribution of corpus must be chargeable against the proportionate share of corpus held in trust for the payment of income to the beneficiary as if the corpus constituted a separate trust.

A power does not fall within the powers described in this paragraph if any person has a power to add to the beneficiary or beneficiaries or to a class of beneficiaries designated to receive the income or corpus, except where such action is to provide for after-born or after-adopted children.

(6) Power to withhold income temporarily. A power to distribute or apply income to or for any current income beneficiary or to accumulate the income for him, provided that any accumulated income must ultimately be payable—

(A) to the beneficiary from whom distribution or application is withheld, to his estate, or to his appointees (or persons named as alternate takers in default of appointment) provided that such beneficiary possesses a power of appointment which does not exclude from the class of possible appointees any person other than the beneficiary, his estate, his creditors, or the creditors of his estate, or

(B) on termination of the trust, or in conjunction with a distribution of corpus which is augmented by such accumulated income, to the current income beneficiaries in shares which have been irrevocably specified in the trust instrument.

Accumulated income shall be considered so payable although it is provided that if any beneficiary does not survive a date of distribution which could reasonably have been expected to occur within the beneficiary's lifetime, the share of the deceased beneficiary is to be paid to his appointees or to one or more designated alternate takers (other than the grantor or the grantor's estate) whose shares have been irrevocably specified. A power does not fall within the powers described in this paragraph if any person has a power to add to the beneficiary or beneficiaries or to a class of beneficiaries designated to receive the income or corpus except where such action is to provide for after-born or after-adopted children.

(7) Power to withhold income during disability of a beneficiary. A power exercisable only during—

(A) the existence of a legal disability of any current income beneficiary, or

(B) the period during which any income beneficiary shall be under the age of 21 years,

to distribute or apply income to or for such beneficiary or to accumulate and add the income to corpus. A power does not fall within the powers described in this paragraph if any person has a power to add to the beneficiary or beneficiaries or to a class of beneficiaries designated to receive the income or corpus, except where such action is to provide for after-born or after-adopted children.

(8) Power to allocate between corpus and income. A power to allocate receipts and disbursements as between corpus and income, even though expressed in broad language.

(c) Exception for certain powers of independent trustees. Subsection (a) shall not apply to a power solely exercisable (without the approval or consent of any other person) by a trustee or trustees, none of whom is the grantor, and no more than half of whom are related or subordinate parties who are subservient to the wishes of the grantor—

(1) to distribute, apportion, or accumulate income to or for a beneficiary or beneficiaries, or to, for, or within a class of beneficiaries; or

(2) to pay out corpus to or for a beneficiary or beneficiaries or to or for a class of beneficiaries (whether or not income beneficiaries).

A power does not fall within the powers described in this subsection if any person has a power to add to the beneficiary or beneficiaries or to a class of beneficiaries designated to receive the income or corpus, except where such action is to provide for after-born or after-adopted children. For periods during which an individual is the spouse of the grantor (within the meaning of section 672(e)(2)), any reference in this subsection to the grantor shall be treated as including a reference to such individual.

(d) Power to allocate income if limited by a standard. Subsection (a) shall not apply to a power solely exercisable (without the approval or consent of any other person) by a trustee or trustees, none of whom is the grantor or spouse living with the grantor, to distribute, apportion, or accumulate income to or for a beneficiary or beneficiaries, or to, for, or within a class of beneficiaries, whether or not the conditions of paragraph (6) or (7) of subsection (b) are satisfied, if such power is limited by a reasonably definite external standard which is set forth in the trust instrument. A power does not fall within the powers described in this subsection if any person has a power to add to the beneficiary or beneficiaries or to a class of beneficiaries designated to receive the income or corpus except where such action is to provide for after-born or after-adopted children.

Regulations

§ 1.674(a)–1 Power to control beneficial enjoyment; scope of section 674.

(a) Under section 674, the grantor is treated as the owner of a portion of trust if the grantor or a nonadverse party has a power, beyond specified limits, to dispose of the beneficial enjoyment of the income or corpus, whether the power is a fiduciary power, a power of appointment, or any other power. Section 674(a) states in general terms that the grantor is treated as the owner in every case in which he or a nonadverse party can affect the beneficial enjoyment of a portion of a trust, the limitations being set forth as exceptions in subsections (b), (c), and (d) of section 674. These exceptions are discussed in detail in §§ 1.674(b)–1 through 1.674(d)–1. Certain limitations applicable to section 674(b), (c), and (d) are set forth in § 1.674(d)–2. Section 674(b) describes powers which are excepted regardless of who holds them. Section 674(c) describes additional powers of trustees which are excepted if at least half the trustees are independent, and if the grantor is not a trustee. Section 674(d) describes a further power which is excepted if it is held by trustees other than the grantor or his spouse (if living with the grantor).

(b) In general terms the grantor is treated as the owner of a portion of a trust if he or a nonadverse party or both has a power to dispose of the beneficial enjoyment of the corpus or income unless the power is one of the following:

(1) *Miscellaneous powers over either ordinary income or corpus.* (i) A power that can only affect the beneficial enjoyment of income (including capital gains) received after a period of time such that the grantor would not be treated as an owner under section 673 if the power were a reversionary interest (section 674(b)(2));

(ii) A testamentary power held by anyone (other than a testamentary power held by the grantor over accumulated income) (section 674(b)(3));

(iii) A power to choose between charitable beneficiaries or to affect the manner of their enjoyment of a beneficial interest (section 674(b)(4));

(iv) A power to allocate receipts and disbursements between income and corpus (section 674(b)(8)).

(2) *Powers of distribution primarily affecting only one beneficiary.* (i) A power to distribute corpus to or for a current income beneficiary, if the distribution must be charged against the share of corpus from which the beneficiary may receive income (section 674(b)(5)(B));

(ii) A power to distribute income to or for a current income beneficiary or to accumulate it either (a) if accumulated income must either be payable to the beneficiary from whom it was withheld or as described in paragraph (b)(6) of § 1.674(b)–1 (section 674(b)(6)); (b) if the power is to apply income to the support of a dependent of the grantor, and the income is not so applied (section 674(b)(1)); or (c) if the beneficiary is under 21 or under a legal disability and accumulated income is added to corpus (section 674(b)(7)).

(3) *Powers of distribution affecting more than one beneficiary.* A power to distribute corpus or income to or among one or more beneficiaries or to accumulate income, either (i) if the power is held by a trustee or trustees other than the grantor, at least half of whom are independent (section 674(c)), or (ii) if the power is limited by a reasonably definite standard in the trust instrument, and in the case of a power over income, if in addition the power is held by a trustee or trustees other than the grantor and the grantor's spouse living with the grantor (section 674(b)(5)(A) and (d)). (These powers include both powers to "sprinkle" income or corpus among current beneficiaries, and powers to shift income or corpus between current beneficiaries and remaindermen; however, certain of the powers described under subparagraph (2) of this paragraph can have the latter effect incidentally.)

(c) See section 671 and §§ 1.671–2 and 1.671–3 for rules for the treatment of income, deductions, and credits when a person is treated as the owner of all or only a portion of a trust.

[T.D. 6500, 25 FR 11814, Nov. 26, 1960]

§ 1.674(b)–1 Excepted powers exercisable by any person.

(a) Paragraph (b)(1) through (8) of this section sets forth a number of powers which may be exercisable by any person without causing the grantor to be treated as an owner of a trust under section 674(a). Further, with the exception of powers described in paragraph (b)(1) of this section, it is immaterial whether these powers are held in the capacity of trustee. It makes no difference under section 674(b) that the person holding the power is the grantor, or a related or subordinate party (with the qualifications noted in paragraph (b)(1) and (3) of this section).

(b) The exceptions referred to in paragraph (a) of this section are as follows (see, however, the limitations set forth in § 1.674(d)–2):

(1) *Powers to apply income to support of a dependent.* Section 674(b)(1) provides, in effect, that regardless of the general rule of section 674(a), the income of a trust will not be considered as taxable to the grantor merely because in the discretion of any person (other than a grantor who is not acting as a trustee or cotrustee) it may be used for the support of a beneficiary whom the grantor is legally obligated to support, except to the extent that it is in fact used for that purpose. See section 677(b) and the regulations thereunder.

(2) *Powers affecting beneficial enjoyment only after a period.* Section 674(b)(2) provides an exception to section 674(a) if the exercise of a power can only affect the beneficial enjoyment of the income of a trust received after a period of time which is such that a grantor would not be treated as an owner under section 673 if the power were a reversionary interest. See §§ 1.673(a)–1 and 1.673(b)–1. For example, if a trust created on January 1, 1955, provides for the payment of income to the grantor's son, and the grantor reserves the power to substitute other beneficiaries of income or corpus in lieu of his son on or after January 1, 1965, the grantor is not treated under section 674 as the owner of the trust with respect to ordinary income received before January 1, 1965. But the grantor will be treated as an owner on and after that date unless the power is relinquished. If the beginning of the period during which the grantor may substitute beneficiaries is postponed, the rules set forth in § 1.673(d)–1 are applicable in order to determine whether the grantor

should be treated as an owner during the period following the postponement.

(3) *Testamentary powers.* Under paragraph (3) of section 674(b) a power in any person to control beneficial enjoyment exercisable only by will does not cause a grantor to be treated as an owner under section 674(a). However, this exception does not apply to income accumulated for testamentary disposition by the grantor or to income which may be accumulated for such distribution in the discretion of the grantor or a nonadverse party, or both, without the approval or consent of any adverse party. For example, if a trust instrument provides that the income is to be accumulated during the grantor's life and that the grantor may appoint the accumulated income by will, the grantor is treated as the owner of the trust. Moreover, if a trust instrument provides that the income is payable to another person for his life, but the grantor has a testamentary power of appointment over the remainder, and under the trust instrument and local law capital gains are added to corpus, the grantor is treated as the owner of a portion of the trust and capital gains and losses are included in that portion. (See § 1.671–3.)

(4) *Powers to determine beneficial enjoyment of charitable beneficiaries.* Under paragraph (4) of section 674(b) a power in any person to determine the beneficial enjoyment of corpus or income which is irrevocably payable (currently or in the future) for purposes specified in section 170(c) (relating to definition of charitable contributions) will not cause the grantor to be treated as an owner under section 674(a). For example, if a grantor creates a trust, the income of which is irrevocably payable solely to educational or other organizations that qualify under section 170(c), he is not treated as an owner under section 674 although he retains the power to allocate the income among such organizations.

(5) *Powers to distribute corpus.* Paragraph (5) of section 674(b) provides an exception to section 674(a) for powers to distribute corpus, subject to certain limitations, as follows:

(i) If the power is limited by a reasonably definite standard which is set forth in the trust instrument, it may extend to corpus distributions to any beneficiary or beneficiaries or class of beneficiaries (whether income beneficiaries or remaindermen) without causing the grantor to be treated as an owner under section 674. See section 674(b)(5)(A). It is not required that the standard consist of the needs and circumstances of the beneficiary. A clearly measurable standard under which the holder of a power is legally accountable is deemed a reasonably definite standard for this purpose. For instance, a power to distribute corpus for the education, support, maintenance, or health of the beneficiary; for his reasonable support and comfort; or to enable him to maintain his accustomed standard of living; or to meet an emergency, would be limited by a reasonably definite standard. However, a power to distribute corpus for the pleasure, desire, or happiness of a beneficiary is not limited by a reasonably definite standard. The entire context of a provision of a trust instrument granting a power must be considered in determining whether the power is limited by a reasonably definite standard. For example, if a trust instrument provides that the determination of the trustee shall be conclusive with respect to the exercise or nonexercise of a power, the power is not limited by a reasonably definite standard. However, the fact that the governing instrument is phrased in discretionary terms is not in itself an indication that no reasonably definite standard exists.

(ii) If the power is not limited by a reasonably definite standard set forth in the trust instrument, the exception applies only if distributions of corpus may be made solely in favor of current income beneficiaries, and any corpus distribution to the current income beneficiary must be chargeable against the proportionate part of corpus held in trust for payment of income to that beneficiary as if it constituted a separate trust (whether or not physically segregated). See section 674(b)(5)(B).

(iii) This subparagraph may be illustrated by the following examples:

Example (1). A trust instrument provides for payment of the income to the grantor's two brothers for life, and for payment of the corpus to the grantor's nephews in equal shares. The grantor reserves the power to distribute corpus to pay medical expenses that may be incurred by his brothers or nephews. The grantor is not treated as an owner by reason of this power because section 674(b)(5)(A) excepts a power, exercisable by any person, to invade corpus for any beneficiary, including a remainderman, if the power is limited by a reasonably definite standard which is set forth in the trust instrument. However, if the power were also exercisable in favor of a person (for example, a sister) who was not otherwise a beneficiary of the trust, section 674(b)(5)(A) would not be applicable.

Example (2). The facts are the same as in example (1) except that the grantor reserves the power to distribute any part of the corpus to his brothers or to his nephews for their happiness. The grantor is treated as the owner of the trust. Paragraph (5)(A) of section 674(b) is inapplicable because the power is not limited by a reasonably definite standard. Paragraph (5)(B) is inapplicable because the power to distribute corpus permits a distribution of corpus to persons other than current income beneficiaries.

Example (3). A trust instrument provides for payment of the income to the grantor's two adult sons in equal shares for 10 years, after which the corpus is to be distributed to his grandchildren in equal shares. The grantor reserves the power to pay over to each son up to one-half of the corpus during the 10-year period, but any such payment shall proportionately reduce subsequent income and corpus payments made to the son receiving the corpus. Thus, if one-half of the corpus is paid to one son, all the income from the remaining half is thereafter payable to the other son. The grantor is not treated as an owner under section 674(a) by reason of this power because it qualifies under the exception of section 674(b)(5)(B).

(6) *Powers to withhold income temporarily.* (i) Section 674(b)(6) excepts a power which, in general, enables the holder merely to effect a postponement in the time when the ordinary income is enjoyed by a current income beneficiary. Specifically, there is excepted a power to distribute or apply ordinary income to or for a current income beneficiary or to accumulate the income, if the accumulated income must ultimately be payable either:

(a) To the beneficiary from whom it was withheld, his estate, or his appointees (or persons designated by name, as a class, or otherwise as alternate takers in default of appointment) under a power of appointment held by the beneficiary which does not exclude from the class of possible appointees any person other than the beneficiary, his estate, his creditors, or the creditors of his estate (section 674(b)(6)(A));

(b) To the beneficiary from whom it was withheld, or if he does not survive a date of distribution which could reasonably be expected to occur within his lifetime, to his appointees (or alternate takers in default of appointment) under any power of appointment, general or special, or if he has no power of appointment to one or more designated alternate takers (other than the grantor of the grantor's estate) whose shares have been irrevocably specified in the trust instrument (section 674(b)(6)(A) and the flush material following); or

(c) On termination of the trust, or in conjunction with a distribution of corpus which is augmented by the accumulated income, to the current income beneficiaries in shares which have been irrevocably specified in the trust instrument, or if any beneficiary does not survive a date of distribution which would reasonably be expected to occur within his lifetime, to his appointees (or alternate takers in default of appointment) under any power of appointment, general or special, or if he has no power of appointment to one or more designated alternate takers (other than the grantor or the grantor's estate) whose shares have been irrevocably specified in the trust instrument (section 674(b)(6)(B) and the flush material following).

In the application of (a) of this subdivision, if the accumulated income of a trust is ultimately payable to the estate of the current income beneficiary or is ultimately payable to his appointees or takers in default of appointment, under a power of the type described in (a) of this subdivision, it need not be payable to the beneficiary from whom it was withheld under any circumstances. Furthermore, if a trust otherwise qualifies for the exception in (a) of this subdivision the trust income will not be considered to be taxable to the grantor under section 677 by reason of the existence of the power of appointment referred to in (a) of this subdivision.) In general, the exception in section 674(b)(6) is not applicable if the power is in substance one to shift ordinary income from one beneficiary to another. Thus, a power will not qualify for this exception if ordinary income may be distributed to beneficiary A, or may be added to corpus which is ultimately payable to beneficiary B, a remainderman who is not a current income beneficiary. However, section 674(b)(6)(B), and (c) of this subdivision, permit a limited power to shift ordinary income among current income beneficiaries, as illustrated in example (1) of this subparagraph.

(ii) The application of section 674(b)(6) may be illustrated by the following examples:

Example (1). A trust instrument provides that the income shall be paid in equal shares to the grantor's two adult daughters but the grantor reserves the power to withhold from either beneficiary any part of that beneficiary's share of income and to add it to the corpus of the trust until the younger daughter reaches the age of 30 years. When the younger daughter reaches the age of 30, the trust is to terminate and the corpus is to be divided equally between the two daughters or their estates. Although exercise of this power may permit the shifting of accumulated income from one beneficiary to the other (since the corpus with the accumulations is to be divided equally) the power is excepted under section 674(b)(6)(B) and subdivision (i)(c) of this subparagraph.

Example (2). The facts are the same as in example (1), except that the grantor of the trust reserves the power to distribute accumulated income to the beneficiaries in such shares as he chooses. The combined powers are not excepted by section 674(b)(6)(B) since income accumulated pursuant to the first power is neither required to be payable only in conjunction with a corpus distribution nor required to be payable in shares specified in the trust instrument. See, however, section 674(c) and § 1.674(c)–1 for the effect of such a power if it is exercisable only by independent trustees.

Example (3). A trust provides for payment of income to the grantor's adult son with the grantor retaining the power to accumulate the income until the grantor's death, when all accumulations are to be paid to the son. If the son predeceases the grantor, all accumulations are, at the death of the grantor, to be paid to his daughter, or if she is not living, to alternate takers (which do not include the grantor's estate) in specified shares. The power is excepted under section 674(b)(6)(A) since the date of distribution (the date of the grantor's death) may, in the usual case, reasonably be expected to occur during the beneficiary's (the son's) lifetime. It is not necessary that the accumulations be payable to the son's estate or his appointees if he should predecease the grantor for this exception to apply.

(7) *Power to withhold income during disability.* Section 674(b)(7) provides an exception for a power which, in general, will permit ordinary income to be withheld during the legal disability of an income beneficiary or while he is under 21. Specifically, there is excepted a power, exercisable only during the existence of a legal disability of any current income beneficiary or the period during which any income beneficiary is under the age of 21 years, to distribute or apply ordinary income to or for that beneficiary or to accumulate the income and add it to corpus. To qualify under this exception it is not necessary that the income ultimately be payable to the income beneficiary from whom it was withheld, his estate, or his appointees; that is, the accumulated income may be added to corpus and ultimately distributed to others. For example, the grantor is not treated as an owner under section 674 if the income of a trust is payable to his son for life, remainder to his grandchildren, although he reserves the power to accumulate income and add it to corpus while his son is under 21.

(8) *Powers to allocate between corpus and income.* Paragraph (8) of section 674(b) provides that a power to allocate receipts and disbursements between corpus and income, even though expressed in broad language, will not cause the grantor to be treated as an owner under the general rule of section 674(a).

[T.D. 6500, 25 FR 11814, Nov. 26, 1960]

§ 1.674(c)–1 Excepted powers exercisable only by independent trustees.

Section 674(c) provides an exception to the general rule of section 674(a) for certain powers that are exercisable by independent trustees. This exception is in addition to those provided for under section 674(b) which may be held by any person including an independent trustee. The powers to which section 674(c) apply are powers (a) to distribute, apportion, or accumulate income to or for a beneficiary or beneficiaries, or to, for, or within a class of beneficiaries, or (b) to pay out corpus to or for a beneficiary or beneficiaries or to or for a class of beneficiaries (whether or not income beneficiaries). In order for such a power to fall within the exception of section 674(c) it must be exercisable solely (without the approval or consent of any other person) by a trustee or trustees none of whom is the grantor and no more than half of whom are related or subordinate parties who are subservient to the wishes of the grantor. (See section 672(c) for definitions of these terms.) An example of the application of section 674(c) is a trust whose income is payable to the grantor's three adult sons with power in an independent trustee to allocate without restriction the amounts of income to be paid to each son each year. Such a power does not cause the grantor to be treated as the owner of the trust. See however, the limitations set forth in § 1.674(d)–2.

[T.D. 6500, 25 FR 11814, Nov. 26, 1960]

§ 1.674(d)–1 Excepted powers exercisable by any trustee other than grantor or spouse.

Section 674(d) provides an additional exception to the general rule of section 674(a) for a power to distribute, apportion, or accumulate income to or for a beneficiary or beneficiaries or to, for, or within a class of beneficiaries, whether or not the conditions of section 674(b)(6) or (7) are satisfied, if the power is solely exercisable (without the approval or consent of any other person) by a trustee or trustees none of whom is the grantor or spouse living with the grantor, and if the power is limited by a reasonably definite external standard set forth in the trust instrument (see paragraph (b)(5) of § 1.674(b)–1 with respect to what constitutes a reasonably definite standard). See, however, the limitations set forth in § 1.674(d)–2.

[T.D. 6500, 25 FR 11814, Nov. 26, 1960]

§ 1.674(d)–2 Limitations on exceptions in section 674(b), (c), and (d).

(a) Power to remove trustee. A power in the grantor to remove, substitute, or add trustees (other than a power exercisable only upon limited conditions which do not exist during the taxable year, such as the death or resignation of, or breach of fiduciary duty by, an existing trustee) may prevent a trust from qualifying under section 674(c) or (d). For example, if a grantor has an unrestricted power to remove an independent trustee and substitute any person including himself as trustee, the trust will not qualify under section 674(c) or (d). On the other hand if the grantor's power to remove, substitute, or add trustees is limited so that its exercise could not alter the trust in a manner that would disqualify it under section 674(c) or (d), as the case may be, the power itself does not disqualify the trust. Thus, for example, a power in the grantor to remove or discharge an independent trustee on the condition that he substitute another independent trustee will not prevent a trust from qualifying under section 674(c).

(b) Power to add beneficiaries. The exceptions described in section 674(b)(5), (6), and (7), (c), and (d), are not applicable if any person has a power to add to the beneficiary or beneficiaries or to a class of beneficiaries designated to receive the income or corpus, except where the action is to provide for after-born or after-adopted children. This limitation does not apply to a power held by a beneficiary to substitute other beneficiaries to succeed to his interest in the trust (so that he would be an adverse party as to the exercise or nonexercise of that power). For example, the limitation does not apply to a power in a beneficiary of a nonspendthrift trust to assign his interest. Nor does the limitation apply to a power held by any person which would qualify as an exception under section 674(b)(3) (relating to testamentary powers).

[T.D. 6500, 25 FR 11814, Nov. 26, 1960]

§ 675. Administrative Powers

The grantor shall be treated as the owner of any portion of a trust in respect of which—

(1) Power to deal for less than adequate and full consideration. A power exercisable by the grantor or a nonadverse party, or both, without the approval or consent of any adverse party enables the grantor or any person to purchase, exchange, or otherwise deal with or dispose of the corpus or the income therefrom for less than an adequate consideration in money or money's worth.

(2) Power to borrow without adequate interest or security. A power exercisable by the grantor or a nonadverse party, or both, enables the grantor to borrow the corpus or income, directly or indirectly, without adequate interest or without adequate security except where a trustee (other than the grantor) is authorized under a general lending power to make loans to any person without regard to interest or security.

(3) Borrowing of the trust funds. The grantor has directly or indirectly borrowed the corpus or income and has not completely repaid the loan, including any interest, before the beginning of the taxable year. The preceding sentence shall not apply to a loan which provides for adequate interest and adequate security, if such loan is made by a trustee other than the grantor and other than a related or subordinate trustee subservient to the grantor. For periods during which an individual is the spouse of the grantor (within the meaning of section 672(e)(2)), any reference in this paragraph to the grantor shall be treated as including a reference to such individual.

(4) General powers of administration. A power of administration is exercisable in a nonfiduciary capacity by any person without the approval or consent of any person in a fiduciary capacity. For purposes of this paragraph, the term "power of administration" means any one or more of the following powers: (A) a power to vote or direct the voting of stock or other securities of a corporation in which the holdings of the grantor and the trust are significant from the viewpoint of voting control; (B) a power to control the investment of the trust funds either by directing investments or reinvestments, or by vetoing proposed investments or reinvestments, to the extent that the trust funds consist of stocks or securities of corporations in which the holdings of the grantor and the trust are significant from the viewpoint of voting control; or (C) a power to reacquire the trust corpus by substituting other property of an equivalent value.

Regulation

§ 1.675–1 Administrative powers.

(a) General rule. Section 675 provides in effect that the grantor is treated as the owner of any portion of a trust if under the terms of the trust instrument or circumstances attendant on its operation administrative control is exercisable primarily for the benefit of the grantor rather than the beneficiaries of the trust. If a grantor retains a power to amend the administrative provisions of a trust instrument which is broad enough to permit an amendment causing the grantor to be treated as the owner of a portion of the trust under section 675, he will be treated as the owner of the portion from its inception. See section 671 and §§ 1.671–2 and 1.671–3 for rules for treatment of items of income, deduction, and credit when a person is treated as the owner of all or only a portion of a trust.

(b) Prohibited controls. The circumstances which cause administrative controls to be considered exercisable primarily for the benefit of the grantor are specifically described in paragraphs (1) through (4) of section 675 as follows:

(1) The existence of a power, exercisable by the grantor or a nonadverse party, or both, without the approval or consent of any adverse party, which enables the grantor or any other person to purchase, exchange, or otherwise deal with or dispose of the corpus or the income of the trust for less than adequate consideration in money or money's worth. Whether the existence of the power itself will constitute the holder an adverse party will depend on the particular circumstances.

(2) The existence of a power exercisable by the grantor or a nonadverse party, or both, which enables the grantor to borrow the corpus or income of the trust, directly or indirectly, without adequate interest or adequate security. However, this paragraph does not apply where a trustee (other than the grantor acting alone) is authorized under a general lending power to make loans to any person without regard to interest or security. A general lending power in the grantor, acting alone as trustee, under which he has power to determine interest rates and the adequacy of security is not in itself an indication that the grantor has power to borrow the corpus or income without adequate interest or security.

(3) The circumstance that the grantor has directly or indirectly borrowed the corpus or income of the trust and has not completely repaid the loan, including any interest, before the beginning of the taxable year. The preceding sentence does not apply to a loan which provides for adequate interest and adequate security, if it is made by a trustee other than the grantor or a related or subordinate trustee subservient to the grantor. See section 672(c) for definition of "a related or subordinate party".

(4) The existence of certain powers of administration exercisable in a nonfiduciary capacity by any nonadverse party without the approval or consent of any person in a fiduciary capacity. The term "powers of administration" means one or more of the following powers:

(i) A power to vote or direct the voting of stock or other securities of a corporation in which the holdings of the grantor and the trust are significant from the viewpoint of voting control;

(ii) A power to control the investment of the trust funds either by directing investments or reinvestments, or by vetoing proposed investments or reinvestments, to the extent that the trust funds consist of stocks or securities of corporations in which the holdings of the grantor and the trust are significant from the viewpoint of voting control; or

(iii) A power to reacquire the trust corpus by substituting other property of an equivalent value.

If a power is exercisable by a person as trustee, it is presumed that the power is exercisable in a fiduciary capacity primarily in the interests of the beneficiaries. This presumption may be rebutted only by clear and convincing proof that the power is not exercisable primarily in the interests of the beneficiaries. If a power is not exercisable by a person as trustee, the determination of whether the power is exercisable in a fiduciary or a nonfiduciary capacity depends on all the terms of the trust and the circumstances surrounding its creation and administration.

(c) Authority of trustee. The mere fact that a power exercisable by a trustee is described in broad language does not indicate that the trustee is authorized to purchase, exchange, or otherwise deal with or dispose of the trust property or income for less than an adequate and full consideration in money or money's worth, or is authorized to lend the trust property or income to the grantor without adequate interest. On the other hand, such authority may be indicated by the actual administration of the trust.

[T.D. 6500, 25 FR 11814, Nov. 26, 1960]

§ 676. Power to Revoke

(a) General rule. The grantor shall be treated as the owner of any portion of a trust, whether or not he is treated as such owner under any other provision of this part, where at any time the power to revest in the grantor title to such portion is exercisable by the grantor or a non-adverse party, or both.

(b) Power affecting beneficial enjoyment only after occurrence of event. Subsection (a) shall not apply to a power the exercise of which can only affect the beneficial enjoyment of the income for a period commencing after the occurrence of an event such that a grantor would not be treated as the owner under section 673 if the power were a reversionary interest. But the grantor may be treated as the owner after the occurrence of such event unless the power is relinquished.

Regulations

§ 1.676(a)–1 Power to revest title to portion of trust property in grantor; general rule.

If a power to revest in the grantor title to any portion of a trust is exercisable by the grantor or a nonadverse party, or both, without the approval or consent of an adverse party, the grantor is treated as the owner of that portion, except as provided in section 676(b) (relating to powers affecting beneficial enjoyment of income only after the expiration of certain periods of time). If the title to a portion of the trust will revest in the grantor upon the exercise of a power by the grantor or a nonadverse party, or both, the grantor is treated as the owner of that portion regardless of whether the power is a power to revoke, to terminate, to alter or amend, or to appoint. See section 671 and §§ 1.671–2 and 1.671–3 for rules for treatment of items of income, deduction, and credit when a person is treated as the owner of all or only a portion of a trust.

[T.D. 6500, 25 FR 11814, Nov. 26, 1960]

§ 1.676(b)–1 Powers exercisable only after a period of time.

Section 676(b) provides an exception to the general rule of section 676(a) when the exercise of a power can only affect the beneficial enjoyment of the income of a trust received after the expiration of a period of time which is such that a grantor would not be treated as the owner of that portion, except as power were a reversionary interest. See §§ 1.673(a)–1 and 1.673(b)–1. Thus, for example, a grantor is excepted from the general rule of section 676(a) with respect to ordinary income if exercise of a power to revest corpus in him cannot affect the beneficial enjoyment of the income received within 10 years after the date of transfer of that portion of the trust. It is immaterial for this purpose that the power is vested at the time of the transfer. However, the grantor is subject to the general rule of section 676(a) after the expiration of the period unless the power is relinquished. Thus, in the above example, the grantor may be treated as the owner and be taxed on all income in the eleventh and succeeding years if exercise of the power can affect beneficial enjoyment of income received in those years. If the beginning of the period during which the grantor may revest is postponed, the rules set forth in § 1.673(d)–1 are applicable to determine whether the grantor should be treated as an owner during the period following the postponement.

[T.D. 6500, 25 FR 11814, Nov. 26, 1960]

§ 677. Income for Benefit of Grantor

(a) General rule. The grantor shall be treated as the owner of any portion of a trust, whether or not he is treated as such owner under section 674, whose income without the approval or consent of any adverse party is, or, in the discretion of the grantor or a nonadverse party, or both, may be—

(1) distributed to the grantor or the grantor's spouse;

(2) held or accumulated for future distribution to the grantor or the grantor's spouse; or

(3) applied to the payment of premiums on policies of insurance on the life of the grantor or the grantor's spouse (except policies of insurance irrevocably payable for a purpose specified in section 170(c) (relating to definition of charitable contributions)).

This subsection shall not apply to a power the exercise of which can only affect the beneficial enjoyment of the income for a period commencing after the occurrence of an event such that the grantor would not be treated as the owner under section 673 if the power were a reversionary interest; but the grantor may be treated as the owner after the occurrence of the event unless the power is relinquished.

(b) Obligations of support. Income of a trust shall not be considered taxable to the grantor under subsection (a) or any other provision of this chapter merely because such income in the discretion of another person, the trustee, or the grantor acting as trustee or co-trustee, may be applied or distributed for the support or maintenance of a beneficiary (other than the grantor's spouse) whom the grantor is legally obligated to support or maintain, except to the extent that such income is so applied or distributed. In cases where the amounts so applied or distributed are paid out of corpus or out of other than income for the taxable year, such amounts shall be considered to be an amount paid or credited within the meaning of paragraph (2) of section 661(a) and shall be taxed to the grantor under section 662.

Regulations

§ 1.677(a)–1 Income for benefit of grantor; general rule.

(a)(1) *Scope.* Section 677 deals with the treatment of the grantor of a trust as the owner of a portion of the trust because he has retained an interest in the income from that portion. For convenience, "grantor" and "spouse" are generally referred to in the masculine and feminine genders, respectively, but if the grantor is a woman the reference to "grantor" is to her and the reference to "spouse" is to her husband. Section 677 also deals with the treatment of the grantor of a trust as the owner of a portion of the trust because the income from property transferred in trust after October 9, 1969, is, or may be, distributed to his spouse or applied to the payment of premiums on policies of insurance on the life of his spouse. However, section 677 does not apply when the income of a trust is taxable to a grantor's spouse under section 71 (relating to alimony and separate maintenance payments) or section 682 (relating to income of an estate or trust in case of divorce, etc.). See section 671–1(b).

(2) *Cross references.* See section 671 and §§ 1.671–2 and 1.671–3 for rules for treatment of items of income, deduction, and credit when a person is treated as the owner of all or a portion of a trust.

(b) Income for benefit of grantor or his spouse; general rule. (1) *Property transferred in trust prior to October 10, 1969.* With respect to property transferred in trust prior to October 10, 1969, the grantor is treated, under section 677, in any taxable year as the owner (whether or not he is treated as an owner under section 674) of a portion of a trust of which the income for the taxable year or for a period not within the exception described in paragraph (e) of this section is, or in the discretion of the grantor or a nonadverse party, or both (without the approval or consent of any adverse party) may be:

(i) Distributed to the grantor;

(ii) Held or accumulated for future distribution to the grantor; or

(iii) Applied to the payment of premiums on policies of insurance on the life of the grantor, except policies of insurance irrevocably payable for a charitable purpose specified in section 170(c).

(2) *Property transferred in trust after October 9, 1969.* With respect to property transferred in trust after October 9, 1969, the grantor is treated, under section 677, in any taxable year as the owner (whether or not he is treated as an owner under section 674) of a portion of a trust of which the income for the taxable year or for a period not within the exception described in paragraph (e) of this section is, or in the discretion of the grantor, or his spouse, or a nonadverse party, or any combination thereof (without the approval or consent of any adverse party other than the grantor's spouse) may be:

(i) Distributed to the grantor or the grantor's spouse;

(ii) Held or accumulated for future distribution to the grantor or the grantor's spouse; or

(iii) Applied to the payment of premiums on policies of insurance on the life of the grantor or the grantor's spouse, except policies of insurance irrevocably payable for a charitable purpose specified in section 170(c).

With respect to the treatment of a grantor as the owner of a portion of a trust solely because its income is, or may be, distributed or held or accumulated for future distribution to a beneficiary who is his spouse or applied to the payment of premiums for insurance on the spouse's life, section 677(a) applies to the income of a trust solely during the period of the marriage of the grantor to a beneficiary. In the case of divorce or separation, see sections 71 and 682 and the regulations thereunder.

(c) Constructive distribution; cessation of interest. Under section 677 the grantor is treated as the owner of a portion of a trust if he has retained any interest which might, without the approval or consent of an adverse party, enable him to have the income from that portion distributed to him at some time either actually or constructively (subject to the exception described in paragraph (e) of this section). In the case of a transfer in trust after October 9, 1969, the grantor is also treated as the owner of a portion of a trust if he has granted or retained any interest which might, without the approval or consent of an adverse party (other than the grantor's spouse), enable his spouse to have the income from the portion at some time, whether or not within the grantor's lifetime, distributed to the spouse either actually or constructively. See paragraph (b)(2) of this section for additional rules relating to the income of a trust prior to the grantor's marriage to a beneficiary. Constructive distribution to the grantor or to his spouse includes payment on behalf of the grantor or his spouse to another in obedience to his or her direction and payment of premiums upon policies of insurance on the grantor's, or his spouse's, life (other than policies of insurance irrevocably payable for charitable purposes specified in section 170(c)). If the grantor (in the case of property transferred prior to Oct. 10, 1969) or the grantor and his spouse (in the case of property transferred after Oct. 9, 1969) are divested permanently and completely of every interest described in this paragraph, the grantor is not treated as an owner under section 677 after that divesting. The word "interest" as used in this paragraph does not include the possibility that the grantor or his spouse might receive back from a beneficiary an interest in a trust by inheritance. Further, with respect to transfers in trust prior to October 10, 1969, the word "interest" does not include the possibility that the grantor might receive back from a beneficiary an interest in a trust as a surviving spouse under a statutory right of election or a similar right.

(d) Discharge of legal obligation of grantor or his spouse. Under section 677 a grantor is, in general, treated as the owner of a portion of a trust whose income is, or in the discretion of the grantor or a nonadverse party, or both, may be applied in discharge of a legal obligation of the grantor (or his spouse in the case of property transferred in trust by the grantor after October 9, 1969). However, see § 1.677(b)–1 for special rules for trusts whose income may not be applied for the discharge of any legal obligation of the grantor or the grantor's spouse other than the support or maintenance of a beneficiary (other than the grantor's spouse) whom the grantor or grantor's spouse is legally obligated to support. See § 301.7701–4(e) of this chapter for rules on the classification of and application of section 677 to an environmental remediation trust.

(e) Exception for certain discretionary rights affecting income. The last sentence of section 677(a) provides that a grantor shall not be treated as the owner when a discretionary right can only affect the beneficial enjoyment of the income of a trust received after a period of time during which a grantor would not be treated as an owner under section 673 if the power were a reversionary interest. See §§ 1.673(a)–1 and 1.673(b)–1. For example, if the ordinary income of a trust is payable to B for 10 years and then in the grantor's discretion income or corpus may be paid to B or to the grantor (or his spouse in the case of property transferred in trust by the grantor after October 9, 1969), the grantor is not treated as an owner with respect to the ordinary income under section 677 during the first 10 years. He will be treated as an owner under section 677 after the expiration of the 10-year period unless the power is relinquished. If the beginning of the period during which the grantor may substitute beneficiaries is postponed, the rules set forth in § 1.673(d)–1 are applicable in determining whether the grantor should be treated as an owner during the period following the postponement.

(f) Accumulation of income. If income is accumulated in any taxable year for future distribution to the grantor (or his spouse in the case of property transferred in trust by the grantor after Oct. 9, 1969), section 677(a)(2) treats the grantor as an owner for that taxable year. The exception set forth in the last sentence of section 677(a) does not apply merely because the grantor (or his spouse in the case of property transferred in trust by the grantor after Oct. 9, 1969) must await the expiration of a period of time before he or she can receive or exercise discretion over previously accumulated income of the trust, even though the period is such that the grantor would not be treated as an owner under section 673 if a reversionary interest were involved. Thus, if income (including capital gains) of a trust is to be accumulated for 10 years and then will be, or at the discretion of the grantor, or his spouse in the case of property transferred in trust after October 9, 1969, or a nonadverse party, may be, distributed to the grantor (or his spouse in the case of property transferred in trust after Oct. 9, 1969), the grantor is treated as the owner of the trust from its inception. If income attributable to transfers after October 9, 1969 is accumulated in any taxable year during the grantor's lifetime for future distribution to his spouse, section 677(a)(2) treats the grantor as an owner for that taxable year even though his spouse may not receive or exercise discretion over such income prior to the grantor's death.

(g) Examples. The application of section 677(a) may be illustrated by the following examples:

Example (1). G creates an irrevocable trust which provides that the ordinary income is to be payable to him for life and that on his death the corpus shall be distributed to B, an unrelated person. Except for the right to receive income, G retains no right or power which would cause him to be treated as an owner under sections 671 through 677. Under the applicable local law capital gains must be applied to corpus. During the taxable year 1970 the trust has the following items of gross income and deductions:

Dividends	$5,000
Capital gain	1,000
Expenses allocable to income	200
Expenses allocable to corpus	100

Since G has a right to receive income he is treated as an owner of a portion of the trust under section 677. Accordingly, he should include the $5,000 of dividends, $200 income expense, and $100 corpus expense in the computation of his taxable income for 1970. He should not include the $1,000 capital gain since that is not attributable to the portion of the trust that he owns. See § 1.671–3(b). The tax consequences of the capital gain are governed by the provisions of subparts A, B, C, and D (section 641 and following), part I, subchapter J, chapter 1 of the Code. Had the trust sustained a capital loss in any amount the loss would likewise not be included in the computation of G's taxable income, but would also be governed by the provisions of such subparts.

Example (2). G creates a trust which provides that the ordinary income is payable to his adult son. Ten years and one day from the date of transfer or on the death of his son, whichever is earlier, corpus is to revert to G. In addition, G retains a discretionary right to receive $5,000 of ordinary income each year. (Absent the exercise of this right all the ordinary income is to be distributed to his son.) G retained no other right or power which would cause him to be treated as an owner under subpart E (section 671 and following). Under the terms of the trust instrument and applicable local law capital gains must be applied to corpus. During the taxable year 1970 the trust had the following items of income and deductions:

Dividends	$10,000
Capital gain	2,000
Expenses allocable to income	400
Expenses allocable to corpus	200

Since the capital gain is held or accumulated for future distributions to G, he is treated under section 677(a)(2) as an owner of a portion of the trust to which the gain is attributable. See § 1.671–3(b).

Therefore, he must include the capital gain in the computation of his taxable income. (Had the trust sustained a capital loss in any amount, G would likewise include that loss in the computation of his taxable income.) In addition, because of G's discretionary right (whether exercised or not) he is treated as the owner of a portion of the trust which will permit a distribution of income to him of $5,000. Accordingly, G includes dividends of $5,208.33 and income expenses of $208.33 in computing his taxable income, determined in the following manner:

Total dividends	$10,000.00
Less: Expenses allocable to income	400.00
Distributable income of the trust	9,600.00
Portion of dividends attributable to G (5,000/9,600 * $10,000)	5,208.33
Portion of income expenses attributable to G (5,000/9, 600 * $400)	208.33
Amount of income subject to discretionary right	5,000.00

In accordance with § 1.671–3(c), G also takes into account $104.17 (5,000/9,600 * $200) of corpus expenses in computing his tax liability. The portion of the dividends and expenses of the trust not attributable to G are governed by the provisions of Subparts A through D.

[T.D. 6500, 25 FR 11814, Nov. 26, 1960, as amended by T.D. 7148, 36 FR 20749, Oct. 29, 1971; T.D. 8668, 61 FR 19191, May 1, 1996]

§ 1.677(b)–1 Trusts for support.

(a) Section 677(b) provides that a grantor is not treated as the owner of a trust merely because its income may in the discretion of any person other than the grantor (except when he is acting as trustee or cotrustee) be applied or distributed for the support or maintenance of a beneficiary (other than the grantor's spouse in the case of income from property transferred in trust after October 9, 1969), such as the child of the grantor, whom the grantor or his spouse is legally obligated to support. If income of the current year of the trust is actually so applied or distributed the grantor may be treated as the owner of any portion of the trust under section 677 to that extent, even though it might have been applied or distributed for other purposes. In the case of property transferred to a trust before October 10, 1969, for the benefit of the grantor's spouse, the grantor may be treated as the owner to the extent income of the current year is actually applied for the support or maintenance of his spouse.

(b) If any amount applied or distributed for the support of a beneficiary, including the grantor's spouse in the case of property transferred in trust before October 10, 1969, whom the grantor is legally obligated to support is paid out of corpus or out of income other than income of the current year, the grantor is treated as a beneficiary of the trust, and the amount applied or distributed is considered to be an amount paid within the meaning of section 661(a)(2), taxable to the grantor under section 662. Thus, he is subject to the other relevant portions of subparts A through D (section 641 and following), part I, subchapter J, chapter 1 of the Code. Accordingly, the grantor may be taxed on an accumulation distribution or a capital gain distribution under subpart D (section 665 and following) of such part I. Those provisions are applied on the basis that the grantor is the beneficiary.

(c) For the purpose of determining the items of income, deduction, and credit of a trust to be included under this section in computing the grantor's tax liability, the income of the trust for the taxable year of distribution will be deemed to have been first distributed. For example, in the case of a trust reporting on the calendar year basis, a distribution made on January 1, 1956, will be deemed to have been made out of ordinary income of the trust for the calendar year 1956 to the extent of the income for that year even though the trust had received no income as of January 1, 1956. Thus, if a distribution of $10,000 is made on January 1, 1956, for the support of the grantor's dependent, the grantor will be treated as the owner of the trust for 1956 to that extent. If the trust received dividends of $5,000 and incurred expenses of $1,000 during that year but subsequent to January 1, he will take into account dividends of $5,000 and expenses of $1,000 in computing his tax liability for 1956. In addition, the grantor will be treated as a beneficiary of the trust with respect to the $6,000 ($10,000 less distributable income of $4,000 (dividends of $5,000 less expenses of $1,000)) paid out of corpus or out of other than income of the current year. See paragraph (b) of this section.

(d) The exception provided in section 677(b) relates solely to the satisfaction of the grantor's legal obligation to support or maintain a beneficiary. Consequently, the general rule of section 677(a) is applicable when in the discretion of the grantor or nonadverse parties income of a trust may be applied in discharge of a grantor's obligations other than his obligation of support or maintenance falling within section 677(b). Thus, if the grantor creates a trust the income of which may in the discretion of a nonadverse party be applied in the payment of the grantor's debts, such as the payment of his rent or other household expenses, he is treated as an owner of the trust regardless of whether the income is actually so applied.

(e) The general rule of section 677(a), and not section 677(b), is applicable if discretion to apply or distribute income of a trust rests solely in the grantor, or in the grantor in conjunction with other persons, unless in either case the grantor has such discretion as trustee or cotrustee.

(f) The general rule of section 677(a), and not section 677(b), is applicable to the extent that income is required, without any discretionary determination, to be applied to the support of a beneficiary whom the grantor is legally obligated to support.

[T.D. 6500, 25 FR 11814, Nov. 26, 1960, as amended by T.D. 7148, 36 FR 20750, Oct. 29, 1971]

§ 678. Person Other than Grantor Treated as Substantial Owner

(a) General rule. A person other than the grantor shall be treated as the owner of any portion of a trust with respect to which:

(1) such person has a power exercisable solely by himself to vest the corpus or the income therefrom in himself, or

(2) such person has previously partially released or otherwise modified such a power and after the release or modification retains such control as would, within the principles of sections 671 to 677, inclusive, subject a grantor of a trust to treatment as the owner thereof.

(b) Exception where grantor is taxable. Subsection (a) shall not apply with respect to a power over income, as originally granted or thereafter modified, if the grantor of the trust or a transferor (to whom section 679 applies) is otherwise treated as the owner under the provisions of this subpart other than this section.

(c) Obligations of support. Subsection (a) shall not apply to a power which enables such person, in the capacity of trustee or co-trustee, merely to apply the income of the trust to the support or maintenance of a person whom the holder of the power is obligated to support or maintain except to the extent that such income is so applied. In cases where the amounts so applied or distributed are paid out of corpus or out of other than income of the taxable year, such amounts shall be considered to be an amount paid or credited within the meaning of paragraph (2) of section 661(a) and shall be taxed to the holder of the power under section 662.

(d) Effect of renunciation or disclaimer. Subsection (a) shall not apply with respect to a power which has been renounced or disclaimed within a reasonable time after the holder of the power first became aware of its existence.

(e) Cross reference. For provision under which beneficiary of trust is treated as owner of the portion of the trust which consists of stock in an S corporation, see section 1361(d).

Regulations

§ 1.678(a)–1 Person other than grantor treated as substantial owner; general rule.

(a) Where a person other than the grantor of a trust has a power exercisable solely by himself to vest the corpus or the income of any portion of a testamentary or inter vivos trust in himself, he is treated under section 678(a) as the owner of that portion, except as provided in section 678(b) (involving taxation of the grantor) and section 678(c) (involving an obligation of support). The holder of such a power also is treated as an owner of the trust even though he has partially released or otherwise modified the power so that he can no longer vest the corpus or income in himself, if he has retained such control of the trust as would, if retained by a grantor, subject the grantor to treatment as the owner under sections 671 to 677, inclusive. See section 671 and §§ 1.671–2 and 1.671–3 for rules for treatment of items of income, deduction, and credit where a person is treated as the owner of all or only a portion of a trust.

(b) Section 678(a) treats a person as an owner of a trust if he has a power exercisable solely by himself to apply the income or corpus for the satisfaction of his legal obligations, other than an obligation to support a dependent (see § 1.678(c)–1 subject to the limitation of section 678(b)). Section 678 does not apply if the power is not exercisable solely by himself. However, see § 1.662(a)–4 for principles applicable to income of a trust which, pursuant to the terms of the trust instrument, is used to satisfy the obligations of a person other than the grantor.

[T.D. 6500, 25 FR 11814, Nov. 26, 1960]

§ 1.678(b)–1 If grantor is treated as the owner.

Section 678(a) does not apply with respect to a power over income, as originally granted or thereafter modified, if the grantor of the trust is treated as the owner under sections 671 to 677, inclusive.

[T.D. 6500, 25 FR 11814, Nov. 26, 1960]

§ 1.678(c)–1 Trusts for support.

(a) Section 678(a) does not apply to a power which enables the holder, in the capacity of trustee or cotrustee, to apply the income of the trust to the support or maintenance of a person whom the holder is obligated to support, except to the extent the income is so applied. See paragraphs (a), (b), and (c) of § 1.677(b)–1 for applicable principles where any amount is applied for the support or maintenance of a person whom the holder is obligated to support.

(b) The general rule in section 678(a) (and not the exception in section 678(c)) is applicable in any case in which the holder of a power exercisable solely by himself is able, in any capacity other than that of trustee or cotrustee, to apply the income in discharge of his obligation of support or maintenance.

(c) Section 678(c) is concerned with the taxability of income subject to a power described in section 678(a). It has no application to the taxability of income which is either required to be applied pursuant to the terms of the trust instrument or is applied pursuant to a power which is not described in section 678(a), the taxability of such income being governed by other provisions of the Code. See § 1.662(a)–4.

[T.D. 6500, 25 FR 11814, Nov. 26, 1960]

§ 1.678(d)–1 Renunciation of power.

Section 678(a) does not apply to a power which has been renounced or disclaimed within a reasonable time after the holder of the power first became aware of its existence.

[Treas. Dec. 6500, 25 FR 11814, Nov. 26, 1960]

§ 679. Foreign Trusts Having One or More United States Beneficiaries

(a) Transferor treated as owner.

(1) In general. A United States person who directly or indirectly transfers property to a foreign trust (other than a trust described in section 6048(a)(3)(B)(ii)) shall be treated as the owner for his taxable year of the portion of such trust attributable to such property if for such year there is a United States beneficiary of any portion of such trust.

(2) Exceptions. Paragraph (1) shall not apply—

(A) Transfers by reason of death. To any transfer by reason of the death of the transferor.

(B) Transfers at fair market value. To any transfer of property to a trust in exchange for consideration of at least the fair market value of the transferred property. For purposes of the preceding sentence, consideration other than cash shall be taken into account at its fair market value.

(3) Certain obligations not taken into account under fair market value exception.

(A) In general. In determining whether paragraph (2)(B) applies to any transfer by a person described in clause (ii) or (iii) of subparagraph (C), there shall not be taken into account—

(i) except as provided in regulations, any obligation of a person described in subparagraph (C), and

(ii) to the extent provided in regulations, any obligation which is guaranteed by a person described in subparagraph (C).

(B) Treatment of principal payments on obligation. Principal payments by the trust on any obligation referred to in subparagraph (A) shall be taken into account on and after the date of the payment in determining the portion of the trust attributable to the property transferred.

(C) Persons described. The persons described in this subparagraph are—

(i) the trust,

(ii) any grantor, owner, or beneficiary of the trust, and

(iii) any person who is related (within the meaning of section 643(i)(2)(B)) to any grantor, owner, or beneficiary of the trust.

(4) Special rules applicable to foreign grantor who later becomes a United States person.

(A) In general. If a nonresident alien individual has a residency starting date within 5 years after directly or indirectly transferring property to a foreign trust, this section and section 6048 shall be applied as if such individual transferred to such trust on the residency starting date an amount equal to the portion of such trust attributable to the property transferred by such individual to such trust in such transfer.

(B) Treatment of undistributed income. For purposes of this section, undistributed net income for periods before such individual's residency starting date shall be taken into account in determining the portion of the trust which is attributable to property transferred by such individual to such trust but shall not otherwise be taken into account.

(C) Residency starting date. For purposes of this paragraph, an individual's residency starting date is the residency starting date determined under section 7701(b)(2)(A).

(5) Outbound trust migrations. If—

(A) an individual who is a citizen or resident of the United States transferred property to a trust which was not a foreign trust, and

(B) such trust becomes a foreign trust while such individual is alive,

then this section and section 6048 shall be applied as if such individual transferred to such trust on the date such trust becomes a foreign trust an amount equal to the portion of such trust attributable to the property previously transferred by such individual to such trust. A rule similar to the rule of paragraph (4)(B) shall apply for purposes of this paragraph.

(b) Trusts acquiring United States beneficiaries. If—

(1) subsection (a) applies to a trust for the transferor's taxable year, and

(2) subsection (a) would have applied to the trust for his immediately preceding taxable year but for the fact that for such preceding taxable year there was no United States beneficiary for any portion of the trust,

then, for purposes of this subtitle, the transferor shall be treated as having income for the taxable year (in addition to his other income for such year) equal to the undistributed net income (at the close of such immediately preceding taxable year) attributable to the portion of the trust referred to in subsection (a).

(c) Trusts treated as having a United States beneficiary.

(1) In general. For purposes of this section, a trust shall be treated as having a United States beneficiary for the taxable year unless—

(A) under the terms of the trust, no part of the income or corpus of the trust may be paid or accumulated during the taxable year to or for the benefit of a United States person, and

(B) if the trust were terminated at any time during the taxable year, no part of the income or corpus of such trust could be paid to or for the benefit of a United States person.

For purposes of subparagraph (A), an amount shall be treated as accumulated for the benefit of a United States person even if the United States person's interest in the trust is contingent on a future event.

(2) Attribution of ownership. For purposes of paragraph (1), an amount shall be treated as paid or accumulated to or for the benefit of a United States person if such amount is paid to or accumulated for a foreign corporation, foreign partnership, or foreign trust or estate, and—

(A) in the case of a foreign corporation, such corporation is a controlled foreign corporation (as defined in section 957(a)),

(B) in the case of a foreign partnership, a United States person is a partner of such partnership, or

(C) in the case of a foreign trust or estate, such trust or estate has a United States beneficiary (within the meaning of paragraph (1)).

(3) Certain United States beneficiaries disregarded. A beneficiary shall not be treated as a United States person in applying this section with respect to any transfer of property to foreign trust if such beneficiary first became a United States person more than 5 years after the date of such transfer.

(4) Special rule in case of discretion to identify beneficiaries. For purposes of paragraph (1)(A), if any person has the discretion (by authority given in the trust agreement, by power of appointment, or otherwise) of making a distribution from the trust to, or for the benefit of, any person, such trust shall be treated as having a beneficiary who is a United States person unless

(A) the terms of the trust specifically identify the class of persons to whom such distributions may be made, and

(B) none of those persons are United States persons during the taxable year.

(5) Certain agreements and understandings treated as terms of the trust. For purposes of paragraph (1)(A), if any United States person who directly or indirectly transfers property to the trust is directly or indirectly involved in any agreement or understanding (whether written, oral, or otherwise) that may result in the income or corpus of the trust being paid or accumulated to or for the benefit of a United States person, such agreement or understanding shall be treated as a term of the trust.

(6) Uncompensated use of trust property treated as a payment. For purposes of this subsection, a loan of cash or marketable securities (or the use of any other trust property) directly or indirectly to or by any United States person (whether or not a beneficiary under the terms of the trust) shall be treated as paid or accumulated for the benefit of a United States person. The preceding sentence shall not apply to the extent that the United States person repays the loan at a market rate of interest (or pays the fair market value of the use of such property) within a reasonable period of time.

(d) Presumption that foreign trust has United States beneficiary. If a United States person directly or indirectly transfers property to a foreign trust (other than a trust described in section 6048(a)(3)(B)(ii)), the Secretary may treat such trust as having a United States beneficiary for purposes of applying this section to such transfer unless such person

(1) submits such information to the Secretary as the Secretary may require with respect to such transfer, and

(2) demonstrates to the satisfaction of the Secretary that such trust satisfies the requirements of subparagraphs (A) and (B) of subsection (c)(1).

(e) Regulations. The Secretary shall prescribe such regulations as may be necessary or appropriate to carry out the purposes of this section.

Regulations

§ 1.679–0 Outline of major topics. [*Omitted. Ed.*]

[T.D. 8955, 66 FR 37889, July 20, 2001]

Proposed § 1.679–0 (REG–124850–08, May 8, 2024) Outline of major topics. [*Omitted. Ed.*]

§ 1.679–1 U.S. transferor treated as owner of foreign trust. [*Omitted. Ed.*]

[T.D. 8955, 66 FR 37889, July 20, 2001]

Proposed § 1.679–1 (REG–124850–08, May 8, 2024) U.S. transferor treated as owner of foreign trust. [*Omitted. Ed.*]

§ 1.679–2 Trusts treated as having a U.S. beneficiary. [*Omitted. Ed.*]

[T.D. 8955, 66 FR 37890, July 20, 2001]

Proposed § 1.679–2 (REG–124850–08, May 8, 2024) Trusts treated as having a U.S. beneficiary. [*Omitted. Ed.*]

§ 1.679–3 Transfers. [*Omitted. Ed.*]

[T.D. 8955, 66 FR 37893, July 20, 2001]

§ 1.679–4 Exceptions to general rule. [*Omitted. Ed.*]

[T.D. 8955, 66 FR 37894, July 20, 2001]

Proposed § 1.679–4 (REG–124850–08, May 8, 2024) Exceptions to general rule. [*Omitted. Ed.*]

§ 1.679–5 Pre-immigration trusts. [*Omitted. Ed.*]

[T.D. 8955, 66 FR 37896, July 20, 2001]

§ 1.679–6 Outbound migrations of domestic trusts. [*Omitted. Ed.*]

[T.D. 8955, 66 FR 37896, July 20, 2001]

§ 1.679–7 Effective dates. [*Omitted. Ed.*]

[T.D. 8955, 66 FR 37897, July 20, 2001]

Proposed § 1.679–7 (REG–124850–08, May 8, 2024) Applicability dates. [*Omitted. Ed.*]

Subpart F. Miscellaneous

§ 681. Limitation on Charitable Deduction

(a) Trade or business income. In computing the deduction allowable under section 642(c) to a trust, no amount otherwise allowable under section 642(c) as a deduction shall be allowed as a deduction with respect to income of a taxable year which is allocable to its unrelated business income for such year. For purposes of the preceding sentence, the term "unrelated business income" means an amount equal to the amount which, if such trust were exempt from tax under section 501(a) by reason of section 501(c)(3), would be computed as its unrelated business taxable income under section 512 (relating to income derived from certain business activities and from certain property acquired with borrowed funds).

(b) Cross reference. For disallowance of certain charitable, etc., deductions otherwise allowable under section 642(c), see sections 508(d) and 4948(c)(4).

Regulations

§ 1.681(a)–1 Limitation on charitable contributions deductions of trusts; scope of section 681.

Under section 681, the unlimited charitable contributions deduction otherwise allowable to a trust under section 642(c) is, in general, subject to percentage limitations, corresponding to those applicable to contributions by an individual under section 170(b)(1)(A) and (B), under the following circumstances;

(a) To the extent that the deduction is allocable to "unrelated business income";

(b) For taxable years beginning before January 1, 1970, if the trust has engaged in a prohibited transaction;

(c) For taxable years beginning before January 1, 1970, if income is accumulated for a charitable purpose and the accumulation is (1) unreasonable, (2) substantially diverted to a noncharitable purpose, or (3) invested against the interests of the charitable beneficiaries.

Further, if the circumstance set forth in paragraph (a) or (c) of this section is applicable, the deduction is limited to income actually paid out for charitable purposes, and is not allowed for income only set aside or to be used for those purposes. If the circumstance set forth in paragraph (b) of this section is applicable, deductions for contributions to the trust may be disallowed. The provisions of section 681 are discussed in detail in §§ 1.681(a)–2 through 1.681(c)–1. For definition of the term "income", see section 643(b) and § 1.643(b)–1.

[T.D. 6500, 25 FR 11814, Nov. 26, 1960, as amended by T.D. 7428, 41 FR 34627, Aug. 16, 1976]

§ 1.681(a)–2 Limitation on charitable contributions deduction of trusts with trade or business income.

(a) In general. No charitable contributions deduction is allowable to a trust under section 642(c) for any taxable year for amounts allocable to the trust's unrelated business income for the taxable year. For the purpose of section 681(a) the term "unrelated business income" of a trust means an amount which would be computed as the trust's unrelated business taxable income under section 512 and the regulations thereunder, if the trust were an organization exempt from tax under section 501(a) by reason of section 501(c)(3). For the purpose of the computation under section 512, the term "unrelated trade or business" includes a trade or business carried on by a partnership of which a trust is a member, as well as one carried on by the trust itself. While the charitable contributions deduction under section 642(c) is entirely disallowed by section 681(a) for amounts allocable to "unrelated business income", a partial deduction is nevertheless allowed for such amounts by the operation of section 512(b)(11), as illustrated in paragraphs (b) and (c) of this section. This partial deduction is subject to the percentage limitations applicable to contributions by an individual under section 170(b)(1)(A) and (B), and is not allowed for amounts set aside or to be used for charitable purposes but not actually paid out during the taxable year. Charitable contributions deductions otherwise allowable under section 170, 545(b)(2), or 642(c) for contributions to a trust are not disallowed solely because the trust has unrelated business income.

(b) Determination of amounts allocable to unrelated business income. In determining the amount for which a charitable contributions deduction would otherwise be allowable under section 642(c) which are allocable to unrelated business income, and therefore not allowable as a deduction, the following steps are taken:

(1) There is first determined the amount which would be computed as the trust's unrelated business taxable income under section 512 and the regulations thereunder if the trust were an organization exempt from tax under section 501(a) by reason of section 501(c)(3), but without taking the charitable contributions deduction allowed under section 512(b)(11).

(2) The amount for which a charitable contributions deduction would otherwise be allowable under section 642(c) is then allocated between the amount determined in subparagraph (1) of this paragraph and any other income of the trust. Unless the facts clearly indicate to the contrary, the allocation to the amount determined in subparagraph (1) of this paragraph is

made on the basis of the ratio (but not in excess of 100 percent) of the amount determined in subparagraph (1) of this paragraph to the taxable income of the trust, determined without the deduction for personal exemption under section 642(b), the charitable contributions deduction under section 642(c), or the deduction for distributions to beneficiaries under section 661(a).

(3) The amount for which a charitable contributions deduction would otherwise be allowable under section 642(c) which is allocable to unrelated business income as determined in subparagraph (2) of this paragraph, and therefore not allowable as a deduction, is the amount determined in subparagraph (2) of this paragraph reduced by the charitable contributions deduction which would be allowed under section 512(b)(11) if the trust were an organization exempt from tax under section 501(a) by reason of section 501(c)(3).

(c) Examples. (1) The application of this section may be illustrated by the following examples, in which it is assumed that the Y charity is not a charitable organization qualifying under section 170(b)(1)(A) (see subparagraph (2) of this paragraph):

Example (1). The X trust has income of $50,000. There is included in this amount a net profit of $31,000 from the operation of a trade or business. The trustee is required to pay half of the trust income to A, an individual, and the balance of the trust income to the Y charity, an organization described in section 170(c)(2). The trustee pays each beneficiary $25,000. Under these facts, the unrelated business income of the trust (computed before the charitable contributions deduction which would be allowed under section 512(b)(11)) is $30,000 ($31,000 less the deduction of $1,000 allowed by section 512(b) (12)). The deduction otherwise allowable under section 642(c) is $25,000, the amount paid to the Y charity. The portion allocable to the unrelated business income (computed as prescribed in paragraph (b)(2) of this section) is $15,000, that is, an amount which bears the same ratio to $25,000 as $30,000 bears to $50,000. The portion allocable to the unrelated business income, and therefore disallowed as a deduction, is $15,000 reduced by $6,000 (20 percent of $30,000, the charitable contributions deduction which would be allowable under section 512(b) (11)), or $9,000.

Example (2). Assume the same facts as in example (1), except that the trustee has discretion as to the portion of the trust income to be paid to each beneficiary, and the trustee pays $40,000 to A and $10,000 to the Y charity. The deduction otherwise allowable under section 642(c) is $10,000. The portion allocable to the unrelated business income computed as prescribed in paragraph (b)(2) of this section is $6,000, that is, an amount which bears the same ratio to $10,000 as $30,000 bears to $50,000. Since this amount does not exceed the charitable contributions deduction which would be allowable under section 512(b)(11) ($6,000, determined as in example (1)), no portion of it is disallowed as a deduction.

Example (3). Assume the same facts as in example (1), except that the terms of the trust instrument require the trustee to pay to the Y charity the trust income, if any, derived from the trade or business, and to pay to A all the trust income derived from other sources. The trustee pays $31,000 to the Y charity and $19,000 to A. The deduction otherwise allowable under section 642(c) is $31,000. Since the entire income from the trade or business is paid to Y charity, the amount allocable to the unrelated business income computed before the charitable contributions deduction under section 512(b)(11) is $30,000 ($31,000 less the deduction of $1,000 allowed by section 512(b)(12)). The amount allocable to the unrelated business income and therefore disallowed as a deduction is $24,000 ($30,000 less $6,000).

Example (4). (i) Under the terms of the trust, the trustee is required to pay half of the trust income to A, an individual, for his life, and the balance of the trust income to the Y charity, an organization described in section 170(c)(2). Capital gains are allocable to corpus and upon A's death the trust is to terminate and the corpus is to be distributed to the Y charity. The trust has taxable income of $50,000 computed without any deduction for personal exemption, charitable contributions, or distributions. The amount of $50,000 includes $10,000 capital gains, $30,000 ($31,000 less the $1,000 deduction allowed under section 512(b)(12)) unrelated business income (computed before the charitable contributions deduction which would be allowed under section 512(b)(11)) and other income of $9,000. The trustee pays each beneficiary $20,000.

(ii) The deduction otherwise allowable under section 642(c) is $30,000 ($20,000 paid to Y charity and $10,000 capital gains allocated to corpus and permanently set aside for charitable purposes). The portion allocable to the unrelated business income is $15,000, that is, an amount which bears the same ratio to $20,000 (the amount paid to Y charity) as $30,000 bears to $40,000 ($50,000 less $10,000 capital gains allocable to corpus). The portion allocable to the unrelated business income, and therefore disallowed as a deduction, is $15,000 reduced by $6,000 (the charitable contributions deduction which would be allowable under section 512(b) (11)), or $9,000.

(2) If, in the examples in subparagraph (1) of this paragraph, the Y charity were a charitable organization qualifying under section 170(b)(1)(A), then the deduction allowable under section 512(b)(11) would be computed at a rate of 30 percent.

[T.D. 6500, 25 FR 11814, Nov. 26, 1960, as amended by T.D. 6605, 27 FR 8097, Aug. 15, 1962]

§ 1.681(b)–1 Cross reference.

For disallowance of certain charitable, etc., deductions otherwise allowable under section 642(c), see sections 508(d) and 4948(c)(4). See also 26 CFR §§ 1.681(b)–1 and 1.681(c)–1 (rev. as of Apr. 1, 1974) for provisions applying before January 1, 1970.

[T.D. 7428, 41 FR 34627, Aug. 16, 1976]

§ 683. Use of Trust as an Exchange Fund

(a) General rule. Except as provided in subsection (b), if property is transferred to a trust in exchange for an interest in other trust property and if the trust would be an investment company (within the meaning of section 351) if it were a corporation, then gain shall be recognized to the transferor.

(b) Exception for pooled income funds. Subsection (a) shall not apply to any transfer to a pooled income fund (within the meaning of section 642(c)(5)).

Regulations

§ 1.683–1 Applicability of provisions; general rule.

Part I (section 641 and following), subchapter J, chapter 1 of the Code, applies to estates and trusts and to beneficiaries only with respect to taxable years which begin after December 31, 1953, and end after August 16, 1954 the date of enactment of the Internal Revenue Code of 1954. In the case of an estate or trust, the date on which a trust is created or amended or on which an estate commences, and the taxable years of beneficiaries, grantors, or decedents concerned are immaterial. This provision applies equally to taxable years of normal and of abbreviated length.

[T.D. 6500, 25 FR 11814, Nov. 26, 1960]

§ 1.683–2 Exceptions.

(a) In the case of any beneficiary of an estate or trust, sections 641 through 682 do not apply to any amount paid, credited, or to be distributed by an estate or trust in any taxable year of the estate or trust which begins before January 1, 1954, or which ends before August 17, 1954. Whether an amount so paid, credited, or to be distributed is to be included in the gross income of a beneficiary is determined with reference to the Internal Revenue Code of 1939. Thus, if a trust in its fiscal year ending June 30, 1954, distributed its current income to a beneficiary on June 30, 1954, the extent to which the distribution is includible in the beneficiary's gross income for his taxable year (the calendar year 1954) and the character of such income will be determined under the Internal Revenue Code of 1939. The Internal Revenue Code of 1954, however, determines the beneficiary's tax liability for a taxable year of the beneficiary to which such Code applies, with respect even to gross income of the beneficiary determined under the Internal Revenue Code of 1939 in accordance with this paragraph. Accordingly, the beneficiary is allowed credits and deductions pursuant to the Internal Revenue Code of 1954 for a taxable year governed by the Internal Revenue Code of 1954. See subparagraph (ii) of example (1) in paragraph (c) of this section.

(b) For purposes of determining the time of receipt of dividends under sections 34 (for purposes of the credit for dividends received on or before December 31, 1964) and 116, the dividends paid, credited, or to be distributed to a beneficiary are deemed to have been received by the beneficiary ratably on the same dates that the dividends were received by the estate or trust.

(c) The application of this section may be illustrated by the following examples:

Example (1). (i) A trust, reporting on the fiscal year basis, receives in its taxable year ending November 30, 1954, dividends on December 3, 1953, and April 3, July 5, and October 4, 1954. It distributes the dividends to A, its sole beneficiary (who reports on the calendar year basis) on November 30, 1954. Since the trust has received dividends in a taxable year ending after July 31, 1954, it will receive a dividend credit under section 34 with respect to dividends received which otherwise qualify under that section, in this case dividends received on October 4, 1954 (i.e., received after July 31, 1954). See section 7851(a)(1)(C). This credit, however, is reduced to the extent the dividends are allocable to the beneficiary as a result of income being paid, credited, or required to be distributed to him. The trust will also be permitted the dividend exclusion under section 116, since it received its dividends in a taxable year ending after July 31, 1954.

(ii) A is entitled to the section 34 credit with respect to the portion of the October 4, 1954, dividends which is distributed to him even though the determination of whether the amount distributed to him is includible in his gross income is made under the Internal Revenue Code of 1939. The credit allowable to the trust is reduced proportionately to the extent A is deemed to have received the October 4 dividends. A is not entitled to a credit with respect to the dividends received by the trust on December 3, 1953, and April 3, and July 5, 1954, because, although he receives after July 31, 1954, the distribution resulting from the trust's receipt of dividends, he is deemed to have received the dividends ratably with the trust on dates prior to July 31, 1954. In determining the exclusion under section 116 to which he is entitled, all the dividends received by the trust in 1954 and distributed to him are aggregated with any other dividends received by him in 1954, since he is deemed to have received such dividends in 1954 and therefore within a taxable year ending after July 31, 1954. He is not, however, entitled to the exclusion for the dividends received by the trust in December 1953.

Example (2). (i) A simple trust reports on the basis of a fiscal year ending July 31. It receives dividends on October 3, 1953, and January 4, April 3, and July 5, 1954. It distributes the dividends to A, its sole beneficiary, on September 1, 1954. The trust, receiving dividends in a taxable year ending prior to August 17, 1954, is entitled neither to the dividend received credit under section 34 nor the dividend exclusion under section 116.

(ii) A (reporting on the calendar year basis) is not entitled to the section 34 credit, because, although he receives after July 31, 1954, the distribution resulting from the trust's receipt of dividends, he is deemed to have received the dividends ratably with the trust, that is, on October 3, 1953, and January 4, April 3, and July 5, 1954. He is, however, entitled to the section 116 exclusion with respect to the dividends received by the trust in 1954 (along with other dividends received by him in 1954) and distributed to him, since he is deemed to have received such dividends on January 4, April 3, and July 5, 1954, each a date in this taxable year ending after July 31, 1954. He is entitled to no exclusion for the dividends received by the trust on October 3, 1953, since he is deemed to receive the resulting distribution on the same date, which falls within a taxable year of his which ends before August 1, 1954, although he is required to include the October 1953 dividends in his 1954 income. See section 164 of the Internal Revenue Code of 1939.

Example (3). A simple trust on a fiscal year ending July 31, 1954, receives dividends August 5 and November 4, 1953. It distributes the dividends to A, its sole beneficiary (who is on a calendar year basis), on September 1, 1954. Neither the trust nor A is entitled to a credit under section 34 or an exclusion under section 116.

[T.D. 6500, 25 FR 11814, Nov. 26, 1960, as amended by T.D. 6777, 29 FR 17809, Dec. 16, 1964]

§ 1.683–3 Application of the 65-day rule of the Internal Revenue Code of 1939. [*Omitted. Ed.*]

[T.D. 6500, 25 FR 11814, Nov. 26, 1960]

§ 684. Recognition of Gain on Certain Transfers to Certain Foreign Trusts and Estates

(a) In General. Except as provided in regulations, in the case of any transfer of property by a United States person to a foreign estate or trust, for purposes of this subtitle, such transfer shall be treated as a sale or exchange for an amount equal to the fair market value of the property transferred, and the transferor shall recognize as gain the excess of—

(1) the fair market value of the property so transferred, over

(2) the adjusted basis (for purposes of determining gain) of such property in the hands of the transferor.

(b) Exception. Subsection (a) shall not apply to a transfer to a trust by a United States person to the extent that any person is treated as the owner of such trust under section 671.

(c) Treatment of Trusts Which Become Foreign Trusts. If a trust which is not a foreign trust becomes a foreign trust, such trust shall be treated for purposes of this section as having transferred, immediately before becoming a foreign trust, all of its assets to a foreign trust.

Regulations

§ 1.684–1 Recognition of gain on transfers to certain foreign trusts and estates.

(a) Immediate recognition of gain—(1) *In general.* Any U.S. person who transfers property to a foreign trust or foreign estate shall be required to recognize gain at the time of the transfer equal to the excess of the fair market value of the property transferred over the adjusted basis (for purposes of determining gain) of such property in the hands of the U.S. transferor unless an exception applies under the provisions of § 1.684–3. The amount of gain recognized is determined on an asset-by-asset basis.

(2) *No recognition of loss.* Under this section a U.S. person may not recognize loss on the transfer of an asset to a foreign trust or foreign estate. A U.S. person may not offset gain realized on the transfer of an appreciated asset to a foreign trust or foreign estate by a loss realized on the transfer of a depreciated asset to the foreign trust or foreign estate.

(b) Definitions. The following definitions apply for purposes of this section:

(1) *U.S. person.* The term U.S. person means a United States person as defined in section 7701(a)(30), and includes a nonresident alien individual who elects under section 6013(g) to be treated as a resident of the United States.

(2) *U.S. transferor.* The term U.S. transferor means any U.S. person who makes a transfer (as defined in § 1.684–2) of property to a foreign trust or foreign estate.

(3) *Foreign trust.* Section 7701(a)(31)(B) defines foreign trust. See also § 301.7701–7 of this chapter.

(4) *Foreign estate.* Section 7701(a)(31)(A) defines foreign estate.

(c) Reporting requirements. A U.S. person who transfers property to a foreign trust or foreign estate must comply with the reporting requirements under section 6048.

(d) Examples. The following examples illustrate the rules of this section. In all examples, A is a U.S. person and FT is a foreign trust. The examples are as follows:

Example (1). Transfer to foreign trust. A transfers property that has a fair market value of 1000X to FT. A's adjusted basis in the property is 400X. FT has no U.S. beneficiary within the meaning of § 1.679–2, and no person is treated as owning any portion of FT. Under paragraph (a)(1) of this section, A recognizes gain at the time of the transfer equal to 600X.

Example (2). Transfer of multiple properties. A transfers property Q, with a fair market value of 1000X, and property R, with a fair market value of 2000X, to FT. At the time of the transfer, A's adjusted basis in property Q is 700X, and A's adjusted basis in property R is 2200X. FT has no U.S. beneficiary within the meaning of § 1.679–2, and no person is treated as owning any portion of FT. Under paragraph (a)(1) of this section, A recognizes the 300X of gain attributable to property Q. Under paragraph (a)(2) of this section, A does not recognize the 200X of loss attributable to property R, and may not offset that loss against the gain attributable to property Q.

Example (3). Transfer for less than fair market value. A transfers property that has a fair market value of 1000X to FT in exchange for 400X of cash. A's adjusted basis in the property is 200X. FT has no U.S. beneficiary within the meaning of § 1.679–2, and no person is treated as owning any portion of FT. Under paragraph (a)(1) of this section, A recognizes gain at the time of the transfer equal to 800X.

Example (4). Exchange of property for private annuity. A transfers property that has a fair market value of 1000X to FT in exchange for FT's obligation to pay A 50X per year for the rest of A's life. A's adjusted basis in the property is 100X. FT has no U.S. beneficiary within the meaning of § 1.679–2, and no person is treated as owning any portion of FT. A is required to recognize gain equal to 900X immediately upon transfer of the property to the trust. This result applies even though A might otherwise have been allowed to defer recognition of gain under another provision of the Internal Revenue Code.

Example (5). Transfer of property to related foreign trust in exchange for qualified obligation. A transfers property that has a fair market value of 1000X to FT in exchange for FT's obligation to make payments to A during the next four years. FT is related to A as defined in § 1.679–1(c)(5). The obligation is treated as a qualified obligation within the meaning of § 1.679–4(d), and no person is treated as owning any portion of FT. A's adjusted basis in the property is 100X. A is required to recognize gain equal to 900X immediately upon transfer of the property to the trust. This result applies even though A might otherwise have been allowed to defer recognition of gain under another provision of the Internal Revenue Code. Section 1.684–3(d) provides rules relating to transfers for fair market value to unrelated foreign trusts.

[T.D. 8956, 66 FR 37899, July 20, 2001]

§ 1.684–2 Transfers.

(a) In general. A transfer means a direct, indirect, or constructive transfer.

(b) Indirect transfers. (1) *In general.* Section 1.679–3(c) shall apply to determine if a transfer to a foreign trust or foreign estate, by any person, is treated as an indirect transfer by a U.S. person to the foreign trust or foreign estate.

(2) *Examples.* The following examples illustrate the rules of this paragraph (b). In all examples, A is a U.S. citizen, FT is a foreign trust, and I is A's uncle, who is a nonresident alien. The examples are as follows:

Example (1). Principal purpose of tax avoidance. A creates and funds FT for the benefit of A's cousin, who is a nonresident alien. FT has no U.S. beneficiary within the meaning of § 1.679–2, and no person is treated as owning any portion of FT. In 2004, A decides to transfer additional property with a fair market value of 1000X and an adjusted basis of 600X to FT. Pursuant to a plan with a principal purpose of avoiding the application of section 684, A transfers the property to I. I subsequently transfers the property to FT. Under paragraph (b) of this section and § 1.679–3(c), A is treated as having transferred the property to FT.

Example (2). U.S. person unable to demonstrate that intermediary acted independently. A creates and funds FT for the benefit of A's cousin, who is a nonresident alien. FT has no U.S. beneficiary within the meaning of § 1.679–2, and no person is treated as owning any portion of FT. On July 1, 2004, A transfers property with a fair market value of 1000X and an adjusted basis of 300X to I, a foreign person. On January 1, 2007, at a time when the fair market value of the property is 1100X, I transfers the property to FT. A is unable to demonstrate to the satisfaction of the Commissioner, under § 1.679–3(c)(2)(ii), that I acted independently of A in making the transfer to FT. Under paragraph (b) of this section and § 1.679–3(c), A is treated as having transferred the property to FT. Under paragraph (b) of this section and § 1.679–3(c)(3), I is treated as an agent of A, and the transfer is deemed to have been made on January 1, 2007. Under § 1.684–1(a), A recognizes gain equal to 800X on that date.

(c) Constructive transfers. Section 1.679–3(d) shall apply to determine if a transfer to a foreign trust or foreign estate is treated as a constructive transfer by a U.S. person to the foreign trust or foreign estate.

(d) Transfers by certain trusts. (1) *In general.* If any portion of a trust is treated as owned by a U.S. person, a transfer of property from that portion of the trust to a foreign trust is treated as a transfer from the owner of that portion to the foreign trust.

(2) *Examples.* The following examples illustrate the rules of this paragraph (d). In all examples, A is a U.S. person, DT is a domestic trust, and FT is a foreign trust. The examples are as follows:

Example (1). Transfer by a domestic trust. On January 1, 2001, A transfers property which has a fair market value of 1000X and an adjusted basis of 200X to DT. A retains the power to revoke DT. On January 1, 2003, DT transfers property which has a fair market value of 500X and an adjusted basis of 100X to FT. At the time of the transfer, FT has no U.S. beneficiary as defined in § 1.679–2 and no person is treated as owning any portion of FT. A is treated as having transferred the property to FT and is required to recognize gain of 400X, under § 1.684–1, at the time of the transfer by DT to FT.

Example (2). Transfer by a foreign trust. On January 1, 2001, A transfers property which has a fair market value of 1000X and an adjusted basis of 200X to FT1. At the time of the transfer, FT1 has a U.S. beneficiary as defined in § 1.679–2 and A is treated as the owner of FT1 under section 679. On January 1, 2003, FT1 transfers property which has a fair market value of 500X and an adjusted basis of 100X to FT2. At the time of the transfer, FT2 has no U.S. beneficiary as defined in § 1.679–2 and no person is treated as owning any portion of FT2. A is treated as having transferred the property to FT2 and is required to recognize gain of 400X, under § 1.684–1, at the time of the transfer by FT1 to FT2.

(e) Deemed transfers when foreign trust no longer treated as owned by a U.S. person. (1) *In general.* If any portion of a foreign trust is treated as owned by a U.S. person under subpart E of part I of subchapter J, chapter 1 of the Internal Revenue Code, and such portion ceases to be treated as owned by that person under such subpart (other than by reason of an actual transfer of property from the trust to which § 1.684–2(d) applies), the U.S. person shall be treated as having transferred, immediately before (but on the same date that) the trust is no longer treated as owned by that U.S. person, the assets of such portion to a foreign trust.

(2) *Examples.* The following examples illustrate the rules of this paragraph (e). In all examples, A is a U.S. citizen and FT is a foreign trust. The examples are as follows:

Example (1). Loss of U.S. beneficiary. (i) On January 1, 2001, A transfers property, which has a fair market value of 1000X and an adjusted basis of 400X, to FT. At the time of the transfer, FT has a U.S. beneficiary within the meaning of § 1.679–2, and A is treated as owning FT under section 679. Under § 1.684–3(a), § 1.684–1 does not cause A to recognize gain at the time of the transfer.

(ii) On July 1, 2003, FT ceases to have a U.S. beneficiary as defined in § 1.679–2(c) and as of that date neither A nor any other person is treated as owning any portion of FT. Pursuant to § 1.679–2(c)(2), if FT ceases to be treated as having a U.S. beneficiary, A will cease to be treated as owner of FT beginning on the first day of the first taxable year following the last taxable year in which there was a U.S. beneficiary. Thus, on January 1, 2004, A ceases to be treated as owner of FT. On that date, the fair market value of the property is 1200X and the adjusted basis is 350X. Under paragraph (e)(1) of this section, A is treated as having transferred the property to FT on January 1, 2004, and must recognize 850X of gain at that time under § 1.684–1.

Example (2). Death of grantor. (i) The initial facts are the same as in paragraph (i) of Example 1.

(ii) On July 1, 2003, A dies, and as of that date no other person is treated as the owner of FT. On that date, the fair market value of the property is 1200X, and its adjusted basis equals 350X. Under paragraph (e)(1) of this section, A is treated as having transferred the property to FT immediately before his death, and generally is required to recognize 850X of gain at that time under § 1.684–1. However, an exception may apply under § 1.684–3(c).

Example (3). Release of a power. (i) On January 1, 2001, A transfers property that has a fair market value of 500X and an adjusted basis of 200X to FT. At the time of the transfer, FT does not have a U.S. beneficiary within the meaning of § 1.679–2. However, A retains the power to revoke the trust. A is treated as the owner of the trust under section 676 and, therefore, under § 1.684–3(a), A is not required to recognize gain under § 1.684–1 at the time of the transfer.

(ii) On January 1, 2007, A releases the power to revoke the trust and, as of that date, neither A nor any other person is treated as owning any portion of FT. On that date, the fair market value of the property is 900X, and its adjusted basis is 200X. Under paragraph (e)(1) of this section, A is treated as having transferred the property to FT on January 1, 2007, and must recognize 700X of gain at that time.

(f) Transfers to entities owned by a foreign trust. Section 1.679–3(f) provides rules that apply with respect to transfers of property by a U.S. person to an entity in which a foreign trust holds an ownership interest.

[T.D. 8956, 66 FR 37900, July 20, 2001]

§ 1.684–3 Exceptions to general rule of gain recognition.

(a) Transfers to grantor trusts. The general rule of gain recognition under § 1.684–1 shall not apply to any transfer of property by a U.S. person to a foreign trust to the extent that any person is treated as the owner of the trust under section 671. Section 1.684–2(e) provides rules regarding a subsequent change in the status of the trust.

(b) Transfers to charitable trusts. The general rule of gain recognition under § 1.684–1 shall not apply to any transfer of property to a foreign trust that is described in section 501(c)(3) (without regard to the requirements of section 508(a)).

(c) Certain transfers at death. (1) *Section 1014 basis.* The general rule of gain recognition under § 1.684–1 shall not apply to any transfer of property to a foreign trust or foreign estate or, in the case of a transfer of property by a U.S. transferor decedent dying in 2010, to a foreign trust, foreign estate, or a nonresident alien, by reason of death of the U.S. transferor, if the basis of the property in the hands of the transferee is determined under section 1014(a).

(2) *Section 1022 basis election.* For U.S. transferor decedents dying in 2010, the general rule of gain recognition under § 1.684–1 shall apply to any transfer of property by reason of death of the U.S. transferor if the basis of the property in the hands of the foreign trust, foreign estate, or the nonresident alien individual is determined under section 1022. The gain on the transfer shall be calculated as set out under § 1.684–1(a), except that adjusted basis will reflect any increases allocated to such property under section 1022.

(d) Transfers for fair market value to unrelated trusts. The general rule of gain recognition under § 1.684–1 shall not apply to any transfer of property for fair market value to a foreign trust that is not a related foreign trust as defined in § 1.679–1(c)(5). Section 1.671–2(e)(2)(ii) defines fair market value.

(e) Transfers to which section 1032 applies. The general rule of gain recognition under § 1.684–1 shall not apply to any transfer of stock (including treasury stock) by a domestic corporation to a foreign trust if the domestic corporation is not required to recognize gain on the transfer under section 1032.

(f) Certain distributions to trusts. For purposes of this section, a transfer does not include a distribution to a trust with respect to an interest held by such trust in an entity other than a trust or an interest in certain investment trusts described in § 301.7701–4(c) of this chapter, liquidating trusts described in § 301.7701–4(d) of this chapter, or environmental remediation trusts described in § 301.7701–4(e) of this chapter.

(g) Examples. The following examples illustrate the rules of this section. In all examples, A is a U.S. citizen and FT is a foreign trust. The examples are as follows:

Example (1). Transfer to owner trust. In 2001, A transfers property which has a fair market value of 1000X and an adjusted basis equal to 400X to FT. At the time of the transfer, FT has a U.S. beneficiary within the meaning of § 1.679–2, and A is treated as owning FT under section 679. Under paragraph (a) of this section, § 1.684–1 does not cause A to recognize gain at the time of the transfer. See § 1.684–2(e) for rules that may require A to recognize gain if the trust is no longer owned by A.

Example (2). Transfer of property at death: Basis determined under section 1014(a). (i) The initial facts are the same as Example 1.

(ii) A dies on July 1, 2004. The fair market value at A's death of all property transferred to FT by A is 1500X. The basis in the property is 400X. A retained the power to revoke FT, thus, the value of all property owned by FT at A's death is includible in A's gross estate for U.S. estate tax purposes. Pursuant to paragraph (c) of this section, A is not required to recognize gain under § 1.684–1 because the basis of the property in the hands of the foreign trust is determined under section 1014(a).

Example (3). Transfer of property at death: Basis not determined under section 1014(a).

(i) The initial facts are the same as Example 1.

(ii) A dies on July 1, 2004. The fair market value at A's death of all property transferred to FT by A is 1500X. The basis in the property is 400X. A retains no power over FT, and FT's basis in the property transferred is not determined under section 1014(a). Under § 1.684–2(e)(1), A is treated as having transferred the property to FT immediately before his death, and must recognize 1100X of gain at that time under § 1.684–1.

Example (4). Transfer of property for fair market value to an unrelated foreign trust. A sells a house with a fair market value of 1000X to FT in exchange for a 30-year note issued by FT. A is not related to FT as defined in § 1.679–1(c)(5). FT is not treated as owned by any person. Pursuant to paragraph (d) of this section, A is not required to recognize gain under § 1.684–1.

[T.D. 8956, 66 FR 37901, July 20, 2001; T.D. 9811, 82 FR 6239, Jan. 19, 2017]

§ 1.684–4 Outbound migrations of domestic trusts.

(a) In general. If a U.S. person transfers property to a domestic trust, and such trust becomes a foreign trust, and neither trust is treated as owned by any person under subpart E of part I of subchapter J, chapter 1 of the Internal Revenue Code, the trust shall be treated for purposes of this section as having transferred all of its assets to a foreign trust and the trust is required to recognize gain on the transfer under § 1.684–1(a). The trust must also comply with the rules of section 6048.

(b) Date of transfer. The transfer described in this section shall be deemed to occur immediately before, but on the same date that, the trust meets the definition of a foreign trust set forth in section 7701(a)(31)(B).

(c) Inadvertent migrations. In the event of an inadvertent migration, as defined in § 301.7701–7(d)(2) of this chapter, a trust may avoid the application of this section by complying with the procedures set forth in § 301.7701–7(d)(2) of this chapter.

(d) Examples. The following examples illustrate the rules of this section. In all examples, A is a U.S. citizen, B is a U.S. citizen, C is a nonresident alien, and T is a trust. The examples are as follows:

Example (1). Migration of domestic trust with U.S. beneficiaries. A transfers property which has a fair market value of 1000X and an adjusted basis equal to 400X to T, a domestic trust, for the benefit of A's children who are also U.S. citizens. B is the trustee of T. On January 1, 2001, while A is still alive, B resigns as trustee and C becomes successor trustee under the terms of the trust. Pursuant to § 301.7701–7(d) of this chapter, T becomes a foreign trust. T has U.S. beneficiaries within the meaning of § 1.679–2 and A is, therefore, treated as owning FT under section 679. Pursuant to § 1.684–3(a), neither A nor T is required to recognize gain at the time of the migration. Section 1.684–2(e) provides rules that may require A to recognize gain upon a subsequent change in the status of the trust.

Example (2). Migration of domestic trust with no U.S. beneficiaries. A transfers property which has a fair market value of 1000X and an adjusted basis equal to 400X to T, a domestic trust for the benefit of A's mother who is not a citizen or resident of the United States. T is not treated as owned by another person. B is the trustee of T. On January 1, 2001, while A is still alive, B resigns as trustee and C becomes successor trustee under the terms of the trust. Pursuant to § 301.7701–7(d) of this chapter, T becomes a foreign trust, FT. FT has no U.S. beneficiaries within the meaning of § 1.679–2 and no person is treated as owning any portion of FT. T is required to recognize gain of 600X on January 1, 2001. Paragraph (c) of this section provides rules with respect to an inadvertent migration of a domestic trust.

[T.D. 8956, 66 FR 37901, July 20, 2001]

§ 1.684–5 Effective date.

(a) Sections 1.684–1 through 1.684–4 apply to transfers of property to foreign trusts and foreign estates after August 7, 2000, except as provided in paragraph (b) of this section.

(b) In the case a U.S. transferor decedent dying in 2010, § 1.684–3(c) applies to transfers of property to foreign trusts, foreign estates, and nonresident aliens after December 31, 2009, and before January 1, 2011.

[T.D. 8956, 66 FR 37902, July 20, 2001; T.D. 9811, 82 FR 6239, Jan. 19, 2017]

§ 685. Treatment of Funeral Trusts

(a) In general. In the case of a qualified funeral trust—

(1) subparts B, C, D, and E shall not apply, and

(2) no deduction shall be allowed by section 642(b).

(b) Qualified funeral trust. For purposes of this subsection, the term "qualified funeral trust" means any trust (other than a foreign trust) if—

(1) the trust arises as a result of a contract with a person engaged in the trade or business of providing funeral or burial services or property necessary to provide such services,

(2) the sole purpose of the trust is to hold, invest, and reinvest funds in the trust and to use such funds solely to make payments for such services or property for the benefit of the beneficiaries of the trust,

(3) the only beneficiaries of such trust are individuals with respect to whom such services or property are to be provided at their death under contracts described in paragraph (1),

(4) the only contributions to the trust are contributions by or for the benefit of such beneficiaries,

(5) the trustee elects the application of this subsection, and

(6) the trust would (but for the election described in paragraph (5)) be treated as owned under subpart E by the purchasers of the contracts described in paragraph (1).

A trust shall not fail to be treated as meeting the requirement of paragraph (6) by reason of the death of an individual but only during the 60-day period beginning on the date of such death.

(c) Application of rate schedule. Section 1(e) shall be applied to each qualified funeral trust by treating each beneficiary's interest in each such trust as a separate trust.

(d) Treatment of amounts refunded to purchaser on cancellation. No gain or loss shall be recognized to a purchaser of a contract described in subsection (b)(1) by reason of any payment from such trust to such purchaser by reason of cancellation of such contract. If any payment referred to in the preceding sentence consists of property other than money, the basis of such property in the hands of such purchaser shall be the same as the trust's basis in such property immediately before the payment.

(e) Simplified reporting. The Secretary may prescribe rules for simplified reporting of all trusts having a single trustee and of trusts terminated during the year.

Part II. Income in Respect of Decedents

§ 691. Recipients of Income in Respect of Decedents

§ 692. Income taxes on members of Armed Forces, astronauts, and victims of certain terrorist attacks on death

§ 691. Recipients of Income in Respect of Decedents

(a) Inclusion in gross income.

(1) General rule. The amount of all items of gross income in respect of a decedent which are not properly includible in respect of the taxable period in which falls the date of his death or a prior period (including the amount of all items of gross income in respect of a prior decedent, if the right to receive such amount was acquired by reason of the death of the prior decedent or by bequest, devise, or inheritance from the prior decedent) shall be included in the gross income, for the taxable year when received, of:

(A) the estate of the decedent, if the right to receive the amount is acquired by the decedent's estate from the decedent;

(B) the person who, by reason of the death of the decedent, acquires the right to receive the amount, if the right to receive the amount is not acquired by the decedent's estate from the decedent; or

(C) the person who acquires from the decedent the right to receive the amount by bequest, devise, or inheritance, if the amount is received after a distribution by the decedent's estate of such right.

(2) Income in case of sale, etc. If a right, described in paragraph (1), to receive an amount is transferred by the estate of the decedent or a person who received such right by reason of the death of the decedent or by bequest, devise, or inheritance from the decedent, there shall be included in the gross income of the estate or such person, as the case may be, for the taxable period in which the transfer occurs, the fair market value of such right at the time of such transfer plus the amount by which any consideration for the transfer exceeds such fair market value. For purposes of this paragraph, the term "transfer" includes sale, exchange, or other disposition, or the satisfaction of an installment obligation at other than face value, but does not include transmission at death to the estate of the decedent or a transfer to a person pursuant to the right of such person to receive such amount by reason of the death of the decedent or by bequest, devise, or inheritance from the decedent.

(3) Character of income determined by reference to decedent. The right, described in paragraph (1), to receive an amount shall be treated, in the hands of the estate of the decedent or any person who acquired such right by reason of the death of the decedent, or by bequest, devise, or inheritance from the decedent, as if it had been acquired by the estate or such person in the transaction in which the right to receive the income was originally derived and the amount includible in gross income under paragraph (1) or (2) shall be considered in the hands of the estate or such person to have the character which it would have had in the hands of the decedent if the decedent had lived and received such amount.

(4) Installment obligations acquired from decedent. In the case of an installment obligation reportable by the decedent on the installment method under section 453, if such obligation is acquired by the decedent's estate from the decedent or by any person by reason of the death of the decedent or by bequest, devise, or inheritance from the decedent—

(A) an amount equal to the excess of the face amount of such obligation over the basis of the obligation in the hands of the decedent (determined under section 453B) shall, for the purpose of paragraph (1), be considered as an item of gross income in respect of the decedent; and

(B) such obligation shall, for purposes of paragraphs (2) and (3), be considered a right to receive an item of gross income in respect of the decedent, but the amount includible in gross income under paragraph (2) shall be reduced by an amount equal to the basis of the obligation in the hands of the decedent (determined under section 453B).

(5) Other rules relating to installment obligations.

(A) In general. In the case of an installment obligation reportable by the decedent on the installment method under section 453, for purposes of paragraph (2)—

(i) the second sentence of paragraph (2) shall be applied by inserting "(other than the obligor)" after "or a transfer to a person",

(ii) any cancellation of such an obligation shall be treated as a transfer, and

(iii) any cancellation of such an obligation occurring at the death of the decedent shall be treated as a transfer by the estate of the decedent (or, if held by a person other than the decedent before the death of the decedent, by such person).

(B) Face amount treated as fair market value in certain cases. In any case to which the first sentence of paragraph (2) applies by reason of subparagraph (A), if the decedent and the obligor were related persons (within the meaning of section 453(f)(1)), the fair market value of the installment obligation shall be treated as not less than its face amount.

(C) Cancellation includes becoming unenforceable. For purposes of subparagraph (A), an installment obligation which becomes unenforceable shall be treated as if it were canceled.

(b) Allowance of deductions and credit. The amount of any deduction specified in section 162, 163, 164, 212, or 611 (relating to deductions for expenses, interest, taxes, and depletion) or credit specified in section 27 (relating to foreign tax credit), in respect of a decedent which is not properly allowable to the decedent in respect of the taxable period in which falls the date of his death, or a prior period, shall be allowed:

(1) Expenses, interest, and taxes. In the case of a deduction specified in section 162, 163, 164, or 212 and a credit specified in section 27, in the taxable year when paid—

(A) to the estate of the decedent; except that

(B) if the estate of the decedent is not liable to discharge the obligation to which the deduction or credit relates, to the person who, by reason of the death of the decedent or by bequest, devise, or inheritance acquires, subject to such obligation, from the decedent an interest in property of the decedent.

(2) Depletion. In the case of the deduction specified in section 611, to the person described in subsection (a)(1)(A), (B), or (C) who, in the manner described therein, receives the income to which the deduction relates, in the taxable year when such income is received.

(c) Deduction for estate tax.

(1) Allowance of deduction.

(A) General rule. A person who includes an amount in gross income under subsection (a) shall be allowed, for the same taxable year, as a deduction an amount which bears the same ratio to the estate tax attributable to the net value for estate tax purposes of all the items described in subsection (a)(1) as the value for estate tax purposes of the items of gross income or portions thereof in respect of which such person included the amount in gross income (or the amount included in gross income, whichever is lower) bears to the value for estate tax purposes of all the items described in subsection (a)(1).

(B) Estates and trusts. In the case of an estate or trust, the amount allowed as a deduction under subparagraph (A) shall be computed by excluding from the gross income of the estate or trust the portion (if any) of the items described in subsection (a)(1) which is properly paid, credited, or to be distributed to the beneficiaries during the taxable year.

(2) Method of computing deduction. For purposes of paragraph (1)—

(A) The term "estate tax" means the tax imposed on the estate of the decedent or any prior decedent under section 2001 or 2101, reduced by the credits against such tax.

(B) The net value for estate tax purposes of all the items described in subsection (a)(1) shall be the excess of the value for estate tax purposes of all the items described in subsection (a)(1) over the deductions from the gross estate in respect of claims which represent the deductions and credit described in subsection (b). Such net value shall be determined with respect to the provisions of section 421(c)(2), relating to the deduction for estate tax with respect to stock options to which part II of subchapter D applies.

(C) The estate tax attributable to such net value shall be an amount equal to the excess of the estate tax over the estate tax computed without including in the gross estate such net value.

(3) Special rule for generation-skipping transfers. In the case of any tax imposed by chapter 13 on a taxable termination or a direct skip occurring as a result of the death of the transferor, there shall be allowed a deduction (under principles similar to the principles of this subsection) for the portion of such tax attributable to items of gross income of the trust which were not properly includible in the gross income of the trust for periods before the date of such termination.

(4) Coordination with capital gain provisions. For purposes of sections 1(h), 1202, and 1211, the amount taken into account with respect to any item described in subsection (a)(1) shall be reduced (but not below zero) by the amount of the deduction allowable under paragraph (1) of this subsection with respect to such item.

(d) Amounts received by surviving annuitant under joint and survivor annuity contract.

(1) Deduction for estate tax. For purposes of computing the deduction under subsection (c)(1)(A), amounts received by a surviving annuitant—

(A) as an annuity under a joint and survivor annuity contract where the decedent annuitant died after the annuity starting date (as defined in section 72(c)(4)), and

(B) during the surviving annuitant's life expectancy period, shall, to the extent included in gross income under section 72, be considered as amounts included in gross income under subsection (a).

(2) Net value for estate tax purposes. In determining the net value for estate tax purposes under subsection (c)(2)(B) for purposes of this subsection, the value for estate tax purposes of the items described in paragraph (1) of this subsection shall be computed—

(A) by determining the excess of the value of the annuity at the date of the death of the deceased annuitant over the total amount excludable from the gross income of the surviving annuitant under section 72 during the surviving annuitant's life expectancy period, and

(B) by multiplying the figure so obtained by the ratio which the value of the annuity for estate tax purposes bears to the value of the annuity at the date of the death of the deceased.

(3) Definitions. For purposes of this subsection—

(A) The term "life expectancy period" means the period beginning with the first day of the first period for which an amount is received by the surviving annuitant under the contract and ending with the close of the taxable year with or in which falls the termination of the life expectancy of the surviving annuitant. For purposes of this subparagraph, the life expectancy of the surviving annuitant shall be determined, as of the date of the death of the deceased annuitant, with reference to actuarial tables prescribed by the Secretary.

(B) The surviving annuitant's expected return under the contract shall be computed, as of the death of the deceased annuitant, with reference to actuarial tables prescribed by the Secretary.

(e) Cross reference. For application of this section to income in respect of a deceased partner, see section 753.

Regulations

§ 1.691(a)–1 Income in respect of a decedent.

(a) Scope of section 691. In general, the regulations under section 691 cover: (1) The provisions requiring that amounts which are not includible in gross income for the decedent's last taxable year or for a prior taxable year be included in the gross income of the estate or persons receiving such income to the extent that such amounts constitute "income in respect of a decedent"; (2) the taxable effect of a transfer of the right to such income; (3) the treatment of certain deductions and credit in respect of a decedent which are not allowable to the decedent for the taxable period ending with his death or for a prior taxable year; (4) the allowance to a recipient of income in respect of a decedent of a deduction for estate taxes attributable to the inclusion of the value of the right to such income in the decedent's estate; (5) special provisions with respect to installment obligations acquired from a decedent and with respect to the allowance of a deduction for estate taxes to a surviving annuitant under a joint and survivor annuity contract; and (6) special provisions relating to installment obligations transmitted at death when prior law applied to the transmission.

(b) General definition. In general, the term "income in respect of a decedent" refers to those amounts to which a decedent was entitled as gross income but which were not properly includible in computing his taxable income for the taxable year ending with the date of his death or for a previous taxable year under the method of accounting employed by the decedent. See the regulations under section 451. Thus, the term includes—

(1) All accrued income of a decedent who reported his income by use of the cash receipts and disbursements method;

(2) Income accrued solely by reason of the decedent's death in case of a decedent who reports his income by use of an accrual method of accounting; and

(3) Income to which the decedent had a contingent claim at the time of his death. See sections 736 and 753 and the regulations thereunder for "income in respect of a decedent" in the case of a deceased partner.

(c) Prior decedent. The term "income in respect of a decedent" also includes the amount of all items of gross income in respect of a prior decedent, if (1) the right to receive such amount was acquired by the decedent by reason of the death of the prior decedent or by bequest, devise, or inheritance from the prior decedent and if (2) the amount of gross income in respect of the prior decedent was not properly includible in computing the decedent's taxable income for the taxable year ending with the date of his death or for a previous taxable year. See example (2) of paragraph (b) of § 1.691(a)–2.

(d) Items excluded from gross income. Section 691 applies only to the amount of items of gross income in respect of a decedent, and items which are excluded from gross income under subtitle A of the Code are not within the provisions of section 691.

(e) Cross reference. For items deemed to be income in respect of a decedent for purposes of the deduction for estate taxes provided by section 691(c), see paragraph (c) of § 1.691(c)–1.

[T.D. 6500, 25 FR 11814, Nov. 26, 1960, as amended by T.D. 6808, 30 FR 3435, March 16, 1965]

§ 1.691(a)–2 Inclusion in gross income by recipients.

(a) Under section 691(a)(1), income in respect of a decedent shall be included in the gross income, for the taxable year when received, of—

(1) The estate of the decedent, if the right to receive the amount is acquired by the decedent's estate from the decedent;

(2) The person who, by reason of the death of the decedent, acquires the right to receive the amount, if the right to receive the amount is not acquired by the decedent's estate from the decedent; or

(3) The person who acquires from the decedent the right to receive the amount by bequest, devise, or inheritance, if the amount is received after a distribution by the decedent's estate of such right.

These amounts are included in the income of the estate or of such persons when received by them whether or not they report income by use of the cash receipts and disbursements methods.

(b) The application of paragraph (a) of this section may be illustrated by the following examples, in each of which it is assumed that the decedent kept his books by use of the cash receipts and disbursements method.

Example (1). The decedent was entitled at the date of his death to a large salary payment to be made in equal annual installments over five years. His estate, after collecting two installments, distributed the right to the remaining installment payments to the residuary legatee of the estate. The estate must include in its gross income the two installments received by it, and the legatee must include in his gross income each of the three installments received by him.

Example (2). A widow acquired, by bequest from her husband, the right to receive renewal commissions on life insurance sold by him in his lifetime, which commissions were payable over a period of years. The widow died before having received all of such commissions, and her son inherited the right to receive the rest of the commissions. The commissions received by the widow were includible in her gross income. The commissions received by the son were not includible in the widow's gross income but must be included in the gross income of the son.

Example (3). The decedent owned a Series E United States savings bond, with his wife as co-owner or beneficiary, but died before the payment of such bond. The entire amount of interest accruing on the bond and not includible in income by the decedent, not just the amount accruing after the death of the decedent, would be treated as income to his wife when the bond is paid.

Example (4). A, prior to his death, acquired 10,000 shares of the capital stock of the X Corporation at a cost of $100 per share. During his lifetime, A had entered into an agreement with X Corporation whereby X Corporation agreed to purchase and the decedent agreed that his executor would sell the 10,000 shares of X Corporation stock owned by him at the book value of the stock at the date of A's death. Upon A's death, the shares are sold by A's executor for $500 a share pursuant to the agreement. Since the sale of stock is consummated after A's death, there is no income in respect of a decedent with respect to the appreciation in value of A's stock to the date of his death. If, in this example, A had in fact sold the stock during his lifetime but payment had not been received before his death, any gain on the sale would constitute income in respect of a decedent when the proceeds were received.

Example (5). (1) A owned and operated an apple orchard. During his lifetime, A sold and delivered 1,000 bushels of apples to X, a canning factory, but did not receive payment before his death. A also entered into negotiations to sell 3,000 bushels of apples to Y, a canning factory, but did not complete the sale before his death. After A's death, the executor received payment from X. He also completed the sale to Y and transferred to Y 1,200 bushels of apples on hand at A's death and harvested and transferred an additional 1,800 bushels. The gain from the sale of apples by A to X constitutes income in respect of a decedent when received. On the other hand, the gain from the sale of apples by the executor to Y does not.

(2) Assume that, instead of the transaction entered into with Y, A had disposed of the 1,200 bushels of harvested apples by delivering them to Z, a cooperative association, for processing and sale. Each year the association commingles the fruit received from all of its members into a pool and assigns to each member a percentage interest in the pool based on the fruit delivered by him. After the fruit is processed and the products are sold, the association distributes the net proceeds from the pool to its members in proportion to their interests in the pool. After A's death, the association made distributions to the executor with respect to A's share of the proceeds from the pool in which A had an interest. Under such circumstances, the proceeds from the disposition of the 1,200 bushels of apples constitute income in respect of a decedent.

[T.D. 6500, 25 FR 11814, Nov. 26, 1960]

§ 1.691(a)–3 Character of gross income.

(a) The right to receive an amount of income in respect of a decedent shall be treated in the hands of the estate, or by the person entitled to receive such amount by bequest, devise, or inheritance from the decedent or by reason of his death, as if it had been acquired in the transaction by which the decedent (or a prior decedent) acquired such right, and shall be considered as having the same character it would have had if the decedent (or a prior decedent) had lived and received such amount. The provisions of section 1014(a), relating to the basis of property acquired from a decedent, and section 1022, relating to the basis of property acquired from certain decedents who died in 2010, do not apply to these amounts in the hands of the estate and such persons. See sections 1014(c) and 1022(f).

(b) The application of paragraph (a) of this section may be illustrated by the following:

(1) If the income would have been capital gain to the decedent, if he had lived and had received it, from the sale of property, held for more than 1 year (6 months for taxable years beginning before 1977; 9 months for taxable years beginning in 1977), the income, when received, shall be treated in the hands of the estate or of such person as capital gain from the sale of the property, held for more than 1 year (6 months for taxable years beginning before 1977; 9 months for taxable years beginning in 1977), in the same manner as if such person had held the property for the period the decedent held it, and had made the sale.

(2) If the income is interest on United States obligations which were owned by the decedent, such income shall be treated as interest on United States obligations in the hands of the person receiving it, for the purpose of determining the credit provided by section 35, as if such person had owned the obligations with respect to which such interest is paid.

(3) If the amounts received would be subject to special treatment under part I (section 1301 and following), subchapter Q, chapter 1 of the Code, relating to income attributable to several taxable years, as in effect for taxable years beginning before January 1, 1964, if the decedent had lived and included such amounts in his gross income, such sections apply with respect to the recipient of the income.

(4) The provisions of sections 632 and 1347, relating to the tax attributable to the sale of certain oil or

gas property and to certain claims against the United States, apply to any amount included in gross income, the right to which was obtained by the decedent by a sale or claim within the provisions of those sections.

(c) Effective/applicability dates. The last two sentences of paragraph (a) of this section apply on and after January 19, 2017. For rules before January 19, 2017, see § 1.691(a)–3 as contained in 26 CFR part 1 revised as of April 1, 2016.

[T.D. 6500, 25 FR 11814, Nov. 26, 1960, as amended by T.D. 6885, 31 FR 7803, June 2, 1966; T.D. 7728, 45 FR 72650, Nov. 3, 1980; T.D. 9811, 82 FR 6239, Jan. 19, 2017]

§ 1.691(a)–4 Transfer of right to income in respect of a decedent.

(a) Section 691(a)(2) provides the rules governing the treatment of income in respect of a decedent (or a prior decedent) in the event a right to receive such income is transferred by the estate or person entitled thereto by bequest, devise, or inheritance, or by reason of the death of the decedent. In general, the transferor must include in his gross income for the taxable period in which the transfer occurs the amount of the consideration, if any, received for the right or the fair market value of the right at the time of the transfer, whichever is greater. Thus, upon a sale of such right by the estate or person entitled to receive it, the fair market value of the right or the amount received upon the sale, whichever is greater, is included in the gross income of the vendor. Similarly, if such right is disposed of by gift, the fair market value of the right at the time of the gift must be included in the gross income of the donor. In the case of a satisfaction of an installment obligation at other than face value, which is likewise considered a transfer under section 691(a)(2), see § 1.691(a)–5.

(b) If the estate of a decedent or any person transmits the right to income in respect of a decedent to another who would be required by section 691(a)(1) to include such income when received in his gross income, only the transferee will include such income when received in his gross income. In this situation, a transfer within the meaning of section 691(a)(2) has not occurred. This paragraph may be illustrated by the following:

(1) If a person entitled to income in respect of a decedent dies before receiving such income, only his estate or other person entitled to such income by bequest, devise, or inheritance from the latter decedent, or by reason of the death of the latter decedent, must include such amount in gross income when received.

(2) If a right to income in respect of a decedent is transferred by an estate to a specific or residuary legatee, only the specific or residuary legatee must include such income in gross income when received.

(3) If a trust to which is bequeathed a right of a decedent to certain payments of income terminates and transfers the right to a beneficiary, only the beneficiary must include such income in gross income when received. If the transferee described in subparagraphs (1), (2), and (3) of this paragraph transfers his right to receive the amounts in the manner described in paragraph (a) of this section, the principles contained in paragraph (a) are applied to such transfer. On the other hand, if the transferee transmits his right in the manner described in this paragraph, the principles of this paragraph are again applied to such transfer.

[T.D. 6500, 25 FR 11814, Nov. 26, 1960]

§ 1.691(a)–5 Installment obligations acquired from decedent.

(a) Section 691(a)(4) has reference to an installment obligation which remains uncollected by a decedent (or a prior decedent) and which was originally acquired in a transaction the income from which was properly reportable by the decedent on the installment method under section 453. Under the provisions of section 691(a)(4), an amount equal to the excess of the face value of the obligation over its basis in the hands of the decedent (determined under section 453(d)(2) and the regulations thereunder) shall be considered an amount of income in respect of a decedent and shall be treated as such. The decedent's estate (or the person entitled to receive such income by bequest or inheritance from the decedent or by reason of the decedent's death) shall include in its gross income when received the same proportion of any payment in satisfaction of such obligations as would be returnable as income by the decedent if he had lived and received such payment. No gain on account of the transmission of such obligations by the decedent's death is required to be reported as income in the return of the decedent for the year of his death. See § 1.691(e)–1 for special provisions relating to the filing of an election to have the provisions of section 691(a)(4) apply in the case of installment obligations in respect of which section 44(d) of the Internal Revenue Code of 1939 (or corresponding provisions of prior law) would have applied but for the filing of a bond referred to therein.

(b) If an installment obligation described in paragraph (a) of this section is transferred within the meaning of section 691(a)(2) and paragraph (a) of § 1.691(a)–4, the entire installment obligation transferred shall be considered a right to income in respect of a decedent but the amount includible in the gross income of the transferor shall be reduced by an amount equal to the basis of the obligation in the hands of the decedent (determined under section 453(d)(2) and the regulations thereunder) adjusted, however, to take into account the receipt of any installment payments after the decedent's death and before such transfer. Thus, the amount includible in the gross income of the transferor shall be the fair market value of such obligation at the time of the transfer or the consideration received for the transfer of the installment obligation, whichever is greater, reduced by the basis of the obligation as described in the preceding sentence. For purposes of this paragraph, the term "transfer" in section 691(a)(2) and paragraph (a) of § 1.691(a)–4 includes the satisfaction of an installment obligation at other than face value.

(c) The application of this section may be illustrated by the following example:

Example. An heir of a decedent is entitled to collect an installment obligation with a face value of $100, a fair market value of $80, and a basis in the hands of the decedent of $60. If the heir collects the obligation at face value, the excess of the amount collected over the basis is considered income in respect of a decedent and includible in the gross income of the heir under section 691(a)(1). In this case, the amount includible would be $40 ($100 less $60). If the heir collects the obligation at $90, an amount other than face value, the entire obligation is considered a right to receive income in respect of a decedent but the amount ordinarily required to be included in the heir's gross income under section 691(a)(2) (namely, the consideration received in satisfaction of the installment obligation or its fair market value, whichever is greater) shall be reduced by the amount of the basis of the obligation in the hands of the decedent. In this case, the amount includible would be $30 ($90 less $60).

[T.D. 6500, 25 FR 11814, Nov. 26, 1960, as amended by T.D. 6808, 30 FR 3435, March 16, 1965]

§ 1.691(b)–1 Allowance of deductions and credit in respect to decedents.

(a) Under section 691(b) the expenses, interest, and taxes described in sections 162, 163, 164, and 212 for which the decedent (or a prior decedent) was liable, which were not properly allowable as a deduction in his last taxable year or any prior taxable year, are allowed when paid—

(1) As a deduction by the estate; or

(2) If the estate was not liable to pay such obligation, as a deduction by the person who by bequest, devise, or inheritance from the decedent or by reason of the death of the decedent acquires, subject to such obligation, an interest in property of the decedent (or the prior decedent).

Similar treatment is given to the foreign tax credit provided by section 33. For the purposes of subparagraph (2) of this paragraph, the right to receive an amount of gross income in respect of a decedent is considered property of the decedent; on the other hand, it is not necessary for a person, otherwise within the provisions of subparagraph (2) of this paragraph, to receive the right to any income in respect of a decedent. Thus, an heir who receives a right to income in respect of a decedent (by reason of the death of the decedent) subject to any income tax imposed by a foreign country during the decedent's life, which tax must be satisfied out of such income, is entitled to the credit provided by section 33 when he pays the tax. If a decedent who reported income by use of the cash receipts and disbursements method owned real property on which accrued taxes had become a lien, and if such property passed directly to the heir of the decedent in a jurisdiction in which real property does not become a part of a decedent's estate, the heir, upon paying such taxes, may take the same deduction under section 164 that would be allowed to the decedent if, while alive, he had made such payment.

(b) The deduction for percentage depletion is allowable only to the person (described in section 691(a)(1)) who receives the income in respect of the decedent to which the deduction relates, whether or not such person receives the property from which such income is derived. Thus, an heir who (by reason of the decedent's death) receives income derived from sales of units of mineral by the decedent (who reported income by use of the cash receipts and disbursements method) shall be allowed the deduction for percentage depletion, computed on the gross income from such number of units as if the heir had the same economic interest in the property as the decedent. Such heir need not also receive any interest in the mineral property other than such income. If the decedent did not compute his deduction for depletion on the basis of percentage depletion, any deduction for depletion to which the decedent was entitled at the date of his death would be allowable in computing his taxable income for his last taxable year, and there can be no deduction in respect of the decedent by any other person for such depletion.

[T.D. 6500, 25 FR 11814, Nov. 26, 1960]

§ 1.691(c)–1 Deduction for estate tax attributable to income in respect of a decedent.

(a) In general. A person who is required to include in gross income for any taxable year an amount of income in respect of a decedent may deduct for the same taxable year that portion of the estate tax imposed upon the decedent's estate which is attributable to the inclusion in the decedent's estate of the right to receive such amount. The deduction is determined as follows:

(1) Ascertain the net value in the decedent's estate of the items which are included under section 691 in computing gross income. This is the excess of the value included in the gross estate on account of the items of gross income in respect of the decedent (see § 1.691(a)–1 and paragraph (c) of this section) over the deductions from the gross estate for claims which represent the deductions and credit in respect of the decedent (see § 1.691(b)–1). But see section 691(d) and paragraph (b) of § 1.691(d)–1 for computation of the special value of a survivor's annuity to be used in computing the net value for estate tax purposes in cases involving joint and survivor annuities.

(2) Ascertain the portion of the estate tax attributable to the inclusion in the gross estate of such net value. This is the excess of the estate tax over the estate tax computed without including such net value in the gross estate. In computing the estate tax without including such net value in the gross estate, any estate tax deduction (such as the marital deduction) which may be based upon the gross estate shall be recomputed so as to take into account the exclusion of such net value from the gross estate. See example (2), paragraph (e) of § 1.691(d)–1.

For purposes of this section, the term "estate tax" means the tax imposed under section 2001 or 2101 (or the corresponding provisions of the Internal Revenue Code of 1939), reduced by the credits against such tax. Each person including in gross income an amount of income in respect of a decedent may deduct as his share of the portion of the estate tax (computed under subparagraph (2) of this paragraph) an amount which bears the same ratio to such portion as the value in the gross estate of the right to the income included by such person in gross income (or the amount included in gross income if lower) bears to the value in the gross estate of all the items of gross income in respect of the decedent.

(b) Prior decedent. If a person is required to include in gross income an amount of income in respect of a prior decedent, such person may deduct for the same taxable year that portion of the estate tax imposed upon the prior decedent's estate which is attributable to the inclusion in the prior decedent's estate of the value of the right to receive such amount. This deduction is computed in the same manner as provided in paragraph (a) of this section and is in addition to the deduction for estate tax imposed upon the decedent's estate which is attributable to the inclusion in the decedent's estate of the right to receive such amount.

(c) Amounts deemed to be income in respect of a decedent. For purposes of allowing the deduction under section 691(c), the following items are also considered to be income in respect of a decedent under section 691(a):

(1) The value for estate tax purposes of stock options in respect of which amounts are includible in gross income under section 421(b) (prior to amendment by section 221(a) of the Revenue Act of 1964), in the case of taxable years ending before January 1, 1964, or under section 422(c)(1), 423(c), or 424(c)(1), whichever is applicable, in the case of taxable years ending after December 31, 1963. See section 421(d)(6) (prior to amendment by sec. 221(a) of the Revenue Act of 1964), in the case of taxable years ending before January 1, 1964, and section 421(c)(2), in the case of taxable years ending after December 31, 1963.

(2) Amounts received by a surviving annuitant during his life expectancy period as an annuity under

a joint and survivor annuity contract to the extent included in gross income under section 72. See section 691(d).

(d) Examples. Paragraphs (a) and (b) of this section may be illustrated by the following examples:

Example (1). X, an attorney who kept his books by use of the cash receipts and disbursements method, was entitled at the date of his death to a fee for services rendered in a case not completed at the time of his death, which fee was valued in his estate at $1,000, and to accrued bond interest, which was valued in his estate at $500. In all, $1,500 was included in his gross estate in respect of income described in section 691(a)(1). There were deducted as claims against his estate $150 for business expenses for which his estate was liable and $50 for taxes accrued on certain property which he owned. In all, $200 was deducted for claims which represent amounts described in section 691(b) which are allowable as deductions to his estate or to the beneficiaries of his estate. His gross estate was $185,000 and, considering deductions of $15,000 and an exemption of $60,000, his taxable estate amounted to $110,000. The estate tax on this amount is $23,700 from which is subtracted a $75 credit for State death taxes leaving an estate tax liability of $23,625. In the year following the closing of X's estate, the fee in the amount of $1,200 was collected by X's son, who was the sole beneficiary of the estate. This amount was included under section 691(a)(1)(C) in the son's gross income. The son may deduct, in computing his taxable income for such year, $260 on account of the estate tax attributable to such income, computed as follows:

(1) (i) Value of income described in section 691(a)(1) included in computing gross estate	$1,500
(ii) Deductions in computing gross estate for claims representing deductions described in § 691(b)	200
(iii) Net value of items described in section 691(a)(1)	1,300
(2) (i) Estate tax	23,625
(ii) Less: Estate tax computed without including $1,300 (item (1)(iii)) in gross estate	23,235
(iii) Portion of estate tax attributable to net value of items described in section 691(a)(1)	390
(3) (i) Value in gross estate of items described in section 691(a)(1) received in taxable year (fee)	1,000
(ii) Value in gross estate of all income items described in section 691(a)(1) (item (1)(i))	1,500
(iii) Part of estate tax deductible on account of receipt of $1,200 fee (1,000/1,500 of $390)	260

Although $1,200 was later collected as the fee, only the $1,000 actually included in the gross estate is used in the above computations. However, to avoid distortion, section 691(c) provides that if the value included in the gross estate is greater than the amount finally collected, only the amount collected shall be used in the above computations. Thus, if the amount collected as the fee were only $500, the estate tax deductible on the receipt of such amount would be 500/1,500 of $390, or $130. With respect to taxable years ending before January 1, 1964, see paragraph (d)(3) of § 1.421–5 for a similar example involving a restricted stock option. With respect to taxable years ending after December 31, 1963, see paragraph (c)(3) of § 1.421–8 for a similar example involving a stock option subject to the provisions of part II of subchapter D.

Example (2). Assume that in example (1) the fee valued at $1,000 had been earned by prior decedent Y and had been inherited by X who died before collecting it. With regard to the son, the fee would be considered income in respect of a prior decedent. Assume further that the fee was valued at $1,000 in Y's estate, that the net value in Y's estate of items described in section 691(a)(1) was $5,000 and that the estate tax imposed on Y's estate attributable to such net value was $550. In such case, the portion of such estate tax attributable to the fee would be 1,000/5,000 of $550, or $110. When the son collects the $1,200 fee, he will receive for the same taxable year a deduction of $110 with respect to the estate tax imposed on the estate of prior decedent Y as well as the deduction of $260 (as computed in example (1)) with respect to the estate tax imposed on the estate of decedent X.

[T.D. 6500, 25 FR 11814, Nov. 26, 1960, as amended by T.D. 6887, 31 FR 8812, June 24, 1966]

§ 1.691(c)–2 Estates and trusts.

(a) In the case of an estate or trust, the deduction prescribed in section 691(c) is determined in the same manner as described in § 1.691(c)–1, with the following exceptions:

(1) If any amount properly paid, credited, or required to be distributed by an estate or trust to a beneficiary consists of income in respect of a decedent received by the estate or trust during the taxable year—

(i) Such income shall be excluded in determining the income in respect of the decedent with respect to which the estate or trust is entitled to a deduction under section 691(c), and

(ii) Such income shall be considered income in respect of a decedent to such beneficiary for purposes of allowing the deduction under section 691(c) to such beneficiary.

(2) For determination of the amount of income in respect of a decedent received by the beneficiary, see sections 652 and 662, and §§ 1.652(b)–2 and 1.662(b)–2. However, for this purpose, distributable net income as defined in section 643(a) and the regulations thereunder shall be computed without taking into account the estate tax deduction provided in section 691(c) and this section. Distributable net income as modified under the preceding sentence shall be applied for other relevant purposes of subchapter J, chapter 1 of the Code, such as the deduction provided by section 651 or 661, or subpart D, part I of subchapter J, relating to excess distributions by trusts.

(3) The rule stated in subparagraph (1) of this paragraph does not apply to income in respect of a decedent which is properly allocable to corpus by the fiduciary during the taxable year but which is distributed to a beneficiary in a subsequent year. The deduction provided by section 691(c) in such a case is allowable only to the estate or trust. If any amount properly paid, credited, or required to be distributed by a trust qualifies as a distribution under section 666, the fact that a portion thereof constitutes income in respect of a decedent shall be disregarded for the purposes of determining the deduction of the trust and of the beneficiaries under section 691(c) since the deduction for estate taxes was taken into consideration in computing the undistributed net income of the trust for the preceding taxable year.

(b) This section shall apply only to amounts properly paid, credited, or required to be distributed in taxable years of an estate or trust beginning after December 31, 1953, and ending after August 16, 1954, except as otherwise provided in paragraph (c) of this section.

(c) In the case of an estate or trust heretofore taxable under the provisions of the Internal Revenue Code of 1939, amounts paid, credited, or to be distributed during its first taxable year subject to the Internal Revenue Code of 1954 which would have been treated as paid, credited, or to be distributed on the last day of the preceding taxable year if the Internal Revenue Code of 1939 were still applicable shall not be subject to the provisions of section 691(c)(1)(B) or this section. See section 683 and the regulations thereunder.

(d) The provisions of this section may be illustrated by the following example, in which it is assumed that the estate and the beneficiary make their returns on the calendar year basis:

Example. (1) The fiduciary of an estate receives taxable interest of $5,500 and income in respect of a decedent of $4,500 during the taxable year. Neither the will of the decedent nor local law requires the allocation to corpus of income in respect of a decedent. The estate tax attributable to the income in respect of a decedent is $1,500. In his discretion, the fiduciary distributes $2,000 (falling within sections 661(a) and 662(a)) to a beneficiary during that year. On these facts the fiduciary and beneficiary are respectively entitled to estate tax deductions of $1,200 and $300, computed as follows:

(2) Distributable net income computed under section 643(a) without regard to the estate tax deduction under section 691(c) is $10,000, computed as follows:

Taxable interest	$5,500
Income in respect of a decedent	4,500
Total	10,000

(3) Inasmuch as the distributable net income of $10,000 exceeds the amount of $2,000 distributed to the beneficiary, the deduction allowable to the estate under section 661(a) and the amount taxable to the beneficiary under section 662(a) is $2,000.

(4) The character of the amounts distributed to the beneficiary under section 662(b) is shown in the following table:

	Taxable interest	*Income in respect of a decedent*	*Total*
Distributable net income	$5,500	$4,500	$10,000
Amount deemed distributed under section 662(b)	1,100	900	2,000

(5) Accordingly, the beneficiary will be entitled to an estate tax deduction of $300 (900/4,500 * $1,500) and the estate will be entitled to an estate tax deduction of $1,200 (3,600/4,500 * $1,500).

(6) The taxable income of the estate is $6,200, computed as follows:

Gross income		$10,000
Less:		
Distributions to the beneficiary	$2,000	
Estate tax deduction under section 691(c)	1,200	
Personal exemption	600	3,800
Taxable income		6,200

[T.D. 6500, 25 FR 11814, Nov. 26, 1960]

§ 1.691(d)–1 Amounts received by surviving annuitant under joint and survivor annuity contract.

(a) In general. Under section 691(d), annuity payments received by a surviving annuitant under a joint and survivor annuity contract (to the extent indicated in paragraph (b) of this section) are treated as income in respect of a decedent under section 691(a) for the purpose of allowing the deduction for estate tax provided for in section 691(c)(1)(A). This section applies only if the deceased annuitant died after December 31, 1953, and after the annuity starting date as defined in section 72(c)(4).

(b) Special value for surviving annuitant's payments. Section 691(d) provides a special value for the surviving annuitant's payments to determine the amount of the estate tax deduction provided for in section 691(c)(1)(A). This special value is determined by multiplying—

(1) The excess of the value of the annuity at the date of death of the deceased annuitant over the total amount excludable from the gross income of the surviving annuitant under section 72 during his life expectancy period (see paragraph (d)(1)(i) of this section) by

(2) A fraction consisting of the value of the annuity for estate tax purposes over the value of the annuity at the date of death of the deceased annuitant.

This special value is used for the purpose of determining the net value for estate tax purposes (see section 691(c)(2)(B) and paragraph (a)(1) of § 1.691(c)–1) and for the purpose of determining the portion of estate tax attributable to the survivor's annuity (see paragraph (a) of § 1.691(c)–1).

(c) Amount of deduction. The portion of estate tax attributable to the survivor's annuity (see paragraph (a) of § 1.691(c)–1) is allowable as a deduction to the surviving annuitant over his life expectancy period. If the surviving annuitant continues to receive annuity payments beyond this period, there is no further deduction under section 691(d). If the surviving annuitant dies before expiration of such period, there is no compensating adjustment for the unused deduction.

(d) Definitions. (1) For purposes of section 691(d) and this section—

(i) The term "life expectancy period" means the period beginning with the first day of the first period for which an amount is received by the surviving annuitant under the contract and ending with the close of the taxable year with or in which falls the termination of the life expectancy of the surviving annuitant.

(ii) The life expectancy of the surviving annuitant shall be determined as of the date of death of the deceased annuitant, with reference to actuarial Table I set forth in § 1.72–9 (but without making any adjustment under paragraph (a)(2) of § 1.72–5).

(iii) The value of the annuity at the date of death of the deceased annuitant shall be the entire value of the survivor's annuity determined by reference to the principles set forth in section 2031 and the regulations thereunder, relating to the valuation of annuities for estate tax purposes.

(iv) The value of the annuity for estate tax purposes shall be that portion of the value determined under subdivision (iii) of this subparagraph which was includible in the deceased annuitant's gross estate.

(2) The determination of the "life expectancy period" of the survivor for purposes of section 691(d) may be illustrated by the following example:

Example. H and W file their income tax returns on the calendar year basis. H dies on July 15, 1955, on which date W is 70 years of age. On August 1, 1955, W receives a monthly payment under a joint and survivor annuity contract. W's life expectancy determined as of the date of H's death is 15 years as determined from Table I in § 1.72–9; thus her life expectancy ends on July 14, 1970. Under the provisions of section 691(d), her life expectancy period begins as of July 1, 1955, and ends as of December 31, 1970, thus giving her a life expectancy period of 15 ½ years.

(e) Examples. The application of section 691(d) and this section may be illustrated by the following examples:

Example (1). (1) H and W, husband and wife, purchased a joint and survivor annuity contract for $203,800 providing for monthly payments of $1,000 starting January 28, 1954, and continuing for their joint lives and for the remaining life of the survivor. H contributed $152,850 and W contributed $50,950 to the cost of the annuity. As of the annuity starting date, January 1, 1954, H's age at his nearest birthday was 70 and W's age at her nearest birthday was 67. H dies on January 1, 1957, and beginning on January 28, 1957, W receives her monthly payments of $1,000. The value of the annuity at the date of H's death is $159,000 (see paragraph (d)(1)(iii) of this section), and the value of the annuity for estate tax purposes (see paragraph (d)(1)(iv) of this section) is $119,250 (152,850/203,800 of $159,000). As of the date of H's death, W's age is 70 and her life expectancy period is 15 years (see paragraph (d) of this section for method of computation). Both H and W reported income by use of the cash receipts and disbursements method and filed income tax returns on the calendar year basis.

(2) The following computations illustrate the application of section 72 in determining the excludable portions of the annuity payments to W during her life expectancy period:

Amount of annuity payments per year (12 x $1,000)	$12,000
Life expectancy of H and W as of the annuity starting date (see section 72(c)(3)(A) and Table II of § 1.72–9 (male, age 70; female, age 67))	19.7
Expected return as of the annuity starting date, January 1, 1954 ($12,000 x 19.7 as determined under section 72(c)(3)(A) and paragraph (b) of § 1.72–5)	$236,400
Investment in the contract as of the annuity starting date, Jan. 1, 1954 (see section 72(c)(1) and paragraph (a) of § 1.72–6)	$203,800
Exclusion ratio (203,800/236,400 as determined under section 72(b) and § 1.72–4) (percent)	86.2
Exclusion per year under section 72 ($12,000 x 86.2 percent)	$10,344
Excludable during W's life expectancy period ($10,344 x 15)	$155,160

(3) For the purpose of computing the deduction for estate tax under section 691(c), the value for estate tax purposes of the amounts includible in W's gross income and considered income in respect of a decedent by virtue of section 691(d)(1) is $2,880. This amount is arrived at in accordance with the formula contained in section 691(d)(2), as follows:

Value of annuity at the date of H's death	$159,000
Total amount excludable from W's gross income under section 72 during W's life expectancy period (see sub-paragraph (2) of this example)	$155,160
Excess	$3,840
Ratio which value of annuity for estate tax purposes bears to value of annuity at date of H's death (119,250/159,000) (percent)	75
Value for estate tax purposes (75 percent of $3,840)	$2,880

This amount ($2,880) is included in the items of income under section 691(a)(1) for the purpose of determining the estate tax attributable to each item under section 691(c)(1)(A). The estate tax determined to be attributable to the item of $2,880 is then allowed as a deduction to W over her 15-year life expectancy period (see example (2) of this paragraph).

Example (2). Assume, in addition to the facts contained in example (1) of this paragraph, that H was an attorney and was entitled at the date of his death to a fee for services rendered in a case not completed at the time of his death, which fee was valued at $1,000, and to accrued bond interest, which was valued at $500. Taking into consideration the annuity payments of example (1), valued at $2,880, a total of $4,380 was included in his gross estate in respect of income described in section 691(a)(1). There were deducted as claims against his estate $280 for business expenses for which his estate was liable and $100 for taxes accrued on certain property which he owned. In all, $380 was deducted for claims which represent amounts described in section 691(b) which are allowable as deductions to his estate or to the beneficiaries of his estate. His gross estate was $404,250 and considering deductions of $15,000, a marital deduction of $119,250 (assuming the annuity to be the only qualifying gift) and an exemption of $60,000, his taxable estate amounted to $210,000. The estate tax on this amount is $53,700 from which is subtracted a $175 credit for State death taxes, leaving an estate tax liability of $53,525. W may deduct, in computing her taxable income during each year of her 15-year life expectancy period, $14.73 on account of the estate tax attributable to the value for estate tax purposes of that portion of the annuity payments considered income in respect of a decedent, computed as follows:

(1)	(i)	Value of income described in section 691(a)(1) included in computing gross estate	$4,380.00
	(ii)	Deductions in computing gross estate for claims representing deductions described in section 691(b)	380.00
	(iii)	Net value of items described in section 691(a)(1)	4,000.00
(2)	(i)	Estate tax	53,525.00
	(ii)	Less: estate tax computed without including $4,000 (item (1)(iii)) in gross estate and by reducing marital deduction by $2,880 (portion of item (1)(iii) allowed as a marital deduction)	53,189.00
	(iii)	Portion of estate tax attributable to net value of income items	336.00
(3)	(i)	Value in gross estate of income attributable to annuity payments	$2,880.00
	(ii)	Value in gross estate of all income items described in section 691(a)(1) (item (1)(i))	4,380.00
	(iii)	Part of estate tax attributable to annuity income (2,880/4,380 of $336)	220.93
	(iv)	Deduction each year on account of estate tax attributable to annuity income ($220.93 ÷ 15 (life expectancy period))	14.73

[T.D. 6500, 25 FR 11814, Nov. 26, 1960]

§ 1.691(e)–1 Installment obligations transmitted at death when prior law applied.

(a) In general. (1) *Application of prior law.* Under section 44(d) of the Internal Revenue Code of 1939 and corresponding provisions of prior law, gains and losses on account of the transmission of installment obligations at the death of a holder of such obligations were required to be reported in the return of the decedent for the year of his death. However, an exception to this rule was provided if there was filed with the Commissioner a bond assuring the return as income of any payment in satisfaction of these obligations in the same proportion as would have been returnable as income by the decedent had he lived and received such payments. Obligations in respect of which such bond was filed are referred to in this section as "obligations assured by bond".

(2) *Application of present law.* Section 691(a)(4) of the Internal Revenue Code of 1954 (effective for taxable years beginning after December 31, 1953, and ending after August 16, 1954) in effect makes the exception which under prior law applied to obligations assured by bond the general rule for obligations

transmitted at death, but contains no requirement for a bond. Section 691(e)(1) provides that if the holder of the installment obligation makes a proper election, the provisions of section 691(a)(4) shall apply in the case of obligations assured by bond. Section 691(e)(1) further provides that the estate tax deduction provided by section 691(c)(1) is not allowable for any amount included in gross income by reason of filing such an election.

(b) Manner and scope of election. (1) *In general.* The election to have obligations assured by bond treated as obligations to which section 691(a)(4) applies shall be made by the filing of a statement with respect to each bond to be released, containing the following information:

(i) The name and address of the decedent from whom the obligations assured by bond were transmitted, the date of his death, and the internal revenue district in which the last income tax return of the decedent was filed.

(ii) A schedule of all obligations assured by the bond on which is listed—

(a) The name and address of the obligors, face amount, date of maturity, and manner of payment of each obligation,

(b) The name, identifying number (provided under section 6109 and the regulations thereunder), and address of each person holding the obligations, and

(c) The name, identifying number, and address, of each person who at the time of the election possesses an interest in each obligation, and a description of such interest.

(iii) The total amount of income in respect of the obligations which would have been reportable as income by the decedent if he had lived and received such payment.

(iv) The amount of income referred to in subdivision (iii) of this subparagraph which has previously been included in gross income.

(v) An unqualified statement, signed by all persons holding the obligations, that they elect to have the provisions of section 691(a)(4) apply to such obligations and that such election shall be binding upon them, all current beneficiaries, and any person to whom the obligations may be transmitted by gift, bequest, or inheritance.

(vi) A declaration that the election is made under the penalties of perjury.

(2) *Filing of statement.* The statement with respect to each bond to be released shall be filed in duplicate with the district director of internal revenue for the district in which the bond is maintained. The statement shall be filed not later than the time prescribed for filing the return for the first taxable year (including any extension of time for such filing) to which the election applies.

(3) *Effect of election.* The election referred to in subparagraph (1) of this paragraph shall be irrevocable. Once an election is made with respect to an obligation assured by bond, it shall apply to all payments made in satisfaction of such obligation which were received during the first taxable year to which the election applies and to all such payments received during each taxable year thereafter, whether the recipient is the person who made the election, a current beneficiary, or a person to whom the obligation may be transmitted by gift, bequest, or inheritance. Therefore, all payments received to which the election applies shall be treated as payments made on installment obligations to which section 691(a)(4) applies. However, the estate tax deduction provided by section 691(c) is not allowable for any such payment. The application of this subparagraph may be illustrated by the following example:

Example. A, the holder of an installment obligation, died in 1952. The installment obligation was transmitted at A's death to B who filed a bond on Form 1132 pursuant to paragraph (c) of § 39.44–5 of Regulations 118 (26 CFR Part 39, 1939 ed.) for the necessary amount. On January 1, 1965, B, a calendar year taxpayer, filed an election under section 691(e) to treat the obligation assured by bond as an obligation to which section 691(a)(4) applies, and B's bond was released for 1964 and subsequent taxable years. B died on June 1, 1965, and the obligation was bequeathed to C. On January 1, 1966, C received an installment payment on the obligation which had been assured by the bond. Because B filed an election with respect to the obligation assured by bond, C is required to treat the proper proportion of the January 1, 1966, payment and all subsequent payments made in satisfaction of this obligation as income in respect of a decedent. However, no estate tax deduction is allowable to C under section 691(c)(1) for any estate tax attributable to the inclusion of the value of such obligation in the estate of either A or B.

(c) Release of bond. If an election according to the provisions of paragraph (b) of this section is filed, the liability under any bond filed under section 44(d) of the 1939 Code (or the corresponding provisions of prior law) shall be released with respect to each taxable year to which such election applies. However, the liability under any such bond for an earlier taxable year to which the election does not apply shall not be released until the district director of internal revenue for the district in which the bond is maintained is assured that the proper portion of each installment payment received in such taxable year has been reported and the tax thereon paid.

[T.D. 6808, 30 FR 3436, March 16, 1965]

§ 1.691(f)–1 Cross reference.

See section 753 and the regulations thereunder for application of section 691 to income in respect of a deceased partner.

[T.D. 6808, 30 FR 3436, March 16, 1965]

§ 692. Income Taxes on Members of Armed Forces, Astronauts, and Victims of Certain Terrorist Attacks on Death

(a) General rule. In the case of any individual who dies while in active service as a member of the Armed Forces of the United States, if such death occurred while serving in a combat zone (as determined under section 112) or as a result of wounds, disease, or injury incurred while so serving—

(1) any tax imposed by this subtitle shall not apply with respect to the taxable year in which falls the date of his death, or with respect to any prior taxable year ending on or after the first day he so served in a combat zone; and

(2) any tax under this subtitle and under the corresponding provisions of prior revenue laws for taxable years preceding those specified in paragraph (1) which is unpaid at the date of his death (including interest, additions to the tax, and additional amounts) shall not be assessed, and if assessed the assessment shall be abated, and if collected shall be credited or refunded as an overpayment.

(b) Individuals in missing status. For purposes of this section, in the case of an individual who was in a missing status within the meaning of section 6013(f)(3)(A), the date of his death shall be treated as being not earlier than the date on which a determination of his death is made under section 556 of title 37 of the United States Code. Except in the case of the combat zone designated for purposes of the Vietnam conflict, the preceding sentence shall not cause subsection (a)(1) to apply for any taxable year beginning more than 2 years after the date designated under section 112 as the date of termination of combatant activities in a combat zone.

(c) Certain military or civilian employees of the United States dying as a result of injuries.

(1) In general. In the case of any individual who dies while a military or civilian employee of the United States, if such death occurs as a result of wounds or injury which was incurred while the individual was a military or civilian employee of the United States and which was incurred in a terroristic or military action, any tax imposed by this subtitle shall not apply—

(A) with respect to the taxable year in which falls the date of his death, and

(B) with respect to any prior taxable year in the period beginning with the last taxable year ending before the taxable year in which the wounds or injury were incurred.

(2) Terroristic or military action. For purposes of paragraph (1), the term "terroristic or military action" means—

(A) any terroristic activity which a preponderance of the evidence indicates was directed against the United States or any of its allies, and

(B) any military action involving the Armed Forces of the United States and resulting from violence or aggression against the United States or any of its allies (or threat thereof).

For purposes of the preceding sentence, the term "military action" does not include training exercises.

(3) Treatment of multinational forces. For purposes of paragraph (2), any multinational force in which the United States is participating shall be treated as an ally of the United States.

(d) Individuals dying as a result of certain attacks.

(1) In general. In the case of a specified terrorist victim, any tax imposed by this chapter shall not apply—

(A) with respect to the taxable year in which falls the date of death, and

(B) with respect to any prior taxable year in the period beginning with the last taxable year ending before the taxable year in which the wounds, injury, or illness referred to in paragraph (3) were incurred.

(2) $10,000 minimum benefit. If, but for this paragraph, the amount of tax not imposed by paragraph (1) with respect to a specified terrorist victim is less than $10,000, then such victim shall be treated as having made a payment against the tax imposed by this chapter for such victim's last taxable year in an amount equal to the excess of $10,000 over the amount of tax not so imposed.

(3) Taxation of certain benefits. Subject to such rules as the Secretary may prescribe, paragraph (1) shall not apply to the amount of any tax imposed by this chapter which would be computed by only taking into account the items of income, gain, or other amounts attributable to—

(A) deferred compensation which would have been payable after death if the individual had died other than as a specified terrorist victim, or

(B) amounts payable in the taxable year which would not have been payable in such taxable year but for an action taken after September 11, 2001.

(4) Specified terrorist victim. For purposes of this subsection, the term 'specified terrorist victim' means any decedent—

(A) who dies as a result of wounds or injury incurred as a result of the terrorist attacks against the United States on April 19, 1995, or September 11, 2001, or

(B) who dies as a result of illness incurred as a result of an attack involving anthrax occurring on or after September 11, 2001, and before January 1, 2002.

Such term shall not include any individual identified by the Attorney General to have been a participant or conspirator in any such attack or a representative of such an individual.

(5) Relief with respect to astronauts. The provisions of this subsection shall apply to any astronaut whose death occurs in the line of duty, except that paragraph (3)(B) shall be applied by using the date of the death of the astronaut rather than September 11, 2001.

Regulation

§ 1.692–1 Abatement of income taxes of certain members of the Armed Forces of the United States upon death. [*Omitted. Ed.*]

[T.D. 6500, 25 FR 11814, Nov. 26, 1960, as amended by T.D. 7543, 43 FR 19392, May 5, 1978]

Subchapter N. Tax Based on Income from Sources Within or Without the United States

Part II. Nonresident Aliens and Foreign Corporations

Subpart A. Nonresident Alien Individuals

§ 877A. Tax Responsibilities of Expatriation

(a) General rules. For purposes of this subtitle

(1) Mark to market. All property of a covered expatriate shall be treated as sold on the day before the expatriation date for its fair market value.

(2) Recognition of gain or loss. In the case of any sale under paragraph (1)

(A) notwithstanding any other provision of this title, any gain arising from such sale shall be taken into account for the taxable year of the sale, and

(B) any loss arising from such sale shall be taken into account for the taxable year of the sale to the extent otherwise provided by this title, except that section 1091 shall not apply to any such loss.

Proper adjustment shall be made in the amount of any gain or loss subsequently realized for gain or loss taken into account under the preceding sentence, determined without regard to paragraph (3).

(3) Exclusion for certain gain.

(A) In general. The amount which would (but for this paragraph) be includible in the gross income of any individual by reason of paragraph (1) shall be reduced (but not below zero) by $600,000.*

(B) Adjustment for inflation.

(i) In general. In the case of any taxable year beginning in a calendar year after 2008, the dollar amount in subparagraph (A) shall be increased by an amount equal to

(I) such dollar amount, multiplied by

(II) the cost-of-living adjustment determined under section 1(f)(3) for the calendar year in which the taxable year begins, by substituting "calendar year 2007" for "calendar year 2016" in subparagraph (A)(ii) thereof.

(ii) Rounding. If any amount as adjusted under clause (i) is not a multiple of $1,000, such amount shall be rounded to the nearest multiple of $1,000.

(b) Election to defer tax.

(1) In general. If the taxpayer elects the application of this subsection with respect to any property treated as sold by reason of subsection (a), the time for payment of the additional tax attributable to such property shall be extended until the due date of the return for the taxable year in which such property is disposed of (or, in the case of property disposed of in a transaction in which gain is not recognized in whole or in part, until such other date as the Secretary may prescribe).

(2) Determination of tax with respect to property. For purposes of paragraph (1), the additional tax attributable to any property is an amount which bears the same ratio to the additional tax imposed by this chapter for the taxable year solely by reason of subsection (a) as the gain taken into account under subsection (a) with respect to such property bears to the total gain taken into account under subsection (a) with respect to all property to which subsection (a) applies.

* Rev. Proc. 2025–32 provides that "[f]or taxable years beginning in 2026, the amount that would be includible in the gross income of a covered expatriate by reason of § 877A(a)(1) is reduced (but not below zero) by $910,000 pursuant to § 877A(a)(3)." *Ed.*

(3) Termination of extension. The due date for payment of tax may not be extended under this subsection later than the due date for the return of tax imposed by this chapter for the taxable year which includes the date of death of the expatriate (or, if earlier, the time that the security provided with respect to the property fails to meet the requirements of paragraph (4), unless the taxpayer corrects such failure within the time specified by the Secretary).

(4) Security.

(A) In general. No election may be made under paragraph (1) with respect to any property unless adequate security is provided with respect to such property.

(B) Adequate security. For purposes of subparagraph (A), security with respect to any property shall be treated as adequate security if

(i) it is a bond which is furnished to, and accepted by, the Secretary, which is conditioned on the payment of tax (and interest thereon), and which meets the requirements of section 6325, or

(ii) it is another form of security for such payment (including letters of credit) that meets such requirements as the Secretary may prescribe.

(5) Waiver of certain rights. No election may be made under paragraph (1) unless the taxpayer makes an irrevocable waiver of any right under any treaty of the United States which would preclude assessment or collection of any tax imposed by reason of this section.

(6) Elections. An election under paragraph (1) shall only apply to property described in the election and, once made, is irrevocable.

(7) Interest. For purposes of section 6601, the last date for the payment of tax shall be determined without regard to the election under this subsection.

(c) Exception for certain property. Subsection (a) shall not apply to

(1) any deferred compensation item (as defined in subsection (d)(4)),

(2) any specified tax deferred account (as defined in subsection (e)(2)), and

(3) any interest in a nongrantor trust (as defined in subsection (f)(3)).

(d) Treatment of deferred compensation items.

(1) Withholding on eligible deferred compensation items.

(A) In general. In the case of any eligible deferred compensation item, the payor shall deduct and withhold from any taxable payment to a covered expatriate with respect to such item a tax equal to 30 percent thereof.

(B) Taxable payment. For purposes of subparagraph (A), the term "taxable payment" means with respect to a covered expatriate any payment to the extent it would be includible in the gross income of the covered expatriate if such expatriate continued to be subject to tax as a citizen or resident of the United States. A deferred compensation item shall be taken into account as a payment under the preceding sentence when such item would be so includible.

* * *

(e) Treatment of specified tax deferred accounts.

(1) Account treated as distributed. In the case of any interest in a specified tax deferred account held by a covered expatriate on the day before the expatriation date

(A) the covered expatriate shall be treated as receiving a distribution of his entire interest in such account on the day before the expatriation date,

(B) no early distribution tax shall apply by reason of such treatment, and

(C) appropriate adjustments shall be made to subsequent distributions from the account to reflect such treatment.

(2) Specified tax deferred account. For purposes of paragraph (1), the term "specified tax deferred account" means an individual retirement plan (as defined in section 7701(a)(37)) other than any arrangement described in subsection (k) or (p) of section 408, a qualified tuition program (as defined in section 529), a qualified ABLE program (as defined in section 529A), a Coverdell education savings account (as defined in section 530), a health savings account (as defined in section 223), and an Archer MSA (as defined in section 220).

(f) Special rules for nongrantor trusts.

(1) In general. In the case of a distribution (directly or indirectly) of any property from a nongrantor trust to a covered expatriate

(A) the trustee shall deduct and withhold from such distribution an amount equal to 30 percent of the taxable portion of the distribution, and

(B) if the fair market value of such property exceeds its adjusted basis in the hands of the trust, gain shall be recognized to the trust as if such property were sold to the expatriate at its fair market value.

(2) Taxable portion. For purposes of this subsection, the term "taxable portion" means, with respect to any distribution, that portion of the distribution which would be includible in the gross income of the covered expatriate if such expatriate continued to be subject to tax as a citizen or resident of the United States.

(3) Nongrantor trust. For purposes of this subsection, the term "nongrantor trust" means the portion of any trust that the individual is not considered the owner of under subpart E of part I of subchapter J. The determination under the preceding sentence shall be made immediately before the expatriation date.

(4) Special rules relating to withholding. For purposes of this subsection

(A) rules similar to the rules of subsection (d)(6) shall apply, and

(B) the covered expatriate shall be treated as having waived any right to claim any reduction under any treaty with the United States in withholding on any distribution to which paragraph (1)(A) applies unless the covered expatriate agrees to such other treatment as the Secretary determines appropriate.

(5) Application. This subsection shall apply to a nongrantor trust only if the covered expatriate was a beneficiary of the trust on the day before the expatriation date.

(g) Definitions and special rules relating to expatriation. For purposes of this section

(1) Covered expatriate.

(A) In general. The term "covered expatriate" means an expatriate who meets the requirements of subparagraph (A), (B), or (C) of section 877(a)(2).*

(B) Exceptions. An individual shall not be treated as meeting the requirements of subparagraph (A) or (B) of section 877(a)(2) if

(i) the individual

(I) became at birth a citizen of the United States and a citizen of another country and, as of the expatriation date, continues to be a citizen of, and is taxed as a resident of, such other country, and

* Rev. Proc. 2025–32 provides that "[f]or calendar year 2026, under § 877A(g)(1)(A), unless an exception under § 877A(g)(1)(B) applies, an individual is a covered expatriate if the individual's 'average annual net income tax' under § 877(a)(2)(A) for the five taxable years ending before the expatriation date is more than $211,000." *Ed.*

(II) has been a resident of the United States (as defined in section 7701(b)(1)(A)(ii)) for not more than 10 taxable years during the 15-taxable year period ending with the taxable year during which the expatriation date occurs, or

(ii) (I) the individual's relinquishment of United States citizenship occurs before such individual attains age 18 ½, and

(II) the individual has been a resident of the United States (as so defined) for not more than 10 taxable years before the date of relinquishment.

(C) Covered expatriates also subject to tax as citizens or residents. In the case of any covered expatriate who is subject to tax as a citizen or resident of the United States for any period beginning after the expatriation date, such individual shall not be treated as a covered expatriate during such period for purposes of subsections (d)(1) and (f) and section 2801.

(2) Expatriate. The term "expatriate" means

(A) any United States citizen who relinquishes his citizenship, and

(B) any long-term resident of the United States who ceases to be a lawful permanent resident of the United States (within the meaning of section 7701(b)(6)).

(3) Expatriation date. The term "expatriation date" means

(A) the date an individual relinquishes United States citizenship, or

(B) in the case of a long-term resident of the United States, the date on which the individual ceases to be a lawful permanent resident of the United States (within the meaning of section 7701(b)(6)).

(4) Relinquishment of citizenship. A citizen shall be treated as relinquishing his United States citizenship on the earliest of

(A) the date the individual renounces his United States nationality before a diplomatic or consular officer of the United States pursuant to paragraph (5) of section 349(a) of the Immigration and Nationality Act (8 U.S.C. 1481(a)(5)),

(B) the date the individual furnishes to the United States Department of State a signed statement of voluntary relinquishment of United States nationality confirming the performance of an act of expatriation specified in paragraph (1), (2), (3), or (4) of section 349(a) of the Immigration and Nationality Act (8 U.S.C. 1481(a)(1)–(4)),

(C) the date the United States Department of State issues to the individual a certificate of loss of nationality, or

(D) the date a court of the United States cancels a naturalized citizen's certificate of naturalization.

Subparagraph (A) or (B) shall not apply to any individual unless the renunciation or voluntary relinquishment is subsequently approved by the issuance to the individual of a certificate of loss of nationality by the United States Department of State.

(5) Long-term resident. The term "long-term resident" has the meaning given to such term by section 877(e)(2).

(6) Early distribution tax. The term "early distribution tax" means any increase in tax imposed under section 72(t), 220(f)(4), 223(f)(4), 409A(a)(1)(B), 529(c)(6), 529A(c)(3), or 530(d)(4).

(h) Other rules.

(1) Termination of deferrals, etc. In the case of any covered expatriate, notwithstanding any other provision of this title

(A) any time period for acquiring property which would result in the reduction in the amount of gain recognized with respect to property disposed of by the taxpayer shall terminate on the day before the expatriation date, and

(B) any extension of time for payment of tax shall cease to apply on the day before the expatriation date and the unpaid portion of such tax shall be due and payable at the time and in the manner prescribed by the Secretary.

(2) Step-up in basis. Solely for purposes of determining any tax imposed by reason of subsection (a), property which was held by an individual on the date the individual first became a resident of the United States (within the meaning of section 7701(b)) shall be treated as having a basis on such date of not less than the fair market value of such property on such date. The preceding sentence shall not apply if the individual elects not to have such sentence apply. Such an election, once made, shall be irrevocable.

(3) Coordination with section 684. If the expatriation of any individual would result in the recognition of gain under section 684, this section shall be applied after the application of section 684.

(i) Regulations. The Secretary shall prescribe such regulations as may be necessary or appropriate to carry out the purposes of this section.

Subchapter O. Gain or Loss on Disposition of Property

Part I. Determination of Amount of And Recognition of Gain or Loss

§ 1001. Determination of Amount of and Recognition of Gain or Loss

(a) Computation of gain or loss. The gain from the sale or other disposition of property shall be the excess of the amount realized therefrom over the adjusted basis provided in section 1011 for determining gain, and the loss shall be the excess of the adjusted basis provided in such section for determining loss over the amount realized.

(b) Amount realized. The amount realized from the sale or other disposition of property shall be the sum of any money received plus the fair market value of the property (other than money) received. In determining the amount realized—

(1) there shall not be taken into account any amount received as reimbursement for real property taxes which are treated under section 164(d) as imposed on the purchaser, and

(2) there shall be taken into account amounts representing real property taxes which are treated under section 164(d) as imposed on the taxpayer if such taxes are to be paid by the purchaser.

(c) Recognition of gain or loss. Except as otherwise provided in this subtitle, the entire amount of the gain or loss, determined under this section, on the sale or exchange of property shall be recognized.

(d) Installment sales. Nothing in this section shall be construed to prevent (in the case of property sold under contract providing for payment in installments) the taxation of that portion of any installment payment representing gain or profit in the year in which such payment is received.

(e) Certain term interests.

(1) In general. In determining gain or loss from the sale or other disposition of a term interest in property, that portion of the adjusted basis of such interest which is determined pursuant to section 1014, 1015, or 1041 (to the extent that such adjusted basis is a portion of the entire adjusted basis of the property) shall be disregarded.

(2) Term interest in property defined. For purposes of paragraph (1), the term "term interest in property" means—

(A) a life interest in property,

(B) an interest in property for a term of years, or

(C) an income interest in a trust.

(3) Exception. Paragraph (1) shall not apply to a sale or other disposition which is a part of a transaction in which the entire interest in property is transferred to any person or persons.

Regulation

§ 1.1001–1 Computation of gain or loss.

(a) General rule. Except as otherwise provided in subtitle A of the Code, the gain or loss realized from the conversion of property into cash, or from the exchange of property for other property differing materially either in kind or in extent, is treated as income or as loss sustained. The amount realized from a sale or other disposition of property is the sum of any money received plus the fair market value of any property (other than money) received. The fair market value of property is a question of fact, but only in rare and extraordinary cases will property be considered to have no fair market value. The general method of computing such gain or loss is prescribed by section 1001(a) through (d) which contemplates that from the amount realized upon the sale or exchange there shall be withdrawn a sum sufficient to restore the adjusted basis prescribed by section 1011 and the regulations thereunder (i.e., the cost or other basis adjusted for receipts, expenditures, losses, allowances, and other items chargeable against and applicable to such cost or other basis). The amount which remains after the adjusted basis has been restored to the taxpayer constitutes the realized gain. If the amount realized upon the sale or exchange is insufficient to restore to the taxpayer the adjusted basis of the property, a loss is sustained to the extent of the difference between such adjusted basis and the amount realized. The basis may be different depending upon whether gain or loss is being computed. For example, see section 1015(a) and the regulations thereunder. Section 1001(e) and paragraph (f) of this section prescribe the method of computing gain or loss upon the sale or other disposition of a term interest in property the adjusted basis (or a portion) of which is determined pursuant, or by reference, to section 1014 (relating to the basis of property acquired from a decedent), section 1015 (relating to the basis of property acquired by gift or by a transfer in trust), or section 1022 (relating to the basis of property acquired from certain decedents who died in 2010). For rules determining the amount realized for purposes of computing the gain or loss upon the sale, exchange, or other disposition of digital assets, as defined in § 1.6045–1(a)(19), other than a digital asset not required to be reported as a digital asset pursuant to § 1.6045–1(c)(8)(ii), (iii), or (iv), see § 1.1001–7.

* * *

(d) Installment sales. In the case of property sold on the installment plan, special rules for the taxation of the gain are prescribed in section 453.

(e) Transfers in part a sale and in part a gift. (1) Where a transfer of property is in part a sale and in part a gift, the transferor has a gain to the extent that the amount realized by him exceeds his adjusted basis in the property. However, no loss is sustained on such a transfer if the amount realized is less than the adjusted basis. For the determination of basis of property in the hands of the transferee, see § 1.1015–4. For the allocation of the adjusted basis of property in the case of a bargain sale to a charitable organization, see § 1.1011–2.

(2) *Examples.* The provisions of subparagraph (1) may be illustrated by the following examples:

Example (1). A transfers property to his son for $60,000. Such property in the hands of A has an adjusted basis of $30,000 (and a fair market value of $90,000). A's gain is $30,000, the excess of $60,000, the amount realized, over the adjusted basis, $30,000. He has made a gift of $30,000, the excess of $90,000, the fair market value, over the amount realized, $60,000.

Example (2). A transfers property to his son for $30,000. Such property in the hands of A has an adjusted basis of $60,000 (and a fair market value of $90,000). A has no gain or loss, and has made a gift of $60,000, the excess of $90,000, the fair market value, over the amount realized, $30,000.

Example (3). A transfers property to his son for $30,000. Such property in A's hands has an adjusted basis of $30,000 (and a fair market value of $60,000). A has no gain and has made a gift of $30,000, the excess of $60,000, the fair market value, over the amount realized, $30,000.

Example (4). A transfers property to his son for $30,000. Such property in A's hands has an adjusted basis of $90,000 (and a fair market value of $60,000). A has sustained no loss, and has made a gift of $30,000, the excess of $60,000, the fair market value, over the amount realized, $30,000.

(f) Sale or other disposition of a term interest in property. (1) *General rule.* Except as otherwise provided in paragraph (f)(3) of this section, for purposes of determining gain or loss from the sale or other disposition after October 9, 1969, of a term interest in property (as defined in paragraph (f)(2) of this section), a taxpayer shall not take into account that portion of the adjusted basis of such interest that is determined pursuant, or by reference, to section 1014 (relating to the basis of property acquired from a decedent), section 1015 (relating to the basis of property acquired by gift or by a transfer in trust), or section 1022 (relating to the basis of property acquired from certain decedents who died in 2010) to the extent that such adjusted basis is a portion of the adjusted uniform basis of the entire property (as defined in § 1.1014–5). Where a term interest in property is transferred to a corporation in connection with a transaction to which section 351 applies and the adjusted basis of the term interest:

(i) Is determined pursuant to sections 1014, 1015, or 1022; and

(ii) Is also a portion of the adjusted uniform basis of the entire property, a subsequent sale or other disposition of such term interest by the corporation will be subject to the provisions of section 1001(e) and this paragraph (f) to the extent that the basis of the term interest so sold or otherwise disposed of is determined by reference to its basis in the hands of the transferor as provided by section 362(a). See paragraph (f)(2) of this section for rules relating to the characterization of stock received by the transferor of a term interest in property in connection with a transaction to which section 351 applies. That portion of the adjusted uniform basis of the entire property that is assignable to such interest at the time of its sale or other disposition shall be determined under the rules provided in § 1.1014–5. Thus, gain or loss realized from a sale or other disposition of a term interest in property shall be determined by comparing the amount of the proceeds of such sale with that part of the adjusted basis of such interest that is not a portion of the adjusted uniform basis of the entire property.

(2) *Term interest defined.* For purposes of section 1001(e) and this paragraph, a "term interest in property" means—

(i) A life interest in property,

(ii) An interest in property for a term of years, or

(iii) An income interest in a trust.

Generally, subdivisions (i), (ii), and (iii) refer to an interest, present or future, in the income from property or the right to use property which will terminate or fail on the lapse of time, on the occurrence of an event or contingency, or on the failure of an event or contingency to occur. Such divisions do not refer to remainder or reversionary interests in the property itself or other interests in the property which will ripen into ownership of the entire property upon termination or failure of a preceding term interest. A "term interest in property" also includes any property received upon a sale or other disposition of a life interest in property, an interest in property for a term of years, or an income interest in a trust by the original holder of such interest, but only to the extent that the adjusted basis of the property received is determined by reference to the adjusted basis of the term interest so transferred.

(3) *Exception.* Paragraph (1) of section 1001(e) and subparagraph (1) of this paragraph shall not apply to a sale or other disposition of a term interest in property as a part of a single transaction in which the entire interest in the property is transferred to a third person or to two or more other persons, including persons who

acquire such entire interest as joint tenants, tenants by the entirety, or tenants in common. See § 1.1014–5 for computation of gain or loss upon such a sale or other disposition where the property has been acquired from a decedent or by gift or transfer in trust.

(4) *Illustrations*. For examples illustrating the application of this paragraph, see paragraph (d) of § 1.1014–5.

* * *

(h) Severances of trusts. (1) *In general.* The severance of a trust (including without limitation a severance that meets the requirements of § 26.2642–6 or of § 26.2654–1(b) of this chapter) is not an exchange of property for other property differing materially either in kind or in extent if—

(i) An applicable state statute or the governing instrument authorizes or directs the trustee to sever the trust; and

(ii) Any non-pro rata funding of the separate trusts resulting from the severance (including non-pro rata funding as described in § 26.2642–6(d)(4) or § 26.2654–1(b)(1)(ii)(C) of this chapter), whether mandatory or in the discretion of the trustee, is authorized by an applicable state statute or the governing instrument.

(2) *Effective/applicability date.* This paragraph (h) applies to severances occurring on or after August 2, 2007. Taxpayers may apply this paragraph (h) to severances occurring on or after August 24, 2004, and before August 2, 2007.

(i) Effective/applicability date. Except as provided in paragraphs (g) and (h) of this section, this section applies on and after January 19, 2017. For rules before January 19, 2017, see § 1.1001–1 as contained in 26 CFR part 1 revised as of April 1, 2016.

[T.D. 6500, 25 FR 11910, Nov. 26, 1960, as amended by T.D. 7142, 36 FR 18950, Sept. 24, 1971; T.D. 7207, 37 FR 20797, Oct. 5, 1972; T.D. 7213, 37 FR 21992, Oct. 18, 1972; T.D. 8517, 59 FR 4807, Feb. 2, 1994; T.D. 8674, 61 FR 30139, June 14, 1996; T.D. 9348, 72 FR 42293, Aug. 2, 2007; T.D. 9729, 80 FR 48250, Aug. 12, 2015; 80 FR 55543, Sept. 16, 2015; T.D. 9811, 82 FR 6240, Jan. 19, 2017; T.D. 10000, 89 FR 56543, July 9, 2024]

Part II. Basis Rules of General Application

§ 1011. Adjusted Basis for Determining Gain or Loss

(a) General rule. The adjusted basis for determining the gain or loss from the sale or other disposition of property, whenever acquired, shall be the basis (determined under section 1012 or other applicable sections of this subchapter and subchapters C (relating to corporate distributions and adjustments), K (relating to partners and partnerships), and P (relating to capital gains and losses)), adjusted as provided in section 1016.

(b) Bargain sale to a charitable organization. If a deduction is allowable under section 170 (relating to charitable contributions) by reason of a sale, then the adjusted basis for determining the gain from such sale shall be that portion of the adjusted basis which bears the same ratio to the adjusted basis as the amount realized bears to the fair market value of the property.

Regulation

§ 1.1011–1 Adjusted basis.

The adjusted basis for determining the gain or loss from the sale or other disposition of property is the cost or other basis prescribed in section 1012 or other applicable provisions of subtitle A of the Code, adjusted to the extent provided in sections 1016, 1017, and 1018 or as otherwise specifically provided for under applicable provisions of internal revenue laws.

[T.D. 6500, 25 FR 11910, Nov. 26, 1960]

§ 1012. Basis of Property—Cost

(a) In general. The basis of property shall be the cost of such property, except as otherwise provided in this subchapter and subchapters C (relating to corporate distributions and adjustments), K (relating to partners and partnerships), and P (relating to capital gains and losses).

(b) Special rule for apportioned real estate taxes. The cost of real property shall not include any amount in respect of real property taxes which are treated under section 164(d) as imposed on the taxpayer.

* * *

Regulations

§ 1.1012–1 Basis of property.

(a) General rule. In general, the basis of property is the cost thereof. The cost is the amount paid for such property in cash or other property. This general rule is subject to exceptions stated in subchapter O (relating to gain or loss on the disposition of property), subchapter C (relating to corporate distributions and adjustments), subchapter K (relating to partners and partnerships), and subchapter P (relating to capital gains and losses), chapter 1 of the Code.

* * *

(c) Sale of stock. (1) *In general.* (i) Except as provided in paragraph (e)(2) of this section (dealing with stock for which the average basis method is permitted), if a taxpayer sells or transfers shares of stock in a corporation that the taxpayer purchased or acquired on different dates or at different prices and the taxpayer does not adequately identify the lot from which the stock is sold or transferred, the stock sold or transferred is charged against the earliest lot the taxpayer purchased or acquired to determine the basis and holding period of the stock. If the earliest lot purchased or acquired is held in a stock certificate that represents multiple lots of stock, and the taxpayer does not adequately identify the lot from which the stock is sold or transferred, the stock sold or transferred is charged against the earliest lot included in the certificate. See paragraphs (c)(2), (c)(3), and (c)(4) of this section for rules on what constitutes an adequate identification.

(ii) A taxpayer must determine the basis of identical stock (within the meaning of paragraph (e)(4) of this section) by averaging the cost of each share if the stock is purchased at separate times on the same calendar day in executing a single trade order and the broker executing the trade provides a single confirmation that reports an aggregate total cost or an average cost per share. However, the taxpayer may determine the basis of the stock by the actual cost per share if the taxpayer notifies the broker in writing of this intent. The taxpayer must notify the broker by the earlier of the date of the sale of any of the stock for which the taxpayer received the confirmation or one year after the date of the confirmation. A broker may extend the one-year period but the taxpayer must notify the broker no later than the date of sale of any of the stock.

(2) *Identification of stock.* An adequate identification is made if it is shown that certificates representing shares of stock from a lot which was purchased or acquired on a certain date or for a certain price were delivered to the taxpayer's transferee. Except as otherwise provided in subparagraph (3) or (4) of this paragraph, such stock certificates delivered to the transferee constitute the stock sold or transferred by the taxpayer. Thus, unless the requirements of subparagraph (3) or (4) of this paragraph are met, the stock sold or transferred is charged to the lot to which the certificates delivered to the transferee belong, whether or not the taxpayer intends, or instructs his broker or other agent, to sell or transfer stock from a lot pur-

chased or acquired on a different date or for a different price.

(3) *Identification on confirmation document.* (i) Where the stock is left in the custody of a broker or other agent, an adequate identification is made if—

(a) At the time of the sale or transfer, the taxpayer specifies to such broker or other agent having custody of the stock the particular stock to be sold or transferred, and

(b) Within a reasonable time thereafter, confirmation of such specification is set forth in a written document from such broker or other agent.

Stock identified pursuant to this subdivision is the stock sold or transferred by the taxpayer, even though stock certificates from a different lot are delivered to the taxpayer's transferee.

(ii) Where a single stock certificate represents stock from different lots, where such certificate is held by the taxpayer rather than his broker or other agent, and where the taxpayer sells a part of the stock represented by such certificate through a broker or other agent, an adequate identification is made if—

(a) At the time of the delivery of the certificate to the broker or other agent, the taxpayer specifies to such broker or other agent the particular stock to be sold or transferred, and

(b) Within a reasonable time thereafter, confirmation of such specification is set forth in a written document from such broker or agent. Where part of the stock represented by a single certificate is sold or transferred directly by the taxpayer to the purchaser or transferee instead of through a broker or other agent, an adequate identification is made if the taxpayer maintains a written record of the particular stock which he intended to sell or transfer.

(4) *Stock held by a trustee, executor, or administrator.* (i) A trustee or executor or administrator of an estate holding stock (not left in the custody of a broker) makes an adequate identification if the trustee, executor, or administrator—

(a) Specifies in writing in the books and records of the trust or estate the particular stock to be sold, transferred, or distributed;

(b) In the case of a distribution, furnishes the distributee with a written document identifying the particular stock distributed; and

(c) In the case of a sale or transfer through a broker or other agent, specifies to the broker or agent the particular stock to be sold or transferred, and within a reasonable time thereafter the broker or agent confirms the specification in a written document.

(ii) The stock the trust or estate identifies under paragraph (c)(4)(i) of this section is the stock treated as sold, transferred, or distributed, even if the trustee, executor, or administrator delivers stock certificates from a different lot.

(5) *Subsequent sales.* If stock identified under subparagraph (3) or (4) of this paragraph as belonging to a particular lot is sold, transferred, or distributed, the stock so identified shall be deemed to have been sold, transferred, or distributed, and such sale, transfer, or distribution will be taken into consideration in identifying the taxpayer's remaining stock for purposes of subsequent sales, transfers, or distributions.

(6) *Bonds.* Paragraphs (1) through (5), (8), and (9) of this section apply to the sale or transfer of bonds.

* * *

(8) *Time for making identification.* For purposes of this paragraph (c), an adequate identification of stock is made at the time of sale, transfer, delivery, or distribution if the identification is made no later than the earlier of the settlement date or the time for settlement required by Rule 15c6–1 under the Securities Exchange Act of 1934, 17 CFR 240.15c6–1 (or its successor). A standing order or instruction for the specific identification of stock is treated as an adequate identification made at the time of sale, transfer, delivery, or distribution.

(9) *Method of writing.* (i) A written confirmation, record, document, instruction, notification, or advice includes a writing in electronic format.

(ii) A broker or agent may include the written confirmation required under this paragraph (c) in an account statement or other document the broker or agent periodically provides to the taxpayer if the broker or agent provides the statement or other document within a reasonable time after the sale or transfer.

(10) *Method for determining basis of stock.* A method of determining the basis of stock, including a

method of identifying stock sold under this paragraph (c) and the average basis method described in paragraph (e) of this section, is not a method of accounting. Therefore, a change in a method of determining the basis of stock is not a change in method of accounting to which sections 446 and 481 apply.

(11) *Effective/applicability date.* Paragraphs (c)(1), (c)(4), (c)(6), (c)(7)(ii), (c)(7)(iii)(a), (c)(8), (c)(9), and (c)(10) of this section apply for taxable years beginning after October 18, 2010.

[T.D. 6500, 25 FR 11910, Nov. 26, 1960, as amended by T.D. 6837, 30 FR 8787, July 13, 1965; T.D. 6887, 31 FR 8814, June 24, 1966; T.D. 6934, 32 FR 15671, 15676, Nov. 14, 1967; T.D. 6984, 33 FR 19176, Dec. 21, 1968; T.D. 7015, 34 FR 9672, June 20, 1969; T.D. 7081, 35 FR 19996, Dec. 31, 1970; T.D. 7129, 36 FR 12736, July 7, 1971; T.D. 7154, 36 FR 24997, Dec. 28, 1971; 36 FR 13208, July 16, 1971; 36 FR 24997, Dec. 28, 1971; T.D. 7213, 37 FR 21992, Oct. 18, 1972; T.D. 7568, 43 FR 47505, Oct. 16, 1978; T.D. 7728, 45 FR 72650, Nov. 3, 1980; T.D. 8517, 59 FR 4807, Feb. 2, 1994; T.D. 8674, 61 FR 30139, June 14, 1996; T.D. 9504, 75 FR 64084, Oct. 18, 2010; T.D. 10000, 89 FR 56545, July 9, 2024]

§ 1.1012–2 Transfers in part a sale and in part a gift.

For rules relating to basis of property acquired in a transfer which is in part a gift and in part a sale, see § 1.170A–4(c), § 1.1011–2(b), and § 1.105–4.

[T.D. 6500, 25 FR 11910, Nov. 26, 1960, as amended by T.D. 7207, 37 FR 20799, Oct. 5, 1972]

§ 1014. Basis of Property Acquired from a Decedent

(a) In general. Except as otherwise provided in this section, the basis of property in the hands of a person acquiring the property from a decedent or to whom the property passed from a decedent shall, if not sold, exchanged, or otherwise disposed of before the decedent's death by such person, be—

(1) the fair market value of the property at the date of the decedent's death, or

(2) in the case of an election under section 2032, its value at the applicable valuation date prescribed by such section,

(3) in the case of an election under section 2032A, its value determined under such section, or

(4) to the extent of the applicability of the exclusion described in section 2031(c), the basis in the hands of the decedent.

(b) Property acquired from the decedent. For purposes of subsection (a), the following property shall be considered to have been acquired from or to have passed from the decedent:

(1) Property acquired by bequest, devise, or inheritance, or by the decedent's estate from the decedent;

(2) Property transferred by the decedent during his lifetime in trust to pay the income for life to or on the order or direction of the decedent, with the right reserved to the decedent at all times before his death to revoke the trust;

(3) In the case of decedents dying after December 31, 1951, property transferred by the decedent during his lifetime in trust to pay the income for life to or on the order or direction of the decedent with the right reserved to the decedent at all times before his death to make any change in the enjoyment thereof through the exercise of a power to alter, amend, or terminate the trust;

(4) Property passing without full and adequate consideration under a general power of appointment exercised by the decedent by will;

(5) In the case of decedents dying after August 26, 1937, and before January 1, 2005, property acquired by bequest, devise, or inheritance or by the decedent's estate from the decedent, if the property consists of stock or securities of a foreign corporation, which with respect to its taxable year next preceding the date of the decedent's death was, under the law applicable to such year, a foreign personal holding company. In such case, the basis shall be the fair market value of such property at the date of the decedent's death or the basis in the hands of the decedent, whichever is lower;

(6) In the case of decedents dying after December 31, 1947, property which represents the surviving spouse's one-half share of community property held by the decedent and the surviving spouse under the community property laws of any State, or possession of the United States or any foreign country, if at least one-half of the whole of the community interest in such property was includible in determining the value of the decedent's gross estate under chapter 11 of subtitle B (section 2001 and following, relating to estate tax) or section 811 of the Internal Revenue Code of 1939;

(7) [Repealed.]

(8) [Repealed.]

(9) In the case of decedents dying after December 31, 1953, property acquired from the decedent by reason of death, form of ownership, or other conditions (including property acquired through the exercise or non-exercise of a power of appointment), if by reason thereof the property is required to be included in determining the value of the decedent's gross estate under chapter 11 of subtitle B or under the Internal Revenue Code of 1939. In such case, if the property is acquired before the death of the decedent, the basis shall be the amount determined under subsection (a) reduced by the amount allowed to the taxpayer as deductions in computing taxable income under this subtitle or prior income tax laws for exhaustion, wear and tear, obsolescence, amortization, and depletion on such property before the death of the decedent. Such basis shall be applicable to the property commencing on the death of the decedent. This paragraph shall not apply to—

(A) annuities described in section 72;

(B) property to which paragraph (5) would apply if the property had been acquired by bequest; and

(C) property described in any other paragraph of this subsection.

(10) Property includible in the gross estate of the decedent under section 2044 (relating to certain property for which marital deduction was previously allowed). In any such case, the last 3 sentences of paragraph (9) shall apply as if such property were described in the first sentence of paragraph (9).

(c) Property representing income in respect of a decedent. This section shall not apply to property which constitutes a right to receive an item of income in respect of a decedent under section 691.

* * *

(e) Appreciated property acquired by decedent by gift within 1 year of death.

(1) In general. In the case of a decedent dying after December 31, 1981, if—

(A) appreciated property was acquired by the decedent by gift during the 1-year period ending on the date of the decedent's death, and

(B) such property is acquired from the decedent by (or passes from the decedent to) the donor of such property (or the spouse of such donor), the basis of such property in the hands of such donor (or spouse) shall be the adjusted basis of such property in the hands of the decedent immediately before the death of the decedent.

(2) Definitions. For purposes of paragraph (1)—

(A) Appreciated property. The term "appreciated property" means any property if the fair market value of such property on the day it was transferred to the decedent by gift exceeds its adjusted basis.

(B) Treatment of certain property sold by estate. In the case of any appreciated property described in subparagraph (A) of paragraph (1) sold by the estate of the decedent or by a trust of which the decedent was the grantor, rules similar to the rules of paragraph (1) shall apply to the extent the donor of such property (or the spouse of such donor) is entitled to the proceeds from such sale.

(f) Basis must be consistent with estate tax return. For purposes of this section—

(1) In general. The basis of any property to which subsection (a) applies shall not exceed

(A) in the case of property the final value of which has been determined for purposes of the tax imposed by chapter 11 on the estate of such decedent, such value, and

(B) in the case of property not described in subparagraph (A) and with respect to which a statement has been furnished under section 6035(a) identifying the value of such property, such value.

(2) Exception. Paragraph (1) shall only apply to any property whose inclusion in the decedent's estate increased the liability for the tax imposed by chapter 11 (reduced by credits allowable against such tax) on such estate.

(3) Determination. For purposes of paragraph (1), the basis of property has been determined for purposes of the tax imposed by chapter 11 if

(A) the value of such property is shown on a return under section 6018 and such value is not contested by the Secretary before the expiration of the time for assessing a tax under chapter 11,

(B) in a case not described in subparagraph (A), the value is specified by the Secretary and such value is not timely contested by the executor of the estate, or

(C) the value is determined by a court or pursuant to a settlement agreement with the Secretary.

(4) Regulations. The Secretary may by regulations provide exceptions to the application of this subsection.

Regulations

§ 1.1014–0 Table of contents. [*Omitted. Ed.*]

[T.D. 9991, Sept. 16, 2024]

§ 1.1014–1 Basis of property acquired from a decedent.

(a) General rule. The purpose of section 1014 is, in general, to provide a basis for property acquired from a decedent that is equal to the value placed upon such property for purposes of the federal estate tax. Accordingly, the general rule is that the basis of property acquired from a decedent is the fair market value of such property at the date of the decedent's death, or, if the decedent's executor so elects, at the alternate valuation date prescribed in section 2032, or in section 811(j) of the Internal Revenue Code (Code) of 1939. However, the basis of property acquired from certain decedents who died in 2010 is determined under section 1022, if the decedent's executor made an election under section 301(c) of the Tax Relief, Unemployment Insurance Reauthorization, and Job Creation Act of 2010, Public Law 111–312 (124 Stat. 3296, 3300 (2010)). See section 1022. Property acquired from a decedent includes, principally, property acquired by bequest, devise, or inheritance, and, in the case of decedents dying after December 31, 1953, property required to be included in determining the value of the decedent's gross estate under any provision of the Code of 1954 or the Code of 1939. For certain property acquired from a decedent, the initial basis of the property must not exceed the property's final value for Federal estate tax purposes. See section 1014(f) and § 1.1014–10 for rules relating to the consistent basis requirement. The general rule governing basis of property acquired from a decedent, as well as other rules prescribed elsewhere in this section, shall have no application if the property is sold, exchanged, or otherwise disposed of before the decedent's death by the person who acquired the property from the decedent. For general rules on the applicable valuation date where the executor of a decedent's estate elects under section 2032, or under section 811(j) of the Code of 1939, to value the decedent's gross estate at the alternate valuation date prescribed in such sections, see § 1.1014–3(e).

* * *

(c) Property to which section 1014 does not apply. Section 1014 has no application to property that constitutes a right to receive an item of income in respect of a decedent under section 691.

(d) Applicability date. This section applies after September 17, 2024. For rules on and before September 17, 2024, see § 1.1014–1 as contained in 26 CFR part 1 revised as of January 19, 2017.

[T.D. 6500, 25 FR 11910, Nov. 26, 1960, as amended by T.D. 6527, 26 FR 413, Jan. 19, 1961; T.D. 6887, 31 FR 8812, June 24, 1966; T.D. 7283, 38 FR 20825, Aug. 3, 1973; T.D. 9811, 82 FR 6240, Jan. 19, 2017; T.D. 9991, 89 FR 76375, Sept. 17, 2024]

§ 1.1014–2 Property acquired from a decedent.

(a) In general. The following property, except where otherwise indicated, is considered to have been acquired from a decedent and the basis thereof is determined in accordance with the general rule in § 1.1014–1:

(1) Without regard to the date of the decedent's death, property acquired by bequest, devise, or inheritance, or by the decedent's estate from the decedent, whether the property was acquired under the decedent's will or under the law governing the descent and distribution of the property of decedents. However, see paragraph (c)(1) of this section if the property was acquired by bequest or inheritance from a decedent dying after August 26, 1937, and if such property consists of stock or securities of a foreign personal holding company.

(2) Without regard to the date of the decedent's death, property transferred by the decedent during his lifetime in trust to pay the income for life to or on the order or direction of the decedent, with the right reserved to the decedent at all times before his death to revoke the trust.

(3) In the case of decedents dying after December 31, 1951, property transferred by the decedent during his lifetime in trust to pay the income for life to or on the order or direction of the decedent with the right reserved to the decedent at all times before his death to make any change in the enjoyment thereof through the exercise of a power to alter, amend, or terminate the trust.

(4) Without regard to the date of the decedent's death, property passing without full and adequate consideration under a general power of appointment exercised by the decedent by will. (See section 2041(b) for definition of general power of appointment.)

(5) In the case of decedents dying after December 31, 1947, property which represents the surviving spouse's one-half share of community property held by the decedent and the surviving spouse under the community property laws of any State, Territory, or possession of the United States or any foreign country, if at least one-half of the whole of the community interest in that property was includible in determining the value of the decedent's gross estate under part III, chapter 11 of the Internal Revenue Code of 1954 (relating to the estate tax) or section 811 of the Internal Revenue Code of 1939. It is not necessary for the application of this subparagraph that an estate tax return be required to be filed for the estate of the decedent or that an estate tax be payable.

* * *

(b) Property acquired from a decedent dying after December 31, 1953. (1) *In general.* In addition to the property described in paragraph (a) of this section, and except as otherwise provided in subparagraph (3) of this paragraph, in the case of a decedent dying after December 31, 1953, property shall also be considered to have been acquired from the decedent to the extent that both of the following conditions are met: (i) The property was acquired from the decedent by reason of death, form of ownership, or other conditions (including property acquired through the exercise or non-exercise of a power of appointment), and (ii) the property is includible in the decedent's gross estate under the provisions of the Internal Revenue Code of 1954, or the Internal Revenue Code of 1939, because of such acquisition. The basis of such property in the hands of the person who acquired it from the decedent shall be determined in accordance with the general rule in § 1.1014–1. See, however, § 1.1014–6 for special adjustments if such property is acquired before the death of the decedent. See also subparagraph (3) of this paragraph for a description of property not within the scope of this paragraph.

(2) *Rules for the application of subparagraph (1) of this paragraph.* Except as provided in § 1.1014–10, it is not necessary for the application of this paragraph (b)(2) that an estate tax return be required to be filed for the estate of the decedent or that an estate tax be payable. It is not necessary for the application of this paragraph that an estate tax return be required to be filed for the estate of the decedent or that an estate tax be payable. Property acquired prior to the death of a

decedent which is includible in the decedent's gross estate, such as property transferred by a decedent in contemplation of death, and property held by a taxpayer and the decedent as joint tenants or as tenants by the entireties is within the scope of this paragraph. Also, this paragraph includes property acquired through the exercise or nonexercise of a power of appointment where such property is includible in the decedent's gross estate. It does not include property not includible in the decedent's gross estate such as property not situated in the United States acquired from a nonresident who is not a citizen of the United States.

(3) *Exceptions to application of this paragraph.* The rules in this paragraph are not applicable to the following property:

(i) Annuities described in section 72;

(ii) Stock or securities of a foreign personal holding company as described in section 1014(b)(5) (see paragraph (c)(1) of this section);

(iii) Property described in any paragraph other than paragraph (9) of section 1014(b). See paragraphs (a) and (c) of this section.

In illustration of subdivision (ii), assume that A acquired by gift stock of a character described in paragraph (c)(1) of this section from a donor and upon the death of the donor the stock was includible in the donor's estate as being a gift in contemplation of death. A's basis in the stock would not be determined by reference to its fair market value at the donor's death under the general rule in section 1014(a). Furthermore, the special basis rules prescribed in paragraph (c)(1) of this section are not applicable to such property acquired by gift in contemplation of death. It will be necessary to refer to the rules in section 1015(a) to determine the basis.

(c) Special basis rules with respect to certain property acquired from a decedent. (1) *Stock or securities of a foreign personal holding company.* The basis of certain stock or securities of a foreign corporation which was a foreign personal holding company with respect to its taxable year next preceding the date of the decedent's death is governed by a special rule. If such stock was acquired from a decedent dying after August 26, 1937, by bequest or inheritance, or by the decedent's estate from the decedent, the basis of the property in the hands of the person who so acquired it (notwithstanding any other provision of section 1014) shall be the fair market value of such property at the date of the decedent's death or the adjusted basis of the stock in the hands of the decedent, whichever is lower.

* * *

[T.D. 6500, 25 FR 11910, Nov. 26, 1960; T.D 9991, 89 FR 76375, Sept. 17, 2024]

§ 1.1014–3 Other basis rules.

(a) Fair market value. For purposes of this section and § 1.1014–1, the value of property as of the date of the decedent's death as appraised for the purpose of the Federal estate tax or the alternate value as appraised for such purpose, whichever is applicable, shall be deemed to be its fair market value. If no estate tax return is required to be filed under section 6018 (or under section 821 or 864 of the Internal Revenue Code of 1939), the value of the property appraised as of the date of the decedent's death for the purpose of State inheritance or transmission taxes shall be deemed to be its fair market value and no alternate valuation date shall be applicable.

* * *

(c) Reinvestments by a fiduciary. The basis of property acquired after the death of the decedent by a fiduciary as an investment is the cost or other basis of such property to the fiduciary, and not the fair market value of such property at the death of the decedent. For example, the executor of an estate purchases stock of X company at a price of $100 per share with the proceeds of the sale of property acquired from a decedent. At the date of the decedent's death the fair market value of such stock was $98 per share. The basis of such stock to the executor or to a legatee, assuming the stock is distributed, is $100 per share.

(d) Reinvestments of property transferred during life. Where property is transferred by a decedent during life and the property is sold, exchanged, or otherwise disposed of before the decedent's death by the person who acquired the property from the decedent, the general rule stated in paragraph (a) of § 1.1014–1 shall not apply to such property. However, in such a case, the basis of any property acquired by such donee in exchange for the original property, or of any property acquired by the donee through reinvesting the proceeds of the sale of the original property, shall be the fair market value of the property thus acquired at the date of the decedent's death (or applicable alternate valuation date) if the property thus acquired is properly included in the decedent's gross estate for Federal estate tax purposes. These rules also apply to property acquired by the donee in any further exchanges or in further reinvestments. For example, on January 1, 1956, the decedent made a gift of real property to a trust for the benefit of his children, reserving to himself the power to revoke the trust at will. Prior to the decedent's death, the trustee sold the real property and invested the proceeds in stock of the Y Company at $50 per share. At the time of the decedent's death, the value of such stock was $75 per share. The corpus of the trust was required to be included in the decedent's gross estate owing to his reservation of the power of revocation. The basis of the Y company stock following the decedent's death is $75 per share. Moreover, if the trustee sold the Y Company stock before the decedent's death for $65 a share and reinvested the proceeds in Z company stock which increased in value to $85 per share at the time of the decedent's death, the basis of the Z company stock following the decedent's death would be $85 per share.

(e) Alternate valuation dates. Section 1014(a) provides a special rule applicable in determining the basis of property described in § 1.1014–2 where

(1) The property is includible in the gross estate of a decedent who died after October 21, 1942, and

(2) The executor elects for estate tax purposes under section 2032, or section 811(j) of the Internal Revenue Code of 1939, to value the decedent's gross estate at the alternate valuation date prescribed in such sections.

In those cases, the value applicable in determining the basis of the property is not the value at the date of the decedent's death but (with certain limitations) the value at the date one year after his death if not distributed, sold, exchanged, or otherwise disposed of in the meantime. If such property was distributed, sold, exchanged, or otherwise disposed of within one year after the date of the decedent's death by the person who acquired it from the decedent, the value applicable in determining the basis is its value as of the date of such distribution, sale, exchange, or other disposition. For illustrations of the operation of this paragraph, see the estate tax regulations under section 2032.

[T.D. 6500, 25 FR 11910, Nov. 26, 1960]

§ 1.1014–4 Uniformity of basis; adjustment to basis.

(a) In general. (1) The basis of property acquired from a decedent, as determined under section 1014(a) or section 1022, is uniform in the hands of every person having possession or enjoyment of the property at any time under the will or other instrument or under the laws of descent and distribution. The principle of uniform basis means that the basis of the property (to which proper adjustments must, of course, be made) will be the same, or uniform, whether the property is possessed or enjoyed by the executor or administrator, the heir, the legatee or devisee, or the trustee or beneficiary of a trust created by a will or an inter vivos trust. In determining the amount allowed or allowable to a taxpayer in computing taxable income as deductions for depreciation or depletion under section 1016(a)(2), the uniform basis of the property shall at all times be used and adjusted. The sale, exchange, or other disposition by a life tenant or remainderman of his interest in property will, for purposes of this section, have no effect upon the uniform basis of the property in the hands of those who acquired it from the decedent. Thus, gain or loss on sale of trust assets by the trustee will be determined without regard to the prior sale of any interest in the property. Moreover, any adjustment for depreciation shall be made to the uniform basis of the property without regard to such prior sale, exchange, or other disposition.

(2) Under the law governing wills and the distribution of the property of decedents, all titles to property acquired by bequest, devise, or inheritance relate back to the death of the decedent, even though the interest of the person taking the title was, at the date of death of the decedent, legal, equitable, vested, contingent, general, specific, residual, conditional, executory, or otherwise. Accordingly, there is a common acquisition date for all titles to property acquired from a decedent within the meaning of section 1014 or section 1022, and, for this reason, a common or uniform basis for all such interests. For example, if distribution of personal property left by a decedent is not made until one year after his death, the basis of such property in the hands of the legatee is its fair market value at the time when the decedent died, and not when the legatee actually received the property. If the bequest is of the residue to trustees in trust, and the executors do not distribute the residue to such trustees until five years after the death

of the decedent, the basis of each piece of property left by the decedent and thus received, in the hands of the trustees, is its fair market value at the time when the decedent dies. If the bequest is to trustees in trust to pay to A during his lifetime the income of the property bequeathed, and after his death to distribute such property to the survivors of a class, and upon A's death the property is distributed to the taxpayer as the sole survivor, the basis of such property, in the hands of the taxpayer, is its fair market value at the time when the decedent died. The purpose of the Code in prescribing a general uniform basis rule for property acquired from a decedent is, on the one hand, to tax the gain, in respect of such property, to him who realizes it (without regard to the circumstances that at the death of the decedent it may have been quite uncertain whether the taxpayer would take or gain anything); and, on the other hand, not to recognize as gain any element of value resulting solely from the circumstance that the possession or enjoyment of the taxpayer was postponed. Such postponement may be, for example, until the administration of the decedent's estate is completed, until the period of the possession or enjoyment of another has terminated, or until an uncertain event has happened. It is the increase or decrease in the value of property reflected in a sale or other disposition which is recognized as the measure of gain or loss.

(3) The principles stated in subparagraphs (1) and (2) of this paragraph do not apply to property transferred by an executor, administrator or trustee, to an heir, legatee, devisee or beneficiary under circumstances such that the transfer constitutes a sale or exchange. In such a case, gain or loss must be recognized by the transferor to the extent required by the revenue laws, and the transferee acquires a basis equal to the fair market value of the property on the date of the transfer. Thus, for example, if the trustee of a trust created by will transfers to a beneficiary, in satisfaction of a specific bequest of $10,000, securities which had a fair market value of $9,000 on the date of the decedent's death (the applicable valuation date) and $10,000 on the date of the transfer, the trust realizes a taxable gain of $1,000 and the basis of the securities in the hands of the beneficiary would be $10,000. As a further example, if the executor of an estate transfers to a trust property worth $200,000, which had a fair market value of $175,000 on the date of the decedent's death (the applicable valuation date), in satisfaction of the decedent's bequest in trust for the benefit of his wife of cash or securities to be selected by the executor in an amount sufficient to utilize the marital deduction to the maximum extent authorized by law (after taking into consideration any other property qualifying for the marital deduction), capital gain in the amount of $25,000 would be realized by the estate and the basis of the property in the hands of the trustees would be $200,000. If, on the other hand, the decedent bequeathed a fraction of his residuary estate to a trust for the benefit of his wife, which fraction will not change regardless of any fluctuations in value of property in the decedent's estate after his death, no gain or loss would be realized by the estate upon transfer of property to the trust, and the basis of the property in the hands of the trustee would be its fair market value on the date of the decedent's death or on the alternate valuation date.

(b) Multiple interests. Where more than one person has an interest in property acquired from a decedent, the basis of such property shall be determined and adjusted without regard to the multiple interests. The basis of computing gain or loss on the sale of any one of such multiple interests shall be determined under § 1.1014–5. Thus, the deductions for depreciation and for depletion allowed or allowable, under sections 167 and 611, to a legal life tenant as if the life tenant were the absolute owner of the property, constitute an adjustment to the basis of the property not only in the hands of the life tenant, but also in the hands of the remainderman and every other person to whom the same uniform basis is applicable. Similarly, the deductions allowed or allowable under sections 167 and 611, both to the trustee and to the trust beneficiaries, constitute an adjustment to the basis of the property not only in the hands of the trustee, but also in the hands of the trust beneficiaries and every other person to whom the uniform basis is applicable. See, however, section 262. Similarly, adjustments in respect of capital expenditures or losses, tax-free distributions, or other distributions applicable in reduction of basis, or other items for which the basis is adjustable are made without regard to which one of the persons to whom the same uniform basis is applicable makes the capital expenditures or sustains the capital losses, or to whom the tax-free or other distributions are made, or to whom the deductions are allowed or allowable. See § 1.1014–6 for adjustments in respect of property acquired from a decedent prior to his death.

(c) Records. The executor or other legal representative of the decedent, the fiduciary of a trust under a will, the life tenant and every other person to whom a uniform basis under this section is applicable, shall maintain records showing in detail all deductions, distributions, or other items for which adjustment to basis is required to be made by sections 1016 and 1017, and shall furnish to the district director such information with respect to those adjustments as he may require.

(d) Effective/applicability date. This section applies on and after January 19, 2017. For rules before January 19, 2017, see § 1.1014–4 as contained in 26 CFR part 1 revised as of April 1, 2016.

[T.D. 6500, 25 FR 11910, Nov. 26, 1960; T.D. 9811, 82 FR 6241, Jan. 19, 2017]

§ 1.1014–5 Gain or loss.

(a) Sale or other disposition of a life interest, remainder interest, or other interest in property acquired from a decedent. (1) Except as provided in paragraph (b) or (c) of this section with respect to the sale or other disposition after October 9, 1969, of a term interest in property, gain or loss from a sale or other disposition of a life interest, remainder interest, or other interest in property acquired from a decedent is determined by comparing the amount of the proceeds with the amount of that part of the adjusted uniform basis which is assignable to the interest so transferred. The adjusted uniform basis is the uniform basis of the entire property adjusted to the date of sale or other disposition of any such interest as required by sections 1016 and 1017. The uniform basis is the unadjusted basis of the entire property determined immediately after the decedent's death under the applicable sections of part II of subchapter O of chapter 1 of the Code.

(2) Except as provided in paragraph (b) of this section, the proper measure of gain or loss resulting from a sale or other disposition of an interest in property acquired from a decedent is so much of the increase or decrease in the value of the entire property as is reflected in such sale or other disposition. Hence, in ascertaining the basis of a life interest, remainder interest, or other interest which has been so transferred, the uniform basis rule contemplates that proper adjustments will be made to reflect the change in relative value of the interests on account of the passage of time.

(3) The factors set forth in the tables contained in § 20.2031–7 or, for certain prior periods, § 20.2031–7A, of part 20 of this chapter (Estate Tax Regulations) shall be used in the manner provided therein in determining the basis of the life interest, the remainder interest, or the term certain interest in the property on the date such interest is sold. The basis of the life interest, the remainder interest, or the term certain interest is computed by multiplying the uniform basis (adjusted to the time of the sale) by the appropriate factor. In the case of the sale of a life interest or a remainder interest, the factor used is the factor (adjusted where appropriate) which appears in the life interest or the remainder interest column of the table opposite the age (on the date of the sale) of the person at whose death the life interest will terminate. In the case of the sale of a term certain interest, the factor used is the factor (adjusted where appropriate) which appears in the term certain column of the table opposite the number of years remaining (on the date of sale) before the term certain interest will terminate.

(b) Sale or other disposition of certain term interests. (1) *In general.* In determining gain or loss from the sale or other disposition after October 9, 1969, of a term interest in property (as defined in § 1.1001–1(f)(2)) the adjusted basis of which is determined pursuant, or by reference, to section 1014 (relating to the basis of property acquired from a decedent), section 1015 (relating to the basis of property acquired by gift or by a transfer in trust), or section 1022 (relating to the basis of property acquired from certain decedents who died in 2010), that part of the adjusted uniform basis assignable under the rules of paragraph (a) of this section to the interest sold or otherwise disposed of shall be disregarded to the extent and in the manner provided by section 1001(e) and § 1.1001–1(f).

(2) *Effective/applicability date.* The provisions of paragraph (b)(1) of this section relating to section 1022 are effective on and after January 19, 2017. For rules before January 19, 2017, see § 1.1014–5 as contained in 26 CFR part 1 revised as of April 1, 2016.

(c) Sale or other disposition of a term interest in a tax-exempt trust. (1) *In general.* In the case of any sale or other disposition by a taxable beneficiary of a term interest (as defined in § 1.1001–1(f)(2)) in a tax-exempt trust (as defined in paragraph (c)(2) of this section) to which section 1001(e)(3) applies, the taxable beneficiary's share of adjusted uniform basis, determined as of (and immediately before) the sale or disposition of that interest, is—

(i) That part of the adjusted uniform basis assignable to the term interest of the taxable beneficiary under the rules of paragraph (a) of this section reduced, but not below zero, by

(ii) An amount determined by applying the same actuarial share applied in paragraph (c)(1)(i) of this section to the sum of—

(A) The trust's undistributed net ordinary income within the meaning of section 664(b)(1) and § 1.664–1(d)(1)(ii)(a)(1) for the current and prior taxable years of the trust, if any; and

(B) The trust's undistributed net capital gains within the meaning of section 664(b)(2) and § 1.664–1(d)(1)(ii)(a)(2) for the current and prior taxable years of the trust, if any.

(2) *Tax-exempt trust defined.* For purposes of this section, the term tax-exempt trust means a charitable remainder annuity trust or a charitable remainder unitrust as defined in section 664.

(3) *Taxable beneficiary defined.* For purposes of this section, the term taxable beneficiary means any person other than an organization described in section 170(c) or exempt from taxation under section 501(a).

(4) *Effective/applicability date.* This paragraph (c) and paragraph (d) Example 7 and Example 8 of this section apply to sales and other dispositions of interests in tax-exempt trusts occurring on or after January 16, 2014, except for sales or dispositions occurring pursuant to a binding commitment entered into before January 16, 2014.

(d) Illustrations. The application of this section may be illustrated by the following examples, in which references are made to the actuarial tables contained in part 20 of this chapter (Estate Tax Regulations):

Example 1. Securities worth $500,000 at the date of decedent's death on January 1, 1971, are bequeathed to his wife, W, for life, with remainder over to his son, S. W is 48 years of age when the life interest is acquired. The estate does not elect the alternate valuation allowed by section 2032. By reference to § 20.2031–7A(c), the life estate factor for age 48, female, is found to be 0.77488 and the remainder factor for such age is found to be 0.22512. Therefore, the present value of the portion of the uniform basis assigned to W's life interest is $387,440 ($500,000 x 0.77488), and the present value of the portion of the uniform basis assigned to S's remainder interest is $112,560 ($500,000 x 0.22512). W sells her life interest to her nephew, A, on February 1, 1971, for $370,000, at which time W is still 48 years of age. Pursuant to section 1001(e), W realizes no loss; her gain is $370,000, the amount realized from the sale. A has a basis of $370,000 which he can recover by amortization deductions over W's life expectancy.

Example 2. The facts are the same as in example (1) except that W retains the life interest for 12 years, until she is 60 years of age, and then sells it to A on February 1, 1983, when the fair market value of the securities has increased to $650,000. By reference to § 20.2031–7A(c), the life estate factor for age 60, female, is found to be 0.63226 and the remainder factor for such age is found to be 0.36774. Therefore, the present value on February 1, 1983, of the portion of the uniform basis assigned to W's life interest is $316,130 ($500,000 x 0.63226) and the present value on that date of the portion of the uniform basis assigned to S's remainder interest is $183,870 ($500,000 x 0.36774). W sells her life interest for $410,969, that being the commuted value of her remaining life interest in the securities as appreciated ($650,000 x 0.63226). Pursuant to section 1001(e), W's gain is $410,969, the amount realized. A has a basis of $410,969 which he can recover by amortization deductions over W's life expectancy.

Example 3. Unimproved land having a fair market value of $18,800 at the date of the decedent's death on January 1, 1970, is devised to A, a male, for life, with remainder over to B, a female. The estate does not elect the alternate valuation allowed by section 2032. On January 1, 1971, A sells his life interest to S for $12,500. S is not related to A or B. At the time of the sale, A is 39 years of age. By reference to § 20.2031–7A(c), the life estate factor for age 39, male, is found to be 0.79854. Therefore, the present value of the portion of the uniform basis assigned to A's life interest is $15,012.55 ($18,800 x 0.79854). This portion is disregarded under section 1001(e). A realizes no loss; his gain is $12,500, the amount realized. S has a basis of

$12,500 which he can recover by amortization deductions over A's life expectancy.

Example 4. The facts are the same as in example (3) except that on January 1, 1971, A and B jointly sell the entire property to S for $25,000 and divide the proceeds equally between them. A and B are not related, and there is no element of gift or compensation in the transaction. By reference to § 20.2031–7A(c), the remainder factor for age 39, male, is found to be 0.20146. Therefore, the present value of the uniform basis assigned to B's remainder interest is $3,787.45 ($18,800 x 0.20146). On the sale A realizes a loss of $2,512.55 ($15,012.55 less $12,500), the portion of the uniform basis assigned to his life interest not being disregarded by reason of section 1001(e)(3). B's gain on the sale is $8,712.55 ($12,500 less $3,787.45). S has a basis in the entire property of $25,000, no part of which, however, can be recovered by amortization deductions over A's life expectancy.

Example 5. (a) Nondepreciable property having a fair market value of $54,000 at the date of decedent's death on January 1, 1971, is devised to her husband, H, for life and, after his death, to her daughter, D, for life, with remainder over to her grandson, G. The estate does not elect the alternate valuation allowed by section 2032. On January 1, 1973, H sells his life interest to D for $32,000. At the date of the sale, H is 62 years of age, and D is 45 years of age. By reference to § 20.2031–7A(c), the life estate factor for age 62, male, is found to be 0.52321. Therefore, the present value on January 1, 1973, of the portion of the adjusted uniform basis assigned to H's life interest is $28,253 ($54,000 x 0.52321). Pursuant to section 1001(e), H realizes no loss; his gain is $32,000, the amount realized from the sale. D has a basis of $32,000 which she can recover by amortization deductions over H's life expectancy.

(b) On January 1, 1976, D sells both life estates to G for $40,000. During each of the years 1973 through 1975, D is allowed a deduction for the amortization of H's life interest. At the date of the sale H is 65 years of age, and D is 48 years of age. For purposes of determining gain or loss on the sale by D, the portion of the adjusted uniform basis assigned to H's life interest and the portion assigned to D's life interest are not taken into account under section 1001(e). However, pursuant to § 1.1001–1(f)(1), D's cost basis in H's life interest, minus deductions for the amortization of such interest, is taken into account. On the sale, D realizes gain of $40,000 minus an amount which is equal to the $32,000 cost basis (for H's life estate) reduced by amortization deductions. G is entitled to amortize over H's life expectancy that part of the $40,000 cost which is attributable to H's life interest. That part of the $40,000 cost which is attributable to D's life interest is not amortizable by G until H dies.

Example 6. Securities worth $1,000,000 at the date of decedent's death on January 1, 1971, are bequeathed to his wife, W, for life, with remainder over to his son, S. W is 48 years of age when the life interest is acquired. The estate does not elect the alternate valuation allowed by section 2032. By reference to § 20.2031–7A(c), the life estate factor for age 48, female, is found to be 0.77488, and the remainder factor for such age is found to be 0.22512. Therefore, the present value of the portion of the uniform basis assigned to W's life interest is $774,880 ($1,000,000 x 0.77488), and the present value of the portion of the uniform basis assigned to S's remainder interest is $225,120 ($1,000,000 x 0.22512). On February 1, 1971, W transfers her life interest to corporation X in exchange for all of the stock of X pursuant to a transaction in which no gain or loss is recognized by reason of section 351. On February 1, 1972, W sells all of her stock in X to S for $800,000. Pursuant to section 1001(e) and § 1.1001–1(f)(2), W realizes no loss; her gain is $800,000, the amount realized from the sale. On February 1, 1972, X sells to N for $900,000 the life interest transferred to it by W. Pursuant to section 1001(e) and § 1.1001–1(f)(1), X realizes no loss; its gain is $900,000, the amount realized from the sale. N has a basis of $900,000 which he can recover by amortization deductions over W's life expectancy.

Example 7. (a) Grantor creates a charitable remainder unitrust (CRUT) on Date 1 in which Grantor retains a unitrust interest and irrevocably transfers the remainder interest to Charity. Grantor is an individual taxpayer subject to income tax. CRUT meets the requirements of section 664 and is exempt from income tax.

(b) Grantor's basis in the shares of X stock used to fund CRUT is $10x. On Date 2, CRUT sells the X stock for $100x. The $90x of gain is exempt from income tax under section 664(c)(1). On Date 3, CRUT uses the $100x proceeds from its sale of the X stock to purchase Y stock. On Date 4, CRUT sells the Y stock for $110x. The $10x of gain on the sale of the Y stock is exempt from income tax under section 664(c)(1). On Date 5, CRUT uses the $110x proceeds from its sale of Y stock to buy Z stock. On Date 5, CRUT's basis in its assets is $110x and CRUT's total undistributed net capital gains are $100x.

(c) Later, when the fair market value of CRUT's assets is $150x and CRUT has no undistributed net ordinary income, Grantor and Charity sell all of their interests in CRUT to a third person. Grantor receives $100x for the retained unitrust interest, and Charity receives $50x for its interest. Because the entire interest in CRUT is transferred to the third person, section 1001(e)(3) prevents section 1001(e)(1) from applying to the transaction. Therefore, Grantor's gain on the sale of the retained unitrust interest in CRUT is determined under section 1001(a), which provides that Grantor's gain on the sale of that interest is the excess of the amount realized, $100x, over Grantor's adjusted basis in the interest.

(d) Grantor's adjusted basis in the unitrust interest in CRUT is that portion of CRUT's adjusted uniform basis that is assignable to Grantor's interest under § 1.1014–5, which is Grantor's actuarial share of the adjusted uniform basis. In this case, CRUT's adjusted uniform basis in its sole asset, the Z stock, is $110x. However, paragraph (c) of this section applies to the transaction. Therefore, Grantor's actuarial share of CRUT's adjusted uniform basis (determined by applying the factors set forth in the tables contained in § 20.2031–7 of this chapter) is reduced by an amount determined by applying the same factors to the sum of CRUT's $0 of undistributed net ordinary income and its $100x of undistributed net capital gains.

(e) In determining Charity's share of the adjusted uniform basis, Charity applies the factors set forth in the tables contained in § 20.2031–7 of this chapter to the full $110x of basis.

Example 8. (a) Grantor creates a charitable remainder annuity trust (CRAT) on Date 1 in which Grantor retains an annuity interest and irrevocably transfers the remainder interest to Charity. Grantor is an individual taxpayer subject to income tax. CRAT meets the requirements of section 664 and is exempt from income tax.

(b) Grantor funds CRAT with shares of X stock having a basis of $50x. On Date 2, CRAT sells the X stock for $150x. The $100x of gain is exempt from income tax under section 664(c)(1). On Date 3, CRAT distributes $10x to Grantor, and uses the remaining $140x of net proceeds from its sale of the X stock to purchase Y stock. Grantor treats the $10x distribution as capital gain, so that CRAT's remaining undistributed net capital gains amount described in section 664(b)(2) and § 1.664–1(d) is $90x.

(c) On Date 4, when the fair market value of CRAT's assets, which consist entirely of the Y stock, is still $140x, Grantor and Charity sell all of their interests in CRAT to a third person. Grantor receives $126x for the retained annuity interest, and Charity receives $14x for its remainder interest. Because the entire interest in CRAT is transferred to the third person, section 1001(e)(3) prevents section 1001(e)(1) from applying to the transaction. Therefore, Grantor's gain on the sale of the retained annuity interest in CRAT is determined under section 1001(a), which provides that Grantor's gain on the sale of that interest is the excess of the amount realized, $126x, over Grantor's adjusted basis in that interest.

(d) Grantor's adjusted basis in the annuity interest in CRAT is that portion of CRAT's adjusted uniform basis that is assignable to Grantor's interest under § 1.1014–5, which is Grantor's actuarial share of the adjusted uniform basis. In this case, CRAT's adjusted uniform basis in its sole asset, the Y stock, is $140x. However, paragraph (c) of this section applies to the transaction. Therefore, Grantor's actuarial share of CRAT's adjusted uniform basis (determined by applying the factors set forth in the tables contained in § 20.2031–7 of this chapter) is reduced by an amount determined by applying the same factors to the sum of CRAT's $0 of undistributed net ordinary income and its $90x of undistributed net capital gains.

(e) In determining Charity's share of the adjusted uniform basis, Charity applies the factors set forth in the tables contained in § 20.2031–7 of this chapter to determine its actuarial share of the full $140x of basis.

[T.D. 6500, 25 FR 11910, Nov. 26, 1960, as amended by T.D. 7142, 36 FR 18951, Sept. 24, 1971; T.D. 8540, 59 FR 30102, June 10, 1994; T.D. 9729, 80 FR 48250, Aug. 12, 2015; 80 FR 55543, Sept. 16, 2015; T.D. 9811, 82 FR 6241, Jan. 19, 2017]

§ 1.1014–6 Special rule for adjustments to basis where property is acquired from a decedent prior to his death.

(a) In general. (1) The basis of property described in section 1014(b)(9) which is acquired from a decedent prior to his death shall be adjusted for depreciation, obsolescence, amortization, and depletion allowed the taxpayer on such property for the period prior to the decedent's death. Thus, in general, the adjusted basis of such property will be its fair market value at the decedent's death, or the applicable alternate valuation date, less the amount allowed (determined with regard to section 1016(a)(2)(B)) to the taxpayer as deductions for exhaustion, wear and tear, obsolescence, amortization, and depletion for the period held by the taxpayer prior to the decedent's death. The deduction allowed for a taxable year in which the decedent dies shall be an amount properly allocable to that part of the year prior to his death. For a discussion of the basis adjustment required by section 1014(b)(9) where property is held in trust, see paragraph (c) of this section.

(2) Where property coming within the purview of subparagraph (1) of this paragraph was held by the decedent and his surviving spouse as tenants by the entirety or as joint tenants with right of survivorship, and joint income tax returns were filed by the decedent and the surviving spouse in which the deductions referred to in subparagraph (1) were taken, there shall be allocated to the surviving spouse's interest in the property that proportion of the deductions allowed for each period for which the joint returns were filed which her income from the property bears to the total income from the property. Each spouse's income from the property shall be determined in accordance with local law.

(3) The application of this paragraph may be illustrated by the following examples:

Example (1). The taxpayer acquired incomeproducing property by gift on January 1, 1954. The property had a fair market value of $50,000 on the date of the donor's death, January 1, 1956, and was included in his gross estate at that amount for estate tax purposes as a transfer in contemplation of death. Depreciation in the amount of $750 per year was allowable for each of the taxable years 1954 and 1955. However, the taxpayer claimed depreciation in the amount of $500 for each of these years (resulting in a reduction in his taxes) and his income tax returns were accepted as filed. The adjusted basis of the property as of the date of the decedent's death is $49,000 ($50,000, the fair market value at the decedent's death, less $1,000, the total of the amounts actually allowed as deductions).

Example (2). On July 1, 1952, H purchased for $30,000 income-producing property which he conveyed to himself and W, his wife, as tenants by the entirety. Under local law each spouse was entitled to one-half of the income therefrom. H died on January 1, 1955, at which time the fair market value of the property was $40,000. The entire value of the property was included in H's gross estate. H and W filed joint income tax returns for the years 1952, 1953, and 1954. The total depreciation allowance for the year 1952 was $500 and for each of the other years 1953 and 1954 was $1,000. One-half of the $2,500 depreciation will be allocated to W. The adjusted basis of the property in W's hands on January 1, 1955, was $38,750 ($40,000, value on the date of H's death, less $1,250, depreciation allocated to W for periods before H's death). However, if, under local law, all of the income from the property was allocable to H, no adjustment under this paragraph would be required and W's basis for the property as of the date of H's death would be $40,000.

(b) Multiple interests in property described in section 1014(b)(9) and acquired from a decedent prior to his death. (1) Where more than one person has an interest in property described in section 1014(b)(9) which was acquired from a decedent before his death, the basis of such property and of each of the several interests therein shall, in general, be determined and adjusted in accordance with the principles contained in §§ 1.1014–4 and 1.1014–5, relating to the uniformity of basis rule. Application of these principles to the determination of basis under section 1014(b)(9) is shown in the remaining subparagraphs of this paragraph in connection with certain commonly encountered situations involving multiple interests in property acquired from a decedent before his death.

(2) Where property is acquired from a decedent before his death, and the entire property is subsequently included in the decedent's gross estate for estate tax purposes, the uniform basis of the property, as well as the basis of each of the several interests in the property, shall be determined by taking into account the basis adjustments required by section 1014(a) owing to such inclusion of the entire property in the decedent's

gross estate. For example, suppose that the decedent transfers property in trust, with a life estate to A, and the remainder to B or his estate. The transferred property consists of 100 shares of the common stock of X Corporation, with a basis of $10,000 at the time of the transfer. At the time of the decedent's death the value of the stock is $20,000. The transfer is held to have been made in contemplation of death and the entire value of the trust is included in the decedent's gross estate. Under section 1014(a), the uniform basis of the property in the hands of the trustee, the life tenant, and the remainderman, is $20,000. If immediately prior to the decedent's death, A's share of the uniform basis of $10,000 was $6,000, and B's share was $4,000, then, immediately after the decedent's death, A's share of the uniform basis of $20,000 is $12,000, and B's share is $8,000.

(3)(i) In cases where, due to the operation of the estate tax, only a portion of property acquired from a decedent before his death is included in the decedent's gross estate, as in cases where the decedent retained a reversion to take effect upon the expiration of a life estate in another, the uniform basis of the entire property shall be determined by taking into account any basis adjustments required by section 1014(a) owing to such inclusion of a portion of the property in the decedent's gross estate. In such cases the uniform basis is the adjusted basis of the entire property immediately prior to the decedent's death increased (or decreased) by an amount which bears the same relation to the total appreciation (or diminution) in value of the entire property (over the adjusted basis of the entire property immediately prior to the decedent's death) as the value of the property included in the decedent's gross estate bears to the value of the entire property. For example, assume that the decedent creates a trust to pay the income to A for life, remainder to B or his estate. The trust instrument further provides that if the decedent should survive A, the income shall be paid to the decedent for life. Assume that the decedent predeceases A, so that, due to the operation of the estate tax, only the present value of the remainder interest is included in the decedent's gross estate. The trust consists of 100 shares of the common stock of X Corporation with an adjusted basis immediately prior to the decedent's death of $10,000 (as determined under section 1015). At the time of the decedent's death, the value of the stock is $20,000, and the value of the remainder interest in the hands of B is $8,000. The uniform basis of the entire property following the decedent's death is $14,000, computed as follows:

Uniform basis prior to decedent's death	$10,000
plus	
Increase in uniform basis (determined by the following formula)	4,000

$$\frac{\text{Increase in uniform basis (to be determined)}}{\$10{,}000 \text{ (total appreciation)}} = \frac{\$8{,}000 \text{ (value of property included in gross estate)}}{\$20{,}000 \text{ (value of entire property)}}$$

Uniform basis under section 1014(a)	14,000

(ii) In cases of the type described in subdivision (i) of this subparagraph, the basis of any interest which is included in the decedent's gross estate may be ascertained by adding to (or subtracting from) the basis of such interest determined immediately prior to the decedent's death the increase (or decrease) in the uniform basis of the property attributable to the inclusion of the interest in the decedent's gross estate. Where the interest is sold or otherwise disposed of at any time after the decedent's death, proper adjustment must be made in order to reflect the change in value of the interest on account of the passage of time, as provided in § 1.1014–5. For an illustration of the operation of this subdivision, see step 6 of the example in § 1.1014–7.

(iii) In cases of the type described in subdivision (i) of this subparagraph (cases where, due to the operation of the estate tax, only a portion of the property is included in the decedent's gross estate), the basis for computing the depreciation, amortization, or depletion allowance shall be the uniform basis of the property determined under section 1014(a). However, the manner of taking into account such allowance computed with respect to such uniform basis is subject to the following limitations:

(a) In cases where the value of the life interest is not included in the decedent's gross estate, the amount of such allowance to the life tenant under section 167(h) (or section 611(b)) shall not exceed (or be less than) the amount which would have been allowable to the life tenant if no portion of the basis of the property was determined under section 1014(a). Proper adjustment shall be made for the amount allowable to the life tenant, as required by section 1016. Thus, an appropriate adjustment shall be made to the uniform basis of the property in the hands of the trustee, to the basis of the life interest in the hands of the life tenant, and to the basis of the remainder in the hands of the remainderman.

(b) Any remaining allowance (that is, the increase in the amount of depreciation, amortization, or depletion allowable resulting from any increase in the uniform basis of the property under section 1014(a)) shall not be allowed to the life tenant. The remaining allowance shall, instead, be allowed to the trustee to the extent that the trustee both (1) is required or permitted, by the governing trust instrument (or under local law), to maintain a reserve for depreciation, amortization, or depletion, and (2) actually maintains such a reserve. If, in accordance with the preceding sentence, the trustee does maintain such a reserve, the remaining allowance shall be taken into account, under section 1016, in adjusting the uniform basis of the property in the hands of the trustee and in adjusting the basis of the remainder interest in the hands of the remainderman, but shall not be taken into account, under section 1016, in determining the basis of the life interest in the hands of the life tenant. For an example of the operation of this subdivision, see paragraph (b) of § 1.1014–7.

(4) In cases where the basis of any interest in property is not determined under section 1014(a), as where such interest (i) is not included in the decedent's gross estate, or (ii) is sold, exchanged or otherwise disposed of before the decedent's death, the basis of such interest shall be determined under other applicable provisions of the Code. To illustrate, in the example shown in subparagraph (3)(i) of this paragraph the basis of the life estate in the hands of A shall be determined under section 1015, relating to the basis of property acquired by gift. If, on the other hand, A had sold his life interest prior to the decedent's death, the basis of the life estate in the hands of A's transferee would be determined under section 1012.

(c) Adjustments for deductions allowed prior to the decedent's death. (1) As stated in paragraph (a) of this section, section 1014(b)(9) requires a reduction in the uniform basis of property acquired from a decedent before his death for certain deductions allowed in respect of such property during the decedent's lifetime. In general, the amount of the reduction in basis required by section 1014(b)(9) shall be the aggregate of the deductions allowed in respect of the property, but shall not include deductions allowed in respect of the property to the decedent himself. In cases where, owing to the operation of the estate tax, only a part of the value of the entire property is included in the decedent's gross estate, the amount of the reduction required by section 1014(b)(9) shall be an amount which bears the same relation to the total of all deductions (described in paragraph (a) of this section) allowed in respect of the property as the value of the property included in the decedent's gross estate bears to the value of the entire property.

(2) The application of this paragraph may be illustrated by the following examples:

Example (1). The decedent creates a trust to pay the income to A for life, remainder to B or his estate. The property transferred in trust consists of an apartment building with a basis of $50,000 at the time of the transfer. The decedent dies 2 years after the transfer is made and the gift is held to have been made in contemplation of death. Depreciation on the property was allowed in the amount of $1,000 annually. At the time of the decedent's death the value of the property is $58,000. The uniform basis of the property in the hands of the trustee, the life tenant, and the remainderman, immediately after the decedent's death is $56,000 ($58,000, fair market value of the property immediately after the decedent's death, reduced by $2,000, deductions for depreciation allowed prior to the decedent's death).

Example (2). The decedent creates a trust to pay the income to A for life, remainder to B or his estate. The trust instrument provides that if the decedent should survive A, the income shall be paid to the decedent for life. The decedent predeceases A and the present value of the remainder interest is included in the decedent's gross estate for estate tax purposes. The property transferred consists of an apartment building with a basis of $110,000 at the time of the transfer. Following the creation of the trust and during the balance of the decedent's life, deductions for depreciation were allowed on the property in the amount of $10,000. At the time of decedent's death the value of the entire property is $150,000, and the value of the remainder interest is $100,000. Accordingly, the uniform basis of the property in the hands of the trustee, the life tenant, and the remainderman, as adjusted under section 1014(b)(9), is $126,666, computed as follows:

Uniform basis prior to decedent's death $100,000

plus

Increase in uniform basis before reduction (determined by the following formula) 33,333

Increase in uniform basis (to be determined)	=	$100,000 (value of property included in gross estate)
$50,000 (total appreciation of property since - time of transfer)		$150,000 (value of entire property)

$133,333

less

Deductions allowed prior to decedent's death—taken into account under section 1014(b)(9) (determined by the following formula) 6,667

Prior deductions taken into account (to be determined)	=	$100,000 (value of property included in gross estate)
$10,000 (total deductions allowed prior to decedent's death)		$150,000 (value of entire property)

Uniform basis under section 1014 126,666

[T.D. 6500, 25 FR 11910, Nov. 26, 1960, as amended by T.D. 6712, 29 FR 3656, March 24, 1964; T.D. 7142, 36 FR 18952, Sept. 24, 1971]

§ 1.1014–7 Example applying rules of §§ 1.1014–4 through 1.1014–6 to case involving multiple interests.

(a) On January 1, 1950, the decedent creates a trust to pay the income to A for life, remainder to B or his estate. The trust instrument provides that if the decedent should survive A, the income shall be paid to the decedent for life. The decedent, who died on January 1, 1955, predeceases A, so that, due to the operation of the estate tax, only the present value of the remainder interest is included in the decedent's gross estate. The trust consists of an apartment building with a basis of $30,000 at the time of transfer. Under the trust instrument the trustee is required to maintain a reserve for depreciation. During the decedent's lifetime depreciation is allowed in the amount of $800 annually. At the time of the decedent's death the value of the apartment building is $45,000. A, the life tenant, is 43 years of age at the time of the decedent's death. Immediately after the decedent's death, the uniform basis of the entire property under section 1014(a) is $32,027; A's basis for the life interest is $15,553; and B's basis for the remainder interest is $16,474, computed as follows:

Step 1. Uniform basis (adjusted) immediately prior to decedent's death:

Basis at time of transfer $30,000

less

Depreciation allowed under section 1016 before decedent's death ($800 x 5) 4,000

26,000

Step 2. Value of property included in decedent's gross estate: 0.40180 (remainder factor, age 43) * $45,000 (value of entire property) 18,081

Step 3. Uniform basis of property under section 1014(a), before reduction required by section 1014(b)(9): Uniform basis (adjusted) prior to decedent's death 26,000

Increase in uniform basis (determined by the following formula) 7,634

Increase in uniform basis (to be determined)	=	$18,081 (value of property included in gross estate)
$19,000 (total appreciation, $45,000-$26,000)		$45,000 (value of entire property)

33,634

Step 4. Uniform basis reduced as required by section 1014(b)(9) for deductions allowed prior to death:

Uniform basis before reduction $33,634

less

Deductions allowed prior to decedent's death—taken into account under section 1014(b)(9) (determined by the following formula) $1,607

Prior deductions taken into account (to be property included determined)	=	$18,081 (value of in gross estate)
$4,000 (total deductions allowed prior to decedent's death)		$45,000 (value of entire property)

32,027

Step 5. A's basis for the life interest at the time of the decedent's death, determined under section 1015:

0.59820 (life factor, age 43)
* $26,000 15,553

Step 6. B's basis for the remainder interest, determined under section 1014(a):

Basis prior to the decedent's death:
0.40180 (remainder factor,
age 43) * $26,000 10,447

plus

Increase in uniform basis
owing to decedent's death:
Increase in uniform basis....................... $7,634

Reduction required by
section 1014(b)(9) 1,607 6,027

16,474

(b) Assume the same facts as in paragraph (a) of this section. Assume further, that following the decedent's death depreciation is allowed in the amount of $1,000 annually. As of January 1, 1964, when A's age is 52, the adjusted uniform basis of the entire property is $23,027; A's basis for the life interest is $9,323; and B's basis for the remainder interest is $13,704, computed as follows:

Step 7. Uniform basis (adjusted) as of January 1, 1964:

Uniform basis determined
under section 1014(a),
reduced as required by
section 1014(b)(9) $32,027

less

Depreciation allowed since
decedent's death ($1,000 * 9).................. 9,000

23,027

Step 8. Allocable share of adjustment for depreciation allowable in the nine years since the decedent's death:

A's interest
0.49587 (life factor, age 52) *
$7,200 ($800, depreciation
attributable to uniform basis
before increase under section
1014(a), * 9) 3,570

B's interest
0.50413 (remainder factor, age 52)
x $7,200 ($800, depreciation
attributable to uniform basis
before increase under section
014(a), * 9) 3,630

plus

$200 (annual depreciation
attributable to increase in
uniform basis under section
1014(a)) * 9 1,800

5,430

Step 9. Tentative bases of A's and B's interests as of January 1, 1964 (before adjustment for depreciation).

A's interest
0.49587 (life factor, age 52) *
$26,000 (adjusted uniform basis
immediately before decedent's death) ... $12,893

B's interest
0.50413 (remainder factor, age 52) *
$26,000 (adjusted uniform basis
immediately before decedent's death) 13,107

plus

Increase in uniform basis
owing to inclusion of
remainder in decedent's
gross estate 6,027

19,134

Step 10. Bases of A's and B's interests as of January 1, 1964.

A
Tentative basis (Step 9) 12,893

less

Allocable depreciation (Step 8)................ 3,570

9,323

B
Tentative basis (Step 9) 19,134

less

Allocable depreciation (Step 8)................ 5,430

13,704

[T.D. 6500, 25 FR 11910, Nov. 26, 1960]

§ 1.1014–8 Bequest, devise, or inheritance of a remainder interest.

(a)(1) Where property is transferred for life, with remainder in fee, and the remainderman dies before the life tenant, no adjustment is made to the uniform basis of the property on the death of the remainderman (see paragraph (a) of § 1.1014–4). However, the basis of the remainderman's heir, legatee, or devisee for the remainder interest is determined by adding to (or subtracting from) the part of the adjusted uniform basis assigned to the remainder interest (determined in accordance with the principles set forth in §§ 1.1014–4 through 1.1014–6) the difference between—

(i) The value of the remainder interest included in the remainderman's estate, and

(ii) The basis of the remainder interest immediately prior to the remainderman's death.

(2) The basis of any property distributed to the heir, legatee, or devisee upon termination of a trust (or legal life estate) or at any other time (unless included in the gross income of the legatee or devisee) shall be determined by adding to (or subtracting from) the adjusted uniform basis of the property thus distributed the difference between—

(i) The value of the remainder interest in the property included in the remainderman's estate, and

(ii) The basis of the remainder interest in the property immediately prior to the remainderman's death.

(b) The provisions of paragraph (a) of this section are illustrated by the following examples:

Example (1). Assume that, under the will of a decedent, property consisting of common stock with a value of $1,000 at the time of the decedent's death is transferred in trust, to pay the income to A for life, remainder to B or to B's estate. B predeceases A and bequeaths the remainder interest to C. Assume that B dies on January 1, 1956, and that the value of the stock originally transferred is $1,600 at B's death. A's age at that time is 37. The value of the remainder interest included in B's estate is $547 (0.34185, remainder factor age 37, * $1,600), and hence $547 is C's basis for the remainder interest immediately after B's death. Assume that C sells the remainder interest on January 1, 1961, when A's age is 42. C's basis for the remainder interest at the time of such sale is $596, computed as follows:

Basis of remainder interest computed with respect to uniform basis of entire property(0.39131, remainder factor age 42, * $1,000, uniform basis of entire property)		$391
plus		
Value of remainder interest included in B's estate	$547	
less		
Basis of remainder interest immediately prior to B's death (0.34185, remainder factor age 37, * $1,000)	342	205
Basis of C's remainder interest at the time of sale		596

Example (2). Assume the same facts as in example (1), except that C does not sell the remainder interest. Upon A's death terminating the trust, C's basis for the stock distributed to him is computed as follows:

Uniform basis of the property, adjusted to date of termination of the trust		$1,000
plus		
Value of remainder interests in the property at the time of B's death	$547	
less		
B's share of uniform basis of the property at the time of his death	342	205
C's basis for the stock distributed to him upon the termination of the trust		1,205

Example (3). Assume the same facts as in example (2), except that the property transferred is depreciable. Assume further that $100 of depreciation was allowed prior to B's death and that $50 of depreciation is allowed between the time of B's death and the termination of the trust. Upon A's death terminating the trust, C's basis for the property distributed to him is computed as follows:

Uniform basis of the property, adjusted to date of termination of the trust:

Uniform basis immediately after decedent's death		$1,000
Depreciation allowed following decedent's death	150	$350
plus		
Value of remainder interest in the property at the time of B's death		547

less		
B's share of uniform basis of the property at the time of his death (0.34185 * $900, uniform basis at B's death)	308	239
C's basis for the property distributed to him upon the termination of the trust		1,089

(c) The rules stated in paragraph (a) of this section do not apply where the basis of the remainder interest in the hands of the remainderman's transferee is determined by reference to its cost to such transferee. See also paragraph (a) of § 1.1014–4. Thus, if, in example (1) of paragraph (b) of this section B sold his remainder interest to C for $547 in cash, C's basis for the stock distributed to him upon the death of A terminating the trust is $547.

[T.D. 6500, 25 FR 11910, Nov. 26, 1960]

§ 1.1014–9 Special rule with respect to DISC stock. [*Omitted. Ed.*]

[T.D. 7283, 38 FR 20825, Aug. 3, 1973]

§ 1.1014–10 Basis of property acquired from a decedent must be consistent with property's Federal estate tax value.

(a) Consistent basis requirement. (1) *General rule.* The consistent basis requirement is the requirement that the initial basis in certain property be equal to or less than the property's final value as determined under paragraph (b)(1) of this section or, if no final value has yet been determined, the property's reported value for Federal estate tax purposes as described in paragraph (b)(2) of this section. The property subject to the consistent basis requirement is referred to in this section as consistent basis property and is described in paragraph (c)(1) of this section.

(2) *Initial basis in consistent basis property and effect of basis adjustments.* The initial basis in consistent basis property is the final value of the property, as determined under paragraph (b)(1) of this section, and, until the final value of this property is determined, the property's initial basis is the reported value, as described in paragraph (b)(2) of this section. The initial basis in consistent basis property may be adjusted pursuant to the operation of section 1014 or other provisions of the Internal Revenue Code (Code) governing basis, as applicable, and those adjustments will not violate the consistent basis requirement in paragraph (a)(1) of this section. For example, the initial basis in consistent basis property may be adjusted for gain recognized by the estate upon distribution of the property and for post-death capital improvements and depreciation. It also may be adjusted in the manner provided in section 1014(d) in the case of DISC stock and in the manner provided under subchapter K or S of chapter 1 of the Code, respectively, in the case of an interest in a partnership or S corporation.

(3) *Duration of consistent basis requirement.* The consistent basis requirement applies as long as the initial basis in consistent basis property is related, in whole or in part, to the property's final value, as determined under paragraph (b)(1) of this section, or, if applicable, the property's reported value, as determined under paragraph (b)(2) of this section. Therefore, regardless of the number of successive owners, the consistent basis requirement continues to apply until the entire property is sold, exchanged, or otherwise disposed of in one or more transactions that result in a recognition event for income tax purposes (whether or not resulting in a gain or loss) or until the entire property becomes includible in another decedent's gross estate. The consistent basis requirement applies whenever there is a taxable event with respect to the property, such as, but not limited to, a sale or exchange, depreciation, or amortization of the property. The expiration of the period of limitations on assessment for an income tax return that uses an incorrect basis in reporting a taxable event with respect to consistent basis property has no effect on the duty to determine basis under the rules of this section for purposes of reporting any subsequent taxable event with respect to the property if the consistent basis requirement continues to apply under the rule of this paragraph (a)(3).

(b) Final value and reported value. (1) *Final value.* The final value of consistent basis property is its fair market value as finally determined for Federal estate tax purposes. That value is—

(i) The value reported on an estate tax return filed with the IRS, once the period of limitations on assessment (see section 6501) of estate tax has expired without that value having been timely adjusted by the IRS; or

(ii) The value determined or specified by the IRS that differs from the value reported on an estate tax return filed with the IRS and the value specified by the IRS for other included property, as defined in paragraph (d)(4) of this section, once the period of limitations on assessment applicable to the estate tax has expired without that value having been timely contested by the executor, as defined in paragraphs (d)(1) and (2) of this section, respectively; or

(iii) The value determined in a written agreement with the IRS, (whether entered into in the course of the administrative proceedings between the estate and the IRS or after the commencement of litigation), once that written agreement has been executed by both the executor and the IRS and is binding on all parties (including, but not limited to, the executor, the IRS, and the beneficiaries); or

(iv) The value determined by a court for the purpose of determining the estate tax liability of the estate, as defined in paragraph (d)(3) of this section, once the court's determination no longer can be appealed to any court.

(2) *Reported value if no final value yet determined.* (i) *In general.* Prior to the determination of the final value in accordance with paragraph (b)(1) of this section, a taxpayer may not claim an initial basis in consistent basis property in excess of the property's value as reported on the Statement described in § 1.6035–1(c)(2) and required under § 1.6035–1 (as supplemented). This value is referred to in this section as the reported value. A value reported on a Statement (or a supplement to the Statement) that either reports a value from an estate tax return filed after the expiration of the period of limitations on assessment applicable to that return, or a value reported for property not reported on the estate tax return, is not a reported value for purposes of this section. See § 1.6035–1(d) regarding an executor's duty to supplement the Statement.

(ii) *Limit on reliance on Statement not reporting final value.* If the final value of consistent basis property is determined (as described in paragraph (b)(1) of this section) before the expiration of the period of limitations on assessment for a taxpayer's income tax return that reports a taxable event with regard to the property, the taxpayer's reliance on a Statement (or a supplement to the Statement) that does not report the final value of the property may result in an income tax deficiency and underpayment. See, however, section 6664 and the corresponding regulations for rules relating to waivers of penalties for certain failures due to reasonable cause.

(3) *Special rules.* (i) *Property subject to debt.* The final value or, if applicable, the reported value of property subject to recourse or non-recourse debt is determined based on the gross value of that property undiminished by the debt, regardless of whether the estate tax return reports the net value (equity of redemption value) of the property or separately reports the gross value of the property and the outstanding debt.

(ii) *Special use property.* The final value or, if applicable, the reported value of special use property with regard to which a recapture event (described in section 2032A(c)(1)) has occurred is increased as provided in section 1016(c) if the qualified heir makes the election under section 1016(c) and pays the amounts required under that section.

(c) Consistent basis property. (1) *Property subject to the consistent basis requirement.*

(i) *In general.* Except as provided in paragraph (c)(2) of this section, consistent basis property is any property

(A) To which section 1014(a) applies;

(B) That is included property, as defined in paragraph (d)(4) of this section, if the decedent's Federal estate tax return is filed after July 31, 2015, and any other property the basis of which is determined, in whole or in part, by reference to the basis of included property (for example, property acquired in a like-kind exchange or an involuntary conversion); and

(C) Whose value increases the estate tax liability, as defined in paragraph (d)(3) of this section, that is payable after the application of allowable credits, as defined in paragraph (d)(5) of this section.

(ii) *Application.* If the decedent's Federal estate tax return is filed on or before July 31, 2015, no included property and no other property described in paragraph (c)(1)(i) of this section is subject to the consistent basis requirement, even if the due date of that return is after July 31, 2015, or if one or more supplements to that return are filed with the IRS after July 31, 2015. If an estate tax liability is payable after the application of allowable credits, all property described in paragraphs (c)(1)(i)(A) and (B) of this section is considered property whose value increases the estate tax liability for purposes of paragraph (c)(1)(i)(C) of this section and, therefore, is subject to the consistent basis requirement, except as provided in paragraph (c)(2) of this section. If, after the application of allowable credits, no estate tax liability is payable, no such property is subject to the consistent basis requirement.

(2) *Property excepted from or not subject to the consistent basis requirement.* Notwithstanding paragraph (c)(1) of this section, the following property either is excepted from or is not subject to the consistent basis requirement—

(i) United States dollars (as defined in paragraph (d)(6) of this section).

(ii) United States dollar-denominated demand deposits.

(iii) Certificates of deposit denominated in United States dollars.

(iv) Cash collateral denominated in United States dollars held by a third party to secure a liability (such as a deposit of purchase money or a security deposit).

(v) Shares of a registered investment company priced in United States dollars that is a money market fund under Rule 2a–7 under the Investment Company Act of 1940 (17 CFR 270.2).

(vi) Life insurance proceeds on the life of the decedent payable in a lump sum in United States dollars.

(vii) Federal, State, and local tax refunds and other refunds payable entirely in United States dollars.

(viii) Notes that are forgiven in full by the decedent upon death, whether or not denominated in United States dollars.

(ix) Household and personal effects for which an appraisal is not required under § 20.2031–6(b) of this chapter.

(x) Property the initial basis of which is not in any way determined with regard to or derived from the property's final value as determined under paragraph (b)(1) of this section or its reported value as determined under paragraph (b)(2) of this section, if applicable. Such property includes but is not limited to—

(A) Annuity contracts subject to section 72 and amounts received as an annuity subject to section 72;

(B) An interest in property that consists entirely of the right to receive an item of income in respect of a decedent as defined in section 691;

(C) Amounts received under installment obligations arising from a transaction for which the installment method for determining gain under section 453 applies;

(D) Appreciated property described in section 1014(e) that is acquired by the decedent within 1 year of death;

(E) Stock of a passive foreign investment company subject to section 1296(i), but only if the basis of such stock is the adjusted basis in the hands of the decedent immediately before the decedent's death; and

(F) Interests in and distributions from retirement plans and deferred compensation plans, including individual retirement arrangements as defined in sections 408 and 408A, that are expressed entirely in United States dollars.

(xi) Any interest in property that qualified for an estate tax marital deduction under section 2056, 2056A, or 2106(a)(3) for which such a deduction was properly claimed, and/or any interest in property that qualified for an estate tax charitable deduction under section 2055 or 2106(a)(2) for which such a deduction was properly claimed, provided that the value of the decedent's entire interest in the included property is wholly deductible and equal to the total amount qualifying for those deductions.

(xii) Property that represents the surviving spouse's one-half share of community property to which section 1014(b)(6) applies, regardless of whether this property is included property as defined in paragraph (d)(4) of this section.

(xiii) Property the basis of which is adjusted in a manner similar to section 1014(a) on the occurrence of a taxable termination that occurs on the death of a trust beneficiary pursuant to section 2654(a)(2) (to the extent the property is not then includible in the gross estate of any person).

(xiv) Any other property that is not described in paragraph (c)(1)(i) of this section or that is identified as excepted property in published guidance in the Federal Register or in the Internal Revenue Bulletin (see § 601.601(d)(2)(ii)(b) of this chapter).

(d) Definitions. The following definitions apply for purposes of this section

(1) Contested. The term contested means to put at issue the value of property in a written communication to the IRS that identifies the specific property, states that the executor does not accept as correct the value of that property as determined or specified by the IRS, and provides the executor's claimed value for that property as determined in accordance with the requirements of section 2031, the corresponding regulations, and other applicable guidance. An issue cannot be contested by a general statement or written communication that does not include each of these specified elements.

(2) Executor. The term executor includes any person described in section 2203, as expanded to include all persons required under section 6018(b) to file an estate tax return.

(3) Estate tax liability. The term estate tax liability means the amount of tax imposed under chapter 11 of the Code (chapter 11).

(4) Included property. The term included property means property the value of which is included in the value of the decedent's gross estate as defined in section 2031 or 2103. Generally, this refers to property whose value is reported on an estate tax return, but it also refers to property whose value otherwise is included in the total value of the gross estate (for example, during examination by the IRS) so that a final value is or will be determined for that property under chapter 11. However, solely for purposes of this section, included property does not refer to unreported property whose value is not reported on an estate tax return and whose value is not otherwise included in the value of the decedent's gross estate as finally determined for Federal estate tax purposes.

(5) Allowable credits. The term allowable credits includes any credit against the estate tax liability allowable by any section of the Code or by reason of any treaty obligation of the United States, provided the estate qualifies for and properly claims the credit by complying with all applicable rules for claiming the credit. For instance, the prorated unified credit under section 2102(b)(3) is an allowable credit for qualifying estates if the estate files all necessary forms or statements required by the IRS to claim that credit.

(6) United States dollars. The term United States dollars means the official currency of the United States. The term United States dollars includes physical bills and coins for which the value of each bill or coin is equivalent to the face amount of that bill or coin. This definition does not include other physical United States bills or coins with numismatic value because these bills and coins typically do not have a value equal to their face value.

(e) Examples. The following examples illustrate the application of this section. In each case, the decedent D was a citizen of the United States, the estate does not elect the alternate valuation method under section 2032, and an estate tax liability is payable after the application of all allowable credits.

Example (1). (i) Final value determined by value on estate tax return. At D's death, D owned (among other assets) a private residence not subject to any debt. D's sole beneficiary is D's child C. The value of the residence is reported on the estate tax return at $300,000. The IRS accepts the return as filed and the period of limitations on assessment of estate tax expires. For purposes of the consistent basis requirement applicable to C, the final value of D's residence is $300,000, and therefore, C's initial basis in the residence is $300,000. See paragraphs (a)(2) and (b)(1)(i) of this section.

(ii) Adjustment of initial basis pursuant to other Code provisions. Several years later, C adds a master suite to the private residence at a cost of $45,000. Pursuant to section 1016(a), C's basis in the residence is increased by $45,000 to $345,000. Subsequently, C sells the residence to an unrelated third party for $450,000. C claims a basis in the residence of $345,000 and reports a gain of $105,000 ($450,000 less $345,000). C has complied with the consistent basis requirement, and C's adjustment to C's initial basis does not violate the consistent basis requirement. See paragraphs (a)(1) and (2) of this section.

Example (2). (i) Final value determined on examination. The facts are the same as in paragraph (e)(1)(i) of this section (Example 1) except that, on examination, the IRS adjusts the value of the residence to $290,000 and that value is not contested before the period of limitations on assessment of estate tax expires. For purposes of the consistent basis requirement applicable to C, the final value of the residence is $290,000, and therefore, C's initial basis in the residence, before taking into account C's subsequent renovations, is

$290,000. See paragraphs (a)(2) and (b)(1)(ii) of this section.

(ii) Reported value if no final value yet determined and reliance on Statement required under § 1.6035–1. Prior to the determination of final value, C sells the residence for $375,000. C reports a gain of $75,000 on C's income tax return, relying on the reported value in a Statement required under § 1.6035–1 and claiming an initial basis of $300,000. C has complied with the consistent basis requirement because C did not claim an initial basis in the residence in excess of its reported value before the final value was determined. However, because C claimed an initial basis in the residence that exceeds the final value, C may have an income tax deficiency and underpayment for the year of the sale if the applicable period of limitations on assessment for C's income tax return has not expired when the final value is determined. See paragraphs (b)(2)(i) and (ii) of this section.

Example (3). (i) Final value determined by agreement. At D's death, D owned 50% of Partnership P, whose sole asset was a rental building with a fair market value of $10 million subject to non-recourse debt of $2 million. D's sole beneficiary is D's child C. The value of D's interest in Partnership P is reported on the estate tax return at $4 million (50% of ($10 million less $2 million)). On examination, the IRS timely adjusts the value of the partnership interest to $5.25 million and the executor of D's estate timely contests that value before the period of limitations on assessment of estate tax expires. Subsequently, the IRS and the executor of D's estate enter into a settlement agreement that provides that the value of D's interest in Partnership P for purposes of the estate tax is $4.5 million. For purposes of the consistent basis requirement applicable to C, the final value of the partnership interest is $4.5 million, and therefore, C's initial basis in the partnership interest is $4.5 million. See paragraphs (a)(2) and (b)(1)(iii) of this section.

(ii) Adjustment of initial basis pursuant to other Code provisions. C's share of Partnership P's liabilities at the date of D's death is $1 million. Under section 742 of the Internal Revenue Code and § 1.742–1 of this part, C's basis in the partnership interest is $5.5 million ($4.5 million initial basis plus C's $1 million share of Partnership P's debt). C later sells the partnership interest for $5 million at a time when C's basis has not changed and C's share of the debt remains $1 million. Under section 752(d), C's amount realized on the sale includes $1 million for the reduction in C's share of partnership liabilities. Therefore, C's total amount realized is $6 million. C reports taxable gain of $0.5 million ($6 million amount realized less $5.5 million basis). C has complied with the consistent basis requirement because C did not claim an initial basis in the partnership interest that exceeds the final value of the interest, as determined under paragraph (b)(1) of this section, and C's adjustment of the initial basis in the partnership interest as reported does not violate the consistent basis requirement. See paragraphs (a)(1) and (2) of this section.

Example (4). (i) Final value determined by court decision. At D's death, D owned (among other assets) a rental property. D's sole beneficiary is D's child C. The value of the rental property is reported on the estate tax return at $1 million. On examination, the IRS determines the value of the rental property to be $1.5 million. A court subsequently determines that the fair market value of the rental property for purposes of the estate tax is $1.3 million and the court's decision becomes final. For purposes of the consistent basis requirement, the final value of the rental property is $1.3 million, and therefore, C's initial basis is $1.3 million. See paragraphs (a)(2) and (b)(1)(iv) of this section.

(ii) Reliance on Statement required under § 1.6035–1 and duration of consistent basis requirement. After the estate tax return is filed and before the final value is determined, C receives a Statement required under § 1.6035–1 showing a reported value of $1 million for the rental property. C claims a depreciation deduction on the first income tax return C files after acquiring the property, relying on the reported value in the Statement required under § 1.6035–1. C has complied with the consistent basis requirement on that return because C did not claim an initial basis in the rental property in excess of its reported value before the final value was determined. C may claim a credit or refund of income tax that may result from the increased depreciation deduction based on the final value of the rental property, but only if the period of limitations for a claim for a credit or refund of income tax for that year has not expired. C must use the final value of $1.3 million to determine C's unadjusted basis in the rental property for all open taxable years. In this case and pursuant to section 1016(a)(2), C's adjusted basis is determined by reducing the rental property's final value of $1.3

million by the greater of the depreciation deductions allowed or allowable based on the final value of $1.3 million for all prior tax years (open and closed). See paragraphs (a)(3), (b)(2)(i) and (ii) of this section.

Example (5). Final value for property subject to debt. At D's death, D's gross estate includes a yacht valued at $750,000, subject to $150,000 non-recourse debt. D's sole beneficiary is D's child C. Pursuant to the rule in § 20.2053–7 of this chapter, the executor of D's estate reports the $600,000 net value of the yacht on the estate tax return ($750,000 less $150,000 debt) and claims no other deduction for the debt. The IRS accepts the return as filed and the period of limitations on assessment of estate tax expires. For purposes of the consistent basis requirement applicable to C, the final value of the yacht is $750,000, and therefore, C's initial basis in the yacht is $750,000. See paragraph (b)(3) of this section.

Example (6). Included property subject to the consistent basis requirement. After exercising due diligence to discover estate assets, the executor of D's estate reports the value of all known property includible in D's gross estate on a timely filed estate tax return and pays the estate tax liability. During examination of the return, the IRS becomes aware of a piece of artwork in the possession of D's child C, the value of which is includible in D's gross estate but is not reported on the estate tax return. The value of the artwork for Federal estate tax purposes is $500,000. Pursuant to the examination, the IRS includes the value of the artwork in the value of D's gross estate, which causes an increase in D's estate tax liability. Neither the inclusion of the artwork in D's gross estate nor the value at which the artwork is included in D's estate is contested by the executor of D's estate before the period of limitation on assessment of estate tax expires. The artwork is subject to the consistent basis requirement and the final value of the artwork is $500,000. Therefore, C's initial basis in the artwork is $500,000. See paragraphs (a)(2) and (c)(1)(i) of this section.

Example (7). (i) Partially deductible property subject to the consistent basis requirement. Pursuant to a bequest in D's will, Trust is established and funded with certain property, the value of which is includible in the gross estate under section 2031. Trust is a charitable remainder annuity trust described in section 664(d)(1). Trust provides that, in each taxable year during the lifetime of D's surviving child C, the trustee must pay to C an annuity of 5% of the initial net fair market value of all property passing to Trust as finally determined for Federal estate tax purposes. Upon the death of C, the trustee must distribute all of the then principal and income of Trust to organizations described in sections 170(c), 2055(a), and 2522(a) of the Code as the trustee selects, in the trustee's sole discretion. Although the executor of D's estate properly claims an estate tax charitable deduction under section 2055(e)(2)(A) for the value of the remainder interest in Trust, D's estate has an estate tax liability after application of all allowable credits. The property passing to Trust is subject to the consistent basis requirement because the value of the property is included in D's gross estate, an estate tax liability is payable after the application of all allowable credits, and the property is not described in paragraph (c)(2) of this section (in particular, the property is not wholly deductible property within the meaning of paragraph (c)(2)(xi) of this section).

(ii) Wholly deductible property not subject to the consistent basis requirement. The facts are the same as in paragraph (e)(7)(i) of this section (Example 7), except that the sole annuity beneficiary of Trust is D's surviving spouse S, and the executor of D's estate properly claims a deduction under section 2056(b)(8) for the value of S's annuity interest. Because the value of D's entire interest in the property passing to Trust qualified for either a charitable deduction under section 2055(e)(2) or a marital deduction under section 2056(b)(8), none of the property passing to Trust will be subject to the consistent basis requirement. See paragraph (c)(2)(xi) of this section.

(iii) Property not wholly deductible property if the sum of marital and charitable deductions allowed for that property is less than the value of the decedent's entire interest in the property. At the time of D's death, D owned 80 shares of voting stock in a closely-held corporation that has 100 shares of voting stock outstanding. D's will directed the executor of D's estate to distribute 40 shares of D's stock to a marital trust and 40 shares of D's stock to a charitable trust. D's executor included the value of D's 80 shares of stock in D's gross estate at $8,000,000 for purposes of the estate tax. Because of discounts applicable in valuing each of the two blocks of only 40 shares of the stock, D's executor correctly claimed a charitable deduction under section 2055(e)(2) of only $3,000,000, and correctly claimed a marital deduction under section 2056(b)(7) of only $3,000,000. D's executor determined that an estate tax was due on D's estate after the application of all allowable credits. The IRS accepted the return as filed and the period of limitations on assessment of estate tax expired. The 40 shares of stock owned by charitable trust and the 40 shares of stock owned by marital trust are not wholly deductible property within the meaning of paragraph (c)(2)(xi) of this section and are subject to the consistent basis requirement.

(f) Applicability date. This section applies to property described in paragraph (c)(1) of this section that is acquired from a decedent or by reason of the death of a decedent if the decedent's Federal estate tax return is filed after September 17, 2024.

[T.D. 9991, Sept. 16, 2024]

§ 1015. Basis of Property Acquired by Gifts and Transfers in Trust

(a) Gifts after December 31, 1920. If the property was acquired by gift after December 31, 1920, the basis shall be the same as it would be in the hands of the donor or the last preceding owner by whom it was not acquired by gift, except that if such basis (adjusted for the period before the date of the gift as provided in section 1016) is greater than the fair market value of the property at the time of the gift, then for the purpose of determining loss the basis shall be such fair market value. If the facts necessary to determine the basis in the hands of the donor or the last preceding owner are unknown to the donee, the Secretary shall, if possible, obtain such facts from such donor or last preceding owner, or any other person cognizant thereof. If the Secretary finds it impossible to obtain such facts, the basis in the hands of such donor or last preceding owner shall be the fair market value of such property as found by the Secretary as of the date or approximate date at which, according to the best information that the Secretary is able to obtain, such property was acquired by such donor or last preceding owner.

(b) Transfer in trust after December 31, 1920. If the property was acquired after December 31, 1920, by a transfer in trust (other than by a transfer in trust by a gift, bequest, or devise), the basis shall be the same as it would be in the hands of the grantor increased in the amount of gain or decreased in the amount of loss recognized to the grantor on such transfer under the law applicable to the year in which the transfer was made.

* * *

(d) Increased basis for gift tax paid.

(1) In general. If—

(A) the property is acquired by gift on or after September 2, 1958, the basis shall be the basis determined under subsection (a), increased (but not above the fair market value of the property at the time of the gift) by the amount of gift tax paid with respect to such gift, or

(B) the property was acquired by gift before September 2, 1958, and has not been sold, exchanged, or otherwise disposed of before such date, the basis of the property shall be increased on such date by the amount of gift tax paid with respect to such gift, but such increase shall not exceed an amount equal to the amount by which the fair market value of the property at the time of the gift exceeded the basis of the property in the hands of the donor at the time of the gift.

(2) Amount of tax paid with respect to gift. For purposes of paragraph (1), the amount of gift tax paid with respect to any gift is an amount which bears the same ratio to the amount of gift tax paid under chapter 12 with respect to all gifts made by the donor for the calendar year (or preceding calendar period) in which such gift is made as the amount of such gift bears to the taxable gifts (as defined in section 2503(a) but computed without the deduction allowed by section 2521) made by the donor during such calendar year or period. For purposes of the preceding sentence, the amount of any gift shall be the amount included with respect to such gift in determining (for the purposes of section 2503(a)) the total amount of gifts made during the calendar year or period, reduced by the amount of any deduction allowed with respect to such gift under section 2522 (relating to charitable deduction) or under section 2523 (relating to marital deduction).

(3) Gifts treated as made one-half by each spouse. For purposes of paragraph (1), where the donor and his spouse elected, under section 2513 to have the gift considered as made one-half by each, the amount of gift tax paid with respect to such gift under chapter 12 shall be the sum of the amounts of tax paid with respect to each half of such gift (computed in the manner provided in paragraph (2)).

(4) Treatment as adjustment to basis. For purposes of section 1016(b), an increase in basis under paragraph (1) shall be treated as an adjustment under section 1016(a).

* * *

(6) Special rule for gifts made after December 31, 1976.

(A) In general. In the case of any gift made after December 31, 1976, the increase in basis provided by this subsection with respect to any gift for the gift tax paid under chapter 12 shall be an amount (not in excess of the amount of tax so paid) which bears the same ratio to the amount of tax so paid as—

(i) the net appreciation in value of the gift, bears to

(ii) the amount of the gift.

(B) Net appreciation. For purposes of paragraph (1), the net appreciation in value of any gift is the amount by which the fair market value of the gift exceeds the donor's adjusted basis immediately before the gift.

(e) Gifts between spouses. In the case of any property acquired by gift in a transfer described in section 1041(a), the basis of such property in the hands of the transferee shall be determined under section 1041(b)(2) and not this section.

Regulations

§ 1.1015–1 Basis of property acquired by gift after December 31, 1920.

(a) General rule. (1) In the case of property acquired by gift after December 31, 1920 (whether by a transfer in trust or otherwise), the basis of the property for the purpose of determining gain is the same as it would be in the hands of the donor or the last preceding owner by whom it was not acquired by gift. The same rule applies in determining loss unless the basis (adjusted for the period prior to the date of gift in accordance with sections 1016 and 1017) is greater than the fair market value of the property at the time of the gift. In such case, the basis for determining loss is the fair market value at the time of the gift.

(2) The provisions of subparagraph (1) of this paragraph may be illustrated by the following example.

Example. A acquires by gift income-producing property which has an adjusted basis of $100,000 at the date of gift. The fair market value of the property at the date of gift is $90,000. A later sells the property for $95,000. In such case there is neither gain nor loss. The basis for determining loss is $90,000; therefore, there is no loss. Furthermore, there is no gain, since the basis for determining gain is $100,000.

(3) If the facts necessary to determine the basis of property in the hands of the donor or the last preceding owner by whom it was not acquired by gift are unknown to the donee, the district director shall, if possible, obtain such facts from such donor or last preceding owner, or any other person cognizant thereof. If the district director finds it impossible to obtain such facts, the basis in the hands of such donor or last preceding owner shall be the fair market value of such property as found by the district director as of the date or approximate date at which, according to the best information the district director is able to obtain, such property was acquired by such donor or last preceding owner. See paragraph (e) of this section for rules relating to fair market value.

(b) Uniform basis; proportionate parts of. Property acquired by gift has a single or uniform basis although more than one person may acquire an interest in such property. The uniform basis of the property remains fixed subject to proper adjustment for items under sections 1016 and 1017. However, the value of the proportionate parts of the uniform basis represented, for instance, by the respective interests of the life tenant and remainderman are adjustable to reflect the change in the relative values of such interest on account of the lapse of time. The portion of the basis attributable to an interest at the time of its sale or other disposition shall be determined under the rules provided in § 1.1014–5. In determining gain or loss from the sale or other disposition after October 9, 1969, of a term interest in property (as defined in § 1.1001–1(f)(2)) the adjusted basis of which is determined pursuant, or by reference, to section 1015, that part of the adjusted uniform basis assignable under the rules of § 1.1014–5(a) to the interest sold or otherwise disposed of shall be disregarded to the extent and in the manner provided by section 1001(e) and § 1.1001–1(f).

(c) Time of acquisition. The date that the donee acquires an interest in property by gift is when the donor relinquishes dominion over the property and not necessarily when title to the property is acquired by the donee. Thus, the date that the donee acquires an interest in property by gift where he is a successor in interest, such as in the case of a remainderman of a life estate or a beneficiary of the distribution of the corpus of a trust, is the date such interests are created by the donor and not the date the property is actually acquired.

(d) Property acquired by gift from a decedent dying after December 31, 1953. If an interest in property was acquired by the taxpayer by gift from a donor dying after December 31, 1953, under conditions which required the inclusion of the property in the donor's gross estate for estate tax purposes, and the property had not been sold, exchanged, or otherwise disposed of by the taxpayer before the donor's death, see the rules prescribed in section 1014 and the regulations thereunder.

(e) Fair market value. For the purposes of this section, the value of property as appraised for the purpose of the Federal gift tax, or, if the gift is not subject to such tax, its value as appraised for the purpose of a State gift tax, shall be deemed to be the fair market value of the property at the time of the gift.

(f) Reinvestments by fiduciary. If the property is an investment by the fiduciary under the terms of the gift (as, for example, in the case of a sale by the fiduciary of property transferred under the terms of the gift, and the reinvestment of the proceeds), the cost or other basis to the fiduciary is taken in lieu of the basis specified in paragraph (a) of this section.

(g) Records. To insure a fair and adequate determination of the proper basis under section 1015, persons making or receiving gifts of property should preserve and keep accessible a record of the facts necessary to determine the cost of the property and, if pertinent, its fair market value as of March 1, 1913, or its fair market value as of the date of the gift.

[T.D. 6500, 25 FR 11910, Nov. 26, 1960, as amended by T.D. 6693, 28 FR 12818, Dec. 3, 1963; T.D. 7142, 36 FR 18952, Sept. 24, 1971]

§ 1.1015–2 Transfer of property in trust after December 31, 1920.

(a) General rule. (1) In the case of property acquired after December 31, 1920, by transfer in trust (other than by a transfer in trust by a gift, bequest, or devise) the basis of property so acquired is the same as it would be in the hands of the grantor increased in the amount of gain or decreased in the amount of loss recognized to the grantor upon such transfer under the law applicable to the year in which the transfer was made. If the taxpayer acquired the property by a transfer in trust, this basis applies whether the property be in the hands of the trustee, or the beneficiary, and whether acquired prior to the termination of the trust and distribution of the property, or thereafter.

(2) The principles stated in paragraph (b) of § 1.1015–1 concerning the uniform basis are applicable in determining the basis of property where more than one person acquires an interest in property by transfer in trust after December 31, 1920.

(b) Reinvestment by fiduciary. If the property is an investment made by the fiduciary (as, for example, in the case of a sale by the fiduciary of property transferred by the grantor, and the reinvestment of the proceeds), the cost or other basis to the fiduciary is taken in lieu of the basis specified in paragraph (a) of this section.

[T.D. 6500, 25 FR 11910, Nov. 26, 1960]

§ 1.1015–3 Gift or transfer in trust before January 1, 1921. [*Omitted. Ed.*]

[T.D. 6500, 25 FR 11910, Nov. 26, 1960]

§ 1.1015–4 Transfers in part a gift and in part a sale.

(a) General rule. Where a transfer of property is in part a sale and in part a gift, the unadjusted basis of the property in the hands of the transferee is the sum of—

(1) Whichever of the following is the greater:

(i) The amount paid by the transferee for the property, or

(ii) The transferor's adjusted basis for the property at the time of the transfer, and

(2) The amount of increase, if any, in basis authorized by section 1015(d) for gift tax paid (see § 1.1015–5).

For determining loss, the unadjusted basis of the property in the hands of the transferee shall not be greater than the fair market value of the property at the time of such transfer. For determination of gain or loss of the transferor, see § 1.1001–1(e) and § 1.1011–2. For special rule where there has been a charitable contribution of less than a taxpayer's entire interest in property, see section 170(e)(2) and § 1.170A–4(c).

(b) Examples. The rule of paragraph (a) of this section is illustrated by the following examples:

Example (1). If A transfers property to his son for $30,000, and such property at the time of the transfer has an adjusted basis of $30,000 in A's hands (and a fair market value of $60,000), the unadjusted basis of the property in the hands of the son is $30,000.

Example (2). If A transfers property to his son for $60,000, and such property at the time of transfer has an adjusted basis of $30,000 in A's hands (and a fair market value of $90,000), the unadjusted basis of such property in the hands of the son is $60,000.

Example (3). If A transfers property to his son for $30,000, and such property at the time of transfer has an adjusted basis in A's hands of $60,000 (and a fair market value of $90,000), the unadjusted basis of such property in the hands of the son is $60,000.

Example (4). If A transfers property to his son for $30,000 and such property at the time of transfer has an adjusted basis of $90,000 in A's hands (and a fair market value of $60,000), the unadjusted basis of the property in the hands of the son is $90,000. However, since the adjusted basis of the property in A's hands at the time of the transfer was greater than the fair market value at that time, for the purpose of determining any loss on a later sale or other disposition of the property by the son its unadjusted basis in his hands is $60,000.

[T.D. 6500, 25 FR 11910, Nov. 26, 1960, as amended by T.D. 6693, 28 FR 12818, Dec. 3, 1963; T.D. 7207, 37 FR 20799, Oct. 5, 1972]

§ 1.1015–5 Increased basis for gift tax paid.

* * *

(c) Special rule for increased basis for gift tax paid in the case of gifts made after December 31, 1976. (1) *In general.* With respect to gifts made after December 31, 1976 (other than gifts between spouses described in section 1015(e)), the increase in basis for gift tax paid is determined under section 1015(d)(6). Under section 1015(d)(6)(A), the increase in basis with respect to gift tax paid is limited to the amount (not in excess of the amount of gift tax paid) that bears the same ratio to the amount of gift tax paid as the net appreciation in value of the gift bears to the amount of the gift.

(2) *Amount of gift.* In general, for purposes of section 1015(d)(6)(A)(ii), the amount of the gift is determined in conformance with the provisions of paragraph (b) of this section. Thus, the amount of the gift is the amount included with respect to the gift in determining (for purposes of section 2503(a)) the total amount of gifts made during the calendar year (or calendar quarter in the case of a gift made on or before December 31, 1981), reduced by the amount of any annual exclusion allowable with respect to the gift under section 2503(b), and any deductions allowed with respect to the gift under section 2522 (relating to the charitable deduction) and section 2523 (relating to the marital deduction). Where more than one gift of a present interest in property is made to the same donee during a calendar year, the annual exclusion shall apply to the earliest of such gifts in point of time.

(3) *Amount of gift tax paid with respect to the gift.* In general, for purposes of section 1015(d)(6), the amount of gift tax paid with respect to the gift is determined in conformance with the provisions of paragraph (b) of this section. Where more than one gift is made by the donor in a calendar year (or quarter in the case of gifts made on or before December 31, 1981), the amount of gift tax paid with respect to any specific gift made during that period is the amount which bears the same ratio to the total gift tax paid for that period (determined after reduction for any gift tax unified credit available under section 2505) as the amount of the gift (computed as described in paragraph (c)(2)

of this section) bears to the total taxable gifts for the period.

(4) *Qualified domestic trusts.* For purposes of section 1015(d)(6), in the case of a qualified domestic trust (QDOT) described in section 2056A(a), any distribution during the noncitizen surviving spouse's lifetime with respect to which a tax is imposed under section 2056A(b)(1)(A) is treated as a transfer by gift, and any estate tax paid on the distribution under section 2056A(b)(1)(A) is treated as a gift tax. The rules under this paragraph apply in determining the extent to which the basis in the assets distributed is increased by the tax imposed under section 2056A(b)(1)(A).

(5) *Examples.* Application of the provisions of this paragraph (c) may be illustrated by the following examples:

Example (1). (i) Prior to 1995, X exhausts X's gift tax unified credit available under section 2505. In 1995, X makes a gift to X's child Y, of a parcel of real estate having a fair market value of $100,000. X's adjusted basis in the real estate immediately before making the gift was $70,000. Also in 1995, X makes a gift to X's child Z, of a painting having a fair market value of $70,000. X timely files a gift tax return for 1995 and pays gift tax in the amount of $55,500, computed as follows:

Value of real estate transferred to Y	$100,000	
Less: Annual exclusion	10,000	
Included amount of gift (C)		$90,000
Value of painting transferred to Z	$70,000	
Less: annual exclusion	10,000	
Included amount of gift		60,000
Total included gifts (D)		$150,000
Total gift tax liability for 1995 gifts (B)		$55,500

(ii) The gift tax paid with respect to the real estate transferred to Y, is determined as follows:

$$\frac{\$90{,}000(C)}{\$150{,}000(D)} * \$55{,}500 = \$33{,}300$$

(iii) (A) The amount by which Y's basis in the real property is increased is determined as follows:

$$\frac{\begin{array}{c}\$30{,}000\\ \text{(net appreciation)}\end{array}}{\begin{array}{c}\$90{,}000\\ \text{(amount of gift)}\end{array}} * \$33{,}300 = \$11{,}000$$

(B) Y's basis in the real property is $70,000 plus $11,100, or $81,100. If x had not exhausted any of X's unified credit, no gift tax would have been paid and, as a result, Y's basis would not be increased.

Example (2). (i) X dies in 1995. X's spouse, Y, is not a United States citizen. In order to obtain the marital deduction for property passing to X's spouse, X established a QDOT in X's will. In 1996, the trustee of the QDOT makes a distribution of principal from the QDOT in the form of shares of stock having a fair market value of $70,000 on the date of distribution. The trustee's basis in the stock (determined under section 1014) is $50,000. An estate tax is imposed on the distribution under section 2056A(b)(1)(A) in the amount $38,500, and is paid. Y's basis in the shares of stock is increased by a portion of the section 2056A estate tax paid determined as follows:

$$\frac{\begin{array}{c}\$20{,}000\\ \text{(net appreciation)}\end{array}}{\begin{array}{c}\$70{,}000\\ \text{(distribution)}\end{array}} * \begin{array}{c}\$38{,}500\\ \text{(section 2056A estate tax)}\end{array} = \$11{,}000$$

(ii) Y's basis in the stock is $50,000 plus $11,000, or $61,000.

(6) *Effective date.* The provisions of this paragraph (c) are effective for gifts made after August 22, 1995.

(d) Treatment as adjustment to basis. Any increase in basis under section 1015(d) and this section shall, for purposes of section 1016(b) (relating to adjustments to a substituted basis), be treated as an adjustment under section 1016(a) to the basis of the donee's property to which such increase applies. See paragraph (p) of § 1.1016–5.

[T.D. 6693, 28 FR 12818, Dec. 3, 1963, as amended by T.D. 7238, 37 FR 28715, Dec. 29, 1972; T.D. 7910, 48 FR 40372, Sept. 7, 1983; T.D. 8612, 60 FR 43537, Aug. 22, 1995]

§ 1016. Adjustments to Basis

(a) General rule. Proper adjustment in respect of the property shall in all cases be made—

(1) for expenditures, receipts, losses, or other items, properly chargeable to capital account, but no such adjustment shall be made

(A) for

(i) taxes or other carrying charges described in section 266; or

(ii) expenditures described in section 173 (relating to circulation expenditures), for which deductions have been taken by the taxpayer in determining taxable income for the taxable year or prior taxable years; or

(B) for mortality, expense, or other reasonable charges incurred under an annuity or life insurance contract;

(2) in respect of any period since February 28, 1913, for exhaustion, wear and tear, obsolescence, amortization, and depletion, to the extent of the amount—

(A) allowed as deductions in computing taxable income under this subtitle or prior income tax laws, and

(B) resulting (by reason of the deductions so allowed) in a reduction for any taxable year of the taxpayer's taxes under this subtitle (other than chapter 2, relating to tax on self-employment income), or prior income, war-profits, or excess-profits tax laws, but not less than the amount allowable under this subtitle or prior income tax laws. Where no method has been adopted under section 167 (relating to depreciation deduction), the amount allowable shall be determined under the straight line method. Subparagraph (B) of this paragraph shall not apply in respect of any period since February 28, 1913, and before January 1, 1952, unless an election has been made under section 1020 (as in effect before the date of the enactment of the Tax Reform Act of 1976). Where for any taxable year before the taxable year 1932 the depletion allowance was based on discovery value or a percentage of income, then the adjustment for depletion for such year shall be based on the depletion which would have been allowable for such year if computed without reference to discovery value or a percentage of income;

* * *

(b) Substituted basis. Whenever it appears that the basis of property in the hands of the taxpayer is a substituted basis, then the adjustments provided in subsection (a) shall be made after first making in respect of such substituted basis proper adjustments of a similar nature in respect of the period during which the property was held by the transferor, donor, or grantor, or during which the other property was held by the person for whom the basis is to be determined. A similar rule shall be applied in the case of a series of substituted bases.

(c) Increase in basis of property on which additional estate tax is imposed.

(1) Tax imposed with respect to entire interest. If an additional estate tax is imposed under section 2032A(c)(1) with respect to any interest in property and the qualified heir makes an election under this subsection with respect to the imposition of such tax, the adjusted basis of such interest shall be increased by an amount equal to the excess of—

(A) the fair market value of such interest on the date of the decedent's death (or the alternate valuation date under section 2032, if the executor of the decedent's estate elected the application of such section), over

(B) the value of such interest determined under section 2032A(a).

(2) Partial dispositions.

(A) In general. In the case of any partial disposition for which an election under this subsection is made, the increase in basis under paragraph (1) shall be an amount—

(i) which bears the same ratio to the increase which would be determined under paragraph (1) (without regard to this paragraph) with respect to the entire interest, as

(ii) the amount of the tax imposed under section 2032A(c)(1) with respect to such disposition bears to the adjusted tax difference attributable to the entire interest (as determined under section 2032A(c)(2)(B)).

(B) Partial disposition. For purposes of subparagraph (A), the term "partial disposition" means any disposition or cessation to which subsection (c)(2)(D), (h)(1)(B), or (i)(1)(B) of section 2032A applies.

(3) Time adjustment made. Any increase in basis under this subsection shall be deemed to have occurred immediately before the disposition or cessation resulting in the imposition of the tax under section 2032A(c)(1).

(4) Special rule in the case of substituted property. If the tax under section 2032A(c)(1) is imposed with respect to qualified replacement property (as defined in section 2032A(h)(3)(B)) or qualified exchange property (as defined in section 2032A(i)(3)), the increase in basis under paragraph (1) shall be made by reference to the property involuntarily converted or exchanged (as the case may be).

(5) Election.

(A) In general. An election under this subsection shall be made at such time and in such manner as the Secretary shall by regulations prescribe. Such an election, once made, shall be irrevocable.

(B) Interest on recaptured amount. If an election is made under this subsection with respect to any additional estate tax imposed under section 2032A(c)(1), for purposes of section 6601 (relating to interest on underpayments), the last date prescribed for payment of such tax shall be deemed to be the last date prescribed for payment of the tax imposed by section 2001 with respect to the estate of the decedent (as determined for purposes of section 6601).

* * *

Regulation

§ 1.1016–1 Adjustments to basis; scope of section.

Section 1016 and §§ 1.1016–2 to 1.1016–10, inclusive, contain the rules relating to the adjustments to be made to the basis of property to determine the adjusted basis as defined in section 1011. However, if the property was acquired from a decedent before his death, see § 1.1014–6 for adjustments on account of certain deductions allowed the taxpayer for the period between the date of acquisition of the property and the date of death of the decedent. If an election has been made under the Retirement-Straight Line Adjustment Act of 1958 (26 U.S.C. 1016 note), see § 1.9001–1 for special rules for determining adjusted basis in the case of a taxpayer who has changed from the retirement to the straightline method of computing depreciation allowances.

[T.D. 6500, 25 FR 11910, Nov. 26, 1960]

Under § 301(a) of the Tax Relief, Unemployment Insurance Reauthorization, and Job Creation Act of 2010 (P.L. 111–312) Section 1022 was eliminated from the Code. However, § 301(c) of the Act provides "[n]otwithstanding sub-section (a), in the case of an estate of a decedent dying after December 31, 2009, and before January 1, 2011, the executor (within the meaning of section 2203 of the Internal Revenue Code of 1986) may elect to apply such Code as though the amendments made by subsection (a) do not apply with respect to chapter 11 of such Code and with respect to property acquired or passing from such decedent . . . ." Therefore, § 1022 is included for those estates where the executor makes such election.

§ 1022. Treatment of Property Acquired from a Decedent Dying after December 31, 2009

(a) In general. *Except as otherwise provided in this section—*

(1) *property acquired from a decedent dying after December 31, 2009, shall be treated for purposes of this subtitle as transferred by gift, and*

(2) *the basis of the person acquiring property from such a decedent shall be the lesser of—*

(A) *the adjusted basis of the decedent, or*

(B) *the fair market value of the property at the date of the decedent's death.*

(b) Basis increase for certain property.

(1) In general. *In the case of property to which this subsection applies, the basis of such property under subsection (a) shall be increased by its basis increase under this subsection.*

(2) Basis increase. *For purposes of this subsection—*

(A) In general. *The basis increase under this subsection for any property is the portion of the aggregate basis increase which is allocated to the property pursuant to this section.*

(B) Aggregate basis increase. *In the case of any estate, the aggregate basis increase under this subsection is $1,300,000.*

(C) Limit increased by unused built-in losses and loss carryovers. *The limitation under subparagraph (B) shall be increased by—*

(i) *the sum of the amount of any capital loss carryover under section 1212(b), and the amount of any net operating loss carryover under section 172, which would (but for the decedent's death) be carried from the decedent's last taxable year to a later taxable year of the decedent, plus*

(ii) *the sum of the amount of any losses that would have been allowable under section 165 if the property acquired from the decedent had been sold at fair market value immediately before the decedent's death.*

(3) Decedent nonresidents who are not citizens of the united states. *In the case of a decedent nonresident not a citizen of the United States—*

(A) *paragraph (2)(B) shall be applied by substituting "$60,000" for "$1,300,000", and*

(B) *paragraph (2)(C) shall not apply.*

(c) Additional basis increase for property acquired by surviving spouse.

(1) In general. *In the case of property to which this subsection applies and which is qualified spousal property, the basis of such property under subsection (a) (as increased under subsection (b)) shall be increased by its spousal property basis increase.*

(2) Spousal property basis increase. *For purposes of this subsection—*

(A) In general. *The spousal property basis increase for property referred to in paragraph (1) is the portion of the aggregate spousal property basis increase which is allocated to the property pursuant to this section.*

(B) Aggregate spousal property basis increase. *In the case of any estate, the aggregate spousal property basis increase is $3,000,000.*

(3) Qualified spousal property. *For purposes of this subsection, the term 'qualified spousal property' means—*

(A) *outright transfer property, and*

(B) *qualified terminable interest property.*

(4) Outright transfer property. *For purposes of this subsection—*

(A) In general. *The term 'outright transfer property' means any interest in property acquired from the decedent by the decedent's surviving spouse.*

(B) Exception. *Subparagraph (A) shall not apply where, on the lapse of time, on the occurrence of an event or contingency, or on the failure of an event or contingency to occur, an interest passing to the surviving spouse will terminate or fail—*

(i) (I) *if an interest in such property passes or has passed (for less than an adequate and full consideration in money or money's worth) from the decedent to any person other than such surviving spouse (or the estate of such spouse), and*

(II) *if by reason of such passing such person (or his heirs or assigns) may possess or enjoy any part of such property after such termination or failure of the interest so passing to the surviving spouse, or*

(ii) *if such interest is to be acquired for the surviving spouse, pursuant to directions of the decedent, by his executor or by the trustee of a trust.*

For purposes of this subparagraph, an interest shall not be considered as an interest which will terminate or fail merely because it is the ownership of a bond, note, or similar contractual obligation, the discharge of which would not have the effect of an annuity for life or for a term.

(C) Interest of spouse conditional on survival for limited period. *For purposes of this paragraph, an interest passing to the surviving spouse shall not be considered as an interest which will terminate or fail on the death of such spouse if—*

(i) *such death will cause a termination or failure of such interest only if it occurs within a period not exceeding 6 months after the decedent's death, or only if it occurs as a result of a common disaster resulting in the death of the decedent and the surviving spouse, or only if it occurs in the case of either such event, and*

(ii) *such termination or failure does not in fact occur.*

(5) Qualified terminable interest property. *For purposes of this subsection—*

(A) In general. *The term 'qualified terminable interest property' means property—*

(i) *which passes from the decedent, and*

(ii) *in which the surviving spouse has a qualifying income interest for life.*

(B) Qualifying income interest for life. *The surviving spouse has a qualifying income interest for life if—*

(i) *the surviving spouse is entitled to all the income from the property, payable annually or at more frequent intervals, or has a usufruct interest for life in the property, and*

(ii) *no person has a power to appoint any part of the property to any person other than the surviving spouse.*

Clause (ii) shall not apply to a power exercisable only at or after the death of the surviving spouse. To the extent provided in regulations, an annuity shall be treated in a manner similar to an income interest in property (regardless of whether the property from which the annuity is payable can be separately identified).

(C) Property includes interest therein. *The term "property" includes an interest in property.*

(D) Specific portion treated as separate property. *A specific portion of property shall be treated as separate property. For purposes of the preceding sentence, the term 'specific portion' only includes a portion determined on a fractional or percentage basis.*

(d) Definitions and special rules for application of subsections (b) and (c).

(1) Property to which subsections (b) and (c) apply.

(A) In general. *The basis of property acquired from a decedent may be increased under subsection (b) or (c) only if the property was owned by the decedent at the time of death.*

(B) Rules relating to ownership.

(i) Jointly held property. *In the case of property which was owned by the decedent and another person as joint tenants with right of survivorship or tenants by the entirety—*

(I) *if the only such other person is the surviving spouse, the decedent shall be treated as the owner of only 50 percent of the property,*

(II) *in any case (to which subclause (I) does not apply) in which the decedent furnished consideration for the acquisition of the property, the decedent shall be treated as the owner to the extent of the portion of the property which is proportionate to such consideration, and*

(III) *in any case (to which subclause (I) does not apply) in which the property has been acquired by gift, bequest, devise, or inheritance by the decedent and any other person as joint tenants with right of survivorship and their interests are not otherwise specified or fixed by law, the decedent shall be treated as the owner to the extent of the value of a fractional part to be determined by dividing the value of the property by the number of joint tenants with right of survivorship.*

(ii) Revocable trusts. *The decedent shall be treated as owning property transferred by the decedent during life to a qualified revocable trust (as defined in section 645(b)(1)).*

(iii) Powers of appointment. *The decedent shall not be treated as owning any property by reason of holding a power of appointment with respect to such property.*

(iv) Community property. *Property which represents the surviving spouse's one-half share of community property held by the decedent and the surviving spouse under the community property laws of any State or possession of the United States or any foreign country shall be treated for purposes of this section as owned by, and acquired from, the decedent if at least one-half of the whole of the community interest in such property is treated as owned by, and acquired from, the decedent without regard to this clause.*

(C) Property acquired by decedent by gift within 3 years of death.

(i) In general. *Subsections (b) and (c) shall not apply to property acquired by the decedent by gift or by inter vivos transfer for less than adequate and full consideration in money or money's worth during the 3-year period ending on the date of the decedent's death.*

(ii) Exception for certain gifts from spouse. *Clause (i) shall not apply to property acquired by the decedent from the decedent's spouse unless, during such 3-year period, such spouse acquired the property in whole or in part by gift or by inter vivos transfer for less than adequate and full consideration in money or money's worth.*

(D) Stock of certain entities. *Subsections (b) and (c) shall not apply to—*

(i) *stock or securities of a foreign personal holding company,*

(ii) *stock of a DISC or former DISC,*

(iii) *stock of a foreign investment company, or*

(iv) *stock of a passive foreign investment company unless such company is a qualified electing fund (as defined in section 1295) with respect to the decedent.*

(2) Fair market value limitation. *The adjustments under subsections (b) and (c) shall not increase the basis of any interest in property acquired from the decedent above its fair market value in the hands of the decedent as of the date of the decedent's death.*

(3) Allocation rules.

(A) In general. *The executor shall allocate the adjustments under subsections (b) and (c) on the return required by section 6018.*

(B) Changes in allocation. *Any allocation made pursuant to subparagraph (A) may be changed only as provided by the Secretary.*

(4) Inflation adjustment of basis adjustment amounts.

(A) In general. *In the case of decedents dying in a calendar year after 2010, the $1,300,000, $60,000, and $3,000,000 dollar amounts in subsections (b) and (c)(2)(B) shall each be increased by an amount equal to the product of—*

(i) *such dollar amount, and*

(ii) *the cost-of-living adjustment determined under section 1(f)(3) for such calendar year, determined by substituting "2009" for "1992" in subparagraph (B) thereof.*

(B) Rounding. *If any increase determined under subparagraph (A) is not a multiple of—*

(i) *$100,000 in the case of the $1,300,000 amount,*

(ii) *$5,000 in the case of the $60,000 amount, and*

(iii) *$250,000 in the case of the $3,000,000 amount,*

such increase shall be rounded to the next lowest multiple thereof.

(e) Property acquired from the decedent. *For purposes of this section, the following property shall be considered to have been acquired from the decedent:*

(1) *Property acquired by bequest, devise, or inheritance, or by the decedent's estate from the decedent.*

(2) *Property transferred by the decedent during his lifetime—*

(A) *to a qualified revocable trust (as defined in section 645(b)(1)), or*

(B) *to any other trust with respect to which the decedent reserved the right to make any change in the enjoyment thereof through the exercise of a power to alter, amend, or terminate the trust.*

(3) *Any other property passing from the decedent by reason of death to the extent that such property passed without consideration.*

(f) Coordination with section 691. *This section shall not apply to property which constitutes a right to receive an item of income in respect of a decedent under section 691.*

(g) Certain liabilities disregarded.

(1) In general. *In determining whether gain is recognized on the acquisition of property—*

(A) *from a decedent by a decedent's estate or any beneficiary other than a tax-exempt beneficiary, and*

(B) *from the decedent's estate by any beneficiary other than a tax-exempt beneficiary,*

and in determining the adjusted basis of such property, liabilities in excess of basis shall be disregarded.

(2) Tax-exempt beneficiary. *For purposes of paragraph (1), the term 'tax-exempt beneficiary' means—*

(A) the United States, any State or political subdivision thereof, any possession of the United States, any Indian tribal government (within the meaning of section 7871), or any agency or instrumentality of any of the foregoing,

(B) an organization (other than a cooperative described in section 521) which is exempt from tax imposed by chapter 1,

(C) any foreign person or entity (within the meaning of section 168(h)(2)), and

(D) to the extent provided in regulations, any person to whom property is transferred for the principal purpose of tax avoidance.

***(h) Regulations.** The Secretary shall prescribe such regulations as may be necessary to carry out the purposes of this section.*

Part III. Common Nontaxable Exchanges

§ 1040. Transfer of Certain Farm, etc., Real Property

(a) General rule. If the executor of the estate of any decedent transfers to a qualified heir (within the meaning of section 2032A(e)(1)) any property with respect to which an election was made under section 2032A, then gain on such transfer shall be recognized to the estate only to the extent that, on the date of such transfer, the fair market value of such property exceeds the value of such property for purposes of chapter 11 (determined without regard to section 2032A).

(b) Similar rule for certain trusts. To the extent provided in regulations prescribed by the Secretary, a rule similar to the rule provided in subsection (a) shall apply where the trustee of a trust (any portion of which is included in the gross estate of the decedent) transfers property with respect to which an election was made under section 2032A.

(c) Basis of property acquired in transfer described in subsection (a) or (b). The basis of property acquired in a transfer with respect to which gain realized is not recognized by reason of subsection (a) or (b) shall be the basis of such property immediately before the transfer increased by the amount of the gain recognized to the estate or trust on the transfer.

§ 1041. Transfers of Property Between Spouses or Incident to Divorce

(a) General rule. No gain or loss shall be recognized on a transfer of property from an individual to (or in trust for the benefit of)—

(1) a spouse, or

(2) a former spouse, but only if the transfer is incident to the divorce.

(b) Transfer treated as gift; transferee has transferor's basis. In the case of any transfer of property described in subsection (a)—

(1) for purposes of this subtitle, the property shall be treated as acquired by the transferee by gift, and

(2) the basis of the transferee in the property shall be the adjusted basis of the transferor.

(c) Incident to divorce. For purposes of subsection (a)(2), a transfer of property is incident to the divorce if such transfer—

(1) occurs within 1 year after the date on which the marriage ceases, or

(2) is related to the cessation of the marriage.

(d) Special rule where spouse is nonresident alien. Subsection (a) shall not apply if the spouse (or former spouse) of the individual making the transfer is a nonresident alien.

(e) Transfers in trust where liability exceeds basis. Subsection (a) shall not apply to the transfer of property in trust to the extent that—

(1) the sum of the amount of the liabilities assumed, plus the amount of the liabilities to which the property is subject, exceeds

(2) the total of the adjusted basis of the property transferred.

Proper adjustment shall be made under subsection (b) in the basis of the transferee in such property to take into account gain recognized by reason of the preceding sentence.

Subchapter P. Capital Gains and Losses

Part III. General Rules for Determining Capital Gains and Losses

§ 1221. Capital Asset Defined

(a) In general. For purposes of this subtitle, the term "capital asset" means property held by the taxpayer (whether or not connected with his trade or business), but does not include—

(1) stock in trade of the taxpayer or other property of a kind which would properly be included in the inventory of the taxpayer if on hand at the close of the taxable year, or property held by the taxpayer primarily for sale to customers in the ordinary course of his trade or business;

(2) property, used in his trade or business, of a character which is subject to the allowance for depreciation provided in section 167, or real property used in his trade or business;

(3) a patent, invention, model or design (whether or not patented), a secret formula or process, a copyright, a literary, musical, or artistic composition, a letter or memorandum, or similar property, held by

(A) a taxpayer whose personal efforts created such property,

(B) in the case of a letter, memorandum, or similar property, a taxpayer for whom such property was prepared or produced, or

(C) a taxpayer in whose hands the basis of such property is determined, for purposes of determining gain from a sale or exchange, in whole or part by reference to the basis of such property in the hands of a taxpayer described in subparagraph (A) or (B);

(4) accounts or notes receivable acquired in the ordinary course of trade or business for services rendered or from the sale of property described in paragraph (1);

(5) a publication of the United States Government (including the Congressional Record) which is received from the United States Government or any agency thereof, other than by purchase at the price at which it is offered for sale to the public, and which is held by—

(A) a taxpayer who so received such publication, or

(B) a taxpayer in whose hands the basis of such publication is determined, for purposes of determining gain from a sale or exchange, in whole or in part by reference to the basis of such publication in the hands of a taxpayer described in subparagraph (A);

(6) any commodities derivative financial instrument held by a commodities derivatives dealer, unless—

(A) it is established to the satisfaction of the Secretary that such instrument has no connection to the activities of such dealer as a dealer, and

(B) such instrument is clearly identified in such dealer's records as being described in subparagraph (A) before the close of the day on which it was acquired, originated, or entered into (or such other time as the Secretary may by regulations prescribe);

(7) any hedging transaction which is clearly identified as such before the close of the day on which it was acquired, originated, or entered into (or such other time as the Secretary may by regulations prescribe); or

(8) supplies of a type regularly used or consumed by the taxpayer in the ordinary course of a trade or business of the taxpayer.

* * *

(b) Definitions and special rules.

* * *

(3) Sale or exchange of self-created musical works. At the election of the taxpayer, paragraphs (1) and (3) of subsection (a) shall not apply to musical compositions or copyrights in musical works sold or exchanged, by a taxpayer described in subsection (a)(3).

* * *

§ 1222. Other Terms Relating to Capital Gains and Losses

For purposes of this subtitle—

(1) Short-term capital gain. The term "short-term capital gain" means gain from the sale or exchange of a capital asset held for not more than 1 year, if and to the extent such gain is taken into account in computing gross income.

(2) Short-term capital loss. The term "short-term capital loss" means loss from the sale or exchange of a capital asset held for not more than 1 year, if and to the extent that such loss is taken into account in computing taxable income.

(3) Long-term capital gain. The term "long-term capital gain" means gain from the sale or exchange of a capital asset held for more than 1 year, if and to the extent such gain is taken into account in computing gross income.

(4) Long-term capital loss. The term "long-term capital loss" means loss from the sale or exchange of a capital asset held for more than 1 year, if and to the extent that such loss is taken into account in computing taxable income.

(5) Net short-term capital gain. The term "net short-term capital gain" means the excess of short-term capital gains for the taxable year over the short-term capital losses for such year.

(6) Net short-term capital loss. The term "net short-term capital loss" means the excess of short-term capital losses for the taxable year over the short-term capital gains for such year.

(7) Net long-term capital gain. The term "net long-term capital gain" means the excess of long-term capital gains for the taxable year over the long-term capital losses for such year.

(8) Net long-term capital loss. The term "net long-term capital loss" means the excess of long-term capital losses for the taxable year over the long-term capital gains for such year.

(9) Capital gain net income. The term "capital gain net income" means the excess of the gains from sales or exchanges of capital assets over the losses from such sales or exchanges.

(10) Net capital loss. The term "net capital loss" means the excess of the losses from sales or exchanges of capital assets over the sum allowed under section 1211. In the case of a corporation, for the purpose of determining losses under this paragraph, amounts which are short-term capital losses under section 1212 shall be excluded.

(11) Net capital gain. The term "net capital gain" means the excess of the net long-term capital gain for the taxable year over the net short-term capital loss for such year.

* * *

§ 1223. Holding Period of Property

For purposes of this subtitle—

* * *

(2) In determining the period for which the taxpayer has held property however acquired there shall be included the period for which such property was held by any other person, if under this chapter such property has, for the purpose of determining gain or loss from a sale or exchange, the same basis in whole or in part in his hands as it would have in the hands of such other person.

* * *

(9) In the case of a person acquiring property from a decedent or to whom property passed from a decedent (within the meaning of section 1014(b)), if—

(A) the basis of such property in the hands of such person is determined under section 1014, and

(B) such property is sold or otherwise disposed of by such person within 1 year after the decedent's death, then such person shall be considered to have held such property for more than 1 year.

(10) If—

(A) property is acquired by any person in a transfer to which section 1040 applies,

(B) such property is sold or otherwise disposed of by such person within 1 year after the decedent's death, and

(C) such sale or disposition is to a person who is a qualified heir (as defined in section 2032A(e)(1)) with respect to the decedent,

then the person making such sale or other disposition shall be considered to have held such property for more than 1 year.

* * *

Chapter 2A. Unearned Income Medicare Contribution

§ 1411. Imposition of Tax

(a) In general. Except as provided in subsection (e)

* * *

(2) Application to estates and trusts. In the case of an estate or trust, there is hereby imposed (in addition to any other tax imposed by this subtitle) for each taxable year a tax of 3.8 percent of the lesser of

(A) the undistributed net investment income for such taxable year, or

(B) the excess (if any) of

(i) the adjusted gross income (as defined in section 67(e)) for such taxable year, over

(ii) the dollar amount at which the highest tax bracket in section 1(e) begins for such taxable year.

(b) Threshold amount. For purposes of this chapter, the term "threshold amount" means

* * *

(3) in any other case, $200,000.

(c) Net investment income. For purposes of this chapter

(1) In general. The term "net investment income" means the excess (if any) of

(A) the sum of

(i) gross income from interest, dividends, annuities, royalties, and rents, other than such income which is derived in the ordinary course of a trade or business not described in paragraph (2),

(ii) other gross income derived from a trade or business described in paragraph (2), and

(iii) net gain (to the extent taken into account in computing taxable income) attributable to the disposition of property other than property held in a trade or business not described in paragraph (2), over

(B) the deductions allowed by this subtitle which are properly allocable to such gross income or net gain.

(2) Trades and businesses to which tax applies. A trade or business is described in this paragraph if such trade or business is

(A) a passive activity (within the meaning of section 469) with respect to the taxpayer, or

(B) a trade or business of trading in financial instruments or commodities (as defined in section 475(e)(2)).

* * *

(d) Modified adjusted gross income. For purposes of this chapter, the term "modified adjusted gross income" means adjusted gross income increased by the excess of

(1) the amount excluded from gross income under section 911(a)(1), over

(2) the amount of any deductions (taken into account in computing adjusted gross income) or exclusions disallowed under section 911(d)(6) with respect to the amounts described in paragraph (1).

(e) Nonapplication of section. This section shall not apply to

* * *

(2) a trust all of the unexpired interests in which are devoted to one or more of the purposes described in section 170(c)(2)(B).

Regulations

§ 1.1411–1 General rules.

(a) General rule. Except as otherwise provided, all Internal Revenue Code (Code) provisions that apply for chapter 1 purposes in determining taxable income (as defined in section 63(a)) of a taxpayer also apply in determining the tax imposed by section 1411.

* * *

(c) Effect of section 1411 and the regulations thereunder for other purposes. The inclusion or exclusion of items of income, gain, loss, or deduction in determining net investment income for purposes of section 1411, and the assignment of items of income, gain, loss, or deduction to a particular category of net investment income under section 1411(c)(1)(A), does not affect the treatment of any item of income, gain, loss, or deduction under any provision of the Code other than section 1411.

(d) Definitions. The following definitions apply for purposes of calculating net investment income under section 1411 and the regulations thereunder

(1) The term gross income from annuities under section 1411(c)(1)(A) includes the amount received as an annuity under an annuity, endowment, or life insurance contract that is includible in gross income as a result of the application of section 72(a) and section 72(b), and an amount not received as an annuity under an annuity contract that is includible in gross income under section 72(e). In the case of a sale of an annuity, to the extent the sales price of the annuity does not exceed its surrender value, the gain recognized would be treated as gross income from an annuity within the meaning of section 1411(c)(1)(A)(i) and § 1.1411–4(a)(1)(i). However, if the sales price of the annuity exceeds its surrender value, the seller would treat the gain equal to the difference between the basis in the annuity and the surrender value as gross income from an annuity described in section 1411(c)(1)(A)(i) and § 1.1411–4(a)(1)(i) and the excess of the sales price over the surrender value as gain from the disposition of property included in section 1411(c)(1)(A)(iii) and § 1.1411–4(a)(1)(iii). The term gross income from annuities does not include amounts paid in consideration for services rendered. For example, distributions from a foreign retirement plan that are paid in the form of an annuity and include investment income that was earned by the retirement plan does not constitute income from an annuity within the meaning of section 1411(c)(1)(A)(i).

* * *

(8) The term net investment income (NII) means net investment income as defined in section 1411(c) and § 1.1411–4, as adjusted pursuant to the rules described in § 1.1411–10(c).

* * *

(10) The term gross income from rents includes amounts paid or to be paid principally for the use of (or the right to use) tangible property.

(11) The term gross income from royalties includes amounts received from mineral, oil, and gas royalties, and amounts received for the privilege of using patents, copyrights, secret processes and formulas, goodwill, trademarks, tradebrands, franchises, and other like property.

* * *

(e) Disallowance of certain credits against the section 1411 tax. Amounts that may be credited against only the tax imposed by chapter 1 of the Code may not be credited against the section 1411 tax imposed by chapter 2A of the Code unless specifically provided in the Code. For example, the foreign income, war profits, and excess profits taxes that are allowed as a foreign tax credit by section 27(a), section 642(a), and section 901, respectively, are not allowed as a credit against the section 1411 tax.

* * *

(g) Effective/applicability date. This section applies to taxable years beginning after December 31, 2013. However, taxpayers may apply this section to taxable years beginning after December 31, 2012, in accordance with paragraph (f) of this section.

[T.D. 9644, 78 FR 72424, Dec. 2, 2013]

§ 1.1411–3 Application to estates and trusts.

(a) Estates and trusts to which tax applies *(1) In general* (i) *General application.* Section 1411 and the regulations thereunder apply to all estates and trusts that are subject to the provisions of part I of subchapter J of chapter 1 of subtitle A of the Internal Revenue Code, unless specifically exempted under paragraph (b) of this section.

(ii) *Calculation of tax.* The tax imposed by section 1411(a)(2) for each taxable year is equal to 3.8 percent of the lesser of

(A) The estate's or trust's undistributed net investment income for such taxable year; or

(B) The excess (if any) of—

(1) The estate's or trust's adjusted gross income (as defined in section 67(e) and as adjusted under § 1.1411–10(e)(2), if applicable) for such taxable year; over

(2) The dollar amount at which the highest tax bracket in section 1(e) begins for such taxable year.

(2) Taxable year of less than twelve months (i) *General rule.* In the case of an estate or trust that has a taxable year consisting of less than twelve months (short taxable year), the dollar amount described in paragraph (a)(1)(ii)(B)(2) of this section is not reduced or prorated.

(ii) *Change of annual accounting period.* Notwithstanding paragraph (a)(2)(i) of this section, an estate or trust that has a short taxable year resulting from a change of annual accounting period (but not from an individual's death) reduces the dollar amount described in paragraph (a)(1)(ii)(B)(2) of this section to an amount that bears the same ratio to that dollar amount as the number of months in the short taxable year bears to twelve.

(3) Rules with respect to CFCs and PFICs. Additional rules in § 1.1411–10 apply to an estate or trust that holds an interest in a controlled foreign corporation (CFC) or a passive foreign investment company (PFIC).

(b) Application to certain trusts and estates *(1) Exception for certain trusts and estates.* The following trusts are not subject to the tax imposed by section 1411:

(i) A trust or decedent's estate all of the unexpired interests in which are devoted to one or more of the purposes described in section 170(c)(2)(B).

(ii) A trust exempt from tax under section 501.

(iii) A charitable remainder trust described in section 664. However, see paragraph (d) of this section for special rules regarding the treatment of annuity or unitrust distributions from such a trust to persons subject to tax under section 1411.

(iv) Any other trust, fund, or account that is statutorily exempt from taxes imposed in subtitle A. For example, see sections 220(e)(1), 223(e)(1), 529(a), and 530(a).

(v) A trust, or a portion thereof, that is treated as a grantor trust under subpart E of part I of subchapter J of chapter 1. However, in the case of any such trust or portion thereof, each item of income or deduction that is included in computing taxable income of a grantor or another person under section 671 is treated as if it had been received by, or paid directly to, the grantor or other person for purposes of calculating such person's net investment income.

(vi) Electing Alaska Native Settlement Trusts subject to taxation under section 646.

(vii) Cemetery Perpetual Care Funds to which section 642(i) applies.

(viii) Foreign trusts (as defined in section 7701(a)(31)(B) and § 301.7701–7(a)(2)) (but see §§ 1.1411–3(e)(3)(ii) and 1.1411–4(e)(1)(ii) for rules related to distributions from foreign trusts to United States beneficiaries).

(ix) Foreign estates (as defined in section 7701(a)(31)(A)) (but see § 1.1411–3(e)(3)(ii) for rules related to distributions from foreign estates to United States beneficiaries).

* * *

[T.D. 9644, 78 FR 72424, 72427, Dec. 2, 2013; 79 FR 18160, April 1, 2014]

Federal Estate Tax

Code and Selected Regulations

SUBTITLE B. ESTATE AND GIFT TAXES

Chapter 11. Estate Tax

Subchapter A. Estates of Citizens or Residents

Part I. Tax Imposed

Introductory Regulations

§ 20.0–1 Introduction.

(a) In general. (1) The regulations in this part (part 20, subchapter B, chapter I, title 26, Code of Federal Regulations) are designated "Estate Tax Regulations." These regulations pertain to (i) the Federal estate tax imposed by chapter 11 of subtitle B of the Internal Revenue Code on the transfer of estates of decedents dying after August 16, 1954, and (ii) certain related administrative provisions of subtitle F of the Code. It should be noted that the application of many of the provisions of these regulations may be affected by the provisions of an applicable death tax convention with a foreign country. Unless otherwise indicated, references in the regulations to the "Internal Revenue Code" or the "Code" are references to the Internal Revenue Code of 1954, as amended, and references to a section or other provision of law are references to a section or other provision of the Internal Revenue Code of 1954, as amended. Unless otherwise provided, the Estate Tax Regulations are applicable to the estates of decedents dying after August 16, 1954, and supersede the regulations contained in part 81, subchapter B, chapter I, title 26, Code of Federal Regulations (1939)(Regulations 105, Estate Tax), as prescribed and made applicable to the Internal Revenue Code of 1954 by Treasury Decision 6091, signed August 16, 1954 (19 FR 5167, Aug. 17, 1954). The regulations in this part do not reflect the amendments made by the Foreign Investors Tax Act of 1966 (80 Stat. 1539).

(2) Section 2208 makes the provisions of chapter 11 of the Code apply to the transfer of the estates of certain decedents dying after September 2, 1958, who were citizens of the United States and residents of a possession thereof at the time of death. Section 2209 makes the provisions of chapter 11 apply to the transfer of the estates of certain other decedents dying after September 14, 1960, who were citizens of the United States and residents of a possession thereof at the time of death. See §§ 20.2208–1 and 20.2209–1. Except as otherwise provided in §§ 20.2208–1 and 20.2209–1, the provisions of these regulations do not apply to the estates of such decedents.

(b) Scope of regulations—(1) *Estates of citizens or residents.* Subchapter A of Chapter 11 of the Code pertains to the taxation of the estate of a person who was a citizen or a resident of the United States at the time of his death. A "resident" decedent is a decedent who, at the time of his death, had his domicile in the United States. The term "United States", as used in the estate tax regulations, includes only the States and the

District of Columbia. The term also includes the Territories of Alaska and Hawaii prior to their admission as States. See section 7701(a)(9). A person acquires a domicile in a place by living there, for even a brief period of time, with no definite present intention of later removing therefrom. Residence without the requisite intention to remain indefinitely will not suffice to constitute domicile, nor will intention to change domicile effect such a change unless accompanied by actual removal. For the meaning of the term "citizen of the United States" as applied in a case where the decedent was a resident of a possession of the United States, see § 20.2208–1. The regulations pursuant to subchapter A are set forth in §§ 20.2001–1 to 20.2056(d)–1.

(2) *Estates of nonresidents not citizens.* Subchapter B of Chapter 11 of the Code pertains to the taxation of the estate of a person who was a nonresident not a citizen of the United States at the time of his death. A "nonresident" decedent is a decedent who, at the time of his death, had his domicile outside the United States under the principles set forth in subparagraph (1) of this paragraph. (See, however, section 2202 with respect to missionaries in foreign service.) The regulations pursuant to subchapter B are set forth in §§ 20.2101–1 to 20.2107–1.

(3) *Miscellaneous substantive provisions.* Subchapter C of Chapter 11 of the Code contains a number of miscellaneous substantive provisions. The regulations pursuant to subchapter C are set forth in §§ 20.2203–1 through 20.2209–1.

(4) *Procedure and administration provisions.* Subtitle F of the Internal Revenue Code contains some sections which are applicable to the Federal estate tax. The regulations pursuant to those sections are set forth in §§ 20.6001–1 to 20.7101–1. Such regulations do not purport to be all the regulations on procedure and administration which are pertinent to estate tax matters. For the remainder of the regulations on procedure and administration which are pertinent to estate tax matters, see part 301 (Regulations on Procedure and Administration) of this chapter.

(c) Arrangement and numbering. Each section of the regulations in this part (other than this section and § 20.0–2) is designated by a number composed of the part number followed by a decimal point (20.); the section of the Internal Revenue Code which it interprets; a hyphen (-); and a number identifying the section. By use of these designations one can ascertain the sections of the regulations relating to a provision of the Code. For example, the regulations pertaining to section 2012 of the Code are designated § 20.2012–1.

[T.D. 6296, 23 FR 4529, June 24, 1958, as amended by T.D. 6526, 26 FR 414, Jan. 19, 1961; T.D. 7238, 37 FR 28717, Dec. 29, 1972; T.D. 7296, 38 FR 34191, Dec. 12, 1973; T.D. 7665, 45 FR 6089, Jan. 25, 1980; T.D. 8522, 59 FR 9646, March 1, 1994; T.D. 9849, 84 FR 9238, March 14, 2019]

§ 20.0–2 General description of tax

(a) Nature of tax. The Federal estate tax is neither a property tax nor an inheritance tax. It is a tax imposed upon the transfer of the entire taxable estate and not upon any particular legacy, devise, or distributive share. Escheat of a decedent's property to the State for lack of heirs is a transfer which causes the property to be included in the decedent's gross estate.

(b) Method of determining tax; estate of citizen or resident. *(1) In general.* Subparagraphs (2) to (5) of this paragraph contain a general description of the method to be used in determining the Federal estate tax imposed upon the transfer of the estate of a decedent who was a citizen or resident of the United States at the time of his death.

(2) Gross estate. The first step in determining the tax is to ascertain the total value of the decedent's gross estate. The value of the gross estate includes the value of all property to the extent of the interest therein of the decedent at the time of his death. (For certain exceptions in the case of real property situated outside the United States, see paragraphs (a) and (c) of § 20.2031–1.) In addition, the gross estate may include property in which the decedent did not have an interest at the time of his death. A decedent's gross estate for Federal estate tax purposes may therefore be very different from the same decedent's estate for local probate purposes. Examples of items which may be included in a decedent's gross estate and not in his probate estate are the following: certain property transferred by the decedent during his lifetime without adequate consideration; property held jointly by the decedent and others; property over which the decedent had a general power of appointment; proceeds of certain policies of insurance on the decedent's life; annuities; and dower or curtesy of a surviving spouse or a statutory estate in lieu thereof. For a detailed expla-

nation of the method of ascertaining the value of the gross estate, see sections 2031 through 2044, and the regulations thereunder.

(3) Taxable estate. The second step in determining the tax is to ascertain the value of the decedent's taxable estate. The value of the taxable estate is determined by subtracting from the value of the gross estate the authorized exemption and deductions. Under various conditions and limitations, deductions are allowable for expenses, indebtedness, taxes, losses, charitable transfers, and transfers to a surviving spouse. For a detailed explanation of the method of ascertaining the value of the taxable estate, see sections 2051 through 2056, and the regulations thereunder.

(4) Gross estate tax. The third step is the determination of the gross estate tax. This is accomplished by the application of certain rates to the value of the decedent's taxable estate. In this connection, see section 2001 and the regulations thereunder.

(5) Net estate tax payable. The final step is the determination of the net estate tax payable. This is done by subtracting from the gross estate tax the authorized credits against tax. Under certain conditions and limitations, credits are allowable for the following (computed in the order stated below):

(i) State death taxes paid in connection with the decedent's estate (section 2011);

(ii) Gift taxes paid on inter-vivos transfers by the decedent of property included in his gross estate (section 2012);

(iii) Foreign death taxes paid in connection with the decedent's estate (section 2014); and

(iv) Federal estate taxes paid on transfers of property to the decedent (section 2013).

Sections 25.2701–5 and 25.2702–6 of this chapter contain rules that provide additional adjustments to mitigate double taxation in cases where the amount of the decedent's gift was previously determined under the special valuation provisions of sections 2701 and 2702. For a detailed explanation of the credits against tax, see sections 2011 through 2016 and the regulations thereunder.

(c) Method of determining tax; estate of nonresident not a citizen. In general, the method to be used in determining the Federal estate tax imposed upon the transfer of an estate of a decedent who was a nonresident not a citizen of the United States is similar to that described in paragraph (b) of this section with respect to the estate of a citizen or resident. Briefly stated, the steps are as follows: First, ascertain the sum of the value of that part of the decedent's "entire gross estate" which at the time of his death was situated in the United States (see §§ 20.2103–1 and 20.2014–1) and, in the case of an estate of an expatriate to which section 2107 applies, any amounts includible in his gross estate under section 2107(b) (see paragraph (b) of § 20.2107–1); second, determine the value of the taxable estate by subtracting from the amount determined under the first step the amount of the allowable deductions (see § 20.2106–1); third, compute the gross estate tax on the taxable estate (see § 20.2106–1); and fourth, subtract from the gross estate tax the total amount of any allowable credits in order to arrive at the net estate tax payable (see § 20.2102–1 and paragraph (c) of § 20.2107–1).

[T.D. 6296, 23 FR 4529, June 24, 1958, as amended by T.D. 6684, 28 FR 11408, Oct. 24, 1963; T.D. 7296, 38 FR 34191, Dec. 12, 1973; T.D. 8395, 57 FR 4254, Feb. 4, 1992]

§ 2001. Imposition and Rate of Tax

(a) Imposition. A tax is hereby imposed on the transfer of the taxable estate of every decedent who is a citizen or resident of the United States.

(b) Computation of Tax. The tax imposed by this section shall be the amount equal to the excess (if any) of—

(1) a tentative tax computed under subsection (c) of—

(A) the amount of the taxable estate, and

(B) the amount of the adjusted taxable gifts, over

(2) the aggregate amount of tax which would have been payable under chapter 12 with respect to gifts made by the decedent after December 31, 1976, if the modifications described in subsection (g) had been applicable at the time of such gifts.

For purposes of paragraph (1)(B), the term "adjusted taxable gifts" means the total amount of the taxable gifts (within the meaning of section 2503) made by the decedent after December 31, 1976, other than gifts which are includible in the gross estate of the decedent.

(c) Rate Schedule.

If the amount with respect to which the tentative tax to be computed is:	*The tentative tax is:*
Not over $10,000	18 percent of such amount.
Over $10,000 but not over $20,000	$1,800, plus 20 percent of the excess of such amount over $10,000
Over $20,000 but not over $40,000	$3,800, plus 22 percent of the excess of such amount over $20,000
Over $40,000 but not over $60,000	$8,200, plus 24 percent of the excess of such amount over $40,000
Over $60,000 but not over $80,000	$13,000, plus 26 percent of the excess of such amount over $60,000
Over $80,000 but not over $100,000	$18,200, plus 28 percent of the excess of such amount over $80,000
Over $100,000 but not over $150,000	$23,800, plus 30 percent of the excess of such amount over $100,000
Over $150,000 but not over $250,000	$38,800, plus 32 percent of the excess of such amount over $150,000
Over $250,000 but not over $500,000	$70,800, plus 34 percent of the excess of such amount over $250,000
Over $500,000 but not over $750,000	$155,800, plus 37 percent of the excess of such amount over $500,000.
Over $750,000 but not over $1,000,000	$248,300, plus 39 percent of the excess of such amount over $750,000.
Over $1,000,000	$345,800, plus 40 percent of the excess of such amount over $1,000,000.

(d) Adjustment for gift tax paid by spouse. For purposes of subsection (b)(2), if—

(1) the decedent was the donor of any gift one-half of which was considered under section 2513 as made by the decedent's spouse, and

(2) the amount of such gift is includible in the gross estate of the decedent,

any tax payable by the spouse under chapter 12 on such gift (as determined under section 2012(d)) shall be treated as a tax payable with respect to a gift made by the decedent.

(e) Coordination of sections 2513 and 2035. If—

(1) the decedent's spouse was the donor of any gift one-half of which was considered under section 2513 as made by the decedent, and

(2) the amount of such gift is includible in the gross estate of the decedent's spouse by reason of section 2035, such gift shall not be included in the adjusted taxable gifts of the decedent for purposes of subsection (b)(1)(B), and the aggregate amount determined under subsection (b)(2) shall be reduced by the amount (if any) determined under subsection (d) which was treated as a tax payable by the decedent's spouse with respect to such gift.

(f) Valuation of gifts.

(1) In general. If the time has expired under section 6501 within which a tax may be assessed under chapter 12 (or under corresponding provisions of prior laws) on—

(A) the transfer of property by gift made during a preceding calendar period (as defined in section 2502(b)); or

(B) an increase in taxable gifts required under section 2701(d),

the value thereof shall, for purposes of computing the tax under this chapter, be the value as finally determined for purposes of chapter 12.

(2) Final determination. For purposes of paragraph (1), a value shall be treated as finally determined for purposes of chapter 12 if—

(A) the value is shown on a return under such chapter and such value is not contested by the Secretary before the expiration of the time referred to in paragraph (1) with respect to such return;

(B) in a case not described in subparagraph (A), the value is specified by the Secretary and such value is not timely contested by the taxpayer; or

(C) the value is determined by a court or pursuant to a settlement agreement with the Secretary.

For purposes of subparagraph (A), the value of an item shall be treated as shown on a return if the item is disclosed in the return, or in a statement attached to the return, in a manner adequate to apprise the Secretary of the nature of such item.

(g) Modifications to tax payable.

(1) Modifications to gift tax payable to reflect different tax rates. For purposes of applying subsection (b)(2) with respect to 1 or more gifts, the rates of tax under subsection (c) in effect at the decedent's death shall, in lieu of the rates of tax in effect at the time of such gifts, be used both to compute—

(A) the tax imposed by chapter 12 with respect to such gifts, and

(B) the credit allowed against such tax under section 2505, including in computing—

(i) the applicable credit amount under section 2505(a)(1), and

(ii) the sum of the amounts allowed as a credit for all preceding periods under section 2505(a)(2).

(2) Modifications to estate tax payable to reflect different basic exclusion amounts. The Secretary shall prescribe such regulations as may be necessary or appropriate to carry out this section with respect to any difference between—

(A) the basic exclusion amount under section 2010(c)(3) applicable at the time of the decedent's death, and

(B) the basic exclusion amount under such section applicable with respect to any gifts made by the decedent.

Regulations

§ 20.2001–1 Valuation of adjusted taxable gifts and section 2701(d) taxable events.

(a) Adjusted taxable gifts made prior to August 6, 1997. For purposes of determining the value of adjusted taxable gifts as defined in section 2001(b), if the gift was made prior to August 6, 1997, the value of the gift may be adjusted at any time, even if the time within which a gift tax may be assessed has expired under section 6501. This paragraph (a) also applies to adjustments involving issues other than valuation for gifts made prior to August 6, 1997.

(b) Adjusted taxable gifts and section 2701(d) taxable events occurring after August 5, 1997. For purposes of determining the amount of adjusted taxable gifts as defined in section 2001(b), if, under section 6501, the time has expired within which a gift tax may be assessed under chapter 12 of the Internal Revenue Code (or under corresponding provisions of prior laws) with respect to a gift made after August 5, 1997, or with respect to an increase in taxable gifts required under section 2701(d) and § 25.2701–4 of this chapter, then the amount of the taxable gift will be the amount as finally determined for gift tax purposes under chapter 12 of the Internal Revenue Code and the amount of the taxable gift may not thereafter be adjusted. The rule of this paragraph (b) applies to adjustments involving all issues relating to the gift, including valuation issues and legal issues involving the interpretation of the gift tax law.

(c) Finally determined. For purposes of paragraph (b) of this section, the amount of a taxable gift as finally determined for gift tax purposes is—

(1) The amount of the taxable gift as shown on a gift tax return, or on a statement attached to the return, if the Internal Revenue Service does not contest such amount before the time has expired under section 6501 within which gift taxes may be assessed;

(2) The amount as specified by the Internal Revenue Service before the time has expired under section 6501 within which gift taxes may be assessed on the gift, if such specified amount is not timely contested by the taxpayer;

(3) The amount as finally determined by a court of competent jurisdiction; or

(4) The amount as determined pursuant to a settlement agreement entered into between the taxpayer and the Internal Revenue Service.

(d) Definitions. For purposes of paragraph (b) of this section, the amount is finally determined by a court of competent jurisdiction when the court enters a final decision, judgment, decree or other order with respect to the amount of the taxable gift that is not subject to appeal. See, for example, section 7481 regarding the finality of a decision by the U.S. Tax Court. Also, for purposes of paragraph (b) of this section, a settlement agreement means any agreement entered into by the Internal Revenue Service and the taxpayer that is binding on both. The term includes a closing agreement under section 7121, a compromise under section 7122, and an agreement entered into in settlement of litigation involving the amount of the taxable gift.

(e) Expiration of period of assessment. For purposes of determining if the time has expired within which a tax may be assessed under chapter 12 of the Internal Revenue Code, see § 301.6501(c)–1(e) and (f) of this chapter.

(f) Effective dates. Paragraph (a) of this section applies to transfers of property by gift made prior to August 6, 1997, if the estate tax return for the donor/decedent's estate is filed after December 3, 1999. Paragraphs (b) through (e) of this section apply to transfers of property by gift made after August 5, 1997, if the gift tax return for the calendar period in which the gift is made is filed after December 3, 1999.

[T.D. 6296, 23 FR 4529, June 24, 1958; T.D. 8845, 64 FR 67769, Dec. 3, 1999]

§ 20.2001–2 Valuation of adjusted taxable gifts for purposes of determining the deceased spousal unused exclusion amount of last deceased spouse.

(a) General rule. Notwithstanding § 20.2001–1(b), §§ 20.2010–2(d) and 20.2010–3(d) provide additional rules regarding the authority of the Internal Revenue Service to examine any gift or other tax return(s), even if the time within which a tax may be as-

* 31 U.S.C. § 192 has been revised and relocated. For the current version, see the Appendix. *Ed.*

sessed under section 6501 has expired, for the purpose of determining the deceased spousal unused exclusion amount available under section 2010(c) of the Internal Revenue Code.

(b) Effective/applicability date. Paragraph (a) of this section applies to the estates of decedents dying on or after June 12, 2015. See 26 CFR 20.2001–2T(a), as contained in 26 CFR part 20, revised as of April 1, 2015, for the rules applicable to estates of decedents dying on or after January 1, 2011, and before June 12, 2015.

[T.D. 9725, 80 FR 34284, June 16, 2015]

§ 2002. Liability for Payment

The tax imposed by this chapter shall be paid by the executor.

Regulation

§ 20.2002–1 Liability for payment of tax.

The Federal estate tax imposed both with respect to the estates of citizens or residents and with respect to estates of nonresidents not citizens is payable by the executor or administrator of the decedent's estate. This duty applies to the entire tax, regardless of the fact that the gross estate consists in part of property which does not come within the possession of the executor or administrator. If there is no executor or administrator appointed, qualified and acting in the United States, any person in actual or constructive possession of any property of the decedent is required to pay the entire tax to the extent of the value of the property in his possession. See section 2203, defining the term "executor". The personal liability of the executor or such other person is described in section 3467 of the Revised Statutes (31 U.S.C. 192)* as follows:

Every executor, administrator, or assignee, or other person, who pays, in whole or in part, any debt due by the person or estate for whom or for which he acts before he satisfies and pays the debts due to the United States from such person or estate, shall become answerable in his own person and estate to the extent of such payments for the debts so due to the United States, or for so much thereof as may remain due and unpaid.

As used in said section, the word "debt" includes a beneficiary's distributive share of an estate. Thus, if the executor pays a debt due by the decedent's estate or distributes any portion of the estate before all the estate tax is paid, he is personally liable, to the extent of the payment or distribution, for so much of the estate tax as remains due and unpaid. In addition, section 6324(a)(2) provides that if the estate tax is not paid when due, then the spouse, transferee, trustee (except the trustee of an employee's trust which meets the requirements of section 401(a)), surviving tenant, person in possession of the property by reason of the exercise, nonexercise, or release of a power of appointment, or beneficiary, who receives, or has on the date of the decedent's death, property included in the gross estate under sections 2034 through 2042, is personally liable for the tax to the extent of the value, at the time of the decedent's death, of such property. See also the following related sections of the Internal Revenue Code: Section 2204, discharge of executor from personal liability; section 2205, reimbursement out of estate; sections 2206 and 2207, liability of life insurance beneficiaries and recipients of property over which decedent had power of appointment; sections 6321 through 6325, concerning liens for taxes; and section 6901(a)(1), concerning the liabilities of transferees and fiduciaries.

[T.D. 6296, 23 FR 4529, June 24, 1958]

Part II. Credits Against Tax

§ 2010. Unified Credit Against Estate Tax

§ 2012. Credit for Gift Tax

§ 2013. Credit for Tax on Prior Transfers

§ 2014. Credit for Foreign Death Taxes

§ 2010. Unified Credit Against Estate Tax

(a) General rule. A credit of the applicable credit amount shall be allowed to the estate of every decedent against the tax imposed by section 2001.

(b) Adjustment to credit for certain gifts made before 1977. The amount of the credit allowable under subsection (a) shall be reduced by an amount equal to 20 percent of the aggregate amount allowed as a specific exemption under section 2521 (as in effect before its repeal by the Tax Reform Act of 1976) with respect to gifts made by the decedent after September 8, 1976.

(c) Applicable Credit Amount.

(1) In General. For purposes of this section, the applicable credit amount is the amount of the tentative tax which would be determined under section 2001(c) if the amount with respect to which such tentative tax is to be computed were equal to the applicable exclusion amount.

(2) Applicable Exclusion Amount. For purposes of this subsection, the applicable exclusion amount is the sum of—

(A) the basic exclusion amount, and

(B) in the case of a surviving spouse, the deceased spousal unused exclusion amount.

(3) Basic Exclusion Amount.

(A) In General. For purposes of this subsection, the basic exclusion amount is $15,000,000.

(B) Inflation Adjustment. In the case of any decedent dying in a calendar year after 2011, the dollar amount in subparagraph (A) shall be increased by an amount equal to—

(i) such dollar amount, multiplied by

(ii) the cost-of-living adjustment determined under section 1(f)(3) for such calendar year by substituting "calendar year 2010" for "calendar year 2016" in subparagraph (A)(ii) thereof.

If any amount as adjusted under the preceding sentence is not a multiple of $10,000, such amount shall be rounded to the nearest multiple of $10,000.*

(4) Deceased Spousal Unused Exclusion Amount. For purposes of this subsection, with respect to a surviving spouse of a deceased spouse dying after December 31, 2010, the term "deceased spousal unused exclusion amount" means the lesser of—

(A) the basic exclusion amount, or

(B) the excess of—

(i) the applicable exclusion amount of the last such deceased spouse of such surviving spouse, over

(ii) the amount with respect to which the tentative tax is determined under section 2001(b)(1) on the estate of such deceased spouse.

(5) Special Rules.

(A) Election required. A deceased spousal unused exclusion amount may not be taken into account by a surviving spouse under paragraph (2) unless the executor of the estate of the deceased spouse files an estate tax return on which such amount is computed and makes an election on such return that such

* Rev. Proc. 2025–32 provides "Section 70106 of the OBBBA amends § 2010(c)(3) by increasing the basic exclusion amount to $15,000,000 for calendar year 2026. The basic exclusion amount is a component of the applicable exclusion amount described in § 2010(c)(2) and is used in determining the applicable credit amount against estate tax described in § 2010(c)(1) . . . ." *Ed.*

amount may be so taken into account. Such election, once made, shall be irrevocable. No election may be made under this subparagraph if such return is filed after the time prescribed by law (including extensions) for filing such return.

(B) Examination of prior returns after expiration of period of limitations with respect to deceased spousal unused exclusion amount. Notwithstanding any period of limitation in section 6501, after the time has expired under section 6501 within which a tax may be assessed under chapter 11 or 12 with respect to a deceased spousal unused exclusion amount, the Secretary may examine a return of the deceased spouse to make determinations with respect to such amount for purposes of carrying out this subsection.

(6) Regulations. The Secretary shall prescribe such regulations as may be necessary or appropriate to carry out this subsection.

(d) Limitation based on amount of tax. The amount of the credit allowed by subsection (a) shall not exceed the amount of the tax imposed by section 2001.

[The following table, though not part of the Internal Revenue Code, is supplied for historical purposes. Ed.]

Unified Credit and Exemption Equivalent for Prior Years

Year	*Unified Credit*	*Exemption Equivalent*
1977	$30,000	$120,667
1978	$34,000	$134,000
1979	$38,000	$147,333
1980	$42,500	$161,563
1981	$47,000	$175,625
1982	$62,800	$225,000
1983	$79,300	$275,000
1984	$96,300	$325,000
1985	$121,800	$400,000
1986	$155,800	$500,000
1987–1997	$192,800	$600,000
1998	$202,050	$625,000
1999	$211,300	$650,000
2000 and 2001	$220,550	$675,000
2002–2003	$345,800	$1,000,000
2004–2005	$555,800	$1,500,000
2006–2008	$780,800	$2,000,000
2009	$1,455,800	$3,500,000
2010 (if no election is made)	$1,730,800	$5,000,000
2011	$1,730,800	$5,000,000
2012	$1,772,800	$5,120,000
2013	$2,045,800	$5,250,000
2014	$2,081,800	$5,340,000

2015	$2,117,800	$5,430,000
2016	$2,125,800	$5,450,000
2017	$2,141,800	$5,490,000
2018	$4,417,800	$11,180,000
2019	$4,505,800	$11,400,000
2020	$4,577,800	$11,580,000
2021	$4,625,800	$11,700,000
2022	$4,769,800	$12,060,000
2023	$5,113,800	$12,920,000
2024	$5,389,800	$13,610,000
2025	$5,541,800	$13,990,000
2026	$5,945,800	$15,000,000

Regulations

§ 20.2010–0 Table of contents. [*Omitted. Ed.*]

[T.D. 9725, 80 FR 34285, June 16, 2015; T.D. 9884, 84 FR 64999, Nov. 26, 2019]

§ 20.2010–1 Unified credit against estate tax; in general.

(a) General rule. Section 2010(a) allows the estate of every decedent a credit against the estate tax imposed by section 2001. The allowable credit is the applicable credit amount. See paragraph (e)(1) of this section for an explanation of the term applicable credit amount.

(b) Special rule in case of certain gifts made before 1977. The applicable credit amount allowable under paragraph (a) of this section must be reduced by an amount equal to 20 percent of the aggregate amount allowed as a specific exemption under section 2521 (as in effect before its repeal by the Tax Reform Act of 1976) for gifts made by the decedent after September 8, 1976, and before January 1, 1977.

(c) Special rule in the case of a difference between the basic exclusion amount applicable to gifts and that applicable at the donor's date of death. Changes in the basic exclusion amount that occur between the date of a donor's gift and the date of the donor's death may cause the basic exclusion amount allowable on the date of a gift to exceed that allowable on the date of death. If the total of the amounts allowable as a credit in computing the gift tax payable on the decedent's post-1976 gifts, within the meaning of section 2001(b)(2), to the extent such credits are based solely on the basic exclusion amount as defined and adjusted in section 2010(c)(3), exceeds the credit allowable within the meaning of section 2010(a) in computing the estate tax, again only to the extent such credit is based solely on such basic exclusion amount, in each case by applying the tax rates in effect at the decedent's death, then the portion of the credit allowable in computing the estate tax on the decedent's taxable estate that is attributable to the basic exclusion amount is the sum of the amounts attributable to the basic exclusion amount allowable as a credit in computing the gift tax payable on the decedent's post-1976 gifts.

(1) *Computational rules.* For purposes of this paragraph (c):

(i) In determining the amounts allowable as a credit:

(A) The amount allowable as a credit in computing gift tax payable for any calendar period may not exceed the tentative tax on the gifts made during that period (section 2505(c)); and

(B) The amount allowable as a credit in computing the estate tax may not exceed the net tentative tax on the taxable estate (section 2010(d)).

(ii) In determining the extent to which an amount allowable as a credit in computing gift tax payable is based solely on the basic exclusion amount:

(A) Any deceased spousal unused exclusion (DSUE) amount available to the decedent is deemed to be applied to gifts made by the decedent before the decedent's basic exclusion amount is applied to those gifts (see §§ 20.2010–3(b) and 25.2505–2(b));

(B) In a calendar period in which the applicable exclusion amount allowable with regard to gifts made during that period includes amounts other than the basic exclusion amount, the allowable basic exclusion amount may not exceed that necessary to reduce the tentative gift tax to zero; and

(C) In a calendar period in which the applicable exclusion amount allowable with regard to gifts made during that period includes amounts other than the basic exclusion amount, the portion of the credit based solely on the basic exclusion amount is that which corresponds to the result of dividing the basic exclusion amount allocable to those gifts by the applicable exclusion amount allocable to those gifts.

(iii) In determining the extent to which an amount allowable as a credit in computing the estate tax is based solely on the basic exclusion amount, the credit is computed as if the applicable exclusion amount were limited to the basic exclusion amount.

(2) *Examples.* All basic exclusion amounts include hypothetical inflation adjustments. Unless otherwise stated, in each example the decedent's date of death is after 2025.

(i) *Example 1.* Individual A (never married) made cumulative post-1976 taxable gifts of $9 million, all of which were sheltered from gift tax by the cumulative total of $11.4 million in basic exclusion amount allowable on the dates of the gifts. The basic exclusion amount on A's date of death is $6.8 million. A was not eligible for any restored exclusion amount pursuant to Notice 2017–15. Because the total of the amounts allowable as a credit in computing the gift tax payable on A's post-1976 gifts (based on the $9 million of basic exclusion amount used to determine those credits) exceeds the credit based on the $6.8 million basic exclusion amount allowable on A's date of death, this paragraph (c) applies, and the credit for purposes of computing A's estate tax is based on a basic exclusion amount of $9 million, the amount used to determine the credits allowable in computing the gift tax payable on A's post-1976 gifts.

(ii) *Example 2.* Assume that the facts are the same as in Example 1 of paragraph (c)(2)(i) of this section except that A made cumulative post-1976 taxable gifts of $4 million. Because the total of the amounts allowable as a credit in computing the gift tax payable on A's post-1976 gifts is less than the credit based on the $6.8 million basic exclusion amount allowable on A's date of death, this paragraph (c) does not apply. The credit to be applied for purposes of computing A's estate tax is based on the $6.8 million basic exclusion amount as of A's date of death, subject to the limitation of section 2010(d).

(iii) *Example 3.* Individual B's predeceased spouse, C, died before 2026, at a time when the basic exclusion amount was $11.4 million. C had made no taxable gifts and had no taxable estate. C's executor elected, pursuant to § 20.2010–2, to allow B to take into account C's $11.4 million DSUE amount. B made no taxable gifts and did not remarry. The basic exclusion amount on B's date of death is $6.8 million. Because the total of the amounts allowable as a credit in computing the gift tax payable on B's post-1976 gifts attributable to the basic exclusion amount (zero) is less than the credit based on the basic exclusion amount allowable on B's date of death, this paragraph (c) does not apply. The credit to be applied for purposes of computing B's estate tax is based on B's $18.2 million applicable exclusion amount, consisting of the $6.8 million basic exclusion amount on B's date of death plus the $11.4 million DSUE amount, subject to the limitation of section 2010(d).

(iv) *Example 4.* Assume the facts are the same as in Example 3 of paragraph (c)(2)(iii) of this section except that, after C's death and before 2026, B makes taxable gifts of $14 million in a year when the basic exclusion amount is $12 million. B is considered to apply the DSUE amount to the gifts before applying B's basic exclusion amount. The amount allowable as a credit in computing the gift tax payable on B's post-1976 gifts for that year ($5,545,800) is the tax on $14 million, consisting of $11.4 million in DSUE amount and $2.6 million in basic exclusion amount. This basic exclusion amount is 18.6 percent of the $14 million exclusion amount allocable to those gifts, with the result that $1,031,519 (0.186 x $5,545,800) of the amount allowable as a credit for that year in computing gift tax payable is based solely on the basic exclusion amount. The amount allowable as a credit based solely on the basic exclusion amount for purposes of computing B's estate tax ($2,665,800) is the tax on the $6.8 million basic exclusion amount on B's date of death. Because the portion of the credit allowable in computing the gift tax payable on B's post-1976 gifts based solely on the basic exclusion amount ($1,031,519) is less than the credit based solely on the basic exclusion amount ($2,665,800) allowable on B's date of death, this paragraph (c) does not apply. The credit to be applied for purposes of computing B's estate tax is based on B's $18.2 million applicable exclusion amount, consisting of the $6.8 million basic exclusion amount on B's date of death plus the $11.4 million DSUE amount, subject to the limitation of section 2010(d).

(3) *[Reserved]*

(d) Credit limitation. The applicable credit amount allowed under paragraph (a) of this section cannot exceed the amount of the estate tax imposed by section 2001.

(e) Explanation of terms. The explanation of terms in this section applies to this section and to §§ 20.2010–2 and 20.2010–3.

(1) *Applicable credit amount.* The term applicable credit amount refers to the allowable credit against estate tax imposed by section 2001 and gift tax imposed by section 2501. The applicable credit amount equals the amount of the tentative tax that would be determined under section 2001(c) if the amount on which such tentative tax is to be computed were equal to the applicable exclusion amount. The applicable credit amount is determined by applying the unified rate schedule in section 2001(c) to the applicable exclusion amount.

(2) *Applicable exclusion amount.* The applicable exclusion amount equals the sum of the basic exclusion amount and, in the case of a surviving spouse, the deceased spousal unused exclusion (DSUE) amount.

(3) *Basic exclusion amount.* Except to the extent provided in paragraph (e)(3)(iii) of this section, the basic exclusion amount is the sum of the amounts described in paragraphs (e)(3)(i) and (ii) of this section.

(i) For any decedent dying in calendar year 2011 or thereafter, $5,000,000; and

(ii) For any decedent dying after calendar year 2011 and before calendar year 2018, $5,000,000 multiplied by the cost-of-living adjustment determined under section 1(f)(3) for the calendar year of the decedent's death by substituting "calendar year 2010" for "calendar year 1992" in section 1(f)(3)(B) and by rounding to the nearest multiple of $10,000. For any decedent dying after calendar year 2017, $5,000,000 multiplied by the cost-of-living adjustment determined under section 1(f)(3) for the calendar year of the decedent's death by substituting "calendar year 2010" for "calendar year 2016" in section 1(f)(3)(A)(ii) and rounded to the nearest multiple of $10,000.

(iii) For any decedent dying after calendar year 2017, and before calendar year 2026, paragraphs (e)(3)(i) and (ii) of this section will be applied by substituting "$10,000,000" for "$5,000,000."

(4) *Deceased spousal unused exclusion (DSUE) amount.* The term DSUE amount refers, generally, to the unused portion of a decedent's applicable exclusion amount to the extent this amount does not exceed the basic exclusion amount in effect in the year of the decedent's death. For the rules on computing the DSUE amount, see §§ 20.2010–2(c) and 20.2010–3(b).

(5) *Last deceased spouse.* The term last deceased spouse means the most recently deceased individual who, at that individual's death after December 31, 2010, was married to the surviving spouse. See §§ 20.2010–3(a) and 25.2505–2(a) for additional rules pertaining to the identity of the last deceased spouse for purposes of determining the applicable exclusion amount of the surviving spouse.

(f) Applicability dates. (1) *In general.* Except as provided in paragraph (f)(2) of this section, this section applies to the estates of decedents dying after June 11, 2015. For the rules applicable to estates of decedents dying after December 31, 2010, and before June 12, 2015, see § 20.2010–1T, as contained in 26 CFR part 20, revised as of April 1, 2015.

(2) *Exceptions.* Paragraphs (c) and (e)(3) of this section apply to estates of decedents dying on and after November 26, 2019. However, paragraph (e)(3) of this section may be applied by estates of decedents dying after December 31, 2017, and before November 26, 2019. For the explanation of the basic exclusion amount applicable to estates of decedents dying after June 11, 2015, and before January 1, 2018, see § 20.2010–1(d)(3), as contained in 26 CFR part 20, revised as of April 1, 2019.

[T.D. 9725, 80 FR 34285, June 16, 2015; T.D. 9884, 84 FR 64999, Nov. 26, 2019]

Proposed § 20.2010–1 (April 27, 2022) Unified credit against estate tax; in general.

Section 20.2010–1 is amended by:

1. Adding paragraph (c)(3); and

2. Revising the first sentence of paragraph (f)(2) and adding a sentence after the second sentence.

The additions and revisions read as follows:

* * * *

(c) * * *

(3) *Exception to the special rule.* (i) *Transfers to which the special rule does not apply.* Except as provided in paragraph (c)(3)(ii) of this section, the special rule of paragraph (c) of this section does not apply to transfers includible in the gross estate, or treated as includible in the gross estate for purposes of section 2001(b), including without limitation the following transfers:

(A) Transfers includible in the gross estate pursuant to section 2035, 2036, 2037, 2038, or 2042, regardless of whether all or any part of the transfer was deductible pursuant to section 2522 or 2523;

(B) Transfers made by enforceable promise to the extent they remain unsatisfied as of the date of death;

(C) Transfers described in § 25.2701–5(a)(4) or § 25.2702–6(a)(1) of this chapter; and

(D) Transfers that would have been described in paragraph (c)(3)(i)(A), (B), or (C) of this section but for the transfer, relinquishment, or elimination of an interest, power, or property, effectuated within 18 months of the date of the decedent's death by the decedent alone, by the decedent in conjunction with any other person, or by any other person.

(ii) *Transfers to which the special rule continues to apply.* Notwithstanding paragraph (c)(3)(i) of this section, the special rule of paragraph (c) of this section applies to the following transfers:

(A) Transfers includible in the gross estate in which the value of the taxable portion of the transfer, determined as of the date of the transfer, was 5 percent or less of the total value of the transfer; and

(B) Transfers, relinquishments, or eliminations described in paragraph (c)(3)(i)(D) of this section effectuated by the termination of the durational period described in the original instrument of transfer by either the mere passage of time or the death of any person.

(iii) *Examples.* In each example, the basic exclusion amount on the date of the gift was $11.4 million, the basic exclusion amount on the date of death is $6.8 million, and both amounts include hypothetical inflation adjustments. The donor's executor does not elect to use the alternate valuation date and, unless otherwise stated, the donor never married and made no other gifts during life.

(A) *Example 1.* Individual A made a completed gift of A's promissory note in the amount of $9 million. The note remained unpaid as of the date of A's death. The assets that are to be used to satisfy the note are part of A's gross estate, with the result that the note is treated as includible in the gross estate for purposes of section 2001(b) and is not included in A's adjusted taxable gifts. Because the note is treated as includible in the gross estate and does not qualify for the 5 percent de minimis rule in paragraph (c)(3)(ii)(A) of this section, the exception to the special rule found in paragraph (c)(3) of this section applies to the gift of the note. The credit to be applied for purposes of computing A's estate tax is based on the $6.8 million basic exclusion amount as of A's date of death, subject to the limitation of section 2010(d). The result would be the same if A or a person empowered to act on A's behalf had paid the note within the 18 months prior to the date of A's death.

(B) *Example 2.* Assume that the facts are the same as in paragraph (c)(3)(iii)(A) of this section (*Example 1*) except that A's promissory note had a value of $2 million and, on the same date that A made the gift of the promissory note, A also made a gift of $9 million in cash. The cash gift was paid immediately, whereas the $2 million note remained unpaid as of the date of A's death. The assets that are to be used to satisfy the note are part of A's gross estate, with the result that the note is treated as includible in the gross estate for purposes of section 2001(b) and is not included in A's adjusted taxable gifts. Because the $2 million note is treated as includible in the gross estate and does not qualify for the 5 percent de minimis rule in paragraph (c)(3)(ii)(A) of this section, the exception to the special rule found in paragraph (c)(3) of this section applies to the gift of the note. On the other hand, the $9 million cash gift was paid immediately, and no portion of that gift is includible or treated as includible in the gross estate. Because the amount allowable as a credit in computing the gift tax payable on A's $9 million cash gift exceeds the credit based on the $6.8 million basic exclusion amount allowable on A's date of death, the special rule of paragraph (c) of this section applies to that gift. The credit to be applied for purposes of computing A's estate tax is based on a basic exclusion amount of $9 million, the amount used to determine the credit allowable in computing the gift tax payable on A's $9 million cash gift.

(C) *Example 3.* Assume that the facts are the same as in paragraph (c)(3)(iii)(A) of this section (*Example 1*) except that, prior to A's gift of the note, the executor of the estate of A's predeceased spouse elected, pursuant to § 20.2010–2, to allow A to take into account the predeceased spouse's $2 million DSUE amount. Assume further that A's promissory note had a value of $2 million on the date of the gift, and that A made a gift of $9 million in cash a few days later. The cash gift was paid immediately, whereas the $2 million note remained unpaid as of the date of A's death. The assets that are to be used to satisfy the note are part of A's gross estate, with the result that the note is treated as includible in the gross estate for purposes of section 2001(b) and is not included in A's adjusted taxable gifts. Because A's DSUE amount was sufficient to shield the gift of the note from gift tax, no basic exclusion amount was applicable to the $2 million gift pursuant to paragraph (c)(1)(ii)(A) of this section and the special rule of paragraph (c) of this section does not apply to that gift. On the other hand, the $9 million cash gift was paid immediately, and no portion of that gift is includible or treated as includible in the gross estate. Because the amount allowable as a credit in computing the gift tax payable on A's $9 million cash gift exceeds the credit based on the $6.8 million basic exclusion amount allowable on A's date of death, the special rule of paragraph (c) of this section applies to that gift. The credit to be applied for purposes of computing A's estate tax is based on A's $11 million applicable exclusion amount, consisting of the $2 million DSUE amount plus the $9 million amount used to determine the credit allowable in computing the gift tax payable on A's $9 million cash gift.

(D) *Example 4.* Individual B transferred $9 million to a grantor retained annuity trust (GRAT), retaining a qualified annuity interest within the meaning of § 25.2702–3(b) of this chapter valued at $8,550,000. The taxable portion of the transfer valued as of the date of the transfer was $450,000. B died during the term of the GRAT. The entire GRAT corpus is includible in the gross estate pursuant to § 20.2036–1(c)(2). Because the value of the taxable portion of the transfer was 5 percent or less of the total value of the transfer determined as of the date of the gift, the 5 percent de minimis rule in paragraph (c)(3)(ii)(A) of this section is met and the exception to the special rule found in paragraph (c)(3) of this section does not apply to the gift. However, because the total of the amounts allowable as a credit in computing the gift tax payable on B's post-1976 gift of $450,000 is less than the credit based on the $6.8 million basic exclusion amount allowable on B's date of death, the special rule of paragraph (c) of this section does not apply to the gift. The credit to be applied for purposes of computing B's estate tax is based on the $6.8 million basic exclusion amount as of B's date of death, subject to the limitation of section 2010(d).

(E) *Example 5.* Assume that the facts are the same as in paragraph (c)(3)(iii)(D) of this section (*Example 4*) except that B's qualified annuity interest is valued at $8 million. The taxable portion of the transfer valued as of the date of the transfer was $1 million. Because the value of the taxable portion of the transfer was more than 5 percent of the total value of the transfer determined as of the date of the gift, the 5 percent de minimis rule in paragraph (c)(3)(ii)(A) of this section is not met and the exception to the special rule found in paragraph (c)(3) of this section applies to the gift. The credit to be applied for purposes of computing B's estate tax is based on the $6.8 million basic exclusion amount as of B's date of death, subject to the limitation of section 2010(d).

(F) *Example 6.* Assume that the facts are the same as in paragraph (c)(3)(iii)(D) of this section (*Example 4*) except that B's qualified annuity interest is valued at $2 million. The taxable portion of the transfer valued as of the date of the transfer was $7 million. B survived the term of the GRAT. Because B survived the original unaltered term of the GRAT, no part of the value of the assets transferred to the GRAT is includible in B's gross estate, and the exception to the special rule found in paragraph (c)(3) of this section does not apply to the gift. Moreover, because the amount allowable as a credit in computing the gift tax payable on B's $7 million gift exceeds the credit based on the $6.8 million basic exclusion amount allowable on B's date of death, the special rule of paragraph (c) of this section applies to the gift. The credit to be applied for purposes of computing B's estate tax is based on a basic exclusion amount of $7 million, the amount used to determine the credit allowable in computing the gift tax payable on B's transfer to the GRAT.

(G) *Example 7.* Individual C transferred $9 million to a grantor retained income trust (GRIT), retaining an income interest valued at $0 pursuant to section 2702(a)(2)(A). The taxable portion of the transfer valued as of the date of the transfer was $9 million. C died during the term of the GRIT. The entire GRIT corpus is includible in C's gross estate pursuant to section 2036(a)(1) because C retained the right to receive all of the income of the GRIT. Because the transferred assets are includible in the gross estate and do not qualify for the 5 percent de minimis rule in paragraph (c)(3)(ii)(A) of this section, the exception to the special rule found in paragraph (c)(3) of this section applies to the gift. The credit to be applied for purposes of computing C's estate tax is based on the $6.8 million basic exclusion amount as of C's date of death, subject to the limitation of section 2010(d).

* * * *

(f) * * *

(2) *Exceptions.* Except as specifically provided in this paragraph (f)(2), paragraphs (c) and (e)(3) of this section apply to estates of decedents dying on or after November 26, 2019. * * * Paragraph (c)(3) of this section is applicable to the estates of decedents dying on or after April 27, 2022.

* * * *

§ 20.2010–2 Portability provisions applicable to estate of a decedent survived by a spouse.

(a) Election required for portability. To allow a decedent's surviving spouse to take into account that decedent's deceased spousal unused exclusion (DSUE) amount, the executor of the decedent's estate must elect portability of the DSUE amount on a timely filed Form 706, "United States Estate (and Generation-Skipping Transfer) Tax Return" (estate tax return). This election is referred to in this section and in § 20.2010–3 as the portability election.

(1) *Timely filing required.* An estate that elects portability will be considered, for purposes of subtitle B and subtitle F of the Internal Revenue Code (Code), to be required to file a return under section 6018(a). Accordingly, the due date of an estate tax return required to elect portability is nine months after the decedent's date of death or the last day of the period covered by an extension (if an extension of time for filing has been obtained). See §§ 20.6075–1 and 20.6081–1 for additional rules relating to the time for filing estate tax returns. An extension of time to elect portability under this paragraph (a) will not be granted under § 301.9100–3 of this chapter to an estate that is required to file an estate tax return under section 6018(a), as determined without regard to this paragraph (a). Such an extension, however, may be available under the procedures applicable under §§ 301.9100–1 and 301.9100–3 of this chapter to an estate that is not required to file a return under section 6018(a), as determined without regard to this paragraph (a).

(2) *Portability election upon filing of estate tax return.* Upon the timely filing of a complete and properly prepared estate tax return, an executor of an estate of a decedent survived by a spouse will have elected portability of the decedent's DSUE amount unless the executor chooses not to elect portability and satisfies the requirement in paragraph (a)(3)(i) of this section. See paragraph (a)(7) of this section for the return requirements related to the portability election.

(3) *Portability election not made; requirements for election not to apply.* The executor of the estate of a decedent survived by a spouse will not make or be considered to make the portability election if either of the following applies:

(i) The executor states affirmatively on a timely filed estate tax return, or in an attachment to that estate tax return, that the estate is not electing portability under section 2010(c)(5). The manner in which the executor may make this affirmative statement on the estate tax return is as set forth in the instructions issued with respect to such form ("Instructions for Form 706").

(ii) The executor does not timely file an estate tax return in accordance with paragraph (a)(1) of this section.

(4) *Election irrevocable.* An executor of the estate of a decedent survived by a spouse who timely files an estate tax return may make or may supersede a portability election previously made, provided that the estate tax return reporting the election or the superseding election is filed on or before the due date of the return, including extensions actually granted. However, see paragraph (a)(6) of this section when contrary elections are made by more than one person permitted to make the election. The portability election, once made, becomes irrevocable once the due date of the estate tax return, including extensions actually granted, has passed.

(5) *Estates eligible to make the election.* An executor may elect portability on behalf of the estate of a decedent survived by a spouse if the decedent dies on or after January 1, 2011. However, an executor of the estate of a nonresident decedent who was not a citizen of the United States at the time of death may not elect portability on behalf of that decedent, and the timely filing of such a decedent's estate tax return will not constitute the making of a portability election.

(6) *Persons permitted to make the election.* (i) *Appointed executor*. An executor or administrator of the estate of a decedent survived by a spouse that is appointed, qualified, and acting within the United States, within the meaning of section 2203 (an appointed executor), may timely file the estate tax return on behalf of the estate of the decedent and, in so doing, elect portability of the decedent's DSUE amount. An appointed executor also may elect not to have portability apply pursuant to paragraph (a)(3) of this section.

(ii) *Non-appointed executor*. If there is no appointed executor, any person in actual or constructive possession of any property of the decedent (a non-appointed executor) may timely file the estate tax return on behalf of the estate of the decedent and, in so doing, elect portability of the decedent's DSUE amount, or, by complying with paragraph (a)(3) of this section, may elect not to have portability apply. A portability election made by a non-appointed executor when there is no appointed executor for that decedent's estate can be superseded by a subsequent contrary election made by an appointed executor of that same decedent's estate on an estate tax return filed on or before the due date of the return, including extensions actually granted. An election to allow portability made by a non-appointed executor cannot be superseded by a contrary election to have portability not apply made by another non-appointed executor of that same decedent's estate (unless such other non-appointed executor is the successor of the non-appointed executor who made the election). See § 20.6018–2 for additional rules relating to persons permitted to file the estate tax return.

(7) *Requirements of return.* (i) *General rule.* An estate tax return will be considered complete and properly prepared for purposes of this section if it is prepared in accordance with the instructions issued for the estate tax return (Instructions for Form 706) and if the requirements of §§ 20.6018–2, 20.6018–3, and 20.6018–4 are satisfied. However, see paragraph (a)(7)(ii) of this section for reduced requirements applicable to certain property of certain estates.

(ii) *Reporting of value not required for certain property* (A) *In general.* A special rule applies with respect to certain property of estates in which the executor is not required to file an estate tax return under section 6018(a), as determined without regard to paragraph (a)(1) of this section. With respect to such an estate, for bequests, devises, or transfers of property included in the gross estate, the value of which is deductible under section 2056 or 2056A (marital deduction property) or under section 2055(a) (charitable deduction property), an executor is not required to report a value for such property on the estate tax return (except to the extent provided in this paragraph (a)(7)(ii)(A)) and will be required to report only the description, ownership, and/or beneficiary of such property, along with all other information necessary to establish the right of the estate to the deduction in accordance with §§ 20.2056(a)–1(b)(i) through (iii) and 20.2055–1(c), as applicable. However, this rule does not apply in certain circumstances as provided in this paragraph (a) and as may be further described in guidance issued from time to time by publication in the Internal Revenue Bulletin (see § 601.601(d)(2)(ii)(b) of this chapter). In particular, this rule does not apply to marital deduction property or charitable deduction property if—

(*1*) The value of such property relates to, affects, or is needed to determine, the value passing from the decedent to a recipient other than the recipient of the marital or charitable deduction property;

(*2*) The value of such property is needed to determine the estate's eligibility for the provisions of sections 2032, 2032A, or another estate or generation-skipping transfer tax provision of the Code for which the value of such property or the value of the gross estate or adjusted gross estate must be known (not including section 1014 of the Code);

(*3*) Less than the entire value of an interest in property includible in the decedent's gross estate is marital deduction property or charitable deduction property; or

(*4*) A partial disclaimer or partial qualified terminable interest property (QTIP) election is made with respect to a bequest, devise, or transfer of property includible in the gross estate, part of which is marital deduction property or charitable deduction property.

(B) *Return requirements when reporting of value not required for certain property*. Paragraph (a)(7)(ii)(A) of this section applies only if the executor exercises due diligence to estimate the fair market value of the gross estate, including the property described in paragraph (a)(7)(ii)(A) of this section. Using the executor's best estimate of the value of properties to which paragraph (a)(7)(ii)(A) of this section applies, the executor must report on the estate tax return, under penalties of perjury, the amount corresponding to the particular range within which falls the executor's best estimate of the total gross estate, in accordance with the Instructions for Form 706.

(C) *Examples*. The following examples illustrate the application of paragraph (a)(7)(ii) of this section. In each example, assume that Husband (H) dies in 2015, survived by his wife (W), that both H and W are U.S. citizens, that H's gross estate does not exceed the excess of the applicable exclusion amount for the year of his death over the total amount of H's adjusted taxable gifts and any specific exemption under section 2521, and that H's executor (E) timely files Form 706 solely to make the portability election.

Example 1. (i) *Facts*. The assets includible in H's gross estate consist of a parcel of real property and bank accounts held jointly with W with rights of survivorship, a life insurance policy payable to W, and a survivor annuity payable to W for her life. H made no taxable gifts during his lifetime.

(ii) *Application*. E files an estate tax return on which these assets are identified on the proper schedule, but E provides no information on the return with regard to the date of death value of these assets in accordance with paragraph (a)(7)(ii)(A) of this section. To establish the estate's entitlement to the marital deduction in accordance with § 20.2056(a)–1(b) (except with regard to establishing the value of the property) and the instructions for the estate tax return, E includes with the estate tax return evidence to verify the title of each jointly held asset, to confirm that W is the sole beneficiary of both the life insurance policy and the survivor annuity, and to verify that the annuity is exclusively for W's life. Finally, E reports on the estate return E's best estimate, determined by exercising due diligence, of the fair market value of the gross estate in accordance with paragraph (a)(7)(ii)(B) of this section. The estate tax return is considered complete and properly prepared and E has elected portability.

Example 2. (i) *Facts*. H's will, duly admitted to probate and not subject to any proceeding to challenge its validity, provides that H's entire estate is to be distributed outright to W. The non-probate assets includible in H's gross estate consist of a life insurance policy payable to H's children from a prior marriage, and H's individual retirement account (IRA) payable to W. H made no taxable gifts during his lifetime.

(ii) *Application*. E files an estate tax return on which all of the assets includible in the gross estate are identified on the proper schedule. In the case of the probate assets and the IRA, no information is provided with regard to date of death value in accordance with paragraph (a)(7)(ii)(A) of this section. However, E attaches a copy of H's will and describes each such asset and its ownership to establish the estate's entitlement to the marital deduction in accordance with the instructions for the estate tax return and § 20.2056(a)–1(b) (except with regard to establishing the value of the property). In the case of the life insurance policy payable to H's children, all of the regular return requirements, including reporting and establishing the fair market value of such asset, apply. Finally, E reports on the estate return E's best estimate, determined by exercising due diligence, of the fair market value of the gross estate in accordance with paragraph (a)(7)(ii)(B) of this section. The estate tax return is considered complete and properly prepared and E has elected portability.

Example 3. (i) *Facts*. H's will, duly admitted to probate and not subject to any proceeding to challenge its validity, provides that 50 percent of the property passing under the terms of H's will is to be paid to a marital trust for W and 50 percent is to be paid to a trust for W and their descendants.

(ii) *Application.* The amount passing to the non-marital trust cannot be verified without knowledge of the full value of the property passing under the will. Therefore, the value of the property of the marital trust relates to or affects the value passing to the trust for W and the descendants of H and W. Accordingly, the general return requirements apply to all of the property includible in the gross estate and the provisions of paragraph (a)(7)(ii) of this section do not apply.

(b) Requirement for DSUE computation on estate tax return. Section 2010(c)(5)(A) requires an executor of a decedent's estate to include a computation of the DSUE amount on the estate tax return to elect portability and thereby allow the decedent's surviving spouse to take into account that decedent's DSUE amount. This requirement is satisfied by the timely filing of a complete and properly prepared estate tax return, as long as the executor has not elected out of portability as described in paragraph (a)(3)(i) of this section. See paragraph (a)(7) of this section for the requirements for a return to be considered complete and properly prepared.

(c) Computation of the DSUE amount. (1) *General rule.* Subject to paragraphs (c)(2) through (4) of this section, the DSUE amount of a decedent with a surviving spouse is the lesser of the following amounts—

(i) The basic exclusion amount in effect in the year of the death of the decedent; or

(ii) The excess of—

(A) The decedent's applicable exclusion amount; over

(B) The sum of the amount of the taxable estate and the amount of the adjusted taxable gifts of the decedent, which together is the amount on which the tentative tax on the decedent's estate is determined under section 2001(b)(1).

(2) *Special rule to consider gift taxes paid by decedent.* Solely for purposes of computing the decedent's DSUE amount, the amount of the adjusted taxable gifts of the decedent referred to in paragraph (c)(1)(ii)(B) of this section is reduced by the amount, if any, on which gift taxes were paid for the calendar year of the gift(s).

(3) *Impact of applicable credits.* An estate's eligibility under sections 2012 through 2015 for credits against the tax imposed by section 2001 does not impact the computation of the DSUE amount.

(4) *Special rule in case of property passing to qualified domestic trust.* (i) *In general.* When property passes for the benefit of a surviving spouse in a qualified domestic trust (QDOT) as defined in section 2056A(a), the DSUE amount of the decedent is computed on the decedent's estate tax return for the purpose of electing portability in the same manner as this amount is computed under paragraph (c)(1) of this section, but this DSUE amount is subject to subsequent adjustments. The DSUE amount of the decedent must be redetermined upon the occurrence of the final distribution or other event (generally, the termination of all QDOTs created by or funded with assets passing from the decedent or the death of the surviving spouse) on which estate tax is imposed under section 2056A. See § 20.2056A–6 for the rules on determining the estate tax under section 2056A. See § 20.2010–3(c)(3) regarding the timing of the availability of the decedent's DSUE amount to the surviving spouse.

(ii) *Surviving spouse becomes a U.S. citizen.* If the surviving spouse becomes a U.S. citizen and if the requirements of section 2056A(b)(12) and the corresponding regulations are satisfied, the estate tax imposed under section 2056A(b)(1) ceases to apply. Accordingly, no estate tax will be imposed under section 2056A either on subsequent QDOT distributions or on the property remaining in the QDOT on the surviving spouse's death and the decedent's DSUE amount is no longer subject to adjustment.

(5) *Examples.* The following examples illustrate the application of this paragraph (c):

Example 1. Computation of DSUE amount. (i) *Facts.* In 2002, having made no prior taxable gift, Husband (H) makes a taxable gift valued at $1,000,000 and reports the gift on a timely filed gift tax return. Because the amount of the gift is equal to the applicable exclusion amount for that year ($1,000,000), $345,800 is allowed as a credit against the tax, reducing the gift tax liability to zero. H dies in 2015, survived by Wife (W). H and W are U.S. citizens and neither has any prior marriage. H's taxable estate is $1,000,000. The executor of H's estate timely files H's estate tax return and elects portability, thereby allowing W to benefit from H's DSUE amount.

(ii) *Application.* The executor of H's estate computes H's DSUE amount to be $3,430,000 (the lesser of the $5,430,000 basic exclusion amount in 2015, or the excess of H's $5,430,000 applicable exclusion amount over the sum of the $1,000,000 taxable estate and the $1,000,000 amount of adjusted taxable gifts).

Example 2. Computation of DSUE amount when gift tax paid. (i) *Facts.* The facts are the same as in Example 1 of this paragraph (c)(5) except that the value of H's taxable gift in 2002 is $2,000,000. After application of the applicable credit amount, H owes gift tax on $1,000,000, the amount of the gift in excess of the applicable exclusion amount for that year. H pays the gift tax owed on the 2002 transfer.

(ii) *Application.* On H's death, the executor of H's estate computes the DSUE amount to be $3,430,000 (the lesser of the $5,430,000 basic exclusion amount in 2015, or the excess of H's $5,430,000 applicable exclusion amount over the sum of the $1,000,000 taxable estate and $1,000,000 of adjusted taxable gifts sheltered from tax by H's applicable credit amount). H's adjusted taxable gifts of $2,000,000 were reduced for purposes of this computation by $1,000,000, the amount of taxable gifts on which gift taxes were paid.

Example 3. Computation of DSUE amount when QDOT created. (i) *Facts.* Husband (H), a U.S. citizen, makes his first taxable gift in 2002, valued at $1,000,000, and reports the gift on a timely filed gift tax return. No gift tax is due because the applicable exclusion amount for that year ($1,000,000) equals the fair market value of the gift. H dies in 2015 with a gross estate of $2,000,000. H's surviving spouse (W) is a resident, but not a citizen, of the United States and, under H's will, a pecuniary bequest of $1,500,000 passes to a QDOT for the benefit of W. H's executor timely files an estate tax return and makes the QDOT election for the property passing to the QDOT, and H's estate is allowed a marital deduction of $1,500,000 under section 2056(d) for the value of that property. H's taxable estate is $500,000. On H's estate tax return, H's executor computes H's preliminary DSUE amount to be $3,930,000 (the lesser of the $5,430,000 basic exclusion amount in 2015, or the excess of H's $5,430,000 applicable exclusion amount over the sum of the $500,000 taxable estate and the $1,000,000 adjusted taxable gifts). No taxable events within the meaning of section 2056A occur during W's lifetime with respect to the QDOT, and W makes no taxable gifts. At all times since H's death, W has been a U.S. resident. In 2017, W dies and the value of the assets of the QDOT is $1,800,000.

(ii) *Application.* H's DSUE amount is redetermined to be $2,130,000 (the lesser of the $5,430,000 basic exclusion amount in 2015, or the excess of H's $5,430,000 applicable exclusion amount over $3,300,000 (the sum of the $500,000 taxable estate augmented by the $1,800,000 of QDOT assets and the $1,000,000 adjusted taxable gifts)).

Example 4. Computation of DSUE amount when surviving spouse with QDOT becomes a U.S. citizen. (i) *Facts.* The facts are the same as in Example 3 of this paragraph (c)(5) except that W becomes a U.S. citizen in 2016 and dies in 2018. The U.S. Trustee of the QDOT notifies the IRS that W has become a U.S. citizen by timely filing a final estate tax return (Form 706-QDT). Pursuant to section 2056A(b)(12), the estate tax under section 2056A no longer applies to the QDOT property.

(ii) *Application.* Because H's DSUE amount no longer is subject to adjustment once W becomes a citizen of the United States, H's DSUE amount is $3,930,000, as it was preliminarily determined as of H's death. Upon W's death in 2018, the value of the QDOT property is includible in W's gross estate.

(d) Authority to examine returns of decedent. The IRS may examine returns of a decedent in determining the decedent's DSUE amount, regardless of whether the period of limitations on assessment has expired for that return. See § 20.2010–3(d) for additional rules relating to the IRS's authority to examine returns. See also section 7602 for the IRS's authority, when ascertaining the correctness of any return, to examine any returns that may be relevant or material to such inquiry.

(e) Effective/applicability date. This section applies to the estates of decedents dying on or after June 12, 2015. See 26 CFR 20.2010–2T, as contained in 26 CFR part 20, revised as of April 1, 2015, for the rule applicable to estates of decedents dying on or after January 1, 2011, and before June 12, 2015.

[T.D. 9725, 80 FR 34285, June 16, 2015]

§ 20.2010–3 Portability provisions applicable to the surviving spouse's estate.

(a) Surviving spouse's estate limited to DSUE amount of last deceased spouse. (1) *In general.* The deceased spousal unused exclusion (DSUE) amount of a decedent, computed under § 20.2010–2(c), is included in determining the surviving spouse's applicable exclusion amount under section 2010(c)(2), provided—

(i) Such decedent is the last deceased spouse of such surviving spouse within the meaning of § 20.2010–1(e)(5) on the date of the death of the surviving spouse; and

(ii) The executor of the decedent's estate elected portability (see § 20.2010–2(a) and (b) for applicable requirements).

(2) *No DSUE amount available from last deceased spouse.* If the last deceased spouse of such surviving spouse had no DSUE amount, or if the executor of such a decedent's estate did not make a portability election, the surviving spouse's estate has no DSUE amount (except as provided in paragraph (b)(1)(ii) of this section) to be included in determining the applicable exclusion amount, even if the surviving spouse previously had a DSUE amount available from another decedent who, prior to the death of the last deceased spouse, was the last deceased spouse of such surviving spouse. See paragraph (b) of this section for a special rule in the case of multiple deceased spouses and a previously applied DSUE amount.

(3) *Identity of last deceased spouse unchanged by subsequent marriage or divorce.* A decedent is the last deceased spouse (as defined in § 20.2010–1(e)(5)) of a surviving spouse even if, on the date of the death of the surviving spouse, the surviving spouse is married to another (then-living) individual. If a surviving spouse marries again and that marriage ends in divorce or an annulment, the subsequent death of the divorced spouse does not end the status of the prior deceased spouse as the last deceased spouse of the surviving spouse. The divorced spouse, not being married to the surviving spouse at death, is not the last deceased spouse as that term is defined in § 20.2010–1(e)(5).

(b) Special rule in case of multiple deceased spouses and previously-applied DSUE amount. (1) *In general.* A special rule applies to compute the DSUE amount included in the applicable exclusion amount of a surviving spouse who previously has applied the DSUE amount of one or more deceased spouses to taxable gifts in accordance with § 25.2505–2(b) and (c). If a surviving spouse has applied the DSUE amount of one or more (successive) last deceased spouses to the surviving spouse's transfers during life, and if any of those last deceased spouses is different from the surviving spouse's last deceased spouse as defined in § 20.2010–1(e)(5) at the time of the surviving spouse's death, then the DSUE amount to be included in determining the applicable exclusion amount of the surviving spouse at the time of the surviving spouse's death is the sum of—

(i) The DSUE amount of the surviving spouse's last deceased spouse as described in paragraph (a)(1) of this section; and

(ii) The DSUE amount of each other deceased spouse of the surviving spouse, to the extent that such amount was applied to one or more taxable gifts of the surviving spouse.

(2) *Example.* The following example, in which all described individuals are U.S. citizens, illustrates the application of this paragraph (b):

Example. (i) *Facts.* Husband 1 (H1) dies in 2011, survived by Wife (W). Neither has made any taxable gifts during H1's lifetime. H1's executor elects portability of H1's DSUE amount. The DSUE amount of H1 as computed on the estate tax return filed on behalf of H1's estate is $5,000,000. In 2012, W makes taxable gifts to her children valued at $2,000,000. W reports the gifts on a timely filed gift tax return. W is considered to have applied $2,000,000 of H1's DSUE amount to the amount of taxable gifts, in accordance with § 25.2505–2(c), and, therefore, W owes no gift tax. W has an applicable exclusion amount remaining in the amount of $8,120,000 ($3,000,000 of H1's remaining DSUE amount plus W's own $5,120,000 basic exclusion amount). W marries Husband 2 (H2) in 2013. H2 dies in 2014. H2's executor elects portability of H2's DSUE amount, which is properly computed on H2's estate tax return to be $2,000,000. W dies in 2015.

(ii) *Application.* The DSUE amount to be included in determining the applicable exclusion amount available to W's estate is $4,000,000, determined by adding the $2,000,000 DSUE amount of H2 and the $2,000,000 DSUE amount of H1 that was applied by W to W's 2012 taxable gifts. The $4,000,000 DSUE amount added to W's $5,430,000 basic exclusion amount (for 2015), causes W's applicable exclusion amount to be $9,430,000.

(c) Date DSUE amount taken into consideration by surviving spouse's estate. (1) *General rule.* A portability election made by an executor of a decedent's estate (see § 20.2010–2(a) and (b) for applicable requirements) generally applies as of the date of the decedent's death. Thus, such decedent's DSUE amount is included in the applicable exclusion amount of the decedent's surviving spouse under section 2010(c)(2) and will be applicable to transfers made by the surviving spouse after the decedent's death (subject to the limitations in paragraph (a) of this section). However, such decedent's DSUE amount will not be included in the applicable exclusion amount of the surviving spouse, even if the surviving spouse had made a transfer in reliance on the availability or computation of the decedent's DSUE amount:

(i) If the executor of the decedent's estate supersedes the portability election by filing a subsequent estate tax return in accordance with § 20.2010–2(a)(4);

(ii) To the extent that the DSUE amount subsequently is reduced by a valuation adjustment or the correction of an error in calculation; or

(iii) To the extent that the surviving spouse cannot substantiate the DSUE amount claimed on the surviving spouse's return.

(2) *Exception when surviving spouse not a U.S. citizen on date of deceased spouse's death.* If a surviving spouse becomes a citizen of the United States after the death of the surviving spouse's last deceased spouse, the DSUE amount of the surviving spouse's last deceased spouse becomes available to the surviving spouse on the date the surviving spouse becomes a citizen of the United States (subject to the limitations in paragraph (a) of this section). However, when the special rule regarding qualified domestic trusts in paragraph (c)(3) of this section applies, the earliest date on which a decedent's DSUE amount may be included in the applicable exclusion amount of such decedent's surviving spouse who becomes a U.S. citizen is as provided in paragraph (c)(3) of this section.

(3) *Special rule when property passes to surviving spouse in a qualified domestic trust.* (i) *In general.* When property passes from a decedent for the benefit of the decedent's surviving spouse in one or more qualified domestic trusts (QDOT) as defined in section 2056A(a) and the decedent's executor elects portability, the DSUE amount available to be included in the applicable exclusion amount of the surviving spouse under section 2010(c)(2) is the DSUE amount of the decedent as redetermined in accordance with § 20.2010–2(c)(4) (subject to the limitations in paragraph (a) of this section). The earliest date on which such decedent's DSUE amount may be included in the applicable exclusion amount of the surviving spouse under section 2010(c)(2) is the date of the occurrence of the final QDOT distribution or final other event (generally, the termination of all QDOTs created by or funded with assets passing from the decedent or the death of the surviving spouse) on which tax under section 2056A is imposed. However, the decedent's DSUE amount as redetermined in accordance with § 20.2010–2(c)(4) may be applied to certain taxable gifts of the surviving spouse. See § 25.2505–2(d)(3)(i).

(ii) *Surviving spouse becomes a U.S. citizen.* If a surviving spouse for whom property has passed from a decedent in one or more QDOTs becomes a citizen of the United States and the requirements in section 2056A(b)(12) and the corresponding regulations are satisfied, then the date on which such decedent's DSUE amount may be included in the applicable exclusion amount of the surviving spouse under section 2010(c)(2) (subject the limitations in paragraph (a) of this section) is the date on which the surviving spouse becomes a citizen of the United States. See § 20.2010–2(c)(4) for the rules for computing the decedent's DSUE amount in the case of a qualified domestic trust.

(d) Authority to examine returns of deceased spouses. For the purpose of determining the DSUE amount to be included in the applicable exclusion amount of a surviving spouse, the Internal Revenue Service (IRS) may examine returns of each of the surviving spouse's deceased spouses whose DSUE amount is claimed to be included in the surviving spouse's applicable exclusion amount, regardless of whether the period of limitations on assessment has expired for any such return. The IRS's authority to examine returns of a deceased spouse applies with respect to each transfer by the surviving spouse to which a DSUE amount is or has been applied. Upon examination, the IRS may adjust or eliminate the DSUE amount reported on such a return of a deceased spouse; however, the IRS may assess additional tax on that return only if that tax is assessed within the period of limitations on assessment under section 6501 applicable to the tax shown on that return. See also section 7602 for the IRS's authority, when ascertaining the correctness of any return, to examine any returns that may be relevant or material to such inquiry. For purposes of these examinations to determine the DSUE amount, the surviving spouse is considered to have a material interest that is affected by the return information of the deceased spouse within the meaning of section 6103(e)(3).

(e) Availability of DSUE amount for estates of nonresidents who are not citizens. The estate of a nonresident surviving spouse who is not a citizen of the United States at the time of such surviving spouse's death shall not take into account the DSUE amount of any deceased spouse of such surviving spouse within the meaning of § 20.2010–1(e)(5) except to the extent allowed under any applicable treaty obligation of the United States. See section 2102(b)(3).

(f) Effective/applicability date. This section applies to the estates of decedents dying on or after June 12, 2015. See 26 CFR 20.2010–3T, as contained in 26 CFR part 20, revised as of April 1, 2015, for the rules applicable to estates of decedents dying on or after January 1, 2011, and before June 12, 2015.

[T.D. 9725, 80 FR 34288, June 16, 2015; T.D. 9884, 84 FR 65000, Nov. 26, 2019]

§ 2012. Credit for Gift Tax

(a) In general. If a tax on a gift has been paid under chapter 12 (sec. 2501 and following), or under corresponding provisions of prior laws, and thereafter on the death of the donor any amount in respect of such gift is required to be included in the value of the gross estate of the decedent for purposes of this chapter, then there shall be credited against the tax imposed by section 2001 the amount of the tax paid on a gift under chapter 12, or under corresponding provisions of prior laws, with respect to so much of the property which constituted the gift as is included in the gross estate, except that the amount of such credit shall not exceed an amount which bears the same ratio to the tax imposed by section 2001 (after deducting from such tax the unified credit provided by section 2010) as the value (at the time of the gift or at the time of the death, whichever is lower) of so much of the property which constituted the gift as is included in the gross estate bears to the value of the entire gross estate reduced by the aggregate amount of the charitable and marital deductions allowed under sections 2055, 2056, and 2106(a)(2).

(b) Valuation reductions. In applying, with respect to any gift, the ratio stated in subsection (a), the value at the time of the gift or at the time of the death, referred to in such ratio, shall be reduced—

(1) by such amount as will properly reflect the amount of such gift which was excluded in determining (for purposes of section 2503(a)), or of corresponding provisions of prior laws, the total amount of gifts made during the calendar quarter (or calendar year if the gift was made before January 1, 1971) in which the gift was made;

(2) if a deduction with respect to such gift is allowed under section 2056(a) (relating to marital deduction), then by the amount of such value, reduced as provided in paragraph (1); and

(3) if a deduction with respect to such gift is allowed under sections 2055 or 2106(a)(2) (relating to charitable deduction), then by the amount of such value, reduced as provided in paragraph (1) of this subsection.

(c) Where gift considered made one-half by spouse. Where the decedent was the donor of the gift but, under the provisions of section 2513, or corresponding provisions of prior laws, the gift was considered as made one-half by his spouse—

(1) the term "the amount of the tax paid on a gift under chapter 12", as used in subsection (a), includes the amounts paid with respect to each half of such gift, the amount paid with respect to each being computed in the manner provided in subsection (d); and

(2) in applying, with respect to such gift, the ratio stated in subsection (a), the value at the time of the gift or at the time of the death, referred to in such ratio, includes such value with respect to each half of such gift, each such value being reduced as provided in paragraph (1) of subsection (b).

(d) Computation of amount of gift tax paid.

(1) Amount of tax. For purposes of subsection (a), the amount of tax paid on a gift under chapter 12, or under corresponding provisions of prior laws, with respect to any gift shall be an amount which bears the same ratio to the total tax paid for the calendar quarter (or calendar year if the gift was made before January 1, 1971) in which the gift was made as the amount of such gift bears to the total amount of taxable gifts (computed without deduction of the specific exemption) for such quarter or year.

(2) Amount of gift. For purposes of paragraph (1), the "amount of such gift" shall be the amount included with respect to such gift in determining (for the purposes of section 2503(a), or of corresponding provisions of prior laws) the total amount of gifts made during such quarter or year, reduced by the amount of any deduction allowed with respect to such gift under section 2522, or under corresponding provisions of prior laws (relating to charitable deduction), or under section 2523 (relating to marital deduction).

(e) Section inapplicable to gifts made after December 31, 1976. No credit shall be allowed under this section with respect to the amount of any tax paid under chapter 12 on any gift made after December 31, 1976.

Regulation

§ 20.2012–1 Credit for gift tax. [*Omitted. Ed.*]
[T.D. 6296, 23 FR 4529, June 24, 1958, as amended by T.D. 7238, 37 FR 28718, Dec. 29, 1972; T.D. 8522, 59 FR 9646, March 1, 1994]

§ 2013. Credit for Tax on Prior Transfers

(a) General rule. The tax imposed by section 2001 shall be credited with all or a part of the amount of the Federal estate tax paid with respect to the transfer of property (including property passing as a result of the exercise or non-exercise of a power of appointment) to the decedent by or from a person (herein designated as a "transferor") who died within 10 years before, or within 2 years after, the decedent's death. If the transferor died within 2 years of the death of the decedent, the credit shall be the amount determined under subsections (b) and (c). If the transferor predeceased the decedent by more than 2 years, the credit shall be the following percentage of the amount so determined—

(1) 80 percent, if within the third or fourth years preceding the decedent's death;

(2) 60 percent, if within the fifth or sixth years preceding the decedent's death;

(3) 40 percent, if within the seventh or eighth years preceding the decedent's death; and

(4) 20 percent, if within the ninth or tenth years preceding the decedent's death.

(b) Computation of credit. Subject to the limitation prescribed in subsection (c), the credit provided by this section shall be an amount which bears the same ratio to the estate tax paid (adjusted as indicated hereinafter) with respect to the estate of the transferor as the value of the property transferred bears to the taxable estate of the transferor (determined for purposes of the estate tax) decreased by any death taxes paid with respect to such estate. For purposes of the preceding sentence, the estate tax paid shall be the Federal estate tax paid increased by any credits allowed against such estate tax under section 2012, or corresponding provisions of prior laws, on account of gift tax, and for any credits allowed against such estate tax under this section on account of prior transfers where the transferor acquired property from a person who died within 10 years before the death of the decedent.

(c) Limitation on credit.

(1) In general. The credit provided in this section shall not exceed the amount by which—

(A) the estate tax imposed by section 2001 or section 2101 (after deducting the credits provided for in sections 2010, 2012, and 2014) computed without regard to this section, exceeds

(B) such tax computed by excluding from the decedent's gross estate the value of such property transferred and, if applicable, by making the adjustment hereinafter indicated.

If any deduction is otherwise allowable under section 2055 or section 2106(a)(2) (relating to charitable deduction) then, for the purpose of the computation indicated in subparagraph (B), the amount of such deduction shall be reduced by that part of such deduction which the value of such property transferred bears to the decedent's entire gross estate reduced by the deductions allowed under sections 2053 and 2054, or section 2106(a)(1) (relating to deduction for expenses, losses, etc.). For purposes of this section, the value of such property transferred shall be the value as provided for in subsection (d) of this section.

(2) Two or more transferors. If the credit provided in this section relates to property received from 2 or more transferors, the limitation provided in paragraph (1) of this subsection shall be computed by aggregating the value of the property so transferred to the decedent. The aggregate limitation so determined shall be apportioned in accordance with the value of the property transferred to the decedent by each transferor.

(d) Valuation of property transferred. The value of property transferred to the decedent shall be the value used for the purpose of determining the Federal estate tax liability of the estate of the transferor but—

(1) there shall be taken into account the effect of the tax imposed by section 2001 or 2101, or any estate, succession, legacy, or inheritance tax, on the net value to the decedent of such property;

(2) where such property is encumbered in any manner, or where the decedent incurs any obligation imposed by the transferor with respect to such property, such encumbrance or obligation shall be taken into account in the same manner as if the amount of a gift to the decedent of such property was being determined; and

(3) if the decedent was the spouse of the transferor at the time of the transferor's death, the net value of the property transferred to the decedent shall be reduced by the amount allowed under section 2056 (relating to marital deductions), as a deduction from the gross estate of the transferor.

(e) Property defined. For purposes of this section, the term "property" includes any beneficial interest in property, including a general power of appointment (as defined in section 2041).

(f) Treatment of additional tax imposed under section 2032A. If section 2032A applies to any property included in the gross estate of the transferor and an additional tax is imposed with respect to such property under section 2032A(c) before the date which is 2 years after the date of the decedent's death, for purposes of this section—

(1) the additional tax imposed by section 2032A(c) shall be treated as a Federal estate tax payable with respect to the estate of the transferor; and

(2) the value of such property and the amount of the taxable estate of the transferor shall be determined as if section 2032A did not apply with respect to such property.

Regulations

§ 20.2013–1 Credit for tax on prior transfers.

(a) In general. A credit is allowed under section 2013 against the Federal estate tax imposed on the present decedent's estate for Federal estate tax paid on the transfer of property to the present decedent from a transferor who died within ten years before, or within two years after, the present decedent's death. See § 20.2013–5 for definition of the terms "property" and "transfer". There is no requirement that the transferred property be identified in the estate of the present decedent or that the property be in existence at the time of the decedent's death. It is sufficient that the transfer of the property was subjected to Federal estate tax in the estate of the transferor and that the transferor died within the prescribed period of time. The executor must submit such proof as may be requested by the district director in order to establish the right of the estate to the credit.

(b) Limitations on credit. The credit for tax on prior transfers is limited to the smaller of the following amounts:

(1) The amount of the Federal estate tax attributable to the transferred property in the transferor's estate, computed as set forth in § 20.2013–2; or

(2) The amount of the Federal estate tax attributable to the transferred property in the decedent's estate, computed as set forth in § 20.2013–3. Rules for valuing property for purposes of the credit are contained in § 20.2013–4.

(c) Percentage reduction. If the transferor died within the two years before, or within the two years after, the present decedent's death, the credit is the smaller of the two limitations described in paragraph (b) of this section. If the transferor predeceased the present decedent by more than two years, the credit is a certain percentage of the smaller of the two limitations described in paragraph (b) of this section, determined as follows:

(1) 80 percent, if the transferor died within the third or fourth years preceding the present decedent's death;

(2) 40 percent, if the transferor died within the fifth or sixth years preceding the present decedent's death;

(3) 40 percent, if the transferor died within the seventh or eighth years preceding the present decedent's death; and

(4) 20 percent, if the transferor died within the ninth or tenth years preceding the present decedent's death.

The word "within" as used in this paragraph means "during". Therefore, if a death occurs on the second anniversary of another death, the first death is considered to have occurred within the two years before the second death. If the credit for tax on prior transfers relates to property received from two or more transferors, the provisions of this paragraph are to be applied separately with respect to the property received from each transferor. See paragraph (d) of example (2) in § 20.2013–6.

(d) Examples. For illustrations of the application of this section, see examples (1) and (2) set forth in § 20.2013–6.

[T.D. 6296, 23 FR 4529, June 24, 1958]

§ 20.2013–2 "First limitation".

(a) The amount of the Federal estate tax attributable to the transferred property in the transferor's estate is the "first limitation." Thus, the credit is limited to an amount, A, which bears the same ratio to B (the "transferor's adjusted Federal estate tax", computed as described in paragraph (b) of this section) as C (the value of the property transferred (see § 20.2013–4)) bears to D (the "transferor's adjusted taxable estate", computed as described in paragraph (c) of this section). Stated algebraically, the "first limitation" (A) equals:

$$\frac{\text{value of transferred property (C)}}{\text{“transferor's adjusted taxable estate” (D)}} * \text{“transferor's adjusted Federal estate tax” (B)}$$

(b) For purposes of the ratio stated in paragraph (a) of this section, the "transferor's adjusted Federal estate tax" referred to as factor "B" is the amount of the Federal estate tax paid with respect to the transferor's estate plus:

(1) Any credit allowed the transferor's estate for gift tax under section 2012, or the corresponding provisions of prior law; and

(2) Any credit allowed the transferor's estate, under section 2013, for tax on prior transfers, but only if the transferor acquired property from a person who died within 10 years before the death of the present decedent.

(c)(1) For purposes of the ratio stated in paragraph (a) of this section, the "transferor's adjusted taxable estate" referred to as factor "D" is the amount of the transferor's taxable estate (or net estate) decreased by the amount of any "death taxes" paid with respect to his gross estate and increased by the amount of the exemption allowed in computing his taxable estate (or net estate). The amount of the transferor's taxable estate (or net estate) is determined in accordance with the provisions of § 20.2051–1 in the case of a citizen or resident of the United States or of § 20.2106–1 in the case of a nonresident not a citizen of the United States (or the corresponding provisions of prior regulations). The term "death taxes" means the Federal estate tax plus all other estate, inheritance, legacy, succession, or similar death taxes imposed by, and paid to, any taxing authority, whether within or without the United States. However, only the net amount of such taxes paid is taken into consideration.

(2) The amount of the exemption depends upon the citizenship and residence of the transferor at the time of his death. Except in the case of a decedent described in section 2209 (relating to certain residents of possessions of the United States who are considered nonresidents not citizens), if the decedent was a citizen or resident of the United States, the exemption is the $60,000 authorized by section 2052 (or the corresponding provisions of prior law). If the decedent was a nonresident not a citizen of the United States, or is considered under section 2209 to have been such a nonresident, the exemption is the $30,000 or $2,000, as the case may be, authorized by section 2106(a)(3) (or the corresponding provisions of prior law), or such larger amount as is authorized by section 2106(a)(3)(B) or may have been allowed as an exemption pursuant to the prorated exemption provisions of an applicable death tax convention. See § 20.2052–1 and paragraph (a)(3) of § 20.2106–1.

(d) If the credit for tax on prior transfers relates to property received from two or more transferors, the provisions of this section are to be applied separately with respect to the property received from each transferor. See paragraph (b) of example (2) in § 20.2013–6.

(e) For illustrations of the application of this section, see examples (1) and (2) set forth in § 20.2013–6.

[T.D. 6296, 23 FR 4529, June 24, 1958; 25 FR 14021, Dec. 31, 1960, as amended at T.D. 7296, 38 FR 34191, Dec. 12, 1973]

§ 20.2013–3 "Second limitation".

(a) The amount of the Federal estate tax attributable to the transferred property in the present decedent's estate is the "second limitation". Thus, the credit is limited to the difference between—

(1) The net estate tax payable (see paragraph (b)(5) or (c), as the case may be, of § 20.0–2) with respect to the present decedent's estate, determined without regard to any credit for tax on prior transfers under section 2013 or any credit for foreign death taxes claimed under the provisions of a death tax convention, and

(2) The net estate tax determined as provided in subparagraph (1) of this paragraph but computed by subtracting from the present decedent's gross estate the value of the property transferred (see § 20.2013–4), and by making only the adjustment indicated in paragraph (b) of this section if a charitable deduction is allowable to the estate of the present decedent.

(b) If a charitable deduction is allowable to the estate of the present decedent under the provisions of section 2055 or section 2106(a)(2) (for estates of nonresidents not citizens), for purposes of determining the tax described in paragraph (a)(2) of this section, the charitable deduction otherwise allowable is reduced by an amount, E, which bears the same ratio to F (the charitable deduction otherwise allowable) as G (the value of the transferred property (see § 20.2013–4)) bears to H (the value of the present decedent's gross estate reduced by the amount of the deductions for expenses, indebtedness, taxes, losses, etc., allowed under the provisions of sections 2053 and 2054 or section 2106(a)(1) (for estates of nonresidents not citizens)). See paragraph (c)(2) of example (1) and paragraph (c)(2) of example (2) in § 20.2013–6.

(c) If the credit for tax on prior transfers relates to property received from two or more transferors, the property received from all transferors is aggregated in determining the limitation on credit under this section (the "second limitation"). However, the limitation so determined is apportioned to the property received from each transferor in the ratio that the property received from each transferor bears to the total property received from all transferors. See paragraph (c) of example (2) in § 20.2013–6.

(d) For illustrations of the application of this section, see examples (1) and (2) set forth in § 20.2013–6.

[T.D. 6296, 23 FR 4529, June 24, 1958; 25 FR 14021, Dec. 31, 1960, as amended at T.D. 7296, 38 FR 34191, Dec. 12, 1973]

§ 20.2013–4 Valuation of property transferred.

(a) For purposes of section 2013 and §§ 20.2013–1 to 20.2013–6, the value of the property transferred to the decedent is the value at which the property was included in the transferor's gross estate for the purpose of the Federal estate tax (see sections 2031, 2032, 2103, and 2107, and the regulations thereunder) reduced as indicated in paragraph (b) of this section. If the decedent received a life estate or a remainder or other limited interest in property that was included in a transferor decedent's gross estate, the value of the interest is determined as of the date of the transferor's death on the basis of recognized valuation principles (see §§ 20.2031–7 (or, for certain prior periods, § 20.2031–7A) and 20.7520–1 through 20.7520–4). The application of this paragraph may be illustrated by the following examples:

Example (1). A died on January 1, 1953, leaving Blackacre to B. The property was included in A's gross estate at a value of $100,000. On January 1, 1955, B sold Blackacre to C for $150,000. B died on February 1, 1955. For purposes of computing the credit against the tax imposed on B's estate, the value of the property transferred to B is $100,000.

Example (2). A died on January 1, 1953, leaving Blackacre to B for life and, upon B's death, remainder to C. At the time of A's death, B was 56 years of age. The property was included in A's gross estate at a value of $100,000. The part of that value attributable to the life estate is $44,688 and the part of that value attributable to the remainder is $55,312 (see § 20.2031–7A(b)). B died on January 1, 1955, and C died on January 1, 1956. For purposes of computing the credit against the tax imposed on B's estate, the value of the property transferred to B is $44,688. For purposes of computing the credit against the tax imposed on C's estate, the value of the property transferred to C is $55,312.

(b) In arriving at the value of the property transferred to the decedent, the value at which the property was included in the transferor's gross estate (see paragraph (a) of this section) is reduced as follows:

(1) By the amount of the Federal estate tax and any other estate, inheritance, legacy, or succession taxes which were payable out of the property transferred to the decedent or which were payable by the decedent in connection with the property transferred to him. For example, if under the transferor's will or local law all death taxes are to be paid out of other property with the result that the decedent receives a bequest free and clear of all death taxes, no reduction is to be made under this subparagraph;

(2) By the amount of any marital deduction allowed the transferor's estate under section 2056 (or under section 812(e) of the Internal Revenue Code of 1939) if the decedent was the spouse of the transferor at the time of the transferor's death;

(3)(i) By the amount of administration expenses in accordance with the principles of § 20.2056(b)–4(d).

(ii) This paragraph (b)(3) applies to transfers from estates of decedents dying on or after December 3, 1999; and

(4)(i) By the amount of any encumbrance on the property or by the amount of any obligation imposed by the transferor and incurred by the decedent with respect to the property, to the extent such charges would be taken into account if the amount of a gift to the decedent of such property were being determined.

(ii) For purposes of this subparagraph, an obligation imposed by the transferor and incurred by the decedent with respect to the property includes a bequest, etc., in lieu of the interest of the surviving spouse under community property laws, unless the interest was, immediately prior to the transferor's death, a mere expectancy. However, an obligation imposed by the transferor and incurred by the decedent with respect to the property does not include a bequest, devise, or other transfer in lieu of dower, curtesy, or of a statutory estate created in lieu of dower or curtesy, or of other marital rights in the transferor's property or estate.

(iii) The application of this subparagraph may be illustrated by the following examples:

Example (1). The transferor devised to the decedent real estate subject to a mortgage. The value of the property transferred to the decedent does not include the amount of the mortgage. If, however, the transferor by his will directs the executor to pay off the mortgage, such payment constitutes an additional amount transferred to the decedent.

Example (2). The transferor bequeathed certain property to the decedent with a direction that the decedent pay $1,000 to X. The value of the property transferred to the decedent is the value of the property reduced by $1,000.

Example (3). The transferor bequeathed certain property to his wife, the decedent, in lieu of her interest in property held by them as community property under the law of the State of their residence. The wife elected to relinquish her community property interest and to take the bequest. The value of the property transferred to the decedent is the value of the property reduced by the value of the community property interest relinquished by the wife.

Example (4). The transferor bequeathed to the decedent his entire residuary estate, out of which certain claims were to be satisfied. The entire distributable income of the transferor's estate (during the period of its administration) was applied toward the satisfaction of these claims and the remaining portion of the claims was satisfied by the decedent out of his own funds. Thus, the decedent received a larger sum upon settlement of the transferor's estate than he was actually bequeathed. The value of the property transferred to the decedent is the value at which such property was included in the transferor's gross estate, reduced by the amount of the estate income and the decedent's own funds paid out in satisfaction of the claims.

[T.D. 6296, 23 FR 4529, June 24, 1958, as amended by T.D. 7077, 35 FR 18461, Dec. 4, 1970; T.D. 7296, 38 FR 34191, Dec. 12, 1973; T.D. 8522, 59 FR 9646, March 1, 1994; T.D. 8540, 59 FR 30151, June 10, 1994; T.D. 8846, 64 FR 67764, Dec. 3, 1999]

§ 20.2013–5 "Property" and "transfer" defined.

(a) For purposes of section 2013 and §§ 20.2013–1 to 20.2013–6, the term "property" means any beneficial interest in property, including a general power of appointment (as defined in section 2041) over property. Thus, the term does not include an interest in property consisting merely of a bare legal title, such as that of a trustee. Nor does the term include a power of appointment over property which is not a general power of appointment (as defined in section 2041). Examples of property, as described in this paragraph, are annuities, life estates, estates for terms of years, vested or contingent remainders and other future interests.

(b) In order to obtain the credit for tax on prior transfers, there must be a transfer of property described in paragraph (a) of this section by or from the transferor to the decedent. The term "transfer" of property by or from a transferor means any passing of property or an interest in property under circumstances which were such that the property or interest was included in the gross estate of the transferor. In this connection, if the decedent receives property as a result of the exercise or nonexercise of a power of appointment, the donee of the power (and not the creator) is deemed to be the transferor of the property if the property subject to the power is includible in the donee's gross estate under section 2041 (relating to powers of appointment). Thus, notwithstanding the designation by local law of the capacity in which the decedent takes, property received from the transferor includes interests in property held by or devolving upon the decedent: (1) As spouse under dower or curtesy laws or laws creating an estate in lieu of dower or curtesy; (2) as surviving tenant of a tenancy by the entirety or joint tenancy with survivorship rights; (3) as beneficiary of the proceeds of life insurance; (4) as survivor under an annuity contract; (5) as donee (possessor) of a general power of appointment (as defined in section 2041); (6) as appointee under the exercise of a general power of appointment (as defined in section 2041); or (7) as remainderman under the release or nonexercise of a power of appointment by reason of which the property is included in the gross estate of the donee of the power under section 2041.

(c) The application of this section may be illustrated by the following example:

Example. A devises Blackacre to B, as trustee, with directions to pay the income therefore to C, his son, for life. Upon C's death, Blackacre is to be sold. C is given a general testamentary power, to appoint one-third of the proceeds, and a testamentary power, which is not a general power, to appoint the remaining two-thirds of the proceeds, to such of the issue of his sister D as he should choose. D has a daughter, E, and a son, F. Upon his death, C exercised his general power by appointing one-third of the proceeds to D and his special power by appointing two-thirds of the proceeds to E. Since B's interest in Blackacre as a trustee is not a beneficial interest, no part of it is "property" for purpose of the credit in B's estate. On the other hand, C's life estate and his testamentary power over the one-third interest in the remainder constitute "property" received from A for purpose of the credit in C's estate. Likewise, D's one-third interest in the remainder received through the exercise of C's general power of appointment is "property" received from C for purpose of the credit in D's estate. No credit is allowed E's estate for the property which passed to her from C since the property was not included in C's gross estate. On the other hand, no credit is allowed in E's estate for property passing to her from A since her interest was not susceptible of valuation at the time of A's death (see § 20.2013–4).

[T.D. 6296, 23 FR 4529, June 24, 1958]

§ 20.2013–6 Examples. [*Omitted. Ed.*]

[T.D. 6296, 23 FR 4529, June 24, 1958; 25 FR 14021, Dec. 31, 1960]

§ 2014. Credit for Foreign Death Taxes

(a) In general. The tax imposed by section 2001 shall be credited with the amount of any estate, inheritance, legacy, or succession taxes actually paid to any foreign country in respect of any property situated within such foreign country and included in the gross estate (not including any such taxes paid with respect to the estate of a person other than the decedent). The determination of the country within which property is situated shall be made in accordance with the rules applicable under subchapter B (sec. 2101 and following) in determining whether property is situated within or without the United States.

(b) Limitations on credit. The credit provided in this section with respect to such taxes paid to any foreign country—

(1) shall not, with respect to any such tax, exceed an amount which bears the same ratio to the amount of such tax actually paid to such foreign country as the value of property which is—

(A) situated within such foreign country,

(B) subjected to such tax, and

(C) included in the gross estate

bears to the value of all property subjected to such tax; and

(2) shall not, with respect to all such taxes, exceed an amount which bears the same ratio to the tax imposed by section 2001 (after deducting from such tax the credits provided by sections 2010 and 2012) as the value of property which is—

(A) situated within such foreign country,

(B) subjected to the taxes of such foreign country, and

(C) included in the gross estate

bears to the value of the entire gross estate reduced by the aggregate amount of the deductions allowed under sections 2055 and 2056.

(c) Valuation of property.

(1) The values referred to in the ratio stated in subsection (b)(1) are the values determined for purposes of the tax imposed by such foreign country.

(2) The values referred to in the ratio stated in subsection (b)(2) are the values determined under this chapter; but, in applying such ratio, the value of any property described in subparagraphs (A), (B), and (C) thereof shall be reduced by such amount as will properly reflect, in accordance with regulations prescribed by the Secretary, the deductions allowed in respect of such property under sections 2055 and 2056 (relating to charitable and marital deductions).

(d) Proof of credit. The credit provided in this section shall be allowed only if the taxpayer establishes to the satisfaction of the Secretary—

(1) the amount of taxes actually paid to the foreign country,

(2) the amount and date of each payment thereof,

(3) the description and value of the property in respect of which such taxes are imposed, and

(4) all other information necessary for the verification and computation of the credit.

(e) Period of limitation. The credit provided in this section shall be allowed only for such taxes as were actually paid and credit therefor claimed within 4 years after the filing of the return required by section 6018, except that—

(1) If a petition for redetermination of a deficiency has been filed with the Tax Court within the time prescribed in section 6213(a), then within such 4-year period or before the expiration of 60 days after the decision of the Tax Court becomes final.

(2) If, under section 6161, an extension of time has been granted for payment of the tax shown on the return, or of a deficiency, then within such 4-year period or before the date of the expiration of the period of the extension.

Refund based on such credit may (despite the provisions of sections 6511 and 6512) be made if claim therefor is filed within the period above provided. Any such refund shall be made without interest.

(f) Additional limitation in cases involving a deduction under section 2053(d). In any case where a deduction is allowed under section 2053(d) for an estate, succession, legacy, or inheritance tax imposed by and actually paid to any foreign country upon a transfer by the decedent for public, charitable, or religious uses described in section 2055, the property described in subparagraphs (A), (B), and (C) of paragraphs (1) and (2) of subsection (b) of this section shall not include any property in respect of which such deduction is allowed under section 2053(d).

(g) Possession of United States deemed a foreign country. For purposes of the credits authorized by this section, each possession of the United States shall be deemed to be a foreign country.

(h) Similar credit required for certain alien residents. Whenever the President finds that—

(1) a foreign country, in imposing estate, inheritance, legacy, or succession taxes, does not allow to citizens of the United States resident in such foreign country at the time of death a credit similar to the credit allowed under subsection (a),

(2) such foreign country, when requested by the United States to do so has not acted to provide such a similar credit in the case of citizens of the United States resident in such foreign country at the time of death, and

(3) it is in the public interest to allow the credit under subsection (a) in the case of citizens or subjects of such foreign country only if it allows such a similar credit in the case of citizens of the United States resident in such foreign country at the time of death,

the President shall proclaim that, in the case of citizens or subjects of such foreign country dying while the proclamation remains in effect, the credit under subsection (a) shall be allowed only if such foreign country allows such a similar credit in the case of citizens of the United States resident in such foreign country at the time of death.

Regulations

§ 20.2014–1 Credit for foreign death taxes.

(a) In general. (1) A credit is allowed under section 2014 against the Federal estate tax for any estate, inheritance, legacy, or succession taxes actually paid to any foreign country (hereinafter referred to as "foreign death taxes"). The credit is allowed only for foreign death taxes paid (i) with respect to property situated within the country to which the tax is paid, (ii) with respect to property included in the decedent's gross estate, and (iii) with respect to the decedent's estate. The credit is allowable to the estate of a decedent who was a citizen of the United States at the time of his death. The credit is also allowable, as provided in paragraph (c) of this section, to the estate of a decedent who was a resident but not a citizen of the United States at the time of his death. The credit is not allowable to the estate of a decedent who was neither a citizen nor a resident of the United States at the time of his death. See paragraph (b)(1) of § 20.0–1 for the meaning of the term "resident" as applied to a decedent. The credit is allowable not only for death taxes paid to foreign countries which are states in the international sense, but also for death taxes paid to possessions or political subdivisions of foreign states. With respect to the estate of a decedent dying after September 2, 1958, the term "foreign country", as used in this section and §§ 20.2014–2 to 20.2014–6, includes a possession of the United States. See §§ 20.2011–1 and 20.2011–2 for the allowance of a credit for death taxes paid to a possession of the United States in the case of a decedent dying before September 3, 1958. No credit is allowable for interest or penalties paid in connection with foreign death taxes.

(2) In addition to the credit for foreign death taxes under section 2014, similar credits are allowed under death tax conventions with certain foreign countries. If credits against the Federal estate tax are allowable under section 2014, or under section 2014 and one or more death tax conventions, for death taxes paid to more than one country, the credits are combined and the aggregate amount is credited against the Federal estate tax, subject to the limitation provided for in paragraph (c) of § 20.2014–4. For application of the credit in cases involving a death tax convention, see § 20.2014–4.

(3) No credit is allowable under section 2014 in connection with property situated outside of the foreign country imposing the tax for which credit is claimed. However, such a credit may be allowable under certain death tax conventions. In the case of a tax imposed by a political subdivision of a foreign country, credit for the tax shall be allowed with respect to property having a situs in that foreign country, even though, under the principles described in this subparagraph, the property has a situs in a political subdivision different from the one imposing the tax. Whether or not particular property of a decedent is situated in the foreign country imposing the tax is determined in accordance with the same principles that would be applied in determining whether or not similar property of a nonresident decedent not a citizen of the United States is situated within the United States for Federal estate tax purposes. See §§ 20.2104–1 and 20.2105–1. For example, under § 20.2104–1 shares of stock are deemed to be situated in the United States only if issued by a domestic corporation. Thus, a share of corporate stock is regarded as situated in the foreign country imposing the tax only if the issuing corporation is incorporated in that country. Further, under § 20.2105–1 amounts receivable as insurance on the life of a nonresident not a citizen of the United States at the time of his death are not deemed situated in the United States. Therefore, in determining the credit under section 2014 in the case of a decedent who was a citizen or resident of the United States, amounts receivable as insurance on the life of the decedent and payable under a policy issued by a corporation incorporated in a foreign country are not deemed situated in such foreign country. In addition, under § 20.2105–1 in the case of an estate of a nonresident not a citizen of the United States who died on or after November 14, 1966, a debt obligation of a domestic corporation is not considered to be situated in the United States if any interest thereon would be treated under section 862(a)(1) as income from sources without the United States by reason of section 861(a)(1)(B) (relating to interest received from a domestic corporation less than 20 percent of whose gross income for a 3-year period was derived from sources within the United States). Accordingly, a debt obligation the primary obligor on which is a corporation incorporated in the foreign country imposing the tax is not considered to be situated in that country if,

under circumstances corresponding to those described in § 20.2105–1 less than 20 percent of the gross income of the corporation for the 3-year period was derived from sources within that country. Further, under § 20.2104–1 in the case of an estate of a nonresident not a citizen of the United States who died before November 14, 1966, a bond for the payment of money is not situated within the United States unless it is physically located in the United States. Accordingly, in the case of the estate of a decedent dying before November 14, 1966, a bond is deemed situated in the foreign country imposing the tax only if it is physically located in that country. Finally, under § 20.2105–1 moneys deposited in the United States with any person carrying on the banking business by or for a nonresident not a citizen of the United States who died before November 14, 1966, and who was not engaged in business in the United States at the time of death are not deemed situated in the United States. Therefore, an account with a foreign bank in the foreign country imposing the tax is not considered to be situated in that country under corresponding circumstances.

(4) Where a deduction is allowed under section 2053(d) for foreign death taxes paid with respect to a charitable gift, the credit for foreign death taxes is subject to further limitations as explained in § 20.2014–7.

(b) Limitations on credit. The credit for foreign death taxes is limited to the smaller of the following amounts:

(1) The amount of a particular foreign death tax attributable to property situated in the country imposing the tax and included in the decedent's gross estate for Federal estate tax purposes, computed as set forth in § 20.2014–2; or

(2) The amount of the Federal estate tax attributable to particular property situated in a foreign country, subjected to foreign death tax in that country, and included in the decedent's gross estate for Federal estate tax purposes, computed as set forth in § 20.2014–3.

(c) Credit allowable to estate of resident not a citizen. (1) In the case of an estate of a decedent dying before November 14, 1966, who was a resident but not a citizen of the United States, a credit is allowed to the estate under section 2014 only if the foreign country of which the decedent was a citizen or subject, in imposing foreign death taxes, allows a similar credit to the estates of citizens of the United States who were resident in that foreign country at the time of death.

(2) In the case of an estate of a decedent dying on or after November 14, 1966, who was a resident but not a citizen of the United States, a credit is allowed to the estate under section 2014 without regard to the similar credit requirement of subparagraph (1) of this paragraph unless the decedent was a citizen or subject of a foreign country with respect to which there is in effect at the time of the decedent's death a Presidential proclamation, as authorized by section 2014(h), reinstating the similar credit requirement. In the case of an estate of a decedent who was a resident of the United States and a citizen or subject of a foreign country with respect to which such a proclamation has been made, and who dies while the proclamation is in effect, a credit is allowed under section 2014 only if that foreign country, in imposing foreign death taxes, allows a similar credit to the estates of citizens of the United States who were resident in that foreign country at the time of death. The proclamation authorized by section 2014(h) for the reinstatement of the similar credit requirement with respect to the estates of citizens or subjects of a specific foreign country may be made by the President whenever he finds that—

(i) The foreign country, in imposing foreign death taxes, does not allow a similar credit to the estates of citizens of the United States who were resident in the foreign country at the time of death,

(ii) The foreign country, after having been requested to do so, has not acted to provide a similar credit to the estates of such citizens, and

(iii) It is in the public interest to allow the credit under section 2014 to the estates of citizens or subjects of the foreign country only if the foreign country allows a similar credit to the estates of citizens of the United States who were resident in the foreign country at the time of death.

The proclamation for the reinstatement of the similar credit requirement with respect to the estates of citizens or subjects of a specific foreign country may be revoked by the President. In that case, a credit is allowed under section 2014, to the estate of a decedent who was a citizen or subject of that foreign country and a resident of the United States at the time of death, without regard to the similar credit requirement if the decedent dies after the proclamation reinstating the similar credit requirement has been revoked.

[T.D. 6296, 23 FR 4529, June 24, 1958, as amended by T.D. 6526, 26 FR 415, Jan. 19, 1961; T.D. 6600, 27 FR 4983, May 29, 1962; T.D. 7296, 38 FR 34192, Dec. 12, 1973]

§ 20.2014–2 "First limitation". [*Omitted. Ed.*]

[T.D. 6296, 23 FR 4529, June 24, 1958, as amended by T.D. 6600, 27 FR 4984, May 29, 1962; T.D. 6684, 28 FR 11408, Oct. 24, 1963; T.D. 7296, 38 FR 34193, Dec. 12, 1973; 39 FR 2090, Jan. 17, 1974]

§ 20.2014–3 "Second limitation". [*Omitted. Ed.*]

[T.D. 6296, 23 FR 4529, June 24, 1958, as amended by T.D. 6600, 27 FR 4984, May 29, 1962; T.D. 7296, 38 FR 34193, Dec. 12, 1973; T.D. 8522, 59 FR 9646, March 1, 1994]

§ 20.2014–4 Application of credit in cases involving a death tax convention. [*Omitted. Ed.*]

[T.D. 6296, 23 FR 4529, June 24, 1958, as amended by T.D. 6742, 29 FR 7928, June 23, 1964; T.D. 7296, 38 FR 34193, Dec. 12, 1973]

§ 20.2014–5 Proof of credit. [*Omitted. Ed.*]

[T.D. 6296, 23 FR 4529, June 24, 1958]

§ 20.2014–6 Period of limitations on credit. [*Omitted. Ed.*]

[T.D. 6296, 23 FR 4529, June 24, 1958]

§ 20.2014–7 Limitation on credit if a deduction for foreign death taxes is allowed under section 2053(d). [*Omitted. Ed.*]

[T.D. 6600, 27 FR 4984, May 27, 1962]

§ 2015. Credit for Death Taxes on Remainders

Where an election is made under section 6163(a) to postpone payment of the tax imposed by section 2001 or 2101, such part of any estate, inheritance, legacy, or succession taxes allowable as a credit under section 2014, as is attributable to a reversionary or remainder interest may be allowed as a credit against the tax attributable to such interest, subject to the limitations on the amount of the credit contained in such sections, if such part is paid, and credit therefor claimed, at any time before the expiration of the time for payment of the tax imposed by section 2001 or 2101 as postponed and extended under section 6163.

Regulation

§ 20.2015–1 Credit for death taxes on remainders.

(a) If the executor of an estate elects under section 6163(a) to postpone the time for payment of any portion of the Federal estate tax attributable to a reversionary or remainder interest in property, credit is allowed under sections 2011 and 2014 against that portion of the Federal estate tax for State death taxes and foreign death taxes attributable to the reversionary or remainder interest if the State death taxes or foreign death taxes are paid and if credit therefor is claimed either—

(1) Within the time provided for in sections 2011 and 2014, or

(2) Within the time for payment of the tax imposed by section 2001 or 2101 as postponed under section 6163(a) and as extended under section 6163(b) (on account of undue hardship) or, if the precedent interest terminated before July 5, 1958, within 60 days after the termination of the preceding interest or interests in the property. The allowance of credit, however, is subject to the other limitations contained in sections 2011 and 2014 and, in the case of the estate of a decedent who was a nonresident not a citizen of the United States, in section 2102(b).

(b) In applying the rule stated in paragraph (a) of this section, credit for State death taxes or foreign death taxes paid within the time provided in sections 2011 and 2014 is applied first to the portion of the Federal estate tax payment of which is not postponed, and any excess is applied to the balance of the Federal estate tax. However, credit for State death taxes or foreign death taxes not paid within the time provided in section 2011 and 2014 is allowable only against the portion of the Federal estate tax attributable to the reversionary or remainder interest, and only for State or foreign death taxes attributable to that interest. If a State death tax or a foreign death tax is imposed upon both a reversionary or remainder interest and upon other property, without a definite apportionment of the tax, the amount of the tax deemed attributable to the reversionary or remainder interest is an amount which bears the same ratio to the total tax as the value of the reversionary or remainder interest bears to the value of the entire property with respect to which the tax was imposed. In applying this ratio, adjustments consistent with those required under paragraph (c) of § 20.6163–1 must be made.

(c) The application of this section may be illustrated by the following examples:

Example (1). One-third of the Federal estate tax was attributable to a remainder interest in real property located in State Y, and two-thirds of the Federal estate tax was attributable to other property located in State X. The payment of the tax attributable to the remainder interest was postponed under the provisions of section 6163(a). The maximum credit allowable for State death taxes under the provisions of section 2011 is $12,000. Therefore, of the maximum credit allowable, $4,000 is attributable to the remainder interest and $8,000 is attributable to the other property. Within the 4-year period provided for in section 2011, inheritance tax in the amount of $9,000 was paid to State X in connection with the other property. With respect to this $9,000, $8,000 (the maximum amount allowable) is allowed as a credit against the Federal estate tax attributable to the other property, and $1,000 is allowed as a credit against the postponed tax. The life estate or other precedent interest expired after July 4, 1958. After the expiration of the 4-year period but before the expiration of the period of postponement elected under section 6163(a) and of the period of extension granted under section 6163(b) for payment of the tax, inheritance tax in the amount of $5,000 was paid to State Y in connection with the remainder interest. As the maximum credit allowable with respect to the remainder interest is $4,000 and $1,000 has already been allowed as a credit, an additional $3,000 will be credited against the Federal estate tax attributable to the remainder interest. It should be noted that if the life estate or other precedent interest had expired after the expiration of the 4-year period but before July 5, 1958, the same result would be reached only if the inheritance tax had been paid to State Y before the expiration of 60 days after the termination of the life estate or other precedent interest.

Example (2). The facts are the same as in example (1), except that within the 4-year period inheritance tax in the amount of $2,500 was paid to State Y with respect to the remainder interest and inheritance tax in the amount of $7,500 was paid to State X with respect to the other property. The amount of $8,000 is allowed as a credit against the Federal estate tax attributable to the other property and the amount of $2,000 is allowed as a credit against the postponed tax. The life estate or other precedent interest expired after July 4, 1958. After the expiration of the 4-year period but before the expiration of the period of postponement elected under section 6163(a) and of the period of extension granted under section 6163(b) for payment of the tax, inheritance tax in the amount of $5,000 was paid to State Y in connection with the remainder interest. As the maximum credit allowable with respect to the remainder interest is $4,000 and $2,000 already has been allowed as a credit, an additional $2,000 will be credited against the Federal estate tax attributable to the remainder interest. It should be noted that if the life estate or other precedent interest had expired after the expiration of the 4-year period but before July 5, 1958, the same result would be reached only if the inheritance tax had been paid to State Y before the expiration of 60 days after the termination of the life estate or other precedent interest.

Example (3). The facts are the same as in example (2), except that no payment was made to State Y within the 4-year period. The amount of $7,500 is allowed as a credit against the Federal estate tax attributable to the other property. After termination of the life interest additional credit will be allowed in the amount of $4,000 against the Federal estate tax attributable to the remainder interest. Since the payment of $5,000 was made to State Y following the expiration of the 4-year period, no part of the payment may be allowed as a credit against the Federal estate tax attributable to the other property.

[T.D. 6296, 23 FR 4529, June 24, 1958, as amended by T.D. 6526, 26 FR 415, Jan. 19, 1961; T.D. 7296, 38 FR 34194, Dec. 12, 1973]

§ 2016. Recovery of Taxes Claimed as Credit

If any tax claimed as a credit under section 2014 is recovered from any foreign country, the executor, or any other person or persons recovering such amount, shall give notice of such recovery to the Secretary at such time and in such manner as may be required by regulations prescribed by him, and the Secretary shall (despite the provisions of section 6501) redetermine the amount of the tax under this chapter and the amount, if any, of the tax due on such redetermination, shall be paid by the executor or such person or persons, as the case may be, on notice and demand. No interest shall be assessed or collected on any amount of tax due on any redetermination by the Secretary, resulting from a refund to the executor of tax claimed as a credit under section 2014, for any period before the receipt of such refund, except to the extent interest was paid by the foreign country on such refund.

Regulation

§ 20.2016–1 Recovery of death taxes claimed as credit.

In accordance with the provisions of section 2016, the executor (or any other person) receiving a refund of any State death taxes or foreign death taxes claimed as a credit under section 2011 or section 2014 shall notify the district director of the refund within 30 days of its receipt. The notice shall contain the following information:

(a) The name of the decedent;

(b) The date of the decedent's death;

(c) The property with respect to which the refund was made;

(d) The amount of the refund, exclusive of interest;

(e) The date of the refund; and

(f) The name and address of the person receiving the refund.

If the refund was in connection with foreign death taxes claimed as a credit under section 2014, the notice shall also contain a statement showing the amount of interest, if any, paid by the foreign country on the refund. Finally, the person filing the notice shall furnish the district director such additional information as he may request. Any Federal estate tax found to be due by reason of the refund is payable by the person or persons receiving it, upon notice and demand, even though the refund is received after the expiration of the period of limitations set forth in section 6501 (see section 6501(c)(5)). If the tax found to be due results from a refund of foreign death tax claimed as a credit under section 2014, such tax shall not bear interest for any period before the receipt of the refund, except to the extent that interest was paid by the foreign country on the refund.

[T.D. 6296, 23 FR 4529, June 24, 1958]

Part III. Gross Estate

§ 2031. Definition of Gross Estate

(a) General. The value of the gross estate of the decedent shall be determined by including to the extent provided for in this part, the value at the time of his death of all property, real or personal, tangible or intangible, wherever situated.

(b) Valuation of unlisted stock and securities. In the case of stock and securities of a corporation the value of which, by reason of their not being listed on an exchange and by reason of the absence of sales thereof, cannot be determined with reference to bid and asked prices or with reference to sales prices, the value thereof shall be determined by taking into consideration, in addition to all other factors, the value of stock or securities of corporations engaged in the same or a similar line of business which are listed on an exchange.

(c) Estate Tax With Respect to Land Subject to a Qualified Conservation Easement.

(1) In general. If the executor makes the election described in paragraph (6), then, except as otherwise provided in this subsection, there shall be excluded from the gross estate the lesser of

(A) the applicable percentage of the value of land subject to a qualified conservation easement, reduced by the amount of any deduction under section 2055(f) with respect to such land, or

(B) $500,000.

(2) Applicable percentage. For purposes of paragraph (1), the term "applicable percentage" means 40 percent reduced (but not below zero) by 2 percentage points for each percentage point (or fraction thereof) by which the value of the qualified conservation easement is less than 30 percent of the value of the land (determined without regard to the value of such easement and reduced by the value of any retained development right (as defined in paragraph (5))). The values taken into account under the preceding sentence shall be such values as of the date of the contribution referred to in paragraph (8)(B).

(3) [Repealed.]

(4) Treatment of certain indebtedness.

(A) In general. The exclusion provided in paragraph (1) shall not apply to the extent that the land is debt-financed property.

(B) Definitions. For purposes of this paragraph—

(i) Debt-financed property. The term "debt-financed property" means any property with respect to which there is an acquisition indebtedness (as defined in clause (ii)) on the date of the decedent's death.

(ii) Acquisition indebtedness. The term "acquisition indebtedness" means, with respect to debt-financed property, the unpaid amount of—

(I) the indebtedness incurred by the donor in acquiring such property,

(II) the indebtedness incurred before the acquisition of such property if such indebtedness would not have been incurred but for such acquisition,

(III) the indebtedness incurred after the acquisition of such property if such indebtedness would not have been incurred but for such acquisition and the incurrence of such indebtedness was reasonably foreseeable at the time of such acquisition, and

(IV) the extension, renewal, or refinancing of an acquisition indebtedness.

(5) Treatment of retained development right.

(A) In general. Paragraph (1) shall not apply to the value of any development right retained by the donor in the conveyance of a qualified conservation easement.

(B) Termination of retained development right. If every person in being who has an interest (whether or not in possession) in the land executes an agreement to extinguish permanently some or all of any development rights (as defined in subparagraph (D)) retained by the donor on or before the date for filing the return of the tax imposed by section 2001, then any tax imposed by section 2001 shall be reduced accordingly. Such agreement shall be filed with the return of the tax imposed by section 2001. The agreement shall bc in such form as the Secretary shall prescribe.

(C) Additional tax. Any failure to implement the agreement described in subparagraph (B) not later than the earlier of—

(i) the date which is 2 years after the date of the decedent's death, or

(ii) the date of the sale of such land subject to the qualified conservation easement,

shall result in the imposition of an additional tax in the amount of the tax which would have been due on the retained development rights subject to such agreement. Such additional tax shall be due and payable on the last day of the 6th month following such date.

(D) Development right defined. For purposes of this paragraph, the term 'development right' means any right to use the land subject to the qualified conservation easement in which such right is retained for any commercial purpose which is not subordinate to and directly supportive of the use of such land as a farm for farming purposes (within the meaning of section 2032A(e)(5)).

(6) Election. The election under this subsection shall be made on or before the due date (including extensions) for filing the return of tax imposed by section 2001 and shall be made on such return. Such an election, once made, shall be irrevocable.

(7) Calculation of estate tax due. An executor making the election described in paragraph (6) shall, for purposes of calculating the amount of tax imposed by section 2001, include the value of any development right (as defined in paragraph (5)) retained by the donor in the conveyance of such qualified conservation easement. The computation of tax on any retained development right prescribed in this paragraph shall be done in such manner and on such forms as the Secretary shall prescribe.

(8) Definitions. For purposes of this subsection—

(A) Land subject to a qualified conservation easement. The term "land subject to a qualified conservation easement" means land—

(i) which is located in the United States or any possession of the United States,

(ii) which was owned by the decedent or a member of the decedent's family at all times during the 3-year period ending on the date of the decedent's death, and

(iii) with respect to which a qualified conservation easement has been made by an individual described in subparagraph (C), as of the date of the election described in paragraph (6).

(B) Qualified conservation easement. The term "qualified conservation easement" means a qualified conservation contribution (as defined in section 170(h)(1)) of a qualified real property interest (as defined in section 170(h)(2)(C)), except that clause (iv) of section 170(h)(4)(A) shall not apply, and the restriction on the use of such interest described in section 170(h)(2)(C) shall include a prohibition on more than a de minimis use for a commercial recreational activity.

(C) Individual described. An individual is described in this subparagraph if such individual is—

(i) the decedent,

(ii) a member of the decedent's family,

(iii) the executor of the decedent's estate, or

(iv) the trustee of a trust the corpus of which includes the land to be subject to the qualified conservation easement.

(D) Member of family. The term "member of the decedent's family" means any member of the family (as defined in section 2032A(e)(2)) of the decedent.

(9) Treatment of easements granted after death. In any case in which the qualified conservation easement is granted after the date of the decedent's death and on or before the due date (including extensions) for filing the return of tax imposed by section 2001, the deduction under section 2055(f) with respect to such easement shall be allowed to the estate but only if no charitable deduction is allowed under chapter 1 to any person with respect to the grant of such easement.

(10) Application of this section to interests in partnerships, corporations, and trusts. This section shall apply to an interest in a partnership, corporation, or trust if at least 30 percent of the entity is owned (directly or indirectly) by the decedent, as determined under the rules described in section 2057(e)(3) (as in effect before its repeal).

(d) Cross Reference. For executor's right to be furnished on request a statement regarding any valuation made by the Secretary within the gross estate, see section 7517.

Regulations

§ 20.2031–0 Table of contents. [*Omitted. Ed.*]

[T.D. 8540, 59 FR 30151, June 10, 1994; T.D. 8819, 64 FR 23211, April 30, 1999; T.D. 8886, 65 FR 36929, June 12, 2000; T.D. 9448, 74 FR 21484, May 7, 2009; T.D. 9540, 76 FR 49612, Aug. 10, 2011; T.D. 9974, 88 FR 37439, June 7, 2023]

§ 20.2031–1 Definition of gross estate; valuation of property.

(a) Definition of gross estate. Except as otherwise provided in this paragraph the value of the gross estate of a decedent who was a citizen or resident of the United States at the time of his death is the total value of the interests described in sections 2033 through 2044. The gross estate of a decedent who died before October 17, 1962, does not include real property situated outside the United States (as defined in paragraph (b)(1) of § 20.0–1). Except as provided in paragraph (c) of this section (relating to the estates of decedents dying after October 16, 1962, and before July 1, 1964), in the case of a decedent dying after October 16, 1962, real property situated outside the United States which comes within the scope of sections 2033 through 2044 is included in the gross estate to the same extent as any other property coming within the scope of those sections. In arriving at the value of the gross estate the interests described in sections 2033 through 2044 are valued as described in this section, §§ 20.2031–2 through 20.2031–9 and § 20.2032–1. The contents of sections 2033 through 2044 are, in general, as follows:

(1) Sections 2033 and 2034 are concerned mainly with interests in property passing through the decedent's probate estate. Section 2033 includes in the decedent's gross estate any interest that the decedent had in property at the time of his death. Section 2034 provides that any interest of the decedent's surviving spouse in the decedent's property, such as dower or curtesy, does not prevent the inclusion of such property in the decedent's gross estate.

(2) Sections 2035 through 2038 deal with interests in property transferred by the decedent during

his life under such circumstances as to bring the interests within the decedent's gross estate. Section 2035 includes in the decedent's gross estate property transferred in contemplation of death, even though the decedent had not interest in, or control over, the property at the time of his death. Section 2036 provides for the inclusion of transferred property with respect to which the decedent retained the income or the power to designate who shall enjoy the income. Section 2037 includes in the decedent's gross estate certain transfers under which the beneficial enjoyment of the property could be obtained only by surviving the decedent. Section 2038 provides for the inclusion of transferred property if the decedent had at the time of his death the power to change the beneficial enjoyment of the property. It should be noted that there is considerable overlap in the application of sections 2036 through 2038 with respect to reserved powers, so that transferred property may be includible in the decedent's gross estate in varying degrees under more than one of those sections.

(3) Sections 2039 through 2042 deal with special kinds of property and powers. Sections 2039 and 2040 concern annuities and jointly held property respectively. Section 2041 deals with powers held by the decedent over the beneficial enjoyment of property not originating with the decedent. Section 2042 concerns insurance under policies on the life of the decedent.

(4) Section 2043 concerns the sufficiency of consideration for transfers made by the decedent during his life. This has a bearing on the amount to be included in the decedent's gross estate under sections 2035 through 2038, and 2041. Section 2044 deals with retroactivity.

(b) Valuation of property in general. The value of every item of property includible in a decedent's gross estate under sections 2031 through 2044 is its fair market value at the time of the decedent's death, except that if the executor elects the alternate valuation method under section 2032, it is the fair market value thereof at the date, and with the adjustments, prescribed in that section. The fair market value is the price at which the property would change hands between a willing buyer and a willing seller, neither being under any compulsion to buy or to sell and both having reasonable knowledge of relevant facts. The fair market value of a particular item of property includible in the decedent's gross estate is not to be determined by a forced sale price. Nor is the fair market value of an item of property to be determined by the sale price of the item in a market other than that in which such item is most commonly sold to the public, taking into account the location of the item wherever appropriate. Thus, in the case of an item of property includible in the decedent's gross estate, which is generally obtained by the public in the retail market, the fair market value of such an item of property is the price at which the item or a comparable item would be sold at retail. For example, the fair market value of an automobile (an article generally obtained by the public in the retail market) includible in the decedent's gross estate is the price for which an automobile of the same or approximately the same description, make, model, age, condition, etc., could be purchased by a member of the general public and not the price for which the particular automobile of the decedent would be purchased by a dealer in used automobiles. Examples of items of property which are generally sold to the public at retail may be found in §§ 20.2031–6 and 20.2031–8. The value is generally to be determined by ascertaining as a basis the fair market value as of the applicable valuation date of each unit of property. For example, in the case of shares of stock or bonds, such unit of property is generally a share of stock or a bond. Livestock, farm machinery, harvested and growing crops must generally be itemized and the value of each item separately returned. Property shall not be returned at the value at which it is assessed for local tax purposes unless that value represents the fair market value as of the applicable valuation date. All relevant facts and elements of value as of the applicable valuation date shall be considered in every case. The value of items of property which were held by the decedent for sale in the course of a business generally should be reflected in the value of the business. For valuation of interests in businesses, see § 20.2031–3. See § 20.2031–2 and §§ 20.2031–4 through 20.2031–8 for further information concerning the valuation of other particular kinds of property. For certain circumstances under which the sale of an item of property at a price below its fair market value may result in a deduction for the estate, see paragraph (d)(2) of § 20.2053–3.

(c) Real property situated outside the United States; gross estate of decedent dying after October 16, 1962, and before July 1, 1964.

(1) *In general.* In the case of decedent dying after October 16, 1962, and before July 1, 1964, the value of real property situated outside the United States (as defined in paragraph (b)(1) of § 20.0–1) is not included in the gross estate of the decedent—

(i) Under section 2033, 2034, 2035(a), 2036(a), 2037(a), or 2038(a) to the extent the real property, or the decedent's interest in it, was acquired by the decedent before February 1, 1962;

(ii) Under section 2040 to the extent such property or interest was acquired by the decedent before February 1, 1962, or was held by the decedent and the survivor in a joint tenancy or tenancy by the entirety before February 1, 1962; or

(iii) Under section 2041(a) to the extent that before February 1, 1962, such property or interest was subject to a general power of appointment (as defined in section 2041) possessed by the decedent.

(2) *Certain property treated as acquired before February 1, 1962.* For purposes of this paragraph real property situated outside the United States (including property held by the decedent and the survivor in a joint tenancy or tenancy by the entirety), or an interest in such property or a general power of appointment in respect of such property, which was acquired by the decedent after January 31, 1962, is treated as acquired by the decedent before February 1, 1962, if

(i) Such property, interest, or power was acquired by the decedent by gift within the meaning of section 2511, or from a prior decedent by devise or inheritance, or by reason of death, form of ownership, or other conditions (including the exercise or nonexercise of a power of appointment); and

(ii) Before February 1, 1962, the donor or prior decedent had acquired the property or his interest therein or had possessed a power of appointment in respect thereof.

(3) *Certain property treated as acquired after January 31, 1962.* For purposes of this paragraph that portion of capital additions or improvements made after January 31, 1962, to real property situated outside the United States is, to the extent that it materially increases the value of the property, treated as real property acquired after January 31, 1962. Accordingly, the gross estate may include the value of improvements on unimproved real property, such as office buildings, factories, houses, fences, drainage ditches, and other capital items, and the value of capital additions and improvements to existing improvements, placed on real property after January 31, 1962, whether or not the value of such real property or existing improvements is included in the gross estate.

[T.D. 6296, 23 FR 4529, June 24, 1958, as amended by T.D. 6684, 28 FR 11408, Oct. 24, 1963; T.D. 6826, 30 FR 7708, June 15, 1965]

§ 20.2031–2 Valuation of stocks and bonds.

(a) In general. The value of stocks and bonds is the fair market value per share or bond on the applicable valuation date.

(b) Based on selling prices. (1) In general, if there is a market for stocks or bonds, on a stock exchange, in an over-the-counter market, or otherwise, the mean between the highest and lowest quoted selling prices on the valuation date is the fair market value per share or bond. If there were no sales on the valuation date but there were sales on dates within a reasonable period both before and after the valuation date, the fair market value is determined by taking a weighted average of the means between the highest and lowest sales on the nearest date before and the nearest date after the valuation date. The average is to be weighted inversely by the respective numbers of trading days between the selling dates and the valuation date. If the stocks or bonds are listed on more than one exchange, the records of the exchange where the stocks or bonds are principally dealt in should be employed if such records are available in a generally available listing or publication of general circulation. In the event that such records are not so available and such stocks or bonds are listed on a composite listing of combined exchanges available in a generally available listing or publication of general circulation, the records of such combined exchanges should be employed. In valuing listed securities, the executor should be careful to consult accurate records to obtain values as of the applicable valuation date. If quotations of unlisted securities are obtained from brokers, or evidence as to their sale is obtained from officers of the issuing companies, copies of the letters furnishing such quotations or evidence of sale should be attached to the return.

(2) If it is established with respect to bonds for which there is a market on a stock exchange, that the highest and lowest selling prices are not available for

the valuation date in a generally available listing or publication of general circulation but that closing selling prices are so available, the fair market value per bond is the mean between the quoted closing selling price on the valuation date and the quoted closing selling price on the trading day before the valuation date. If there were no sales on the trading day before the valuation date but there were sales on a date within a reasonable period before the valuation date, the fair market value is determined by taking a weighted average of the quoted closing selling price on the valuation date and the quoted closing selling price on the nearest date before the valuation date. The closing selling price for the valuation date is to be weighted by the number of trading days between the previous selling date and the valuation date. If there were no sales within a reasonable period before the valuation date but there were sales on the valuation date, the fair market value is the closing selling price on such valuation date. If there were no sales on the valuation date but there were sales on dates within a reasonable period both before and after the valuation date, the fair market value is determined by taking a weighted average of the quoted closing selling prices on the nearest date before and the nearest date after the valuation date. The average is to be weighted inversely by the respective numbers of trading days between the selling dates and the valuation date. If the bonds are listed on more than one exchange, the records of the exchange where the bonds are principally dealt in should be employed. In valuing listed securities, the executor should be careful to consult accurate records to obtain values as of the applicable valuation date.

(3) The application of this paragraph may be illustrated by the following examples:

Example (1). Assume that sales of X Company common stock nearest the valuation date (Friday, June 15) occurred two trading days before (Wednesday, June 13) and three trading days after (Wednesday, June 20) and on these days the mean sale prices per share were $10 and $15, respectively. The price of $12 is taken as representing the fair market value of a share of X Company common stock as of the valuation date

$$[(3 * 10) + (2 * 15)]/5.$$

Example (2). Assume the same facts as in example (1) except that the mean sale prices per share on June 13, and June 20 were $15 and $10, respectively. The price of $13 is taken as representing the fair market value of a share of X Company common stock as of the valuation date

$$\frac{(3 * 15) + (2 * 10)}{5}$$

Example (3). Assume the decedent died on Sunday, October 7, and that Saturday and Sunday were not trading days. If sales of X Company common stock occurred on Friday, October 5, at mean sale prices per share of $20 and on Monday, October 8, at mean sale prices per share of $23, the price of $21.50 is taken as representing the fair market value of a share of X Company common stock as of the valuation date

$$\frac{(1 * 20) + (23 * 1)}{2}$$

Example (4). Assume that on the valuation date (Tuesday, April 3, 1973) the closing selling price of a listed bond was $25 per bond and that the highest and lowest selling prices are not available in a generally available listing or publication of general circulation for that date. Assume further, that the closing selling price of the same listed bond was $21 per bond on the day before the valuation date (Monday, April 2, 1973). Thus, under paragraph (b)(2) of this section the price of $23 is taken as representing the fair market value per bond as of the valuation date

$$\frac{(25 + 21)}{2}$$

Example (5). Assume the same facts as in example (4) except that there were no sales on the day before the valuation date. Assume further, that there were sales on Thursday, March 29, 1973, and that the closing selling price on that day was $23. The price of $24.50 is taken as representing the fair market value per bond as of the valuation date

$$\frac{(1 * 23) + (3 * 25)}{4}$$

Example (6). Assume that no bonds were traded on the valuation date (Friday, April 20). Assume further, that sales of bonds nearest the valuation date occurred two trading days before (Wednesday, April 18) and three trading days after (Wednesday, April 25) the valuation date and that on these two days the closing selling prices per bond were $29 and $22, respectively.

The highest and lowest selling prices are not available for these dates in a generally available listing or publication of general circulation. Thus, under paragraph (b)(2) of this section, the price of $26.20 is taken as representing the fair market value of a bond as of the valuation date

$$\frac{(3 * 29) + (2 * 22)}{5}$$

(c) Based on bid and asked prices. If the provisions of paragraph (b) of this section are inapplicable because actual sales are not available during a reasonable period beginning before and ending after the valuation date, the fair market value may be determined by taking the mean between the bona fide bid and asked prices on the valuation date, or if none, by taking a weighted average of the means between the bona fide bid and asked prices on the nearest trading date before and the nearest trading date after the valuation date, if both such nearest dates are within a reasonable period. The average is to be determined in the manner described in paragraph (b) of this section.

(d) Based on incomplete selling prices or bid and asked prices. If the provisions of paragraphs (b) and (c) of this section are inapplicable because no actual sale prices or bona fide bid and asked prices are available on a date within a reasonable period before the valuation date, but such prices are available on a date within a reasonable period after the valuation date, or vice versa, then the mean between the highest and lowest available sale prices or bid and asked prices may be taken as the value.

(e) Where selling prices or bid and asked prices do not reflect fair market value. If it is established that the value of any bond or share of stock determined on the basis of selling or bid and asked prices as provided under paragraphs (b), (c), and (d) of this section does not reflect the fair market value thereof, then some reasonable modification of that basis or other relevant facts and elements of value are considered in determining the fair market value. Where sales at or near the date of death are few or of a sporadic nature, such sales alone may not indicate fair market value. In certain exceptional cases, the size of the block of stock to be valued in relation to the number of shares changing hands in sales may be relevant in determining whether selling prices reflect the fair market value of the block of stock to be valued. If the executor can show that the block of stock to be valued is so large in relation to the actual sales on the existing market that it could not be liquidated in a reasonable time without depressing the market, the price at which the block could be sold as such outside the usual market, as through an underwriter, may be a more accurate indication of value than market quotations. Complete data in support of any allowance claimed due to the size of the block of stock being valued shall be submitted with the return. On the other hand, if the block of stock to be valued represents a controlling interest, either actual or effective, in a going business, the price at which other lots change hands may have little relation to its true value.

(f) Where selling prices or bid and asked prices are unavailable. If the provisions of paragraphs (b), (c), and (d) of this section are inapplicable because actual sale prices and bona fide bid and asked prices are lacking, then the fair market value is to be determined by taking the following factors into consideration:

(1) In the case of corporate or other bonds, the soundness of the security, the interest yield, the date of maturity, and other relevant factors; and

(2) In the case of shares of stock, the company's net worth, prospective earning power and dividend-paying capacity, and other relevant factors.

Some of the "other relevant factors" referred to in subparagraphs (1) and (2) of this paragraph are: The good will of the business; the economic outlook in the particular industry; the company's position in the industry and its management; the degree of control of the business represented by the block of stock to be valued; and the values of securities of corporations engaged in the same or similar lines of business which are listed on a stock exchange. However, the weight to be accorded such comparisons or any other evidentiary factors considered in the determination of a value depends upon the facts of each case. In addition to the relevant factors described above, consideration shall also be given to nonoperating assets, including proceeds of life insurance policies payable to or for the benefit of the company, to the extent such nonoperating assets have not been taken into account in the determination of net worth, prospective earning power and dividend-earning capacity. Complete financial and other data upon which the valuation is based should be submitted with the return, including copies of reports of any examinations of the company made by accountants, engineers, or any technical experts as of or near the applicable valuation date.

(g) Pledged securities. The full value of securities pledged to secure an indebtedness of the decedent is included in the gross estate. If the decedent had a trading account with a broker, all securities belonging to the decedent and held by the broker at the date of death must be included at their fair market value as of the applicable valuation date. Securities purchased on margin for the decedent's account and held by a broker must also be returned at their fair market value as of the applicable valuation date. The amount of the decedent's indebtedness to a broker or other person with whom securities were pledged is allowed as a deduction from the gross estate in accordance with the provisions of § 20.2053–1 or § 20.2106–1 (for estates of nonresidents not citizens).

(h) Securities subject to an option or contract to purchase. Another person may hold an option or a contract to purchase securities owned by a decedent at the time of his death. The effect, if any, that is given to the option or contract price in determining the value of the securities for estate tax purposes depends upon the circumstances of the particular case. Little weight will be accorded a price contained in an option or contract under which the decedent is free to dispose of the underlying securities at any price he chooses during his lifetime. Such is the effect, for example, of an agreement on the part of a shareholder to purchase whatever shares of stock the decedent may own at the time of his death. Even if the decedent is not free to dispose of the underlying securities at other than the option or contract price, such price will be disregarded in determining the value of the securities unless it is determined under the circumstances of the particular case that the agreement represents a bona fide business arrangement and not a device to pass the decedent's shares to the natural objects of his bounty for less than an adequate and full consideration in money or money's worth. See section 2703 and the regulations at § 25.2703 of this chapter for special rules involving options and agreements (including contracts to purchase) entered into (or substantially modified after) October 8, 1990.

(i) Stock sold "ex-dividend." In any case where a dividend is declared on a share of stock before the decedent's death but payable to stock holders of record on a date after his death and the stock is selling "ex-dividend" on the date of the decedent's death, the amount of the dividend is added to the ex-dividend quotation in determining the fair market value of the stock as of the date of the decedent's death.

(j) Application of chapter 14. See section 2701 and the regulations at § 25.2701 of this chapter for special rules for valuing the transfer of an interest in a corporation and for the treatment of unpaid qualified payments at the death of the transferor or an applicable family member. See section 2704(b) and the regulations at § 25.2704–2 of this chapter for special valuation rules involving certain restrictions on liquidation rights created after October 8, 1990.

[T.D. 6296, 23 FR 4529, June 24, 1958; 25 FR 14021, Dec. 31, 1960, as amended by T.D. 7312, 39 FR 14948, April 29, 1974; T.D. 7327, 39 FR 35354, Oct. 1, 1974; T.D. 7432, 41 FR 38769, Sept. 13, 1976; T.D. 8395, 57 FR 4254, Feb. 4, 1992; 71 FR 2147, Jan. 13, 2006]

§ 20.2031–3 Valuation of interests in businesses.

The fair market value of any interest of a decedent in a business, whether a partnership or a proprietorship, is the net amount which a willing purchaser whether an individual or a corporation, would pay for the interest to a willing seller, neither being under any compulsion to buy or to sell and both having reasonable knowledge of relevant facts. The net value is determined on the basis of all relevant factors including—

(a) A fair appraisal as of the applicable valuation date of all the assets of the business, tangible and intangible, including good will;

(b) The demonstrated earning capacity of the business; and

(c) The other factors set forth in paragraphs (f) and (h) of § 20.2031–2 relating to the valuation of corporate stock, to the extent applicable. Special attention should be given to determining an adequate value of the good will of the business in all cases in which the decedent has not agreed, for an adequate and full consideration in money or money's worth, that his interest passes at his death to, for example, his surviving partner or partners. Complete financial and other data upon which the valuation is based should be submitted with the return, including copies of reports of examinations of the business made by accountants, engineers, or any technical experts as of or near the applicable valuation date. See section 2701 and the regulations at § 25.2701 of this chapter for special rules for valuing the transfer of an interest in a partnership and for the treatment of unpaid qualified payments at the death of the transferor or an applicable family member. See section 2703 and the regulations at § 25.2703 of this chapter for special rules involving options and agreements (including contracts to purchase) entered into (or substantially modified after) October 8, 1990. See section 2704(b) and the regulations at § 25.2704–2 of this chapter for special valuation rules involving certain restrictions on liquidation rights created after October 8, 1990.

[T.D. 8395, 57 FR 4254, Feb. 4, 1992]

§ 20.2031–4 Valuation of notes.

The fair market value of notes, secured or unsecured, is presumed to be the amount of unpaid principal, plus interest accrued to the date of death, unless the executor establishes that the value is lower or that the notes are worthless. However, items of interest shall be separately stated on the estate tax return. If not returned at face value, plus accrued interest, satisfactory evidence must be submitted that the note is worth less than the unpaid amount (because of the interest rate, date of maturity, or other cause), or that the note is uncollectible, either in whole or in part (by reason of the insolvency of the party or parties liable, or for other cause), and that any property pledged or mortgaged as security is insufficient to satisfy the obligation.

[T.D. 6296, 23 FR 4529, June 24, 1958]

Proposed § 20.2031–4 (Aug. 20, 1985) Valuation of notes.

LR–165–84 provides that § 20.2031–4 is amended by adding a new sentence at the end to read as follows:

See § 20.7872–1 for special rules in the case of gift loans (within the meaning of § 1.7872–4(B)) made after June 6, 1984.

§ 20.2031–5 Valuation of cash on hand or on deposit.

The amount of cash belonging to the decedent at the date of his death, whether in his possession or in the possession of another, or deposited with a bank, is included in the decedent's gross estate. If bank checks outstanding at the time of the decedent's death and given in discharge of bona fide legal obligations of the decedent incurred for an adequate and full consideration in money or money's worth are subsequently honored by the bank and charged to the decedent's account, the balance remaining in the account may be returned, but only if the obligations are not claimed as deductions from the gross estate.

[T.D. 6296, 23 FR 4529, June 24, 1958]

§ 20.2031–6 Valuation of household and personal effects.

(a) General rule. The fair market value of the decedent's household and personal effects is the price which a willing buyer would pay to a willing seller, neither being under any compulsion to buy or to sell and both having reasonable knowledge of relevant facts. A room by room itemization of household and personal effects is desirable. All the articles should be named specifically, except that a number of articles contained in the same room, none of which has a value in excess of $100, may be grouped. A separate value should be given for each article named. In lieu of an itemized list, the executor may furnish a written statement, containing a declaration that it is made under penalties of perjury, setting forth the aggregate value as appraised by a competent appraiser or appraisers of recognized standing and ability, or by a dealer or dealers in the class of personalty involved.

(b) Special rule in cases involving a substantial amount of valuable articles. Notwithstanding the provisions of paragraph (a) of this section, if there are included among the household and personal effects articles having marked artistic or intrinsic value of a total value in excess of $3,000 (e.g., jewelry, furs, silverware, paintings, etchings, engravings, antiques, books, statuary, vases, oriental rugs, coin or stamp collections), the appraisal of an expert or experts, under oath, shall be filed with the return. The appraisal shall be accompanied by a written statement of the executor containing a declaration that it is made under the penalties of perjury as to the completeness of the itemized list of such property and as to the disinterested character and the qualifications of the appraiser or appraisers.

(c) Disposition of household effects prior to investigation. If it is desired to effect distribution or sale of any portion of the household or personal effects of the decedent in advance of an investigation by an officer of the Internal Revenue Service, information to that effect shall be given to the district director. The statement to the district director shall be accompanied by an appraisal of such property, under oath, and by a written statement of the executor, containing a declaration that it is made under the penalties of perjury, regarding the completeness of the list of such property and the qualifications of the appraiser, as heretofore described. If a personal inspection by an officer of the Internal Revenue Service is not deemed necessary, the executor will be so advised. This procedure is designed to facilitate disposition of such property and to obviate future expense and inconvenience to the estate by affording the district director an opportunity to make an investigation should one be deemed necessary prior to sale or distribution.

(d) Additional rules if an appraisal involved. If, pursuant to paragraphs (a), (b), and (c) of this section, expert appraisers are employed, care should be taken to see that they are reputable and of recognized competency to appraise the particular class of property involved. In the appraisal, books in sets by standard authors should be listed in separate groups. In listing paintings having artistic value, the size, subject, and artist's name should be stated. In the case of oriental rugs, the size, make, and general condition should be given. Sets of silverware should be listed in separate groups. Groups or individual pieces of silverware should be weighed and the weights given in troy ounces. In arriving at the value of silverware, the appraisers should take into consideration its antiquity, utility, desirability, condition, and obsolescence.

[T.D. 6296, 23 FR 4529, June 24, 1958]

§ 20.2031–7 Valuation of annuities, interests for life or term of years, and remainder or reversionary interests.

(a) In general. Except as otherwise provided in paragraph (b) of this section and § 20.7520–3(b) (pertaining to certain limitations on the use of prescribed tables), the fair market value of annuities, life estates, terms of years, remainders, and reversionary interests for estates of decedents is the present value of such interests, determined under paragraph (d) of this section. The regulations in this and in related sections provide tables with standard actuarial factors and examples that illustrate how to use the tables to compute the present value of ordinary annuity, life, and remainder interests in property. These sections also refer to standard and special actuarial factors that may be necessary to compute the present value of similar interests in more unusual fact situations.

(b) Commercial annuities and insurance contracts. The value of annuities issued by companies regularly engaged in their sale, and of insurance policies on the lives of persons other than the decedent, is determined under § 20.2031–8. See § 20.2042–1 with respect to insurance policies on the decedent's life.

(c) Actuarial valuations. The present value of annuities, interests for life or a term of years, and remainder or reversionary interests for estates of decedents for which the valuation date of the gross estate is on or after June 1, 2023, is determined under paragraph (d) of this section. The present value of annuities, interests for life or a term of years, and remainder or reversionary interests for estates of decedents for which the valuation date of the gross estate is before June 1, 2023, is determined (subject to paragraph (d)(3) of this section) under the following sections:

Valuation Dates		*Applicable Regulations*
After	*Before*	
—	01-01-52	§ 20.2031–7A(a)
12-31-51	01-01-71	§ 20.2031–7A(b)
12-31-70	12-01-83	§ 20.2031–7A(c)
11-30-83	05-01-89	§ 20.2031–7A(d)
04-30-89	05-01-99	§ 20.2031–7A(e)
04-30-99	05-01-09	§ 20.2031–7A(f)
04-30-09	06-01-23	§ 20.2031–7A(g)

(d) Actuarial valuations on or after June 1, 2023 (1) *In general.* Except as otherwise provided in paragraph (b) of this section and § 20.7520–3(b) (pertaining to certain limitations on the use of prescribed tables), if the valuation date for the gross estate of the decedent is on or after June 1, 2023, the fair market value of annuities, interests for life or a term of years, and remainder or reversionary interests is the present value determined by using standard or special section 7520 actuarial factors. Many of these standard factors are derived by using the actuarial formulas provided in paragraph (d)(2) of this section, the appropriate section 7520 interest rate, and, if applicable, the mortality component for the valuation date of the interest that is being valued. For purposes of the computations described in this section, the age of an individual is the age of that individual at the individual's nearest birthday. For the convenience of taxpayers, paragraph (d)(2) of this section provides for published tables of factors for specific types of interests. These published tables provide factors for rates from 0.2 to 20 percent, inclusive, at intervals of two-tenths of one percent. In general, appropriate factors instead may be computed directly from the actuarial formulas provided in paragraph (d)(2) of this section. In some cases, specific examples in this part and IRS publications illustrate approximation methods (for example, interpolation) for obtaining factors when the required valuation rate falls between two listed rates (such as in the case of a pooled income fund's rate of return or a unitrust's adjusted payout rate). Exact methods of obtaining the applicable actuarial factors are allowed, such as through software using the actual rate of return and the actuarial formulas provided in paragraph (d)(2) of this section, provided that the taxpayer uses at least the same number of decimal places as are provided in the published tables. The approximation method provided in this part, again using at least the same number of decimal places as provided in this part, must be used if more exact methods are not available. See §§ 20.7520–1 through 20.7520–4. The selected method must be applied consistently in valuing all interests in the same property.

(2) *Specific interests* (i) *Pooled income funds and charitable remainder trusts*. The fair market value of a remainder interest in a pooled income fund, as defined in § 1.642(c)–5 of this chapter, is its value determined under § 1.642(c)–6(e) of this chapter. The fair market value of a remainder interest in a charitable remainder annuity trust, as defined in § 1.664–2(a) of this chapter, is the present value determined under § 1.664–2(c) of this chapter. The fair market value of a remainder interest in a charitable remainder unitrust, as defined in § 1.664–3 of this chapter, is its present value determined under § 1.664–4(e) of this chapter. The fair market value of a life interest or an interest for a term of years in a charitable remainder unitrust is the fair market value of the property as of the date of valuation less the fair market value of the remainder interest on that date determined under § 1.664–4(e)(4) and (5) of this chapter.

(ii) *Ordinary remainder and reversionary interests* (A) *Remainder and reversionary interests for a term of years.* If the interest to be valued is a remainder or reversionary interest to take effect after a definite number of years, the present value of the interest is computed by multiplying the value of the property by the appropriate remainder factor (that corresponds to the applicable section 7520 interest rate and the stated term). The factor for an ordinary remainder interest following a term certain may be found using the formula in Figure 1 to this paragraph (d)(2)(ii)(A) and computing the result to at least six decimal places. For the convenience of taxpayers, actuarial factors have been computed by the IRS and appear in Table B. Table B can be found on the IRS website at *https://www.irs.gov/retirement-plans/actuarial-tables* (or a corresponding URL as may be updated from time to time). Table B is referenced and explained in IRS Publication 1457, Actuarial Valuations Version 4A, which will be available within a reasonable time after June 1, 2023. The remainder factors from Table B also can be found in paragraph (d)(6) of this section, but only for interest rates from 4.2 to 14 percent, inclusive. For information about obtaining special factors for other situations, see paragraph (d)(4) of this section.

Figure 1 to paragraph (d)(2)(ii)(A) – Formula for determining term certain remainder factors

$$\left(\frac{1}{1+i}\right)^n$$

where:

n = the term of years; and

i = the interest rate specified under section 7520 of the Internal Revenue Code.

(B) *Remainder and reversionary interests dependent on the life of one individual.* If the interest to be valued is a remainder or reversionary interest to take effect after the death of one individual, the present value of the interest is computed by multiplying the value of the property by the appropriate remainder factor (that corresponds to the applicable section 7520 interest rate and the age of the measuring life of the life interest that precedes the remainder interest). The factor for an ordinary remainder interest following the death of one individual may be found using the formula in Figure 2 to this paragraph (d)(2)(ii)(B) and computing the result to at least five decimal places. The prescribed mortality table is Table 2010CM as set forth in paragraph (d)(7)(ii) of this section, or for periods before June 1, 2023, the appropriate table found in § 20.2031–7A. For the convenience of taxpayers, actuarial factors have been computed by the IRS and appear in Table S. Table S currently is available, at no charge, electronically via the IRS website at *https://www.irs.gov/retirement-plans/actuarial-tables* (or a corresponding URL as may be updated from time to time). Table S is referenced and explained by IRS Publication 1457, Actuarial Valuations Version 4A, which will be available within a reasonable time after June 1, 2023. For information about obtaining special factors for other situations, see paragraph (d)(4) of this section.

Figure 2 to paragraph (d)(2)(ii)(B) – Formula for determining single life remainder factors

$$\left(1+\frac{i}{2}\right)\sum_{t=0}^{\infty} v^{t+1}\left({}_{t+1}q_x - {}_{t}q_x\right)$$

where:

i = the applicable interest rate under section 7520 of the Internal Revenue Code;

v = 1 / (1 + i) ;

${}_tq_x = 1 - \frac{l_{x+t}}{l_x}$;

x = the age of the measuring life (determined as age at nearest birthday); and

l_x = the number associated with age x as set forth in the prescribed mortality table, representing the number of persons alive at age x.

(iii) *Ordinary interests for a term of years and ordinary interests for life.* If the interest to be valued is the right of a person to receive the income of certain property, or to the use of certain property, for a term of years or for the life of one individual, the present value of the interest is computed by multiplying the value of the property by the appropriate actuarial factor for an interest for a term of years or for a life (that corresponds to the applicable section 7520 interest rate and the durational period). The actuarial factor for an ordinary income interest for a term certain may be found by subtracting from 1.000000 the factor for an ordinary remainder interest following the same term certain that is determined under the formula in paragraph (d)(2)(ii)(A) of this section. For the convenience of taxpayers, actuarial factors have been computed by the IRS and appear in the "Income Interest" column of Table B which can be found on the IRS website at *https://www.irs.gov/retirement-plans/actuarial-tables* (or a corresponding URL as may be updated from time to time). The actuarial factor for an ordinary income interest for the life of one individual may be found by subtracting from 1.00000 the factor for an ordinary remainder interest following the life of the same individual that is determined in paragraph (d)(2)(ii)(B) of this section. For the convenience of taxpayers, actuarial factors have been computed by the IRS and appear in the "Life Estate" column of Table S. Table S (applicable when the valuation date is on or after June 1, 2023) can be found on the IRS website at *https://www.irs.gov/retirement-plans/actuarial-tables*. Tables B and S are referenced and explained by *IRS Publication 1457, Actuarial Valuations Version 4A*. See § 20.2031–7A or earlier versions of Publication 1457 for valuation of interests before June 1, 2023. For information about obtaining special factors for other situations, see paragraph (d)(4) of this section.

(iv) *Annuities.* (A) If the interest to be valued is the right of a person to receive an annuity that is payable at the end of each year for a term of years or for the life of one individual, the present value of the interest is computed by multiplying the aggregate amount payable annually by the appropriate annuity factor (that corresponds to the applicable section 7520 interest rate and annuity period). The appropriate annuity factor for an annuity payable for a term of years is computed by subtracting from 1.000000 the factor for an ordinary remainder interest following the same term certain that is determined under the formula in paragraph (d)(2)(ii)(A) of this section and then dividing the result by the applicable section 7520 interest rate expressed to at least four decimal places. For the convenience of taxpayers, actuarial factors have been computed by the IRS and appear in the "Annuity" column of Table B which can be found on the IRS website at *https://www.irs.gov/retirement-plans/actuarial-tables* (or a corresponding URL as may be updated from time to time). The appropriate annuity factor for an annuity payable for the life of one individual is computed by subtracting from 1.00000 the factor for an ordinary remainder interest following the life of the same individual that is determined under the formula in paragraph (d)(2)(ii)(B) of this section and then dividing the result by the applicable section 7520 interest rate expressed to at least four decimal places. For the convenience of taxpayers, actuarial factors have been computed by the IRS and appear in the "Annuity" column of Table S. Table S (applicable when the valuation date is on or after June 1, 2023) can be found on the IRS website at *https://www.irs.gov/retirement-plans/actuarial-tables*. Tables B and S are referenced and explained in *IRS Publication 1457, Actuarial Valuations Version 4A*. See § 20.2031–7A or earlier versions of Publication 1457 for valuation of interests before June 1, 2023. For information about obtaining special factors for other situations, see paragraph (d)(4) of this section.

(B) If the annuity is payable at the end of semiannual, quarterly, monthly, or weekly periods, the product obtained by multiplying the annuity factor by the aggregate amount payable annually is then multiplied by the applicable adjustment factor at the appropriate interest rate component for payments made at the end of the specified periods. The applicable adjustment factor may be found using the formula in Figure 3 to this paragraph (d)(2)(iv)(B) and calculating the result to at least four decimal places. For the convenience of taxpayers, actuarial factors have been computed by the IRS and appear in Table K. Table K, which is referenced and explained by Publication 1457, can be found on the IRS website at *https://www.irs.gov/retirement-plans/actuarial-tables*. The provisions of this paragraph (d)(2)(iv)(B) are illustrated by the example in paragraph (d)(2)(iv)(B)(2) of this section.

Figure 3 to paragraph (d)(2)(iv)(B) – Formula for determining annuity adjustment factor at the end of the specified period

$$\frac{i}{p\left[(1+i)^{(1/p)}-1\right]}$$

where:

p = the number of payments per year; and

i = the interest rate specified under section 7520 of the Internal Revenue Code.

(*1*) *Sample factors from actuarial Tables S and K.* For purposes of the example in paragraph (d)(2)(iv)(B)(*2*) of this section, the following factors from Tables S and K will be used:

TABLE 2 TO PARAGRAPH (d)(2)(iv)(B)(*1*) FACTORS FROM TABLE S—BASED ON TABLE 2010CM			
Interest at 3.2 Percent			
Age	Annuity	Life Estate	Remainder
75	9.4053	0.30097	0.69903

TABLE 2 TO PARAGRAPH (d)(2)(iv)(B)(*1*) FACTORS FROM TABLE S—BASED ON TABLE 2010CM			
Factors from Table K Adjustment Factors for Annuities Payable at the End of Each Interval			
Interest Rate	Semi-Annually	Quarterly	Monthly
3.2%	1.0079	1.0119	1.0146

(2) *Example.* At the time of the decedent's death, the survivor/annuitant, age 75, is entitled to receive an annuity of $15,000 per year for life payable in equal monthly installments at the end of each month. The section 7520 rate for the month in which the decedent died is 3.2 percent. Under Table S, the annuity factor at 3.2 percent for an individual aged 75 is 9.4053. Under Table K, the adjustment factor under the column for payments made at the end of each monthly period at the rate of 3.2 percent is 1.0146. The aggregate annual amount, $15,000, is multiplied by the factor 9.4053 and the product then is multiplied by 1.0146. The present value of the annuity at the date of the decedent's death is, therefore, $143,139.26 ($15,000 x 9.4053 x 1.0146).

(C) If an annuity is payable at the beginning of annual, semiannual, quarterly, monthly, or weekly periods for a term of years, the value of the annuity is computed by multiplying the aggregate amount payable annually by the annuity factor described in paragraph (d)(2)(iv)(A) of this section; and the product so obtained then is multiplied by the applicable adjustment factor at the appropriate interest rate component for payments made at the beginning of specified periods. The applicable adjustment factor may be found using the formula in Figure 4 to this paragraph (d)(2)(iv)(C) and calculating the result to at least four decimal places. For the convenience of taxpayers, actuarial factors have been computed by the IRS and appear in Table J. Table J, which is referenced and explained by Publication 1457, can be found on the IRS website at *https://www.irs.gov/retirement-plans/actuarial-tables*. If an annuity is payable at the beginning of annual, semiannual, quarterly, monthly, or weekly periods for one or more lives, the value of the annuity is the sum of the first payment plus the present value of a similar annuity, the first payment of which is not to be made until the end of the payment period, determined as provided in paragraph (d)(2)(iv)(B) of this section.

Figure 4 to paragraph (d)(2)(iv)(C) – Formula for determining annuity adjustment factor at the beginning of the specified period

$$\frac{i}{p\left[(1-v)^{(1/p)}\right]}$$

where:

p = the number of payments per year;

v = 1 / (1 + i); and

i = the interest rate specified under section 7520 of the Internal Revenue Code.

(v) *Annuity and unitrust interests for a term of years or until the prior death of an individual.* See § 25.2512–5(d)(2)(v) of this chapter for examples explaining how to compute the present value of an annuity or unitrust interest that is payable until the earlier of the lapse of a term of years or the death of an individual.

(3) *Transitional rule.* If a decedent dies after April 30, 2019, and on or before June 1, 2023, the fair market value of annuities, interests for life or a term of years, and remainder or reversionary interests based on one or more measuring lives included in the gross estate of the decedent is their present value determined under this section by using the section 7520 interest rate for the month in which the valuation date occurs (see §§ 20.7520–1(b) and 20.7520–2(a)(2)) and factors derived from the selected mortality table, either Table 2010CM in paragraph (d)(7)(ii) of this section

or Table 2000CM in § 20.2031–7A(g)(4), at the option of the donor or the decedent's executor, as the case may be. If any previously filed estate tax return is supplemented to use the actuarial factors based on Table 2010CM, the supplemental return must state at the top "AMENDED PURSUANT TO TD 9974." For the convenience of taxpayers, actuarial factors based on Table 2010CM appear in the current version of Table S, and actuarial factors based on Table 2000CM appear in the previous version of Table S. Both versions of Table S will be available as provided in paragraph (d)(4) of this section. The decedent's executor must consistently use the same mortality basis with respect to each interest (income, remainder, partial, etc.) in the same property, and with respect to all transfers occurring on the same valuation date. For example, gift and income tax charitable deductions with respect to the same transfer must be determined based on factors with the same mortality basis, and all assets includible in the gross estate and/or estate tax deductions claimed must be valued based on factors with the same mortality basis.

(4) *Publications and actuarial computations by the Internal Revenue Service.* The factor for determining the present value of a remainder interest that is dependent on the termination of the life of one individual may be computed by using the formula in paragraph (d)(2)(ii)(B) of this section to derive a remainder factor from the appropriate mortality table expressed to at least five decimal places. For the convenience of taxpayers, actuarial factors have been computed by the IRS and appear in Table S. The remainder factor for determining the present value of a remainder interest following a term certain may be computed by using the formula in paragraph (d)(2)(ii)(A) of this section expressed to at least six decimal places. For the convenience of taxpayers, actuarial factors have been computed by the IRS and appear in Table B. Adjustment factors for term certain annuities payable at the beginning of each interval may be computed by using the formula in paragraph (d)(2)(iv)(C) of this section expressed to at least four decimal places. For the convenience of taxpayers, actuarial factors have been computed by the IRS and appear in Table J. Adjustment factors for annuities payable at the end of each interval may be computed by using the formula in paragraph (d)(2)(iv)(B) of this section expressed to at least four decimal places. For the convenience of taxpayers, actuarial factors have been computed by the IRS and appear in Table K. These tables currently are available, at no charge, electronically via the IRS website at *https://www.irs.gov/retirement-plans/actuarial-tables* (or a corresponding URL as may be updated from time to time). *IRS Publication 1457, Actuarial Valuations Version 4A (2023)*, references and explains the factors contained in the actuarial tables and also includes examples that illustrate how to compute many special factors for more unusual situations. This publication will be available within a reasonable time after June 1, 2023. Tables B, J, and K also can be found in paragraph (d)(6) of this section, but only for interest rates from 4.2 to 14 percent, inclusive. If a special factor is required in the case of an actual decedent, the special factor may be calculated by the executor using the actuarial formulas in paragraph (d)(2) of this section or the executor may request a ruling to obtain the factor from the Internal Revenue Service. The request for a ruling must be accompanied by a recitation of the facts including a statement of the date of birth for each measuring life, the date of the decedent's death, any other applicable dates, and a copy of the will, trust, or other relevant documents. A request for a ruling must comply with the instructions for requesting a ruling published periodically in the Internal Revenue Bulletin (see §§ 601.201 and 601.601(d)(2)(ii)(b) of this chapter) and must include payment of the required user fee.

(5) *Examples.* The provisions of this section are illustrated by the examples in this paragraph (d)(5). For purposes of these examples, the following factors from Tables S, B, and K will be used:

Table 3 to paragraph (d)(5)

Factors from Table S—Based on Table 2010CM			
Interest at 3.2 Percent			
Age	Annuity	Life Estate	Remainder
31	23.8334	0.76267	0.23733
46	20.0146	0.64047	0.35953
Interest at 4.6 Percent			
Age	Annuity	Life Estate	Remainder
65	11.7691	0.54138	0.45862
Factors from Table B			
Annuity, Income, and Remainder Interests for a Term Certain			
Interest at 2.6 Percent			
Years	Annuity	Income Interest	Remainder
5	4.6325	0.120445	0.879555
Factors from Table K			
Adjustment Factors for Annuities Payable at the End of Each Interval			
Interest Rate	Semi-Annually	Quarterly	Monthly
2.6%	1.0065	1.0097	1.0119
3.2%	1.0079	1.0119	1.0146

(i) *Example 1*: Remainder payable at an individual's death. The decedent, or the decedent's estate, was entitled to receive certain property worth $50,000 upon the death of A, to whom the income was bequeathed for life. At the time of the decedent's death, A was 65 years and 5 months old. In the month in which the decedent died, the section 7520 rate was 4.6 percent. Under Table S, the remainder factor at 4.6 percent for determining the present value of the remainder interest due at the death of a person aged 65, A's age at A's nearest birthday to the date of the decedent's death, is 0.45862. The present value of the remainder interest at the date of the decedent's death is, therefore, $22,931 ($50,000 times 0.45862).

(ii) *Example 2*: Income payable for an individual's life. A's parent bequeathed an income interest in property to A for life, with the remainder interest passing to B at A's death. At the time of the parent's death, the value of the property was $50,000 and A was 30 years and 10 months old. The section 7520 rate at the time of the parent's death was 3.2 percent. Under Table S, the factor at 3.2 percent for determining the present value of the life estate given to a person aged 31, A's age at A's nearest birthday to the date of the decedent's death, is 0.76267. The present value of A's income interest at the time of the parent's death is, therefore, $38,133.50 ($50,000.00 x 0.76267).

(iii) *Example 3*: Annuity payable for an individual's life. A purchased an annuity for the benefit of both A and B. Under the terms of the annuity contract, at A's death, a survivor annuity of $10,000 per year, payable in equal semiannual installments made at the end of each interval is payable to B for life. At A's death, B was 45 years and 7 months old. Also, at A's death, the section 7520 rate was 3.2 percent. Under Table S, the factor at 3.2 percent for determining the present value of an annuity interest payable until the death of a person age 46 (B's age at B's nearest birthday to the date of A's death) is 20.0146. The adjustment factor from Table K at an interest rate of 3.2 percent for semi-annual annuity payments made at the end of the period is 1.0079. The present value of the annuity at the date of A's death is, therefore, $201,727.15 ($10,000 x 20.0146 x 1.0079).

(iv) *Example 4*: Annuity payable for a term of years. The decedent, or the decedent's estate, was entitled to receive an annuity of $10,000 per year payable in equal quarterly installments at the end of each quarter throughout a term certain. At the time of the decedent's death, the section 7520 rate was 2.6 percent. A quarterly payment had been made immediately prior to the decedent's death and payments were to continue for 5 more years. Under Table B for the interest rate of 2.6 percent, the factor for the present value of an annuity with a term of 5 years is 4.6325. The adjustment factor from Table K at an interest rate of 2.6 percent for quarterly annuity payments made at the end of the quarter is 1.0097. The present value of the annuity is, therefore, $46,774.35 ($10,000 x 4.6325 x 1.0097).

(6) *Actuarial Table B, Table J, and Table K where the valuation date is after April 30, 1989.* Except as provided in § 20.7520–3(b) (pertaining to certain limitations on prescribed tables), for determination of the present value of an interest that is dependent on a term of years, the tables in this paragraph (d)(6) must be used in the application of the provisions of this section when the section 7520 interest rate component is between 4.2 and 14 percent.

Table B

Term Certain Remainder Factors Applicable After April 30, 1989

Interest Rate

Years	4.2%	4.4%	4.6%	4.8%	5.0%	5.2%	5.4%	5.6%	5.8%	6.0%
1	.959693	.957854	.956023	.954198	.952381	.950570	.948767	.946970	.945180	.943396
2	.921010	.917485	.913980	.910495	.907029	.903584	.900158	.896752	.893364	.889996
3	.883887	.878817	.873786	.868793	.863838	.858920	.854040	.849197	.844390	.839619
4	.848260	.841779	.835359	.829001	.822702	.816464	.810285	.804163	.798100	.792094
5	.814069	.806302	.798623	.791031	.783526	.776106	.768771	.761518	.754348	.747258
6	.781257	.772320	.763501	.754801	.746215	.737744	.729384	.721135	.712994	.704961
7	.749766	.739770	.729925	.720230	.710681	.701277	.692015	.682893	.673908	.665057
8	.719545	.708592	.697825	.687242	.676839	.666613	.656561	.646679	.636964	.627412
9	.690543	.678728	.667137	.655765	.644609	.633663	.622923	.612385	.602045	.591898
10	.662709	.650122	.637798	.625730	.613913	.602341	.591009	.579910	.569041	.558395
11	.635997	.622722	.609750	.597071	.584679	.572568	.560729	.549157	.537846	.526788
12	.610362	.596477	.582935	.569724	.556837	.544266	.532001	.520035	.508361	.496969
13	.585760	.571339	.557299	.543630	.530321	.517363	.504745	.492458	.480492	.468839
14	.562150	.547259	.532790	.518731	.505068	.491790	.478885	.466343	.454151	.442301
15	.539491	.524195	.509360	.494972	.481017	.467481	.454350	.441612	.429255	.417265
16	.517746	.502102	.486960	.472302	.458112	.444374	.431072	.418194	.405723	.393646
17	.496877	.480941	.465545	.450670	.436297	.422408	.408987	.396017	.383481	.371364
18	.476849	.460671	.445071	.430028	.415521	.401529	.388033	.375016	.362458	.350344
19	.457629	.441256	.425498	.410332	.395734	.381681	.368153	.355129	.342588	.330513
20	.4391863	.422659	.406786	.391538	.376889	.362815	.349291	.336296	.323807	.311805
21	.421481	.404846	.388897	.373605	.358942	.344881	.331396	.318462	.306056	.294155
22	.404492	.387783	.371794	.356494	.341850	.327834	.314417	.301574	.289278	.277505
23	.388188	.371440	.355444	.340166	.325571	.311629	.298309	.285581	.273420	.261797
24	.372542	.355785	.339813	.324586	.310068	.296225	.283025	.270437	.258431	.246979
25	.357526	.340791	.324869	.309719	.295303	.281583	.268525	.256096	.344263	.232999
26	.343115	.326428	.310582	.295533	.281241	.267664	.254768	.242515	.230873	.219810
27	.329285	.312670	.296923	.281998	.267848	.254434	.241715	.229654	.218216	.207368
28	.316012	.299493	.283866	.269082	.255094	.241857	.299331	.217475	.206253	.195630
29	.303275	.286870	.271382	.256757	.242946	.229902	.217582	.205943	.194947	.184557
30	.291051	.274780	.259447	.244997	.231377	.218538	.206434	.195021	.184260	.174110
31	.279319	.263199	.248038	.233776	.220359	.207736	.195858	.184679	.174158	.164255
32	.268061	.252106	.237130	.223069	.209866	.197468	.185823	.174886	.164611	.154957
33	.257256	.241481	.226702	.212852	.199873	.187707	.176303	.165612	.155587	.146186
34	.246887	.231304	.216732	.203103	.190355	.178429	.167270	.156829	.147058	.137912
35	.236935	.221556	.207201	.193801	.181290	.169609	.158701	.148512	.138996	.130105
36	.227385	.212218	.198089	.184924	.172657	.161255	.150570	.140637	.131376	.122841
37	.218220	.203274	.189377	.176454	.164436	.153256	.142856	.133179	.124174	.115793
38	.209424	.194707	.181049	.168373	.156605	.145681	.135537	.126116	.117367	.109239
39	.200983	.186501	.173087	.160661	.149148	.138480	.128593	.119428	.110933	.103056
40	.192882	.178641	.165475	.153302	.142046	.131635	.122004	.113095	.104851	.097222
41	.185107	.171112	.158198	.146281	.135282	.125128	.115754	.107098	.099103	.091719
42	.177646	.163900	.151241	.139581	.128840	.118943	.109823	.101418	.093670	.086527
43	.170486	.156992	.144590	.133188	.122704	.113064	.104197	.096040	.088535	.081630
44	.163614	.150376	.138231	.127088	.116861	.107475	.098858	.090947	.083682	.077009
45	.157019	.144038	.132152	.121267	.111297	.102163	.093793	.086124	.079094	.072650
46	.150690	.137968	.126340	.115713	.105997	.097113	.088988	.081557	.074758	.068538
47	.144616	.132153	.120784	.110413	.100949	.092312	.084429	.077232	.070660	.064658
48	.138787	.126583	.115473	.105356	.096142	.087749	.080103	.073136	.066786	.060998
49	.133193	.121248	.110395	.100530	.091564	.083412	.075999	.069258	.063125	.057546
50	.127824	.116138	.105540	.095926	.087204	.079289	.072106	.065585	.059665	.054288
51	.122672	.111243	.100898	.091532	.083051	.075370	.068411	.062107	.056394	.051215
52	.117728	.106555	.096461	.087340	.079096	.071644	.064907	.058813	.053302	.048316
53	.112982	.102064	.092219	.083340	.075330	.068103	.061581	.055695	.050380	.045582
54	.108428	.097763	.088164	.079523	.071743	.064737	.058426	.052741	.047618	.043001
55	.104058	.093642	.084286	.075880	.068326	.061537	.055433	.049944	.145008	.040567
56	.099864	.089696	.080580	.072405	.065073	.058495	.052593	.047296	.042541	.038271
57	.095839	.085916	.077036	.069089	.061974	.055604	.049898	.044787	.040208	.036105
58	.091976	.082295	.073648	.065924	.059023	.052855	.047342	.042412	.038004	.034061
59	.088268	.078826	.070409	.062905	.056212	.050243	.044916	.040163	.035921	.032133
60	.084710	.075504	.067313	.060024	.053536	.047759	.042615	.038033	.033952	.030314

Table B
Term Certain Remainder Factors Applicable After April 30, 1989
Interest Rate

Years	6.2%	6.4%	6.6%	6.8%	7.0%	7.2%	7.4%	7.6%	7.8%	8.0%
1	.941620	.939850	.938086	.936330	.934579	.932836	.931099	.929368	.927644	.925926
2	.886647	.883317	.880006	.876713	.873439	.870183	.866945	.863725	.860523	.857339
3	.834885	.830185	.825521	.820892	.816298	.811738	.807211	.802718	.798259	.793832
4	.786144	.780249	.774410	.768626	.762895	.757218	.751593	.746021	.740500	.835030
5	.740248	.733317	.726464	.719687	.712986	.706360	.699808	.693328	.686920	.680583
6	.697032	.689208	.681486	.673864	.666342	.658918	.651590	.644357	.637217	.630170
7	.656339	.647752	.639292	.630959	.622750	.614662	.606694	.598845	.591111	.583490
8	.618022	.608789	.599711	.590786	.582009	.573379	.564892	.556547	.548340	.540269
9	.581942	.572170	.562581	.553170	.543934	.534868	.525971	.517237	.508664	.500249
10	.547968	.537754	.527750	.517950	.508349	.498944	.489731	.480704	.471859	.463193
11	.515977	.505408	.495075	.484972	.475093	.465433	.455987	.446750	.437717	.428883
12	.485854	.475007	.464423	.454093	.444012	.434173	.424569	.415196	.406046	.397114
13	.457490	.446436	.435669	.425181	.414964	.405012	.395316	.385870	.376666	.367698
14	.430781	.419582	.408695	.398109	.387817	.377810	.368078	.358615	.349412	.340461
15	.405632	.394344	.383391	.372762	.362446	.352434	.342717	.333285	.324130	.315242
16	.381951	.370624	.359654	.349028	.338735	.328763	.319103	.309745	.300677	.291890
17	.359653	.348331	.337386	.326805	.316574	.306682	.297117	.287867	.278921	.270269
18	.338656	.327379	.316498	.305997	.295864	.286084	.276645	.267534	.258739	.250249
19	.318885	.307687	.296902	.286514	.276508	.266870	.257584	.248638	.240018	.231712
20	.300268	.289179	.278520	.268272	.258419	.248946	.239836	.231076	.222651	.214548
21	.282739	.271785	.261276	.251191	.241513	.232225	.223311	.214755	.206541	.198656
22	.266232	.255437	.245099	.235197	.225713	.216628	.207925	.199586	.191596	.183941
23	.250689	.240073	.229924	.220222	.210947	.202078	.193598	.185489	.177733	.170315
24	.236054	.225632	.215689	.206201	.197147	.188506	.180259	.172387	.164873	.157699
25	.222273	.212060	.202334	.193072	.184249	.175845	.167839	.160211	.152943	.146018
26	.209297	.199305	.189807	.180779	.172195	.164035	.156275	.148895	.141877	.135202
27	.197078	.187317	.178056	.169269	.160930	.153017	.145507	.138379	.131611	.125187
28	.185572	.176049	.167031	.158491	.150402	.142740	.135482	.128605	.122088	.115914
29	.174739	.165460	.156690	.148400	.140563	.133153	.126147	.119521	.113255	.107328
30	.164537	.155507	.146989	.138951	.131367	.124210	.117455	.111079	.105060	.099377
31	.154932	.146154	.137888	.130104	.122773	.115868	.109362	.103233	.097458	.092016
32	.145887	.137362	.129351	.121820	.114741	.108085	.101827	.095942	.090406	.085200
33	.137370	.129100	.121342	.114064	.107235	.100826	.094811	.089165	.083865	.078889
34	.129350	.121335	.113830	.106802	.100219	.094054	.088278	.082867	.077797	.073045
35	.121798	.114036	.106782	.100001	.093663	.087737	.082196	.077014	.072168	.067635
36	.114688	.107177	.100171	.093634	.087535	.081844	.076532	.071574	.066946	.062625
37	.107992	.100730	.093969	.087673	.081809	.076347	.071259	.066519	.062102	.057986
38	.101688	.094671	.088151	.082090	.076457	.071219	.066349	.061821	.057609	.053690
39	.095751	.088977	.082693	.076864	.071455	.066436	.061778	.057454	.053440	.049713
40	.090161	.083625	.077573	.071970	.066780	.061974	.057521	.053396	.049573	.046031
41	.084897	.078595	.072770	.067387	.062412	.057811	.053558	.049625	.045987	.042621
42	.079941	.073867	.068265	.063097	.058329	.053929	.049868	.046120	.042659	.039464
43	.075274	.069424	.064038	.059079	.054513	.050307	.046432	.042862	.039572	.036541
44	.070880	.065248	.060074	.055318	.050946	.046928	.043233	.039835	.036709	.033834
45	.066742	.061323	.056354	.051796	.047613	.043776	.040254	.037021	.034053	.031328
46	.062845	.057635	.052865	.048498	.044499	.040836	.037480	.034406	.031589	.029007
47	.059176	.054168	.049592	.045410	.041587	.038093	.034898	.031976	.029303	.026859
48	.055722	.050910	.046522	.042519	.038867	.035535	.032493	.029717	.027183	.024869
49	.052469	.047848	.043641	.039812	.036324	.033148	.030255	.027618	.025216	.023027
50	.049405	.044970	.040939	.037277	.033948	.030922	.028170	.025668	.023392	.021321
51	.046521	.042265	.038405	.034903	.031727	.028845	.026229	.023855	.021699	.019742
52	.043805	.039722	.036027	.032681	.029651	.026907	.024422	.022170	.020129	.018280
53	.041248	.037333	.033796	.030600	.027711	.025100	.022739	.020604	.018673	.016925
54	.038840	.053087	.031704	.028652	.025899	.023414	.021172	.019149	.017322	.015672
55	.036572	.032977	.029741	.026828	.024204	.021842	.019714	.017796	.016068	.014511
56	.034437	.030993	.027900	.025119	.022621	.020375	.018355	.016539	.014906	.013436
57	.032427	.029129	.026172	.023520	.021141	.019006	.017091	.015371	.013827	.012441
58	.030534	.027377	.024552	.022023	.019758	.017730	.015913	.014285	.012827	.011519
59	.028751	.025730	.023032	.020620	.018465	.016539	.014817	.013276	.011899	.010666
60	.027073	.024183	.021606	.019307	.017257	.015428	.013796	.012339	.011038	.009876

Table B
Term Certain Remainder Factors Applicable After April 30, 1989
Interest Rate

Years	8.2%	8.4%	8.6%	8.8%	9.0%	9.2%	9.4%	9.6%	9.8%	10.0%
1	.924214	.922509	.920810	.919118	.917431	.915751	.914077	.912409	.910747	.909091
2	.854172	.851023	.847892	.844777	.841680	.838600	.835536	.832490	.829460	.826446
3	.789438	.785077	.780747	.776450	.772183	.767948	.763744	.759571	.755428	.751315
4	.729610	.724241	.718920	.713649	.708425	.703250	.698121	.693039	.688003	.683013
5	.674316	.668119	.661989	.655927	.649931	.644001	.638136	.632335	.626597	.620921
6	.623213	.616346	.609566	.602874	.596267	.589745	.583305	.576948	.570671	.564474
7	.575982	.568585	.561295	.554112	.547034	.540059	.533186	.526412	.519737	.513158
8	.532331	.524524	.516846	.509294	.501866	.494560	.487373	.480303	.473349	.466507
9	.491988	.483879	.475917	.468101	.460428	.452894	.445496	.438233	.431101	.424098
10	.454703	.446383	.438230	.430240	.422411	.414738	.407218	.399848	.392624	.385543
11	.420243	.411792	.403526	.395441	.387533	.379797	.372228	.364826	.357581	.350494
12	.388394	.379882	.371571	.363457	.355535	.347799	.340245	.332869	.325666	.318631
13	.358960	.350445	.342147	.334060	.326179	.318497	.311010	.303713	.296559	.289664
14	.331756	.323288	.315052	.307040	.299246	.291664	.284287	.277110	.270127	.263331
15	.306613	.298236	.290103	.282206	.274538	.267092	.259860	.252838	.246017	.239392
16	.283376	.275126	.267130	.259381	.251870	.244589	.237532	.203691	.224059	.217629
17	.261901	.253806	.245976	.238401	.231073	.223983	.217123	.210485	.204061	.197845
18	.242052	.234139	.226497	.219119	.211994	.205113	.198467	.192048	.185848	.179859
19	.223708	.215995	.208561	.201396	.194490	.187832	.181414	.175226	.169260	.163508
20	.206754	.199257	.192045	.185107	.178431	.172007	.165826	.159878	.154153	.148644
21	.191085	.183817	.176837	.170135	.163698	.157516	.151578	.145874	.140395	.135131
22	.176604	.169573	.162834	.156374	.150182	.144245	.138554	.133097	.127864	.122846
23	.163220	.156432	.149939	.143726	.137781	.132093	.126649	.121439	.116452	.111678
24	.150850	.144310	.138065	.132101	.126405	.120964	.115767	.110802	.106058	.101526
25	.139418	.133128	.127132	.121416	.115969	.110773	.105820	.101097	.096592	.092296
26	.128852	.122811	.117064	.111596	.106393	.101441	.096727	.092241	.087971	.083905
27	.119087	.113295	.107794	.102570	.097608	.092894	.088416	.084162	.080119	.076278
28	.110062	.104515	.099258	.094274	.089548	.085068	.080819	.076790	.072968	.069343
29	.101721	.096416	.091398	.086649	.082155	.077901	.073875	.070064	.066456	.063039
30	.094012	.088945	.084160	.079640	.075371	.071338	.067527	.063927	.060524	.057309
31	.086887	.082053	.077495	.073199	.069148	.065328	.061725	.058327	.055122	.052099
32	.080302	.085694	.071358	.067278	.063438	.059824	.056422	.053218	.050202	.047362
33	.074216	.069829	.065708	.061837	.058200	.054784	.051574	.048557	.045722	.043057
34	.068592	.064418	.060504	.056835	.053395	.050168	.047142	.044304	.041641	.039143
35	.063394	.159426	.055713	.052238	.048986	.045942	.043092	.040423	.037924	.035584
36	.058589	.054821	.051301	.048013	.044941	.042071	.039389	.036882	.034539	.032349
37	.054149	.050573	.047239	.044130	.041231	.038527	.036005	.033652	.031457	.029408
38	.050045	.046654	.043498	.040560	.037826	.035281	.032911	.030704	.028649	.026735
39	.046253	.043039	.040053	.037280	.034703	.032309	.030083	.028015	.026092	.024304
40	.042747	.039703	.036881	.034264	.031838	.029587	.027498	.025561	.023763	.022095
41	.039508	.036627	.033961	.031493	.029209	.027094	.025136	.023322	.021642	.020086
42	.036514	.033789	.031271	.028946	.026797	.024811	.022976	.021279	.019711	.018260
43	.033746	.031170	.028795	.026605	.024584	.022721	.021002	.019415	.017951	.016600
44	.031189	.028755	.026515	.024453	.022555	.020807	.019197	.017715	.016349	.015091
45	.028825	.026527	.024415	.022475	.020692	.019054	.017548	.016163	.014890	.013719
46	.026641	.024471	.022482	.020657	.018984	.017449	.016040	.014747	.013561	.012472
47	.024622	.022575	.020701	.018986	.017416	.015978	.014662	.013456	.012351	.011338
48	.022856	.020825	.019062	.017451	.015978	.014632	.013402	.012277	.011248	.010307
49	.021031	.019212	.017552	.016039	.014659	.013400	.012250	.011202	.010244	.009370
50	.019437	.017723	.016163	.014742	.013449	.012271	.011198	.010221	.009330	.008519
51	.017964	.016350	.014883	.013550	.012338	.011237	.010236	.009325	.008497	.007744
52	.016603	.015083	.013704	.012454	.011319	.010290	.009356	.008508	.007739	.007040
53	.015345	.013914	.012619	.011446	.010385	.009423	.008552	.007763	.007048	.006400
54	.014185	.012836	.011620	.010521	.009527	.008629	.007817	.007083	.006419	.005818
55	.013107	.011841	.010699	.009670	.008741	.007902	.007146	.006463	.005846	.005289
56	.012114	.010923	.009852	.008888	.008019	.007237	.006532	.005897	.005324	.004809
57	.011196	.010077	.009072	.008169	.007357	.006627	.005971	.005380	.004849	.004371
58	.010347	.009296	.008354	.007508	.006749	.006069	.005458	.004909	.004416	.003974
59	.009563	.008576	.007692	.006901	.006192	.005557	.004989	.004479	.004022	.003613
60	.008838	.007911	.007083	.006343	.005681	.005089	.004560	.004087	.003663	.003284

Table B

Term Certain Remainder Factors Applicable After April 30, 1989

Interest Rate

Years	10.2%	10.4%	10.6%	10.8%	11.0%	11.2%	11.4%	11.6%	11.8%	12.0%
1	.907441	.905797	.904159	.902527	.900901	.899281	.897666	.896057	.894454	.892857
2	.823449	.820468	.817504	.814555	.811622	.808706	.805804	.802919	.800049	.797194
3	.747232	.743178	.739153	.735158	.731191	.727253	.723343	.719461	.715607	.711780
4	.678069	.673168	.668312	.663500	.658731	.654005	.649321	.644679	.640078	.635518
5	.615307	.609754	.604261	.598827	.593451	.588134	.582873	.577669	.572520	.567427
6	.558355	.552313	.546348	.540457	.534641	.528897	.523225	.517625	.512093	.506631
7	.506674	.500284	.493985	.487777	.481658	.475627	.469682	.463821	.458044	.452349
8	.459777	.453156	.446641	.440232	.433926	.427722	.421617	.415610	.409700	.403883
9	.417221	.410467	.403835	.397322	.390925	.384642	.378472	.372411	.366458	.360610
10	.378603	.371800	.365131	.358593	.352184	.345901	.339741	.333701	.327780	.321973
11	.343560	.336775	.330137	.323640	.317283	.311062	.304974	.299016	.293184	.287476
12	.311760	.305050	.298496	.292094	.285841	.279732	.273765	.267935	.262240	.256675
13	.282904	.276313	.269888	.263623	.257514	.251558	.245749	.240085	.234561	.229174
14	.256719	.250284	.244022	.237927	.231995	.226221	.220601	.215130	.209804	.204620
15	.232957	.226706	.220634	.214735	.209004	.203436	.198026	.192769	.187661	.182696
16	.211395	.205350	.199489	.193804	.188292	.182946	.177761	.172732	.167854	.163122
17	.191828	.186005	.180369	.174914	.169633	.164520	.159570	.154778	.150138	.145644
18	.174073	.168483	.163083	.157864	.152822	.147950	.143241	.138690	.134291	.130040
19	.157961	.152612	.147453	.142477	.137678	.133048	.128582	.124274	.120117	.116107
20	.143340	.138235	.133321	.128589	.124034	.119648	.115424	.111357	.107439	.103667
21	.130073	.125213	.120543	.116055	.111742	.107597	.103612	.099782	.096100	.092560
22	.118033	.113418	.108990	.104743	.100669	.096760	.093009	.089410	.085957	.082643
23	.107108	.102733	.098544	.094533	.090693	.087014	.083491	.080117	.076884	.073788
24	.097195	.093056	.089100	.085319	.081705	.078250	.074947	.071789	.068770	.065882
25	.088198	.084289	.080560	.077003	.073608	.070369	.067278	.064327	.061511	.058823
26	.080035	.076349	.072839	.069497	.066314	.063281	.060393	.057641	.055019	.052521
27	.072627	.069157	.065858	.062723	.059742	.056908	.054213	.051650	.049212	.046894
28	.065905	.062642	.059547	.056609	.053822	.051176	.048665	.046281	.044018	.041869
29	.059804	.056741	.053840	.051091	.048488	.046022	.043685	.041470	.039372	.037383
30	.054269	.051396	.048680	.046111	.043683	.041386	.039214	.037160	.035216	.033378
31	.049246	.046554	.044014	.041617	.039354	.037218	.035201	.033297	.031500	.029802
32	.044688	.042169	.039796	.037560	.035454	.033469	.031599	.029836	.028175	.026609
33	.040552	.038196	.035982	.033899	.031940	.030098	.028365	.026735	.025201	.023758
34	.036798	.034598	.032533	.030595	.028775	.027067	.025463	.023956	.022541	.021212
35	.033392	.031339	.029415	.027613	.025924	.024341	.022857	.021466	.020162	.018940
36	.030301	.028387	.026596	.024921	.023355	.021889	.020518	.019235	.018034	.016910
37	.027497	.025712	.024047	.022492	.021040	.019684	.018418	.017236	.016131	.015098
38	.024952	.023290	.021742	.020300	.018955	.017702	.016533	.015444	.014428	.013481
39	.022642	.021096	.019658	.018321	.017077	.015919	.014841	.013839	.012905	.012036
40	.020546	.019109	.017774	.016535	.015384	.014316	.013323	.012400	.011543	.010747
41	.018645	.017309	.016071	.014923	.013860	.012874	.011959	.011111	.010325	.009595
42	.016919	.015678	.014531	.013469	.012486	.011577	.010735	.009956	.009235	.008567
43	.015353	.014201	.013138	.012156	.011249	.010411	.009637	.008922	.008260	.007649
44	.013932	.012864	.011879	.010971	.010134	.009362	.008651	.007994	.007389	.006830
45	.012642	.011652	.010740	.009902	.009130	.008419	.007765	.007163	.006609	.006098
46	.011472	.010554	.009711	.008937	.008225	.007571	.006971	.006419	.005911	.005445
47	.010410	.009560	.008780	.008065	.007410	.006809	.006257	.005752	.005287	.004861
48	.009447	.008659	.007939	.007279	.006676	.006123	.005617	.005154	.004729	.004340
49	.008572	.007844	.007178	.006570	.006014	.005506	.005042	.004618	.004230	.003875
50	.007779	.007105	.006490	.005929	.005418	.004952	.004526	.004138	.003784	.003460
51	.007059	.006435	.005868	.005351	.004881	.004453	.004063	.003708	.003384	.003089
52	.006406	.005829	.005306	.004830	.004397	.004005	.003647	.003322	.003027	.002758
53	.005813	.005280	.004797	.004359	.003962	.003601	.003274	.002977	.002708	.002463
54	.005275	.004783	.004337	.003934	.003569	.003238	.002939	.002668	.002422	.002199
55	.004786	.004332	.003922	.003551	.003215	.002912	.002638	.002390	.002166	.001963
56	.004343	.003924	.003546	.003205	.002897	.002619	.002368	.002142	.001938	.001753
57	.003941	.003554	.003206	.002892	.002610	.002355	.002126	.001919	.001733	.001565
58	.003577	.003220	.002899	.002610	.002351	.002118	.001908	.001720	.001550	.001398
59	.003246	.002916	.002621	.002356	.002118	.001905	.001713	.001541	.001387	.001248
60	.002945	.002642	.002370	.002126	.001908	.001713	.001538	.001381	.001240	.001114

Table B
Term Certain Remainder Factors Applicable After April 30, 1989
Interest Rate

Years	12.2%	12.4%	12.6%	12.8%	13.0%	13.2%	13.4%	13.6%	13.8%	14.0%
1	.891266	.889680	.888099	.886525	.884956	.883392	.881834	.880282	.878735	.877193
2	.794354	.791530	.788721	.785926	.783147	.780382	.777632	.774896	.772175	.769468
3	.707981	.704208	.700462	.696743	.693050	.689383	.685742	.682127	.678536	.674972
4	.630999	.626520	.622080	.617680	.613319	.608996	.604711	.600464	.596254	.592080
5	.562388	.557402	.552469	.547589	.542760	.537982	.533255	.528577	.523949	.519369
6	.501237	.495909	.490648	.485451	.480319	.475249	.470242	.465297	.460412	.455587
7	.446735	.441200	.435744	.430364	.425061	.419831	.414676	.409592	.404580	.399637
8	.398160	.392527	.386984	.381529	.376160	.370876	.365675	.360557	.355518	.350559
9	.354866	.349223	.343680	.338235	.332885	.327629	.322465	.317391	.312406	.307508
10	.316280	.310697	.305222	.299853	.294588	.289425	.284361	.279394	.274522	.269744
11	.281889	.276421	.271068	.265827	.260698	.255676	.250759	.245945	.241232	.236617
12	.251238	.245926	.240735	.235663	.230706	.225862	.221128	.216501	.211979	.207559
13	.223920	.218795	.213797	.208921	.204165	.199525	.194998	.190582	.186273	.182069
14	.199572	.194658	.189873	.185213	.180677	.176258	.171956	.167766	.163685	.159710
15	.177872	.173183	.168626	.164196	.159891	.155705	.151637	.147681	.143835	.140096
16	.158531	.154077	.149757	.145564	.141496	.137549	.133718	.130001	.126393	.122892
17	.141293	.137080	.132999	.129046	.125218	.121510	.117917	.114438	.111066	.107800
18	.125930	.121957	.118116	.114403	.110812	.107341	.103984	.100737	.097598	.094561
19	.112237	.108503	.104899	.101421	.098064	.094824	.091696	.088677	.085762	.082948
20	.100033	.096533	.093161	.089912	.086782	.083767	.080861	.078061	.075362	.072762
21	.089156	.085883	.082736	.079709	.076798	.073999	.071306	.068716	.066224	.063826
22	.079462	.076408	.073478	.070664	.067963	.065370	.062880	.060489	.058193	.055988
23	.070821	.067979	.065255	.062646	.060144	.057747	.055450	.053247	.051136	.049112
24	.063121	.060480	.057953	.055537	.053225	.051014	.048898	.046873	.044935	.043081
25	.056257	.053807	.051468	.049235	.047102	.045065	.043119	.041261	.039486	.037790
26	.050140	.047871	.045709	.043648	.041683	.039810	.038024	.036321	.034698	.033149
27	.044688	.042590	.040594	.038695	.036888	.035168	.033531	.031973	.030490	.029078
28	.039829	.037892	.036052	.034304	.032644	.031067	.029569	.028145	.026793	.025507
29	.035498	.033711	.032017	.030411	.028889	.027444	.026075	.024776	.023544	.022375
30	.031638	.029992	.028435	.026960	.025565	.024244	.022994	.021810	.020689	.019627
31	.028198	.026684	.025253	.023901	.022624	.021417	.020277	.019199	.018180	.017217
32	.025132	.023740	.022427	.021189	.020021	.018920	.017881	.016900	.015975	.015102
33	.022399	.021121	.019917	.018785	.017718	.016714	.015768	.014877	.014038	.013248
34	.019964	.018791	.017689	.016653	.015680	.014765	.013905	.013096	.012336	.011621
35	.017793	.016718	.015709	.014763	.013876	.013043	.012261	.011528	.010840	.010194
36	.015858	.014873	.013951	.013088	.012279	.011522	.010813	.010148	.009525	.008942
37	.014134	.013233	.012390	.011603	.010867	.010178	.009535	.008933	.008370	.007844
38	.012597	.011773	.011004	.010286	.009617	.008992	.008408	.007864	.007355	.006880
39	.011227	.010474	.009772	.009119	.008510	.007943	.007415	.006922	.006463	.006035
40	.010007	.009319	.008679	.008084	.007531	.007017	.006538	.006093	.005679	.005294
41	.008919	.008291	.007708	.007167	.006665	.006199	.005766	.005364	.004991	.004644
42	.007949	.007376	.006845	.006354	.005898	.005476	.005085	.004722	.004386	.004074
43	.007084	.006562	.006079	.005633	.005219	.004837	.004484	.004157	.003854	.003573
44	.006314	.005838	.005399	.004993	.004619	.004273	.003954	.003659	.003386	.003135
45	.005628	.005194	.004795	.004427	.004088	.003775	.003487	.003221	.002976	.002750
46	.005016	.004621	.004258	.003924	.003617	.003335	.003075	.002835	.002615	.002412
47	.004470	.004111	.003782	.003479	.003201	.002946	.002711	.002496	.002298	.002116
48	.003984	.003658	.003359	.003084	.002833	.002602	.002391	.002197	.002019	.001856
49	.003551	.003254	.002983	.002734	.002507	.002299	.002108	.001934	.001774	.001628
50	.003165	.002895	.002649	.002424	.002219	.002031	.001859	.001702	.001559	.001428
51	.002821	.002576	.002353	.002149	.001963	.001794	.001640	.001499	.001370	.001253
52	.002514	.002292	.002089	.001905	.001737	.001585	.001446	.001319	.001204	.001099
53	.002241	.002039	.001856	.001689	.001538	.001400	.001275	.001161	.001058	.000964
54	.001997	.001814	.001648	.001497	.001361	.001237	.001124	.001022	.000930	.000846
55	.001780	.001614	.001463	.001327	.001204	.001093	.000991	.000900	.000817	.000742
56	.001586	.001436	.001300	.001177	.001066	.000965	.000874	.000792	.000718	.000651
57	.001414	.001277	.001154	.001043	.000943	.000853	.000771	.000697	.000631	.000571
58	.001260	.001136	.001025	.000925	.000835	.000753	.000680	.000614	.000554	.000501
59	.001123	.001011	.000910	.000820	.000739	.000665	.000600	.000540	.000487	.000439
60	.001001	.000900	.000809	.000727	.000654	.000588	.000529	.000476	.000428	.000385

Table J

Adjustment Factors for Term Certain Annuities Payable at the Beginning of Each Interval Applicable After April 30, 1989

Frequency of payments

Interest Rate	Annually	Semi Annually	Quarterly	Monthly	Weekly
4.2	1.0420	1.0314	1.0261	1.0226	1.0213
4.4	1.0440	1.0329	1.0274	1.0237	1.0223
4.6	1.0460	1.0344	1.0286	1.0247	1.0233
4.8	1.0480	1.0359	1.0298	1.0258	1.0243
5.0	1.0500	1.0373	1.0311	1.0269	1.0253
5.2	1.0520	1.0388	1.0323	1.0279	1.0263
5.4	1.0540	1.0403	1.0335	1.0290	1.0273
5.6	1.0560	1.0418	1.0348	1.0301	1.0283
5.8	1.0580	1.0433	1.0360	1.0311	1.0293
6.0	1.0600	1.0448	1.0372	1.0322	1.0303
6.2	1.0620	1.0463	1.0385	1.0333	1.0313
6.4	1.0640	1.0478	1.0397	1.0343	1.0323
6.6	1.0660	1.0492	1.0409	1.0354	1.0333
6.8	1.0680	1.0507	1.0422	1.0365	1.0343
7.0	1.0700	1.0522	1.0434	1.0375	1.0353
7.2	1.0720	1.0537	1.0446	1.0386	1.0363
7.4	1.0740	1.0552	1.0458	1.0396	1.0373
7.6	1.0760	1.0567	1.0471	1.0407	1.0383
7.8	1.0780	1.0581	1.0483	1.0418	1.0393
8.0	1.0800	1.0596	1.0495	1.0428	1.0403
8.2	1.0820	1.0611	1.0507	1.0439	1.0413
8.4	1.0840	1.0626	1.0520	1.0449	1.0422
8.6	1.0860	1.0641	1.0532	1.0460	1.0432
8.8	1.0880	1.0655	1.0544	1.0471	1.0442
9.0	1.0900	1.0670	1.0556	1.0481	1.0452
9.2	1.0920	1.0685	1.0569	1.0492	1.0462
9.4	1.0940	1.0700	1.0581	1.0502	1.0472
9.6	1.0960	1.0715	1.0593	1.0513	1.0482
9.8	1.0980	1.0729	1.0605	1.0523	1.0492
10.0	1.1000	1.0744	1.0618	1.0534	1.0502
10.2	1.1020	1.0759	1.0630	1.0544	1.0512
10.4	1.1040	1.0774	1.0642	1.0555	1.0521
10.6	1.1060	1.0788	1.0654	1.0565	1.0531
10.8	1.1080	1.0803	1.0666	1.0576	1.0541
11.0	1.1100	1.0818	1.0679	1.0586	1.0551
11.2	1.1120	1.0833	1.0691	1.0597	1.0561
11.4	1.1140	1.0847	1.0703	1.0607	1.0571
11.6	1.1160	1.0862	1.0715	1.0618	1.0581
11.8	1.1180	1.0877	1.0727	1.0628	1.0590
12.0	1.1200	1.0892	1.0739	1.0639	1.0600
12.2	1.1220	1.0906	1.0752	1.0649	1.0610
12.4	1.1240	1.0921	1.0764	1.0660	1.0620
12.6	1.1260	1.0936	1.0776	1.0670	1.0630
12.8	1.1280	1.0950	1.0788	1.0681	1.0639
13.0	1.3000	1.0965	1.0800	1.0691	1.0649
13.2	1.1320	1.0980	1.0812	1.0701	1.0659
13.4	1.1340	1.0994	1.0824	1.0712	1.0669
13.6	1.1360	1.1009	1.0836	1.0722	1.0679
13.8	1.1380	1.1024	1.0849	1.0733	1.0688
14.0	1.1400	1.1309	1.0861	1.0743	1.0698

Table K

Adjustment Factors For Annuities Payable At The End Of Each Interval Applicable After April 30, 1989

(Frequency of Payments)

Interest Rate	Annually	Semi Annually	Quarterly	Monthly	Weekly
4.2	1.0000	1.0104	1.0156	1.0191	1.0205
4.4	1.0000	1.0109	1.0164	1.0200	1.0214
4.6	1.0000	1.0114	1.0171	1.0209	1.0224
4.8	1.0000	1.0119	1.0178	1.0218	1.0234
5.0	1.0000	1.0123	1.0186	1.0227	1.0243
5.2	1.0000	1.0128	1.0193	1.0236	1.0253
5.4	1.0000	1.0133	1.0200	1.0245	1.0262
5.6	1.0000	1.0138	1.0208	1.0254	1.0272
5.8	1.0000	1.0143	1.0215	1.0263	1.0282
6.0	1.0000	1.0148	1.0222	1.0272	1.0291
6.2	1.0000	1.0153	1.0230	1.0281	1.0301
6.4	1.0000	1.0158	1.0237	1.0290	1.0311
6.6	1.0000	1.0162	1.0244	1.0299	1.0320
6.8	1.0000	1.0167	1.0252	1.0308	1.0330
7.0	1.0000	1.0172	1.0259	1.0317	1.0339
7.2	1.0000	1.0177	1.0266	1.0326	1.0349
7.4	1.0000	1.0182	1.0273	1.0335	1.0358
7.6	1.0000	1.0187	1.0281	1.0344	1.0368
7.8	1.0000	1.0191	1.0288	1.0353	1.0378
8.0	1.0000	1.0196	1.0295	1.0362	1.0387
8.2	1.0000	1.0201	1.0302	1.0370	1.0397
8.4	1.0000	1.0206	1.0310	1.0379	1.0406
8.6	1.0000	1.0211	1.0317	1.0388	1.0416
8.8	1.0000	1.0215	1.0324	1.0397	1.0425
9.0	1.0000	1.0220	1.0331	1.0406	1.0435
9.2	1.0000	1.0225	1.0339	1.0415	1.0444
9.4	1.0000	1.0230	1.0346	1.0424	1.0454
9.6	1.0000	1.0235	1.0353	1.0433	1.0463
9.8	1.0000	1.0239	1.0360	1.0442	1.0473
10.0	1.0000	1.0244	1.0368	1.0450	1.0482
10.2	1.0000	1.0249	1.0375	1.0459	1.0492
10.4	1.0000	1.0254	1.0382	1.0468	1.0501
10.6	1.0000	1.0258	1.0389	1.0477	1.0511
10.8	1.0000	1.0263	1.0396	1.0486	1.0520
11.0	1.0000	1.0268	1.0404	1.0495	1.0530
11.2	1.0000	1.0273	1.0411	1.0503	1.0539
11.4	1.0000	1.0277	1.0418	1.0512	1.0549
11.6	1.0000	1.0282	1.0425	1.0521	1.0558
11.8	1.0000	1.0287	1.0432	1.0530	1.0568
12.0	1.0000	1.0292	1.0439	1.0539	1.0577
12.2	1.0000	1.0296	1.0447	1.0548	1.0587
12.4	1.0000	1.0301	1.0454	1.0556	1.0596
12.6	1.0000	1.0306	1.0461	1.0565	1.0605
12.8	1.0000	1.0310	1.0468	1.0574	1.0615
13.0	1.0000	1.0315	1.0475	1.0583	1.0624
13.2	1.0000	1.0320	1.0482	1.0591	1.0634
13.4	1.0000	1.0324	1.0489	1.0600	1.0643
13.6	1.0000	1.0329	1.0496	1.0609	1.0652
13.8	1.0000	1.0334	1.0504	1.0618	1.0662
14.0	1.0000	1.0339	1.0511	1.0626	1.0671

(7) *Actuarial Table S and Table 2010CM where the valuation date is on or after June 1, 2023* (i) *Determination of required factors*. Except as provided in § 20.7520–3(b) (pertaining to certain limitations on the use of prescribed tables), for determination of the present value of a remainder interest that is dependent on the termination of a life interest, where the valuation date is on or after June 1, 2023, actuarial remainder factors computed to at least five decimal places directly by using the formula in paragraph (d)(2)(ii)(B) of this section, Table 2010CM, and the section 7520 rate are used in the application of the provisions of this section. For the convenience of taxpayers, the actuarial factors, when the section 7520 interest rate component is from 0.2 to 20 percent, inclusive, have been computed by the IRS and can be found in Table S. Table S currently is available, at no charge, electronically via the IRS website at *https://www.irs.gov/retirement-plans/actuarial-tables*. Table S is also referenced and explained by IRS Publication 1457, Actuarial Valuations Version 4A, which will be available within a reasonable time after June 1, 2023.

(ii) *Table 2010CM*.

Age x	l_x	Age x	l_x	Age x	l_x
0	100,000.00	37	97,193.66	74	71,177.55
1	99,382.28	38	97,058.84	75	69,174.83
2	99,341.16	39	96,915.25	76	67,044.59
3	99,313.80	40	96,761.20	77	64,773.93
4	99,292.72	41	96,595.51	78	62,366.05
5	99,276.45	42	96,416.30	79	59,795.50
6	99,261.55	43	96,220.61	80	57,080.84
7	99,248.33	44	96,005.41	81	54,213.71
8	99,236.50	45	95,768.60	82	51,205.27
9	99,226.09	46	95,509.98	83	48,059.88
10	99,217.03	47	95,229.06	84	44,808.51
11	99,208.80	48	94,923.45	85	41,399.79
12	99,199.98	49	94,589.88	86	37,895.25
13	99,188.21	50	94,225.50	87	34,313.98
14	99,170.64	51	93,828.33	88	30,700.82
15	99,145.34	52	93,398.01	89	27,106.68
16	99,111.91	53	92,934.52	90	23,586.75
17	99,070.69	54	92,438.08	91	20,198.02
18	99,021.50	55	91,907.95	92	16,996.17
19	98,964.16	56	91,342.02	93	14,032.08
20	98,898.61	57	90,737.24	94	11,348.23
21	98,824.20	58	90,090.97	95	8,975.661
22	98,741.32	59	89,401.06	96	6,931.559
23	98,652.16	60	88,665.95	97	5,218.261
24	98,559.87	61	87,883.66	98	3,823.642
25	98,466.80	62	87,051.88	99	2,722.994
26	98,373.71	63	86,167.86	100	1,882.108

Age x	l_x	Age x	l_x	Age x	l_x
27	98,280.09	64	85,226.77	101	1,261.083
28	98,185.51	65	84,221.59	102	818.2641
29	98,089.05	66	83,142.34	103	513.7236
30	97,989.90	67	81,978.28	104	311.8784
31	97,887.47	68	80,728.83	105	183.0200
32	97,781.58	69	79,387.95	106	103.8046
33	97,672.13	70	77,957.53	107	56.91106
34	97,559.20	71	76,429.84	108	30.17214
35	97,442.53	72	74,797.63	109	15.47804
36	97,321.14	73	73,049.33	110	0.000000

(e) Applicability date. This section applies on and after June 1, 2023.

[T.D. 8540, 59 FR 30152, June 10, 1994 T.D. 8819, 64 FR 23212, April 30, 1999; T.D. 8886, 65 FR 36929, June 12, 2000; T.D. 9448, 74 FR 21484, May 7, 2009; T.D. 9540, 76 FR 49612, Aug. 10, 2011; T.D. 9974, 88 FR 37439, June 7, 2023]

§ 20.2031–7A Valuation of annuities, interests for life or a term of years, and remainder or reversionary interests for estates of decedents for which the valuation date of the gross estate is before June 1, 2023.

(a) Valuation of annuities, interests for life or term of years, and remainder or reversionary interests for estates of decedents for which the valuation date of the gross estate is before January 1, 1952. [*Omitted. Ed.*]

(b) Valuation of annuities, interests for life or term of years, and remainder or reversionary interests for estates of decedents for which the valuation date of the gross estate is after December 31, 1951, and before January 1, 1971. [*Omitted. Ed.*]

(c) Valuation of annuities, interests for life or term of years, and remainder or reversionary interests for estates of decedents for which the valuation date of the gross estate is after December 31, 1970, and before December 1, 1983. [*Omitted. Ed.*]

(d) Valuation of annuities, interests for life or term of years, and remainder or reversionary interests for estates of decedents for which the valuation date of the gross estate is after November 30, 1983, and before May 1, 1989. [*Omitted. Ed.*]

(e) Valuation of annuities, interests for life or term of years, and remainder or reversionary interests for estates of decedents for which the valuation date of the gross estate is after April 30, 1989, and before May 1, 1999. [*Omitted. Ed.*]

(f) Valuation of annuities, interests for life or term of years, and remainder or reversionary interests for estates of decedents for which the valuation date of the gross estate is after April 30,1999, and before May 1, 2009. [*Omitted. Ed.*]

(g) Valuation of annuities, interests for life or a term of years, and remainder or reversionary interests for estates of decedents for which the valuation date of the gross estate is on or after May 1, 2009, and before June 1, 2023 (1) *In general.* Except as otherwise provided in §§ 20.2031–7(b) and 20.7520–3(b) (pertaining to certain limitations on the use of prescribed tables), if the valuation date for the gross estate of the decedent is on or after May 1, 2009, and before June 1, 2023, the fair market value of annuities, interests for life or a term of years, and remainder or reversionary interests is the present value of the interests determined by using standard or special section 7520 actuarial factors and the valuation methodology described in § 20.2031–7(d). These factors are derived by using the appropriate section 7520 interest rate and, if applicable, the mortality component for the valuation date of the interest that is being valued. See §§ 20.7520–1 through 20.7520–4. See paragraph (g)(4) of this section for determination of the appropriate table for use in valuing these interests.

(2) *Transitional rules.* (i) If a decedent dies on or after May 1, 2009, and if, on May 1, 2009, the dece-

dent was under a mental disability so that the disposition of the decedent's property could not be changed, and the decedent dies on or before June 1, 2023, either without having regained the ability to dispose of the decedent's property or within 90 days of the date on which the decedent first regains that ability, the fair market value of annuities, interests for life or a term of years, and remainder or reversionary interests included in the gross estate of the decedent is their present value determined either under this section or under the corresponding section applicable at the time the decedent first became subject to the mental disability, at the option of the decedent's executor. For example, see paragraph (d) of this section.

(ii) If a decedent dies on or after May 1, 2009, and before July 1, 2009, the fair market value of annuities, interests for life or a term of years, and remainder or reversionary interests based on one or more measuring lives included in the gross estate of the decedent is their present value determined under this section by using the section 7520 interest rate for the month in which the valuation date occurs (see §§ 20.7520–1(b) and 20.7520–2(a)(2)) and the appropriate actuarial tables under either paragraph (f)(4) or (g)(4) of this section, at the option of the decedent's executor.

(iii) For purposes of paragraphs (g)(2)(i) and (ii) of this section, where the decedent's executor is given the option to use the appropriate actuarial tables under either paragraph (f)(4) or (g)(4) of this section, the decedent's executor must consistently use the same mortality basis with respect to each interest (income, remainder, partial, etc.) in the same property, and with respect to all transfers occurring on the same valuation date. For example, gift and income tax charitable deductions with respect to the same transfer must be determined based on factors with the same mortality basis, and all assets includible in the gross estate and/or estate tax deductions claimed must be valued based on factors with the same mortality basis.

(iv) If a decedent dies after April 30, 2019, and before June 1, 2023, the fair market value of annuities, interests for life or a term of years, and remainder or reversionary interests based on one or more measuring lives included in the gross estate is their present value determined under § 20.2031–7(d)(3).

(3) *Publications and actuarial computations by the Internal Revenue Service.* The factor for determining the present value of a remainder interest that is dependent on the termination of the life of one individual may be computed by using the formula in § 20.2031–7(d)(2)(ii)(B) to derive a remainder factor from the appropriate mortality table expressed to at least five decimal places. For the convenience of taxpayers, actuarial factors have been computed by the IRS and appear in Table S. The factor for determining the present value of a remainder interest following a term certain may be computed by using the formula in § 20.2031–7(d)(2)(ii)(A) expressed to at least six decimal places. For the convenience of taxpayers, actuarial factors have been computed by the IRS and appear in Table B. Adjustment factors for term certain annuities payable at the beginning of each interval may be computed by using the formula in § 20.2031–7(d)(2)(iv)(C) expressed to at least four decimal places. For the convenience of taxpayers, actuarial factors have been computed by the IRS and appear in Table J. Adjustment factors for annuities payable at the end of each interval may be computed by using the formula in § 20.2031–7(d)(2)(iv)(B) expressed to at least four decimal places. For the convenience of taxpayers, actuarial factors have been computed by the IRS and appear in Table K. These tables are referenced and explained by IRS Publication 1457, Actuarial Values Version 3A (2009). Publication 1457 includes examples that illustrate how to compute many special factors for more unusual situations. The actuarial tables are available, at no charge, electronically via the IRS website at https://www.irs.gov/retirement-plans/actuarial-tables (or a corresponding URL as may be updated from time to time). Table S also can be found in paragraph (g)(4) of this section, but only for interest rates from 0.2 to 14 percent, inclusive. Tables B, J, and K also can be found in § 20.2031–7(d)(6), but only for interest rates from 4.2 to 14 percent, inclusive. If a special factor is required in the case of an actual decedent, the special factor may be calculated by the executor using the actuarial formulas in § 20.2031–7(d)(2) or the executor may request a ruling to obtain the factor from the Internal Revenue Service. The request for a ruling must be accompanied by a recitation of the facts including a statement of the date of birth for each measuring life, the date of the decedent's death, any other applicable dates, and a copy of the will, trust, or other relevant documents. A request for a ruling must comply with the instructions for requesting a ruling published periodically in the Internal Revenue Bulletin (see §§ 601.201 and

601.601(d)(2)(ii)(b) of this chapter) and must include payment of the required user fee.

(4) *Actuarial tables.* Except as provided in § 20.7520–3(b) (pertaining to certain limitations on the use of prescribed tables), actuarial factors based on Table 2000CM must be used in the application of the provisions of this section. The factor for determining the present value of a remainder interest that is dependent on the termination of the life of one individual may be computed by using the formula in § 20.2031–7(d)(2)(ii)(B) to derive a remainder factor from the appropriate mortality table to at least five decimal places. For the convenience of taxpayers, actuarial factors, when the section 7520 interest rate component is from 0.2 to 20 percent, inclusive, have been computed by the IRS and appear in Table S (applicable on and after May 1, 2009, and before June 1, 2023). These actuarial tables, as referenced and explained by IRS Publication 1457, Actuarial Valuations Version 3A, are available, at no charge, electronically via the IRS website at *https://www.irs.gov/retirement-plans/actuarial-tables*. Table S (notwithstanding the lack of the applicable termination date in its heading), where the section 7520 interest rate component is from 0.2 to 14 percent, inclusive, and Table 2000CM are as follows:

Table S. Based on Life Table 2000CM Single Life Remainder Factors Applicable On or After May 1, 2009 [*Omitted. Ed.*]

Table 2000 CM [*Omitted. Ed.*]

(5) Applicability dates. Paragraphs (g)(1) through (4) of this section apply on and after May 1, 2009, and before June 1, 2023.

[T.D. 6296, 23 FR 4529, June 24, 1958, as amended by T.D. 7077, 35 FR 18461, Dec. 4, 1970; T.D. 7955, 49 FR 19992, May 11, 1984; T.D. 8540, 59 FR 30102, 30103, 30151, 30152, June 10, 1994; T.D. 8819, 64 FR 23211, 23212, April 30, 1999; 64 FR 33195, June 22, 1999; T.D. 8886, 65 FR 36943, June 12, 2000; T.D. 9448, 74 FR 21484, 21509, May 7, 2009; T.D. 9540, 76 FR 49637, Aug. 10, 2011; T.D. 9974, 88 FR 37439, 37445, June 7, 2023]

§ 20.2031–8 Valuation of certain life insurance and annuity contracts; valuation of shares in an open-end investment company.

(a) Valuation of certain life insurance and annuity contracts. (1) The value of a contract for the payment of an annuity, or an insurance policy on the life of a person other than the decedent, issued by a company regularly engaged in the selling of contracts of that character is established through the sale by that company of comparable contracts. An annuity payable under a combination annuity contract and life insurance policy on the decedent's life (e.g., a "retirement income" policy with death benefit) under which there was no insurance element at the time of the decedent's death (see paragraph (d) of § 20.2039–1) is treated like a contract for the payment of an annuity for purposes of this section.

(2) As valuation of an insurance policy through sale of comparable contracts is not readily ascertainable when, at the date of the decedent's death, the contract has been in force for some time and further premium payments are to be made, the value may be approximated by adding to the interpolated terminal reserve at the date of the decedent's death the proportionate part of the gross premium last paid before the date of the decedent's death which covers the period extending beyond that date. If, however, because of the unusual nature of the contract such an approximation is not reasonable close to the full value of the contract, this method may not be used.

(3) The application of this section may be illustrated by the following examples. In each case involving an insurance contract, it is assumed that there are no accrued dividends or outstanding indebtedness on the contract.

Example (1). X purchased from a life insurance company a joint and survivor annuity contract under the terms of which X was to receive payments of $1,200 annually for his life and, upon X's death, his wife was to receive payments of $1,200 annually for her life. Five years after such purchase, when his wife was 50 years of age, X died. The value of the annuity contract at the date of X's death is the amount which the company would charge for an annuity providing for the payment of $1,200 annually for the life of a female 50 years of age.

Example (2). Y died holding the incidents of ownership in a life insurance policy on the life of his wife. The policy was one on which no further payments were to be made to the company (e.g., a single premium policy or a paid-up policy). The value of the insurance policy at the date of Y's death is the amount which the company would charge for a single premium contract of the same specified amount on the life of a person of the age of the insured.

Example (3). Z died holding the incidents of ownership in a life insurance policy on the life of his wife. The policy was an ordinary life policy issued nine years and four months prior to Z's death and at a time when Z's wife was 35 years of age. The gross annual premium is $2,811 and the decedent died four months after the last premium due date. The value of the insurance policy at the date of Z's death is computed as follows:

Terminal reserve at end of tenth year	$14,601.00
Terminal reserve at end of ninth year	$12,965.00
Increase	$ 1,636.00
One-third of such increase (Z having died four months following the last preceding premium due date) is	$545.33
Terminal reserve at end of ninth year	12,965.00
Interpolated terminal reserve at date of Z's death	13,510.33
Two-thirds of gross premium (2/3 x $2,811)	1,874.00
Value of the insurance policy	$15,384.33

(b) Valuation of shares in an open-end investment company. (1) The fair market value of a share in an open-end investment company (commonly known as a "mutual fund") is the public redemption price of a share. In the absence of an affirmative showing of the public redemption price in effect at the time of death, the last public redemption price quoted by the company for the date of death shall be presumed to be the applicable public redemption price, If the alternative valuation method under 2032 is elected, the last public redemption price quoted by the company for the alternative valuation date shall be the applicable redemption price. If there is no public redemption price quoted by the company for the applicable valuation date (e.g., the valuation date is a Saturday, Sunday, or holiday), the fair market value of the mutual fund share is the last public redemption price quoted by the company for the first day preceding the applicable valuation date for which there is a quotation. In any case where a dividend is declared on a share in an open-end investment company before the decedent's death but payable to shareholders of record on a date after his death and the share is quoted "ex-dividend" on the date of the decedent's death, the amount of the dividend is added to the ex-dividend quotation in determining the fair market value of the share as of the date of the decedent's death. As used in this paragraph, the term "open-end investment company" includes only a company which on the applicable valuation date was engaged in offering its shares to the public in the capacity of an open-end investment company.

(2) The provisions of this paragraph shall apply with respect to estates of decedents dying after August 16, 1954.

[T.D. 6680, 28 FR 10872, Oct. 10, 1963, as amended by T.D. 7319, 39 FR 26723, July 23, 1974]

§ 20.2031–9 Valuation of other property.

The valuation of any property not specifically described in §§ 20.2031–2 to 20.2031–8 is made in accordance with the general principles set forth in § 20.2031–1. For example, a future interest in property not subject to valuation in accordance with the actuarial principles set forth in § 20.2031–7 is to be valued in accordance with the general principles set forth in § 20.2031–1.

[T.D. 6296, 23 FR 4529, June 24, 1958]

§ 2032. Alternate Valuation

(a) General. The value of the gross estate may be determined, if the executor so elects, by valuing all the property included in the gross estate as follows:

(1) In the case of property distributed, sold, exchanged, or otherwise disposed of, within 6 months after the decedent's death such property shall be valued as of the date of distribution, sale, exchange, or other disposition.

(2) In the case of property not distributed, sold, exchanged, or otherwise disposed of, within 6 months after the decedent's death such property shall be valued as of the date 6 months after the decedent's death.

(3) Any interest or estate which is affected by mere lapse of time shall be included at its value as of the time of death (instead of the later date) with adjustment for any difference in its value as of the later date not due to mere lapse of time.

(b) Special rules. No deduction under this chapter of any item shall be allowed if allowance for such item is in effect given by the alternate valuation provided by this section. Wherever in any other subsection or section of this chapter reference is made to the value of property at the time of the decedent's death, such reference shall be deemed to refer to the value of such property used in determining the value of the gross estate. In case of an election made by the executor under this section, then—

(1) for purposes of the charitable deduction under section 2055 or 2106(a)(2), any bequest, legacy, devise, or transfer enumerated therein, and

(2) for the purpose of the marital deduction under section 2056, any interest in property passing to the surviving spouse,

shall be valued as of the date of the decedent's death with adjustment for any difference in value (not due to mere lapse of time or the occurrence or nonoccurrence of a contingency) of the property as of the date 6 months after the decedent's death (substituting, in the case of property distributed by the executor or trustee, or sold, exchanged, or otherwise disposed of, during such 6-month period, the date thereof).

(c) Election must decrease gross estate and estate tax. No election may be made under this section with respect to an estate unless such election will decrease—

(1) the value of the gross estate, and

(2) the sum of the tax imposed by this chapter and the tax imposed by chapter 13 with respect to property includible in the decedent's gross estate (reduced by credits allowable against such taxes).

(d) Election.

(1) In general. The election provided for in this section shall be made by the executor on the return of the tax imposed by this chapter. Such election, once made, shall be irrevocable.

(2) Exception. No election may be made under this section if such return is filed more than 1 year after the time prescribed by law (including extensions) for filing such return.

Regulation

§ 20.2032–1 Alternate valuation.

(a) In general. In general, section 2032 provides for the valuation of a decedent's gross estate at a date other than the date of the decedent's death. More specifically, if an executor elects the alternate valuation method under section 2032, the property included in the decedent's gross estate on the date of his death is valued as of whichever of the following dates is applicable:

(1) Any property distributed, sold, exchanged, or otherwise disposed of within 6 months (1 year, if the decedent died on or before December 31, 1970) after the decedent's death is valued as of the date on which it is first distributed, sold, exchanged, or otherwise disposed of;

(2) Any property not distributed, sold, exchanged, or otherwise disposed of within 6 months (1 year, if the decedent died on or before December 31, 1970) after the decedent's death is valued as of the date 6 months (1 year, if the decedent died on or before December 31, 1970) after the date of the decedent's death;

(3) Any property, interest, or estate which is affected by mere lapse of time is valued as of the date of the decedent's death, but adjusted for any difference in its value not due to mere lapse of time as of the date 6 months (1 year, if the decedent died on or before December 31, 1970) after the decedent's death, or as of the date of its distribution, sale, exchange, or other disposition, whichever date first occurs.

(b) Method and effect of election. (1) *In general.* The election to use the alternate valuation method is made on the return of tax imposed by section 2001. For purposes of this paragraph (b), the term return of tax imposed by section 2001 means the last estate tax return filed by the executor on or before the due date of the return (including extensions of time to file actually granted) or, if a timely return is not filed, the first estate tax return filed by the executor after the due date, provided the return is filed no later than 1 year after the due date (including extensions of time to file actually granted). Once the election is made, it is irrevocable, provided that an election may be revoked on a subsequent return filed on or before the due date of the return (including extensions of time to file actually granted). The election may be made only if it will decrease both the value of the gross estate and the sum (reduced by allowable credits) of the estate tax and the generation-skipping transfer tax payable by reason of the decedent's death with respect to the property includible in the decedent's gross estate. If the election is made, the alternate valuation method applies to all property included in the gross estate and cannot be applied to only a portion of the property.

(2) *Protective election.* If, based on the return of tax as filed, use of the alternate valuation method would not result in a decrease in both the value of the gross estate and the sum (reduced by allowable credits) of the estate tax and the generation-skipping transfer tax liability payable by reason of the decedent's death with respect to the property includible in the decedent's gross estate, a protective election may be made to use the alternate valuation method if it is subsequently determined that such a decrease would occur. A protective election is made on the return of tax imposed by section 2001. The protective election is irrevocable as of the due date of the return (including extensions of time actually granted). The protective election becomes effective on the date on which it is determined that use of the alternate valuation method would result in a decrease in both the value of the gross estate and in the sum (reduced by allowable credits) of the estate tax and generation-skipping transfer tax liability payable by reason of the decedent's death with respect to the property includible in the decedent's gross estate.

(3) *Requests for extension of time to make the election.* A request for an extension of time to make the election or protective election pursuant to §§ 301.9100–1 and 301.9100–3 of this chapter will not be granted unless the return of tax imposed by section 2001 is filed no later than 1 year after the due date of the return (including extensions of time actually granted).

(c) Meaning of "distributed, sold, exchanged, or otherwise disposed of". (1) The phrase "distributed, sold, exchanged, or otherwise disposed of" comprehends all possible ways by which property ceases to form a part of the gross estate. For example, money on hand at the date of the decedent's death which is thereafter used in the payment of funeral expenses, or which is thereafter invested, falls within the term "otherwise disposed of." The term also includes the surrender of a stock certificate for corporate assets in complete or partial liquidation of a corporation pursuant to section 331. The term does not, however, extend to transactions which are mere changes in form. Thus, it does not include a transfer of assets to a corporation in exchange for its stock in a transaction with respect to which no gain or loss would be recognizable for income tax purposes under section 351. Nor does it include an exchange of stock or securities in a corporation for stock or securities in the same corporation or another corporation in a transaction, such as a merger, recapitalization, reorganization or other transaction described in section 368(a) or 355, with respect to which no gain or loss is recognizable for income tax purposes under section 354 or 355.

(2) Property may be "distributed" either by the executor, or by a trustee of property included in the gross estate under section 2035 through 2038, or section 2041. Property is considered as "distributed" upon the first to occur of the following:

(i) The entry of an order or decree of distribution, if the order or decree subsequently becomes final;

(ii) The segregation or separation of the property from the estate or trust so that it becomes unqualifiedly subject to the demand or disposition of the distributee; or

(iii) The actual paying over or delivery of the property to the distributee.

(3) Property may be "sold, exchanged, or otherwise disposed of" by: (i) The executor; (ii) a trustee or other donee to whom the decedent during his lifetime transferred property included in his gross estate under sections 2035 through 2038, or section 2041; (iii) an heir

or devisee to whom title to property passes directly under local law; (iv) a surviving joint tenant or tenant by the entirety; or (v) any other person. If a binding contract for the sale, exchange, or other disposition of property is entered into, the property is considered as sold, exchanged, or otherwise disposed of on the effective date of the contract, unless the contract is not subsequently carried out substantially in accordance with its terms. The effective date of a contract is normally the date it is entered into (and not the date it is consummated, or the date legal title to the property passes) unless the contract specifies a different effective date.

(d) "Included property" and "excluded property". If the executor elects the alternate valuation method under section [2032], all property interests existing at the date of decedent's death which form a part of his gross estate as determined under sections 2033 through 2044 are valued in accordance with the provisions of this section. Such property interests are referred to in this section as "included property". Furthermore, such property interests remain "included property" for the purpose of valuing the gross estate under the alternate valuation method even though they change in form during the alternate valuation period by being actually received, or disposed of, in whole or in part, by the estate. On the other hand, property earned or accrued (whether received or not) after the date of the decedent's death and during the alternate valuation period with respect to any property interest existing at the date of the decedent's death, which does not represent a form of "included property" itself or the receipt of "included property" is excluded in valuing the gross estate under the alternate valuation method. Such property is referred to in this section as "excluded property". Illustrations of "included property" and "excluded property" are contained in the subparagraphs (1) to (4) of this paragraph:

(1) *Interest-bearing obligations.* Interest-bearing obligations, such as bonds or notes, may comprise two elements of "included property" at the date of the decedent's death, namely, (i) the principal of the obligation itself, and (ii) interest accrued to the date of death. Each of these elements is to be separately valued as of the applicable valuation date. Interest accrued after the date of death and before the subsequent valuation date constitutes "excluded property". However, any part payment or principal made between the date of death and the subsequent valuation date, or any advance payment of interest for a period after the subsequent valuation date made during the alternate valuation period which has the effect of reducing the value of the principal obligation as of the subsequent valuation date, will be included in the gross estate, and valued as of the date of such payment.

(2) *Leased property.* The principles set forth in subparagraph (1) of this paragraph with respect to interest-bearing obligations also apply to leased realty or personalty which is included in the gross estate and with respect to which an obligation to pay rent has been reserved. Both the realty or personalty itself and the rents accrued to the date of death constitute "included property", and each is to be separately valued as of the applicable valuation date. Any rent accrued after the date of death and before the subsequent valuation date is "excluded property". Similarly, the principle applicable with respect to interest paid in advance is equally applicable with respect to advance payments of rent.

(3) *Noninterest-bearing obligations.* In the case of noninterest-bearing obligations sold at a discount, such as savings bonds, the principal obligation and the discount amortized to the date of death are property interests existing at the date of death and constitute "included property". The obligation itself is to be valued at the subsequent valuation date without regard to any further increase in value due to amortized discount. The additional discount amortized after death and during the alternate valuation period is the equivalent of interest accruing during that period and is, therefore, not to be included in the gross estate under the alternate valuation method.

(4) *Stock of a corporation.* Shares of stock in a corporation and dividends declared to stockholders of record on or before the date of the decedent's death and not collected at the date of death constitute "included property" of the estate. On the other hand, ordinary dividends out of earnings and profits (whether in cash, shares of the corporation, or other property) declared to stockholders of record after the date of the decedent's death are "excluded property" and are not to be valued under the alternate valuation method. If, however, dividends are declared to stockholders of record after the date of the decedent's death with the effect that the shares of stock at the subsequent valuation date do not reasonably represent the same

"included property" of the gross estate as existed at the date of the decedent's death, the dividends are "included property", except to the extent that they are out of earnings of the corporation after the date of the decedent's death. For example, if a corporation makes a distribution in partial liquidation to stockholders of record during the alternate valuation period which is not accompanied by a surrender of a stock certificate for cancellation, the amount of the distribution received on stock included in the gross estate is itself "included property", except to the extent that the distribution was out of earnings and profits since the date of the decedent's death. Similarly, if a corporation, in which the decedent owned a substantial interest and which possessed at the date of the decedent's death accumulated earnings and profits equal to its paid-in capital, distributed all of its accumulated earnings and profits as a cash dividend to shareholders of record during the alternate valuation period, the amount of the dividends received on stock includible in the gross estate will be included in the gross estate under the alternate valuation method. Likewise, a stock dividend distributed under such circumstances is "included property".

(e) Illustrations of "included property" and "excluded property". The application of paragraph (d) of this section may be further illustrated by the following example in which it is assumed that the decedent died on January 1, 1955:

Description	*Subsequent valuation date*	*Alternate value*	*Value at date of death*
Bond, par value $1,000 bearing interest at 4 percent payable quarterly on Feb. 1, May 1, Aug. 1, and Nov. 1. Bond distributed to legatee on Mar. 1, 1955	Mar. 1, 1955	$1,000.00	1,000.00
Interest coupon of $10 attached to bond and not cashed at date of death although due and payable Nov. 1, 1954. Cashed by executor on Feb. 1, 1955	Feb. 1, 1955	10.00	10.00
Interest accrued from Nov. 1, 1954, to Jan. 1, 1955, collected on Feb. 1, 1955	Feb. 1, 1955	6.67	6.67
Real estate, not disposed of within year following death. Rent of $300 due at the end of each quarter, Feb. 1, May 1, Aug. 1, and Nov. 1	Jan. 1, 1956	11,000.00	12,000.00
Rent due for quarter ending Nov. 1, 1954, but not collected until Feb. 1, 1955	Feb. 1, 1955	300.00	300.00
Rent accrued for November and December 1954, collected on Feb. 1, 1955	Feb. 1, 1955	200.00	200.00
Common stock, X Corporation, 500 shares, not disposed of within year following decedent's death	Jan. 1, 1956	47,500.00	50,000.00
Dividend of $2 per share declared Dec. 10, 1954, and paid on Jan. 10, 1955, to holders of record on Dec. 30, 1954	Jan. 10, 1955	1,000.00	1,000.00

(f) Mere lapse of time. In order to eliminate changes in value due only to mere lapse of time, section 2032(a)(3) provides that any interest or estate "affected by mere lapse of time" is included in a decedent's gross estate under the alternate valuation method at its value as of the date of the decedent's death, but with adjustment for any difference in its value as of the subsequent valuation date not due to mere lapse of time. Properties, interests, or estates which are "affected by mere lapse of time" include patents, estates for the life of a person other than the decedent, remainders, reversions, and other like properties, interests, or estates. The phrase "affected by mere lapse of time" has no reference to obligations for the payment of money, whether or not interest-bearing, the value of which changes with the passing of time. However, such an obligation, like any other property, may become affected by lapse of time when made the subject of a bequest or transfer which itself is creative of an interest or estate so affected. The application of this paragraph is illustrated in subparagraphs (1) and (2) of this paragraph:

(1) *Life estates, remainders, and similar interests* (i) *In general.* The values of life estates, remainders, and similar interests are to be obtained by applying the methods prescribed in § 20.2031–7, using the age of each person, the duration of whose life may affect the value of the interest, as of the date of the decedent's death, and the value of the property as of the alternate valuation date.

(ii) Sample factors from actuarial Table S. The present value of a remainder interest dependent on the termination of one life is determined by using the formula in § 20.2031–7(d)(2)(ii)(B) to derive a remainder factor from the appropriate mortality table to at least five decimal places. For the convenience of taxpayers, actuarial factors have been computed by the IRS and appear in Table S. Table S can be found on the IRS website at *https://www.irs.gov/retirement-plans/actuarial-tables* (or a corresponding URL as may be updated from time to time). For purposes of the example in paragraph (e)(5)(iii) of this section, the following relevant factors from Table S is used:

Factors from Table S—Based on Table 2010CM			
Interest at 4.2 Percent			
Age	Annuity	Life Estate	Remainder
65	12.2128	0.51294	0.48706
Interest at 4.6 Percent			
Age	Annuity	Life Estate	Remainder
65	11.7691	0.54138	0.45862

(iii) *Example.* Assume that the decedent, or the decedent's estate, was entitled to receive certain property worth $50,000 upon the death of A, who was entitled to the income for life. At the time of the decedent's death, A was 65 years and 5 months old, and the section 7520 rate was 4.6 percent. The value of the decedent's remainder interest at the date of the decedent's death would be, as illustrated in § 20.2031–7(d)(5)(i) (Example 1), $22,931.00 ($50,000 x 0.45862). On the date that is 6 months after the decedent's death, A was 65 years and 11 months old, and the section 7520 rate was 4.2 percent. If, because of economic conditions, the property declined in value and was worth only $40,000 on the date that was 6 months after the date of the decedent's death, and the decedent's executor elected to use the alternate valuation date, the value of the remainder interest would be $19,482.40 ($40,000 x 0.48706). When the alternate valuation date is elected, the age of A, and other aspects of valuation which change by reason of the mere passage of time, is determined as of the date of the decedent's death, while the value of the property and the relevant section 7520 interest rate is determined as of the alternate valuation date. Thus, the computation uses A's age of 65 years old at the date of the decedent's death, even though A would be closest to 66 years old on the alternate valuation date.

(2) *Patents.* To illustrate the alternate valuation of a patent, assume that the decedent owned a patent which, on the date of the decedent's death, had an unexpired term of ten years and a value of $78,000. Six months after the date of the decedent's death, the patent was sold, because of lapse of time and other causes, for $60,000. The alternate value thereof would be obtained by dividing $60,000 by 0.95 (ratio of the remaining life of the patent at the alternate date to the remaining life of the patent at the date of the decedent's death), and would, therefore, be $63,157.89.

(g) Effect of election on deductions. If the executor elects the alternate valuation method under section 2032, any deduction for administration expenses under section 2053(b) (pertaining to property not subject to claims) or losses under section 2054 (or section 2106(a)(1), relating to estates of nonresidents not citizens) is allowed only to the extent that it is not otherwise in effect allowed in determining the value of the gross estate. Furthermore, the amount of any charitable deduction under section 2055 (or section 2106(a)(2), relating to the estates of nonresidents not citizens) or the amount of any marital deduction under section 2056 is determined by the value of the property with respect to which the deduction is allowed as of the date of the decedent's death, adjusted, however, for any difference in its value as of the date 6 months (1 year, if the decedent died on or before December 31, 1970) after death, or as of the date of its distribution, sale, exchange, or other disposition, whichever first occurs. However, no such adjustment may take into account any difference in value due to lapse of time or to the occurrence or nonoccurrence of a contingency.

(h) Applicability date. Paragraph (b) of this section is applicable to decedents dying on or after January 4, 2005. However, pursuant to section 7805(b)(7), taxpayers may elect to apply paragraph (b) of this section retroactively if the period of limitations for filing a claim for a credit or refund of Federal estate or generation-skipping transfer tax under section 6511 has not expired. Paragraph (f)(1) of this section applies on and after June 1, 2023.

[T.D. 6296, 23 FR 4529, June 24, 1958, as amended by T.D. 7238, 37 FR 28718, Dec. 29, 1972; T.D. 7955, 49 FR 19995, May 11, 1984; T.D. 8540, 59 FR 30103, June 10, 1994; T.D. 8819, 64 FR 23229, April 30, 1999; T.D. 9172, 70 FR 296, Jan. 4, 2005; T.D. 9448, 74 FR 21509, May 7, 2009; T.D. 9449, 74 FR 27080, June 8, 2009; T.D. 9974, 88 FR 37446, June 7, 2023]

§ 2032A. Valuation of Certain Farm, Etc., Real Property

(a) Value based on use under which property qualifies.

(1) General rule. If—

(A) the decedent was (at the time of his death) a citizen or resident of the United States, and

(B) the executor elects the application of this section and files the agreement referred to in subsection (d)(2),

then, for purposes of this chapter, the value of qualified real property shall be its value for the use under which it qualifies, under subsection (b), as qualified real property.

(2) Limitation on aggregate reduction in fair market value. The aggregate decrease in the value of qualified real property taken into account for purposes of this chapter which results from the application of paragraph (1) with respect to any decedent shall not exceed $750,000.

(3) Inflation adjustment. In the case of estates of decedents dying in a calendar year after 1998, the $750,000 amount contained in paragraph (2) shall be increased by an amount equal to—

(A) $750,000, multiplied by

(B) the cost-of-living adjustment determined under section 1(f)(3) for such calendar year by substituting "calendar year 1997" for "calendar year 2016" in subparagraph (A)(ii) thereof.

If any amount as adjusted under the preceding sentence is not a multiple of $10,000, such amount shall be rounded to the next lowest multiple of $10,000.*

(b) Qualified real property.

(1) In general. For purposes of this section, the term "qualified real property" means real property located in the United States which was acquired from or passed from the decedent to a qualified heir of the decedent and which, on the date of the decedent's death, was being used for a qualified use by the decedent or a member of the decedent's family, but only if—

(A) 50 percent or more of the adjusted value of the gross estate consists of the adjusted value of real or personal property which—

(i) on the date of the decedent's death, was being used for a qualified use by the decedent or a member of the decedent's family, and

(ii) was acquired from or passed from the decedent to a qualified heir of the decedent.

* Rev. Proc. 2025–32 provides that "[f]or an estate of a decedent dying in calendar year 2026, if the executor elects to use the special use valuation method under § 2032A for qualified real property, the aggregate decrease in the value of qualified real property resulting from electing to use § 2032A for purposes of the estate tax cannot exceed $1,460,000." *Ed.*

(B) 25 percent or more of the adjusted value of the gross estate consists of the adjusted value of real property which meets the requirements of subparagraphs (A)(ii) and (C),

(C) during the 8-year period ending on the date of the decedent's death there have been periods aggregating 5 years or more during which—

(i) such real property was owned by the decedent or a member of the decedent's family and used for a qualified use by the decedent or a member of the decedent's family, and

(ii) there was material participation by the decedent or a member of the decedent's family in the operation of the farm or other business, and

(D) such real property is designated in the agreement referred to in subsection (d)(2).

(2) Qualified use. For purposes of this section, the term "qualified use" means the devotion of the property to any of the following:

(A) use as a farm for farming purposes, or

(B) use in a trade or business other than the trade or business of farming.

(3) Adjusted value. For purposes of paragraph (1), the term "adjusted value" means—

(A) in the case of the gross estate, the value of the gross estate for purposes of this chapter (determined without regard to this section), reduced by any amounts allowable as a deduction under paragraph (4) of section 2053(a), or

(B) in the case of any real or personal property, the value of such property for purposes of this chapter (determined without regard to this section), reduced by any amounts allowable as a deduction in respect of such property under paragraph (4) of section 2053(a).

(4) Decedents who are retired or disabled.

(A) In general. If, on the date of the decedent's death, the requirements of paragraph (1)(C)(ii) with respect to the decedent for any property are not met, and the decedent—

(i) was receiving old-age benefits under title II of the Social Security Act for a continuous period ending on such date, or

(ii) was disabled for a continuous period ending on such date,

then paragraph (1)(C)(ii) shall be applied with respect to such property by substituting "the date on which the longer of such continuous periods began" for "the date of the decedent's death" in paragraph (1)(C).

(B) Disabled defined. For purposes of subparagraph (A), an individual shall be disabled if such individual has a mental or physical impairment which renders him unable to materially participate in the operation of the farm or other business.

(C) Coordination with recapture. For purposes of subsection (c)(6)(B)(i), if the requirements of paragraph (1)(C)(ii) are met with respect to any decedent by reason of subparagraph (A), the period ending on the date on which the continuous period taken into account under subparagraph (A) began shall be treated as the period immediately before the decedent's death.

(5) Special rules for surviving spouses.

(A) In general. If property is qualified real property with respect to a decedent (hereinafter in this paragraph referred to as the "first decedent") and such property was acquired from or passed from the first decedent to the surviving spouse of the first decedent, for purposes of applying this subsection and subsection (c) in the case of the estate of such surviving spouse, active management of the farm or other business by the surviving spouse shall be treated as material participation by such surviving spouse in the operation of such farm or business.

(B) Special rule. For the purposes of subparagraph (A), the determination of whether property is qualified real property with respect to the first decedent shall be made without regard to subparagraph (D) of paragraph (1) and without regard to whether an election under this section was made.

(C) Coordination with paragraph (4). In any case in which to do so will enable the requirements of paragraph (1)(C)(ii) to be met with respect to the surviving spouse, this subsection and subsection (c) shall be applied by taking into account any application of paragraph (4).

(c) Tax treatment of dispositions and failures to use for qualified use.

(1) Imposition of additional estate tax. If, within 10 years after the decedent's death and before the death of the qualified heir—

(A) the qualified heir disposes of any interest in qualified real property (other than by a disposition to a member of his family), or

(B) the qualified heir ceases to use for the qualified use the qualified real property which was acquired (or passed) from the decedent,

then, there is hereby imposed an additional estate tax.

(2) Amount of additional tax.

(A) In general. The amount of the additional tax imposed by paragraph (1) with respect to any interest shall be the amount equal to the lesser of—

(i) the adjusted tax difference attributable to such interest, or

(ii) the excess of the amount realized with respect to the interest (or, in any case other than a sale or exchange at arm's length, the fair market value of the interest) over the value of the interest determined under subsection (a).

(B) Adjusted tax difference attributable to interest. For purposes of subparagraph (A), the adjusted tax difference attributable to an interest is the amount which bears the same ratio to the adjusted tax difference with respect to the estate (determined under subparagraph (C)) as—

(i) the excess of the value of such interest for purposes of this chapter (determined without regard to subsection (a)) over the value of such interest determined under subsection (a), bears to

(ii) a similar excess determined for all qualified real property.

(C) Adjusted tax difference with respect to the estate. For purposes of subparagraph (B), the term "adjusted tax difference with respect to the estate" means the excess of what would have been the estate tax liability but for subsection (a) over the estate tax liability. For purposes of this subparagraph, the term "estate tax liability" means the tax imposed by section 2001 reduced by the credits allowable against such tax.

(D) Partial dispositions. For purposes of this paragraph, where the qualified heir disposes of a portion of the interest acquired by (or passing to) such heir (or a predecessor qualified heir) or there is a cessation of use of such a portion—

(i) the value determined under subsection (a) taken into account under subparagraph (A)(ii) with respect to such portion shall be its pro rata share of such value of such interest, and

(ii) the adjusted tax difference attributable to the interest taken into account with respect to the transaction involving the second or any succeeding portion shall be reduced by the amount of the tax imposed by this subsection with respect to all prior transactions involving portions of such interest.

(E) Special rule for disposition of timber. In the case of qualified woodland to which an election under subsection (e)(13)(A) applies, if the qualified heir disposes of (or severs) any standing timber on such qualified woodland—

(i) such disposition (or severance) shall be treated as a disposition of a portion of the interest of the qualified heir in such property, and

(ii) the amount of the additional tax imposed by paragraph (1) with respect to such disposition shall be an amount equal to the lesser of—

(I) the amount realized on such disposition (or, in any case other than a sale or exchange at arm's length, the fair market value of the portion of the interest disposed or severed), or

(II) the amount of additional tax determined under this paragraph (without regard to this subparagraph) if the entire interest of the qualified heir in the qualified woodland had been disposed of, less the sum of the amount of the additional tax imposed with respect to all prior transactions involving such woodland to which this subparagraph applied.

For purposes of the preceding sentence, the disposition of a right to sever shall be treated as the disposition of the standing timber. The amount of additional tax imposed under paragraph (1) in any case in which a qualified heir disposes of his entire interest in the qualified woodland shall be reduced by any amount determined under this subparagraph with respect to such woodland.

(3) Only 1 additional tax imposed with respect to any 1 portion. In the case of an interest acquired from (or passing from) any decedent, if subparagraph (A) or (B) of paragraph (1) applies to any portion of an interest, subparagraph (B) or (A), as the case may be, of paragraph (1) shall not apply with respect to the same portion of such interest.

(4) Due date. The additional tax imposed by this subsection shall become due and payable on the day which is 6 months after the date of the disposition or cessation referred to in paragraph (1).

(5) Liability for tax; furnishing of bond. The qualified heir shall be personally liable for the additional tax imposed by this subsection with respect to his interest unless the heir has furnished bond which meets the requirements of subsection (e)(11).

(6) Cessation of qualified use. For purposes of paragraph (1)(B), real property shall cease to be used for the qualified use if—

(A) such property ceases to be used for the qualified use set forth in subparagraph (A) or (B) of subsection (b)(2) under which the property qualified under subsection (b), or

(B) during any period of 8 years ending after the date of the decedent's death and before the date of the death of the qualified heir, there had been periods aggregating more than 3 years during which—

(i) in the case of periods during which the property was held by the decedent, there was no material participation by the decedent or any member of his family in the operation of the farm or other business, and

(ii) in the case of periods during which the property was held by any qualified heir, there was no material participation by such qualified heir or any member of his family in the operation of the farm or other business.

(7) Special rules.

(A) No tax if use begins within 2 years. If the date on which the qualified heir begins to use the qualified real property (hereinafter in this subparagraph referred to as the commencement date) is before the date 2 years after the decedent's death—

(i) no tax shall be imposed under paragraph (1) by reason of the failure by the qualified heir to so use such property before the commencement date, and

(ii) the 10-year period under paragraph (1) shall be extended by the period after the decedent's death and before the commencement date.

(B) Active management by eligible qualified heir treated as material participation. For purposes of paragraph (6)(B)(ii), the active management of a farm or other business by—

(i) an eligible qualified heir, or

(ii) a fiduciary of an eligible qualified heir described in clause (ii) or (iii) of subparagraph (C),

shall be treated as material participation by such eligible qualified heir in the operation of such farm or business. In the case of an eligible qualified heir described in clause (ii), (iii), or (iv) of subparagraph (C), the preceding sentence shall apply only during periods during which such heir meets the requirements of such clause.

(C) Eligible qualified heir. For purposes of this paragraph, the term "eligible qualified heir" means a qualified heir who—

(i) is the surviving spouse of the decedent,

(ii) has not attained the age of 21,

(iii) is disabled (within the meaning of subsection (b)(4)(B)), or

(iv) is a student.

(D) Student. For purposes of subparagraph (C), an individual shall be treated as a student with respect to periods during any calendar year if (and only if) such individual is a student (within the meaning of section 152(f)(2)) for such calendar year.

(E) Certain rents treated as qualified use. For purposes of this subsection, a surviving spouse or lineal descendant of the decedent shall not be treated as failing to use qualified real property in a qualified use solely because such spouse or descendant rents such property to a member of the family of such spouse or descendant on a net cash basis. For purposes of the preceding sentence, a legally adopted child of an individual shall be treated as the child of such individual by blood.

(8) Qualified conservation contribution is not a disposition. A qualified conservation contribution (as defined in section 170(h)) by gift or otherwise shall not be deemed a disposition under subsection (c)(1)(A).

(d) Election; agreement.

(1) Election. The election under this section shall be made on the return of the tax imposed by section 2001. Such election shall be made in such manner as the Secretary shall by regulations prescribe. Such an election, once made, shall be irrevocable.

(2) Agreement. The agreement referred to in this paragraph is a written agreement signed by each person in being who has an interest (whether or not in possession) in any property designated in such agreement consenting to the application of subsection (c) with respect to such property.

(3) Modification of election and agreement to be permitted. The Secretary shall prescribe procedures which provide that in any case in which the executor makes an election under paragraph (1) (and submits the agreement referred to in paragraph (2)) within the time prescribed therefor, but—

(A) the notice of election, as filed, does not contain all required information, or

(B) signatures of 1 or more persons required to enter into the agreement described in paragraph (2) are not included on the agreement as filed, or the agreement does not contain all required information, the executor will have a reasonable period of time (not exceeding 90 days) after notification of such failures to provide such information or signatures.

(e) Definitions; special rules. For purposes of this section—

(1) Qualified heir. The term "qualified heir" means, with respect to any property, a member of the decedent's family who acquired such property (or to whom such property passed) from the decedent. If a qualified heir disposes of any interest in qualified real property to any member of his family, such member shall thereafter be treated as the qualified heir with respect to such interest.

(2) Member of family. The term "member of the family" means, with respect to any individual, only—

(A) an ancestor of such individual,

(B) the spouse of such individual,

(C) a lineal descendant of such individual, of such individual's spouse, or of a parent of such individual, or

(D) the spouse of any lineal descendant described in subparagraph (C).

For purposes of the preceding sentence, a legally adopted child of an individual shall be treated as the child of such individual by blood.

(3) Certain real property included. In the case of real property which meets the requirements of subparagraph (C) of subsection (b)(1), residential buildings and related improvements on such real property occupied on a regular basis by the owner or lessee of such real property or by persons employed by such owner or lessee for the purpose of operating or maintaining such real property, and roads, buildings, and other structures and improvements functionally related to the qualified use shall be treated as real property devoted to the qualified use.

(4) Farm. The term "farm" includes stock, dairy, poultry, fruit, furbearing animal, and truck farms, plantations, ranches, nurseries, ranges, greenhouses or other similar structures used primarily for the raising of agricultural or horticultural commodities, and orchards and woodlands.

(5) Farming purposes. The term "farming purposes" means—

(A) cultivating the soil or raising or harvesting any agricultural or horticultural commodity (including the raising, shearing, feeding, caring for, training, and management of animals) on a farm;

(B) handling, drying, packing, grading, or storing on a farm any agricultural or horticultural commodity in its unmanufactured state, but only if the owner, tenant, or operator of the farm regularly produces more than one-half of the commodity so treated; and

(C)(i) the planting, cultivating, caring for, or cutting of trees, or

(ii) the preparation (other than milling) of trees for market.

(6) Material participation. Material participation shall be determined in a manner similar to the manner used for purposes of paragraph (1) of section 1402(a) (relating to net earnings from self-employment).

(7) Method of valuing farms.

(A) In general. Except as provided in subparagraph (B), the value of a farm for farming purposes shall be determined by dividing—

(i) the excess of the average annual gross cash rental for comparable land used for farming purposes and located in the locality of such farm over the average annual State and local real estate taxes for such comparable land, by

(ii) the average annual effective interest rate for all new Federal Land Bank loans.

For purposes of the preceding sentence, each average annual computation shall be made on the basis of the 5 most recent calendar years ending before the date of the decedent's death.

(B) Value based on net share rental in certain cases.

(i) In general. If there is no comparable land from which the average annual gross cash rental may be determined but there is comparable land from which the average net share rental may be determined, subparagraph (A)(i) shall be applied by substituting "average annual net share rental" for "average annual gross cash rental".

(ii) Net share rental. For purposes of this paragraph, the term "net share rental" means the excess of—

(I) the value of the produce received by the lessor of the land on which such produce is grown, over

(II) the cash operating expenses of growing such produce which, under the lease, are paid by the lessor.

(C) Exception. The formula provided by subparagraph (A) shall not be used—

(i) where it is established that there is no comparable land from which the average annual gross cash rental may be determined, or

(ii) where the executor elects to have the value of the farm for farming purposes determined and that there is no comparable land from which the average net share rental may be determined under paragraph (8).

(8) Method of valuing closely held business interests, etc. In any case to which paragraph (7)(A) does not apply, the following factors shall apply in determining the value of any qualified real property:

(A) The capitalization of income which the property can be expected to yield for farming or closely held business purposes over a reasonable period of time under prudent management using traditional cropping patterns for the area, taking into account soil capacity, terrain configuration, and similar factors,

(B) The capitalization of the fair rental value of the land for farmland or closely held business purposes,

(C) Assessed land values in a State which provides a differential or use value assessment law for farmland or closely held business,

(D) Comparable sales of other farm or closely held business land in the same geographical area far enough removed from a metropolitan or resort area so that nonagricultural use is not a significant factor in the sales price, and

(E) Any other factor which fairly values the farm or closely held business value of the property.

(9) Property acquired from decedent. Property shall be considered to have been acquired from or to have passed from the decedent if—

(A) such property is so considered under section 1014(b) (relating to basis of property acquired from a decedent),

(B) such property is acquired by any person from the estate, or

(C) such property is acquired by any person from a trust (to the extent such property is includible in the gross estate of the decedent).

(10) Community property. If the decedent and his surviving spouse at any time held qualified real property as community property, the interest of the surviving spouse in such property shall be taken into account under this section to the extent necessary to provide a result under this section with respect to such property which is consistent with the result which would have obtained under this section if such property had not been community property.

(11) Bond in lieu of personal liability. If the qualified heir makes written application to the Secretary for determination of the maximum amount of the additional tax which may be imposed by subsection (c) with respect to the qualified heir's interest, the Secretary (as soon as possible, and in any event within 1 year after the making of such application) shall notify the heir of such maximum amount. The qualified heir, on furnishing a bond in such amount and for such period as may be required, shall be discharged from personal liability for any additional tax imposed by subsection (c) and shall be entitled to a receipt or writing showing such discharge.

(12) Active management. The term "active management" means the making of the management decisions of a business (other than the daily operating decisions).

(13) Special rules for woodlands.

(A) In general. In the case of any qualified woodland with respect to which the executor elects to have this subparagraph apply, trees growing on such woodland shall not be treated as a crop.

(B) Qualified woodland. The term "qualified woodland" means any real property which—

(i) is used in timber operations, and

(ii) is an identifiable area of land such as an acre or other area for which records are normally maintained in conducting timber operations.

(C) Timber operations. The term "timber operations" means—

(i) the planting, cultivating, caring for, or cutting of trees, or

(ii) the preparation (other than milling) of trees for market.

(D) Election. An election under subparagraph (A) shall be made on the return of the tax imposed by section 2001. Such election shall be made in such manner as the Secretary shall by regulations prescribe. Such an election, once made, shall be irrevocable.

(14) Treatment of replacement property acquired in section 1031 or 1033 transactions.

(A) In general. In the case of any qualified replacement property, any period during which there was ownership, qualified use, or material participation with respect to the replaced property by the decedent or any member of his family shall be treated as a period during which there was such ownership, use, or material participation (as the case may be) with respect to the qualified replacement property.

(B) Limitation. Subparagraph (A) shall not apply to the extent that the fair market value of the qualified replacement property (as of the date of its acquisition) exceeds the fair market value of the replaced property (as of the date of its disposition).

(C) Definitions. For purposes of this paragraph—

(i) Qualified replacement property. The term "qualified replacement property" means any real property which is—

(I) acquired in an exchange which qualifies under section 1031, or

(II) the acquisition of which results in the nonrecognition of gain under section 1033.

Such term shall only include property which is used for the same qualified use as the replaced property was being used before the exchange.

(ii) Replaced property. The term "replaced property" means—

(I) the property transferred in the exchange which qualifies under section 1031, or

(II) the property compulsorily or involuntarily converted (within the meaning of section 1033).

(f) Statute of limitations. If qualified real property is disposed of or ceases to be used for a qualified use, then—

(1) the statutory period for the assessment of any additional tax under subsection (c) attributable to such disposition or cessation shall not expire before the expiration of 3 years from the date the Secretary is notified (in such manner as the Secretary may by regulations prescribe) of such disposition or cessation (or if later in the case of an involuntary conversion or exchange to which subsection (h) or (i) applies, 3 years from the date the Secretary is notified of the replacement of the converted property or of an intention not to replace or of the exchange of property), and

(2) such additional tax may be assessed before the expiration of such 3-year period notwithstanding the provisions of any other law or rule of law which would otherwise prevent such assessment.

(g) Application of this section and section 6324B to interests in partnerships, corporations, and trusts. The Secretary shall prescribe regulations setting forth the application of this section and section 6324B in the case of an interest in a partnership, corporation, or trust which, with respect to the decedent, is an interest in a closely held business (within the meaning of paragraph (1) of section 6166(b)). For purposes of the preceding sentence, an interest in a discretionary trust all the beneficiaries of which are qualified heirs shall be treated as a present interest.

(h) Special rules for involuntary conversions of qualified real property.

(1) Treatment of converted property.

(A) In general. If there is an involuntary conversion of an interest in qualified real property—

(i) no tax shall be imposed by subsection (c) on such conversion if the cost of the qualified replacement property equals or exceeds the amount realized on such conversion, or

(ii) if clause (i) does not apply, the amount of the tax imposed by subsection (c) on such conversion shall be the amount determined under subparagraph (B).

(B) Amount of tax where there is not complete reinvestment. The amount determined under this subparagraph with respect to any involuntary conversion is the amount of the tax which (but for this subsection) would have been imposed on such conversion reduced by an amount which—

(i) bears the same ratio to such tax, as

(ii) the cost of the qualified replacement property bears to the amount realized on the conversion.

(2) Treatment of replacement property. For purposes of subsection (c)—

(A) any qualified replacement property shall be treated in the same manner as if it were a portion of the interest in qualified real property which was involuntarily converted; except that with respect to such qualified replacement property the 10-year period under paragraph (1) of subsection (c) shall be extended by any period, beyond the 2-year period referred to in section 1033(a)(2)(B)(i), during which the qualified heir was allowed to replace the qualified real property,

(B) any tax imposed by subsection (c) on the involuntary conversion shall be treated as a tax imposed on a partial disposition, and

(C) paragraph (6) of subsection (c) shall be applied—

(i) by not taking into account periods after the involuntary conversion and before the acquisition of the qualified replacement property, and

(ii) by treating material participation with respect to the converted property as material participation with respect to the qualified replacement property.

(3) Definitions and special rules. For purposes of this subsection—

(A) Involuntary conversion. The term "involuntary conversion" means a compulsory or involuntary conversion within the meaning of section 1033.

(B) Qualified replacement property. The term "qualified replacement property" means—

(i) in the case of an involuntary conversion described in section 1033(a)(1), any real property into which the qualified real property is converted, or

(ii) in the case of an involuntary conversion described in section 1033(a)(2), any real property purchased by the qualified heir during the period specified in section 1033(a)(2)(B) for purposes of replacing the qualified real property.

Such term only includes property which is to be used for the qualified use set forth in subparagraph (A) or (B) of subsection (b)(2) under which the qualified real property qualified under subsection (a).

(4) Certain rules made applicable. The rules of the last sentence of section 1033(a)(2)(A) shall apply for purposes of paragraph (3)(B)(ii).

(i) Exchanges of qualified real property.

(1) Treatment of property exchanged.

(A) Exchanges solely for qualified exchange property. If an interest in qualified real property is exchanged solely for an interest in qualified exchange property in a transaction which qualifies under section 1031, no tax shall be imposed by subsection (c) by reason of such exchange.

(B) Exchanges where other property received. If an interest in qualified real property is exchanged for an interest in qualified exchange property and other property in a transaction which qualifies under section 1031, the amount of the tax imposed by subsection (c) by reason of such exchange shall be the amount of tax which (but for this subparagraph) would have been imposed on such exchange under subsection (c)(1), reduced by an amount which—

(i) bears the same ratio to such tax, as

(ii) the fair market value of the qualified exchange property bears to the fair market value of the qualified real property exchanged.

For purposes of clause (ii) of the preceding sentence, fair market value shall be determined as of the time of the exchange.

(2) Treatment of qualified exchange property. For purposes of subsection (c)—

(A) any interest in qualified exchange property shall be treated in the same manner as if it were a portion of the interest in qualified real property which was exchanged,

(B) any tax imposed by subsection (c) by reason of the exchange shall be treated as a tax imposed on a partial disposition, and

(C) paragraph (6) of subsection (c) shall be applied by treating material participation with respect to the exchanged property as material participation with respect to the qualified exchange property.

(3) Qualified exchange property. For purposes of this subsection, the term "qualified exchange property" means real property which is to be used for the qualified use set forth in subparagraph (A) or (B) of subsection (b)(2) under which the real property exchanged therefor originally qualified under subsection (a).

Regulations

§ 20.2032A–3 Material participation requirements for valuation of certain farm and closely-held business real property.

(a) In general. Under section 2032A, an executor may, for estate tax purposes, make a special election concerning valuation of qualified real property (as defined in section 2032A(b)) used as a farm for farming purposes or in another trade or business. If this election is made, the property will be valued on the basis of its value for its qualified use in farming or the other trade or business, rather than its fair market value determined on the basis of highest and best use (irrespective of whether its highest and best use is the use in farming or other business). For the special valuation rules of section 2032A to apply, the deceased owner and/or a member of the owner's family (as defined in section 2032A(e)(2)) must materially participate in the operation of the farm or other business. Whether the required material participation occurs is a factual determination, and the types of activities and financial risks which will support such a finding will vary with the mode of ownership of both the property itself and of any business in which it is used. Passively collecting rents, salaries, draws, dividends, or other income from the farm or other business is not sufficient for material participation, nor is merely advancing capital and reviewing a crop plan or other business proposal and financial reports each season or business year.

(b) Types of qualified property. (1) *In general.* Real property valued under section 2032A must pass from the decedent to a qualified heir or be acquired from the decedent by a qualified heir. The real property may be owned directly or may be owned indirectly through ownership of an interest in a corporation, a partnership, or a trust. Where the ownership is indirect, however, the decedent's interest in the business must, in addition to meeting the tests for qualification under section 2032A, qualify under the tests of section 6166(b)(1) as an interest in a closely-held business on the date of the decedent's death and for sufficient other time (combined with periods of direct ownership) to equal at least 5 years of the 8 year period preceding the death. All specially valued property must be used in a trade or business. Directly owned real property that is leased by a decedent to a separate closely held business is considered to be qualified real property, but only if the separate business qualifies as a closely held business under section 6166(b)(1) with respect to the decedent on the date of his or her death and for sufficient other time (combined with periods during which the property was operated as a proprietorship) to equal at least 5 years of the 8 year period preceding the death. For example, real property owned by the decedent and leased to a farming corporation or partnership owned and operated entirely by the decedent and fewer than 15 members of the decedent's family is eligible for special use valuation. Under section 2032A, the term trade or business applies only to an active business such as a manufacturing, mercantile, or service enterprise, or to the raising of agricultural or horticultural commodities, as distinguished from passive investment activities. The mere passive rental of property "to a party other than a member of the decedent's family" will not qualify. The decedent "or a member of the decedent's family" must own an equity interest in the farm operation. A trade or business is not necessarily present even though an office and regular hours are maintained for management of income producing assets, as the term "business" is not as broad under section 2032A as under section 162. Additionally, no trade or business is present in the case of activities not engaged in for profit. See section 183.

(2) *Structures and other real property improvements.* Qualified real property includes residential buildings and other structures and real property improvements occupied or used on a regular basis by the owner or lessee of real property (or by employees of the owner or lessee) for the purpose of operating the farm or other closely held business. A farm residence occupied by the decedent owner of the specially valued property is considered to be occupied for the purpose of operating the farm even though a family member (not the decedent) was the person materially participating in the operation of the farm as required under section 2032A(b)(1)(C).

(c) Period material participation must last. The required participation must last—

(1) For periods totalling 5 years or more during the 8 years immediately preceding the date of the decedent's death; and

(2) For periods totalling 5 years or more during any 8 year period ending after the date of the decedent's

death (up to a maximum of 15 years after decedent's death, when the additional estate tax provisions of section 2032A(c) cease to apply).

In determining whether the material participation requirement is satisfied, no exception is made for periods during which real property is held by the decedent's estate. Additionally, contemporaneous material participation by 2 or more family members during a period totalling a year will not result in that year being counted as 2 or more years for purposes of satisfying the requirements of this paragraph (c). Death of a qualified heir (as defined in section 2032A(e)(1)) before the requisite time has passed ends any material participation requirement for that heir's portion of the property as to the original decedent's estate if the heir received a separate, joint or other undivided property interest from the decedent. If qualified heirs receive successive interests in specially valued property (e.g. life estate and remainder interests) from the decedent, the material participation requirement does not end with respect to any part of the property until the death of the last qualified heir (or, if earlier, the expiration of 15 years from the date of the decedent's death). The requirements of section 2032A will fully apply to an heir's estate if an election under this section is made for the same property by the heir's executor. In general, to determine whether the required participation has occurred, brief periods (e.g., periods of 30 days or less) during which there was no material participation may be disregarded. This is so only if these periods were both preceded and followed by substantial periods (e.g. periods of more than 120 days) in which there was uninterrupted material participation. See paragraph (e)(1) of this section which provides a special rule for periods when little or no activity is necessary to manage fully a farm.

(d) Period property must be owned by decedent and family members. Only real property which is actually owned by any combination of the decedent, members of the decedent's family, and qualified closely held businesses for periods totalling at least 5 of the 8 years preceding the date of decedent's death may be valued under section 2032A. For example, replacement property acquired in like-kind exchange under section 1031 is considered to be owned only from the date on which the replacement property is actually acquired. On the other hand, replacement property acquired as a result of an involuntary conversion in a transfer that would meet the requirements of section 2032A(h) if it occurred after the date of the decedent's death is considered to have been owned from the date in which the involuntarily converted property was acquired. Property transferred from a proprietorship to a corporation or a partnership during the 8-year period ending on the date of the decedent's death is considered to be continuously owned to the extent of the decedent's equity interest in the corporation or partnership if, (1) the transfer meets the requirements of section 351 or 721, respectively, and (2) the decedent's interest in the corporation or partnership meets the requirements for indirectly held property contained in paragraph (b)(1) of this section. Likewise, property transferred to a trust is considered to be continuously owned if the beneficial ownership of the trust property is such that the requirements of section 6166(b)(1)(C) would be so satisfied if the property were owned by a corporation and all beneficiaries having vested interests in the trust were shareholders in the corporation. Any periods following the transfer during which the interest in the corporation, partnership, or trust does not meet the requirements of section 6166(b)(1) may not be counted for purposes of satisfying the ownership requirements of this paragraph (d).

(e) Required activities. (1) *In general.* Actual employment of the decedent (or of a member of the decedent's family) on a substantially full-time basis (35 hours a week or more) or to any lesser extent necessary personally to manage fully the farm or business in which the real property to be valued under section 2032A is used constitutes material participation. For example, many farming operations require only seasonal activity. Material participation is present as long as all necessary functions are performed even though little or no actual activity occurs during nonproducing seasons. In the absence of this direct involvement in the farm or other business, the activities of either the decedent or family members must meet the standards prescribed in this paragraph and those prescribed in the regulations issued under section 1402(a)(1). Therefore, if the participant (or participants) is self-employed with respect to the farm or other trade or business, his or her income from the farm or other business must be earned income for purposes of the tax on self-employment income before the participant is considered to be materially participating under section 2032A. Payment of the self-employment tax is not conclusive as to the presence of material participation. If no self-employment taxes have been paid, however, material participation is presumed not to have occurred unless the executor demonstrates to the satisfaction of the Internal Revenue Service that material participation did in fact occur and informs the Service of the reason no such tax was paid. In addition, all such taxes (including interest and penalties) determined to be due must be paid. In determining whether the material participation requirement is satisfied, the activities of each participant are viewed separately from the activities of all other participants, and at any given time, the activities of at least one participant must be material. If the involvement is less than full-time, it must be pursuant to an arrangement providing for actual participation in the production or management of production where the land is used by any nonfamily member, or any trust or business entity, in farming or another business. The arrangement may be oral or written, but must be formalized in some manner capable of proof. Activities not contemplated by the arrangement will not support a finding of material participation under section 2032A, and activities of any agent or employee other than a family member may not be considered in determining the presence of material participation. Activities of family members are considered only if the family relationship existed at the time the activities occurred.

(2) *Factors considered.* No single factor is determinative of the presence of material participation, but physical work and participation in management decisions are the principal factors to be considered. As a minimum, the decedent and/or a family member must regularly advise or consult with the other managing party on the operation of the business. While they need not make all final management decisions alone, the decedent and/or family members must participate in making a substantial number of these decisions. Additionally, production activities on the land should be inspected regularly by the family participant, and funds should be advanced and financial responsibility assumed for a substantial portion of the expense involved in the operation of the farm or other business in which the real property is used. In the case of a farm, the furnishing by the owner or other family members of a substantial portion of the machinery, implements, and livestock used in the production activities is an important factor to consider in finding material participation. With farms, hotels, or apartment buildings, the operation of which qualifies as a trade or business, the participating decedent or heir's maintaining his or her principal place of residence on the premises is a factor to consider in determining whether the overall participation is material. Retention of a professional farm manager will not by itself prevent satisfaction of the material participation requirement by the decedent and family members. However, the decedent and/ or a family member must personally materially participate under the terms of arrangement with the professional farm manager to satisfy this requirement.

(f) Special rules for corporations, partnerships, and trusts. (1) *Required arrangement.* With indirectly owned property as with property that is directly owned, there must be an arrangement calling for material participation in the business by the decedent owner or a family member. Where the real property is indirectly owned, however, even full-time involvement must be pursuant to an arrangement between the entity and the decedent or family member specifying the services to be performed. Holding an office in which certain material functions are inherent may constitute the necessary arrangement for material participation. Where property is owned by a trust, the arrangement will generally be found in one or more of four situations. First, the arrangement may result from appointment as a trustee. Second, the arrangement may result from an employer-employee relationship in which the participant is employed by a qualified closely held business owned by the trust in a position requiring his or her material participation in its activities. Third, the participants may enter into a contract with the trustees to manage, or take part in managing, the real property for the trust. Fourth, where the trust agreement expressly grants the management rights to the beneficial owner, that grant is sufficient to constitute the arrangement required under this section.

(2) *Required activities.* The same participation standards apply under section 2032A where property is owned by a qualified closely held business as where the property is directly owned. In the case of a corporation, a partnership, or a trust where the participating decedent and/or family members are employees and thereby not subject to self-employment income taxes, they are to be viewed as if they were self-employed, and their activities must be activities that would subject them to self-employment income taxes were they

so. Where property is owned by a corporation, a partnership or a trust, participation in the management and operation of the real property itself as a component of the closely held business is the determinative factor. Nominally holding positions as a corporate officer or director and receiving a salary therefrom or merely being listed as a partner and sharing in profits and losses will not alone support a finding of material participation. This is so even though, as partners, the participants pay self-employment income taxes on their distributive shares of partnership earnings under § 1.1402(a)–2. Further, it is especially true for corporate directors in states where the board of directors need not be an actively functioning entity or need only act informally. Corporate offices held by an owner are, however, factors to be considered with all other relevant facts in judging the degree of participation. When real property is directly owned and is leased to a corporation or partnership in which the decedent owns an interest which qualified as an interest in a trade or business within the meaning of section 6166(b)(1), the presence of material participation is determined by looking at the activities of the participant with regard to the property in whatever capacity rendered. During any periods when qualified real property is held by an estate, material participation is to be determined in the same manner as if the property were owned by a trust.

(g) Examples. The rules for determining material participation may be illustrated by the following examples. Additional illustrations may be found in examples (1) through (6) in § 1.1402(a)–4.

Example (1). A, the decedent, actively operated his 100-acre farm on a full-time basis for 20 years. He then leased it to B for the 10 years immediately preceding his death. By the terms of the lease, A was to consult with B on where crops were to be planted, to supervise marketing of the crop, and to share equally with B in expenses and earnings. A was present on the farm each spring for consultation; however, once planting was completed, he left for his retirement cottage where he remained until late summer, at which time he returned to the farm to supervise the marketing operation. A at all times maintained the farm home in which he had lived for the time he had owned the farm and lived there when at the farm. In light of his activities, assumption of risks, and valuable knowledge of proper techniques for the particular land gained over 20 years of full-time farming on the land involved, A is deemed to have materially participated in the farming business.

Example (2). D is the 70-year old widow of farmer C. She lives on a farm for which special valuation has been elected and has lived there for 20 years. D leases the land to E under an arrangement calling for her participation in the operation of the farm. D annually raises a vegetable garden, chickens, and hogs. She also inspects the tobacco fields (which produce approximately 50 percent of farm income) weekly and informs E if she finds any work that needs to be done. D and E share expenses and income equally. Other decisions such as what fields to plant and when to plant and harvest crops are left to E, but D does occasionally make suggestions. During the harvest season, D prepares and serves meals for all temporary farm help. D is deemed to participate materially in the farm operations based on her farm residence and her involvement with the main money crop.

Example (3). Assume that D in example (2) moved to a nursing home 1 year after her husband's death. E completely operated the farm for her for 6 years following her move. If E is not a member of D's family, material participation ceases when D moves; however, if E is a member of D's family, E's material participation will prevent disqualification even if D owns the property. Further, upon D's death, the section 203A valuation could be elected for her estate if E were a member of her family and the other requirements of section 203A were satisfied.

Example (4). F, a qualified heir, owned a specially valued farm. He contracted with G to manage the farm for him as F, a lawyer, lived and worked 15 miles away in a nearby town. F supplied all machinery and equipment and assumed financial responsibility for the expenses of the farm operation. The contract specified that G was to submit a crop plan and a list of expenses and earnings for F's approval. It also called for F to inspect the farm regularly and to approve all expenditures over $100. In practice, F visited the farm weekly during the growing season to inspect and discuss operations. He actively participated in making important management decisions such as what fields to plant or pasture and how to utilize the subsidy program. F is deemed to have materially participated in the farm operation as his personal involvement amounted to more than managing an investment. Had F not regularly inspected the farm and participated in management decisions, however, he would not be considered to be materially participating. This would be true even though F did assume financial responsibility for the operation and did review annual crop plans.

Example (5). Decedent I owned 90 percent of all outstanding stock of X Corporation, a qualified closely-held business which owns real property to be specially valued. I held no formal position in the corporation and there was no arrangement for him to participate in daily business operations. I regularly spent several hours each day at the corporate offices and made decisions on many routine matters. I is not deemed to have materially participated in the X Corporation despite his activity because there was no arrangement requiring him to act in the manner in which he did.

Example (6). Decedent J was a senior partner in the law firm of X, Y, and Z, which is a qualified closely held business owning the building in which its offices are located. J ceased to practice law actively 5 years before his death in 1977; however, he remained a full partner and annually received a share of firm profits. J is not deemed to have materially participated under section 2032A even though he still may have reported his distributive share of partnership income for self-employment income tax purposes if the payments were not made pursuant to any retirement agreement. This is so because J does not meet the requirement of actual personal material participation.

Example (7). K, the decedent, owned a tree farm. He contracted with L, a professional forester, to manage the property for him as K, a doctor, lived and worked in a town 50 miles away. The activities of L are not considered in determining whether K materially participated in the tree farm operation. During the 5 years preceding K's death, there was no need for frequent inspections of the property or consultation concerning it, inasmuch as most of the land had been reforested and the trees were in the beginning stages of their growing cycle. However, once every year, L submitted for K's approval a proposed plan for the management of the property over the next year. K actively participated in making important management decisions, such as where and whether a pre-commercial thinning should be conducted, whether the timber was adequately protected from fire and disease, whether fire lines needed to be plowed around the new trees, and whether boundary lines were properly maintained around the property. K inspected the property at least twice every year and assumed financial responsibility for the expenses of the tree farm. K also reported his income from the tree farm as earned income for purposes of the tax on self-employment income. Over a period of several years, K had harvested and marketed timber from certain tracts of the tree farm and had supervised replanting of the areas where trees were removed. K's history of harvesting, marketing, and replanting of trees showed him to be in the business of tree farming rather than merely passively investing in timber land. If the history of K's tree farm did not show such an active business operation, however, the tree farm would not qualify for special use valuation. In light of all these facts, K is deemed to have materially participated in the farm as his personal involvement amounted to more than managing an investment.

Example (8). Decedent M died on January 1, 1978, owning a farm for which special use valuation under section 2032A has been elected. M owned the farm real property for 15 years before his death. During the 4 years preceding M's death (January 1, 1974 through December 31, 1977), the farm was rented to N, a non-family member, and neither M nor any member of his family materially participated in the farming operation. From January 1, 1970, until December 31, 1973, both M and his daughter, O, materially participated in the farming operation. The material participation requirement of section 2032A(b)(1)(C)(ii) is not satisfied because material participation did not occur for periods aggregating at least 5 different years of the 8 years preceding M's death.

[T.D. 7710, 45 FR 50739, July 31, 1980; T.D. 7786, 46 FR 43036, Aug. 26, 1981]

§ 20.2032A–4 Method of valuing farm real property.

(a) In general. Unless the executor of the decedent's estate elects otherwise under section 2032A(e)(7)(B)(ii) or fails to document comparable rented farm property meeting the requirements of this section, the value of the property which is used for farming purposes and which is subject to an election under section 2032A is determined by—

(1) Subtracting the average annual state and local real estate taxes on actual tracts of comparable real property in the same locality from the average annual gross cash rental for that same comparable property, and

(2) Dividing the result so obtained by the average annual effective interest rate charged on new Federal land bank loans.

The computation of each average annual amount is to be based on the 5 most recent calendar years ending before the date of the decedent's death.

(b) Gross cash rental. (1) *Generally.* Gross cash rental is the total amount of cash received for the use of actual tracts of comparable farm real property in the same locality as the property being specially valued during the period of one calendar year. This amount is not diminished by the amount of any expenses or liabilities associated with the farm operation or the lease. See, paragraph (d) of this section for a definition of comparable property and rules for property on which buildings or other improvements are located and farms including multiple property types. Only rentals from tracts of comparable farm property which are rented solely for an amount of cash which is not contingent upon production are acceptable for use in valuing real property under section 2032A(e)(7). The rentals considered must result from an arm's-length transaction as defined in this section. Additionally, rentals received under leases which provide for payment solely in cash are not acceptable as accurate measures of cash rental value if involvement by the lessor (or a member of the lessor's family who is other than a lessee) in the management or operation of the farm to an extent which amounts to material participation under the rules of section 2032A is contemplated or actually occurs. In general, therefore, rentals for any property which qualifies for special use valuation cannot be used to compute gross cash rentals under this section because the total amount received by the lessor does not reflect the true cash rental value of the real property.

(2) *Special rules*—(i) *Documentation required of executor.* The executor must identify to the Internal Revenue Service actual comparable property for all specially valued property and cash rentals from that property if the decedent's real property is valued under section 2032A(e)(7). If the executor does not identify such property and cash rentals, all specially valued real property must be valued under the rules of section 2032A(e)(8) if special use valuation has been elected. See, however, § 20.2032A–8(d) for a special rule for estates electing section 2032A treatment on or before August 30, 1980

(ii) *Arm's-length transaction required.* Only those cash rentals which result from a lease entered into in an arm's-length transaction are acceptable under section 2032A(e)(7). For these purposes, lands leased from the Federal government, or any state or local government, which are leased for less than the amount that would be demanded by a private individual leasing for profit are not leased in an arm's-length transaction. Additionally, leases between family members (as defined in section 2032A(e)(2)) which do not provide a return on the property commensurate with that received under leases between unrelated parties in the locality are not acceptable under this section.

(iii) *In-kind rents, statements of appraised rental value, and area averages.* Rents which are paid wholly or partly in kind (e.g., crop shares) may not be used to determine the value of real property under section 2032A(e)(7). Likewise, appraisals or other statements regarding rental value as well as area-wide averages of rentals (i.e., those compiled by the United States Department of Agriculture) may not be used under section 2032A(e)(7) because they are not true measures of the actual cash rental value of comparable property in the same locality as the specially valued property.

(iv) *Period for which comparable real property must have been rented solely for cash.* Comparable real property rented solely for cash must be identified for each of the five calendar years preceding the year of the decedent's death if section 2032A(e)(7) is used to value the decedent's real property. Rentals from the same tract of comparable property need not be used for each of these 5 years, however, provided an actual tract of property meeting the requirements of this section is identified for each year.

(v) *Leases under which rental of personal property is included.* No adjustment to the rents actually received by the lessor is made for the use of any farm equipment or other personal property the use of which is included under a lease for comparable real property unless the lease specifies the amount of the total rental attributable to the personal property and that amount is reasonable under the circumstances.

(c) State and local real estate taxes. For purposes of the farm valuation formula under section 2032A(e)(7) state and local taxes are taxes which are assessed by a state or local government and which are allowable deductions under section 164. However, only those taxes on the comparable real property from which cash rentals are determined may be used in the formula valuation.

(d) Comparable real property defined. Comparable real property must be situated in the same locality as the specially valued property. This requirement is not to be viewed in terms of mileage or political divisions alone, but rather is to be judged according to generally accepted real property valuation rules. The determination of properties which are comparable is a factual one and must be based on numerous factors, no one of which is determinative. It will, therefore, frequently be necessary to value farm property in segments where there are different uses or land characteristics included in the specially valued farm. For example, if section 2032A(e)(7) is used, rented property on which comparable buildings or improvements are located must be identified for specially valued property on which buildings or other real property improvements are located. In cases involving multiple areas or land characteristics, actual comparable property for each segment must be used, and the rentals and taxes from all such properties combined (using generally accepted real property valuation rules) for use in the valuation formula given in this section. However, any premium or discount resulting from the presence of multiple uses or other characteristics in one farm is also to be reflected. All factors generally considered in real estate valuation are to be considered in determining comparability under section 2032A. While not intended as an exclusive list, the following factors are among those to be considered in determining comparability—

(1) Similarity of soil as determined by any objective means, including an official soil survey reflected in a soil productivity index;

(2) Whether the crops grown are such as would deplete the soil in a similar manner;

(3) The types of soil conservation techniques that have been practiced on the two properties;

(4) Whether the two properties are subject to flooding;

(5) The slope of the land;

(6) In the case of livestock operations, the carrying capacity of the land;

(7) Where the land is timbered, whether the timber is comparable to that on the subject property;

(8) Whether the property as a whole is unified or whether it is segmented, and where segmented, the availability of the means necessary for movement among the different segments;

(9) The number, types, and conditions of all buildings and other fixed improvements located on the properties and their location as it affects efficient management and use of property and value per se; and

(10) Availability of, and type of, transportation facilities in terms of costs and of proximity of the properties to local markets.

(e) Effective interest rate defined. (1) *Generally.* The annual effective interest rate on new Federal land bank loans is the average billing rate charged on new agricultural loans to farmers and ranchers in the farm credit district in which the real property to be valued under section 2032A is located, adjusted as provided in paragraph (e)(2) of this section. This rate is to be a single rate for each district covering the period of one calendar year and is to be computed to the nearest one-hundredth of one percent. In the event that the district billing rates of interest on such new agricultural loans change during a year, the rate for that year is to be weighted to reflect the portion of the year during which each such rate was charged. If a district's billing rate on such new agricultural loans varies according to the amount of the loan, the rate applicable to a loan in an amount resulting from dividing the total dollar amount of such loans closed during the year by the total number of the loans closed is to be used under section 2032A. Applicable rates may be obtained from the district director of internal revenue.

(2) *Adjustment to billing rate of interest.* The billing rate of interest determined under this paragraph is to be adjusted to reflect the increased cost of borrowing resulting from the required purchase of land bank association stock. For section 2032A purposes, the rate of required stock investment is the average of the percentages of the face amount of new agricultural loans to farmers and ranchers required to be invested in such stock by the applicable district bank during the year. If this percentage changes during a year, the average is to be adjusted to reflect the period when each percentage requirement was effective. The percentage is viewed

as a reduction in the loan proceeds actually received from the amount upon which interest is charged.

(3) *Example.* The determination of the effective interest rate for any year may be illustrated as follows:

Example. District X of the Federal land bank system charged an 8 percent billed interest rate on new agricultural loans for 8 months of the year, 1976, and an 8.75 percent rate for 4 months of the year. The average billing rate was, therefore, 8.25 percent [(1.08 * 8/12) + (1.0875 * 4/12) = 1.0825]. The district required stock equal to 5 percent of the face amount of the loan to be purchased as a precondition to receiving a loan. Thus, the borrower only received 95 percent of the funds upon which he paid interest. The applicable annual interest rate for 1976 of 8.68 percent is computed as follows:

8.25 percent * 1.00 (total loan amount) = 8.25 percent (billed interest rate) divided by 0.95 (percent of loan proceeds received by borrower) = 8.68 percent (effective interest rate for 1976).

[T.D. 7710, 45 FR 50742, July 31, 1980]

§ 20.2032A–8 Election and agreement to have certain property valued under section 2032A for estate tax purposes.

(a) Election of special use valuation. (1) *In general.* An election under section 2032A is made as prescribed in paragraph (a)(3) of this section and on Form 706, United States Estate Tax Return. Once made, this election is irrevocable; however, see paragraph (d) of this section for a special rule for estates for which elections are made on or before August 30, 1980. Under section 2032A(a)(2), special use valuation may not reduce the value of the decedent's estate by more than $500,000. This election is available only if, at the time of death, the decedent was a citizen or resident of the United States.

(2) *Elections to specially value less than all qualified real property included in an estate.* An election under section 2032A need not include all real property included in an estate which is eligible for special use valuation, but sufficient property to satisfy the threshold requirements of section 2032A(b)(1)(B) must be specially valued under the election. If joint or undivided interests (e.g. interests as joint tenants or tenants in common) in the same property are received from a decedent by qualified heirs, an election with respect to one heir's joint or undivided interest need not include any other heir's interest in the same property if the electing heir's interest plus other property to be specially valued satisfy the requirements of section 2032A(b)(1)(B). If successive interests (e.g. life estates and remainder interests) are created by a decedent in otherwise qualified property, an election under section 2032A is available only with respect to that property (or portion thereof) in which qualified heirs of the decedent receive all of the successive interests, and such an election must include the interests of all of those heirs. For example, if a surviving spouse receives a life estate in otherwise qualified property and the spouse's brother receives a remainder interest in fee, no part of the property may be valued pursuant to an election under section 2032A. Where successive interests in specially valued property are created, remainder interests are treated as being received by qualified heirs only if such remainder interests are not contingent upon surviving a nonfamily member or are not subject to divestment in favor of a nonfamily member.

(3) *Time and manner of making election.* An election under this section is made by attaching to a timely filed estate tax return the agreement described in paragraph (c)(1) of this section and a notice of election which contains the following information:

(i) The decedent's name and taxpayer identification number as they appear on the estate tax return;

(ii) The relevant qualified use;

(iii) The items of real property shown on the estate tax return to be specially valued pursuant to the election (identified by schedule and item number);

(iv) The fair market value of the real property to be specially valued under section 2032A and its value based on its qualified use (both values determined without regard to the adjustments provided by section 2032A(b)(3)(B));

(v) The adjusted value (as defined in section 2032A(b)(3)(B)) of all real property which is used in a qualified use and which passes from the decedent to a qualified heir and the adjusted value of all real property to be specially valued;

(vi) The items of personal property shown on the estate tax return that pass from the decedent to a qualified heir and are used in a qualified use under section

2032A (identified by schedule and item number) and the total value of such personal property adjusted as provided under section 2032A(b)(3)(B);

(vii) The adjusted value of the gross estate, as defined in section 2032A(b)(3)(A);

(viii) The method used in determining the special value based on use;

(ix) Copies of written appraisals of the fair market value of the real property;

(x) A statement that the decedent and/or a member of his or her family has owned all specially valued real property for at least 5 years of the 8 years immediately preceding the date of the decedent's death;

(xi) Any periods during the 8-year period preceding the date of the decedent's death during which the decedent or a member of his or her family did not own the property, use it in a qualified use, or materially participate in the operation of the farm or other business within the meaning of section 2032A(e)(6);

(xii) The name, address, taxpayer identification number, and relationship to the decedent of each person taking an interest in each item of specially valued property, and the value of the property interests passing to each such person based on both fair market value and qualified use;

(xiii) Affidavits describing the activities constituting material participation and the identity of the material participant or participants; and

(xiv) A legal description of the specially valued property.

If neither an election nor a protective election is timely made, special use valuation is not available to the estate. See sections 2032A(d)(1), 6075(a), and 6081(a).

(b) Protective election. A protective election may be made to specially value qualified real property. The availability of special use valuation pursuant to this election is contingent upon values as finally determined (or agreed to following examination of a return) meeting the requirements of section 2032A. A protective election does not, however, extend the time for payment of any amount of tax. Rules for such extensions are contained in sections 6161, 6163, 6166, and 6166A. The protective election is to be made by a notice of election filed with a timely estate tax return stating that a protective election under section 2032A is being made pending final determination of values. This notice is to include the following information:

(1) The decedent's name and taxpayer identification number as they appear on the estate tax return;

(2) The relevant qualified use; and

(3) The items of real and personal property shown on the estate tax return which are used in a qualified use, and which pass to qualified heirs (identified by schedule and item number). If it is found that the estate qualifies for special use valuation based upon values as finally determined (or agreed to following examination of a return), an additional notice of election must be filed within 60 days after the date of such determination. This notice must set forth the information required under paragraph (a)(3) of this section and is to be attached, together with the agreement described in paragraph (c)(1) of this section, to an amended estate tax return. The new return is to be filed with the Internal Revenue Service office where the original return was filed.

(c) Agreement to special valuation by persons with an interest in property. (1) *In general.* The agreement required under section 2032A(a)(1)(B) and (d)(2) must be executed by all parties who have any interest in the property being valued based on its qualified use as of the date of the decedent's death. In the case of a qualified heir, the agreement must express consent to personal liability under section 2032A(c) in the event of certain early dispositions of the property or early cessation of the qualified use. See section 2032A(c)(6). In the case of parties (other than qualified heirs) with interests in the property, the agreement must express consent to collection of any additional estate tax imposed under section 2032A(c) from the qualified property. The agreement is to be in a form that is binding on all parties having an interest in the property. It must designate an agent with satisfactory evidence of authority to act for the parties to the agreement in all dealings with the Internal Revenue Service on matters arising under section 2032A and must indicate the address of that agent.

(2) *Persons having an interest in designated property.* An interest in property is an interest which, as of the date of the decedent's death, can be asserted under applicable local law so as to affect the disposition of the specially valued property by the estate. Any person

in being at the death of the decedent who has any such interest in the property, whether present or future, or vested or contingent, must enter into the agreement. Included among such persons are owners of remainder and executory interests, the holders of general or special powers of appointment, beneficiaries of a gift over in default of exercise of any such power, co-tenants, joint tenants and holders of other undivided interests when the decedent held only a joint or undivided interest in the property or when only an undivided interest is specially valued, and trustees of trusts holding any interest in the property. An heir who has the power under local law to caveat (challenge) a will and thereby affect disposition of the property is not, however, considered to be a person with an interest in property under section 2032A solely by reason of that right. Likewise, creditors of an estate are not such persons solely by reason of their status as creditors.

(3) *Consent on behalf of interested party.* If any person required to enter into the agreement provided for by paragraph (c)(1) either desires that an agent act for him or her or cannot legally bind himself or herself due to infancy or other incompetency, or to death before the election under section 2032A is timely exercised, a representative authorized under local law to bind such person in an agreement of this nature is permitted to sign the agreement on his or her behalf.

(4) *Duties of agent designated in agreement.* The Internal Revenue Service will contact the agent designated in the agreement under paragraph (c)(1) on all matters relating to continued qualification under section 2032A of the specially valued real property and on all matters relating to the special lien arising under section 6324B. It is the duty of the agent as attorney-in-fact for the parties with interests in the specially valued property to furnish the Service with any requested information and to notify the Service of any disposition or cessation of qualified use of any part of the property.

(d) Special rule for estates for which elections under section 2032A are made on or before August 30, 1980. [*Omitted. Ed.*]

[T.D. 7710, 45 FR 50743, July 31, 1980; T.D. 7786, 46 FR 43037, Aug. 26, 1981]

§ 2033. Property in which the Decedent Had an Interest

The value of the gross estate shall include the value of all property to the extent of the interest therein of the decedent at the time of his death.

Regulation

§ 20.2033–1 Property in which the decedent had an interest.

(a) In general. The gross estate of a decedent who was a citizen or resident of the United States at the time of his death includes under section 2033 the value of all property, whether real or personal, tangible or intangible, and wherever situated, beneficially owned by the decedent at the time of his death. (For certain exceptions in the case of real property situated outside the United States, see paragraphs (a) and (c) of § 20.2031–1.) Real property is included whether it came into the possession and control of the executor or administrator or passed directly to heirs or devisees. Various statutory provisions which exempt bonds, notes, bills, and certificates of indebtedness of the Federal Government or its agencies and the interest thereon from taxation are generally not applicable to the estate tax, since such tax is an excise tax on the transfer of property at death and is not a tax on the property transferred.

(b) Miscellaneous examples. A cemetery lot owned by the decedent is part of his gross estate, but its value is limited to the salable value of that part of the lot which is not designed for the interment of the decedent and the members of his family. Property subject to homestead or other exemptions under local law is included in the gross estate. Notes or other claims held by the decedent are likewise included even though they are cancelled by the decedent's will. Interest and rents accrued at the date of the decedent's death constitute a part of the gross estate. Similarly, dividends which are payable to the decedent or his estate by reason of the fact that on or before the date of the decedent's death he was a stockholder of record (but which have not been collected at death) constitutes a part of the gross estate.

[T.D. 6296, 23 FR 4529, June 24, 1958, as amended by T.D. 6684, 28 FR 11409, Oct. 24, 1963]

§ 2034. Dower or Curtesy Interests

The value of the gross estate shall include the value of all property to the extent of any interest therein of the surviving spouse, existing at the time of the decedent's death as dower or curtesy, or by virtue of a statute creating an estate in lieu of dower or curtesy.

Regulation

§ 20.2034–1 Dower or curtesy interests.

A decedent's gross estate includes under section 2034 any interest in property of the decedent's surviving spouse existing at the time of the decedent's death as dower or curtesy, or any interest created by statute in lieu thereof (although such other interest may differ in character from dower or curtesy). Thus, the full value of property is included in the decedent's gross estate, without deduction of such an interest of the surviving husband or wife, and without regard to when the right to such an interest arose.

[T.D. 6296, 23 FR 4529, June 24, 1958]

§ 2035. Adjustments for Certain Gifts Made Within 3 Years of Decedent's Death

(a) Inclusion of certain property in gross estate. If—

(1) the decedent made a transfer (by trust or otherwise) of an interest in any property, or relinquished a power with respect to any property, during the 3-year period ending on the date of the decedent's death, and

(2) the value of such property (or an interest therein) would have been included in the decedent's gross estate under section 2036, 2037, 2038, or 2042 if such transferred interest or relinquished power had been retained by the decedent on the date of his death,

the value of the gross estate shall include the value of any property (or interest therein) which would have been so included.

(b) Inclusion of gift tax on gifts made during 3 years before decedent's death. The amount of the gross estate (determined without regard to this subsection) shall be increased by the amount of any tax paid under chapter 12 by the decedent or his estate on any gift made by the decedent or his spouse during the 3-year period ending on the date of the decedent's death.

(c) Other rules relating to transfers within 3 years of death.

(1) In general. For purposes of—

(A) section 303(b) (relating to distributions in redemption of stock to pay death taxes),

(B) section 2032A (relating to special valuation of certain farms, etc., real property), and

(C) subchapter C of chapter 64 (relating to lien for taxes),

the value of the gross estate shall include the value of all property to the extent of any interest therein of which the decedent has at any time made a transfer, by trust or otherwise, during the 3-year period ending on the date of the decedent's death.

(2) Coordination with section 6166. An estate shall be treated as meeting the 35 percent of adjusted gross estate requirement of section 6166(a)(1) only if the estate meets such requirement both with and without the application of paragraph (1).

(3) Marital and small transfers. Paragraph (1) shall not apply to any transfer (other than a transfer with respect to a life insurance policy) made during a calendar year to any donee if the decedent was not required by section 6019 (other than by reason of section 6019(2)) to file any gift tax return for such year with respect to transfers to such donee.

(d) Exception. Subsection (a) shall not apply to any bona fide sale for an adequate and full consideration in money or money's worth.

(e) Treatment of certain transfers from revocable trusts. For purposes of this section and section 2038, any transfer from any portion of a trust during any period that such portion was treated under section 676 as owned by the decedent by reason of a power in the grantor (determined without regard to section 672(e)) shall be treated as a transfer made directly by the decedent.

§ 2036. Transfers with Retained Life Estate

(a) General rule. The value of the gross estate shall include the value of all property to the extent of any interest therein of which the decedent has at any time made a transfer (except in case of a bona fide sale for an adequate and full consideration in money or money's worth), by trust or otherwise, under which he has retained for his life or for any period not ascertainable without reference to his death or for any period which does not in fact end before his death—

(1) the possession or enjoyment of, or the right to the income from, the property, or

(2) the right, either alone or in conjunction with any person, to designate the persons who shall possess or enjoy the property or the income therefrom.

(b) Voting rights.

(1) In general. For purposes of subsection (a)(1), the retention of the right to vote (directly or indirectly) shares of stock of a controlled corporation shall be considered to be a retention of the enjoyment of transferred property.

(2) Controlled corporation. For purposes of paragraph (1), a corporation shall be treated as a controlled corporation if, at any time after the transfer of the property and during the 3-year period ending on the date of the decedent's death, the decedent owned (with the application of section 318), or had the right (either alone or in conjunction with any person) to vote, stock possessing at least 20 percent of the total combined voting power of all classes of stock.

(3) Coordination with section 2035. For purposes of applying section 2035 with respect to paragraph (1), the relinquishment or cessation of voting rights shall be treated as a transfer of property made by the decedent.

(c) Limitation on application of general rule. This section shall not apply to a transfer made before March 4, 1931; nor to a transfer made after March 3, 1931, and before June 7, 1932, unless the property transferred would have been includible in the decedent's gross estate by reason of the amendatory language of the joint resolution of March 3, 1931 (46 Stat. 1516).

Regulations

§ 20.2036–1 Transfers with retained life estate.

(a) In general. A decedent's gross estate includes under section 2036 the value of any interest in property transferred by the decedent after March 3, 1931, whether in trust or otherwise, except to the extent that the transfer was for an adequate and full consideration in money or money's worth (see § 20.2043–1), if the decedent retained or reserved—

(1) For his life;

(2) For any period not ascertainable without reference to his death (if the transfer was made after June 6, 1932); or

(3) For any period which does not in fact end before his death:

(i) The use, possession, right to income, or other enjoyment of the transferred property.

(ii) The right, either alone or in conjunction with any other person or persons, to designate the person or persons who shall possess or enjoy the transferred property or its income (except that, if the transfer was made before June 7, 1932, the right to designate must be retained by or reserved to the decedent alone).

(b) Meaning of terms. (1) A reservation by the decedent "for any period not ascertainable without reference to his death" may be illustrated by the following examples:

(i) A decedent reserved the right to receive the income from transferred property in quarterly payments, with the proviso that no part of the income between the last quarterly payment and the date of the decedent's death was to be received by the decedent or his estate; and

(ii) A decedent reserved the right to receive the income, annuity, or other payment from transferred property after the death of another person who was in fact enjoying the income, annuity, or other payment at the time of the decedent's death. In such a case, the amount to be included in the decedent's gross estate under this section does not include the value of the outstanding interest of the other person as determined in paragraphs (c)(1)(i) and (c)(2)(ii) of this section. See also, paragraphs (c)(1)(ii) *Example 1* and (c)(2)(iv) *Example 8* of this section. If the other person predeceased the decedent, the reservation by the decedent may be considered to be either for life, or for a period that does not in fact end before death.

(2) The "use, possession, right to the income, or other enjoyment of the transferred property" is considered as having been retained by or reserved to the decedent to the extent that the use, possession, right to the income, or other enjoyment is to be applied toward the discharge of a legal obligation of the decedent, or otherwise for his pecuniary benefit. The term "legal obligation" includes a legal obligation to support a dependent during the decedent's lifetime.

(3) The phrase "right * * * to designate the person or persons who shall possess or enjoy the transferred property or the income therefrom" includes a reserved power to designate the person or persons to receive the income from the transferred property, or to possess or enjoy nonincome-producing property, during the decedent's life or during any other period described in paragraph (a) of this section. With respect to such a power, it is immaterial (i) whether the power was exercisable alone or only in conjunction with another person or persons, whether or not having an adverse interest; (ii) in what capacity the power was exercisable by the decedent or by another person or persons in conjunction with the decedent; and (iii) whether the exercise of the power was subject to a contingency beyond the decedent's control which did not occur before his death (e.g., the death of another person during the decedent's lifetime). The phrase, however, does not include a power over the transferred property itself which does not affect the enjoyment of the income received or earned during the decedent's life. (See, however, section 2038 for the inclusion of property in the gross estate on account of such a power.) Nor does the phrase apply to a power held solely by a person other than the decedent. But, for example, if the decedent reserved the unrestricted power to remove or discharge a trustee at any time and appoint himself as trustee, the decedent is considered as having the powers of the trustee.

(c) Retained or reserved interest. (1) *Amount included in gross estate.* (i) *In general.* If the decedent retained or reserved an interest or right with respect to all of the property transferred by him, the amount to be included in his gross estate under section 2036 is the value of the entire property, less only the value of any outstanding income interest which is not subject to the decedent's interest or right and which is actually being enjoyed by another person at the time of the decedent's death. If the decedent retained or reserved an interest or right with respect to a part only of the property transferred by him, the amount to be included in his gross estate under section 2036 is only a corresponding proportion of the amount described in the preceding sentence. An interest or right is treated as having been retained or reserved if at the time of the transfer there was an understanding, express, or implied, that the interest or right would later be conferred. If this section applies to an interest retained by the decedent in a trust or otherwise and the terms of the trust or other governing instrument provide that, after the decedent's death, payments the decedent was receiving during life are to continue to be made to the decedent's estate for a specified period (as opposed to payments that were payable to the decedent prior to the decedent's death but were not actually paid until after the decedent's death), such payments that become payable after the decedent's death are not includible in the decedent's gross estate under section 2033 because they are properly reflected in the value of the trust corpus included under this section. Payments that become payable to the decedent prior to the decedent's date of death, but are not paid until after the decedent's date of death, are includible in the decedent's gross estate under section 2033.

(ii) *Examples.* The application of paragraph (c)(1)(i) of this section is illustrated in the following examples:

Example (1). Decedent (D) creates an irrevocable inter vivos trust. The terms of the trust provide that all of the trust income is to be paid to D and D's child, C, in equal shares during their joint lives and, on the death of the first to die of D and C, all of the trust income is to be paid to the survivor. On the death of the survivor of D and C, the remainder is to be paid to another individual, F. Subsequently, D dies survived by C. Fifty percent of the value of the trust corpus is includible in D's gross estate under section 2036(a)(1) because, under the terms of the trust, D retained the right to receive one-half of the trust income for D's life. In addition, the excess (if any) of the value of the remaining 50 percent of the trust corpus, over the present value of C's outstanding life estate in that 50 percent of trust corpus, also is includible in D's gross estate under section 2036(a)(1), because D retained the right to receive all of the trust income for such time as D survived C. If C had predeceased D, then 100 percent of the trust corpus would have been includible in D's gross estate.

Example (2). D transferred D's personal residence to D's child (C), but retained the right to use the residence for a term of years. D dies during the term. At D's death, the fair market value of the personal residence is includible in D's gross estate under section 2036(a)(1) because D retained the right to use the residence for a period that did not in fact end before D's death.

(2) *Retained annuity, unitrust, and other income interests in trusts.* (i) *In general.* This paragraph (c)(2) applies to a grantor's retained use of an asset held in trust or a retained annuity, unitrust, or other interest in any trust (other than a trust constituting an employee benefit) including without limitation the following (collectively referred to in this paragraph (c)(2) as "trusts"): Certain charitable remainder trusts (collectively CRTs) such as a charitable remainder annuity trust (CRAT) within the meaning of section 664(d)(1), a charitable remainder unitrust (CRUT) within the meaning of section 664(d)(2) or (d)(3), and any charitable remainder trust that does not qualify under section 664(d), whether because the CRT was created prior to 1969, there was a defect in the drafting of the CRT, there was no intention to qualify the CRT for the charitable deduction, or otherwise; other trusts established by a grantor (collectively GRTs) such as a grantor retained annuity trust (GRAT) paying out a qualified annuity interest within the meaning of § 25.2702–3(b) of this chapter, a grantor retained unitrust (GRUT) paying out a qualified unitrust interest within the meaning of § 25.2702–3(c) of this chapter; and various other forms of grantor retained income trusts (GRITs) whether or not the grantor's retained interest is a qualified interest as defined in section 2702(b), including without limitation a qualified personal residence trust (QPRT) within the meaning of § 25.2702–5(c) of this chapter and a personal residence trust (PRT) within the meaning of § 25.2702–5(b) of this chapter. If a decedent transferred property into such a trust and retained or reserved the right to use such property, or the right to an annuity, unitrust, or other interest in such trust with respect to the property decedent so transferred for decedent's life, any period not ascertainable without reference to the decedent's death, or for a period that does not in fact end before the decedent's death, then the decedent's right to use the property or the retained annuity, unitrust, or other interest (whether payable from income and/or principal) constitutes the retention of the possession or enjoyment of, or the right to the income from, the property for purposes of section 2036. The portion of the trust's corpus includible in the decedent's gross estate for Federal estate tax purposes is that portion of the trust corpus necessary to provide the decedent's retained use or retained annuity, unitrust, or other payment (without reducing or invading principal). In the case of a retained annuity or unitrust, the portion of the trust's corpus includible in the decedent's gross estate is that portion of the trust corpus necessary to generate sufficient income to satisfy the retained annuity or unitrust (without reducing or invading principal),

using the interest rates provided in section 7520 and the adjustment factors prescribed in § 20.2031–7 (or § 20.2031–7A), if applicable. The computation is illustrated in paragraph (c)(2)(iv), Examples 1, 2, and 3 of this section. The portion of the trust's corpus includible in the decedent's gross estate under section 2036, however, shall not exceed the fair market value of the trust's corpus at the decedent's date of death.

(ii) *Decedent's retained annuity following a current annuity interest of another person.* If the decedent retained the right to receive an annuity or other payment (rather than income) after the death of the current recipient of that interest, then the amount includible in the decedent's gross estate under this section is the amount of trust corpus required to produce sufficient income to satisfy the entire annuity or other payment the decedent would have been entitled to receive if the decedent had survived the current recipient (thus, also including the portion of that entire amount payable to the decedent before the current recipient's death), reduced by the present value of the current recipient's interest. However, the amount includible shall not be less than the amount of corpus required to produce sufficient income to satisfy the annuity or other payment the decedent was entitled, at the time of the decedent's death, to receive for each year. In addition, in no event shall the amount includible exceed the value of the trust corpus on the date of death. Finally, in calculating the present value of the current recipient's interest, the exhaustion of trust corpus test described in § 20.7520–3(b)(2) (exhaustion test) is not to be applied, even in cases where § 20.7520–3(b)(2) would otherwise require it to be applied. The following steps implement this computation.

(A) *Step 1*: Determine the fair market value of the trust corpus on the decedent's date of death.

(B) *Step 2*: Determine, in accordance with paragraph (c)(2)(i) of this section, the amount of corpus required to generate sufficient income to pay the annuity, unitrust, or other payment (determined on the date of the decedent's death) payable to the decedent for the trust year in which the decedent's death occurred.

(C) *Step 3*: Determine, in accordance with paragraph (c)(2)(i) of this section, the amount of corpus required to generate sufficient income to pay the annuity, unitrust, or other payment that the decedent would have been entitled to receive for each trust year if the decedent had survived the current recipient.

(D) *Step 4*: Determine the present value of the current recipient's annuity, unitrust, or other payment (without applying the exhaustion test).

(E) *Step 5*: Reduce the amount determined in Step 3 by the amount determined in Step 4, but not to below the amount determined in Step 2.

(F) *Step 6*: The amount includible in the decedent's gross estate under this section is the lesser of the amounts determined in Step 5 and Step 1.

(iii) *Graduated retained interests.* (A) *In general.* For purposes of this section, a graduated retained interest is the grantor's reservation of a right to receive an annuity, unitrust, or other payment as described in paragraph (c)(2)(i) of this section, payable at least annually, that increases (but does not decrease) over a period of time, not more often than annually.

(B) *Other definitions.* (*1*) *Base amount.* The base amount is the amount of corpus required to generate the annuity, unitrust, or other payment payable for the trust year in which the decedent's death occurs. See paragraph (c)(2)(i) of this section for the calculation of the base amount.

(*2*) *Periodic addition.* The periodic addition in a graduated retained interest for each year after the year in which decedent's death occurs is the amount (if any) by which the annuity, unitrust, or other payment that would have been payable for that year if the decedent had survived exceeds the total amount of payments that would have been payable for the year immediately preceding that year. For example, assume the trust instrument provides that the grantor is to receive an annual annuity payable to the grantor or the grantor's estate for a 5-year term. The initial annual payment is $100,000, and each succeeding annual payment is to be 120 percent of the amount payable for the preceding year. Assuming the grantor dies in the second year of the trust (whether before or after the due date of the second annual payment), the periodic additions for years 3, 4, and 5 of the trust are as follows:

	(1) Annual payment	(2) Prior year payment	(1–2) Periodic addition
Year 3	144,000	120,000	24,000
Year 4	172,800	144,000	28,800
Year 5	207,360	172,800	34,560

(3) *Corpus amount.* For each trust year in which a periodic addition occurs (increase year), the corpus amount is the amount of trust corpus which, starting from the decedent's date of death, is necessary to generate an amount of income sufficient to pay the periodic addition, beginning in the increase year and continuing in perpetuity, without reducing or invading principal. For each year with a periodic addition, the corpus amount required as of the decedent's date of death is the product of two factors: The first is the result of dividing the periodic addition (adjusted for payments made more frequently than annually, if applicable, and for payments due at the beginning, rather than the end, of a payment period (see Table K or J of § 20.2031–7(d)(6)) by the section 7520 rate (periodic addition/rate)); and the second is 1 divided by the sum of 1 and the section 7520 rate raised to the T power (1/(1 + rate)[caret]T). The second factor applies a present value discount to reflect the period beginning with the date of death and ending on the last day of the trust year immediately before the year for which the periodic addition is first payable.

(i) The corpus amount is determined as follows:

$$\frac{\text{(Periodic Addition) X (Adjustment Factor)}}{\text{Section 7520 Rate}} \quad * \quad \frac{1}{\text{(1+ Section 7520 Rate)}^{T}}$$

(ii) The adjustment factor, if applicable, is the factor for payments made more frequently than annually and for payments due at the beginning, rather than the end, of a calendar period (see Table K or J of § 20.2031–7(d)(6)). T equals the time period in years from the decedent's date of death through the last day of the trust year immediately before the year for which the periodic addition is first payable.

(C) *Amount includible.* The amount includible in the gross estate in the case of a graduated retained interest is the sum of the base amount and the corpus amount for each year for which a periodic addition is first payable. The sum of these amounts represents the amount of trust principal that would be necessary to generate the annual payments that would have been paid to the decedent if the decedent had survived and had continued to receive the graduated retained interest. The amount of trust corpus includible in a decedent's gross estate under this section, however, shall not exceed the fair market value of the trust corpus on the decedent's date of death. The provisions of this section also apply to graduated retained interests in transferred property not held in trust.

(iv) *Examples.* The application of paragraphs (c)(2)(i), (c)(2)(ii), and (c)(2)(iii) of this section is illustrated in the following examples:

(A) *Example 1.* (1) Decedent (D) transferred $100,000 to an inter vivos trust that qualifies as a CRAT under section 664(d)(1). The trust agreement provides for an annuity of $7,500 to be paid each year to D for D's life, then to D's child (C) for C's life, with the remainder to be distributed upon the survivor's death to N, a charitable organization described in sections 170(c), 2055(a), and 2522(a). The annuity is payable to D or C, as the case may be, annually on each December 31st. D dies in September 2006, survived by C who was then age 40. On D's death, the value of the trust assets was $300,000 and the section 7520 interest rate was 6 percent. D's executor does not elect to use the alternate valuation date.

(2) The amount of corpus with respect to which D retained the right to the income, and thus the amount includible in D's gross estate under section 2036, is that amount of corpus necessary to yield the annual annuity payment to D (without reducing or invading principal). In this case, the formula for determining the amount of corpus necessary to yield the annual annuity payment to D is: annual annuity/section 7520 interest rate = amount includible under section 2036. The amount of corpus necessary to yield the annual annuity is $7,500/.06 = $125,000. Therefore, $125,000 is includible in D's gross estate under section 2036(a)(1). (The result would be the same if D had retained an interest in the CRAT for a term of years and had died during the term. The result also would be the same if D had irrevocably relinquished D's annuity interest less than 3 years prior to D's death because of the application of section 2035.) If, instead, the trust agreement had provided that D could revoke C's annuity interest

or change the identity of the charitable remainderman, see section 2038 with regard to the portion of the trust to be included in the gross estate on account of such a retained power to revoke. Under the facts presented, section 2039 does not apply to include any amount in D's gross estate by reason of this retained annuity. See § 20.2039–1(e).

(B) *Example 2.* (1) D transferred $100,000 to a GRAT in which D's annuity is a qualified interest described in section 2702(b). The trust agreement provides for an annuity of $12,000 per year to be paid to D for a term of ten years or until D's earlier death. The annuity amount is payable in twelve equal installments at the end of each month. At the expiration of the term of years or on D's earlier death, the remainder is to be distributed to D's child (C). D dies prior to the expiration of the ten-year term. On the date of D's death, the value of the trust assets is $300,000 and the section 7520 interest rate is 6 percent. D's executor does not elect to use the alternate valuation date.

(2) The amount of corpus with respect to which D retained the right to the income, and thus the amount includible in D's gross estate under section 2036, is that amount of corpus necessary to yield the annual annuity payment to D (without reducing or invading principal). In this case, the formula for determining the amount of corpus necessary to yield the annual annuity payment to D is: annual annuity (adjusted for monthly payments)/section 7520 interest rate = amount includible under section 2036. The Table K adjustment factor for monthly annuity payments in this case is 1.0272. Thus, the amount of corpus necessary to yield the annual annuity is ($12,000 x 1.0272)/.06 = $205,440. Therefore, $205,440 is includible in D's gross estate under section 2036(a)(1). If, instead, the trust agreement had provided that the annuity was to be paid to D during D's life and to D's estate for the balance of the 10-year term if D died during that term, then the portion of trust corpus includible in D's gross estate would still be as calculated in this paragraph. It is not material whether payments are made to D's estate after D's death. Under the facts presented, section 2039 does not apply to include any amount in D's gross estate by reason of this retained annuity. See § 20.2039–1(e).

(C) *Example 3.* (1) D created a CRUT within the meaning of section 664(d)(2). The trust instrument directs the trustee to hold, invest, and reinvest the corpus of the trust and to pay to D for D's life, and then to D's child (C) for C's life, in equal quarterly installments payable at the end of each calendar quarter, an amount equal to 6 percent of the fair market value of the trust as valued on December 15 of the prior taxable year of the trust. At the termination of the trust, the then-remaining corpus, together with any and all accrued income, is to be distributed to N, a charitable organization described in sections 170(c), 2055(a), and 2522(a). D dies six years later, survived by C, who was then age 55. The value of the trust assets on D's death was $300,000. D's executor does not elect to use the alternate valuation date and D's executor does not choose to use the section 7520 interest rate for either of the two months prior to D's death.

(2) The amount of the corpus with respect to which D retained the right to the income, and thus the amount includible in D's gross estate under section 2036(a)(1), is that amount of corpus necessary to yield the unitrust payments as interest on the corpus. In this case, such amount of corpus is determined by dividing the trust's equivalent income interest rate by the section 7520 rate (which was 5.4 percent at the time of D's death). The equivalent income interest rate is determined by dividing the trust's adjusted payout rate by the excess of 1 over the adjusted payout rate. Based on Table F(5.4) in § 1.664–4(e)(6)(iii) of this chapter, the appropriate adjusted payout rate for the trust at D's death is 5.807 percent (6 percent x 0.967769). Thus, the equivalent income interest rate is 6.165 percent (5.807 percent/(1–5.807 percent)). The ratio of the equivalent interest rate to the assumed interest rate under section 7520 is 114.17 percent (6.165 percent/5.4 percent). Because this exceeds 100 percent, D's retained payout interest exceeds a full income interest in the trust, and D effectively retained the income from all the assets transferred to the trust. Accordingly, because D retained for life an interest at least equal to the right to all income from all the property transferred by D to the CRUT, the entire value of the corpus of the CRUT is includible in D's gross estate under section 2036(a)(1). (The result would be the same if D had retained, instead, an interest in the CRUT for a term of years and had died during the term.) Under the facts presented, section 2039 does not apply to include any amount in D's gross estate by reason of D's retained unitrust interest. See § 20.2039–1(e).

(3) If, instead, D had retained the right to a unitrust amount having an adjusted payout for which the cor-

responding equivalent interest rate would have been less than the 5.4 percent assumed interest rate of section 7520, then a correspondingly reduced proportion of the trust corpus would be includible in D's gross estate under section 2036(a)(1). Alternatively, if the interest retained by D was instead only one-half of the 6 percent unitrust interest, then the amount included in D's estate would be the amount needed to produce a 3 percent unitrust interest. All of the results in this paragraph (c)(2)(iv)(C)(3) (Example 3) would be the same if the trust had been a grantor retained unitrust instead of a CRUT.

(D) *Example 4*. During life, D established a 15-year GRIT for the benefit of individuals who are not members of D's family within the meaning of section 2704(c)(2). D retained the right to receive all of the net income from the GRIT, payable annually, during the GRIT's term. D dies during the GRIT's term. D's executor does not elect to use the alternate valuation date. In this case, the GRIT's corpus is includible in D's gross estate under section 2036(a)(1) because D retained the right to receive all of the income from the GRIT for a period that did not in fact end before D's death. If, instead, D had retained the right to receive 60 percent of the GRIT's net income, then 60 percent of the GRIT's corpus would have been includible in D's gross estate under section 2036. Under the facts presented, section 2039 does not apply to include any amount in D's gross estate by reason of D's retained interest. See § 20.2039–1(e).

(E) *Example 5*. In 2003, D transferred $10X to a pooled income fund that conforms to Rev. Proc. 88–53, 1988–2 CB 712 (1988) in exchange for 1 unit in the fund. D is to receive all of the income from that 1 unit during D's life. Upon D's death, D's child (C), is to receive D's income interest for C's life. In 2008, D dies. D's executor does not elect to use the alternate valuation date. In this case, the fair market value of D's 1 unit in the pooled income fund is includible in D's gross estate under section 2036(a)(1) because D retained the right to receive all of the income from that unit for a period that did not in fact end before D's death. See § 601.601(d)(2)(ii)(b) of this chapter.

(F) *Example 6*. D transferred D's personal residence to a trust that met the requirements of a qualified personal residence trust (QPRT) as set forth in § 25.2702–5(c) of this chapter. Pursuant to the terms of the QPRT, D retained the right to use the residence for 10 years or until D's prior death. D dies before the end of the term. D's executor does not elect to use the alternate valuation date. In this case, the fair market value of the QPRT's assets on the date of D's death are includible in D's gross estate under section 2036(a)(1) because D retained the right to use the residence for a period that did not in fact end before D's death.

(G) *Example 7*. (1) On November 1, year N, D transfers assets valued at $2,000,000 to a GRAT. Under the terms of the GRAT, the trustee is to pay to D an annuity for a 5-year term that is a qualified interest described in section 2702(b). The annuity amount is to be paid annually at the end of each trust year, on October 31st. The first annual payment is to be $100,000. Each succeeding payment is to be 120 percent of the amount paid in the preceding year. Income not distributed in any year is to be added to principal. If D dies during the 5-year term, the payments are to be made to D's estate for the balance of the GRAT term. At the end of the 5-year term, the trust is to terminate and the corpus is to be distributed to C, D's child. D dies on January 31st of the third year of the GRAT term. On the date of D's death, the value of the trust corpus is $3,200,000, the section 7520 interest rate is 6.8 percent, and the adjustment factor from Table K of § 20.2031–7 is 1.0000. D's executor does not elect to value the gross estate as of the alternate valuation date pursuant to section 2032.

(2) The amount includible in D's gross estate under section 2036(a)(1) as described in paragraph (c)(2)(iii)(C) of this section is determined and illustrated as follows:

A GRAT Year	*B* Annual Annuity Payment	*C* Periodic Addition	*D* Required Principal: C * Adj. Factor/0.068	*E* Deferral Period: Death to GRAT Year	*F* Present Value Factor: $1/(1+.068)^E$	*G* Corpus Amount at Death D * F
3	144,000	n/a	2,117,647	n/a	n/a	2,117,647
4	172,800	28,800	423,529	0.747945	0.951985	403,193
5	207,360	34,560	508,235	1.747945	0.891372	453,026
					Total:	2,973,866

(3) Specifically:

(A) *Column A.* First, determine the year of the trust term during which the decedent's death occurs, and the number of subsequent years remaining in the trust term for which the decedent retained or reserved an interest. In this example, D dies during year 3, with two additional years remaining in the term.

(B) *Column B.* Under the formula specified in the trust, the annuity payment to be made on October 31st of the 3rd year of the trust term is $144,000. Using that same formula, determine the annuity amounts for years 4 and 5.

(C) *Column C.* Determine the periodic addition for year 4 and year 5 by subtracting the annuity amount for the preceding year from the annuity amount for that year; the periodic addition for that year is the amount of the increase in the annuity amount for that year.

(D) *Columns D through G for year 3.* For the year of the decedent's death (year 3), determine the principal required to produce the annuity amount (Column D) by multiplying the annuity amount (Column B) by the adjustment factor (in this case 1.0000) and by dividing the product by the applicable interest rate under section 7520. Because this is the year of decedent's death and reflects the annuity amount payable to the decedent in that year, there is no deferral, so this is also the Base Amount (the amount of corpus required to produce the annuity for year 3) (Column G).

(E) *Columns D through G for years 4 and 5.* For each succeeding year of the trust term during which the periodic addition will not be payable until a year subsequent to the year of the decedent's death, determine the principal required to produce the periodic addition payable for that year (Column D) by multiplying the periodic addition (Column C) by the adjustment factor and by dividing the product by the applicable interest rate under section 7520. Compute the factors to reflect the length of the deferral period (Column E) and the present value (Column F) as described in paragraph (c)(2)(iii)(B)(3) of this section. Multiply the amount of corpus in Column D by the factors in Columns E and F to determine the Corpus Amount for that year (Column G).

(F) *Column G total.* The sum of the amounts in Column G represents the total amount includable in the gross estate (but not in excess of the fair market value of the trust on the decedent's date of death).

(iv) An illustration of the amount of trust corpus (as of the decedent's death) necessary to produce the scheduled payments is as follows:

<table>
<tr><th></th><th></th><th>Year 3</th><th>Year 4</th><th>Year 5</th><th>Corpus Amount</th></tr>
<tr><td>2nd Periodic Addition</td><td>$34,560</td><td colspan="2">Deferral Period</td><td>$453,026</td><td>$453,026</td></tr>
<tr><td>1st Periodic Addition</td><td>$28,800</td><td>Deferral Period</td><td colspan="2">$403,193</td><td>$403,193</td></tr>
<tr><td>Annuity in year of death</td><td>$144,000</td><td colspan="3">$2,117,647</td><td>$2,117,647</td></tr>
<tr><td colspan="5">Total amount (sum) included in gross estate</td><td>$2,973,866</td></tr>
</table>

(v) A total corpus amount (as defined in paragraph (c)(2)(iii)(B)(3) of this section) of $2,973,866 constitutes the principal required as of decedent's date of death to produce (without reducing or invading principal) the annual payments that D would have received if D had survived and had continued to receive the retained annuity. Therefore, $2,973,866 of the trust corpus is includible in D's gross estate under section 2036(a)(1). The remaining $226,134 of the trust corpus is not includible in D's gross estate under section 2036(a)(1). The result would be the same if D's retained annuity instead had been payable to D for a term of 5 years, or until D's prior death, at which time the GRAT would have terminated and the trust corpus would have become payable to another.

(vi) If, instead, D's annuity was to have been paid on a monthly or quarterly basis, then the periodic addition would have to be adjusted as provided in paragraph (c)(2)(iii)(B)(3) of this section. Specifically, in Column D of the Table for years 4 and 5 in this example, the amount of the principal required would be computed by multiplying the periodic addition by the appropriate factor from Table K or J of § 20.2031–7(d)(6) before dividing as indicated and computing the amounts in Columns E through G. In addition, Column D in year 3 also would have to be so adjusted. Under the facts presented, section 2039 does not apply to include any amount in D's gross estate by reason of this retained interest. See § 20.2039–1(e).

(H) *Example (8)*. (1) D creates an irrevocable inter vivos trust. The terms of the trust provide that an annuity of $10,000 per year is to be paid to D and C, D's child, in equal shares during their joint lives. On the death of the first to die of D and C, the entire $10,000 annuity is to be paid to the survivor for life. On the death of the survivor of D and C, the remainder is to be paid to another individual, F. Subsequently, D dies survived by C. On D's date of death, the fair market value of the trust is $120,000 and the section 7520 rate is 7 percent. At the date of D's death, the amount of trust corpus needed to produce D's annuity interest ($5,000 per year) is $71,429 ($5,000/0.07). In addition, assume the present value of C's right to receive $5,000 annually for the remainder of C's life is $40,000. The portion of the trust corpus includible in D's gross estate under section 2036(a)(1) is $102,857, determined as follows:

(2) *Step 1*: Fair market value of corpus.. $120,000

(3) *Step 2*: Corpus required to produce D's date of death annuity ($5,000/0.07)......... 71,429

(4) *Step 3*: Corpus required to produce D's annuity if D had survived C ($10,000/0.07).. 142,857

(5) *Step 4*: Present value of C's interest.. 40,000

(6) *Step 5*: The amount determined in Step 3, reduced by the amount determined in Step 4, but not to below the amount determined in Step 2 ($142,857–$40,000, but not less than $71,429)........................... 102,857

(7) *Step 6*: The lesser of the amounts determined in Steps 5 and 1 ($102,857 or $120,000)... 102,857

(3) *Effective/applicability dates*. Paragraphs (a) and (c)(1)(i) of this section are applicable to the estates of decedents dying after August 16, 1954. Paragraphs (c)(1)(ii) and (c)(2) of this section apply to the estates of decedents dying on or after July 14, 2008. All but the last two sentences at the end of paragraph (c)(1)(i) of this section are applicable to the estates of decedents dying after August 16, 1954. The first, second, and sixth sentences in paragraph (c)(2)(i) of this section and all but the introductory text, Example 7, and Example 8 of paragraph (c)(2)(iv) of this section are applicable to the estates of decedent's dying on or after July 14, 2008. Paragraph (b)(1)(ii) of this section, the last two sentences at the end of paragraph (c)(1)(i) of this section, Example 1 of paragraph (c)(1)(ii) of this section, the third, fourth, and fifth sentences in paragraph (c)(2)(i) of this section; paragraph (c)(2)(ii) of this section; paragraph (c)(2)(iii) of this section; and the introductory text, Example 7, and Example 8 of paragraph (c)(2)(iv) of this section are applicable to the estates of decedents dying on or after November 8, 2011.

[T.D. 6296, 23 FR 4529, June 24, 1958, as amended by T.D. 6501, 25 FR 10869, Nov. 16, 1960; T.D. 9414, 73 FR 40177, July 14, 2008; 73 FR 44648, July 31, 2008; T.D. 9555, 76 FR 69128, Nov. 8, 2011; T.D. 9974, 88 FR 37447, June 7, 2023]

Proposed § 20.2036–2 (LR–181–76, Aug. 3, 1983) Special treatment of retained voting rights

(a) In general. For purposes of section 2036(a)(1) and § 20.2036–1(a), the retention of the right to vote (directly or indirectly) shares of stock of a controlled corporation is a retention of the enjoyment of the transferred property if:

(1) The transfer was made after June 22, 1976;

(2) The corporation was a controlled corporation at any time after transfer of that stock; and

(3) The corporation was a controlled corporation at any time during the three-year period ending on the decedent's death.

The rule of this section does not require inclusion of stock in the gross estate if the transferred stock has no voting rights or if the donor has not retained voting rights in the stock transferred. Thus, for example, if a person owning 100 percent of the voting and nonvoting stock of a corporation transfers the nonvoting stock, that person shall not be treated as having retained the enjoyment of the property transferred merely because of voting rights in the stock retained. Stock carrying voting rights that will vest only when conditions occur, such as preferred stock which gains voting rights only if no dividends are paid, is subject to this section. However, if the decedent's right to vote such stock is only in a fiduciary capacity (e.g., because the decedent is trustee of a trust to which the stock has been transferred), such stock is subject to this section only if, after the transfer by the decedent, the conditions occur that give the decedent the right to vote the stock. Stock that possesses voting rights in only extraordinary matters, such as mergers or liquidations shall be subject to this section unless the decedent's retention of voting rights is only in a fiduciary capacity.

(b) Relinquishment or cessation of voting rights within three years of death. In general, the relinquishment or cessation of retained voting rights shall be treated as a "transfer of property" for purposes of section 2035 (transfer within three years of death) if:

(1) The voting rights were retained in a transfer made after June 22, 1976: and

(2) The corporation was a controlled corporation at some point in time occurring after the transfer, before the relinquishment or cessation of voting rights, and within three years of death.

However, to the extent that a relinquishment of voting rights is in exchange for voting rights in another controlled corporation, the relinquishment shall not be treated as a "transfer of property" for purposes of section 2035. See paragraph (e)(3) of this section for the treatment of voting rights in such other corporation.

(c) Meaning of right to vote. For purposes of this section, the term "right to vote" means the power to vote, whether exercisable alone or in conjunction with other persons. The capacity in which the decedent can exercise voting power is immaterial. Accordingly, a fiduciary power exercisable as trustee, co-trustee, or as officer of a corporation is a right to vote stock within the meaning of this section. For purposes of section 2036(b)(1) and § 20.2036–2(a), the constructive ownership rules of section 318 shall not be used to attribute the retention of voting rights to the decedent. Therefore, the fact that a relative of the decedent is trustee of a trust to which the decedent has transferred stock shall not in itself require a finding that the decedent indirectly retained the right to vote that stock. However, any arrangement to shift formal voting power away from the decedent will not be treated for this purpose as a relinquishment of all voting rights if, in substance, the decedent has retained voting power. Moreover, voting power shall be deemed retained in cases where there is any agreement with the decedent, express or implied, that the shareholder, or other holder of the power to vote stock, either will vote the stock in a specified manner or will not vote the stock. If the decedent has the power to obtain the right to vote, such as where he may appoint himself as trustee of a trust holding the stock, the decedent has retained the right to vote for purposes of section 2036.

(d) Meaning of controlled corporation. (1) *In general.* For purposes of this section, the term "controlled corporation" means a corporation in which the decedent, with application of the constructive ownership rules of section 318, is deemed to own or have a right to vote stock possessing at least 20 percent of the total combined voting power of all classes of stock.

(2) *Computations.* (i) *Total combined voting power of all classes of stock.* For purposes of this paragraph, the total combined voting power of all classes of stock shall include only stock that currently has voting power. Stock that may vote only on extraordinary matters, such as mergers or liquidations, shall be disregarded. Similarly, treasury stock and stock that is authorized but unissued shall be disregarded.

(ii) *Decedent's percentage of total combined voting power.* For purposes of this paragraph, in determining whether the voting power possessed by the decedent is a least 20 percent of the total combined voting power of all classes of stock, consideration will be given to all the facts and circumstances. Generally, the percentage of voting power possessed by a person in a corporation may be determined by reference to the power of stock to vote for the election of directors. Instruments that do not have voting rights shall be disregarded. Instruments having no voting rights but which may be converted into voting stock shall be disregarded until such conversion occurs. Instruments carrying voting rights that will vest only when conditions, the occurrence of which is indeterminate, have been met will be disregarded until the conditions have occurred which cause the voting rights to vest. An example of such an instrument is preferred stock which gains voting rights only if no dividends are paid.

(iii) *Example.* The following example illustrates the application of paragraphs (d)(1) through (d)(2)(ii) of this section.

Example. A corporation has three classes of stock outstanding, consisting of 40 shares of class A voting stock, 50 shares of class B voting stock, and 60 shares of class C preferred stock which is nonvoting except for extraordinary matters or unless the arrearages in dividends exceed a specified amount. Assume for purposes of this example that except for extraordinary business matters, the voting stock's only voting power is the right to vote in the election of directors. The class A stockholders are entitled to elect 7 of the 10 corporate directors, and the class B stockholders are entitled to elect the other 3 of the 10 directors. Thus, the class A stock (as a class) possesses 70 percent of the total combined voting power of all classes of stock, and the class B stock (as a class) possesses 30 percent of such voting power. At the time of D 's death, D has voting rights in 9 shares of class A stock directly; and with the constructive ownership rules of section 318, D is deemed to have voting rights in 3 additional shares of class A stock. D has no interest in the class B stock and owns all 60 shares of the class C stock. Thus, D is deemed to possess 21 percent ((9+3) shares/40 shares x 70 percent) of the total combined voting power of all classes of stock. By reason of such voting power, the corporation is a controlled corporation within the meaning of this section.

(e) Direct versus indirect retention of voting rights. (1) *Direct transfers.* Subject to the limitations contained in paragraph (a) of this section, if the decedent transfers stock of a controlled corporation (except in case of a bona fide sale for adequate and full consideration in money or money's worth), the retention of voting rights in the stock transferred shall require a portion of the fair market value of the stock to be included in the gross estate. For purposes of this paragraph (e)(1), transfers of stock in exchange for, in whole or in part, either property donated by the decedent or property for which the decedent supplied the purchase consideration, will not be considered a bona fide sale for adequate and full consideration. The amount included in the gross estate under this paragraph (e)(1) shall be an amount, not less than zero, equal to the fair market value at death of the stock transferred less the value of any consideration the decedent received in exchange.

(2) *Indirect transfer.* Section 2036 applies to indirect as well as direct transfers. The acquisition of voting rights in stock acquired through the exercise of other instruments transferred by the decedent (such as through the exercise of warrants or options, or the conversion rights on convertible nonvoting stock or indebtedness) shall cause the stock to be treated as acquired with consideration furnished by the decedent and an indirect transfer by the decedent. If a third party makes a transfer to the trust and the consideration for the transfer was furnished by the decedent, the transfer by the third party to the trust will be treated as a transfer by the decedent to the trust. In addition, if the decedent makes a transfer by gift to a trust, and the trust subsequently acquires stock in which the decedent has voting rights, then for purposes of section 2036(a), the transaction will be treated as an indirect transfer of stock by the decedent (irrespective of whether the acquisition of the stock can be traced to the gift). The amount included in the gross estate in such a case is equal to the fair market value at death of the portion of the stock acquired with funds provided by the decedent. In the case of a purchase of stock from a third party by a trust, the stock shall be treated as purchased with funds provided by the decedent to the extent there are funds in the trust treated as provided by the decedent. For this purpose, the portion of the funds in the trust treated as provided by the decedent shall be determined after each addition to the trust and is equal to a fraction. The numerator of the fraction is the sum of—

(i) The total value of the trust immediately prior to the latest addition multiplied by the fraction of such value treated as provided by the decedent because of prior additions, and

(ii) The amount of the latest addition to the extent provided by the decedent. The denominator of the fraction is the total value of the trust immediately after the latest addition.

(3) *Exchange of voting rights.* For purposes of this section, if a decedent is deemed to have retained the right to vote shares of stock of a controlled corporation in a transfer occurring after June 22, 1976, the subsequent relinquishment of those voting rights in exchange for voting rights in other stock of a controlled corporation, shall be treated as a retention of voting rights in such other stock. Furthermore, for purposes of section 2036(a), such other stock shall be treated

as property transferred by the decedent. For example, if a person transfers stock in ABC Corporation (a controlled corporation) after June 22, 1976, to a trust for which that person is a trustee—thus retaining voting rights in a fiduciary capacity—and the trust later sells the ABC Corporation stock, using the proceeds to purchase stock in XYZ Corporation (a controlled corporation), that person will be treated as having retained the right to vote the shares of XYZ Corporation. In such a transaction, the shares of XYZ Corporation shall be treated as transferred by that person. If the stock in XYZ Corporation is acquired directly from the decedent, the amount included in the gross estate shall be determined under paragraph (e)(1) of this section. If the stock in XYZ Corporation is acquired from someone other than the decedent, the amount included in the decedent's gross estate shall be determined under paragraph (e)(2) of this section.

(4) *Examples.* The following examples illustrate the application of section 2043 and paragraphs (e)(1) and (e)(2) of this section.

Example (1). During 1977, D transferred by gift $100,000 cash to a trust. During 1979, D transferred to the trust 1000 shares of ABC Corporation voting stock worth $100,000. The 1979 transfer was in exchange for $50,000 cash and D retained voting rights in all the stock transferred. Assume that at some time after the stock transfer, ABC Corporation is a controlled corporation within the meaning of this section. D dies during 1981, at which time the stock is worth $150,000. As a result of the stock transfer, the amount included in D's gross estate under section 2036 is $100,000, computed as follows:

Fair market value of instruments at death	$150,000
Less consideration received by D	50,000
Amount included in D's gross estate	100,000

Example (2). The facts are the same as in example (1) except that the 1979 transfer to the trust (1000 shares of ABC Corporation) was in exchange for $100,000 cash. As a result of the stock transfer, the amount included in D's gross estate under section 2036 is $50,000, computed as follows:

Fair market value of instruments at death	$150,000
Less consideration received by D	100,000
Amount included in D's gross estate	50,000

The 1979 transfer is not considered a bona fide sale for adequate and full consideration in money or money's worth since D provided the consideration by virtue of his 1977 transfer to the trust.

Example (3). During 1979, D transferred by gift 1000 shares of ABC Corporation voting stock worth $100,000 to his wife W. During 1980, W made a gift of the same stock to a trust. Assume that D becomes trustee of the trust and hence acquires the right to vote the stock in that capacity. Assume further that, at some time after D's transfer, ABC Corporation is a controlled corporation within the meaning of this section. D dies during 1981, at which time the stock is worth $150,000. The full $150,000 is included in D's gross estate under section 2036.

Example (4). During 1979, D transferred by gift $90,000 to a trust that already had $90,000 of funds, all of which is attributable to contributions by persons other than D. During 1980, the trust purchased at full fair market value 1000 shares of ABC Corporation voting stock worth $100,000, at which time, because of appreciation, the value of the trust was $210,000. Assume that D acquires the right to vote the stock as trustee of the trust and that at some time after the stock purchase, ABC Corporation is a controlled corporation within the meaning of this section. D dies during 1981, at which time the stock is worth $150,000. Pursuant to paragraph (e)(2) of this section, at the time of the stock purchase, $105,000 (50 percent of $210,000) of funds in the trust were funds supplied by D, $100,000 of which are treated as used to purchase the stock. Accordingly, the amount included in D's gross estate under section 2036, $150,000, is the value at death of the portion of the stock acquired with funds provided by D.

§ 2037. Transfers Taking Effect at Death

(a) General rule. The value of the gross estate shall include the value of all property to the extent of any interest therein of which the decedent has at any time after September 7, 1916, made a transfer (except in case of a bona fide sale for an adequate and full consideration in money or money's worth), by trust or otherwise, if—

(1) possession or enjoyment of the property can, through ownership of such interest, be obtained only by surviving the decedent, and

(2) the decedent has retained a reversionary interest in the property (but in the case of a transfer made before October 8, 1949, only if such reversionary interest arose by the express terms of the instrument of transfer), and the value of such reversionary interest immediately before the death of the decedent exceeds 5 percent of the value of such property.

(b) Special rules. For purposes of this section, the term "reversionary interest" includes a possibility that property transferred by the decedent—

(1) may return to him or his estate, or

(2) may be subject to a power of disposition by him,

but such term does not include a possibility that the income alone from such property may return to him or become subject to a power of disposition by him. The value of a reversionary interest immediately before the death of the decedent shall be determined (without regard to the fact of the decedent's death) by usual methods of valuation, including the use of tables of mortality and actuarial principles, under regulations prescribed by the Secretary. In determining the value of a possibility that property may be subject to a power of disposition by the decedent, such possibility shall be valued as if it were a possibility that such property may return to the decedent or his estate. Notwithstanding the foregoing, an interest so transferred shall not be included in the decedent's gross estate under this section if possession or enjoyment of the property could have been obtained by any beneficiary during the decedent's life through the exercise of a general power of appointment (as defined in section 2041) which in fact was exercisable immediately before the decedent's death.

Regulation

§ 20.2037–1 Transfers taking effect at death.

(a) In general. A decedent's gross estate includes under section 2037 the value of any interest in property transferred by the decedent after September 7, 1916, whether in trust or otherwise, except to the extent that the transfer was for an adequate and full consideration in money or money's worth (see § 20.2043–1), if—

(1) Possession or enjoyment of the property could, through ownership of the interest, have been obtained only by surviving the decedent,

(2) The decedent had retained a possibility (referred to in this section as a "reversionary interest") that the property, other than the income alone, would return to the decedent or his estate or would be subject to a power of disposition by him, and

(3) The value of the reversionary interest immediately before the decedent's death exceeded 5 percent of the value of the entire property. However, if the transfer was made before October 8, 1949, section 2037 is applicable only if the reversionary interest arose by the express terms of the instrument of transfer and not by operation of law (see paragraph (f) of this section). See also paragraph (g) of this section with respect to transfers made between November 11, 1935, and January 29, 1940. The provisions of section 2037 do not apply to transfers made before September 8, 1916.

(b) Condition of survivorship. As indicated in paragraph (a) of this section, the value of an interest in transferred property is not included in a decedent's gross estate under section 2037 unless possession or enjoyment of the property could, through ownership of such interest, have been obtained only by surviving the decedent. Thus, property is not included in the decedent's gross estate if, immediately before the decedent's death, possession or enjoyment of the property could have been obtained by any beneficiary either by surviving the decedent or through the occurrence of some other event such as the expiration of a term of years. However, if a consideration of the terms and circumstances of the transfer as a whole indicates that the "other event" is unreal and if the death of the decedent does, in fact, occur before the "other event", the beneficiary will be considered able to possess or enjoy the property only by surviving the decedent. Notwithstanding the foregoing, an interest in transferred property is not includible in a decedent's gross estate under section 2037 if possession or enjoyment of the property could have been obtained by any beneficiary during the decedent's life through the exercise of a general power of appointment (as defined in section 2041) which in fact was exercisable immediately before the decedent's death. See examples (5) and (6) in paragraph (e) of this section.

(c) Retention of reversionary interest. (1) As indicated in paragraph (a) of this section, the value of an interest in transferred property is not included in a decedent's gross estate under section 2037 unless the decedent had retained a reversionary interest in the property, and the value of the reversionary interest immediately before the death of the decedent exceeded 5 percent of the value of the property.

(2) For purposes of section 2037, the term "reversionary interest" includes a possibility that property transferred by the decedent may return to him or his estate and a possibility that property transferred by the decedent may become subject to a power of disposition by him. The term is not used in a technical sense, but has reference to any reserved right under which the transferred property shall or may be returned to the grantor. Thus, it encompasses an interest arising either by the express terms of the instrument of transfer or by operation of law. (See, however, paragraph (f) of this section with respect to transfers made before October 8, 1949.) The term "reversionary interest" does not include rights to income only, such as the right to receive the income from a trust after the death of another person. (However, see section 2036 for the inclusion of property in the gross estate on account of such rights.) Nor does the term "reversionary interest" include the possibility that the decedent during his lifetime might have received back an interest in transferred property by inheritance through the estate of another person. Similarly, a statutory right of a spouse to receive a portion of whatever estate a decedent may leave at the time of his death is not a "reversionary interest".

(3) For purposes of this section, the value of the decedent's reversionary interest is computed as of the moment immediately before his death, without regard to whether or not the executor elects the alternate valuation method under section 2032 and without regard to the fact of the decedent's death. The value is ascertained in accordance with recognized valuation principles for determining the value for estate tax purposes of future or conditional interests in property. (See §§ 20.2031–1, 20.2031–7, and 20.2031–9). For example, if the decedent's reversionary interest was subject to an outstanding life estate in his wife, his interest is valued according to the actuarial rules set forth in § 20.2031–7. On the other hand, if the decedent's reversionary interest was contingent on the death of his wife without issue surviving and if it cannot be shown that his wife is incapable of having issue (so that his interest is not subject to valuation according to the actuarial rules in § 20.2031–7), his interest is valued according to the general rules set forth in § 20.2031–1. A possibility that the decedent may be able to dispose of property under certain conditions is considered to have the same value as a right of the decedent to the return of the property under those same conditions.

(4) In order to determine whether or not the decedent retained a reversionary interest in transferred property of a value in excess of 5 percent, the value of the reversionary interest is compared with the value of the transferred property, including interests therein which are not dependent upon survivorship of the decedent. For example, assume that the decedent, A, transferred property in trust with the income payable to B for life and with the remainder payable to C if A predeceases B, but with the property to revert to A if B predeceases A. Assume further that A does, in fact, predecease B. The value of A's reversionary interest immediately before his death is compared with the value of the trust corpus, without deduction of the value of B's outstanding life estate. If, in the above example, A had retained a reversionary interest in one-half only of the trust corpus, the value of his reversionary interest would be compared with the value of one-half of the trust corpus, again without deduction of any part of the value of B's outstanding life estate.

(d) Transfers partly taking effect at death. If separate interests in property are transferred to one or more beneficiaries, paragraphs (a) to (c) of this section are to be separately applied with respect to each interest. For example, assume that the decedent transferred an interest in Blackacre to A which could be possessed or enjoyed only by surviving the decedent, and that the decedent transferred an interest in Blackacre to B which could be possessed or enjoyed only on the occurrence of some event unrelated to the decedent's death. Assume further that the decedent retained a reversionary interest in Blackacre of a value in excess of 5 percent. Only the value of the interest transferred to A is includible in the decedent's gross estate. Similar results would obtain if possession or enjoyment of the entire property could have been obtained only by surviving the decedent, but the decedent had retained a reversionary interest in a part only of such property.

(e) Examples. The provisions of paragraphs (a) to (d) of this section may be further illustrated by the following examples. It is assumed that the transfers were made on or after October 8, 1949; for the significance of this date, see paragraphs (f) and (g) of this section:

Example (1). The decedent transferred property in trust with the income payable to his wife for life and, at her death, remainder to the decedent's then surviving children, or if none, to the decedent or his estate. Since each beneficiary can possess or enjoy the property without surviving the decedent, no part of the property is includible in the decedent's gross estate under section 2037, regardless of the value of the decedent's reversionary interest. (However, see section 2033 for inclusion of the value of the reversionary interest in the decedent's gross estate.)

Example (2). The decedent transferred property in trust with the income to be accumulated for the decedent's life, and at his death, principal and accumulated income to be paid to the decedent's then surviving issue, or, if none, to A or A's estate. Since the decedent retained no reversionary interest in the property, no part of the property is includible in the decedent's gross estate, even though possession or enjoyment of the property could be obtained by the issue only by surviving the decedent.

Example (3). The decedent transferred property in trust with the income payable to his wife for life and with the remainder payable to the decedent or, if he is not living at his wife's death, to his daughter or her estate. The daughter cannot obtain possession or enjoyment of the property without surviving the decedent. Therefore, if the decedent's reversionary interest immediately before his death exceeded 5 percent of the value of the property, the value of the property, less the value of the wife's outstanding life estate, is includible in the decedent's gross estate.

Example (4). The decedent transferred property in trust with the income payable to his wife for life and with the remainder payable to his son or, if the son is not living at the wife's death, to the decedent or, if the decedent is not then living, to X or X's estate. Assume that the decedent was survived by his wife, his son, and X. Only X cannot obtain possession or enjoyment of the property without surviving the decedent. Therefore, if the decedent's reversionary interest immediately before his death exceeded 5 percent of the value of the property, the value of X's remainder interest (with reference to the time immediately after the decedent's death) is includible in the decedent's gross estate.

Example (5). The decedent transferred property in trust with the income to be accumulated for a period of 20 years or until the decedent's prior death, at which time the principal and accumulated income was to be paid to the decedent's son if then surviving. Assume that the decedent does, in fact, die before the expiration of the 20-year period. If, at the time of the transfer, the decedent was 30 years of age, in good health, etc., the son will be considered able to possess or enjoy the property without surviving the decedent. If, on the other hand, the decedent was 70 years of age at the time of the transfer, the son will not be considered able to possess or enjoy the property without surviving the decedent. In this latter case, if the value of the decedent's reversionary interest (arising by operation of law) immediately before his death exceeded 5 percent of the value of the property, the value of the property is includible in the decedent's gross estate.

Example (6). The decedent transferred property in trust with the income to be accumulated for his life and, at his death, the principal and accumulated income to be paid to the decedent's then surviving children. The decedent's wife was given the unrestricted power to alter, amend, or revoke the trust. Assume that the wife survived the decedent but did not, in fact, exercise her power during the decedent's lifetime. Since possession or enjoyment of the property could have been obtained by the wife during the decedent's lifetime under the exercise of a general power of appointment, which was, in fact, exercisable immediately before the decedent's death, no part of the property is includible in the decedent's gross estate.

(f) Transfers made before October 8, 1949. [*Omitted. Ed.*]

* * *

(g) Transfers made after November 11, 1935, and before January 29, 1940. [*Omitted. Ed.*]

* * *

[T.D. 6296, 23 FR 4529, June 24, 1958]

§ 2038. Revocable Transfers

(a) In general. The value of the gross estate shall include the value of all property—

(1) Transfers after June 22, 1936. To the extent of any interest therein of which the decedent has at any time made a transfer (except in case of a bona fide sale for an adequate and full consideration in money or money's worth), by trust or otherwise, where the enjoyment thereof was subject at the date of his death to any change through the exercise of a power (in whatever capacity exercisable) by the decedent alone or by the decedent in conjunction with any other person (without regard to when or from what source the decedent acquired such power), to alter, amend, revoke, or terminate, or where any such power is relinquished during the 3-year period ending on the date of the decedent's death.

(2) Transfers on or before June 22, 1936. To the extent of any interest therein of which the decedent has at any time made a transfer (except in case of a bona fide sale for an adequate and full consideration in money or money's worth), by trust or otherwise, where the enjoyment thereof was subject at the date of his death to any change through the exercise of a power, either by the decedent alone or in conjunction with any person, to alter, amend, or revoke, or where the decedent relinquished any such power during the 3-year period ending on the date of the decedent's death. Except in the case of transfers made after June 22, 1936, no interest of the decedent of which he has made a transfer shall be included in the gross estate under paragraph (1) unless it is includible under this paragraph.

(b) Date of existence of power. For purposes of this section, the power to alter, amend, revoke, or terminate shall be considered to exist on the date of the decedent's death even though the exercise of the power is subject to a precedent giving of notice or even though the alteration, amendment, revocation, or termination takes effect only on the expiration of a stated period after the exercise of the power, whether or not on or before the date of the decedent's death notice has been given or the power has been exercised. In such cases proper adjustment shall be made representing the interests which would have been excluded from the power if the decedent had lived, and for such purpose, if the notice has not been given or the power has not been exercised on or before the date of his death, such notice shall be considered to have been given, or the power exercised, on the date of his death.

Regulation

§ 20.2038–1 Revocable transfers.

(a) In general. A decedent's gross estate includes under section 2038 the value of any interest in property transferred by the decedent, whether in trust or otherwise, if the enjoyment of the interest was subject at the date of the decedent's death to any change through the exercise of a power by the decedent to alter, amend, revoke, or terminate, or if the decedent relinquished such a power in contemplation of death. However, section 2038 does not apply—

(1) To the extent that the transfer was for an adequate and full consideration in money or money's worth (see § 20.2043–1);

(2) If the decedent's power could be exercised only with the consent of all parties having an interest (vested or contingent) in the transferred property, and if the power adds nothing to the rights of the parties under local law; or

(3) To a power held solely by a person other than the decedent. But, for example, if the decedent had the unrestricted power to remove or discharge a trustee at any time and appoint himself trustee, the decedent is considered as having the powers of the trustee. However, this result would not follow if he only had the power to appoint himself trustee under limited conditions which did not exist at the time of his death. (See last two sentences of paragraph (b) of this section.)

Except as provided in this paragraph, it is immaterial in what capacity the power was exercisable by the decedent or by another person or persons in conjunction with the decedent; whether the power was exercisable alone or only in conjunction with another person or persons, whether or not having an adverse interest (unless the transfer was made before June 2, 1924; see paragraph (d) of this section); and at what time or from what source the decedent acquired his power (unless the transfer was made before June 23, 1936; see paragraph (c) of this section). Section 2038 is applicable to any power affecting the time or manner of enjoyment of property or its income, even though the identity of the beneficiary is not affected. For example, section 2038 is applicable to a power reserved by the grantor of a trust to accumulate income or distribute it to A, and to distribute corpus to A, even though the remainder is vested in A or his estate, and no other person has any beneficial interest in the trust. However, only the value of an interest in property subject to a power to which section 2038 applies is included in the decedent's gross estate under section 2038.

(b) Date of existence of power. A power to alter, amend, revoke, or terminate will be considered to have existed at the date of the decedent's death even though the exercise of the power was subject to a precedent giving of notice or even though the alteration, amendment, revocation, or termination would have taken effect only on the expiration of a stated period after the exercise of the power, whether or not on or before the date of the decedent's death notice had been given or the power had been exercised. In determining the value of the gross estate in such cases, the full value of the property transferred subject to the power is discounted for the period required to elapse between the date of the decedent's death and the date upon which the alteration, amendment, revocation, or termination could take effect. In this connection, see especially § 20.2031–7. However, section 2038 is not applicable to a power the exercise of which was subject to a contingency beyond the decedent's control which did not occur before his death (e.g., the death of another person during the decedent's life). See, however, section 2036(a)(2) for the inclusion of property in the decedent's gross estate on account of such a power.

(c) Transfers made before June 23, 1936. [*Omitted. Ed.*]

* * *

(d) Transfers made before June 2, 1924. [*Omitted. Ed.*]

* * *

(e) Powers relinquished in contemplation of death. (1) *In general.* If a power to alter, amend, revoke, or terminate would have resulted in the inclusion of an interest in property in a decedent's gross estate under section 2038 if it had been held until the decedent's death, the relinquishment of the power in contemplation of the decedent's death within 3 years before his death results in the inclusion of the same interest in property in the decedent's gross estate, except to the extent that the power was relinquished for an adequate and full consideration in money or money's worth (see § 20.2043–1). For the meaning of the phrase "in contemplation of death", see paragraph (c) of § 20.2035–1.

(2) *Transfers before June 23, 1936.* In the case of a transfer made before June 23, 1936, section 2038 applies only to a relinquishment made by the decedent. However, in the case of a transfer made after June 22, 1936, section 2038 also applies to a relinquishment made by a person or persons holding the power in conjunction with the decedent, if the relinquishment was made in contemplation of the decedent's death and had the effect of extinguishing the power.

(f) Effect of disability to relinquish power in certain cases. Notwithstanding anything to the contrary in paragraphs (a) through (e) of this section the provisions of this section do not apply to a transfer if—

(1) The relinquishment on or after January 1, 1940, and on or before December 31, 1947, of the power would, by reason of section 1000(e), of the Internal Revenue Code of 1939, be deemed not a transfer of property for the purpose of the gift tax under chapter 4 of the Internal Revenue Code of 1939, and

(2) The decedent was, for a continuous period beginning on or before September 30, 1947, and ending with his death, after August 16, 1954, under a mental disability to relinquish a power.

For the purpose of the foregoing provision, the term "mental disability" means mental incompetence, in fact, to release the power whether or not there was an adjudication of incompetence. Such provision shall apply even though a guardian could have released the power for the decedent. No interest shall be allowed or paid on any overpayment allowable under section 2038(c) with respect to amounts paid before August 7, 1959.

[T.D. 6296, 23 FR 4529, June 24, 1958, as amended by T.D. 6600, 27 FR 4985, May 29, 1962]

§ 2039. Annuities

(a) General. The gross estate shall include the value of an annuity or other payment receivable by any beneficiary by reason of surviving the decedent under any form of contract or agreement entered into after March 3, 1931 (other than as insurance under policies on the life of the decedent), if, under such contract or agreement, an annuity or other payment was payable to the decedent, or the decedent possessed the right to receive such annuity or payment, either alone or in conjunction with another for his life or for any period not ascertainable without reference to his death or for any period which does not in fact end before his death.

(b) Amount includible. Subsection (a) shall apply to only such part of the value of the annuity or other payment receivable under such contract or agreement as is proportionate to that part of the purchase price therefor contributed by the decedent. For purposes of this section, any contribution by the decedent's employer or former employer to the purchase price of such contract or agreement (whether or not to an employee's trust or fund forming part of a pension, annuity, retirement, bonus or profit sharing plan) shall be considered to be contributed by the decedent if made by reason of his employment.

Regulations

§ 20.2039–1 Annuities.

(a) In general. A decedent's gross estate includes under section 2039(a) and (b) the value of an annuity or other payment receivable by any beneficiary by reason of surviving the decedent under certain agreements or plans to the extent that the value of the annuity or other payment is attributable to contributions made by the decedent or his employer. Sections 2039(a) and (b), however, have no application to an amount which constitutes the proceeds of insurance under a policy on the decedent's life. Paragraph (b) of this section describes the agreements or plans to which section 2039(a) and (b) applies; paragraph (c) of this section provides rules for determining the amount includible in the decedent's gross estate; paragraph (d) of this section distinguishes proceeds of life insurance; and paragraph (e) of this section distinguishes annuity, unitrust, and other interests retained by a decedent in certain trusts.

The fact that an annuity or other payment is not includible in a decedent's gross estate under section 2039(a) and (b) does not mean that it is not includible under some other section of part III of subchapter A of chapter 11. However, see section 2039(c) and (d) and § 20.2039–2 for rules relating to the exclusion from a decedent's gross estate of annuities and other payments under certain "qualified plans." Further, the fact that an annuity or other payment may be includible under section 2039(a) will not preclude the application of another section of chapter 11 with regard to that interest. For annuity interests in trust, see paragraph (e)(1) of this section.

(b) Agreements or plans to which section 2039(a) and (b) applies. (1) Section 2039(a) and (b) applies to the value of an annuity or other payment receivable by any beneficiary under any form of contract or agreement entered into after March 3, 1931, under which—

(i) An annuity or other payment was payable to the decedent, either alone or in conjunction with another person or persons, for his life or for any period not ascertainable without reference to his death or for any period which does not in fact end before his death, or

(ii) The decedent possessed, for his life or for any period not ascertainable without reference to his death or for any period which does not in fact end before his death, the right to receive such an annuity or other payment, either alone or in conjunction with another person or persons.

The term "annuity or other payment" as used with respect to both the decedent and the beneficiary has reference to one or more payments extending over any period of time. The payments may be equal or unequal, conditional or unconditional, periodic or sporadic. The term "contract or agreement" includes any arrangement, understanding or plan, or any combination of arrangements, understandings or plans arising by reason of the decedent's employment. An annuity or other payment "was payable" to the decedent if, at the time of his death, the decedent was in fact receiving an annuity or other payment, whether or not he had an enforceable right to have payments continued. The decedent "possessed the right to receive" an annuity or other payment if, immediately before his death, the decedent had an enforceable right to receive payments at some time in the future, whether or not, at the time of his death, he had a present right to receive payments. In connection with the preceding sentence, the decedent will be regarded as having had "an enforceable right to receive payments at some time in the future" so long as he had complied with his obligations under the contract or agreement up to the time of his death. For the meaning of the phrase "for his life or for any period not ascertainable without reference to his death or for any period which does not in fact end before his death", see section 2036 and § 20.2036–1.

(2) The application of this paragraph is illustrated and more fully explained in the following examples. In each example: (i) It is assumed that all transactions occurred after March 3, 1931, and (ii) the amount stated to be includible in the decedent's gross estate is determined in accordance with the provisions of paragraph (c) of this section.

Example (1). The decedent purchased an annuity contract under the terms of which the issuing company agreed to pay an annuity to the decedent for his life and, upon his death, to pay a specified lump sum to his designated beneficiary. The decedent was drawing his annuity at the time of his death. The amount of the lump sum payment to the beneficiary is includible in the decedent's gross estate under section 2039(a) and (b).

Example (2). Pursuant to a retirement plan, the employer made contributions to a fund which was to provide the employee, upon his retirement at age 60, with an annuity for life, and which was to provide the employee's wife, upon his death after retirement, with a similar annuity for life. The benefits under the plan were completely forfeitable during the employee's life, but upon his death after retirement, the benefits to the wife were forfeitable only upon her remarriage. The employee had no right to originally designate or to ever change the employer's designation of the surviving beneficiary. The retirement plan at no time met the requirements of section 401(a) (relating to qualified plans). Assume that the employee died at age 61 after the employer started payment of his annuity as described above. The value of the wife's annuity is includible in the decedent's gross estate under section 2039(a) and (b). Includibility in this case is based on the fact that the annuity to the decedent "was payable" at the time of his death. The fact that the decedent's annuity was forfeitable is of no consequence since, at the time of his death, he was in fact receiving payments under the plan. Nor is it important that the decedent had no right to choose the surviving beneficiary. The element of forfeitability in the wife's annuity may be taken into account only with respect to the valuation of the annuity in the decedent's gross estate.

Example (3). Pursuant to a retirement plan, the employer made contributions to a fund which was to provide the employee, upon his retirement at age 60, with an annuity of $100 per month for life, and which was to provide his designated beneficiary, upon the employee's death after retirement, with a similar annuity for life. The plan also provided that (a) upon the employee's separation from service before retirement, he would have a nonforfeitable right to receive a reduced annuity starting at age 60, and (b) upon the employee's death before retirement, a lump sum payment representing the amount of the employer's contributions credited to the employee's account would be paid to the designated beneficiary. The plan at no time met the requirements of section 401(a) (relating to qualified plans). Assume that the employee died at age 49 and that the designated beneficiary was paid the specified lump sum payment. Such amount is includible in the decedent's gross estate under section 2039(a) and (b). Since immediately before his death, the employee had an enforceable right to receive an annuity commencing at age 60, he is considered to have "possessed the right to receive" an annuity as that term is used in section 2039(a). If, in this example, the employee would not be entitled to any benefits in the event of his separation from service before retirement for any reason other than death, the result would be the same so long as the decedent had complied with his obligations under the contract up to the time of his death. In such case, he is considered to have had, immediately before his death, an enforceable right to receive an annuity commencing at age 60.

Example (4). Pursuant to a retirement plan, the employee made contributions to a fund which was to provide the employee, upon his retirement at age 60, with an annuity for life, and which was to provide his designated beneficiary, upon the employee's death after retirement, with a similar annuity for life. The plan provided, however, that no benefits were payable in the event of the employee's death before retirement. The retirement plan at no time met the requirements of section 401(a) (relating to qualified plans). Assume that the employee died at age 59 but that the employer nevertheless started payment of an annuity in a slightly reduced amount to the designated beneficiary. The value of the annuity is not includible in the decedent's gross estate under section 2039(a) and (b). Since the employee died before reaching the retirement age, the employer was under no obligation to pay the annuity to the employee's designated beneficiary. Therefore, the annuity was not paid under a "contract or agreement" as that term is used in section 2039(a). If, however, it can be established that the employer has consistently paid an annuity under such circumstances, the annuity will be considered as having been paid under a "contract or agreement".

Example (5). The employer made contributions to a retirement fund which were credited to the employee's individual account. Under the plan, the employee was to receive one-half the amount credited to his account upon his retirement at age 60, and his designated beneficiary was to receive the other one-half upon the employee's death after retirement. If the employee should die before reaching the retirement age, the entire amount credited to his account at such time was to be paid to the designated beneficiary. The retirement plan at no time met the requirements of section 401(a) (relating to qualified plans). Assume that the employee received one-half the amount credited to his account upon reaching the retirement age and that he died shortly thereafter. Since the employee received all that he was entitled to receive under the plan before his death, no amount was payable to him for his life or for any period not ascertainable without reference to his death, or for any period which did not in fact end before his death. Thus, the amount of the payment to the designated beneficiary is not includible in the decedent's gross estate under section 2039(a) and (b). If, in this example, the employee died before reaching the retirement age, the amount of the payment to the designated beneficiary would be includible in the decedent's gross estate under section 2039(a) and (b). In this latter case, the decedent possessed the right to receive lump sum payment for a period which did not in fact end before his death.

Example (6). The employer made contributions to two different funds set up under two different plans. One plan was to provide the employee upon his retirement at age 60, with an annuity for life, and the other plan was to provide the employee's designated beneficiary, upon the employee's death, with a similar annuity for life. Each plan was established at a different time and each plan was administered separately in every respect. Neither plan at any time met the requirements of section 401(a) (relating to qualified plans). The value of the designated beneficiary's annuity is includible in the employee's gross estate. All rights and benefits accruing to an employee and to others by reason of the employment (except rights and benefits accruing under certain plans meeting the requirements of section 401(a) (see § 20.2039–2)) are considered together in determining whether or not section 2039(a) and (b) applies. The scope of section 2039(a) and (b) cannot be limited by indirection.

(c) Amount includible in the gross estate. The amount to be included in a decedent's gross estate under section 2039(a) and (b) is an amount which bears the same ratio to the value at the decedent's death of the annuity or other payment receivable by the beneficiary as the contribution made by the decedent, or made by his employer (or former employer) for any reason connected with his employment, to the cost of the contract or agreement bears to its total cost. In applying this ratio, the value at the decedent's death of the annuity or other payment is determined in accordance with the rules set forth in §§ 20.2031–1, 20.2031–7, 20.2031–8, and 20.2031–9. The application of this paragraph may be illustrated by the following examples:

Example (1). On January 1, 1945, the decedent and his wife each contributed $15,000 to the purchase price of an annuity contract under the terms of which the issuing company agreed to pay an annuity to the decedent and his wife for their joint lives and to continue the annuity to the survivor for his life. Assume that the value of the survivor's annuity at the decedent's death (computed under § 20.2031–8) is $20,000. Since the decedent contributed one-half of the cost of the contract, the amount to be included in his gross estate under section 2039(a) and (b) is $10,000.

Example (2). Under the terms of an employment contract entered into on January 1, 1945, the employer and the employee made contributions to a fund which was to provide the employee, upon his retirement at age 60, with an annuity for life, and which was to provide his designated beneficiary, upon the employee's death after retirement, with a similar annuity for life. The retirement fund at no time formed part of a plan meeting the requirements of section 401(a) (relating to qualified plans). Assume that the employer and the employee each contributed $5,000 to the retirement fund. Assume further, that the employee died after retirement at which time the value of the survivor's annuity was $8,000. Since the employer's contributions were made by reason of the decedent's employment, the amount to be included in his gross estate under section 2039(a) and (b) is the entire $8,000. If, in the above example, only the employer made contributions to the fund, the amount to be included in the gross estate would still be $8,000.

(d) Insurance under policies on the life of the decedent. If an annuity or other payment receivable by a beneficiary under a contract or agreement is in substance the proceeds of insurance under a policy on the life of the decedent, section 2039(a) and (b) does not apply. For the extent to which such an annuity or other payment is includable in a decedent's gross estate, see section 2042 and § 20.2042–1. A combination annuity contract and life insurance policy on the decedent's life (e.g., a "retirement income" policy with death benefits) which matured during the decedent's lifetime so that there was no longer an insurance element under the contract at the time of the decedent's death is subject to the provisions of section 2039(a) and (b). On the other hand, the treatment of a combination annuity contract and life insurance policy on the decedent's life which did not mature during the decedent's lifetime depends upon the nature of the contract at the time of the decedent's death. The nature of the contract is generally determined by the relation of the reserve value of the policy to the value of the death benefit at the time of the decedent's death. If the decedent dies before the reserve value equals the death benefit, there is still an insurance element under the contract. The contract is therefore considered, for estate tax purposes, to be an insurance policy subject to the provisions of section 2042. However, if the decedent dies after the reserve value equals the death benefit, there is no longer an insurance element under the contract. The contract is therefore considered to be a contract for an annuity or other payment subject to the provisions of section 2039(a) and (b) or some other section of part III of subchapter A of chapter 11. Notwithstanding the relation of the reserve value to the value of the death benefit, a contract under which the death benefit could never exceed the total premiums paid, plus interest, contains no insurance element.

Example. Pursuant to a retirement plan established January 1, 1945, the employer purchased a contract from an insurance company which was to provide the employee, upon his retirement at age 65, with an annuity of $100 per month for life, and which was to provide his designated beneficiary, upon the employee's death after retirement, with a similar annuity for life. The contract further provided that if the employee should die before reaching the retirement age, a lump sum payment of $20,000 would be paid to his designated beneficiary in lieu of the annuity described above. The plan at no time met the requirements of section 401(a) (relating to qualified plans). Assume that the reserve value of the contract at the retirement age would be $20,000. If the employee died after reaching the retirement age, the death benefit to the designated beneficiary would constitute an annuity, the value of which would be includable in the employee's gross estate under section 2039(a) and (b). If, on the other hand, the employee died before reaching his retirement age, the death benefit to the designated beneficiary would constitute insurance under a policy on the life of the decedent since the reserve value would be less than the death benefit. Accordingly, its includability would depend upon section 2042 and § 20.2042–1.

(e) No application to certain trusts. Section 2039 shall not be applied to include in a decedent's gross estate all or any portion of a trust (other than a trust constituting an employee benefit, but including those described in the following sentence) if the decedent retained a right to use property of the trust or retained an annuity, unitrust, or other interest in the trust, in either case as described in section 2036. Such trusts include without limitation the following (collectively referred to in this paragraph (e) as "trusts"): certain charitable remainder trusts (collectively CRTs) such as a charitable remainder annuity trust (CRAT) within the meaning of section 664(d)(1), a charitable remainder unitrust (CRUT) within the meaning of section 664(d)(2) or (d)(3), and any other charitable remainder trust that does not qualify under section 664(d), whether because the CRT was created prior to 1969, there was a defect in the drafting of the CRT, there was no intention to qualify the CRT for the charitable deduction, or otherwise; other trusts established by a grantor (collectively GRTs) such as a grantor retained annuity trust (GRAT) paying out a qualified annuity interest within the meaning of § 25.2702–3(b) of this chapter, a grantor retained unitrust (GRUT) paying out a qualified unitrust interest within the meaning of § 25.2702–3(c) of this chapter; and various forms of grantor retained income trusts (GRITs) whether or not the grantor's retained interest is a qualified interest as defined in section 2702(b), including without limitation a qualified personal residence trust (QPRT) within the meaning of § 25.2702–5(c) of this chapter and a personal residence trust (PRT) within the meaning of § 25.2702–5(b) of this chapter. For purposes of determining the extent to which a retained interest causes all or a portion of a trust to be included in a decedent's gross estate, see § 20.2036–1(c)(1), (2), and (3).

(f) Effective/applicability dates. The first, second, and fourth sentences in paragraph (a) of this section are applicable to the estates of decedents dying after August 16, 1954. The fifth sentence of paragraph (a) of this section is applicable to the estates of decedents dying on or after October 27, 1972, and to the estates of decedents for which the period for filing a claim for credit or refund of an estate tax overpayment ends on or after October 27, 1972. The third, sixth, and seventh sentences of paragraph (a) of this section and all of paragraph (e) of this section are applicable to the estates of decedents dying on or after July 14, 2008.

[T.D. 6296, 23 FR 4529, June 24, 1958; 25 FR 14021, Dec. 31, 1960, as amended by T.D. 7416, 41 FR 14514, April 6, 1976; T.D. 9414, 73 FR 40178, July 14, 2008]

§ 20.2039–1T Limitations and repeal of estate tax exclusion for qualified plans and individual retirement plans (IRAs) (temporary). [*Omitted. Ed.*]

[T.D. 8073, 51 FR 4335, Feb. 4, 1986]

§ 20.2039–2 Annuities under "qualified plans" and section 403(b) annuity contracts. [*Omitted. Ed.*]

[T.D. 6296, 23 FR 4529, June 24, 1958, as amended by T.D. 6526, 26 FR 416, Jan. 19, 1961; T.D. 6666, 28 FR 7251, July 16, 1963; T.D. 7043, 35 FR 8480, June 2, 1970; T.D. 7416, 41 FR 14514, April 6, 1976; T.D. 7428, 41 FR 34628, Aug. 16, 1976; T.D. 7562, 43 FR 38820, Aug. 31, 1978; T.D. 7761, 46 FR 7303, Jan. 23, 1981; T.D. 8540, 59 FR 30103, June 10, 1994]

§ 20.2039–3 Lump sum distributions under "qualified plans;" decedents dying after December 31, 1976, and before January 1, 1979. [*Omitted. Ed.*]

[T.D. 7761, 46 FR 7304, Jan. 23, 1981]

§ 20.2039–4 Lump sum distributions from "qualified plans;" decedents dying after December 31, 1978. [*Omitted. Ed.*]

[T.D. 7761, 46 FR 7304, Jan. 23, 1981; amended by T.D. 7956, 49 FR 20283, May 14, 1984]

§ 20.2039–5 Annuities under individual retirement plans. [*Omitted. Ed.*]

[T.D. 7761, 46 FR 7305, Jan. 23, 1981; 46 FR 17191, Mar. 18, 1981; T.D. 8540, 59 FR 30103, June 10, 1994]

§ 2040. Joint Interests

(a) General rule. The value of the gross estate shall include the value of all property to the extent of the interest therein held as joint tenants with right of survivorship by the decedent and any other person, or as tenants by the entirety by the decedent and spouse, or deposited, with any person carrying on the banking business, in their joint names and payable to either or the survivor, except such part thereof as may be shown to have originally belonged to such other person and never to have been received or acquired by the latter from the decedent for less than an adequate and full consideration in money or money's worth: Provided, That where such property or any part thereof, or part of the consideration with which such property was acquired, is shown to have been at any time acquired by such other person from the decedent for less than an adequate and full consideration in money or money's worth, there shall be excepted only such part of the value of such property as is proportionate to the consideration furnished by such other person: Provided further, That where any property has been acquired by gift, bequest, devise, or inheritance, as a tenancy by the entirety by the decedent and spouse, then to the extent of one-half of the value thereof, or, where so acquired by the decedent and any other person as joint tenants with right of survivorship and their interests are not otherwise specified or fixed by law, then to the extent of the value of a fractional part to be determined by dividing the value of the property by the number of joint tenants with right of survivorship.

(b) Certain joint interests of husband and wife.

(1) Interests of spouse excluded from gross estate. Notwithstanding subsection (a), in the case of any qualified joint interest, the value included in the gross estate with respect to such interest by reason of this section is one-half of the value of such qualified joint interest.

(2) Qualified joint interest defined. For purposes of paragraph (1), the term "qualified joint interest" means any interest in property held by the decedent and the decedent's spouse as—

(A) tenants by the entirety, or

(B) joint tenants with right of survivorship, but only if the decedent and the spouse of the decedent are the only joint tenants.

Regulation

§ 20.2040–1 Joint interests.

(a) In general. A decedent's gross estate includes under section 2040 the value of property held jointly at the time of the decedent's death by the decedent and another person or persons with right of survivorship, as follows:

(1) To the extent that the property was acquired by the decedent and the other joint owner or owners by gift, devise, bequest, or inheritance, the decedent's fractional share of the property is included.

(2) In all other cases, the entire value of the property is included except such part of the entire value as is attributable to the amount of the consideration in money or money's worth furnished by the other joint owner or owners. See § 20.2043–1 with respect to adequacy of consideration. Such part of the entire value is that portion of the entire value of the property at the decedent's death or at the alternate valuation date described in section 2032 which the consideration in money or money's worth furnished by the other joint owner or owners bears to the total cost of acquisition and capital additions. In determining the consideration furnished by the other joint owner or owners, there is taken into account only that portion of such consideration which is shown not to be attributable to money or other property acquired by the other joint owner or owners from the decedent for less than a full and adequate consideration in money or money's worth.

The entire value of jointly held property is included in a decedent's gross estate unless the executor submits facts sufficient to show that property was not acquired entirely with consideration furnished by the decedent, or was acquired by the decedent and the other joint owner or owners by gift, bequest, devise, or inheritance.

(b) Meaning of "property held jointly". Section 2040 specifically covers property held jointly by the decedent and any other person (or persons), property held by the decedent and spouse as tenants by the entirety, and a deposit of money, or a bond or other instrument, in the name of the decedent and any other person and payable to either or the survivor. The section applies to all classes of property, whether real or personal, and regardless of when the joint interests were created. Furthermore, it makes no difference that the survivor takes the entire interest in the property by right of survivorship and that no interest therein forms a part of the decedent's estate for purposes of administration. The section has no application to property held by the decedent and any other person (or persons) as tenants in common.

(c) Examples. The application of this section may be explained in the following examples in each of which it is assumed that the other joint owner or owners survived the decedent:

(1) If the decedent furnished the entire purchase price of the jointly held property, the value of the entire property is included in his gross estate;

(2) If the decedent furnished a part only of the purchase price, only a corresponding portion of the value of the property is so included;

(3) If the decedent furnished no part of the purchase price, no part of the value of the property is so included;

(4) If the decedent, before the acquisition of the property by himself and the other joint owner, gave the

latter a sum of money or other property which thereafter became the other joint owner's entire contribution to the purchase price, then the value of the entire property is so included, notwithstanding the fact that the other property may have appreciated in value due to market conditions between the time of the gift and the time of the acquisition of the jointly held property;

(5) If the decedent, before the acquisition of the property by himself and the other joint owner, transferred to the latter for less than an adequate and full consideration in money or money's worth other income-producing property, the income from which belonged to and became the other joint owner's entire contribution to the purchase price, then the value of the jointly held property less that portion attributable to the income which the other joint owner did furnish is included in the decedent's gross estate;

(6) If the property originally belonged to the other joint owner and the decedent purchased his interest from the other joint owner, only that portion of the value of the property attributable to the consideration paid by the decedent is included;

(7) If the decedent and his spouse acquired the property by will or gift as tenants by the entirety, one-half of the value of the property is included in the decedent's gross estate; and

(8) If the decedent and his two brothers acquired the property by will or gift as joint tenants, one-third of the value of the property is so included.

[T.D. 6296, 23 FR 4529, June 24, 1958]

§ 2041. Powers of Appointment

(a) In general. The value of the gross estate shall include the value of all property.

(1) Powers of appointment created on or before October 21, 1942. To the extent of any property with respect to which a general power of appointment created on or before October 21, 1942, is exercised by the decedent—

(A) by will, or

(B) by a disposition which is of such nature that if it were a transfer of property owned by the decedent, such property would be includible in the decedent's gross estate under sections 2035 to 2038, inclusive;

but the failure to exercise such a power or the complete release of such a power shall not be deemed an exercise thereof. If a general power of appointment created on or before October 21, 1942, has been partially released so that it is no longer a general power of appointment, the exercise of such power shall not be deemed to be the exercise of a general power of appointment if—

(i) such partial release occurred before November 1, 1951, or

(ii) the donee of such power was under a legal disability to release such power on October 21, 1942, and such partial release occurred not later than 6 months after the termination of such legal disability.

(2) Powers created after October 21, 1942. To the extent of any property with respect to which the decedent has at the time of his death a general power of appointment created after October 21, 1942, or with respect to which the decedent has at any time exercised or released such a power of appointment by a disposition which is of such nature that if it were a transfer of property owned by the decedent, such property would be includible in the decedent's gross estate under sections 2035 to 2038, inclusive. For purposes of this paragraph (2), the power of appointment shall be considered to exist on the date of the decedent's death even though the exercise of the power is subject to a precedent giving of notice or even though the exercise of the power takes effect only on the expiration of a stated period after its exercise, whether or not on or before the date of the decedent's death notice has been given or the power has been exercised.

(3) Creation of another power in certain cases. To the extent of any property with respect to which the decedent—

(A) by will, or

(B) by a disposition which is of such nature that if it were a transfer of property owned by the decedent such property would be includible in the decedent's gross estate under section 2035, 2036, or 2037,

exercises a power of appointment created after October 21, 1942, by creating another power of appointment which under the applicable local law can be validly exercised so as to postpone the vesting of any estate or interest in such property, or suspend the absolute ownership or power of alienation of such property, for a period ascertainable without regard to the date of the creation of the first power.

(b) Definitions. For purposes of subsection (a)—

(1) General power of appointment. The term "general power of appointment" means a power which is exercisable in favor of the decedent, his estate, his creditors, or the creditors of his estate; except that—

(A) A power to consume, invade, or appropriate property for the benefit of the decedent which is limited by an ascertainable standard relating to the health, education, support, or maintenance of the decedent shall not be deemed a general power of appointment.

(B) A power of appointment created on or before October 21, 1942, which is exercisable by the decedent only in conjunction with another person shall not be deemed a general power of appointment.

(C) In the case of a power of appointment created after October 21, 1942, which is exercisable by the decedent only in conjunction with another person—

(i) If the power is not exercisable by the decedent except in conjunction with the creator of the power—such power shall not be deemed a general power of appointment.

(ii) If the power is not exercisable by the decedent except in conjunction with a person having a substantial interest in the property, subject to the power, which is adverse to exercise of the power in favor of the decedent—such power shall not be deemed a general power of appointment. For the purposes of this clause a person who, after the death of the decedent, may be possessed of a power of appointment (with respect to the property subject to the decedent's power) which he may exercise in his own favor shall be deemed as having an interest in the property and such interest shall be deemed adverse to such exercise of the decedent's power.

(iii) If (after the application of clauses (i) and (ii)) the power is a general power of appointment and is exercisable in favor of such other person—such power shall be deemed a general power of appointment only in respect of a fractional part of the property subject to such power, such part to be determined by dividing the value of such property by the number of such persons (including the decedent) in favor of whom such power is exercisable.

For purposes of clauses (ii) and (iii), a power shall be deemed to be exercisable in favor of a person if it is exercisable in favor of such person, his estate, his creditors, or the creditors of his estate.

(2) Lapse of power. The lapse of a power of appointment created after October 21, 1942, during the life of the individual possessing the power shall be considered a release of such power. The preceding sentence shall apply with respect to the lapse of powers during any calendar year only to the extent that the property, which could have been appointed by exercise of such lapsed powers, exceeded in value, at the time of such lapse, the greater of the following amounts:

(A) $5,000, or

(B) 5 percent of the aggregate value, at the time of such lapse, of the assets out of which, or the proceeds of which, the exercise of the lapsed powers could have been satisfied.

(3) Date of creation of power. For purposes of this section, a power of appointment created by a will executed on or before October 21, 1942, shall be considered a power created on or before such date if the person executing such will dies before July 1, 1949, without having republished such will, by codicil or otherwise, after October 21, 1942.

Regulations

§ 20.2041–1 Powers of appointment; in general.

(a) Introduction. A decedent's gross estate includes under section 2041 the value of property in respect of which the decedent possessed, exercised, or released certain powers of appointment. This section contains rules of general application; § 20.2041–2 contains rules specifically applicable to general powers of appointment created on or before October 21, 1942; and § 20.2041–3 sets forth specific rules applicable to powers of appointment created after October 21, 1942.

(b) Definition of "power of appointment". (1) *In general.* The term "power of appointment" includes all powers which are in substance and effect powers of appointment regardless of the nomenclature used in creating the power and regardless of local property law connotations. For example, if a trust instrument provides that the beneficiary may appropriate or consume the principal of the trust, the power to consume or appropriate is a power of appointment. Similarly, a power given to a decedent to affect the beneficial enjoyment of trust property or its income by altering, amending, or revoking the trust instrument or terminating the trust is a power of appointment. If the community property laws of a State confer upon the wife a power of testamentary disposition over property in which she does not have a vested interest she is considered as having a power of appointment. A power in a donee to remove or discharge a trustee and appoint himself may be a power of appointment. For example, if under the terms of a trust instrument, the trustee or his successor has the power to appoint the principal of the trust for the benefit of individuals including himself, and the decedent has the unrestricted power to remove or discharge the trustee at any time and appoint any other person including himself, the decedent is considered as having a power of appointment. However, the decedent is not considered to have a power of appointment if he only had the power to appoint a successor, including himself, under limited conditions which did not exist at the time of his death, without an accompanying unrestricted power of removal. Similarly, a power to amend only the administrative provisions of a trust instrument, which cannot substantially affect the beneficial enjoyment of the trust property or income, is not a power of appointment. The mere power of management, investment, custody of assets, or the power to allocate receipts and disbursements as between income and principal, exercisable in a fiduciary capacity, whereby the holder has no power to enlarge or shift any of the beneficial interests therein except as an incidental consequence of the discharge of such fiduciary duties is not a power of appointment. Further, the right in a beneficiary of a trust to assent to a periodic accounting, thereby relieving the trustee from further accountability, is not a power of appointment if the right of assent does not consist of any power or right to enlarge or shift the beneficial interest of any beneficiary therein.

(2) *Relation to other sections.* For purposes of §§ 20.2041–1 to 20.2041–3, the term "power of appointment" does not include powers reserved by the decedent to himself within the concept of sections 2036 through 2038. (See §§ 20.2036–1 to 20.2038–1.) No provision of section 2041 or of §§ 20.2041–1 to 20.2041–3 is to be construed as in any way limiting the application of any other section of the Internal Revenue Code or of these regulations. The power of the owner of a property interest already possessed by him to dispose of his interest, and nothing more, is not a power of appointment, and the interest is includable in his gross estate to the extent it would be includable under section 2033 or some other provision of part III of subchapter A of chapter 11. For example, if a trust created by S provides for payment of the income to A for life with power in A to appoint the remainder by will and, in default of such appointment for payment of the income to A's widow, W, for her life and for payment of the remainder to A's estate, the value of A's interest in the remainder is includable in his gross estate under section 2033 regardless of its includability under section 2041.

(3) *Powers over a portion of property.* If a power of appointment exists as to part of an entire group of assets or only over a limited interest in property, section 2041 applies only to such part or interest. For example, if a trust created by S provides for the payment of income to A for life, then to W for life, with power in A to appoint the remainder by will and in default of appointment for payment of the remainder to B or his estate, and if A dies before W, section 2041 applies only to the value of the remainder interest excluding

W's life estate. If A dies after W, section 2041 would apply to the value of the entire property. If the power were only over one-half the remainder interest, section 2041 would apply only to one-half the value of the amounts described above.

(c) Definition of "general power of appointment". (1) *In general.* The term "general power of appointment" as defined in section 2041(b)(1) means any power of appointment exercisable in favor of the decedent, his estate, his creditors, or the creditors of his estate, except (i) joint powers, to the extent provided in §§ 20.2041–2 and 20.2041–3, and (ii) certain powers limited by an ascertainable standard, to the extent provided in subparagraph (2) of this paragraph. A power of appointment exercisable to meet the estate tax, or any other taxes, debts, or charges which are enforceable against the estate, is included within the meaning of a power of appointment exercisable in favor of the decedent's estate, his creditors, or the creditors of his estate. A power of appointment exercisable for the purpose of discharging a legal obligation of the decedent or for his pecuniary benefit is considered a power of appointment exercisable in favor of the decedent or his creditors. However, for purposes of §§ 20.2041–1 to 20.2041–3, a power of appointment not otherwise considered to be a general power of appointment is not treated as a general power of appointment merely by reason of the fact that an appointee may, in fact, be a creditor of the decedent or his estate. A power of appointment is not a general power if by its terms it is either—

(a) Exercisable only in favor of one or more designated persons or classes other than the decedent or his creditors, or the decedent's estate or the creditors of his estate, or

(b) Expressly not exercisable in favor of the decedent or his creditors, or the decedent's estate or the creditors of his estate.

A decedent may have two powers under the same instrument, one of which is a general power of appointment and the other of which is not. For example, a beneficiary may have a power to withdraw trust corpus during his life, and a testamentary power to appoint the corpus among his descendants. The testamentary power is not a general power of appointment.

(2) *Powers limited by an ascertainable standard.* A power to consume, invade, or appropriate income or corpus, or both, for the benefit of the decedent which is limited by an ascertainable standard relating to the health, education, support, or maintenance of the decedent is, by reason of section 2041(b)(1)(A), not a general power of appointment. A power is limited by such a standard if the extent of the holder's duty to exercise and not to exercise the power is reasonably measurable in terms of his needs for health, education, or support (or any combination of them). As used in this subparagraph, the words "support" and "maintenance" are synonymous and their meaning is not limited to the bare necessities of life. A power to use property for the comfort, welfare, or happiness of the holder of the power is not limited by the requisite standard. Examples of powers which are limited by the requisite standard are powers exercisable for the holder's "support," "support in reasonable comfort," "maintenance in health and reasonable comfort," "support in his accustomed manner of living," "education, including college and professional education," "health," and "medical, dental, hospital and nursing expenses and expenses of invalidism." In determining whether a power is limited by an ascertainable standard, it is immaterial whether the beneficiary is required to exhaust his other income before the power can be exercised.

(3) *Certain powers under wills of decedents dying between January 1 and April 2, 1948.* Section 210 of the Technical Changes Act of 1953 provides that if a decedent died after December 31, 1947, but before April 3, 1948, certain property interests described therein may, if the decedent's surviving spouse so elects, be accorded special treatment in the determination of the marital deduction to be allowed the decedent's estate under the provisions of section 812(e) of the Internal Revenue Code of 1939. See § 81.47a(h) of Regulations 105 (26 CFR (1939) 81.47a(h)). The section further provides that property affected by the election shall, for the purpose of inclusion in the surviving spouse's gross estate, be considered property with respect to which she has a general power of appointment. Therefore, notwithstanding any other provision of law or of §§ 20.2041–1 to 20.2041–3, if the present decedent (in her capacity as surviving spouse of a prior decedent) has made an election under section 210 of the Technical Changes Act of 1953, the property which was the subject of the election shall be considered as property with respect to which the present decedent has a general power of appointment

created after October 21, 1942, exercisable by deed or will, to the extent it was treated as an interest passing to the surviving spouse and not passing to any other person for the purpose of the marital deduction in the prior decedent's estate.

(d) Definition of "exercise". Whether a power of appointment is in fact exercised may depend upon local law. For example, the residuary clause of a will may be considered under local law as an exercise of a testamentary power of appointment in the absence of evidence of a contrary intention drawn from the whole of the testator's will. However, regardless of local law, a power of appointment is considered as exercised for purposes of section 2041 even though the exercise is in favor of the taker in default of appointment, and irrespective of whether the appointed interest and the interest in default of appointment are identical or whether the appointee renounces any right to take under the appointment. A power of appointment is also considered as exercised even though the disposition cannot take effect until the occurrence of an event after the exercise takes place, if the exercise is irrevocable and, as of the time of the exercise, the condition was not impossible of occurrence. For example, if property is left in trust to A for life, with a power in B to appoint the remainder by will, and B dies before A, exercising his power by appointing the remainder to C if C survives A, B is considered to have exercised his power if C is living at B's death. On the other hand, a testamentary power of appointment is not considered as exercised if it is exercised subject to the occurrence during the decedent's life of an express or implied condition which did not in fact occur. Thus, if in the preceding example, C dies before B, B's power of appointment would not be considered to have been exercised. Similarly, if a trust provides for income to A for life, remainder as A appoints by will, and A appoints a life estate in the property to B and does not otherwise exercise his power, but B dies before A, A's power is not considered to have been exercised.

(e) Time of creation of power. A power of appointment created by will is, in general, considered as created on the date of the testator's death. However, section 2041(b)(3) provides that a power of appointment created by a will executed on or before October 21, 1942, is considered a power created on or before that date if the testator dies before July 1, 1949, without having republished the will, by codicil or otherwise, after October 21, 1942. A power of appointment created by an inter vivos instrument is considered as created on the date the instrument takes effect. Such a power is not considered as created at some future date merely because it is not exercisable on the date the instrument takes effect, or because it is revocable, or because the identity of its holders is not ascertainable until after the date the instrument takes effect. However, if the holder of a power exercises it by creating a second power, the second power is considered as created at the time of the exercise of the first. The application of this paragraph may be illustrated by the following examples:

Example (1). A created a revocable trust before October 22, 1942, providing for payment of income to B for life with remainder as B shall appoint by will. Even though A dies after October 21, 1942, without having exercised his power of revocation, B's power of appointment is considered a power created before October 22, 1942.

Example (2). C created an irrevocable inter vivos trust before October 22, 1942, naming T as trustee and providing for payment of income to D for life with remainder to E. T was given the power to pay corpus to D and the power to appoint a successor trustee. If T resigns after October 21, 1942, and appoints D as successor trustee, D is considered to have a power of appointment created before October 22, 1942.

Example (3). F created an irrevocable inter vivos trust before October 22, 1942, providing for payment of income to G for life with remainder as G shall appoint by will, but in default of appointment income to H for life with remainder as H shall appoint by will. If G died after October 21, 1942, without having exercised his power of appointment, H's power of appointment is considered a power created before October 22, 1942, even though it was only a contingent interest until G's death.

Example (4). If in example (3) above G had exercised his power of appointment by creating a similar power in J, J's power of appointment would be considered a power created after October 21, 1942.

[T.D. 6296, 23 FR 4529, June 24, 1958, as amended by T.D. 6582, 26 FR 11861, Dec. 12, 1961]

§ 20.2041–2 Powers of appointment created on or before October 21, 1942. [*Omitted. Ed.*]

[T.D. 6296, 23 FR 4529, June 24, 1958]

§ 20.2041–3 Powers of appointment created after October 21, 1942.

(a) In general. (1) Property subject to a power of appointment created after October 21, 1942, is includable in the gross estate of the holder of the power under varying conditions depending on whether the power is (i) general in nature, (ii) possessed at death, or (iii) exercised or released. See paragraphs (b), (c), and (d) of § 20.2041–1 for the definition of various terms used in this section. See paragraph (c) of this section for the rules applicable to determine the extent to which joint powers created after October 21, 1942, are to be treated as general powers of appointment.

(2) If the power is a general power of appointment, the value of an interest in property subject to such a power is includable in a decedent's gross estate under section 2041(a)(2) if either—

(i) The decedent has the power at the time of his death (and the interest exists at the time of his death), or

(ii) The decedent exercised or released the power, or the power lapsed, under the circumstances and to the extent described in paragraph (d) of this section.

(3) If the power is not a general power of appointment, the value of property subject to the power is includable in the holder's gross estate under section 2041(a)(3) only if it is exercised to create a further power under certain circumstances (see paragraph (e) of this section).

(b) Existence of power at death. For purposes of section 2041(a)(2), a power of appointment is considered to exist on the date of a decedent's death even though the exercise of the power is subject to the precedent giving of notice, or even though the exercise of the power takes effect only on the expiration of a stated period after its exercise, whether or not on or before the decedent's death notice has been given or the power has been exercised. However, a power which by its terms is exercisable only upon the occurrence during the decedent's lifetime of an event or a contingency which did not in fact take place or occur during such time is not a power in existence on the date of the decedent's death. For example, if a decedent was given a general power of appointment exercisable only after he reached a certain age, only if he survived another person, or only if he died without descendants, the power would not be in existence on the date of the decedent's death if the condition precedent to its exercise had not occurred.

(c) Joint powers created after October 21, 1942. The treatment of a power of appointment created after October 21, 1942, which is exercisable only in conjunction with another person is governed by section 2041(b)(1)(C), which provides as follows:

(1) Such a power is not considered a general power of appointment if it is not exercisable by the decedent except with the consent or joinder of the creator of the power.

(2) Such power is not considered a general power of appointment if it is not exercisable by the decedent except with the consent or joinder of a person having a substantial interest in the property subject to the power which is adverse to the exercise of the power in favor of the decedent, his estate, his creditors, or the creditors of his estate. An interest adverse to the exercise of a power is considered as substantial if its value in relation to the total value of the property subject to the power is not insignificant. For this purpose, the interest is to be valued in accordance with the actuarial principles set forth in § 20.2031–7 or, if it is not susceptible to valuation under those provisions, in accordance with the general principles set forth in § 20.2031–1. A taker in default of appointment under a power has an interest which is adverse to an exercise of the power. A coholder of the power has no adverse interest merely because of his joint possession of the power nor merely because he is a permissible appointee under a power. However, a coholder of a power is considered as having an adverse interest where he may possess the power after the decedent's death and may exercise it at that time in favor of himself, his estate, his creditors, or the creditors of his estate. Thus, for example, if X, Y, and Z held a power jointly to appoint among a group of persons which includes themselves and if on the death of X the power will pass to Y and Z jointly, then Y and Z are considered to have interests adverse to the exercise of the power in favor of X. Similarly, if on Y's death the power will pass to Z, Z is considered to have an interest adverse to the exercise of the power in favor of Y. The application of this subparagraph may be further illustrated by the follow-

ing additional examples in each of which it is assumed that the value of the interest in question is substantial:

Example (1). The decedent and R were trustees of a trust under the terms of which the income was to be paid to the decedent for life and then to M for life, and the remainder was to be paid to R. The trustees had power to distribute corpus to the decedent. Since R's interest was substantially adverse to an exercise of the power in favor of the decedent the latter did not have a general power of appointment. If M and the decedent were the trustees, M's interest would likewise have been adverse.

Example (2). The decedent and L were trustees of a trust under the terms of which the income was to be paid to L for life and then to M for life, and the remainder was to be paid to the decedent. The trustees had power to distribute corpus to the decedent during L's life. Since L's interest was adverse to an exercise of the power in favor of the decedent, the decedent did not have a general power of appointment. If the decedent and M were the trustees, M's interest would likewise have been adverse.

Example (3). The decedent and L were trustees of a trust under the terms of which the income was to be paid to L for life. The trustees could designate whether corpus was to be distributed to the decedent or to A after L's death. L's interest was not adverse to an exercise of the power in favor of the decedent, and the decedent therefore had a general power of appointment.

(3) A power which is exercisable only in conjunction with another person, and which after application of the rules set forth in subparagraphs (1) and (2) of this paragraph constitutes a general power of appointment, will be treated as though the holders of the power who are permissible appointees of the property were joint owners of property subject to the power. The decedent, under this rule, will be treated as possessed of a general power of appointment over an aliquot share of the property to be determined with reference to the number of joint holders, including the decedent, who (or whose estates or creditors) are permissible appointees. Thus, for example, if X, Y, and Z hold an unlimited power jointly to appoint among a group of persons, including themselves, but on the death of X the power does not pass to Y and Z jointly, then Y and Z are not considered to have interests adverse to the exercise of the power in favor of X. In this case X is considered to possess a general power of appointment as to one-third of the property subject to the power.

(d) Releases, lapses, and disclaimers of general powers of appointment. (1) Property subject to a general power of appointment created after October 21, 1942, is includable in the gross estate of a decedent under section 2041(a)(2) even though he does not have the power at the date of his death, if during his life he exercised or released the power under circumstances such that, if the property subject to the power had been owned and transferred by the decedent, the property would be includable in the decedent's gross estate under section 2035, 2036, 2037, or 2038. Further, section 2041(b)(2) provides that the lapse of a power of appointment is considered to be a release of the power to the extent set forth in subparagraph (3) of this paragraph. A release of a power of appointment need not be formal or express in character. The principles set forth in § 20.2041–2 for determining the application of the pertinent provisions of sections 2035 through 2038 to a particular exercise of a power of appointment are applicable for purposes of determining whether or not an exercise or release of a power of appointment created after October 21, 1942, causes the property to be included in a decedent's gross estate under section 2041(a)(2). If a general power of appointment created after October 21, 1942, is partially released, a subsequent exercise or release of the power under circumstances described in the first sentence of this subparagraph, or its possession at death will nevertheless cause the property subject to the power to be included in the gross estate of the holder of the power.

(2) Section 2041(a)(2) is not applicable to the complete release of a general power of appointment created after October 21, 1942, whether exercisable during life or by will, if the release was not made in contemplation of death within the meaning of section 2035, and if after the release the holder of the power retained no interest in or control over the property subject to the power which would cause the property to be included in his gross estate under sections 2036 through 2038 if the property had been transferred by the holder.

(3) The failure to exercise a power of appointment created after October 21, 1942, within a specified time, so that the power lapses, constitutes a release of the power. However, section 2041(b)(2) provides

that such a lapse of a power of appointment during any calendar year during the decedent's life is treated as a release for purposes of inclusion of property in the gross estate under section 2041(a)(2) only to the extent that the property which could have been appointed by exercise of the lapsed power exceeds the greater of (i) $5,000 or (ii) 5 percent of the aggregate value, at the time of the lapse, of the assets out of which, or the proceeds of which, the exercise of the lapsed power could have been satisfied. For example, assume that A transferred $200,000 worth of securities in trust providing for payment of income to B for life with remainder to B's issue. Assume further that B was given a noncumulative right to withdraw $10,000 a year from the principal of the trust fund (which neither increased nor decreased in value prior to B's death). In such case, the failure of B to exercise his right of withdrawal will not result in estate tax with respect to the power to withdraw $10,000 which lapses each year before the year of B's death. At B's death there will be included in his gross estate the $10,000 which he was entitled to withdraw for the year in which his death occurs less any amount which he may have taken during that year. However, if in the above example B had possessed the right to withdraw $15,000 of the principal annually, the failure to exercise such power in any year will be considered a release of the power to the extent of the excess of the amount subject to withdrawal over 5 percent of the trust fund (in this example, $5,000, assuming that the trust fund is worth $200,000 at the time of the lapse). Since each lapse is treated as though B had exercised dominion over the trust property by making a transfer of principal reserving the income therefrom for his life, the value of the trust property (but only to the extent of the excess of the amount subject to withdrawal over 5 percent of the trust fund) is includable in B's gross estate (unless before B's death he has disposed of his right to the income under circumstances to which sections 2035 through 2038 would not be applicable). The extent to which the value of the trust property is included in the decedent's gross estate is determined as provided in subparagraph (4) of this paragraph.

(4) The purpose of section 2041(b)(2) is to provide a determination, as of the date of the lapse of the power, of the proportion of the property over which the power lapsed which is an exempt disposition for estate tax purposes and the proportion which, if the other requirements of sections 2035 through 2038 are satisfied, will be considered as a taxable disposition. Once the taxable proportion of any disposition at the date of lapse has been determined, the valuation of that proportion as of the date of the decedent's death (or, if the executor has elected the alternate valuation method under section 2032, the value as of the date therein provided), is to be ascertained in accordance with the principles which are applicable to the valuation of transfers of property by the decedent under the corresponding provisions of sections 2035 through 2038. For example, if the life beneficiary of a trust had a right exercisable only during one calendar year to draw down $50,000 from the corpus of a trust, which he did not exercise, and if at the end of the year the corpus was worth $800,000, the taxable portion over which the power lapsed is $10,000 (the excess of $50,000 over 5 percent of the corpus), or 1/80 of the total value. On the decedent's death, if the total value of the corpus of the trust (excluding income accumulated after the lapse of the power) on the applicable valuation date was $1,200,000, $15,000 (1/80 of $1,200,000) would be includable in the decedent's gross estate. However, if the total value was then $600,000, only $7,500 (1/80 of $600,000) would be includable.

(5) If the failure to exercise a power, such as a right of withdrawal, occurs in more than a single year, the proportion of the property over which the power lapsed which is treated as a taxable disposition will be determined separately for each such year. The aggregate of the taxable proportions for all such years, valued in accordance with the above principles, will be includable in the gross estate by reason of the lapse. The includable amount, however, shall not exceed the aggregate value of the assets out of which, or the proceeds of which, the exercise of the power could have been satisfied, valued as of the date of the decedent's death (or, if the executor has elected the alternate valuation method under section 2032, the value as of the date therein provided).

(6)(i) A disclaimer or renunciation of a general power of appointment created in a transfer made after December 31, 1976, is not considered to be the release of the power if the disclaimer or renunciation is a qualified disclaimer as described in section 2518 and the corresponding regulations. For rules relating to when the transfer creating the power occurs, see § 25.2518–2(c)(3) of this chapter. If the disclaimer or renunciation is not a qualified disclaimer, it is considered a release of the power by the disclaimant.

(ii) The disclaimer or renunciation of a general power of appointment created in a taxable transfer before January 1, 1977, in the person disclaiming is not considered to be a release of the power. The disclaimer or renunciation must be unequivocal and effective under local law. A disclaimer is a complete and unqualified refusal to accept the rights to which one is entitled. There can be no disclaimer or renunciation of a power after its acceptance. In the absence of facts to the contrary, the failure to renounce or disclaim within a reasonable time after learning of its existence will be presumed to constitute an acceptance of the power. In any case where a power is purported to be disclaimed or renounced as to only a portion of the property subject to the power, the determination as to whether or not there has been a complete and unqualified refusal to accept the rights to which one is entitled will depend on all the facts and circumstances of the particular case, taking into account the recognition and effectiveness of such a disclaimer under local law. Such rights refer to the incidents of the power and not to other interests of the decedent in the property. If effective under local law, the power may be disclaimed or renounced without disclaiming or renouncing such other interests.

(iii) The first and second sentences of paragraph (d)(6)(i) of this section are applicable for transfers creating the power to be disclaimed made on or after December 31, 1997.

(e) Successive powers. (1) Property subject to a power of appointment created after October 21, 1942, which is not a general power, is includable in the gross estate of the holder of the power under section 2041(a)(3) if the power is exercised, and if both of the following conditions are met:

(i) If the exercise is (a) by will, or (b) by a disposition which is of such nature that if it were a transfer of property owned by the decedent, the property would be includable in the decedent's gross estate under sections 2035 through 2037; and

(ii) If the power is exercised by creating another power of appointment which, under the terms of the instruments creating and exercising the first power and under applicable local law, can be validly exercised so as to (a) postpone the vesting of any estate or interest in the property for a period ascertainable without regard to the date of the creation of the first power, or (b) (if the applicable rule against perpetuities is stated in terms of suspension of ownership or of the power of alienation, rather than of vesting) suspend the absolute ownership or the power of alienation of the property for a period ascertainable without regard to the date of the creation of the first power.

(2) For purposes of the application of section 2041(a)(3), the value of the property subject to the second power of appointment is considered to be its value unreduced by any precedent or subsequent interest which is not subject to the second power. Thus, if a decedent has a power to appoint by will $100,000 to a group of persons consisting of his children and grandchildren and exercises the power by making an outright appointment of $75,000 and by giving one appointee a power to appoint $25,000, no more than $25,000 will be includable in the decedent's gross estate under section 2041(a)(3). If, however, the decedent appoints the income from the entire fund to a beneficiary for life with power in the beneficiary to appoint the remainder by will, the entire $100,000 will be includable in the decedent's gross estate under section 2041(a)(3) if the exercise of the second power can validly postpone the vesting of any estate or interest in the property or can suspend the absolute ownership or power of alienation of the property for a period ascertainable without regard to the date of the creation of the first power.

(f) Examples. The application of this section may be further illustrated by the following examples, in each of which it is assumed, unless otherwise stated, that S has transferred property in trust after October 21, 1942, with the remainder payable to R at L's death, and that neither L nor R has any interest in or power over the enjoyment of the trust property except as is indicated separately in each example:

Example (1). Income is directed to be paid to L during his lifetime at the end of each year, if living. L has an unrestricted power during his lifetime to cause the income to be distributed to any other person, but no power to cause it to be accumulated. At L's death, no part of the trust property is includable in L's gross estate since L had a power to dispose of only his income interest, a right otherwise possessed by him.

Example (2). Income is directed to be accumulated during L's life but L has a noncumulative power to distribute $10,000 of each year's income to himself. Unless L's power is limited to himself. Unless L's power is limited by an ascertainable standard (relating to his health, etc.), as defined in paragraph (c)(2) of § 20.2041–1, he has a general power of appointment over $10,000 of each year's income, the lapse of which may cause a portion of any income not distributed to be included in his gross estate under section 2041. See subparagraphs (3), (4), and (5) of paragraph (d) of this section. Thus, if the trust income during the year amounts to $20,000, L's failure to distribute any of the income to himself constitutes a lapse as to $5,000 (i.e., the amount by which $10,000 exceeds $5,000). If L's power were cumulative (i.e., if the power did not lapse at the end of each year but lapsed only by reason of L's death), the total accumulations which L chose not to distribute to himself immediately before his death would be includable in his gross estate under section 2041.

Example (3). L is entitled to all the income during his lifetime and has an unrestricted power to cause corpus to be distributed to himself. L had a general power of appointment over the corpus of the trust, and the entire corpus as of the time of his death is includable in his gross estate under section 2041.

Example (4). Income was payable to L during his lifetime. R has an unrestricted power to cause corpus to be distributed to L. R dies before L. In such case, R has only a power to dispose of his remainder interest, the value of which is includable in his gross estate under section 2033, and nothing in addition would be includable under section 2041. If in this example R's remainder were contingent on his surviving L, nothing would be includable in his gross estate under either section 2033 or 2041. While R would have a power of appointment, it would not be a general power.

Example (5). Income was payable to L during his lifetime. R has an unrestricted power to cause corpus to be distributed to himself. R dies before L. While the value of R's remainder interest is includable in his gross estate under section 2033, R also has a general power of appointment over the entire trust corpus. Under such circumstances, the entire value of the trust corpus is includable in R's gross estate under section 2041.

[T.D. 6296, 23 FR 4529, June 24, 1958; 25 FR 14021, Dec. 31, 1960; T.D. 8095, 51 FR 28367, Aug. 7, 1986; T.D. 8744, 62 FR 68184, Dec. 31, 1997]

§ 2042. Proceeds of Life Insurance

The value of the gross estate shall include the value of all property—

(1) Receivable by the executor. To the extent of the amount receivable by the executor as insurance under policies on the life of the decedent.

(2) Receivable by other beneficiaries. To the extent of the amount receivable by all other beneficiaries as insurance under policies on the life of the decedent with respect to which the decedent possessed at his death any of the incidents of ownership, exercisable either alone or in conjunction with any other person. For purposes of the preceding sentence, the term "incident of ownership" includes a reversionary interest (whether arising by the express terms of the policy or other instrument or by operation of law) only if the value of such reversionary interest exceeded 5 percent of the value of the policy immediately before the death of the decedent. As used in this paragraph, the term "reversionary interest" includes a possibility that the policy, or the proceeds of the policy, may return to the decedent or his estate, or may be subject to a power of disposition by him. The value of a reversionary interest at any time shall be determined (without regard to the fact of the decedent's death) by usual methods of valuation, including the use of tables of mortality and actuarial principles, pursuant to regulations prescribed by the Secretary. In determining the value of a possibility that the policy or proceeds thereof may be subject to a power of disposition by the decedent, such possibility shall be valued as if it were a possibility that such policy or proceeds may return to the decedent or his estate.

Regulation

§ 20.2042–1 Proceeds of life insurance.

(a) In general. (1) Section 2042 provides for the inclusion in a decedent's gross estate of the proceeds of insurance on the decedent's life (i) receivable by or for the benefit of the estate (see paragraph (b) of this section) and (ii) receivable by other beneficiaries (see paragraph (c) of this section). The term "insurance" refers to life insurance of every description, including death benefits paid by fraternal beneficial societies operating under the lodge system.

(2) Proceeds of life insurance which are not includable in the gross estate under section 2042 may, depending upon the facts of the particular case, be includable under some other section of part III of subchapter A of chapter 11. For example, if the decedent possessed incidents of ownership in an insurance policy on his life but gratuitously transferred all rights in the policy in contemplation of death, the proceeds would be includable under section 2035. Section 2042 has no application to the inclusion in the gross estate of the value of rights in an insurance policy on the life of a person other than the decedent, or the value of rights in a combination annuity contract and life insurance policy on the decedent's life (i.e., a "retirement income" policy with death benefit or an "endowment" policy) under which there was no insurance element at the time of the decedent's death (see paragraph (d) of § 20.2039–1).

(3) Except as provided in paragraph (c)(6), the amount to be included in the gross estate under section 2042 is the full amount receivable under the policy. If the proceeds of the policy are made payable to a beneficiary in the form of an annuity for life or for a term of years, the amount to be included in the gross estate is the one sum payable at death under an option which could have been exercised either by the insured or by the beneficiary, or if no option was granted, the sum used by the insurance company in determining the amount of the annuity.

(b) Receivable by or for the benefit of the estate. (1) Section 2042 requires the inclusion in the gross estate of the proceeds of insurance on the decedent's life receivable by the executor or administrator, or payable to the decedent's estate. It makes no difference whether or not the estate is specifically named as the beneficiary under the terms of the policy. Thus, if under the terms of an insurance policy the proceeds are receivable by another beneficiary but are subject to an obligation, legally binding upon the other beneficiary, to pay taxes, debts, or other charges enforceable against the estate, then the amount of such proceeds required for the payment in full (to the extent of the beneficiary's obligation) of such taxes, debts, or other charges is includable in the gross estate. Similarly, if the decedent purchased an insurance policy in favor of another person or a corporation as collateral security for a loan or other accommodation, its proceeds are considered to be receivable for the benefit of the estate. The amount of the loan outstanding at the date of the decedent's death, with interest accrued to that date, will be deductible in determining the taxable estate. See § 20.2053–4.

(2) If the proceeds of an insurance policy made payable to the decedent's estate are community assets under the local community property law and, as a result, one-half of the proceeds belongs to the decedent's spouse, then only one-half of the proceeds is considered to be receivable by or for the benefit of the decedent's estate.

(c) Receivable by other beneficiaries. (1) Section 2042 requires the inclusion in the gross estate of the proceeds of insurance on the decedent's life not receivable by or for the benefit of the estate if the decedent possessed at the date of his death any of the incidents of ownership in the policy, exercisable either alone or in conjunction with any other person. However, if the decedent did not possess any of such incidents of ownership at the time of his death nor transfer them in contemplation of death, no part of the proceeds would be includible in his gross estate under section 2042. Thus, if the decedent owned a policy of insurance on his life and, 4 years before his death, irrevocably assigned his entire interest in the policy to his wife retaining no reversionary interest therein (see subparagraph (3) of this paragraph), the proceeds of the policy would not be includible in his gross estate under section 2042.

(2) For purposes of this paragraph, the term "incidents of ownership" is not limited in its meaning to ownership of the policy in the technical legal sense. Generally speaking, the term has reference to the right of the insured or his estate to the economic benefits of the policy. Thus, it includes the power to change

the beneficiary, to surrender or cancel the policy, to assign the policy, to revoke an assignment, to pledge the policy for a loan, or to obtain from the insurer a loan against the surrender value of the policy, etc. See subparagraph (6) of this paragraph for rules relating to the circumstances under which incidents of ownership held by a corporation are attributable to a decedent through his stock ownership.

(3) The term "incidents of ownership" also includes a reversionary interest in the policy or its proceeds, whether arising by the express terms of the policy or other instrument or by operation of law, but only if the value of the reversionary interest immediately before the death of the decedent exceeded 5 percent of the value of the policy.

As used in this subparagraph, the term "reversionary interest" includes a possibility that the policy or its proceeds may return to the decedent or his estate and a possibility that the policy or its proceeds may become subject to a power of disposition by him. In order to determine whether or not the value of a reversionary interest immediately before the death of the decedent exceeded 5 percent of the value of the policy, the principles contained in paragraph (c)(3) and (4) of § 20.2037–1, insofar as applicable, shall be followed under this subparagraph. In that connection, there must be specifically taken into consideration any incidents of ownership held by others immediately before the decedent's death which would affect the value of the reversionary interest. For example, the decedent would not be considered to have a reversionary interest in the policy of a value in excess of 5 percent if the power to obtain the cash surrender value existed in some other person immediately before the decedent's death and was exercisable by such other person alone and in all events. The terms "reversionary interest" and "incidents of ownership" do not include the possibility that the decedent might receive a policy or its proceeds by inheritance through the estate of another person, or as a surviving spouse under a statutory right of election or a similar right.

(4) A decedent is considered to have an "incident of ownership" in an insurance policy on his life held in trust if, under the terms of the policy, the decedent (either alone or in conjunction with another person or persons) has the power (as trustee or otherwise) to change the beneficial ownership in the policy or its proceeds, or the time or manner of enjoyment thereof, even though the decedent has no beneficial interest in the trust. Moreover, assuming the decedent created the trust, such a power may result in the inclusion in the decedent's gross estate under section 2036 or 2038 of other property transferred by the decedent to the trust if, for example, the decedent has the power to surrender the insurance policy and if the income otherwise used to pay premiums on the policy would become currently payable to a beneficiary of the trust in the event that the policy were surrendered.

(5) As an additional step in determining whether or not a decedent possessed any incidents of ownership in a policy or any part of a policy, regard must be given to the effect of the State or other applicable law upon the terms of the policy. For example, assume that the decedent purchased a policy of insurance on his life with funds held by him and his surviving wife as community property, designating their son as beneficiary but retaining the right to surrender the policy. Under the local law, the proceeds upon surrender would have inured to the marital community. Assuming that the policy is not surrendered and that the son receives the proceeds on the decedent's death, the wife's transfer of her one-half interest in the policy was not considered absolute before the decedent's death. Upon the wife's prior death, one-half of the value of the policy would have been included in her gross estate. Under these circumstances, the power of surrender possessed by the decedent as agent for his wife with respect to one-half of the policy is not, for purposes of this section, an "incident of ownership", and the decedent is, therefore, deemed to possess an incident of ownership in only one-half of the policy.

(6) In the case of economic benefits of a life insurance policy on the decedent's life that are reserved to a corporation of which the decedent is the sole or controlling stockholders, the corporations' incidents of ownership will not be attributed to the decedent through his stock ownership to the extent the proceeds of the policy are payable to the corporation. Any proceeds payable to a third party for a valid business purpose, such as in satisfaction of a business debt of the corporation, so that the net worth of the corporation is increased by the amount of such proceeds, shall be deemed to be payable to the corporation for purposes of the preceding sentence. See § 20.2031–2(f) for a rule providing that the proceeds of certain life insurance policies shall be considered in determining the

value of the decedent's stock. Except as hereinafter provided with respect to a group-term life insurance policy, if any part of the proceeds of the policy are not payable to or for the benefit of the corporation, and thus are not taken into account in valuing the decedent's stock holdings in the corporation for purposes of section 2031, any incidents of ownership held by the corporation as to that part of the proceeds will be attributed to the decedent through his stock ownership where the decedent is the sole or controlling stockholder. Thus, for example, if the decedent is the controlling stockholder in a corporation, and the corporation owns a life insurance policy on his life, the proceeds of which are payable to the decedent's spouse, the incidents of ownership held by the corporation will be attributed to the decedent through his stock ownership and the proceeds will be included in his gross estate under section 2042. If in this example the policy proceeds had been payable 40 percent to decedent's spouse and 60 percent to the corporation, only 40 percent of the proceeds would be included in decedent's gross estate under section 2042. For purposes of this subparagraph, the decedent will not be deemed to be the controlling stockholder of a corporation unless, at the time of his death, he owned stock possessing more than 50 percent of the total combined voting power of the corporation. Solely for purposes of the preceding sentence, a decedent shall be considered to be the owner of only the stock with respect to which legal title was held, at the time of his death, by (i) the decedent (or his agent or nominee); (ii) the decedent and another person jointly (but only the proportionate number of shares which corresponds to the portion of the total consideration which is considered to be furnished by the decedent for purposes of section 2040 and the regulations thereunder); and (iii) by a trustee of a voting trust (to the extent of the decedent's beneficial interest therein) or any other trust with respect to which the decedent was treated as an owner under subpart E, part I, subchapter J, chapter 1 of the Code immediately prior to his death. In the case of group-term life insurance, as defined in the regulations under section 79, the power to surrender or cancel a policy held by a corporation shall not be attributed to any decedent through his stock ownership.

[T.D. 6296, 23 FR 4529, June 24, 1958; 25 FR 14021, Dec. 31, 1960 as amended by T.D. 7312, 39 FR 14949, April 29, 1974; T.D. 7623, 44 FR 28800, May 17, 1979]

§ 2043. Transfers for Insufficient Consideration

(a) In general. If any one of the transfers, trusts, interests, rights, or powers enumerated and described in sections 2035 to 2038, inclusive, and section 2041 is made, created, exercised, or relinquished for a consideration in money or money's worth, but is not a bona fide sale for an adequate and full consideration in money or money's worth, there shall be included in the gross estate only the excess of the fair market value at the time of death of the property otherwise to be included on account of such transaction, over the value of the consideration received therefor by the decedent.

(b) Marital rights not treated as consideration.

(1) In general. For purposes of this chapter, a relinquishment or promised relinquishment of dower or curtesy, or of a statutory estate created in lieu of dower or curtesy, or of other marital rights in the decedent's property or estate, shall not be considered to any extent a consideration "in money or money's worth".

(2) Exception. For purposes of section 2053 (relating to expenses, indebtedness, and taxes), a transfer of property which satisfies the requirements of paragraph (1) of section 2516 (relating to certain property settlements) shall be considered to be made for an adequate and full consideration in money or money's worth.

Regulation

§ 20.2043–1 Transfers for insufficient consideration.

(a) In general. The transfers, trusts, interests, rights or powers enumerated and described in sections 2035 through 2038 and section 2041 are not subject to the Federal estate tax if made, created, exercised, or relinquished in a transaction which constituted a bona fide sale for an adequate and full consideration in money or money's worth. To constitute a bona fide sale for an adequate and full consideration in money or money's worth, the transfer must have been made in good faith, and the price must have been an adequate and full equivalent reducible to a money value. If the price was less than such a consideration, only the excess of the fair market value of the property (as of the applicable valuation date) over the price received by the decedent is included in ascertaining the value of his gross estate.

(b) Marital rights and support obligations. For purposes of chapter 11, a relinquishment or promised relinquishment or dower, curtesy, or of a statutory estate created in lieu of dower or curtesy, or of other marital rights in the decedent's property or estate, is not to any extent a consideration in "money or money's worth."

[T.D. 6296, 23 FR 4529, June 24, 1958]

§ 2044. Certain Property for Which Marital Deduction was Previously Allowed

(a) General rule. The value of the gross estate shall include the value of any property to which this section applies in which the decedent had a qualifying income interest for life.

(b) Property to which this section applies. This section applies to any property if—

(1) a deduction was allowed with respect to the transfer of such property to the decedent—

(A) under section 2056 by reason of subsection (b)(7) thereof, or

(B) under section 2523 by reason of subsection (f) thereof, and

(2) section 2519 (relating to dispositions of certain life estates) did not apply with respect to a disposition by the decedent of part or all of such property.

(c) Property treated as having passed from decedent. For purposes of this chapter and chapter 13, property includible in the gross estate of the decedent under subsection (a) shall be treated as property passing from the decedent.

Regulations

§ 20.2044–1 Certain property for which marital deduction was previously allowed.

(a) In general. Section 2044 generally provides for the inclusion in the gross estate of property in which the decedent had a qualifying income interest for life and for which a deduction was allowed under section 2056(b)(7) or 2523(f). The value of the property included in the gross estate under section 2044 is not reduced by the amount of any section 2503(b) exclusion that applied to the transfer creating the interest. See section 2207A, regarding the right of recovery against the persons receiving the property that is applicable in certain cases.

(b) Passed from. For purposes of section 1014 and chapters 11 and 13 of subtitle B of the Internal Revenue Code, property included in a decedent's gross estate under section 2044 is considered to have been acquired from or to have passed from the decedent to the person receiving the property upon the decedent's death. Thus, for example, the property is treated as passing from the decedent for purposes of determining the availability of the charitable deduction under section 2055, the marital deduction under section 2056, and special use valuation under section 2032A. In addition, the tax imposed on property includible under section 2044 is eligible for the installment payment of estate tax under section 6166.

(c) Presumption. Unless established to the contrary, section 2044 applies to the entire value of the trust at the surviving spouse's death. If a marital deduction is taken on either the estate or gift tax return with respect to the transfer which created the qualifying income interest, it is presumed that the deduction was allowed for purposes of section 2044. To avoid the inclusion of property in the decedent-spouse's gross estate under this section, the executor of the spouse's estate must establish that a deduction was not taken for the transfer which created the qualifying income interest. For example, to establish that a deduction was not taken, the executor may produce a copy of the estate or gift tax return filed with respect to the transfer by the first spouse or the first spouse's estate establishing that no deduction was taken under section 2523(f) or section 2056(b)(7). In addition, the executor may establish that no return was filed on the original transfer by the decedent because the value of the first spouse's gross estate was below the threshold requirement for filing under section 6018. Similarly, the executor could establish that the transfer creating the decedent's qualifying income interest for life was made before the effective date of section 2056(b)(7) or section 2523(f).

(d) Amount included. (1) *In general.* The amount included under this section is the value of the entire interest in which the decedent had a qualifying income interest for life, determined as of the date of the decedent's death (or the alternate valuation date, if applicable). If, in connection with the transfer of property that created the decedent's qualifying income interest for life, a deduction was allowed under section 2056(b)(7) or section 2523(f) for less than the entire interest in the property (i.e., for a fractional or percentage share of the entire interest in the transferred property), the amount includible in the decedent's gross estate under this section is equal to the fair market value of the entire interest in the property on the date of the decedent's death (or the alternate valuation date, if applicable) multiplied by the fractional or percentage share of the interest for which the deduction was taken.

(2) *Inclusion of income.* If any income from the property for the period between the date of the transfer creating the decedent-spouse's interest and the date of the decedent-spouse's death has not been distributed before the decedent-spouse's death, the undistributed income is included in the decedent-spouse's gross estate under this section to the extent that the income is not so included under any other section of the Internal Revenue Code.

(3) *Reduction of includible share in certain cases.* If only a fractional or percentage share is includible under this section, the includible share is appropriately reduced if—

(i) The decedent-spouse's interest was in a trust and distributions of principal were made to the spouse during the spouse's lifetime;

(ii) The trust provides that the distributions are to be made from the qualified terminable interest share of the trust; and

(iii) The executor of the decedent-spouse's estate can establish the reduction in that share based on the fair market value of the trust assets at the time of each distribution.

(4) *Interest in previously severed trust.* If the decedent-spouse's interest was in a trust consisting of only qualified terminable interest property and the trust was severed (in compliance with § 20.2056(b)–7(b) or § 25.2523(f)–1(b) of this chapter) from a trust that, after the severance, held only property that was not qualified terminable interest property, only the value of the property in the severed portion of the trust is includible in the decedent-spouse's gross estate.

(e) Examples. The following examples illustrate the principles in paragraphs (a) through (d) of this section, where the decedent, D, was survived by spouse, S.

Example (1). Inclusion of trust subject to election. Under D's will, assets valued at $800,000 in D's gross estate (net of debts, expenses and other charges, including death taxes, payable from the property) passed in trust with income payable to S for life. Upon S's death, the trust principal is to be distributed to D's children. D's executor elected under section 2056(b)(7) to treat the entire trust property as qualified terminable interest property and claimed a marital deduction of $800,000. S made no disposition of the income interest during S's lifetime under section 2519. On the date of S's death, the fair market value of the trust property was $740,000. S's executor did not elect the alternate valuation date. The amount included in S's gross estate pursuant to section 2044 is $740,000.

Example (2). Inclusion of trust subject to partial election. The facts are the same as in Example 1, except that D's executor elected under section 2056(b)(7) with respect to only 50 percent of the value of the trust ($400,000). Consequently, only the equivalent portion of the trust is included in S's gross estate; i.e., $370,000 (50 percent of $740,000).

Example (3). Spouse receives qualifying income interest in a fraction of trust income. Under D's will, assets valued at $800,000 in D's gross estate (net of debts, expenses and other charges, including death taxes, payable from the property) passed in trust with 20 percent of the trust income payable to S for S's life. The will provides that the trust principal is to be distributed to D's children upon S's death. D's executor elected to deduct, pursuant to section 2056(b)(7), 50 percent of the amount for which the election could be made; i.e., $80,000 (50 percent of 20 percent of $800,000). Consequently, on the death of S, only the equivalent portion of the trust is included in S's gross estate; i.e., $74,000 (50 percent of 20 percent of $740,000).

Example (4). Distribution of corpus during spouse's lifetime. The facts are the same as in Example 3, except that S was entitled to receive all the trust income but the executor of D's estate elected under section 2056(b)(7) with respect to only 50 percent of the value of the trust ($400,000). Pursuant to authority in the will, the trustee made a discretionary distribution of $100,000 of principal to S in 1995 and charged the entire distribution to the qualified terminable interest share. Immediately prior to the distribution, the fair market value of the trust property was $1,100,000 and the qualified terminable interest portion of the trust was 50 percent. Immediately after the distribution, the qualified terminable interest portion of the trust was 45 percent ($450,000 divided by $1,000,000). Provided S's executor can establish the relevant facts, the amount included in S's gross estate is $333,000 (45 percent of $740,000).

Example (5). Spouse assigns a portion of income interest during life. Under D's will, assets valued at $800,000 in D's gross estate (net of debts, expenses and other charges, including death taxes, payable from the property) passed in trust with all the income payable to S, for S's life. The will provides that the trust principal is to be distributed to D's children upon S's death. D's executor elected under section 2056(b)(7) to treat the entire trust property as qualified terminable interest property and claimed a marital deduction of $800,000. During the term of the trust, S transfers to C the right to 40 percent of the income from the trust for S's life. Because S is treated as transferring the entire remainder interest in the trust corpus under section 2519 (as well as 40 percent of the income interest under section 2511), no part of the trust is includible in S's gross estate under section 2044. However, if S retains until death an income interest in 60 percent of the trust corpus (which corpus is treated pursuant to section 2519 as having been transferred by S for both gift and estate tax purposes), 60 percent of the property will be includible in S's gross estate under section 2036(a) and a corresponding adjustment is made in S's adjusted taxable gifts.

Example (6). Inter vivos trust subject to election under section 2523(f). D transferred $800,000 to a trust providing that trust income is to be paid annually to S, for S's life. The trust provides that upon S's death, $100,000 of principal is to be paid to X charity and the remaining principal distributed to D's children. D elected to treat all of the property transferred to the trust as qualified terminable interest property under section 2523(f). At the time of S's death, the fair market value of the trust is $1,000,000. S's executor does not elect the alternate valuation date. The amount included in S's gross estate is $1,000,000; i.e., the fair market value at S's death of the entire trust property. The $100,000 that passes to X charity on S's death is treated as a transfer by S to X charity for purposes of section 2055. Therefore, S's estate is allowed a charitable deduction for the $100,000 transferred from the trust to the charity to the same extent that a deduction would be allowed by section 2055 for a bequest by S to X charity.

Example (7). Spousal interest in the form of an annuity. D died prior to October 24, 1992, the effective date of the Energy Policy Act of 1992 (Pub.L. 102–486). See § 20.2056(b)–7(e). Under D's will, assets valued at $500,000 in D's gross estate (net of debts, expenses and other charges, including death taxes, payable from the property) passed in trust pursuant to which an annuity of $20,000 a year was payable to S for S's life. Trust income not paid to S as an annuity is to be accumulated in the trust and may not be distributed during S's lifetime. D's estate deducted $200,000 under section 2056(b)(7) and § 20.2056(b)–7(e)(2). S did not assign any portion of S's interest during S's life. At the time of S's death, the value of the trust property is $800,000. S's executor does not elect the alternate valuation date. The amount included in S's gross estate pursuant to section 2044 is $320,000 ([$200,000/$500,000] * $800,000).

Example (8). Inclusion of trust property when surviving spouse dies before first decedent's estate tax return is filed. D dies on July 1, 1997. Under the terms of D's will, a trust is established for the benefit of D's spouse, S. The will provides that S is entitled to receive the income from that portion of the trust that the executor elects to treat as qualified terminable interest property. The remaining portion of the trust passes as of D's date of death to a trust for the benefit of C, D's child. The trust terms otherwise provide S with a qualifying income interest for life under section 2056(b)(7)(B)(ii). S dies on February 10, 1998. On April 1, 1998, D's executor files D's estate tax return on which an election is made to treat a portion of the trust as qualified terminable interest property under section 2056(b)(7). S's estate tax return is filed on November 10, 1998. The value on the date of S's death of the portion of the trust for which D's executor made a QTIP election is includible in S's gross estate under section 2044.

[T.D. 8522, 59 FR 9646, March 1, 1994; T.D. 8779, 63 FR 44393, Aug. 19, 1998]

§ 20.2044–2 Effective dates.

Except as specifically provided in Example 7 of § 20.2044–1(e), the provisions of § 20.2044–1 are effective with respect to estates of a decedent-spouse dying after March 1, 1994. With respect to estates of decedent-spouses dying on or before such date, taxpayers may rely on any reasonable interpretation of the statutory provisions. For these purposes, the provisions of § 20.2044–1 (as well as project LR–211–76, 1984–1 C.B., page 598, see § 601.601(d)(2)(ii)(b) of this chapter), are considered a reasonable interpretation of the statutory provisions.

[T.D. 8522, 59 FR 9647, March 1, 1994]

§ 2045. Prior Interests

Except as otherwise specifically provided by law, sections 2034 to 2042, inclusive, shall apply to the transfers, trusts, estates, interests, rights, powers, and relinquishment of powers, as severally enumerated and described therein, whenever made, created, arising, existing, exercised, or relinquished.

Regulation

§ 20.2045–1 Applicability to pre-existing transfers or interests.

Sections 2034 through 2042 are applicable regardless of when the interests and events referred to in those sections were created or took place, except as otherwise provided in those sections and the regulations thereunder.

[T.D. 6334, 23 FR 8904, Nov. 15, 1958; 25 FR 14021, Dec. 31, 1960; T.D. 8522, 59 FR 9646, March 1, 1994]

§ 2046. Disclaimers

For provisions relating to the effect of a qualified disclaimer for purposes of this chapter, see section 2518.

Regulation

§ 20.2046–1 Disclaimed property.

(a) This section shall apply to the disclaimer or renunciation of an interest in the person disclaiming by a transfer made after December 31, 1976. For rules relating to when the transfer creating the interest occurs, see § 25.2518–2(c)(3) and (c)(4) of this chapter. If a qualified disclaimer is made with respect to such a transfer, the Federal estate tax provisions are to apply with respect to the property interest disclaimed as if the interest had never been transferred to the person making the disclaimer. See section 2518 and the corresponding regulations for rules relating to a qualified disclaimer.

(b) The first and second sentences of this section are applicable for transfers creating the interest to be disclaimed made on or after December 31, 1997.

[T.D. 8095, 51 FR 28368, Aug. 7, 1986; T.D. 8744, 62 FR 68184, Dec. 31, 1997]

Part IV. Taxable Estate

§ 2051. Definition of Taxable Estate

§ 2053. Expenses, Indebtedness, and Taxes

§ 2054. Losses

§ 2051. Definition of Taxable Estate

For purposes of the tax imposed by section 2001, the value of the taxable estate shall be determined by deducting from the value of the gross estate the deductions provided for in this part.

Regulation

§ 20.2051–1 Definition of taxable estate.

(a) General rule. The taxable estate of a decedent who was a citizen or resident (see § 20.0–1(b)(1)) of the United States at death is determined by subtracting the total amount of the deductions authorized by sections 2053 through 2058 from the total amount which must be included in the gross estate under sections 2031 through 2044. These deductions are in general as follows—

(1) Funeral and administration expenses and claims against the estate (including certain taxes and charitable pledges) (section 2053).

(2) Losses from casualty or theft during the administration of the estate (section 2054).

(3) Charitable transfers (section 2055).

(4) The marital deduction (section 2056).

(5) Qualified domestic trusts (section 2056A).

(6) Family-owned business interests (section 2057) to the extent applicable to estates of decedents.

(7) State death taxes (section 2058) to the extent applicable to estates of decedents.

(b) Special rules. See section 2106 and the corresponding regulations for special rules regarding the computation of the taxable estate of a decedent who was not a citizen or resident of the United States. See also § 1.642(g)–1 of this chapter concerning the disallowance for income tax purposes of certain deductions allowed for estate tax purposes.

(c) Effective/applicability date. This section applies to the estates of decedents dying on or after October 20, 2009.

[T.D. 6296, 23 FR 4529, June 24, 1958; T.D. 9468, 74 FR 53657, Oct. 20, 2009]

§ 2053. Expenses, Indebtedness, and Taxes

(a) General rule. For purposes of the tax imposed by section 2001, the value of the taxable estate shall be determined by deducting from the value of the gross estate such amounts—

(1) for funeral expenses,

(2) for administration expenses,

(3) for claims against the estate, and

(4) for unpaid mortgages on, or any indebtedness in respect of, property where the value of the decedent's interest therein, undiminished by such mortgage or indebtedness, is included in the value of the gross estate,

as are allowable by the laws of the jurisdiction, whether within or without the United States, under which the estate is being administered.

(b) Other administration expenses. Subject to the limitations in paragraph (1) of subsection (c), there shall be deducted in determining the taxable estate amounts representing expenses incurred in administering property not subject to claims which is included in the gross estate to the same extent such amounts would be allowable as a deduction under subsection (a) if such property were subject to claims, and such amounts are paid before the expiration of the period of limitation for assessment provided in section 6501.

(c) Limitations.

(1) Limitations applicable to subsections (a) and (b).

(A) Consideration for claims. The deduction allowed by this section in the case of claims against the estate, unpaid mortgages, or any indebtedness shall, when founded on a promise or agreement, be limited to the extent that they were contracted bona fide and for an adequate and full consideration in money or money's worth; except that in any case in which any such claim is founded on a promise or agreement of the decedent to make a contribution or gift to or for the use of any donee described in section 2055 for the purposes specified therein, the deduction for such claims shall not be so limited, but shall be limited to the extent that it would be allowable as a deduction under section 2055 if such promise or agreement constituted a bequest.

(B) Certain taxes. Any income taxes on income received after the death of the decedent, or property taxes not accrued before his death, or any estate, succession, legacy, or inheritance taxes, shall not be deductible under this section.

(C) Certain claims by remaindermen. No deduction shall be allowed under this section for a claim against the estate by a remainderman relating to any property described in section 2044.

(D) Section 6166 interest. No deduction shall be allowed under this section for any interest payable under section 6601 on any unpaid portion of the tax imposed by section 2001 for the period during which an extension of time for payment of such tax is in effect under section 6166.

(2) Limitations applicable only to subsection (a). In the case of the amounts described in subsection (a), there shall be disallowed the amount by which the deductions specified therein exceed the value, at the time of the decedent's death, of property subject to claims, except to the extent that such deductions represent amounts paid before the date prescribed for the filing of the estate tax return. For purposes of this section, the term "property subject to claims" means property includible in the gross estate of the decedent which, or the avails of which, would under the applicable law, bear the burden of the payment of such deductions in the final adjustment and settlement of the estate, except that the value of the property shall be reduced by the amount of the deduction under section 2054 attributable to such property.

(d) Certain foreign death taxes.

(1) In general. Notwithstanding the provisions of subsection (c)(1)(B), for purposes of the tax imposed by section 2001, the value of the taxable estate may be determined, if the executor so elects before the expiration of the period of limitation for assessment provided in section 6501, by deducting from the value of the gross estate the amount (as determined in accordance with regulations prescribed by the Secretary) of any estate, succession, legacy, or inheritance tax imposed by and actually paid to any foreign country, in respect of any property situated within such foreign country and included in the gross estate of a citizen or resident of the United States, upon a transfer by the decedent for public, charitable, or religious uses described in section 2055. The determination under this paragraph of the country within which property is situated shall be made in accordance with the rules applicable under subchapter B (sec. 2101 and following) in determining whether property is situated within or without the United States. Any election under this paragraph shall be exercised in accordance with regulations prescribed by the Secretary.

(2) Condition for allowance of deduction. No deduction shall be allowed under paragraph (1) for a foreign death tax specified therein unless the decrease in the tax imposed by section 2001 which results from the deduction provided in paragraph (1) will inure solely for the benefit of the public, charitable, or religious transferees described in section 2055 or section 2106(a)(2). In any case where the tax imposed by section 2001 is equitably apportioned among all the transferees of property included in the gross estate, including those described in sections 2055 and 2106(a)(2) (taking into account any exemptions, credits, or deductions allowed by this chapter), in determining such decrease, there shall be disregarded any decrease in the Federal estate tax which any transferees other than those described in sections 2055 and 2106(a)(2) are required to pay.

(3) Effect on credit for foreign death taxes of deduction under this subsection.

(A) Election. An election under this subsection shall be deemed a waiver of the right to claim a credit, against the Federal estate tax, under a death tax convention with any foreign country for any tax or portion thereof in respect of which a deduction is taken under this subsection.

(B) Cross reference. See section 2014(f) for the effect of a deduction taken under this paragraph on the credit for foreign death taxes.

(e) Marital rights. For provisions treating certain relinquishments of marital rights as consideration in money or money's worth, see section 2043(b)(2).

Regulations

§ 20.2053–1 Deductions for expenses, indebtedness, and taxes; in general.

(a) General rule. In determining the taxable estate of a decedent who was a citizen or resident of the United States at death, there are allowed as deductions under section 2053(a) and (b) amounts falling within the following two categories (subject to the limitations contained in this section and in §§ 20.2053–2 through 20.2053–10)—

(1) *First category.* Amounts which are payable out of property subject to claims and which are allowable by the law of the jurisdiction, whether within or without the United States, under which the estate is being administered for—

(i) Funeral expenses;

(ii) Administration expenses;

(iii) Claims against the estate (including taxes to the extent set forth in § 20.2053–6 and charitable pledges to the extent set forth in § 20.2053–5); and

(iv) Unpaid mortgages on, or any indebtedness in respect of, property, the value of the decedent's interest in which is included in the value of the gross estate undiminished by the mortgage or indebtedness.

As used in this subparagraph, the phrase "allowable by the law of the jurisdiction" means allowable by the law governing the administration of decedents' estates. The phrase has no reference to amounts allowable as deductions under a law which imposes a State death tax. See further §§ 20.2053–2 through 20.2053–7.

(2) *Second category.* Amounts representing expenses incurred in administering property which is included in the gross estate but which is not subject to claims and which—

(i) Would be allowed as deductions in the first category if the property being administered were subject to claims; and

(ii) Were paid before the expiration of the period of limitation for assessment provided in section 6501.

See further § 20.2053–8.

(b) Provisions applicable to both categories. (1) *In general.* If the item is not one of those described in paragraph (a) of this section, it is not deductible merely because payment is allowed by the local law. If the amount which may be expended for the particular purpose is limited by the local law no deduction in excess of that limitation is permissible.

(2) *Bona fide requirement.* (i) *In general.* Amounts allowed as deductions under section 2053(a) and (b) must be expenses and claims that are bona fide in nature. No deduction is permissible to the extent it is founded on a transfer that is essentially donative in character (a mere cloak for a gift or bequest) except to the extent the deduction is for a claim that would be allowable as a deduction under section 2055 as a charitable bequest.

(ii) *Claims and expenses involving family members.* Factors indicative (but not necessarily determinative) of the bona fide nature of a claim or expense involving a family member of a decedent, a related entity, or a beneficiary of a decedent's estate or revocable trust, in relevant instances, may include, but are not limited to, the following—

(A) The transaction underlying the claim or expense occurs in the ordinary course of business, is negotiated at arm's length, and is free from donative intent.

(B) The nature of the claim or expense is not related to an expectation or claim of inheritance.

(C) The claim or expense originates pursuant to an agreement between the decedent and the family member, related entity, or beneficiary, and the agreement is substantiated with contemporaneous evidence.

(D) Performance by the claimant is pursuant to the terms of an agreement between the decedent and the family member, related entity, or beneficiary and the performance and the agreement can be substantiated.

(E) All amounts paid in satisfaction or settlement of a claim or expense are reported by each party for Federal income and employment tax purposes, to the extent appropriate, in a manner that is consistent with the reported nature of the claim or expense.

(iii) *Definitions.* The following definitions apply for purposes of this paragraph (b)(2):

(A) Family members include the spouse of the decedent; the grandparents, parents, siblings, and lineal descendants of the decedent or of the decedent's spouse; and the spouse and lineal descendants of any such grandparent, parent, and sibling. Family members include adopted individuals.

(B) A related entity is an entity in which the decedent, either directly or indirectly, had a beneficial ownership interest at the time of the decedent's death or at any time during the three-year period ending on the decedent's date of death. Such an entity, however, shall not include a publicly-traded entity nor shall it include a closely-held entity in which the combined beneficial interest, either direct or indirect, of the decedent and the decedent's family members, collectively, is less than 30 percent of the beneficial ownership interests (whether voting or non-voting and whether an interest in stock, capital and/or profits), as determined at the time a claim described in this section is being asserted. Notwithstanding the foregoing, an entity in which the decedent, directly or indirectly, had any managing interest (for example, as a general partner of a partnership or as a managing member of a limited liability company) at the time of the decedent's death shall be considered a related entity.

(C) Beneficiaries of a decedent's estate include beneficiaries of a trust of the decedent.

(3) *Court decrees and settlements.* (i) *Court decree.* If a court of competent jurisdiction over the administration of an estate reviews and approves expenditures for funeral expenses, administration expenses, claims against the estate, or unpaid mortgages (referred to in this section as a "claim or expense"), a final judicial decision in that matter may be relied upon to establish the amount of a claim or expense that is otherwise deductible under section 2053 and these regulations provided that the court actually passes upon the facts on which deductibility depends. If the court does not pass upon those facts, its decree may not be relied upon to establish the amount of the claim or expense that is otherwise deductible under section 2053. It must appear that the court actually passed upon the merits of the claim. This will be presumed in all cases of an active and genuine contest. If the result reached appears to be unreasonable, this is some evidence that there was not such a contest, but it may be rebutted by proof to the contrary. Any amount meeting the requirements of this paragraph (b)(3)(i) is deductible to the extent it actually has been paid or will be paid, subject to any applicable limitations in this section.

(ii) *Claims and expenses where court approval not required under local law.* A deduction for the amount of a claim or expense that is otherwise deductible under section 2053 and these regulations will not be denied under section 2053 solely because a local court decree has not been entered with respect to such amount, provided that no court decree is required under applicable law to determine the amount or allowability of the claim or expense.

(iii) *Consent decree.* A local court decree rendered by consent may be relied on to establish the amount of a claim or expense that is otherwise deductible under section 2053 and these regulations provided that the consent resolves a bona fide issue in a genuine contest. Consent given by all parties having interests adverse to that of the claimant will be presumed to resolve a bona fide issue in a genuine contest. Any amount meeting the requirements of this paragraph (b)(3)(iii) is deductible to the extent it actually has been paid or will be paid, subject to any applicable limitations in this section.

(iv) *Settlements.* A settlement may be relied on to establish the amount of a claim or expense (whether contingent or noncontingent) that is otherwise deductible under section 2053 and these regulations, provided that the settlement resolves a bona fide issue in a genuine contest and is the product of arm's-length negotiations by parties having adverse interests with respect to the claim or expense. A deduction will not be denied for a settlement amount paid by an estate if the estate can establish that the cost of defending or contesting the claim or expense, or the delay associated with litigating the claim or expense, would impose a higher burden on the estate than the payment of the amount paid to settle the claim or expense. Nevertheless, no deduction will be allowed for amounts paid in settlement of an unenforceable claim. For this purpose, to the extent a claim exceeds an applicable limit under local law, the claim is deemed to be unenforceable. However, as long as the enforceability of the claim is at issue in a bona fide dispute, the claim will not be deemed to be unenforceable for this purpose. Any amount meeting the requirements of this paragraph (b)(3)(iv) is deductible to the extent it actually has been paid or will be paid, subject to any applicable limitations in this section.

(v) *Additional rules.* Notwithstanding paragraph (b)(3)(i) through (iv) of this section, additional rules may apply to the deductibility of certain claims and expenses. See § 20.2053–2 for additional rules regarding the deductibility of funeral expenses. See § 20.2053–3 for additional rules regarding the deductibility of administration expenses. See § 20.2053–4 for additional rules regarding the deductibility of claims against the estate. See § 20.2053–7 for additional rules regarding the deductibility of unpaid mortgages.

(4) *Examples.* Unless otherwise provided, assume that the amount of any claim or expense is paid out of property subject to claims and is paid within the time prescribed for filing the "United States Estate (and Generation-Skipping Transfer) Tax Return," Form 706. The following examples illustrate the application of this paragraph (b):

Example (1). Consent decree at variance with the law of the State. Decedent's (D's) estate is probated in State. D's probate estate is valued at $100x. State law provides that the executor's commission shall not exceed 3 percent of the probate estate. A consent decree is entered allowing the executor's commission in the amount of $5x. The estate pays the executor's commission in the amount of $5x. For purposes of section 2053, the executor may deduct only $3x of the $5x expense paid for the executor's commission because the amount approved by the consent decree in excess of $3x is in excess of the applicable limit for executor's commissions under local law. Therefore, for purposes of section 2053, the consent decree may not be relied upon to establish the amount of the expense for the executor's commission.

Example (2). Decedent's (D's) estate is probated in State. State law grants authority to an executor to administer an estate without court approval, so long as notice of and a right to object to a proposed action is provided to interested persons. The executor of D's estate (E) proposes to sell property of the estate in order to pay the debts of D. E gives requisite notice to all interested parties and no interested person objects. E sells the real estate and pays a real estate commission of $20x to a professional real estate agent. The amount of the real estate commission paid does not exceed the applicable limit under State law. Provided that the sale of the property was necessary to pay D's debts, expenses of administration, or taxes, to preserve the estate, or to effect distribution, the executor may deduct the $20x expense for the real estate commission under section 2053 even though no court decree was entered approving the expense.

Example (3). Claim by family member. For a period of three years prior to D's death, D's niece (N) provides accounting and bookkeeping services on D's behalf. N is a CPA and provides similar accounting and bookkeeping services to unrelated clients. At the end of each month, N presents an itemized bill to D for services rendered. The fees charged by N conform to the prevailing market rate for the services rendered and are comparable to the fees N charges other clients for similar services. The amount due is timely paid each month by D and is properly reported for Federal income and employment tax purposes by N. In the six months prior to D's death, D's poor health prevents D from making payments to N for the amount due. After D's death, N asserts a claim against the estate for $25x, an amount representing the amount due for the six-month period prior to D's death. D's estate pays

$25x to N in satisfaction of the claim before the return is timely filed and N properly reports the $25x received by E for income tax purposes. Barring any other relevant facts or circumstances, E may rely on the following factors to establish that the claim is bona fide: (1) N's claim for services rendered arose in the ordinary course of business, as N is a CPA performing similar services for other clients; (2) the fees charged were deemed to be negotiated at arm's length, as the fees were consistent with the fees N charged for similar services to unrelated clients; (3) the billing records and the records of D's timely payments to N constitute contemporaneous evidence of an agreement between D and N for N's bookkeeping services; and (4) the amount of the payments to N is properly reported by N for Federal income and employment tax purposes. E may deduct the amount paid to N in satisfaction of the claim.

(c) Provision applicable to first category only. Deductions of the first category (described in paragraph (a)(1) of this section) are limited under section 2053(a) to amounts which would be property allowable out of property subject to claims by the law of the jurisdiction under which the decedent's estate is being administered. Further, the total allowable amount of deductions of the first category is limited by section 2053(c)(2) to the sum of—

(1) The value of property included in the decedent's gross estate and subject to claims, plus

(2) Amounts paid, out of property not subject to claims against the decedent's estate, within 9 months (15 months in the case of the estate of a decedent dying before January 1, 1971) after the decedent's death (the period within which the estate tax return must be filed under section 6075), or within any extension of time for filing the return granted under section 6081.

The term "property subject to claims" is defined in section 2053(c)(2) as meaning the property includible in the gross estate which, or the avails of which, under the applicable law, would bear the burden of the payment of these deductions in the final adjustment and settlement of the decedent's estate. However, for the purposes of this definition, the value of property subject to claims is first reduced by the amount of any deduction allowed under section 2054 for any losses from casualty or theft incurred during the settlement of the estate attributable to such property. The application of this paragraph may be illustrated by the following examples:

Example (1). The only item in the gross estate is real property valued at $250,000 which the decedent and his surviving spouse held as tenants by the entirety. Under the local law this real property is not subject to claims. Funeral expenses of $1,200 and debts of the decedent in the amount of $1,500 are allowable under local law. Before the prescribed date for filing the estate tax return, the surviving spouse paid the funeral expenses and $1,000 of the debts. The remaining $500 of the debts was paid by her after the prescribed date for filing the return. The total amount allowable as deductions under section 2053 is limited to $2,200, the amount paid prior to the prescribed date for filing the return.

Example (2). The only two items in the gross estate were a bank deposit of $20,000 and insurance in the amount of $150,000. The insurance was payable to the decedent's surviving spouse and under local law was not subject to claims. Funeral expenses of $1,000 and debts in the amount of $29,000 were allowable under local law. A son was executor of the estate and before the prescribed date for filing the estate tax return he paid the funeral expenses of $9,000 of the debts, using therefor $5,000 of the bank deposit and $5,000 supplied by the surviving spouse. After the prescribed date for filing the return, the executor paid the remaining $20,000 of the debts, using for that purpose the $15,000 left in the bank account plus an additional $5,000 supplied by the surviving spouse. The total amount allowable as deductions under section 2053 is limited to $25,000 ($20,000 of property subject to claims plus the $5,000 additional amount which, before the prescribed date for filing the return, was paid out of property not subject to claims).

(d) Amount deductible. (1) *General rule.* To take into account properly events occurring after the date of a decedent's death in determining the amount deductible under section 2053 and these regulations, the deduction for any claim or expense described in paragraph (a) of this section is limited to the total amount actually paid in settlement or satisfaction of that item (subject to any applicable limitations in this section). However, see paragraph (d)(4) of this section for the rules for deducting certain ascertainable amounts; see § 20.2053–4(b) and (c) for the rules regarding the deductibility of certain claims against the estate; and see

§ 20.2053–7 for the rules regarding the deductibility of unpaid mortgages and other indebtedness.

(2) *Application of post-death events.* In determining whether and to what extent a deduction under section 2053 is allowable, events occurring after the date of a decedent's death will be taken into consideration—

(i) Until the expiration of the applicable period of limitations on assessment prescribed in section 6501 (including without limitation at all times during which the running of the period of limitations is suspended); and

(ii) During subsequent periods, in determining the amount (if any) of an overpayment of estate tax due in connection with a claim for refund filed within the time prescribed in section 6511(a).

(3) *Reimbursements.* A deduction is not allowed to the extent that a claim or expense described in paragraph (a) of this section is or could be compensated for by insurance or otherwise could be reimbursed. If the executor is able to establish that only a partial reimbursement could be collected, then only that portion of the potential reimbursement that reasonably could have been expected to be collected will reduce the estate's deductible portion of the total claim or expense. An executor may certify that the executor neither knows nor reasonably should have known of any available reimbursement for a claim or expense described in section 2053(a) or (b) on the estate's United States Estate (and Generation-Skipping Transfer) Tax Return (Form 706), in accordance with the instructions for that form. A potential reimbursement will not reduce the deductible amount of a claim or expense to the extent that the executor, on Form 706 and in accordance with the instructions for that form, provides a reasonable explanation for his or her reasonable determination that the burden of necessary collection efforts in pursuit of a right of reimbursement would outweigh the anticipated benefit from those efforts. Nevertheless, even if a reasonable explanation is provided, subsequent events (including without limitation an actual reimbursement) occurring within the period described in § 20.2053–1(d)(2) will be considered in determining the amount (if any) of a reduction under this paragraph (d)(3) in the deductible amount of a claim or expense.

(4) *Exception for certain ascertainable amounts.*

(i) *General rule.* A deduction will be allowed for a claim or expense that satisfies all applicable requirements even though it is not yet paid, provided that the amount to be paid is ascertainable with reasonable certainty and will be paid. For example, executors' commissions and attorneys' fees that are not yet paid, and that meet the requirements for deductibility under § 20.2053–3(b) and (c), respectively, are deemed to be ascertainable with reasonable certainty and may be deducted if such expenses will be paid. However, no deduction may be taken upon the basis of a vague or uncertain estimate. To the extent a claim or expense is contested or contingent, such a claim or expense cannot be ascertained with reasonable certainty.

(ii) *Effect of post-death events.* A deduction under this paragraph (d)(4) will be allowed to the extent the Commissioner is reasonably satisfied that the amount to be paid is ascertainable with reasonable certainty and will be paid. In making this determination, the Commissioner will take into account events occurring after the date of a decedent's death. To the extent the amount for which a deduction was claimed does not satisfy the requirements of this paragraph (d)(4), and is not otherwise deductible, the deduction will be disallowed by the Commissioner. If a deduction is claimed on Form 706 for an amount that is not yet paid and the deduction is disallowed in whole or in part (or if no deduction is claimed on Form 706), then if the claim or expense subsequently satisfies the requirements of this paragraph (d)(4) or is paid, relief may be sought by filing a claim for refund. To preserve the estate's right to claim a refund for amounts becoming deductible after the expiration of the period of limitation for the filing of a claim for refund, a protective claim for refund may be filed in accordance with paragraph (d)(5) of this section.

(5) *Protective claim for refund.* (i) *In general.* A protective claim for refund under this section may be filed at any time before the expiration of the period of limitation prescribed in section 6511(a) for the filing of a claim for refund to preserve the estate's right to claim a refund by reason of claims or expenses that are not paid or do not otherwise meet the requirements of deductibility under section 2053 and these regulations until after the expiration of the period of limitation for filing a claim for refund. Such a protective claim shall be made in accordance with guidance that may be provided from time to time by publication in the

Internal Revenue Bulletin (see § 601.601(d)(2)(ii)(b)). Although the protective claim need not state a particular dollar amount or demand an immediate refund, a protective claim must identify each outstanding claim or expense that would have been deductible under section 2053(a) or (b) if such item already had been paid and must describe the reasons and contingencies delaying the actual payment of the claim or expense. Action on protective claims will proceed after the executor has notified the Commissioner within a reasonable period that the contingency has been resolved and that the amount deductible under § 20.2053–1 has been established.

(ii) *Effect on marital and charitable deduction.* To the extent that a protective claim for refund is filed with respect to a claim or expense that would have been deductible under section 2053(a) or (b) if such item already had been paid and that is payable out of a share that meets the requirements for a charitable deduction under section 2055 or a marital deduction under section 2056 or section 2056A, or from a combination thereof, neither the charitable deduction nor the marital deduction shall be reduced by the amount of such claim or expense until the amount is actually paid or meets the requirements of paragraph (d)(4) of this section for deducting certain ascertainable amounts or the requirements of § 20.2053–4(b) or (c) for deducting certain claims against the estate.

(6) [Reserved]

(7) *Examples.* Assume that the amounts described in section 2053(a) are payable out of property subject to claims and are allowable by the law of the jurisdiction governing the administration of the estate, whether the applicable jurisdiction is within or outside of the United States. Assume that the claims against the estate are not deductible under § 20.2053–4(b) or (c). Also assume, unless otherwise provided, that none of the limitations on the amount of the deduction described in this section apply to the deduction claimed under section 2053. The following examples illustrate the application of this paragraph (d):

Example (1). Amount of expense ascertainable. Decedent's (D's) estate was probated in State. State law provides that the personal representative shall receive compensation equal to 2.5 percent of the value of the probate estate. The executor (E) may claim a deduction for estimated fees equal to 2.5 percent of D's probate estate on the Form 706 filed for D's estate under the rule for deducting certain ascertainable amounts set forth in paragraph (d)(4) of this section, provided that the estimated amount will be paid. However, the Commissioner will disallow the deduction upon examination of the estate's Form 706 to the extent that the amount for which a deduction was claimed no longer satisfies the requirements of paragraph (d)(4) of this section. If this occurs, E may file a protective claim for refund in accordance with paragraph (d)(5) of this section in order to preserve the estate's right to claim a refund for the amount of the fee that is subsequently paid or that subsequently meets the requirements of paragraph (d)(4) of this section for deducting certain ascertainable amounts.

Example (2). Amount of claim not ascertainable. Prior to death, Decedent (D) is sued by Claimant (C) for $100x in a tort proceeding and responds asserting affirmative defenses available to D under applicable local law. C and D are unrelated. D subsequently dies and D's Form 706 is due before a final judgment is entered in the case. The executor of D's estate (E) may not claim a deduction with respect to C's claim on D's Form 706 under the special rule contained in paragraph (d)(4) of this section because the deductible amount cannot be ascertained with reasonable certainty. However, E may file a timely protective claim for refund in accordance with paragraph (d)(5) of this section in order to preserve the estate's right to subsequently claim a refund at the time a final judgment is entered in the case and the claim is either paid or meets the requirements of paragraph (d)(4) of this section for deducting certain ascertainable amounts.

Example (3). Amount of claim payable out of property qualifying for marital deduction. The facts are the same as in Example 2 except that the applicable credit amount, under section 2010, against the estate tax was fully consumed by D's lifetime gifts, D is survived by Spouse (S), and D's estate passes entirely to S in a bequest that qualifies for the marital deduction under section 2056. Even though any amount D's estate ultimately pays with respect to C's claim will be paid from the assets qualifying for the marital deduction, in filing Form 706, E need not reduce the amount of the marital deduction claimed on D's Form 706. Instead, pursuant to the protective claim for refund filed by E, the marital deduction will be reduced by the claim once a final judgment is entered in the case. At that time, a deduction will be allowed for the amount that is either paid or meets the requirements of paragraph (d)(4) of this section for deducting certain ascertainable amounts.

(e) Disallowance of double deductions. See section 642(g) and § 1.642(g)–1 with respect to the disallowance for income tax purposes of certain deductions unless the right to take such deductions for estate tax purposes is waived.

(f) Effective/applicability date. This section applies to the estates of decedents dying on or after October 20, 2009.

[T.D. 6296, 23 FR 4529, June 24, 1958, as amended by T.D. 7238, 37 FR 28719, Dec. 29, 1972; T.D. 9468, 74 FR 53657, Oct. 20, 2009; 74 FR 61525, Nov. 25, 2009]

Proposed § 20.2053–1 (June 28, 2022) Deductions for expenses, indebtedness, and taxes; in general.

Section 20.2053–1 is amended by:

1. Adding paragraph (d)(6).

2. Revising the introductory text of paragraph (d)(7).

3. In paragraph (d)(7), Examples 1 through 3 are designated as paragraphs (d)(7)(i) through (iii), respectively.

4. In newly designated paragraphs (d)(7)(i) and (ii):

i. Removing "ascertainable," and adding "ascertainable." in its place.

ii. Adding a sentence to the end of the paragraphs.

5. In newly designated paragraph (d)(7)(iii):

i. Removing "deduction," and "Example 2" and adding "deduction." and "paragraph (d)(7)(ii) of this section (Example 2)" in their places, respectively.

ii. Revising the last sentence of the paragraph.

6. Adding paragraphs (d)(7)(iv) through (vi).

7. Revising paragraph (f).

The additions and revisions read as follows:

(d) * * *

(6) *Limitation on amount deductible.* (i) *Claims and expenses paid after the grace period.* (A) *Definitions.* The following definitions apply for purposes of this paragraph (d):

(1) *Grace period.* The grace period is the period beginning on the date of the decedent's death and extending through the third anniversary of that date.

(2) *Post-grace-period payment.* A post-grace-period payment is the amount of a claim or expense described in paragraph (a) of this section not paid or to be paid before the end of the grace period.

(B) *General rule.* To the extent that a post-grace-period payment otherwise meets the requirements for deductibility of a claim or expense under section 2053 and the regulations in this part thereunder, the amount deductible under section 2053 is limited to the present value, as of the decedent's date of death, of that amount. The present value of each post-grace-period payment is calculated by discounting it from the payment date or expected date of payment to the decedent's date of death. The applicable discount rate is the applicable Federal rate determined under section 1274(d) for the month in which the decedent's death occurs, compounded annually. The length of time from the decedent's date of death to the date of payment or expected date of payment will determine whether the Federal rate applicable to that payment is the Federal mid-term rate or the Federal long-term rate. The Internal Revenue Service publishes the applicable Federal rates for each month in the Internal Revenue Bulletin (see § 601.601(d)(2)(ii) of this chapter). Any reasonable assumptions and methodology in regard to time period measurements may be used to calculate, in accordance with paragraph (d)(6)(ii) of this section, the present value of the post-grace-period payment(s).

(ii) *Calculating present value of amounts paid or payable.* (A) *Single post-grace-period payment.* The amount deductible under section 2053 for a single post-grace-period payment is computed by calculating the present value of such payment as follows:

$$\text{Amount of future payment x } [1 / (1 + i)]^t$$

Where:

t is the amount of time (expressed in years and fractions of years) from the day after the decedent's date of death to the payment date or expected date of payment; and

i is the applicable discount rate.

(B) *Multiple post-grace-period payments.* The amount deductible under section 2053 for multiple post-grace-period payments is computed by calculating the present value of each such payment using the formula in paragraph (d)(6)(ii)(A) of this section; the sum of the discounted amounts of the post-grace-period payments is the amount that is deductible for such payments.

(C) *Multiple payment dates occurring during and after the grace period.* A claim or expense described in paragraph (a) of this section may have at least one payment date or expected date of payment during the grace period and at least one payment date or expected date of payment after the grace period. For such a claim or expense, the amount deductible under section 2053 is computed by calculating the present value of each separate post-grace-period payment using the formula in paragraph (d)(6)(ii)(A) of this section, and adding the total of these discounted amounts to any amount of the claim or expense having a payment date or expected date of payment during the grace period. Any amount having a payment date or expected date of payment during the grace period is not discounted in arriving at the amount deductible.

(iii) *Discounting when actual date of payment is unknown.* With regard to a post-grace-period payment that may be deducted in advance of payment under paragraph (d)(4) of this section or § 20.2053–4(b) or (c), the amount deductible must be determined by computing the present value of the amount of that post-grace-period payment as if that amount will be paid on the expected date of payment. The expected date of payment in settlement or satisfaction of a claim or expense must be determined using all information reasonably available to the taxpayer to make a fair and reasonable estimate of the expected date or dates of payment. For amounts deductible under § 20.2053–4(b) or (c), the expected date or dates of payment must be identified in a written appraisal document of a person that is qualified by knowledge and experience to appraise the claim being valued. *See* § 20.2053–4(b)(1)(iv) and (c)(1)(iv). However, the computation of present value is subject to adjustment if, within the period described in paragraph (d)(2) of this section, the actual date or dates of payment become known and differ from the estimated date or dates of payment. *See* paragraph (d)(6)(vi) of this section.

(iv) *Statement supporting present value computation required.* A deduction under section 2053 for a claim or expense that is required to be discounted to present value under paragraph (d)(6)(i) of this section must be supported by a statement to be filed with the Form 706 showing the computation of the present value of that item, including, if applicable, the basis for the determination of the expected date(s) of payment.

(v) *Ordering rule.* In computing the amount deductible for a claim or expense under paragraph (d) of this section, the amount deductible for a claim or expense (otherwise determined under paragraphs (d)(1) through (4) of this section) is discounted to present value under paragraph (d)(6) of this section before applying the limits in § 20.2053–4(b)(2) and (c).

(vi) *Effect of post-death events.* If a deduction is claimed for the present value of a post-grace-period payment, the claimed deduction is subject to adjustment to reflect any post-death events affecting the amount of such post-grace-period payment and any change in the expected or actual date of payment. *See* paragraph (d)(2) of this section for the period during which post-death events are taken into account.

(vii) *Exceptions.* The rule in paragraph (d)(6)(i) of this section does not apply to unpaid principal of mortgages and other indebtedness deductible under § 20.2053–7.

(7) *Examples.* Assume that the amounts described in section 2053(a) are payable out of property subject to claims and are allowable by the law of the jurisdiction governing the administration of the estate, whether the applicable jurisdiction is within or outside of the United States. Assume that, unless otherwise provided, the claims against the estate are not deductible under § 20.2053–4(b) or (c) and all amounts are paid during the grace period. The following examples illustrate the application of this paragraph (d):

(i) * * * However, any amounts that will not be paid on or before the third anniversary of the date of D's death (that is, are not paid during the grace period) are subject to the present value limitation in paragraph (d)(6) of this section.

(ii) * * * If the amount of the claim will not be paid on or before the third anniversary of the date of D's death (that is, the amount is not paid during the grace period), the amount deductible is subject to the present value limitation in paragraph (d)(6) of this section.

(iii) * * * At that time, a deduction will be allowed for the amount that is either paid or meets the requirements of paragraph (d)(4) of this section for deducting certain ascertainable amounts, subject to the present value limitation in paragraph (d)(6) of this section, if applicable.

(iv) *Example 4: Discounting amount paid more than three years after decedent's date of death.* The facts are the same as in paragraph (d)(7)(ii) of this section (*Example 2*) except that E files a timely protective claim for refund in accordance with paragraph (d)(5) of this section to preserve the estate's right to claim a refund, a final judgment in the amount of $100x is entered against and paid by the estate precisely five years after D's date of death, and the applicable Federal (mid-term) rate determined under section 1274(d) for the month in which D's date of death occurs, compounded annually, is 2.00%. Within a reasonable period of time after the final judgment is entered, E notifies the Commissioner that the contingency has been resolved. E may claim a deduction for the present value of the amount paid in satisfaction of the claim as of D's date of death. Under the facts in this paragraph (d)(7)(iv), the present value of the amount paid in five years equals $\$100x/(1 + .0200)^5$ or $100x/1.104081 or $90.57x.

(v) *Example 5: Discounting amount to be paid when actual date of payment not known.* The facts are the same as in paragraph (d)(7)(ii) of this section (*Example 2*) except that the claim is deductible under § 20.2053–4(c) because all amounts deducted by the estate under that paragraph do not exceed $500,000. E obtains a written appraisal document meeting the requirements of § 20.2053–4(c)(iv) and reasonably determines that the future value of the claim is $300,000 (that is, before discounting the claim to its present value). E determines, after considering all available information and making reasonable assumptions, that the expected date of payment of the claim is Date X, which is reflected in the appraisal. Date X is a date after the third anniversary of D's date of death. E may claim a deduction for the present value of the claim as of D's date of death, determined by discounting $300,000 for the period from the date of death to Date X, using the applicable Federal rate determined under section 1274(d) for the month in which D's death occurs, compounded annually.

(vi) *Example 6: Discounting amount to be paid for series of payments payable over a period that does not end on or before the third anniversary of the decedent's death.* Pursuant to the terms of a divorce and separation agreement entered on June 1 of Year 1, Decedent (D) is obligated to make annual payments of $100x to Claimant (C) on September 1 of year 1 and each September 1st thereafter until D has made a total of 10 such payments. D dies on December 1 of Year 5 after having made the first five annual payments required under the agreement. The applicable Federal (mid-term) rate determined under section 1274(d) for the month in which D's death occurs, compounded annually, is 2.00%. The executor of D's estate (E) may claim a deduction with respect to C's claim on D's Form 706 under the special rule contained in paragraph (d)(4) of this section because the deductible amount can be ascertained with reasonable certainty. E computes the discounted deductible amount of the claim by adding the undiscounted amount of the three payments that will be made before the third anniversary of D's death ($300x) to the discounted amounts of the two payments that will be made after the third anniversary of D's death. Accordingly, the amount deductible for the claim equals $483.866x ($300x + $92.843x + $91.023x). The individual calculations for the present values of the payments in the last two years of the payment obligation are shown in table 1 to this paragraph (d)(7)(vi).

TABLE 1 TO PARAGRAPH (d)(7)(vi)

	(1)	(2)	(3)	(4)	(5)
	t	1 + i	1/(1 + i)	$[1/(1 + i)]^t$	$[1/(1 + i)]^t \times 100x$
Year 9	3.75	1.0200	0.980392	0.928430	92.843x
Year 10	4.75	1.0200	0.980392	0.910226	91.023x

* * * *

(f) Applicability date. The rules of this section apply to the estates of decedents dying on or after [*date of publication of the final rule in the Federal Register*].

§ 20.2053–2 Deduction for funeral expenses.

Such amounts for funeral expenses are allowed as deductions from a decedent's gross estate as (a) are actually expended, (b) would be properly allowable out of property subject to claims under the laws of the local jurisdiction, and (c) satisfy the requirements of paragraph (c) of § 20.2053–1. A reasonable expenditure for a tombstone, monument, or mausoleum, or for a burial lot, either for the decedent or his family, including a reasonable expenditure for its future care, may be deducted under this heading, provided such an expenditure is allowable by the local law. Included in funeral expenses is the cost of transportation of the person bringing the body to the place of burial.

[T.D. 6296, 23 FR 4529, June 24, 1958]

§ 20.2053–3 Deduction for expenses of administering estate.

(a) In general. The amounts deductible from a decedent's gross estate as "administration expenses" of the first category (see paragraphs (a) and (c) of § 20.2053–1) are limited to such expenses as are actually and necessarily, incurred in the administration of the decedent's estate; that is, in the collection of assets, payment of debts, and distribution of property to the persons entitled to it. The expenses contemplated in the law are such only as attend the settlement of an estate and the transfer of the property of the estate to individual beneficiaries or to a trustee, whether the trustee is the executor or some other person. Expenditures not essential to the proper settlement of the estate, but incurred for the individual benefit of the heirs, legatees, or devisees, may not be taken as deductions. Administration expenses include (1) executor's commissions; (2) attorney's fees; and (3) miscellaneous expenses. Each of these classes is considered separately in paragraphs (b) through (d) of this section.

(b) Executor's commissions. (1) Executors' commissions are deductible to the extent permitted by § 20.2053–1 and this section, but no deduction may be taken if no commissions are to be paid. In addition, the amount of the commissions claimed as a deduction must be in accordance with the usually accepted standards and practice of allowing such an amount in estates of similar size and character in the jurisdiction in which the estate is being administered, or any deviation from the usually accepted standards or range of amounts (permissible under applicable local law) must be justified to the satisfaction of the Commissioner.

(2) A bequest or devise to the executor in lieu of commissions is not deductible. If, however, the terms of the will set forth the compensation payable to the executor for services to be rendered in the administration of the estate, a deduction may be taken to the extent that the amount so fixed does not exceed the compensation allowable by the local law or practice and to the extent permitted by § 20.2053–1.

(3) Except to the extent that a trustee is in fact performing services with respect to property subject to claims which would normally be performed by an executor, amounts paid as trustees' commissions do not constitute expenses of administration under the first category, and are only deductible as expenses of the second category to the extent provided in § 20.2053–8.

(c) Attorney's fees. (1) Attorney's fees are deductible to the extent permitted by § 20.2053–1 and this section. Further, the amount of the fees claimed as a deduction may not exceed a reasonable remuneration for the services rendered, taking into account the size and character of the estate, the law and practice in the jurisdiction in which the estate is being administered, and the skill and expertise of the attorneys.

(2) A deduction for attorneys' fees incurred in contesting an asserted deficiency or in prosecuting a claim for refund should be claimed at the time the deficiency is contested or the refund claim is prosecuted. A deduction for reasonable attorney's fees actually incurred in contesting an asserted deficiency or in prosecuting a claim for refund will be allowed to the extent permitted by § 20.2053–1 even though the deduction, as such, was not claimed on the estate tax return or in the claim for refund. A deduction for these fees shall not be denied, and the sufficiency of a claim for refund shall not be questioned, solely by reason of the fact that the amount of the fees to be paid was not established at the time that the right to the deduction was claimed.

(3) Attorneys' fees incurred by beneficiaries incident to litigation as to their respective interests are not deductible if the litigation is not essential to the proper settlement of the estate within the meaning of paragraph (a) of this section. An attorney's fee not meeting

this test is not deductible as an administration expense under section 2053 and this section, even if it is approved by a probate court as an expense payable or reimbursable by the estate.

(d) Miscellaneous administration expenses. (1) Miscellaneous administration expenses include such expenses as court costs, surrogates' fees, accountants' fees, appraisers' fees, clerk hire, etc. Expenses necessarily incurred in preserving and distributing the estate, including the cost of storing or maintaining property of the estate if it is impossible to effect immediate distribution to the beneficiaries, are deductible to the extent permitted by § 20.2053–1. Expenses for preserving and caring for the property may not include outlays for additions or improvements; nor will such expenses be allowed for a longer period than the executor is reasonably required to retain the property.

(2) Expenses for selling property of the estate are deductible to the extent permitted by § 20.2053–1 if the sale is necessary in order to pay the decedent's debts, expenses of administration, or taxes, to preserve the estate, or to effect distribution. The phrase "expenses for selling property" includes brokerage fees and other expenses attending the sale, such as the fees of an auctioneer if it is reasonably necessary to employ one. Where an item included in the gross estate is disposed of in a bona fide sale (including a redemption) to a dealer in such items at a price below its fair market value, for purposes of this paragraph there shall be treated as an expense for selling the item whichever of the following amounts is the lesser: (i) The amount by which the fair market value of the property on the applicable valuation date exceeds the proceeds of the sale, or (ii) the amount by which the fair market value of the property on the date of the sale exceeds the proceeds of the sale. The principles used in determining the value at which an item of property is included in the gross estate shall be followed in arriving at the fair market value of the property for purposes of this paragraph. See §§ 20.2031–1 through 20.2031–9.

(3) Expenses incurred in defending the estate against claims described in section 2053(a)(3) are deductible to the extent permitted by § 20.2053–1 if the expenses are incurred incident to the assertion of defenses to the claim available under the applicable law, even if the estate ultimately does not prevail. For purposes of this paragraph (d)(3), "expenses incurred in defending the estate against claims" include costs relating to the arbitration and mediation of contested issues, costs associated with defending the estate against claims (whether or not enforceable), and costs associated with reaching a negotiated settlement of the issues.

(e) Effective/applicability date. This section applies to the estates of decedents dying on or after October 20, 2009.

[T.D. 6296, 23 FR 4529, June 24, 1958, as amended by T.D. 6826, 30 FR 7708, June 15, 1965; 44 FR 23525, April 20, 1979; T.D. 9468, 74 FR 53660, Oct. 20, 2009]

Proposed § 20.2053–3 (June 28, 2022) Deduction for expenses of administering estate.

Section 20.2053–3 is amended by:

1. Redesignating paragraphs (d) and (e) as paragraphs (e) and (f), respectively.

2. Adding a new paragraph (d).

3. Revising newly redesignated paragraph (f).

The additions and revisions read as follows:

(d) Interest expense incurred in administering the estate

(1) *Interest payable under section 6601 on unpaid tax.* (i) *Section 6166 interest.* As used in paragraph (d)(1) of this section, the phrase "section 6166 interest" means interest payable under section 6601 on unpaid estate tax deferred under section 6166. This includes interest accruing on an installment or other payment under section 6166 during the period of an extension of time for making that payment under section 6161(a)(2)(B). Section 6166 interest is not deductible pursuant to section 2053(c)(1)(D).

(ii) *Non-section 6166 interest.* As used in paragraph (d)(1) of this section, the phrase "non-section 6166 interest" means interest payable under section 6601 or under state or local law other than section 6166 interest. Non-section 6166 interest that accrues on or after the decedent's date of death on any unpaid tax or penalties may be deductible to the extent permitted by § 20.2053–1 and this section. For purposes of paragraph (d)(1) of this section, penalties include any unpaid additions to tax, additional taxes, and penalties. When non-section 6166 interest accrues on unpaid estate tax deferred under section 6161 or section 6163, the interest expense is actually and necessarily incurred in the administration of the estate for purposes of paragraph (a) of this section because the extension was based on a demonstrated need to defer payment. When non-section 6166 interest accrues on and after the date of a decedent's death on any unpaid tax or penalties in connection with an underpayment of tax or a deficiency, the interest expense generally is actually and necessarily incurred in the administration of the estate for purposes of paragraph (a) of this section.

(iii) *Exception.* Notwithstanding paragraph (d)(1)(ii) of this section, non-section 6166 interest accruing on unpaid tax and penalties on and after the decedent's date of death, whether in connection with a deferral, underpayment, or deficiency, is not actually and necessarily incurred in the administration of the estate for purposes of paragraph (a) of this section and is not deductible to the extent the interest expense is attributable to an executor's negligence, disregard of applicable rules or regulations (including careless, reckless, or intentional disregard of rules or regulations) as defined in § 1.6662–3(b)(2) of this chapter, or fraud with intent to evade tax. Interest expense is attributable to an executor's negligence, disregard of applicable rules or regulations, or fraud with intent to evade tax to the extent that the underlying deferral, underpayment, or deficiency, is attributable to such conduct by the executor. Similarly, even when the underlying deferral, underpayment, or deficiency is not attributable to such conduct by the executor, the interest expense is attributable to an executor's negligence, disregard of the rules or regulations, or fraud with intent to evade tax to the extent the subsequent accrual of interest is attributable to such conduct by the executor.

(iv) *Examples.* The following examples illustrate the application of this paragraph (d)(1). In each example, the decedent (D) dies on October 1, Year 1, and the estate tax return is due July 1 of the following calendar year, Year 2. In each example, except as expressly stated, there is no negligence, disregard of applicable rules or regulations, or fraud on the part of the executor.

(A) *Example 1.* On July 1, Year 2, the executor of D's estate (E) timely files the estate tax return based on values determined in good faith and pays $500,000, which is the estate tax shown on the return. Upon examination, the Internal Revenue Service (IRS) makes an adjustment to the value of an asset includible in the gross estate, resulting in a $25,000 increase in estate tax due. E initially contests the adjustment, but eventually agrees to the assessment of the deficiency in the amount of $25,000. Interest on the deficiency is payable under section 6601 in the amount of $X. E makes a payment in satisfaction of the assessed deficiency and interest. For purposes of paragraph (a) of this section, the interest expense in the amount of $X is considered actually and necessarily incurred in the administration of D's estate, and its deduction reduces the amount of the deficiency.

(B) *Example 2.* The executor of D's estate (E) files the estate tax return and pays the estate tax shown on the return ($500,000) on July 1 of Year 3, one year after the due date. On August 1, Year 3, the IRS assesses interest on the unpaid tax under section 6601 in the amount of $X, assesses late filing and late payment penalties in accordance with section 6651 in the amount of $Y, and issues a notice and demand for payment of $X and $Y. On August 1, Year 4, E makes payment to the IRS of $Z, which is the total amount due for $X and $Y, as well as interest that accrued on these amounts from August 1, Year 3, to August 1, Year 4, payable under section 6601. The facts establish that E's failure to timely file the return and timely pay the tax and failure to pay the assessed interest and penalties within the period provided in the notice and demand is a result of E's disregard of the rules for filing the return and paying the tax and any assessed penalties. Under the facts in this paragraph (d)(1)(iv)(B), neither the interest payable under section 6601 that accrued on the unpaid tax before notice and demand nor the interest that accrued on the unpaid tax and penalties after notice and demand is an expense that is actually and necessarily incurred in the administration of D's estate for purposes of paragraph (a) of this section.

(C) *Example 3.* Prior to D's death, the IRS had assessed an income tax deficiency against D for the 2009 tax period in the amount of $75,000, and penalties in the amount of $X. The assessed tax and penalties remained unpaid on D's date of death. On July 1, Year 2, the executor of D's estate (E) timely files the estate tax return and timely pays the estate tax shown on the return to be due. On the same date, E also pays all claims against and liabilities of the estate, except for the assessed income tax deficiency and penalties for the 2009 tax period. Despite E's awareness that the estate had sufficient liquidity and funds to satisfy all estate liabilities, including the 2009 income tax deficiency and penalties, E does not pay the assessed income tax deficiency, penalties, and accrued interest until July 1, Year 4. E's failure to pay the assessed income tax deficiency and penalties for the 2009 tax period is a result of E's disregard of applicable rules or regulations. Even though the underlying income tax deficiency is not attributable to E's negligence, disregard of applicable rules, or fraud with intent to evade tax, the interest that accrued after July 1, Year 2, on the assessed deficiency and penalties is attributable to E's disregard of applicable rules or regulations. Accordingly, the post-July 1, Year 2, interest is not an expense that is actually and necessarily incurred in the administration of D's estate.

(2) *Interest expense on certain loan obligations of the estate.* Interest on a loan entered into by the estate to facilitate the payment of the estate's tax and other liabilities or the administration of the estate may be deductible depending on all the facts and circumstances. To be a deductible administration expense, interest expense must arise from an instrument or contractual arrangement that constitutes indebtedness under applicable income tax regulations and general principles of Federal tax law. In addition, the interest expense and the loan to which interest expense relates must satisfy the requirement of § 20.2053–1(b)(2) that they are bona fide in nature based on all the facts and circumstances. Further, both the loan to which the interest expense relates and the loan terms must be actually and necessarily incurred in the administration of the decedent's estate and must be essential to the proper settlement of the decedent's estate. See paragraph (a) of this section. If the facts and circumstances establish that the interest expense arises from an instrument or contractual arrangement that constitutes indebtedness under general principles of Federal tax law, factors that collectively may support a finding that the interest expense also satisfies the additional requirements under § 20.2053–1(b)(2) and paragraph (a) of this section include, but are not limited to, the following:

(i) The interest rate on and the terms of the underlying loan (whether between related or unrelated parties), including any prepayment penalty, are reasonable given all the facts and circumstances and comparable to an arms-length loan transaction;

(ii) The underlying loan is entered into by an executor of the decedent's estate acting in the capacity of executor or, if no executor is appointed and acting, the person accountable for satisfying the liabilities of the estate;

(iii) The lender properly includes amounts of paid and/or accrued interest (including original issue discount as determined under sections 1271 through 1275 and the regulations in this part under those sections, such as original issue discount attributable to stated interest that is treated as part of the stated redemption price at maturity because it is not payable at least annually) in gross income for Federal income tax purposes, particularly if the lender is a family member of the decedent, a related entity, or a beneficiary of the decedent's estate or trust (as defined in § 20.2053–1(b)(2)(iii));

(iv) The loan proceeds are used to satisfy estate liabilities that are essential to the proper settlement of the estate, including, but not limited to, the Federal estate tax liability;

(v) The loan term and payment schedule correspond to the estate's anticipated ability to make the payments under, and to satisfy, the loan, and the loan term does not extend beyond what is reasonably necessary;

(vi) The only practical alternatives to the loan are the sale of estate assets at prices that are significantly below-market, the forced liquidation of an entity that conducts an active trade or business, or some similar financially undesirable course of action;

(vii) The underlying loan is entered into when the estate's liquid assets are insufficient to satisfy estate liabilities, the estate does not have control (within the meaning of section 2701(b)(2)) of an entity that has liquid assets sufficient to satisfy estate liabilities, the estate has no power to direct or compel an entity in which it has an interest to sell liquid assets to enable the estate to satisfy its liabilities, and the estate's assets are expected to generate sufficient cash flow or liquidity to make the payments required under the loan;

(viii) The estate's illiquidity does not occur after the decedent's death as a result of the decedent's testamentary estate plan to create illiquidity; similarly, the illiquidity does not occur post-death as a deliberate result of the action or inaction of the executor who then had both knowledge or reason to know of the estate tax liability and a reasonable alternative to that action or inaction that could have avoided or mitigated the illiquidity;

(ix) The lender is not a beneficiary of a substantial portion of the value of the estate, and is not an entity over which such a beneficiary has control (within the meaning of section 2701(b)(2)) or the right to compel or direct the making of the loan;

(x) The lender or lenders are not beneficiaries of the estate whose individual share of liability under the loan is substantially similar to his or her share of the estate; and

(xi) The decedent's estate has no right of recovery of estate tax against, or of contribution from, the person loaning the funds.

* * * *

(f) Applicability date. The rules of this section apply to the estates of decedents dying on or after [*date of publication of the final rule in the Federal Register*].

§ 20.2053–4 Deduction for claims against the estate.

(a) In general. (1) *General rule.* For purposes of this section, liabilities imposed by law or arising out of contracts or torts are deductible if they meet the applicable requirements set forth in § 20.2053–1 and this section. To be deductible, a claim against a decedent's estate must represent a personal obligation of the decedent existing at the time of the decedent's death. Except as otherwise provided in paragraphs (b) and (c) of this section and to the extent permitted by § 20.2053–1, the amounts that may be deducted as claims against a decedent's estate are limited to the amounts of bona fide claims that are enforceable against the decedent's estate (and are not unenforceable when paid) and claims that—

(i) Are actually paid by the estate in satisfaction of the claim; or

(ii) Meet the requirements of § 20.2053–1(d)(4) for deducting certain ascertainable amounts.

(2) *Effect of post-death events.* Events occurring after the date of a decedent's death shall be considered in determining whether and to what extent a deduction is allowable under section 2053. See § 20.2053–1(d)(2).

(b) Exception for claims and counterclaims in related matter. (1) *General rule.* If a decedent's gross estate includes one or more claims or causes of action and there are one or more claims against the decedent's estate in the same or a substantially-related matter, or, if a decedent's gross estate includes a particular asset and there are one or more claims against the decedent's estate integrally related to that particular asset, the executor may deduct on the estate's United States Estate (and Generation-Skipping Transfer) Tax Return (Form 706) the current value of the claim or claims against the estate, even though payment has not been made, provided that—

(i) Each such claim against the estate otherwise satisfies the applicable requirements set forth in § 20.2053–1;

(ii) Each such claim against the estate represents a personal obligation of the decedent existing at the time of the decedent's death;

(iii) Each such claim is enforceable against the decedent's estate (and is not unenforceable when paid);

(iv) The value of each such claim against the estate is determined from a "qualified appraisal" performed by a "qualified appraiser" within the meaning of section 170 of the Internal Revenue Code and the corresponding regulations;

(v) The value of each such claim against the estate is subject to adjustment for post-death events; and

(vi) The aggregate value of the related claims or assets included in the decedent's gross estate exceeds 10 percent of the decedent's gross estate.

(2) *Limitation on deduction.* The deduction under this paragraph (b) is limited to the value of the related claims or particular assets included in decedent's gross estate.

(3) *Effect of post-death events.* If, under this paragraph (b), a deduction is claimed on Form 706 for a claim against the estate and, during the period described in § 20.2053–1(d)(2), the claim is paid or meets the requirements of § 20.2053–1(d)(4) for deducting certain ascertainable amounts, the claimed deduction is subject to adjustment to reflect, and may not exceed, the amount paid on the claim or the amount meeting the requirements of § 20.2053–1(d)(4). If, under this paragraph (b), a deduction is claimed on Form 706 for a claim against the estate and, during the period described in § 20.2053–1(d)(2), the claim remains unpaid (and does not meet the requirements of § 20.2053–1(d)(4) for deducting certain ascertainable amounts), the claimed deduction is subject to ad-

justment to reflect, and may not exceed, the current valuation of the claim. A valuation of the claim will be considered current if it reflects events occurring after the decedent's death. With regard to any amount in excess of the amount deductible under this paragraph (b), an estate may preserve the estate's right to claim a refund for claims that are paid or that meet the requirements of § 20.2053–(1)(d)(4) after the expiration of the period of limitation for filing a claim for refund by filing a protective claim for refund in accordance with the rules in § 20.2053–1(d)(5).

(c) Exception for claims totaling not more than $500,000. (1) *General rule.* An executor may deduct on Form 706 the current value of one or more claims against the estate even though payment has not been made on the claim or claims to the extent that—

(i) Each such claim against the estate otherwise satisfies the applicable requirements for deductibility set forth in § 20.2053–1;

(ii) Each such claim against the estate represents a personal obligation of the decedent existing at the time of the decedent's death;

(iii) Each such claim is enforceable against the decedent's estate (and is not unenforceable when paid);

(iv) The value of each such claim against the estate is determined from a "qualified appraisal" performed by a "qualified appraiser" within the meaning of section 170 of the Internal Revenue Code and the corresponding regulations;

(v) The total amount deducted by the estate under this paragraph (c) does not exceed $500,000;

(vi) The full value of each claim, rather than just a portion of that amount, must be deductible under this paragraph (c) and, for this purpose, the full value of each such claim is deemed to be the unpaid amount of that claim that is not deductible after the application of §§ 20.2053–1 and 20.2053–4(b); and

(vii) The value of each claim deducted under this paragraph (c) is subject to adjustment for post-death events.

(2) *Effect of post-death events.* If, under this paragraph (c), a deduction is claimed for a claim against the estate and, during the period described in § 20.2053–1(d)(2), the claim is paid or meets the requirements of § 20.2053–1(d)(4) for deducting certain ascertainable amounts, the amount of the allowable deduction for that claim is subject to adjustment to reflect, and may not exceed, the amount paid on the claim or the amount meeting the requirements of § 20.2053–1(d)(4). If, under this paragraph (c), a deduction is claimed for a claim against the estate and, during the period described in § 20.2053–1(d)(2), the claim remains unpaid (and does not meet the requirements of § 20.2053–1(d)(4) for deducting certain ascertainable amounts), the amount of the allowable deduction for that claim is subject to adjustment to reflect, and may not exceed, the current value of the claim. The value of the claim will be considered current if it reflects events occurring after the decedent's death. To claim a deduction for amounts in excess of the amount deductible under this paragraph (c), the estate may preserve the estate's right to claim a refund for claims that are not paid or that do not meet the requirements of § 20.2053–1(d)(4) until after the expiration of the period of limitation for the filing of a claim for refund by filing a protective claim for refund in accordance with the rules in § 20.2053–1(d)(5).

(3) *Examples.* The following examples illustrate the application of this paragraph (c). Assume that the value of each claim is determined from a "qualified appraisal" performed by a "qualified appraiser" and reflects events occurring after the death of the decedent (D). Also assume that each claim represents a personal obligation of D that existed at D's death, that each claim is enforceable against the decedent's estate (and is not unenforceable when paid), and that each claim otherwise satisfies the requirements for deductibility of § 20.2053–1.

Example (1). There are three claims against the estate of the decedent (D) that are not paid and are not deductible under § 20.2053–1(d)(4) or paragraph (b) of this section: $25,000 of Claimant A, $35,000 of Claimant B, and $1,000,000 of Claimant C. The executor of D's estate (E) may not claim a deduction under this paragraph with respect to any portion of the claim of Claimant C because the value of that claim exceeds $500,000. E may claim a deduction under this paragraph for the total amount of the claims filed by Claimant A and Claimant B ($60,000) because the aggregate value of the full amount of those claims does not exceed $500,000.

Example (2). There are three claims against the estate of the decedent (D) that are not paid and are not deductible under § 20.2053–1(d)(4) or paragraph (b) of this section; specifically, a separate $200,000 claim of each of three claimants, A, B and C. The executor of D's estate (E) may claim a deduction under this paragraph for any two of these three claims because the aggregate value of the full amount of any two of the claims does not exceed $500,000. E may not deduct any part of the value of the remaining claim under this paragraph because the aggregate value of the full amount of all three claims would exceed $500,000.

Example (3). As a result of an automobile accident involving the decedent (D) and A, D's gross estate includes a claim against A that is valued at $750,000. In the same matter, A files a counterclaim against D's estate that is valued at $1,000,000. A's claim against D's estate is not paid and is not deductible under § 20.2053–1(d)(4). All other section 2053 claims and expenses of D's estate have been paid and are deductible. The executor of D's estate (E) deducts $750,000 of A's claim against the estate under § 20.2053–4(b). E may claim a deduction under this paragraph (c) for the total value of A's claim not deducted under § 20.2053–4(b), or $250,000. If, instead, the value of A's claim against D's estate is $1,500,000, so that the amount not deductible under § 20.2053–4(b) exceeds $500,000, no deduction is available under this paragraph (c).

(d) Special rules. (1) *Potential and unmatured claims.* Except as provided in § 20.2053–1(d)(4) and in paragraphs (b) and (c) of this section, no estate tax deduction may be taken for a claim against the decedent's estate while it remains a potential or unmatured claim. Claims that later mature may be deducted (to the extent permitted by § 20.2053–1) in connection with a timely claim for refund. To preserve the estate's right to claim a refund for claims that mature and become deductible after the expiration of the period of limitation for filing a claim for refund, a protective claim for refund may be filed in accordance with § 20.2053–1(d)(5). See § 20.2053–1(b)(3) for rules relating to the treatment of court decrees and settlements.

(2) *Contested claims.* Except as provided in paragraphs (b) and (c) of this section, no estate tax deduction may be taken for a claim against the decedent's estate to the extent the estate is contesting the decedent's liability. Contested claims that later mature may be deducted (to the extent permitted by § 20.2053–1) in connection with a claim for refund filed within the time prescribed in section 6511(a). To preserve the estate's right to claim a refund for claims that mature and become deductible after the expiration of the period of limitation for filing a claim for refund, a protective claim for refund may be filed in accordance with § 20.2053–1(d)(5). See § 20.2053–1(b)(3) for rules relating to the treatment of court decrees and settlements.

(3) *Claims against multiple parties.* If the decedent or the decedent's estate is one of two or more parties against whom the claim is being asserted, the estate may deduct only the portion of the total claim due from and paid by the estate, reduced by the total of any reimbursement received from another party, insurance, or otherwise. The estate's deductible portion also will be reduced by the contribution or other amount the estate could have collected from another party or an insurer but which the estate declines or fails to attempt to collect. See further § 20.2053–1(d)(3).

(4) *Unenforceable claims.* Claims that are unenforceable prior to or at the decedent's death are not deductible, even if they are actually paid. Claims that become unenforceable during the administration of the estate are not deductible to the extent that they are paid (or will be paid) after they become unenforceable. However, see § 20.2053–1(b)(3)(iv) regarding a claim whose enforceability is at issue.

(5) *Claims founded upon a promise.* Except with regard to pledges or subscriptions (see § 20.2053–5), section 2053(c)(1)(A) provides that the deduction for a claim founded upon a promise or agreement is limited to the extent that the promise or agreement was bona fide and in exchange for adequate and full consideration in money or money's worth; that is, the promise or agreement must have been bargained for at arm's length and the price must have been an adequate and full equivalent reducible to a money value.

(6) *Recurring payments.* (i) *Noncontingent obligations.* If a decedent is obligated to make recurring payments on an enforceable and certain claim that satisfies the requirements for deductibility under this section and the payments are not subject to a contingency, the amount of the claim will be deemed ascertainable with reasonable certainty for purposes of the rule for deducting certain ascertainable amounts set forth in § 20.2053–1(d)(4). If the recurring payments

will be paid, a deduction will be allowed under the rule for deducting certain ascertainable amounts set forth in § 20.2053–1(d)(4) (subject to any applicable limitations in § 20.2053–1). Recurring payments for purposes of this section exclude those payments made in connection with a mortgage or indebtedness described in and governed by § 20.2053–7. If a decedent's obligation to make a recurring payment is contingent on the death or remarriage of the claimant and otherwise satisfies the requirements of this paragraph (d)(6)(i), the amount of the claim (measured according to actuarial principles, using factors set forth in the transfer tax regulations or otherwise provided by the IRS) will be deemed ascertainable with reasonable certainty for purposes of the rule for deducting certain ascertainable amounts set forth in § 20.2053–1(d)(4).

(ii) *Contingent obligations.* If a decedent has a recurring obligation to pay an enforceable and certain claim but the decedent's obligation is subject to a contingency or is not otherwise described in paragraph (d)(6)(i) of this section, the amount of the claim is not ascertainable with reasonable certainty for purposes of the rule for deducting certain ascertainable amounts set forth in § 20.2053–1(d)(4). Accordingly, the amount deductible is limited to amounts actually paid by the estate in satisfaction of the claim in accordance with § 20.2053–1(d)(1) (subject to any applicable limitations in § 20.2053–1).

(iii) *Purchase of commercial annuity to satisfy recurring obligation to pay.* If a decedent has a recurring obligation (whether or not contingent) to pay an enforceable and certain claim and the estate purchases a commercial annuity from an unrelated dealer in commercial annuities in an arm's-length transaction to satisfy the obligation, the amount deductible by the estate (subject to any applicable limitations in § 20.2053–1) is the sum of—

(A) The amount paid for the commercial annuity, to the extent that the amount paid is not refunded, or expected to be refunded, to the estate;

(B) Any amount actually paid to the claimant by the estate prior to the purchase of the commercial annuity; and

(C) Any amount actually paid to the claimant by the estate in excess of the annuity amount as is necessary to satisfy the recurring obligation.

(7) *Examples.* The following examples illustrate the application of paragraph (d) of this section. Except as is otherwise provided in the examples, assume—

(i) A claim satisfies the applicable requirements set forth in § 20.2053–1 and paragraph (a) of this section, is payable from property subject to claims, and the amount of the claim is not subject to any other applicable limitations in § 20.2053–1;

(ii) A claim is not deductible under paragraphs (b) or (c) of this section as an exception to the general rule contained in paragraph (a) of this section; and

(iii) The claimant (C) is not a family member, related entity or beneficiary of the estate of decedent (D) and is not the executor (E).

Example (1). Contested claim, single defendant, no decision. D is sued by C for $100x in a tort proceeding and responds asserting affirmative defenses available to D under applicable local law. D dies and E is substituted as defendant in the suit. D's Form 706 is due before a judgment is reached in the case. D's gross estate exceeds $100x. E may not take a deduction on Form 706 for the claim against the estate. However, E may claim a deduction under § 20.2053–3(c) or § 20.2053–3(d)(3) for expenses incurred in defending the estate against the claim if the expenses have been paid in accordance with § 20.2053–1(d)(1) or if the expenses meet the requirements of § 20.2053–1(d)(4) for deducting certain ascertainable amounts. E may file a protective claim for refund before the expiration of the period of limitation prescribed in section 6511(a) in order to preserve the estate's right to claim a refund, if the amount of the claim will not be paid or cannot be ascertained with reasonable certainty by the expiration of this limitation period. If payment is subsequently made pursuant to a court decision or a settlement, the payment, as well as expenses incurred incident to the claim and not previously deducted, may be deducted and relief may be sought in connection with a timely-filed claim for refund.

Example (2). Contested claim, single defendant, final court decree and payment. The facts are the same as in Example 1 except that, before the Form 706 is timely filed, the court enters a decision in favor of C, no timely appeal is filed, and payment is made. E may claim a deduction on Form 706 for the amount paid in satisfaction of the claim against the estate pursuant to the final decision of the local court, including any interest accrued prior to D's death. In addition, E may claim a deduction under § 20.2053–3(c) or § 20.2053–3(d)(3) for expenses incurred in defending the estate against the claim and in processing payment of the claim if the expenses have been paid in accordance with § 20.2053–1(d)(1) or if the expenses meet the requirements of § 20.2053–1(d)(4) for deducting certain ascertainable amounts.

Example (3). Contested claim, single defendant, settlement and payment. The facts are the same as in Example 1 except that a settlement is reached between E and C for $80x and payment is made before Form 706 is timely filed. E may claim a deduction on Form 706 for the amount paid to C ($80x) in satisfaction of the claim against the estate. In addition, E may claim a deduction under § 20.2053–3(c) or § 20.2053–3(d)(3) for expenses incurred in defending the estate, reaching a settlement, and processing payment of the claim if the expenses have been paid in accordance with § 20.2053–1(d)(1) or if the expenses meet the requirements of § 20.2053–1(d)(4) for deducting certain ascertainable amounts.

Example (4). Contested claim, multiple defendants. The facts are the same as in Example 1 except that the suit filed by C lists D and an unrelated third-party (K) as defendants. If the claim against the estate is not resolved prior to the time the Form 706 is filed, E may not take a deduction for the claim on Form 706. If payment is subsequently made of D's share of the claim pursuant to a court decision holding D liable for 40 percent of the amount due and K liable for 60 percent of the amount due, then E may claim a deduction for the amount paid in satisfaction of the claim against the estate representing D's share of the liability as assigned by the court decree ($40x), plus any interest on that share accrued prior to D's death. If the court decision finds D and K jointly and severally liable for the entire $100x and D's estate pays the entire $100x but could have reasonably collected $50x from K in reimbursement, E may claim a deduction of $50x together with the interest on $50x accrued prior to D's death. In both instances, E also may claim a deduction under § 20.2053–3(c) or § 20.2053–3(d)(3) for expenses incurred and not previously deducted in defending the estate against the claim and processing payment of the amount due from D if the expenses have been paid in accordance with § 20.2053–1(d)(1) or if the expenses meet the requirements of § 20.2053–1(d)(4) for deducting certain ascertainable amounts.

Example (5). Contested claim, multiple defendants, settlement and payment. The facts are the same as in Example 1 except that the suit filed by C lists D and an unrelated third-party (K) as defendants. D's estate settles with C for $10x and payment is made before Form 706 is timely filed. E may take a deduction on Form 706 for the amount paid to C ($10x) in satisfaction of the claim against the estate. In addition, E may claim a deduction under § 20.2053–3(c) or § 20.2053–3(d)(3) for expenses incurred in defending the estate, reaching a settlement, and processing payment of the claim if the expenses have been paid in accordance with § 20.2053–1(d)(1) or if the expenses meet the requirements of § 20.2053–1(d)(4) for deducting certain ascertainable amounts.

Example (6). Mixed claims. During life, D contracts with C to perform specific work on D's home for $75x. Under the contract, additional work must be approved in advance by D. C performs additional work and sues D for $100x for work completed including the $75x agreed to in the contract. D dies and D's Form 706 is due before a judgment is reached in the case. E accepts liability of $75x but contests liability of $25x. E may take a deduction of $75x on Form 706 if the amount has been paid or meets the requirements of § 20.2053–1(d)(4) for deducting certain ascertainable amounts. In addition, E may claim a deduction under § 20.2053–3(c) or § 20.2053–3(d)(3) for expenses incurred in defending the estate against the claim if the expenses have been paid or if the expenses meet the requirements of § 20.2053–1(d)(4) for deducting certain ascertainable amounts. E may file a protective claim for refund before the expiration of the period of limitation prescribed in section 6511(a) in order to preserve the estate's right to claim a refund for any amount in excess of $75x that is subsequently paid to resolve the claim against the estate. To the extent that any unpaid expenses incurred in defending the estate against the claim are not deducted as an ascertainable amount pursuant to § 20.2053–1(d)(4), they may be included in the protective claim for refund.

Example (7). Claim having issue of enforceability. D is sued by C for $100x in a tort proceeding in which there is an issue as to whether the claim is barred by the applicable period of limitations. After D's death but prior to the decision of the court, a settlement meeting the requirements of § 20.2053–1(b)(3)(iv) is reached between E and C in the amount of $50x. E pays C this amount before the Form 706 is timely filed. E may take a deduction on Form 706 for the amount paid to C ($50x) in satisfaction of the claim. If, subsequent to E's payment to C, facts develop to indicate that the claim was, in fact, unenforceable, the deduction will not be denied provided the enforceability of the claim was at issue in a bona dispute at the time of the payment. See § 20.2053–1(b)(3)(iv). A deduction may be available under § 20.2053–3(d)(3) for expenses incurred in defending the estate, reaching a settlement, and processing payment of the claim if the expenses have been paid in accordance with § 20.2053–1(d)(1) or if the expenses meet the requirements of § 20.2053–1(d)(4) for deducting certain ascertainable amounts.

Example (8). Noncontingent and recurring obligation to pay, binding on estate. D's property settlement agreement incident to D's divorce, signed three years prior to D's death, obligates D or D's estate to pay to S, D's former spouse, $20x per year until S's death or remarriage. Prior to D's death, D made payments in accordance with the agreement and, after D's death, E continues to make the payments in accordance with the agreement. D's obligation to pay S under the property settlement agreement is deemed to be a claim against the estate that is ascertainable with reasonable certainty for purposes of § 20.2053–1(d)(4). To the extent the obligation to make the recurring payment is a claim that will be paid, E may deduct the amount of the claim (measured according to actuarial principles, using factors set forth in the transfer tax regulations or otherwise provided by the IRS) under the rule for deducting certain ascertainable amounts set forth in § 20.2053–1(d)(4).

Example (9). Recurring obligation to pay, estate purchases a commercial annuity in satisfaction. D's settlement agreement with T, the claimant in a suit against D, signed three years prior to D's death, obligates D or D's estate to pay to T $20x per year for 10 years, provided that T does not reveal the details of the claim or of the settlement during that period. D dies in Year 1. In Year 2, D's estate purchases a commercial annuity from an unrelated issuer of commercial annuities, XYZ, to fund the obligation to T. E may deduct the entire amount paid to XYZ to obtain the annuity, even though the obligation to T was contingent.

(e) Interest on claim. (1) Subject to any applicable limitations in § 20.2053–1, the interest on a deductible claim is itself deductible as a claim under section 2053 to the extent of the amount of interest accrued at the decedent's death (even if the executor elects the alternate valuation method under section 2032), but only to the extent of the amount of interest actually paid or meeting the requirements of § 20.2053–1(d)(4) for deducting certain ascertainable amounts.

(2) Post-death accrued interest may be deductible in appropriate circumstances either as an estate tax administration expense under section 2053 or as an income tax deduction.

(f) Effective/applicability date. This section applies to the estates of decedents dying on or after October 20, 2009.

[T.D. 6296, 23 FR 4529, June 24, 1958; T.D. 9468, 74 FR 53660, Oct. 20, 2009; 74 FR 61525, Nov. 25, 2009]

Proposed § 20.2053–4 (June 28, 2022) Deduction for claims against the estate.

Section 20.2053–4 is amended by:

1. Revising paragraphs (b)(1)(iv), (b)(2), and (c)(1)(iv) and (v), the second sentence of paragraph (c)(3), paragraph (d)(5), and paragraph (d)(7)(iii) introductory text.

2. In paragraph (d)(7)(iii), Examples 1 through 9 are designated as paragraphs (d)(7)(iii)(A) through (I), respectively.

3. In newly designated paragraph (d)(7)(iii)(A), removing "decision," and "§ 20.2053–3(c) or § 20.2053–3(d)(3)" adding "decision." and "§ 20.2053–3(c) or (d)(3)" in their places, respectively.

4. In newly designated paragraphs (d)(7)(iii)(B) and (C), removing "payment,", "Example 1", and "§ 20.2053–3(c) or § 20.2053–3(d)(3)" and adding "payment.", "paragraph (d)(7)(iii)(A) of this section (Example 1)", and "§ 20.2053–3(c) or (d)(3)" in their places, respectively.

5. In newly designated paragraph (d)(7)(iii)(D), removing "defendants,", "Example 1", and "§ 20.2053–3(c) or § 20.2053–3(d)(3)" and adding "defendants.", "paragraph (d)(7)(iii)(A) of this sec-

tion (Example 1)", and "§ 20.2053–3(c) or (d)(3)" in their places, respectively.

6. In newly designated paragraph (d)(7)(iii)(E), removing "payment,", "Example 1", and "§ 20.2053–3(c) or § 20.2053–3(d)(3)" and adding "payment.", "paragraph (d)(7)(iii)(A) of this section (Example 1)", and "§ 20.2053–3(c) or (d)(3)" in their places, respectively.

7. In newly designated paragraph (d)(7)(iii)(F), removing "claims," and "§ 20.2053–3(c) or § 20.2053–3(d)(3)" and adding "claims." and "§ 20.2053–3(c) or (d)(3)" in their places, respectively.

8. In newly designated paragraph (d)(7)(iii)(G), removing "enforceability," and adding "enforceability." in its place.

9. In newly designated paragraph (d)(7)(iii)(H), removing "estate," and adding "estate." in its place.

10. In newly designated paragraph (d)(7)(iii)(I), removing "satisfaction," and adding "satisfaction." in its place.

11. Adding paragraph (d)(7)(iii)(J).

12. Revising paragraph (f).

The additions and revisions read as follows:

* * * *

(b) * * *

(1) * * *

(iv) The value of each such claim against the estate is supported by a written appraisal document to be filed with the Form 706, *United States Estate (and Generation-Skipping Transfer) Tax Return*, or successor form, and the written appraisal document

(A) Adequately reflects post-death events that have occurred prior to the date on which a deduction is claimed on an estate's Form 706;

(B) Reports, considers, and appropriately weighs all relevant facts and elements of value as are known or are reasonably determinable at the time of the appraisal, including the underlying facts of the claim against the estate, potential litigating risks, and the current status of the claim and procedural history;

(C) Takes into account post-death events reasonably anticipated to occur;

(D) Identifies an expected date or dates of payment (for purposes of determining the applicability of the present value limitation in § 20.2053–1(d)(6));

(E) Explains in detail the methods and analysis that support the appraisal's conclusions;

(F) Is prepared, signed under penalties of perjury, and dated by a person who is qualified by knowledge and experience to appraise the claim being valued and is not a family member of the decedent, a related entity, or a beneficiary of the decedent's estate or revocable trust (as those terms are defined in § 20.2053–1(b)(2)(iii)), a family member of a beneficiary or a related entity as to a beneficiary (as those terms would be defined in § 20.2053–1(b)(2)(iii) if references therein to the decedent were replaced with a reference to such beneficiary, and without regard to the limitations in § 20.2053–1(b)(2)(iii) based on the decedent's date of death), or an employee or other owner of any of them; and

(G) Includes a statement providing the basis for the person's qualifications to appraise the claim being valued;

* * * *

(2) *Limitation on deduction.* The deduction under this paragraph (b) is limited to the value of the related claims or particular assets included in decedent's gross estate. *See* § 20.2053–1(d)(6)(v) for the impact of the present value limitation.

* * * *

(c) * * *

(1) * * *

(iv) The value of each such claim against the estate is supported by a written appraisal document to be filed with the Form 706, *United States Estate (and Generation-Skipping Transfer) Tax Return*, or successor form, and the written appraisal document

(A) Adequately reflects post-death events that have occurred prior to the date on which a deduction is claimed on an estate's Form 706;

(B) Reports, considers and appropriately weighs all relevant facts and elements of value as are known or reasonably determinable at the time of the appraisal, including the underlying facts of the claim against the estate, potential litigating risks, and the current status of the claim and procedural history;

(C) Takes into account post-death events reasonably anticipated to occur;

(D) Identifies an expected date or dates of payment (for purposes of determining the applicability of the present value limitation in § 20.2053–1(d)(6));

(E) Explains in detail the methods and analysis that support the appraisal's conclusions;

(F) Is prepared, signed under penalties of perjury, and dated by a person who is qualified by knowledge and experience to appraise the claim being valued, and is not a family member of the decedent, a related entity, or a beneficiary of the decedent's estate or revocable trust (as those terms are defined in § 20.2053–1(b)(2)(iii)), a family member of a beneficiary or a related entity as to a beneficiary (as those terms would be defined in § 20.2053–1(b)(2)(iii) if references therein to the decedent were replaced with a reference to such beneficiary, and without regard to the limitations in § 20.2053–1(b)(2)(iii) based on the decedent's date of death), or an employee or other owner of any of them; and

(G) Includes a statement providing the basis for the person's qualifications to appraise the claim being valued;

(v) The total amount deducted by the estate under paragraph (c) of this section does not exceed $500,000 (see § 20.2053–1(d)(6)(v) for the impact of the present value limitation);

* * * *

(3) * * * Assume that each claim is paid within three years after the decedent's death, and that the value of each claim is determined from a written appraisal document that meets the requirements of paragraph (c)(1)(iv) of this section. * * *

(d) * * *

(5) *Claims founded upon a promise.* (i) *In general.* To be deductible, a claim founded on a promise must represent a personal obligation of the decedent existing at the time of the decedent's death, and the claim must be enforceable against the decedent's estate. In addition, except with regard to pledges or subscriptions (*see* § 20.2053–5), the deduction for a claim founded upon a promise or agreement is limited to the extent that the promise or agreement was bona fide and in exchange for adequate and full consideration in money or money's worth; that is, the promise or agreement must have been bargained for at arm's length and the price must have been an adequate and full equivalent reducible to money value.

(ii) *Decedent's promise to guarantee a debt.* A deduction for a claim founded upon a decedent's agreement to guarantee a debt of another is a claim founded on a promise and is subject to the limitation in paragraph (d)(5)(i) of this section. For purposes of section 2053, a decedent's agreement to guarantee a debt of an entity in which the decedent had an interest at the time the guarantee was given satisfies the requirement that the agreement be in exchange for adequate and full consideration in money or money's worth if, at the time the guarantee was given, the decedent had control (within the meaning of section 2701(b)(2)) of the entity. Alternatively, this requirement is satisfied to the extent the maximum liability of the decedent under the guarantee did not exceed, at the time the guarantee was given, the fair market value of the decedent's interest in the entity. The bona fide nature of the decedent's agreement to guarantee a debt of a family member, a related entity, or a beneficiary (as defined in § 20.2053–1(b)(2)(iii)) is determined in accordance with § 20.2053–1(b)(2)(ii). For a claim otherwise deductible under this paragraph (d)(5)(ii), the estate's right of contribution or reimbursement will reduce the amount deductible in accordance with § 20.2053–1(d)(3). Payments made pursuant to the decedent's guarantee of a debt are deductible only to the extent that the debt for which the guarantee is given has not been taken into account in computing the value of the gross estate under § 20.2053–7 or otherwise.

* * * *

(7) * * *

(iii) The claimant (C) is not a family member, related entity, or beneficiary of the estate of decedent (D), unless otherwise provided, and is not the executor (E).

* * * *

(J) *Example 10: Guarantee.* On Date 1, D entered into a guarantee agreement with Bank (C) to secure financing for a closely-held business (LLC) in which D had a controlling interest. LLC was solvent at the time LLC executed a promissory note in the amount of $100x in favor of C. Prior to D's death, LLC became insolvent and stopped making payments on the note. After D's death, C filed a claim against D's estate for payment of the remaining balance due under the note and E paid the full amount due. Although E had a right of contribution against LLC for primary payment of the indebtedness, LLC was insolvent and no part of the debt was collectible at the time E deducted the payment. D's estate may deduct the amount paid to C in satisfaction of D's liability under the guarantee agreement. The guarantee agreement is considered to have been contracted for an adequate and full consideration in money or money's worth. The result would be the same if D did not have control of LLC as long as the fair market value of D's interest in the LLC on Date 1 was at least $100x.

* * * *

(f) Applicability date. The rules of this section apply to the estates of decedents dying on or after [*date of publication of the final rule in the Federal Register*].

§ 20.2053–5 Deductions for charitable, etc., pledges or subscriptions.

(a) A pledge or a subscription, evidenced by a promissory note or otherwise, even though enforceable against the estate, is deductible (subject to any applicable limitations in § 20.2053–1) only to the extent that—

(1) Liability therefor[e] was contracted bona fide and for an adequate and full consideration in cash or its equivalent, or

(2) It would have constituted an allowable deduction under section 2055 (relating to charitable, etc., deductions) if it had been a bequest.

(b) Effective/applicability date. This section applies to the estates of decedents dying on or after October 20, 2009.

[T.D. 6296, 23 FR 4529, June 24, 1958; T.D. 9468, 74 FR 53664, Oct. 20, 2009]

§ 20.2053–6 Deduction for taxes.

(a) In general. (1) Taxes are deductible in computing a decedent's gross estate—

(i) Only as claims against the estate (except to the extent that excise taxes may be allowable as administration expenses);

(ii) Only to the extent not disallowed by section 2053(c)(1)(B) and this section; and

(iii) Subject to any applicable limitations in § 20.2053–1.

(2) See §§ 20.2053–9 and 20.2053–10 with respect to the deduction allowed for certain state and foreign death taxes.

(b) Property taxes. Property taxes are not deductible unless they accrued before the decedent's death. However, they are not deductible merely because they have accrued in an accounting sense. Property taxes in order to be deductible must be an enforceable obligation of the decedent at the time of his death.

(c) Death taxes. (1) For the estates of decedents dying on or before December 31, 2004, no estate, succession, legacy or inheritance tax payable by reason of the decedent's death is deductible, except as provided in §§ 20.2053–9 and 20.2053–10 with respect to certain state and foreign death taxes on transfers for charitable, etc., uses. However, see sections 2011 and 2014 and the corresponding regulations with respect to credits for death taxes.

(2) For the estates of decedents dying after December 31, 2004, see section 2058 to determine the deductibility of state death taxes.

(d) Gift taxes. Unpaid gift taxes on gifts made by a decedent before his death are deductible. If a gift is considered as made one-half by the decedent and one-half by his spouse under section 2513, the entire amount of the gift tax, unpaid at the decedent's death, attributable to a gift in fact made by the decedent is deductible. No portion of the tax attributable to a gift in fact made by the decedent's spouse is deductible except to the extent that the obligation is enforced against the decedent's estate and his estate has no effective right of contribution against his spouse. (See section 2012 and § 20.2012–1 with respect to credit for gift taxes paid upon gifts of property included in a decedent's gross estate.)

(e) Excise taxes. Excise taxes incurred in selling property of a decedent's estate are deductible as an expense of administration if the sale is necessary in order to (1) pay the decedent's debts, expenses of administration, or taxes, (2) preserve the estate, or (3) effect distribution. Excise taxes incurred in distributing property of the estate in kind are also deductible.

(f) Income taxes. Unpaid income taxes are deductible if they are on income property includible in an income tax return of the decedent for a period before his death. Taxes on income received after the decedent's death are not deductible. If income received by a decedent during his lifetime is included in a joint income tax return filed by the decedent and his spouse, or by the decedent's estate and his surviving spouse, the portion of the joint liability for the period covered by the return for which a deduction will be allowed is the amount for which the decedent's estate would be liable under local law, as between the decedent and his spouse, after enforcement of any effective right of reimbursement or contribution. In the absence of evidence to the contrary, the deductible amount is presumed to be an amount bearing the same ratio to the total joint tax liability for the period covered by the return that the amount of income tax for which the decedent would have been liable if he had filed a separate return for that period bears to the total of the amounts for which the decedent and his spouse would have been liable if they had both filed separate returns for that period. Thus, in the absence of evidence to the contrary, the deductible amount equals:

$$\frac{\text{Decedent's separate tax}}{\text{Both separate taxes}} * \text{Joint tax.}$$

However, the deduction cannot in any event exceed the lesser of—

(1) The decedent's liability for the period (as determined in this paragraph) reduced by the amounts already contributed by the decedent toward payment of the joint liability, or

(2) If there is an enforceable agreement between the decedent and his spouse or between the executor and the spouse relative to the payment of the joint liability, the amount which pursuant to the agreement is to be contributed by the estate toward payment of the joint liability. If the decedent's estate and his surviving spouse are entitled to a refund on account of an overpayment of a joint income tax liability, the overpayment is an asset includible in the decedent's gross estate under section 2033 in the amount to which the estate would be entitled under local law, as between the estate and the surviving spouse. In the absence of evidence to the contrary, the includible amount is presumed to be the amount by which the decedent's contributions toward payment of the joint tax exceeds his liability determined in accordance with the principles set forth in this paragraph (other than subparagraph (1) of this paragraph).

(g) Post-death adjustments of deductible tax liability. Post-death adjustments increasing a tax liability accrued prior to the decedent's death, including increases of taxes deducted under this section, will increase the amount of the deduction available under section 2053(a)(3) for that tax liability. Similarly, any refund subsequently determined to be due to and received by the estate or its successor in interest with respect to taxes deducted by the estate under this section reduce the amount of the deduction taken for that tax liability under section 2053(a)(3). Expenses associated with defending the estate against the increase in tax liability or with obtaining the refund may be deductible under § 20.2053–3(d)(3). A protective claim for refund of estate taxes may be filed before the expiration of the period of limitation for filing a claim for refund in order to preserve the estate's right to claim a refund if the amount of a deductible tax liability may be affected by such an adjustment or refund. The application of this section may be illustrated by the following examples:

Example 1. Increase in tax due. After the decedent's death, the Internal Revenue Service examines the gift tax return filed by the decedent in the year before the decedent's death and asserts a deficiency of $100x. The estate pays attorney's fees of $30x in a non-frivolous defense against the increased deficiency. The final determination of the deficiency, in the amount of $90x, is paid by the estate prior to the expiration of the limitation period for filing a claim for refund. The estate may deduct $90x under section 2053(a)(3) and $30x under § 20.2053–3(c)(2) or (d)(3) in connection with a timely claim for refund.

Example 2. Refund of taxes paid. Decedent's estate timely files D's individual income tax return for the year in which the decedent died. The estate timely pays the entire amount of the tax due, $50x, as shown on that return. The entire $50x was attributable to income received prior to the decedent's death. Decedent's estate subsequently discovers an error on the income tax return and timely files a claim for refund of income tax. Decedent's estate receives a refund of $10x. The estate is allowed a deduction of only $40x under section 2053(a)(3) for the income tax liability accrued prior to the decedent's death. If D's estate had claimed a deduction of $50x on D's United States

Estate (and Generation-Skipping Transfer) Tax Return (Form 706), the deduction claimed under section 2053(a)(3) will be allowed only to the extent of $40x upon examination by the Commissioner.

(h) Effective/applicability date. This section applies to the estates of decedents dying on or after October 20, 2009.

[T.D. 6296, 23 FR 4529, June 24, 1958; T.D. 9468, 74 FR 53664, Oct. 20, 2009]

§ 20.2053–7 Deduction for unpaid mortgages.

A deduction is allowed from a decedent's gross estate of the full unpaid amount of a mortgage upon, or of any other indebtedness in respect of, any property of the gross estate, including interest which had accrued thereon to the date of death, provided the value of the property, undiminished by the amount of the mortgage or indebtedness, is included in the value of the gross estate. If the decedent's estate is liable for the amount of the mortgage or indebtedness, the full value of the property subject to the mortgage or indebtedness must be included as part of the value of the gross estate; the amount of the mortgage or indebtedness being in such case allowed as a deduction. But if the decedent's estate is not so liable, only the value of the equity of redemption (or the value of the property, less the mortgage or indebtedness) need be returned as part of the value of the gross estate. In no case may the deduction on account of the mortgage or indebtedness exceed the liability therefor contracted bona fide and for an adequate and full consideration in money or money's worth. See § 20.2043–1. Only interest accrued to the date of the decedent's death is allowable even though the alternate valuation method under section 2032 is selected. In any case where real property situated outside the United States no deduction may be taken of any mortgage thereon or any other indebtedness does not form a part of the gross estate, in respect thereof.

[T.D. 6296, 23 FR 4529, June 24, 1958 as amended by T.D. 6684, 28 FR 11409, Oct. 24, 1963]

§ 20.2053–8 Deduction for expenses in administering property not subject to claims.

(a) Expenses incurred in administering property included in a decedent's gross estate but not subject to claims fall within the second category of deductions set forth in § 20.2053–1, and may be allowed as deductions if they—

(1) Would be allowed as deductions in the first category if the property being administered were subject to claims; and

(2) Were paid before the expiration of the period of limitation for assessment provided in section 6501.

Usually, these expenses are incurred in connection with the administration of a trust established by a decedent during his lifetime. They may also be incurred in connection with the collection of other assets or the transfer or clearance of title to other property included in a decedent's gross estate for estate tax purposes but not included in his probate estate.

(b) These expenses may be allowed as deductions only to the extent that they would be allowed as deductions under the first category if the property were subject to claims. See § 20.2053–3. The only expenses in administering property not subject to claims which are allowed as deductions are those occasioned by the decedent's death and incurred in settling the decedent's interest in the property or vesting good title to the property in the beneficiaries. Expenses not coming within the description in the preceding sentence but incurred on behalf of the transferees are not deductible.

(c) The principles set forth in paragraphs (b), (c), and (d) of § 20.2053–3 (relating to the allowance of executor's commissions, attorney's fees, and miscellaneous administration expenses of the first category) are applied in determining the extent to which trustee's commissions, attorney's and accountant's fees, and miscellaneous administration expenses are allowed in connection with the administration of property not subject to claims.

(d) The application of this section may be illustrated by the following examples:

Example (1). In 1940, the decedent made an irrevocable transfer of property to the X Trust Company, as trustee. The instrument of transfer provided that the trustee should pay the income from the property to the decedent for the duration of his life and upon his death, distribute the corpus of the trust among designated beneficiaries. The property was included in the decedent's gross estate under the provisions of section 2036. Three months after the date of death, the trustee distributed the trust corpus among the beneficiaries, except for $6,000 which it withheld. The amount withheld represented $5,000 which it retained as trustee's commissions in connection with the termination of the trust and $1,000 which it had paid to an attorney for representing it in connection with the termination. Both the trustee's commissions and the attorney's fees were allowable under the law of the jurisdiction in which the trust was being administered, were reasonable in amount, and were in accord with local custom. Under these circumstances, the estate is allowed a deduction of $6,000.

Example (2). In 1945, the decedent made an irrevocable transfer of property to Y Trust Company, as trustee. The instrument of transfer provided that the trustee should pay the income from the property to the decedent during his life. If the decedent's wife survived him, the trust was to continue for the duration of her life, with Y Trust Company and the decedent's son as co-trustees, and with income payable to the decedent's wife for the duration of her life. Upon the death of both the decedent and his wife, the corpus is to be distributed among designated remaindermen. The decedent was survived by his wife. The property was included in the decedent's gross estate under the provisions of section 2036. In accordance with local custom, the trustee made an accounting to the court as of the date of the decedent's death. Following the death of the decedent, a controversy arose among the remaindermen as to their respective rights under the instrument of transfer, and a suit was brought in court to which the trustee was made a party. As part of the accounting, the court approved the following expenses which the trustee had paid within 3 years following the date of death: $10,000, trustee's commissions; $5,000, accountant's fees; $25,000, attorney's fees; and $2,500, representing fees paid to the guardian of a remainderman who was a minor. The trustee's commissions and accountant's fees were for services in connection with the usual issues involved in a trust accounting as also were one-half of the attorney's and guardian's fees. The remainder of the attorney's and guardian's fees were for services performed in connection with the suit brought by the remaindermen. The amount allowed as a deduction is the $28,750 ($10,000, trustee's commissions; $5,000, accountant's fees; $12,500, attorney's fees; and $1,250, guardian's fees) incurred as expenses in connection with the usual issues involved in a trust accounting. The remaining expenses are not allowed as deductions since they were incurred on behalf of the transferees.

Example (3). Decedent in 1950 made an irrevocable transfer of property to the Z Trust Company, as trustee. The instrument of transfer provided that the trustee should pay the income from the property to the decedent's wife for the duration of her life. If the decedent survived his wife the trust corpus was to be returned to him but if he did not survive her, then upon the death of the wife, the trust corpus was to be distributed among their children. The decedent predeceased his wife and the transferred property, less the value of the wife's outstanding life estate, was included in his gross estate under the provisions of section 2037 since his reversionary interest therein immediately before his death was in excess of 5 percent of the value of the property. At the wife's request, the court ordered the trustee to render an accounting of the trust property as of the date of the decedent's death. No deduction will be allowed the decedent's estate for any of the expenses incurred in connection with the trust accounting, since the expenses were incurred on behalf of the wife.

Example (4). If, in the preceding example, the decedent died without other property and no executor or administrator of his estate was appointed, so that it was necessary for the trustee to prepare an estate tax return and participate in its audit, or if the trustee required accounting proceedings for its own protection in accordance with local custom, trustees', attorneys', and guardians' fees in connection with the estate tax or accounting proceedings would be deductible to the same extent that they would be deductible if the property were subject to claims. Deductions incurred under similar circumstances by a surviving joint tenant or the recipient of life insurance proceeds would also be deductible.

[T.D. 6296, 23 FR 4529, June 24, 1958]

§ 20.2053–9 Deduction for certain State death taxes.

(a) General rule. A deduction is allowed a decedent's estate under section 2053(d) for the amount of any estate, succession, legacy, or inheritance tax imposed by a State, Territory, or the District of Columbia, or, in the case of a decedent dying before September 3, 1958, a possession of the United States upon a transfer by the decedent for charitable, etc., uses described in section 2055 or 2106(a)(2) (relating to the estates of nonresidents not citizens), but only if (1) the conditions stated in paragraph (b) of this section are met, and (2) an election is made in accordance with the provisions of paragraph (c) of this section. See section 2011(e) and § 20.2011–2 for the effect which the allowance of this deduction has upon the credit for State death taxes. However, see section 2058 to determine the deductibility of state death taxes by estates to which section 2058 is applicable.

(b) Condition for allowance of deduction. (1) The deduction is not allowed unless either—

(i) The entire decrease in the Federal estate tax resulting from the allowance of the deduction inures solely to the benefit of a charitable, etc., transferee described in section 2055 or 2106(a)(2), or

(ii) The Federal estate tax is equitably apportioned among all the transferees (including the decedent's surviving spouse and the charitable, etc., transferees) of property included in the decedent's gross estate.

For allowance of the credit, it is sufficient if either of these conditions is satisfied. Thus, in a case where the entire decrease in Federal estate tax inures to the benefit of a charitable transferee, the deduction is allowable even though the Federal estate tax is not equitably apportioned among all the transferees of property included in the decedent's gross estate. Similarly, if the Federal estate tax is equitably apportioned among all the transferees of property included in the decedent's gross estate, the deduction is allowable even though a noncharitable transferee receives some benefit from the allowance of the deduction.

(2) For purposes of this paragraph, the Federal estate tax is considered to be equitably apportioned among all the transferees (including the decedent's surviving spouse and the charitable, etc., transferees) of property included in the decedent's gross estate only if each transferee's share of the tax is based upon the net amount of his transfer subjected to the tax (taking into account any exemptions, credits, or deductions allowed by chapter 11). See examples (2) through (5) of paragraph (e) of this section.

(c) Exercise of election. The election to take a deduction for a state death tax imposed upon a transfer for charitable, etc., uses shall be exercised by the executor by the filing of a written notification to that effect with the Commissioner. The notification shall be filed before the expiration of the period of limitation for assessment provided in section 6501 (usually 3 years from the last day for filing the return). The election may be revoked by the executor by the filing of a written notification to that effect with the Commissioner at any time before the expiration of such period.

(d) Amount of State death tax imposed upon a transfer. If a State death tax is imposed upon the transfer of the decedent's entire estate and not upon the transfer of a particular share thereof, the State death tax imposed upon a transfer for charitable, etc., uses is deemed to be an amount, E, which bears the same ratio to F (the amount of the State death tax imposed with respect to the transfer of the entire estate) as G (the value of the charitable, etc., transfer, reduced as provided in the next sentence) bears to H (the total value of the properties, interests, and benefits subjected to the State death tax received by all persons interested in the estate, reduced as provided in the last sentence of this paragraph). In arriving at amount G of the ratio, the value of the charitable, etc., transfer is reduced by the amount of any deduction or exclusion allowed with respect to such property in determining the amount of the State death tax. In arriving at amount H of the ratio, the total value of the properties, interests, and benefits subjected to State death tax received by all persons interested in the estate is reduced by the amount of all deductions and exclusions allowed in determining the amount of the State death tax on account of the nature of a beneficiary or a beneficiary's relationship to the decedent.

(e) Examples. The application of this section may be illustrated by the following examples:

Example (1). The decedent's gross estate was valued at $200,000. He bequeathed $90,000 to a nephew, $10,000 to Charity A, and the remainder of his estate to Charity B. State inheritance tax in the amount of $13,500 was imposed upon the bequest to the nephew, $1,500 upon the bequest to Charity A, and $15,000 upon the bequest to Charity B. Under the will and local law, each legatee is required to pay the State inheritance tax on his bequest, and the Federal estate tax is to be paid out of the residuary estate. Since the entire burden of paying the Federal estate tax falls on Charity B, it follows that the decrease in the Federal estate tax resulting from the allowance of deductions for State death taxes in the amounts of $1,500 and $15,000 would inure solely for the benefit of Charity B. Therefore, deductions of $1,500 and $15,000 are allowable under section 2053(d). If, in this example, the State death taxes as well as the Federal estate tax were to be paid out of the residuary estate, the result would be the same.

Example (2). The decedent's gross estate was valued at $350,000. Expenses, indebtedness, etc., amounted to $50,000. The entire estate was bequeathed in equal shares to a son, a daughter, and Charity C. State inheritance tax in the amount of $2,000 was imposed upon the bequest to the son, $2,000 upon the bequest to the daughter, and $5,000 upon the bequest to Charity C. Under the will and local law, each legatee is required to pay his own State inheritance tax and his proportionate share of the Federal estate tax determined by taking into consideration the net amount of his bequest subjected to the tax. Since each legatee's share of the Federal estate tax is based upon the net amount of his bequest subjected to the tax (note that the deductions under sections 2053(d) and 2055 will have the effect of reducing Charity C's proportionate share of the tax), the tax is considered to be equitably apportioned. Thus, a deduction of $5,000 is allowable under section 2053(d). This deduction together with a deduction of $95,000 under section 2055 (charitable deduction) will mean that none of Charity C's bequest is subjected to Federal estate tax. Hence, the son and the daughter will bear the entire estate tax.

Example (3). The decedent bequeathed his property in equal shares, after payment of all expenses, to a son, a daughter, and a charity. State inheritance tax of $2,000 was imposed upon the bequest to the son, $2,000 upon the bequest to the daughter, and $15,000 upon the bequest to the charity. Under the will and local law, each beneficiary pays the State inheritance tax on his bequest and the Federal estate tax is to be paid out of the estate as an administration expense. If the deduction for State death tax on the charitable bequest is allowed in this case, some portion of the decrease in the Federal estate tax would inure to the benefit of the son and the daughter. The Federal estate tax is not considered to be equitably apportioned in this case since each legatee's share of the Federal estate tax is not based upon the net amount of his bequest subjected to the tax (note that the deductions under sections 2053(d) and 2055 will not have the effect of reducing the charity's proportionate share of the tax). Inasmuch as some of the decrease in the Federal estate tax payable would inure to the benefit of the son and the daughter, and inasmuch as there is no equitable apportionment of the tax, no deduction is allowable under section 2053(d).

Example (4). The decedent bequeathed his entire residuary estate in trust to pay the income to X for life with remainder to charity. The State imposed inheritance taxes of $2,000 upon the bequest to X and $10,000 upon the bequest to charity. Under the will and local law, all State and Federal taxes are payable out of the residuary estate and therefore they would reduce the amount which would become the corpus of the trust. If the deduction for the State death tax on the charitable bequest is allowed in this case, some portion of the decrease in the Federal estate tax would inure to the benefit of X since the allowance of the deduction would increase the size of the corpus from which X is to receive the income for life. Also, the Federal estate tax is not considered to be equitably apportioned in this case since each legatee's share of the Federal estate tax is not based upon the net amount of his bequest subjected to the tax (note that the deductions under sections 2053(d) and 2055 will not have the effect of reducing the charity's proportionate share of the tax). Inasmuch as some of the decrease in the Federal estate tax payable would inure to the benefit of X, and inasmuch as there is no equitable apportionment of the tax, no deduction is allowable under section 2053(d).

Example (5). The decedent's gross estate was valued at $750,000. Expenses, indebtedness, etc., amounted to $500,000. The decedent bequeathed $350,000 of his estate to his surviving spouse and the remainder of his estate equally to his son and Charity D. State inheritance tax in the amount of $7,000 was imposed upon the bequest to the surviving spouse, $26,250 upon the bequest to the son, and $26,250 upon the bequest to Charity D. The will was silent concerning the payment of taxes. In such a case, the local law provides that each legatee shall pay his own State inheritance tax. The local law further provides for an apportionment of the Federal estate tax among the legatees of the estate. Under the apportionment provisions, the surviving spouse is not required to bear any part of the Federal estate tax with respect to her $350,000 bequest. It should be noted, however, that the marital deduction allowed to the decedent's estate by reason of the bequest to the surviving spouse is limited to $343,000 ($350,000 bequest less $7,000 State inheritance tax payable by the surviving spouse). Thus, the bequest to the surviving spouse is subjected to the Federal estate tax in the net amount of $7,000. If the deduction for State death tax on the charitable bequest is allowed in this case, some portion of the decrease in the Federal estate tax would inure to the benefit of the son. The Federal estate tax is not considered to be equitably apportioned in this case since each legatee's share of the Federal estate tax is not based upon the net amount of his bequest subjected to the tax (note that the surviving spouse is to pay no tax). Inasmuch as some of the decrease in the Federal estate tax payable would inure to the benefit of the son, and inasmuch as there is no equitable apportionment of the tax, no deduction is allowable under section 2053(d).

(f) Effective/applicability date. (1) The last sentence of paragraph (a) of this section applies to the estates of decedents dying on or after October 20, 2009, to which section 2058 is applicable.

(2) The other provisions of this section apply to the estates of decedents dying on or after October 20, 2009, to which section 2058 is not applicable.

[T.D. 6296, 23 FR 4529, June 24, 1958, as amended by T.D. 6526, 26 FR 417, Jan. 19, 1961; T.D. 6666, 28 FR 7251, July 16, 1963; T.D. 9468, 74 FR 53664, Oct. 20, 2009]

§ 20.2053–10 Deduction for certain foreign death taxes.

(a) General rule. A deduction is allowed the estate of a decedent dying on or after July 1, 1955, under section 2053(d) for the amount of any estate, succession, legacy, or inheritance tax imposed by and actually paid to any foreign country, in respect of any property situated within such foreign country and included in the gross estate of a citizen or resident of the United States, upon a transfer by the decedent for charitable, etc., uses described in section 2055, but only if (1) the conditions stated in paragraph (b) of this section are met, and (2) an election is made in accordance with the provisions of paragraph (c) of this section. The determination of the country within which property is situated is made in accordance with the rules contained in sections 2104 and 2105 in determining whether property is situated within or without the United States. See section 2014(f) and § 20.2014–7 for the effect which the allowance of this deduction has upon the credit for foreign death taxes.

(b) Condition for allowance of deduction. (1) The deduction is not allowed unless either—

(i) The entire decrease in the Federal estate tax resulting from the allowance of the deduction inures solely to the benefit of a charitable, etc., transferee described in section 2055, or

(ii) The Federal estate tax is equitably apportioned among all the transferees (including the decedent's surviving spouse and the charitable, etc., transferees) of property included in the decedent's gross estate.

For allowance of the deduction, it is sufficient if either of these conditions is satisfied. Thus, in a case where the entire decrease in Federal estate tax inures to the benefit of a charitable transferee, the deduction is allowable even though the Federal estate tax is not equitably apportioned among all the transferees of property included in the decedent's gross estate. Similarly, if the Federal estate tax is equitably apportioned among all the transferees of property included in the decedent's gross estate, the deduction is allowable even though a noncharitable transferee receives some benefit from the allowance of the deduction.

(2) For purposes of this paragraph, the Federal estate tax is considered to be equitably apportioned among all the transferees (including the decedent's surviving spouse and the charitable, etc., transferees) of property included in the decedent's gross estate only if each transferee's share of the tax is based upon the net amount of his transfer subjected to the tax (taking into account any exemptions, credits, or deductions allowed by chapter 11). See examples (2) through (5) of paragraph (e) of § 20.2053–9.

(c) Exercise of election. The election to take a deduction for a foreign death tax imposed upon a transfer for charitable, etc., uses shall be exercised by the executor by the filing of a written notification to that effect with the Commissioner of internal revenue in whose district the estate tax return for the decedent's estate was filed. An election to take the deduction for foreign death taxes is deemed to be a waiver of the right to claim a credit under a treaty with any foreign country for any tax or portion thereof claimed as a deduction under this section. The notification shall be filed before the expiration of the period of limitation for assessment provided in section 6501 (usually 3 years from the last day for filing the return). The election may be revoked by the executor by the filing of a written notification to that effect with the Commissioner at any time before the expiration of such period.

(d) Amount of foreign death tax imposed upon a transfer. If a foreign death tax is imposed upon the transfer of the entire part of the decedent's estate subject to such tax and not upon the transfer of a particular share thereof, the foreign death tax imposed upon a transfer for charitable, etc., uses is deemed to be an amount, J, which bears the same ratio to K (the amount of the foreign death tax imposed with respect to the transfer of the entire part of the decedent's estate subject to such tax) as M (the value of the charitable, etc., transfer, reduced as provided in the next sentence) bears to N (the total value of the properties, interests, and benefits subjected to the foreign death tax received by all persons interested in the estate, reduced as provided in the last sentence of this paragraph). In arriving at amount M of the ratio, the value of the charitable, etc., transfer is reduced by the amount of any deduction or exclusion allowed with respect to such property in determining the amount of the foreign death tax. In arriving at amount N of the ratio, the total value of the properties, interests, and benefits subjected to foreign death tax received by all persons interested in the estate is reduced by the amount of all deductions and exclusions allowed in determining the amount of the foreign death tax on account of the nature of a beneficiary or a beneficiary's relationship to the decedent.

(e) Effective/applicability date. This section applies to the estates of decedents dying on or after October 20, 2009.

[T.D. 6600, 27 FR 4985, May 29, 1962; T.D. 9468, 74 FR 53665, Oct. 20, 2009]

§ 2054. Losses

For purposes of the tax imposed by section 2001, the value of the taxable estate shall be determined by deducting from the value of the gross estate losses incurred during the settlement of estates arising from fires, storms, shipwrecks, or other casualties, or from theft, when such losses are not compensated for by insurance or otherwise.

Regulation

§ 20.2054–1 Deduction for losses from casualties or theft.

A deduction is allowed for losses incurred during the settlement of the estate arising from fires, storms, shipwrecks, or other casualties, or from theft, if the losses are not compensated for by insurance or otherwise. If the loss is partly compensated for, the excess of the loss over the compensation may be deducted. Losses which are not of the nature described are not deductible. In order to be deductible a loss must occur during the settlement of the estate. If a loss with respect to an asset occurs after its distribution to the distributee it may not be deducted. Notwithstanding the foregoing, no deduction is allowed under this section if the estate has waived its right to take such a deduction pursuant to the provisions of section 642(g) in order to permit its allowance for income tax purposes. See further § 1.642(g)–1.

[T.D. 6296, 23 FR 4529, June 24, 1958]

§ 2055. Transfers for Public, Charitable, and Religious Uses

(a) In general. For purposes of the tax imposed by section 2001, the value of the taxable estate shall be determined by deducting from the value of the gross estate the amount of all bequests, legacies, devises, or transfers—

(1) to or for the use of the United States, any State, any political subdivision thereof, or the District of Columbia, for exclusively public purposes;

(2) to or for the use of any corporation organized and operated exclusively for religious, charitable, scientific, literary, or educational purposes, including the encouragement of art, or to foster national or international amateur sports competition (but only if no part of its activities involve the provision of athletic facilities or equipment), and the prevention of cruelty to children or animals, no part of the net earnings of which inures to the benefit of any private stockholder or individual, which is not disqualified for tax exemption under section 501(c)(3) by reason of attempting to influence legislation, and which does not participate in, or intervene in (including the publishing or distributing of statements), any political campaign on behalf of (or in opposition to) any candidate for public office;

(3) to a trustee or trustees, or a fraternal society, order, or association operating under the lodge system, but only if such contributions or gifts are to be used by such trustee or trustees, or by such fraternal society, order, or association, exclusively for religious, charitable, scientific, literary, or educational purposes, or for the prevention of cruelty to children or animals, such trust, fraternal society, order, or association would not be disqualified for tax exemption under section 501(c)(3) by reason of attempting to influence legislation, and such trustee or trustees, or such fraternal society, order, or association, does not participate in, or intervene in (including the publishing or distributing of statements), any political campaign on behalf of (or in opposition to) any candidate for public office;

(4) to or for the use of any veterans' organization incorporated by Act of Congress, or of its departments or local chapters or posts, no part of the net earnings of which inures to the benefit of any private shareholder or individual, or

(5) to an employee stock ownership plan if such transfer qualifies as a qualified gratuitous transfer of qualified employer securities within the meaning of section 664(g).

For purposes of this subsection, the complete termination before the date prescribed for the filing of the estate tax return of a power to consume, invade, or appropriate property for the benefit of an individual before such power has been exercised by reason of the death of such individual or for any other reason shall be considered and deemed to be a qualified disclaimer with the same full force and effect as though he had filed such qualified disclaimer. Rules similar to the rules of section 501(j) shall apply for purposes of paragraph (2).

(b) Powers of appointment. Property includible in the decedent's gross estate under section 2041 (relating to powers of appointment) received by a donee described in this section shall, for purposes of this section, be considered a bequest of such decedent.

(c) Death taxes payable out of bequests. If the tax imposed by section 2001, or any estate, succession, legacy, or inheritance taxes, are, either by the terms of the will, by the law of the jurisdiction under which the estate is administered, or by the law of the jurisdiction imposing the particular tax, payable in whole or in part out of the bequests, legacies, or devises otherwise deductible under this section, then the amount deductible under this section shall be the amount of such bequests, legacies, or devises reduced by the amount of such taxes.

(d) Limitation on deduction. The amount of the deduction under this section for any transfer shall not exceed the value of the transferred property required to be included in the gross estate.

(e) Disallowance of deductions in certain cases.

(1) No deduction shall be allowed under this section for a transfer to or for the use of an organization or trust described in section 508(d) or 4948(c)(4) subject to the conditions specified in such sections.

(2) Where an interest in property (other than an interest described in section 170(f)(3)(B)) passes or has passed from the decedent to a person, or for a use, described in subsection (a), and an interest (other than an interest which is extinguished upon the decedent's death) in the same property passes or has passed (for less than an adequate and full consideration in money or money's worth) from the decedent to a person, or for a use, not described in subsection (a), no deduction shall be allowed under this section for the interest which passes or has passed to the person, or for the use, described in subsection (a) unless—

(A) in the case of a remainder interest, such interest is in a trust which is a charitable remainder annuity trust or a charitable remainder unitrust (described in section 664) or a pooled income fund (described in section 642(c)(5)), or

(B) in the case of any other interest, such interest is in the form of a guaranteed annuity or is a fixed percentage distributed yearly of the fair market value of the property (to be determined yearly).

(3) Reformations to comply with paragraph (2).

(A) In general. A deduction shall be allowed under subsection (a) in respect of any qualified reformation.

(B) Qualified reformation. For purposes of this paragraph, the term "qualified reformation" means a change of a governing instrument by reformation, amendment, construction, or otherwise which changes a reformable interest into a qualified interest but only if—

(i) any difference between—

(I) the actuarial value (determined as of the date of the decedent's death) of the qualified interest, and

(II) the actuarial value (as so determined) of the reformable interest, does not exceed 5 percent of the actuarial value (as so determined) of the reformable interest,

(ii) in the case of—

(I) a charitable remainder interest, the nonremainder interest (before and after the qualified reformation) terminated at the same time, or

(II) any other interest, the reformable interest and the qualified interest are for the same period, and

(iii) such change is effective as of the date of the decedent's death.

A nonremainder interest (before reformation) for a term of years in excess of 20 years shall be treated as satisfying subclause (I) of clause (ii) if such interest (after reformation) is for a term of 20 years.

(C) Reformable interest. For purposes of this paragraph—

(i) In general. The term "reformable interest" means any interest for which a deduction would be allowable under subsection (a) at the time of the decedent's death but for paragraph (2).

(ii) Beneficiary's interest must be fixed. The term "reformable interest" does not include any interest unless, before the remainder vests in possession, all payments to persons other than an organization described in subsection (a) are expressed either in specified dollar amounts or a fixed percentage of the fair market value of the property. For purposes of determining whether all such payments are expressed as a fixed percentage of the fair market value of the property, section 664(d)(3) shall be taken into account.

(iii) Special rule where timely commencement of reformation. Clause (ii) shall not apply to any interest if a judicial proceeding is commenced to change such interest into a qualified interest not later than the 90th day after—

(I) if an estate tax return is required to be filed, the last date (including extensions) for filing such return, or

(II) if no estate tax return is required to be filed, the last date (including extensions) for filing the income tax return for the 1st taxable year for which such a return is required to be filed by the trust.

(iv) Special rule for will executed before January 1, 1979, etc. In the case of any interest passing under a will executed before January 1, 1979, or under a trust created before such date, clause (ii) shall not apply.

(D) Qualified interest. For purposes of this paragraph, the term "qualified interest" means an interest for which a deduction is allowable under subsection (a).

(E) Limitation. The deduction referred to in subparagraph (A) shall not exceed the amount of the deduction which would have been allowable for the reformable interest but for paragraph (2).

(F) Special rule where income beneficiary dies. If (by reason of the death of any individual, or by termination or distribution of a trust in accordance with the terms of the trust instrument) by the due date for filing the estate tax return (including any extension thereof) a reformable interest is in a wholly charitable trust or passes directly to a person or for a use described in subsection (a), a deduction shall be allowed for such reformable interest as if it had met the requirements of paragraph (2) on the date of the decedent's death. For purposes of the preceding sentence, the term "wholly charitable trust" means a charitable trust which, upon the allowance of a deduction, would be described in section 4947(a)(1).

(G) Statute of limitations. The period for assessing any deficiency of any tax attributable to the application of this paragraph shall not expire before the date 1 year after the date on which the Secretary is notified that such reformation (or other proceeding pursuant to subparagraph (J)) has occurred.

(H) Regulations. The Secretary shall prescribe such regulations as may be necessary to carry out the purposes of this paragraph, including regulations providing such adjustments in the application of the provisions of section 508 (relating to special rules relating to section 501(c)(3) organizations), subchapter J (relating to estates, trusts, beneficiaries, and decedents), and chapter 42 (relating to private foundations) as may be necessary by reason of the qualified reformation.

(I) Reformations permitted in case of remainder interests in residence or farm, pooled income funds, etc. The Secretary shall prescribe regulations (consistent with the provisions of this paragraph) permitting reformations in the case of any failure—

(i) to meet the requirements of section 170(f)(3)(B) (relating to remainder interests in personal residence or farm, etc.), or

(ii) to meet the requirements of section 642(c)(5).

(J) Void or reformed trust in cases of insufficient remainder interests. In the case of a trust that would qualify (or could be reformed to qualify pursuant to subparagraph (B)) but for failure to satisfy the requirement of paragraph (1)(D) or (2)(D) of section 664(d), such trust may be—

(i) declared null and void ab initio, or

(ii) changed by reformation, amendment, or otherwise to meet such requirement by reducing the payout rate or the duration (or both) of any noncharitable beneficiary's interest to the extent necessary to satisfy such requirement, pursuant to a proceeding that is commenced within the period required in subparagraph (C)(iii). In a case described in clause (i), no deduction shall be allowed under this title for any transfer to the trust and any transactions entered into by the trust prior to being declared void shall be treated as entered into by the transferor.

(4) Works of art and their copyrights treated as separate properties in certain cases.

(A) In general. In the case of a qualified contribution of a work of art, the work of art and the copyright on such work of art shall be treated as separate properties for purposes of paragraph (2).

(B) Work of art defined. For purposes of this paragraph, the term "work of art" means any tangible personal property with respect to which there is a copyright under Federal law.

(C) Qualified contribution defined. For purposes of this paragraph, the term "qualified contribution" means any transfer of property to a qualified organization if the use of the property by the organization is related to the purpose or function constituting the basis for its exemption under section 501.

(D) Qualified organization defined. For purposes of this paragraph, the term "qualified organization" means any organization described in section 501(c)(3) other than a private foundation (as defined in section 509). For purposes of the preceding sentence, a private operating foundation (as defined in section 4942(j)(3)) shall not be treated as a private foundation.

(5) Contributions to donor advised funds. A deduction otherwise allowed under subsection (a) for any contribution to a donor advised fund (as defined in section 4966(d)(2)) shall only be allowed if—

(A) the sponsoring organization (as defined in section 4966(d)(1)) with respect to such donor advised fund is not—

(i) described in paragraph (3) or (4) of subsection (a), or

(ii) a type III supporting organization (as defined in section 4943(f)(5)(A)) which is not a functionally integrated type III supporting organization (as defined in section 4943(f)(5)(B)), and

(B) the taxpayer obtains a contemporaneous written acknowledgment (determined under rules similar to the rules of section 170(f)(8)(C)) from the sponsoring organization (as so defined) of such donor advised fund that such organization has exclusive legal control over the assets contributed.

(f) Special rule for irrevocable transfers of easements in real property. A deduction shall be allowed under subsection (a) in respect of any transfer of a qualified real property interest (as defined in section 170(h)(2)(C)) which meets the requirements of section 170(h) (without regard to paragraph (4)(A) thereof).

(g) Cross references.

(1) For option as to time for valuation for purpose of deduction under this section, see section 2032.

(2) For treatment of certain organizations providing child care, see section 501(k).

(3) For exemption of gifts and bequests to or for the benefit of Library of Congress, see section 5 of the Act of March 3, 1925, as amended (2 U.S.C. 161).

(4) For treatment of gifts and bequests for the benefit of the Naval Historical Center as gifts or bequests to or for the use of the United States, see section 8622 of title 10, United States Code.

(5) For treatment of gifts and bequests to or for the benefit of National Park Foundation as gifts or bequests to or for the use of the United States, see section 8 of the Act of December 18, 1967 (16 U.S.C. 191).

(6) For treatment of gifts, devises, or bequests accepted by the Secretary of State, the Director of the International Communication Agency, or the Director of the United States International Development Cooperation Agency as gifts, devises, or bequests to or for the use of the United States, see section 25 of the State Department Basic Authorities Act of 1956.

(7) For treatment of gifts or bequests of money accepted by the Attorney General for credit to "Commissary Funds, Federal Prisons" as gifts or bequests to or for the use of the United States, see section 4043 of title 18, United States Code.

(8) For payment of tax on gifts and bequests of United States obligations to the United States, see section 3113(e) of title 31, United States Code.

(9) For treatment of gifts and bequests for benefit of the Naval Academy as gifts or bequests to or for the use of the United States, see section 8473 of title 10, United States Code.

(10) For treatment of gifts and bequests for benefit of the Naval Academy Museum as gifts or bequests to or for the use of the United States, see section 8474 of title 10, United States Code.

(11) For exemption of gifts and bequests received by National Archives Trust Fund Board, see section 2308 of title 44, United States Code.

(12) For treatment of gifts and bequests to or for the use of Indian tribal governments (or their subdivisions), see section 7871.

Regulations

§ 20.2055–1 Deduction for transfers for public, charitable, and religious uses; in general.

(a) General rule. A deduction is allowed under section 2055(a) from the gross estate of a decedent who was a citizen or resident of the United States at the time of his death for the value of property included in the decedent's gross estate and transferred by the decedent during his lifetime or by will—

(1) To or for the use of the United States, any State, Territory, any political subdivision thereof, or the District of Columbia, for exclusively public purposes;

(2) To or for the use of any corporation or association organized and operated exclusively for religious, charitable, scientific, literary, or educational purposes (including the encouragement of art and for the prevention of cruelty to children or animals), if no part of the net earnings of the corporation or association inures to the benefit of any private stockholder or individual (other than as a legitimate object of such purposes), if the organization is not disqualified for tax exemption under section 501(c)(3) by reason of attempting to influence legislation, and if, in the case of transfers made after December 31, 1969, it does not participate in, or intervene in (including the publishing or distributing of statements), any political campaign on behalf of or in opposition to any candidate for public office.

(3) To a trustee or trustees, or a fraternal society, order, or association operating under the lodge system, if the transferred property is to be used exclusively for religious, charitable, scientific, literary, or educational purposes (or for the prevention of cruelty to children or animals), if no substantial part of the activities of such transferee is carrying on propaganda, or otherwise attempting, to influence legislation, and if, in the case of transfers made after December 31, 1969, such transferee does not participate in, or intervene in (including the publishing or distributing of statements), any political campaign on behalf of any candidate for public office; or

(4) To or for the use of any veterans' organization incorporated by act of Congress, or of any of its departments, local chapters, or posts, no part of the net earnings of which inures to the benefit of any private shareholder or individual.

The deduction is not limited, in the case of estates of citizens or residents of the United States, to transfers to domestic corporations or associations, or to trustees for use within the United States. Nor is the deduction subject to percentage limitations such as are applicable to the charitable deduction under the income tax. An organization will not be considered to meet the requirements of subparagraph (2) or (3) of this paragraph if such organization engages in any activity which would cause it to be classified as an "action" organization under paragraph (c)(3) of § 1.501(c)(3)–1 of this chapter (Income Tax Regulations). See §§ 20.2055–4 and 20.2055–5 for rules relating to the disallowance of deductions to trusts and organizations which engage in certain prohibited transactions or whose governing instruments do not contain certain specified requirements.

(b) Powers of appointment. (1) *General rule.* A deduction is allowable under section 2055(b) for the value of property passing to or for the use of a transferee described in paragraph (a) of this section by the exercise, failure to exercise, release or lapse of a power of appointment by reason of which the property is includible in the decedent's gross estate under section 2041.

(2) *Certain bequests subject to power of appointment.* For the allowance of a deduction in the case of a bequest in trust where the decedent's surviving spouse (i) was over 80 years of age at the date of decedent's death, (ii) was entitled for life to all of the net income from the trust, and (iii) had a power of appointment over the corpus of the trust exercisable by will in favor of, among others, a charitable organization, see section 2055(b)(2). See also section 6503(e) for suspension of the period of limitations for assessment or collection of any deficiency attributable to the allowance of the deduction.

(c) Submission of evidence. In establishing the right of the estate to the deduction authorized by section 2055, the executor should submit the following with the return:

(1) A copy of any instrument in writing by which the decedent made a transfer of property in his lifetime the value of which is required by statute to be included in his gross estate, for which a deduction under section 2055 is claimed. If the instrument is of record the copy should be certified, and if not of record, the copy should be verified.

(2) A written statement by the executor containing a declaration that it is made under penalties of perjury and stating whether any action has been instituted to construe or to contest the decedent's will or any provision thereof affecting the charitable deduction claimed and whether, according to his information and belief, any such action is designed or contemplated.

The executor shall also submit such other documents or evidence as may be requested by the district director.

(d) Cross references. (1) See section 2055(f) for certain cross references relating to section 2055.

(2) For treatment of bequests accepted by the Secretary of State or the Secretary of Commerce, for the purpose of organizing and holding an international conference to negotiate a Patent Corporation Treaty, as bequests to or for the use of the United States, see section 3 of Joint Resolution of December 24, 1969 (Public Law 91–160, 83 Stat. 443).

(3) For treatment of bequests accepted by the Secretary of the Department of Housing and Urban Development, for the purpose of aiding or facilitating the work of the Department, as bequests to or for the use of the United States, see section 7(k) of the Department of Housing and Urban Development Act (42 U.S.C. 3535), as added by section 905 of Public Law 91–609 (84 Stat. 1809).

(4) For treatment of certain property accepted by the Chairman of the Administrative Conference of the United States, for the purposes of aiding and facilitating the work of the Conference, as a devise or bequest to the United States, see 5 U.S.C. 575(c)(12), as added by section 1(b) of the Act of October 21, 1972 (Public Law 92–526, 86 Stat. 1048).

(5) For treatment of the Board for International Broadcasting as a corporation described in section 2055(a)(2), see section 7 of the Board for International Broadcasting Act of 1973 (Public Law 93–129, 87 Stat. 459).

[T.D. 6296, 23 FR 4529, June 24, 1958; 25 FR 14021, Dec. 31, 1960 as amended by T.D. 8318, 39 FR 25452, July 11, 1974; T.D. 8308, 55 FR 35593, Aug. 31, 1990]

§ 20.2055–2 Transfers not exclusively for charitable purposes.

(a) Remainders and similar interests. If a trust is created or property is transferred for both a charitable and a private purpose, deduction may be taken of the value of the charitable beneficial interest only insofar as that interest is presently ascertainable, and hence severable from the noncharitable interest. Thus, in the case of decedent's dying before January 1, 1970, if money or property is placed in trust to pay the income to an individual during his life, or for a term of years, and then to pay the principal to a charitable organization, the present value of the remainder is deductible. See paragraph (e) of this section for limitations applicable to decedent's dying after December 31, 1969. See paragraph (f) of this section for rules relating to valuation of partial interests in property passing for charitable purposes.

(b) Transfers subject to a condition or a power. (1) If, as of the date of a decedent's death, a transfer for charitable purposes is dependent upon the performance of some act or the happening of a precedent event in order that it might become effective, no deduction is allowable unless the possibility that the charitable transfer will not become effective is so remote as to be negligible. If an estate or interest has passed to, or is vested in, charity at the time of a decedent's death and the estate or interest would be defeated by the subsequent performance of some act or the happening of some event, the possibility of occurrence of which appeared at the time of the decedent's death to be so remote as to be negligible, the deduction is allowable. If the legatee, devisee, donee, or trustee is empowered to divert the property or fund, in whole or in part, to a use or purpose which would have rendered it, to the extent that it is subject to such power, not deductible had it been directly so bequeathed, devised, or given by the decedent, the deduction will be limited to that portion, if any, of the property or fund which is exempt from an exercise of the power.

(2) The application of this paragraph may be illustrated by the following examples:

Example (1). In 1965, A dies leaving certain property in trust in which charity is to receive the income for the life of his widow. The assets placed in trust by the decedent consist of stock in a corporation the fiscal policies of which are controlled by the decedent and his family. The trustees of the trust and the remaindermen are members of the decedent's family, and the governing instrument contains no adequate guarantee of the request income to the charitable organization. Under such circumstances, no deduction will be allowed. Similarly, if the trustees are not members of the decedent's family but have no power to sell or otherwise dispose of the closely held stock, or otherwise insure the requisite enjoyment of income to the charitable organization, no deduction will be allowed.

Example (2). C dies leaving a tract of land to a city government for as long as the land is used by the city for a public park. If the city accepts the tract and if, on the date of C's death, the possibility that the city will not use the land for a public park is so remote as to be negligible, a deduction will be allowed.

(c) Disclaimers. (1) *Decedents dying after December 31, 1976.* In the case of a bequest, devise, or transfer made by a decedent dying after December 31, 1976, the amount of a bequest, devise or transfer for which a deduction is allowable under section 2055 includes an interest which falls into the bequest, devise or transfer as the result of either—

(i) A qualified disclaimer (see section 2518 and the corresponding regulations for rules relating to a qualified disclaimer), or

(ii) The complete termination of a power to consume, invade, or appropriate property for the benefit of an individual by reason of the death of such individual or for any other reason, if the termination occurs within the period of time (including extensions) for filing the decedent's Federal estate tax return and before such power has been exercised.

(2) *Decedents dying before January 1, 1977.* In the case of a bequest, devise or transfer made by a decedent dying before January 1, 1977, the amount of a bequest, devise or transfer, for which a deduction is allowable under section 2055 includes an interest which falls into the bequest, devise or transfer as a result of either—

(i) A disclaimer of a bequest, devise, transfer, or power, if the disclaimer is made within 9 months (15 months if the decedent died on or before December 31, 1970) after the decedent's death (the period of time within which the estate tax return must be filed under section 6075) or within any extension of time for filing the return granted pursuant to section 6081, and the disclaimer is irrevocable at the time the deduction is allowed, or

(ii) The complete termination of a power to consume, invade, or appropriate property for the benefit of an individual (whether the termination occurs by reason of the death of the individual, or otherwise) if the termination occurs within the period described in paragraph (c)(2)(i) of this section and before the power has been exercised. Ordinarily, a disclaimer made by a person not under any legal disability will be considered irrevocable when filed with the probate court. A disclaimer is a complete and unqualified refusal to accept the right to which one is entitled. Thus, if a beneficiary uses these rights for his own purposes, as by receiving a consideration for his formal disclaimer, he has not refused the rights to which he was entitled. There can be no disclaimer after an acceptance of these rights, expressly or impliedly. The disclaimer of a power is to be distinguished from the release or exercise of a power. The release or exercise of a power by the donee of the power in favor of a person or object described in paragraph (a) of § 20.2055–1 does not result in any deduction under section 2055 in the estate of the donor of a power (but see paragraph (b)(1) of § 20.2055–1 with respect to the donee's estate).

(d) Payments in compromise. If a charitable organization assigns or surrenders a part of a transfer to it pursuant to a compromise agreement in settlement of a controversy, the amount so assigned or surrendered is not deductible as a transfer to that charitable organization.

(e) Limitation applicable to decedents dying after December 31, 1969. (1) *Disallowance of deduction.* (i) *In general.* In the case of decedents dying after December 31, 1969, where an interest in property passes or has passed from the decedent for charitable purposes and an interest (other than an interest which is extinguished upon the decedent's death) in the same property passes or has passed from the decedent for private purposes (for less than an adequate and full consideration in money or money's worth) after October 9, 1969, no deduction is allowed under section 2055 for the value of the interest which passes or has passed for charitable purposes unless the interest in property is a deductible interest described in subparagraph (2) of this paragraph. The principles of section 2056 and the regulations thereunder shall apply for purposes of determining under this paragraph (e)(1)(i) whether an interest in property passes or has passed from the decedent. If however, as of the date of a decedent's death, a transfer for a private purpose is dependent upon the performance of some act on the happening of a precedent event in order that it might become effective, an interest in property will be considered to pass for a private purpose unless the possibility of occurrence of such act or event is so remote as to be negligible. The application of this paragraph (e)(1)(i) may be illustrated by the following examples, in each of which it is assumed that the interest in property which passes for private purposes does not pass for an adequate and full consideration in money or money's worth:

Example (1). In 1973, H creates a trust which is to pay the income of the trust to W for her life, the reversionary interest in the trust being retained by H. H predeceases W in 1975. H's will provide that the residue of his estate (including the reversionary interest in the trust) is to be transferred to charity. For purposes of this paragraph (e)(1)(i), interests in the same property have passed from H for charitable purposes and for private purposes.

Example (2). In 1973, H creates a trust which is to pay the income of the trust to W for her life and upon termination of the life estate to transfer the remainder to S. S predeceases W in 1975. S's will provides that the residue of his estate (including the remainder interest in the trust) is to be transferred to charity. For purposes of this paragraph (e)(1)(i), interests in the same property have not passed from H or S for charitable purposes and for private purposes.

Example (3). H transfers Blackacre to A by gift, reserving the right to the rentals of Blackacre for a term of 20 years. H dies within the 20-year term, bequeathing the right to the remaining rentals to charity. For purposes of this subparagraph the term "property" refers to Blackacre, and the right to rentals from Blackacre consist of an interest in Blackacre. An interest in Blackacre has passed from H for charitable purposes and for private purposes.

Example (4). H bequeaths the residue of his estate in trust for the benefit of A and a charity. An annuity of $5,000 a year is to be paid to charity for 20 years. Upon termination of the 20-year term the corpus is to be distributed to A if living. However, if A should die during the 20-year term, the corpus is to be distributed to charity upon termination of the term. An interest in the residue of the estate has passed from H for charitable purposes. In addition, an interest in the residue of the estate has passed from H for private purposes, unless the possibility that A will survive the 20-year term is so remote as to be negligible.

Example (5). H bequeaths the residue of his estate in trust. Under the terms of the trust an annuity of $5,000 a year is to be paid to charity for 20 years. Upon termination of the term, the corpus is to pass to such of A's children and their issue as A may appoint. However, if A should die during the 20-year term without exercising the power of appointment, the corpus is to be distributed to charity upon termination of the term. Since the possible appointees include private persons, an interest in the residue of the estate is considered to have passed from H for private purposes.

Example (6). H devises Blackacre to X Charity. Under applicable local law, W, H's widow, is entitled to elect a dower interest in Blackacre. W elects to take her dower interest in Blackacre. For purposes of this paragraph (e)(1)(i), interests in the same property have passed from H for charitable purposes and for private purposes. If, however, W does not elect to take her dower interest in Blackacre, then, for purposes of this paragraph (e)(1)(i), interests in the same property have not passed from H for charitable purposes and for private purposes.

(ii) *Works of art and copyrights treated as separate properties.* (a) *In general.* For purposes of paragraphs (e)(1)(i) and (e)(2) of this section, in the case of decedents dying after December 31, 1981, if a decedent makes a qualified contribution of a work of art, the work of art and the copyright on such work of art shall be treated as separate properties. Thus, a deduction is allowable under section 2055 for a qualified contribution of a work of art, whether or not the related copyright is simultaneously transferred to a charitable organization.

(b) *Work of art defined.* For purposes of paragraph (e)(1)(ii)(a) of this section, the term "work of art" means any tangible personal property with respect to which a copyright exists under Federal law.

(c) *Qualified contribution defined.* For purposes of paragraph (e)(1)(ii)(a) of this section, the term "qualified contribution" means any transfer of property to a qualified organization (as defined in paragraph (e)(1)(ii)(d) of this section) if the use of the property by the organization is related to the purpose or function constituting the basis for its exemption under section 501. The rules contained in § 1.170A–4(b)(3) shall apply in determining if the use of property by an organization is related to such purpose or function.

(d) *Qualified organization defined.* For purposes of paragraph (e)(1)(ii)(c) of this section, the term "qualified organization" means any organization described in section 501(c)(3) other than a private foundation (as defined in section 509). A private operating foundation (as defined in section 4942(j)(3)) shall be considered a qualified organization under this paragraph.

(e) *Examples.* The application of paragraphs (e)(1)(i) and (e)(1)(ii)(a) through (d) of this section may be illustrated by the following examples:

Example (1). A, an artist, died in 1983. A work of art created by A and the copyright interest in that work of art were included in A's estate. Under the terms of A's will, the work of art is transferred to X charity, the only charitable beneficiary under A's will. X has no suitable use for the work of art and sells it. It is determined under the rules of § 1.170A–4(b)(3) that the property is put to an unrelated use by X charity. Therefore, the rule of paragraph (e)(1)(ii)(a), which treats works of art and their copyrights as separate properties, does not apply because the transfer of the work of art to X is not a qualified contribution. To determine whether paragraph (e)(1)(i) of this section applies to disallow a deduction under section 2055, it must be determined which interests are treated as passing to X under local law.

(i) If under local law A's will is treated as fully transferring both the work of art and the copyright interest to X, then paragraph (e)(1)(i) of this section does not apply to disallow a deduction under section 2055 for the value of the work of art and the copyright interest.

(ii) If under local law A's will is treated as transferring only the work of art to X, and the copyright interest is treated as part of the residue of the estate, no deduction is allowable under section 2055 to A's estate for the value of the work of art because the transfer of the work of art is not a qualified contribution and paragraph (e)(1)(i) of this section applies to disallow the deduction.

Example (2). B, a collector of art, purchased a work of art from an artist who retained the copyright interest. B died in 1983. Under the terms of B's will the work of art is given to Y charity. Since B did not own the copyright interest, paragraph (e)(1)(i) of this section does not apply to disallow a deduction under section 2055 for the value of the work of art, regardless of whether or not the contribution is a qualified contribution under paragraph (e)(1)(ii)(c) of this section.

(2) *Deductible interests.* A deductible interest for purposes of subparagraph (1) of this paragraph is a charitable interest in property where—

(i) *Undivided portion of decedent's entire interest.* The charitable interest is an undivided portion, not in trust, of the decedent's entire interest in property. An undivided portion of a decedent's entire interest in property must consist of a fraction or percentage of each and every substantial interest or right owned by the decedent in such property and must extend over the entire term of the decedent's interest in such property and in other property into which such property is converted. For example, if the decedent transferred a life estate in an office building to his wife for her life and retained a reversionary interest in the office building, the devise by the decedent of one-half of that reversionary interest to charity while his wife is still alive will not be considered the transfer of a deductible interest; because an interest in the same property has already passed from the decedent for private purposes, the reversionary interest will not be considered the decedent's entire interest in the property. If, on the other hand, the decedent had been given a life estate in Blackacre for the life of his wife and the decedent had no other interest in Blackacre at any time during his life, the devise by the decedent of one-half of that life estate to charity would be considered the transfer of a deductible interest; because the life estate would be considered the decedent's entire interest in the property, the devise would be of an undivided portion of such entire interest. An undivided portion of a decedent's entire interest in the property includes an interest in property whereby the charity is given the right, as a tenant in common with the decedent's devisee or legatee, to possession, dominion, and control of the property for a portion of each year appropriate to its interest in such property. However, except as provided in paragraphs (e)(2)(ii), (iii), and (iv) of this section, for purposes of this subdivision a charitable contribution of an interest in property not in trust where the decedent transfers some specific rights to one party and transfers other substantial rights to another party will not be considered a contribution of an undivided portion of the decedent's entire interest in property. A bequest to charity made on or before December 17, 1980, of an open space easement in gross in perpetuity shall be considered the transfer to charity of an undivided portion of the decedent's entire interest in the property. For the definition of an open space easement in gross in perpetuity, see § 1.170A–7(b)(1)(ii) of this chapter (Income Tax Regulations).

(ii) *Remainder interest in personal residence.* The charitable interest is a remainder interest, not in trust, in a personal residence. Thus, for example, if the decedent devises to charity a remainder interest in a personal residence and bequeaths to his surviving spouse a life estate in such property, the value of the remainder interest is deductible under section 2055. For purposes of this subdivision, the term "personal residence" means any property which was used by the decedent as his personal residence even though it was not used as his principal residence. For example, a decedent's vacation home may be a personal residence for purposes of this subdivision. The term "personal residence" also includes stock owned by the decedent as a tenant-stockholder in a cooperative housing corporation (as those terms are defined in section 216(b)(1) and (2)) if the dwelling which the decedent was entitled to occupy as such stockholder was used by him as his personal residence.

(iii) *Remainder interest in a farm.* The charitable interest is a remainder interest, not in trust, in a farm. Thus, for example, if the decedent devises to charity a remainder interest in a farm and bequeaths to his daughter a life estate in such property, the value of the remainder interest is deductible under section 2055. For purposes of this subdivision, the term "farm" means any land used by the decedent or his tenant for the production of crops, fruits, or other agricultural products or for the sustenance of livestock. The term "livestock" includes cattle, hogs, horses, mules, donkeys, sheep, goats, captive furbearing animals, chickens, turkeys, pigeons, and other poultry. A farm includes the improvements thereon.

(iv) *Qualified conservation contribution.* The charitable interest is a qualified conservation contribution. For the definition of a qualified conservation contribution, see § 1.170A–14.

(v) *Charitable remainder trusts and pooled income funds.* The charitable interest is a remainder interest in a trust which is a charitable remainder annuity trust, as defined in section 664(d)(1) and § 1.664–2 of this chapter; a charitable remainder unitrust, as defined in section 664(d)(2) and (3) and § 1.664–3 of this chapter; or a pooled income fund, as defined in section 642(c)(5) and § 1.642(c)–5 of this chapter. The charitable organization to or for the use of which the remainder interest passes must meet the requirements of both section 2055(a) and section 642(c)(5)(A), section 664(d)(1)(C), or section 664(d)(2)(C), whichever applies. For example, the charitable organization to which the remainder interest in a charitable remainder annuity trust passes may not be a foreign corporation.

(vi) *Guaranteed annuity interest.* (a) The charitable interest is a guaranteed annuity interest, whether or not such interest is in trust. For purposes of this subdivision (vi), the term "guaranteed annuity interest" means the right pursuant to the instrument of transfer to receive a guaranteed annuity. A guaranteed annuity is an arrangement under which a determinable amount is paid periodically, but not less often than annually, for a specified term of years or for the life or lives of certain individuals, each of whom must be living at the date of death of the decedent and can be ascertained at such date. Only one or more of the following individuals may be used as measuring lives: the decedent's spouse, and an individual who, with respect to all remainder beneficiaries (other than charitable organizations described in section 170, 2055, or 2522), is either a lineal ancestor or the spouse of a lineal ancestor of those beneficiaries. A trust will satisfy the requirement that all noncharitable remainder beneficiaries are lineal descendants of the individual who is the measuring life, or that individual's spouse, if there is less than a 15% probability that individuals who are not lineal descendants will receive any trust corpus. This probability must be computed, based on the current applicable Life Table contained in § 20.2031–7, as of the date of the decedent's death taking into account the interests of all primary and contingent remainder beneficiaries who are living at that time. An interest payable for a specified term of years can qualify as a guaranteed annuity interest even if the governing instrument contains a savings clause intended to ensure compliance with a rule against perpetuities. The savings clause must utilize a period for vesting of 21 years after the deaths of measuring lives who are selected to maximize, rather than limit, the term of the trust. The rule in this paragraph that a charitable interest may be payable for the life or lives of only certain specified individuals does not apply in the case of a charitable guaranteed annuity interest payable under a charitable remainder trust described in section 664. An amount is determinable if the exact amount which must be paid under the conditions specified in the instrument of transfer can be ascertained as of the appropriate valuation date. For example, the amount to be paid may be a stated sum for a term of years, or for the life of the decedent's spouse, at the expiration of which it may be changed by a specified amount, but it may not be redetermined by reference to a fluctuating index such as the cost of living index. In further illustration, the amount to be paid may be expressed in terms of a fraction or a percentage of the net fair market value, as finally determined for Federal estate tax purposes, of the residue of the estate on the appropriate valuation date, or it may be expressed in terms of a fraction or percentage of the cost of living index on the appropriate valuation date.

(b) A charitable interest is a guaranteed annuity interest only if it is a guaranteed annuity interest in every respect. For example, if the charitable interest is the right to receive from a trust each year a payment equal to the lesser of a sum certain or a fixed percentage of the net fair market value of the trust assets, determined annually, such interest is not a guaranteed annuity interest.

(c) Where a charitable interest in the form of a guaranteed annuity interest is not in trust, the interest will be considered a guaranteed annuity interest only if it is to be paid by an insurance company or by an organization regularly engaged in issuing annuity contracts.

(d) Where a charitable interest in the form of a guaranteed annuity interest is in trust, the governing instrument of the trust may provide that income of the trust which is in excess of the amount required to pay the guaranteed annuity interest shall be paid to or for the use of a charity. Nevertheless, the amount of the deduction under section 2055 shall be limited to the fair market value of the guaranteed annuity interest as determined under paragraph (f)(2)(iv) of this section.

(e) Where a charitable interest in the form of a guaranteed annuity interest is in trust and the present value, on the appropriate valuation date, of all the income interests for a charitable purpose exceeds 60 percent of the aggregate fair market value of all amounts in such trust (after the payment of estate taxes and all other liabilities), the charitable interest will not be considered a guaranteed annuity interest unless the governing instrument of the trust prohibits both the acquisition and the retention of assets which would give rise to a tax under section 4944 if the trustee had acquired such assets.

(f) Where a charitable interest in the form of a guaranteed annuity interest is in trust, the charitable interest generally is not a guaranteed annuity interest if any amount may be paid by the trust for a private purpose before the expiration of all the charitable annuity interests. There are two exceptions to this general rule. First, the charitable interest is a guaranteed annuity interest if the amount payable for a private purpose is in the form of a guaranteed annuity interest and the trust's governing instrument does not provide for any preference or priority in the payment of the private annuity as opposed to the charitable annuity. Second, the charitable interest is a guaranteed annuity interest if under the trust's governing instrument the amount that may be paid for a private purpose is payable only from a group of assets that are devoted exclusively to private purposes and to which section 4947(a)(2) is inapplicable by reason of section 4947(a)(2)(B). For purposes of this paragraph (e)(2)(vi)(f), an amount is not paid for a private purpose if it is paid for an adequate and full consideration in money or money's worth. See § 53.4947–1(c) of this chapter for rules relating to the inapplicability of section 4947(a)(2) to segregated amounts in a split-interest trust.

(g) Neither the requirement in (e) of this subdivision (vi) for a prohibition in the governing instrument against the retention of assets which would give rise to a tax under section 4944 if the trustee had acquired the assets nor the provisions of (f) of this subdivision (vi) shall apply to—

(1) A trust executed on or before May 21, 1972, if—

(i) The trust is irrevocable on such date,

(ii) The trust is revocable on such date and the decedent dies within 3 years after such date without having amended any dispositive provision of the trust after such date, or

(iii) The trust is revocable on such date and no dispositive provision of the trust is amended within a period ending 3 years after such date and the decedent is, at the end of such 3-year period and at all times thereafter, under a mental disability (as defined in § 1.642(c)–2(b)(3)(ii) of this chapter) to amend the trust, or

(2) A will executed on or before May 21, 1972, if—

(i) The testator dies within 3 years after such date without having amended any dispositive provision of the will after such date, by codicil or otherwise,

(ii) The testator at no time after such date has the right to change the provisions of the will which pertain to the trust, or

(iii) No dispositive provision of the will is amended by the decedent, by codicil or otherwise, within a period ending 3 years after such date and the decedent is, at the end of such 3-year period and at all times thereafter, under a mental disability (as defined in § 1.642(c)–2(b)(3)(ii) of this chapter) to amend the will by codicil or otherwise.

(h) For purposes of this subdivision (vi) and paragraph (f) of this section, the term "appropriate valuation date" means the date of death or the alternate valuation date determined pursuant to an election under section 2032.

(i) For rules relating to certain governing instrument requirements and to the imposition of certain excise taxes where the guaranteed annuity interest is in trust and for rules governing payment of private income interests by split-interest trusts, see section 4947(a)(2) and (b)(3)(A), and the regulations thereunder.

(vii) *Unitrust interest.* (a) The charitable interest is a unitrust interest, whether or not such interest is in trust. For purposes of this subdivision (vii), the term "unitrust interest" means the right pursuant to the instrument of transfer to receive payment, not less often than annually, of a fixed percentage of the net fair market value, determined annually, of the property which funds the unitrust interest. In computing the net fair market value of the property which funds the unitrust interest, all assets and liabilities shall be taken into account without regard to whether particular items are taken into account in determining the income from the property. The net fair market value of the property which funds the unitrust interest may be determined on any one date during the year or by taking the average of valuations made on more than one date during the year, provided that the same valuation date or dates and valuation methods are used each year. Where the charitable interest is a unitrust interest to be paid by a trust and the governing instrument of the trust does not specify the valuation date or dates, the trustee shall select such date or dates and shall indicate his selection on the first return on Form 1041 which the trust is required to file. Payments under a unitrust interest may be paid for a specified term of years or for the life or lives of specified individuals, each of whom must be living at the date of death of the decedent and can be ascertained at such date. Only one or more of the following individuals may be used as measuring lives: the decedent's spouse, and an individual who, with respect to all remainder beneficiaries (other than charitable organizations described in section 170, 2055, or 2522), is either a lineal ancestor or the spouse of a lineal ancestor of those beneficiaries. A trust will satisfy the requirement that all noncharitable remainder beneficiaries are lineal descendants of the individual who is the measuring life, or that individual's spouse, if there is less than a 15% probability that individuals who are not lineal descendants will receive any trust corpus. This probability must be computed, based on the current applicable Life Table contained in § 20.2031–7, as of the date of the decedent's death taking into account the interests of all primary and contingent remainder beneficiaries who are living at that time. An interest payable for a specified term of years can qualify as a unitrust interest even if the governing instrument contains a savings clause intended to ensure compliance with a rule against perpetuities. The savings clause must utilize a period for vesting of 21 years after the deaths of measuring lives who are selected to maximize, rather than limit, the term of the trust. The rule in this paragraph that a charitable interest may be payable for the life or lives of only certain specified individuals does not apply in the case of a charitable unitrust interest payable under a charitable remainder trust described in section 664.

(b) A charitable interest is a unitrust interest only if it is a unitrust interest in every respect. For example, if the charitable interest is the right to receive from a trust each year a payment equal to the lesser of a sum certain or a fixed percentage of the net fair market value of the trust assets, determined annually, such interest is not a unitrust interest.

(c) Where a charitable interest in the form of a unitrust interest is not in trust, the interest will be considered a unitrust interest only if it is to be paid by an insurance company or by an organization regularly engaged in issuing interests otherwise meeting the requirements of a unitrust interest.

(d) Where a charitable interest in the form of a unitrust interest is in trust, the governing instrument of the trust may provide that income of the trust which is in excess of the amount required to pay the unitrust interest shall be paid to or for the use of a charity. Nevertheless, the amount of the deduction under section 2055 shall be limited to the fair market value of the unitrust interest as determined under paragraph (f)(2)(v) of this section.

(e) Where a charitable interest in the form of a unitrust interest is in trust, the charitable interest generally is not a unitrust interest if any amount may be paid by the trust for a private purpose before the expiration of all the charitable unitrust interests. There are two exceptions to this general rule. First, the charitable interest is a unitrust interest if the amount payable for a private purpose is in the form of a unitrust interest and the trust's governing instrument does not provide for any preference or priority in the payment of the private unitrust interest as opposed to the charitable unitrust interest. Second, the charitable interest is a unitrust interest if under the trust's governing instrument the amount that may be paid for a private purpose is payable only from a group of assets that are devoted exclusively to private purposes and to which section 4947(a)(2) is inapplicable by reason of section 4947(a)(2)(B). For purposes of this paragraph (e)(2)(vii)(e), an amount is not paid for a private purpose if it is paid for an adequate and full consideration in money or money's worth. See § 53.4947–1(c) of this chapter for rules relating to the inapplicability of section 4947(a)(2) to segregated amounts in a split-interest trust.

(f) For rules relating to certain governing instrument requirements and to the imposition of certain excise taxes where the unitrust interest is in trust and for rules governing payment of private income interests by a split-interest trust, see section 4947(a)(2) and (b)(3)(A), and the regulations thereunder.

(3) *Effective/applicability date.* The provisions of this paragraph apply only in the case of decedents dying after December 31, 1969, except that they do not apply—

(i) In the case of property passing under the terms of a will executed on or before October 9, 1969—

(a) If the decedent dies after October 9, 1969, but before October 9, 1972, without having amended any dispositive provision of the will after October 9, 1969, by codicil or otherwise,

(b) If the decedent dies after October 9, 1969, and at no time after that date had the right to change the portions of the will which pertain to the passing of the property to, or for the use of, an organization described in section 2055(a), or

(c) If no dispositive provision of the will is amended by the decedent, by codicil or otherwise, after October 9, 1969, and before October 9, 1972, and the decedent is on October 9, 1972, and at all times thereafter under a mental disability (as defined in § 1.642(c)–2(b)(3)(ii) of this chapter (Income Tax Regulations)) to amend the will by codicil or otherwise, or

(ii) In the case of property transferred in trust on or before October 9, 1969—

(a) If the decedent dies after October 9, 1969, but before October 9, 1972, without having amended, after October 9, 1969, any dispositive provision of the instrument governing the disposition of the property,

(b) If the property transferred was an irrevocable interest to, or for the use of, an organization described in section 2055(a), or

(c) If no dispositive provision of the instrument governing the disposition of the property is amended by the decedent after October 9, 1969, and before October 9, 1972, and the decedent is on October 9, 1972, and at all times thereafter under a mental disability (as defined in § 1.642(c)–2(b)(3)(ii) of this chapter) to change the disposition of the property, and (iii)(A) The rule in paragraphs (e)(2)(vi)(a) and (e)(2)(vii)(a) of this section that guaranteed annuity interests or unitrust interests, respectively, may be payable for a specified term of years or for the life or lives of only certain individuals generally is effective in the case of transfers pursuant to wills and revocable trusts when the decedent dies on or after April 4, 2000. Two exceptions from the application of the rule in paragraphs (e)(2)(vi)(a) and (e)(2)(vii)(a) of this section are provided for transfers pursuant to a will or revocable trust executed on or before April 4, 2000. One exception is for a decedent who dies on or before July 5, 2001, without having republished the will (or amended the trust) by codicil or otherwise. The other exception is for a decedent who was, on April 4, 2000, under a mental disability that prevented a change in the disposition of the decedent's property, and who either does not regain competence to dispose of such property before the date of death, or dies prior to the later of 90 days after the date on which the decedent first regains competence, or July 5, 2001, without having republished the will (or amended the trust) by codicil or otherwise. If a guaranteed annuity interest or unitrust interest created pursuant to a will or revocable trust when the decedent dies on or after April 4, 2000, uses an individual other than one permitted in paragraphs (e)(2)(vi)(a) and (e)(2)(vii)(a) of this section, and the interest does not qualify for this transitional relief, the interest may be reformed into a lead interest payable for a specified term of years. The term of years is determined by taking the factor for valuing the annuity or unitrust interest for the named individual measuring life and identifying the term of years (rounded up to the next whole year) that corresponds to the equivalent term of years factor for an annuity or unitrust interest. A judicial reformation must be commenced prior to the later of July 5, 2001, or the date prescribed by section 2055(e)(3)(C)(iii). Any judicial reformation must be completed within a reasonable time after it is commenced. A non-judicial reformation is permitted if effective under state law, provided it is completed by the date on which a judicial reformation must be commenced. In the alternative, if a court, in a proceeding that is commenced on or before July 5, 2001, declares any transfer made pursuant to a will or revocable trust where the decedent dies on or after April 4, 2000, and on or before March 6, 2001, null and void ab initio, the Internal Revenue Service will treat such transfers in a manner similar to that described in section 2055(e)(3)(J).

(B) The appropriate annuity factor for an annuity payable for a term of years is computed by subtracting from 1.000000 the factor for an ordinary remainder interest following the same term certain that is determined under the formula in § 20.2031–7(d)(2)(ii)(A) and then dividing the result by the applicable section 7520 interest rate, expressing the annuity factor to at least four decimal places. For the convenience of taxpayers, actuarial factors have been computed by the IRS and appear in the "Annuity" column of Table B. The appropriate annuity factor for an annuity payable for the life of one individual is computed by subtracting from 1.00000 the factor for an ordinary remainder interest following the life of the same individual that is determined under the formula in § 20.2031–7(d)(2)(ii)(B) and then dividing the result by the applicable section 7520 interest rate expressed to at least four decimal places. For the convenience of taxpayers, actuarial factors have been computed by the IRS and appear in the "Annuity" column of Table S. Tables B and S can be found on the IRS website at *https://www.irs.gov/retirement-plans/actuarial-tables* (or a corresponding URL as may be updated from time to time). For purposes of the example in paragraph (e)(3)(iii)(C) of this section, the following relevant factors from Tables B and S are used:

Factors from Table B			
Annuity, Income, and Remainder Interests for a Term Certain			
Interest at 3.2 Percent			
Years	Annuity	Income Interest	Remainder
37	21.5068	0.688218	0.311782
38	21.8089	0.697886	0.302114

Factors from Table S—Based on Table 2010CM			
Interest at 3.2 Percent			
Age	Annuity	Life Estate	Remainder
40	21.7045	0.69454	0.30546

(C) The following example illustrates how to determine the term of years for a reformed interest as discussed in paragraph (e)(3)(iii)(A) of this section. Assume an annuity interest payable for the life of an individual age 40 at the time of the transfer on or after June 1, 2023, with an interest rate of 3.2 percent under section 7520. Under Table S, the annuity factor at 3.2 percent for the life of an individual age 40 is 21.7045. Based on Table B at 3.2 percent, the factor 21.7045 corresponds to a term of years between 37 and 38 years. Accordingly, the annuity interest must be reformed into an interest payable for a term of 38 years.

(4) *Amendment of dispositive provisions.* For purposes of subparagraphs (2) and (3) of this paragraph, an amendment shall generally be considered as one which amends the dispositive provisions of a will or trust if it results in a change in the persons to whom the funds are to be given or makes changes in the conditions under which the funds are given. Examples of amendments which do not amend the dispositive provisions of a will or trust include the substitution of one fiduciary for another to act in the capacity of executor or trustee and the change in the name of a legatee or beneficiary by reason of the legatee's or beneficiary's marriage. On the other hand, examples of amendments which do amend the dispositive provisions of a will or trust include an increase or decrease in the amount of a general bequest, an amendment which increases or decreases the power of a trustee to determine an allocation of income or corpus in such a way as to change the beneficiaries of the funds or a beneficiary's share of the funds, or a change in the allocation of, or in the right to allocate, receipts and expenditures between income and principal in such a way as to change the beneficiaries of the funds or a beneficiary's share of the funds.

(5) *Amendment of wills providing for pour-over into trusts.* For purposes of subparagraphs (2) and (3) of this paragraph, an amendment of a dispositive provision of a trust to which assets are to be transferred under a will shall be considered a dispositive amendment of such will.

(f) Valuation of charitable interest. (1) *In general.* The amount of the deduction in the case of a contribution of a partial interest in property to which this section applies is the fair market value of the partial interest at the appropriate valuation date, as defined in paragraph (e)(2)(vi)(h) of this section. The fair market value of an annuity, life estate, term for years, remainder, reversion, (or) unitrust interest is its present value.

(2) *Certain decedents dying after July 31, 1969.* In the case of a transfer of an interest described in subdivision (v), (vi), or (vii) of paragraph (e)(2) of this section by decedents dying after July 31, 1969, the present value of such interest is to be determined under the following rules:

(i) The present value of a remainder interest in a charitable remainder annuity trust is to be determined under § 1.664–2(c) of this chapter (Income Tax Regulations).

(ii) The present value of a remainder interest in a charitable remainder unitrust is to be determined under § 1.664–4 of this chapter.

(iii) The present value of a remainder interest in a pooled income fund is to be determined under § 1.642(c)–6 of this chapter.

(iv) The present value of a guaranteed annuity interest described in paragraph (e)(2)(vi) of this section is to be determined under § 20.2031–7 or, for certain prior periods, § 20.2031–7A, except that, if the annuity is issued by a company regularly engaged in the sale of annuities, the present value is to be determined under § 20.2031–8. If by reason of all the conditions and circumstances surrounding a transfer of an income interest in property in trust it appears that the charity may not receive the beneficial enjoyment of the interest, a deduction will be allowed under section 2055 only for the minimum amount it is evident the charity will receive.

Example (1). In 1975, B dies bequeathing $20,000 in trust with the requirement that a designated charity be paid a guaranteed annuity interest (as defined in paragraph (e)(2)(vi) of this section) of $4,100 a year, payable annually at the end of each year, for a period of 6 years and that the remainder be paid to his children. The fair market value of an annuity of $4,100 a year for a period of 6 years is $20,160.93 ($4,100x4.9173), as determined under Table B in § 20.2031–7A(d). The deduction with respect to the guaranteed annuity interest will be limited to $20,000, which is the minimum amount it is evident the charity will receive.

Example (2). In 1975, C dies bequeathing $40,000 in trust with the requirement that D, an individual, and X Charity be paid simultaneously guaranteed annuity interests (as defined in paragraph (e)(2)(vi) of this section) of $5,000 a year each, payable annually at the end of each year, for a period of 5 years and that the remainder be paid to C's children. The fair market value of two annuities of $5,000 each a year for a period of 5 years is $42,124 ([$5,000x4.2124]x2), as determined under Table B in § 20.2031–7A(d). The trust instrument provides that in the event the trust fund is insufficient to pay both annuities in a given year, the trust fund will be evenly divided between the charitable and private annuitants. The deduction with respect to the charitable annuity will be limited to $20,000, which is the minimum amount it is evident the charity will receive.

Example (3). In 1975, D dies bequeathing $65,000 in trust with the requirement that a guaranteed annuity interest (as defined in paragraph (e)(2)(vi) of this section) of $5,000 a year, payable annually at the end of each year, be paid to Y Charity for a period of 10 years and that a guaranteed annuity interest (as defined in paragraph (e)(2)(vi) of this section) of $5,000 a year, payable annually at the end of each year, be paid to W, his widow, aged 62, for 10 years or until her prior death. The annuities are to be paid simultaneously, and the remainder is to be paid to D's children. The fair market value of the private annuity is $33,877 ($5,000 x 6.7754), as determined pursuant to § 20.2031–7A(c) and by the use of factors involving one life and a term of years as published in Publication 723A (12–70). The fair market value of the charitable annuity is $36,800.50 ($5,000 x 7.3601), as determined under Table B in § 20.2031–7A(d). It is not evident from the governing instrument of the trust or from local law that the trustee would be required to apportion the trust fund between the widow and charity in the event the fund were insufficient to pay both annuities in a given year. Accordingly, the deduction with respect to the charitable annuity will be limited to $31,123 ($65,000 less $33,877 [the value of the private annuity]), which is the minimum amount it is evident the charity will receive.

(v) The present value of a unitrust interest described in paragraph (e)(2)(vii) of this section is to be determined by subtracting the present value of all interests in the transferred property other than the unitrust interest from the fair market value of the transferred property.

(3) *Certain decedents dying before August 1, 1969.* In the case of decedents dying before August 1, 1969, the present value of an interest described in subparagraph (2) of this paragraph is to be determined under § 20.2031–7 except that, if the interest is an annuity issued by a company regularly engaged in the sale of annuities, the present value is to be determined under § 20.2031–8.

(4) *Other decedents.* The present value of an interest not described in paragraph (f)(2) of this section is to be determined under § 20.2031–7(d) in the case of decedents where the valuation date of the gross estate is on or after June 1, 2023, or under § 20.2031–7A in the case of decedents where the valuation date of the gross estate is before June 1, 2023.

(5) *Special computations.* If the interest transferred is such that its present value is to be determined by a special computation, a request for a special factor, accompanied by a statement of the date of birth and sex of each individual the duration of whose life may affect the value of the interest, and by copies of the relevant instruments, may be submitted by the fiduciary to the Commissioner who may, if conditions permit, supply the factor requested. If the Commissioner furnishes the factor, a copy of the letter supplying the factor must be attached to the tax return in which the deduction is claimed. If the Commissioner does not furnish the factor, the claim for deduction must be supported by a full statement of the computation of the present value made in accordance with the principles set forth in this paragraph.

(6) *Applicability date.* Paragraphs (e)(3)(iii) and (f)(4) of this section apply on and after June 1, 2023.

[T.D. 6296, 23 FR 4529, June 24, 1958, as amended by T.D. 7238, 37 FR 28719, Dec. 29, 1972; T.D. 7318, 39 FR 25453, July 11, 1974, 39 FR 26154, July 17, 1974; T.D. 7340, 40 FR 1240, Jan. 7, 1975; T.D. 7955, 49 FR 19995, May 11, 1984; T.D. 7957, 49 FR 20811, May 17, 1984; T.D. 8069, 51 FR 1507, Jan. 14, 1986; 51 FR 5322, Feb. 13, 1986; 51 FR 6219, Feb. 21, 1986; T.D. 8095, 51 FR 28368, Aug. 7, 1986; 51 FR 32071, Sept. 9, 1986; T.D. 8540, 59 FR 30103, 30170, June 10, 1994; T.D. 8819, 64 FR 23222, 23229, April 30, 1999; 64 FR 33196, June 22, 1999; T.D. 8886, 65 FR 36943, June 12, 2000; T.D. 8923, 66 FR 1042, Jan. 5, 2001; T.D. 9068, 68 FR 40131, July 7, 2003; T.D. 9448, 74 FR 21510, May 7, 2009; T.D. 9540, 76 FR 49637, Aug. 10, 2011; T.D. 9974, 88 FR 37447, June 7, 2023]

§ 20.2055–3 Effect of death taxes and administration expenses.

(a) Death taxes. (1) If under the terms of the will or other governing instruments, the law of the jurisdiction under which the estate is administered, or the law of the jurisdiction imposing the particular tax, the Federal estate tax, or any estate, succession, legacy, or inheritance tax is payable in whole or in part out of any property the transfer of which would otherwise be allowable as a deduction under section 2055, section 2055(c) provides that the sum deductible is the amount of the transferred property reduced by the amount of the tax. Section 2055(c) in effect provides that the deduction is based on the amount actually available for charitable uses, that is, the amount of the fund remaining after the payment of all death taxes. Thus, if $50,000 is bequeathed for a charitable purpose and is subjected to a State inheritance tax of $5,000, payable out of the $50,000, the amount deductible is $45,000. If a life estate is bequeathed to an individual with remainder over to a charitable organization, and by the local law the inheritance tax upon the life estate is paid out of the corpus with the result that the charitable organization will be entitled to receive only the amount of the fund less the tax, the deduction is limited to the present value, as of the date of the testator's death, of the remainder of the fund so reduced. If a testator bequeaths his residuary estate, or a portion of it, to charity, and his will contains a direction that certain inheritance taxes, otherwise payable from legacies upon which they were imposed, shall be payable out of the residuary estate, the deduction may not exceed the bequest to charity thus reduced pursuant to the direction of the will. If a residuary estate, or a portion of it, is bequested to charity, and by the local law the Federal estate tax is payable out of the residuary estate, the deduction may not exceed that portion of the residuary estate bequeathed to charity as reduced by the Federal estate tax. The return should fully disclose the computation of the amount to be deducted. If the amount to be deducted is dependent upon the amount of any death tax which has not been paid before the filing of the return, there should be submitted with the return a computation of that tax.

(2) It should be noted that if the Federal estate tax is payable out of a charitable transfer so that the amount of the transfer otherwise passing to charity is reduced by the amount of the tax, the resultant decrease in the amount passing to charity will further reduce the allowable deduction. In such a case, the amount of the charitable deduction can be obtained only by a series of trial-and-error computations, or by a formula. If, in addition, interdependent State and Federal taxes are involved, the computation becomes highly complicated. Examples of methods of computation of the charitable deduction and the marital deduction (with which similar problems are encountered) in various situations are contained in supplemental instructions to the estate tax return.

(3) For the allowance of a deduction to a decedent's estate for certain State death taxes imposed upon charitable transfers, see section 2053(d) and § 20.2053–9.

(b) Administration expenses. (1) *Definitions.* (i) *Management expenses.* Estate management expenses are expenses that are incurred in connection with the investment of estate assets or with their preservation or maintenance during a reasonable period of administration. Examples of these expenses could include investment advisory fees, stock brokerage commissions, custodial fees, and interest.

(ii) *Transmission expenses.* Estate transmission expenses are expenses that would not have been incurred but for the decedent's death and the consequent necessity of collecting the decedent's assets, paying the decedent's debts and death taxes, and distributing the decedent's property to those who are entitled to receive it. Estate transmission expenses include any administration expense that is not a management expense. Examples of these expenses could include executor commissions and attorney fees (except to the extent of commissions or fees specifically related to investment, preservation, and maintenance of the assets), probate fees, expenses incurred in construction proceedings and defending against will contests, and appraisal fees.

(iii) *Charitable share.* The charitable share is the property or interest in property that passed from the decedent for which a deduction is allowable under section 2055(a) with respect to all or part of the property interest. The charitable share includes, for example, bequests to charitable organizations and bequests to a charitable lead unitrust or annuity trust, a charitable remainder unitrust or annuity trust, and a pooled income fund, described in section 2055(e)(2). The charitable share also includes the income produced by the property or interest in property during the period of administration if the income, under the terms of the governing instrument or applicable local law, is payable to the charitable organization or is to be added to the principal of the property interest passing in whole or in part to the charitable organization.

(2) *Effect of transmission expenses.* For purposes of determining the charitable deduction, the value of the charitable share shall be reduced by the amount of the estate transmission expenses paid from the charitable share.

(3) *Effect of management expenses attributable to the charitable share.* For purposes of determining the charitable deduction, the value of the charitable share shall not be reduced by the amount of the estate management expenses attributable to and paid from the charitable share. Pursuant to section 2056(b)(9), however, the amount of the allowable charitable deduction shall be reduced by the amount of any such management expenses that are deducted under section 2053 on the decedent's federal estate tax return.

(4) *Effect of management expenses not attributable to the charitable share.* For purposes of determining the charitable deduction, the value of the charitable share shall be reduced by the amount of the estate management expenses paid from the charitable share but attributable to a property interest not included in the charitable share.

(5) *Example.* The following example illustrates the application of this paragraph (b):

Example. The decedent, who dies in 2000, leaves his residuary estate, after the payment of debts, expenses, and estate taxes, to a charitable remainder unitrust that satisfies the requirements of section 664(d). During the period of administration, the estate incurs estate transmission expenses of $400,000. The residue of the estate (the charitable share) must be reduced by the $400,000 of transmission expenses and by the Federal and State estate taxes before the present value of the remainder interest passing to charity can be determined in accordance with the provisions of § 1.664–4 of this chapter. Because the estate taxes are payable out of the residue, the computation of the estate taxes and the allowable charitable deduction are interrelated. See paragraph (a)(2) of this section.

(6) *Cross reference.* See § 20.2056(b)–4(d) for additional examples applicable to the treatment of administration expenses under this paragraph (b).

(7) *Effective date.* The provisions of this paragraph (b) apply to estates of decedents dying on or after December 3, 1999.

[T.D. 6296, 23 FR 4529, June 24, 1958; T.D. 8846, 64 FR 67765, Dec. 3, 1999; 64 FR 71022, Dec. 20, 1999]

§ 20.2055–4 Disallowance of charitable, etc., deductions because of "prohibited transactions" in the case of decedents dying before January 1, 1970. [*Omitted. Ed.*]

[T.D. 6296, 23 FR 4529, June 24, 1958; 25 FR 14021, Dec. 31, 1960 as amended by T.D. 7318, 39 FR 25456, July 11, 1974]

§ 20.2055–5 Disallowance of charitable, etc., deductions in the case of decedents dying after December 31, 1969.

(a) Organizations subject to section 507(c) tax. Section 508(d)(1) provides that, in the case of decedents dying after December 31, 1969, a deduction which would otherwise be allowable under section 2055 for the value of property transferred by the decedent to or for the use of an organization upon which the tax provided by section 507(c) has been imposed shall not be allowed if the transfer is made by the decedent after notification is made under section 507(a) or if the decedent is a substantial contributor (as defined in section 507(d)(2)) who dies on or after the first day on which action is taken by such organization that culminates in the imposition of the tax under section 507(c). This paragraph does not apply if the entire amount of the unpaid portion of the tax imposed by section 507(c) is abated under section 507(g) by the Commissioner or his delegate.

(b) Taxable private foundations, section 4947 trusts, etc. (1) *In general.* Section 508(d)(2) provides that, in the case of decedents dying after December 31, 1969, a deduction which would otherwise be allowable under section 2055 for the value of property transferred by the decedent shall not be allowed if the transfer is made to or for the use of—

(i) A private foundation or a trust described in section 4947(a)(2) in a taxable year of such organization for which such organization fails to meet the governing instrument requirements of section 508(e) (determined without regard to section 508(e)(2)(B) and (C)), or

(ii) Any organization in a period for which it is not treated as an organization described in section 501(c)(3) by reason of its failure to give notification under section 508(a) of its status to the Commissioner.

For additional rules, see § 1.508–2(b)(1) of this chapter (Income Tax Regulations).

(2) *Transfers not covered by section 508(d)(2)(A)*—(i) *In general.* Any deduction which would otherwise be allowable under section 2055 for the value of property transferred by a decedent dying after December 31, 1969, will not be disallowed under section 508(d)(2)(A) and subparagraph (1)(i) of this paragraph—

(a) In the case of property passing under the terms of a will executed on or before October 9, 1969—

(1) If the decedent dies after October 9, 1969, but before October 9, 1972, without having amended any dispositive provision of the will after October 9, 1969, by codicil or otherwise,

(2) If the decedent dies after October 9, 1969, and at no time after that date had the right to change the portions of the will which pertain to the passing of the property to, or for the use of, an organization described in section 2055(a), or

(3) If no dispositive provision of the will is amended by the decedent, by codicil or otherwise, after October 9, 1969, and before October 9, 1972, and the decedent is on October 9, 1972, and at all times thereafter under a mental disability (as defined in § 1.642(c)–2(b)(3)(ii) of this chapter) to amend the will by codicil or otherwise, or

(b) In the case of property transferred in trust on or before October 9, 1969—

(1) If the decedent dies after October 9, 1969, but before October 9, 1972, without having amended, after October 9, 1969, any dispositive provision of the instrument governing the disposition of the property,

(2) If the property transferred was an irrevocable interest to, or for the use of, an organization described in section 2055(a), or

(3) If no dispositive provision of the instrument governing the disposition of the property is amended by the decedent after October 9, 1969, and before October 9, 1972, and the decedent is on October 9, 1972, and at all times thereafter under a mental disability (as defined in § 1.642(c)–2(b)(3)(ii) of this chapter) to change the disposition of the property.

(ii) *Amendment of dispositive provisions.* For purposes of subdivision (i) of this subparagraph, the provisions of paragraph (e)(4) and (5) of § 20.2055–2 shall apply in determining whether an amendment will be considered as one which amends the dispositive provisions of a will or trust.

(c) Foreign organization with substantial support from foreign sources. Section 4948(c)(4) provides that, in the case of decedents dying after December 31, 1969, a deduction which would otherwise be allowable under section 2055 for the value of property transferred by the decedent to or for the use of a foreign organization which has received substantially all of its support (other than gross investment income) from sources without the United States shall not be allowed if the transfer is made (1) after the date on which the Commissioner has published notice that he has notified such organization that it has engaged in a prohibited transaction, or (2) in a taxable year of such organization for which it is not exempt from taxation under section 501(a) because it has engaged in a prohibited transaction after December 31, 1969.

[T.D. 7318, 39 FR 25456, July 11, 1974]

§ 20.2055–6 Disallowance of double deduction in the case of qualified terminable interest property.

No deduction is allowed from the decedent's gross estate under section 2055 for property with respect to which a deduction is allowed by reason of section 2056(b)(7). See section 2056(b)(9) and § 20.2056(b)–9.

[T.D. 8522, 59 FR 9647, March 1, 1994]

§ 2056. Bequests, Etc., to Surviving Spouse

(a) Allowance of marital deduction. For purposes of the tax imposed by section 2001, the value of the taxable estate shall, except as limited by subsection (b), be determined by deducting from the value of the gross estate an amount equal to the value of any interest in property which passes or has passed from the decedent to his surviving spouse, but only to the extent that such interest is included in determining the value of the gross estate.

(b) Limitation in the case of life estate or other terminable interest.

(1) General rule. Where, on the lapse of time, on the occurrence of an event or contingency, or on the failure of an event or contingency to occur, an interest passing to the surviving spouse will terminate or fail, no deduction shall be allowed under this section with respect to such interest—

(A) if an interest in such property passes or has passed (for less than an adequate and full consideration in money or money's worth) from the decedent to any person other than such surviving spouse (or the estate of such spouse); and

(B) if by reason of such passing such person (or his heirs or assigns) may possess or enjoy any part of such property after such termination or failure of the interest so passing to the surviving spouse;

and no deduction shall be allowed with respect to such interest (even if such deduction is not disallowed under subparagraphs (A) and (B))—

(C) if such interest is to be acquired for the surviving spouse, pursuant to directions of the decedent, by his executor or by the trustee of a trust.

For purposes of this paragraph, an interest shall not be considered as an interest which will terminate or fail merely because it is the ownership of a bond, note, or similar contractual obligation, the discharge of which would not have the effect of an annuity for life or for a term.

(2) Interest in unidentified assets. Where the assets (included in the decedent's gross estate) out of which, or the proceeds of which, an interest passing to the surviving spouse may be satisfied include a particular asset or assets with respect to which no deduction would be allowed if such asset or assets passed from the decedent to such spouse, then the value of such interest passing to such spouse shall, for purposes of subsection (a), be reduced by the aggregate value of such particular assets.

(3) Interest of spouse conditional on survival for limited period. For purposes of this subsection, an interest passing to the surviving spouse shall not be considered as an interest which will terminate or fail on the death of such spouse if—

(A) such death will cause a termination or failure of such interest only if it occurs within a period not exceeding 6 months after the decedent's death, or only if it occurs as a result of a common disaster resulting in the death of the decedent and the surviving spouse, or only if it occurs in the case of either such event; and

(B) such termination or failure does not in fact occur.

(4) Valuation of interest passing to surviving spouse. In determining for purposes of subsection (a) the value of any interest in property passing to the surviving spouse for which a deduction is allowed by this section—

(A) there shall be taken into account the effect which the tax imposed by section 2001, or any estate, succession, legacy, or inheritance tax, has on the net value to the surviving spouse of such interest; and

(B) where such interest or property is encumbered in any manner, or where the surviving spouse incurs any obligation imposed by the decedent with respect to the passing of such interest, such encumbrance or obligation shall be taken into account in the same manner as if the amount of a gift to such spouse of such interest were being determined.

(5) Life estate with power of appointment in surviving spouse. In the case of an interest in property passing from the decedent, if his surviving spouse is entitled for life to all the income from the entire interest, or all the income from a specific portion thereof, payable annually or at more frequent intervals, with power in the surviving spouse to appoint the entire interest, or such specific portion (exercisable in favor of such surviving spouse, or of the estate of such surviving spouse, or in favor of either, whether or not in each case the power is exercisable in favor of others), and with no power in any other person to appoint any part of the interest, or such specific portion, to any person other than the surviving spouse—

(A) the interest or such portion thereof so passing shall, for purposes of subsection (a), be considered as passing to the surviving spouse, and

(B) no part of the interest so passing shall, for purposes of paragraph (1)(A), be considered as passing to any person other than the surviving spouse.

This paragraph shall apply only if such power in the surviving spouse to appoint the entire interest, or such specific portion thereof, whether exercisable by will or during life, is exercisable by such spouse alone and in all events.

(6) Life insurance or annuity payments with power of appointment in surviving spouse. In the case of an interest in property passing from the decedent consisting of proceeds under a life insurance, endowment, or annuity contract, if under the terms of the contract such proceeds are payable in installments or are held by the insurer subject to an agreement to pay interest thereon (whether the proceeds, on the termination of any interest payments, are payable in a lump sum or in annual or more frequent installments), and such installment or interest payments are payable annually or at more frequent intervals, commencing not later than 13 months after the decedent's death, and all amounts, or a specific portion of all such amounts, payable during the life of the surviving spouse are payable only to such spouse, and such spouse has the power to appoint all amounts, or such specific portion, payable under such contract (exercisable in favor of such surviving spouse, or of the estate of such surviving spouse, or in favor of either, whether or not in each case the power is exercisable in favor of others), with no power in any other person to appoint such amounts to any person other than the surviving spouse—

(A) such amounts shall, for purposes of subsection (a), be considered as passing to the surviving spouse, and

(B) no part of such amounts shall, for purposes of paragraph (1)(A), be considered as passing to any person other than the surviving spouse.

This paragraph shall apply only if, under the terms of the contract, such power in the surviving spouse to appoint such amounts, whether exercisable by will or during life, is exercisable by such spouse alone and in all events.

(7) Election with respect to life estate for surviving spouse.

(A) In general. In the case of qualified terminable interest property—

(i) for purposes of subsection (a), such property shall be treated as passing to the surviving spouse, and

(ii) for purposes of paragraph (1)(A), no part of such property shall be treated as passing to any person other than the surviving spouse.

(B) Qualified terminable interest property defined. For purposes of this paragraph—

(i) In general. The term "qualified terminable interest property" means property—

(I) which passes from the decedent,

(II) in which the surviving spouse has a qualifying income interest for life, and

(III) to which an election under this paragraph applies.

(ii) Qualifying income interest for life. The surviving spouse has a qualifying income interest for life if—

(I) the surviving spouse is entitled to all the income from the property, payable annually or at more frequent intervals, or has a usufruct interest for life in the property, and

(II) no person has a power to appoint any part of the property to any person other than the surviving spouse.

Subclause (II) shall not apply to a power exercisable only at or after the death of the surviving spouse. To the extent provided in regulations, an annuity shall be treated in a manner similar to an income interest in property (regardless of whether the property from which the annuity is payable can be separately identified).

(iii) Property includes interest therein. The term "property" includes an interest in property.

(iv) Specific portion treated as separate property. A specific portion of property shall be treated as separate property.

(v) Election. An election under this paragraph with respect to any property shall be made by the executor on the return of tax imposed by section 2001. Such an election, once made, shall be irrevocable.

(C) Treatment of survivor annuities. In the case of an annuity included in the gross estate of the decedent under section 2039 (or, in the case of an interest in an annuity arising under the community property laws of a State, included in the gross estate of the decedent under section 2033) where only the surviving spouse has the right to receive payments before the death of such surviving spouse—

(i) the interest of such surviving spouse shall be treated as a qualifying income interest for life, and

(ii) the executor shall be treated as having made an election under this subsection with respect to such annuity unless the executor otherwise elects on the return of tax imposed by section 2001.

An election under clause (ii), once made, shall be irrevocable.

(8) Special rule for charitable remainder trusts.

(A) In general. If the surviving spouse of the decedent is the only beneficiary of a qualified charitable remainder trust who is not a charitable beneficiary nor an ESOP beneficiary, paragraph (1) shall not apply to any interest in such trust which passes or has passed from the decedent to such surviving spouse.

(B) Definitions. For purposes of subparagraph (A)—

(i) Charitable beneficiary. The term "charitable beneficiary" means any beneficiary which is an organization described in section 170(c).

(ii) ESOP beneficiary. The term "ESOP beneficiary" means any beneficiary which is an employee stock ownership plan (as defined in section 4975(e)(7)) that holds a remainder interest in qualified employer securities (as defined in section 664(g)(4)) to be transferred to such plan in a qualified gratuitous transfer (as defined in section 664(g)(1)).

(iii) Qualified charitable remainder trust. The term "qualified charitable remainder trust" means a charitable remainder annuity trust or a charitable remainder unitrust (described in section 664).

(9) Denial of double deduction. Nothing in this section or any other provision of this chapter shall allow the value of any interest in property to be deducted under this chapter more than once with respect to the same decedent.

(10) Specific portion. For purposes of paragraphs (5), (6), and (7)(B)(iv), the term "specific portion" only includes a portion determined on a fractional or percentage basis.

(c) Definition. For purposes of this section, an interest in property shall be considered as passing from the decedent to any person if and only if—

(1) such interest is bequeathed or devised to such person by the decedent;

(2) such interest is inherited by such person from the decedent;

(3) such interest is the dower or curtesy interest (or statutory interest in lieu thereof) of such person as surviving spouse of the decedent;

(4) such interest has been transferred to such person by the decedent at any time;

(5) such interest was, at the time of the decedent's death, held by such person and the decedent (or by them and any other person) in joint ownership with right of survivorship;

(6) the decedent had a power (either alone or in conjunction with any person) to appoint such interest and if he appoints or has appointed such interest to such person, or if such person takes such interest in default on the release or nonexercise of such power; or

(7) such interest consists of proceeds of insurance on the life of the decedent receivable by such person.

Except as provided in paragraph (5) or (6) of subsection (b), where at the time of the decedent's death it is not possible to ascertain the particular person or persons to whom an interest in property may pass from the decedent, such interest shall, for purposes of subparagraphs (A) and (B) of subsection (b)(1), be considered as passing from the decedent to a person other than the surviving spouse.

(d) Disallowance of marital deduction where surviving spouse not United States citizen.

(1) In general. Except as provided in paragraph (2), if the surviving spouse of the decedent is not a citizen of the United States—

(A) no deduction shall be allowed under subsection (a), and

(B) section 2040(b) shall not apply.

(2) Marital deduction allowed for certain transfers in trust.

(A) In general. Paragraph (1) shall not apply to any property passing to the surviving spouse in a qualified domestic trust.

(B) Special rule. If any property passes from the decedent to the surviving spouse of the decedent, for purposes of subparagraph (A), such property shall be treated as passing to such spouse in a qualified domestic trust if—

(i) such property is transferred to such a trust before the date on which the return of the tax imposed by this chapter is made, or

(ii) such property is irrevocably assigned to such a trust under an irrevocable assignment made on or before such date which is enforceable under local law.

(3) Allowance of credit to certain spouses. If—

(A) property passes to the surviving spouse of the decedent (hereinafter in this paragraph referred to as the "first decedent"),

(B) without regard to this subsection, a deduction would be allowable under subsection (a) with respect to such property, and

(C) such surviving spouse dies and the estate of such surviving spouse is subject to the tax imposed by this chapter,

the Federal estate tax paid (or treated as paid under section 2056A(b)(7)) by the first decedent with respect to such property shall be allowed as a credit under section 2013 to the estate of such surviving spouse and the amount of such credit shall be determined under such section without regard to when the first decedent died and without regard to subsection (d)(3) of such section.

(4) Special rule where resident spouse becomes citizen. Paragraph (1) shall not apply if—

(A) the surviving spouse of the decedent becomes a citizen of the United States before the day on which the return of the tax imposed by this chapter is made, and

(B) such spouse was a resident of the United States at all times after the date of the death of the decedent and before becoming a citizen of the United States.

(5) Reformations permitted.

(A) In general. In the case of any property with respect to which a deduction would be allowable under subsection (a) but for this subsection, the determination of whether a trust is a qualified domestic trust shall be made—

(i) as of the date on which the return of the tax imposed by this chapter is made, or

(ii) if a judicial proceeding is commenced on or before the due date (determined with regard to extensions) for filing such return to change such trust into a trust which is a qualified domestic trust, as of the time when the changes pursuant to such proceeding are made.

(B) Statute of limitations. If a judicial proceeding described in subparagraph (A)(ii) is commenced with respect to any trust, the period for assessing any deficiency of tax attributable to any failure of such trust to be a qualified domestic trust shall not expire before the date 1 year after the date on which the Secretary is notified that the trust has been changed pursuant to such judicial proceeding or that such proceeding has been terminated.

Regulations

§ 20.2056–0 Table of contents. [*Omitted. Ed.*]

[T.D. 8522, 59 FR 9647, March 1, 1994; T.D. 8612, 60 FR 43538, Aug. 22, 1995]

§ 20.2056(a)–1 Marital deduction; in general.

(a) In general. A deduction is allowed under section 2056 from the gross estate of a decedent for the value of any property interest which passes from the decedent to the decedent's surviving spouse if the interest is a deductible interest as defined in § 20.2056(a)–2. With respect to decedents dying in certain years, a deduction is allowed under section 2056 only to the extent that the total of the deductible interests does not exceed the applicable limitations set forth in paragraph (c) of this section. The deduction allowed under section 2056 is referred to as the marital deduction. See also sections 2056(d) and 2056A for special rules applicable in the case of decedents dying after November 10, 1988, if the decedent's surviving spouse is not a citizen of the United States at the time of the decedent's death. In such cases, the marital deduction may not be allowed unless the property passes to a qualified domestic trust as described in section 2056A(a).

(b) Requirements for marital deduction. (1) *In general.* To obtain the marital deduction with respect to any property interest, the executor must establish the following facts—

(i) The decedent was survived by a spouse (see § 20.2056(c)–2(e));

(ii) The property interest passed from the decedent to the spouse (see §§ 20.2056(b)–5 through

20.2056(b)–8 and 20.2056(c)–1 through 20.2056(c)–3);

(iii) The property interest is a deductible interest (see § 20.2056(a)–2); and

(iv) The value of the property interest (see § 20.2056(b)–4).

(2) *Burden of establishing requisite facts.* The executor must provide the facts relating to any applicable limitation on the amount of the allowable marital deduction under § 20.2056(a)–1(c), and must submit proof necessary to establish any fact required under paragraph (b)(1), including any evidence requested by the district director.

(c) Marital deduction; limitation on aggregate deductions. (1) *Estates of decedents dying before 1977.* In the case of estates of decedents dying before January 1, 1977, the marital deduction is limited to one-half of the value of the adjusted gross estate, as that term was defined under section 2056(c)(2) prior to repeal by the Economic Recovery Tax Act of 1981.

(2) *Estates of decedents dying after December 31, 1976, and before January 1, 1982.* Except as provided in § 2002(d)(1) of the Tax Reform Act of 1976 (Pub.L. 94–455), in the case of decedents dying after December 31, 1976, and before January 1, 1982, the marital deduction is limited to the greater of—

(i) $250,000; or

(ii) One-half of the value of the decedent's adjusted gross estate, adjusted for inter vivos gifts to the spouse as prescribed by section 2056(c)(1)(B) prior to repeal by the Economic Recovery Tax Act of 1981 (Pub.L. 97–34).

(3) *Estates of decedents dying after December 31, 1981.* In the case of estates of decedents dying after December 31, 1981, the marital deduction is limited as prescribed in paragraph (c)(2) of this section if the provisions of § 403(e)(3) of Pub.L. 97–34 are satisfied.

[T.D. 6296, 23 FR 4529, June 24, 1958; 25 FR 14021, Dec. 31, 1960; T.D. 8095, 51 FR 28368, Aug. 7, 1986; T.D. 8522, 59 FR 9648, March 1, 1994]

§ 20.2056(a)–2 Marital deduction; "deductible interests" and "nondeductible interests".

(a) In general. Property interests which passed from a decedent to his surviving spouse fall within two general categories: (1) Those with respect to which the marital deduction is authorized, and (2) those with respect to which the marital deduction is not authorized. These categories are referred to in this section and other sections of the regulations under section 2056 as "deductible interests" and "nondeductible interests", respectively (see paragraph (b) of this section). Subject to any applicable limitations set forth in § 20.2056(a)–1(c), the amount of the marital deduction is the aggregate value of the deductible interests.

(b) Deductible interests. An interest passing to a decedent's surviving spouse is a "deductible interest" if it does not fall within one of the following categories of "nondeductible interests";

(1) Any property interest which passed from the decedent to his surviving spouse is a "nondeductible interest" to the extent it is not included in the decedent's gross estate.

(2) If a deduction is allowed under section 2053 (relating to deductions for expenses and indebtedness) by reason of the passing of a property interest from the decedent to his surviving spouse, such interest is, to the extent of the deduction under section 2053, a "nondeductible interest." Thus, a property interest which passed from the decedent to his surviving spouse in satisfaction of a deductible claim of the spouse against the estate is, to the extent of the claim, a "nondeductible interest" (see § 20.2056(b)–4). Similarly, amounts deducted under section 2053(a)(2) for commissioners allowed to the surviving spouse as executor are "nondeductible interests". As to the valuation, for the purpose of the marital deduction, of any property interest which passed from the decedent to his surviving spouse subject to a mortgage or other encumbrance, see § 20.2056(b)–4.

(3) If during settlement of the estate a loss deductible under section 2054 occurs with respect to a property interest, then that interest is, to the extent of the deductible loss, a "nondeductible interest" for the purpose of the marital deduction.

(4) A property interest passing to a decedent's surviving spouse which is a "terminable interest", as defined in § 20.2056(b)–1, is a "nondeductible interest" to the extent specified in that section.

[T.D. 6296, 23 FR 4529, June 24, 1958; T.D. 8522, 59 FR 9649, March 1, 1994]

§ 20.2056(b)–1 Marital deduction; limitation in case of life estate or other "terminable interest".

(a) In general. Section 2056(b) provides that no marital deduction is allowed with respect to certain property interests, referred to generally as "terminable interests", passing from a decedent to his surviving spouse. The phrase "terminable interest" is defined in paragraph (b) of this section. However, the fact that an interest in property passing to a decedent's surviving spouse is a "terminable interest" makes it nondeductible only (1) under the circumstances described in paragraph (c) of this section, and (2) if it does not come within one of the exceptions referred to in paragraph (d) of this section.

(b) "Terminable interests". A "terminable interest" in property is an interest which will terminate or fail on the lapse of time or on the occurrence or the failure to occur of some contingency. Life estates, terms for years, annuities, patents, and copyrights are therefore terminable interests. However, a bond, note, or similar contractual obligation, the discharge of which would not have the effect of an annuity or a term for years, is not a terminable interest.

(c) Nondeductible terminable interests. (1) A property interest which constitutes a terminable interest, as defined in paragraph (b) of this section, is nondeductible if—

(i) Another interest in the same property passed from the decedent to some other person for less than an adequate and full consideration in money or money's worth, and

(ii) By reason of its passing, the other person or his heirs or assigns may possess or enjoy any part of the property after the termination or failure of the spouse's interest.

(2) Even though a property interest which constitutes a terminable interest is not nondeductible by reason of the rules stated in subparagraph (1) of this paragraph, such an interest is nondeductible if—

(i) The decedent has directed his executor or a trustee to acquire such an interest for the decedent's surviving spouse (see further paragraph (f) of this section), or

(ii) Such an interest passing to the decedent's surviving spouse may be satisfied out of a group of assets which includes a nondeductible interest (see further § 20.2056(b)–2). In this case, however, full nondeductibility may not result.

(d) Exceptions. A property interest passing to a decedent's surviving spouse is deductible (if it is not otherwise disqualified under § 20.2056(a)–2) even though it is a terminable interest, and even though an interest therein passed from the decedent to another person, if it is a terminable interest only because—

(1) It is conditioned on the spouse's surviving for a limited period, in the manner described in § 20.2056(b)–3;

(2) It is a right to income for life with a general power of appointment, meeting the requirements set forth in § 20.2056(b)–5;

(3) It consists of life insurance or annuity payments held by the insurer with a general power of appointment in the spouse, meeting the requirements set forth in § 20.2056(b)–6;

(4) It is qualified terminable interest property, meeting the requirements set forth in § 20.2056(b)–7; or

(5) It is an interest in a qualified charitable remainder trust in which the spouse is the only noncharitable beneficiary, meeting the requirements set forth in § 20.2056(b)–8.

(e) Miscellaneous principles. (1) In determining whether an interest passed from the decedent to some other person, it is immaterial whether interests in the same property passed to the decedent's spouse and another person at the same time, or under the same instrument.

(2) In determining whether an interest in the same property passed from the decedent both to his surviving spouse and to some other person, a distinction is to be drawn between "property", as such term is used in section 2056, and an "interest in property". The term "property" refers to the underlying property in which various interests exist; each such interest is not for this purpose to be considered as "property".

(3) Whether or not an interest is nondeductible because it is a terminable interest is to be determined by reference to the property interests which actually passed from the decedent. Subsequent conversions of the property are immaterial for this purpose. Thus, where a decedent bequeathed his estate to his wife

for life with remainder to his children, the interest which passed to his wife is a nondeductible interest, even though the wife agrees with the children to take a fractional share of the estate in fee in lieu of the life interest in the whole, or sells the life estate for cash, or acquires the remainder interest of the children either by purchase or gift.

(4) The terms passed from the decedent, passed from the decedent to his surviving spouse and passed from the decedent to a person other than his surviving spouse are defined in §§ 20.2056(c)–1 through 20.2056(c)–3.

(f) Direction to acquire a terminable interest. No marital deduction is allowed with respect to a property interest which a decedent directs his executor or a trustee to convert after his death into a terminable interest for his surviving spouse. The marital deduction is not allowed even though no interest in the property subject to the terminable interest passes to another person and even though the interest would otherwise come within the exceptions described in §§ 20.2056(b)–5 and 20.2056(b)–6 (relating to life estates and life insurance and annuity payments with powers of appointment). However, a general investment power, authorizing investments in both terminable interests and other property, is not a direction to invest in a terminable interest.

(g) Examples. The application of this section may be illustrated by the following examples. In each example, it is assumed that the executor made no election under section 2056(b)(7) (even if under the specific facts the election would have been available), that any property interest passing from the decedent to a person other than the surviving spouse passed for less than full and adequate consideration in money or money's worth, and that section 2056(b)(8) is inapplicable.

Example (1). H (the decedent) devised real property to W (his surviving wife) for life, with remainder to A and his heirs. The interest which passed from H to W is a nondeductible interest since it will terminate upon her death and A (or his heirs or assigns) will thereafter possess or enjoy the property.

Example (2). H bequeathed the residue of his estate in trust for the benefit of W and A. The trust income is to be paid to W for life, and upon her death the corpus is to be distributed to A or his issue. However, if A should die without issue, leaving W surviving, the corpus is then to be distributed to W. The interest which passed from H to W is a nondeductible interest since it will terminate in the event of her death if A or his issue survive, and A or his issue will thereafter possess or enjoy the property.

Example (3). H during his lifetime purchased an annuity contract providing for payments to himself for life and then to W for life if she should survive him. Upon the death of the survivor of H and W, the excess, if any, of the cost of the contract over the annuity payments theretofore made was to be refunded to A. The interest which passed from H to W is a nondeductible interest since A may possess or enjoy a part of the property following the termination of the interest of W. If, however, the contract provided for no refund upon the death of the survivor of H and W, or provided that any refund was to go to the estate of the survivor, then the interest which passed from H to W is (to the extent it is included in H's gross estate) a deductible interest.

Example (4). H, in contemplation of death, transferred a residence to A for life with remainder to W provided W survives A, but if W predeceases A, the property is to pass to B and his heirs. If it is assumed that H died during A's lifetime, and the value of the residence was included in determining the value of his gross estate, the interest which passed from H to W is a nondeductible interest since it will terminate if W predeceases A and the property will thereafter be possessed or enjoyed by B (or his heirs or assigns). This result is not affected by B's assignment of his interest during H's lifetime, whether made in favor of W or another person, since the term "assigns" (as used in section 2056(b)(1)(B)) includes such an assignee. However, if it is assumed that A predeceased H, the interest of B in the property was extinguished, and, viewed as of the time of the subsequent death of H, the interest which passed from him to W is the entire interest in the property and, therefore, a deductible interest.

Example (5). H transferred real property to A by gift (reserving the right to the rentals) of the property for a term of 20 years. H died within the 20-year term, bequeathing the right to the remaining rentals to a trust for the benefit of W. The terms of the trust satisfy the five conditions stated in § 20.2056(b)–5, so that the property interest which passed in trust is considered to have passed from H to W. However, the interest is a nondeductible interest since it will terminate upon the expiration of the term and A will thereafter possess or enjoy the property.

Example (6). H bequeathed a patent to W and A as tenants in common. In this case, the interest of W will terminate upon the expiration of the term of the patent, but possession or enjoyment of the property by A must necessarily cease at the same time. Therefore, since A's possession or enjoyment cannot outlast the termination of W's interest, the latter is a deductible interest.

Example (7). A decedent bequeathed $100,000 to his wife, subject to a direction to his executor to use the bequest for the purchase of an annuity for the wife. The bequest is a nondeductible interest.

Example (8). Assume that pursuant to local law an allowance for support is payable to the decedent's surviving spouse during the period of the administration of the decedent's estate, but that upon her death or remarriage during such period her right to any further allowance will terminate. Assume further that the surviving spouse is sole beneficiary of the decedent's estate. Under such circumstances, the allowance constitutes a deductible interest since any part of the allowance not receivable by the surviving spouse during her lifetime will pass to her estate under the terms of the decedent's will. If, in this example, the decedent bequeathed only one-third of his residuary estate to his surviving spouse, then two-thirds of the allowance for support would constitute a nondeductible terminable interest.

[T.D. 6296, 23 FR 4529, June 24, 1958; T.D. 8522, 59 FR 9649, March 1, 1994]

§ 20.2056(b)–2 Marital deduction; interest in unidentified assets.

(a) In general. Section 2056(b)(2) provides that if an interest passing to a decedent's surviving spouse may be satisfied out of assets (or their proceeds) which include a particular asset that would be a nondeductible interest if it passed from the decedent to his spouse, the value of the interest passing to the spouse is reduced, for the purpose of the marital deduction, by the value of the particular asset.

(b) Application of section 2056(b)(2). In order for section 2056(b)(2) to apply, two circumstances must coexist, as follows:

(1) The property interest which passed from the decedent to his surviving spouse must be payable out of a group of assets included in the gross estate. Examples of property interests payable out of a group of assets are a general legacy, a bequest of the residue of the decedent's estate or of a proportion of the residue, and a right to a share of the corpus of a trust upon its termination.

(2) The group of assets out of which the property interest is payable must include one or more particular assets which, if passing specifically to the surviving spouse, would be nondeductible interests. Therefore, section 2056(b)(2) is not applicable merely because the group of assets includes a terminable interest, but would only be applicable if the terminable interest were nondeductible under the provisions of § 20.2056(b)–1.

(c) Interest nondeductible if circumstances present. If both of the circumstances set forth in paragraph (b) of this section are present, the property interest payable out of the group of assets is (except as to any excess of its value over the aggregate value of the particular asset or assets which would not be deductible if passing specifically to the surviving spouse) a nondeductible interest.

(d) Example. The application of this section may be illustrated by the following example:

Example. A decedent bequeathed one-third of the residue of his estate to his wife. The property passing under the decedent's will included a right to the rentals of an office building for a term of years, reserved by the decedent under a deed of the building by way of gift to his son. The decedent did not make a specific bequest of the right to such rentals. Such right, if passing specifically to the wife, would be a nondeductible interest (see example (5) of paragraph (g) of § 20.2056(b)–1). It is assumed that the value of the bequest of one-third of the residue of the estate to the wife was $85,000, and that the right to the rentals was included in the gross estate at a value of $60,000. If the decedent's executor had the right under the decedent's will or local law to assign the entire lease in satisfaction of the bequest, the bequest is a nondeductible interest to the extent of $60,000. If the executor could only assign a one-third interest in the lease in satisfaction of the bequest, the bequest is a nondeductible interest to the extent of $20,000. If the decedent's will provided that his wife's bequest could not be satisfied with a nondeductible interest, the entire bequest is a deductible interest. If, in this example, the asset in question had been foreign real estate not included in the decedent's gross estate, the results would be the same.

[T.D. 6296, 23 FR 4529, June 24, 1958; T.D. 8522, 59 FR 9649, March 1, 1994]

§ 20.2056(b)–3 Marital deduction; interest of spouse conditioned on survival for limited period.

(a) In general. Generally, no marital deduction is allowable if the interest passing to the surviving spouse is a terminable interest as defined in paragraph (b) of § 20.2056(b)(1). However, section 2056(b)(3) provides an exception to this rule so as to allow a deduction if (1) the only condition under which it will terminate is the death of the surviving spouse within 6 months after the decedent's death, or her death as a result of a common disaster which also resulted in the decedent's death, and (2) the condition does not in fact occur.

(b) Six months' survival. If the only condition which will cause the interest taken by the surviving spouse to terminate is the death of the surviving spouse and the condition is of such nature that it can occur only within 6 months following the decedent's death, the exception provided by section 2056(b)(3) will apply, provided the condition does not in fact occur. However, if the condition (unless it relates to death as a result of a common disaster) is one which may occur either within the 6-month period or thereafter, the exception provided by section 2056(b)(3) will not apply.

(c) Common disaster. If a property interest passed from the decedent to his surviving spouse subject to the condition that she does not die as a result of a common disaster which also resulted in the decedent's death, the exception provided by section 2056(b)(3) will not be applied in the final audit of the return if there is still a possibility that the surviving spouse may be deprived of the property interest by operation of the common disaster provision as given effect by the local law.

(d) Examples. The application of this section may be illustrated by the following examples:

Example (1). A decedent bequeathed his entire estate to his spouse on condition that she survive him by 6 months. In the event his spouse failed to survive him by 6 months, his estate was to go to his niece and her heirs. The decedent was survived by his spouse. It will be observed that, as of the time of the decedent's death, it was possible that the niece would, by reason of the interest which passed to her from the decedent possess or enjoy the estate after the termination of the interest which passed to the spouse. Hence, under the general rule set forth in § 20.2056(b)–1, the interest which passed to the spouse would be regarded as a nondeductible interest. If the surviving spouse in fact died within 6 months after the decedent's death, that general rule is to be applied, and the interest which passed to the spouse is a nondeductible interest. However, if the spouse in fact survived the decedent by 6 months, thus extinguishing the interest of the niece, the case comes within the exception provided by section 2056(b)(3), and the interest which passed to the spouse is a deductible interest. (It is assumed for the purpose of this example that no other factor which would cause the interest to be nondeductible is present.)

Example (2). The facts are the same as in example (1) except that the will provided that the estate was to go to the niece either in case the decedent and his spouse should both die as a result of a common disaster, or in case the spouse should fail to survive the decedent by 3 months. It is assumed that the decedent was survived by his spouse. In this example, the interest which passed from the decedent to his surviving spouse is to be regarded as a nondeductible interest if the surviving spouse in fact died either within 3 months after the decedent's death or as a result of a common disaster which also resulted in the decedent's death. However, if the spouse in fact survived the decedent by 3 months, and did not thereafter die as a result of a common disaster which also resulted in the decedent's death, the exception provided under section 2056(b)(3) will apply and the interest will be deductible.

Example (3). The facts are the same as in example (1) except that the will provided that the estate was to go to the niece if the decedent and his spouse should both die as a result of a common disaster and if the spouse failed to survive the decedent by 3 months. If the spouse in fact survived the decedent by 3 months, the interest of the niece is extinguished, and the interest passing to the spouse is a deductible interest.

Example (4). A decedent devised and bequeathed his residuary estate to his wife if she was living on the date of distribution of his estate. The devise and bequest is a nondeductible interest even though distribution took place within 6 months after the decedent's death and the surviving spouse in fact survived the date of distribution.

[T.D. 6296, 23 FR 4529, June 24, 1958]

§ 20.2056(b)–4 Marital deduction; valuation of interest passing to surviving spouse.

(a) In general. The value, for the purpose of the marital deduction, of any deductible interest which passed from the decedent to his surviving spouse is to be determined as of the date of the decedent's death, except that if the executor elects the alternate valuation method under section 2032 the valuation is to be determined as of the date of the decedent's death but with the adjustment described in paragraph (a)(3) of § 20.2032–1. The marital deduction may be taken only with respect to the net value of any deductible interest which passed from the decedent to his surviving spouse, the same principles being applicable as if the amount of a gift to the spouse were being determined.

(b) Property interest subject to an encumbrance or obligation. If a property interest passed from the decedent to his surviving spouse subject to a mortgage or other encumbrance, or if an obligation is imposed upon the surviving spouse by the decedent in connection with the passing of a property interest, the value of the property interest is to be reduced by the amount of the mortgage, other encumbrance, or obligation. However, if under the terms of the decedent's will or under local law the executor is required to discharge, out of other assets of the decedent's estate, a mortgage or other encumbrance on property passing from the decedent to his surviving spouse, or is required to reimburse the surviving spouse for the amount of the mortgage or other encumbrance, the payment or reimbursement constitutes an additional interest passing to the surviving spouse. The passing of a property interest subject to the imposition of an obligation by the decedent does not include a bequest, devise, or transfer in lieu of dower, curtesy, or of a statutory estate created in lieu of dower or curtesy, or of other marital rights in the decedent's property or estate. The passing of a property interest subject to the imposition of an obligation by the decedent does, however, include a bequest, etc., in lieu of the interest of his surviving spouse under community property laws unless such interest was, immediately prior to the decedent's death, a mere expectancy. The following examples are illustrative of property interests which passed from the decedent to his surviving spouse subject to the imposition of an obligation by the decedent:

Example (1). A decedent devised a residence valued at $25,000 to his wife, with a direction that she pay $5,000 to his sister. For the purpose of the marital deduction, the value of the property interest passing to the wife is only $20,000.

Example (2). A decedent devised real property to his wife in satisfaction of a debt owing to her. The debt is a deductible claim under section 2053. Since the wife is obligated to relinquish the claim as a condition to acceptance of the devise, the value of the devise is, for the purpose of the marital deduction, to be reduced by the amount of the claim.

Example (3). A decedent bequeathed certain securities to his wife in lieu of her interest in property held by them as community property under the law of the State of their residence. The wife elected to relinquish her community property interest and to take the bequest. For the purpose of the marital deduction, the value of the bequest is to be reduced by the value of the community property interest relinquished by the wife.

(c) Effect of death taxes. (1) In the determination of the value of any property interest which passed from the decedent to his surviving spouse, there must be taken into account the effect which the Federal estate tax, or any estate, succession, legacy, or inheritance tax, has upon the net value to the surviving spouse of the property interest.

(2) For example, assume that the only bequest to the surviving spouse is $100,000 and the spouse is required to pay a State inheritance tax in the amount of $1,500. If no other death taxes affect the net value of the bequest, the value, for the purpose of the marital deduction, is $98,500.

(3) As another example, assume that a decedent devised real property to his wife having a value for Federal estate tax purposes of $100,000 and also be-

queathed to her a nondeductible interest for life under a trust. The State of residence valued the real property at $90,000 and the life interest at $30,000, and imposed an inheritance tax (at graduated rates) of $4,800 with respect to the two interests. If it is assumed that the inheritance tax on the devise is required to be paid by the wife, the amount of tax to be ascribed to the devise is:

(90,000 + 120,000) * $4,800 = $3,600.

Accordingly, if no other death taxes affect the net value of the bequest, the value, for the purpose of the marital deduction, is $100,000 less $3,600, or $96,400.

(4) If the decedent bequeaths his residuary estate, or a portion of it, to his surviving spouse, and his will contains a direction that all death taxes shall be payable out of the residuary estate, the value of the bequest, for the purpose of the marital deduction, is based upon the amount of the residue as reduced pursuant to such direction, if the residuary estate, or a portion of it, is bequeathed to the surviving spouse, and by the local law the Federal estate tax is payable out of the residuary estate, the value of the bequest, for the purpose of the marital deduction, may not exceed its value as reduced by the Federal estate tax. Methods of computing the deduction, under such circumstances, are set forth in supplemental instructions to the estate tax return.

(d) Effect of administration expenses. (1) *Definitions.* (i) *Management expenses.* Estate management expenses are expenses that are incurred in connection with the investment of estate assets or with their preservation or maintenance during a reasonable period of administration. Examples of these expenses could include investment advisory fees, stock brokerage commissions, custodial fees, and interest.

(ii) *Transmission expenses.* Estate transmission expenses are expenses that would not have been incurred but for the decedent's death and the consequent necessity of collecting the decedent's assets, paying the decedent's debts and death taxes, and distributing the decedent's property to those who are entitled to receive it. Estate transmission expenses include any administration expense that is not a management expense. Examples of these expenses could include executor commissions and attorney fees (except to the extent of commissions or fees specifically related to investment, preservation, and maintenance of the assets), probate fees, expenses incurred in construction proceedings and defending against will contests, and appraisal fees.

(iii) *Marital share.* The marital share is the property or interest in property that passed from the decedent for which a deduction is allowable under section 2056(a). The marital share includes the income produced by the property or interest in property during the period of administration if the income, under the terms of the governing instrument or applicable local law, is payable to the surviving spouse or is to be added to the principal of the property interest passing to, or for the benefit of, the surviving spouse.

(2) *Effect of transmission expenses.* For purposes of determining the marital deduction, the value of the marital share shall be reduced by the amount of the estate transmission expenses paid from the marital share.

(3) *Effect of management expenses attributable to the marital share.* For purposes of determining the marital deduction, the value of the marital share shall not be reduced by the amount of the estate management expenses attributable to and paid from the marital share. Pursuant to section 2056(b)(9), however, the amount of the allowable marital deduction shall be reduced by the amount of any such management expenses that are deducted under section 2053 on the decedent's Federal estate tax return.

(4) *Effect of management expenses not attributable to the marital share.* For purposes of determining the marital deduction, the value of the marital share shall be reduced by the amount of the estate management expenses paid from the marital share but attributable to a property interest not included in the marital share.

(5) *Examples.* The following examples illustrate the application of this paragraph (d):

Example (1). The decedent dies after 2006 having made no lifetime gifts. The decedent makes a bequest of shares of ABC Corporation stock to the decedent's child. The bequest provides that the child is to receive the income from the shares from the date of the decedent's death. The value of the bequeathed shares on the decedent's date of death is $3,000,000. The residue of the estate is bequeathed to a trust for which the executor properly makes an election under section 2056(b)(7) to treat as qualified terminable interest property. The value of the residue on the decedent's date of death, before the payment of administration expenses and Federal and State estate taxes, is $6,000,000. Under applicable local law, the executor has the discretion to pay administration expenses from the income or principal of the residuary estate. All estate taxes are to be paid from the residue. The State estate tax equals the State death tax credit available under section 2011.

During the period of administration, the estate incurs estate transmission expenses of $400,000, which the executor charges to the residue. For purposes of determining the marital deduction, the value of the residue is reduced by the Federal and State estate taxes and by the estate transmission expenses. If the transmission expenses are deducted on the Federal estate tax return, the marital deduction is $3,500,000 ($6,000,000 minus $400,000 transmission expenses and minus $2,100,000 Federal and State estate taxes). If the transmission expenses are deducted on the estate's Federal income tax return rather than on the estate tax return, the marital deduction is $3,011,111 ($6,000,000 minus $400,000 transmission expenses and minus $2,588,889 Federal and State estate taxes).

Example (2). The facts are the same as in Example 1, except that, instead of incurring estate transmission expenses, the estate incurs estate management expenses of $400,000 in connection with the residue property passing for the benefit of the spouse. The executor charges these management expenses to the residue. In determining the value of the residue passing to the spouse for marital deduction purposes, a reduction is made for Federal and State estate taxes payable from the residue but no reduction is made for the estate management expenses. If the management expenses are deducted on the estate's income tax return, the net value of the property passing to the spouse is $3,900,000 ($6,000,000 minus $2,100,000 Federal and State estate taxes). A marital deduction is claimed for that amount, and the taxable estate is $5,100,000.

Example (3). The facts are the same as in Example 1, except that the estate management expenses of $400,000 are incurred in connection with the bequest of ABC Corporation stock to the decedent's child. The executor charges these management expenses to the residue. For purposes of determining the marital deduction, the value of the residue is reduced by the Federal and State estate taxes and by the management expenses. The management expenses reduce the value of the residue because they are charged to the property passing to the spouse even though they were incurred with respect to stock passing to the child. If the management expenses are deducted on the estate's Federal income tax return, the marital deduction is $3,011,111 ($6,000,000 minus $400,000 management expenses and minus $2,588,889 Federal and State estate taxes). If the management expenses are deducted on the estate's Federal estate tax return, rather than on the estate's Federal income tax return, the marital deduction is $3,500,000 ($6,000,000 minus $400,000 management expenses and minus $2,100,000 in Federal and State estate taxes).

Example (4). The decedent, who dies in 2000, has a gross estate of $3,000,000. Included in the gross estate are proceeds of $150,000 from a policy insuring the decedent's life and payable to the decedent's child as beneficiary. The applicable credit amount against the tax was fully consumed by the decedent's lifetime gifts. Applicable State law requires the child to pay any estate taxes attributable to the life insurance policy. Pursuant to the decedent's will, the rest of the decedent's estate passes outright to the surviving spouse. During the period of administration, the estate incurs estate management expenses of $150,000 in connection with the property passing to the spouse. The value of the property passing to the spouse is $2,850,000 ($3,000,000 less the insurance proceeds of $150,000 passing to the child). For purposes of determining the marital deduction, if the management expenses are deducted on the estate's income tax return, the marital deduction is $2,850,000 ($3,000,000 less $150,000) and there is a resulting taxable estate of $150,000 ($3,000,000 less a marital deduction of $2,850,000). Suppose, instead, the management expenses of $150,000 are deducted on the estate's estate tax return under section 2053 as expenses of administration. In such a situation, claiming a marital deduction of $2,850,000 would be taking a deduction for the same $150,000 in property under both sections 2053 and 2056 and would shield from estate taxes the $150,000 in insurance proceeds passing to the decedent's child. Therefore, in accordance with section 2056(b)(9), the marital deduction is limited to $2,700,000, and the resulting taxable estate is $150,000.

Example (5). The decedent dies after 2006 having made no lifetime gifts. The value of the decedent's residuary estate on the decedent's date of death is $3,000,000, before the payment of administration expenses and Federal and State estate taxes. The decedent's will provides a formula for dividing the decedent's residuary estate between two trusts to reduce the estate's Federal estate taxes to zero. Under the formula, one trust, for the benefit of the decedent's child, is to be funded with that amount of property equal in value to so much of the applicable exclusion amount under section 2010 that would reduce the estate's Federal estate tax to zero. The other trust, for the benefit of the surviving spouse, satisfies the requirements of section 2056(b)(7) and is to be funded with the remaining property in the estate. The State estate tax equals the State death tax credit available under section 2011. During the period of administration, the estate incurs transmission expenses of $200,000. The transmission expenses of $200,000 reduce the value of the residue to $2,800,000. If the transmission expenses are deducted on the Federal estate tax return, then the formula divides the residue so that the value of the property passing to the child's trust is $1,000,000 and the value of the property passing to the marital trust is $1,800,000. The allowable marital deduction is $1,800,000. The applicable exclusion amount shields from Federal estate tax the entire $1,000,000 passing to the child's trust so that the amount of Federal and State estate taxes is zero. Alternatively, if the transmission expenses are deducted on the estate's Federal income tax return, the formula divides the residue so that the value of the property passing to the child's trust is $800,000 and the value of the property passing to the marital trust is $2,000,000. The allowable marital deduction remains $1,800,000. The applicable exclusion amount shields from Federal estate tax the entire $800,000 passing to the child's trust and $200,000 of the $2,000,000 passing to the marital trust so that the amount of Federal and State estate taxes remains zero.

Example (6). The facts are the same as in Example 5, except that the decedent's will provides that the child's trust is to be funded with that amount of property equal in value to the applicable exclusion amount under section 2010 allowable to the decedent's estate. The residue of the estate, after the payment of any debts, expenses, and Federal and State estate taxes, is to pass to the marital trust. The applicable exclusion amount in this case is $1,000,000, so the value of the property passing to the child's trust is $1,000,000. After deducting the $200,000 of transmission expenses, the residue of the estate is $1,800,000 less any estate taxes. If the transmission expenses are deducted on the Federal estate tax return, the allowable marital deduction is $1,800,000, the taxable estate is zero, and the Federal and State estate taxes are zero. Alternatively, if the transmission expenses are deducted on the estate's Federal income tax return, the net value of the property passing to the spouse is $1,657,874 ($1,800,000 minus $142,106 estate taxes). A marital deduction is claimed for that amount, the taxable estate is $1,342,106, and the Federal and State estate taxes total $142,106.

Example (7). The decedent, who dies in 2000, makes an outright pecuniary bequest of $3,000,000 to the decedent's surviving spouse, and the residue of the estate, after the payment of all debts, expenses, and Federal and State estate taxes, passes to the decedent's child. Under the terms of the applicable local law, a beneficiary of a pecuniary bequest is not entitled to any income on the bequest. During the period of administration, the estate pays estate transmission expenses from the income earned by the property that will be distributed to the surviving spouse in satisfaction of the pecuniary bequest. The income earned on this property is not part of the marital share. Therefore, the allowable marital deduction is $3,000,000, unreduced by the amount of the estate transmission expenses.

(6) *Effective date.* The provisions of this paragraph (d) apply to estates of decedents dying on or after December 3, 1999.

(e) Remainder interests. If the income from property is made payable to another individual for life, or for a term of years, with remainder absolutely to the surviving spouse or to her estate, the marital deduction is based upon the present value of the remainder. The present value of the remainder is to be determined in accordance with the rules stated in § 20.2031–7. For example, if the surviving spouse is to receive $50,000 upon the death of a person aged 31 years, the present value of the remainder is $14,466. If the remainder is such that its value is to be determined by a special computation (see paragraph (b) of § 20.2031–7), a request for a specific factor may be submitted to the Commissioner. The request should be accompanied by a statement of the date of birth of each person, the duration of whose life may affect the value of the remainder, and copies of the relevant instruments. The Commissioner may, if conditions permit, supply the factor requested. If the Commissioner does not furnish the factor, the claim for deduction must be supported by a full statement of the computation of the present value made in accordance with the principles set forth in the applicable paragraphs of § 20.2031–7.

[T.D. 6296, 23 FR 4529, June 24, 1958; 25 FR 14021, Dec. 31, 1960, as amended by T.D. 8522, 59 FR 9649, March 1, 1994; T.D. 8540, 59 FR 30103, June 10, 1994; T.D. 8846, 64 FR 67765, Dec. 3, 1999; 64 FR 71022, Dec. 20, 1999]

§ 20.2056(b)–5 Marital deduction; life estate with power of appointment in surviving spouse.

(a) In general. Section 2056(b)(5) provides that if an interest in property passes from the decedent to his surviving spouse (whether or not in trust) and the spouse is entitled for life to all the income from the entire interest or all the income from a specific portion of the entire interest, with a power in her to appoint the entire interest or the specific portion, the interest which passes to her is a deductible interest, to the extent that it satisfies all five of the conditions set forth below (see paragraph (b) of this section if one or more of the conditions is satisfied as to only a portion of the interest):

(1) The surviving spouse must be entitled for life to all of the income from the entire interest or a specific portion of the entire interest, or to a specific portion of all the income from the entire interest.

(2) The income payable to the surviving spouse must be payable annually or at more frequent intervals.

(3) The surviving spouse must have the power to appoint the entire interest or the specific portion to either herself or her estate.

(4) The power in the surviving spouse must be exercisable by her alone and (whether exercisable by will or during life) must be exercisable in all events.

(5) The entire interest or the specific portion must not be subject to a power in any other person to appoint any part to any person other than the surviving spouse.

(b) Specific portion; deductible amount. If either the right to income or the power of appointment passing to the surviving spouse pertains only to a specific portion of a property interest passing from the decedent, the marital deduction is allowed only to the extent that the rights in the surviving spouse meet all of the five conditions described in paragraph (a) of this section. While the rights over the income and the power must coexist as to the same interest in property, it is not necessary that the rights over the income or the power as to such interest be in the same proportion. However, if the rights over income meeting the required conditions set forth in paragraph (a)(1) and (2) of the section extend over a smaller share of the property interest than the share with respect to which the power of appointment requirements set forth in paragraph (a)(3) through (5) of this section are satisfied, the deductible interest is limited to the smaller share. Correspondingly, if a power of appointment meeting all the requirements extends to a smaller portion of the property interest than the portion over which the income rights pertain, the deductible interest cannot exceed the value of the portion to which such power of appointment applies. Thus, if the decedent leaves to his surviving spouse the right to receive annually all of the income from a particular property interest and a power of appointment meeting the specifications prescribed in paragraph (a)(3) through (5) of this section as to only one-half of the property interest, then only one-half of the property interest is treated as a deductible interest. Correspondingly, if the income interest of the spouse satisfying the requirements extends to only one-fourth of the property interest and a testamentary power of appointment satisfying the requirements extends to all of the property interest, then only one-fourth of the interest in the spouse qualifies as a deductible interest. Further, if the surviving spouse has no right to income from a specific portion of a property interest but a testamentary power of appointment which meets the necessary conditions over the entire interest, then none of the interest qualifies for the deduction. In addition, if, from the time of the decedent's death, the surviving spouse has a power of appointment meeting all of the required conditions over three-fourths of the entire property interest and the prescribed income rights over the entire interest, but with a power in another person to appoint one-half of the entire interest, the value of the interest in the surviving spouse over only one-half of the property interest will qualify as a deductible interest.

(c) Meaning of specific portion. (1) *In general.* Except as provided in paragraphs (c)(2) and (c)(3) of this section, a partial interest in property is not treated as a specific portion of the entire interest. In addition, any specific portion of an entire interest in property is nondeductible to the extent the specific portion is subject to invasion for the benefit of any person other than the surviving spouse, except in the case of a deduction allowable under section 2056(b)(5), relating to the exercise of a general power of appointment by the surviving spouse.

(2) *Fraction or percentage share.* Under section 2056(b)(10), a partial interest in property is treated as a specific portion of the entire interest if the rights of the surviving spouse in income, and the required rights as to the power described in § 20.2056(b)–5(a), constitute a fractional or percentage share of the entire property interest, so that the surviving spouse's interest reflects its proportionate share of the increase or decrease in the value of the entire property interest to which the income rights and the power relate. Thus, if the spouse's right to income and the spouse's power extend to a specified fraction or percentage of the property, or the equivalent, the interest is in a specific portion of the property. In accordance with paragraph (b) of this section, if the spouse has the right to receive the income from a specific portion of the trust property (after applying paragraph (c)(3) of this section) but has a power of appointment over a different specific portion of the property (after applying paragraph (c)(3) of this section), the marital deduction is limited to the lesser specific portion.

(3) *Special rule in the case of estates of decedents dying on or before October 24, 1992, and certain decedents dying after October 24, 1992, with wills or revocable trusts executed on or prior to that date.*

(i) In the case of estates of decedents within the purview of the effective date and transitional rules contained in paragraphs (c)(3)(ii) and (iii) of this section:

(A) A specific sum payable annually, or at more frequent intervals, out of the property and its income that is not limited by the income of the property is treated as the right to receive the income from a specific portion of the property. The specific portion, for purposes of paragraph (c)(2) of this section, is the portion of the property that, assuming the interest rate generally applicable for the valuation of annuities at the time of the decedent's death, would produce income equal to such payments. However, a pecuniary amount payable annually to a surviving spouse is not treated as a right to the income from a specific portion of the trust property for purposes of this paragraph (c)(3)(i)(A) if any person other than the surviving spouse may receive, during the surviving spouse's lifetime, any distribution of the property. To determine the applicable interest rate for valuing annuities, see sections 2031 and 7520 and the regulations under those sections.

(B) The right to appoint a pecuniary amount out of a larger fund (or trust corpus) is considered the right to appoint a specific portion of such fund or trust for purposes of paragraph (c)(2) in an amount equal to such pecuniary amount.

(ii) The rules contained in paragraphs (c)(3)(i)(A) and (B) of this section apply with respect to estates of decedents dying on or before October 24, 1992.

(iii) The rules contained in paragraphs (c)(3)(i)(A) and (B) of this section apply in the case of decedents dying after October 24, 1992, if property passes to the spouse pursuant to a will or revocable trust agreement executed on or before October 24, 1992, and either—

(A) On that date, the decedent was under a mental disability to change the disposition of the property and did not regain competence to dispose of such property before the date of death; or

(B) The decedent dies prior to October 24, 1995.

(iv) Notwithstanding paragraph (c)(3)(iii) of this section, paragraphs (c)(3)(i)(A) and (B) of this section do not apply if the will or revocable trust is amended after October 24, 1992, in any respect that increases the amount of the transfer qualifying for the marital deduction or alters the terms by which the interest so passes to the surviving spouse of the decedent.

(4) *Local law.* A partial interest in property is treated as a specific portion of the entire interest if it is shown that the surviving spouse has rights under local law that are identical to those the surviving spouse would have acquired had the partial interest been expressed in terms satisfying the requirements of paragraph (c)(2) (or paragraph (c)(3) if applicable) of this section.

(5) *Examples.* The following examples illustrate the application of paragraphs (a) through (c)(4) of this section:

Example (1). Spouse entitled to the lesser of an annuity or a fraction of trust income. The decedent, D, died prior to October 24, 1992. D bequeathed in trust 500 identical shares of X company stock, valued for estate tax purposes at $500,000. The trust provides that during the lifetime of D's spouse, S, the trustee is to pay annually to S the lesser of one-half of the trust income or $20,000. Any trust income not paid to S is to be accumulated in the trust and may not be distributed during S's lifetime. S has a testamentary general power of appointment over the entire trust principal. The applicable interest rate for valuing annuities as of D's date of death under section 7520 is 10 percent. For purposes of paragraphs (a) through (c) of this section, S is treated as receiving all of the income from the lesser of—

(i) One half of the stock ($250,000); or

(ii) $200,000, the specific portion of the stock which, as determined in accordance with § 20.2056(b)–5(c)(3)(i)(A), would produce annual income of $20,000 (20,000/.10). Accordingly, the marital deduction is limited to $200,000 (200,000/500,000 or 2/5 of the value of the trust).

Example (2). Spouse possesses power and income interest over different specific portions of trust. The facts are the same as in Example 1 except that S's testamentary general power of appointment is exercisable over only 1/4 of the trust principal. Consequently, under section 2056(b)(5), the marital deduction is allowable only for the value of 1/4 of the trust ($125,000); i.e., the lesser of the value of the portion with respect to which S is deemed to be entitled to all of the income (2/5 of the trust or $200,000), or the value of the portion with respect to which S possesses the requisite power of appointment (1/4 of the trust or $125,000).

Example (3). Power of appointment over pecuniary amount. The decedent, D, died prior to October 24, 1992. D bequeathed property valued at $400,000 for estate tax purposes in trust. The trustee is to pay annually to D's spouse, S, one-fourth of the trust income. Any trust income not paid to S is to be accumulated in the trust and may not be distributed during S's lifetime. The will gives S a testamentary general power of appointment over the sum of $160,000. Because D died prior to October 24, 1992, S's power of appointment over $160,000 is treated as a power of appointment over a specific portion of the entire trust interest. The marital deduction allowable under section 2056(b)(5) is limited to $100,000; that is, the lesser of—

(1) The value of the trust corpus ($400,000);

(2) The value of the trust corpus over which S has a power of appointment ($160,000); or

(3) That specific portion of the trust with respect to which S is entitled to all the income ($100,000).

Example (4). Power of appointment over shares of stock constitutes a power over a specific portion. Under D's will, 250 shares of Y company stock were bequeathed in trust pursuant to which all trust income was payable annually to S, D's spouse, for life. S was given a testamentary general power of appointment over 100 shares of stock. The trust provides that if the trustee sells the Y company stock, S's general power of appointment is exercisable with respect to the sale proceeds or the property in which the proceeds are reinvested. Because the amount of property represented by a single share of stock would be altered if the corporation split its stock, issued stock dividends, made a distribution of capital, etc., a power to appoint 100 shares at the time of S's death is not necessarily a power to appoint the entire interest that the 100 shares represented on the date of D's death. If it is shown that, under local law, S has a general power to appoint not only the 100 shares designated by D but also 100/250 of any distributions by the corporation that are included in trust principal, the requirements of paragraph (c)(2) of this section are satisfied and S is treated as having a general power to appoint 100/250 of the entire interest in the 250 shares. In that case, the marital deduction is limited to 40 percent of the trust principal. If local law does not give S that power, the 100 shares would not constitute a specific portion under § 20.2056(b)–5(c) (including § 20.2056(b)–5(c)(3)(i)(B)). The nature of the asset is such that a change in the capitalization of the corporation could cause an alteration in the original value represented by the shares at the time of D's death and, thus, it does not represent a specific portion of the trust.

(d) Meaning of entire interest. Because a marital deduction is allowed for each separate qualifying interest in property passing from the decedent to the decedent's surviving spouse (subject to any applicable limitations in § 20.2056(a)–1(c)), for purposes of paragraphs (a) and (b) of this section, each property interest with respect to which the surviving spouse received any rights is considered separately in determining whether the surviving spouse's rights extend to the entire interest or to a specific portion of the entire interest. A property interest which consists of several identical units of property (such as a block of 250 shares of stock, whether the ownership is evidenced by one or several certificates) is considered one property interest, unless certain of the units are to be segregated and accorded different treatment, in which case each segregated group of items is considered a separate property interest. The bequest of a specified sum of money constitutes the bequest of a separate property interest if immediately following distribution by the executor and thenceforth it, and the investments made with it, must be so segregated or accounted for as to permit its identification as a separate item of property. The application of this paragraph may be illustrated by the following examples:

Example (1). The decedent transferred to a trustee three adjoining farms, Blackacre, Whiteacre, and Greenacre. His will provided that during the lifetime of the surviving spouse the trustee should pay her all of the income from the trust. Upon her death, all of Blackacre, a one-half interest in Whiteacre, and a one-third interest in Greenacre were to be distributed to the person or persons appointed by her in her will. The surviving spouse is considered as being entitled to all of the income from the entire interest in Blackacre, all of the income from the entire interest in Whiteacre, and all of the income from the entire interest in Greenacre. She also is considered as having a power of appointment over the entire interest in Blackacre, over one-half of the entire interest in Whiteacre, and over one-third of the entire interest in Greenacre.

Example (2). The decedent bequeathed $250,000 to C, as trustee. C is to invest the money and pay all of the income from the investments to W, the decedent's surviving spouse, annually. W was given a general power, exercisable by will, to appoint one-half of the corpus of the trust. Here, immediately following distribution by the executor, the $250,000 will be sufficiently segregated to permit its identification as a separate item, and the $250,000 will constitute an entire property interest. Therefore, W has a right to income and a power of appointment such that one-half of the entire interest is a deductible interest.

Example (3). The decedent bequeathed 100 shares of Z corporation stock to D, as trustee. W, the decedent's surviving spouse, is to receive all of the income of the trust annually and is given a general power, exercisable by will, to appoint out of the trust corpus the sum of $25,000. In this case the $25,000 is not, immediately following distribution, sufficiently segregated to permit its identification as a separate item of property in which the surviving spouse has the entire interest. Therefore, the $25,000 does not constitute the entire interest in a property for the purpose of paragraphs (a) and (b) of this section.

(e) Application of local law. In determining whether or not the conditions set forth in paragraph (a)(1) through (5) of this section are satisfied by the instrument of transfer, regard is to be had to the applicable provisions of the law of the jurisdiction under which the interest passes and, if the transfer is in trust, the applicable provisions of the law governing the administration of the trust. For example, silence of a trust instrument as to the frequency of payment will not be regarded as a failure to satisfy the condition set forth in paragraph (a)(2) of this section that income must be payable to the surviving spouse annually or more frequently unless the applicable law permits payment to be made less frequently than annually. The principles outlined in this paragraph and paragraphs (f) and (g) of this section which are applied in determining whether transfers in trust meet such conditions are equally applicable in ascertaining whether, in the case of interests not in trust, the surviving spouse has the equivalent in rights over income and over the property.

(f) Right to income. (1) If an interest is transferred in trust, the surviving spouse is "entitled for life to all of the income from the entire interest or a specific portion of the entire interest", for the purpose of the condition set forth in paragraph (a)(1) of this section, if the effect of the trust is to give her substantially that degree of beneficial enjoyment of the trust property during her life which the principles of the law of trusts accord to a person who is unqualifiedly designated as the life beneficiary of a trust. Such degree of enjoyment is given only if it was the decedent's intention, as manifested by the terms of the trust instrument and the surrounding circumstances, that the trust should produce for the surviving spouse during her life such an income, or that the spouse should have such use of the trust property as is consistent with the value of the trust corpus and with its preservation. The designation of the spouse as sole income beneficiary for life of the entire interest or a specific portion of the entire interest will be sufficient to qualify the trust unless the terms of the trust and the surrounding circumstances considered as a whole evidence an intention to deprive the spouse of the requisite degree of enjoyment. In determining whether a trust evidences that intention, the treatment required or permitted with respect to individual items must be considered in relation to the entire system provided for the administration of the trust. In addition, the surviving spouse's interest shall meet the condition set forth in paragraph (a)(1) of this section if the spouse is entitled to income as determined by applicable local law that provides for a reasonable apportionment between the income and remainder beneficiaries of the total return of the trust and that meets the requirements of § 1.643(b)–1 of this chapter.

(2) If the over-all effect of a trust is to give to the surviving spouse such enforceable rights as will preserve to her the requisite degree of enjoyment, it is immaterial whether that result is effected by rules specifically stated in the trust instrument, or, in their absence, by the rules for the management of the trust property and the allocation of receipts and expenditures supplied by the State law. For example, a provision in the trust instrument for amortization of bond premium by appropriate periodic charges to interest will not disqualify the interest passing in trust even though there is no State law specifically authorizing amortization, or there is a State law denying amortization which is applicable only in the absence of such a provision in the trust instrument.

(3) In the case of a trust, the rules to be applied by the trustee in allocation of receipts and expenses between income and corpus must be considered in relation to the nature and expected productivity of the assets passing in trust, the nature and frequency of occurrence of the expected receipts, and any provisions as to change in the form of investments. If it is evident from the nature of the trust assets and the rules provided for management of the trust that the allocation to income of such receipts as rents, ordinary cash dividends, and interest will give to the spouse the substantial enjoyment during life required by the statute, provisions that such receipts as stock dividends and proceeds from the conversion of trust assets shall be treated as corpus will not disqualify the interest passing in trust. Similarly, provision for a depletion charge against income in the case of trust assets which are subject to depletion will not disqualify the interest passing in trust, unless the effect is to deprive the spouse of the requisite beneficial enjoyment. The same principle is applicable in the case of depreciation, trustees' commissions, and other charges.

(4) Provisions granting administrative powers to the trustee will not have the effect of disqualifying an interest passing in trust unless the grant of powers evidences the intention to deprive the surviving spouse of the beneficial enjoyment required by the statute. Such an intention will not be considered to exist if the entire terms of the instrument are such that the local courts will impose reasonable limitations upon the exercise of the powers. Among the powers which if subject to reasonable limitations will not disqualify the interest passing in trust are the power to determine the allocation or apportionment of receipts and disbursements between income and corpus, the power to apply the income or corpus for the benefit of the spouse, and the power to retain the assets passing to the trust. For example, a power to retain trust assets which consist substantially of unproductive property will not disqualify the interest if the applicable rules for the administration of the trust require, or permit the spouse to require, that the trustee either make the property productive or convert it within a reasonable time. Nor will such a power disqualify the interest if the applicable rules for administration of the trust require the trustee to use the degree of judgment and care in the exercise of the power which a prudent man would use if he were owner of the trust assets. Further, a power to retain a residence or other property for the personal use of the spouse will not disqualify the interest passing in trust.

(5) An interest passing in trust will not satisfy the condition set forth in paragraph (a)(1) of this section that the surviving spouse be entitled to all the income if the primary purpose of the trust is to safeguard property without providing the spouse with the required beneficial enjoyment. Such trusts include not only trusts which expressly provide for the accumulation of the income but also trusts which indirectly accomplish a similar purpose. For example, assume that the corpus of a trust consists substantially of property which is not likely to be income producing during the life of the surviving spouse and that the spouse cannot compel the trustee to convert or otherwise deal with the property as described in subparagraph (4) of this paragraph. An interest passing to such a trust will not qualify unless the applicable rules for the administration require, or permit the spouse to require, that the trustee

provide the required beneficial enjoyment such as by payments to the spouse out of other assets of the trust.

(6) If a trust is created during the decedent's life, it is immaterial whether or not the interest passing in trust satisfied the conditions set forth in paragraph (a)(1) through (5) of this section prior to the decedent's death. If a trust may be terminated during the life of the surviving spouse, under her exercise of a power of appointment or by distribution of the corpus to her, the interest passing in trust satisfies the condition set forth in paragraph (a)(1) of this section (that the spouse be entitled to all the income) if she (i) is entitled to the income until the trust terminates, or (ii) has the right, exercisable in all events, to have the corpus distributed to her at any time during her life.

(7) An interest passing in trust fails to satisfy the condition set forth in paragraph (a)(1) of this section, that the spouse be entitled to all the income, to the extent that the income is required to be accumulated in whole or in part or may be accumulated in the discretion of any person other than the surviving spouse; to the extent that the consent of any person other than the surviving spouse is required as a condition precedent to distribution of the income; or to the extent that any person other than the surviving spouse has the power to alter the terms of the trust so as to deprive her of her right to the income. An interest passing in trust will not fail to satisfy the condition that the spouse be entitled to all the income merely because its terms provide that the right of the surviving spouse to the income shall not be subject to assignment, alienation, pledge, attachment or claims of creditors.

(8) In the case of an interest passing in trust, the terms "entitled for life" and "payable annually or at more frequent intervals," as used in the conditions set forth in paragraph (a)(1) and (2) of this section, require that under the terms of the trust the income referred to must be currently (at least annually; see paragraph (e) of this section) distributable to the spouse or that she must have such command over the income that it is virtually hers. Thus, the conditions in paragraph (a)(1) and (2) of this section are satisfied in this respect if, under the terms of the trust instrument, the spouse has the right exercisable annually (or more frequently) to require distribution to herself of the trust income, and otherwise the trust income is to be accumulated and added to corpus. Similarly, as respects the income for the period between the last distribution date and the date of the spouse's death, it is sufficient if that income is subject to the spouse's power to appoint. Thus, if the trust instrument provides that income accrued or undistributed on the date of the spouse's death is to be disposed of as if it had been received after her death, and if the spouse has a power of appointment over the trust corpus, the power necessarily extends to the undistributed income.

(9) An interest is not to be regarded as failing to satisfy the conditions set forth in paragraph (a)(1) and (2) of this section (that the spouse be entitled to all the income and that it be payable annually or more frequently) merely because the spouse is not entitled to the income from estate assets for the period before distribution of those assets by the executor, unless the executor is, by the decedent's will, authorized or directed to delay distribution beyond the period reasonably required for administration of the decedent's estate. As to the valuation of the property interest passing to the spouse in trust where the right to income is expressly postponed, see § 20.2056(b)–4.

(g) Power of appointment in surviving spouse. (1) The conditions set forth in paragraph (a)(3) and (4) of this section, that is, that the surviving spouse must have a power of appointment exercisable in favor of herself or her estate and exercisable alone and in all events are not met unless the power of the surviving spouse to appoint the entire interest or a specific portion of it falls within one of the following categories:

(i) A power so to appoint fully exercisable in her own favor at any time following the decedent's death (as, for example, an unlimited power to invade); or

(ii) A power so to appoint exercisable in favor of her estate. Such a power, if exercisable during life, must be fully exercisable at any time during life, or, if exercisable by will, must be fully exercisable irrespective of the time of her death (subject in either case to the provisions of § 20.2053(b)–3, relating to interests conditioned on survival for a limited period); or

(iii) A combination of the powers described under subdivisions (i) and (ii) of this subparagraph. For example, the surviving spouse may, until she attains the age of 50 years, have a power to appoint to herself and thereafter have a power to appoint to her estate. However, the condition that the spouse's power must be exercisable in all events is not satisfied unless irrespective of when the surviving spouse may die the entire interest or a specific portion of it will at the time of her death be subject to one power or the other (subject to the exception in § 20.2053(b)–3, relating to interests contingent on survival for a limited period).

(2) The power of the surviving spouse must be a power to appoint the entire interest or a specific portion of it as unqualified owner (and free of the trust if a trust is involved, or free of the joint tenancy if a joint tenancy is involved) or to appoint the entire interest or a specific portion of it as a part of her estate (and free of the trust if a trust is involved), that is, in effect, to dispose of it to whomsoever she pleases. Thus, if the decedent devised property to a son and the surviving spouse as joint tenants with right of survivorship and under local law the surviving spouse has a power of severance exercisable without consent of the other joint tenant, and by exercising this power could acquire a one-half interest in the property as a tenant in common, her power of severance will satisfy the conditions set forth in paragraph (a)(3) of this section that she have a power of appointment in favor of herself or her estate. However, if the surviving spouse entered into a binding agreement with the decedent to exercise the power only in favor of their issue, that condition is not met. An interest passing in trust will not be regarded as failing to satisfy the condition merely because takers in default of the surviving spouse's exercise of the power are designated by the decedent. The decedent may provide that, in default of exercise of the power, the trust shall continue for an additional period.

(3) A power is not considered to be a power exercisable by a surviving spouse alone and in all events as required by paragraph (a)(4) of this section if the exercise of the power in the surviving spouse to appoint the entire interest or a specific portion of it to herself or to her estate requires the joinder or consent of any other person. The power is not "exercisable in all events", if it can be terminated during the life of the surviving spouse by any event other than her complete exercise or release of it. Further, a power is not "exercisable in all events" if it may be exercised for a limited purpose only. For example, a power which is not exercisable in the event of the spouse's remarriage is not exercisable in all events. Likewise, if there are any restrictions, either by the terms of the instrument or under applicable local law, on the exercise of a power to consume property (whether or not held in trust) for the benefit of the spouse, the power is not exercisable in all events. Thus, if a power of invasion is exercisable only for the spouse's support, or only for her limited use, the power is not exercisable in all events. In order for a power of invasion to be exercisable in all events, the surviving spouse must have the unrestricted power exercisable at any time during her life to use all or any part of the property subject to the power, and to dispose of it in any manner, including the power to dispose of it by gift (whether or not she has power to dispose of it by will).

(4) The power in the surviving spouse is exercisable in all events only if it exists immediately following the decedent's death. For example, if the power given to the surviving spouse is exercisable during life, but cannot be effectively exercised before distribution of the assets by the executor, the power is not exercisable in all events. Similarly, if the power is exercisable by will, but cannot be effectively exercised in the event the surviving spouse dies before distribution of the assets by the executor, the power is not exercisable in all events. However, an interest will not be disqualified by the mere fact that, in the event the power is exercised during administration of the estate, distribution of the property to the appointee will be delayed for the period of administration. If the power is in existence at all times following the decedent's death, limitations of a formal nature will not disqualify an interest. Examples of formal limitations on a power exercisable during life are requirements that an exercise must be in a particular form, that it must be filed with a trustee during the spouse's life, that reasonable notice must be given, or that reasonable intervals must elapse between successive partial exercises. Examples of formal limitations on a power exercisable by will are that it must be exercised by a will executed by the surviving spouse after the decedent's death or that exercise must be by specific reference to the power.

(5) If the surviving spouse has the requisite power to appoint to herself or her estate, it is immaterial that she also has one or more lesser powers. Thus, if she has a testamentary power to appoint to her estate, she may also have a limited power of withdrawal or of appointment during her life. Similarly, if she has an unlimited power of withdrawal, she may have a limited testamentary power.

(h) Requirement of survival for a limited period. A power of appointment in the surviving spouse will not be treated as failing to meet the requirements of paragraph (a)(3) of this section even though the power may terminate, if the only conditions which would cause the termination are those described in paragraph (a) of § 20.2056(b)–3, and if those conditions do not in fact occur. Thus, the entire interest or a specific portion of it will not be disqualified by reason of the fact that the exercise of the power in the spouse is subject to a condition of survivorship described in § 20.2056(b)–3 if the terms of the condition, that is, the survivorship of the surviving spouse, or the failure to die in a common disaster, are fulfilled.

(i) [Reserved]

(j) Existence of a power in another. Paragraph (a)(5) of this section provides that a transfer described in paragraph (a) is nondeductible to the extent that the decedent created a power in the trustee or in any other person to appoint a part of the interest to any person other than the surviving spouse. However, only powers in other persons which are in opposition to that of the surviving spouse will cause a portion of the interest to fail to satisfy the condition set forth in paragraph (a)(5) of this section. Thus, a power in a trustee to distribute corpus to or for the benefit of a surviving spouse will not disqualify the trust. Similarly, a power to distribute corpus to the spouse for the support of minor children will not disqualify the trust if she is legally obligated to support such children. The application of this paragraph may be illustrated by the following examples:

Example (1). Assume that a decedent created a trust, designating his surviving spouse as income beneficiary for life with an unrestricted power in the spouse to appoint the corpus during her life. The decedent further provided that in the event the surviving spouse should die without having exercised the power, the trust should continue for the life of his son with a power in the son to appoint the corpus. Since the power in the son could become exercisable only after the death of the surviving spouse, the interest is not regarded as failing to satisfy the condition set forth in paragraph (a)(5) of this section.

Example (2). Assume that the decedent created a trust, designating his surviving spouse as income beneficiary for life and as donee of a power to appoint by will the entire corpus. The decedent further provided that the trustee could distribute 30 percent of the corpus to the decedent's son when he reached the age of 35 years. Since the trustee has a power to appoint 30 percent of the entire interest for the benefit of a person other than the surviving spouse, only 70 percent of the interest placed in trust satisfied the condition set forth in paragraph (a)(5) of this section. If, in this case, the surviving spouse had a power, exercisable by her will, to appoint only one-half of the corpus as it was constituted at the time of her death, it should be noted that only 35 percent of the interest placed in the trust would satisfy the condition set forth in paragraph (a)(3) of this section.

[T.D. 6296, 23 FR 4529, June 24, 1958; T.D. 8522, 59 FR 9649, March 1, 1994; T.D. 9102, 69 FR 20, Jan. 2, 2004]

§ 20.2056(b)–6 Marital deduction; life insurance or annuity payments with power of appointment in surviving spouse.

(a) In general. Section 2056(b)(6) provides that an interest in property passing from a decedent to his surviving spouse, which consists of proceeds held by an insurer under the terms of a life insurance, endowment, or annuity contract, is a "deductible interest" to the extent that it satisfies all five of the following conditions (see paragraph (b) of this section if one or more of the conditions is satisfied as to only a portion of the proceeds):

(1) The proceeds, or a specific portion of the proceeds, must be held by the insurer subject to an agreement either to pay the entire proceeds or a specific portion thereof in installments, or to pay interest thereon, and all or a specific portion of the installments or interest payable during the life of the surviving spouse must be payable only to her.

(2) The installments or interest payable to the surviving spouse must be payable annually, or more frequently, commencing not later than 13 months after the decedent's death.

(3) The surviving spouse must have the power to appoint all or a specific portion of the amounts so held by the insurer to either herself or her estate.

(4) The power in the surviving spouse must be exercisable by her alone and (whether exercisable by will or during life) must be exercisable in all events.

(5) The amounts or the specific portion of the amounts payable under such contract must not be sub-

ject to a power in any other person to appoint any part thereof to any person other than the surviving spouse.

(b) Specific portion; deductible interest. If the right to receive interest or installment payments or the power of appointment passing to the surviving spouse pertains only to a specific portion of the proceeds held by the insurer, the marital deduction is allowed only to the extent that the rights of the surviving spouse in the specific portion meet the five conditions described in paragraph (a) of this section. While the rights to interest, or to receive payment in installments, and the power must coexist as to the proceeds of the same contract, it is not necessary that the rights to each be in the same proportion. If the rights to interest meeting the required conditions set forth in paragraph (a)(1) and (2) of this section extend over a smaller share of the proceeds than the share with respect to which the power of appointment requirements set forth in paragraph (a)(3) through (5) of this section are satisfied, the deductible interest is limited to the smaller share. Similarly, if the portion of the proceeds payable in installments is a smaller portion of the proceeds than the portion to which the power of appointment meeting such requirements relates, the deduction is limited to the smaller portion. In addition, if a power of appointment meeting all the requirements extends to a smaller portion of the proceeds than the portion over which the interest or installment rights pertain, the deductible interest cannot exceed the value of the portion to which such power of appointment applies. Thus, if the contract provides that the insurer is to retain the entire proceeds and pay all of the interest thereon annually to the surviving spouse and if the surviving spouse has a power of appointment meeting the specifications prescribed in paragraph (a)(3) through (5) of this section, as to only one-half of the proceeds held, then only one-half of the proceeds may be treated as a deductible interest. Correspondingly, if the rights of the spouse to receive installment payments or interest satisfying the requirements extend to only one-fourth of the proceeds and a testamentary power of appointment satisfying the requirements of paragraph (a)(3) through (5) of this section extends to all of the proceeds, then only one-fourth of the proceeds qualifies as a deductible interest. Further, if the surviving spouse has no right to installment payments (or interest) over any portion of the proceeds but a testamentary power of appointment which meets the necessary conditions over the entire remaining proceeds, then none of the proceeds qualifies for the deduction. In addition, if, from the time of the decedent's death, the surviving spouse has a power of appointment meeting all of the required conditions over three-fourths of the proceeds and the right to receive interest from the entire proceeds, but with a power in another person to appoint one-half of the entire proceeds, the value of the interest in the surviving spouse over only one-half of the proceeds will qualify as a deductible interest.

(c) Applicable principles. (1) The principles set forth in paragraph (c) of § 20.2056(b)–5 for determining what constitutes a "specific portion of the entire interest" for the purpose of section 2056(b)(5) are applicable in determining what constitutes a "specific portion of all such amounts" for the purpose of section 2056(b)(6). However, the interest in the proceeds passing to the surviving spouse will not be disqualified by the fact that the installment payments or interest to which the spouse is entitled or the amount of the proceeds over which the power of appointment is exercisable may be expressed in terms of a specific sum rather than a fraction or a percentage of the proceeds provided it is shown that such sums are a definite or fixed percentage or fraction of the total proceeds.

(2) The provisions of paragraph (a) of this section are applicable with respect to a property interest which passed from the decedent in the form of proceeds of a policy of insurance upon the decedent's life, a policy of insurance upon the life of a person who predeceased the decedent, a matured endowment policy, or an annuity contract, but only in case the proceeds are to be held by the insurer. With respect to proceeds under any such contract which are to be held by a trustee, with power of appointment in the surviving spouse, see § 20.2056(b)–5. As to the treatment of proceeds not meeting the requirements of § 20.2056(b)–5 or of this section, see § 20.2056(a)–2.

(3) In the case of a contract under which payments by the insurer commenced during the decedent's life, it is immaterial whether or not the conditions in subparagraphs (1) through (5) of paragraph (a) of this section were satisfied prior to the decedent's death.

(d) Payments of installments or interest. The conditions in subparagraphs (1) and (2) of paragraph (a) of this section relative to the payments of installments or interest to the surviving spouse are satisfied if, under the terms of the contract, the spouse has the right exercisable annually (or more frequently) to require distribution to herself of installments of the proceeds or a specific portion thereof, as the case may be, and otherwise such proceeds or interest are to be accumulated and held by the insurer pursuant to the terms of the contract. A contract which otherwise requires the insurer to make annual or more frequent payments to the surviving spouse following the decedent's death, will not be disqualified merely because the surviving spouse must comply with certain formalities in order to obtain the first payment. For example, the contract may satisfy the conditions in subparagraphs (1) and (2) of paragraph (a) of this section even though it requires the surviving spouse to furnish proof of death before the first payment is made. The condition in paragraph (a)(1) of this section is satisfied where interest on the proceeds or a specific portion thereof is payable, annually or more frequently, for a term, or until the occurrence of a specified event, following which the proceeds or a specific portion thereof are to be paid in annual or more frequent installments.

(e) Powers of appointment. (1) In determining whether the terms of the contract satisfy the conditions in subparagraph (3), (4), or (5) of paragraph (a) of this section relating to a power of appointment in the surviving spouse or any other person, the principles stated in § 20.2056(b)–5 are applicable. As stated in § 20.2056(b)–5, the surviving spouse's power to appoint is "exercisable in all events" only if it is in existence immediately following the decedent's death, subject, however, to the operation of § 20.2056(b)–3 relating to interests conditioned on survival for a limited period.

(2) For examples of formal limitations on the power which will not disqualify the contract, see paragraph (g)(4) of § 20.2056(b)–5. If the power is exercisable from the moment of the decedent's death, the contract is not disqualified merely because the insurer may require proof of the decedent's death as a condition to making payment to the appointee. If the submission of proof of the decedent's death is a condition to the exercise of the power, the power will not be considered "exercisable in all events" unless in the event the surviving spouse had died immediately following the decedent, her power to appoint would have been considered to exist at the time of her death, within the meaning of section 2041(a)(2). See paragraph (b) of § 20.2041–3.

(3) It is sufficient for the purposes of the condition in paragraph (a)(3) of this section that the surviving spouse have the power to appoint amounts held by the insurer to herself or her estate if the surviving spouse has the unqualified power, exercisable in favor of herself or her estate, to appoint amounts held by the insurer which are payable after her death. Such power to appoint need not extend to installments or interest which will be paid to the spouse during her life. Further, the power to appoint need not be a power to require payment in a single sum. For example, if the proceeds of a policy are payable in installments, and if the surviving spouse has the power to direct that all installments payable after her death be paid to her estate, she has the requisite power.

(4) It is not necessary that the phrase "power to appoint" be used in the contract. For example, the condition in paragraph (a)(3) of this section that the surviving spouse have the power to appoint amounts held by the insurer to herself or her estate is satisfied by terms of a contract which give the surviving spouse a right which is, in substance and effect, a power to appoint to herself or her estate, such as a right to withdraw the amount remaining in the fund held by the insurer, or a right to direct that any amount held by the insurer under the contract at her death shall be paid to her estate.

[T.D. 6296, 23 FR 4529, June 24, 1958]

§ 20.2056(b)–7 Election with respect to life estate for surviving spouse.

(a) In general. Subject to section 2056(d), a marital deduction is allowed under section 2056(b)(7) with respect to estates of decedents dying after December 31, 1981, for qualified terminable interest property as defined in paragraph (b) of this section. All of the property for which a deduction is allowed under this paragraph (a) is treated as passing to the surviving spouse (for purposes of § 20.2056(a)–1), and no part of the property is treated as passing to any person other than the surviving spouse (for purposes of § 20.2056(b)–1).

(b) Qualified terminable interest property. (1) *In general.* Section 2056(b)(7)(B)(i) provides the definition of qualified terminable interest property.

(i) Terminable interests described in section 2056(b)(1)(C) cannot qualify as qualified terminable interest property. Thus, if the decedent directs the executor to purchase a terminable interest with estate assets, the terminable interest acquired will not qualify as qualified terminable interest property.

(ii) For purposes of section 2056(b)(7)(B)(i), the term property generally means the entire interest in property (within the meaning of § 20.2056(b)–5(d)) or a specific portion of the entire interest (within the meaning of § 20.2056(b)–5(c)).

(2) *Property for which an election may be made.* (i) *In general.* The election may relate to all or any part of property that meets the requirements of section 2056(b)(7)(B)(i), provided that any partial election must be made with respect to a fractional or percentage share of the property so that the elective portion reflects its proportionate share of the increase or decrease in value of the entire property for purposes of applying sections 2044 or 2519. The fraction or percentage may be defined by formula.

(ii) *Division of trusts.* (A) *In general.* A trust may be divided into separate trusts to reflect a partial election that has been made, or is to be made, if authorized under the governing instrument or otherwise permissible under local law. Any such division must be accomplished no later than the end of the period of estate administration. If, at the time of the filing of the estate tax return, the trust has not yet been divided, the intent to divide the trust must be unequivocally signified on the estate tax return.

(B) *Manner of dividing and funding trust.* The division of the trust must be done on a fractional or percentage basis to reflect the partial election. However, the separate trusts do not have to be funded with a pro rata portion of each asset held by the undivided trust.

(C) *Local law.* A trust may be divided only if the fiduciary is required, either by applicable local law or by the express or implied provisions of the governing instrument, to divide the trust on the basis of the fair market value of the assets of the trust at the time of the division.

(3) *Persons permitted to make the election.* The election referred to in section 2056(b)(7)(B)(i)(III) must be made by the executor that is appointed, qualified, and acting within the United States, within the meaning of section 2203, regardless of whether the property with respect to which the election is to be made is in the executor's possession. If there is no executor appointed, qualified, and acting within the United States, the election may be made by any person with respect to property in the actual or constructive possession of that person and may also be made by that person with respect to other property not in the actual or constructive possession of that person if the person in actual or constructive possession of such other property does not make the election. For example, in the absence of an appointed executor, the trustee of an inter vivos trust (that is included in the gross estate of the decedent) can make the election.

(4) *Manner and time of making the election*—(i) *In general.* The election referred to in section 2056(b)(7)(B)(i)(III) and (v) is made on the return of tax imposed by section 2001 (or section 2101). For purposes of this paragraph, the term return of tax imposed by section 2001 means the last estate tax return filed by the executor on or before the due date of the return, including extensions or, if a timely return is not filed, the first estate tax return filed by the executor after the due date.

(ii) *Election irrevocable.* The election, once made, is irrevocable, provided that an election may be revoked or modified on a subsequent return filed on or before the due date of the return, including extensions actually granted. If an executor appointed under local law has made an election on the return of tax imposed by section 2001 (or section 2101) with respect to one or more properties, no subsequent election may be made with respect to other properties included in the gross estate after the return of tax imposed by section 2001 is filed. An election under section 2056(b)(7)(B)(v) is separate from any elections made under section 2056A(a)(3).

(c) Protective elections. (1) *In general.* A protective election may be made to treat property as qualified terminable interest property only if, at the time the federal estate tax return is filed, the executor of the decedent's estate reasonably believes that there is a bona fide issue that concerns whether an asset is includible in the decedent's gross estate, or the amount or nature of the property the surviving spouse is entitled to receive, i.e., whether property that is includible is eligible for the qualified terminable interest property election. The protective election must identify either the specific asset, group of assets, or trust to which the election applies and the specific basis for the protective election.

(2) *Protective election irrevocable.* The protective election, once made on the return of tax imposed by section 2001, cannot be revoked. For example, if a protective election is made on the basis that a bona fide question exists regarding the inclusion of a trust corpus in the gross estate and it is later determined that the trust corpus is so includible, the protective election becomes effective with respect to the trust corpus and cannot thereafter be revoked.

(d) Qualifying income interest for life. (1) *In general.* Section 2056(b)(7)(B)(ii) provides the definition of qualifying income interest for life. For purposes of section 2056(b)(7)(B)(ii)(II), the surviving spouse is included within the prohibited class of powerholders referred to therein. A power under applicable local law that permits the trustee to adjust between income and principal to fulfill the trustee's duty of impartiality between the income and remainder beneficiaries that meets the requirements of § 1.643(b)–1 of this chapter will not be considered a power to appoint trust property to a person other than the surviving spouse.

(2) *Entitled for life to all income.* The principles of § 20.2056(b)–5(f), relating to whether the spouse is entitled for life to all of the income from the entire interest, or a specific portion of the entire interest, apply in determining whether the surviving spouse is entitled for life to all of the income from the property regardless of whether the interest passing to the spouse is in trust.

(3) *Contingent income interests.* (i) An income interest for a term of years, or a life estate subject to termination upon the occurrence of a specified event (e.g., remarriage), is not a qualifying income interest for life. However, a qualifying income interest for life that is contingent upon the executor's election under section 2056(b)(7)(B)(v) will not fail to be a qualifying income interest for life because of such contingency or because the portion of the property for which the election is not made passes to or for the benefit of persons other than the surviving spouse. This paragraph (d)(3)(i) applies with respect to estates of decedents whose estate tax returns are due after February 18, 1997. This paragraph (d)(3)(i) also applies to estates of decedents whose estate tax returns were due on or before February 18, 1997, that meet the requirements of paragraph (d)(3)(ii) of this section.

(ii) Estates of decedents whose estate tax returns were due on or before February 18, 1997, that did not make the election under section 2056(b)(7)(B)(v) because the surviving spouse's income interest in the property was contingent upon the election or because the nonelected portion of the property was to pass to a beneficiary other than the surviving spouse are granted an extension of time to make the QTIP election if the following requirements are satisfied:

(A) The period of limitations on filing a claim for credit or refund under section 6511(a) has not expired.

(B) A claim for credit or refund is filed on Form 843 with a revised Recapitulation and Schedule M, Form 706 (or 706NA) that signifies the QTIP election. Reference to this section should be made on the Form 843.

(C) The following statement is included with the Form 843: "The undersigned certifies that the property with respect to which the QTIP election is being made will be included in the gross estate of the surviving spouse as provided in section 2044 of the Internal Revenue Code, in determining the federal estate tax liability on the spouse's death." The statement must be signed, under penalties of perjury, by the surviving spouse, the surviving spouse's legal representative (if the surviving spouse is legally incompetent), or the surviving spouse's executor (if the surviving spouse is deceased).

(4) *Income between last distribution date and date of spouse's death.* An income interest does not fail to constitute a qualifying income interest for life solely because income between the last distribution date and the date of the surviving spouse's death is not required to be distributed to the surviving spouse or to the estate of the surviving spouse. See § 20.2044–1 relating to the inclusion of such undistributed income in the gross estate of the surviving spouse.

(5) *Pooled income funds.* An income interest in a pooled income fund described in section 642(c)(5) constitutes a qualifying income interest for life for purposes of section 2056(b)(7)(B)(ii).

(6) *Power to distribute principal to spouse.* An income interest in a trust will not fail to constitute a qualifying income interest for life solely because the trustee has a power to distribute principal to or for the benefit of the surviving spouse. The fact that property

distributed to a surviving spouse may be transferred by the spouse to another person does not result in a failure to satisfy the requirement of section 2056(b)(7)(B)(ii)(II). However, if the surviving spouse is legally bound to transfer the distributed property to another person without full and adequate consideration in money or money's worth, the requirement of section 2056(b)(7)(B)(ii)(II) is not satisfied.

(e) Annuities payable from trusts in the case of estates of decedents dying on or before October 24, 1992, and certain decedents dying after October 24, 1992, with wills or revocable trusts executed on or prior to that date. [*Omitted. Ed.*]

* * *

(f) Joint and survivor annuities. [Reserved]

(g) Application of local law. The provisions of local law are taken into account in determining whether the conditions of section 2056(b)(7)(B)(ii)(I) are satisfied. For example, silence of a trust instrument as to the frequency of payment is not regarded as a failure to satisfy the requirement that the income must be payable to the surviving spouse annually or more frequently unless applicable local law permits payments less frequently.

(h) Examples. The following examples illustrate the application of paragraphs (a) through (g) of this section. In each example, it is assumed that the decedent, D, was survived by S, D's spouse and that, unless stated otherwise, S is not the trustee of any trust established for S's benefit.

Example (1). Life estate in residence. D owned a personal residence valued at $250,000 for estate tax purposes. Under D's will, the exclusive and unrestricted right to use the residence (including the right to continue to occupy the property as a personal residence or to rent the property and receive the income) passes to S for life. At S's death, the property passes to D's children. Under applicable local law, S must consent to any sale of the property. If the executor elects to treat all of the personal residence as qualified terminable interest property, the deductible interest is $250,000, the value of the residence for estate tax purposes.

Example (2). Power to make property productive. D's will established a trust funded with property valued for estate tax purposes at $500,000. The assets include both income producing assets and non-productive assets. S was given the power, exercisable annually, to require distribution of all of the trust income to herself. No trust property may be distributed during S's lifetime to any person other than S. Applicable local law permits S to require that the trustee either make the trust property productive or sell the property and reinvest in productive property within a reasonable time after D's death. If the executor elects to treat all of the trust as qualified terminable interest property, the deductible interest is $500,000. If the executor elects to treat only 20 percent of the trust as qualified terminable interest property, the deductible interest is $100,000, i.e., 20 percent of $500,000.

Example (3). Power of distribution over fraction of trust income. The facts are the same as in Example 2 except that S is given the right exercisable annually for S's lifetime to require distribution to herself of only 50 percent of the trust income for life. The remaining trust income is to be accumulated or distributed among S and the decedent's children in the trustee's discretion. The maximum amount that D's executor may elect to treat as qualified terminable interest property is $250,000; i.e., the estate tax value of the trust ($500,000) multiplied by the percentage of the trust in which S has a qualifying income interest for life (50 percent). If D's executor elects to treat only 20 percent of the portion of the trust in which S has a qualifying income interest as qualified terminable interest property, the deductible interest is $50,000, i.e., 20 percent of $250,000.

Example (4). Power to distribute trust corpus to other beneficiaries. D's will established a trust providing that S is entitled to receive at least annually all the trust income. The trustee is given the power to use annually during S's lifetime $5,000 from the trust for the maintenance and support of S's minor child, C. Any such distribution does not necessarily relieve S of S's obligation to support and maintain C. S does not have a qualifying income interest for life in any portion of the trust because the bequest fails to satisfy the condition that no person have a power, other than a power the exercise of which takes effect only at or after S's death, to appoint any part of the property to any person other than S. The trust would also be nondeductible under section 2056(b)(7) if S, rather than the trustee, held the power to appoint a portion of the principal to C. However, in the latter case, if S made a qualified disclaimer (within the meaning of section 2518) of the power to appoint to C, the trust could qualify for the marital deduction pursuant to section 2056(b)(7), assuming that the power is personal to S and S's disclaimer terminates the power. Similarly, in either case, if C made a qualified disclaimer of C's right to receive distributions from the trust, the trust would qualify under section 2056(b)(7), assuming that C's disclaimer effectively negates the trustee's power under local law.

Example (5). Spouse's income interest terminable on remarriage. D's will established a trust providing that all of the trust income is payable at least annually to S for S's lifetime, provided that, if S remarries, S's interest in the trust will pass to X. The trust is not deductible under section 2056(b)(7). S's income interest is not a qualifying income interest for life because it is not for life but, rather, is terminable upon S's remarriage.

Example (6). Spouse's qualifying income interest for life contingent on executor's election. D's will established a trust providing that S is entitled to receive the income, payable at least annually, from that portion of the trust that the executor elects to treat as qualified terminable interest property. The portion of the trust which the executor does not elect to treat as qualified terminable interest property passes as of D's date of death to a trust for the benefit of C, D's child. Under these facts, the executor is not considered to have a power to appoint any part of the trust property to any person other than S during S's life.

Example (7). Formula partial election. D's will established a trust funded with the residue of D's estate. Trust income is to be paid annually to S for life, and the principal is to be distributed to D's children upon S's death. S has the power to require that all the trust property be made productive. There is no power to distribute trust property during S's lifetime to any person other than S. D's executor elects to deduct a fractional share of the residuary estate under section 2056(b)(7). The election specifies that the numerator of the fraction is the amount of deduction necessary to reduce the Federal estate tax to zero (taking into account final estate tax values) and the denominator of the fraction is the final estate tax value of the residuary estate (taking into account any specific bequests or liabilities of the estate paid out of the residuary estate). The formula election is of a fractional share. The value of the share qualifies for the marital deduction even though the executor's determinations to claim administration expenses as estate or income tax deductions and the final estate tax values will affect the size of the fractional share.

Example (8). Formula partial election. The facts are the same as in Example 7 except that, rather than defining a fraction, the executor's formula states: "I elect to treat as qualified terminable interest property that portion of the residuary trust, up to 100 percent, necessary to reduce the Federal estate tax to zero, after taking into account the available unified credit, final estate tax values and any liabilities and specific bequests paid from the residuary estate." The formula election is of a fractional share. The share is equivalent to the fractional share determined in Example 7.

Example (9). Severance of QTIP trust. D's will established a trust funded with the residue of D's estate. Trust income is to be paid annually to S for life, and the principal is to be distributed to D's children upon S's death. S has the power to require that all of the trust property be made productive. There is no power to distribute trust property during S's lifetime to any person other than S. D's will authorizes the executor to make the election under section 2056(b)(7) only with respect to the minimum amount of property necessary to reduce estate taxes on D's estate to zero, authorizes the executor to divide the residuary estate into two separate trusts to reflect the election, and authorizes the executor to charge any payment of principal to S to the qualified terminable interest trust. S is the sole beneficiary of both trusts during S's lifetime. The authorizations in the will do not adversely affect the allowance of the marital deduction. Only the property remaining in the marital deduction trust, after payment of principal to S, is subject to inclusion in S's gross estate under section 2044 or subject to gift tax under section 2519.

Example (10). Payments to spouse from individual retirement account. S is the life beneficiary of sixteen remaining annual installments payable from D's individual retirement account. The terms of the account provide for the payment of the account balance in nineteen annual installments that commenced when D reached age 70 ½. Each installment is equal to all the income earned on the remaining principal in the account plus a share of the remaining principal equal to 1/19 in the first year, 1/18 in the second year, 1/17 in the third year, etc. Under the terms of the account, S has no right to withdraw any other amounts from the account. Any payments remaining after S's death pass to D's children. S's interest in the account qualifies as a qualifying income interest for life under section 2056(b)(7)(B)(ii), without regard to the provisions of section 2056(b)(7)(C).

Example (11). Spouse's interest in trust in the form of an annuity. D died prior to October 24, 1992. D's will established a trust funded with income producing property valued at $500,000 for estate tax purposes. The trustee is required by the trust instrument to pay $20,000 a year to S for life. Trust income in excess of the annuity amount is to be accumulated in the trust and may not be distributed during S's lifetime. S's lifetime annuity interest is treated as a qualifying income interest for life. If the executor elects to treat the entire portion of the trust in which S has a qualifying income interest as qualified terminable interest property, the value of the deductible interest is (assuming that 10 percent is the applicable interest rate under section 7520 for valuing annuities on the appropriate valuation date) $200,000, because that amount would yield an income to S of $20,000 a year.

Example (12). Value of spouse's annuity exceeds value of trust corpus. The facts are the same as in Example 11 except that the trustee is required to pay S $70,000 a year for life. If the executor elects to treat the entire portion of the trust in which S has a qualifying income interest as qualified terminable interest property, the value of the deductible interest is $500,000, which is the lesser of the entire value of the property ($500,000), or the amount of property that (assuming a 10 percent interest rate) would yield an income to S of $70,000 a year ($700,000).

Example (13). Pooled income fund. D's will provides for a bequest of $200,000 to a pooled income fund described in section 642(c)(5), designating S as the income beneficiary for life. If D's executor elects to treat the entire $200,000 as qualified terminable interest property, the deductible interest is $200,000.

Example (14). Funding severed QTIP trusts. D's will established a trust satisfying the requirements of section 2056(b)(7). Pursuant to the authority in D's will and § 20.2056(b)–7(b)(2)(ii), D's executor indicates on the Federal estate tax return that an election under section 2056(b)(7) is being made with respect to 50 percent of the trust, and that the trust will subsequently be divided to reflect the partial election on the basis of the fair market value of the property at the time of the division. D's executor funds the trust at the end of the period of estate administration. At that time, the property available to fund the trusts consists of 100 shares of X Corporation stock with a current value of $400,000 and 200 shares of Y Corporation stock with a current value of $400,000. D may fund each trust with the stock of either or both corporations, in any combination, provided that the aggregate value of the stock allocated to each trust is $400,000.

[T.D. 8522, 59 FR 9651, March 1, 1994; T.D. 8779, 63 FR 44393, Aug. 19, 1998; T.D. 9102, 69 FR 21, Jan. 2, 2004]

§ 20.2056(b)–8 Special rule for charitable remainder trusts.

(a) In general. (1) *Surviving spouse only noncharitable beneficiary.* With respect to estates of decedents dying after December 31, 1981, subject to section 2056(d), if the surviving spouse of the decedent is the only noncharitable beneficiary of a charitable remainder annuity trust or a charitable remainder unitrust described in section 664 (qualified charitable remainder trust), section 2056(b)(1) does not apply to the interest in the trust that is transferred to the surviving spouse. Thus, the value of the annuity or unitrust interest passing to the spouse qualifies for a marital deduction under section 2056(b)(8) and the value of the remainder interest qualifies for a charitable deduction under section 2055. If an interest in property qualifies for a marital deduction under section 2056(b)(8), no election may be made with respect to the property under section 2056(b)(7). For purposes of this section, the term non-charitable beneficiary means any beneficiary of the qualified charitable remainder trust other than an organization described in section 170(c).

(2) *Interest for life or term of years.* The surviving spouse's interest need not be an interest for life to qualify for a marital deduction under section 2056(b)(8). However, for purposes of section 664, an annuity or unitrust interest payable to the spouse for a term of years cannot be payable for a term that exceeds 20 years.

(3) *Payment of state death taxes.* A deduction is allowed under section 2056(b)(8) even if the transfer to the surviving spouse is conditioned on the spouse's payment of state death taxes, if any, attributable to the qualified charitable remainder trust. See § 20.2056(b)–

4(c) for the effect of such a condition on the amount of the deduction allowable.

(b) Charitable remainder trusts where the surviving spouse is not the only noncharitable beneficiary. In the case of a charitable remainder trust where the decedent's spouse is not the only noncharitable beneficiary (for example, where the noncharitable interest is payable to the decedent's spouse for life and then to another individual for life), the qualification of the interest as qualified terminable interest property is determined solely under section 2056(b)(7) and not under section 2056(b)(8). Accordingly, if the decedent died on or before October 24, 1992, or the trust otherwise comes within the purview of the transitional rules contained in § 20.2056(b)–7(e)(5), the spousal annuity or unitrust interest may qualify under § 20.2056(b)–7(e) as a qualifying income interest for life.

[T.D. 8522, 59 FR 9653, March 1, 1994]

§ 20.2056(b)–9 Denial of double deduction.

The value of an interest in property may not be deducted for Federal estate tax purposes more than once with respect to the same decedent. For example, where a decedent transfers a life estate in a farm to the spouse with a remainder to charity, the entire property is, pursuant to the executor's election under section 2056(b)(7), treated as passing to the spouse. The entire value of the property qualifies for the marital deduction. No part of the value of the property qualifies for a charitable deduction under section 2055 in the decedent's estate.

[T.D. 8522, 59 FR 9654, March 1, 1994]

§ 20.2056(b)–10 Effective dates.

Except as specifically provided in §§ 20.2056(b)–5(c)(3)(ii) and (iii), 20.2056(b)–7(d)(3), 20.2056(b)–7(e)(5), and 20.2056(b)–8(b), the provisions of §§ 20.2056(b)–5(c), 20.2056(b)–7, 20.2056(b)–8, and 20.2056(b)–9 are applicable with respect to estates of decedents dying after March 1, 1994. With respect to decedents dying on or before such date, the executor of the decedent's estate may rely on any reasonable interpretation of the statutory provisions. In addition, the rule in the last sentence of § 20.2056(b)–5(f)(1) and the rule in the last sentence of § 20.2056(b)–7(d)(1) regarding the effect on the spouse's right to income if applicable local law provides for the reasonable apportionment between the income and remainder beneficiaries of the total return of the trust are applicable with respect to trusts for taxable years ending after January 2, 2004.

[T.D. 8522, 59 FR 9654, March 1, 1994; T.D. 8779, 63 FR 44393, Aug. 19, 1998; T.D. 9102, 69 FR 21, Jan. 2, 2004]

§ 20.2056(c)–1 Marital deduction; definition of passed from the decedent.

(a) In general. The following rules are applicable in determining the person to whom any property interest "passed from the decedent":

(1) Property interests devolving upon any person (or persons) as surviving coowner with the decedent under any form of joint ownership under which the right of survivorship existed are considered as having passed from the decedent to such person (or persons).

(2) Property interests at any time subject to the decedent's power to appoint (whether alone or in conjunction with any person) are considered as having passed from the decedent to the appointee under his exercise of the power, or, in case of the lapse, release or nonexercise of the power, as having passed from the decedent to the taker in default of exercise.

(3) The dower or curtesy interest (or statutory interest in lieu thereof) of the decedent's surviving spouse is considered as having passed from the decedent to his spouse.

(4) The proceeds of insurance upon the life of the decedent are considered as having passed from the decedent to the person who, at the time of the decedent's death, was entitled to receive the proceeds.

(5) Any property interest transferred during life, bequeathed or devised by the decedent, or inherited from the decedent, is considered as having passed to the person to whom he transferred, bequeathed, or devised the interest, or to the person who inherited the interest from him.

(6) The survivor's interest in an annuity or other payment described in section 2039 (see §§ 20.2039–1 and 20.2039–2) is considered as having passed from the decedent to the survivor only to the extent that the value of such interest is included in the decedent's gross estate under that section. If only a portion of the entire annuity or other payment is included in the decedent's gross estate and the annuity or other payment is payable to more than one beneficiary, then the value of the interest considered to have passed to

each beneficiary is that portion of the amount payable to each beneficiary that the amount of the annuity or other payment included in the decedent's gross estate bears to the total value of the annuity or other payment payable to all beneficiaries.

(b) Expectant interest in property under community property laws. If before the decedent's death the decedent's surviving spouse had merely an expectant interest in property held by her and the decedent under community property laws, that interest is considered as having passed from the decedent to the spouse.

[T.D. 6296, 23 FR 4529, June 24, 1958; T.D. 8522, 59 FR 9654, March 1, 1994]

§ 20.2056(c)–2 Marital deduction; definition of passed from the decedent to his surviving spouse.

(a) In general. In general, the definition stated in § 20.2056(c)–1 is applicable in determining the property interests which "passed from the decedent to his surviving spouse". Special rules are provided, however, for the following:

(1) In the case of certain interests with income for life to the surviving spouse with power of appointment in her (see § 20.2056(b)–5);

(2) In the case of certain interests with income for life to the surviving spouse that the executor elects to treat as qualified terminable interest property (see § 20.2056(b)–7);

(3) In the case of proceeds held by the insurer under a life insurance, endowment, or annuity contract with power of appointment in the surviving spouse (see § 20.2056(b)–6);

(4) In case of the disclaimer of an interest by the surviving spouse or by any other person (see § 20.2056(d)–1);

(5) In case of an election by the surviving spouse (see paragraph (c) of this section); and

(6) In case of a controversy involving the decedent's will, see paragraph (d) of this section.

A property interest is treated as passing to the surviving spouse only if it passes to the spouse as beneficial owner, except to the extent otherwise provided in §§ 20.2056(b)–5 through 20.2056(b)–7. For this purpose, where a property interest passed from the decedent in trust, such interest is considered to have passed from him to his surviving spouse to the extent of her beneficial interest therein. The deduction may not be taken with respect to a property interest which passed to such spouse merely as trustee, or subject to a binding agreement by the spouse to dispose of the interest in favor of a third person. An allowance or award paid to a surviving spouse pursuant to local law for her support during the administration of the decedent's estate constitutes a property interest passing from the decedent to his surviving spouse. In determining whether or not such an interest is deductible, however, see generally the terminable interest rules of § 20.2056(b)–1 and especially example (8) of paragraph (g) of that section.

(b) Examples. The following illustrate the provisions of paragraph (a) of this section:

(1) A property interest bequeathed in trust by H (the decedent) is considered as having passed from him to W (his surviving spouse)—

(i) If the trust income is payable to W for life and upon her death the corpus is distributable to her executors or administrators;

(ii) If W is entitled to the trust income for a term of years following which the corpus is to be paid to W or her estate;

(iii) If the trust income is to be accumulated for a term of years or for W's life and the augmented fund paid to W or her estate; or

(iv) If the terms of the transfer satisfy the requirements of § 20.2056(b)–5 or § 20.2056(b)–7.

(2) If H devised property—

(i) To A for life with remainder absolutely to W or her estate, the remainder interest is considered to have passed from H to W;

(ii) To W for life with remainder to her estate, the entire property is considered as having passed from H to W; or

(iii) Under conditions which satisfy the provisions of § 20.2056(b)–5 or § 20.2056(b)–7, the entire property is considered as having passed from H to W.

(3) Proceeds of insurance upon the life of H are considered as having passed from H to W if the terms of the contract—

(i) Meet the requirements of § 20.2056(b)–6;

(ii) Provide that the proceeds are payable to W in a lump sum;

(iii) Provide that the proceeds are payable in installments to W for life and after her death any remaining installments are payable to her estate;

(iv) Provide that interest on the proceeds is payable to W for life and upon her death the principal amount is payable to her estate; or

(v) Provide that the proceeds are payable to a trustee under an arrangement whereby the requirements of section 20.2056(b)–5 or 20.2056(b)–7 are satisfied.

(c) Effect of election by surviving spouse. This paragraph contains rules applicable if the surviving spouse may elect between a property interest offered to her under the decedent's will or other instrument and a property interest to which she is otherwise entitled (such as dower, a right in the decedent's estate, or her interest under community property laws) of which adverse disposition was attempted by the decedent under the will or other instrument. If the surviving spouse elects to take against the will or other instrument, then the property interests offered thereunder are not considered as having "passed from the decedent to his surviving spouse" and the dower or other property interest retained by her is considered as having so passed (if it otherwise so qualifies under this section). If the surviving spouse elects to take under the will or other instrument, then the dower or other property interest relinquished by her is not considered as having "passed from the decedent to his surviving spouse" (irrespective of whether it otherwise comes within the definition stated in paragraph (a) of this section) and the interest taken under the will or other instrument is considered as having so passed (if it otherwise so qualifies). As to the valuation of the property interest taken under the will or other instrument, see paragraph (b) of § 20.2056(b)–4.

(d) Will contests. (1) If as a result of a controversy involving the decedent's will, or involving any bequest or devise thereunder, his surviving spouse assigns or surrenders a property interest in settlement of the controversy, the interest so assigned or surrendered is not considered as having "passed from the decedent to his surviving spouse."

(2) If as a result of the controversy involving the decedent's will, or involving any bequest or devise thereunder, a property interest is assigned or surrendered to the surviving spouse, the interest so acquired will be regarded as having "passed from the decedent to his surviving spouse" only if the assignment or surrender as a bona fide recognition of enforceable rights of the surviving spouse in the decedent's estate. Such a bona fide recognition will be presumed where the assignment or surrender was pursuant to a decision of a local court upon the merits in an adversary proceeding following a genuine and active contest. However, such a decree will be accepted only to the extent that the court passed upon the facts upon which deductibility of the property interest depends. If the assignment or surrender was pursuant to a decree rendered by consent, or pursuant to an agreement not to contest the will or not to probate the will, it will not necessarily be accepted as a bona fide evaluation of the rights of the spouse.

(e) Survivorship. If the order of deaths of the decedent and his spouse cannot be established by proof, a presumption (whether supplied by local law, the decedent's will, or otherwise) that the decedent was survived by his spouse will be recognized as satisfying paragraph (b)(1) of § 20.2056(a)–1, but only to the extent that it has the effect of giving to the spouse an interest in property includible in her gross estate under part III of subchapter A of chapter 11. Under these circumstances, if an estate tax return is required to be filed for the estate of the decedent's spouse, the marital deduction will not be allowed in the final audit of the estate tax return of the decedent's estate with respect to any property interest which has not been finally determined to be includible in the gross estate of his spouse.

[T.D. 6296, 23 FR 4529, June 24, 1958; T.D. 8522, 59 FR 9654, March 1, 1994]

§ 20.2056(c)–3 Marital deduction; definition of "passed from the decedent to a person other than his surviving spouse".

The expression "passed from the decedent to a person other than his surviving spouse" refers to any property interest which, under the definition stated in § 20.2056(c)–1 is considered as having "passed from the decedent" and which under the rules referred to in § 20.2056(c)–2 is not considered as having "passed from the decedent to his surviving spouse." Interests which passed to a person other than the surviving spouse include interests so passing under the decedent's exercise, release, or nonexercise of a nontaxable power to appoint. It is immaterial whether the property interest which passed from the decedent to a person other than his surviving spouse is included in the decedent's gross estate. The term "person other than his surviving spouse" includes the possible unascertained takers of a property interest, as, for example, the members of a class to be ascertained in the future. As another example, assume that the decedent created a power of appointment over a property interest, which does not come within the purview of § 20.2056(b)–5 or § 20.2056(b)–6. In such a case, the term "person other than his surviving spouse" refers to the possible appointees and possible takers in default (other than the spouse) of such property interest. Whether or not there is a possibility that the "person other than his surviving spouse" (or the heirs or assigns of such person) may possess or enjoy the property following termination or failure of the interest therein which passed from the decedent to his surviving spouse is to be determined as of the time of the decedent's death.

[T.D. 6296, 23 FR 4529, June 24, 1958; T.D. 8522, 59 FR 9654, March 1, 1994]

§ 20.2056(d)–1 Marital deduction; special rules for marital deduction if surviving spouse is not a United States citizen.

Rules pertaining to the application of section 2056(d), including certain transition rules, are contained in §§ 20.2056A–1 through 20.2056A–13.

[T.D. 8612, 60 FR 43538, Aug. 22, 1995]

§ 20.2056(d)–2 Marital deduction; effect of disclaimers of post-December 31, 1976 transfers.

(a) Disclaimer by a surviving spouse. If a surviving spouse disclaims an interest in property passing to such spouse from the decedent, which interest was created in a transfer made after December 31, 1976, the effectiveness of the disclaimer will be determined by section 2518 and the corresponding regulations. For rules relating to when the transfer creating the interest occurs, see § 25.2518–2(c)(3) and (c)(4) of this chapter. If a qualified disclaimer is determined to have been made by the surviving spouse, the property interest disclaimed is treated as if such interest had never been transferred to the surviving spouse.

(b) Disclaimer by a person other than a surviving spouse. If an interest in property passes from a decedent to a person other than the surviving spouse, and the interest is created in a transfer made after December 31, 1976, and—

(1) The person other than the surviving spouse makes a qualified disclaimer with respect to such interest; and

(2) The surviving spouse is entitled to such interest in property as a result of such disclaimer, the disclaimed interest is treated as passing directly from the decedent to the surviving spouse. For rules relating to when the transfer creating the interest occurs, see § 25.2518–2(c)(3) and (c)(4) of this chapter.

(c) Effective date. The first and second sentences of paragraphs (a) and (b) of this section are applicable for transfers creating the interest to be disclaimed made on or after December 31, 1997.

[T.D. 6296, 23 FR 4529, June 24, 1958; T.D. 8095, 51 FR 28368, Aug. 7, 1986; T.D. 8612, 60 FR 43538, Aug. 22, 1995; T.D. 8744, 62 FR 68184, Dec. 31, 1997]

§ 20.2056(d)–3 Marital deduction; effect of disclaimers of pre-January 1, 1977 transfers. [*Omitted. Ed.*]

[T.D. 8095, 51 FR 28368, Aug. 7, 1986; T.D. 8612, 60 FR 43538, Aug. 22, 1995]

§ 2056A. Qualified Domestic Trust

(a) Qualified domestic trust defined. For purposes of this section and section 2056(d), the term "qualified domestic trust" means, with respect to any decedent, any trust if—

(1) the trust instrument—

(A) except as provided in regulations prescribed by the Secretary, requires that at least 1 trustee of the trust be an individual citizen of the United States or a domestic corporation, and

(B) provides that no distribution (other than a distribution of income) may be made from the trust unless a trustee who is an individual citizen of the United States or a domestic corporation has the right to withhold from such distribution the tax imposed by this section on such distribution,

(2) such trust meets such requirements as the Secretary may by regulations prescribe to ensure the collection of any tax imposed by subsection (b), and

(3) an election under this section by the executor of the decedent applies to such trust.

(b) Tax treatment of trust.

(1) Imposition of estate tax. There is hereby imposed an estate tax on—

(A) any distribution before the date of the death of the surviving spouse from a qualified domestic trust, and

(B) the value of the property remaining in a qualified domestic trust on the date of the death of the surviving spouse.

(2) Amount of tax.

(A) In general. In the case of any taxable event, the amount of the estate tax imposed by paragraph (1) shall be the amount equal to—

(i) the tax which would have been imposed under section 2001 on the estate of the decedent if the taxable estate of the decedent had been increased by the sum of—

(I) the amount involved in such taxable event, plus

(II) the aggregate amount involved in previous taxable events with respect to qualified domestic trusts of such decedent, reduced by

(ii) the tax which would have been imposed under section 2001 on the estate of the decedent if the taxable estate of the decedent had been increased by the amount referred to in clause (i)(II).

(B) Tentative tax where tax of decedent not finally determined.

(i) In general. If the tax imposed on the estate of the decedent under section 2001 is not finally determined before the taxable event, the amount of the tax imposed by paragraph (1) on such event shall be determined by using the highest rate of tax in effect under section 2001 as of the date of the decedent's death.

(ii) Refund of excess when tax finally determined. If—

(I) the amount of the tax determined under clause (i), exceeds

(II) the tax determined under subparagraph (A) on the basis of the final determination of the tax imposed by section 2001 on the estate of the decedent,

such excess shall be allowed as a credit or refund (with interest) if claim therefor is filed not later than 1 year after the date of such final determination.

(C) Special rule where decedent has more than 1 qualified domestic trust. If there is more than 1 qualified domestic trust with respect to any decedent, the amount of the tax imposed by paragraph (1) with respect to such trusts shall be determined by using the highest rate of tax in effect under section 2001 as of the date of the decedent's death (and the provisions of paragraph (3)(B) shall not apply) unless, pursuant to a designation made by the decedent's executor, there is 1 person—

(i) who is an individual citizen of the United States or a domestic corporation and is responsible for filing all returns of tax imposed under paragraph (1) with respect to such trusts and for paying all tax so imposed, and

(ii) who meets such requirements as the Secretary may by regulations prescribe.

(3) Certain lifetime distributions exempt from tax.

(A) Income distributions. No tax shall be imposed by paragraph (1)(A) on any distribution of income to the surviving spouse.

(B) Hardship exemption. No tax shall be imposed by paragraph (1)(A) on any distribution to the surviving spouse on account of hardship.

(4) Tax where trust ceases to qualify. If any qualified domestic trust ceases to meet the requirements of paragraphs (1) and (2) of subsection (a), the tax imposed by paragraph (1) shall apply as if the surviving spouse died on the date of such cessation.

(5) Due date.

(A) Tax on distributions. The estate tax imposed by paragraph (1)(A) shall be due and payable on the 15th day of the 4th month following the calendar year in which the taxable event occurs; except that the estate tax imposed by paragraph (1)(A) on distributions during the calendar year in which the surviving spouse dies shall be due and payable not later than the date on which the estate tax imposed by paragraph (1)(B) is due and payable.

(B) Tax at death of spouse. The estate tax imposed by paragraph (1)(B) shall be due and payable on the date 9 months after the date of such death.

(6) Liability for tax. Each trustee shall be personally liable for the amount of the tax imposed by paragraph (1). Rules similar to the rules of section 2204 shall apply for purposes of the preceding sentence.

(7) Treatment of tax. For purposes of section 2056(d), any tax paid under paragraph (1) shall be treated as a tax paid under section 2001 with respect to the estate of the decedent.

(8) Lien for tax. For purposes of section 6324, any tax imposed by paragraph (1) shall be treated as an estate tax imposed under this chapter with respect to a decedent dying on the date of the taxable event (and the property involved shall be treated as the gross estate of such decedent).

(9) Taxable event. The term "taxable event" means the event resulting in tax being imposed under paragraph (1).

(10) Certain benefits allowed.

(A) In general. If any property remaining in the qualified domestic trust on the date of the death of the surviving spouse is includible in the gross estate of such spouse for purposes of this chapter (or would be includible if such spouse were a citizen or resident of the United States), any benefit which is allowable (or would be allowable if such spouse were a citizen or resident of the United States) with respect to such property to the estate of such spouse under section 2014, 2032, 2032A, 2055, 2056, 2058, or 6166 shall be allowed for purposes of the tax imposed by paragraph (1)(B).

(B) Section 303. If the estate of the surviving spouse meets the requirements of section 303 with respect to any property described in subparagraph (A), for purposes of section 303, the tax imposed by paragraph (1)(B) with respect to such property shall be treated as a Federal estate tax payable with respect to the estate of the surviving spouse.

(C) Section 6161(a)(2). The provisions of section 6161(a)(2) shall apply with respect to the tax imposed by paragraph (1)(B), and the reference in such section to the executor shall be treated as a reference to the trustees of the trust.

(11) Special rule where distribution tax paid out of trust. For purposes of this subsection, if any portion of the tax imposed by paragraph (1)(A) with respect to any distribution is paid out of the trust, an amount equal to the portion so paid shall be treated as a distribution described in paragraph (1)(A).

(12) Special rule where spouse becomes citizen. If the surviving spouse of the decedent becomes a citizen of the United States and if—

(A) such spouse was a resident of the United States at all times after the date of the death of the decedent and before such spouse becomes a citizen of the United States,

(B) no tax was imposed by paragraph (1)(A) with respect to any distribution before such spouse becomes such a citizen, or

(C) such spouse elects—

(i) to treat any distribution on which tax was imposed by paragraph (1)(A) as a taxable gift made by such spouse for purposes of—

(I) section 2001, and

(II) determining the amount of the tax imposed by section 2501 on actual taxable gifts made by such spouse during the year in which the spouse becomes a citizen or any subsequent year, and

(ii) to treat any reduction in the tax imposed by paragraph (1)(A) by reason of the credit allowable under section 2010 with respect to the decedent as a credit allowable to such surviving spouse under section 2505 for purposes of determining the amount of the credit allowable under section 2505 with respect to taxable gifts made by the surviving spouse during the year in which the spouse becomes a citizen or any subsequent year,

paragraph (1)(A) shall not apply to any distributions after such spouse becomes such a citizen (and paragraph (1)(B) shall not apply).

(13) Coordination with section 1015. For purposes of section 1015, any distribution on which tax is imposed by paragraph (1)(A) shall be treated as a transfer by gift, and any tax paid under paragraph (1)(A) shall be treated as a gift tax.

(14) Coordination with terminable interest rules. Any interest in a qualified domestic trust shall not be treated as failing to meet the requirements of paragraph (5) or (7) of section 2056(b) merely by reason of any provision of the trust instrument permitting the withholding from any distribution of an amount to pay the tax imposed by paragraph (1) on such distribution.

(15) No tax on certain distributions. No tax shall be imposed by paragraph (1) on any distribution to the surviving spouse to the extent such distribution is to reimburse such surviving spouse for any tax imposed by subtitle A on any item of income of the trust to which such surviving spouse is not entitled under the terms of the trust.

(c) Definitions. For purposes of this section—

(1) Property includes interest therein. The term "property" includes an interest in property.

(2) Income. Except as provided in regulations, the term "income" has the meaning given to such term by section 643(b).

(3) Trust. To the extend provided in regulations prescribed by the Secretary, the term "trust" includes other arrangements which have substantially the same effect as a trust.

(d) Election. An election under this section with respect to any trust shall be made by the executor on the return of the tax imposed by section 2001. Such an election, once made, shall be irrevocable. No election may be made under this section on any return if such return is filed more than one year after the time prescribed by law (including extensions) for filing such return.

(e) Regulations. The Secretary shall prescribe such regulations as may be necessary or appropriate to carry out the purposes of this section, including regulations under which there may be treated as a qualified domestic trust any annuity or other payment which is includible in the decedent's gross estate and is by its terms payable for life or a term of years.

Regulations

§ 20.2056A–0 Table of contents. [*Omitted. Ed.*]

[T.D. 8612, Aug. 21, 1995, amend T.D. 8686, Nov. 27, 1996]

Proposed § 20.2056A–0 (REG–119683–22, Aug. 21, 2024) Table of contents [*Omitted. Ed.*]

§ 20.2056A–1 Restrictions on allowance of marital deduction if surviving spouse is not a United States citizen.

(a) General rule. Subject to the special rules provided in section 7815(d)(14) of the Omnibus Budget Reconciliation Act of 1989 (Pub.L. 101–239; 103 Stat. 2106), in the case of a decedent dying after November 10, 1988, the federal estate tax marital deduction is not allowed for property passing to or for the benefit of a surviving spouse who is not a United States citizen at the date of the decedent's death (whether or not the surviving spouse is a resident of the United States) unless—

(1) The property passes from the decedent to (or pursuant to)—

(i) A qualified domestic trust (QDOT) described in section 2056A and § 20.2056A–2;

(ii) A trust that, although not meeting all of the requirements for a QDOT, is reformed after the decedent's death to meet the requirements of a QDOT (see § 20.2056A–4(a));

(iii) The surviving spouse not in trust (e.g., by outright bequest or devise, by operation of law, or pursuant to the terms of an annuity or other similar plan or arrangement) and, prior to the date that the estate tax return is filed and on or before the last date prescribed by law that the QDOT election may be made (no more than one year after the time prescribed by law, including extensions, for filing the return), the surviving spouse either actually transfers the property to a QDOT or irrevocably assigns the property to a QDOT (see § 20.2056A–4(b)); or

(iv) A plan or other arrangement that would have qualified for the marital deduction but for section 2056(d)(1)(A), and whose payments are not assignable or transferable to a QDOT, if the requirements of § 20.2056A–4(c) are met; and

(2) The executor makes a timely QDOT election under § 20.2056A–3.

(b) Marital deduction allowed if resident spouse becomes citizen. For purposes of section 2056(d)(1) and paragraph (a) of this section, the surviving spouse is treated as a citizen of the United States at the date of the decedent's death if the requirements of section 2056(d)(4) are satisfied. For purposes of section 2056(d)(4)(A) and notwithstanding § 20.2056A–3(a), a return filed prior to the due date (including extensions) is considered filed on the last date that the return is required to be filed (including extensions), and a late return filed at any time after the due date is considered filed on the date that it is actually filed. A surviving spouse is a resident only if the spouse is a resident under chapter 11 of the Internal Revenue Code. See § 20.0–1(b)(1). The status of the spouse as a resident under section 7701(b) is not relevant to this determination except to the extent that the income tax residency of the spouse is pertinent in applying § 20.0–1(b)(1).

(c) Special rules in the case of certain transfers subject to estate and gift tax treaties. Under section 7815(d)(14) of the Omnibus Budget Reconciliation Act of 1989 (Pub.L. 101–239, 103 Stat. 2106) certain special rules apply in the case of transfers governed by certain estate and gift tax treaties to which the United States is a party. In the case of the estate of, or gift by, an individual who was not a citizen or resident of the United States but was a resident of a foreign country with which the United States has a tax treaty with respect to estate, inheritance, or gift taxes, the amendments made by section 5033 of the Technical and Miscellaneous Revenue Act of 1988 (Pub.L. 100–647, 102 Stat. 3342) do not apply to the extent such amendments would be inconsistent with the provisions of such treaty relating to estate, inheritance, or gift tax marital deductions. Under this rule, the estate may choose either the statutory deduction under section 2056A or the marital deduction allowed under the treaty. Thus, the estate may not avail itself of both the marital deduction under the treaty and the marital deduction under the QDOT provisions of section 2056A and chapter 11 of the Internal Revenue Code with respect to the remainder of the marital property that is not deductible under the treaty.

[T.D. 8612, 60 FR 43539, Aug. 22, 1995]

§ 20.2056A–2 Requirements for qualified domestic trust.

(a) In general. In order to qualify as a qualified domestic trust (QDOT), the requirements of paragraphs (b) and (c) of this section, and the requirements of § 20.2056A–2T(d), must be satisfied. The executor of the decedent's estate and the U.S. Trustee shall establish in such manner as may be prescribed by the Commissioner on the estate tax return and applicable instructions that these requirements have been satisfied or are being complied with. In order to constitute a QDOT, the trust must be maintained under the laws of a state of the United States or the District of Columbia, and the administration of the trust must be governed by the laws of a particular state of the United States or the District of Columbia. For purposes of this paragraph (a), a trust is maintained under the laws of a state of the United States or the District of Columbia if the records of the trust (or copies thereof) are kept in that state (or the District of Columbia). The trust may be established pursuant to an instrument executed under either the laws of a state of the United States or the District of Columbia or pursuant to an instrument executed under the laws of a foreign jurisdiction, such as a foreign will or trust, provided that such foreign instrument designates the law of a particular state of the United States or the District of Columbia as governing the administration of the trust, and such designation is effective under the law of the designated jurisdiction. In addition, the trust must constitute an ordinary trust, as defined in § 301.7701–4(a) of this chapter, and not any other type of entity. For purposes of this paragraph, a trust will not fail to constitute an ordinary trust solely because of the nature of the assets transferred to that trust, regardless of its classification under §§ 301.7701–2 through 301.7701–4 of this chapter.

(b) Qualified marital interest requirements. (1) *Property passing to QDOT.* If property passes from a decedent to a QDOT, the trust must qualify for the federal estate tax marital deduction under section 2056(b)(5) (life estate with power of appointment), section 2056(b)(7) (qualified terminable interest property, including joint and survivor annuities under section 2056(b)(7)(C)), or section 2056(b)(8) (surviving spouse is the only noncharitable beneficiary of a charitable remainder trust), or meet the requirements of an estate trust as defined in § 20.2056(c)–2(b)(1)(i) through (iii).

(2) *Property passing outright to spouse.* If property does not pass from a decedent to a QDOT, but passes to a noncitizen surviving spouse in a form that meets the requirements for a marital deduction without regard to section 2056(d)(1)(A), and that is not described in paragraph (b)(1) of this section, the surviving spouse must either actually transfer the property, or irrevocably assign the property, to a trust (whether created by the decedent, the decedent's executor or by the surviving spouse) that meets the requirements of paragraph (c) of this section and the requirements of § 20.2056A–2T(d) (pertaining, respectively, to statutory requirements and regulatory requirements imposed to ensure collection of tax) prior to the filing of the estate tax return for the decedent's estate and on or before the last date prescribed by law that the QDOT election may be made (see § 20.2056A–3(a)).

(3) *Property passing under a nontransferable plan or arrangement.* If property does not pass from a decedent to a QDOT, but passes under a plan or other arrangement that meets the requirements for a marital deduction without regard to section 2056(d)(1)(A) and whose payments are not assignable or transferable (see § 20.2056A–4(c)), the property is treated as meeting the requirements of this section, and the requirements of § 20.2056A–2T(d), if the requirements of § 20.2056A–4(c) are satisfied. In addition, where an annuity or similar arrangement is described above except that it is assignable or transferable, see § 20.2056A–4(b)(7).

(c) Statutory requirements. The requirements of section 2056A(a)(1)(A) and (B) must be satisfied. For purposes of that section, a domestic corporation is a corporation that is created or organized under the laws of the United States or under the laws of any state of the United States or the District of Columbia. The trustee required under that section is referred to herein as the "U.S. Trustee".

(d) Additional requirements to ensure collection of the section 2056A estate tax. (1) *Security and other arrangements for payment of estate tax imposed under section 2056A(b)(1)*—(i) *QDOTs with assets in excess of $2 million.* If the fair market value of the assets passing, treated, or deemed to have passed to the QDOT (or in the form of a QDOT), determined without reduction for any indebtedness with respect to the assets, as finally determined for federal estate tax purposes, exceeds $2 million as of the date of the decedent's death or, if applicable, the alternate valuation date (adjusted as provided in paragraph (d)(1)(iii) of this section), the trust instrument must meet the requirements of either paragraph (d)(1)(i)(A), (B), or (C) of this section at all times during the term of the QDOT. The QDOT may alternate between any of the arrangements provided in paragraphs (d)(1)(i)(A), (B), and (C) of this section provided that, at any given time, one of the arrangements must be operative. See paragraph (d)(1)(iii) of this section for the definition of finally determined. The QDOT may provide that the trustee has the discretion to use any one of the security arrangements or may provide that the trustee is limited to using only one or two of the arrangements specified in the trust instrument. A trust instrument that specifically states that the trust must be administered in compliance with paragraph (d)(1)(i)(A), (B), or (C) of this section is treated as meeting the requirements of paragraphs (d)(1)(i)(A), (B), or (C) of this section for purposes of paragraphs (d)(1)(i) and, if applicable, (d)(1)(ii) of this section.

(A) *Bank Trustee.* Except as otherwise provided in paragraph (d)(6)(ii) or (iii) of this section, the trust instrument must provide that whenever the Bank Trustee security alternative is used for the QDOT, at least one U.S. Trustee must be a bank as defined in section 581. Alternatively, except as otherwise provided in paragraph (d)(6)(ii) or (iii) of this section, at least one trustee must be a United States branch of a foreign bank, provided that, in such cases, during the entire term of the QDOT a U.S. Trustee must act as a trustee with the foreign bank trustee.

(B) *Bond.* Except as otherwise provided in paragraph (d)(6)(ii) or (iii) of this section, the trust instrument must provide that whenever the bond security arrangement alternative is used for the QDOT, the U.S. Trustee must furnish a bond in favor of the Internal Revenue Service in an amount equal to 65 percent of the fair market value of the trust assets (determined without regard to any indebtedness with respect to the assets) as of the date of the decedent's death (or alternate valuation date, if applicable), as finally determined for federal estate tax purposes (and as further adjusted as provided in paragraph (d)(1)(iv) of this section). If, after examination of the estate tax return, the fair market value of the trust assets, as originally reported on the estate tax return, is adjusted (pursuant to a judicial proceeding or otherwise) resulting in a final determination of the value of the assets as reported on the return, the U.S. Trustee has a reasonable period of time (not exceeding sixty days after the conclusion of the proceeding or other action resulting in a final determination of the value of the assets) to adjust the amount of the bond accordingly. But see, paragraph (d)(1)(i)(D) of this section for a special rule in the case of a substantial undervaluation of QDOT assets. Unless an alternate arrangement under paragraph (d)(1)(i)(A), (B), or (C) of this section, or an arrangement prescribed under paragraph (d)(4) of this section, is provided, or the trust is otherwise no longer subject to the requirements of section 2056A pursuant to section 2056A(b)(12), the bond must remain in effect until the trust ceases to function as a QDOT and any tax liability finally determined to be due under section 2056A(b) is paid, or is finally determined to be zero.

* * *

(C) *Letter of credit.* Except as otherwise provided in paragraph (d)(6)(ii) or (iii) of this section, the trust instrument must provide that whenever the letter of credit security arrangement is used for the QDOT, the U.S. Trustee must furnish an irrevocable letter of credit issued by a bank as defined in section 581, a United States branch of a foreign bank, or a foreign bank with a confirmation by a bank as defined in section 581. The letter of credit must be for an amount equal to 65 percent of the fair market value of the trust assets (determined without regard to any indebtedness with respect to the assets) as of the date of the decedent's death (or alternate valuation date, if applicable), as finally determined for federal estate tax purposes (and as further adjusted as provided in paragraph (d)(1)(iv) of this section). If, after examination of the estate tax return, the fair market value of the trust assets, as originally reported on the estate tax return, is adjusted (pursuant to a judicial proceeding or otherwise) resulting in a final determination of the value of the assets as reported on the return, the U.S. Trustee has a reasonable period of time (not exceeding 60 days after the conclusion of the proceeding or other action resulting in a final determination of the value of the assets) to adjust the amount of the letter of credit accordingly. But see, paragraph (d)(1)(i)(D) of this section for a special rule in the case of a substantial undervaluation of QDOT assets. Unless an alternate arrangement under paragraph (d)(1)(i)(A), (B), or (C) of this section, or an arrangement prescribed under paragraph (d)(4) of this section, is provided, or the trust is otherwise no longer subject to the requirements of section 2056A pursuant to section 2056A(b)(12), the letter of credit must remain in effect until the trust ceases to function as a QDOT and any tax liability finally determined to be due under section 2056A(b) is paid or is finally determined to be zero.

* * *

[T.D. 8612, 60 FR 43540, Aug. 22, 1995; T.D. 8686, 61 FR 60553, Nov. 29, 1996]

Proposed § 20.2056A–2 (REG–119683–22, Aug. 21, 2024) Requirements for qualified domestic trust.

Section 20.2056A–2 is amended by:

1. Revising the first sentence of paragraph (a);

2. Revising paragraph (b)(2);

3. Revising the first sentence of paragraph (b)(3);

4. Removing the fourth sentence of paragraph (d)(1)(i)(B)(1) and adding in its place two new sentences;

5. Revising the ninth and tenth sentences of paragraph (d)(1)(i)(B)(2);

6. Revising the first sentence of paragraph (d)(1)(i)(B)(4), and adding a new sentence at the end of the paragraph;

7. Removing the fourth sentence of paragraph (d)(1)(i)(C)(1) and adding in its place two new sentences;

8. Revising the first, fourteenth, and fifteenth sentences of paragraph (d)(1)(i)(C)(2);

9. Revising the first, tenth, and eleventh sentences of paragraph (d)(1)(i)(C)(3);

10. Revising the first sentence of paragraph (d)(1)(i)(C)(5), and adding a new sentence at the end of the paragraph;

11. Revising paragraph (d)(1)(iii);

12. Revising the paragraph heading of paragraph (d)(6);

13. Deleting paragraph (d)(6)(i);

14. Redesignating paragraphs (d)(6)(ii) and (iii) as paragraphs (d)(6)(i) and (ii) respectively; and

15. Adding paragraph (e).

The revisions and addition read as follows:

§ 20.2056A–2 Requirements for qualified domestic trust.

(a) In general. To qualify as a qualified domestic trust (QDOT), the requirements of paragraphs (b) through (d) of this section must be satisfied. * * *

(b) * * *

(2) Property passing outright to spouse. If property does not pass from a decedent to a QDOT, but passes to a noncitizen surviving spouse in a form that meets the requirements for a marital deduction without regard to section 2056(d)(1)(A), and that is not described in paragraph (b)(1) of this section, the surviving spouse must either actually transfer the property, or irrevocably assign the property, to a trust (whether created by the decedent, by the decedent's executor, or by the surviving spouse) that meets the requirements of paragraphs (c) and (d) of this section (pertaining, respectively, to statutory requirements and regulatory requirements imposed to ensure collection of tax) prior to the filing of the estate tax return for the decedent's estate and on or before the last date prescribed by law that the QDOT election may be made (see § 20.2056A–3(a)).

(3) * * * If property does not pass from a decedent to a QDOT, but passes under a plan or other arrangement that meets the requirements for a marital deduction without regard to section 2056(d)(1)(A) and whose payments are not assignable or transferable (see § 20.2056A–4(c)), the property is treated as meeting the requirements of this section, and the requirements of § 20.2056A–2(d), if the requirements of § 20.2056A–4(c) are satisfied. * * *

* * * * *

(d) * * *

(1) * * *

(i) * * *

(B) * * *

(1) * * * Any notice of failure to renew is required to be sent to the Estate Tax Advisory Group of the Internal Revenue Service. See IRS Publication 4235, Collection Advisory Offices Contact Information, or as otherwise provided in IRS forms and instructions or on https://www.irs.gov, to determine the correct ad-

dress to use when submitting the required documentation. * * *

(2) * * * All notices required to be sent to the Internal Revenue Service under this instrument should be sent to the Estate Tax Advisory Group of the Internal Revenue Service. See IRS Publication 4235, Collection Advisory Offices Contact Information, or as otherwise provided in IRS forms and instructions or on https://www.irs.gov, to determine the correct address to use when submitting the required documentation. * * *

* * * * *

(4) * * * The bond is to be filed (separately from the decedent's Federal estate tax return) by submitting it directly to the Estate Tax Advisory Group of the Internal Revenue Service on or before the later of the filing date or due date of the decedent's Federal estate tax return (Form 706 or 706-NA) unless an extension for filing the bond is granted under § 301.9100 of this chapter. * * * See IRS Publication 4235, Collection Advisory Offices Contact Information, or as otherwise provided in IRS forms and instructions or on https://www.irs.gov, to determine the correct address to use when submitting the required documentation.

(C) * * *

(1) * * * Any notice of failure to renew or closure of a U.S. branch of a foreign bank required to be sent to the Internal Revenue Service must be sent to the Estate Tax Advisory Group of the Internal Revenue Service. See IRS Publication 4235, Collection Advisory Offices Contact Information, or as otherwise provided in the IRS forms and instructions or on https://www.irs.gov, to determine the correct address to use when submitting the required documentation. * * *

(2) * * * The letter of credit must be made in the following form (or in the form that is the same as the following form in all material respects), or an alternative form that the Commissioner prescribes by guidance published in the Internal Revenue Bulletin (see § 601.601(d)(2) of this chapter):

[Issue Date]

To: Internal Revenue Service

Attention: Estate Tax Advisory Group. (See IRS Publication 4235, Collection Advisory Offices Contact Information, or as otherwise provided in IRS forms and instructions or on https://www.irs.gov, to determine the correct address to use when submitting the required documentation). * * *

Except where otherwise stated herein, this Letter of Credit is subject to the most recent revision of the Uniform Customs and Practice for Documentary Credits published by the International Chamber of Commerce (ICC), which can be found on https://www.iccwbo.org. If we notify you of our election not to consider this Letter of Credit renewed and the expiration date occurs during an interruption of business described in the most recent revision of that publication, unless you had consented to cancellation prior to the expiration date, the bank hereby specifically agrees to effect payment if this Letter of Credit is drawn against within 30 days after the resumption of business. * * *

(3) Form of confirmation. If the requirements of this paragraph (d)(1)(i)(C) are satisfied by the issuance of a letter of credit by a foreign bank with confirmation by a bank as defined in section 581, the confirmation must be made in the following form (or in a form that is the same as the following form in all material respects), or an alternative form that the Commissioner prescribes by guidance published in the Internal Revenue Bulletin (see § 601.601(d)(2) of this chapter):

[Issue Date]

To: Internal Revenue Service

Attention: Estate Tax Advisory Group. (See IRS Publication 4235, Collection Advisory Offices Contact Information, or as otherwise provided in IRS forms and instructions or on https://www.irs.gov, to determine the correct address to use when submitting the required documentation). * * *

Except where otherwise stated herein, this Confirmation is subject to the most recent version of the Uniform Customs and Practice for Documentary Credits published by the International Chamber of Commerce (ICC), which can be found on https://www.iccwbo.org. If we notify you of our election not to consider this Confirmation renewed and the expiration date occurs during an interruption of business described in the most recent version of that publication, unless you had consented to cancellation prior to the expiration date, the bank hereby specifically agrees to effect payment if this Confirmation is drawn against within 30 days after the resumption of business. * * *

* * * * *

(5) Procedure. The letter of credit (and confirmation, if applicable) is to be filed separately from the decedent's Federal estate tax return (Form 706 or Form 706-NA) by submitting it directly to the Estate Tax Advisory Group of the Internal Revenue Service on or before the later of the filing date or the due date of the decedent's Federal estate tax return (unless an extension for filing the letter of credit is granted under § 301.9100 of this chapter). * * * See IRS Publication 4235, Collection Advisory Offices Contact Information, or as otherwise provided in IRS forms and instructions or on https://www.irs.gov, to determine the correct address to use when submitting the required documentation.

* * * * *

(iii) Definition of finally determined (A) In general. For purposes of § 20.2056A–2(d)(1)(i) and (ii), the fair market value of assets is the fair market value of those assets as finally determined for Federal estate tax purposes. That value is

(1) The value reported on an estate tax return filed with the Internal Revenue Service, once the period of limitations on assessment (see section 6501) of estate tax has expired without that value having been timely adjusted by the Internal Revenue Service;

(2) The value determined or specified by the Internal Revenue Service for unreported property, or for reported property where the value determined or specified by the Internal Revenue Service differs from the value reported on an estate tax return filed with the Internal Revenue Service, once the period of limitations on assessment applicable to the estate tax has expired without that value having been timely contested by the executor;

(3) The value determined in a written agreement with the Internal Revenue Service (whether entered into during the course of the administrative proceedings between the estate and the Internal Revenue Service or after the commencement of litigation) once that written agreement has been executed by both the executor and the Internal Revenue Service and is binding on all parties (including, but not limited to, the executor, the Internal Revenue Service, and the beneficiaries); or

(4) The value determined by a court for the purpose of determining the estate tax liability of the estate, once the court's determination no longer can be appealed to any court.

(B) Contested and Executor defined. For purposes of this paragraph (d)(1)(iii), the term contested means to put at issue the value of property in a written communication to the Internal Revenue Service that identifies the specific property, states that the executor does not accept as correct the value of that property as determined or specified by the Internal Revenue Service, and provides the executor's claimed value for that property as determined in accordance with the requirements of section 2031, the corresponding regulations, and other applicable guidance. An issue cannot be contested by a general protective statement or written communication that does not include each of these specified elements. For purposes of this paragraph (d)(1)(iii), the term executor includes any person described in section 2203, as expanded to include all persons required under section 6018(b) to file an estate tax return.

* * * * *

(6) Special rules.

* * * * *

(e) Applicability date. This section applies with respect to estates of decedents dying on or after [the date of publication of final regulations in the Federal Register].

§ 20.2056A–3 QDOT election.

(a) General rule. Subject to the time period prescribed in section 2056A(d), the election to treat a trust as a QDOT must be made on the last federal estate tax return filed before the due date (including extensions of time to file actually granted) or, if a timely return is not filed, on the first federal estate tax return filed after the due date. The election, once made, is irrevocable.

(b) No partial elections. An election to treat a trust as a QDOT may not be made with respect to a specific portion of an entire trust that would otherwise qualify for the marital deduction but for the application of section 2056(d). However, if the trust is actually severed in accordance with the applicable requirements of § 20.2056(b)–7(b)(2)(ii) prior to the due date for the election, a QDOT election may be made for any one or more of the severed trusts.

(c) Protective elections. A protective election may be made to treat a trust as a QDOT only if at the time the federal estate tax return is filed, the executor of the decedent's estate reasonably believes that there is a bona fide issue that concerns either the residency or citizenship of the decedent, the citizenship of the surviving spouse, whether an asset is includible in the decedent's gross estate, or the amount or nature of the property the surviving spouse is entitled to receive. For example, if at the time the federal estate tax return is filed either the estate is involved in a bona fide will contest, there is uncertainty regarding the inclusion in the gross estate of an asset which, if includible, would be eligible for the QDOT election, or there is uncertainty regarding the status of the decedent as a resident alien or a nonresident alien for estate tax purposes, or a similar uncertainty regarding the citizenship status of the surviving spouse, a protective QDOT election may be made. The protective election is in addition to, and is not in lieu of, the requirements set forth in § 20.2056A–4. The protective QDOT election must be made on a written statement signed by the executor under penalties of perjury and must be attached to the return described in paragraph (a) of this section, and must identify the specific assets to which the protective election refers and the specific basis for the protective election. However, the protective election may otherwise be defined by means of a formula (such as the minimum amount necessary to reduce the estate tax to zero). Once made, the protective election is irrevocable. For example, if a protective election is made because a bona fide question exists as to the includibility of an asset in the decedent's gross estate and it is later finally determined that the asset is so includible, the protective election becomes effective with respect to the asset and cannot thereafter be revoked.

(d) Manner of election. The QDOT election under paragraph (a) of this section is made in the form and manner set forth in the decedent's estate tax return, including applicable instructions.

[T.D. 8612, 60 FR 43540, Aug. 22, 1995]

§ 20.2056A–4 Procedures for conforming marital trusts and nontrust marital transfers to the requirements of a qualified domestic trust. [*Omitted. Ed.*]

[T.D. 8612, Aug. 21, 1995; amend T.D. 8819, Apr. 29, 1999; T.D. 9448, May 1, 2009; T.D. 9540, Aug. 9, 2011; T.D. 9974, June 1, 2023]

Proposed § 20.2056A–4 (REG–119683–22, Aug. 21, 2024) Procedures for conforming marital trusts and nontrust marital transfers to the requirements of a qualified domestic trust. [*Omitted. Ed.*]

§ 20.2056A–5 Imposition of section 2056A estate tax.

(a) In general. An estate tax is imposed under section 2056A(b)(1) on the occurrence of a taxable event, as defined in section 2056A(b)(9). The tax is generally equal to the amount of estate tax that would have been imposed if the amount involved in the taxable event had been included in the decedent's taxable estate and had not been deductible under section 2056. See section 2056A(b)(3) and paragraph (c) of this section for certain exceptions from taxable events.

(b) Amounts subject to tax. (1) *Distribution of principal during the spouse's lifetime.* If a taxable event occurs during the noncitizen surviving spouse's lifetime, the amount on which the section 2056A estate tax is imposed is the amount of money and the fair market value of the property that is the subject of the distribution (including property distributed from the trust pursuant to the exercise of a power of appointment), including any amount withheld from the distribution by the U.S. Trustee to pay the tax. If, however, the tax is not withheld by the U.S. Trustee but is paid by the U.S. Trustee out of other assets of the QDOT, an amount equal to the tax so paid is treated as an additional distribution to the spouse in the year that the tax is paid.

(2) *Death of surviving spouse.* If a taxable event occurs as a result of the death of the surviving spouse, the amount subject to tax is the fair market value of the trust assets on the date of the spouse's death (or alternate valuation date if applicable). See also section 2032A. Any corpus portion amounts, within the meaning of § 20.2056A–4(c)(4)(i), remaining in a QDOT upon the surviving spouse's death, are subject to tax under section 2056A(b)(1)(B), as well as any residual payments resulting from a nonassignable plan or arrangement that, upon the surviving spouse's death, are payable to the spouse's estate or to successor beneficiaries.

(3) *Trust ceases to qualify as QDOT.* If a taxable event occurs as a result of the trust ceasing to qualify as a QDOT (for example, the trust ceases to have at least one U.S. Trustee), the amount subject to tax is

the fair market value of the trust assets on the date of disqualification.

(c) Distributions and dispositions not subject to tax. (1) *Distributions of principal on account of hardship.* Section 2056A(b)(3)(B) provides an exemption from the section 2056A estate tax for distributions to the surviving spouse on account of hardship. A distribution of principal is treated as made on account of hardship if the distribution is made to the spouse from the QDOT in response to an immediate and substantial financial need relating to the spouse's health, maintenance, education, or support, or the health, maintenance, education, or support of any person that the surviving spouse is legally obligated to support. A distribution is not treated as made on account of hardship if the amount distributed may be obtained from other sources that are reasonably available to the surviving spouse; e.g., the sale by the surviving spouse of personally owned, publicly traded stock or the cashing in of a certificate of deposit owned by the surviving spouse. Assets such as closely held business interests, real estate and tangible personalty are not considered sources that are reasonably available to the surviving spouse. Although a hardship distribution of principal is exempt from the section 2056A estate tax, it must be reported on Form 706-QDT even if it is the only distribution that occurred during the filing period. See § 20.2056A–11 regarding filing requirements for Form 706-QDT.

(2) *Distributions of income to the surviving spouse.* Section 2056A(b)(3)(A) provides an exemption from the section 2056A estate tax for distributions of income to the surviving spouse. In general, for purposes of section 2056A(b)(3)(A), the term income has the same meaning as is provided in section 643(b), except that income does not include capital gains. In addition, income does not include any other item that would be allocated to corpus under applicable local law governing the administration of trusts irrespective of any specific trust provision to the contrary. However, distributions made to the surviving spouse as the income beneficiary in conformance with applicable local law that defines the term income as a unitrust amount (or permits a right to income to be satisfied by such an amount), or that permits the trustee to adjust between principal and income to fulfill the trustee's duty of impartiality between income and principal beneficiaries, will be considered distributions of trust income if applicable local law provides for a reasonable apportionment between the income and remainder beneficiaries of the total return of the trust and meets the requirements of § 1.643(b)–1 of this chapter. In cases where there is no specific statutory or case law regarding the allocation of such items under the law governing the administration of the QDOT, the allocation under this paragraph (c)(2) will be governed by general principles of law (including but not limited to any uniform state acts, such as the Uniform Principal and Income Act, or any Restatements of applicable law). Further, except as provided in this paragraph (c)(2) or in administrative guidance published by the Internal Revenue Service, income does not include items constituting income in respect of a decedent (IRD) under section 691. However, in cases where a QDOT is designated by the decedent as a beneficiary of a pension or profit sharing plan described in section 401(a) or an individual retirement account or annuity described in section 408, the proceeds of which are payable to the QDOT in the form of an annuity, any payments received by the QDOT may be allocated between income and corpus using the method prescribed under § 20.2056A–4(c) for determining the corpus and income portion of an annuity payment.

(3) *Certain miscellaneous distributions and dispositions.* Certain miscellaneous distributions and dispositions of trust assets are exempt from the section 2056A estate tax, including but not limited to the following—

(i) Payments for ordinary and necessary expenses of the QDOT (including bond premiums and letter of credit fees);

(ii) Payments to applicable governmental authorities for income tax or any other applicable tax imposed on the QDOT (other than a payment of the section 2056A estate tax due on the occurrence of a taxable event as described in paragraph (b) of this section);

(iii) Dispositions of trust assets by the trustees (such as sales, exchanges, or pledging as collateral) for full and adequate consideration in money or money's worth; and

(iv) Pursuant to section 2056A(b)(15), amounts paid from the QDOT to reimburse the surviving spouse for any tax imposed on the spouse under Subtitle A of the Internal Revenue Code on any item of income of the QDOT to which the surviving spouse is not entitled under the terms of the trust. Such distributions include (but are not limited to) amounts paid from the QDOT to reimburse the spouse for income taxes paid by the spouse (either by actual payment or through withholding) with respect to amounts received from a nonassignable annuity or other arrangement that are transferred by the spouse to a QDOT pursuant to § 20.2056A–4(c)(3); and income taxes paid by the spouse (either by actual payment or through withholding) with respect to amounts received in a lump sum distribution from a qualified plan if the lump sum distribution is assigned by the surviving spouse to a QDOT. For purposes of this paragraph (c)(3)(iv), the amount of attributable tax eligible for reimbursement is the difference between the actual income tax liability of the spouse and the spouse's income tax liability determined as if the item had not been included in the spouse's gross income in the applicable taxable year.

[T.D. 8612, 60 FR 43546, Aug. 22, 1995; T.D. 9102, 69 FR 21, Jan. 2, 2004]

§ 20.2056A–6 Amount of tax.

(a) Definition of tax. Section 2056A(b)(2) provides for the computation of the section 2056A estate tax. For purposes of sections 2056A(b)(2)(A)(i) and (ii), in determining the tax that would have been imposed under section 2001 on the estate of the first decedent, the rates in effect on the date of the first decedent's death are used. For this purpose, the provisions of section 2001(c)(2) (pertaining to phaseout of graduated rates and unified credit) apply. In addition, for purposes of sections 2056A(b)(2)(A)(i) and (ii), the tax which would have been imposed by section 2001 on the estate of the decedent means the net tax determined under section 2001 or 2101, as the case may be, after allowance of any allowable credits, including the unified credit allowable under section 2010, the credit for state death taxes under section 2011, the credit for tax on prior transfers under section 2013, and the credit for foreign death taxes under section 2014. See paragraph (b)(4) of this section regarding the application of the credits under sections 2011 and 2014. In the case of a decedent nonresident not a citizen of the United States, the applicable credits are determined under section 2102. The estate tax (net of any applicable credits) imposed under section 2056A(b)(1) constitutes an estate tax for purposes of section 691(c)(2)(A).

(b) Benefits allowed in determining amount of section 2056A estate tax. (1) *General rule.* Section 2056A(b)(10) provides for the allowance of certain benefits in computing the section 2056A estate tax. Except as provided in this section, the rules of each of the credit, deduction and deferral provisions, as provided in the Internal Revenue Code must be complied with.

(2) *Treatment as resident.* For purposes of section 2056A(b)(10)(A), a noncitizen spouse is treated as a resident of the United States for purposes of determining whether the QDOT property is includible in the spouse's gross estate under chapter 11 of the Internal Revenue Code, and for purposes of determining whether any of the credits, deductions or deferral provisions are allowable with respect to the QDOT property to the estate of the spouse.

(3) *Special rule in the case of trusts described in section 2056(b)(8).* In the case of a QDOT in which the spouse's interest qualifies for a marital deduction under section 2056(b)(8), the provisions of section 2056A(b)(10)(A) apply in determining the allowance of a charitable deduction in computing the section 2056A estate tax, notwithstanding that the QDOT is not includible in the spouse's gross estate.

(4) *Credit for state and foreign death taxes.* If the assets of the QDOT are included in the surviving spouse's gross estate for federal estate tax purposes, or would have been so includible if the spouse had been a United States resident, and state or foreign death taxes are paid by the spouse's estate with respect to the QDOT, the taxes paid by the spouse's estate with respect to the QDOT are creditable, to the extent allowable under section 2011 or 2014, as applicable, in computing the section 2056A estate tax. In addition, state or foreign death taxes previously paid by the decedent/transferor's estate are also creditable in computing the section 2056A estate tax to the extent allowable under sections 2011 and 2014. Specifically, the tax that would have been imposed on the decedent's estate if the taxable estate had been increased by the value of the QDOT assets on the spouse's death plus the amount involved in prior taxable events (section 2056A(b)(2)(A)(i)), is determined after allowance of a credit equal to the lesser of the state or foreign death tax previously paid by the decedent's estate, or the amount prescribed under section 2011(b) or 2014(b) computed based on a taxable estate increased by such

amounts. Similarly, the tax that would have been imposed on the decedent's estate if the taxable estate had been increased only by the amount involved in prior taxable events (section 2056A(b)(2)(A)(ii)) is determined after allowance of a credit equal to the lesser of the state or foreign death tax previously paid by the decedent's estate, or the amount prescribed under section 2011(b) or 2014(b) computed based on a taxable estate increased by the amount involved in such prior taxable events. See paragraph (d), Example 2, of this section.

(5) *Alternate valuation and special use valuation.* (i) *In general.* In order to claim the benefits of alternate valuation under section 2032, or special use valuation under section 2032A, for purposes of computing the section 2056A estate tax, an election must be made on the Form 706-QDT that is filed with respect to the balance remaining in the QDOT upon the death of the surviving spouse. In addition, the separate requirements for making the section 2032 and/or section 2032A elections under those sections and the regulations thereunder must be complied with except that, for this purpose, the surviving spouse is treated as a resident of the United States regardless of the surviving spouse's actual residency status. Solely for purposes of this paragraph (b)(5), the citizenship of the first decedent is immaterial.

(ii) *Alternate valuation.* For purposes of the alternate valuation election under section 2032, the election may not be made unless the election decreases both the value of the property remaining in the QDOT upon the death of the surviving spouse and the net amount of section 2056A estate tax due. Once made, the election is irrevocable.

(iii) *Special use valuation.* For purposes of section 2032A, the Designated Filer (in the case of multiple QDOTs) or the U.S. Trustee may elect to value certain farm and closely held business real property at its farm or business use value, rather than its fair market value, if all of the requirements under section 2032A and the applicable regulations are met, except that, for this purpose, the surviving spouse is treated as a resident of the United States regardless of the spouse's actual residency status. The total value of property valued under section 2032A in the QDOT cannot be decreased from fair market value by more than $750,000.

(c) Miscellaneous rules. See sections 2056A(b)(2)(B)(i) and 2056A(b)(2)(C) for special rules regarding the appropriate rate of tax. See section 2056A(b)(2)(B)(ii) for provisions regarding a credit or refund with respect to the section 2056A estate tax.

(d) Examples. [*Omitted. Ed.*]

* * *

[T.D. 8612, 60 FR 43547, Aug. 22, 1995]

§ 20.2056A–7 Allowance of prior transfer credit under section 2013. [*Omitted. Ed.*]

[T.D. 8612, 60 FR 43549, Aug. 22, 1995]

§ 20.2056A–8 Special rules for joint property.

(a) Inclusion in gross estate. (1) *General rule.* If property is held by the decedent and the surviving spouse of the decedent as joint tenants with right of survivorship, or as tenants by the entirety, and the surviving spouse is not a United States citizen (or treated as a United States citizen) at the time of the decedent's death, the property is subject to inclusion in the decedent's gross estate in accordance with the rules of section 2040(a) (general rule for includibility of joint interests), and section 2040(b) (special rule for includibility of certain joint interests of husbands and wives) does not apply. Accordingly, the rules contained in section 2040(a) and § 20.2040–1 govern the extent to which such joint interests are includible in the gross estate of a decedent who was a citizen or resident of the United States. Under § 20.2040–1(a)(2), the entire value of jointly held property is included in the decedent's gross estate unless the executor submits facts sufficient to show that property was not entirely acquired with consideration furnished by the decedent, or was acquired by the decedent and the other joint owner by gift, bequest, devise or inheritance. If the decedent is a nonresident not a citizen of the United States, the rules of this paragraph (a)(1) apply pursuant to sections 2103, 2031, 2040(a), and 2056(d)(1)(B).

(2) *Consideration furnished by surviving spouse.* For purposes of applying section 2040(a), in determining the amount of consideration furnished by the surviving spouse, any consideration furnished by the decedent with respect to the property before July 14, 1988, is treated as consideration furnished by the surviving spouse to the extent that the consideration was treated as a gift to the spouse under section 2511, or to the extent that the decedent elected to treat the transfer

as a gift to the spouse under section 2515 (to the extent applicable). For purposes of determining whether the consideration was a gift by the decedent under section 2511, it is presumed that the decedent was a citizen of the United States at the time the consideration was so furnished to the spouse. The special rule of this paragraph (a)(2) is applicable only if the donor spouse predeceases the donee spouse and not if the donee spouse predeceases the donor spouse. In cases where the donee spouse predeceases the donor spouse, any portion of the consideration treated as a gift to the donee spouse/decedent on the creation of the tenancy (or subsequently thereafter), regardless of the date the tenancy was created, is not treated as consideration furnished by the donee spouse/decedent for purposes of section 2040(a).

(3) *Amount allowed to be transferred to QDOT.* If, as a result of the application of the rules described above, only a portion of the value of a jointly-held property interest is includible in a decedent's gross estate, only that portion that is so includible may be transferred to a QDOT under section 2056(d)(2). See § 20.2056A–4(b)(1) and (d), Example 3.

(b) Surviving spouse becomes citizen. Paragraph (a) of this section does not apply if the surviving spouse meets the requirements of section 2056(d)(4). For the definition of resident in applying section 2056(d)(4), see § 20.0–1(b).

(c) Examples. The provisions of this section are illustrated by the following examples:

Example (1). In 1987, D, a United States citizen, purchases real property and takes title in the names of D and S, D's spouse (a noncitizen, but a United States resident), as joint tenants with right of survivorship. In accordance with § 25.2511–1(h)(5) of this chapter, one-half of the value of the property is a gift to S. D dies in 1995. Because S is not a United States citizen, the provisions of section 2040(a) are determinative of the extent to which the real property is includible in D's gross estate. Because the joint tenancy was established before July 14, 1988, and under the applicable provisions of the Internal Revenue Code and regulations the transfer was treated as a gift of one-half of the property, one-half of the value of the property is deemed attributable to consideration furnished by S for purposes of section 2040(a). Accordingly, only one-half of the value of the property is includible in D's gross estate under section 2040(a).

Example (2). The facts are the same as in Example 1, except that S dies in 1995 survived by D who is not a citizen of the United States. For purposes of applying section 2040(a), D's gift to S on the creation of the tenancy is not treated as consideration furnished by S toward the acquisition of the property. Accordingly, since S made no other contributions with respect to the property, no portion of the property is includible in S's gross estate.

Example (3). The facts are the same as in Example 1, except that D and S purchase real property in 1990 making the down payment with funds from a joint bank account. All subsequent mortgage payments and improvements are paid from the joint bank account. The only funds deposited in the joint bank account are the earnings of D and S. It is established that D earned approximately 60% of the funds and S earned approximately 40% of the funds. D dies in 1995. The establishment of S's contribution to the joint bank account is sufficient to show that S contributed 40% of the consideration for the property. Thus, under paragraph § 20.2040–1(a)(2), 60% of the value of the property is includible in D's gross estate.

[T.D. 8612, 60 FR 43549, Aug. 22, 1995]

§ 20.2056A–9 Designated filer.

Section 2056A(b)(2)(C) provides special rules where more than one QDOT is established with respect to a decedent. The designation of a person responsible for filing a return under section 2056A(b)(2)(C)(i) (the Designated Filer) must be made on the decedent's federal estate tax return, or on the first Form 706-QDT that is due and is filed by its prescribed date, including extensions. The Designated Filer must be a U.S. Trustee. If the U.S. Trustee is an individual, that individual must have a tax home (as defined in section 911(d)(3)) in the United States. At least sixty days before the due date for filing the tax returns for all of the QDOTs, the U.S. Trustee(s) of each of the QDOTs must provide to the Designated Filer all of the necessary information relating to distributions from their respective QDOTs. The section 2056A estate tax due from each QDOT is allocated on a pro rata basis (based on the ratio of the amount of each respective distribution constituting a taxable event to the amount of all such distributions), unless a different allocation is required under the terms of the governing instrument or under local law. Unless the decedent has provided for a successor Designated Filer, if the Designated Filer ceases to qualify as a U.S. Trustee, or otherwise becomes unable to serve as the Designated Filer, the remaining trustees of each QDOT must select a qualifying successor Designated Filer (who is also a U.S. Trustee) prior to the due date for the filing of Form 706-QDT (including extensions). The selection is to be indicated on the Form 706-QDT. Failure to select a successor Designated Filer will result in the application of section 2056A(b)(2)(C).

[T.D. 8612, 60 FR 43550, Aug. 22, 1995]

§ 20.2056A–10 Surviving spouse becomes citizen after QDOT established.

(a) Section 2056A estate tax no longer imposed under certain circumstances. Section 2056A(b)(12) provides that a QDOT is no longer subject to the imposition of the section 2056A estate tax if the surviving spouse becomes a citizen of the United States and the following conditions are satisfied—

(1) The spouse either was a United States resident (for the definition of resident for this purpose, see § 20.2056A–1(b)) at all times after the death of the decedent and before becoming a United States citizen, or no taxable distributions are made from the QDOT before the spouse becomes a United States citizen (regardless of the residency status of the spouse); and

(2) The U.S. Trustee(s) of the QDOT notifies the Internal Revenue Service and certifies in writing that the surviving spouse has become a United States citizen. Notice is to be made by filing a final Form 706-QDT on or before April 15th of the calendar year following the year in which the surviving spouse becomes a United States citizen, unless an extension of time for filing is granted under section 6081.

(b) Special election by spouse. If the surviving spouse becomes a United States citizen and the spouse is not a United States resident at all times after the death of the decedent and before becoming a United States citizen, and a tax was previously imposed under section 2056A(b)(1)(A) with respect to any distribution from the QDOT before the surviving spouse becomes a United States citizen, the estate tax imposed under section 2056A(b)(1) does not apply to distributions after the spouse becomes a citizen if—

(1) The spouse elects to treat any taxable distribution from the QDOT prior to the spouse's election as a taxable gift made by the spouse for purposes of section 2001(b)(1)(B) (referring to adjusted taxable gifts), and for purposes of determining the amount of the tax imposed by section 2501 on actual taxable gifts made by the spouse during the year in which the spouse becomes a citizen or in any subsequent year;

(2) The spouse elects to treat any previous reduction in the section 2056A estate tax by reason of the decedent's unified credit (under either section 2010 or section 2102(c)) as a reduction in the spouse's unified credit under section 2505 for purposes of determining the amount of the credit allowable with respect to taxable gifts made by the surviving spouse during the taxable year in which the spouse becomes a citizen, or in any subsequent year; and

(3) The elections referred to in this paragraph (b) are made by timely filing a Form 706-QDT on or before April 15th of the year following the year in which the surviving spouse becomes a citizen (unless an extension of time for filing is granted under section 6081) and attaching notification of the election to the return.

[T.D. 8612, 60 FR 43550, Aug. 22, 1995]

§ 20.2056A–11 Filing requirements and payment of the section 2056A estate tax.

(a) Distributions during surviving spouse's life. Section 2056A(b)(5)(A) provides the due date for payment of the section 2056A estate tax imposed on distributions during the spouse's lifetime. An extension of not more than 6 months may be obtained for the filing of Form 706-QDT under section 6081(a) if the conditions specified therein are satisfied. See also § 20.2056A–5(c)(1) regarding the requirements for filing a Form 706-QDT in the case of a distribution to the surviving spouse on account of hardship, and § 20.2056A–2T(d)(3) regarding the requirements for filing Form 706-QDT in the case of the required annual statement.

(b) Tax at death of surviving spouse. Section 2056A(b)(5)(B) provides the due date for payment of the section 2056A estate tax imposed on the death of the spouse under section 2056A(b)(1)(B). An extension of not more than 6 months may be obtained for the filing of the Form 706-QDT under section 6081(a), if the conditions specified therein are satisfied. The obtaining of an extension of time to file under section 6081(a) does not extend the time to pay the section 2056A estate tax as prescribed under section 2056A(b)(5)(B).

(c) Extension of time for paying section 2056A estate tax. (1) *Extension of time for paying tax under section 6161(a)(2).* Pursuant to sections 2056A(b)(10)(C) and 6161(a)(2), upon a showing of reasonable cause, an extension of time for a reasonable period beyond the due date may be granted to pay any part of the estate tax that is imposed upon the surviving spouse's death under section 2056A(b)(1)(B) and shown on the final Form 706-QDT, or any part of any installments of such tax payable under section 6166 (including any part of a deficiency prorated to any installment under such section). The extension may not exceed 10 years from the date prescribed for payment of the tax (or in the case of an installment or part of a deficiency prorated to an installment, if later, not beyond the date that is 12 months after the due date for the last installment). Such extension may be granted by the district director or the director of the service center where the Form 706-QDT is filed.

(2) *Extension of time for paying tax under section 6161(a)(1).* An extension of time beyond the due date to pay any part of the estate tax imposed on lifetime distributions under section 2056A(b)(1)(A), or imposed at the death of the surviving spouse under section 2056A(b)(1)(B), may be granted for a reasonable period of time, not to exceed 6 months (12 months in the case of the estate tax imposed under section 2056A(b)(1)(B) at the surviving spouse's death), by the district director or the director of the service center where the Form 706-QDT is filed.

(d) Liability for tax. Under section 2056A(b)(6), each trustee (and not solely the U.S. Trustee(s)) of a QDOT is personally liable for the amount of the estate tax imposed in the case of any taxable event under section 2056A(b)(1). In the case of multiple QDOTs with respect to the same decedent, each trustee of a QDOT is personally liable for the amount of the section 2056A estate tax imposed on any taxable event with respect to that trustee's QDOT, but is not personally liable for tax imposed with respect to taxable events involving QDOTs of which that person is not a trustee. However, the assets of any QDOT are subject to collection by the Internal Revenue Service for any tax resulting from a taxable event with respect to any other QDOT established with respect to the same decedent. The trustee may also be personally liable as a withholding agent under section 1461 or other applicable provisions of the Internal Revenue Code.

[T.D. 8612, 60 FR 43551, Aug. 22, 1995]

Proposed § 20.2056A–11 (REG–119683–22, Aug. 21, 2024) Filing requirements and payment of the section 2056A estate tax.

Section 20.2056A–11 is amended by:

1. Revising the final sentence of paragraph (a);

2. Revising the final sentence of paragraph (c)(1);

3. Revising paragraph (c)(2); and

4. Adding paragraph (e).

The revisions and addition read as follows:

§ 20.2056A–11 Filing requirements and payment of the section 2056A estate tax.

(a) * * * See also § 20.2056A–5(c)(1) regarding the requirements for filing a Form 706-QDT in the case of a distribution to the surviving spouse on account of hardship, and § 20.2056A–2(d)(3) regarding the requirements for filing Form 706-QDT in the case of the required annual statement.

* * * * *

(c) * * *

(1) * * * Such extension may be granted by the Advisory Group Managers (or their delegate or designee or as otherwise provided in IRS forms and instructions or on https://www.irs.gov).

(2) Extension of time for paying tax under section 6161(a)(1). An extension of time beyond the due date to pay any part of the estate tax imposed on lifetime distributions under section 2056A(b)(1)(A), or imposed at the death of the surviving spouse under section 2056A(b)(1)(B), or imposed at the termination of the QDOT (such as on the death or resignation of the U.S. trustee), may be granted for a reasonable period of time, not to exceed 6 months (12 months in the case of the estate tax imposed under section 2056A(b)(1)(B) at the surviving spouse's death), by the Advisory Group Managers (or their delegate or designee or as otherwise provided in IRS forms and instructions or on https://www.irs.gov).

* * * * *

(e) Applicability date. This section applies with respect to estates of decedents dying on or after [the date of publication of the final regulations in the Federal Register].

§ 20.2056A–12 Increased basis for section 2056A estate tax paid with respect to distribution from a QDOT.

Under section 2056A(b)(13), in the case of any distribution from a QDOT on which an estate tax is imposed under section 2056A(b)(1)(A), the distribution is treated as a transfer by gift for purposes of section 1015, and any estate tax paid under section 2056A(b)(1)(A) is treated as a gift tax. See § 1.1015–5(c)(4) and (5) of this chapter for rules for determining the amount by which the basis of the distributed property is increased.

[T.D. 8612, 60 FR 43551, Aug. 22, 1995]

§ 20.2056A–13 Effective dates.

Except as provided in this section, the provisions of §§ 20.2056A–1 through 20.2056A–12 are applicable with respect to estates of decedents dying after August 22, 1995. The rule in the fourth sentence of § 20.2056A–5(c)(2) regarding unitrusts and distributions of income to the surviving spouse in conformance with applicable local law is applicable to trusts for taxable years ending after January 2, 2004.

[T.D. 8612, 60 FR 43551, Aug. 22, 1995; T.D. 9102, 69 FR 21, Jan. 2, 2004]

Proposed § 20.2056A–13 (REG–119683–22, Aug. 21, 2024) Applicability dates.

Section 20.2056A–13 is amended by revising the section heading and the first sentence to read as follows:

§ 20.2056A–13 Applicability dates.

Except as provided in this section and in §§ 20.2056A–2(e), 20.2056A–4(e), and

20.2056A–11(e), the provisions of §§ 20.5056A–1 through 20.2056A–12 are applicable with respect to estates of decedents dying on or after August 22, 1995.
* * *

§ 2057. [Repealed]

§ 2058. State Death Taxes

(a) Allowance of Deduction. For purposes of the tax imposed by section 2001, the value of the taxable estate shall be determined by deducting from the value of the gross estate the amount of any estate, inheritance, legacy, or succession taxes actually paid to any State or the District of Columbia, in respect of any property included in the gross estate (not including any such taxes paid with respect to the estate of a person other than the decedent).

(b) Period of Limitations. The deduction allowed by this section shall include only such taxes as were actually paid and deduction therefor claimed before the later of—

(1) 4 years after the filing of the return required by section 6018, or

(2) if—

(A) a petition for redetermination of a deficiency has been filed with the Tax Court within the time prescribed in section 6213(a), the expiration of 60 days after the decision of the Tax Court becomes final,

(B) an extension of time has been granted under section 6161 or 6166 for payment of the tax shown on the return, or of a deficiency, the date of the expiration of the period of the extension, or

(C) a claim for refund or credit of an overpayment of tax imposed by this chapter has been filed within the time prescribed in section 6511, the latest of the expiration of—

(i) 60 days from the date of mailing by certified mail or registered mail by the Secretary to the taxpayer of a notice of the disallowance of any part of such claim,

(ii) 60 days after a decision by any court of competent jurisdiction becomes final with respect to a timely suit instituted upon such claim, or

(iii) 2 years after a notice of the waiver of disallowance is filed under section 6532(a)(3).

Notwithstanding sections 6511 and 6512, refund based on the deduction may be made if the claim for refund is filed within the period provided in the preceding sentence. Any such refund shall be made without interest.

Subchapter B. Estates of Nonresidents Not Citizens

§ 2101. Tax Imposed

(a) Imposition. Except as provided in section 2107, a tax is hereby imposed on the transfer of the taxable estate (determined as provided in section 2106) of every decedent nonresident not a citizen of the United States.

(b) Computation of tax. The tax imposed by this section shall be the amount equal to the excess (if any) of—

(1) a tentative tax computed under section 2001(c) on the sum of—

(A) the amount of the taxable estate, and

(B) the amount of the adjusted taxable gifts, over

(2) a tentative tax computed under section 2001(c) on the amount of the adjusted taxable gifts.

(c) Adjustments for taxable gifts.

(1) Adjusted taxable gifts defined. For purposes of this section, the term "adjusted taxable gifts" means the total amount of the taxable gifts (within the meaning of section 2503 as modified by section 2511) made by the decedent after December 31, 1976, other than gifts which are includible in the gross estate of the decedent.

(2) Adjustment for certain gift tax. For purposes of this section, the rules of section 2001(d) shall apply.

Regulation

§ 20.2101–1 Estates of nonresidents not citizens; tax imposed.

(a) Imposition of tax. Section 2101 imposes a tax on the transfer of the taxable estate of a nonresident who is not a citizen of the United States at the time of death. In the case of estates of decedents dying after November 10, 1988, the tax is computed at the same rates as the tax that is imposed on the transfer of the taxable estate of a citizen or resident of the United States in accordance with the provisions of sections 2101(b) and (c). For the meaning of the terms resident, nonresident, and United States, as applied to a decedent for purposes of the estate tax, see § 20.0–1(b)(1) and (2). For the liability of the executor for the payment of the tax, see section 2002. For special rules as to the phaseout of the graduated rates and unified credit, see sections 2001(c)(2) and 2101(b).

(b) Special rates in the case of certain decedents. In the case of an estate of a nonresident who was not a citizen of the United States and who died after December 31, 1976, and on or before November 10, 1988, the tax on the nonresident's taxable estate is computed using the formula provided under section 2101(b), except that the rate schedule in paragraph (c) of this section is to be used in lieu of the rate schedule in section 2001(c).

* * *

[T.D. 6296, 23 FR 4529, June 24, 1958, as amended by T.D. 7296, 38 FR 34194, Dec. 12, 1973; T.D. 8612, 60 FR 43551, Aug. 22, 1995]

§ 2102. Credits Against Tax

(a) In general. The tax imposed by section 2101 shall be credited with the amounts determined in accordance with sections 2012 and 2013 (relating to gift tax and tax on prior transfers).

(b) Unified credit.

(1) In general. A credit of $13,000 shall be allowed against the tax imposed by section 2101.

(2) Residents of possessions of the United States. In the case of a decedent who is considered to be a "nonresident not a citizen of the United States" under section 2209, the credit under this subsection shall be the greater of—

(A) $13,000, or

(B) that proportion of $46,800 which the value of that part of the decedent's gross estate which at the time of his death is situated in the United States bears to the value of his entire gross estate wherever situated.

(3) Special rules.

(A) Coordination with treaties. To the extent required under any treaty obligation of the United States, the credit allowed under this subsection shall be equal to the amount which bears the same ratio to the applicable credit amount in effect under section 2010(c) for the calendar year which includes the date of death as the value of the part of the decedent's gross estate which at the time of his death is situated in the United States bears to the value of his entire gross estate wherever situated. For purposes of the preceding sentence, property shall not be treated as situated in the United States if such property is exempt from the tax imposed by this subchapter under any treaty obligation of the United States.

(B) Coordination with gift tax unified credit. If a credit has been allowed under section 2505 with respect to any gift made by the decedent, each dollar amount contained in paragraph (1) or (2) or subparagraph (A) of this paragraph (whichever applies) shall be reduced by the amount so allowed.

(4) Limitation based on amount of tax. The credit allowed under this subsection shall not exceed the amount of the tax imposed by section 2101.

(5) Application of other credits. For purposes of subsection (a), sections 2012 and 2013, inclusive, shall be applied as if the credit allowed under this subsection were allowed under section 2010.

Regulation

§ 20.2102–1 Estates of nonresidents not citizens; credits against tax.

(a) In general. In arriving at the net estate tax payable with respect to the transfer of an estate of a nonresident who was not a citizen of the United States at the time of his death, the following credits are subtracted from the tax imposed by section 2101:

(1) The State death tax credit under section 2011, to the extent permitted by section 2102(b) and paragraph (b) of this section;

(2) The gift tax credit under section 2012; and

(3) The credit under section 2013 for tax on prior transfers.

Except as provided in section 2102(b) and paragraph (b) of this section (relating to a special limitation on the amount of the credit for State death taxes), the amount of each of these credits is determined in the same manner as that prescribed for its determination in the case of estates of citizens or residents of the United States. See §§ 20.2011–1 through 20.2013–6. Subject to the additional special limitation contained in section 2102(b) in the case of section 2015, the provisions of sections 2015 and 2016, relating respectively to the credit for death taxes on remainders and the recovery of taxes claimed as a credit, are applicable with respect to the credit for State death taxes in the case of the estates of nonresidents not citizens. However, no credit is allowed under section 2014 for foreign death taxes.

(b) Special limitation. (1) *In general.* In the case of estates of decedents dying on or after November 14, 1966, other than estates the estate tax treatment of which is subject to a Presidential proclamation made pursuant to section 2108(a), the maximum credit allowable under section 2011 for State death taxes against the tax imposed by section 2101 on the transfer of estates of nonresidents not citizens of the United States is an amount which bears the same ratio to the maximum credit computed as provided in section 2011(b) (and without regard to this special limitation) as the value of the property (determined in the same manner as that prescribed in paragraph (b) of § 20.2031–1 for the estates of citizens or residents of the United States) in respect of which a State death tax was actually paid and which is included in the gross estate under section 2103 or, if applicable, section 2107(b) bears to the value (as so determined) of the total gross estate under section 2103 or 2107(b). For purposes of this special limitation, the term "State death taxes" means the taxes described in section 2011(a) and paragraph (a) of § 20.2011–1.

(2) *Illustrations.* The application of this paragraph may be illustrated by the following examples:

Example (1). A, a nonresident not a citizen of the United States, died on February 15, 1967, owning real property in State Z valued at $50,000 and stock in various domestic corporations valued at $100,000 and not subject to death taxes in any State. State Z's inheritance tax actually paid with respect to the real property in State Z is $2,000. A's taxable estate for Federal estate tax purposes is $110,000, in respect of which the maximum credit under section 2011 would be $720 in the absence of the special limitation contained in section 2102(b). However, under section 2102(b) and this paragraph the amount of the maximum credit allowable in respect to A's estate for State death taxes is limited to the amount which bears the same ratio to $720 (the maximum credit computed as provided in section 2011(b)) as $50,000 (the value of the property in respect of which a State death tax was actually paid and which is included in A's gross estate under section 2103) bears to $150,000 (the value of A's total gross estate under section 2103). Accordingly, the maximum credit allowable under section 2102 and this section for all State death taxes actually paid is $240 ($720 * $50,000/$150,000).

Example (2). B, a nonresident not a citizen of the United States, died on January 15, 1967, owning real property in State X valued at $100,000, real property in State Y valued at $200,000, and stock in various domestic corporations valued at $300,000 and not subject to death taxes in any State. States X and Y both imposed inheritance taxes. State X has, in addition to its inheritance tax, an estate tax equal to the amount by which the maximum State death tax credit allowable to an estate against its Federal estate tax exceeds the amount of the inheritance tax imposed by State X plus the amount of death taxes paid to other States. State Y has no estate tax. The amount of the inheritance tax actually paid to State X with respect to the real property situated in State X is $4,000; the amount of the inheritance tax actually paid to State Y with respect to the real property situated in State Y is $9,000. B's taxable estate for Federal estate tax purposes is $550,000, in respect of which the maximum credit under section 2011 would be $14,400 in the absence of the special limitation contained in section 2102(b). However, under section 2102(b) and this paragraph the amount of the maximum credit allowable in respect of B's estate for State death taxes is limited to the amount which bears the same ratio to $14,400 (the maximum credit computed as provided in section 2011(b)) as $300,000 (the value of the property in respect of which a State death tax was actually paid and which is included in B's gross estate under section 2103) bears to $600,000 (the value of B's total gross estate under section 2103). Accordingly, the maximum credit allowable under section 2102 and this section for all State death taxes actually paid is $7,200 ($14,400 * $300,000/$600,000), and the estate tax of State X is not applicable to B's estate.

(c) Unified credit. (1) *In general.* Subject to paragraph (c)(2) of this section, in the case of estates of decedents dying after November 10, 1988, a unified credit of $13,000 is allowed against the tax imposed by section 2101 subject to the limitations of section 2102(c).

(2) *When treaty is applicable.* To the extent required under any treaty obligation of the United States, the estate of a nonresident not a citizen of the United States is allowed the unified credit permitted to a United States citizen or resident of $192,800, multiplied by the proportion that the total gross estate of the decedent situated in the United States bears to the decedent's total gross estate wherever situated.

(3) *Certain residents of possessions.* In the case of a decedent who is considered to be a nonresident not a citizen of the United States under section 2209, there is allowed a unified credit equal to the greater of $13,000, or $46,800 multiplied by the proportion that the decedent's gross estate situated in the United States bears to the total gross estate of the decedent wherever situated.

[T.D. 6296, 23 FR 4529, June 24, 1958; T.D. 7296, 38 FR 34194, Dec. 12, 1973; T.D. 8612, 60 FR 43552, Aug. 22, 1995]

§ 2103. Definition of Gross Estate

For the purpose of the tax imposed by section 2101, the value of the gross estate of every decedent nonresident not a citizen of the United States shall be that part of his gross estate (determined as provided in section 2031) which at the time of his death is situated in the United States.

Regulation

§ 20.2103–1 Estates of nonresidents not citizens; "entire gross estate".

The "entire gross estate" wherever situated of a nonresident who was not a citizen of the United States at the time of his death is made up in the same way as the "gross estate" of a citizen or resident of the United States. See §§ 20.2031–1 through 20.2044–1. See paragraphs (a) and (c) of § 20.2031–1 for the circumstances under which real property situated outside the United States is excluded from the gross estate of a citizen or resident of the United States. However, except as provided in section 2107(b) with respect to the estates of certain expatriates, in the case of a nonresident not a citizen, only that part of the entire gross estate which on the date of the decedent's death is situated in the United States is included in his taxable estate. In fact, property situated outside the United States need not be disclosed on the return unless section 2107 is applicable, certain deductions are claimed, or information is specifically requested. See §§ 20.2106–1, 20.2106–2, and 20.2107–1. For a description of property considered to be situated in the United States, see § 20.2104–1. For a description of property considered to be situated outside the United States, see § 20.2105–1.

[T.D. 6296, 23 FR 4529, June 24, 1958, as amended by T.D. 7296, 38 FR 34195, Dec. 12, 1973]

§ 2104. Property Within the United States

(a) Stock in corporation. For purposes of this subchapter shares of stock owned and held by a nonresident not a citizen of the United States shall be deemed property within the United States only if issued by a domestic corporation.

(b) Revocable transfers and transfers within 3 years of death. For purposes of this subchapter, any property of which the decedent has made a transfer, by trust or otherwise, within the meaning of sections 2035 to 2038, inclusive, shall be deemed to be situated in the United States, if so situated either at the time of the transfer or at the time of the decedent's death.

(c) Debt obligations. For purposes of this subchapter, debt obligations of—

(1) a United States person, or

(2) the United States, a State or any political subdivision thereof, or the District of Columbia,

owned and held by a nonresident not a citizen of the United States shall be deemed property within the United States. Deposits with a domestic branch of a foreign corporation, if such branch is engaged in the commercial banking business, shall, for purposes of this subchapter, be deemed property within the United States. This subsection shall not apply to a debt obligation to which section 2105(b) applies.

Regulation

§ 20.2104–1 Estates of nonresidents not citizens; property within the United States.

(a) In general. Property of a nonresident who was not a citizen of the United States at the time of his death is considered to be situated in the United States if it is—

(1) Real property located in the United States.

(2) Tangible personal property located in the United States, except certain works of art on loan for exhibition (see paragraph (b) of § 20.2105–1).

(3) In the case of an estate of a decedent dying before November 14, 1966, written evidence of intangible personal property which is treated as being the property itself, such as a bond for the payment of money, if it is physically located in the United States; except that this subparagraph shall not apply to obligations of the United States (but not its instrumentalities) issued before March 1, 1941, if the decedent was not engaged in business in the United States at the time of his death. See section 2106(c).

(4) Except as specifically provided otherwise in this section or in § 20.2105–1 (which specific exceptions, in the case of estates of decedents dying on or after November 14, 1966, cause this subparagraph to have relatively limited applicability), intangible personal property the written evidence of which is not treated as being the property itself, if it is issued by or enforceable against a resident of the United States or a domestic corporation or governmental unit.

(5) Shares of stock issued by a domestic corporation, irrespective of the location of the certificates (see, however, paragraph (i) of § 20.2105–1 for a special rule with respect to certain withdrawable accounts in savings and loan or similar associations).

(6) In the case of an estate of a decedent dying before November 14, 1966, moneys deposited in the United States by or for the decedent with any person carrying on the banking business, if the decedent was engaged in business in the United States at the time of his death.

(7) In the case of an estate of a decedent dying on or after November 14, 1966, except as specifically provided otherwise in paragraph (d), (i), (j), (*l*), or (m) of § 20.2105–1, any debt obligation, including a bank deposit, the primary obligor of which is—

(i) A United States person (as defined in section 7701(a)(30)), or

(ii) The United States, a State or any political subdivision thereof, the District of Columbia, or any agency or instrumentality of any such government.

This paragraph applies irrespective of whether the written evidence of the debt obligation is treated as being the property itself or whether the decedent was engaged in business in the United States at the time of his death. For purposes of this subparagraph and paragraphs (k), (*l*), and (m) of § 20.2105–1, a debt obligation on which there are two or more primary obligors shall be apportioned among such obligors, taking into account to the extent appropriate under all the facts and circumstances any choate or inchoate rights of contribution existing among such obligors with respect to the indebtedness. The term "agency or instrumentality," as used in paragraph (a)(7)(ii) of this section does not include a possession of the United States or an agency or instrumentality of a possession. Currency is not a debt obligation for purposes of this subparagraph.

(8) In the case of an estate of a decedent dying on or after January 1, 1970, except as specifically provided otherwise in paragraph (i) or (*l*) of § 20.2105–1, deposits with a branch in the United States of a foreign corporation, if the branch is engaged in the commercial banking business, whether or not the decedent was engaged in business in the United States at the time of his death.

(b) Transfers. Property of which the decedent has made a transfer taxable under sections 2035 through 2038 is deemed to be situated in the United States if it is determined, under the provisions of paragraph (a) of this section, to be so situated either at the time of the transfer or at the time of the decedent's death. See §§ 20.2035–1 through 20.2038–1.

(c) Death tax convention. It should be noted that the situs rules described in this section may be modified for various purposes under the provisions of an applicable death tax convention with a foreign country.

[T.D. 6296, 23 FR 4529, June 24, 1958, 25 FR 14021, Dec. 31, 1960, as amended by T.D. 7296, 38 FR 34195, Dec. 12, 1973; T.D. 7321, 39 FR 29597, Aug. 16, 1974]

§ 2105. Property Without the United States

(a) Proceeds of life insurance. For purposes of this subchapter, the amount receivable as insurance on the life of a nonresident not a citizen of the United States shall not be deemed property within the United States.

(b) Bank deposits and certain other debt obligations. For purposes of this subchapter, the following shall not be deemed property within the United States—

(1) amounts described in section 871(i)(3), if any interest thereon would not be subject to tax by reason of section 871(i)(1) were such interest received by the decedent at the time of his death,

(2) deposits with a foreign branch of a domestic corporation or domestic partnership, if such branch is engaged in the commercial banking business,

(3) debt obligations, if, without regard to whether a statement meeting the requirements of section 871(h)(5) has been received, any interest thereon would be eligible for the exemption from tax under section 871(h)(1) were such interest received by the decedent at the time of his death, and

(4) obligations which would be original issue discount obligations as defined in section 871(g)(1) but for subparagraph (B)(i) thereof, if any interest thereon (were such interest received by the decedent at the time of his death) would not be effectively connected with the conduct of a trade or business within the United States.

Notwithstanding the preceding sentence, if any portion of the interest on an obligation referred to in paragraph (3) would not be eligible for the exemption referred to in paragraph (3) by reason of section 871(h)(4) if the interest were received by the decedent at the time of his death, then an appropriate portion (as determined in a manner prescribed by the Secretary) of the value (as determined for purposes of this chapter) of such debt obligation shall be deemed property within the United States.

(c) Works of art on loan for exhibition. For purposes of this subchapter, works of art owned by a nonresident not a citizen of the United States shall not be deemed property within the United States if such works of art are—

(1) imported into the United States solely for exhibition purposes,

(2) loaned for such purposes, to a public gallery or museum, no part of the net earnings of which inures to the benefit of any private stockholder or individual, and

(3) at the time of the death of the owner, on exhibition, or en route to or from exhibition, in such a public gallery or museum.

* * *

Regulation

§ 20.2105–1 Estates of nonresidents not citizens; property without the United States.

Property of a nonresident who was not a citizen of the United States at the time of his death is considered to be situated outside the United States if it is—

(a)(1) Real property located outside the United States, except to the extent excludable from the entire gross estate wherever situated under § 20.2103–1.

(2) Tangible personal property located outside the United States.

(b) Works of art owned by the decedent if they were—

(1) Imported into the United States solely for exhibition purposes,

(2) Loaned for those purposes to a public gallery or museum, no part of the net earnings of which inures to the benefit of any private shareholder or individual, and

(3) At the time of the death of the owner, on exhibition, or en route to or from exhibition, in such a public gallery or museum.

(c) In the case of an estate of a decedent dying before November 14, 1966, written evidence of intangible personal property which is treated as being the property itself, such as a bond for the payment of money, if it is not physically located in the United States.

(d) Obligations of the United States issued before March 1, 1941, even though physically located in the United States, if the decedent was not engaged in business in the United States at the time of his death.

(e) Except as specifically provided otherwise in this section or in § 20.2104–1, intangible personal property the written evidence of which is not treated as being the property itself, if it is not issued by or enforceable against a resident of the United States or a domestic corporation or governmental unit.

(f) Shares of stock issued by a corporation which is not a domestic corporation, regardless of the location of the certificates.

(g) Amounts receivable as insurance on the decedent's life.

(h) In the case of an estate of a decedent dying before November 14, 1966, moneys deposited in the United States by or for the decedent with any person carrying on the banking business, if the decedent was not engaged in business in the United States at the time of his death.

(i) In the case of an estate of a decedent dying on or after November 14, 1966, and before January 1, 1976, any amount deposited in the United States which is described in section 861(c) (relating to certain bank deposits, withdrawable accounts, and amounts held by an insurance company under an agreement to pay interest), if any interest thereon, were such interest received by the decedent at the time of his death, would be treated under section 862(a)(1) as income from sources without the United States by reason of section 861(a)(1)(A) (relating to interest on amounts described in section 861(c) which is not effectively connected with the conduct of a trade or business within the United States) and the regulations thereunder. If such interest would be treated by reason of those provisions as income from sources without the United States only in part, the amount described in section 861(c) shall be considered situated outside the United States in the same proportion as the part of the interest which would be treated as income from sources without the United States bears to the total amount of the interest. This paragraph applies whether or not the decedent was engaged in business in the United States at the time of his death, and, except with respect to amounts described in section 861(c)(3) (relating to amounts held by an insurance company under an agreement to pay interest), whether or not the deposit or other amount is in fact interest bearing.

(j) In the case of an estate of a decedent dying on or after November 14, 1966, deposits with a branch outside of the United States of a domestic corporation or domestic partnership, if the branch is engaged in the commercial banking business. This paragraph applies whether or not the decedent was engaged in business in the United States at the time of his death, and whether or not the deposits, upon withdrawal, are payable in currency of the United States.

(k) In the case of an estate of a decedent dying on or after November 14, 1966, except as specifically provided otherwise in paragraph (a)(8) of § 20.2104–1 with respect to estates of decedents dying on or after January 1, 1970, any debt obligation, including a bank deposit, the primary obligor of which is neither—

(1) A United States person (as defined in section 7701(a)(30)), nor

(2) The United States, a State or any political subdivision thereof, the District of Columbia, or any agency or instrumentality of any such government.

This paragraph applies irrespective of whether the written evidence of the debt obligation is treated as being the property itself or whether the decedent was engaged in business in the United States at the time of his death. See paragraph (a)(7) of § 20.2104–1 for the treatment of a debt obligation on which there are two or more primary obligors. The term "agency or instrumentality," as used in subparagraph (2) of this paragraph, does not include a possession of the United States or an agency or instrumentality of a possession. Currency is not a debt obligation for purposes of this paragraph.

(l) In the case of an estate of a decedent dying on or after November 14, 1966, any debt obligation to the extent that the primary obligor on the debt obligation is a domestic corporation, if any interest thereon, were the interest received from such obligor by the decedent at the time of his death, would be treated under section 862(a)(1) as income from sources without the United States by reason of section 861(a)(1)(B) (relating to interest received from a domestic corporation less than 20 percent of whose gross income for a 3-year period was derived from sources within the United States) and the regulations thereunder. For such purposes the 3-year period referred to in section 861(a)(1)(B) is the period of 3 years ending with the close of the domestic corporation's last taxable year terminating before the decedent's death. This paragraph applies whether or not (1) the obligation is in fact interest bearing, (2) the written evidence of the debt obligation is treated as being the property itself, or (3) the decedent was engaged in business in the United States at the time of his death. See paragraph (a)(7) of § 20.2104–1 for the treatment of a debt obligation on which there are two or more primary obligors.

(m)(1) In the case of an estate of a decedent dying after December 31, 1972, except as otherwise provided in paragraph (m)(2) of this section any debt obligation to the extent that the primary obligor on the debt obligation is a domestic corporation or domestic partnership, if any interest thereon, were the interest received from such obligor by the decedent at the time of his death, would be treated under section 862(a)(1) as income from sources without the United States by reason of section 861(a)(1)(G) (relating to interest received on certain debt obligations with respect to which elections have been made under section 4912(c)) and the regulations thereunder. This paragraph applies whether or not (i) the obligation is in fact interest bearing, (ii) the written evidence of the debt obligation is treated as being the property itself, or (iii) the decedent was engaged in business in the United States at the time of his death. See paragraph (a)(7) of § 20.2104–1 for the treatment of a debt obligation on which there are two or more primary obligors.

(2) In the case of an estate of a decedent dying before January 1, 1974, this paragraph does not apply to any debt obligation of a foreign corporation assumed by a domestic corporation which is treated under section 4912(c)(2) as issued by such domestic corporation during 1973.

[T.D. 6296, 23 FR 4529, June 24, 1958, as amended by T.D. 6684, 28 FR 11410, Oct. 24, 1963; T.D. 7296, 38 FR 34196, Dec. 12, 1973; T.D. 7321, 39 FR 29597, Aug. 16, 1974]

§ 2106. Taxable Estate

(a) Definition of taxable estate. For purposes of the tax imposed by section 2101, the value of the taxable estate of every decedent nonresident not a citizen of the United States shall be determined by deducting from the value of that part of his gross estate which at the time of his death is situated in the United States—

(1) Expenses, losses, indebtedness, and taxes. That proportion of the deductions specified in sections 2053 and 2054 (other than the deductions described in the following sentence) which the value of such part bears to the value of his entire gross estate, wherever situated. Any deduction allowable under section 2053 in the case of a claim against the estate which was founded on a promise or agreement but was not contracted for an adequate and full consideration in money or money's worth shall be allowable under this paragraph to the extent that it would be allowable as a deduction under paragraph (2) if such promise or agreement constituted a bequest.

(2) Transfers for public, charitable, and religious uses.

(A) In general. The amount of all bequests, legacies, devises, or transfers (including the interest which falls into any such bequest, legacy, devise, or transfer as a result of an irrevocable disclaimer of a bequest, legacy, devise, transfer, or power, if the disclaimer is made before the date prescribed for the filing of the estate tax return)—

(i) to or for the use of the United States, any State, any political subdivision thereof, or the District of Columbia, for exclusively public purposes;

(ii) to or for the use of any domestic corporation organized and operated exclusively for religious, charitable, scientific, literary, or educational purposes, including the encouragement of art and the prevention of cruelty to children or animals, no part of the net earnings of which inures to the benefit of any private stockholder or individual, which is not disqualified for tax exemption under section 501(c)(3) by reason of attempting to influence legislation, and which does not participate in, or intervene in (including the publishing or distributing of statements), any political campaign on behalf of (or in opposition to) any candidate for public office; or

(iii) to a trustee or trustees, or a fraternal society, order, or association operating under the lodge system, but only if such contributions or gifts are to be used within the United States by such trustee or trustees, or by such fraternal society, order, or association, exclusively for religious, charitable, scientific, literary, or educational purposes, or for the prevention of cruelty to children or animals, such trust, fraternal society, order, or association would not be disqualified for tax exemption under section 501(c)(3) by reason of attempting to influence legislation, and such trustee or trustees, or such fraternal society, order, or association, does not participate in, or intervene in (including the publishing or distributing of statements), any political campaign on behalf of (or in opposition to) any candidate for public office;

(B) Powers of appointment. Property includible in the decedent's gross estate under section 2041 (relating to powers of appointment) received by a donee described in this paragraph shall, for purposes of this paragraph, be considered a bequest of such decedent.

(C) Death taxes payable out of bequests. If the tax imposed by section 2101, or any estate, succession, legacy, or inheritance taxes, are, either by the terms of the will, by the law of the jurisdiction under which the estate is administered, or by the law of the jurisdiction imposing the particular tax, payable in whole or in part out of the bequests, legacies, or devises otherwise deductible under this paragraph, then the amount deductible under this paragraph shall be the amount of such bequests, legacies, or devises reduced by the amount of such taxes.

(D) Limitation on deduction. The amount of the deduction under this paragraph for any transfer shall not exceed the value of the transferred property required to be included in the gross estate.

(E) Disallowance of deductions in certain cases. The provisions of section 2055(e) shall be applied in the determination of the amount allowable as a deduction under this paragraph.

(F) Cross references.

(i) For option as to time for valuation for purposes of deduction under this section, see section 2032.

(ii) For exemption of certain bequests for the benefit of the United States and for rules of construction for certain bequests, see section 2055(g).

(iii) For treatment of gifts and bequests to or for the use of Indian tribal governments (or their subdivisions), see section 7871.

(3) Marital deduction. The amount which would be deductible with respect to property situated in the United States at the time of the decedent's death under the principles of section 2056.

(4) State death taxes. The amount which bears the same ratio to the State death taxes as the value of the property, as determined for purposes of this chapter, upon which State death taxes were paid and which is included in the gross estate under section 2103 bears to the value of the total gross estate under section 2103. For purposes of this paragraph, the term "State death taxes" means the taxes described in section 2058(a).

(b) Condition of allowance of deductions. No deduction shall be allowed under paragraphs (1) and (2) of subsection (a) in the case of a nonresident not a citizen of the United States unless the executor includes in the return required to be filed under section 6018 the value at the time of his death of that part of the gross estate of such nonresident not situated in the United States.

Regulations

§ 20.2106–1 Estates of nonresidents not citizens; taxable estate; deductions in general.

(a) The taxable estate of a nonresident who was not a citizen of the United States at the time of his death is determined by adding the value of that part of his gross estate which, at the time of his death, is situated in the United States and, in the case of an estate to which section 2107 (relating to expatriation to avoid tax) applies, any amounts includible in his gross estate under section 2107(b), and then subtracting from the sum thereof the total amount of the following deductions:

(1) The deductions allowed in the case of estates of decedents who were citizens or residents of the United States under sections 2053 and 2054 (see §§ 20.2053–1 through 20.2053–9 and § 20.2054–1) for expenses, indebtedness and taxes, and for losses, to the extent provided in § 20.2106–2.

(2) A deduction computed in the same manner as the one allowed under section 2055 (see §§ 20.2055–1 through 20.2055–5) for charitable, etc., transfers, except—

(i) That the deduction is allowed only for transfers to corporations and associations created or organized in the United States, and to trustees for use within the United States, and

(ii) That the provisions contained in paragraph (c)(2) of § 20.2055–2 relating to termination of a power to consume are not applicable.

(3) Subject to the special rules set forth at § 20.2056A–1(c), the amount which would be deductible with respect to property situated in the United States at the time of the decedent's death under the principles of section 2056. Thus, if the surviving spouse of the decedent is a citizen of the United States at the time of the decedent's death, a marital deduction is allowed with respect to the estate of the decedent if all other applicable requirements of section 2056 are satisfied. If the surviving spouse of the decedent is not a citizen of the United States at the time of the decedent's death, the provisions of section 2056, including specifically the provisions of section 2056(d) and (unless section 2056(d)(4) applies) the provisions of section 2056A (QDOTs) must be satisfied.

(b) Section 2106(b) provides that no deduction is allowed under paragraph (a)(1) or (2) of this section unless the executor discloses in the estate tax return the value of that part of the gross estate not situated in the United States. See § 20.2105–1. Such part must be valued as of the date of the decedent's death, or if the alternate valuation method under section 2032 is elected, as of the applicable valuation date.

[T.D. 6296, 23 FR 5429, June 24, 1958, as amended by T.D. 6526, 26 FR 417, Jan. 19, 1961; T.D. 7296, 38 FR 34197, Dec. 12, 1973; T.D. 7318, 39 FR 25457, July 11, 1974; T.D. 8612, 60 FR 43552, Aug. 22, 1995]

§ 20.2106–2 Estates of nonresidents not citizens; deductions for expenses, losses, etc.

(a) In computing the taxable estate of a nonresident who was not a citizen of the United States at the time of his death, deductions are allowed under sections 2053 and 2054 for expenses, indebtedness and taxes, and for losses, to the following extent:

(1) A pledge or subscription is deductible if it is an enforceable claim against the estate and if it would constitute an allowable deduction under paragraph (a)

(2) of § 20.2106–1, relating to charitable, etc., transfers, if it had been a bequest.

(2) That proportion of other deductions under sections 2053 and 2054 is allowed which the value of that part of the decedent's gross estate situated in the United States at the time of his death bears to the value of the decedent's entire gross estate wherever situated. It is immaterial whether the amounts to be deducted were incurred or expended within or without the United States. For purposes of this subparagraph, an amount which is includible in the decedent's gross estate under section 2107(b) with respect to stock in a foreign corporation shall be included in the value of the decedent's gross estate situated in the United States.

No deduction is allowed under this paragraph unless the value of the decedent's entire gross estate is disclosed in the estate tax return. See paragraph (b) of § 20.2106–1.

(b) In order that the Internal Revenue Service may properly pass upon the items claimed as deductions, the executor should submit a certified copy of the schedule of liabilities, claims against the estate, and expenses of administration filed under any applicable foreign death duty act. If no such schedule was filed, the executor should submit a certified copy of the schedule of these liabilities, claims and expenses filed with the foreign court in which administration was had. If the items of deduction allowable under section 2106(a)(1) were not included in either such schedule, or if no such schedules were filed, then there should be submitted a written statement of the foreign executor containing a declaration that it is made under the penalties of perjury setting forth the facts relied upon as entitling the estate to the benefit of the particular deduction or deductions.

[T.D. 6296, 23 FR 4529, June 24, 1958; 25 FR 14021, Dec. 31, 1960, as amended by T.D. 7296, 38 FR 34197, Dec. 12, 1973; T.D. 8612, 60 FR 43552, Aug. 22, 1995]

§ 2107. Expatriation to Avoid Tax

(a) Treatment of expatriates. A tax computed in accordance with the table contained in section 2001 is hereby imposed on the transfer of the taxable estate, determined as provided in section 2106, of every decedent nonresident not a citizen of the United States if the date of death occurs during a taxable year with respect to which the decedent is subject to tax under section 877(b).

(b) Gross estate. For purposes of the tax imposed by subsection (a), the value of the gross estate of every decedent to whom subsection (a) applies shall be determined as provided in section 2103, except that—

(1) if such decedent owned (within the meaning of section 958(a)) at the time of his death 10 percent or more of the total combined voting power of all classes of stock entitled to vote of a foreign corporation, and

(2) if such decedent owned (within the meaning of section 958(a)), or is considered to have owned (by applying the ownership rules of section 958(b)), at the time of his death, more than 50 percent of—

(A) the total combined voting power of all classes of stock entitled to vote of such corporation, or

(B) the total value of the stock of such corporation,

then that proportion of the fair market value of the stock of such foreign corporation owned (within the meaning of section 958(a)) by such decedent at the time of his death, which the fair market value of any assets owned by such foreign corporation and situated in the United States, at the time of his death, bears to the total fair market value of all assets owned by such foreign corporation at the time of his death, shall be included in the gross estate of such decedent. For purposes of the preceding sentence, a decedent shall be treated as owning stock of a foreign corporation at the time of his death if, at the time of a transfer, by trust or otherwise, within the meaning of sections 2035 to 2038, inclusive, he owned such stock.

(c) Credits.

(1) Unified credit.

(A) In general. A credit of $13,000 shall be allowed against the tax imposed by subsection (a).

(B) Limitation based on amount of tax. The credit allowed under this paragraph shall not exceed the amount of the tax imposed by subsection (a).

(2) Credit for foreign death taxes.

(A) In general. The tax imposed by subsection (a) shall be credited with the amount of any estate, inheritance, legacy, or succession taxes actually paid to any foreign country in respect of any property which is included in the gross estate solely by reason of subsection (b).

(B) Limitation on credit. The credit allowed by subparagraph (A) for such taxes paid to a foreign country shall not exceed the lesser of—

(i) the amount which bears the same ratio to the amount of such taxes actually paid to such foreign country as the value of the property subjected to such taxes by such foreign country and included in the gross estate solely by reason of subsection (b) bears to the value of all property subjected to such taxes by such foreign country, or

(ii) such property's proportionate share of the excess of—

(I) the tax imposed by subsection (a), over

(II) the tax which would be imposed by section 2101 but for this section.

(C) Proportionate share. In the case of property which is included in the gross estate solely by reason of subsection (b), such property's proportionate share is the percentage which the value of such property bears to the total value of all property included in the gross estate solely by reason of subsection (b).

(3) Other credits. The tax imposed by subsection (a) shall be credited with the amounts determined in accordance with subsections (a) and (b) of section 2102. For purposes of subsection (a) of section 2102, sections 2012 and 2013, inclusive, shall be applied as if the credit allowed under paragraph (1) were allowed under section 2010.

(d) Burden of proof. If the Secretary establishes that it is reasonable to believe that an individual's loss of United States citizenship would, but for this section, result in a substantial reduction in the estate, inheritance, legacy, and succession taxes in respect of the transfer of his estate, the burden of proving that such loss of citizenship did not have for one of its principal purposes the avoidance of taxes under this subtitle or subtitle A shall be on the executor of such individual's estate.

(e) Cross reference. For comparable treatment of long-term lawful permanent residents who ceased to be taxed as residents, see section 877(e).

Regulation

§ 20.2107–1 Expatriation to avoid tax.

(a) Rate of tax. The tax imposed by section 2107(a) on the transfer of the taxable estates of certain nonresident expatriate decedents who were formerly citizens of the United States is computed in accordance with the table contained in section 2001, relating to the rate of the tax imposed on the transfer of the taxable estates of decedents who were citizens or residents of the United States. Except for any amounts included in the gross estate solely by reason of section 2107(b) and paragraph (b)(1)(ii) and (iii) of this section, the value of the taxable estate to be used in this computation is determined as provided in section 2106 and § 20.2106–1. The decedents to which section 2107(a) and this section apply are described in paragraph (d) of this section.

(b) Gross estate. (1) *Determination of value.* (i) *General rule.* Except as provided in subdivision (ii) of this subparagraph with respect to stock in certain foreign corporations, for purposes of the tax imposed by section 2107(a) the value of the gross estate of every estate the transfer of which is subject to the tax imposed by that section is determined as provided in section 2103 and § 20.2103–1.

(ii) *Amount includible with respect to stock in certain foreign corporations.* If at the time of his death a nonresident expatriate decedent the transfer of whose estate is subject to the tax imposed by section 2107(a)—

(a) Owned (within the meaning of section 958(a) and the regulations thereunder) 10 percent or more of the total combined voting power of all classes of stock entitled to vote in a foreign corporation, and

(b) Owned (within the meaning of section 958(a) and the regulations thereunder), or is considered to have owned (by applying the ownership rules of section 958(b) and the regulations thereunder), more than 50 percent of the total combined voting power of all classes of stock entitled to vote in such foreign corporation, then section 2107(b) requires the inclusion in the decedent's gross estate, in addition to amounts otherwise includible therein under subdivision (i) of this subparagraph, of an amount equal to that proportion of the fair market value (determined at the time of the decedent's death or, if so elected by the executor of the decedent's estate, on the alternate valuation date as provided in section 2032) of the stock in such foreign corporation owned (within the meaning of section 958(a) and the regulations thereunder) by the decedent at the time of his death, which the fair market value of any assets owned by such foreign corporation and situated in the United States, at the time of his death, bears to the total fair market value of all assets owned by such foreign corporation at the time of his death.

(iii) *Rules of application.* (a) In determining the proportion of the fair market value of the stock which is includible in the gross estate under subdivision (ii) of this subparagraph, the fair market value of the foreign corporation's assets situated in the United States and of its total assets shall be determined without reduction for any outstanding liabilities of the corporation.

(b) For purposes of subdivision (ii) of this subparagraph, the foreign corporation's assets which are situated in the United States shall be all its property which, by applying the provisions of sections 2104, 2105, and §§ 20.2104–1 and 20.2105–1, would be considered to be situated in the United States if such property were property of a nonresident who was not a citizen of the United States.

(c) For purposes of subdivision (ii)(a) of this subparagraph, a decedent is treated as owning stock in a foreign corporation at the time of his death to the extent he owned (within the meaning of section 958(a) and the regulations thereunder) the stock at the time he made a transfer of the stock in a transfer described in sections 2035 to 2038, inclusive (relating respectively to transfers made in contemplation of death, transfers with a retained life estate, transfers taking effect at death, and revocable transfers). For purposes of subdivision (ii)(b) of this subparagraph, a decedent is treated as owning stock in a foreign corporation at the time of his death to the extent he owned (within the meaning of section 958(a) and the regulations thereunder), or is considered to have owned (by applying the ownership rules of section 958(b) and the regulations thereunder), the stock at the time he made a transfer of the stock in a transfer described in sections 2035 to 2038, inclusive. In applying the proportion rule of section 2107(b) and subdivision (ii) of this subparagraph where a decedent is treated as owning stock in a foreign corporation at the time of his death by reason of having transferred his interest in such stock in a transfer described in sections 2035 to 2038, inclusive, the proportionate value of the interest includible in his gross estate is based upon the value as of the applicable valuation date described in section 2031 or 2032 of the amount, determined as of the date of transfer, of his interest in the stock. See example (2) in subparagraph (2) of this paragraph.

(d) For purposes of applying subdivision (ii)(b) of this subparagraph, the same shares of stock may not be counted more than once. See example (2) in subparagraph (2) of this paragraph.

(e) The principles applied in paragraph (b) of § 1.957–1 of this chapter (Income Tax Regulations) for determining what constitutes total combined voting power of all classes of stock entitled to vote in a foreign corporation for purposes of section 957(a) shall be applied in determining what constitutes total combined voting power of all classes of stock entitled to vote in a foreign corporation for purposes of section 2107(b) and subdivision (ii) of this subparagraph. In applying such principles under this paragraph changes in language shall be made, where necessary, in order to treat the nonresident expatriate decedent, rather than U.S. shareholders, as owning such total combined voting power.

(2) *Illustrations.* The application of this paragraph may be illustrated by the following examples:

Example (1). (a) At the time of his death, H, a nonresident expatriate decedent the transfer of whose estate is subject to the tax imposed by section 2107(a), owned a 60-percent interest in M Company, a foreign partnership, which in turn owned stock issued by N Corporation, a foreign corporation. The stock in N Corporation held by M Company, which constituted 50 percent of the total combined voting power of all classes of stock entitled to vote in N Corporation, was valued at $50,000 at the time of H's death. In addition, W, H's wife, also a nonresident not a citizen of the United States, owned at the time of H's death stock in N Corporation constituting 25 percent of the total combined voting power of all classes of stock entitled to vote in that corporation. The fair market value of the assets of N Corporation which, at the time of H's death, were situated in the United States constituted 40 percent of the fair market value of all assets of that corporation. It is assumed for purposes of this example that the executor of H's estate has not elected to value the estate on the alternate valuation date provided in section 2032.

(b) The test contained in subparagraph (1)(ii)(a) of this paragraph is met since at the time of his death H indirectly owned (within the meaning of section 958(a) and the regulations thereunder) 30 percent (60 percent of 50 percent) of the total combined voting power of all classes of stock entitled to vote in N Corporation; and the test contained in subparagraph (1)(ii)(b) of this paragraph is met since at such time H owned or is considered to have owned (within the meaning of section 958 (a) and (b) and the regulations thereunder) 55 percent of the total combined voting power of all classes of stock entitled to vote in N Corporation (having constructive ownership of his wife's 25 percent, in addition to his own indirect ownership of 30 percent, of the total combined voting power). Accordingly, $12,000 is included in H's gross estate by reason of section 2107(b) and this paragraph. This $12,000 is the amount which is equal to 40 percent (the percentage of the fair market value of N Corporation's asset which were situated within the United States at H's death) of $30,000 (the fair market value of the stock then owned by H within the meaning of section 958(a) and the regulations thereunder, i.e., H's 60-percent interest in the $50,000 fair market value of stock held by M Company).

Example (2). (a) Assume the same facts as those given in example (1) except that H made a transfer to W in contemplation of his death (within the meaning of section 2035) of his 60-percent interest in M Company, that on the date of the transfer M Company held stock in N Corporation constituting 80 percent of the total combined voting power of all classes of stock entitled to vote in that corporation (rather than the 50 percent of total combined voting power held by M Company on the date of H's death), and that the 80 percent of total combined voting power owned by M Company on the date of the transfer is valued at $70,000 on that date and at $85,000 at the time of H's death. It is assumed for purposes of this example that the 60-percent interest in M Company was held by W at the time of H's death.

(b) The test contained in subparagraph (1)(ii)(a) of this paragraph is met since, under subparagraph (1)(iii)(c) of this paragraph, H is treated as owning (within the meaning of section 958(a) and the regulations thereunder), at the time of his death, the 48 percent (60 percent of 80 percent) of the total combined voting power of all classes of stock entitled to vote in N Corporation represented by his transferred interest in M Company; and the test contained in subparagraph (1)(ii)(b) of this paragraph is met since, under that subparagraph and subparagraph (1)(iii)(c) of this paragraph, H is treated as owning (within the meaning of section 958 (a) or (b)), at the time of his death, 73 percent (48 percent plus 25 percent) of the total combined voting power of all classes of stock entitled to vote in N Corporation. Accordingly, $20,400 is included in H's gross estate by reason of section 2107(b) and this paragraph. This $20,400 is the amount which is equal to 40 percent (the percentage of the fair market value of N Corporation's assets which were situated within the United States at H's death) of $51,000 (the fair market value at the time of H's death of the transferred interest which under subparagraph (1)(iii)(c) of this paragraph H is considered to own within the meaning of section 958(a) and the regulations thereunder at that time, i.e., the 60-percent interest in the $85,000 fair market value at that time of the 80-percent total combined voting power held by M Company on the date of transfer).

(c) The fact that the stock in N Corporation owned by M Company is considered under subparagraph (1)(ii)(b) of this paragraph to be owned by H for two independent reasons (i.e., under section 958(a) and the regulations thereunder, because H transferred his 60-percent interest in M Company to W in contemplation of death, and under section 958(b) and the regulations thereunder, because H is considered to own the stock in N Corporation indirectly owned by his wife, W, by reason of her ownership of such transferred interest) does not cause the shares of stock represented by the transferred interest in M Company to be counted twice in determining whether the test contained in that subparagraph is met. See subparagraph (1)(iii)(d) of this paragraph.

Example (3). (a) At the time of his death, H, a nonresident expatriate decedent the transfer of whose estate is subject to the tax imposed by section 2107(a), owned a 40-percent beneficial interest in a domestic trust; at that time he also directly owned stock in P Corporation, a foreign corporation, constituting 15 percent of the total combined voting power of all classes of stock entitled to vote in that corporation. The trust owned stock in P Corporation constituting 51 percent of the total combined voting power of all classes of stock entitled to vote in that corporation. The stock in P Corporation owned directly by H was valued at $20,000 on the alternate valuation date determined pursuant to an election under section 2032. The fair market value of the assets of P Corporation which, at the time of H's death, were situated in the United States constituted 20 percent of the fair market value of all assets of that corporation.

(b) By reason of section 958(b)(2) and the regulations thereunder, the trust is considered to own all the stock entitled to vote in P Corporation since it owns more than 50 percent of the total combined voting power of all classes of stock entitled to vote in that corporation. The test contained in subparagraph (1)(ii)(a) of this paragraph is met since at the time of his death H owned (within the meaning of section 958(a) and the regulations thereunder) 15 percent of the total combined voting power of all classes of stock entitled to vote in P Corporation; the stock in P Corporation owned by the trust is not considered to have been owned by H under section 958(a)(2) since the trust is not a foreign trust. In addition, the test contained in subparagraph (1)(ii)(b) of this paragraph is met since at the time of his death H owned or is considered to have owned (within the meaning of section 958(a) and (b) and the regulations thereunder) 55 percent of the total combined voting power of all classes of stock entitled to vote in that corporation (his 15 percent directly owned plus his 40 percent (40 percent of 100 percent) considered to be owned). Accordingly, $4,000 is included in H's gross estate by reason of section 2107(b) and this paragraph. This $4,000 is the amount which is equal to 20 percent (the percentage of the fair market value of P Corporation's assets which were situated within the United States at H's death) of $20,000 (the fair market value of the stock then owned by H within the meaning of section 958(a) and the regulations thereunder). In addition, the value of H's interest in the domestic trust is included in his gross estate under section 2103 to the extent it constitutes property having a situs in the United States.

(c) Credits. Credits against the tax imposed by section 2107(a) are allowed for any amounts determined in accordance with section 2102 and § 20.2102–1 (relating to credits against the estate tax for State death taxes, gift tax, and tax on prior transfers). In computing the special limitation on the credit for State death taxes contained in section 2102(b) and paragraph (b) of § 20.2102–1, amounts included in the gross estate under section 2107(b) and paragraph (b)(1) of this section are to be taken into account.

(d) Decedents to whom the tax imposed by section 2107(a) applies. (1) *General rule.* The tax imposed by section 2107(a) applies to the transfer of the taxable estate of every decedent nonresident not a citizen of the United States dying on or after November 14, 1966, who lost his U.S. citizenship after March 8, 1965, and within the 10-year period ending with the date of his death, except in the case of the estate of a decedent whose loss of U.S. citizenship either—

(i) Resulted from the application of section 301(b), 350, or 355 of the Immigration and Nationality Act, as amended (8 U.S.C. 1401(b), 1482, or 1487); or

(ii) Did not have for one of its principal purposes (but not necessarily its only principal purpose) the avoidance of Federal income, estate, or gift tax.

Section 301(b) of the Immigration and Nationality Act provides generally that a U.S. citizen, who is born outside the United States of parents one of whom is an alien and the other is a U.S. citizen who was physically present in the United States for a specified period, shall lose his U.S. citizenship if, within a specified period preceding the age of 28 years, he fails to be continuously physically present in the United States for at least 5 years. Section 350 of that Act provides that under certain circumstances a person, who at birth acquired the nationality of the United States and of a foreign country and who has voluntarily sought or claimed benefits of the nationality of any foreign country, shall lose his U.S. nationality if, after attaining the age of 22 years, he has a continuous residence for 3 years in the foreign country of which he is a national by birth. Section 355 of that Act provides that a person having U.S. nationality, who is under 21 years of age and whose residence is in a foreign country with or under the legal custody of a parent who loses his U.S. nationality under specified circumstances, shall lose his U.S. nationality if he has or acquires the nationality of that foreign country and attains the age of 25 years without having established his residence in the United States. Section 2107 and this section do not apply to the transfer of any estate the estate tax treatment of which is subject to a Presidential proclamation made pursuant to section 2108(a) (relating to the application of pre-1967 estate tax provisions in the case of a foreign country which imposes a more burdensome tax than the United States).

(2) *Burden of proof.* (i) *General rule.* In determining for purposes of subparagraph (1)(ii) of this paragraph whether a principal purpose for the loss of U.S. citizenship by a decedent was the avoidance of Federal income, estate, or gift tax, the Commissioner must first establish that it is reasonable to believe that the decedent's loss of U.S. citizenship would, but for section 2107 and this section, result in a substantial reduction in the sum of (a) the Federal estate tax and (b) all estate, inheritance, legacy, and succession taxes imposed by foreign countries and political subdivisions thereof, in respect of the transfer of the decedent's estate. Once the Commissioner has so established, the burden of proving that the loss of citizenship by the decedent did not have for one of its principal purposes the avoidance of Federal income, estate, or gift tax shall be on the executor of the decedent's estate.

(ii) *Tentative determination of substantial reduction in Federal and foreign death taxes.* In the absence of complete factual information, the Commissioner may make a tentative determination, based on the information available, that the decedent's loss of U.S. citizenship would, but for section 2107 and this section, result in a substantial reduction in the sum of the Federal and foreign death taxes described in subdivision (i)(a) and (b) of this subparagraph. This tentative determination may be based upon the fact that the laws of the foreign country of which the decedent became a citizen and the laws of the foreign country of which the decedent was a resident at the time of his death, including the laws of any political subdivisions of those foreign countries, would ordinarily result, in the case of an estate of a nonexpatriate decedent having the same citizenship and residence as the decedent, in liability for total death taxes under such laws substantially lower than the amount of the Federal estate tax which would be imposed on the transfer of a comparable estate of a citizen of the United States. In the absence of a preponderance of evidence to the contrary, this tentative determination shall be sufficient to establish that it is reasonable to believe that the decedent's loss of U.S. citizenship would, but for section 2107 and this section, result in a substantial reduction in the sum of the Federal and foreign death taxes described in subdivision (i)(a) and (b) of this subparagraph.

[T.D. 7296, 38 FR 34197, Dec. 12, 1973]

§ 2108. Application of Pre-1967 Estate Tax Provisions [*Omitted. Ed.*]

Subchapter C. Miscellaneous

§ 2201. Combat Zone-Related Deaths of Members of the Armed Forces, Deaths of Astronauts, and Deaths of Victims of Certain Terrorist Attacks

(a) In general. Unless the executor elects not to have this section apply, in applying sections 2001 and 2101 to the estate of a qualified decedent, the rate schedule set forth in subsection (c) shall be deemed to be the rate schedule set forth in section 2001(c).

(b) Qualified decedent. For purposes of this section, the term "qualified decedent" means—

(1) any citizen or resident of the United States dying while in active service of the Armed Forces of the United States, if such decedent—

(A) was killed in action while serving in a combat zone, as determined under section 112(c), or

(B) died as a result of wounds, disease, or injury suffered while serving in a combat zone (as determined under section 112(c)), and while in the line of duty, by reason of a hazard to which such decedent was subjected as an incident of such service,

(2) any specified terrorist victim (as defined in section 692(d)(4)), and

(3) any astronaut whose death occurs in the line of duty.

(c) Rate schedule.

If the amount with respect to which the tentative tax to be computed is:	***The tentative tax is:***
Not over $150,000	1 percent of the amount by which such amount exceeds $100,000.
Over $150,000 but not over $200,000	$500 plus 2 percent of the excess over $150,000.
Over $200,000 but not over $300,000	$1,500 plus 3 percent of the excess over $200,000.
Over $300,000 but not over $500,000	$4,500 plus 4 percent of the excess over $300,000.
Over $500,000 but not over $700,000	$12,500 plus 5 percent of the excess over $500,000.
Over $700,000 but not over $900,000	$22,500 plus 6 percent of the excess over $700,000.
Over $900,000 but not over $1,100,000	$34,500 plus 7 percent of the excess over $900,000.
Over $1,100,000 but not over $1,600,000	$48,500 plus 8 percent of the excess over $1,100,000.
Over $1,600,000 but not over $2,100,000	$88,500 plus 9 percent of the excess over $1,600,000.
Over $2,100,000 but not over $2,600,000	$133,500 plus 10 percent of the excess over $2,100,000.
Over $2,600,000 but not over $3,100,000	$183,500 plus 11 percent of the excess over $2,600,000.
Over $3,100,000 but not over $3,600,000	$238,500 plus 12 percent of the excess over $3,100,000.
Over $3,600,000 but not over $4,100,000	$298,500 plus 13 percent of the excess over $3,600,000.
Over $4,100,000 but not over $5,100,000	$363,500 plus 14 percent of the excess over $4,100,000.

Over $5,100,000 but not over $6,100,000	$503,500 plus 15 percent of the excess over $5,100,000.
Over $6,100,000 but not over $7,100,000	$653,500 plus 16 percent of the excess over $6,100,000.
Over $7,100,000 but not over $8,100,000	$813,500 plus 17 percent of the excess over $7,100,000.
Over $8,100,000 but not over $9,100,000	$983,500 plus 18 percent of the excess over $8,100,000.
Over $9,100,000 but not over $10,100,000	$1,163,500 plus 19 percent of the excess over $9,100,000.
Over $10,100,000	$1,353,500 plus 20 percent of the excess over $10,100,000.

(d) Determination of unified credit. In the case of an estate to which this section applies, subsection (a) shall not apply in determining the credit under section 2010.

§ 2203. Definition of Executor

The term "executor" wherever it is used in this title in connection with the estate tax imposed by this chapter means the executor or administrator of the decedent, or, if there is no executor or administrator appointed, qualified, and acting within the United States, then any person in actual or constructive possession of any property of the decedent.

Regulation

§ 20.2203–1 Definition of executor.

The term "executor" means the executor or administrator of the decedent's estate. However, if there is no executor or administrator appointed, qualified and acting within the United States, the term means any person in actual or constructive possession of any property of the decedent. The term "person in actual or constructive possession of any property of the decedent" includes, among others, the decedent's agents and representatives; safe-deposit companies, warehouse companies, and other custodians of property in this country; brokers holding, as collateral, securities belonging to the decedent; and debtors of the decedent in this country.

[T.D. 6296, 23 FR 4529, June 24, 1958]

§ 2204. Discharge of Fiduciary from Personal Liability

(a) General rule. If the executor makes written application to the Secretary for determination of the amount of the tax and discharge from personal liability therefor, the Secretary (as soon as possible, and in any event within 9 months after the making of such application, or, if the application is made before the return is filed, then within 9 months after the return is filed, but not after the expiration of the period prescribed for the assessment of the tax in section 6501) shall notify the executor of the amount of the tax. The executor, on payment of the amount of which he is notified (other than any amount the time for payment of which is extended under section 6161, 6163, or 6166), and on furnishing any bond which may be required for any amount for which the time for payment is extended, shall be discharged from personal liability for any deficiency in tax thereafter found to be due and shall be entitled to a receipt or writing showing such discharge.

(b) Fiduciary other than the executor. If a fiduciary (not including a fiduciary in respect of the estate of a nonresident decedent) other than the executor makes written application to the Secretary for determination of the amount of any estate tax for which the fiduciary may be personally liable, and for discharge from personal liability therefor, the Secretary upon the discharge of the executor from personal liability under subsection (a), or upon the expiration of 6 months after the making of such application by the fiduciary, if later, shall notify the fiduciary (1) of the amount of such tax for which it has been determined the fiduciary is liable, or (2) that it has been determined that the fiduciary is not liable for any such tax. Such application shall be accompanied by a copy of the instrument, if any, under which such fiduciary is acting, a description of the property held by the fiduciary, and such other information for purposes of carrying out the provisions of this section as the Secretary may require by regulations. On payment of the amount of such tax for which it has been determined the fiduciary is liable (other than any amount the time for payment of which has been extended under section 6161, 6163, or 6166), and on furnishing any bond which may be required for any amount for which the time for payment has been extended, or on receipt by him of notification of a determination that he is not liable for any such tax, the fiduciary shall be discharged from personal liability for any deficiency in such tax thereafter found to be due and shall be entitled to a receipt or writing evidencing such discharge.

(c) Special lien under section 6324A. For purposes of the second sentence of subsection (a) and the last sentence of subsection (b), an agreement which meets the requirements of section 6324A (relating to special lien for estate tax deferred under section 6166) shall be treated as the furnishing of bond with respect to the amount for which the time for payment has been extended under section 6166.

(d) Good faith reliance of gift tax returns. If the executor in good faith relies on gift tax returns furnished under section 6103(e)(3) for determining the decedent's adjusted taxable gifts, the executor shall be discharged from personal liability with respect to any deficiency of the tax imposed by this chapter which is attributable to adjusted taxable gifts which—

(1) are made more than 3 years before the date of the decedent's death, and

(2) are not shown on such returns.

Regulations

§ 20.2204–1 Discharge of executor from personal liability.

(a) General rule. The executor of a decedent's estate may make written application to the applicable internal revenue officer with whom the estate tax return is required to be filed, as provided in § 20.6091–1, for a determination of the Federal estate tax and for a discharge of personal liability therefrom. Within 9 months after receipt of the application, or if the application is made before the return is filed then within 9 months after the return is filed, the executor will be notified of the amount of the tax and, upon payment thereof, he will be discharged from personal liability for any deficiency in the tax thereafter found to be due. If no such notification is received, the executor is discharged at the end of such 9 month period from personal liability for any deficiency thereafter found to be due. The discharge of the executor from personal liability under this section applies only to him in his personal capacity and to his personal assets. The discharge is not applicable to his liability as executor to the extent of the assets of the estate in his possession or control. Further, the discharge is not to operate as a release of any part of the gross estate from the lien for estate tax for any deficiency that may thereafter be determined to be due.

(b) Special rule in the case of extension of time for payment of tax. In addition to the provisions of paragraph (a) of this section, an executor of the estate of a decedent dying after December 31, 1970, may make written application to be discharged from personal liability for the amount of Federal estate tax for which the time for payment has been extended under section 6161, 6163, or 6166. In such a case, the executor will be notified of the amount of bond, if any, to be furnished within 9 months after receipt of the application, or, if the application is made before the return is filed, within 9 months after the return is filed. The amount of any bond required under the provisions of this paragraph shall not exceed the amount of tax the payment of which has been extended. Upon furnishing the bond in the form required under § 301.7101–1 of this chapter (Regulations on Procedure and Administration), or upon receipt of the notification that no bond is required, the executor will be discharged from personal liability for the tax the payment of which has been extended. If no notification is received, the executor is discharged at the end of such 9 month period from personal liability for the tax the payment of which has been extended.

[T.D. 6296, 23 FR 4529, June 24, 1958; as amended by T.D. 7238, 37 FR 28720, Dec. 29, 1972; T.D. 7941, 49 FR 4468, Feb. 7, 1984]

§ 20.2204–2 Discharge of fiduciary other than executor from personal liability.

(a) A fiduciary (not including a fiduciary of the estate of a nonresident decedent), other than the executor, who as a fiduciary holds, or has held at any time since the decedent's death, property transferred to the fiduciary from a decedent dying after December 31, 1970, or his estate, may make written application to the applicable internal revenue officer with whom the estate tax return is required to be filed, as provided in § 20.6091–1, for a determination of the Federal estate tax liability with respect to such property and for a discharge of personal liability therefrom. The application must be accompanied by a copy of the instrument, if any, under which the fiduciary is acting, a description of all the property transferred to the fiduciary from the decedent or his estate, and any other information that would be relevant to a determination of the fiduciary's tax liability.

(b) Upon the discharge of the executor from personal liability under § 20.2204–1, or, if later, within 6 months after the receipt of the application filed by a fiduciary pursuant to the provisions of paragraph (a) of this section, such fiduciary will be notified either (1) of the amount of tax for which it has been determined the fiduciary is liable, or (2) that it has been determined that the fiduciary is not liable for any such tax. The fiduciary will also be notified of the amount of bond, if any, to be furnished for any Federal estate tax for which the time for payment has been extended under section 6161, 6163, or 6166. The amount of any bond required under the provisions of this paragraph shall not exceed the amount of tax the payment of which has been so extended. Upon payment of the amount for which it has been determined the fiduciary is liable, and upon furnishing any bond required under this paragraph in the form specified under § 301.7101–1 of this chapter (Regulations on Procedure and Administration), or upon receipt by the fiduciary of notification of a determination that he is not liable for such tax or that a bond is not required, the fiduciary will be discharged from personal liability for any deficiency in the tax thereafter found to be due. If no such notification is received, the fiduciary is discharged at the end of such 6 months (or upon discharge of the executor, if later) from personal liability for any deficiency thereafter found to be due. The discharge of the fiduciary from personal liability under this section applies only to him in his personal capacity and to his personal assets. The discharge is not applicable to his liability as a fiduciary (such as a trustee) to the extent of the assets of the estate in his possession or control. Further, the discharge is not to operate as a release of any part of the gross estate from the lien for estate tax for any deficiency that may thereafter be determined to be due.

[T.D. 7238, 37 FR 28720, Dec. 29, 1972]

§ 20.2204–3 Special rules for estates of decedents dying after December 31, 1976; special lien under section 6324A.

For purposes of §§ 20.2204–1(b) and 20.2204–2(b), in the case of a decedent dying after December 31, 1976, if the executor elects a special lien in favor of the United States under section 6324A, relating to special lien for estate taxes deferred under sections 6166 or 6166A (as in effect prior to its repeal by the Economic Recovery Tax Act of 1981), such lien shall be treated as the furnishing of a bond with respect to the amount for which the time for payment has been extended under section 6166. If an election has been made under section 6324A, the executor may not thereafter substitute a bond pursuant to section 2204 in lieu of that lien. If a bond has been supplied under section 2204, however, the executor may, by filing a proper notice of election and agreement, substitute a lien under section 6324A for any part or all of such bond. See §§ 20.6324A–1 and 301.6324A–1 for rules relating to a special lien under section 6324A.

[T.D. 7941, 49 FR 4468, Feb. 7, 1984]

§ 2205. Reimbursement out of Estate

If the tax or any part thereof is paid by, or collected out of, that part of the estate passing to or in the possession of any person other than the executor in his capacity as such, such person shall be entitled to reimbursement out of any part of the estate still undistributed or by a just and equitable contribution by the persons whose interest in the estate of the decedent would have been reduced if the tax had been paid before the distribution of the estate or whose interest is subject to equal or prior liability for the payment of taxes, debts, or other charges against the estate, it being the purpose and intent of this chapter that so far as is practicable and unless otherwise directed by the will of the decedent the tax shall be paid out of the estate before its distribution.

Regulation

§ 20.2205–1 Reimbursement out of estate.

If any portion of the tax is paid by or collected out of that part of the estate passing to, or in the possession of, any person other than the duly qualified executor or administrator, that person may be entitled to reimbursement, either out of the undistributed estate or by contribution from other beneficiaries whose shares or interests in the estate would have been reduced had the tax been paid before distribution of the estate, or whose shares or interests are subject either to an equal or prior liability for the payment of taxes, debts, or other charges against the estate. For specific provisions giving the executor the right to reimbursement from life insurance beneficiaries and from recipients of property over which the decedent had a power of appointment, see sections 2206 and 2207. These provisions, however, are not designed to curtail the right of the district director to collect the tax from any person, or out of any property, liable for its payment. The district director cannot be required to apportion the tax among the persons liable nor to enforce any right of reimbursement or contribution.

[T.D. 6296, 23 FR 4529, June 24, 1958]

§ 2206. Liability of Life Insurance Beneficiaries

Unless the decedent directs otherwise in his will, if any part of the gross estate on which tax has been paid consists of proceeds of policies of insurance on the life of the decedent receivable by a beneficiary other than the executor, the executor shall be entitled to recover from such beneficiary such portion of the total tax paid as the proceeds of such policies bear to the taxable estate. If there is more than one such beneficiary, the executor shall be entitled to recover from such beneficiaries in the same ratio. In the case of such proceeds receivable by the surviving spouse of the decedent for which a deduction is allowed under section 2056 (relating to marital deduction), this section shall not apply to such proceeds except as to the amount thereof in excess of the aggregate amount of the marital deductions allowed under such section.

Regulation

§ 20.2206–1 Liability of life insurance beneficiaries.

With respect to the right of the district director to collect the tax without regard to the provisions of section 2206, see § 20.2205–1.

[T.D. 6296, 23 FR 4529, June 24, 1958]

§ 2207. Liability of Recipient of Property over Which Decedent Had Power of Appointment

Unless the decedent directs otherwise in his will, if any part of the gross estate on which the tax has been paid consists of the value of property included in the gross estate under section 2041, the executor shall be entitled to recover from the person receiving such property by reason of the exercise, nonexercise, or release of a power of appointment such portion of the total tax paid as the value of such property bears to the taxable estate. If there is more than one such person, the executor shall be entitled to recover from such persons in the same ratio. In the case of such property received by the surviving spouse of the decedent for which a deduction is allowed under section 2056 (relating to marital deduction), this section shall not apply to such property except as to the value thereof reduced by an amount equal to the excess of the aggregate amount of the marital deductions allowed under section 2056 over the amount of proceeds of insurance upon the life of the decedent receivable by the surviving spouse for which proceeds a marital deduction is allowed under such section.

Regulation

§ 20.2207–1 Liability of recipient of property over which decedent had power of appointment.

With respect to the right of the district director to collect the tax without regard to the provisions of section 2207, see § 20.2205–1.

[T.D. 6296, 23 FR 4529, June 24, 1958]

§ 2207A. Right of Recovery in the Case of Certain Marital Deduction Property

(a) Recovery with respect to estate tax.

(1) In general. If any part of the gross estate consists of property the value of which is includible in the gross estate by reason of section 2044 (relating to certain property for which marital deduction was previously allowed), the decedent's estate shall be entitled to recover from the person receiving the property the amount by which—

(A) the total tax under this chapter which has been paid, exceeds

(B) the total tax under this chapter which would have been payable if the value of such property had not been included in the gross estate.

(2) Decedent may otherwise direct. Paragraph (1) shall not apply with respect to any property to the extent that the decedent in his will (or a revocable trust) specifically indicates an intent to waive any right of recovery under this subchapter with respect to such property.

(b) Recovery with respect to gift tax. If for any calendar year tax is paid under chapter 12 with respect to any person by reason of property treated as transferred by such person under section 2519, such person shall be entitled to recover from the person receiving the property the amount by which—

(1) the total tax for such year under chapter 12, exceeds

(2) the total tax which would have been payable under such chapter for such year if the value of such property had not been taken into account for purposes of chapter 12.

(c) More than one recipient of property. For purposes of this section, if there is more than one person receiving the property, the right of recovery shall be against each such person.

(d) Taxes and interest. In the case of penalties and interest attributable to additional taxes described in subsections (a) and (b), rules similar to subsections (a), (b), and (c) shall apply.

Regulations

§ 20.2207A–1 Right of recovery of estate taxes in the case of certain marital deduction property.

(a) In general. (1) *Right of recovery from person receiving the property.* If the gross estate includes the value of property that is includible by reason of section 2044 (relating to certain property in which the decedent had a qualifying income interest for life under sections 2056(b)(7) or 2523(f)), the estate of the surviving spouse is entitled to recover from the person receiving the property (as defined in paragraph (d) of this section) the amount of Federal estate tax attributable to that property. The right of recovery arises when the Federal estate tax with respect to the property includible in the gross estate by reason of section 2044 is paid by the estate. There is no right of recovery from any person for the property received by that person for which a deduction was allowed from the gross estate if no tax is attributable to that property.

(2) *Failure to exercise right of recovery.* Failure of an estate to exercise a right of recovery under this section upon a transfer subject to section 2044 is treated as a transfer for Federal gift tax purposes of the unrecovered amounts from the persons who would benefit from the recovery to the persons from whom the

recovery could have been obtained. See § 25.2511–1 of this chapter. The transfer is considered made when the right of recovery is no longer enforceable under applicable law. A delay in the exercise of the right of recovery without payment of sufficient interest is a below-market loan. Section 1.7872–5T of the Temporary Income Tax regulations describes factors that are used to determine, based on the facts and circumstances of a particular case, whether a loan otherwise subject to imputation under section 7872 (relating to the treatment of below-market loans) is exempted from its provisions.

(3) *Waiver of right of recovery.* The provisions of § 20.2207A–1(a)(2) do not apply to the extent that the surviving spouse's will provides that a recovery shall not be made or to the extent that the beneficiaries cannot otherwise compel recovery. Thus, e.g., if the surviving spouse gives the executor of the estate discretion to waive the right of recovery and the executor waives the right, no gift occurs under § 25.2511–1 of this chapter if the persons who would benefit from the recovery cannot compel the executor to exercise the right of recovery.

(b) Amount of estate tax attributable to property includible under section 2044. The amount of Federal estate tax attributable to property includible in the gross estate under section 2044 is the amount by which the total Federal estate tax (including penalties and interest attributable to the tax) under chapter 11 of the Internal Revenue Code that has been paid, exceeds the total Federal estate tax (including penalties and interest attributable to the tax) under chapter 11 of the Internal Revenue Code that would have been paid if the value of the property includible in the gross estate by reason of section 2044 had not been so included.

(c) Amount of estate tax attributable to a particular property. An estate's right of recovery with respect to a particular property is an amount equal to the amount determined in paragraph (b) of this section multiplied by a fraction. The numerator of the fraction is the value for Federal estate tax purposes of the particular property included in the gross estate by reason of section 2044, less any deduction allowed with respect to the property. The denominator of the fraction is the total value of all properties included in the gross estate by reason of section 2044, less any deductions allowed with respect to those properties.

(d) Person receiving the property. If the property is in a trust at the time of the decedent's death, the person receiving the property is the trustee and any person who has received a distribution of the property prior to the expiration of the right of recovery if the property does not remain in trust. This paragraph (d) does not affect the right, if any, under local law, of any person with an interest in property to reimbursement or contribution from another person with an interest in the property.

(e) Example. The following example illustrates the application of paragraphs (a) through (d) of this section.

Example. D died in 1994. D's will created a trust funded with certain income producing assets included in D's gross estate at $1,000,000. The trust provides that all the income is payable to D's wife, S, for life, remainder to be divided equally among their four children. In computing D's taxable estate, D's executor deducted, pursuant to section 2056(b)(7), $1,000,000. Assume that S received no other property from D and that S died in 1996. Assume further that S made no section 2519 disposition of the property, that the property was included in S's gross estate at a value of $1,080,000, and that S's will contained no provision regarding section 2207A(a). The tax attributable to the property is equal to the amount by which the total Federal estate tax (including penalties and interest) paid by S's estate exceeds the Federal estate tax (including penalties and interest) that would have been paid if S's gross estate had been reduced by $1,080,000. That amount of tax may be recovered by S's estate from the trust. If, at the time S's estate seeks reimbursement, the trust has been distributed to the four children, S's estate is also entitled to recover the tax from the children.

[T.D. 8522, 59 FR 9654, March 1, 1994; T.D. 9077, 68 FR 42594, July 18, 2003]

§ 20.2207A–2 Effective date.

The provisions of § 20.2207A–1 are effective with respect to estates of decedents dying after March 1, 1994. With respect to estates of decedent dying on or before such date, the executor of the decedent's estate may rely on any reasonable interpretation of the statutory provisions. For these purposes, the provisions of § 20.2207A–1 (as well as project LR–211–76, 1984–1 C.B., page 598, see § 601.601(d)(2)(ii)(b) of this chapter), are considered a reasonable interpretation of the statutory provisions.

[T.D. 8522, 59 FR 9655, March 1, 1994]

§ 25.2207A–1 Right of recovery of gift taxes in the case of certain marital deduction property.

(a) In general. If an individual is treated as transferring an interest in property by reason of section 2519, the individual or the individual's estate is entitled to recover from the person receiving the property (as defined in paragraph (e) of this section) the amount of gift tax attributable to that property. The value of property to which this paragraph (a) applies is the value of all interests in the property other than the qualifying income interest. There is no right of recovery from any person for the property received by that person for which a deduction was allowed from the total amount of gifts, if no Federal gift tax is attributable to the property. The right of recovery arises at the time the Federal gift tax is actually paid by the transferor subject to section 2519.

(b) Failure of a person to exercise the right of recovery. (1) The failure of a person to exercise a right of recovery provided by section 2207A(b) upon a lifetime transfer subject to section 2519 is treated as a transfer for Federal gift tax purposes of the unrecovered amounts to the person(s) from whom the recovery could have been obtained. See § 25.2511–1. The transfer is considered to be made when the right to recovery is no longer enforceable under applicable law and is treated as a gift even if recovery is impossible. A delay in the exercise of the right of recovery without payment of sufficient interest is a below-market loan. Section 1.7872–5T of this chapter describes factors that are used to determine, based on the facts and circumstances of a particular case, whether a loan otherwise subject to imputation under section 7872 (relating to the treatment of below-market loans) is exempted from its provisions.

(2) The transferor subject to section 2519 may execute a written waiver of the right of recovery arising under section 2207A before that right of recovery becomes unenforceable. If a waiver is executed, the transfer of the unrecovered amounts by the transferor is considered to be made on the later of—

(i) The date of the valid and irrevocable waiver rendering the right of recovery no longer enforceable; or

(ii) The date of the payment of the tax by the transferor.

(c) Amount of gift tax attributable to all properties. The amount of Federal gift tax attributable to all properties includible in the total amount of gifts under section 2519 made during the calendar year is the amount by which the total Federal gift tax for the calendar year (including penalties and interest attributable to the tax) under chapter 12 of the Internal Revenue Code which has been paid, exceeds the total Federal gift tax for the calendar year (including penalties and interest attributable to the tax) under chapter 12 of the Internal Revenue Code which would have been paid if the value of the properties includible in the total amount of gifts by reason of section 2519 had not been included.

(d) Amount of gift tax attributable to a particular property. A person's right of recovery with respect to a particular property is an amount equal to the amount determined in paragraph (c) of this section multiplied by a fraction. The numerator of the fraction is the value of the particular property included in the total amount of gifts made during the calendar year by reason of section 2519, less any deduction allowed with respect to the property. The denominator of the fraction is the total value of all properties included in the total amount of gifts made during the calendar year by reason of section 2519, less any deductions allowed with respect to those properties.

(e) Person receiving the property. If the property is in a trust at the time of the transfer, the person receiving the property is the trustee, and any person who has received a distribution of the property prior to the expiration of the right of recovery if the property does not remain in trust. This paragraph (e) does not affect the right, if any, under local law, of any person with an interest in property to reimbursement or contribution from another person with an interest in the property.

(f) Example. The following example illustrates the application of paragraphs (a) through (e) of this section.

Example. D created an inter vivos trust during 1994 with certain income producing assets valued at $1,000,000. The trust provides that all income is payable to D's wife, S, for S's life, with the remainder at S's death to be divided equally among their four children. In computing taxable gifts during calendar year 1994, D deducted, pursuant to section 2523(f), $1,000,000 from the total amount of gifts made. In addition, assume that S received no other transfers from D and that S made a gift during 1996 of the entire life interest to one of the children, at which time the value of trust assets was $1,080,000 and the value of S's life interest was $400,000. Although the entire value of the trust assets ($1,080,000) is, pursuant to sections 2511 and 2519, included in the total amount of S's gifts for calendar year 1996, S is only entitled to reimbursement for the Federal gift tax attributable to the value of the remainder interest, that is, the Federal gift tax attributable to $680,000 ($1,080,000 less $400,000). The Federal gift tax attributable to $680,000 is equal to the amount by which the total Federal gift tax (including penalties and interest) paid for the calendar year exceeds the federal gift tax (including penalties and interest) that would have been paid if the total amount of gifts during 1996 had been reduced by $680,000. That amount of tax may be recovered by S from the trust.

[T.D. 8522, 59 FR 9655, March 1, 1994; T.D. 9077, 68 FR 42595, July 18, 2003]

§ 25.2207A–2 Effective date.

The provisions of § 25.2207A–1 are effective with respect to dispositions made after March 1, 1994. With respect to gifts made on or before such date, the donor may rely on any reasonable interpretation of the statutory provisions. For these purposes, the provisions of § 25.2207A–1 (as well as project LR–211–76, 1984–1 C.B., page 598, see § 601.601(d)(2)(ii)(b) of this chapter), are considered a reasonable interpretation of the statutory provisions.

[T.D. 8522, 59 FR 9656, March 1, 1994]

§ 2207B. Right of Recovery Where Decedent Retained

(a) Estate tax.

(1) In general. If any part of the gross estate on which tax has been paid consists of the value of property included in the gross estate by reason of section 2036 (relating to transfers with retained life estate), the decedent's estate shall be entitled to recover from the person receiving the property the amount which bears the same ratio to the total tax under this chapter which has been paid as—

(A) the value of such property, bears to

(B) the taxable estate.

(2) Decedent may otherwise direct. Paragraph (1) shall not apply with respect to any property to the extent that the decedent in his will (or a revocable trust) specifically indicates an intent to waive any right of recovery under this subchapter with respect to such property.

(b) More than one recipient. For purposes of this section, if there is more than 1 person receiving the property, the right of recovery shall be against each such person.

(c) Penalties and interest. In the case of penalties and interest attributable to the additional taxes described in subsection (a), rules similar to the rules of subsections (a) and (b) shall apply.

(d) No right of recovery against charitable remainder trusts. No person shall be entitled to recover any amount by reason of this section from a trust to which section 664 applies (determined without action).

§ 2208. Certain Residents of Possessions Considered Citizens of the United States

A decedent who was a citizen of the United States and a resident of a possession thereof at the time of his death shall, for purposes of the tax imposed by this chapter, be considered a "citizen" of the United States within the meaning of that term wherever used in this title unless he acquired his United States citizenship solely by reason of (1) his being a citizen of such possession of the United States, or (2) his birth or residence within such possession of the United States.

Regulation

§ 20.2208–1 Certain residents of possessions considered citizens of the United States.

As used in this part, the term "citizen of the United States" is considered to include a decedent dying after September 2, 1958, who, at the time of his death, was domiciled in a possession of the United States and was a United States citizen, and who did not acquire his United States citizenship solely by reason of his being a citizen of such possession or by reason of his birth or residence within such possession. The estate of such a decedent is, therefore, subject to the tax imposed by section 2001. See paragraph (a)(2) of § 20.0–1 and § 20.2209–1 for further information relating to the application of the Federal estate tax to the estates of decedents who were residents of possessions of the United States. The application of this section may be illustrated by the following example and the examples set forth in § 20.2209–1:

Example. A, a citizen of the United States by reason of his birth in the United States at San Francisco, established residence in Puerto Rico and acquired a Puerto Rican citizenship. A died on September 4, 1958, while a citizen and domiciliary of Puerto Rico. A's estate is, by reason of the provisions of section 2208, subject to the tax imposed by section 2001 inasmuch as his United States citizenship is based on birth in the United States and is not based solely on being a citizen of a possession or solely on birth or residence in a possession.

[T.D. 6526, 26 FR 417, Jan. 19, 1961]

§ 2209. Certain Residents of Possessions Considered Nonresidents Not Citizens of the United States

A decedent who was a citizen of the United States and a resident of a possession thereof at the time of his death shall, for purposes of the tax imposed by this chapter, be considered a 'nonresident not a citizen of the United States' within the meaning of that term wherever used in this title, but only if such person acquired his United States citizenship solely by reason of (1) his being a citizen of such possession of the United States, or (2) his birth or residence within such possession of the United States.

Regulation

§ 20.2209–1 Certain residents of possessions considered nonresidents not citizens of the United States.

As used in this part, the term "nonresident not a citizen of the United States" is considered to include a decedent dying after September 14, 1960, who, at the time of his death, was domiciled in a possession of the United States and was a United States citizen, and who acquired his United States citizenship solely by reason of his being a citizen of such possession or by reason of his birth or residence within such possession. The estate of such a decedent is, therefore, subject to the tax imposed by section 2101 which is the tax applicable in the case of a "nonresident not a citizen of the United States." See paragraph (a)(2) of § 20.0–1 and § 20.2208–1 for further information relating to the application of the Federal estate tax to the estates of decedents who were residents of possessions of the United States. The application of this section may be illustrated by the following examples and the example set forth in § 20.2208–1. In each of the following examples the decedent is deemed a "nonresident not a citizen of the United States" and his estate is subject to the tax imposed by section 2101 since the decedent died after September 14, 1960, but would not have been so deemed and subject to such tax if the decedent had died on or before September 14, 1960.

Example (1). C, who acquired his United States citizenship under section 5 of the Act of March 2, 1917 (39 Stat. 953), by reason of being a citizen of Puerto Rico, died in Puerto Rico on October 1, 1960, while domiciled therein. C is considered to have acquired his United States citizenship solely by reason of his being a citizen of Puerto Rico.

Example (2). E, whose parents were United States citizens by reason of their birth in Boston, was born in the Virgin Islands on March 1, 1927. On September 30, 1960, he died in the Virgin Islands while domiciled therein. E is considered to have acquired his United States citizenship solely by reason of his birth in the

Virgin Islands (section 306 of the Immigration and Nationality Act (66 Stat. 237, 8 U.S.C. 1406)).

Example (3). N, who acquired United States citizenship by reason of being a native of the Virgin Islands and a resident thereof on June 28, 1932 (section 306 of the Immigration and Nationality Act (66 Stat. 237, 8 U.S.C. 1406)), died on October 1, 1960, while domiciled in the Virgin Islands. N is considered to have acquired his United States citizenship solely by reason of his birth or residence in the Virgin Islands.

Example (4). P, a former Danish citizen, who on January 17, 1917, resided in the Virgin Islands, made the declaration to preserve his Danish citizenship required by Article 6 of the treaty entered into on August 4, 1916, between the United States and Denmark. Subsequently P acquired United States citizenship when he renounced such declaration before a court of record (section 306 of the Immigration and Nationality Act (66 Stat. 237, 8 U.S.C. 1406)). P died on October 1, 1960, while domiciled in the Virgin Islands. P is considered to have acquired his United States citizenship solely by reason of his birth or residence in the Virgin Islands.

Example (5). R, a former French citizen, acquired his United States citizenship through naturalization proceedings in a court located in the Virgin Islands after having qualified for citizenship by residing in the Virgin Islands for 5 years. R died on October 1, 1960, while domiciled in the Virgin Islands. R is considered to have acquired his United States citizenship solely by reason of his birth or residence within the Virgin Islands.

[T.D. 6526, 26 FR 418, Jan. 19, 1961]

Under § 301(a) of the Tax Relief, Unemployment Insurance Reauthorization, and Job Creation Act of 2010 (P.L. 111–312) § 2210 was eliminated from the Code. However, § 301(c) of the Act provides "[n]otwithstanding sub-section (a), in the case of an estate of a decedent dying after December 31, 2009, and before January 1, 2011, the executor (within the meaning of section 2203 of the Internal Revenue Code of 1986) may elect to apply such Code as though the amendments made by subsection (a) do not apply with respect to chapter 11 of such Code and with respect to property acquired or passing from such decedent . . . ." Therefore, § 2210 is included for those estates where the executor makes such election.

§ 2210. Termination.

(a) In general. *Except as provided in subsection (b), this chapter shall not apply to the estates of decedents dying after December 31, 2009.*

(b) Certain distributions from qualified domestic trusts. *In applying section 2056A with respect to the surviving spouse of a decedent dying before January 1, 2010—*

(1) *section 2056A(b)(1)(A) shall not apply to distributions made after December 31, 2020, and*

(2) *section 2056A(b)(1)(B) shall not apply after December 31, 2009.*

Federal Gift Tax

Code and Selected Regulations

SUBTITLE B. ESTATE AND GIFT TAXES

Chapter 12. Gift Tax

Subchapter A. Determination of Tax Liability

Regulation

§ 25.0–1 Introduction.

(a) In general. (1) The regulations in this part are designated "Gift Tax Regulations." These regulations pertain to (i) the gift tax imposed by chapter 12 of subtitle B of the Internal Revenue Code on the transfer of property by gift by individuals in the calendar year 1955, in subsequent calendar years beginning before the calendar year 1971, in calendar quarters beginning with the first calendar quarter of calendar year 1971 through the last calendar quarter of the calendar year 1981, and in calendar years beginning with the calendar year 1982, and (ii) certain related administrative provisions of subtitle F of the Code. It should be noted that the application of some of the provisions of these regulations may be affected by the provisions of an applicable gift tax convention with a foreign country. Unless otherwise indicated, references in these regulations to the "Internal Revenue Code" or the "Code" are references to the Internal Revenue Code of 1954, as amended, and references to a section or other provision of law are references to a section or other provision of the Internal Revenue Code of 1954, as amended. The Gift Tax Regulations are applicable to the transfer of property by gift by individuals in calendar years 1955 through 1970, in calendar quarters beginning with the first calendar quarter of calendar year 1971 through the last calendar quarter of the calendar year 1981, and in calendar years beginning with the calendar year 1982, and supersede the regulations contained in Part 86, Subchapter B, Chapter 1, Title 26, Code of Federal Regulations (1939) (Regulations 108, Gift Tax (8 FR 10858)), as prescribed and made applicable to the Internal Revenue Code of 1954 by Treasury Decision 6091, signed August 16, 1954 (19 FR 5167, Aug. 17, 1954).

(2) Section 2501(b) makes the provisions of Chapter 12 of the Code apply in the case of gifts made after September 2, 1958, by certain citizens of the United States who were residents of a possession thereof at the time the gifts were made. Section 2501(c) makes the provisions of Chapter 12 apply in the case of gifts made after September 14, 1960, by certain other citizens of the United States who were residents of a possession thereof at the time the gifts were made. See paragraphs (c) and (d) of § 25.2501–1. Except as otherwise provided in paragraphs (c) and (d) of § 25.2501–1, the provisions of these regulations do not apply to the making of gifts by such citizens.

(b) Nature of tax. The gift tax is not a property tax. It is a tax imposed upon the transfer of property by individuals. It is not applicable to transfers by corporations or persons other than individuals. However, see paragraph (h)(1) of § 25.2511–1 with respect to the extent to which a transfer by or to a corporation is considered a transfer by or to its shareholders.

(c) Scope of regulations. (1) *Determination of tax liability.* Subchapter A of Chapter 12 of the Code pertains to the determination of tax liability. The regulations pursuant to Subchapter A are set forth in §§ 25.2501–1 through 25.2504–2. Sections 25.2701–5 and 25.2702–6 contain rules that provide additional adjustments to mitigate double taxation where the amount of the transferor's property was previously determined under the special valuation provisions of sections 2701 and 2702.

(2) *Transfer.* Subchapter B of Chapter 12 and Chapter 14 of the Internal Revenue Code pertain to the transfers which constitute the making of gifts and the valuation of those transfers. The regulations pursuant to subchapter B are set forth in §§ 25.2511–1 through 25.2518–3. The regulations pursuant to Chapter 14 are set forth in §§ 25.2701–1 through 25.2704–3.

(3) *Deductions.* Subchapter C of Chapter 12 of the Code pertains to the deductions which are allowed in determining the amount of taxable gifts. The regulations pursuant to Subchapter C are set forth in §§ 25.2521–1 through 25.2524–1.

(4) *Procedure and administration provisions.* Subtitle F of the Internal Revenue Code contains some sections which are applicable to the gift tax. The regulations pursuant to those sections are set forth in §§ 25.6001–1 through 25.7101–1. Such regulations do not purport to be all the regulations on procedure and administration which are pertinent to gift tax matters. For the remainder of the regulations on procedure and administration which are pertinent to gift tax matters, see Part 301 of this chapter (Regulations on Procedure and Administration).

(d) Arrangement and numbering. Each section of the regulations in this part (other than this section) is designated by a number composed of the part number followed by a decimal point (25.); the section of the Internal Revenue Code which it interprets; a hyphen (-); and a number identifying this section. By use of these designations one can ascertain the sections of the regulations relating to a provision of the Code. For example, the regulations pertaining to section 2521 of the Code are designated § 25.2521–1.

[T.D. 6334, 23 FR 8904, Nov. 15, 1958, as amended by T.D. 6542, 26 FR 548, Jan. 20, 1961; T.D. 7238, 37 FR 28725, Dec. 29, 1972; 45 FR 6089, Jan. 25, 1980; T.D. 7910, 48 FR 40371, Sept. 7, 1983; T.D. 8395, 57 FR 4254, Feb. 4, 1992]

§ 2501. Imposition of Tax

(a) Taxable transfers.

(1) General rule. A tax, computed as provided in section 2502, is hereby imposed for each calendar year on the transfer of property by gift during such calendar year by any individual, resident or nonresident.

(2) Transfers of intangible property. Except as provided in paragraph (3), paragraph (1) shall not apply to the transfer of intangible property by a nonresident not a citizen of the United States.

(3) Exception.

(A) Certain individuals. Paragraph (2) shall not apply in the case of a donor to whom section 877(b) applies for the taxable year which includes the date of the transfer.

(B) Credit for foreign gift taxes. The tax imposed by this section solely by reason of this paragraph shall be credited with the amount of any gift tax actually paid to any foreign country in respect of any gift which is taxable under this section solely by reason of this paragraph.

(4) Transfers to political organizations. Paragraph (1) shall not apply to the transfer of money or other property to a political organization (within the meaning of section 527(e)(1)) for the use of such organization.

(5) Transfers of certain stock.

(A) In general. In the case of a transfer of stock in a foreign corporation described in subparagraph (B) by a donor to whom section 877(b) applies for the taxable year which includes the date of the transfer—

(i) section 2511(a) shall be applied without regard to whether such stock is situated within the United States, and

(ii) the value of such stock for purposes of this chapter shall be its U.S.-asset value determined under subparagraph (C).

(B) Foreign corporation described. A foreign corporation is described in this subparagraph with respect to a donor if—

(i) the donor owned (within the meaning of section 958(a)) at the time of such transfer 10 percent or more of the total combined voting power of all classes of stock entitled to vote of the foreign corporation, and

(ii) such donor owned (within the meaning of section 958(a)), or is considered to have owned (by applying the ownership rules of section 958(b)), at the time of such transfer, more than 50 percent of—

(I) the total combined voting power of all classes of stock entitled to vote of such corporation, or

(II) the total value of the stock of such corporation.

(C) U.S.-asset value. For purposes of subparagraph (A), the U.S.-asset value of stock shall be the amount which bears the same ratio to the fair market value of such stock at the time of transfer as—

(i) the fair market value (at such time) of the assets owned by such foreign corporation and situated in the United States, bears to

(ii) the total fair market value (at such time) of all assets owned by such foreign corporation.

(6) Transfers to certain exempt organizations. Paragraph (1) shall not apply to the transfer of money or other property to an organization described in paragraph (4), (5), or (6) of section 501(c) and exempt from tax under section 501(a), for the use of such organization.

(b) Certain residents of possessions considered citizens of the United States. A donor who is a citizen of the United States and a resident of a possession thereof shall, for purposes of the tax imposed by this chapter, be considered a "citizen" of the United States within the meaning of that term wherever used in this title unless he acquired his United States citizenship solely by reason of (1) his being a citizen of such possession of the United States, or (2) his birth or residence within such possession of the United States.

(c) Certain residents of possessions considered nonresidents not citizens of the United States. A donor who is a citizen of the United States and a resident of a possession thereof shall, for purposes of the tax imposed by this chapter, be considered a "nonresident not a citizen of the United States" within the meaning of that term wherever used in this title, but only if such donor acquired his United States citizenship solely by reason of (1) his being a citizen of such possession of the United States, or (2) his birth or residence within such possession of the United States.

(d) Cross references.

(1) For increase in basis of property acquired by gift for gift tax paid, see section 1015(d).

(2) For exclusion of transfers of property outside the United States by a nonresident who is not a citizen of the United States, see section 2511(a).

Regulation

§ 25.2501–1 Imposition of tax.

(a) In general. (1) The tax applies to all transfers by gift of property, wherever situated, by an individual who is a citizen or resident of the United States, to the extent the value of the transfers exceeds the amount of the exclusions authorized by section 2503 and the deductions authorized by sections 2521 (as in effect prior to its repeal by the Tax Reform Act of 1976), 2522, and 2523. For each "calendar period" (as defined in § 25.2502–1(c)(1)), the tax described in this paragraph (a) is imposed on the transfer of property by gift during such calendar period. For gift tax rules related to an ABLE account established under section 529A, see § 1.529A–4 of this chapter.

(2) The tax does not apply to a transfer by gift of intangible property before January 1, 1967, by a nonresident not a citizen of the United States, unless the donor was engaged in business in the United States during the calendar year in which the transfer was made.

(3)(i) The tax does not apply to any transfer by gift of intangible property on or after January 1, 1967, by a nonresident not a citizen of the United States (whether or not he was engaged in business in the United States), unless the donor is an expatriate who lost his U.S. citizenship after March 8, 1965, and within the 10-year period ending with the date of transfer, and the loss of citizenship—

(a) Did not result from the application of section 301(b), 350, or 355 of the Immigration and Nationality Act, as amended (8 U.S.C. 1401(b), 1482, or 1487). (For a summary of these sections, see paragraph (d)(1) of § 20.2107–1 of this chapter (estate tax regulations)), and

(b) Had for one of its principal purposes (but not necessarily its only principal purpose) the avoidance of Federal income, estate, or gift tax.

(ii) In determining for purposes of subdivision (i)(b) of this subparagraph whether a principal purpose for the loss of U.S. citizenship by a donor was the avoidance of Federal income, estate, or gift tax, the Commissioner must first establish that it is reasonable to believe that the donor's loss of U.S. citizenship would, but for section 2501(a)(3) and this subparagraph, result in a substantial reduction for the calendar period (as defined in § 25.2502–1)(c)(1) in the sum of (a) the Federal gift tax and (b) all gift taxes imposed by foreign countries and political subdivisions thereof, in respect of the transfer of property by gift. Once the Commissioner has so established, the burden of proving that the loss of citizenship by the donor did not have for one of its principal purposes the avoidance of Federal income, estate, or gift tax shall be on the donor. In the absence of complete factual information, the Commissioner may make a tentative determination, based on the information available, that the donor's loss of U.S. citizenship would, but for section 2501(a)(3) and this subparagraph, result in a substantial reduction for the calendar period in the sum of the Federal and foreign gift taxes described in (a) and (b) of this subdivision on the transfer of property by gift. This tentative determination may be based upon the fact that the laws of the foreign country of which the donor became a citizen and the laws of the foreign country of which the donor was a resident at the time of the transfer, including the laws of any political subdivision of those foreign countries, would ordinarily result, in the case of a nonexpatriate donor having the same citizenship and residence as the donor, in liability for total gift taxes under such laws for the calendar period substantially lower than the amount of the Federal gift tax which would be imposed for such period on an amount of comparable gifts by a citizen of the United States. In the absence of a preponderance of evidence to the contrary, this tentative determination shall be sufficient to establish that it is reasonable to believe that the donor's loss of U.S. citizenship would, but for section 2501(a)(3) and this subparagraph, result in a substantial reduction for the calendar period in the sum of the Federal and foreign gift taxes described in (a) and (b) of this subdivision on the transfer of property by gift.

(4) For additional rules relating to the application of the tax to transfers by nonresidents not citizens of the United States, see section 2511 and § 25.2511–3.

(5) The general rule of this paragraph (a) shall not apply to a transfer after May 7, 1974, of money or other property to a political organization for the use of that organization. However, this exception to the general rule applies solely to a transfer to a political organization as defined in section 527(e)(1) and including a newsletter fund to the extent provided under section 527(g). The general rule governs a transfer of property to an organization other than a political organization as so defined.

(b) Resident. A resident is an individual who has his domicile in the United States at the time of the gift. For this purpose the United States includes the States and the District of Columbia. The term also includes the Territories of Alaska and Hawaii prior to admission as a State. See section 7701(a)(9). All other individuals are nonresidents. A person acquires a domicile in a place by living there, for even a brief period of time, with no definite present intention of moving therefrom. Residence without the requisite intention to remain indefinitely will not constitute domicile, nor will intention to change domicile effect such a change unless accompanied by actual removal.

(c) Certain residents of possessions considered citizens of the United States. As used in this part, the term "citizen of the United States" includes a person who makes a gift after September 2, 1958 and who, at the time of making the gift, was domiciled in a possession of the United States and was a United States citizen, and who did not acquire his United States citizenship solely by reason of his being a citizen of such possession or by reason of his birth or residence within such possession. The gift of such a person is, therefore, subject to the tax imposed by section 2501 in the same manner in which a gift made by a resident of the United States is subject to the tax. See paragraph (a) of § 25.01 and paragraph (d) of this section for further information relating to the application of the Federal gift tax to gifts made by persons who were residents of possessions of the United States. The application of this paragraph may be illustrated by the following example and the examples set forth in paragraph (d) of this section:

Example. A, a citizen of the United States by reason of his birth in the United States at San Francisco, established residence in Puerto Rico and acquired Puerto Rican citizenship. A makes a gift of stock of a Spanish corporation on September 4, 1958, while a citizen and domiciliary of Puerto Rico. A's gift is, by reason of the provisions of section 2501(b) subject to the tax imposed by section 2501 inasmuch as his United States citizenship is based on birth in the United States and is not based solely on being a citizen of a possession or solely on birth or residence in a possession.

(d) Certain residents of possessions considered nonresidents not citizens of the United States. As used in this part, the term "nonresident not a citizen of the United States" includes a person who makes a gift after September 14, 1960, and who at the time of making the gift, was domiciled in a possession of the United States and was a United States citizen, and who acquired his United States citizenship solely by reason of his being a citizen of such possession or by reason of his birth or residence within such possession. The gift of such a person, is, therefore, subject to the tax imposed by section 2501 in the same manner in which a gift is subject to the tax when made by a donor who is a "nonresident not a citizen of the United States." See paragraph (a) of § 25.01 and paragraph (c) of this section for further information relating to the application of the Federal gift tax to gifts made by persons who were residents of possessions of the United States. The application of this paragraph may be illustrated by the following examples and the example set forth in paragraph (c) of this section. In each of the following examples the person who makes the gift is deemed a "nonresident not a citizen of the United States" and his gift is subject to the tax imposed by section 2501 in the same manner in which a gift is subject to the tax when made by a donor who is a nonresident not a citizen of the United States, since he made the gift after September 14, 1960, but would not have been so deemed and subject to such tax if the person who made the gift had made it on or before September 14, 1960.

Example (1). C, who acquired his United States citizenship under section 5 of the Act of March 2, 1917 (39 Stat. 953), by reason of being a citizen of Puerto Rico, while domiciled in Puerto Rico makes a gift on October 1, 1960, of real estate located in New York. C is considered to have acquired his United States citizenship solely by reason of his being a citizen of Puerto Rico.

Example (2). E, whose parents were United States citizens by reason of their birth in Boston, was born in the Virgin Islands on March 1, 1927. On September 30, 1960, while domiciled in the Virgin Islands, he made a gift of tangible personal property situated in Kansas. E is considered to have acquired his United States citizenship solely by reason of his birth in the Virgin Islands (section 306 of the Immigration and Nationality Act (66 Stat. 237, 8 U.S.C. 1406)).

Example (3). N, who acquired United States citizenship by reason of being a native of the Virgin Islands and a resident thereof on June 28, 1932 (section 306 of the Immigration and Nationality Act (66 Stat. 237, 8 U.S.C. 1406)), made a gift on October 1, 1960, at which time he was domiciled in the Virgin Islands, of tangible personal property situated in Wisconsin. N is considered to have acquired his United States citizenship solely by reason of his birth or residence in the Virgin Islands.

Example (4). P, a former Danish citizen, who on January 17, 1917, resided in the Virgin Islands, made the declaration to preserve his Danish citizenship required by Article 6 of the treaty entered into on August 4, 1916, between the United States and Denmark. Subsequently P acquired United States citizenship when he renounced such declaration before a court of record (section 306 of the Immigration and Nationality Act (66 Stat. 237, 8 U.S.C. 1406)). P, while domiciled in the Virgin Islands, made a gift on October 1, 1960, of tangible personal property situated in California, P is considered to have acquired his United States citizenship solely by reason of his birth of residence in the Virgin Islands.

Example (5). R, a former French citizen, acquired his United States citizenship through naturalization proceedings in a court located in the Virgin Islands after having qualified for citizenship by residing in the Virgin Islands for 5 years. R, while domiciled in the Virgin Islands, made a gift of tangible personal property situated in Hawaii on October 1, 1960. R is considered to have acquired his United States citizenship solely by reason of his birth or residence within the Virgin Islands.

[T.D. 6334, 23 FR 8904, Nov. 15, 1958, as amended by T.D. 6542, 26 FR 549, Jan. 20, 1961; T.D. 7238, 37 FR 28725, Dec. 29, 1972; T.D. 7296, 38 FR 34201, Dec. 12, 1973; T.D. 7871, 45 FR 8004, Feb. 6, 1980; T.D. 7910, 48 FR 40371, Sept. 7, 1983; T.D. 9923, 85 FR 74047, Nov. 19, 2020]

§ 2502. Rate of Tax

(a) Computation of Tax. The tax imposed by section 2501 for each calendar year shall be an amount equal to the excess of—

(1) a tentative tax, computed under section 2001(c), on the aggregate sum of the taxable gifts for such calendar year and for each of the preceding calendar periods, over

(2) a tentative tax, computed under such section, on the aggregate sum of the taxable gifts for each of the preceding calendar periods.

(b) Preceding calendar period. Whenever used in this title in connection with the gift tax imposed by this chapter, the term "preceding calendar period" means—

(1) calendar years 1932 and 1970 and all calendar years intervening between calendar year 1932 and calendar year 1970,

(2) the first calendar quarter of calendar year 1971 and all calendar quarters intervening between such calendar quarter and the first calendar quarter of calendar year 1982, and

(3) all calendar years after 1981 and before the calendar year for which the tax is being computed.

For purposes of paragraph (1), the term "calendar year 1932" includes only that portion of such year after June 6, 1932.

(c) Tax to be paid by donor. The tax imposed by section 2501 shall be paid by the donor.

Regulations

§ 25.2502–1 Rate of tax.

(a) Computation of tax. The rate of tax is determined by the total of all gifts made by the donor during the calendar period and all the preceding calendar periods since June 6, 1932. See § 25.2502–1(c)(1) for the definition of "calendar period" and § 25.2502–1(c)(2) for the definition of "preceding calendar periods." The following six steps are to be followed in computing the tax:

(1) *First step.* Ascertain the amount of the "taxable gifts" (as defined in § 25.2503–1) for the calendar period for which the return is being prepared.

(2) *Second step.* Ascertain "the aggregate sum of the taxable gifts for each of the preceding calendar periods" (as defined in § 25.2504–1), considering only those gifts made after June 6, 1932.

(3) *Third step.* Ascertain the total amount of the taxable gifts, which is the sum of the amounts determined in the first and second steps. See § 25.2702–6 for an adjustment to the total amount of an individu-

al's taxable gifts where the individual's current taxable gifts include the transfer of certain interests in trust that were previously valued under the provisions of section 2702.

(4) *Fourth step.* Compute the tentative tax on the total amount of taxable gifts (as determined in the third step) using the rate schedule in effect at the time the gift (for which the return is being filed) is made.

(5) *Fifth step.* Compute the tentative tax on the aggregate sum of the taxable gifts for each of the preceding calendar periods (as determined in the second step), using the same rate schedule set forth in the fourth step of this paragraph (a).

(6) *Sixth step.* Subtract the amount determined in the fifth step from the amount determined in the fourth step. The amount remaining is the gift tax for the calendar period for which the return is being prepared.

(b) Rate of tax. The tax is computed in accordance with the rate schedule in effect at the time the gift was made as set forth in section 2001(c) or corresponding provisions of prior law.

(c) Definitions. (1) The term "calendar period" means:

(i) Each calendar year for the calendar years 1932 (but only that portion of such year after June 6, 1932) through 1970;

(ii) Each calendar quarter for the first calendar quarter of the calendar year 1971 through the last calendar quarter of calendar year 1981; or (iii) Each calendar year for the calendar year 1982 and each succeeding calendar year.

(2) The term "preceding calendar periods" means all calendar periods ending prior to the calendar period for which the tax is being computed.

(d) Examples. The following examples illustrate the application of this section with respect to gifts made by citizens or residents of the United States:

Example (1). Assume that in 1955 the donor made taxable gifts, as ascertained under the first step (paragraph (a)(2) of this section), of $62,500 and that there were no taxable gifts for prior years, with the result that the amount ascertainable under the third step is $62,500. Under the fourth step a tax is computed on this amount. Reference to the tax rate schedule in effect in the year 1955 discloses that the tax on this amount is $7,650.

Example (2). A donor makes gifts (other than gifts of future interests in property) during the calendar year 1955 of $30,000 to A and $33,000 to B. Two exclusions of $3,000 each are allowable, in accordance with the provisions of section 2503(b), which results in included gifts for 1955 of $57,000. Specific exemption was claimed and allowed in a total amount of $50,000 in the donor's gift tax returns for the calendar years 1934 and 1935 so there remains no specific exemption available for the donor to claim for 1955. The total amount of gifts made by the donor during preceding years, after excluding $5,000 for each donee for each calendar year in accordance with the provisions of section 1003(b)(1) of the 1939 Code, is computed as follows:

Calendar year 1934	$120,000
Calendar year 1935	25,000
Total amount of included gifts for preceding calendar years	$145,000

The aggregate sum of the taxable gifts for preceding calendar years is $115,000, which is determined by deducting a specific exemption of $30,000 from $145,000, the total amount of included gifts for preceding calendar years. The deduction from the 1934 and 1935 gifts for the specific exemption cannot exceed $30,000 for purposes of computing the tax on the 1955 gifts even though a specific exemption in a total amount of $50,000 was allowed in computing the donor's gift tax liability for 1934 and 1935. (See paragraph (b) of § 25.2504–1.) The computation of the tax for the calendar year 1955 (following the steps set forth in paragraph (a) of this section) is shown below:

(1) Amount of taxable gifts for year	$57,000
(2) Total amount of taxable gifts for preceding years	$115,000
(3) Total taxable gifts	$172,000
(4) Tax computed on item 3 (in accordance with the rate schedule effect for the year 1955)	$ 31,725
(5) Tax computed on item 2 (using same rate schedule)	$18,900
(6) Tax for year 1955 (item 4 minus item 5)	$12,825

Example (3). (i) *Facts.* During the calendar year 1955, H makes the following gifts of present interests:

To his daughter	$40,000
To his son	$5,000
To W, his wife	$5,000
To a charitable organization	$10,000

The gifts to W qualify for the marital deduction, and, pursuant to the provisions of section 2513 (see § 25.2513–1), H and W consent to treat the gifts to third parties as having been made one-half by each spouse. The amount of H's taxable gifts for preceding years is $50,000. Only $25,000 of H's specific exemption provided under section 2521, which was in effect at the time, was claimed and allowed in preceding years. H's remaining specific exemption of $5,000 is claimed for the calendar year of 1955. See § 25.2521–1. W made no gifts during the calendar year 1955 nor during any preceding calendar year. W claims sufficient specific exemption on her return to eliminate tax liability.

(ii) *Computation of H's tax for the calendar year 1955*—(a) *H's taxable gifts for year.*

Total gifts of H		$60,000
Less: Portion of items to be reported by spouse (one-half of total gifts to daughter, son and charity)		27,500
Balance		32,500
Less: Exclusions (three of $3,000 each for daughter, wife and charity and one of $2,500 for son)		11,500
Total included amount		21,000
Less: Deductions:		
Charity	$2,000	
Marital	2,000	
Specific exemption	5,000	
Total deductions		9,000
Amount of taxable gifts for year		12,000

(b) *Computation of tax.* The steps set forth in paragraph (a) of this section are followed.

(1) Amount of taxable gifts for year	$12,000
(2) Total taxable gifts for preceding years	50,000
(3) Total taxable gifts (item (1) plus item (2))	62,000
(4) Tax computed on item (3) (in accordance with the rate schedule in effect for the year 1955)	7,545
(5) Tax computed in item (2) (in accordance with the rate schedule in effect for the year 1955)	5,250
(6) Tax for the calendar year (item (4) minus item (5))	2,295

(iii) *Computation of W's tax for calendar year 1955*—(a) *W's taxable gifts for year.*

Total gifts of W		0
Less: Portion of items to be reported by spouse		0
Balance		0
Gifts of spouse to be included		$27,500
Total gifts for year		27,500
Less: Exclusions (two of $3,000 each for daughter and charity and one of $2,500 for son)		$8,500
Balance		19,000
Less—Deductions:		
Charity		$2,000
Marital		0
Specific exemption		17,000
Total deductions		$19,000
Amount of taxable gifts for year		0

(b) *Computation of tax.* Since W had no "taxable gifts" during the year, there is no tax.

Example (4). (i) *Facts.* The facts are the same as in example (3) except that W made outright gifts of $10,000 to her niece and $20,000 to H at various times during the year. The amount of taxable gifts made by W in preceding calendar years is $75,000, and only $20,000 of her specific exemption provided under section 2521, which was in effect at the time, was claimed and allowed for preceding years. See § 25.2521–1. The remaining specific exemption of $10,000 is claimed for the calendar year 1955.

(ii) *Computation of H's tax for the calendar year 1955*—(a) *H's taxable gifts for year.*

Total gifts of H	$60,000
Less: Portion of items to be reported by spouse	27,500
Balance	32,500
Gifts of spouse to be included	5,000
Total gifts for year	37,500

Less: Exclusions ($11,500 as shown in example (3) plus $3,000 exclusion for gift to niece) 14,500

Total included amount of gifts for year...... 23,000

Deductions:

Charity $2,000

Marital 2,000

Specific exemption 5,000

Total deductions 9,000

Amount of taxable gifts for year 14,000

(b) *Computation of tax.*

(1) Amount of taxable gifts for year $14,000

(2) Total taxable gifts for preceding years 50,000

(3) Total taxable gifts (item (1) plus item (2)).. 64,000

(4) Tax computed on item (3) 7,965

(5) Tax computed on item (2) 5,250

(6) Tax for year (item (4) minus item (5)).. 2,715

(iii) *Computation of W's tax for the calendar year 1955*—(a) *W's taxable gifts for year.*

Total gifts of W $30,000

Less: Portion of item—to be reported by spouse (one-half of gift to niece) 5,000

Balance... 25,000

Gifts of spouse to be included.................... 27,500

Total gifts for year..................................... 52,500

Less: Exclusions (four of $3,000 each for daughter, husband, niece and charity, and one of $2,500 for son) ... $14,500

Total included amount of gifts for year...... 38,000

Deductions:

Charity $2,000

Marital 10,000

Specific exemption 10,000

Total deductions 22,000

Amount of taxable gifts for year............. $16,000

(b) *Computation of tax.*

(1) Amount of taxable gifts for year 16,000

(2) Total taxable gifts for preceding years 75,000

(3) Total taxable gifts 91,000

(4) Tax computed on item (3) 13,635

(5) Tax computed on item (2) 10,275

(6) Tax for year (item (4) minus item (5))... 3,360

Example (5). A makes gifts (other than gifts of future interests in property) to B in the first quarter of 1971 of $43,000 and in the second quarter of 1971 of $60,000. A gave to C in the second quarter of 1971 land valued at $11,000. The full amount of A's specific exemption provided under section 2521 was claimed and allowed in 1956. In 1966, A made taxable gifts totaling $21,000 on which gift tax was timely paid and no other taxable gifts were made by A in any other year preceding 1971. The gift tax return due for the first calendar quarter of 1971 was timely filed and the tax paid. With respect to the gifts made to B in 1971, the $3,000 annual gift tax exclusion provided by section 2503(b) is applied in its entirety against the $43,000 gift made to B in the first quarter and therefore is not available to offset the $60,000 gift made to B in the second quarter. (See § 25.2503–2(b).) A further $3,000 annual gift tax exclusion is available, however, to offset the $11,000 gift made to C in the second quarter of 1971. The computation of the gift tax for the second calendar quarter of 1971 due on August 15, 1971 (following the steps set forth in paragraph (a) of this section) is shown below:

(1) Amount of taxable gifts for the second calendar quarter of 1971 ($60,000 + $11,000 - $3,000) $68,000

(2) Total amount of taxable gifts for preceding calendar periods ($43,000 - $3,000 + $21,000) 61,000

(3) Total taxable gifts 129,000

(4) Tax computed on item 3 (in accordance with rate schedule in effect for the year 1971)........................ 22,050

(5) Tax computed on item 2 (using same rate schedule).......................... 7,335

(6) Tax for second calendar quarter of 1971 (item 4 minus item 5)....... 14,715

Example (6). A makes gifts (other than gifts of future interests in property) during the calendar year 1982 of $160,000 to B and $100,000 to C. Two exclusions of $10,000 each are allowable, in accordance with the provisions of section 2503(b), which results in taxable gifts for 1982 of $240,000. In the first calendar quarter of 1978, A made taxable gifts totaling $100,000 on which gift tax was paid. For the calendar year 1969, A made taxable gifts totaling $50,000. The full amount of A's specific exemption provided under section 2521, which was in effect at the time, was claimed and allowed in 1968. The computation of the gift tax for the calendar period 1982 (following the steps set forth in paragraph (a) of this section) is shown below.

(1) Amount of taxable gifts for the calendar year 1982, $240,000.

(2) Total amount of taxable gifts for preceding calendar periods ($100,000 + $50,000), $150,000.

(3) Total taxable gifts, $390,000.

(4) Tax computed on item 3 (in accordance with the rate schedule in effect for the year 1982), $118,400.

(5) Tax computed on item 2 (using same rate schedule), $38,800.

(6) Tax for year 1982 (Item 4 minus item 5), $79,600.

[T.D. 6334, 23 FR 8904, Nov. 15, 1958, as amended by T.D. 7238, 37 FR 28725, Dec. 29, 1972; T.D. 7910, 48 FR 40371, Sept. 7, 1983; T.D. 8395, 57 FR 4255, Feb. 4, 1992]

§ 25.2502–2 Donor primarily liable for tax.

Section 2502(d) provides that the donor shall pay the tax. If the donor dies before the tax is paid the amount of the tax is a debt due the United States from the decedent's estate and his executor or administrator is responsible for its payment out of the estate. (See § 25.6151–1 for the time and place for paying the tax.) If there is no duly qualified executor or administrator, the heirs, legatees, devisees, and distributees are liable for and required to pay the tax to the extent of the value of their inheritances, bequests, devises, or distributive shares of the donor's estate. If a husband and wife effectively signify consent, under section 2513, to have gifts made to a third party during any "calendar period" (as defined in § 25.2502–1(c)(1)) considered as made one-half by each, the liability with respect to the gift tax of each spouse for that calendar period is joint and several (see § 25.2513–4). As to the personal liability of the donee, see paragraph (b) of § 301.6324–1 of this chapter (Regulations on Procedure and Administration). As to the personal liability of the executor or administrator, see section 3467 of the Revised Statutes (31 U.S.C. 192),* which reads as follows:

> Every executor, administrator, or assignee, or other person, who pays, in whole or in part, any debt due by the person or estate for whom or for which he acts before he satisfies and pays the debts due to the United States from such person or estate, shall become answerable in his own person and estate to the extent of such payments for the debts so due to the United States, or for so much thereof as may remain due and unpaid.

As used in such section 3467, the word "debt" includes a beneficiary's distributive share of an estate. Thus if an executor pays a debt due by the estate which is being administered by him or distributes any portion of the estate before there is paid all of the gift tax which he has a duty to pay, the executor is personally liable, to the extent of the payment or distribution, for so much of the gift tax as remains due and unpaid.

[T.D. 7238, 37 FR 28726, Dec. 29, 1972, as amended by T.D. 7910, 48 FR 40371, Sept. 7, 1983]

§ 2503. Taxable Gifts

(a) General definition. The term "taxable gifts" means the total amount of gifts made during the calendar year, less the deductions provided in subchapter C (section 2522 and following).

(b) Exclusion from gifts.

(1) In general. In the case of gifts (other than gifts of future interests in property) made to any person by the donor during the calendar year, the first $10,000 of such gifts to such person shall not, for purposes of subsection (a), be included in the total amount of gifts made during such year. Where there has been a transfer to any person of a present interest in property, the possibility that such interest may be diminished by the exercise of a power shall be disregarded in applying this subsection, if no part of such interest will at any time pass to any other person.

* 31 U.S.C. § 192 has been revised and relocated. For the current version, see the Appendix. *Ed.*

(2) Inflation adjustment. In the case of gifts made in a calendar year after 1998, the $10,000 amount contained in paragraph (1) shall be increased by an amount equal to—

(A) $10,000, multiplied by

(B) the cost-of-living adjustment determined under section 1(f)(3) for such calendar year by substituting "calendar year 1997" for "calendar year 2016" in subparagraph (A)(ii) thereof.

If any amount as adjusted under the preceding sentence is not a multiple of $1,000, such amount shall be rounded to the next lowest multiple of $1,000.*

(c) Transfer for the benefit of minor. No part of a gift to an individual who has not attained the age of 21 years on the date of such transfer shall be considered a gift of a future interest in property for purposes of subsection (b) if the property and the income therefrom—

(1) may be expended by, or for the benefit of, the donee before his attaining the age of 21 years, and

(2) will to the extent not so expended—

(A) pass to the donee on his attaining the age of 21 years, and

(B) in the event the donee dies before attaining the age of 21 years, be payable to the estate of the donee or as he may appoint under a general power of appointment as defined in section 2514(c).

(d) [Repealed.]

(e) Exclusion for certain transfers for educational expenses or medical expenses.

(1) In general. Any qualified transfer shall not be treated as a transfer of property by gift for purposes of this chapter.

(2) Qualified transfer. For purposes of this subsection, the term "qualified transfer" means any amount paid on behalf of an individual—

(A) as tuition to an educational organization described in section 170(b)(1)(A)(ii) for the education or training of such individual, or

(B) to any person who provides medical care (as defined in section 213(d)) with respect to such individual as payment for such medical care.

(f) Waiver of certain pension rights. If any individual waives, before the death of a participant, any survivor benefit, or right to such benefit, under section 401(a)(11) or 417, such waiver shall not be treated as a transfer of property by gift for purposes of this chapter.

(g) Treatment of certain loans of artworks.

(1) In general. For purposes of this subtitle, any loan of a qualified work of art shall not be treated as a transfer (and the value of such qualified work of art shall be determined as if such loan had not been made) if—

(A) such loan is to an organization described in section 501(c)(3) and exempt from tax under section 501(c) (other than a private foundation), and

(B) the use of such work by such organization is related to the purpose or function constituting the basis for its exemption under section 501.

(2) Definitions. For purposes of this section—

(A) Qualified work of art. The term "qualified work of art" means any archaeological, historic, or creative tangible personal property.

* Rev. Proc. 2025–32 provides that "[f]or calendar year 2026, the first $19,000 of gifts to any person (other than gifts of future interests in property) are not included in the total amount of taxable gifts under § 2503 made during that year." *Ed.*

(B) Private foundation. The term "private foundation" has the meaning given such term by section 509, except that such term shall not include any private operating foundation (as defined in section 4942(j)(3)).

Regulations

§ 25.2503–1 General definitions of "taxable gifts" and of "total amount of gifts."

The term "taxable gifts" means the "total amount of gifts" made by the donor during the "calendar period" (as defined in § 25.2502–1(c)(1)) less the deductions provided for in sections 2521 (as in effect before its repeal by the Tax Reform Act of 1976), 2522, and 2523 (specific exemption, charitable, etc., gifts and the marital deduction, respectively). The term "total amount of gifts" means the sum of the values of the gifts made during the calendar period less the amounts excludable under section 2503(b). See § 25.2503–2. The entire value of any gift of a future interest in property must be included in the total amount of gifts for the calendar period in which the gift is made. See § 25.2503–3.

[T.D. 7238, 37 FR 28727, Dec. 29, 1972, as amended by T.D. 7910, 48 FR 40373, Sept. 7, 1983]

§ 25.2503–2 Exclusions from gifts.

(a) Gifts made after December 31, 1981. Except as provided in paragraph (f) of this section (involving gifts to a noncitizen spouse), the first $10,000 of gifts made to any one donee during the calendar year 1982 or any calendar year thereafter, except gifts of future interests in property as defined in §§ 25.2503–3 and 25.2503–4, is excluded in determining the total amount of gifts for the calendar year. In the case of a gift in trust the beneficiary of the trust is the donee.

(b) Gifts made after December 31, 1970 and before January 1, 1982. In computing taxable gifts for the calendar quarter, in the case of gifts (other than gifts of future interests in property) made to any person by the donor during any calendar quarter of the calendar year 1971 or any subsequent calendar year, $3,000 of such gifts to such person less the aggregate of the amounts of such gifts to such person during all preceding calendar quarters of any such calendar year shall not be included in the total amount of gifts made during such quarter. Thus, the first $3,000 of gifts made to any one donee during the calendar year 1971 or any calendar year thereafter, except gifts of future interests in property as defined in §§ 25.2503–3 and 25.2503–4, is excluded in determining the total amount of gifts for a calendar quarter. In the case of a gift in trust the beneficiary of the trust is the donee. The application of this paragraph may be illustrated by the following examples:

Example (1). A made a gift of $3,000 to B on January 8, 1971, and on April 20, 1971, gave B an additional gift of $10,000. A made no other gifts in 1971. The total amount of gifts made by A during the second quarter of 1971 is $10,000 because the $3,000 exclusion provided by section 2503(b) is first applied to the January 8th gift.

Example (2). A gave $2,000 to B on January 8, 1971, and on April 20, 1971, gave him $10,000. The total amount of gifts made by A during the second quarter of 1971 is $9,000 because only $2,000 of the $3,000 exclusion provided by section 2503(b) was applied against the January 8th gift; $1,000 was available to offset other gifts (except gifts of a future interest) made to B during 1971.

(c) Gifts made before January 1, 1971. The first $3,000 of gifts made to any one donee during the calendar year 1955, or 1970, or any calendar year intervening between calendar year 1955 and calendar year 1970, except gifts of future interests in property as defined in §§ 25.2503–3 and 25.2503–4, is excluded in determining the total amount of gifts for the calendar year. In the case of a gift in trust the beneficiary of the trust is the donee.

(d) Transitional rule. The increased annual gift tax exclusion as defined in section 2503(b) shall not apply to any gift subject to a power of appointment granted under an instrument executed before September 12, 1981, and not amended on or after that date, provided that: (1) The power is exercisable after December 31, 1981, (2) the power is expressly defined in terms of, or by reference to, the amount of the gift tax exclusion under section 2503(b) (or the corresponding provision of prior law), and (3) there is not enacted a State law applicable to such instrument which construes the power of appointment as referring to the increased annual gift tax exclusion provided by the Economic Recovery Tax Act of 1981.

(e) Examples. The provisions of paragraph (d) of this section may be illustrated by the following examples:

Example (1). A executed an instrument to create a trust for the benefit of B on July 2, 1981. The trust granted to B the power, for a period of 90 days after any transfer of cash to the trust, to withdraw from the trust the lesser of the amount of the transferred cash or the amount equal to the section 2503(b) annual gift tax exclusion. The trust was not amended on or after September 12, 1981. No state statute has been enacted which construes the power of appointment as referring to the increased annual gift tax exclusion provided by the Economic Recovery Tax Act of 1981. Accordingly, the maximum annual gift tax exclusion applicable to any gift subject to the exercise of the power of appointment is $3,000.

Example (2). Assume the same facts as in example (1) except that the power of appointment granted in the trust refers to section 2503(b) as amended at any time. The maximum annual gift tax exclusion applicable to any gift subject to the exercise of the power of appointment is $10,000.

(f) Special rule in the case of gifts made on or after July 14, 1988, to a spouse who is not a United States citizen. (1) *In general.* Subject to the special rules set forth at § 20.2056A–1(c) of this chapter, in the case of gifts made on or after July 14, 1988, if the donee of the gift is the donor's spouse and the donee spouse is not a citizen of the United States at the time of the gift, the first $100,000 of gifts made during the calendar year to the donee spouse (except gifts of future interests) is excluded in determining the total amount of gifts for the calendar year. The rule of this paragraph (f) applies regardless of whether the donor is a citizen or resident of the United States for purposes of chapter 12 of the Internal Revenue Code.

(2) *Gifts made after June 29, 1989.* In the case of gifts made after June 29, 1989, the $100,000 exclusion provided in paragraph (f)(1) of this section applies only if the gift in excess of the otherwise applicable annual exclusion is in a form that qualifies for the gift tax marital deduction under section 2523(a) but for the provisions of section 2523(i)(1) (disallowing the marital deduction if the donee spouse is not a United States citizen.) See § 25.2523(i)–1(d), Example 4.

(3) *Effective date.* This paragraph (f) is effective with respect to gifts made after August 22, 1995.

[T.D. 6334, 23 FR 8904, Nov. 15, 1958, as amended by T.D. 7238, 37 FR 28727, Dec. 29, 1972; T.D. 7910, 48 FR 40371, Sept. 7, 1983; T.D. 7978, 49 FR 38541, Oct. 1, 1984; T.D. 8612, 60 FR 43552, Aug. 22, 1995]

§ 25.2503–3 Future interests in property.

(a) No part of the value of a gift of a future interest may be excluded in determining the total amount of gifts made during the "calendar period" (as defined in § 25.2502–1(c)(1)). "Future interest" is a legal term, and includes reversions, remainders, and other interests or estates, whether vested or contingent, and whether or not supported by a particular interest or estate, which are limited to commence in use, possession, or enjoyment at some future date or time. The term has no reference to such contractual rights as exist in a bond, note (though bearing no interest until maturity), or in a policy of life insurance, the obligations of which are to be discharged by payments in the future. But a future interest or interests in such contractual obligations may be created by the limitations contained in a trust or other instrument of transfer used in effecting a gift. A contribution to an ABLE account established under section 529A is not a future interest.

(b) An unrestricted right to the immediate use, possession, or enjoyment of property or the income from property (such as a life estate or term certain) is a present interest in property. An exclusion is allowable with respect to a gift of such an interest (but not in excess of the value of the interest). If a donee has received a present interest in property, the possibility that such interest may be diminished by the transfer of a greater interest in the same property to the donee through the exercise of a power is disregarded in computing the value of the present interest, to the extent that no part of such interest will at any time pass to any other person (see example (4) of paragraph (c) of this section). For an exception to the rule disallowing an exclusion for gifts of future interests in the case of certain gifts to minors, see § 25.2503–4.

(c) The operation of this section may be illustrated by the following examples:

Example (1). Under the terms of a trust created by A the trustee is directed to pay the net income to B, so long as B shall live. The trustee is authorized in his discretion to withhold payments of income during any period he deems advisable and add such income to the trust corpus. Since B's right to receive the income payments is subject to the trustee's discretion, it is not a present interest and no exclusion is allowable with respect to the transfer in trust.

Example (2). C transfers certain insurance policies on his own life to a trust created for the benefit of D. Upon C's death the proceeds of the policies are to be invested and the net income therefrom paid to D during his lifetime. Since the income payments to D will not begin until after C's death the transfer in trust represents a gift of a future interest in property against which no exclusion is allowable.

Example (3). Under the terms of a trust created by E the net income is to be distributed to E's three children in such shares as the trustee, in his uncontrolled discretion deems advisable. While the terms of the trust provide that all of the net income is to be distributed, the amount of income any one of the three beneficiaries will receive rests entirely within the trustee's discretion and cannot be presently ascertained. Accordingly, no exclusions are allowable with respect to the transfers to the trust.

Example (4). Under the terms of a trust the net income is to be paid to F for life, with the remainder payable to G on F's death. The trustee has the uncontrolled power to pay over the corpus to F at any time. Although F's present right to receive the income may be terminated, no other person has the right to such income interest. Accordingly, the power in the trustee is disregarded in determining the value of F's present interest. The power would not be disregarded to the extent that the trustee during F's life could distribute corpus to persons other than F.

Example (5). The corpus of a trust created by J consists of certain real property, subject to a mortgage. The terms of the trust provide that the net income from the property is to be used to pay the mortgage. After the mortgage is paid in full the net income is to be paid to K during his lifetime. Since K's right to receive the income payments will not begin until after the mortgage is paid in full the transfer in trust represents a gift of a future interest in property against which no exclusion is allowable.

Example (6). L pays premiums on a policy of insurance on his life, all the incidents of ownership in the policy (including the right to surrender the policy) are vested in M. The payment of premiums by L constitutes a gift of a present interest in property.

[T.D. 6334, 23 FR 8904, Nov. 15, 1958, as amended by T.D. 7238, 37 FR 28727, Dec. 29, 1972; T.D. 7910, 48 FR 40371, Sept. 7, 1983; T.D. 9923, 85 FR 74047, Nov. 19, 2020]

§ 25.2503–4 Transfer for the benefit of a minor.

(a) Section 2503(c) provides that no part of a transfer for the benefit of a donee who has not attained the age of 21 years on the date of the gift will be considered a gift of a future interest in property if the terms of the transfer satisfy all of the following conditions:

(1) Both the property itself and its income may be expended by or for the benefit of the donee before he attains the age of 21 years;

(2) Any portion of the property and its income not disposed of under subparagraph (1) of this paragraph will pass to the donee when he attains the age of 21 years; and

(3) Any portion of the property and its income not disposed of under subparagraph (1) of this paragraph will be payable either to the estate of the donee or as he may appoint under a general power of appointment as defined in section 2514(c) if he dies before attaining the age of 21 years.

(b) Either a power of appointment exercisable by the donee by will or a power of appointment exercisable by the donee during his lifetime will satisfy the conditions set forth in paragraph (a)(3) of this section. However, if the transfer is to qualify for the exclusion under this section, there must be no restrictions of substance (as distinguished from formal restrictions of the type described in paragraph (g)(4) of § 25.2523(e)–1 by the terms of the instrument of transfer on the exercise of the power by the donee. However, if the minor is given a power of appointment exercisable during lifetime or is given a power of appointment exercisable by will, the fact that under the local law a minor is under a disability to exercise an inter vivos power or to execute a will does not cause the transfer to fail to satisfy the conditions of section 2503(c). Further, a transfer does not fail to satisfy the conditions of section 2503(c) by reason of the mere fact that—

(1) There is left to the discretion of a trustee the determination of the amounts, if any, of the income or property to be expended for the benefit of the minor and the purpose for which the expenditure is to be made, provided there are no substantial restrictions under the terms of the trust instrument on the exercise of such discretion;

(2) The donee, upon reaching age 21, has the right to extend the term of the trust; or

(3) The governing instrument contains a disposition of the property or income not expended during the donee's minority to persons other than the donee's estate in the event of the default of appointment by the donee.

(c) A gift to a minor which does not satisfy the requirements of section 2503(c) may be either a present or a future interest under the general rules of § 25.2503–3. Thus, for example, a transfer of property in trust with income required to be paid annually to a minor beneficiary and corpus to be distributed to him upon his attaining the age of 25 is a gift of a present interest with respect to the right to income but is a gift of a future interest with respect to the right to corpus.

[T.D. 6334, 23 FR 8904, Nov. 15, 1958]

Proposed § 25.2503–5 (EE–7–78, July 14, 1981) Individual retirement plan for spouse.

(a) In general. For purposes of section 2503 (b), and payment made by an individual for the benefit of his or her spouse—

(1) To individual retirement account described in section 408(a),

(2) To an individual retirement subaccount described in § 1.220–1(b)(3),

(3) For an individual retirement annuity described in section 408(b), or

(4) For a retirement bond described in section 409,

shall not be considered a gift of a future interest in property to the extent that such payment is allowable as a deduction under section 220 for the taxable year for which the contribution is made. Thus, for example, if individual A paid $900 to an individual retirement account for 1980 on behalf of A's spouse, B, of which $875 was deductible, $875 would not be a gift of a future interest.

(b) Effective date. Paragraph (a) of this section is effective for transfers made after December 31, 1976.

§ 25.2503–6 Exclusion for certain qualified transfer for tuition or medical expenses.

(a) In general. Section 2503(e) provides that any qualified transfer after December 31, 1981, shall not be treated as a transfer of property by gift for purposes of Chapter 12 of Subtitle B of the Code. Thus, a qualified transfer on behalf of any individual is excluded in determining the total amount of gifts in calendar year 1982 and subsequent years. This exclusion is available in addition to the $10,000 annual gift tax exclusion. Furthermore, an exclusion for a qualified transfer is permitted without regard to the relationship between the donor and the donee. A contribution to an ABLE account established under section 529A is not a qualified transfer.

(b) Qualified transfers. (1) *Definition.* For purposes of this paragraph, the term "qualified transfer" means any amount paid on behalf of an individual—

(i) As tuition to a qualifying educational organization for the education or training of that individual, or

(ii) To any person who provides medical care with respect to that individual as payment for the qualifying medical expenses arising from such medical care.

(2) *Tuition expenses.* For purposes of paragraph (b)(1)(i) of this section, a qualifying educational organization is one which normally maintains a regular faculty and curriculum and normally has a regularly enrolled body of pupils or students in attendance at the place where its educational activities are regularly carried on. See section 170(b)(1)(A)(ii) and the regulations thereunder. The unlimited exclusion is permitted for tuition expenses of full-time or part-time students paid directly to the qualifying educational organization providing the education. No unlimited exclusion is permitted for amounts paid for books, supplies, dormitory fees, board, or other similar expenses which do not constitute direct tuition costs.

(3) *Medical expenses.* For purposes of paragraph (b)(1)(ii) of this section, qualifying medical expenses are limited to those expenses defined in section 213(d) (section 213(e) prior to January 1, 1984) and include expenses incurred for the diagnosis, cure, mitigation,

treatment or prevention of disease, or for the purpose of affecting any structure or function of the body or for transportation primarily for and essential to medical care. In addition, the unlimited exclusion from the gift tax includes amounts paid for medical insurance on behalf of any individual. The unlimited exclusion from the gift tax does not apply to amounts paid for medical care that are reimbursed by the donee's insurance. Thus, if payment for a medical expense is reimbursed by the donee's insurance company, the donor's payment for that expense, to the extent of the reimbursed amount, is not eligible for the unlimited exclusion from the gift tax and the gift is treated as having been made on the date the reimbursement is received by the donee.

(c) Examples. The provisions of paragraph (b) of this section may be illustrated by the following examples.

Example (1). In 1982, A made a tuition payment directly to a foreign university on behalf of B. A had no legal obligation to make this payment. The foreign university is described in section 170(b)(1)(A)(ii) of the Code. A's tuition payment is exempt from the gift tax under section 2503(e) of the Code.

Example (2). A transfers $100,000 to a trust the provisions of which state that the funds are to be used for tuition expenses incurred by A's grandchildren. A's transfer to the trust is a completed gift for Federal gift tax purposes and is not a direct transfer to an educational organization as provided in paragraph (b)(2) of this section and does not qualify for the unlimited exclusion from gift tax under section 2503(e).

Example (3). C was seriously injured in an automobile accident in 1982. D, who is unrelated to C, paid C's various medical expenses by checks made payable to the physician. D also paid the hospital for C's hospital bills. These medical and hospital expenses were types described in section 213 of the Code and were not reimbursed by insurance or otherwise. Because the medical and hospital bills paid in 1982 for C were medical expenses within the meaning of section 213 of the Code, and since they were paid directly by D to the person rendering the medical care, they are not treated as transfers subject to the gift tax.

Example (4). Assume the same facts as in example (2) except that instead of making the payments directly to the medical service provided, D reimbursed C for the medical expenses which C had previously paid. The payments made by D to C do not qualify for the exclusion under section 2503(e) of the Code and are subject to the gift tax on the date the reimbursement is received by C to the extent the reimbursement and all other gifts from D to C during the year of the reimbursement exceed the $10,000 annual exclusion provided in section 2503(b).

[T.D. 7978, 49 FR 38541, Oct. 1, 1984; T.D. 7978, 49 FR 39843, Oct. 11, 1984; T.D. 9923, 85 FR 74047, Nov. 19, 2020]

§ 2504. Taxable Gifts for Preceding Calendar Periods

(a) In general. In computing taxable gifts for preceding calendar periods for purposes of computing the tax for any calendar year—

(1) there shall be treated as gifts such transfers as were considered to be gifts under the gift tax laws applicable to the calendar period in which the transfers were made,

(2) there shall be allowed such deductions as were provided for under such laws, and

(3) the specific exemption in the amount (if any) allowable under section 2521 (as in effect before its repeal by the Tax Reform Act of 1976) shall be applied in all computations in respect of preceding calendar periods ending before January 1, 1977, for purposes of computing the tax for any calendar year.

(b) Exclusions from gifts for preceding calendar periods. In the case of gifts made to any person by the donor during preceding calendar periods, the amount excluded, if any, by the provisions of gift tax laws applicable to the periods in which the gifts were made shall not, for purposes of subsection (a), be included in the total amount of the gifts made during such preceding calendar periods.

(c) Valuation of gifts. If the time has expired under section 6501 within which a tax may be assessed under this chapter 12 (or under corresponding provisions of prior laws) on—

(1) the transfer of property by gift made during a preceding calendar period (as defined in section 2502(b)); or

(2) an increase in taxable gifts required under section 2701(d),

the value thereof shall, for purposes of computing the tax under this chapter, be the value as finally determined (within the meaning of section 2001(f)(2)) for purposes of this chapter.

(d) Net gifts. The term "net gifts" as used in corresponding provisions of prior laws shall be read as "taxable gifts" for purposes of this chapter.

Regulations

§ 25.2504–1 Taxable gifts for preceding calendar periods.

(a) In order to determine the correct gift tax liability for any calendar period it is necessary to ascertain the correct amount, if any, of the aggregate sum of the taxable gifts for each of the "preceding calendar periods" (as defined in § 25.2502–1(c)(2)). See paragraph (a) of § 25.2502–1. The term "aggregate sum of the taxable gifts for each of the preceding calendar periods" means the correct aggregate of such gifts, not necessarily that returned for those calendar periods and in respect of which tax was paid. All transfers that constituted gifts in prior calendar periods under the laws, including the provisions of law relating to exclusions from gifts, in effect at the time the transfers were made are included in determining the amount of taxable gifts for preceding calendar periods. The deductions other than for the specific exemption (see paragraph (b) of this section) allowed by the laws in effect at the time the transfers were made also are taken into account in determining the aggregate sum of the taxable gifts for preceding calendar periods. (The allowable exclusion from a gift is $5,000 for years before 1939, $4,000 for the calendar years 1939 through 1942, $3,000 for the calendar years 1943 through 1981, and $10,000 thereafter.)

(b) In determining the aggregate sum of the taxable gifts for the "preceding calendar periods" (as defined in § 25.2502–1(c)(2)), the total of the amounts allowed as deductions for the specific exemption, under section 2521 (as in effect prior to its repeal by the Tax Reform Act of 1976) and the corresponding provisions of prior laws, shall not exceed $30,000. Thus, if the only prior gifts by a donor were made in 1940 and 1941 (at which time the specific exemption allowable was $40,000), and if in the donor's returns for those years the donor claimed deductions totaling $40,000 for the specific exemption and reported taxable gifts totaling $110,000, then in determining the aggregate sum of the taxable gifts for the preceding calendar periods, the deductions for the specific exemption cannot exceed $30,000, and the donor's taxable gifts for such periods will be $120,000 (instead of the $110,000 reported on the donor's returns). (The allowable deduction for the specific exemption was $50,000 for calendar years before 1936, $40,000 for calendar years 1936 through 1942, and $30,000 for 1943 through 1976.)

(c) If the donor and the donor's spouse consented to have gifts made to third parties considered as made one-half by each spouse, pursuant to the provisions of section 2513 or section 1000(f) of the Internal Revenue Code of 1939 (which corresponds to Section 2513), these provisions shall be taken into account in determining the aggregate sum of the taxable gifts for the preceding calendar periods (under paragraph (a) of this section).

(d) If interpretations of the gift tax law in preceding calendar periods resulted in the erroneous inclusion of property for gift tax purposes that should have been excluded, or the erroneous exclusion of property that should have been included, adjustments must be made in order to arrive at the correct aggregate of taxable gifts for the preceding calendar periods (under paragraph (a) of this section). However, see section 1000(e) and (g) of the 1939 Code relating to certain discretionary trusts and reciprocal trusts. However, see § 25.2504–2(b) regarding certain gifts made after August 5, 1997.

[T.D. 6334, 23 FR 8904, Nov. 15, 1958, as amended by T.D. 7238, 37 FR 28727, Dec. 29, 1972; T.D. 7910, 48 FR 40373, Sept. 7, 1983; T.D. 8845, 64 FR 67770, Dec. 3, 1999]

§ 25.2504–2 Determination of gifts for preceding calendar periods.

(a) Gifts made before August 6, 1997. If the time has expired within which a tax may be assessed under chapter 12 of the Internal Revenue Code (or under corresponding provisions of prior laws) on the transfer of property by gift made during a preceding calendar period, as defined in § 25.2502–1(c)(2), the gift was made prior to August 6, 1997, and a tax has been assessed or paid for such prior calendar period, the value of the gift, for purposes of arriving at the correct amount of the taxable gifts for the preceding calendar periods (as defined under § 25.2504–1(a)), is the value used in computing the tax for the last preceding calendar period for which a tax was assessed or paid under chapter 12 of the Internal Revenue Code or the corresponding provisions of prior laws. However, this rule does not apply where no tax was paid or assessed for the prior calendar period. Furthermore, this rule does not apply to adjustments involving issues other than valuation. See § 25.2504–1(d).

(b) Gifts made or section 2701(d) taxable events occurring after August 5, 1997. If the time has expired under section 6501 within which a gift tax may be assessed under chapter 12 of the Internal Revenue Code (or under corresponding provisions of prior laws) on the transfer of property by gift made during a preceding calendar period, as defined in § 25.2502–1(c)(2), or with respect to an increase in taxable gifts required under section 2701(d) and § 25.2701–4, and the gift was made, or the section 2701(d) taxable event occurred, after August 5, 1997, the amount of the taxable gift or the amount of the increase in taxable gifts, for purposes of determining the correct amount of taxable gifts for the preceding calendar periods (as defined in § 25.2504–1(a)), is the amount that is finally determined for gift tax purposes (within the meaning of § 20.2001–1(c) of this chapter) and such amount may not be thereafter adjusted. The rule of this paragraph (b) applies to adjustments involving all issues relating to the gift including valuation issues and legal issues involving the interpretation of the gift tax law. For purposes of determining if the time has expired within which a gift tax may be assessed, see § 301.6501(c)–1(e) and (f) of this chapter.

(c) Examples. The following examples illustrate the rules of paragraphs (a) and (b) of this section:

Example (1). (i) *Facts.* In 1996, A transferred closely-held stock in trust for the benefit of B, A's child. A timely filed a Federal gift tax return reporting the 1996 transfer to B. No gift tax was assessed or paid as a result of the gift tax annual exclusion and the application of A's available unified credit. In 2001, A transferred additional closely-held stock to the trust. A's Federal gift tax return reporting the 2001 transfer was timely filed and the transfer was adequately disclosed under § 301.6501(c)–1(f)(2) of this chapter. In computing the amount of taxable gifts, A claimed annual exclusions with respect to the transfers in 1996 and 2001. In 2003, A transfers additional property to B and timely files a Federal gift tax return reporting the gift.

(ii) *Application of the rule limiting adjustments to prior gifts.* Under section 2504(c), in determining A's 2003 gift tax liability, the amount of A's 1996 gift can be adjusted for purposes of computing prior taxable gifts, since that gift was made prior to August 6, 1997, and therefore, the provisions of paragraph (a) of this section apply. Adjustments can be made with respect to the valuation of the gift and legal issues presented (for example, the availability of the annual exclusion with respect to the gift). However, A's 2001 transfer was adequately disclosed on a timely filed gift tax return and, thus, under paragraph (b) of this section, the amount of the 2001 taxable gift by A may not be adjusted (either with respect to the valuation of the gift or any legal issue) for purposes of computing prior taxable gifts in determining A's 2003 gift tax liability.

Example (2). (i) *Facts.* In 1996, A transferred closely-held stock to B, A's child. A timely filed a Federal gift tax return reporting the 1996 transfer to B and paid gift tax on the value of the gift reported on the return. On August 1, 1997, A transferred additional closely-held stock to B in exchange for a promissory note signed by B. Also, on September 10, 1997, A transferred closely-held stock to C, A's other child. On April 15, 1998, A timely filed a gift tax return for 1997 reporting the September 10, 1997, transfer to C and, under § 301.6501(c)–1(f)(2) of this chapter, adequately disclosed that transfer and paid gift tax with respect to the transfer. However, A believed that the transfer to B on August 1, 1997, was for full and adequate consideration and A did not report the transfer to B on the 1997 Federal gift tax return. In 2002, A transfers additional property to B and timely files a Federal gift tax return reporting the gift.

(ii) *Application of the rule limiting adjustments to prior gifts.* Under section 2504(c), in determining A's 2002 gift tax liability, the value of A's 1996 gift cannot be adjusted for purposes of computing the value of prior taxable gifts, since that gift was made prior to August 6, 1997, and a timely filed Federal gift tax return was filed on which a gift tax was assessed and paid. However, A's prior taxable gifts can be adjusted to reflect the August 1, 1997, transfer because, although a gift tax return for 1997 was timely filed and gift tax was paid, under § 301.6501(c)–1(f) of this chapter the period for assessing gift tax with respect to the August 1, 1997, transfer did not commence to run since that transfer was not adequately disclosed on the 1997 gift tax return. Accordingly, a gift tax may be assessed with respect to the August 1, 1997, transfer and the amount of the gift would be reflected in prior taxable gifts for purposes of computing A's gift tax liability for 2002. A's September 10, 1997, transfer to C was adequately disclosed on a timely filed gift tax return and, thus, under paragraph (b) of this section, the amount of the September 10, 1997, taxable gift by A may not be adjusted for purposes of computing prior taxable gifts in determining A's 2002 gift tax liability.

Example (3). (i) *Facts.* In 1994, A transferred closely-held stock to B and C, A's children. A timely filed a Federal gift tax return reporting the 1994 transfers to B and C and paid gift tax on the value of the gifts reported on the return. Also in 1994, A transferred closely-held stock to B in exchange for a bona fide promissory note signed by B. A believed that the transfer to B in exchange for the promissory note was for full and adequate consideration and A did not report that transfer to B on the 1994 Federal gift tax return. In 2002, A transfers additional property to B and timely files a Federal gift tax return reporting the gift.

(ii) *Application of the rule limiting adjustments to prior gifts.* Under section 2504(c), in determining A's 2002 gift tax liability, the value of A's 1994 gifts cannot be adjusted for purposes of computing prior taxable gifts because those gifts were made prior to August 6, 1997, and a timely filed Federal gift tax return was filed with respect to which a gift tax was assessed and paid, and the period of limitations on assessment has expired. The provisions of paragraph (a) of this section apply to the 1994 transfers. However, for purposes of determining A's adjusted taxable gifts in computing A's estate tax liability, the gifts may be adjusted. See § 20.2001–1(a) of this chapter.

(d) Effective dates. Paragraph (a) of this section applies to transfers of property by gift made prior to August 6, 1997. Paragraphs (b) and (c) of this section apply to transfers of property by gift made after August 5, 1997, if the gift tax return for the calendar period in which the transfer is reported is filed after December 3, 1999.

[T.D. 6334, 23 FR 8904, Nov. 15, 1958, as amended by T.D. 7238, 37 FR 28728, Dec. 29, 1972; T.D. 7910, 48 FR 40374, Sept. 7, 1983; T.D. 8845, 64 FR 67770, Dec. 3, 1999]

§ 2505. Unified Credit Against Gift Tax

(a) General Rule. In the case of a citizen or resident of the United States, there shall be allowed as a credit against the tax imposed by section 2501 for each calendar year an amount equal to—

(1) the applicable credit amount in effect under section 2010(c) which would apply if the donor died as of the end of the calendar year, reduced by

(2) the sum of the amounts allowable as a credit to the individual under this section for all preceding calendar periods.

For purposes of applying paragraph (2) for any calendar year, the rates of tax in effect under section 2502(a)(2) for such calendar year shall, in lieu of the rates of tax in effect for preceding calendar periods, be used in determining the amounts allowable as a credit under this section for all preceding calendar periods.

(b) Adjustment to credit for certain gifts made before 1977. The amount allowable under subsection (a) shall be reduced by an amount equal to 20 percent of the aggregate amount allowed as a specific exemption under section 2521 (as in effect before its repeal by the Tax Reform Act of 1976) with respect to gifts made by the individual after September 8, 1976.

(c) Limitation based on amount of tax. The amount of the credit allowed under subsection (a) for any calendar year shall not exceed the amount of the tax imposed by section 2501 for such calendar year.

Regulations

§ 25.2505–0 Table of contents. [*Omitted. Ed.*]

[T.D. 9725, 80 FR 34290, June 16, 2015]

§ 25.2505–1 Unified credit against gift tax; in general.

(a) General rule. Section 2505(a) allows a citizen or resident of the United States a credit against the tax imposed by section 2501 for each calendar year. The allowable credit is the applicable credit amount in effect under section 2010(c) that would apply if the donor died as of the end of the calendar year, reduced by the sum of the amounts allowable as a credit against the gift tax due for all preceding calendar periods. See §§ 25.2505–2, 20.2010–1, and 20.2010–2 for additional rules and definitions related to determining the applicable credit amount in effect under section 2010(c).

(b) Applicable rate of tax. In determining the amounts allowable as a credit against the gift tax due for all preceding calendar periods, the unified rate schedule under section 2001(c) in effect for such calendar year applies instead of the rates of tax actually in effect for preceding calendar periods. See sections 2505(a) and 2502(a)(2).

(c) Special rule in case of certain gifts made before 1977. The applicable credit amount allowable under paragraph (a) of this section must be reduced by an amount equal to 20 percent of the aggregate amount allowed as a specific exemption under section 2521 (as in effect before its repeal by the Tax Reform Act of 1976) for gifts made by the decedent after September 8, 1976, and before January 1, 1977.

(d) Credit limitation. The applicable credit amount allowed under paragraph (a) of this section for any calendar year shall not exceed the amount of the tax imposed by section 2501 for such calendar year.

(e) Effective/applicability date. This section applies to gifts made on or after June 12, 2015. See 26 CFR 25.2505–1T, as contained in 26 CFR part 25, revised as of April 1, 2015, for the rules applicable to gifts made on or after January 1, 2011, and before June 12, 2015.

[T.D. 9725, 80 FR 34290, June 16, 2015]

§ 25.2505–2 Gifts made by a surviving spouse having a DSUE amount available.

(a) Donor who is surviving spouse is limited to DSUE amount of last deceased spouse. (1) *In general.* In computing a surviving spouse's gift tax liability with regard to a transfer subject to the tax imposed by section 2501 (taxable gift), a deceased spousal unused exclusion (DSUE) amount of a decedent, computed under § 20.2010–2(c), is included in determining the surviving spouse's applicable exclusion amount under section 2010(c)(2), provided:

(i) Such decedent is the last deceased spouse of such surviving spouse within the meaning of § 20.2010–1(e)(5) at the time of the surviving spouse's taxable gift; and

(ii) The executor of the decedent's estate elected portability (see § 20.2010–2(a) and (b) for applicable requirements).

(2) *No DSUE amount available from last deceased spouse.* If on the date of the surviving spouse's taxable gift the last deceased spouse of such surviving spouse had no DSUE amount or if the executor of the estate of such last deceased spouse did not elect portability, the surviving spouse has no DSUE amount (except as and to the extent provided in paragraph (c)(1)(ii) of this section) to be included in determining his or her applicable exclusion amount, even if the surviving spouse previously had a DSUE amount available from another decedent who, prior to the death of the last deceased spouse, was the last deceased spouse of such surviving spouse. See paragraph (c) of this section for a special rule in the case of multiple deceased spouses.

(3) *Identity of last deceased spouse unchanged by subsequent marriage or divorce.* A decedent is the last deceased spouse (as defined in § 20.2010–1(e)(5)) of a surviving spouse even if, on the date of the surviving spouse's taxable gift, the surviving spouse is married to another (then-living) individual. If a surviving spouse marries again and that marriage ends in divorce or an annulment, the subsequent death of the divorced spouse does not end the status of the prior deceased spouse as the last deceased spouse of the surviving

spouse. The divorced spouse, not being married to the surviving spouse at death, is not the last deceased spouse as that term is defined in § 20.2010–1(e)(5).

(b) Manner in which DSUE amount is applied. If a donor who is a surviving spouse makes a taxable gift and a DSUE amount is included in determining the surviving spouse's applicable exclusion amount under section 2010(c)(2), such surviving spouse will be considered to apply such DSUE amount to the taxable gift before the surviving spouse's own basic exclusion amount.

(c) Special rule in case of multiple deceased spouses and previously-applied DSUE amount. (1) *In general.* A special rule applies to compute the DSUE amount included in the applicable exclusion amount of a surviving spouse who previously has applied the DSUE amount of one or more deceased spouses. If a surviving spouse applied the DSUE amount of one or more (successive) last deceased spouses to the surviving spouse's previous lifetime transfers, and if any of those last deceased spouses is different from the surviving spouse's last deceased spouse as defined in § 20.2010–1(e)(5) at the time of the current taxable gift by the surviving spouse, then the DSUE amount to be included in determining the applicable exclusion amount of the surviving spouse that will be applicable at the time of the current taxable gift is the sum of—

(i) The DSUE amount of the surviving spouse's last deceased spouse as described in paragraph (a)(1) of this section; and

(ii) The DSUE amount of each other deceased spouse of the surviving spouse to the extent that such amount was applied to one or more previous taxable gifts of the surviving spouse.

(2) *Example.* The following example, in which all described individuals are U.S. citizens, illustrates the application of this paragraph (c):

Example. (i) *Facts.* Husband 1 (H1) dies in 2011, survived by Wife (W). Neither has made any taxable gifts during H1's lifetime. H1's executor elects portability of H1's deceased spousal unused exclusion (DSUE) amount. The DSUE amount of H1 as computed on the estate tax return filed on behalf of H1's estate is $5,000,000. In 2012, W makes taxable gifts to her children valued at $2,000,000. W reports the gifts on a timely filed gift tax return. W is considered to have applied $2,000,000 of H1's DSUE amount to the 2012 taxable gifts, in accordance with paragraph (b) of this section, and, therefore, W owes no gift tax. W is considered to have an applicable exclusion amount remaining in the amount of $8,120,000 ($3,000,000 of H1's remaining DSUE amount plus W's own $5,120,000 basic exclusion amount). In 2013, W marries Husband 2 (H2). H2 dies on June 30, 2015. H2's executor elects portability of H2's DSUE amount, which is properly computed on H2's estate tax return to be $2,000,000.

(ii) *Application.* The DSUE amount to be included in determining the applicable exclusion amount available to W for gifts during the second half of 2015 is $4,000,000, determined by adding the $2,000,000 DSUE amount of H2 and the $2,000,000 DSUE amount of H1 that was applied by W to W's 2012 taxable gifts. Thus, W's applicable exclusion amount during the balance of 2015 is $9,430,000 ($4,000,000 DSUE plus $5,430,000 basic exclusion amount for 2015).

(d) Date DSUE amount taken into consideration by donor who is a surviving spouse. (1) *General rule.* A portability election made by an executor of a decedent's estate (see § 20.2010–2(a) and (b) for applicable requirements) generally applies as of the date of such decedent's death. Thus, the decedent's DSUE amount is included in the applicable exclusion amount of the decedent's surviving spouse under section 2010(c)(2) and will be applicable to transfers made by the surviving spouse after the decedent's death (subject to the limitations in paragraph (a) of this section). However, such decedent's DSUE amount will not be included in the applicable exclusion amount of the surviving spouse, even if the surviving spouse had made a taxable gift in reliance on the availability or computation of the decedent's DSUE amount:

(i) If the executor of the decedent's estate supersedes the portability election by filing a subsequent estate tax return in accordance with § 20.2010–2(a)(4);

(ii) To the extent that the DSUE amount subsequently is reduced by a valuation adjustment or the correction of an error in calculation; or

(iii) To the extent that the DSUE amount claimed on the decedent's return cannot be determined.

(2) *Exception when surviving spouse not a U.S. citizen on date of deceased spouse's death.* If a surviving spouse becomes a citizen of the United States after the death of the surviving spouse's last deceased spouse, the DSUE amount of the surviving spouse's last deceased spouse becomes available to the surviving spouse on the date the surviving spouse becomes a citizen of the United States (subject to the limitations in paragraph (a) of this section). However, when the special rule regarding qualified domestic trusts in paragraph (d)(3) of this section applies, the earliest date on which a decedent's DSUE amount may be included in the applicable exclusion amount of such decedent's surviving spouse who becomes a U.S. citizen is as provided in paragraph (d)(3) of this section.

(3) *Special rule when property passes to surviving spouse in a qualified domestic trust.* (i) *In general.* When property passes from a decedent for the benefit of the decedent's surviving spouse in one or more qualified domestic trusts (QDOT) as defined in section 2056A(a) and the decedent's executor elects portability, the DSUE amount available to be included in the applicable exclusion amount of the surviving spouse under section 2010(c)(2) is the DSUE amount of the decedent as redetermined in accordance with § 20.2010–2(c)(4) (subject to the limitations in paragraph (a) of this section). The earliest date on which such decedent's DSUE amount may be included in the applicable exclusion amount of the surviving spouse under section 2010(c)(2) is the date of the occurrence of the final QDOT distribution or final other event (generally, the termination of all QDOTs created by or funded with assets passing from the decedent or the death of the surviving spouse) on which tax under section 2056A is imposed. However, the decedent's DSUE amount as redetermined in accordance with § 20.2010–2(c)(4) may be applied to the surviving spouse's taxable gifts made in the year of the surviving spouse's death or, if the terminating event occurs prior to the surviving spouse's death, then in the year of that terminating event and/or in any subsequent year during the surviving spouse's life.

(ii) *Surviving spouse becomes a U.S. citizen.* If a surviving spouse for whom property has passed from a decedent in one or more QDOTs becomes a citizen of the United States and the requirements in section 2056A(b)(12) and the corresponding regulations are satisfied, then the date on which such decedent's DSUE amount may be included in the applicable exclusion amount of the surviving spouse under section 2010(c)(2) (subject to the limitations in paragraph (a) of this section) is the date on which the surviving spouse becomes a citizen of the United States. See § 20.2010–2(c)(4) for the rules for computing the decedent's DSUE amount in the case of a qualified domestic trust.

(iii) *Example.* The following example illustrates the application of this paragraph (d)(3):

Example. (i) *Facts.* Husband (H), a U.S. citizen, dies in 2011 having made no taxable gifts during his lifetime. H's gross estate is $3,000,000. H's wife (W) is not a citizen of the United States and, under H's will, a pecuniary bequest of $2,000,000 passes to a QDOT for the benefit of W. H's executor timely files an estate tax return and makes the QDOT election for the property passing to the QDOT, and H's estate is allowed a marital deduction of $2,000,000 under section 2056(d) for the value of that property. H's taxable estate is $1,000,000. On H's estate tax return, H's executor computes H's preliminary DSUE amount to be $4,000,000. No taxable events within the meaning of section 2056A occur during W's lifetime with respect to the QDOT, and W resides in the United States at all times after H's death. W makes a taxable gift of $1,000,000 to X in 2012 and a taxable gift of $1,000,000 to Y in January 2015, in each case from W's own assets rather than from the QDOT. W dies in September 2015, not having married again, when the value of the assets of the QDOT is $2,200,000.

(ii) *Application.* H's DSUE amount is redetermined to be $1,800,000 (the lesser of the $5,000,000 basic exclusion amount for 2011, or the excess of H's $5,000,000 applicable exclusion amount over $3,200,000 (the sum of the $1,000,000 taxable estate augmented by the $2,200,000 of QDOT assets)). On W's gift tax return filed for 2012, W cannot apply any DSUE amount to the gift made to X. However, because W's gift to Y was made in the year that W died, W's executor will apply $1,000,000 of H's redetermined DSUE amount to the gift on W's gift tax return filed for 2015. The remaining $800,000 of H's redetermined DSUE amount is included in W's applicable exclusion amount to be used in computing W's estate tax liability.

(e) Authority to examine returns of deceased spouses. For the purpose of determining the DSUE amount to be included in the applicable exclusion amount of a surviving spouse, the Internal Revenue Service (IRS) may examine returns of each of the surviving spouse's deceased spouses whose DSUE amount is claimed to be included in the surviving spouse's applicable exclusion amount, regardless of whether the period of limitations on assessment has expired for any such return. The IRS's authority to examine returns of a deceased spouse applies with respect to each transfer by the surviving spouse to which a DSUE amount is or has been applied. Upon examination, the IRS may adjust or eliminate the DSUE amount reported on such a return of a deceased spouse; however, the IRS may assess additional tax on that return only if that tax is assessed within the period of limitations on assessment under section 6501 applicable to the tax shown on that return. See also section 7602 for the IRS's authority, when ascertaining the correctness of any return, to examine any returns that may be relevant or material to such inquiry.

(f) Availability of DSUE amount for nonresidents who are not citizens. A nonresident surviving spouse who was not a citizen of the United States at the time of making a transfer subject to tax under chapter 12 of the Internal Revenue Code shall not take into account the DSUE amount of any deceased spouse except to the extent allowed under any applicable treaty obligation of the United States. See section 2102(b)(3).

(g) Effective/applicability date. This section applies to gifts made on or after June 12, 2015. See 26 CFR 25.2505–2T, as contained in 26 CFR part 25, revised as of April 1, 2015, for the rules applicable to gifts made on or after January 1, 2011, and before June 12, 2015.

[T.D. 9725, 80 FR 34290, June 16, 2015; T.D. 9884, 85 FR 6803, Feb. 6, 2020]

Subchapter B. Transfers

§ 2511. Transfers in General

(a) Scope. Subject to the limitations contained in this chapter, the tax imposed by section 2501 shall apply whether the transfer is in trust or otherwise, whether the gift is direct or indirect, and whether the property is real or personal, tangible or intangible; but in the case of a nonresident not a citizen of the United States, shall apply to a transfer only if the property is situated within the United States.

(b) Intangible property. For purposes of this chapter, in the case of a nonresident not a citizen of the United States who is excepted from the application of section 2501(a)(2)—

(1) shares of stock issued by a domestic corporation, and

(2) debt obligations of—

(A) a United States person, or

(B) the United States, a State or any political subdivision thereof, or the District of Columbia,

which are owned and held by such nonresident shall be deemed to be property situated within the United States.

Regulations

§ 25.2511–1 Transfers in general.

(a) The gift tax applies to a transfer by way of gift whether the transfer is in trust or otherwise, whether the gift is direct or indirect, and whether the property is real or personal, tangible or intangible. For example, a taxable transfer may be effected by the creation of a trust, the forgiving of a debt, the assignment of a judgment, the assignment of the benefits of an insurance policy, or the transfer of cash, certificates of deposit, or Federal, State or municipal bonds. Statutory provisions which exempt bonds, notes, bills and certificates of indebtedness of the Federal Government or its agencies and the interest thereon from taxation are not applicable to the gift tax, since the gift tax is an excise tax on the transfer, and is not a tax on the subject of the gift.

(b) In the case of a gift by a nonresident not a citizen of the United States—

(1) If the gift was made on or after January 1, 1967, by a donor who was not an expatriate to whom section 2501(a)(2) was inapplicable on the date of the gift by reason of section 2501(a)(3) and paragraph (a)(3) of § 25.2501–1, or

(2) If the gift was made before January 1, 1967, by a donor who was not engaged in business in the United States during the calendar year in which the gift was made, the gift tax applies only if the gift consisted of real property or tangible personal property situated within the United States at the time of the transfer. See §§ 25.2501–1 and 25.2511–3.

(c)(1) The gift tax also applies to gifts indirectly made. Thus, any transaction in which an interest in property is gratuitously passed or conferred upon another, regardless of the means or device employed, constitutes a gift subject to tax. See further § 25.2512–8 relating to transfers for insufficient consideration. However, in the case of a transfer creating an interest in property (within the meaning of § 25.2518–2(c)(3) and (c)(4)) made after December 31, 1976, this paragraph (c)(1) shall not apply to the donee if, as a result of a qualified disclaimer by the donee, the interest passes to a different donee. Nor shall it apply to a donor if, as a result of a qualified disclaimer by the donee, a completed transfer of an interest in property is not effected. See section 2518 and the corresponding regulations for rules relating to a qualified disclaimer.

(2) In the case of taxable transfers creating an interest in the person disclaiming made before January 1, 1977, where the law governing the administration of the decedent's estate gives a beneficiary, heir, or next-of-kin a right completely and unqualifiedly to refuse to accept ownership of property transferred from a decedent (whether the transfer is effected by the decedent's will or by the law of descent and distribution), a refusal to accept ownership does not constitute the making of a gift if the refusal is made within a reasonable time after knowledge of the existence of the transfer. The refusal must be unequivocal and effective under the local law. There can be no refusal of ownership of property after its acceptance. In the absence of the facts to the contrary, if a person fails to refuse to accept a transfer to him of ownership of a decedent's property within a reasonable time after learning of the existence of the transfer, he will be presumed to have accepted the property. Where the local law does not permit such a refusal, any disposition by the beneficiary, heir, or next-of-kin whereby ownership is transferred gratuitously to another constitutes the making of a gift by the beneficiary, heir, or next-of-kin. In any case where a refusal is purported to relate to only a part of the property, the determination of whether or not there has been a complete and unqualified refusal to accept ownership will depend on all of the facts and circumstances in each particular case, taking into account the recognition and effectiveness of such a purported refusal under the local law. In illustration, if Blackacre was devised to A under the decedent's will (which also provided that all lapsed legacies and devises shall go to B, the residuary beneficiary), and under the local law A could refuse to accept ownership in which case title would be considered as never having passed to A, A's refusal to accept Blackacre within a reasonable time of learning of the devise will not constitute the making of a gift by A to B. However, if a decedent who owned Greenacre died intestate with C and D as his only heirs, and under local law the heir of a decedent cannot, by refusal to accept, prevent himself from becoming an owner of intestate property, any gratuitous disposition by C (by whatever term it is known) whereby he gives up his ownership of a portion of

Greenacre and D acquires the whole thereof constitutes the making of a gift by C to D.

(3) The fourth sentence of paragraph (c)(1) of this section is applicable for transfers creating an interest to be disclaimed made on or after December 31, 1997.

(d) If a joint income tax return is filed by a husband and wife for a taxable year, the payment by one spouse of all or part of the income tax liability for such year is not treated as resulting in a transfer that is subject to gift tax. The same rule is applicable to the payment of gift tax for a "calendar period" (as defined in § 25.2502–1(c)(1)) in the case of a husband and wife who have consented to have the gifts made considered as made half by each of them in accordance with the provisions of section 2513.

(e) If a donor transfers by gift less than his entire interest in property, the gift tax is applicable to the interest transferred. The tax is applicable, for example, to the transfer of an undivided half interest in property, or to the transfer of a life estate when the grantor retains the remainder interest, or vice versa. However, if the donor's retained interest is not susceptible of measurement on the basis of generally accepted valuation principles, the gift tax is applicable to the entire value of the property subject to the gift. Thus if a donor, aged 65 years, transfers a life estate in property to A, aged 25 years, with remainder to A's issue, or in default of issue, with reversion to the donor, the gift tax will normally be applicable to the entire value of the property.

(f) If a donor is the owner of only a limited interest in property, and transfers his entire interest, the interest is in every case to be valued by the rules set forth in §§ 25.2512–1 through 25.2512–7. If the interest is a remainder or reversion or other future interest, it is to be valued on the basis of actuarial principles set forth in § 25.2512–5, or if it is not susceptible of valuation in that manner, in accordance with the principles set forth in § 25.2512–1.

(g)(1) Donative intent on the part of the transferor is not an essential element in the application of the gift tax to the transfer. The application of the tax is based on the objective facts of the transfer and the circumstances under which it is made, rather than on the subjective motives of the donor. However, there are certain types of transfers to which the tax is not applicable. It is applicable only to a transfer of a beneficial interest in property. It is not applicable to a transfer of bare legal title to a trustee. A transfer by a trustee of trust property in which he has no beneficial interest does not constitute a gift by the trustee (but such a transfer may constitute a gift by the creator of the trust, if until the transfer he had the power to change the beneficiaries by amending or revoking the trust). The gift tax is not applicable to a transfer for a full and adequate consideration in money or money's worth, or to ordinary business transactions, described in § 25.2512–8.

(2) If a trustee has a beneficial interest in trust property, a transfer of the property by the trustee is not a taxable transfer if it is made pursuant to a fiduciary power the exercise or nonexercise of which is limited by a reasonably fixed or ascertainable standard which is set forth in the trust instrument. A clearly measurable standard under which the holder of a power is legally accountable is such a standard for this purpose. For instance, a power to distribute corpus for the education, support, maintenance, or health of the beneficiary; for his reasonable support and comfort; to enable him to maintain his accustomed standard of living; or to meet an emergency, would be such a standard. However, a power to distribute corpus for the pleasure, desire, or happiness of a beneficiary is not such a standard. The entire context of a provision of a trust instrument granting a power must be considered in determining whether the power is limited by a reasonably definite standard. For example, if a trust instrument provides that the determination of the trustee shall be conclusive with respect to the exercise or nonexercise of a power, the power is not limited by a reasonably definite standard. However, the fact that the governing instrument is phrased in discretionary terms is not in itself an indication that no such standard exists.

(h) The following are examples of transactions resulting in taxable gifts and in each case it is assumed that the transfers were not made for an adequate and full consideration in money or money's worth:

(1) A transfer of property by a corporation to B is a gift to B from the stockholders of the corporation. If B himself is a stockholder, the transfer is a gift to him from the other stockholders but only to the extent it exceeds B's own interest in such amount as a shareholder. A transfer of property by B to a corporation generally represents gifts by B to the other individual shareholders of the corporation to the extent of their proportionate interests in the corporation. However,

there may be an exception to this rule, such as a transfer made by an individual to a charitable, public, political or similar organization which may constitute a gift to the organization as a single entity, depending upon the facts and circumstances in the particular case.

(2) The transfer of property to B if there is imposed upon B the obligation of paying a commensurate annuity to C is a gift to C.

(3) The payment of money or the transfer of property to B in consideration of B's promise to render a service to C is a gift to C, or to both B and C, depending on whether the service to be rendered to C is or is not an adequate and full consideration in money or money's worth for that which is received by B. See section 2512(b) and the regulations thereunder.

(4) If A creates a joint bank account for himself and B (or a similar type of ownership by which A can regain the entire fund without B's consent), there is a gift to B when B draws upon the account for his own benefit, to the extent of the amount drawn without any obligation to account for a part of the proceeds to A. Similarly, if A purchases a United States savings bond registered as payable to "A or B," there is a gift to B when B surrenders the bond for cash without any obligation to account for a part of the proceeds to A.

(5) If A with his own funds purchases property and has the title conveyed to himself and B as joint owners, with rights of survivorship (other than a joint ownership described in example (4) but which rights may be defeated by either party severing his interest, there is a gift to B in the amount of half the value of the property. However, see § 25.2515–1 relative to the creation of a joint tenancy (or tenancy by the entirety) between husband and wife in real property with rights of survivorship which, unless the donor elects otherwise is not considered as a transfer includible for Federal gift tax purposes at the time of the creation of the joint tenancy. See § 25.2515–2 with respect to determining the extent to which the creation of a tenancy by the entirety constitutes a taxable gift if the donor elects to have the creation of the tenancy so treated. See also § 25.2523(d)–1 with respect to the marital deduction allowed in the case of the creation of a joint tenancy or a tenancy by the entirety.

(6) If A is possessed of a vested remainder interest in property, subject to being divested only in the event he should fail to survive one or more individuals or the happening of some other event, an irrevocable assignment of all or any part of his interest would result in a transfer includible for Federal gift tax purposes. See especially § 25.2512–5 for the valuation of an interest of this type.

(7) If A, without retaining a power to revoke the trust or to change the beneficial interests therein, transfers property in trust whereby B is to receive the income for life and at his death the trust is to terminate and the corpus is to be returned to A, provided A survives, but if A predeceases B the corpus is to pass to C, A has made a gift equal to the total value of the property less the value of his retained interest. See § 25.2512–5 for the valuation of the donor's retained interest.

(8) If the insured purchases a life insurance policy, or pays a premium on a previously issued policy, the proceeds of which are payable to a beneficiary or beneficiaries other than his estate, and with respect to which the insured retains no reversionary interest in himself or his estate and no power to revest the economic benefits in himself or his estate or to change the beneficiaries or their proportionate benefits (or if the insured relinquishes by assignment, by designation of a new beneficiary or otherwise, every such power that was retained in a previously issued policy), the insured has made a gift of the value of the policy, or to the extent of the premium paid, even though the right of the assignee or beneficiary to receive the benefits is conditioned upon his surviving the insured. For the valuation of life insurance policies see § 25.2512–6.

(9) Where property held by a husband and wife as community property is used to purchase insurance upon the husband's life and a third person is revocably designated as beneficiary and under the State law the husband's death is considered to make absolute the transfer by the wife, there is a gift by the wife at the time of the husband's death of half the amount of the proceeds of such insurance.

(10) If under a pension plan (pursuant to which he has an unqualified right to an annuity) an employee has an option to take either a retirement annuity for himself alone or a smaller annuity for himself with a survivorship annuity payable to his wife, an irrevocable election by the employee to take the reduced annuity in order that an annuity may be paid, after the employee's death, to his wife results in the making of

a gift. However, see section 2517 and the regulations thereunder for the exemption from gift tax of amounts attributable to employers' contributions under qualified plans and certain other contracts.

[T.D. 6334, 23 FR 8904, Nov. 15, 1958, as amended by T.D. 6542, 26 FR 550, Jan. 20, 1961; T.D. 7150, 36 FR 22900, Dec. 2, 1971; T.D. 7238, 37 FR 28728, Dec. 29, 1972; T.D. 7296, 38 FR 34202, Dec. 12, 1973; T.D. 7910, 48 FR 40374, Sept. 7, 1983; T.D. 8095, 51 FR 28369, Aug. 7, 1986; T.D. 8540, 59 FR 30103, June 10, 1994; T.D. 8744, 62 FR 68185, Dec. 31, 1997]

§ 25.2511–2 Cessation of donor's dominion and control.

(a) The gift tax is not imposed upon the receipt of the property by the donee, nor is it necessarily determined by the measure of enrichment resulting to the donee from the transfer, nor is it conditioned upon ability to identify the donee at the time of the transfer. On the contrary, the tax is a primary and personal liability of the donor, is an excise upon his act of making the transfer, is measured by the value of the property passing from the donor, and attaches regardless of the fact that the identity of the donee may not then be known or ascertainable. For gift tax rules related to an ABLE account established under section 529A, see § 1.529A–4 of this chapter.

(b) As to any property, or part thereof or interest therein, of which the donor has so parted with dominion and control as to leave in him no power to change its disposition, whether for his own benefit or for the benefit of another, the gift is complete. But if upon a transfer of property (whether in trust or otherwise) the donor reserves any power over its disposition, the gift may be wholly incomplete, or may be partially complete and partially incomplete, depending upon all the facts in the particular case. Accordingly, in every case of a transfer of property subject to a reserved power, the terms of the power must be examined and its scope determined. For example, if a donor transfers property to another in trust to pay the income to the donor or accumulate it in the discretion of the trustee, and the donor retains a testamentary power to appoint the remainder among his descendants, no portion of the transfer is a completed gift. On the other hand, if the donor had not retained the testamentary power of appointment, but instead provided that the remainder should go to X or his heirs, the entire transfer would be a completed gift. However, if the exercise of the trustee's power in favor of the grantor is limited by a fixed or ascertainable standard (see paragraph (g)(2) of § 25.2511–1), enforceable by or on behalf of the grantor, then the gift is incomplete to the extent of the ascertainable value of any rights thus retained by the grantor.

(c) A gift is incomplete in every instance in which a donor reserves the power to revest the beneficial title to the property in himself. A gift is also incomplete if and to the extent that a reserved power gives the donor the power to name new beneficiaries or to change the interests of the beneficiaries as between themselves unless the power is a fiduciary power limited by a fixed or ascertainable standard. Thus, if an estate for life is transferred but, by an exercise of a power, the estate may be terminated or cut down by the donor to one of less value, and without restriction upon the extent to which the estate may be so cut down, the transfer constitutes an incomplete gift. If in this example the power was confined to the right to cut down the estate for life to one for a term of five years, the certainty of an estate for not less than that term results in a gift to that extent complete.

(d) A gift is not considered incomplete, however, merely because the donor reserves the power to change the manner or time of enjoyment. Thus, the creation of a trust the income of which is to be paid annually to the donee for a period of years, the corpus being distributable to him at the end of the period, and the power reserved by the donor being limited to a right to require that, instead of the income being so payable, it should be accumulated and distributed with the corpus to the donee at the termination of the period, constitutes a completed gift.

(e) A donor is considered as himself having a power if it is exercisable by him in conjunction with any person not having a substantial adverse interest in the disposition of the transferred property or the income therefrom. A trustee, as such, is not a person having an adverse interest in the disposition of the trust property or its income.

(f) The relinquishment or termination of a power to change the beneficiaries of transferred property, occurring otherwise than by the death of the donor (the statute being confined to transfers by living donors), is regarded as the event that completes the gift and causes the tax to apply. For example, if A transfers property in trust for the benefit of B and C but reserves the power as trustee to change the proportionate interests of B and C, and if A thereafter has another person appointed trustee in place of himself, such later relinquishment of the power by A to the new trustee completes the gift of the transferred property, whether or not the new trustee has a substantial adverse interest. The receipt of income or of other enjoyment of the transferred property by the transferee or by the beneficiary (other than by the donor himself) during the interim between the making of the initial transfer and the relinquishment or termination of the power operates to free such income or other enjoyment from the power, and constitutes a gift of such income or of such other enjoyment taxable as of the "calendar period" (as defined in § 25.2502–1(c)(1)) of its receipt. If property is transferred in trust to pay the income to A for life with remainder to B, powers to distribute corpus to A, and to withhold income from A for future distribution to B, are powers to change the beneficiaries of the transferred property.

(g) If a donor transfers property to himself as trustee (or to himself and some other person, not possessing a substantial adverse interest, as trustees), and retains no beneficial interest in the trust property and no power over it except fiduciary powers, the exercise or nonexercise of which is limited by a fixed or ascertainable standard, to change the beneficiaries of the transferred property, the donor has made a completed gift and the entire value of the transferred property is subject to the gift tax.

(h) If a donor delivers a properly indorsed stock certificate to the donee or the donee's agent, the gift is completed for gift tax purposes on the date of delivery. If the donor delivers the certificate to his bank or broker as his agent, or to the issuing corporation or its transfer agent, for transfer into the name of the donee, the gift is completed on the date the stock is transferred on the books of the corporation.

(i) [Reserved]

(j) If the donor contends that a power is of such nature as to render the gift incomplete, and hence not subject to the tax as of the calendar period (as defined in § 25.2502–1(c)(1)) of the initial transfer, see § 301.6501(c)–1(f)(5) of this chapter.

[T.D. 6334, 23 FR 8904, Nov. 15, 1958, as amended by T.D. 7238, 37 FR 28728, Dec. 29, 1972; T.D. 7910, 48 FR 40374, Sept. 7, 1983; T.D. 8845, 64 FR 67771, Dec. 3, 1999; T.D. 9923, 85 FR 74047, Nov. 19, 2020]

§ 25.2511–3 Transfers by nonresidents not citizens.

(a) In general. Sections 2501 and 2511 contain rules relating to the taxation of transfers of property by gift by a donor who is a nonresident not a citizen of the United States. (See paragraph (b) of § 25.2501–1 for the definition of the term "resident" for purposes of the gift tax.) As combined these rules are:

(1) The gift tax applies only to the transfer of real property and tangible personal property situated in the United States at the time of the transfer if either—

(i) The gift was made on or after January 1, 1967, by a nonresident not a citizen of the United States who was not an expatriate to whom section 2501(a)(2) was inapplicable on the date of the gift by reason of section 2501(a)(3) and paragraph (a)(3) of § 25.2501–1, or

(ii) The gift was made before January 1, 1967, by a nonresident not a citizen of the United States who was not engaged in business in the United States during the calendar year in which the gift was made.

(2) The gift tax applies to the transfer of all property (whether real or personal, tangible or intangible) situated in the United States at the time of the transfer if either—

(i) The gift was made on or after January 1, 1967, by a nonresident not a citizen of the United States who was an expatriate to whom section 2501(a)(2) was inapplicable on the date of the gift by reason of section 2501(a)(3) and paragraph (a)(3) of § 25.2501–1, or

(ii) The gift was made before January 1, 1967, by a nonresident not a citizen of the United States who was engaged in business in the United States during the calendar year in which the gift was made.

(b) Situs of property. For purposes of applying the gift tax to the transfer of property owned and held by a nonresident not a citizen of the United States at the time of the transfer—

(1) Real property and tangible personal property. Real property and tangible personal property constitute property within the United States only if they are physically situated therein.

(2) Intangible personal property. Except as provided otherwise in subparagraphs (3) and (4) of this paragraph, intangible personal property constitutes property within the United States if it consists of a property right issued by or enforceable against a resident of the United States or a domestic corporation (public or private), irrespective of where the written evidence of the property is physically located at the time of the transfer.

(3) Shares of stock. Irrespective of where the stock certificates are physically located at the time of the transfer—

(i) Shares of stock issued by a domestic corporation constitute property within the United States, and

(ii) Shares of stock issued by a corporation which is not a domestic corporation constitute property situated outside the United States.

(4) Debt obligations. (i) In the case of gifts made on or after January 1, 1967, a debt obligation, including a bank deposit, the primary obligor of which is a United States person (as defined in section 7701(a)(30)), the United States, a State, or any political subdivision thereof, the District of Columbia, or any agency or instrumentality of any such government constitutes property situated within the United States. This subdivision applies—

(a) In the case of a debt obligation of a domestic corporation, whether or not any interest on the obligation would be treated under section 862(a)(1) as income from sources without the United States by reason of section 861(a)(1)(B) (relating to interest received from a domestic corporation less than 20 percent of whose gross income for a 3-year period was derived from sources within the United States) and the regulations thereunder;

(b) In the case of an amount described in section 861(c) (relating to certain bank deposits, withdrawable accounts, and amounts held by an insurance company under an agreement to pay interest), whether or not any interest thereon would be treated under section 862(a)(1) as income from sources without the United States by reason of section 861(a)(1)(A) (relating to interest on amounts described in section 861(c) which is not effectively connected with the conduct of a trade or business within the United States) and the regulations thereunder;

(c) In the case of a deposit with a domestic corporation or domestic partnership, whether or not the deposit is with a foreign branch thereof engaged in the commercial banking business; and

(d) Irrespective of where the written evidence of the debt obligation is physically located at the time of the transfer.

For purposes of this subdivision, a debt obligation on which there are two or more primary obligors shall be apportioned among such obligors, taking into account to the extent appropriate under all the facts and circumstances any choate or inchoate rights of contribution existing among such obligors with respect to the indebtedness. The term "agency or instrumentality", as used in this subdivision, does not include a possession of the United States or an agency or instrumentality of a possession.

(ii) In the case of gifts made on or after January 1, 1967, a debt obligation, including a bank deposit, not deemed under subdivision (i) of this subparagraph to be situated within the United States, constitutes property situated outside the United States.

(iii) In the case of gifts made before January 1, 1967, a debt obligation the written evidence of which is treated as being the property itself constitutes property situated within the United States if the written evidence of the obligation is physically located in the United States at the time of the transfer, irrespective of who is the primary obligor on the debt. If the written evidence of the obligation is physically located outside the United States, the debt obligation constitutes property situated outside the United States.

(iv) Currency is not a debt obligation for purposes of this subparagraph.

[T.D. 6334, 23 FR 8904, Nov. 15, 1958, as amended by T.D. 6542, 26 FR 549, Jan. 20, 1961; T.D. 7238, 37 FR 28728, Dec. 29, 1972; T.D. 7296, 38 FR 34202, Dec. 12, 1973]

§ 2512. Valuation of Gifts

(a) If the gift is made in property, the value thereof at the date of the gift shall be considered the amount of the gift.

(b) Where property is transferred for less than an adequate and full consideration in money or money's worth, then the amount by which the value of the property exceeded the value of the consideration shall be deemed a gift, and shall be included in computing the amount of gifts made during the calendar year.

(c) Cross reference. For individual's right to be furnished on request a statement regarding any valuation made by the Secretary of a gift by that individual, see section 7517.

Regulations

§ 25.2512–0 Table of contents. [*Omitted. Ed.*]

[T.D. 8540, 59 FR 30173, June 10, 1994; T.D. 8819, 64 FR 23223, April 30, 1999; T.D. 8886, 65 FR 36940, June 12, 2000; T.D. 9448, 74 FR 21512, May 7, 2009; T.D. 9540, 76 FR 49639, Aug. 10, 2011; T.D. 9974, 88 FR 37451, June 7, 2023]

§ 25.2512–1 Valuation of property; in general.

Section 2512 provides that if a gift is made in property, its value at the date of the gift shall be considered the amount of the gift. The value of the property is the price at which such property would change hands between a willing buyer and a willing seller, neither being under any compulsion to buy or to sell, and both having reasonable knowledge of relevant facts. The value of a particular item of property is not the price that a forced sale of the property would produce. Nor is the fair market value of an item of property the sale price in a market other than that in which such item is most commonly sold to the public, taking into account the location of the item wherever appropriate. Thus, in the case of an item of property made the subject of a gift, which is generally obtained by the public in the retail market, the fair market value of such an item of property is the price at which the item or a comparable item would be sold at retail. For example, the value of an automobile (an article generally obtained by the public in the retail market) which is the subject of a gift, is the price for which an automobile of the same or approximately the same description, make, model, age, condition, etc., could be purchased by a member of the general public and not the price for which the particular automobile of the donor would be purchased by a dealer in used automobiles. Examples of items of property which are generally sold to the public at retail may be found in § 25.2512–6. The value is generally to be determined by ascertaining as a basis the fair market value at the time of the gift of each unit of the property. For example, in the case of shares of stocks or bonds, such unit of property is generally a share or a bond. Property shall not be returned at the value at which it is assessed for local tax purposes unless that value represents the fair market value thereof on the date of the gift. All relevant facts and elements of value as of the time of the gift shall be considered. Where the subject of a gift is an interest in a business, the value of items of property in the inventory of the business generally should be reflected in the value of the business. For valuation of interests in businesses, see § 25.2512–3. See § 25.2512–2 and §§ 25.2512–4 through 25.2512–6 for further information concerning the valuation of other particular kinds of property. See section 2701 and the regulations at § 25.2701 for special rules for valuing transfers of an interest in a corporation or a partnership and for the treatment of unpaid qualified payments at the subsequent transfer of an applicable retained interest by the transferor or by an applicable family member. See section 2704(b) and the regulations at § 25.2704–2 for special valuation rules where an interest in property is subject to an applicable restriction.

[T.D. 6334, 23 FR 8904, Nov. 15, 1958, as amended by T.D. 6826, 30 FR 7709, June 15, 1965; T.D. 8395, 57 FR 4255, Feb. 4, 1992]

§ 25.2512–2 Stocks and bonds.

(a) In general. The value of stocks and bonds is the fair market value per share or bond on the date of the gift.

(b) Based on selling prices. (1) In general, if there is a market for stocks or bonds, on a stock exchange, in an over-the-counter market or otherwise, the mean between the highest and lowest quoted selling prices on the date of the gift is the fair market value per share or bond. If there were no sales on the date of the gift but there were sales on dates within a reasonable period both before and after the date of the gift, the fair market value is determined by taking a weighted average of the means between the highest and lowest sales on the nearest date before and the nearest date after the date of the gift. The average is to be weighted inversely by the respective numbers of trading days between the selling dates and the date of the gift. If the stocks or bonds are listed on more than one exchange, the records of the exchange where the stocks or bonds are principally dealt in should be employed if such records are available in a generally available listing or publication of general circulation. In the event that such records are not so available and such stocks or bonds are listed on a composite listing of combined exchanges available in a generally available listing or publication of general circulation, the records of such combined exchanges should be employed. In valuing listed securities, the donor should be careful to consult accurate records to obtain values as of the date of the gift. If quotations of unlisted securities are obtained from brokers, or evidence as to their sale is obtained from the officers of the issuing companies, copies of letters furnishing such quotations or evidence of sale should be attached to the return.

(2) If it is established with respect to bonds for which there is a market on a stock exchange, that the highest and lowest selling prices are not available for the date of the gift in a generally available listing or publication of general circulation but that closing prices are so available, the fair market value per bond is the mean between the quoted closing selling price on the date of the gift and the quoted closing selling price on the trading day before the date of the gift. If there were no sales on the trading day before the date of the gift but there were sales on dates within a reasonable period before the date of the gift, the fair market value is determined by taking a weighted average of the quoted closing selling prices on the date of the gift and the nearest date before the date of the gift. The closing selling price for the date of the gift is to be weighted by the respective number of trading days between the previous selling date and the date of the gift. If there were no sales within a reasonable period before the date of the gift but there were sales on the date of the gift, the fair market value is the closing selling price on the date of the gift. If there were no sales on the date of the gift but there were sales within a reasonable period both before and after the date of the gift, the fair market value is determined by taking a weighted average of the quoted closing selling prices on the nearest date before and the nearest date after the date of the gift. The average is to be weighed inversely by the respective numbers of trading days between the selling dates and the date of the gift. If the bonds are listed on more than one exchange, the records of the exchange where the bonds are principally dealt in should be employed. In valuing listed securities, the donor should be careful to consult accurate records to obtain values as of the date of the gift.

(3) The application of this paragraph may be illustrated by the following examples:

Example (1). Assume that sales of stock nearest the date of the gift (Friday, June 15) occurred two trading days before (Wednesday, June 13) and three trading days after (Wednesday, June 20) and on these days the mean sale prices per share were $10 and $15, respectively. The price of $12 is taken as representing the fair market value of a share of stock as of the date of the gift

$$\frac{(3 * 10) \quad + \quad (2 * 15)}{5}$$

Example (2). Assume the same facts as in example 1 except that the mean sale prices per share on June 13 and June 20 were $15 and $10 respectively. The price of $13 is taken as representing the fair market value of a share of stock as of the date of the gift

$$\frac{(3 * 15) \quad + \quad (2 * 10)}{5}$$

Example (3). Assume that on the date of the gift (Tuesday, April 3, 1973) the closing selling price of certain listed bonds was $25 per bond and that the highest and lowest selling prices are not available in a generally available listing or publication of general circulation for that date. Assume further, that the closing selling price of such bonds was $21 per bond on the day before the date of the gift (Monday, April 2, 1973). Thus, under paragraph (b)(2) of this section, the price of $23 is taken as representing the fair market value per bond as of the date of the gift

$$\frac{(25 \quad + \quad 21)}{2}$$

Example (4). Assume the same facts as in example 3 except that there were no sales on the day before the date of the gift. Assume further, that there were sales on Thursday, March 29, 1973, and that the closing selling price on that day was $23. The price of $24.50

is taken as representing the fair market value per bond as of the date of the gift

$$\frac{(1 * 23) \quad + \quad (3 * 25)}{4}$$

Example (5). Assume that no bonds were traded on the date of the gift (Friday, April 20). Assume further, that sales of bonds nearest the date of the gift occurred two trading days before (Wednesday, April 18) and three trading days after (Wednesday, April 25) the date of the gift and that on these two days the closing selling prices per bond were $29 and $22, respectively. The highest and lowest selling prices are not available for these dates in a generally available listing or publication of general circulation. Thus, under paragraph (b)(2) of this section the price of $26.20 is taken as representing the fair market value of a bond as of the date of the gift

$$\frac{(3 * 29) \quad + \quad (2 * 22)}{5}$$

(c) Based on bid and asked prices. If the provisions of paragraph (b) of this section are inapplicable because actual sales are not available during reasonable period beginning before and ending after the date of the gift, the fair market value may be determined by taking the mean between the bona fide bid and asked prices on the date of the gift, or if none, by taking a weighted average of the means between the bona fide bid and asked prices on the nearest trading date before and the nearest trading date after the date of the gift, if both such nearest dates are within a reasonable period. The average is to be determined in the manner described in paragraph (b) of this section.

(d) Where selling prices and bid and asked prices are not available for dates both before and after the date of gift. If the provisions of paragraphs (b) and (c) of this section are inapplicable because no actual sale prices or quoted bona fide bid and asked prices are available on a date within a reasonable period before the date of the gift, but such prices are available on a date within a reasonable period after the date of the gift, or vice versa, then the mean between the highest and lowest available sale prices or bid and asked prices may be taken as the value.

(e) Where selling prices or bid and asked prices do not represent fair market value. In cases in which it is established that the value per bond or share of any security determined on the basis of the selling or bid and asked prices as provided under paragraphs (b), (c), and (d) of this section does not represent the fair market value thereof, then some reasonable modification of the value determined on that basis or other relevant facts and elements of value shall be considered in determining fair market value. Where sales at or near the date of the gift are few or of a sporadic nature, such sales alone may not indicate fair market value. In certain exceptional cases, the size of the block of securities made the subject of each separate gift in relation to the number of shares changing hands in sales may be relevant in determining whether selling prices reflect the fair market value of the block of stock to be valued. If the donor can show that the block of stock to be valued, with reference to each separate gift, is so large in relation to the actual sales on the existing market that it could not be liquidated in a reasonable time without depressing the market, the price at which the block could be sold as such outside the usual market, as through an underwriter, may be a more accurate indication of value than market quotations. Complete data in support of any allowance claimed due to the size of the block of stock being valued should be submitted with the return. On the other hand, if the block of stock to be valued represents a controlling interest, either actual or effective, in a going business, the price at which other lots change hands may have little relation to its true value.

(f) Where selling prices or bid and asked prices are unavailable. If the provisions of paragraphs (b), (c), and (d) of this section are inapplicable because actual sale prices and bona fide bid and asked prices are lacking, then the fair market value is to be determined by taking the following factors into consideration:

(1) In the case of corporate or other bonds, the soundness of the security, the interest yield, the date of maturity, and other relevant factors; and

(2) In the case of shares of stock, the company's net worth, prospective earning power and dividend-paying capacity, and other relevant factors.

Some of the "other relevant factors" referred to in subparagraphs (1) and (2) of this paragraph are: The goodwill of the business; the economic outlook in the particular industry; the company's position in the industry and its management; the degree of control of the business represented by the block of stock to be valued; and the values of securities of corporations engaged in the same or similar lines of business which are listed on a stock exchange. However, the weight to be accorded such comparisons or any other evidentiary factors considered in the determination of a value depends upon the facts of each case. Complete financial and other data upon which the valuation is based should be submitted with the return, including copies of reports of any examinations of the company made by accountants, engineers, or any technical experts as of or near the date of the gift.

[T.D. 6334, 23 FR 8904, Nov. 15, 1958; 25 FR 14021, Dec. 31, 1960, as amended by T.D. 7327, 39 FR 35355, Oct. 1, 1974; T.D. 7432, 41 FR 38769, Sept. 13, 1976]

§ 25.2512–3 Valuation of interest in businesses.

(a) Care should be taken to arrive at an accurate valuation of any interest in a business which the donor transfers without an adequate and full consideration in money or money's worth. The fair market value of any interest in a business, whether a partnership or a proprietorship, is the net amount which a willing purchaser, whether an individual or a corporation, would pay for the interest to a willing seller, neither being under any compulsion to buy or to sell and both having reasonable knowledge of the relevant facts. The net value is determined on the basis of all relevant factors including—

(1) A fair appraisal as of the date of the gift of all the assets of the business, tangible and intangible, including good will;

(2) The demonstrated earning capacity of the business; and

(3) The other factors set forth in paragraph (f) of § 25.2512–2 relating to the valuation of corporate stock, to the extent applicable.

Special attention should be given to determining an adequate value of the good will of the business. Complete financial and other data upon which the valuation is based should be submitted with the return, including copies of reports of examinations of the business made by accountants, engineers, or any technical experts as of or near the date of the gift.

(b) [Reserved]

[T.D. 6334, 23 FR 8904, Nov. 15, 1958]

§ 25.2512–4 Valuation of notes.

The fair market value of notes, secured or unsecured, is presumed to be the amount of unpaid principal, plus accrued interest to the date of the gift, unless the donor establishes a lower value. Unless returned at face value, plus accrued interest, it must be shown by satisfactory evidence that the note is worth less than the unpaid amount (because of the interest rate, or date of maturity, or other cause), or that the note is uncollectible in part (by reason of the insolvency of the party or parties liable, or for other cause), and that the property, if any, pledged or mortgaged as security is insufficient to satisfy it.

[T.D. 6334, 23 FR 8904, Nov. 15, 1958]

Proposed § 25.2512–4 (April 8, 1986) Valuation of notes.

LR–189–84 provides that § 25.2512–4 is revised to read as follows:

The fair market value of notes, secured or unsecured, is presumed to be the amount of unpaid principal, plus accrued interest to the date of the gift, unless the donor establishes a lower value. The fair market value of a debt instrument (as defined in § 1.1275–1(b)) whose issue price is determined under section 1273(b)(1), (2), or (3), or section 1274 is presumed to be its revised issue price (as defined in § 1.1275–1(h)). Unless returned at this value, it must be shown by satisfactory evidence that the note is worth less than the unpaid amount (because of the interest rate, or date of maturity, or other cause), or that the note is uncollectible in part (by reason of the insolvency of the party or parties liable, or for other cause), and that the property, if any, pledged or mortgaged as security is insufficient to satisfy it. See § 25.2512–8 and § 1.1012–2 for special rules relating to certain sales or exchanges of property. See § 25.7872–1 for special rules in the case of gift loans (within the meaning of § 1.7872–4(b)) made after June 6, 1984.

§ 25.2512–5 Valuation of annuities, unitrust interests, interests for life or term of years, and remainder or reversionary interests.

(a) In general. Except as otherwise provided in paragraph (b) of this section and § 25.7520–3(b), the fair market value of annuities, unitrust interests, life estates, terms of years, remainders, and reversions transferred by gift is the present value of the interests determined under paragraph (d) of this section.

Section 20.2031–7 of this chapter (Estate Tax Regulations) and related sections provide tables with standard actuarial factors and examples that illustrate how to use the tables to compute the present value of ordinary annuity, life, and remainder interests in property. These sections also refer to standard and special actuarial factors that may be necessary to compute the present value of similar interests in more unusual fact situations. These factors and examples are also generally applicable for gift tax purposes in computing the values of taxable gifts.

(b) Commercial annuities and insurance contracts. The value of life insurance contracts and contracts for the payment of annuities issued by companies regularly engaged in their sale is determined under § 25.2512–6.

(c) Actuarial valuations. The present value of annuities, interests for life or a term of years, and remainder or reversionary interests transferred by gift on or after June 1, 2023, is determined under paragraph (d) of this section. The present value of annuities, interests for life or a term of years, and remainder or reversionary interests transferred by gift before June 1, 2023, is determined (subject to paragraph (d)(3) of this section) under the following sections:

Valuation Dates		*Applicable Regulations*
After	*Before*	
—	01-01-52	§ 25.2512–5A(a)
12-31-51	01-01-71	§ 25.2512–5A(b)
12-31-70	12-01-83	§ 25.2512–5A(c)
11-30-83	05-01-89	§ 25.2512–5A(d)
04-30-89	05-01-99	§ 25.2512–5A(e)
04-30-99	05-01-09	§ 25.2512–5A(f)
04-30-09	06-01-23	§ 25.2512–5A(g)

(d) Actuarial valuations on or after June 1, 2023 (1) *In general.* Except as otherwise provided in paragraph (b) of this section and § 25.7520–3(b) (relating to exceptions to the use of prescribed tables under certain circumstances), the fair market value of annuities, interests for life or a term of years, and remainder or reversionary interests transferred on or after June 1, 2023, is the present value of such interests determined under paragraph (d)(2) of this section and by using standard or special section 7520 actuarial factors. Many of these factors are derived by using the actuarial formulas provided in § 20.2031–7(d)(2) of this chapter, appropriate section 7520 interest rate, and, if applicable, the mortality component for the valuation date of the interest that is being valued. For purposes of the computations described in this section, the age of an individual is the age of that individual at the individual's nearest birthday. For the convenience of taxpayers, paragraph (d)(2) of this section provides for published tables of factors for specific types of interests. These published tables provide factors for rates from 0.2 to 20 percent, inclusive, at intervals of two-tenths of one percent. In general, appropriate factors instead may be computed directly from the actuarial formulas provided in § 20.2031–7(d)(2) of this chapter. In some cases, specific examples in this part and IRS publications illustrate approximation methods (for example, interpolation) for obtaining factors when the required valuation rate falls between two listed rates (such as in the case of a pooled income fund's rate of return or a unitrust's adjusted payout rate). Exact methods of obtaining the applicable actuarial factors are allowed, such as through software using the actual rate of return and the actuarial formulas provided in § 20.2031–7(d)(2) of this chapter. When using either an exact method or the approximation method, the resulting actuarial factor must be expressed with at least the same number of decimal places as that used in this part. The approximation method provided in this part must be used if more exact methods are not available. See §§ 25.7520–1 through 25.7520–4. The selected method must be applied consistently in valuing all interests in the same property. The fair market value of a qualified annuity interest described in section 2702(b)(1) and a qualified unitrust interest described in section 2702(b)(2) is the present value of such interests determined under § 25.7520–1(c).

(2) *Specific interests.* When the donor transfers property in trust or otherwise and retains an interest therein, generally, the value of the gift is the value of the property transferred less the value of the donor's retained interest. However, if the donor transfers property after October 8, 1990, to or for the benefit of a member of the donor's family, the value of the gift is the value of the property transferred less the value of the donor's retained interest as determined under section 2702. If the donor assigns or relinquishes an annuity, an interest for life or a term of years, a remainder or reversionary interest that the donor holds

by virtue of a transfer previously made by the donor or another, the value of the gift is the value of the interest transferred. However, see section 2519 for a special rule in the case of the assignment of an income interest by a person who received the interest from a spouse.

(i) *Pooled income funds and charitable remainder trusts*. The fair market value of a remainder interest in a pooled income fund, as defined in § 1.642(c)–5 of this chapter, is its value determined under § 1.642(c)–6(e) of this chapter (see § 1.642(c)–6A of this chapter for certain prior periods). The fair market value of a remainder interest in a charitable remainder annuity trust, as described in § 1.664–2(a) of this chapter, is its present value determined under § 1.664–2(c) of this chapter. The fair market value of a remainder interest in a charitable remainder unitrust, as defined in § 1.664–3 of this chapter, is its present value determined under § 1.664–4(e) of this chapter. The fair market value of a life interest or term for years interest in a charitable remainder unitrust is the fair market value of the property as of the date of transfer less the fair market value of the remainder interest, determined under § 1.664–4(e)(4) and (5) of this chapter.

(ii) *Ordinary remainder and reversionary interests* (A) Remainder and reversionary interests after a term of years. If the interest to be valued is a remainder or reversionary interest to take effect after a definite number of years, the present value of the interest is computed by multiplying the value of the property by the appropriate remainder factor (that corresponds to the applicable section 7520 interest rate and the stated term). The factor for an ordinary remainder interest following a term certain may be found using the formula in § 20.2031–7(d)(2)(ii)(A) of this chapter and computing the result to at least six decimal places. For the convenience of taxpayers, actuarial factors have been computed by the IRS and appear in Table B. Table B can be found on the IRS website at *https://www.irs.gov/retirement-plans/actuarial-tables* (or a corresponding URL as may be updated from time to time). Table B is referenced and explained in IRS Publication 1457, Actuarial Valuations Version 4A, which will be available within a reasonable time after June 1, 2023. The remainder factors from Table B also can be found in paragraph (d)(6) of this section, but only for interest rates from 4.2 to 14 percent, inclusive. For information about obtaining special factors for other situations, see paragraph (d)(4) of this section.

(B) Remainder and reversionary interests dependent on the life of one individual. If the interest to be valued is a remainder or reversionary interest to take effect after the death of one individual, the present value of the interest is computed by multiplying the value of the property by the appropriate remainder factor (that corresponds to the applicable section 7520 interest rate and the age of the measuring life of the life interest that precedes the remainder interest). The factor for an ordinary remainder interest following the death of one individual may be found by using the formula in § 20.2031–7(d)(2)(ii)(B) of this chapter to derive a remainder factor from the appropriate mortality table to at least five decimal places. For the convenience of taxpayers, actuarial factors have been computed by the IRS and appear in Table S. Table S currently is available, at no charge, electronically via the IRS website at *https://www.irs.gov/retirement-plans/actuarial-tables* (or a corresponding URL as may be updated from time to time). Table S is referenced and explained by IRS Publication 1457, Actuarial Valuations Version 4A, which will be available within a reasonable time after June 1, 2023. For information about obtaining special factors for other situations, see paragraph (d)(4) of this section.

(iii) *Ordinary interests for a term of years and life interests*. If the interest to be valued is the right of a person to receive the income of certain property, or to the use of certain property, for a term of years or for the life of one individual, the present value of the interest is computed by multiplying the value of the property by the appropriate actuarial factor for an interest for a term of years or for a life interest (that corresponds to the applicable section 7520 interest rate and the durational period). The actuarial factor for an ordinary income interest for a term certain may be found by subtracting from 1.000000 the factor for an ordinary remainder interest following the same term certain that is determined under the formula in § 20.2031–7(d)(2)(ii)(A) of this chapter. For the convenience of taxpayers, actuarial factors have been computed by the IRS and appear in the "Income Interest" column of Table B which can be found on the IRS website at *https://www.irs.gov/retirement-plans/actuarial-tables* (or a corresponding URL as may be updated from time to time). The actuarial factor for an ordinary income interest for the life of one individual may be found by subtracting from 1.00000 the factor for an ordinary remainder interest following the life of the same individual that is determined in § 20.2031–7(d)(2)(ii)(B) of this chapter. For the convenience of taxpayers, actuarial factors have been computed by the IRS and appear in the "Life Estate" column of Table S. Table S (applicable when the valuation date is on or after June 1, 2023) can be found on the IRS website at *https://www.irs.gov/retirement-plans/actuarial-tables*. Tables B and S are referenced and explained by IRS Publication 1457, Actuarial Valuations Version 4A. See § 20.2031–7A of this chapter or earlier versions of Publication 1457 for valuation of interests before June 1, 2023. For information about obtaining special factors for other situations, see paragraph (d)(4) of this section.

(iv) *Annuities*. (A) If the interest to be valued is the right of a person to receive an annuity that is payable at the end of each year for a term of years or for the life of one individual, the present value of the interest is computed by multiplying the aggregate amount payable annually by the appropriate annuity factor (that corresponds to the applicable section 7520 interest rate and annuity period). The appropriate annuity factor for an annuity payable for a term of years is computed by subtracting from 1.000000 the factor for an ordinary remainder interest following the same term certain that is determined under the formula in § 20.2031–7(d)(2)(ii)(A) of this chapter and then dividing the result by the applicable section 7520 interest rate expressed to at least four decimal places. For the convenience of taxpayers, actuarial factors have been computed by the IRS and appear in the "Annuity" column of Table B which can be found on the IRS website at *https://www.irs.gov/retirement-plans/actuarial-tables* (or a corresponding URL as may be updated from time to time). The appropriate annuity factor for an annuity payable for the life of one individual is computed by subtracting from 1.00000 the factor for an ordinary remainder interest following the life of the same individual that is determined in § 20.2031–7(d)(2)(ii)(B) of this chapter and then dividing the result by the applicable section 7520 interest rate expressed to at least four decimal places. For the convenience of taxpayers, actuarial factors have been computed by the IRS and appear in the "Annuity" column of Table S. Table S (applicable when the valuation date is on or after June 1, 2023) can be found on the IRS website at *https://www.irs.gov/retirement-plans/actuarial-tables*. Tables B and S are referenced and explained in IRS Publication 1457, Actuarial Valuations Version 4A. See § 20.2031–7A of this chapter or earlier versions of Publication 1457 for valuation of interests before June 1, 2023. For information about obtaining special factors for other situations, see paragraph (d)(4) of this section.

(B) If the annuity is payable at the end of semiannual, quarterly, monthly, or weekly periods, the product obtained by multiplying the annuity factor by the aggregate amount payable annually then is multiplied by the applicable adjustment factor at the appropriate interest rate component for payments made at the end of the specified period. The applicable adjustment factor may be found using the formula in § 20.2031–7(d)(2)(iv)(B) of this chapter expressed to at least four decimal places. For the convenience of taxpayers, actuarial factors have been computed by the IRS and appear in Table K. Table K, which is referenced and explained by Publication 1457, can be found on the IRS website at *https://www.irs.gov/retirement-plans/actuarial-tables*. The provisions of this paragraph (d)(2)(iv)(B) are illustrated by the example in paragraph (d)(2)(iv)(B)(2) of this section.

(1) *Sample factors from actuarial Tables S and K.* For purposes of the example in paragraph (d)(2)(iv)(B)(2) of this section, the relevant factors from Tables S and K are:

Factors from Table S—Based on Table 2010CM			
Interest at 3.2 Percent			
Age	Annuity	Life Estate	Remainder
68	12.2552	0.39217	0.60783
Factors from Table K			
Adjustment Factors for Annuities Payable at the End of Each Interval			
Interest Rate	Semi-Annually	Quarterly	Monthly
3.2%	1.0079	1.0119	1.0146

(2) *Example.* On July 1 of a year after 2021, the donor agrees to pay the annuitant the sum of $10,000 per year, payable in equal semiannual installments at the end of each period. The semiannual installments are to be made on each December 31st and June 30th. The annuity is payable until the annuitant's death. On the date of the agreement, the annuitant is 68 years and 5 months old. The donee annuitant's age is treated as 68 for purposes of computing the present value of the annuity. The section 7520 rate on the date of the agreement is 3.2 percent. Under Table S, the factor at 3.2 percent for determining the present value of an annuity payable until the death of a person aged 68 is 12.2552. The adjustment factor from Table K in the column for payments made at the end of each semiannual period at the rate of 3.2 percent is 1.0079. The aggregate annual amount of the annuity, $10,000, is multiplied by the factor 12.2552 and the product is multiplied by 1.0079. The present value of the donee's annuity is, therefore, $123,520.16 ($10,000 x 12.2552 x 1.0079).

(C) If an annuity is payable at the beginning of annual, semiannual, quarterly, monthly, or weekly periods for a term of years, the value of the annuity is computed by multiplying the aggregate amount payable annually by the annuity factor described in paragraph (d)(2)(iv)(A) of this section; and the product so obtained then is multiplied by the applicable adjustment factor at the appropriate interest rate component for payments made at the beginning of specified periods. The applicable adjustment factor may be found using the formula in § 20.2031–7(d)(2)(iv)(C) of this chapter expressed to at least four decimal places. For the convenience of taxpayers, actuarial factors have been computed by the IRS and appear in Table J. Table J, which is referenced and explained by Publication 1457, can be found on the IRS website at *https://www.irs.gov/retirement-plans/actuarial-tables*. If an annuity is payable at the beginning of annual, semiannual, quarterly, monthly, or weekly periods for one or more lives, the value of the annuity is the sum of the first payment and the present value of a similar annuity, the first payment of which is not to be made until the end of the payment period, determined as provided in paragraph (d)(2)(iv)(B) of this section.

(v) *Annuity and unitrust interests for a term of years or until the prior death of an individual* (A) *Annuity interests* (1) *In general.* (i) The present value of an annuity interest that is payable until the earlier to occur of the lapse of a specific number of years or the death of an individual may be computed with the use of commutation factors and an applicable adjustment factor. The commutation factors are computed directly with the set of formulas in Figure 1 to this paragraph (d)(2)(v)(A)(1)(i). The prescribed mortality table is Table 2010CM as set forth in § 20.2031–7(d)(7)(ii) of this chapter, or for periods before June 1, 2023, the appropriate table found in § 20.2031–7A of this chapter. For the convenience of taxpayers, commutation factors have been computed by the IRS and appear in Table H. Table H currently is available, at no charge, electronically via the IRS website at *https://www.irs.gov/retirement-plans/actuarial-tables* (or a corresponding URL as may be updated from time to time). Table H is referenced and explained by IRS Publication 1457, Actuarial Valuations Version 4A, which will be available within a reasonable time after June 1, 2023.

Figure 1 to paragraph (d)(2)(v)(A)(*1*)(*i*)– Formulas for determining commutation factors

$$D_x = v^x \cdot l_x$$

$$N_{x+1} = \sum_{t=1}^{\infty} D_{x+t}$$

$$M_x = \sum_{t=0}^{\infty} v^{x+t+1} \cdot d_{x+t}$$

$$\mathring{N}_x = N_{x+1} + \frac{1}{2} M_x$$

$$\overline{M}_x = (1 + \frac{i}{2}) \cdot M_x$$

where:

i = the applicable interest rate under Section 7520 of the Internal Revenue Code;

v = 1 / (1 + i);

d_x = $l_x - l_{x+1}$;

x = is the age of the measuring life (determined as age at nearest birthday); and

l_x = the number associated with age x as set forth in the prescribed mortality table, representing the number of persons alive at age x.

(ii) The applicable adjustment factor for annuities that are payable at the end of semiannual, quarterly, monthly, or weekly periods is computed by use of the formula in § 20.2031–7(d)(2)(iv)(B) of this chapter expressed to at least four decimal places. For the convenience of taxpayers, actuarial factors have been computed by the IRS and appear in Table K. Table K can be found on the IRS website at *https://www.irs.gov/retirement-plans/actuarial-tables*. For purposes of the example in paragraph (d)(2)(v)(A)(2) of this section, the relevant factors from Tables H(2.8) and K are:

Factors from Table H(2.8)			
Commutation Factors—Based on Table 2010CM			
Interest at 2.8 Percent			
Age (x)	D_x	N_x-factor	M_x-factor
60	16,911.03	271,994.3	9,295.187
70	11,280.80	133,677.8	7,537.826
Factors from Table K			
Adjustment Factors for Annuities Payable at the End of Each Interval			
Interest Rate	Semi-Annually	Quarterly	Monthly
2.8%	1.0070	1.0104	1.0128

(2) *Example*. The donor transfers $100,000 into a trust on January 1, 2022 and retains the right to receive an annuity from the trust in the amount of $10,000 per year, payable in equal semiannual installments at the end of each period. The semiannual installments are to be made on each June 30th and December 31st. The annuity is payable for 10 years or until the donor's prior death. At the time of the transfer, the donor is 59 years and 6 months old. The donor's age is deemed to be 60 for purposes of computing the present value of the retained annuity. If the section 7520 rate for the month in which the transfer occurred is 2.8 percent, the present value of the donor's retained annuity interest for the shorter of life or term would be is $82,363.54, determined in Figure 2 to this paragraph (d)(2)(v)(A)(2).

Figure 2 to paragraph (d)(2)(v)(A)(2) – Illustration of calculation of present value of the donor's retained annuity interest for the shorter of life or term

A.	Initial age	60
B.	Plus: Term of years	10
C.	Sum (Terminal age)	70
D.	$\mathring{N}_x$ factor, Table H(2.8), age 60	271,994.30
E.	Less: $\mathring{N}_x$ factor, Table H(2.8), age 70	133,677.80
F.	Difference	138,316.50
G.	D_x factor, Table H(2.8), age 60	16,911.03
H.	Required Annuity Factor: F / G	8.1791
I.	Table K factor, semiannual payments at 2.8%	1.0070
J.	Annual Annuity Amount	$10,000
K.	Present value of retained interest: H x I x J	$82,363.54

(B) *Unitrust interests* (1) *In general.* (i) The present value of a unitrust interest that is payable until the earlier to occur of the lapse of a specific number of years or the death of an individual may be computed with the use of an adjusted payout rate factor and unitrust commutation factors. The payout rate adjustment factor is determined by applying the formula in § 1.664–4(e)(6)(ii) of this chapter for the section 7520 interest rate applicable to the transfer and computing the result to at least six decimal places. For the convenience of taxpayers, payout rate adjustment factors have been computed by the IRS, for interest rates from 0.2 to 20 percent, inclusive, and appear in Tables F(0.2) through F(20.0). The unitrust commutation factors may be computed directly with the set of formulas in Figure 3 to this paragraph (d)(2)(v)(B)(1)(i). For the convenience of taxpayers, actuarial factors have been computed by the IRS and appear in Table Z. Tables F and Z can be found on the IRS website at *https://www.irs.gov/retirement-plans/actuarial-tables*.

Figure 3 to paragraph (d)(2)(v)(B)(*1*)(*i*) – Formulas for determining unitrust commutation factors

$$^{u}D_x = {^{u}v^{x}} \cdot l_x$$

$$^{u}N_{x+1} = \sum_{t=1}^{\infty} {^{u}D_{x+t}}$$

$$^{u}M_x = \sum_{t=0}^{\infty} {^{u}v^{x+t+1}} \cdot d_{x+t}$$

$$^{u}\mathring{N}_x = {^{u}N_{x+1}} + \frac{1}{2}\,{^{u}M_x}$$

$$^{u}\bar{M}_x = (1 + \frac{^{u}i}{2}) \cdot {^{u}M_x}$$

where:

r = the adjusted payout rate;

^{u}v = 1 - r;

^{u}i = r / (1 – r);

d_x = $l_x - l_{x+1}$;

x = is the age of the measuring life (determined as age at nearest birthday); and

l_x = the number associated with age x as set forth in the prescribed mortality table, representing the number of persons alive at age x.

(ii) For purposes of the example in paragraph (d)(2)(v)(B)(2) of this section, the relevant factors from Tables F(3.4), Z(4.8), and Z(5.0) are:

Factors From Table F(3.4)			
Factors for Computing Adjusted Payout Rates for Unitrusts			
Interest at 3.4 Percent			
# of Months from Annual Valuation to First Payout		Adjustment Factors for Payments at End of Period	
At Least	But Less Than	Annual	Semiannual
6	7	0.983422	0.975270
Factors from Table Z(4.8)			
Unitrust Commutation Factors—Based on Table 2010CM			
Adjusted Payout Rate of 4.8 Percent			
Age (x)	${}^{u}D_x$	${}^{u}N_x$-factor	${}^{u}M_x$-factor
60	4,634.189	58,509.09	1,684.151
70	2,491.406	24,541.74	1,254.007
Factors from Table Z(5.0)			
Unitrust Commutation Factors—Based on Table 2010CM			
Adjusted Payout Rate of 5.0 Percent			
Age (x)	${}^{u}D_x$	${}^{u}N_x$-factor	${}^{u}M_x$-factor
60	4,084.822	50,451.77	1,429.466
70	2,150.356	20,823.44	1,054.386

(2) *Example of interpolation.* The donor who, as of the nearest birthday, is 60 years old, transfers $100,000 to a unitrust on January 1st of a year after 2021. The trust instrument requires that each year the trust pay to the donor, in equal semiannual installments on June 30th and December 31st, 5 percent of the fair market value of the trust assets, valued as of January 1st of that year, for 10 years or until the prior death of the donor. The section 7520 rate for the January in which the transfer occurred is 3.4 percent. Under Table F(3.4), the appropriate adjustment factor is 0.975270 for semiannual payments payable at the end of the semiannual period. The adjusted payout rate is 4.876 percent (5% x 0.975270). The present value of the donor's retained interest is $37,419.00 determined in paragraphs (d)(2)(v)(B)(2)(i) through (iii) of this section. Using Table Z, the method required is to prepare two computations, one at a payout rate of 4.8 percent, and one at 5.0 percent, and interpolate between these two in order to get the result at the adjusted payout rate of 4.876 percent. As an alternative to using an interpolation method, it also is acceptable to compute the remainder factor directly from the root actuarial formulas using the actual adjusted payout rate of 4.876%.

(i) Determine the terminal age, as illustrated in Figure 4 to this paragraph (d)(2)(v)(B)(2)(i).

A.	Initial age	60
B.	Plus: Term of years	10
C.	Sum (Terminal age)	70

(ii) Determine the Payout Interest Factor at the Table Z payout rates immediately below and above the adjusted payout rate, as illustrated in Figure 5 to this paragraph (d)(2)(v)(B)(2)(ii).

Figure 5 to paragraph (d)(2)(v)(B)(2)(*ii*)–Illustration of determination of payout interest factors

D.	Payout Rate	4.80%	5.00%
E.	Equivalent Interest Rate Factor: D / (1 - D)	0.05042	0.05263
F.	$^{u}\mathring{N}_x$ factor, Table Z, age 60	58,509.09	50,451.77
G.	Less: $^{u}\mathring{N}_x$ factor, TableZ, age 70	24,541.74	20,823.44
H.	Difference	33,967.35	29,628.33
I.	$^{u}D_x$ factor, Table Z, age 60	4,634.189	4,084.822
J.	Intermediate Factor: H / I	7.32973	7.25327
K.	Payout Interest Factor: E x J	0.36956	0.38174

(iii) Interpolate between the Payout Interest Factors at 4.8% and 5.0% to determine the Payout Interest Factor at the adjusted rate of 4.876%, as illustrated in Figure 6 to this paragraph (d)(2)(v)(B)(2)(iii).

Figure 6 to paragraph (d)(2)(v)(B)(2)(*iii*)–Illustration of interpolation

L.	Payout Interest Factor at 5.00%	0.38174
M.	Less: Payout Interest Factor at 4.8%	0.36956
N.	Difference: L - M	0.01218
O.	Adjusted Payout Rate	4.876%

P. Interpolation Adjustment:

$$\frac{5.00\% - 4.876\%}{5.00\% - 4.80\%} = \frac{z}{0.01218}$$

$$\frac{5.00\% - 4.876\%}{5.00\% - 4.80\%} \cdot 0.01218 = z = 0.00755$$

Q.	Payout Interest Factor at 5.00%	0.38174
R.	Less: Interpolation Adjustment z	0.00755
S.	Interpolated Payout Interest Factor: Q - R	0.37419
T.	Amount Transferred	$100,000
U.	Present Value of Retained Payout Interest: S x T	$37,419

(3) *Transitional rule.* If the valuation date of a transfer of property by gift is after April 30, 2019, and on or before June 1, 2023, the fair market value of the interest transferred is determined by using the section 7520 interest rate for the month in which the valuation date occurs (see §§ 25.7520–1(b) and 25.7520–2(a)(2)) and the appropriate actuarial factors derived from the selected mortality table, either Table 2010CM in § 20.2031–7(d)(7)(ii) of this chapter or Table 2000CM in § 20.2031–7A(g)(4) of this chapter, at the option of the donor or the decedent's executor, as the case may be. If any previously filed gift tax return is supplemented to use the actuarial factors based on Table 2010CM, the supplemental return must state at the top "AMENDED PURSUANT TO TD 9974." For the convenience of taxpayers, actuarial factors based on Table 2010CM appear in the current version of Table S, and actuarial factors based on Table 2000CM appear in the previous version of Table S. Both versions of Table S will be available as provided in paragraph (d)(4) of this section. With respect to each individual transaction, the donor must consistently use the same mortality basis with respect to each interest (income, remainder, partial, etc.) in the same property, and with

respect to all transfers occurring on the same valuation date. For example, gift and income tax charitable deductions with respect to the same transfer must be determined based on factors with the same mortality basis, and all assets includible in the gross estate and/or estate tax deductions claimed must be valued based on factors with the same mortality basis.

(4) *Publications and actuarial computations by the Internal Revenue Service.* The factor for determining the present value of a remainder interest that is dependent on the termination of the life of one individual may be computed by using the formula in § 20.2031–7(d)(2)(ii)(B) of this chapter to derive a remainder factor from the appropriate mortality table expressed to at least five decimal places. For the convenience of taxpayers, actuarial factors have been computed by the IRS and appear in Table S. The factor for determining the present value of a remainder interest following a term certain may be computed by using the formula in § 20.2031–7(d)(2)(ii)(A) of this chapter expressed to at least six decimal places. For the convenience of taxpayers, actuarial factors have been computed by the IRS and appear in Table B. Adjustment factors for term certain annuities payable at the beginning of each interval may be computed by using the formula in § 20.2031–7(d)(2)(iv)(C) of this chapter expressed to at least four decimal places. For the convenience of taxpayers, actuarial factors have been computed by the IRS and appear in Table J. Adjustment factors for annuities payable at the end of each interval may be computed by using the formula in § 20.2031–7(d)(2)(iv)(B) of this chapter expressed to at least four decimal places. For the convenience of taxpayers, actuarial factors have been computed by the IRS and appear in Table K. These tables currently are available, at no charge, electronically via the IRS website at *https://www.irs.gov/retirement-plans/actuarial-tables* (or a corresponding URL as may be updated from time to time). IRS Publication 1457, Actuarial Valuations Version 4A (2023), references and explains the factors contained in the actuarial tables and also includes examples that illustrate how to compute many special factors for more unusual situations. This publication will be available within a reasonable time after June 1, 2023. Tables B, J, and K also can be found in § 20.2031–7(d)(6) of this chapter, but only for interest rates from 4.2 to 14 percent, inclusive. If a particular factor is required, that factor may be calculated by the taxpayer using the actuarial formula in § 20.2031–7(d)(2) of this chapter or the taxpayer may request a ruling to obtain the factor from the Internal Revenue Service. The request for a ruling must be accompanied by a recitation of the facts including a statement of the date of birth for each measuring life, the date of the gift, any other applicable dates, and a copy of the will, trust, or other relevant documents. A request for a ruling must comply with the instructions for requesting a ruling published periodically in the Internal Revenue Bulletin (see Rev. Proc. 2023–1, 2023–1 I.R.B. 1, or successor revenue procedures, and §§ 601.201 and 601.601(d)(2)(ii)(b) of this chapter) and must include payment of the required user fee.

(e) Applicability date. This section applies on and after June 1, 2023.

[T.D. 8540, 59 FR 30174, June 10, 1994; T.D. 8819, 64 FR 23224, April 30, 1999; T.D. 8886, 65 FR 36940, June 12, 2000; 65 FR 39470, June 26, 2000; 65 FR 52163, Aug. 28, 2000; 65 FR 58222, Sept. 28, 2000; T.D. 9448, 74 FR 21512, May 7, 2009; T.D. 9540, 76 FR 49639, Aug. 10, 2011; T.D. 9974, 88 FR 37451, June 7, 2023]

§ 25.2512–5A Valuation of annuities, interests for life or a term of years, and remainder or reversionary interests transferred before June 1, 2023.

(a) Valuation of annuities, interests for life or term of years, and remainder or reversionary interests transferred before January 1, 1952. [*Omitted. Ed.*]

(b) Valuation of annuities, interests for life or term of years, and remainder or reversionary interests transferred after December 31, 1951, and before January 1, 1971. [*Omitted. Ed.*]

(c) Valuation of annuities, interests for life or term of years, and remainder or reversionary interests transferred after December 31, 1970, and before December 1, 1983. [*Omitted. Ed.*]

(d) Valuation of annuities, interests for life or term of years, and remainder or reversionary interests transferred after November 30, 1983, and before May 1, 1989. [*Omitted. Ed.*]

(e) Valuation of annuities, unitrust interests, interests for life or term of years, and remainder or

reversionary interests transferred after April 30, 1989, and before May 1, 1999. [*Omitted. Ed.*]

(f) Valuation of annuities, unitrust interests, interests for life or term of years, and remainder or reversionary interests transferred after April 30, 1999, and before May 1, 2009 [*Omitted. Ed.*]

(g) Valuation of annuities, interests for life or a term of years, and remainder or reversionary interests transferred on or after May 1, 2009, and before June 1, 2023 (1) *In general.* Except as otherwise provided in §§ 25.2512–5(b) and 25.7520–3(b) (pertaining to certain limitations on the use of prescribed tables), if the valuation date of the transferred interest is on or after May 1, 2009, and before June 1, 2023, the fair market value of annuities, interests for life or a term of years, and remainder or reversionary interests transferred by gift is the present value of the interests determined by using standard or special section 7520 actuarial factors and the valuation methodology described in § 25.2512–5(d). Sections 20.2031–7(d)(6) and 20.2031–7A(g)(4) of this chapter and related sections provide tables with standard actuarial factors and examples that illustrate how to use the tables to compute the present value of ordinary annuity, life, term, and remainder interests in property. Sections 20.2031–7(d)(6) and 20.2031–7A(g)(4) of this chapter also refer to standard and special actuarial factors that may be necessary to compute the present value of similar interests in more unusual fact situations. These factors and examples also generally are applicable for gift tax purposes in computing the values of taxable gifts.

(2) *Transitional rule.* (i) If the valuation date of a transfer of property by gift is on or after May 1, 2009, and before July 1, 2009, the fair market value of the interest transferred is determined by using the section 7520 interest rate for the month in which the valuation date occurs (see §§ 25.7520–1(b) and 25.7520–2(a)(2)) and the appropriate actuarial tables under either § 20.2031–7A(f)(4) or (g)(4) of this chapter, at the option of the donor.

(ii) For purposes of paragraph (g)(2)(i) of this section, where the donor is given the option to use either of two appropriate actuarial tables, the donor must consistently use the same mortality basis with respect to each interest (income, remainder, partial, etc.) in the same property, and with respect to all transfers occurring on the same valuation date. For example, gift and income tax charitable deductions with respect to the same transfer must be determined based on factors with the same mortality basis, and all assets includible in the gross estate and/or estate tax deductions claimed must be valued based on factors with the same mortality basis.

(iii) If the valuation date of a transfer of property by gift is after April 30, 2019, and before June 1, 2023, the fair market value of the interest transferred is determined under § 25.2512–5(d)(3).

(3) *Publications and actuarial computations by the Internal Revenue Service.* The factor for determining the present value of a remainder interest that is dependent on the termination of the life of one individual may be computed by using the formula in § 20.2031–7(d)(2)(ii)(B) of this chapter to derive a remainder factor from the appropriate mortality table to at least five decimal places. For the convenience of taxpayers, actuarial factors have been computed by the IRS and appear in Table S. The factor for determining the present value of a remainder interest following a term certain may be computed by using the formula in § 20.2031–7(d)(2)(ii)(A) of this chapter expressed to at least six decimal places. For the convenience of taxpayers, actuarial factors have been computed by the IRS and appear in Table B. Adjustment factors for term certain annuities payable at the beginning of each interval may be computed by using the formula in § 20.2031–7(d)(2)(iv)(C) of this chapter expressed to at least four decimal places. For the convenience of taxpayers, actuarial factors have been computed by the IRS and appear in Table J. Adjustment factors for annuities payable at the end of each interval may be computed by using the formula in § 20.2031–7(d)(2)(iv)(B) of this chapter expressed to at least four decimal places. For the convenience of taxpayers, actuarial factors have been computed by the IRS and appear in Table K. These tables are referenced and explained by IRS Publication 1457, Actuarial Values Version 3A, (2009). Publication 1457 includes examples that illustrate how to compute many special factors for more unusual situations. The actuarial tables are available, at no charge, electronically via the IRS website at *https://www.irs.gov/retirement-plans/actuarial-tables* (or a corresponding URL as may be updated from time to time). Table S also can be found in § 20.2031–7A(g)(4) of this chapter, but only for interest rates from 0.2

to 14 percent, inclusive. Tables B, J, and K also can be found in § 20.2031–7(d)(6) of this chapter, but only for interest rates from 4.2 to 14 percent, inclusive. If a particular factor is required in the case of a completed gift, that factor may be calculated by the donor using the actuarial formulas in § 20.2031–7(d)(2) of this chapter or the donor may request a ruling to obtain the factor from the Internal Revenue Service. The request for a ruling must be accompanied by a recitation of the facts including a statement of the date of birth for each measuring life, the date of the gift, any other applicable dates, and a copy of the will, trust, or other relevant documents. A request for a ruling must comply with the instructions for requesting a ruling published periodically in the Internal Revenue Bulletin (see §§ 601.201 and 601.601(d)(2)(ii)(b) of this chapter) and must include payment of the required user fee.

(4) *Applicability dates*. Paragraphs (g)(1) through (3) of this section apply on and after May 1, 2009, and before June 1, 2023.

[T.D. 6334, 23 FR 8904, Nov. 15, 1958; 25 FR 14021, Dec. 31, 1960, as amended by T.D. 7077, 35 FR 18464, Dec. 4, 1970; 35 FR 18965, Dec. 15, 1970; T.D. 7955, 49 FR 19995, May 11, 1984; T.D. 8395, 57 FR 4255, Feb. 4, 1992; T.D. 8540, 59 FR 30103, 30173, 30174, June 10, 1994; T.D. 8819, 64 FR 23226, April 30, 1999; T.D. 8886, 65 FR 36943, June 12, 2000; T.D. 9448, 74 FR 21515, May 7, 2009; T.D. 9540, 76 FR 49641, Aug. 10, 2011; T.D. 9974, 88 FR 37459, June 7, 2023]

§ 25.2512–6 Valuation of certain life insurance and annuity contracts; valuation of shares in an open-end investment company.

(a) Valuation of certain life insurance and annuity contracts. The value of a life insurance contract or of a contract for the payment of an annuity issued by a company regularly engaged in the selling of contracts of that character is established through the sale of the particular contract by the company, or through the sale by the company of comparable contracts. As valuation of an insurance policy through sale of comparable contracts is not readily ascertainable when the gift is of a contract which has been in force for some time and on which further premium payments are to be made, the value may be approximated by adding to the interpolated terminal reserve at the date of the gift the proportionate part of the gross premium last paid before the date of the gift which covers the period extending beyond that date. If, however, because of the unusual nature of the contract such approximation is not reasonably close to the full value, this method may not be used. The following examples, so far as relating to life insurance contracts, are of gifts of such contracts on which there are no accrued dividends or outstanding indebtedness.

Example (1). A donor purchases from a life insurance company for the benefit of another a life insurance contract or a contract for the payment of an annuity. The value of the gift is the cost of the contract.

Example (2). An annuitant purchased from a life insurance company a single payment annuity contract by the terms of which he was entitled to receive payments of $1,200 annually for the duration of his life. Five years subsequent to such purchase, and when of the age of 50 years, he gratuitously assigns the contract. The value of the gift is the amount which the company would charge for an annuity contract providing for the payment of $1,200 annually for the life of a person 50 years of age.

Example (3). A donor owning a life insurance policy on which no further payments are to be made to the company (e.g., a single premium policy or paid-up policy) makes a gift of the contract. The value of the gift is the amount which the company would charge for a single premium contract of the same specified amount on the life of a person of the age of the insured.

Example (4). A gift is made four months after the last premium due date of an ordinary life insurance policy issued nine years and four months prior to the gift thereof by the insured, who was 35 years of age at date of issue. The gross annual premium is $2,811. The computation follows:

Terminal reserve at end of tenth year	$14,601.00
Terminal reserve at end of ninth year	12,965.00
Increase	1,636.00
One-third of such increase (the gift having been made four months following the last preceding premium due date), is	545.33
Terminal reserve at end of ninth year	12,965.00
Interpolated terminal reserve at date of gift	13,510.33

Two-thirds of gross premium ($2,811)	1,874.00
Value of the gift	15,384.33

Example (5). A donor purchases from a life insurance company for $15,198, a joint and survivor annuity contract which provides for the payment of $60 a month to the donor during his lifetime, and then to his sister for such time as she may survive him. The premium which would have been charged by the company for an annuity of $60 monthly payable during the life of the donor alone is $10,690. The value of the gift is $4,508 ($15,198 less $10,690).

(b) Valuation of shares in an open-end investment company. (1) The fair market value of a share in an open-end investment company (commonly known as a "mutual fund") is the public redemption price of a share. In the absence of an affirmative showing of the public redemption price in effect at the time of the gift, the last public redemption price quoted by the company for the date of the gift shall be presumed to be the applicable public redemption price. If there is no public redemption price quoted by the company for the date of the gift (e.g., the date of the gift is a Saturday, Sunday, or holiday), the fair market value of the mutual fund share is the last public redemption price quoted by the company for the first day preceding the date of the gift for which there is a quotation. As used in this paragraph the term "open-end investment company" includes only a company which on the date of the gift was engaged in offering its shares to the public in the capacity of an open-end investment company.

(2) The provisions of this paragraph shall apply with respect to gifts made after December 31, 1954.

[T.D. 6334, 23 FR 8904, Nov. 15, 1958, as amended by T.D. 6542, 26 FR 549, Jan. 20, 1961; T.D. 6680, 28 FR 10872, Oct. 10, 1963; T.D. 7319, 39 FR 26723, July 23, 1974]

§ 25.2512–7 Effect of excise tax.

If jewelry, furs or other property, the purchase of which is subject to an excise tax, is purchased at retail by a taxpayer and made the subject of gifts within a reasonable time after purchase, the purchase price, including the excise tax, is considered to be the fair market value of the property on the date of the gift, in the absence of evidence that the market price of similar articles has increased or decreased in the meantime. Under other circumstances, the excise tax is taken into account in determining the fair market value of property to the extent, and only to the extent, that it affects the price at which the property would change hands between a willing buyer and a willing seller, as provided in § 25.2512–1.

[T.D. 6334, 23 FR 8904, Nov. 15, 1958]

§ 25.2512–8 Transfers for insufficient consideration.

Transfers reached by the gift tax are not confined to those only which, being without a valuable consideration, accord with the common law concept of gifts, but embrace as well sales, exchanges, and other dispositions of property for a consideration to the extent that the value of the property transferred by the donor exceeds the value in money or money's worth of the consideration given therefor. However, a sale, exchange, or other transfer of property made in the ordinary course of business (a transaction which is bona fide, at arm's length, and free from any donative intent), will be considered as made for an adequate and full consideration in money or money's worth. A consideration not reducible to a value in money or money's worth, as love and affection, promise of marriage, etc., is to be wholly disregarded, and the entire value of the property transferred constitutes the amount of the gift. Similarly, a relinquishment or promised relinquishment of dower or curtesy, or of a statutory estate created in lieu of dower or curtesy, or of other marital rights in the spouse's property or estate, shall not be considered to any extent a consideration "in money or money's worth." See, however, section 2516 and the regulations thereunder with respect to certain transfers incident to a divorce. See also sections 2701, 2702, 2703 and 2704 and the regulations at §§ 25.2701–0 through 25.2704–3 for special rules for valuing transfers of business interests, transfers in trust, and transfers pursuant to options and purchase agreements.

[T.D. 6334, 23 FR 8904, Nov. 15, 1958; T.D. 8395, 57 FR 4255, Feb. 4, 1992]

Proposed § 25.2512–8 (April 8, 1986) Valuation of notes.

LR–189–84 provides that § 25.2512–8 is revised to read as follows:

Transfers reached by the gift tax are not confined to those only which, being without a valuable consideration, accord with the common law concept of gifts, but embrace as well sales, exchanges, and other dispositions of property for a consideration to the extent that the value of the property transferred by the donor differs from the value in money or money's worth of the consideration given therefor. However, a sale, exchange, or other transfer of property made in the ordinary course of business (a transaction which is bona fide, at arm's length, and free from any donative intent), will be considered as made for consideration in money or money's worth equal to the value of the property transferred. If the buyer issues one or more debt instruments as all or a part of the consideration for the property, then the property and the debt instruments shall be valued in accordance with the rules set forth in § 1.1012–2. A consideration not reducible to a value in money or money's worth, as love and affection, promise of marriage, etc., is to be wholly disregarded, and the entire value of the property transferred constitutes the amount of the gift. Similarly, a relinquishment or promised relinquishment of dower or curtesy, or of a statutory estate created in lieu of dower or curtesy, or of other material rights in the spouse's property or estate, shall not be considered to any extent a consideration "in money or money's worth." See, however, section 2516 and the regulations thereunder with respect to certain transfers incident to a divorce.

§ 2513. Gift by Husband or Wife to Third Party

(a) Considered as made one-half by each.

(1) In general. A gift made by one spouse to any person other than his spouse shall, for the purposes of this chapter, be considered as made one-half by him and one-half by his spouse, but only if at the time of the gift each spouse is a citizen or resident of the United States. This paragraph shall not apply with respect to a gift by a spouse of an interest in property if he creates in his spouse a general power of appointment, as defined in section 2514(c), over such interest. For purposes of this section, an individual shall be considered as the spouse of another individual only if he is married to such individual at the time of the gift and does not remarry during the remainder of the calendar year.

(2) Consent of both spouses. Paragraph (1) shall apply only if both spouses have signified (under the regulations provided for in subsection (b)) their consent to the application of paragraph (1) in the case of all such gifts made during the calendar year by either while married to the other.

(b) Manner and time of signifying consent.

(1) Manner. A consent under this section shall be signified in such manner as is provided under regulations prescribed by the Secretary.

(2) Time. Such consent may be so signified at any time after the 15th day of April following the close of such year, unless before such 15th day no return has been filed for such year by either spouse, in which case the consent may not be signified after a return for such year is filed by either spouse.

(A) The consent may not be signified after the 15th day of April following the close of such year, unless before such 15th day no return has been filed for such year by either spouse, in which case the consent may not be signified after a return for such year is filed by either spouse.

(B) The consent may not be signified after a notice of deficiency with respect to the tax for such year has been sent to either spouse in accordance with section 6212(a).

(c) Revocation of consent. Revocation of a consent previously signified shall be made in such manner as is provided under regulations prescribed by the Secretary, but the right to revoke a consent previously signified with respect to a calendar year—

(1) shall not exist after the 15th day of April following the close of such year if the consent was signified on or before such 15th day, and

(2) shall not exist if the consent was not signified under after such 15th day.

(d) Joint and several liability for tax. If the consent required by subsection (a)(2) is signified with respect to a gift made in any calendar year, the liability with respect to the entire tax imposed by this chapter of each spouse for such year shall be joint and several.

Regulations

§ 25.2513–1 Gifts by husband or wife to third party considered as made one-half by each.

(a) A gift made by one spouse to a person other than his (or her) spouse may, for the purpose of the gift tax, be considered as made one-half by his spouse, but only if at the time of the gift each spouse was a citizen or resident of the United States. For purposes of this section, an individual is to be considered as the spouse of another individual only if he was married to such individual at the time of the gift and does not remarry during the remainder of the "calendar period" (as defined in § 25.2502–1(c)(1)).

(b) The provisions of this section will apply to gifts made during a particular "calendar period" (as defined in § 25.2502–1(c)(1)) only if both spouses signify their consent to treat all gifts made to third parties during that calendar period by both spouses while married to each other as having been made one-half by each spouse. As to the manner and time for signifying consent, see § 25.2513–2. Such consent, if signified with respect to any calendar period, is effective with respect to all gifts made to third parties during such calendar period except as follows:

(1) If the consenting spouses were not married to each other during a portion of the calendar period, the consent is not effective with respect to any gifts made during such portion of the calendar period. Where the consent is signified by an executor or administrator of a deceased spouse, the consent is not effective with respect to gifts made by the surviving spouse during the portion of the calendar period that his spouse was deceased.

(2) If either spouse was a nonresident not a citizen of the United States during any portion of the calendar period, the consent is not effective with respect to any gift made during that portion of the calendar period.

(3) The consent is not effective with respect to a gift by one spouse of a property interest over which he created in his spouse a general power of appointment (as defined in section 2514(c)).

(4) If one spouse transferred property in part to his spouse and in part to third parties, the consent is effective with respect to the interest transferred to third parties only insofar as such interest is ascertainable at the time of the gift and hence severable from the interest transferred to his spouse. See § 25.2512–5 for the principles to be applied in the valuation of annuities, life estates, terms for years, remainders and reversions.

(5) The consent applies alike to gifts made by one spouse alone and to gifts made partly by each spouse, provided such gifts were to third parties and do not fall within any of the exceptions set forth in subparagraphs (1) through (4) of this paragraph. The consent may not be applied only to a portion of the property interest constituting such gifts. For example, a wife may not treat gifts made by her spouse from his separate property to third parties as having been made one-half by her if her spouse does not consent to treat gifts made by her to third parties during the same calendar period as having been made one-half by him. If the consent is effectively signified on either the husband's return or the wife's return, all gifts made by the spouses to third parties (except as described in subparagraphs (1) through (4) of this paragraph), during the calendar period will be treated as having been made one-half by each spouse.

(c) If a husband and wife consent to have the gifts made to third party donees considered as made one-half by each spouse, and only one spouse makes gifts during the "calendar period" (as defined in § 25.2502–1(c)(1)), the other spouse is not required to file a gift tax return provided: (1) The total value of the gifts made to each third party donee since the beginning of the calendar year is not in excess of $20,000 ($6,000 for calendar years prior to 1982), and (2) no portion of the property transferred constitutes a gift of a future interest. If a transfer made by either spouse during the calendar period to a third-party represents a gift of a future interest in property and the spouses consent to have the gifts considered as made one-half by each, a gift tax return for such calendar period must be filed by each spouse regardless of the value of the transfer.

(See § 25.2503–3 for the definition of a future interest.)

(d) The following examples illustrate the application of this section relating to the requirements for the filing of a return, assuming that a consent was effectively signified:

(1) A husband made gifts valued at $7,000 during the second quarter of 1971 to a third party and his wife made no gifts during this time. Each spouse is required to file a return for the second calendar quarter of 1971.

(2) A husband made gifts valued at $5,000 to each of two third parties during the year 1970 and his wife made no gifts. Only the husband is required to file a return. (See § 25.6019–2.)

(3) During the third quarter of 1971, a husband made gifts valued at $5,000 to a third party, and his wife made gifts valued at $2,000 to the same third party. Each spouse is required to file a return for the third calendar quarter of 1971.

(4) A husband made gifts valued at $5,000 to a third party and his wife made gifts valued at $3,000 to another third party during the year 1970. Only the husband is required to file a return for the calendar year 1970. (See § 25.6019–2.)

(5) A husband made gifts valued at $2,000 during the first quarter of 1971 to third parties which represented gifts of future interests in property (see § 25.2503–3), and his wife made no gifts during such calendar quarter. Each spouse is required to file a return for the first calendar quarter of 1971.

[T.D. 6334, 23 FR 8904, Nov. 15, 1958, as amended by T.D. 7238, 37 FR 28729, Dec. 29, 1972; T.D. 7910, 48 FR 40374, Sept. 7, 1983]

§ 25.2513–2 Manner and time of signifying consent.

(a)(1) Consent to the application of the provisions of section 2513 with respect to a "calendar period" (as defined in § 25.2502–1(c)(1)) shall, in order to be effective, be signified by both spouses. If both spouses file gift tax returns within the time for signifying consent, it is sufficient if—

(i) The consent of the husband is signified on the wife's return, and the consent of the wife is signified on the husband's return;

(ii) The consent of each spouse is signified on his own return; or

(iii) The consent of both spouses is signified on one of the returns.

If only one spouse files a gift tax return within the time provided for signifying consent, the consent of both spouses shall be signified on that return. However, wherever possible, the notice of the consent is to be shown on both returns and it is preferred that the notice be executed in the manner described in subdivision (i) of this subparagraph. The consent may be revoked only as provided in § 25.2513–3. If one spouse files more than one gift tax return for a calendar period on or before the due date of the return, the last return so filed shall, for the purpose of determining whether a consent has been signified, be considered as the return. (See §§ 25.6075–1 and 25.6075–2 for the due date of a gift tax return.)

(2) For gifts made after December 31, 1970, and before January 1, 1982, subject to the limitations of paragraph (b) of this section, the consent signified on a return filed for a calendar quarter will be effective for a previous calendar quarter of the same calendar year for which no return was filed because the gifts made during such previous calendar quarter did not exceed the annual exclusion provided by section 2503(b), if the gifts in such previous calendar quarter are listed on that return. Thus, for example, if A gave $2,000 to his son in the first quarter of 1972 (and filed no return because of section 2503(b)) and gave a further $4,000 to such son in the last quarter of the year, A and his spouse could signify consent to the application of section 2513 on the return filed for the fourth quarter and have it apply to the first quarter as well, provided that the $2,000 gift is listed on such return.

(b)(1) With respect to gifts made after December 31, 1981, or before January 1, 1971, the consent may be signified at any time following the close of the calendar year, subject to the following limitations:

(i) The consent may not be signified after the 15th day of April following the close of the calendar year, unless before such 15th day no return has been filed for the year by either spouse, in which case the consent may not be signified after a return for the year is filed by either spouse; and

(ii) The consent may not be signified for a calendar year after a notice of deficiency in gift tax for that year has been sent to either spouse in accordance with the provisions of section 6212(a).

(2) With respect to gifts made after December 31, 1970 and before January 1, 1982, the consent may be signified at any time following the close of the calendar quarter in which the gift was made, subject to the following limitations:

(i) The consent may not be signified after the 15th day of the second month following the close of such calendar quarter, unless before such 15th day, no return has been filed for such calendar quarter by either spouse, in which case the consent may not be signified after a return for such calendar quarter is filed by either spouse; and

(ii) The consent may not be signified after a notice of deficiency with respect to the tax for such calendar quarter has been sent to either spouse in accordance with section 6212(a).

(c) The executor or administrator of a deceased spouse, or the guardian or committee of a legally incompetent spouse, as the case may be, may signify the consent.

(d) If the donor and spouse consent to the application of section 2513, the return or returns for the "calendar period" (as defined in § 25.2502–1(c)(1)) must set forth, to the extent provided thereon, information relative to the transfers made by each spouse.

[T.D. 6334, 23 FR 8904, Nov. 15, 1958, as amended by T.D. 7238, 37 FR 28730, Dec. 29, 1972; T.D. 7910, 48 FR 40374, 40375, Sept. 7, 1983]

§ 25.2513–3 Revocation of consent.

(a)(1) With respect to gifts made after December 31, 1981, or before January 1, 1971, if the consent to the application of the provisions of section 2513 for a calendar year was effectively signified on or before the 15th day of April following the close of the calendar year, either spouse may revoke the consent by filing in duplicate a signed statement of revocation, but only if the statement is filed on or before such 15th day of April. Therefore, a consent that was not effectively signified until after the 15th day of April following the close of the calendar year to which it applies may not be revoked.

(2) With respect to gifts made after December 31, 1970, and before January 1, 1982, if the consent to the application of the provisions of section 2513 for a calendar quarter was effectively signified on or before the 15th day of the second month following the close of such calendar quarter, either spouse may revoke the consent by filing in duplicate a signed statement of revocation, but only if the statement is filed on or before such 15th day of the second month following the close of such calendar quarter. Therefore, a consent that was not effectively signified until after the 15th day of the second month following the close of the calendar quarter to which it applies may not be revoked.

(b) Except as provided in paragraph (b) of § 301.6091–1 of this chapter (relating to handcarried documents), the statement referred to in paragraph (a) of this section shall be filed with the internal revenue officer with whom the gift tax return is required to be filed, or with whom the gift tax return would be required to be filed if a return were required.

[T.D. 6334, 23 FR 8904, Nov. 15, 1958, as amended by T.D. 7012, 34 FR 7691, May, 15, 1969; T.D. 7238, 37 FR 28730, Dec. 29, 1972; T.D. 7910, 48 FR 40375, Sept. 7, 1983]

§ 25.2513–4 Joint and several liability for tax.

If consent to the application of the provisions of section 2513 is signified as provided in § 25.2513–2, and not revoked as provided in § 25.2513–3, the liability with respect to the entire gift tax of each spouse for such "calendar period" (as defined in § 25.2502–1(c)(1)) is joint and several. See paragraph (d) of § 25.2511–1.

[T.D. 6334, 23 FR 8904, Nov. 15, 1958, as amended by T.D. 7238, 37 FR 28730, Dec. 29, 1972; T.D. 7910, 48 FR 40375, Sept. 7, 1983]

§ 2514. Powers of Appointment

(a) Powers created on or before October 21, 1942. An exercise of a general power of appointment created on or before October 21, 1942, shall be deemed a transfer of property by the individual possessing such power; but the failure to exercise such a power or the complete release of such a power shall not be deemed an exercise thereof. If a general power of appointment created on or before October 21, 1942, has been partially released so that it is no longer a general power of appointment, the subsequent exercise of such power shall not be deemed to be the exercise of a general power of appointment if—

(1) such partial release occurred before November 1, 1951, or

(2) the donee of such power was under a legal disability to release such power on October 21, 1942, and such partial release occurred not later than six months after the termination of such legal disability.

(b) Powers created after October 21, 1942. The exercise or release of a general power of appointment created after October 21, 1942, shall be deemed a transfer of property by the individual possessing such power.

(c) Definition of general power of appointment. For purposes of this section, the term "general power of appointment" means a power which is exercisable in favor of the individual possessing the power (hereafter in this subsection referred to as the "possessor"), his estate, his creditors, or the creditors of his estate; except that—

(1) A power to consume, invade, or appropriate property for the benefit of the possessor which is limited by an ascertainable standard relating to the health, education, support, or maintenance of the possessor shall not be deemed a general power of appointment.

(2) A power of appointment created on or before October 21, 1942, which is exercisable by the possessor only in conjunction with another person shall not be deemed a general power of appointment.

(3) In the case of a power of appointment created after October 21, 1942, which is exercisable by the possessor only in conjunction with another person—

(A) if the power is not exercisable by the possessor except in conjunction with the creator of the power—such power shall not be deemed a general power of appointment;

(B) if the power is not exercisable by the possessor except in conjunction with a person having a substantial interest, in the property subject to the power, which is adverse to exercise of the power in favor of the possessor—such power shall not be deemed a general power of appointment. For the purposes of this subparagraph a person who, after the death of the possessor, may be possessed of a power of appointment (with respect to the property subject to the possessor's power) which he may exercise in his own favor shall be deemed as having an interest in the property and such interest shall be deemed adverse to such exercise of the possessor's power;

(C) if (after the application of subparagraphs (A) and (B)) the power is a general power of appointment and is exercisable in favor of such other person—such power shall be deemed a general power of appointment only in respect of a fractional part of the property subject to such power, such part to be determined by dividing the value of such property by the number of such persons (including the possessor) in favor of whom such power is exercisable.

For purposes of subparagraphs (B) and (C), a power shall be deemed to be exercisable in favor of a person if it is exercisable in favor of such person, his estate, his creditors, or the creditors of his estate.

(d) Creation of another power in certain cases. If a power of appointment created after October 21, 1942, is exercised by creating another power of appointment which, under the applicable local law, can be validly exercised so as to postpone the vesting of any estate or interest in the property which was subject to the first power, or suspend the absolute ownership or power of alienation of such property, for a period ascertainable without regard to the date of the creation of the first power, such exercise of the first power shall, to the extent of the property subject to the second power, be deemed a transfer of property by the individual possessing such power.

(e) Lapse of power. The lapse of a power of appointment created after October 21, 1942, during the life of the individual possessing the power shall be considered a release of such power. The rule of the preceding sentence shall apply with respect to the lapse of powers during any calendar year only to the extent that the property which could have been appointed by exercise of such lapsed powers exceeds in value the greater of the following amounts:

(1) $5,000, or

(2) 5 percent of the aggregate value of the assets out of which, or the proceeds of which, the exercise of the lapsed powers could be satisfied.

(f) Date of creation of power. For purposes of this section a power of appointment created by a will executed on or before October 21, 1942, shall be considered a power created on or before such date if the person executing such will dies before July 1, 1949, without having republished such will, by codicil or otherwise, after October 21, 1942.

Regulations

§ 25.2514–1 Transfers under power of appointment.

(a) Introductory. (1) Section 2514 treats the exercise of a general power of appointment created on or before October 21, 1942, as a transfer of property for purposes of the gift tax. The section also treats as a transfer of property the exercise or complete release of a general power of appointment created after October 21, 1942, and under certain circumstances the exercise of a power of appointment (not a general power of appointment) created after October 21, 1942, by the creation of another power of appointment. See paragraph (d) of § 25.2514–3. Under certain circumstances, also, the failure to exercise a power of appointment created after October 21, 1942, within a specified time, so that the power lapses, constitutes a transfer of property. Paragraphs (b) through (e) of this section contain definitions of certain terms used in §§ 25.2514–2 and 25.2514–3. See § 25.2514–2 for specific rules applicable to certain powers created on or before October 21, 1942. See § 25.2514–3 for specific rules applicable to powers created after October 21, 1942.

(b) Definition of "power of appointment". (1) *In general.* The term "power of appointment" includes all powers which are in substance and effect powers of appointment received by the donee of the power from another person, regardless of the nomenclature used in creating the power and regardless of local property law connotations. For example, if a trust instrument provides that the beneficiary may appropriate or consume the principal of the trust, the power to consume or appropriate is a power of appointment. Similarly, a power given to a donee to affect the beneficial enjoyment of a trust property or its income by altering, amending or revoking the trust instrument or terminating the trust is a power of appointment. A power in a donee to remove or discharge a trustee and appoint himself may be a power of appointment. For example, if under the terms of a trust instrument, the trustee or his successor has the power to appoint the principal of the trust for the benefit of individuals including himself, and A, another person, has the unrestricted power to remove or discharge the trustee at any time and appoint any other person, including himself, A is considered as having a power of appointment. However, he would not be considered to have a power of appointment if he only had the power to appoint a successor, including himself, under limited conditions which did not exist at the time of exercise, release or lapse of the trustee's power, without an accompanying unrestricted power of removal. Similarly, a power to amend only the administrative provisions of a trust instrument, which cannot substantially affect the beneficial enjoyment of the trust property or income, is not a power of appointment. The mere power of management, investment, custody of assets, or the power to allocate receipts and disbursements as between income and principal, exercisable in a fiduciary capacity, whereby the holder has no power to enlarge or shift any of the beneficial interests therein except as an incidental consequence of the discharge of such fiduciary duties is not a power of appointment. Further, the right in a beneficiary of a trust to assent to a periodic accounting, thereby relieving the trustee from further accountability, is not a power of appointment if the right of assent does not consist of any power or right to enlarge or shift the beneficial interest of any beneficiary therein.

(2) *Relation to other sections.* For purposes of §§ 25.2514–1 through 25.2514–3, the term "power of appointment" does not include powers reserved by a donor to himself. No provision of section 2514 or of §§ 25.2514–1 through 25.2514–3 is to be construed as in any way limiting the application of any other section of the Internal Revenue Code or of these regulations. The power of the owner of a property interest already possessed by him to dispose of his interest, and nothing more, is not a power of appointment, and the interest is includible in the amount of his gifts to

the extent it would be includible under section 2511 or other provisions of the Internal Revenue Code. For example, if a trust created by S provides for payment of the income to A for life with power in A to appoint the entire trust property by deed during her lifetime to a class consisting of her children, and a further power to dispose of the entire corpus by will to anyone, including her estate, and A exercises the inter vivos power in favor of her children, she has necessarily made a transfer of her income interest which constitutes a taxable gift under section 2511(a), without regard to section 2514. This transfer also results in a relinquishment of her general power to appoint by will which constitutes a transfer under section 2514 if the power was created after October 21, 1942.

(3) *Powers over a portion of property.* If a power of appointment exists as to part of an entire group of assets or only over a limited interest in property, section 2514 applies only to such part or interest.

(c) Definition of "general power of appointment". (1) *In general.* The term "general power of appointment" as defined in section 2514(c) means any power of appointment exercisable in favor of the person possessing the power (referred to as the "possessor"), his estate, his creditors, or the creditors of his estate, except (i) joint powers, to the extent provided in §§ 25.2514–2 and 25.2514–3 and (ii) certain powers limited by an ascertainable standard, to the extent provided in subparagraph (2) of this paragraph. A power of appointment exercisable to meet the estate tax, or any other taxes, debts, or charges which are enforceable against the possessor or his estate, is included within the meaning of a power of appointment exercisable in favor of the possessor, his estate, his creditors, or the creditors of his estate. A power of appointment exercisable for the purpose of discharging a legal obligation of the possessor or for his pecuniary benefit is considered a power of appointment exercisable in favor of the possessor or his creditors. However, for purposes of §§ 25.2514–1 through 25.2514–3, a power of appointment not otherwise considered to be a general power of appointment is not treated as a general power of appointment merely by reason of the fact that an appointee may, in fact, be a creditor of the possessor or his estate. A power of appointment is not a general power if by its terms it is either—

(a) Exercisable only in favor of one or more designated persons or classes other than the possessor or his creditors, or the possessor's estate, or the creditors of his estate, or

(b) Expressly not exercisable in favor of the possessor or his creditors, the possessor's estate, or the creditors of his estate.

A beneficiary may have two powers under the same instrument, one of which is a general power of appointment and the other of which is not. For example, a beneficiary may have a general power to withdraw a limited portion of trust corpus during his life, and a further power exercisable during his lifetime to appoint the corpus among his children. The latter power is not a general power of appointment (but its exercise may result in the exercise of the former power; see paragraph (d) of this section).

(2) *Powers limited by an ascertainable standard.* A power to consume, invade, or appropriate income or corpus, or both, for the benefit of the possessor which is limited by an ascertainable standard relating to the health, education, support, or maintenance of the possessor is, by reason of section 2514(c)(1), not a general power of appointment. A power is limited by such a standard if the extent of the possessor's duty to exercise and not to exercise the power is reasonably measurable in terms of his needs for health, education, or support (or any combination of them). As used in this subparagraph, the words "support" and "maintenance" are synonymous and their meaning is not limited to the bare necessities of life. A power to use property for the comfort, welfare, or happiness of the holder of the power is not limited by the requisite standard. Examples of powers which are limited by the requisite standard are powers exercisable for the holder's "support," "support in reasonable comfort," "maintenance in health and reasonable comfort," "support in his accustomed manner of living," "education, including college and professional education," "health," and "medical, dental, hospital and nursing expenses and expenses of invalidism." In determining whether a power is limited by an ascertainable standard, it is immaterial whether the beneficiary is required to exhaust his other income before the power can be exercised.

(3) *Certain powers under wills of decedents dying between January 1 and April 2, 1948.* Section 210 of the Technical Changes Act of 1953 provides that if a decedent died after December 31, 1947, but before April 3, 1948, certain property interests described

therein may, if the decedent's surviving spouse so elects, be accorded special treatment in the determination of the marital deduction to be allowed the decedent's estate under the provisions of section 812(e) of the Internal Revenue Code of 1939. See paragraph (h) of § 81.47a of Regulations 105 (26 CFR (1939) 81.47a(h)). The section further provides that property affected by the election shall be considered property with respect to which the surviving spouse has a general power of appointment. Therefore, notwithstanding any other provision of law or of §§ 25.2514–1 through 25.2514–3, if the surviving spouse has made an election under section 210 of the Technical Changes Act of 1953, the property which was the subject of the election shall be considered as property with respect to which she has a general power of appointment created after October 21, 1942, exercisable by deed or will, to the extent it was treated as an interest passing to the surviving spouse and not passing to any other person for the purpose of the marital deduction in the prior decedent's estate.

(d) Definition of "exercise." Whether a power of appointment is in fact exercised may depend upon local law. However, regardless of local law, a power of appointment is considered as exercised for purposes of section 2514 even though the exercise is in favor of the taker in default of appointment, and irrespective of whether the appointed interest and the interest in default of appointment are identical or whether the appointee renounces any right to take under the appointment. A power of appointment is also considered as exercised even though the disposition cannot take effect until the occurrence of an event after the exercise takes place, if the exercise is irrevocable and, as of the time of the exercise, the condition was not impossible of occurrence. For example, if property is left in trust to A for life, with a power in A to appoint the remainder by an instrument filed with the trustee during his life, and A exercises his power by appointing the remainder to B in the event that B survives A, A is considered to have exercised his power if the exercise was irrevocable. Furthermore, if a person holds both a presently exercisable general power of appointment and a presently exercisable nongeneral power of appointment over the same property, the exercise of the nongeneral power is considered the exercise of the general power only to the extent that immediately after the exercise of the nongeneral power the amount of money or property subject to being transferred by the exercise of the general power is decreased. For example, assume A has a noncumulative annual power to withdraw the greater of $5,000 or 5 percent of the value of a trust having a value of $300,000 and a lifetime nongeneral power to appoint all or a portion of the trust corpus to A's child or grandchildren. If A exercises the nongeneral power by appointing $150,000 to A's child, the exercise of the nongeneral power is treated as the exercise of the general power to the extent of $7,500 (maximum exercise of general power before the exercise f the nongeneral power, 5% of $300,000 or $15,000, less maximum exercise of the general power after the exercise of the nongeneral power, 5% of $150,000 or $7,500).

(e) Time of creation of power. A power of appointment created by will is, in general, considered as created on the date of the testator's death. However, section 2514(f) provides that a power of appointment created by a will executed on or before October 21, 1942, is considered a power created on or before that date if the testator dies before July 1, 1949, without having republished the will, by codicil or otherwise, after October 21, 1942. A power of appointment created by an inter vivos instrument is considered as created on the date the instrument takes effect. Such a power is not considered as created at some future date merely because it is not exercisable on the date the instrument takes effect, or because it is revocable, or because the identity of its holders is not ascertainable until after the date the instrument takes effect. However, if the holder of a power exercises it by creating a second power, the second power is considered as created at the time of the exercise of the first. The application of this paragraph may be illustrated by the following examples:

Example (1). A created a revocable trust before October 22, 1942, providing for payment of income to B for life with remainder as B shall appoint by deed or will. Even though A dies after October 21, 1942, without having exercised his power of revocation, B's power of appointment is considered a power created before October 22, 1942.

Example (2). C created an irrevocable inter vivos trust before October 22, 1942, naming T as trustee and providing for payment of income to D for life with remainder to E. T was given the power to pay corpus to D and the power to appoint a successor trustee. If

T resigns after October 21, 1942, and appoints D as successor trustee, D is considered to have a power of appointment created before October 22, 1942.

Example (3). F created an irrevocable inter vivos trust before October 22, 1942, providing for payment of income to G for life with remainder as G shall appoint by deed or will, but in default of appointment income to H for life with remainder as H shall appoint by deed or will. If G died after October 21, 1942, without having exercised his power of appointment, H's power of appointments is considered a power created before October 22, 1942, even though it was only a contingent interest until G's death.

Example (4). If in example (3) above G had exercised by will his power of appointment, by creating a similar power in J, J's power of appointment would be considered a power created after October 21, 1942.

[T.D. 6334, 23 FR 8904, Nov. 15, 1958, as amended by T.D. 6582, 26 FR 11861, Dec. 12, 1961; T.D. 9757, 46 FR 6929, Jan. 22, 1981]

§ 25.2514–2 Powers of appointment created on or before October 21, 1942. [*Omitted. Ed.*]

[T.D. 6334, 23 FR 8904, Nov. 15, 1958]

§ 25.2514–3 Powers of appointment created after October 21, 1942.

(a) In general. The exercise, release, or lapse (except as provided in paragraph (c) of this section) of a general power of appointment created after October 21, 1942, is deemed to be a transfer of property by the individual possessing the power. The exercise of a power of appointment that is not a general power is considered to be a transfer if it is exercised to create a further power under certain circumstances (see paragraph (d) of this section). See paragraph (c) of § 25.2514–1 for the definition of various terms used in this section. See paragraph (b) of this section for the rules applicable to determine the extent to which joint powers created after October 21, 1942, are to be treated as general powers of appointment.

(b) Joint powers created after October 21, 1942. The treatment of a power of appointment created after October 21, 1942, which is exercisable only in conjunction with another person is governed by section 2514(c)(3), which provides as follows:

(1) Such a power is not considered as a general power of appointment if it is not exercisable by the possessor except with the consent or joinder of the creator of the power.

(2) Such power is not considered as a general power of appointment if it is not exercisable by the possessor except with the consent or joinder of a person having a substantial interest in the property subject to the power which is adverse to the exercise of the power in favor of the possessor, his estate, his creditors, or the creditors of his estate. An interest adverse to the exercise of a power is considered as substantial if its value in relation to the total value of the property subject to the power is not insignificant. For this purpose, the interest is to be valued in accordance with the actuarial principles set forth in § 25.2512–5 or, if it is not susceptible to valuation under those provisions, in accordance with the general principles set forth in § 25.2512–1. A taker in default of appointment under a power has an interest which is adverse to an exercise of the power. A coholder of the power has no adverse interest merely because of his joint possession of the power nor merely because he is a permissible appointee under a power. However, a coholder of a power is considered as having an adverse interest where he may possess the power after the possessor's death and may exercise it at that time in favor of himself, his estate, his creditors, or the creditors of his estate. Thus, for example, if X, Y, and Z held a power jointly to appoint among a group of persons which includes themselves and if on the death of X the power will pass to Y and Z jointly, then Y and Z are considered to have interests adverse to the exercise of the power in favor of X. Similarly, if on Y's death the power will pass to Z, Z is considered to have an interest adverse to the exercise of the power in favor of Y. The application of this subparagraph may be further illustrated by the following examples in each of which it is assumed that the value of the interest in question is substantial:

Example (1). The taxpayer and R are trustees of a trust under which the income is to be paid to the taxpayer for life and then to M for life, and R is remainderman. The trustees have power to distribute corpus to the taxpayer. Since R's interest is substantially adverse to an exercise of the power in favor of the taxpayer, the latter does not have a general power of appointment. If M and the taxpayer were trustees, M's interest would likewise be adverse.

Example (2). The taxpayer and L are trustees of a trust under which the income is to be paid to L for life and then to M for life, and the taxpayer is remainderman. The trustees have power to distribute corpus to the taxpayer during L's life. Since L's interest is adverse to an exercise of the power in favor of the taxpayer, the taxpayer does not have a general power of appointment. If the taxpayer and M were trustees, M's interest would likewise be adverse.

Example (3). The taxpayer and L are trustees of a trust under which the income is to be paid to L for life. The trustees can designate whether corpus is to be distributed to the taxpayer or to A after L's death. L's interest is not adverse to an exercise of the power in favor of the taxpayer, and the taxpayer therefore has a general power of appointment.

(3) A power which is exercisable only in conjunction with another person, and which after application of the rules set forth in subparagraphs (1) and (2) of this paragraph, constitutes a general power of appointment, will be treated as though the holders of the power who are permissible appointees of the property were joint owners of property subject to the power. The possessor, under this rule, will be treated as possessed of a general power of appointment over an aliquot share of the property to be determined with reference to the number of joint holders, including the possessor, who (or whose estates or creditors) are permissible appointees. Thus, for example, if X, Y, and Z hold an unlimited power jointly to appoint among a group of persons, including themselves, but on the death of X the power does not pass to Y and Z jointly, then Y and Z are not considered to have interests adverse to the exercise of the power in favor of X. In this case, X is considered to possess a general power of appointment as to one-third of the property subject to the power.

(c) Partial releases, lapses, and disclaimers of general powers of appointment created after October 21, 1942. (1) *Partial release of power.* The general principles set forth in § 25.2511–2 for determining whether a donor of property (or of a property right or interest) has divested himself of all or any portion of his interest therein to the extent necessary to effect a completed gift are applicable in determining whether a partial release of a power of appointment constitutes a taxable gift. Thus, if a general power of appointment is partially released so that thereafter the donor may still appoint among a limited class of persons not including himself the partial release does not effect a complete gift, since the possessor of the power has retained the right to designate the ultimate beneficiaries of the property over which he holds the power and since it is only the termination of such control which completes a gift.

(2) *Powers partially released before June 1, 1951.* If a general power of appointment created after October 21, 1942, was partially released prior to June 1, 1951, so that it no longer represented a general power of appointment, as defined in paragraph (c) of § 25.2514–1, the subsequent exercise, release, or lapse of the partially released power at any time thereafter will not constitute the exercise or release of a general power of appointment. For example, assume that A created a trust in 1943 under which B possessed a general power of appointment. By an instrument executed in 1948 such general power of appointment was reduced in scope by B to an excepted power. The inter vivos exercise in 1955, or in any "calendar period" (as defined in § 25.2502–1(c)(1)) thereafter, of such excepted power is not considered an exercise or release of a general power of appointment for purposes of the gift tax.

(3) *Power partially released after May 31, 1951.* If a general power of appointment created after October 21, 1942, was partially released after May 31, 1951, the subsequent exercise, release or a lapse of the power at any time thereafter, will constitute the exercise or release of a general power of appointment for gift tax purposes.

(4) *Release or lapse of power.* A release of a power of appointment need not be formal or express in character. For example, the failure to exercise a general power of appointment created after October 21, 1942, within a specified time so that the power lapses, constitutes a release of the power. In any case where the possessor of a general power of appointment is incapable of validly exercising or releasing a power, by reason of minority, or otherwise, and the power may not be validly exercised or released on his behalf, the failure to exercise or release the power is not a lapse of the power. If a trustee has in his capacity as trustee a power which is considered as a general power of appointment, his resignation or removal as trustee will cause a lapse of his power. However, section 2514(e) provides that a lapse during any calendar year is considered as a release so as to be subject to the gift tax only to the extent that the property which could have been appointed by exercise of the lapsed power of ap-

pointment exceeds the greater of (i) $5,000, or (ii) 5 percent of the aggregate value, at the time of the lapse, of the assets out of which, or the proceeds of which, the exercise of the lapsed power could be satisfied. For example, if an individual has a noncumulative right to withdraw $10,000 a year from the principal of a trust fund, the failure to exercise this right of withdrawal in a particular year will not constitute a gift if the fund at the end of the year equals or exceeds $200,000. If, however, at the end of the particular year the fund should be worth only $100,000, the failure to exercise the power will be considered a gift to the extent of $5,000, the excess of $10,000 over 5 percent of a fund of $100,000. Where the failure to exercise a power, such as a right of withdrawal, occurs in more than a single year, the value of the taxable transfer will be determined separately for each year.

(5) *Disclaimer of power created after December 31, 1976.* A disclaimer or renunciation of a general power of appointment created in a transfer made after December 31, 1976, is not considered a release of the power for gift tax purposes if the disclaimer or renunciation is a qualified disclaimer as described in section 2518 and the corresponding regulations. For rules relating to when a transfer creating the power occurs, see § 25.2518–2(c)(3). If the disclaimer or renunciation is not a qualified disclaimer, it is considered a release of the power.

(6) *Disclaimer of power created before January 1, 1977.* A disclaimer or renunciation of a general power of appointment created in a taxable transfer before January 1, 1977, in the person disclaiming is not considered a release of the power. The disclaimer or renunciation must be unequivocal and effective under local law. A disclaimer is a complete and unqualified refusal to accept the rights to which one is entitled. There can be no disclaimer or renunciation of a power after its acceptance. In the absence of facts to the contrary, the failure to renounce or disclaim within a reasonable time after learning of the existence of a power shall be presumed to constitute an acceptance of the power. In any case where a power is purported to be disclaimed or renounced as to only a portion of the property subject to the power, the determination as to whether there has been a complete and unqualified refusal to accept the rights to which one is entitled will depend on all the facts and circumstances of the particular case, taking into account the recognition and effectiveness of such a disclaimer under local law. Such rights refer to the incidents of the power and not to other interests of the possessor of the power in the property. If effective under local law, the power may be disclaimed or renounced without disclaiming or renouncing such other interests.

(7) The first and second sentences of paragraph (c)(5) of this section are applicable for transfers creating the power to be disclaimed made on or after December 31, 1997.

(d) Creation of another power in certain cases. Paragraph (d) of section 2514 provides that there is a transfer for purposes of the gift tax of the value of property (or of property rights or interests) with respect to which a power of appointment, which is not a general power of appointment, created after October 21, 1942, is exercised by creating another power of appointment which, under the terms of the instruments creating and exercising the first power and under applicable local law, can be validly exercised so as to (1) postpone the vesting of any estate or interest in the property for a period ascertainable without regard to the date of the creation of the first power, or (2) (if the applicable rule against perpetuities is stated in terms of suspensions of ownership or of the power of alienation, rather than of vesting) suspend the absolute ownership or the power of alienation of the property for a period ascertainable without regard to the date of the creation of the first power. For the purpose of section 2514(d), the value of the property subject to the second power of appointment is considered to be its value unreduced by any precedent or subsequent interest which is not subject to the second power. Thus, if a donor has a power to appoint $100,000 among a group consisting of his children or grandchildren and during his lifetime exercises the power by making an outright appointment of $75,000 and by giving one appointee a power to appoint $25,000, no more than $25,000 will be considered a gift under section 2514(d). If, however, the donor appoints the income from the entire fund to a beneficiary for life with power in the beneficiary to appoint the remainder, the entire $100,000 will be considered a gift under section 2514(d), if the exercise of the second power can validly postpone the vesting of any estate or interest in the property or can suspend the absolute ownership or power of alienation of the property for a period ascertainable without regard to the date of the creation of the first power.

(e) Examples. The application of this section may be further illustrated by the following examples in each of which it is assumed, unless otherwise stated, that S has transferred property in trust after October 21, 1942, with the remainder payable to R at L's death, and that neither L nor R has any interest in or power over the enjoyment of the trust property except as is indicated separately in each example:

Example (1). The income is payable to L for life. L has the power to cause the income to be paid to R. The exercise of the right constitutes the making of a transfer of property under section 2511. L's power does not constitute a power of appointment since it is only a power to dispose of his income interest, a right otherwise possessed by him.

Example (2). The income is to be accumulated during L's life. L has the power to have the income distributed to himself. If L's power is limited by an ascertainable standard (relating to health, etc.) as defined in paragraph (c)(2) of § 25.2514–1, the lapse of such power will not constitute a transfer of property for gift tax purposes. If L's power is not so limited, its lapse or release during L's lifetime may constitute a transfer of property for gift tax purposes. See especially paragraph (c)(4) of § 25.2514–3.

Example (3). The income is to be paid to L for life. L has a power, exercisable at any time, to cause the corpus to be distributed to himself. L has a general power of appointment over the remainder interest, the release of which constitutes a transfer for gift tax purposes of the remainder interest. If in this example L had a power to cause the corpus to be distributed only to X, L would have a power of appointment which is not a general power of appointment, the exercise or release of which would not constitute a transfer of property for purposes of the gift tax. Although the exercise or release of the nongeneral power is not taxable under this section, see § 25.2514–1(b)(2) for the gift tax consequences of the transfer of the life income interest.

Example (4). The income is payable to L for life. R has the right to cause the corpus to be distributed to L at any time. R's power is not a power of appointment, but merely a right to dispose of his remainder interest, a right already possessed by him. In such a case, the exercise of the right constitutes the making of a transfer of property under section 2511 of the value, if any, of his remainder interest. See paragraph (e) of § 25.2511–1.

Example (5). The income is to be paid to L. R has the right to appoint the corpus to himself at any time. R's general power of appointment over the corpus includes a general power to dispose of L's income interest therein. The lapse or release of R's general power over the income interest during his life may constitute the making of a transfer of property. See especially paragraph (c)(4) of § 25.2514–3.

[T.D. 6334, 23 FR 8904, Nov. 15, 1958, as amended by T.D. 7238, 37 FR 28730, Dec. 29, 1972; T.D. 7776, 46 FR 27642, May 21, 1981; T.D. 7910, 48 FR 40375, Sept. 7, 1983; T.D. 8095, 51 FR 28370, Aug. 7, 1986; T.D. 8744, 62 FR 68185, Dec. 31, 1997]

§ 2515. Treatment of Generation-Skipping Transfer Tax

In the case of any taxable gift which is a direct skip (within the meaning of chapter 13), the amount of such gift shall be increased by the amount of any tax imposed on the transferor under chapter 13 with respect to such gift.

[There are no regulations relating to the current § 2515. The following relate to repealed § 2515, which dealt with the gift tax consequences of the creation and termination of tenancies by the entirety in real property. Ed.]

Selected Regulations to Repealed § 2515 (Tenancies by the Entirety in Real Property)

§ 25.2515–1 Tenancies by the entirety; in general.

(a) Scope. (1) *In general.* This section and §§ 25.2515–2 through 25.2515–4 do not apply to the creation of a tenancy by the entirety after December 31, 1981, and do not reflect changes made to the Internal Revenue Code by sections 702(k)(1)(A) of the Revenue Act of 1978, or section 2002(c)(2) of the Tax Reform Act of 1976.

(2) *Special rule in the case of tenancies created after July 13, 1988, if the donee spouse is not a United States citizen.* Under section 2523(i)(3), applicable (subject to the special treaty rule contained

in Public Law 101–239, section 7815(d)(14)) in the case of tenancies by the entirety and joint tenancies created between spouses after July 13, 1988, if the donee spouse is not a citizen of the United States, the principles contained in section 2515 and §§ 25.2515–1 through 25.2515–4 apply in determining the gift tax consequences with respect to the creation and termination of the tenancy, except that the election provided in section 2515(a) (prior to repeal by the Economic Recovery Tax Act of 1981) and § 25.2515–2 (relating to the donor's election to treat the creation of the tenancy as a transfer for gift tax purposes) does not apply.

(3) *Nature of.* An estate by the entirety in real property is essentially a joint tenancy between husband and wife with the right of survivorship. As used in this section and §§ 25.2515–2 through 25.2515–4, the term "tenancy by the entirety" includes a joint tenancy between husband and wife in real property with right of survivorship, or a tenancy which accords to the spouses rights equivalent thereto regardless of the term by which such a tenancy is described in local property law.

(b) Gift upon creation of tenancy by the entirety; in general. During calendar years prior to 1955 the contribution made by a husband or wife in the creation of a tenancy by the entirety constituted a gift to the extent that the consideration furnished by either spouse exceeded the value of the rights retained by that spouse. The contribution made by either or both spouses in the creation of such a tenancy during the calendar year 1955, any calendar year beginning before January 1, 1971, or any calendar quarter beginning after December 31, 1970, is not deemed a gift by either spouse, regardless of the proportion of the total consideration furnished by either spouse, unless the donor spouse elects (see § 25.2515–2) under section 2515(c) to treat such transaction as a gift in the calendar quarter or calendar year in which the transaction is effected. See § 25.2502–1(c)(1) for the definition of calendar quarter. However, there is a gift upon the termination of such a tenancy, other than by the death of a spouse, if the proceeds received by one spouse on termination of the tenancy are larger than the proceeds allocable to the consideration furnished by that spouse to the tenancy. The creation of a tenancy by the entirety takes place if (1) a husband or his wife purchases property and causes the title thereto to be conveyed to themselves as tenants by the entirety, (2) both join in such a purchase, or (3) either or both cause to be created such a tenancy in property already owned by either or both of them. The rule prescribed herein with respect to the creation of a tenancy by the entirety applies also to contributions made in the making of additions to the value of such a tenancy (in the form of improvements, reductions in the indebtedness, or otherwise), regardless of the proportion of the consideration furnished by each spouse. See § 25.2516–1 for transfers made pursuant to a property settlement agreement incident to divorce.

* * *

[T.D. 6334, 23 FR 8904, Nov. 15, 1958, as amended by T.D. 7238, 37 FR 28731, Dec. 29, 1972; T.D. 8522, 59 FR 9656, March 1, 1994]

§ 25.2515–2 Tenancies by the entirety; transfers treated as gifts; manner of election and valuation.

* * *

(b) If the donor spouse exercises the election as provided in paragraph (a) of this section, the amount of the gift at the creation of the tenancy is the amount of his contribution to the tenancy less the value of his retained interest in it, determined as follows:

(1) If under the law of the jurisdiction governing the rights of the spouses, either spouse, acting alone, can bring about a severance of his or her interest in the property, the value of the donor's retained interest is one-half the value of the property.

(2) If, under the law of the jurisdiction governing the rights of the spouses each is entitled to share in the income or other enjoyment of the property but neither, acting alone, may defeat the right of the survivor of them to the whole of the property, the amount of retained interest of the donor is determined by use of the appropriate actuarial factors for the spouses at their respective attained ages at the time the transaction is effected.

* * *

[T.D. 6334, 23 FR 8904, Nov. 15, 1958, as amended by T.D. 7150, 36 FR 22900, Dec. 2, 1971; T.D. 7238, 37 FR 28731, Dec. 29, 1972; T.D. 8540, 59 FR 30177, June 10, 1994]

§ 25.2515–3 Termination of tenancy by the entirety; cases in which entire value of gift is determined under section 2515(b). [*Omitted. Ed.*]

[T.D. 6334, 23 FR 8904, Nov. 15, 1958, as amended by T.D. 7238, 37 FR 28732, Dec. 29, 1972]

§ 25.2515–4 Termination of tenancy by entirety; cases in which none, or a portion only, of value of gift is determined under section 2515(b). [*Omitted. Ed.*]

[T.D. 6334, 23 FR 8904, Nov. 15, 1958, as amended by T.D. 7238, 37 FR 28732, Dec. 29, 1972]

§ 2516. Certain Property Settlements

Where husband and wife enter into a written agreement relative to their marital and property rights and divorce occurs within the 3-year period beginning on the date 1 year before such agreement is entered into (whether or not such agreement is approved by the divorce decree), any transfers of property or interests in property made pursuant to such agreement—

(1) to either spouse in settlement of his or her marital or property rights, or

(2) to provide a reasonable allowance for the support of issue of the marriage during minority,

shall be deemed to be transfers made for a full and adequate consideration in money or money's worth.

Regulations

§ 25.2516–1 Certain property settlements.

(a) Section 2516 provides that transfers of property or interests in property made under the terms of a written agreement between spouses in settlement of their marital or property rights are deemed to be for an adequate and full consideration in money or money's worth and, therefore, exempt from the gift tax (whether or not such agreement is approved by a divorce decree), if the spouses obtain a final decree of divorce from each other within two years after entering into the agreement.

(b) See paragraph (b) of § 25.6019–3 for the circumstances under which information relating to property settlements must be disclosed on the transferor's gift tax return for the "calendar period" (as defined in § 25.2502–1(c)(1)) in which the agreement becomes effective.

[T.D. 6334, 23 FR 8904, Nov. 15, 1958, as amended by T.D. 7238, 37 FR 28732, Dec. 29, 1972; T.D. 7910, 48 FR 40375, Sept. 7, 1983]

§ 25.2516–2 Transfers in settlement of support obligations.

Transfers to provide a reasonable allowance for the support of children (including legally adopted children) of a marriage during minority are not subject to the gift tax if made pursuant to an agreement which satisfies the requirements of section 2516.

[T.D. 6334, 23 FR 8904, Nov. 15, 1958]

§ 2518. Disclaimers

(a) General rule. For purposes of this subtitle, if a person makes a qualified disclaimer with respect to any interest in property, this subtitle shall apply with respect to such interest as if the interest had never been transferred to such person.

(b) Qualified disclaimer defined. For purposes of subsection (a), the term "qualified disclaimer" means an irrevocable and unqualified refusal by a person to accept an interest in property but only if—

(1) such refusal is in writing,

(2) such writing is received by the transferor of the interest, his legal representative, or the holder of the legal title to the property to which the interest relates not later than the date which is 9 months after the later of—

(A) the day on which the transfer creating the interest in such person is made, or

(B) the day on which such person attains age 21,

(3) such person has not accepted the interest or any of its benefits, and

(4) as a result of such refusal, the interest passes without any direction on the part of the person making the disclaimer and passes either—

(A) to the spouse of the decedent, or

(B) to a person other than the person making the disclaimer.

(c) Other rules. For purposes of subsection (a)—

(1) Disclaimer of undivided portion of interest. A disclaimer with respect to an undivided portion of an interest which meets the requirements of the preceding sentence shall be treated as a qualified disclaimer of such portion of the interest.

(2) Powers. A power with respect to property shall be treated as an interest in such property.

(3) Certain transfers treated as disclaimers. A written transfer of the transferor's entire interest in the property—

(A) which meets requirements similar to the requirements of paragraphs (2) and (3) of subsection (b), and

(B) which is to a person or persons who would have received the property had the transferor made a qualified disclaimer (within the meaning of subsection (b)),

shall be treated as a qualified disclaimer.

Regulations

§ 25.2518–1 Qualified disclaimers of property; in general.

(a) Applicability. (1) *In general.* The rules described in this section, § 25.2518–2, and § 25.2518–3 apply to the qualified disclaimer of an interest in property which is created in the person disclaiming by a transfer made after December 31, 1976. In general, a qualified disclaimer is an irrevocable and unqualified refusal to accept the ownership of an interest in property. For rules relating to the determination of when a transfer creating an interest occurs, see § 25.2518–2(c)(3) and (4).

(2) *Example.* The provisions of paragraph (a)(1) of this section may be illustrated by the following example:

Example. W creates an irrevocable trust on December 10, 1968, and retains the right to receive the income for life. Upon the death of W, which occurs after December 31, 1976, the trust property is distributable to W's surviving issue, per stirpes. The transfer creating the remainder interest in the trust occurred in 1968. See § 25.2511–1(c)(2). Therefore, section 2518 does not apply to the disclaimer of the remainder interest because the transfer creating the interest was made prior to January 1, 1977. If, however, W had caused the gift to be incomplete by also retaining the power to designate the person or persons to receive the trust principal at death, and, as a result, no transfer (within the meaning of § 25.2511–1(c)(2)) of the remainder interest was made at the time of the creation of the trust, section 2518 would apply to any disclaimer made after W's death with respect to an interest in the trust property.

(3) Paragraph (a)(1) of this section is applicable for transfers creating the interest to be disclaimed made on or after December 31, 1997.

(b) Effect of a qualified disclaimer. If a person makes a qualified disclaimer as described in section 2518(b) and § 25.2518–2, for purposes of the Federal estate, gift, and generation-skipping transfer tax provisions, the disclaimed interest in property is treated as if it had never been transferred to the person making the qualified disclaimer. Instead, it is considered as passing directly from the transferor of the property to the person entitled to receive the property as a result of the disclaimer. Accordingly, a person making a qualified disclaimer is not treated as making a gift. Similarly, the value of a decedent's gross estate for purposes of the Federal estate tax does not include the value of property with respect to which the decedent, or the decedent's executor or administrator on behalf of the decedent, has made a qualified disclaimer. If the disclaimer is not a qualified disclaimer, for the purposes of the Federal estate, gift, and generation-skipping transfer tax provisions, the disclaimer is disregarded and the disclaimant is treated as having received the interest.

(c) Effect of local law. (1) *In general.* (i) *Interests created before 1982.* A disclaimer of an interest created in a taxable transfer before 1982 which otherwise meets the requirements of a qualified disclaimer under section 2518 and the corresponding regulations but which, by itself, is not effective under applicable local law to divest ownership of the disclaimed property from the disclaimant and vest it in another, is nevertheless treated as a qualified disclaimer under section 2518 if, under applicable local law, the disclaimed interest in property is transferred, as a result of attempting the disclaimer, to another person without any direction on the part of the disclaimant. An interest in property will not be considered to be transferred without any direction on the part of the disclaimant if, under applicable local law, the disclaimant has any discretion (whether or not such discretion is exercised) to determine who will receive such interest. Actions by the disclaimant which are required under local law merely to divest ownership of the property from the disclaimant and vest ownership in another person will not disqualify the disclaimer for purposes of section 2518(a). See § 25.2518–2(d)(1) for rules relating to the immediate vesting of title in the disclaimant.

(ii) *Interests created after 1981.* [Reserved]

(2) *Creditor's claims.* The fact that a disclaimer is voidable by the disclaimant's creditors has no effect on the determination of whether such disclaimer constitutes a qualified disclaimer. However, a disclaimer that is wholly void or that is voided by the disclaimant's creditors cannot be a qualified disclaimer.

(3) *Examples.* The provisions of paragraphs (c)(1) and (2) of this section may be illustrated by the following examples:

Example (1). F dies testate in State Y on June 17, 1978. G and H are beneficiaries under the will. The will provides that any disclaimed property is to pass to the residuary estate. H has no interest in the residuary estate. Under the applicable laws of State Y, a disclaimer must be made within 6 months of the death of the testator. Seven months after F's death, H disclaimed the real property H received under the will. The disclaimer statute of State Y has a provision stating that an untimely disclaimer will be treated as an assignment of the interest disclaimed to those persons who would have taken had the disclaimer been valid. Pursuant to this provision, the disclaimed property became part of the residuary estate. Assuming the remaining requirements of section 2518 are met, H has made a qualified disclaimer for purposes of section 2518(a).

Example (2). Assume the same facts as in example (1) except that the law of State Y does not treat an ineffective disclaimer as a transfer to alternative takers. H assigns the disclaimed interest by deed to those who would have taken had the disclaimer been valid. Under these circumstances, H has not made a qualified disclaimer for purposes of section 2518(a) because the disclaimant directed who would receive the property.

Example (3). Assume the same facts as in example (1) except that the law of State Y requires H to pay a transfer tax in order to effectuate the transfer under the ineffective disclaimer provision. H pays the transfer tax. H has made a qualified disclaimer for purposes of section 2518(a).

(d) Cross-reference. For rules relating to the effect of qualified disclaimers on the estate tax charitable and marital deductions, see §§ 20.2055–2(c) and 20.2056(d)–1 respectively. For rules relating to the effect of a qualified disclaimer of a general power of appointment, see § 20.2041–3(d).

[T.D. 8095, 51 FR 28370, Aug. 7, 1986; T.D. 8744, 62 FR 68185, Dec. 31, 1997]

§ 25.2518–2 Requirements for a qualified disclaimer.

(a) In general. For the purposes of section 2518(a), a disclaimer shall be a qualified disclaimer only if it satisfies the requirements of this section. In general, to be a qualified disclaimer—

(1) The disclaimer must be irrevocable and unqualified:

(2) The disclaimer must be in writing;

(3) The writing must be delivered to the person specified in paragraph (b)(2) of this section within the time limitations specified in paragraph (c)(1) of this section;

(4) The disclaimant must not have accepted the interest disclaimed or any of its benefits; and

(5) The interest disclaimed must pass either to the spouse of the decedent or to a person other than the disclaimant without any direction on the part of the person making the disclaimer.

(b) Writing. (1) *Requirements.* A disclaimer is a qualified disclaimer only if it is in writing. The writing must identify the interest in property disclaimed and be signed either by the disclaimant or by the disclaimant's legal representative.

(2) *Delivery.* The writing described in paragraph (b)(1) of this section must be delivered to the transferor of the interest, the transferor's legal representative, the holder of the legal title to the property to which the interest relates, or the person in possession of such property.

(c) Time limit. (1) *In general.* A disclaimer is a qualified disclaimer only if the writing described in paragraph (b)(1) of this section is delivered to the persons described in paragraph (b)(2) of this section no later than the date which is 9 months after the later of—

(i) The date on which the transfer creating the interest in the disclaimant is made, or

(ii) The day on which the disclaimant attains age 21.

(2) *A timely mailing of a disclaimer treated as a timely delivery.* Although section 7502 and the regulations under that section apply only to documents to be filed with the Service, a timely mailing of a disclaimer to the person described in paragraph (b)(2) of this section is treated as a timely delivery if the mailing requirements under paragraphs (c)(1), (c)(2) and (d) of § 301.7502–1 are met. Further, if the last day of the period specified in paragraph (c)(1) of this section falls on Saturday, Sunday or a legal holiday (as defined in paragraph (b) of § 301.7503–1), then the delivery of the writing described in paragraph (b)(1) of this section shall be considered timely if delivery is made on the first succeeding day which is not Saturday, Sunday or a legal holiday. See paragraph (d)(3) of this section for rules applicable to the exception for individuals under 21 years of age.

(3) *Transfer.* (i) For purposes of the time limitation described in paragraph (c)(1)(i) of this section, the 9-month period for making a disclaimer generally is to be determined with reference to the transfer creating the interest in the disclaimant. With respect to inter vivos transfers, a transfer creating an interest occurs when there is a completed gift for Federal gift tax purposes regardless of whether a gift tax is imposed on the completed gift. Thus, gifts qualifying for the gift tax annual exclusion under section 2503(b) are regarded as transfers creating an interest for this purpose. With respect to transfers made by a decedent at death or transfers that become irrevocable at death, the transfer creating the interest occurs on the date of the decedent's death, even if an estate tax is not imposed on the transfer. For example, a bequest of foreign-situs property by a nonresident alien decedent is regarded as a transfer creating an interest in property even if the transfer would not be subject to estate tax. If there is a transfer creating an interest in property during the transferor's lifetime and such interest is later included in the transferor's gross estate for estate tax purposes (or would have been included if such interest were subject to estate tax), the 9-month period for making the qualified disclaimer is determined with reference to the earlier transfer creating the interest. In the case of a general power of appointment, the holder of the power has a 9-month period after the transfer creating the power in which to disclaim. If a person to whom any interest in property passes by reason of the exercise, release, or lapse of a general power desires to make a qualified disclaimer, the disclaimer must be made within a 9-month period after the exercise, release, or lapse regardless of whether the exercise, release, or lapse is subject to estate or gift tax. In the case of a nongeneral power of appointment, the holder of the power, permissible appointees, or takers in default of appointment must disclaim within a 9-month period after the original transfer that created or authorized the creation of the power. If the transfer is for the life of an income beneficiary with succeeding interests to other persons, both the life tenant and the other remaindermen, whether their interests are vested or contingent, must disclaim no later than 9 months after the original transfer creating an interest. In the case of a remainder interest in property which an executor elects to treat

as qualified terminable interest property under section 2056(b)(7), the remainderman must disclaim within 9 months of the transfer creating the interest, rather than 9 months from the date such interest is subject to tax under section 2044 or 2519. A person who receives an interest in property as the result of a qualified disclaimer of the interest must disclaim the previously disclaimed interest no later than 9 months after the date of the transfer creating the interest in the preceding disclaimant. Thus, if A were to make a qualified disclaimer of a specific bequest and as a result of the qualified disclaimer the property passed as part of the residue, the beneficiary of the residue could make a qualified disclaimer no later than 9 months after the date of the testator's death. See paragraph (d)(3) of this section for the time limitation rule with reference to recipients who are under 21 years of age.

(ii) Sentences 1 through 10 and 12 of paragraph (c)(3)(i) of this section are applicable for transfers creating the interest to be disclaimed made on or after December 31, 1997.

(4) *Joint property.* (i) *Interests in joint tenancy with right of survivorship or tenancies by the entirety.* Except as provided in paragraph (c)(4)(iii) of this section (with respect to joint bank, brokerage, and other investment accounts), in the case of an interest in a joint tenancy with right of survivorship or a tenancy by the entirety, a qualified disclaimer of the interest to which the disclaimant succeeds upon creation of the tenancy must be made no later than 9 months after the creation of the tenancy regardless of whether such interest can be unilaterally severed under local law. A qualified disclaimer of the survivorship interest to which the survivor succeeds by operation of law upon the death of the first joint tenant to die must be made no later than 9 months after the death of the first joint tenant to die regardless of whether such interest can be unilaterally severed under local law and, except as provided in paragraph (c)(4)(ii) of this section (with respect to certain tenancies created on or after July 14, 1988), such interest is deemed to be a one-half interest in the property. (See, however, section 2518(b)(2)(B) for a special rule in the case of disclaimers by persons under age 21.) This is the case regardless of the portion of the property attributable to consideration furnished by the disclaimant and regardless of the portion of the property that is included in the decedent's gross estate under section 2040 and regardless of whether the interest can be unilaterally severed under local law. See paragraph (c)(5), Examples (7) and (8), of this section.

(ii) *Certain tenancies in real property between spouses created on or after July 14, 1988.* In the case of a joint tenancy between spouses or a tenancy by the entirety in real property created on or after July 14, 1988, to which section 2523(i)(3) applies (relating to the creation of a tenancy where the spouse of the donor is not a United States citizen), the surviving spouse may disclaim any portion of the joint interest that is includible in the decedent's gross estate under section 2040. See paragraph (c)(5), Example (9), of this section.

(iii) *Special rule for joint bank, brokerage, and other investment accounts (e.g., accounts held at mutual funds) established between spouses or between persons other than husband and wife.* In the case of a transfer to a joint bank, brokerage, or other investment account (e.g., an account held at a mutual fund), if a transferor may unilaterally regain the transferor's own contributions to the account without the consent of the other cotenant, such that the transfer is not a completed gift under § 25.2511–1(h)(4), the transfer creating the survivor's interest in the decedent's share of the account occurs on the death of the deceased cotenant. Accordingly, if a surviving joint tenant desires to make a qualified disclaimer with respect to funds contributed by a deceased cotenant, the disclaimer must be made within 9 months of the cotenant's death. The surviving joint tenant may not disclaim any portion of the joint account attributable to consideration furnished by that surviving joint tenant. See paragraph (c)(5), Examples (12), (13), and (14), of this section, regarding the treatment of disclaimed interests under sections 2518, 2033 and 2040.

(iv) *Effective date.* This paragraph (c)(4) is applicable for disclaimers made on or after December 31, 1997.

(5) *Examples.* The provisions of paragraphs (c)(1) through (c)(4) of this section may be illustrated by the following examples. For purposes of the following examples, assume that all beneficiaries are over 21 years of age.

Example (1). On May 13, 1978, in a transfer which constitutes a completed gift for Federal gift tax purposes, A creates a trust in which B is given a lifetime interest in the income from the trust. B is also given a nongeneral testamentary power of appointment over the corpus of the trust. The power of appointment may be exercised in favor of any of the issue of A and B. If there are no surviving issue at B's death or if the power is not exercised, the corpus is to pass to E. On May 13, 1978, A and B have two surviving children, C and D. If A, B, C or D wishes to make a qualified disclaimer, the disclaimer must be made no later than 9 months after May 13, 1978.

Example (2). Assume the same facts as in example (1) except that B is given a general power of appointment over the corpus of the trust. B exercises the general power of appointment in favor of C upon B's death on June 17, 1989. C may make a qualified disclaimer no later than 9 months after June 17, 1989. If B had died without exercising the general power of appointment, E could have made a qualified disclaimer no later than 9 months after June 17, 1989.

Example (3). F creates a trust on April 1, 1978, in which F's child G is to receive the income from the trust for life. Upon G's death, the corpus of the trust is to pass to G's child H. If either G or H wishes to make a qualified disclaimer, it must be made no later than 9 months after April 1, 1978.

Example (4). A creates a trust on February 15, 1978, in which B is named the income beneficiary for life. The trust further provides that upon B's death the proceeds of the trust are to pass to C, if then living. If C predeceases D, the proceeds shall pass to D or D's estate. To have timely disclaimers for purposes of section 2518, B, C, and D must disclaim their respective interests no later than 9 months after February 15, 1978.

Example (5). A, a resident of State Q, dies on January 10, 1979, devising certain real property to B. The disclaimer laws of State Q require that a disclaimer be made within a reasonable time after a transfer. B disclaims the entire interest in real property on November 10, 1979. Although B's disclaimer may be effective under State Q law, it is not a qualified disclaimer under section 2518 because the disclaimer was made later than 9 months after the taxable transfer to B.

Example (6). A creates a revocable trust on June 1, 1980, in which B and C are given the income interest for life. Upon the death of the last income beneficiary, the remainder interest is to pass to D. The creation of the trust is not a completed gift for Federal gift tax purposes, but each distribution of trust income to B and C is a completed gift at the date of distribution. B and C must disclaim each income distribution no later than 9 months after the date of the particular distribution. In order to disclaim an income distribution in the form of a check, the recipient must return the check to the trustee uncashed along with a written disclaimer. A dies on September 1, 1982, causing the trust to become irrevocable, and the trust corpus is includible in A's gross estate for Federal estate tax purposes under section 2038. If B or C wishes to make a qualified disclaimer of his income interest, he must do so no later than 9 months after September 1, 1982. If D wishes to make a qualified disclaimer of his remainder interest, he must do so no later than 9 months after September 1, 1982.

Example (7). On February 1, 1990, A purchased real property with A's funds. Title to the property was conveyed to "A and B, as joint tenants with right of survivorship." Under applicable state law, the joint interest is unilaterally severable by either tenant. B dies on May 1, 1998, and is survived by A. On January 1, 1999, A disclaims the one-half survivorship interest in the property to which A succeeds as a result of B's death. Assuming that the other requirements of section 2518(b) are satisfied, A has made a qualified disclaimer of the one-half survivorship interest (but not the interest retained by A upon the creation of the tenancy, which may not be disclaimed by A). The result is the same whether or not A and B are married and regardless of the proportion of consideration furnished by A and B in purchasing the property.

Example (8). Assume the same facts as in Example (7) except that A and B are married and title to the property was conveyed to "A and B, as tenants by the entirety." Under applicable state law, the tenancy cannot be unilaterally severed by either tenant. Assuming that the other requirements of section 2518(b) are satisfied, A has made a qualified disclaimer of the one-half survivorship interest (but not the interest retained by A upon the creation of the tenancy, which may not be disclaimed by A). The result is the same regardless of the proportion of consideration furnished by A and B in purchasing the property.

Example (9). On March 1, 1989, H and W purchase a tract of vacant land which is conveyed to them as tenants by the entirety. The entire consideration is paid by H. W is not a United States citizen. H dies on June

1, 1998. W can disclaim the entire joint interest because this is the interest includible in H's gross estate under section 2040(a). Assuming that W's disclaimer is received by the executor of H's estate no later than 9 months after June 1, 1998, and the other requirements of section 2518(b) are satisfied, W's disclaimer of the property would be a qualified disclaimer. The result would be the same if the property was held in joint tenancy with right of survivorship that was unilaterally severable under local law.

Example (10). In 1986, spouses A and B purchased a personal residence taking title as tenants by the entirety. B dies on July 10, 1998. A wishes to disclaim the one-half undivided interest to which A would succeed by right of survivorship. If A makes the disclaimer, the property interest would pass under B's will to their child C. C, an adult, and A resided in the residence at B's death and will continue to reside there in the future. A continues to own a one-half undivided interest in the property. Assuming that the other requirements of section 2518(b) are satisfied, A may make a qualified disclaimer with respect to the one-half undivided survivorship interest in the residence if A delivers the written disclaimer to the personal representative of B's estate by April 10, 1999, since A is not deemed to have accepted the interest or any of its benefits prior to that time and A's occupancy of the residence after B's death is consistent with A's retained undivided ownership interest. The result would be the same if the property was held in joint tenancy with right of survivorship that was unilaterally severable under local law.

Example (11). H and W, husband and wife, reside in state X, a community property state. On April 1, 1978, H and W purchase real property with community funds. The property is not held by H and W as jointly owned property with rights of survivorship. H and W hold the property until January 3, 1985, when H dies. H devises his portion of the property to W. On March 15, 1985, W disclaims the portion of the property devised to her by H. Assuming all the other requirements of section 2518(b) have been met, W has made a qualified disclaimer of the interest devised to her by H. However, W could not disclaim the interest in the property that she acquired on April 1, 1978.

Example (12). On July 1, 1990, A opens a bank account that is held jointly with B, A's spouse, and transfers $50,000 of A's money to the account. A and B are United States citizens. A can regain the entire account without B's consent, such that the transfer is not a completed gift under § 25.2511–1(h)(4). A dies on August 15, 1998, and B disclaims the entire amount in the bank account on October 15, 1998. Assuming that the remaining requirements of section 2518(b) are satisfied, B made a qualified disclaimer under section 2518(a) because the disclaimer was made within 9 months after A's death at which time B had succeeded to full dominion and control over the account. Under state law, B is treated as predeceasing A with respect to the disclaimed interest. The disclaimed account balance passes through A's probate estate and is no longer joint property includible in A's gross estate under section 2040. The entire account is, instead, includible in A's gross estate under section 2033. The result would be the same if A and B were not married.

Example (13). The facts are the same as Example (12), except that B, rather than A, dies on August 15, 1998. A may not make a qualified disclaimer with respect to any of the funds in the bank account, because A furnished the funds for the entire account and A did not relinquish dominion and control over the funds.

Example (14). The facts are the same as Example (12), except that B disclaims 40 percent of the funds in the account. Since, under state law, B is treated as predeceasing A with respect to the disclaimed interest, the 40 percent portion of the account balance that was disclaimed passes as part of A's probate estate, and is no longer characterized as joint property. This 40 percent portion of the account balance is, therefore, includible in A's gross estate under section 2033. The remaining 60 percent of the account balance that was not disclaimed retains its character as joint property and, therefore, is includible in A's gross estate as provided in section 2040(b). Therefore, 30 percent (1/2 * 60 percent) of the account balance is includible in A's gross estate under section 2040(b), and a total of 70 percent of the aggregate account balance is includible in A's gross estate. If A and B were not married, then the 40 percent portion of the account subject to the disclaimer would be includible in A's gross estate as provided in section 2033 and the 60 percent portion of the account not subject to the disclaimer would be includible in A's gross estate as provided in section 2040(a), because A furnished all of the funds with respect to the account.

(d) No acceptance of benefits. (1) *Acceptance.* A qualified disclaimer cannot be made with respect to an interest in property if the disclaimant has accepted the interest or any of its benefits, expressly or impliedly, prior to making the disclaimer. Acceptance is manifested by an affirmative act which is consistent with ownership of the interest in property. Acts indicative of acceptance include using the property or the interest in property; accepting dividends, interest, or rents from the property; and directing others to act with respect to the property or interest in property. However, merely taking delivery of an instrument of title, without more, does not constitute acceptance. Moreover, a disclaimant is not considered to have accepted property merely because under applicable local law title to the property vests immediately in the disclaimant upon the death of a decedent. The acceptance of one interest in property will not, by itself, constitute an acceptance of any other separate interests created by the transferor and held by the disclaimant in the same property. In the case of residential property, held in joint tenancy by some or all of the residents, a joint tenant will not be considered to have accepted the joint interest merely because the tenant resided on the property prior to disclaiming his interest in the property. The exercise of a power of appointment to any extent by the donee of the power is an acceptance of its benefits. In addition, the acceptance of any consideration in return for making the disclaimer is an acceptance of the benefits of the entire interest disclaimed.

(2) *Fiduciaries.* If a beneficiary who disclaims an interest in property is also a fiduciary, actions taken by such person in the exercise of fiduciary powers to preserve or maintain the disclaimed property shall not be treated as an acceptance of such property or any of its benefits. Under this rule, for example, an executor who is also a beneficiary may direct the harvesting of a crop or the general maintenance of a home. A fiduciary, however, cannot retain a wholly discretionary power to direct the enjoyment of the disclaimed interest. For example, a fiduciary's disclaimer of a beneficial interest does not meet the requirements of a qualified disclaimer if the fiduciary exercised or retains a discretionary power to allocate enjoyment of that interest among members of a designated class. See paragraph (e) of this section for rules relating to the effect of directing the redistribution of disclaimed property.

(3) *Under 21 years of age.* A beneficiary who is under 21 years of age has until 9 months after his twenty-first birthday in which to make a qualified disclaimer of his interest in property. Any actions taken with regard to an interest in property by a beneficiary or a custodian prior to the beneficiary's twenty-first birthday will not be an acceptance by the beneficiary of the interest.

(4) *Examples.* The provisions of paragraphs (d)(1), (2) and (3) of this section may be illustrated by the following examples:

Example (1). On April 9, 1977, A established a trust for the benefit of B, then age 22. Under the terms of the trust, the current income of the trust is to be paid quarterly to B. Additionally, one half the principal is to be distributed to B when B attains the age of 30 years. The balance of the principal is to be distributed to B when B attains the age of 40 years. Pursuant to the terms of the trust, B received a distribution of income on June 30, 1977. On August 1, 1977, B disclaimed B's right to receive both the income from the trust and the principal of the trust, B's disclaimer of the income interest is not a qualified disclaimer for purposes of section 2518(a) because B accepted income prior to making the disclaimer. B's disclaimer of the principal, however, does satisfy section 2518(b)(3). See also § 25.2518–3 for rules relating to the disclaimer of less than an entire interest in property.

Example (2). B is the recipient of certain property devised to B under the will of A. The will stated that any disclaimed property was to pass to C. B and C entered into negotiations in which it was decided that B would disclaim all interest in the real property that was devised to B. In exchange, C promised to let B live in the family home for life. B's disclaimer is not a qualified disclaimer for purposes of section 2518(a) because B accepted consideration for making the disclaimer.

Example (3). A received a gift of Blackacre on December 25, 1978. A never resided on Blackacre but when property taxes on Blackacre became due on July 1, 1979, A paid them out of personal funds. On August 15, 1979, A disclaimed the gift of Blackacre. Assuming all the requirements of section 2518(b) have been met, A has made a qualified disclaimer of Blackacre. Merely paying the property taxes does not constitute an acceptance of Blackacre even though A's personal funds were used to pay the taxes.

Example (4). A died on February 15, 1978. Pursuant to A's will, B received a farm in State Z. B requested the executor to sell the farm and to give the proceeds to B. The executor then sold the farm pursuant to B's request. B then disclaimed $50,000 of the proceeds from the sale of the farm. B's disclaimer is not a qualified disclaimer. By requesting the executor to sell the farm B accepted the farm even though the executor may not have been legally obligated to comply with B's request. See also § 25.2518–3 for rules relating to the disclaimer of less than an entire interest in property.

Example (5). Assume the same facts as in example (4) except that instead of requesting the executor to sell the farm, B pledged the farm as security for a short-term loan which was paid off prior to distribution of the estate. B then disclaimed his interest in the farm. B's disclaimer is not a qualified disclaimer. By pledging the farm as security for the loan, B accepted the farm.

Example (6). A delivered 1,000 shares of stock in Corporation X to B as a gift on February 1, 1980. A had the shares registered in B's name on that date. On April 1, 1980, B disclaimed the interest in the 1,000 shares. Prior to making the disclaimer, B did not pledge the shares, accept any dividends or otherwise commit any acts indicative of acceptance. Assuming the remaining requirements of section 2518 are satisfied, B's disclaimer is a qualified disclaimer.

Example (7). On January 1, 1980, A created an irrevocable trust in which B was given a testamentary general power of appointment over the trust's corpus. B executed a will on June 1, 1980, in which B provided for the exercise of the power of appointment. On September 1, 1980, B disclaimed the testamentary power of appointment. Assuming the remaining requirements of section 2518(b) are satisfied, B's disclaimer of the testamentary power of appointment is a qualified disclaimer.

Example (8). H and W reside in X, a community property state. On January 1, 1981, H and W purchase a residence with community funds. They continue to reside in the house until H dies testate on February 1, 1990. Although H could devise his portion of the residence to any person, H devised his portion of the residence to W. On September 1, 1990, W disclaims the portion of the residence devised to her pursuant to H's will but continues to live in the residence. Assuming the remaining requirements of section 2518(b) are satisfied, W's disclaimer is a qualified disclaimer under section 2518(a). W's continued occupancy of the house prior to making the disclaimer will not by itself be treated as an acceptance of the benefits of the portion of the residence devised to her by H.

Example (9). In 1979, D established a trust for the benefit of D's minor children E and F. Under the terms of the trust, the trustee is given the power to make discretionary distributions of current income and corpus to both children. The corpus of the trust is to be distributed equally between E and F when E becomes 35 years of age. Prior to attaining the age of 21 years on April 8, 1982, E receives several distributions of income from the trust. E receives no distributions of income between April 8, 1982 and August 15, 1982, which is the date on which E disclaims all interest in the income from the trust. As a result of the disclaimer the income will be distributed to F. If the remaining requirements of section 2518 are met, E's disclaimer is a qualified disclaimer under section 2518(a). To have a qualified disclaimer of the interest in corpus, E must disclaim the interest no later than 9 months after April 8, 1982, E's 21st birthday.

Example (10). Assume the same facts as in example (9) except that E accepted a distribution of income on May 13, 1982. E's disclaimer is not a qualified disclaimer under section 2518 because by accepting an income distribution after attaining the age of 21, E accepted benefits from the income interest.

Example (11). F made a gift of 10 shares of stock to G as custodian for H under the State X Uniform Gifts to Minors Act. At the time of the gift, H was 15 years old. At age 18, the local age of majority, the 10 shares were delivered to and registered in the name of H. Between the receipt of the shares and H's 21st birthday, H received dividends from the shares. Within 9 months of attaining age 21, H disclaimed the 10 shares. Assuming H did not accept any dividends from the shares after attaining age 21, the disclaimer by H is a qualified disclaimer under section 2518.

(e) Passage without direction by the disclaimant of beneficial enjoyment of disclaimed interest. (1) *In general.* A disclaimer is not a qualified disclaimer unless the disclaimed interest passes without any direction on the part of the disclaimant to a person other than the disclaimant (except as provided in paragraph (e)(2) of this section). If there is an express or implied agreement that the disclaimed interest in property is to be given or bequeathed to a person specified by the disclaimant, the disclaimant shall be treated as directing the transfer of the property interest. The requirements of a qualified disclaimer under section 2518 are not satisfied if—

(i) The disclaimant, either alone or in conjunction with another, directs the redistribution or transfer of the property or interest in property to another person (or has the power to direct the redistribution or transfer of the property or interest in property to another person unless such power is limited by an ascertainable standard); or

(ii) The disclaimed property or interest in property passes to or for the benefit of the disclaimant as a result of the disclaimer (except as provided in paragraph (e)(2) of this section).

If a power of appointment is disclaimed, the requirements of this paragraph (e)(1) are satisfied so long as there is no direction on the part of the disclaimant with respect to the transfer of the interest subject to the power or with respect to the transfer of the power to another person. A person may make a qualified disclaimer of a beneficial interest in property even if after such disclaimer the disclaimant has a fiduciary power to distribute to designated beneficiaries, but only if the power is subject to an ascertainable standard. See examples (11) and (12) of paragraph (e)(5) of this section.

(2) *Disclaimer by surviving spouse.* In the case of a disclaimer made by a decedent's surviving spouse with respect to property transferred by the decedent, the disclaimer satisfies the requirements of this paragraph (e) if the interest passes as a result of the disclaimer without direction on the part of the surviving spouse either to the surviving spouse or to another person. If the surviving spouse, however, retains the right to direct the beneficial enjoyment of the disclaimed property in a transfer that is not subject to Federal estate and gift tax (whether as trustee or otherwise), such spouse will be treated as directing the beneficial enjoyment of the disclaimed property, unless such power is limited by an ascertainable standard. See examples (4), (5), and (6) in paragraph (e)(5) of this section.

(3) *Partial failure of disclaimer.* If a disclaimer made by a person other than the surviving spouse is not effective to pass completely an interest in property to a person other than the disclaimant because—

(i) The disclaimant also has a right to receive such property as an heir at law, residuary beneficiary, or by any other means; and

(ii) The disclaimant does not effectively disclaim these rights, the disclaimer is not a qualified disclaimer with respect to the portion of the disclaimed property which the disclaimant has a right to receive. If the portion of the disclaimed interest in property which the disclaimant has a right to receive is not severable property or an undivided portion of the property, then the disclaimer is not a qualified disclaimer with respect to any portion of the property. Thus, for example, if a disclaimant who is not a surviving spouse receives a specific bequest of a fee simple interest in property and as a result of the disclaimer of the entire interest, the property passes to a trust in which the disclaimant has a remainder interest, then the disclaimer will not be a qualified disclaimer unless the remainder interest in the property is also disclaimed. See § 25.2518–3(a)(1)(ii) for the definition of severable property.

(4) *Effect of precatory language.* Precatory language in a disclaimer naming takers of disclaimed property will not be considered as directing the redistribution or transfer of the property or interest in property to such persons if the applicable State law gives the language no legal effect.

(5) *Examples.* The provisions of this paragraph (e) may be illustrated by the following examples:

Example (1). A, a resident of State X, died on July 30, 1978. Pursuant to A's will, B, A's son and heir at law, received the family home. In addition, B and C each received 50 percent of A's residuary estate. B disclaimed the home. A's will made no provision for the distribution of property in the case of a beneficiary's disclaimer. Therefore, pursuant to the disclaimer laws of State X, the disclaimed property became part of the residuary estate. Because B's 50 percent share of the residuary estate will be increased by 50 percent of the value of the family home, the disclaimed property will not pass solely to another person. Consequently, B's disclaimer of the family home is a qualified disclaimer only with respect to the 50 percent portion that passes solely to C. Had B also disclaimed B's 50 percent interest in the residuary estate, the disclaimer would have been a qualified disclaimer under section 2518 of the entire interest in the home (assuming the remaining requirements of a qualified disclaimer were satisfied). Similarly, if under the laws of State X, the disclaimer has the effect of divesting B of all interest in the home, both as devisee and as a beneficiary of the residuary estate, including any property resulting from its sale, the disclaimer would be a qualified disclaimer of B's entire interest in the home.

Example (2). D, a resident of State Y, died testate on June 30, 1978. E, an heir at law of D, received specific bequests of certain severable personal property from D. E disclaimed the property transferred by D under the will. The will made no provision for the distribution of property in the case of a beneficiary's disclaimer. The disclaimer laws of State Y provide that such property shall pass to the decedent's heirs at law in the same manner as if the disclaiming beneficiary had died immediately before the testator's death. Because State Y's law treats E as predeceasing D, the property disclaimed by E does not pass to E as an heir at law or otherwise. Consequently, if the remaining requirements of section 2518(b) are satisfied, E's disclaimer is a qualified disclaimer under section 2518(a).

Example (3). Assume the same facts as in example (2) except that State Y has no provision treating the disclaimant as predeceasing the testator. E's disclaimer satisfies section 2518 (b)(4) only to the extent that E does not have a right to receive the property as an heir at law. Had E disclaimed both the share E received under D's will and E's intestate share, the requirement of section 2518(b)(4) would have been satisfied.

Example (4). B died testate on February 13, 1980. B's will established both a marital trust and a nonmarital trust. The decedent's surviving spouse, A, is an income beneficiary of the marital trust and has a testamentary general power of appointment over its assets. A is also an income beneficiary of the nonmarital trust, but has no power to appoint or invade the corpus. The provisions of the will specify that any portion of the marital trust disclaimed is to be added to the nonmarital trust. A disclaimed 30 percent of the marital trust. (See § 25.2518–3(b) for rules relating to the disclaimer of an undivided portion of an interest in property.) Pursuant to the will, this portion of the marital trust property was transferred to the nonmarital trust without any direction on the part of A. This disclaimer by A satisfies section 2518(b)(4).

Example (5). Assume the same facts as in example (4) except that A, the surviving spouse, has both an income interest in the nonmarital trust and a testamentary nongeneral power to appoint among designated beneficiaries. This power is not limited by an ascertainable standard. The requirements of section 2518(b)(4) are not satisfied unless A also disclaims the nongeneral power to appoint the portion of the trust corpus that is attributable to the property that passed to the nonmarital trust as a result of A's disclaimer. Assuming that the fair market value of the disclaimed property on the date of the disclaimer is $250,000 and that the fair market value of the nonmarital trust (including the disclaimed property) immediately after the disclaimer is $750,000, A must disclaim the power to appoint one-third of the nonmarital trust's corpus. The result is the same regardless of whether the nongeneral power is testamentary or inter vivos.

Example (6). Assume the same facts as in example (4) except that A has both an income interest in the nonmarital trust and a power to invade corpus if needed for A's health or maintenance. In addition, an independent trustee has power to distribute to A any portion of the corpus which the trustee determines to be desirable for A's happiness. Assuming the other requirements of section 2518 are satisfied, A may make a qualified disclaimer of interests in the marital trust without disclaiming any of A's interests in the nonmarital trust.

Example (7). B died testate on June 1, 1980. B's will created both a marital trust and a nonmarital trust. The decedent's surviving spouse, C, is an income beneficiary of the marital trust and has a testamentary general power of appointment over its assets. C is an income beneficiary of the nonmarital trust, and additionally has the noncumulative right to withdraw yearly the greater of $5,000 or 5 percent of the aggregate value of the principal. The provisions of the will specify that any portion of the marital trust disclaimed is to be added to the nonmarital trust. C disclaims 50 percent of the marital trust corpus. Pursuant to the will, this amount is transferred to the nonmarital trust. Assuming the remaining requirements of section 2518(b) are satisfied, C's disclaimer is a qualified disclaimer.

Example (8). A, a resident of State X, died on July 19, 1979. A was survived by a spouse B, and three children, C, D, and E. Pursuant to A's will, B received one-half of A's estate and the children received equal shares of the remaining one-half of the estate. B disclaimed the entire interest B had received. The will made no provisions for the distribution of property in the case of a beneficiary's disclaimer. The disclaimer laws of State X provide that under these circumstances disclaimed property passes to the decedent's heirs at law in the same manner as if the disclaiming beneficiary had died immediately before the testator's death. As a result, C, D, and E are A's only remaining heirs at law, and will divide the disclaimed property equally among themselves. B's disclaimer includes language stating that "it is my intention that C, D, and E will share equally in the division of this property as a result of my disclaimer." State X considers these to be precatory words and gives them no legal effect. B's disclaimer meets all other requirements imposed by State X on disclaimers, and is considered an effective disclaimer under which the property will vest solely in C, D, and E in equal shares without any further action required by B. Therefore, B is not treated as directing the redistribution or transfer of the property. If the remaining requirements of section 2518 are met, B's disclaimer is a qualified disclaimer.

Example (9). C died testate on January 1, 1979. According to C's will, D was to receive 1/3 of the residuary estate with any disclaimed property going to E. D was also to receive a second 1/3 of the residuary estate with any disclaimed property going to F. Finally, D was to receive a final 1/3 of the residuary estate with any disclaimed property going to G. D specifically states that he is disclaiming the interest in which the disclaimed property is designated to pass to E. D has effectively directed that the disclaimed property will pass to E and therefore D's disclaimer is not a qualified disclaimer under section 2518(a).

Example (10). Assume the same facts as in example (9) except that C's will also states that D was to receive Blackacre and Whiteacre. C's will further provides that if D disclaimed Blackacre then such property was to pass to E and that if D disclaimed Whiteacre then Whiteacre was to pass to F. D specifically disclaims Blackacre with the intention that it pass to E. Assuming the other requirements of section 2518 are met, D has made a qualified disclaimer of Blackacre. Alternatively, D could disclaim an undivided portion of both Blackacre and Whiteacre. Assuming the other requirements of section 2518 are met, this would also be a qualified disclaimer.

Example (11). G creates an irrevocable trust on February 16, 1983, naming H, I and J as the income beneficiaries for life and F as the remainderman. F is also named the trustee and as trustee has the discretionary power to invade the corpus and make discretionary distributions to H, I or J during their lives. F disclaims the remainder interest on August 8, 1983, but retains his discretionary power to invade the corpus. F has not made a qualified disclaimer because F retains the power to direct enjoyment of the corpus and the retained fiduciary power is not limited by an ascertainable standard.

Example (12). Assume the same facts as in example (11) except that F may only invade the corpus to make distributions for the health, maintenance or support of H, I or J during their lives. If the other requirements of section 2518(b) are met, F has made a qualified disclaimer of the remainder interest because the retained fiduciary power is limited by an ascertainable standard.

[T.D. 8095, 51 FR 28371, Aug. 7, 1986; 51 FR 31939, Sept. 8, 1986; T.D. 8744, 62 FR 68185, Dec. 31, 1997]

§ 25.2518–3 Disclaimer of less than an entire interest.

(a) Disclaimer of a partial interest. (1) *In general.* (i) *Interest.* If the requirements of this section are met, the disclaimer of all or an undivided portion of any separate interest in property may be a qualified disclaimer even if the disclaimant has another interest in the same property. In general, each interest in property that is separately created by the transferor is treated as a separate interest. For example, if an income interest in securities is bequeathed to A for life, then to B for life, with the remainder interest in such securities bequeathed to A's estate, and if the remaining requirements of section 2518(b) are met, A could make a qualified disclaimer of either the income interest or the remainder, or an undivided portion of either interest. A could not, however, make a qualified disclaimer of the income interest for a certain number of years. Further, where local law merges interests separately created by the transferor, a qualified disclaimer will be allowed only if there is a disclaimer of the entire merged interest or an undivided portion of such merged interest. See example (12) in paragraph (d) of this section. See § 25.2518–3(b) for rules relating to the disclaimer of an undivided portion. Where the merger of separate interests would occur but for the creation by the transferor of a nominal interest (as defined in paragraph (a)(1)(iv) of this section), a qualified disclaimer will be allowed only if there is a disclaimer of all the separate interests, or an undivided portion of all such interests, which would have merged but for the nominal interest.

(ii) *Severable property.* A disclaimant shall be treated as making a qualified disclaimer of a separate interest in property if the disclaimer relates to severable property and the disclaimant makes a disclaimer which would be a qualified disclaimer if such property were the only property in which the disclaimant had an interest. If applicable local law does not recognize a purported disclaimer of severable property, the disclaimant must comply with the requirements of paragraph (c)(1) of § 25.2518–1 in order to make a qualified disclaimer of the severable property. Severable property is property which can be divided into separate parts each of which, after severance, maintains a complete and independent existence. For example, a legatee of shares of corporate stock may accept some shares of the stock and make a qualified disclaimer of the remaining shares.

(iii) *Powers of appointment.* A power of appointment with respect to property is treated as a separate interest in such property and such power of appointment with respect to all or an undivided portion of such property may be disclaimed independently from any other interests separately created by the transferor in the property if the requirements of section 2518(b) are met. See example (21) of paragraph (d) of this section. Further, a disclaimer of a power of appointment with respect to property is a qualified disclaimer only if any right to direct the beneficial enjoyment of the property which is retained by the disclaimant is limited by an ascertainable standard. See example (9) of paragraph (d) of this section.

(iv) *Nominal interest.* A nominal interest is an interest in property created by the transferor that—

(A) Has an actuarial value (as determined under § 20.2031–7) of less than 5 percent of the total value of the property at the time of the taxable transfer creating the interest,

(B) Prevents the merger under local law or two or more other interests created by the transferor, and

(C) Can be clearly shown from all the facts and circumstances to have been created primarily for the purpose of preventing the merger of such other interests.

Factors to be considered in determining whether an interest is created primarily for the purpose of preventing merger include (but are not limited to) the following: the relationship between the transferor and the interest holder; the age difference between the interest holder and the beneficiary whose interests would have merged; the interest holder's state of health at the time of the taxable transfer; and, in the case of a contingent remainder, any other factors which indicate that the possibility of the interest vesting as a fee simple is so remote as to be negligible.

(2) *In trust.* A disclaimer is not a qualified disclaimer under section 2518 if the beneficiary disclaims income derived from specific property transferred in trust while continuing to accept income derived from the remaining properties in the same trust unless the disclaimer results in such property being removed from the trust and passing, without any direction on the part of the disclaimant, to persons other than the disclaimant or to the spouse of the decedent. Moreover, a disclaimer of both an income interest and a remainder interest in specific trust assets is not a qualified disclaimer if the beneficiary retains interests in other trust property unless, as a result of the disclaimer, such assets are removed from the trust and pass, without any direction on the part of the disclaimant, to persons other than the disclaimant or to the spouse of the decedent. The disclaimer of an undivided portion of an interest in a trust may be a qualified disclaimer. See also paragraph (b) of this section for rules relating to the disclaimer of an undivided portion of an interest in property.

(b) Disclaimer of undivided portion. A disclaimer of an undivided portion of a separate interest in property which meets the other requirements of a qualified disclaimer under section 2518(b) and the corresponding regulations is a qualified disclaimer. An undivided portion of a disclaimant's separate interest in property must consist of a fraction or percentage of each and every substantial interest or right owned by the disclaimant in such property and must extend over the entire term of the disclaimant's interest in such property and in other property into which such property is converted. A disclaimer of some specific rights while retaining other rights with respect to an interest in the property is not a qualified disclaimer of an undivided portion of the disclaimant's interest in property. Thus, for example, a disclaimer made by the devisee of a fee simple interest in Blackacre is not a qualified disclaimer if the disclaimant disclaims a remainder interest in Blackacre but retains a life estate.

(c) Disclaimer of a pecuniary amount. A disclaimer of a specific pecuniary amount out of a pecuniary or nonpecuniary bequest or gift which satisfies the other requirements of a qualified disclaimer under section 2518(b) and the corresponding regulations is a qualified disclaimer provided that no income or other benefit of the disclaimed amount inures to the benefit of the disclaimant either prior to or subsequent to the disclaimer. Thus, following the disclaimer of a specific pecuniary amount from a bequest or gift, the amount disclaimed and any income attributable to such amount must be segregated from the portion of the gift or bequest that was not disclaimed. Such a segregation of assets making up the disclaimer of a pecuniary amount must be made on the basis of the fair market value of the assets on the date of the disclaimer or on a basis that is fairly representative of value changes that may have occurred between the date of transfer and the date of the disclaimer. A pecuniary amount distributed to the disclaimant from the bequest or gift prior to the disclaimer shall be treated as a distribution of corpus from the bequest or gift. However, the acceptance of a distribution from the gift or bequest shall also be considered to be an acceptance of a proportionate amount of income earned by the bequest or gift. The proportionate share of income considered to be accepted by the disclaimant shall be determined at the time of the disclaimer according to the following formula:

$$\frac{\text{Total amount of distributions received by the disclaimant out of the gift or bequest}}{\text{Total Value of the gift or bequest on the date of transfer}} * \text{Total amount of income earned by the gift or bequest between date of transfer and date of disclaimer}$$

See examples (17), (18), and (19) in § 25.2518–3(d) for illustrations of the rules set forth in this paragraph (c).

(d) Examples. The provisions of this section may be illustrated by the following examples:

Example (1). A, a resident of State Q, died on August 1, 1978. A's will included specific bequests of 100 shares of stock in X corporation; 200 shares of stock in Y corporation; 500 shares of stock in Z corporation; personal effects consisting of paintings, home furnishings, jewelry, and silver, and a 500 acre farm consisting of a residence, various outbuildings, and 500 head of cattle. The laws of State Q provide that a disclaimed interest passes in the same manner as if the disclaiming beneficiary had died immediately before the testator's death. Pursuant to A's will, B was to receive both the personal effects and the farm. C was to receive all the shares of stock in Corporation X and Y and D was to receive all the shares of stock in Corporation Z. B disclaimed 2 of the paintings and all the jewelry, C disclaimed 50 shares of Y corporation stock, and D disclaimed 100 shares of Z corporation stock. If the remaining requirements of section 2518(b) and the corresponding regulations are met, each of these disclaimers is a qualified disclaimer for purposes of section 2518(a).

Example (2). Assume the same facts as in example (1) except that D disclaimed the income interest in the shares of Z corporation stock while retaining the remainder interest in such shares. D's disclaimer is not a qualified disclaimer.

Example (3). Assume the same facts as in example (1) except that B disclaimed 300 identified acres of the 500 acres. Assuming that B's disclaimer meets the remaining requirements of section 2518(b), it is a qualified disclaimer.

Example (4). Assume the same facts as in example (1) except that A devised the income from the farm to B for life and the remainder interest to C. B disclaimed 40 percent of the income from the farm. Assuming that it meets the remaining requirements of section 2518(b), B's disclaimer of an undivided portion of the income is a qualified disclaimer.

Example (5). E died on September 13, 1978. Under the provisions of E's will, E's shares of stock in X, Y, and Z corporations were to be transferred to a trust. The trust provides that all income is to be distributed currently to F and G in equal parts until F attains the age of 45 years. At that time the corpus of the trust is to be divided equally between F and G. F disclaimed the income arising from the shares of X stock. G disclaimed 20 percent of G's interest in the trust. F's disclaimer is not a qualified disclaimer because the X stock remains in the trust. If the remaining requirements of section 2518(b) are met, G's disclaimer is a qualified disclaimer.

Example (6). Assume the same facts as in example (5) except that F disclaimed both the income interest and the remainder interest in the shares of X stock. F's disclaimer results in the X stock being transferred out of the trust to G without any direction on F's part. F's disclaimer is a qualified disclaimer under section 2518(b).

Example (7). Assume the same facts as in example (5) except that F is only an income beneficiary of the trust. The X stock remains in the trust after F's disclaimer of the income arising from the shares of X stock. F's disclaimer is not a qualified disclaimer under section 2518.

Example (8). Assume the same facts as in example (5) except that F disclaimed the entire income interest in the trust while retaining the interest F has in corpus. Alternatively, assume that G disclaimed G's entire corpus interest while retaining G's interest in the income from the trust. If the remaining requirements of section 2518(b) are met, either disclaimer will be a qualified disclaimer.

Example (9). G creates an irrevocable trust on May 13, 1980, with H, I, and J as the income beneficiaries. In addition, H, who is the trustee, holds the power to invade corpus for H's health, maintenance, support and happiness and a testamentary power of appointment over the corpus. In the absence of the exercise of the power of appointment, the property passes to I and J in equal shares. H disclaimed the power to invade corpus for H's health, maintenance, support and happiness. Because H retained the testamentary power to appoint the property in the corpus, H's disclaimer is not a qualified disclaimer. If H also disclaimed the testamentary power of appointment, H's disclaimer would have been a qualified disclaimer.

Example (10). E creates an irrevocable trust on May 1, 1980, in which D is the income beneficiary for life. Subject to the trustee's discretion, E's children, A, B, and C, have the right to receive corpus during D's lifetime. The remainder passes to D if D survives A, B, C, and all their issue. D also holds an inter vivos power to appoint the trust corpus to A, B, and C. On September 1, 1980, D disclaimed the remainder interest. D's disclaimer is not a qualified disclaimer because D retained the power to direct the use and enjoyment of corpus during D's life.

Example (11). Under H's will, a trust is created from which W is to receive all of the income for life. The trustee has the power to invade the trust corpus for the support or maintenance of D during the life of W. The trust is to terminate at W's death, at which time the trust property is to be distributed to D. D makes a timely disclaimer of the right to corpus during W's lifetime, but does not disclaim the remainder interest. D's disclaimer is a qualified disclaimer assuming the remaining requirements of section 2518 are met.

Example (12). Under the provisions of G's will A received a life estate in a farm, and was the sole beneficiary of property in the residuary estate. The will also provided that the remainder interest in the farm pass to the residuary estate. Under local law A's interests merged to give A a fee simple in the farm. A made a timely disclaimer of the life estate. A's disclaimer of a partial interest is not a qualified disclaimer under section 2518(a). If A makes a disclaimer of the entire merged interest in the farm or an undivided portion of such merged interest then A would be making a qualified disclaimer assuming all the other requirements of section 2518(b) are met.

Example (13). A, a resident of State Z, dies on September 3, 1980. Under A's will, Blackacre is devised to C for life, then to D for 1 month, remainder to C. Had A not created D's interest, State Z law would have merged C's life estate and the remainder to C to create a fee simple interest in C. Assume that the actuarial value of D's interest is less than 5 percent of the total value of Blackacre on the date of A's death. Further assume that facts and circumstances (particularly the duration of D's interest) clearly indicate that D's interest was created primarily for the purpose of preventing the merger of C's two interests in Blackacre. D's interest in Blackacre is a nominal interest and C's two interests will, for purposes of making a qualified disclaimer, be considered to have merged. Thus, C cannot make a qualified disclaimer of his remainder while retaining the life estate. C can, however, make a qualified disclaimer of both of these interests entirely or an undivided portion of both.

Example (14). A, a resident of State X, dies on October 12, 1978. Under A's will, Blackacre was devised to B for life, then to C for life if C survives B, remainder to B's estate. On the date of A's death, B and C are both 8 year old grandchildren of A. In addition, C is in good health. The actual value of C's interest is less than 5 percent of the total value of Blackacre on the date of A's death. No facts are present which would indicate that the possibility of C's contingent interest vesting is so remote as to be negligible. Had C's contingent life estate not been created, B's life estate and remainder interests would have merged under local law to give B a fee simple interest in Blackacre. Although C's interest prevents the merger of B's two interests and has an actual value of less than 5 percent, C's interest is not a nominal interest within the meaning of § 25.2518–3(a)(1)(iv) because the facts and circumstances do not clearly indicate that the interest was created primarily for the purpose of preventing the merger of other interests in the property. Assuming all the other requirements of section 2518(b) are met, B can make a qualified disclaimer of the remainder while retaining his life estate.

Example (15). In 1981, A transfers $60,000 to a trust created for the benefit of B who was given the income interest for life and who also has a testamentary nongeneral power of appointment over the corpus. A transfers an additional $25,000 to the trust on June 1, 1984. At that time the trust corpus (exclusive of the $25,000 transfer) has a fair market value of $75,000. On January 1, 1985, B disclaims the right to receive income attributable to 25 percent of the corpus

$$\frac{\text{\$25,000 (1984 transfer)}}{\text{\$100,000 (Fair market value after of corpus immediately the 1984 transfer)}} = 25\%$$

Assuming that no distributions were made to B attributable to the $25,000, B's disclaimer is a qualified disclaimer for purposes of section 2518(a) if all the remaining requirements of section 2518(b) are met.

Example (16). Under the provisions of B's will, A is left an outright cash legacy of $50,000 and has no other interest in B's estate. A timely disclaimer by A of any stated dollar amount is a qualified disclaimer under section 2518(a).

Example (17). D bequeaths his brokerage account to E. The account consists of stocks and bonds and a cash amount earning interest. The total value of the cash and assets in the account on the date of D's death is $100,000. Four months after D's death, E makes a withdrawal of cash from the account for personal use amounting to $40,000. Eight months after D's death, E disclaims $60,000 of the account without specifying any particular assets or cash. The cumulative fair market value of the stocks and bonds in the account on the date of the disclaimer is equal to the value of such stocks and bonds on the date of D's death. The income earned by the account between the date of D's death and the date of E's disclaimer was $20,000. The amount of income earned by the account that E accepted by withdrawing $40,000 from the account prior to the disclaimer is determined by applying the formula set forth in § 25.2518–3(c) as follows:

$$\frac{\$40,000}{\$100,000} * \$20,000 = \$8,000$$

E is considered to have accepted $8,000 of the income earned by the account. If (i) the $60,000 disclaimed by E and the $12,000 of income earned prior to the disclaimer which is attributable to that amount are segregated from the $8,000 of income E is considered to have accepted, (ii) E does not accept any benefits of the $72,000 so segregated, and (iii) the other requirements of section 2518 (b) are met, then E's disclaimer of $60,000 from the account is a qualified disclaimer.

Example (18). A bequeathed his residuary estate to B. The residuary estate had a value of $1 million on the date of A's death. Six months later, B disclaimed $200,000 out of this bequest. B received distributions of all the income from the entire estate during the period of administration. When the estate was distributed, B received the entire residuary estate except for $200,000 in cash. B did not make a qualified disclaimer since he accepted the benefits of the $200,000 during the period of estate administration.

Example (19). Assume the same facts as in example (18) except that no income was paid to B and the value of the residuary estate on the date of the disclaimer (including interest earned from date of death) was $1.5 million. In addition, as soon as B's disclaimer was made, the executor of A's estate set aside assets worth $300,000

$$\frac{\$200,000}{\$1,000,000} * \$1,500,000$$

and the interest earned after the disclaimer on that amount in a separate fund so that none of the income was paid to B. B's disclaimer is a qualified disclaimer under section 2518(a).

Example (20). A bequeathed his residuary estate to B. B disclaims a fractional share of the residuary estate. Any disclaimed property will pass to A's surviving spouse, W. The numerator of the fraction disclaimed is the smallest amount which will allow A's estate to pass free of Federal estate tax and the denominator is the value of the residuary estate. B's disclaimer is a qualified disclaimer.

Example (21). A created a trust on July 1, 1979. The trust provides that all current income is to be distributed equally between B and C for the life of B. B also is given a testamentary general power of appointment over the corpus. If the power is not exercised, the corpus passes to C or C's heirs. B disclaimed the testamentary power to appoint an undivided one-half of the trust corpus. Assuming the remaining requirements of section 2518(b) are satisfied, B's disclaimer is a qualified disclaimer under section 2518(a).

[T.D. 8095, 51 FR 28375, Aug. 7, 1986; 51 FR 31939, Sept. 8, 1986; T.D. 8540, 59 FR 30103, June 10, 1994]

§ 2519. Dispositions of Certain Life Estates

(a) General rule. For purposes of this chapter and chapter 11, any disposition of all or part of a qualifying income interest for life in any property to which this section applies shall be treated as a transfer of all interests in such property other than the qualifying income interest.

(b) Property to which this subsection applies. This section applies to any property if a deduction was allowed with respect to the transfer of such property to the donor—

(1) under section 2056 by reason of subsection (b)(7) thereof, or

(2) under section 2523 by reason of subsection (f) thereof.

(c) Cross reference. For right of recovery for gift tax in the case of property treated as transferred under this section, see section 2207A(b).

Regulations

§ 25.2519–1 Dispositions of certain life estates.

(a) In general. If a donee spouse makes a disposition of all or part of a qualifying income interest for life in any property for which a deduction was allowed under section 2056(b)(7) or section 2523(f) for the transfer creating the qualifying income interest, the donee spouse is treated for purposes of chapters 11 and 12 of subtitle B of the Internal Revenue Code as transferring all interests in property other than the qualifying income interest. For example, if the donee spouse makes a disposition of part of a qualifying income interest for life in trust corpus, the spouse is treated under section 2519 as making a transfer subject to chapters 11 and 12 of the entire trust other than the qualifying income interest for life. Therefore, the donee spouse is treated as making a gift under section 2519 of the entire trust less the qualifying income interest, and is treated for purposes of section 2036 as having transferred the entire trust corpus, including that portion of the trust corpus from which the retained income interest is payable. A transfer of all or a portion of the income interest of the spouse is a transfer by the spouse under section 2511. See also section 2702 for special rules applicable in valuing the gift made by the spouse under section 2519.

(b) Presumption. Unless the donee spouse establishes to the contrary, section 2519 applies to the entire trust at the time of the disposition. If a deduction is taken on either the estate or gift tax return with respect to the transfer which created the qualifying income interest, it is presumed that the deduction was allowed for purposes of section 2519. To avoid the application of section 2519 upon a transfer of all or part of the donee spouse's income interest, the donee spouse must establish that a deduction was not taken for the transfer of property which created the qualifying income interest. For example, to establish that a deduction was not taken, the donee spouse may produce a copy of the estate or gift tax return filed with respect to the transfer creating the qualifying income interest for life establishing that no deduction was taken under section 2056(b)(7) or section 2523(f). In addition, the donee spouse may establish that no return was filed on the original transfer by the donor spouse because the value of the first spouse's gross estate was below the threshold requirement for filing under section 6018. Similarly, the donee spouse could establish that the transfer creating the qualifying income interest for life was made before the effective date of section 2056(b)(7) or section 2523(f), whichever is applicable.

(c) Amount treated as a transfer. (1) *In general.* The amount treated as a transfer under this section upon a disposition of all or part of a qualifying income interest for life in qualified terminable interest property is equal to the fair market value of the entire property subject to the qualifying income interest, determined on the date of the disposition (including any accumulated income and not reduced by any amount excluded from total gifts under section 2503(b) with respect to the transfer creating the interest), less the value of the qualifying income interest in the property on the date of the disposition. The gift tax consequences of the disposition of the qualifying income interest are determined separately under § 25.2511–2. See paragraph (c)(4) of this section for the effect of gift tax that the donee spouse is entitled to recover under section 2207A.

(2) *Disposition of interest in property with respect to which a partial election was made.* If, in connection with the transfer of property that created the spouse's qualifying income interest for life, a deduction was allowed under section 2056(b)(7) or section 2523(f) for less than the entire interest in the property (i.e., for a fractional or percentage share of the entire interest in the transferred property) the amount treated as a transfer by the donee spouse under this section is equal to the fair market value of the entire property subject to the qualifying income interest on the date of the disposition, less the value of the qualifying income interest for life, multiplied by the fractional or percentage share of the interest for which the deduction was taken.

(3) *Reduction for distributions charged to nonelective portion of trust.* The amount determined under paragraph (c)(2) of this section (if applicable) is appropriately reduced if—

(i) The donee spouse's interest is in a trust and distributions of principal have been made to the donee spouse;

(ii) The trust provides that distributions of principal are made first from the qualified terminable interest share of the trust; and

(iii) The donee spouse establishes the reduction in that share based on the fair market value of the trust assets at the time of each distribution.

(4) *Effect of gift tax entitled to be recovered under section 2207A on the amount of the transfer.* The amount treated as a transfer under paragraph (c)(1) of this section is further reduced by the amount the donee spouse is entitled to recover under section 2207A(b) (relating to the right to recover gift tax attributable to the remainder interest). If the donee spouse is entitled to recover gift tax under section 2207A(b), the amount of gift tax recoverable and the value of the remainder interest treated as transferred under section 2519 are determined by using the same interrelated computation applicable for other transfers in which the transferee assumes the gift tax liability. The gift tax consequences of failing to exercise the right of recovery are determined separately under § 25.2207A–1(b).

(5) *Interest in previously severed trust.* If the donee spouse's interest is in a trust consisting of only qualified terminable interest property, and the trust was previously severed (in compliance with § 20.2056(b)–7(b)(2)(ii) of this chapter or § 25.2523(f)–1(b)(3)(ii) from a trust that, after the severance, held only property that was not qualified terminable interest property, only the value of the property in the severed portion of the trust at the time of the disposition is treated as transferred under this section.

(d) Identification of property transferred. If only part of the property in which a donee spouse has a qualifying income interest for life is qualified terminable interest property, the donee spouse is, in the case of a disposition of all or part of the income interest within the meaning of section 2519, deemed to have transferred a pro rata portion of the entire qualified terminable interest property for purposes of this section.

(e) Exercise of power of appointment. The exercise by any person of a power to appoint qualified terminable interest property to the donee spouse is not treated as a disposition under section 2519, even though the donee spouse subsequently disposes of the appointed property.

(f) Conversion of qualified terminable interest property. The conversion of qualified terminable interest property into other property in which the donee spouse has a qualifying income interest for life is not, for purposes of this section, treated as a disposition of the qualifying income interest. Thus, the sale and reinvestment of assets of a trust holding qualified terminable interest property is not a disposition of the qualifying income interest, provided that the donee spouse continues to have a qualifying income interest for life in the trust after the sale and reinvestment. Similarly, the sale of real property in which the spouse possesses a legal life estate and thus meets the requirements of qualified terminable interest property, followed by the transfer of the proceeds into a trust which also meets the requirements of qualified terminable interest property, or by the reinvestment of the proceeds in income producing property in which the donee spouse has a qualifying income interest for life, is not considered a disposition of the qualifying income interest. On the other hand, the sale of qualified terminable interest property, followed by the payment to the donee spouse of a portion of the proceeds equal to the value of the donee spouse's income interest, is considered a disposition of the qualifying income interest.

(g) Examples. The following examples illustrate the application of paragraphs (a) through (f) of this section. Except as provided otherwise in the examples, assume that the decedent, D, was survived by spouse, S, that in each example the section 2503(b) exclusion has already been fully utilized for each year with respect to the donee in question, that section 2503(e) is not applicable to the amount deemed transferred, and that the gift taxes on the amount treated as transferred under paragraph (c) are offset by S's unified credit. The examples are as follows:

Example (1). Transfer of the spouse's life estate in residence. Under D's will, a personal residence valued for estate tax purposes at $250,000 passes to S for life, and after S's death to D's children. D's executor made a valid election to treat the property as qualified terminable interest property. During 1995, when the fair market value of the property is $300,000 and the value of S's life interest in the property is $100,000, S makes a gift of S's entire interest in the property to D's children. Pursuant to section 2519, S makes a gift in the amount of $200,000 (i.e., the fair market value of the qualified terminable interest property of $300,000 less the fair market value of S's qualifying income interest in the property of $100,000). In addition, under section 2511, S makes a gift of $100,000 (i.e., the fair market value of S's income interest in the property). See § 25.2511–2.

Example (2). Sale of spouse's life estate. The facts are the same as in Example 1 except that during 1995, S sells S's interest in the property to D's children for $100,000. Pursuant to section 2519, S makes a gift of $200,000 ($300,000 less $100,000 value of the qualifying income interest in the property). S does not make a gift of the income interest under section 2511, because the consideration received for S's income interest is equal to the value of the income interest.

Example (3). Transfer of income interest in trust subject to partial election. D's will established a trust valued for estate tax purposes at $500,000, all of the income of which is payable annually to S for life. After S's death, the principal of the trust is to be distributed to D's children. Assume that only 50 percent of the trust was treated as qualified terminable interest property. During 1995, S makes a gift of all of S's interest in the trust to D's children at which time the fair market value of the trust is $400,000 and the fair market value of S's life income interest in the trust is $100,000. Pursuant to section 2519, S makes a gift of $150,000 (the fair market value of the qualified terminable interest property, 50 percent of $400,000, less the $50,000 income interest in the qualified terminable interest property). S also makes a gift pursuant to section 2511 of $100,000 (i.e., the fair market value of S's life income interest).

Example (4). Transfer of a portion of income interest in trust subject to a partial election. The facts are the same as in Example 3 except that S makes a gift of only 40 percent of S's interest in the trust. Pursuant to section 2519, S makes a gift of $150,000 (i.e., the fair market value of the qualified terminable interest property, 50 percent of $400,000, less the $50,000 value of S's qualified income interest in the qualified terminable interest property). S also makes a gift pursuant to section 2511 of $40,000 (i.e., the fair market value of 40 percent of S's life income interest). See also section 2702 for additional rules that may affect the value of the total amount of S's gift under section 2519 to take into account the fact that S's 30 percent retained income interest attributable to the qualifying income interest is valued at zero under that section, thereby increasing the value of S's section 2519 gift to $180,000. In addition, under § 25.2519–1(d), S's disposition of 40 percent of the income interest is deemed to be a transfer of a pro rata portion of the qualified terminable interest property. Thus, assuming no further lifetime dispositions by S, 30 percent (60 percent of 50 percent) of the trust property is included in S's gross estate under section 2036 and an adjustment is made to S's adjusted taxable gifts under section 2001(b)(1)(B). If S later disposes of all or a portion of the retained income interest, see § 25.2702–6.

Example (5). Transfer of a portion of spouse's interest in a trust from which corpus was previously distributed to the spouse. D's will established a trust valued for estate tax purposes at $500,000, all of the income of which is payable annually to S for life. The trustee is granted the discretion to distribute trust principal to S. All appointments of principal must be made from the portion of the trust subject to the section 2056(b)(7) election. After S's death, the principal of the trust is to be distributed to D's children. The executor makes the section 2056(b)(7) election with respect to 50 percent of the trust. In 1994, pursuant to the terms of D's will, the trustee distributed $50,000 of principal to S and charged the entire distribution to the qualified terminable interest portion of the trust.

Immediately prior to the distribution, the value of the entire trust was $550,000 and the value of the qualified terminable interest portion was $275,000 (50 percent of $550,000). Provided S can establish the above facts, the qualified terminable interest portion of the trust immediately after the distribution is $225,000 or 45 percent of the value of the trust ($225,000/ $500,000). In 1996, when the value of the trust is $400,000 and the value of S's income interest is $100,000, S makes a transfer of 40 percent of S's income interest. S's gift under section 2519 is $135,000; i.e., the fair market value of the qualified terminable interest property, 45 percent of $400,000 ($180,000), less the value of the income interest in the qualified terminable interest property, $45,000 (45 percent of $100,000). S also makes a gift under section 2511 of $40,000; i.e., the fair market value of 40 percent of S's income interest. S's disposition of 40 percent of the income interest is deemed to be a transfer under section 2519 of the entire 45 percent portion of the remainder subject to the section 2056(b)(7) election. Since S retained 60 percent of the income interest, 27 percent (60 percent of 45 percent) of the trust property is includible in S's gross estate under section 2036. See also section 2702 and Example 4 as to the principles applicable in valuing S's gift under section 2702 and adjusted taxable gifts upon S's subsequent death.

Example (6). Transfer of Spousal Annuity Payable From Trust. D died prior to October 24, 1992. D's will established a trust valued for estate tax purposes at $500,000. The trust instrument required the trustee to pay an annuity to S of $20,000 a year for life. All the trust income other than the amounts paid to S as an annuity are to be accumulated in the trust and may not be distributed during S's lifetime to any person other than S. After S's death, the principal of the trust is to be distributed to D's children. Because D died prior to the effective date of section 1941 of the Energy Policy Act of 1992, S's annuity interest qualifies as a qualifying income interest for life. Under § 20.2056(b)–7(e) of this chapter, based on an applicable 10 percent interest rate, 40 percent of the property, or $200,000, is the value of the deductible interest. During 1996, S makes a gift of the annuity interest to D's children at which time the fair market value of the trust is $800,000 and the fair market value of S's annuity interest in the trust is $100,000. Pursuant to section 2519, S is treated as making a gift of $220,000 (the fair market value of the qualified terminable interest property, 40 percent of $800,000 ($320,000), less the $100,000 annuity interest in the qualified terminable interest property). S is also treated pursuant to section 2511 as making a gift of $100,000 (the fair market value of S's annuity interest).

[T.D. 8522, 59 FR 9656, March 1, 1994; T.D. 9077, 68 FR 42595, July 18, 2003]

§ 25.2519–2 Effective date.

Except as specifically provided in § 25.2519–1(g), Example 6, the provisions of § 25.2519–1 are effective with respect to gifts made after March 1, 1994. With respect to gifts made on or before such date, the donee spouse of a section 2056(b)(7) or section 2523(f) transfer may rely on any reasonable interpretation of the statutory provisions. For these purposes, the provisions of § 25.2519–1 (as well as project LR–211–76, 1984–1 C.B., page 598, see § 601.601(d)(2)(ii)(b) of this chapter), are considered a reasonable interpretation of the statutory provisions.

[T.D. 8522, 59 FR 9658, March 1, 1994]

Subchapter C. Deductions

§ 2522. Charitable and Similar Gifts

(a) Citizens or residents. In computing taxable gifts for the calendar year, there shall be allowed as a deduction in the case of a citizen or resident the amount of all gifts made during such year to or for the use of—

(1) the United States, any State, or any political subdivision thereof, or the District of Columbia, for exclusively public purposes;

(2) a corporation, or trust, or community chest, fund, or foundation, organized and operated exclusively for religious, charitable, scientific, literary, or educational purposes, or to foster national or international amateur sports competition (but only if no part of its activities involve the provision of athletic facilities or equipment), including the encouragement of art and the prevention of cruelty to children or animals, no part of the net earnings of which inures to the benefit of any private shareholder or individual, which is not disqualified for tax exemption under section 501(c)(3) by reason of attempting to influence legislation, and which does not participate in, or intervene in (including the publishing or distributing of statements), any political campaign on behalf of (or in opposition to) any candidate for public office;

(3) a fraternal society, order, or association, operating under the lodge system, but only if such gifts are to be used exclusively for religious, charitable, scientific, literary, or educational purposes, including the encouragement of art and the prevention of cruelty to children or animals;

(4) posts or organizations of war veterans, or auxiliary units or societies of any such posts or organizations, if such posts, organizations, units, or societies are organized in the United States or any of its possessions, and if no part of their net earnings inures to the benefit of any private shareholder or individual.

Rules similar to the rules of section 501(j) shall apply for purposes of paragraph (2).

(b) Nonresidents. In the case of a nonresident not a citizen of the United States, there shall be allowed as a deduction the amount of all gifts made during such year to or for the use of—

(1) the United States, any State, or any political subdivision thereof, or the District of Columbia, for exclusively public purposes;

(2) a domestic corporation organized and operated exclusively for religious, charitable, scientific, literary, or educational purposes, including the encouragement of art and the prevention of cruelty to children or animals, no part of the net earnings of which inures to the benefit of any private shareholder or individual, which is not disqualified for tax exemption under section 501(c)(3) by reason of attempting to influence legislation, and which does not participate in, or intervene in (including the publishing or distributing of statements), any political campaign on behalf of (or in opposition to) any candidate for public office;

(3) a trust, or community chest, fund, or foundation, organized and operated exclusively for religious, charitable, scientific, literary, or educational purposes, including the encouragement of art and the prevention of cruelty to children or animals, no substantial part of the activities of which is carrying on propaganda, or otherwise attempting, to influence legislation, and which does not participate in, or intervene in (including the publishing or distributing of statements), any political campaign on behalf of (or in opposition to) any candidate for public office; but only if such gifts are to be used within the United States exclusively for such purposes;

(4) a fraternal society, order, or association, operating under the lodge system, but only if such gifts are to be used within the United States exclusively for religious, charitable, scientific, literary, or educational purposes, including the encouragement of art and the prevention of cruelty to children or animals;

(5) posts or organizations of war veterans, or auxiliary units or societies of any such posts or organizations, if such posts, organizations, units, or societies are organized in the United States or any of its possessions, and if no part of their net earnings inures to the benefit of any private shareholder or individual.

(c) Disallowance of deductions in certain cases.

(1) No deduction shall be allowed under this section for a gift to or for the use of an organization or trust described in section 508(d) or 4948(c)(4) subject to the conditions specified in such sections.

(2) Where a donor transfers an interest in property (other than an interest described in section 170(f)(3)(B)) to a person, or for a use, described in subsection (a) or (b) and an interest in the same property is retained by the donor, or is transferred or has been transferred (for less than an adequate and full consideration in money or money's worth) from the donor to a person, or for a use, not described in subsection (a) or (b), no deduction shall be allowed under this section for the interest which is, or has been transferred to the person, or for the use, described in subsection (a) or (b), unless—

(A) in the case of a remainder interest, such interest is in a trust which is a charitable remainder annuity trust or a charitable remainder unitrust (described in section 664) or a pooled income fund (described in section 642(c)(5)), or

(B) in the case of any other interest, such interest is in the form of a guaranteed annuity or is a fixed percentage distributed yearly of the fair market value of the property (to be determined yearly).

(3) Rules similar to the rules of section 2055(e)(4) shall apply for purposes of paragraph (2).

(4) Reformations to comply with paragraph (2).

(A) In general. A deduction shall be allowed under subsection (a) in respect of any qualified reformation (within the meaning of section 2055(e)(3)(B)).

(B) Rules similar to section 2055(e)(3) to apply. For purposes of this paragraph, rules similar to the rules of section 2055(e)(3) shall apply.

(5) Contributions to donor advised funds. A deduction otherwise allowed under subsection (a) for any contribution to a donor advised fund (as defined in section 4966(d)(2)) shall only be allowed if—

(A) the sponsoring organization (as defined in section 4966(d)(1)) with respect to such donor advised fund is not—

(i) described in paragraph (3) or (4) of subsection (a), or

(ii) a type III supporting organization (as defined in section 4943(f)(5)(A)) which is not a functionally integrated type III supporting organization (as defined in section 4943(f)(5)(B)), and

(B) the taxpayer obtains a contemporaneous written acknowledgment (determined under rules similar to the rules of section 170(f)(8)(C)) from the sponsoring organization (as so defined) of such donor advised fund that such organization has exclusive legal control over the assets contributed.

(d) Special rule for irrevocable transfers of easements in real property. A deduction shall be allowed under subsection (a) in respect of any transfer of a qualified real property interest (as defined in section 170(h)(2)(C)) which meets the requirements of section 170(h) (without regard to paragraph (4)(A) thereof).

(e) Special rules for fractional gifts.

(1) Denial of deduction in certain cases.

(A) In general. No deduction shall be allowed for a contribution of an undivided portion of a taxpayer's entire interest in tangible personal property unless all interests in the property are held immediately before such contribution by—

(i) the taxpayer, or

(ii) the taxpayer and the donee.

(B) Exceptions. The Secretary may, by regulation, provide for exceptions to subparagraph (A) in cases where all persons who hold an interest in the property make proportional contributions of an undivided portion of the entire interest held by such persons.

(2) Recapture of deduction in certain cases; addition to tax.

(A) In general. The Secretary shall provide for the recapture of an amount equal to any deduction allowed under this section (plus interest) with respect to any contribution of an undivided portion of a taxpayer's entire interest in tangible personal property—

(i) in any case in which the donor does not contribute all of the remaining interests in such property to the donee (or, if such donee is no longer in existence, to any person described in section 170(c)) on or before the earlier of—

(I) the date that is 10 years after the date of the initial fractional contribution, or

(II) the date of the death of the donor, and

(ii) in any case in which the donee has not, during the period beginning on the date of the initial fractional contribution and ending on the date described in clause (i)—

(I) had substantial physical possession of the property, and

(II) used the property in a use which is related to a purpose or function constituting the basis for the organizations' exemption under section 501.

(B) Addition to tax. The tax imposed under this chapter for any taxable year for which there is a recapture under subparagraph (A) shall be increased by 10 percent of the amount so recaptured.

(C) Initial fractional contribution. For purposes of this paragraph, the term "initial fractional contribution" means, with respect to any donor, the first gift of an undivided portion of the donor's entire interest in any tangible personal property for which a deduction is allowed under subsection (a) or (b).

(f) Cross references.

(1) For treatment of certain organizations providing child care, see section 501(k).

(2) For exemption of certain gifts to or for the benefit of the United States and for rules of construction with respect to certain bequests, see section 2055(f).

(3) For treatment of gifts to or for the use of Indian tribal governments (or their subdivisions), see section 7871.

Regulations

§ 25.2522(a)–1 Charitable and similar gifts; citizens or residents.

(a) In determining the amount of taxable gifts for the "calendar period" (as defined in § 25.2502–1(c)(1)) there may be deducted, in the case of a donor who was a citizen or resident of the United States at the time the gifts were made, all gifts included in the "total amount of gifts" made by the donor during the calendar period (see section 2503 and the regulations thereunder) and made to or for the use of:

(1) The United States, any State, Territory, or any political subdivision thereof, or the District of Columbia, for exclusively public purposes.

(2) Any corporation, trust, community chest, fund, or foundation organized and operated exclusively for religious charitable, scientific, literary, or educational purposes, including the encouragement of art and the prevention of cruelty to children or animals, if no part of the net earnings of the organization inures to the benefit of any private shareholder or individual, if it is not disqualified for tax exemption under section 501(c)(3) by reason of attempting to influence legislation, and if, in the case of gifts made after December 31, 1969, it does not participate in, or intervene in (including the publishing or distributing of statements), any political campaign on behalf of or in opposition to any candidate for public office.

(3) A fraternal society, order, or association, operating under the lodge system, provided the gifts are to be used by the society, order or association exclusively for one or more of the purposes set forth in subparagraph (2) of this paragraph.

(4) Any post or organization of war veterans or auxiliary unit or society thereof, if organized in the United States or any of its possessions, and if no part of its net earnings inures to the benefit of any private shareholder or individual.

The deduction is not limited to gifts for use within the United States, or to gifts to or for the use of domestic corporations, trusts, community chests, funds, or foundations, or fraternal societies, orders, or associations operating under the lodge system. An organization will not be considered to meet the requirements of subparagraph (2) of this paragraph, or of paragraph (b)(2) or (3) of this section, if such organization engages in any activity which would cause it to be classified as an "action" organization under paragraph (c)(3) of § 1.501(c)(3)–1 of this chapter (Income Tax Regulations). For the deductions for charitable and similar gifts made by a nonresident who was not a citizen of the United States at the time the gifts were made, see § 25.2522(b)–1. See §§ 25.2522(c)–1 and 25.2522(c)–2 for rules relating to the disallowance of deductions to trusts and organizations which engage in certain prohibited transactions or whose governing instruments do not contain certain specified requirements.

(b) The deduction under section 2522 is not allowed for a transfer to a corporation, trust, community chest, fund, or foundation unless the organization or trust meets the following four tests:

(1) It must be organized and operated exclusively for one or more of the specified purposes.

(2) It must not be disqualified for tax exemption under section 501(c)(3) by reason of attempting to influence legislation.

(3) In the case of gifts made after December 31, 1969, it must not participate in, or intervene in (including the publishing or distributing of statements), any political campaign on behalf of any candidate for public office.

(4) Its net earnings must not inure in whole or in part to the benefit of private shareholders or individuals other than as legitimate objects of the exempt purposes.

For further limitations see § 25.2522(c)–1, relating to gifts to trusts and organizations which have engaged in a prohibited transaction described in section 681(b)(2) or section 503(c).

(c) In order to prove the right to the charitable, etc., deduction provided by section 2522 the donor must submit such data as may be requested by the Internal Revenue Service. As to the extent the deductions provided by this section are allowable, see section 2524.

[T.D. 6334, 23 FR 8904, Nov. 15, 1958, as amended by T.D. 7012, 34 FR 7691, May 15, 1969; T.D. 7238, 37 FR 28733, Dec. 29, 1972; T.D. 7318, 39 FR 25457, July 11, 1974; T.D. 7910, 48 FR 40375, Sept. 7, 1983; T.D. 8308, 55 FR 35594, Aug. 31, 1990]

§ 25.2522(b)–1 Charitable and similar gifts; nonresidents not citizens.

(a) The deduction for charitable and similar gifts, in the case of a nonresident who was not a citizen of the United States at the time he made the gifts, is governed by the same rules as those applying to gifts by citizens or residents, subject, however, to the following exceptions:

(1) If the gifts are made to or for the use of a corporation, the corporation must be one created or organized under the laws of the United States or of any State or Territory thereof.

(2) If the gifts are made to or for the use of a trust, community chest, fund or foundation, or a fraternal society, order or association operating under the lodge system, the gifts must be for use within the United States exclusively for religious, charitable, scientific,

literary or educational purposes, including the encouragement of art and the prevention of cruelty to children or animals.

(b) [Reserved]

[T.D. 6334, 23 FR 8904, Nov. 15, 1958]

§ 25.2522(c)–1 Disallowance of charitable, etc., deductions because of "prohibited transactions" in the case of gifts made before January 1, 1970. [*Omitted. Ed.*]

[T.D. 6334, 23 FR 8904, Nov. 15, 1958; 25 FR 14021, Dec. 31, 1960, as amended by T.D. 7318, 39 FR 25458, July 11, 1974]

§ 25.2522(c)–2 Disallowance of charitable, etc., deductions in the case of gifts made after December 31, 1969.

(a) Organizations subject to section 507(c) tax. Section 508(d)(1) provides that, in the case of gifts made after December 31, 1969, a deduction which would otherwise be allowable under section 2522 for a gift to or for the use of an organization upon which the tax provided by section 507(c) has been imposed shall not be allowed if the gift is made by the donor after notification is made under section 507(a) or if the donor is a substantial contributor (as defined in section 507(d)(2)) who makes such gift in his taxable year (as defined in section 441) which includes the first day on which action is taken by such organization that culminates in the imposition of the tax under section 507(c) and any subsequent taxable year. This paragraph does not apply if the entire amount of the unpaid portion of the tax imposed by section 507(c) is abated under section 507(g) by the Commissioner or his delegate.

(b) Taxable private foundations, section 4947 trusts, etc. Section 508(d)(2) provides that, in the case of gifts made after December 31, 1969, a deduction which would otherwise be allowable under section 2522 shall not be allowed if the gift is made to or for the use of—

(1) A private foundation or a trust described in section 4947(a)(2) in a taxable year of such organization for which such organization fails to meet the governing instrument requirements of section 508(e) (determined without regard to section 508(e)(2)(B) and (C)), or

(2) Any organization in a period for which it is not treated as an organization described in section 501(c) (3) by reason of its failure to give notification under section 508(a) of its status to the Commissioner.

For additional rules, see § 1.508–2(b)(1) of this chapter (Income Tax Regulations).

(c) Foreign organizations with substantial support from foreign sources. Section 4948(c)(4) provides that, in the case of gifts made after December 31, 1969, a deduction which would otherwise be allowable under section 2522 for a gift to or for the use of a foreign organization which has received substantially all of its support (other than gross investment income) from sources without the United States shall not be allowed if the gift is made (1) after the date on which the Commissioner has published notice that he has notified such organization that it has engaged in a prohibited transaction, or (2) in a taxable year of such organization for which it is not exempt from taxation under section 501(a) because it has engaged in a prohibited transaction after December 31, 1969.

[T.D. 7318, 39 FR 25458, July 11, 1974]

§ 25.2522(c)–3 Transfers not exclusively for charitable, etc., purposes in the case of gifts made after July 31, 1969.

(a) Remainders and similar interests. If a trust is created or property is transferred for both a charitable and a private purpose, deduction may be taken of the value of the charitable beneficial interest only insofar as that interest is presently ascertainable, and hence severable from the noncharitable interest.

(b) Transfers subject to a condition or a power. (1) If, as of the date of the gift, a transfer for charitable purposes is dependent upon the performance of some act or of the happening of a precedent event in order that it might become effective, no deduction is allowable unless the possibility that the charitable transfer will not become effective is so remote as to be negligible. If an estate or interest has passed to, or is vested in, charity on the date of the gift and the estate or interest would be defeated by the performance of some act or the happening of some event, the possibility of occurrence of which appeared on such date to be so remote as to be negligible, the deduction is allowable. If the donee or trustee is empowered to divert the property or fund, in whole or in part, to a use or purpose which would have rendered it, to the extent that it is subject to such power, not deductible had it been directly so given by the donor, the deduction will be limited to that portion, if any, of the property or fund which is exempt from an exercise of the power.

(2) The application of this paragraph may be illustrated by the following examples:

Example (1). In 1965, A transfers certain property in trust in which charity is to receive the income for his life. The assets placed in trust by the donor consist of stock in a corporation the fiscal policies of which are controlled by the donor and his family. The trustees of the trust and the remainderman are members of the donor's family and the governing instrument contains no adequate guarantee of the requisite income to the charitable organization. Under such circumstances, no deduction will be allowed. Similarly, if the trustees are not members of the donor's family but have no power to sell or otherwise dispose of the closely held stock, or otherwise insure the requisite enjoyment of income to the charitable organization, no deduction will be allowed.

Example (2). C transfers a tract of land to a city government for as long as the land is used by the city for a public park. If on the date of gift the city does plan to use the land for a public park and the possibility that the city will not use the land for a public park is so remote as to be negligible, a deduction will be allowed.

(c) Transfers of partial interest in property. (1) *Disallowance of deduction.* (i) *In general.* If a donor transfers an interest in property after July 31, 1969, for charitable purposes and an interest in the same property is retained by the donor, or is transferred or has been transferred for private purposes after such date (for less than an adequate and full consideration in money or money's worth), no deduction is allowed under section 2522 for the value of the interest which is transferred or has been transferred for charitable purposes unless the interest in property is a deductible interest described in subparagraph (2) of this paragraph. The principles that are used in applying section 2523 and the regulations thereunder shall apply for purposes of determining under this paragraph (c)(1)(i) whether an interest in property is retained by the donor, or is transferred or has been transferred by the donor. If, however, as of the date of the gift, a retention of any interest by a donor, or a transfer for a private purpose, is dependent upon the performance of some act or the happening of a precedent event in order that it may become effective, an interest in property will be considered retained by the donor, or transferred for a private purpose, unless the possibility of occurrence of such act or event is so remote as to be negligible. The application of this paragraph (c)(1)(i) may be illustrated by the following examples, in each of which it is assumed that the property interest which is transferred for private purposes is not transferred for an adequate and full consideration in money or money's worth:

Example (1). In 1973, H creates a trust which is to pay the income of the trust to W for her life, the reversionary interest in the trust being retained by H. In 1975, H gives the reversionary interest to charity, while W is still living. For purposes of this paragraph (c)(1)(i), interests in the same property have been transferred by H for charitable purposes and for private purposes.

Example (2). In 1973, H creates a trust which is to pay the income of the trust to W for her life and upon termination of the life estate to transfer the remainder to S. In 1975, S gives his remainder interest to charity, while W is still living. For purposes of this paragraph (c)(1)(i), interests in the same property have not been transferred by H or S for charitable purposes and for private purposes.

Example (3). H transfers Blackacre to A by gift, reserving the right to the rentals of Blackacre for a term of 20 years. After 4 years H transfers the right to the remaining rentals to charity. For purposes of this paragraph (c)(1)(i) the term "property" refers to Blackacre, and the right to rentals from Blackacre consist of an interest in Blackacre. An interest in Blackacre has been transferred by H for charitable purposes and for private purposes.

Example (4). H transfers property in trust for the benefit of A and a charity. An annuity of $5,000 a year is to be paid to charity for 20 years. Upon termination of the 20-year term the corpus is to be distributed to A if living. However, if A should die during the 20-year term, the corpus is to be distributed to charity upon termination of the term. An interest in property has been transferred by H for charitable purposes. In addition, an interest in the same property has been transferred by H for private purposes unless the possibility that A will survive the 20-year term is so remote as to be negligible.

Example (5). H transfers property in trust, under the terms of which an annuity of $5,000 a year is to be paid to charity for 20 years. Upon termination of the term, the corpus is to pass to such of A's children and their issue as A may appoint. However, if A should die during the 20-year term without exercising the power of appointment, the corpus is to be distributed to charity upon termination of the term. Since the possible appointees include private persons, an interest in the corpus of the trust is considered to have been transferred by H for private purposes.

(ii) *Works of art and copyright treated as separate properties.* For purposes of paragraphs (c)(1)(i) and (c)(2) of this section, rules similar to the rules in § 20.2055–2(e)(1)(ii) shall apply in the case of transfers made after December 31, 1981.

(2) *Deductible interests.* A deductible interest for purposes of subparagraph (1) of this paragraph is a charitable interest in property where—

(i) *Undivided portion of donor's entire interest.* The charitable interest is an undivided portion, not in trust, of the donor's entire interest in property. An undivided portion of a donor's entire interest in property must consist of a fraction or percentage of each and every substantial interest or right owned by the donor in such property and must extend over the entire term of the donor's interest in such property and in other property into which such property is converted. For example, if the donor gave a life estate in an office building to his wife for her life and retained a reversionary interest in the office building, the gift by the donor of one-half of that reversionary interest to charity while his wife is still alive will not be considered the transfer of a deductible interest; because an interest in the same property has already passed from the donor for private purposes, the reversionary interest will not be considered the donor's entire interest in the property. If, on the other hand, the donor had been given a life estate in Blackacre for the life of his wife and the donor had no other interest in Blackacre on or before the time of gift, the gift by the donor of one-half of that life estate to charity would be considered the transfer of a deductible interest; because the life estate would be considered the donor's entire interest in the property, the gift would be of an undivided portion of such entire interest. An undivided portion of a donor's entire interest in property includes an interest in property whereby the charity is given the right, as a tenant in common with the donor, to possession, dominion, and control of the property for a portion of each year appropriate to its interest in such property. However, except as provided in paragraphs (c)(2)(ii), (iii), and (iv) of this section, for purposes of this subdivision a charitable contribution of an interest in property not in trust where the decedent transfers some specific rights to one party and transfers other substantial rights to another party will not be considered a contribution of an undivided portion of the decedent's entire interest in property. A gift to charity made on or before December 17, 1980, of an open space easement in gross in perpetuity shall be considered the transfer to charity of an undivided portion of the donor's entire interest in property.

(ii) *Remainder interest in a personal residence.* The charitable interest is an irrevocable remainder interest, not in trust, in a personal residence. Thus, for example, if the donor gives to charity a remainder interest in a personal residence and retains an estate in such property for life or a term of years the value of such remainder interest is deductible under section 2522. For purposes of this subdivision, the term "personal residence" means any property which is used by the donor as his personal residence even though it is not used as his principal residence. For example, a donor's vacation home may be a personal residence for purposes of this subdivision. The term "personal residence" also includes stock owned by the donor on the date of gift as a tenant-stockholder in a cooperative housing corporation (as those terms are defined in section 216(b)(1) and (2)) if the dwelling which the donor is entitled to occupy as such stockholder is used by him as his personal residence.

(iii) *Remainder interest in a farm.* The charitable interest is an irrevocable remainder interest, not in trust, in a farm. Thus, for example, if the donor gives to charity a remainder interest in a farm and retains an estate in such property for life or a term of years, the value of such remainder interest is deductible under section 2522. For purposes of this subdivision, the term "farm" means any land used by the donor or his tenant for the production of crops, fruits, or other agricultural products or for the sustenance of livestock. The term "livestock" includes cattle, hogs, horses, mules, donkeys, sheep, goats, captive fur-bearing animals, chickens, turkeys, pigeons, and other poultry. A farm includes the improvements thereon.

(iv) *Qualified Conservation Contribution.* The charitable interest is a qualified conservation contribution. For the definition of a qualified conservation contribution, see § 1.170A–14.

(v) *Charitable remainder trust and pooled income funds.* The charitable interest is a remainder interest in a trust which is a charitable remainder annuity trust, as defined in section 664(d)(1) and § 1.664–2 of this chapter; a charitable remainder unitrust, as defined in section 664(d)(2) and (3) and § 1.664–3 of this chapter; or a pooled income fund, as defined in section 642(c)(5) and § 1.642(c)–5 of this chapter. The charitable organization to or for the use of which the remainder interest is transferred must meet the requirements of both section 2522(a) or (b) and section 642(c)(5)(A), section 664(d)(1)(C), or section 664(d)(2)(C), whichever applies. For example, the charitable organization to which the remainder interest in a charitable remainder annuity trust is transferred may not be a foreign corporation.

(vi) *Guaranteed annuity interest.* (a) The charitable interest is a guaranteed annuity interest, whether or not such interest is in trust. For purposes of this paragraph (c)(2)(vi), the term "guaranteed annuity interest" means an irrevocable right pursuant to the instrument of transfer to receive a guaranteed annuity. A guaranteed annuity is an arrangement under which a determinable amount is paid periodically, but not less often than annually, for a specified term of years or for the life or lives of certain individuals, each of whom must be living at the date of the gift and can be ascertained at such date. Only one or more of the following individuals may be used as measuring lives: the donor, the donor's spouse, and an individual who, with respect to all remainder beneficiaries (other than charitable organizations described in section 170, 2055, or 2522), is either a lineal ancestor or the spouse of a lineal ancestor of those beneficiaries. A trust will satisfy the requirement that all noncharitable remainder beneficiaries are lineal descendants of the individual who is the measuring life, or that individual's spouse, if there is less than a 15% probability that individuals who are not lineal descendants will receive any trust corpus. This probability must be computed, based on the current applicable Life Table contained in § 20.2031–7, at the time property is transferred to the trust taking into account the interests of all primary and contingent remainder beneficiaries who are living at that time. An interest payable for a specified term of years can qualify as a guaranteed annuity interest even if the governing instrument contains a savings clause intended to ensure compliance with a rule against perpetuities. The savings clause must utilize a period for vesting of 21 years after the deaths of measuring lives who are selected to maximize, rather than limit, the term of the trust. The rule in this paragraph that a charitable interest may be payable for the life or lives of only certain specified individuals does not apply in the case of a charitable guaranteed annuity interest payable under a charitable remainder trust described in section 664. An amount is determinable if the exact amount which must be paid under the conditions specified in the instrument of transfer can be ascertained as of the date of gift. For example, the amount to be paid may be a stated sum for a term or years, or for the life of the donor, at the expiration of which it may be changed by a specified amount, but it may not be redetermined by reference to a fluctuating index such as the cost of living index. In further illustration, the amount to be paid may be expressed as a fraction or percentage of the cost of living index on the date of gift.

(b) A charitable interest is a guaranteed annuity interest only if it is a guaranteed annuity interest in every respect. For example, if the charitable interest is the right to receive from a trust each year a payment equal to the lesser of a sum certain or a fixed percentage of the net fair market value of the trust assets, determined annually, such interest is not a guaranteed annuity interest.

(c) Where a charitable interest in the form of a guaranteed annuity interest is not in trust, the interest will be considered a guaranteed annuity interest only if it is to be paid by an insurance company or by an organization regularly engaged in issuing annuity contracts.

(d) Where a charitable interest in the form of a guaranteed annuity interest is in trust, the governing instrument of the trust may provide that income of the trust which is in excess of the amount required to pay the guaranteed annuity interest shall be paid to or for the use of a charity. Nevertheless, the amount of the deduction under section 2522 shall be limited to the fair market value of the guaranteed annuity interest as determined under paragraph (d)(2)(iv) of this section.

(e) Where a charitable interest in the form of a guaranteed annuity interest is in trust and the present value on the date of gift of all income interests for a charitable purpose exceeds 60 percent of the aggregate fair market value of all amounts in such trust (after the payment of liabilities), the charitable interest will not be considered a guaranteed annuity interest unless the governing instrument of the trust prohibits both the acquisition and the retention of assets which would give rise to a tax under section 4944 if the trustee had acquired such assets. The requirement in this (e) for a prohibition in the governing instrument against the retention of assets which would give rise to a tax under section 4944 if the trustee had acquired the assets shall not apply to a gift made on or before May 21, 1972.

(f) Where a charitable interest in the form of a guaranteed annuity interest is in trust, and the gift of such interest is made after May 21, 1972, the charitable interest generally is not a guaranteed annuity interest if any amount may be paid by the trust for a private purpose before the expiration of all the charitable annuity interests. There are two exceptions to this general rule. First, the charitable interest is a guaranteed annuity interest if the amount payable for a private purpose is in the form of a guaranteed annuity interest and the trust's governing instrument does not provide for any preference or priority in the payment of the private annuity as opposed to the charitable annuity. Second, the charitable interest is a guaranteed annuity interest if under the trust's governing instrument the amount that may be paid for a private purpose is payable only from a group of assets that are devoted exclusively to private purposes and to which section 4947(a)(2) is inapplicable by reason of section 4947(a)(2)(B). For purposes of this paragraph (c)(2)(vi)(f), an amount is not paid for a private purpose if it is paid for an adequate and full consideration in money or money's worth. See § 53.4947–1(c) of this chapter for rules relating to the inapplicability of section 4947(a)(2) to segregated amounts in a split-interest trust.

(g) For rules relating to certain governing instrument requirements and to the imposition of certain excise taxes where the guaranteed annuity interest is in trust and for rules governing payment of private income interests by a split-interest trust, see section 4947(a)(2) and (b)(3)(A), and the regulations thereunder.

(vii) *Unitrust interest.* (a) The charitable interest is a unitrust interest, whether or not such interest is in trust. For purposes of this paragraph (c)(2)(vii), the term "unitrust interest" means an irrevocable right pursuant to the instrument of transfer to receive payment, not less often than annually, of a fixed percentage of the net fair market value, determined annually, of the property which funds the unitrust interest. In computing the net fair market value of the property which funds the unitrust interest, all assets and liabilities shall be taken into account without regard to whether particular items are taken into account in determining the income from the property. The net fair market value of the property which funds the unitrust interest may be determined on any one date during the year or by taking the average of valuations made on more than one date during the year, provided that the same valuation date or dates and valuation methods are used each year. Where the charitable interest is a unitrust interest to be paid by a trust and the governing instrument of the trust does not specify the valuation date or dates, the trustee shall select such date or dates and shall indicate his selection on the first return on Form 1041 which the trust is required to file. Payments under a unitrust interest may be paid for a specified term of years or for the life or lives of certain individuals, each of whom must be living at the date of the gift and can be ascertained at such date. Only one or more of the following individuals may be used as measuring lives: the donor, the donor's spouse, and an individual who, with respect to all remainder beneficiaries (other than charitable organizations described in section 170, 2055, or 2522), is either a lineal ancestor or the spouse of a lineal ancestor of those beneficiaries. A trust will satisfy the requirement that all noncharitable remainder beneficiaries are lineal descendants of the individual who is the measuring life, or that individual's spouse, if there is less than a 15% probability that individuals who are not lineal descendants will receive any trust corpus. This probability must be computed, based on the current applicable Life Table contained in § 20.2031–7, at the time property is transferred to the trust taking into account the interests of all primary and contingent remainder beneficiaries who are living at that time. An interest payable for a specified term of years can qualify as a unitrust interest even if the governing instrument contains a savings clause intended to ensure compliance with a rule against perpetuities. The savings clause must utilize a period for vesting of

21 years after the deaths of measuring lives who are selected to maximize, rather than limit, the term of the trust. The rule in this paragraph that a charitable interest may be payable for the life or lives of only certain specified individuals does not apply in the case of a charitable unitrust interest payable under a charitable remainder trust described in section 664.

(b) A charitable interest is a unitrust interest only if it is a unitrust interest in every respect. For example, if the charitable interest is the right to receive from a trust each year a payment equal to the lesser of a sum certain or a fixed percentage of the net fair market value of the trust assets, determined annually, such interest is not a unitrust interest.

(c) Where a charitable interest in the form of a unitrust interest is not in trust, the interest will be considered a unitrust interest only if it is to be paid by an insurance company or by an organization regularly engaged in issuing interests otherwise meeting the requirements of a unitrust interest.

(d) Where a charitable interest in the form of a unitrust interest is in trust, the governing instrument of the trust may provide that income of the trust which is in excess of the amount required to pay the unitrust interest shall be paid to or for the use of a charity. Nevertheless, the amount of the deduction under section 2522 shall be limited to the fair market value of the unitrust interest as determined under paragraph (d)(2)(v) of this section.

(e) Where a charitable interest in the form of a unitrust interest is in trust, the charitable interest generally is not a unitrust interest if any amount may be paid by the trust for a private purpose before the expiration of all the charitable unitrust interests. There are two exceptions to this general rule. First, the charitable interest is a unitrust interest if the amount payable for a private purpose is in the form of a unitrust interest and the trust's governing instrument does not provide for any preference or priority in the payment of the private unitrust interest as opposed to the charitable unitrust interest. Second, the charitable interest is a unitrust interest if under the trust's governing instrument the amount that may be paid for a private purpose is payable only from a group of assets that are devoted exclusively to private purposes and to which section 4947(a)(2) is inapplicable by reason of section 4947(a)(2)(B). For purposes of this paragraph (c)(2)(vii)(e), an amount is not paid for a private purpose if it is paid for an adequate and full consideration in money or money's worth. See § 53.4947–1(c) of this chapter for rules relating to the inapplicability of section 4947(a)(2) to segregated amounts in a split-interest trust.

(f) For rules relating to certain governing instrument requirements and to the imposition of certain excise taxes where the unitrust interest is in trust and for rules governing payment of private income interests by a split-interest trust, see sections 4947(a)(2) and (b)(3)(A), and the regulations thereunder.

(d) Valuation of charitable interest. (1) *In general.* The amount of the deduction in the case of a contribution of a partial interest in property to which this section applies is the fair market value of the partial interest on the date of gift. The fair market value of an annuity, life estate, term for years, remainder, reversion or unitrust interest is its present value.

(2) *Certain transfers after July 31, 1969.* In the case of a transfer after July 31, 1969, of an interest described in paragraph (c)(2)(v), (vi), or (vii) of this section, the present value of such interest is to be determined under the following rules:

(i) The present value of a remainder interest in a charitable remainder annuity trust is to be determined under § 1.664–2(c) of this chapter (Income Tax Regulations).

(ii) The present value of a remainder interest in a charitable remainder unitrust is to be determined under § 1.664–4 of this chapter.

(iii) The present value of a remainder interest in a pooled income fund is to be determined under § 1.642(c)–6 of this chapter.

(iv) The present value of a guaranteed annuity interest described in paragraph (c)(2)(vi) of this section is to be determined under § 25.2512–5, except that, if the annuity is issued by a company regularly engaged in the sale of annuities, the present value is to be determined under § 25.2512–6. If by reason of all the conditions and circumstances surrounding a transfer of an income interest in property in trust it appears that the charity may not receive the beneficial enjoyment of the interest, a deduction will be allowed under section 2522 only for the minimum amount it is evident the charity will receive.

(A) *Example 1.* In 1975, B transfers $20,000 in trust with the requirement that a designated charity be paid a guaranteed annuity interest (as defined in paragraph (c)(2)(vi) of this section) of $4,100 a year, payable annually at the end of each year for a period of 6 years and that the remainder be paid to his children. The fair market value of an annuity of $4,100 a year for a period of 6 years is $20,160.93 ($4,100 x 4.9173), as determined under § 25.2512–5A(c). The deduction with respect to the guaranteed annuity interest will be limited to $20,000, which is the minimum amount it is evident the charity will receive.

(B) *Example 2.* In 1975, C transfers $40,000 in trust with the requirement that D, an individual, and X Charity be paid simultaneously guaranteed annuity interests (as defined in paragraph (c)(2)(vi) of this section) of $5,000 a year each, payable annually at the end of each year, for a period of 5 years and that the remainder be paid to C's children. The fair market value of two annuities of $5,000 each a year for a period of 5 years is $42,124 ([$5,000 x 4.2124] x 2), as determined under § 25.2512–5A(c). The trust instrument provides that in the event the trust fund is insufficient to pay both annuities in a given year, the trust fund will be evenly divided between the charitable and private annuitants. The deduction with respect to the charitable annuity will be limited to $20,000, which is the minimum amount it is evident the charity will receive.

(C) *Example 3* (1) Factors. The appropriate annuity factor for an annuity payable for a term of years is computed by subtracting from 1.000000 the factor for an ordinary remainder interest following the same term certain that is determined under the formula in § 20.2031–7(d)(2)(ii)(A) of this chapter and then dividing the result by the applicable section 7520 interest rate expressed to at least four decimal places. For the convenience of taxpayers, annuity factors have been computed by the IRS and appear in the "Annuity" column of Table B. The actuarial commutation factors can be computed directly by using the formulas in § 25.2512–5(d)(2)(v)(A)(1), the section 7520 rate, and Table 2010CM as set forth in § 20.2031–7(d)(7)(ii) of this chapter. For the convenience of taxpayers, actuarial factors have been computed by the IRS and appear in Table H. Tables B and H can be found on the IRS website at *https://www.irs.gov/retirement-plans/actuarial-tables* (or a corresponding URL as may be updated from time to time). For purposes of the example in paragraph (d)(2)(iv)(C)(2) of this section, the relevant factors from Tables B and H are:

Factors from Table B			
Annuity, Income, and Remainder Interests for a Term Certain			
Interest at 2.8 Percent			
Years	Annuity	Income Interest	Remainder
10	8.6179	0.241302	0.758698
Factors from Table H(2.8)			
Commutation Factors—Based on Table 2010CM			
Interest at 2.8 Percent			
Age (x)	D_x	N_x-factor	M_x-factor
60	16,911.03	271,994.3	9,295.187
70	11,280.80	133,677.8	7,537.826

(2) *Application.* In a year after 2023, D transfers $65,000 in trust with the requirement that a guaranteed annuity interest (as defined in paragraph (c)(2)(vi) of this section) of $5,000 a year, payable annually at the end of each year, be paid to Y Charity for a period of 10 years and that a guaranteed annuity interest (as defined in paragraph (c)(2)(vi) of this section) of $5,000 a year, payable annually at the end of each year, be paid to W, D's wife, aged 60, for 10 years or until her prior death. The annuities are to be paid simultaneously, and the remainder is to be paid to D's children. The section 7520 interest rate for the date of transfer is 2.8 percent, and the taxpayer elects not to use the interest rate from either of the two preceding months. The fair market value of the private annuity is $40,895.50 ($5,000 x 8.1791), as determined pursuant

to § 25.2512–5(d)(2)(v)(A) and by the use of factors derived from Table H and illustrated in paragraph (d)(2)(iv)(C)(3) of this section. The fair market value of the charitable annuity is $43,089.50 ($5,000 x 8.6179), determined using the annuity factor from Table B. It is not evident from the governing instrument of the trust or from local law that the trustee would be required to apportion the trust fund between the wife and charity in the event the fund were insufficient to pay both annuities in a given year. Accordingly, the deduction with respect to the charitable annuity will be limited to $24,104.50 ($65,000 less $40,895.50 [the value of the private annuity]), which is the minimum amount it is evident the charity will receive.

(3) Actuarial factor. In paragraph (d)(2)(iv)(C)(2) of this section, the actuarial factor for determining the value of the private annuity is derived by the use of factors involving one life and a term of years. The factor is determined as illustrated in Figure 1 to this paragraph (d)(2)(iv)(C)(3).

Figure 1 to paragraph (d)(2)(iv)(C)(3) – Illustration of calculation of annuity factor for shorter of term or life

A.	Initial age	60
B.	Plus: Term of years	10
C.	Sum (Terminal age)	70
D.	$\overset{\circ}{N}_x$ factor, Table H(2.8), age 60	271,994.30
E.	Less: $\overset{\circ}{N}_x$ factor, Table H(2.8), age 70	133,677.80
F.	Difference	138,316.50
G.	D_x factor, Table H(2.8), age 60	16,911.03
H.	Required Annuity Factor: F / G	8.1791

(v) The present value of a unitrust interest described in paragraph (c)(2)(vii) of this section is to be determined by subtracting the present value of all interests in the transferred property other than the unitrust interest from the fair market value of the transferred property.

(3) *Other transfers*. The present value of an interest not described in paragraph (d)(2) of this section is to be determined under § 25.2512–5.

(4) *Special computations*. If the interest transferred is such that its present value is to be determined by a special computation, a request for a special factor, accompanied by a statement of the date of birth and sex of each individual the duration of whose life may affect the value of the interest, and by copies of the relevant instruments, may be submitted by the donor to the Commissioner who may, if conditions permit, supply the factor requested. If the Commissioner furnishes the factor, a copy of the letter supplying the factor must be attached to the tax return in which the deduction is claimed. If the Commissioner does not furnish the factor, the claim for deduction must be supported by a full statement of the computation of the present value made in accordance with the principles set forth in this paragraph.

(e) Guaranteed annuity and unitrust interests reformed as an interest for a term of years (1) *In general*. The rules in paragraphs (c)(2)(vi)(a) and (c)(2)(vii)(a) of this section that guaranteed annuity interests or unitrust interests, respectively, may be payable for a specified term of years or for the life or lives of only certain individuals applies to transfers made on or after April 4, 2000. If a transfer is made on or after April 4, 2000, that uses an individual other than one permitted in paragraphs (c)(2)(vi)(a) and (c)(2)(vii)(a) of this section, the interest may be reformed into a lead interest payable for a specified term of years. The term of years is determined by taking the factor for valuing the annuity or unitrust interest for the named individual measuring life and identifying the term of years (rounded up to the next whole year) that corresponds to the equivalent term of years factor for an annuity or unitrust interest. See paragraph (e)(4) of this section for an example.

(2) *Judicial and non-judicial reformations*. A judicial reformation must be commenced prior to October

15th of the year following the year in which the transfer is made and must be completed within a reasonable time after it is commenced. A non-judicial reformation is permitted if effective under state law, provided it is completed by the date on which a judicial reformation must be commenced. In the alternative, if a court, in a proceeding that is commenced on or before July 5, 2001, declares any transfer, made on or after April 4, 2000, and on or before March 6, 2001, null and void ab initio, the Internal Revenue Service will treat such transfers in a manner similar to that described in section 2055(e)(3)(J).

(3) *Sample factors from actuarial Tables B and S.* The appropriate annuity factor for an annuity payable for a term of years is computed by subtracting from 1.000000 the factor for an ordinary remainder interest following the same term certain that is determined under the formula in § 20.2031–7(d)(2)(ii)(A) of this chapter and then dividing the result by the applicable section 7520 interest rate expressed to at least four decimal places. For the convenience of taxpayers, actuarial factors have been computed by the IRS and appear in the "Annuity" column of Table B. The appropriate annuity factor for an annuity payable for the life of one individual is computed by subtracting from 1.00000 the factor for an ordinary remainder interest following the life of the same individual that is determined under the formula in § 20.2031–7(d)(2)(ii)(B) of this chapter and then dividing the result by the applicable section 7520 interest rate expressed to at least four decimal places. For the convenience of taxpayers, actuarial factors have been computed by the IRS and appear in the "Annuity" column of Table S. Tables B and S can be found on the IRS website at *https://www.irs.gov/retirement-plans/actuarial-tables*. For purposes of the example in paragraph (e)(4) of this section, the relevant factors from Tables B and S are:

Factors from Table B			
Annuity, Income, and Remainder Interests for a Term Certain			
Interest at 2.4 Percent			
Years	Annuity	Income Interest	Remainder
38	24.7471	0.593929	0.406071
39	25.1436	0.603447	0.396553
Factors from Table S—Based on Table 2010CM			
Interest at 2.4 Percent			
Age	Annuity	Life Estate	Remainder
40	24.9063	0.59775	0.40225

(4) *Example.* An annuity interest payable for the life of an individual age 40 at the time of the transfer that occurs on or after June 1, 2023, assuming an interest rate of 2.4 percent under section 7520, has an annuity factor reported in Table S of 24.9063. Based on Table B at 2.4 percent, the factor 24.9063 corresponds to a term of years between 38 and 39 years. Accordingly, the annuity interest must be reformed into an interest payable for a term of 39 years. (To determine the value of a charitable remainder interest payable after this annuity interest, the taxpayer then must satisfy the test illustrated in § 25.7520–3(b)(2)(v)(E).)

(f) Applicability date. This section applies only to gifts made after July 31, 1969.

[T.D. 7318, 39 FR 25458, July 11, 1974; 39 FR 26154, July 17, 1974, as amended by T.D. 7340, 40 FR 1240, Jan. 7, 1975; T.D. 7955, 49 FR 19998, May 11, 1984; T.D. 7957, 49 FR 20812, May 17, 1984; T.D. 8069, 51 FR 1507, Jan. 14, 1986; 51 FR 5323, Feb. 13, 1986; 51 FR 6319, Feb. 21, 1986; T.D. 8540, 59 FR 30103, 30177, June 10, 1994; T.D. 8630, 60 FR 63919, Dec. 13, 1995; 61 FR 7992, March 1, 1996; T.D. 8923, 66 FR 1043, Jan. 5, 2001; T.D. 9068, 68 FR 40132, July 7, 2003; T.D. 9448, 74 FR 21515, May 7, 2009; T.D. 9540, 76 FR 49641, Aug. 10, 2011; T.D. 9974, 88 FR 37460, June 7, 2023]

§ 25.2522(c)–4 Disallowance of double deduction in the case of qualified terminable interest property.

No deduction is allowed under section 2522 for the transfer of an interest in property if a deduction is taken from the total amount of gifts with respect to that property by reason of section 2523(f). See § 25.2523(h)–1.

[T.D. 8522, 59 FR 9658, March 1, 1994]

§ 25.2522(d)–1 Additional cross references.

(a) See section 14 of the Wild and Scenic Rivers Act (Public Law 90–542, 82 Stat. 918) for provisions relating to the claim and allowance of the value of certain easements as a gift under section 2522.

(b) For treatment of gifts accepted by the Secretary of State or the Secretary of Commerce, for the purpose of organizing and holding an international conference to negotiate a Patent Corporation Treaty, as gifts to or for the use of the United States, see section 3 of Joint Resolution of December 24, 1969 (Public Law 91–160, 83 Stat. 443).

(c) For treatment of gifts accepted by the Secretary of the Department of Housing and Urban Development, for the purpose of aiding or facilitating the work of the Department, as gifts to or for the use of the United States, see section 7(k) of the Department of Housing and Urban Development Act (42 U.S.C. 3535), as added by section 905 of Public Law 91–609 (84 Stat. 1809).

(d) For treatment of certain property accepted by the Chairman of the Administrative Conference of the United States, for the purpose of aiding and facilitating the work of the Conference, as gifts to the United States, see 5 U.S.C. 575(c)(12), as added by section 1(b) of the Act of October 21, 1972 (Public Law 92–526, 86 Stat. 1048).

(e) For treatment of the Board for International Broadcasting as a corporation described in section 2522(a)(2), see section 7 of the Board for International Broadcasting Act of 1973 (Public Law 93–129, 87 Stat. 459).

[T.D. 7318, 39 FR 25461, July 11, 1974]

§ 2523. Gift to Spouse

(a) Allowance of deduction. Where a donor transfers during the calendar year by gift an interest in property to a donee who at the time of the gift is the donor's spouse, there shall be allowed as a deduction in computing taxable gifts for the calendar year an amount with respect to such interest equal to its value.

(b) Life estate or other terminable interest. Where, on the lapse of time, on the occurrence of an event or contingency, or on the failure of an event or contingency to occur, such interest transferred to the spouse will terminate or fail, no deduction shall be allowed with respect to such interest—

(1) if the donor retains in himself, or transfers or has transferred (for less than an adequate and full consideration in money or money's worth) to any person other than such donee spouse (or the estate of such spouse), an interest in such property, and if by reason of such retention or transfer the donor (or his heirs or assigns) or such person (or his heirs or assigns) may possess or enjoy any part of such property after such termination or failure of the interest transferred to the donee spouse; or

(2) if the donor immediately after the transfer to the donee spouse has a power to appoint an interest in such property which he can exercise (either alone or in conjunction with any person) in such manner that the appointee may possess or enjoy any part of such property after such termination or failure of the interest transferred to the donee spouse. For purposes of this paragraph, the donor shall be considered as having immediately after the transfer to the donee spouse such power to appoint even though such power cannot be exercised until after the lapse of time, upon the occurrence of an event or contingency, or on the failure of an event or contingency to occur.

An exercise or release at any time by the donor, either alone or in conjunction with any person, of a power to appoint an interest in property, even though not otherwise a transfer, shall, for purposes of paragraph (1), be considered as a transfer by him. Except as provided in subsection (e), where at the time of the transfer it is impossible to ascertain the particular person or persons who may receive from the donor an interest in property so transferred by him, such interest shall, for purposes of paragraph (1), be considered as transferred to a person other than the donee spouse.

(c) Interest in unidentified assets. Where the assets out of which, or the proceeds of which, the interest transferred to the donee spouse may be satisfied include a particular asset or assets with respect to which no deduction would be allowed if such asset or assets were transferred from the donor to such spouse, then the value of the interest transferred to such spouse shall, for purposes of subsection (a), be reduced by the aggregate value of such particular assets.

(d) Joint interests. If the interest is transferred to the donee spouse as sole joint tenant with the donor or as tenant by the entirety, the interest of the donor in the property which exists solely by reason of the possibility that the donor may survive the donee spouse, or that there may occur a severance of the tenancy, shall not be considered for purposes of subsection (b) as an interest retained by the donor in himself.

(e) Life estate with power of appointment in donee spouse. Where the donor transfers an interest in property, if by such transfer his spouse is entitled for life to all of the income from the entire interest, or all the income from a specific portion thereof, payable annually or at more frequent intervals, with power in the donee spouse to appoint the entire interest, or such specific portion (exercisable in favor of such donee spouse, or of the estate of such donee spouse, or in favor of either, whether or not in each case the power is exercisable in favor of others), and with no power in any other person to appoint any part of such interest, or such portion, to any person other than the donee spouse—

(1) the interest, or such portion, so transferred shall, for purposes of subsection (a) be considered as transferred to the donee spouse, and

(2) no part of the interest, or such portion, so transferred shall, for purposes of subsection (b)(1), be considered as retained in the donor or transferred to any person other than the donee spouse.

This subsection shall apply only if, by such transfer, such power in the donee spouse to appoint the interest, or such portion, whether exercisable by will or during life, is exercisable by such spouse alone and in all events. For purposes of this subsection, the term "specific portion" only includes a portion determined on a fractional or percentage basis.

(f) Election with respect to life estate for donee spouse.

(1) In general. In the case of qualified terminable interest property—

(A) for purposes of subsection (a), such property shall be treated as transferred to the donee spouse, and

(B) for purposes of subsection (b)(1), no part of such property shall be considered as retained in the donor or transferred to any person other than the donee spouse.

(2) Qualified terminable interest property. For purposes of this subsection, the term "qualified terminable interest property" means any property—

(A) which is transferred by the donor spouse,

(B) in which the donee spouse has a qualifying income interest for life, and

(C) to which an election under this subsection applies.

(3) Certain rules made applicable. For purposes of this subsection, rules similar to the rules of clauses (ii), (iii), and (iv) of section 2056(b)(7)(B) shall apply and the rules of section 2056(b)(10) shall apply.

(4) Election.

(A) Time and manner. An election under this subsection with respect to any property shall be made on or before the date prescribed by section 6075(b) for filing a gift tax return with respect to the transfer (determined without regard to section 6019(2)) and shall be made in such manner as the Secretary shall by regulations prescribe.

(B) Election irrevocable. An election under this subsection, once made, shall be irrevocable.

(5) Treatment of interest retained by donor spouse.

(A) In general. In the case of any qualified terminable interest property—

(i) such property shall not be includible in the gross estate of the donor spouse, and

(ii) any subsequent transfer by the donor spouse of an interest in such property shall not be treated as a transfer for purposes of this chapter.

(B) Subparagraph (A) not to apply after transfer by donee spouse. Subparagraph (A) shall not apply with respect to any property after the donee spouse is treated as having transferred such property under section 2519, or such property is includible in the donee spouse's gross estate under section 2044.

(6) Treatment of joint and survivor annuities. In the case of a joint and survivor annuity where only the donor spouse and donee spouse have the right to receive payments before the death of the last spouse to die—

(A) the donee spouse's interest shall be treated as a qualifying income interest for life,

(B) the donor spouse shall be treated as having made an election under this subsection with respect to such annuity unless the donor spouse otherwise elects on or before the date specified in paragraph (4)(A),

(C) paragraph (5) and section 2519 shall not apply to the donor spouse's interest in the annuity, and

(D) if the donee spouse dies before the donor spouse, no amount shall be includible in the gross estate of the donee spouse under section 2044 with respect to such annuity.

An election under subparagraph (B), once made, shall be irrevocable.

(g) Special rule for charitable remainder trusts.

(1) In general. If, after the transfer, the donee spouse is the only beneficiary who is not a charitable beneficiary (other than the donor) of a qualified charitable remainder trust, subsection (b) shall not apply to the interest in such trust which is transferred to the donee spouse.

(2) Definitions. For purposes of paragraph (1), the terms "charitable beneficiary" and "qualified charitable remainder trust" have the meanings given to such terms by section 2056(b)(8)(B).

(h) Denial of double deduction. Nothing in this section or any other provision of this chapter shall allow the value of any interest in property to be deducted under this chapter more than once with respect to the same donor.

(i) Disallowance of marital deduction where spouse not citizen. If the spouse of the donor is not a citizen of the United States—

(1) no deduction shall be allowed under this section,

(2) section 2503(b) shall be applied with respect to gifts which are made by the donor to such spouse and with respect to which a deduction would be allowable under this section but for paragraph (1) by substituting "$100,000" for "$10,000",* and

(3) the principles of sections 2515 and 2515A (as such sections were in effect before their repeal by the Economic Recovery Tax Act of 1981) shall apply, except that the provisions of such section 2515 providing for an election shall not apply.

This subsection shall not apply to any transfer resulting from the acquisition of rights under a joint and survivor annuity described in subsection (f)(6).

* Rev. Proc. 2025–32 provides that "[f]or calendar year 2026, the first $194,000 . . . of gifts to a spouse who is not a citizen of the United States (other than gifts of future interests in property) are not included in the total amount of taxable gifts under §§ 2503 and 2523(i)(2) made during that year." *Ed.*

Regulations

§ 25.2523(a)–1 Gift to spouse; in general.

(a) In general. In determining the amount of taxable gifts for the calendar quarter (with respect to gifts made after December 31, 1970, and before January 1, 1982), or calendar year (with respect to gifts made before January 1, 1971, or after December 31, 1981), a donor may deduct the value of any property interest transferred by gift to a donee who at the time of the gift is the donor's spouse, except as limited by paragraphs (b) and (c) of this section. See § 25.2502–1(c)(1) for the definition of calendar quarter. This deduction is referred to as the marital deduction. In the case of gifts made prior to July 14, 1988, no marital deduction is allowed with respect to a gift if, at the time of the gift, the donor is a nonresident not a citizen of the United States. Further, in the case of gifts made on or after July 14, 1988, no marital deduction is allowed (regardless of the donor's citizenship or residence) for transfers to a spouse who is not a citizen of the United States at the time of the transfer. However, for certain special rules applicable in the case of estate and gift tax treaties, see section 7815(d)(14) of Public Law 101–239. The donor must submit any evidence necessary to establish the donor's right to the marital deduction.

(b) "Deductible interests" and "nondeductible interests". (1) *In general.* The property interests transferred by a donor to his spouse consist of either transfers with respect to which the marital deduction is authorized (as described in subparagraph (2) of this paragraph) or transfers with respect to which the marital deduction is not authorized (as described in subparagraph (3) of this paragraph). These transfers are referred to in this section and in §§ 25.2523(b)–1 through 25.2523(f)–1 as "deductible interests" and "nondeductible interests", respectively.

(2) *"Deductible interest".* A property interest transferred by a donor to his spouse is a "deductible interest" if it does not fall within either class of "nondeductible interests" described in subparagraph (3) of this paragraph.

(3) *"Nondeductible interests".* (i) A property interest transferred by a donor to his spouse which is a "terminable interest", as defined in § 25.2523(b)–1, is a "nondeductible interest" to the extent specified in that section.

(ii) Any property interest transferred by a donor to the donor's spouse is a nondeductible interest to the extent it is not required to be included in a gift tax return for a calendar quarter (for gifts made after December 31, 1970, and before January 1, 1982) or calendar year (for gifts made before January 1, 1971, or after December 31, 1981).

(c) Computation. (1) *In general.* The amount of the marital deduction depends upon when the interspousal gifts are made, whether the gifts are terminable interests, whether the limitations of § 25.2523(f)–1A (relating to gifts of community property before January 1, 1982) are applicable, and whether § 25.2523(f)–1 (relating to the election with respect to life estates) is applicable, and (with respect to gifts made on or after July 14, 1988) whether the donee spouse is a citizen of the United States (see section 2523(i)).

(2) *Gifts prior to January 1, 1977.* Generally, with respect to gifts made during a calendar quarter prior to January 1, 1977, the marital deduction allowable under section 2523 is 50 percent of the aggregate value of the deductible interests. See section 2524 for an additional limitation on the amount of the allowable deduction.

(3) *Gifts after December 31, 1976, and before January 1, 1982.* Generally, with respect to gifts made during a calendar quarter beginning after December 31, 1976, and ending prior to January 1, 1982, the marital deduction allowable under section 2523 is computed as a percentage of the deductible interests in those gifts. If the aggregate amount of deductions for such gifts is $100,000 or less, a deduction is allowed for 100 percent of the deductible interests. No deduction is allowed for otherwise deductible interests in an aggregate amount that exceeds $100,000 and is equal to or less than $200,000. For deductible interests in excess of $200,000, the deduction is limited to 50 percent of such deductible interests. If a donor remarries, the computations in this paragraph (c)(3) are made on the basis of aggregate gifts to all persons who at the time of the gifts are the donor's spouse. See section 2524 for an additional limitation on the amount of the allowable deduction.

(4) *Gifts after December 31, 1981.* Generally, with respect to gifts made during a calendar year beginning

after December 31, 1981 (other than gifts made on or after July 14, 1988, to a spouse who is not a United States citizen on the date of the transfer), the marital deduction allowable under section 2523 is 100 percent of the aggregate value of the deductible interests. See section 2524 for an additional limitation on the amount of the allowable deduction, and section 2523(i) regarding disallowance of the marital deduction for gifts to a spouse who is not a United States citizen.

(d) Examples. The following examples (in which it is assumed that the donors have previously utilized any specific exemptions provided by section 2521 for gifts prior to January 1, 1977) illustrate the application of paragraph (c) of this section and the interrelationship of sections 2523 and 2503.

Example (1). A donor made a transfer by gift of $6,000 cash to his spouse on December 25, 1971. The donor made no other transfers during 1971. The amount of the marital deduction for the fourth calendar quarter of 1971 is $3,000 (one-half of $6,000); the amount of the annual exclusion under section 2503(b) is $3,000; and the amount of taxable gifts is zero ($6,000 - $3,000 (annual exclusion) - $3,000 (marital deduction)).

Example (2). A donor made transfers by gift to his spouse of $3,000 cash on January 1, 1971, and $3,000 cash on May 1, 1971. The donor made no other transfers during 1971. For the first calendar quarter of 1971 the marital deduction is zero because the amount excluded under section 2503(b) is $3,000, and the amount of taxable gifts is also zero. For the second calendar quarter of 1971 the marital deduction is $1,500 (one-half of $3,000), and the amount of taxable gifts is $1,500 ($3,000 - $1,500 (marital deduction)). Under section 2503(b) no amount of the second $3,000 gift may be excluded because the entire $3,000 annual exclusion was applied against the gift made in the first calendar quarter of 1971.

Example (3). A donor made a transfer by gift to his spouse of $10,000 cash on April 1, 1972. The donor made no other transfers during 1972. For the second calendar quarter of 1972 the amount of the marital deduction is $5,000 (one-half of $10,000); the amount excluded under section 2503(b) is $3,000; the amount of taxable gifts is $2,000 ($10,000 - $3,000 (annual exclusion) - $5,000 (marital deduction)).

Example (4). A donor made transfers by gift to his spouse of $2,000 cash on January 1, 1971, $2,000 cash on April 5, 1971, and $10,000 cash on December 1, 1971. The donor made no other transfers during 1971. For the first calendar quarter of 1971 the marital deduction is zero because the amount excluded under section 2503(b) is $2,000, and the amount of taxable gifts is also zero. For the second calendar quarter of 1971 the marital deduction is $1,000 (one-half of $2,000) (see section 2524); the amount excluded under section 2503(b) is $1,000 because $2,000 of the $3,000 annual exclusion was applied against the gift made in the first calendar quarter of 1971; and the amount of taxable gifts is zero ($2,000 - $1,000 (annual exclusion) - $1,000 (marital deduction)). For the fourth calendar quarter of 1971, the marital deduction is $5,000 (one-half of $10,000); the amount excluded under section 2503(b) is zero because the entire $3,000 annual exclusion was applied against the gifts made in the first and second calendar quarters of 1971; and the amount of taxable gifts is $5,000 ($10,000 - $5,000 (marital deduction)).

Example (5). A donor made transfers by gift to his spouse of $2,000 cash on January 10, 1972, $2,000 cash on May 1, 1972, and a remainder interest valued at $16,000 on June 1, 1972. The donor made no other transfers during 1972. For the first calendar quarter of 1972, the marital deduction is zero because $2,000 is excluded under section 2503(b), and the amount of taxable gifts is also zero. For the second calendar quarter of 1972 the marital deduction is $9,000 (one-half of $16,000 plus one-half of $2,000); the amount excluded under section 2503(b) is $1,000 because $2,000 of the $3,000 annual exclusion was applied against the gift made in the first calendar quarter of 1971; and the amount of taxable gifts is $8,000 ($18,000 - $1,000 (annual exclusion) - $9,000 (marital deduction)).

Example (6). A donor made transfers by gift to his spouse of $2,000 cash on January 1, 1972, a remainder interest valued at $16,000 on January 5, 1972, and $2,000 cash on April 30, 1972. The donor made no other transfers during 1972. For the first calendar quarter of 1972, the marital deduction is $9,000 (one-half of $16,000 plus one-half of $2,000); the amount excluded under section 2503(b) is $2,000; and the amount of taxable gifts is $7,000 ($18,000 - $2,000 (annual exclusion) - $9,000 (marital deduction)). For the second calendar quarter of 1972 the marital deduction is

$1,000 (one-half of $2,000); the amount excluded under section 2503(b) is $1,000 because $2,000 of the $3,000 annual exclusion was applied against the gift of the present interest in the first calendar quarter of 1971; and the amount of taxable gifts is zero ($2,000 - $1,000 (annual exclusion) - $1,000 (marital deduction)).

Example (7). A donor made a transfer by gift to his spouse of $12,000 cash on July 1, 1955. The donor made no other transfers during 1955. For the calendar year 1955 the amount of the marital deduction is $6,000 (one-half of $12,000); the amount excluded under section 2503(b) is $3,000; and the amount of taxable gifts is $3,000 ($12,000 - $3,000 (annual exclusion) - $6,000 (marital deduction)).

Example (8). A donor made a transfer by gift to the donor's spouse, a United States citizen, of $200,000 cash on January 1, 1995. The donor made no other transfers during 1995. For calendar year 1995, the amount excluded under section 2503(b) is $10,000; the marital deduction is $190,000; and the amount of taxable gifts is zero ($200,000 - $10,000 (annual exclusion) - $190,000 (marital deduction)).

(e) Valuation. If the income from property is made payable to the donor or another individual for life or for a term of years, with remainder to the donor's spouse or to the estate of the donor's spouse, the marital deduction is computed (pursuant to § 25.2523(a)–1(c)) with respect to the present value of the remainder, determined under section 7520. The present value of the remainder (that is, its value as of the date of gift) is to be determined in accordance with the rules stated in § 25.2512–5 or, for certain prior periods, § 25.2512–5A. See the example in paragraph (d) of § 25.2512–5. If the remainder is such that its value is to be determined by a special computation, a request for a specific factor, accompanied by a statement of the dates of birth of each person, the duration of whose life may affect the value of the remainder, and by copies of the relevant instruments may be submitted by the donor to the Commissioner who, if conditions permit, may supply the factor requested. If the Commissioner does not furnish the factor, the claim for deduction must be supported by a full statement of the computation of the present value, made in accordance with the principles set forth in § 25.2512–5(d) or, for certain prior periods, § 25.2512–5A.

[T.D. 6334, 23 FR 8904, Nov. 15, 1958, as amended by T.D. 7012, 34 FR 7691, May 15, 1969; T.D. 7238, 37 FR 28733, Dec. 29, 1972; T.D. 7955, 49 FR 19998, May 11, 1984; T.D. 8522, 59 FR 9658, March 1, 1994; T.D. 8540, 59 FR 30103, June 10, 1994; 60 FR 16382, March 30, 1995]

§ 25.2523(b)–1 Life estate or other terminable interest.

(a) In general. (1) The provisions of section 2523(b) generally disallow a marital deduction with respect to certain property interests (referred to generally as terminable interests and defined in paragraph (a)(3) of this section) transferred to the donee spouse under the circumstances described in paragraph (a)(2) of this section, unless the transfer comes within the purview of one of the exceptions set forth in § 25.2523(d)–1 (relating to certain joint interests); § 25.2523(e)–1 (relating to certain life estates with powers of appointment); § 25.2523(f)–1 (relating to certain qualified terminable interest property); or § 25.2523(g)–1 (relating to certain qualified charitable remainder trusts).

(2) If a donor transfers a terminable interest in property to the donee spouse, the marital deduction is disallowed with respect to the transfer if the donor spouse also—

(i) Transferred an interest in the same property to another donee (see paragraph (b) of this section), or

(ii) Retained an interest in the same property in himself (see paragraph (c) of this section), or

(iii) Retained a power to appoint an interest in the same property (see paragraph (d) of this section).

Notwithstanding the preceding sentence, the marital deduction is disallowed under these circumstances only if the other donee, the donor, or the possible appointee, may, by reason of the transfer or retention, possess or enjoy any part of the property after the termination or failure of the interest therein transferred to the donee spouse.

(3) For purposes of this section, a distinction is to be drawn between "property," as such term is used in section 2523, and an "interest in property." The "property" referred to is the underlying property in which various interests exist; each such interest is not, for this purpose, to be considered as "property." A "terminable interest" in property is an interest which will ter-

minate or fail on the lapse of time or on the occurrence or failure to occur of some contingency. Life estates, terms for years, annuities, patents, and copyrights are therefore terminable interests. However, a bond, note, or similar contractual obligation, the discharge of which would not have the effect of an annuity or term for years, is not a terminable interest.

(b) Interest in property which another donee may possess or enjoy. (1) Section 2523(b) provides that no marital deduction shall be allowed with respect to the transfer to the donee spouse of a "terminable interest" in property, in case—

(i) The donor transferred (for less than an adequate and full consideration in money or money's worth) an interest in the same property to any person other than the donee spouse (or the estate of such spouse), and

(ii) By reason of such transfer, such person (or his heirs or assigns) may possess or enjoy any part of such property after the termination or failure of the interest therein transferred to the donee spouse.

(2) In determining whether the donor transferred an interest in property to any person other than the donee spouse, it is immaterial whether the transfer to the person other than the donee spouse was made at the same time as the transfer to such spouse, or at any earlier time.

(3) Except as provided in § 25.2523(e)–1 or § 25.2523(f)–1, if at the time of the transfer it is impossible to ascertain the particular person or persons who may receive a property interest transferred by the donor, such interest is considered as transferred to a person other than the donee spouse for the purpose of section 2523(b). This rule is particularly applicable in the case of the transfer of a property interest by the donor subject to a reserved power. See § 25.2511–2. Under this rule, any property interest over which the donor reserved a power to revest the beneficial title in himself, or over which the donor reserved the power to name new beneficiaries or to change the interests of the beneficiaries as between themselves, is for the purpose of section 2523(b), considered as transferred to a "person other than the donee spouse." The following examples, in which it is assumed that the donor did not make an election under sections 2523(f)(2)(C) and (f)(4), illustrate the application of the provisions of this paragraph (b)(3):

Example (1). If a donor transferred property in trust naming his wife as the irrevocable income beneficiary for 10 years, and providing that, upon the expiration of that term, the corpus should be distributed among his wife and children in such proportions as the trustee should determine, the right to the corpus, for the purpose of the marital deduction, is considered as transferred to a "person other than the donee spouse."

Example (2). If, in the above example, the donor had provided that, upon the expiration of the 10-year term, the corpus was to be paid to his wife, but also reserved the power to revest such corpus in himself, the right to corpus, for the purpose of the marital deduction, is considered as transferred to a "person other than the donee spouse."

(4) The term "person other than the donee spouse" includes the possible unascertained takers of a property interest, as, for example, the members of a class to be ascertained in the future. As another example, assume that the donor created a power of appointment over a property interest, which does not come within the purview of § 25.2523(e)–1. In such a case, the term "person other than the donee spouse" refers to the possible appointees and takers in default (other than the spouse) of such property interest.

(5) An exercise or release at any time by the donor (either alone or in conjunction with any person) of a power to appoint an interest in property, even though not otherwise a transfer by him is considered as a transfer by him in determining, for the purpose of section 2523(b), whether he transferred an interest in such property to a person other than the donee spouse.

(6) The following examples illustrate the application of this paragraph. In each example, it is assumed that the donor made no election under sections 2523(f)(2)(C) and (f)(4) and that the property interest that the donor transferred to a person other than the donee spouse is not transferred for adequate and full consideration in money or money's worth:

Example (1). H (the donor) transferred real property to W (his wife) for life, with remainder to A and his heirs. No marital deduction may be taken with respect to the interest transferred to W, since it will terminate upon her death and A (or his heirs or assigns) will thereafter possess or enjoy the property.

Example (2). H transferred property for the benefit of W and A. The income was payable to W for life and upon her death the principal was to be distributed to A or his issue. However, if A should die without issue, leaving W surviving, the principal was then to be distributed to W. No marital deduction may be taken with respect to the interest transferred to W, since it will terminate in the event of his issue will thereafter possess or enjoy the property.

Example (3). H purchased for $100,000 a life annuity for W. If the annuity payments made during the life of W should be less than $100,000, further payments were to be made to A. No marital deduction may be taken with respect to the interest transferred to W; since A may possess or enjoy a part of the property following the termination of W's interest. If, however, the contract provided for no continuation of payments, and provided for no refund upon the death of W, or provided that any refund was to go to the estate of W, then a marital deduction may be taken with respect to the gift.

Example (4). H transferred property to A for life with remainder to W provided W survives A, but if W predeceases A, the property is to pass to B and his heirs. No marital deduction may be taken with respect to the interest transferred to W.

Example (5). H transferred real property to A, reserving the right to the rentals of the property for a term of 20 years. H later transferred the right to the remaining rentals to W. No marital deduction may be taken with respect to the interest since it will terminate upon the expiration of the balance of the 20-year term and A will thereafter possess or enjoy the property.

Example (6). H transferred a patent to W and A as tenants in common. In this case, the interest of W will terminate upon the expiration of the term of the patent, but possession and enjoyment of the property by A must necessarily cease at the same time. Therefore, since A's possession or enjoyment cannot outlast the termination of W's interest, the provisions of section 2523(b) do not disallow the marital deduction with respect to the interest.

(c) Interest in property which the donor may possess or enjoy. (1) Section 2523(b) provides that no marital deduction is allowed with respect to the transfer to the donee spouse of a "terminable interest" in property, if—

(i) The donor retained in himself an interest in the same property, and

(ii) By reason of such retention, the donor (or his heirs or assigns) may possess or enjoy any part of the property after the termination or failure of the interest transferred to the donee spouse. However, as to a transfer to the donee spouse as sole joint tenant with the donor or as tenant by the entirety, see § 25.2523(d)–1.

(2) In general, the principles illustrated by the examples under paragraph (b) of this section are applicable in determining whether the marital deduction may be taken with respect to a property interest transferred to the donee spouse subject to the retention by the donor of an interest in the same property. The application of this paragraph may be further illustrated by the following example, in which it is assumed that the donor made no election under sections 2523(f)(2)(C) and (f)(4).

Example. The donor purchased three annuity contracts for the benefit of his wife and himself. The first contract provided for payments to the wife for life, with refund to the donor in case the aggregate payments made to the wife were less than the cost of the contract. The second contract provided for payments to the donor for life, and then to the wife for life if she survived the donor. The third contract provided for payments to the donor and his wife for their joint lives and then to the survivor of them for life. No marital deduction may be taken with respect to the gifts resulting from the purchases of the contracts since, in the case of each contract, the donor may possess or enjoy a part of the property after the termination or failure of the interest transferred to the wife.

(d) Interest in property over which the donor retained a power to appoint. (1) Section 2523(b) provides that no marital deduction is allowed with respect to the transfer to the donee spouse of a terminable interest in property if—

(i) The donor had, immediately after the transfer, a power to appoint an interest in the same property, and

(ii) The donor's power was exercisable (either alone or in conjunction with any person) in such manner that the appointee may possess or enjoy any part of the property after the termination or failure of the interest transferred to the donee spouse.

(2) For the purposes of section 2523(b), the donor is to be considered as having, immediately after the transfer to the donee spouse, such a power to appoint even though the power cannot be exercised until after the lapse of time, upon the occurrence of an event or contingency, or upon the failure of an event or contingency to occur. It is immaterial whether the power retained by the donor was a taxable power of appointment under section 2514.

(3) The principles illustrated by the examples under paragraph (b) of this section are generally applicable in determining whether the marital deduction may be taken with respect to a property interest transferred to the donee spouse subject to retention by the donor of a power to appoint an interest in the same property. The application of this paragraph may be further illustrated by the following example:

Example. The donor, having a power of appointment over certain property, appointed a life estate to his spouse. No marital deduction may be taken with respect to such transfer, since, if the retained power to appoint the remainder interest is exercised, the appointee thereunder may possess or enjoy the property after the termination or failure of the interest taken by the donee spouse.

[T.D. 6334, 23 FR 8904, Nov. 15, 1958; T.D. 8522, 59 FR 9659, March 1, 1994]

§ 25.2523(c)–1 Interest in unidentified assets.

(a) Section 2523(c) provides that if an interest passing to a donee spouse may be satisfied out of a group of assets (or their proceeds) which include a particular asset that would be a nondeductible interest if it passed from the donor to his spouse, the value of the interest passing to the spouse is reduced, for the purpose of the marital deduction, by the value of the particular asset.

(b) In order for this section to apply, two circumstances must coexist, as follows:

(1) The property interest transferred to the donee spouse must be payable out of a group of assets. An example of a property interest payable out of a group of assets is a right to a share of the corpus of a trust upon its termination.

(2) The group of assets out of which the property interest is payable must include one or more particular assets which, if transferred by the donor to the donee spouse, would not qualify for the marital deduction. Therefore, section 2523(c) is not applicable merely because a group of assets includes a terminable interest, but would only be applicable if the terminable interest were nondeductible under the provisions of § 25.2523(b)–1.

(c) If both of the circumstances set forth in paragraph (b) of this section exist, only a portion of the property interest passing to the spouse is a deductible interest. The portion qualifying as a deductible interest is an amount equal to the excess, if any, of the value of the property interest passing to the spouse over the aggregate value of the asset (or assets) that if transferred to the spouse would not qualify for the marital deduction. See paragraph (c) of § 25.2523(a)–1 to determine the percentage of the deductible interest allowable as a marital deduction. The application of this section may be illustrated by the following example:

Example. H was absolute owner of a rental property and on July 1, 1950, transferred it to A by gift, reserving the income for a period of 20 years. On July 1, 1955, he created a trust to last for a period of 10 years. H was to receive the income from the trust and at the termination of the trust the trustee is to turn over to H's wife, W, property having a value of $100,000. The trustee has absolute discretion in deciding which properties in the corpus he shall turn over to W in satisfaction of the gift to her. The trustee received two items of property from H. Item (1) consisted of shares of corporate stock. Item (2) consisted of the right to receive the income from the rental property during the unexpired portion of the 20-year term. Assume that at the termination of the trust on July 1, 1965, the value of the right to the rental income for the then unexpired term of 5 years (item (2)) will be $30,000. Since item (2) is a nondeductible interest and the trustee can turn it over to W in partial satisfaction of her gift, only $70,000 of the $100,000 receivable by her on July 1, 1965, will be considered as property with respect to which a marital deduction is allowable. The present value on July 1, 1955, of the right to receive $70,000 at the end of 10 years is $49,624.33 as determined under § 25.2512–5A(c). The value of the property qualifying for the marital deduction, therefore, is $49,624.33 and a marital deduction is allowed for one-half of that amount, or $24,812.17.

[T.D. 6334, 23 FR 8904, Nov. 15, 1958; 25 FR 14021, Dec. 31, 1960, as amended by T.D. 8522, 59 FR 9659,

March 1, 1994; T.D. 8540, 59 FR 30103, June 10, 1994]

§ 25.2523(d)–1 Joint interests.

Section 2523(d) provides that if a property interest is transferred to the donee spouse as sole joint tenant with the donor or as a tenant by the entirety, the interest of the donor in the property which exists solely by reason of the possibility that the donor may survive the donee spouse, or that there may occur a severance of the tenancy, is not for the purposes of section 2523(b), to be considered as an interest retained by the donor in himself. Under this provision, the fact that the donor may, as surviving tenant, possess or enjoy the property after the termination of the interest transferred to the donee spouse does not preclude the allowance of the marital deduction with respect to the latter interest. Thus, if the donor purchased real property in the name of the donor and the donor's spouse as tenants by the entirety or as joint tenants with rights of survivorship, a marital deduction is allowable with respect to the value of the interest of the donee spouse in the property (subject to the limitations set forth in § 25.2523(a)–1). See paragraph (c) of § 25.2523(b)–1, and section 2524.

[T.D. 6334, 23 FR 8904, Nov. 15, 1958, as amended by T.D. 7238, 37 FR 28734, Dec. 29, 1972; T.D. 8522, 59 FR 9659, March 1, 1994]

§ 25.2523(e)–1 Marital deduction; life estate with power of appointment in donee spouse.

(a) In general. Section 2523(e) provides that if an interest in property is transferred by a donor to his spouse (whether or not in trust) and the spouse is entitled for life to all the income from a specific portion of the entire interest, with a power in her to appoint the entire interest of all the income from interest or the specific portion, the interest transferred to her is a deductible interest, to the extent that it satisfies all five of the conditions set forth below (see paragraph (b) of this section if one or more of the conditions is satisfied as to only a portion of the interest):

(1) The donee spouse must be entitled for life to all of the income from the entire interest or a specific portion of the entire interest, or to a specific portion of all the income from the entire interest.

(2) The income payable to the donee spouse must be payable annually or at more frequent intervals.

(3) The donee spouse must have the power to appoint the entire interest of the specific portion to either herself or her estate.

(4) The power in the donee spouse must be exercisable by her alone and (whether exercisable by will or during life) must be exercisable in all events.

(5) The entire interest or the specific portion must not be subject to a power in any other person to appoint any part to any person other than the donee spouse.

(b) Specific portion; deductible amount. If either the right to income or the power of appointment given to the donee spouse pertains only to a specific portion of a property interest, the portion of the interest which qualifies as a deductible interest is limited to the extent that the rights in the donee spouse meet all of the five conditions described in paragraph (a) of this section. While the rights over the income and the power must coexist as to the same interest in property, it is not necessary that the rights over the income or the power as to such interest be in the same proportion. However, if the rights over income meeting the required conditions set forth in paragraph (a)(1) and (2) of this section extend over a smaller share of the property interest than the share with respect to which the power of appointment requirements set forth in paragraph (a)(3) through (5) of this section are satisfied, the deductible interest is limited to the smaller share. Conversely, if a power of appointment meeting all the requirements extends to a smaller portion of the property interest than the portion over which the income rights pertain, the deductible interest cannot exceed the value of the portion to which such power of appointment applies. Thus, if the donor gives to the donee spouse the right to receive annually all of the income from a particular property interest and a power of appointment meeting the specifications prescribed in paragraph (a)(3) through (5) of this section as to only one-half of the property interest, then only one-half of the property interest is treated as a deductible interest. Correspondingly, if the income interest of the spouse satisfying the requirements extends to only one-fourth of the property interest and a testamentary power of appointment satisfying the requirements extends to all of the property interest, then only one-fourth of the interest in the spouse qualifies as a deductible interest. Further, if the donee spouse has no right to income from a specific portion of a property interest but a testamentary power of appointment which meets the necessary conditions over the entire interest, then none of the interest qualifies for the deduction. In addition, if, from the time of the transfer, the donee spouse has a power of appointment meeting all of the required conditions over three-fourths of the entire property interest and the prescribed income rights over the entire interest, but with a power in another person to appoint one-half of the entire interest, the value of the interest in the donee spouse over only one-half of the property interest will qualify as a deductible interest.

(c) Meaning of specific portion. (1) *In general.* Except as provided in paragraphs (c)(2) and (c)(3) of this section, a partial interest in property is not treated as a specific portion of the entire interest. In addition, any specific portion of an entire interest in property is nondeductible to the extent the specific portion is subject to invasion for the benefit of any person other than the donee spouse, except in the case of a deduction allowable under section 2523(e), relating to the exercise of a general power of appointment by the donee spouse.

(2) *Fraction or percentage share.* Under section 2523(e), a partial interest in property is treated as a specific portion of the entire interest if the rights of the donee spouse in income, and the required rights as to the power described in § 25.2523(e)–1(a), constitute a fractional or percentage share of the entire property interest, so that the donee spouse's interest reflects its proportionate share of the increase or decrease in the value of the entire property interest to which the income rights and the power relate. Thus, if the spouse's right to income and the spouse's power extend to a specified fraction or percentage of the property, or its equivalent, the interest is in a specific portion of the property. In accordance with paragraph (b) of this section, if the spouse has the right to receive the income from a specific portion of the trust property (after applying paragraph (c)(3) of this section) but has a power of appointment over a different specific portion of the property (after applying paragraph (c)(3) of this section), the marital deduction is limited to the lesser specific portion.

(3) *Special rule in the case of gifts made on or before October 24, 1992.* In the case of gifts within the purview of the effective date rule contained in paragraph (c)(3)(iii) of this section:

(i) A specific sum payable annually, or at more frequent intervals, out of the property and its income that is not limited by the income of the property is treated as the right to receive the income from a specific portion of the property. The specific portion, for purposes of paragraph (c)(2) of this section, is the portion of the property that, assuming the interest rate generally applicable for the valuation of annuities at the time of the donor's gift, would produce income equal to such payments. However, a pecuniary amount payable annually to a donee spouse is not treated as a right to the income from a specific portion of trust property for purposes of this paragraph (c)(3)(i) if any person other than the donee spouse may receive, during the donee spouse's lifetime, any distribution of the property. To determine the applicable interest rate for valuing annuities, see sections 2512 and 7520 and the regulations under those sections.

(ii) The right to appoint a pecuniary amount out of a larger fund (or trust corpus) is considered the right to appoint a specific portion of such fund or trust in an amount equal to such pecuniary amount.

(iii) The rules contained in paragraphs (c)(3)(i) and (ii) of this section apply with respect to gifts made on or before October 24, 1992.

(4) *Local law.* A partial interest in property is treated as a specific portion of the entire interest if it is shown that the donee spouse has rights under local law that are identical to those the donee spouse would have acquired had the partial interest been expressed in terms satisfying the requirements of paragraph (c)(2) of this section (or paragraph (c)(3) of this section if applicable).

(5) *Examples.* The following examples illustrate the application of paragraphs (b) and (c) of this section, where D, the donor, transfers property to D's spouse, S:

Example (1). Spouse entitled to the lesser of an annuity or a fraction of trust income. Prior to October 24, 1992, D transferred in trust 500 identical shares of X Company stock, valued for gift tax purposes at $500,000. The trust provided that during the lifetime of D's spouse, S, the trustee is to pay annually to S the lesser of one-half of the trust income or $20,000. Any trust income not paid to S is to be accumulated in the trust and may not be distributed during S's lifetime. S has a testamentary general power of appointment over the entire trust principal. The applicable interest rate for valuing annuities as of the date of D's gift under section 7520 is 10 percent. For purposes of paragraphs (a) through (c) of this section, S is treated as receiving all of the income from the lesser of one-half of the stock ($250,000), or $200,000, the specific portion of the stock which, as determined in accordance with § 25.2523(e)–1(c)(3)(i) of this chapter, would produce annual income of $20,000 (20,000/.10). Accordingly, the marital deduction is limited to $200,000 (200,000/500,000 or 2/5 of the value of the trust.)

Example (2). Spouse possesses power and income interest over different specific portions of trust. The facts are the same as in Example 1 except that S's testamentary general power of appointment is exercisable over only 1/4 of the trust principal. Consequently, under section 2523(e), the marital deduction is allowable only for the value of 1/4 of the trust ($125,000); i.e., the lesser of the value of the portion with respect to which S is deemed to be entitled to all of the income (2/5 of the trust or $200,000), or the value of the portion with respect to which S possesses the requisite power of appointment (1/4 of the trust or $125,000).

Example (3). Power of appointment over shares of stock constitutes a power over a specific portion. D transferred 250 identical shares of Y company stock to a trust under the terms of which trust income is to be paid annually to S, during S's lifetime. S was given a testamentary general power of appointment over 100 shares of stock. The trust provides that if the trustee sells the Y company stock, S's general power of appointment is exercisable with respect to the sale proceeds or the property in which the proceeds are reinvested. Because the amount of property represented by a single share of stock would be altered if the corporation split its stock, issued stock dividends, made a distribution of capital, etc., a power to appoint 100 shares at the time of S's death is not necessarily a power to appoint the entire interest that the 100 shares represented on the date of D's gift. If it is shown that, under local law, S has a general power to appoint not only the 100 shares designated by D but also 100/250 of any distributions by the corporation that are included in trust principal, the requirements of paragraph (c)(2) of this section are satisfied and S is treated as having a general power to appoint 100/250 of the entire interest in the 250 shares. In that case, the marital deduction is limited to 40 percent of the trust principal. If local law does not give S that power, the 100 shares would not constitute a specific portion under § 25.2523(e)–1(c) (including § 25.2523(e)–1(c)(3)(ii)). The nature of the asset is such that a change in the capitalization of the corporation could cause an alteration in the original value represented by the shares at the time of the transfer and is thus not a specific portion of the trust.

(d) Definition of "entire interest". Since a marital deduction is allowed for each qualifying separate interest in property transferred by the donor to the donee spouse, for purposes of paragraphs (a) and (b) of this section, each property interest with respect to which the donee spouse received some rights is considered separately in determining whether her rights extend to the entire interest or to a specific portion of the entire interest. A property interest which consists of several identical units of property (such as a block of 250 shares of stock, whether the ownership is evidenced by one or several certificates) is considered one property interest, unless certain of the units are to be segregated and accorded different treatment, in which case each segregated group of items is considered a separate property interest. The bequest of a specified sum of money constitutes the bequest of a separate property interest if immediately following the transfer and thenceforth it, and the investments made with it, must be so segregated or accounted for as to permit its identification as a separate item of property. The application of this paragraph may be illustrated by the following examples:

Example (1). The donor transferred to a trustee three adjoining farms, Blackacre, Whiteacre, and Greenacre. The trust instrument provided that during the lifetime of the donee spouse the trustee should pay her all of the income from the trust. Upon her death, all of Blackacre, a one-half interest in Whiteacre, and a one-third interest in Greenacre were to be distributed to the person or persons appointed by her in her will. The donee spouse is considered as being entitled to all of the income from the entire interest in Blackacre, all of the income from the entire interest in Whiteacre, and all of the income from the entire interest in Greenacre. She also is considered as having a power of appointment over the entire interest in Blackacre, over one-half of the entire interest in Whiteacre, and over one-third of the entire interest in Greenacre.

Example (2). The donor transferred $250,000 to C, as trustee. C is to invest the money and pay all of the income from the investments to W, the donor's spouse, annually. W was given a general power, exercisable by will, to appoint one-half of the corpus of the trust. Here, immediately following establishment of the trust, the $250,000 will be sufficiently segregated to permit its identification as a separate item, and the $250,000 will constitute an entire property interest. Therefore, W has a right to income and a power of appointment such that one-half of the entire interest is a deductible interest.

Example (3). The donor transferred 100 shares of Z Corporation stock to D, as trustee. W, the donor's spouse, is to receive all of the income of the trust annually and is given a general power, exercisable by will, to appoint out of the trust corpus the sum of $25,000. In this case the $25,000 is not, immediately following establishment of the trust, sufficiently segregated to permit its identification as a separate item of property in which the donee spouse has the entire interest. Therefore, the $25,000 does not constitute the entire interest in a property for the purpose of paragraphs (a) and (b) of this section.

(e) Application of local law. In determining whether or not the conditions set forth in paragraph (a)(1) through (5) of this section are satisfied by the instrument of transfer, regard is to be had to the applicable provisions of the law of the jurisdiction under which the interest passes and, if the transfer is in trust, the applicable provisions of the law governing the administration of the trust. For example, silence of a trust instrument as to the frequency of payment will not be regarded as a failure to satisfy the condition set forth in paragraph (a)(2) of this section that income must be payable to the donee spouse annually or more frequently unless the applicable law permits payment to be made less frequently than annually. The principles outlined in this paragraph and paragraphs (f) and (g) of this section which are applied in determining whether transfers in trust meet such conditions are equally applicable in ascertaining whether, in the case of interests not in trust, the donee spouse has the equivalent in rights over income and over the property.

(f) Right to income. (1) If an interest is transferred in trust, the donee spouse is "entitled for life to all of the income from the entire interest or a specific portion of the entire interest," for the purpose of the condition set forth in paragraph (a)(1) of this section, if the effect of the trust is to give her substantially that degree of beneficial enjoyment of the trust property during her life which the principles of the law of trust accord to a person who is unqualifiedly designated as the life beneficiary of a trust. Such degree of enjoyment is given only if it was the donor's intention, as manifested by the terms of the trust instrument and the surrounding circumstances, that the trust should produce for the donee spouse during her life such an income, or that the spouse should have such use of the trust property as is consistent with the value of the trust corpus and with its preservation. The designation of the spouse as sole income beneficiary for life of the entire interest or a specific portion of the entire interest will be sufficient to qualify the trust unless the terms of the trust and the surrounding circumstances considered as a whole evidence an intention to deprive the spouse of the requisite degree of enjoyment. In determining whether a trust evidences that intention, the treatment required or permitted with respect to individual items must be considered in relation to the entire system provided for the administration of the trust. In addition, the spouse's interest shall meet the condition set forth in paragraph (a)(1) of this section if the spouse is entitled to income as defined or determined by applicable local law that provides for a reasonable apportionment between the income and remainder beneficiaries of the total return of the trust and that meets the requirements of § 1.643(b)–1 of this chapter.

(2) If the over-all effect of a trust is to give to the donee spouse such enforceable rights as will preserve to her the requisite degree of enjoyment, it is immaterial whether that result is effected by rules specifically stated in the trust instrument, or, in their absence, by the rules for the management of the trust property and the allocation of receipts and expenditures supplied by the State law. For example, a provision in the trust instrument for amortization of bond premium by appropriate periodic charges to interest will not disqualify the interest transferred in trust even though there is no State law specifically authorizing amortization or there is a State law denying amortization which is applicable only in the absence of such a provision in the trust instrument.

(3) In the case of a trust, the rules to be applied by the trustee in allocation of receipts and expenses between income and corpus must be considered in relation to the nature and expected productivity of the assets transferred in trust, the nature and frequency

of occurrence of the expected receipts, and any provisions as to change in the form of investments. If it is evident from the nature of the trust assets and the rules provided for management of the trust that the allocation to income of such receipts as rents, ordinary cash dividends and interest will give to the spouse the substantial enjoyment during life required by the statute, provisions that such receipts as stock dividends and proceeds from the conversion of trust assets shall be treated as corpus will not disqualify the interest transferred in trust. Similarly, provision for a depletion charge against income in the case of trust assets which are subject to depletion will not disqualify the interest transferred in trust, unless the effect is to deprive the spouse of the requisite beneficial enjoyment. The same principle is applicable in the case of depreciation, trustees' commissions, and other charges.

(4) Provisions granting administrative powers to the trustees will not have the effect of disqualifying an interest transferred in trust unless the grant of powers evidences the intention to deprive the donee spouse of the beneficial enjoyment required by the statute. Such an intention will not be considered to exist if the entire terms of the instrument are such that the local courts will impose reasonable limitations upon the exercise of the powers. Among the powers which if subject to reasonable limitations will not disqualify the interest transferred in trust are the power to determine the allocation or apportionment of receipts and disbursements between income and corpus, the power to apply the income or corpus for the benefit of the spouse, and the power to retain the assets transferred to the trust. For example, a power to retain trust assets which consist substantially of unproductive property will not disqualify the interest if the applicable rules for the administration of the trust require, or permit the spouse to require, that the trustee either make the property productive or convert it within a reasonable time. Nor will such a power disqualify the interest if the applicable rules for administration of the trust require the trustee to use the degree of judgment and care in the exercise of the power which a prudent man would use if he were owner of the trust assets. Further, a power to retain a residence for the spouse or other property for the personal use of the spouse will not disqualify the interest transferred in trust.

(5) An interest transferred in trust will not satisfy the condition set forth in paragraph (a)(1) of this section that the donee spouse be entitled to all the income if the primary purpose of the trust is to safeguard property without providing the spouse with the required beneficial enjoyment. Such trusts include not only trusts which expressly provide for the accumulation of the income but also trusts which indirectly accomplish a similar purpose. For example, assume that the corpus of a trust consists substantially of property which is not likely to be income producing during the life of the donee spouse and that the spouse cannot compel the trustee to convert or otherwise deal with the property as described in subparagraph (4) of this paragraph. An interest transferred to such a trust will not qualify unless the applicable rules for the administration require, or permit the spouse to require, that the trustee provide the required beneficial enjoyment, such as by payments to the spouse out of other assets of the trust.

(6) If a trust may be terminated during the life of the donee spouse, under her exercise of a power of appointment or by distribution of the corpus to her, the interest transferred in trust satisfies the condition set forth in paragraph (a)(1) of this section (that the spouse be entitled to all the income) if she (i) is entitled to the income until the trust terminates, or (ii) has the right, exercisable in all events, to have the corpus distributed to her at any time during her life.

(7) An interest transferred in trust fails to satisfy the condition set forth in paragraph (a)(1) of this section, that the spouse be entitled to all the income, to the extent that the income is required to be accumulated in whole or in part or may be accumulated in the discretion of any person other than the donee spouse; to the extent that the consent of any person other than the donee spouse is required as a condition precedent to distribution of the income; or to the extent that any person other than the donee spouse has the power to alter the terms of the trust so as to deprive her of her right to the income. An interest transferred in trust will not fail to satisfy the condition that the spouse be entitled to all the income merely because its terms provide that the right of the donee spouse to the income shall not be subject to assignment, alienation, pledge, attachment or claims of creditors.

(8) In the case of an interest transferred in trust, the terms "entitled for life" and "payable annually or at more frequent intervals", as used in the conditions set forth in paragraph (a)(1) and (2) of this section, require that under the terms of the trust the income referred to

must be currently (at least annually; see paragraph (e) of this section) distributable to the spouse or that she must have such command over the income that it is virtually hers. Thus, the conditions in paragraph (a)(1) and (2) of this section are satisfied in this respect if, under the terms of the trust instrument, the donee spouse has the right exercisable annually (or more frequently) to require distribution to herself of the trust income, and otherwise the trust income is to be accumulated and added to corpus. Similarly, as respects the income for the period between the last distribution date and the date of the spouse's death, it is sufficient if that income is subject to the spouse's power to appoint. Thus, if the trust instrument provides that income accrued or undistributed on the date of the spouse's death is to be disposed of as if it had been received after her death, and if the spouse has a power of appointment over the trust corpus, the power necessarily extends to the undistributed income.

(g) Power of appointment in donee spouse. (1) The conditions set forth in paragraph (a)(3) and (4) of this section, that is, that the donee spouse must have a power of appointment exercisable in favor of herself or her estate and exercisable alone and in all events, are not met unless the power of the donee spouse to appoint the entire interest or a specific portion of it falls within one of the following categories:

(i) A power so to appoint fully exercisable in her own favor at any time during her life (as, for example, an unlimited power to invade); or

(ii) A power so to appoint exercisable in favor of her estate. Such a power, if exercisable during life, must be fully exercisable at any time during life, or if exercisable by will, must be fully exercisable irrespective of the time of her death; or

(iii) A combination of the powers described under subdivisions (i) and (ii) of this subparagraph. For example, the donee spouse may, until she attains the age of 50 years, have a power to appoint to herself and thereafter have a power to appoint to her estate. However, the condition that the spouse's power must be exercisable in all events is not satisfied unless irrespective of when the donee spouse may die the entire interest or a specific portion of it will at the time of her death be subject to one power or the other.

(2) The power of the donee spouse must be a power to appoint the entire interest or a specific portion of it as unqualified owner (and free of the trust if a trust is involved, or free of the joint tenancy if a joint tenancy is involved) or to appoint the entire interest or a specific portion of it as a part of her estate (and free of the trust if a trust is involved), that is, in effect, to dispose of it to whomsoever she pleases. Thus, if the donor transferred property to a son and the donee spouse as joint tenants with right of survivorship and under local law the donee spouse has a power of severance exercisable without consent of the other joint tenant, and by exercising this power could acquire a one-half interest in the property as a tenant in common, her power of severance will satisfy the condition set forth in paragraph (a)(3) of this section that she have a power of appointment in favor of herself or her estate. However, if the donee spouse entered into a binding agreement with the donor to exercise the power only in favor of their issue, that condition is not met. An interest transferred in trust will not be regarded as failing to satisfy the condition merely because takers in default of the donee spouse's exercise of the power are designated by the donor. The donor may provide that, in default of exercise of the power, the trust shall continue for an additional period.

(3) A power is not considered to be a power exercisable by a donee spouse alone and in all events as required by paragraph (a)(4) of this section if the exercise of the power in the donee spouse to appoint the entire interest or a specific portion of it to herself or to her estate requires the joinder or consent of any other person. The power is not "exercisable in all events", if it can be terminated during the life of the donee spouse by any event other than her complete exercise or release of it. Further, a power is not "exercisable in all events" if it may be exercised for a limited purpose only. For example, a power which is not exercisable in the event of the spouse's remarriage is not exercisable in all events. Likewise, if there are any restrictions, either by the terms of the instrument or under applicable local law, on the exercise of a power to consume property (whether or not held in trust) for the benefit of the spouse, the power is not exercisable in all events. Thus, if a power of invasion is exercisable only for the spouse's support, or only for her limited use, the power is not exercisable in all events. In order for a power of invasion to be exercisable in all events, the donee spouse must have the unrestricted power exercisable at any time during her life to use all or any part

of the property subject to the power, and to dispose of it in any manner, including the power to dispose of it by gift (whether or not she has power to dispose of it by will).

(4) If the power is in existence at all times following the transfer of the interest, limitations of a formal nature will not disqualify the interest. Examples of formal limitations on a power exercisable during life are requirements that an exercise must be in a particular form, that it must be filed with a trustee during the spouse's life, that reasonable notice must be given, or that reasonable intervals must elapse between successive partial exercises. Examples of formal limitations on a power exercisable by will are that it must be exercised by a will executed by the donee spouse after the making of the gift or that exercise must be by specific reference to the power.

(5) If the donee spouse has the requisite power to appoint to herself or her estate, it is immaterial that she also has one or more lesser powers. Thus, if she has a testamentary power to appoint to her estate, she may also have a limited power of withdrawal or of appointment during her life. Similarly, if she has an unlimited power of withdrawal, she may have a limited testamentary power.

(h) Existence of a power in another. Paragraph (a)(5) of this section provides that a transfer described in paragraph (a) is nondeductible to the extent that the donor created a power in the trustee or in any other person to appoint a part of the interest to any person other than the donee spouse. However, only powers in other persons which are in opposition to that of the donee spouse will cause a portion of the interest to fail to satisfy the condition set forth in paragraph (a)(5) of this section. Thus, a power in a trustee to distribute corpus to or for the benefit of the donee spouse will not disqualify the trust. Similarly, a power to distribute corpus to the spouse for the support of minor children will not disqualify the trust if she is legally obligated to support such children. The application of this paragraph may be illustrated by the following examples:

Example (1). Assume that a donor created a trust, designating his spouse as income beneficiary for life with an unrestricted power in the spouse to appoint the corpus during her life. The donor further provided that in the event the donee spouse should die without having exercised the power, the trust should continue for the life of his son with a power in the son to appoint the corpus. Since the power in the son could become exercisable only after the death of the donee spouse, the interest is not regarded as failing to satisfy the condition set forth in paragraph (a)(5) of this section.

Example (2). Assume that the donor created a trust, designating his spouse as income beneficiary for life and as donee of a power to appoint by will the entire corpus. The donor further provided that the trustee could distribute 30 percent of the corpus to the donor's son when he reached the age of 35 years. Since the trustee has a power to appoint 30 percent of the entire interest for the benefit of a person other than the donee spouse, only 70 percent of the interest placed in trust satisfied the condition set forth in paragraph (a)(5) of this section. If, in this case, the donee spouse had a power, exercisable by her will, to appoint only one-half of the corpus as it was constituted at the time of her death, it should be noted that only 35 percent of the interest placed in the trust would satisfy the condition set forth in paragraph (a)(3) of this section.

[T.D. 6334, 23 FR 8904, Nov. 15, 1958, as amended by T.D. 6542, 26 FR 552, Jan. 20, 1961, as amended by T.D. 8522, 59 FR 9659, March 1, 1994; T.D. 9102, 69 FR 21, Jan. 2, 2004]

§ 25.2523(f)–1 Election with respect to life estate transferred to donee spouse.

(a) In general. (1) With respect to gifts made after December 31, 1981, subject to section 2523(i), a marital deduction is allowed under section 2523(a) for transfers of qualified terminable interest property. Qualified terminable interest property is terminable interest property described in section 2523(b)(1) that satisfies the requirements of section 2523(f)(2) and this section. Terminable interests that are described in section 2523(b)(2) cannot qualify as qualified terminable interest property. Thus, if the donor retains a power described in section 2523(b)(2) to appoint an interest in qualified terminable interest property, no deduction is allowable under section 2523(a) for the property.

(2) All of the property for which a deduction is allowed under this paragraph (a) is treated as passing to the donee spouse (for purposes of § 25.2523(a)–1), and no part of the property is treated as retained by the donor or as passing to any person other than the donee spouse (for purposes of § 25.2523(b)–1(b)).

(b) Qualified terminable interest property. (1) *Definition.* Section 2523(f)(2) provides the definition of qualified terminable interest property.

(2) *Meaning of property.* For purposes of section 2523(f)(2), the term property generally means an entire interest in property (within the meaning of § 25.2523(e)–1(d)) or a specific portion of the entire interest (within the meaning of § 25.2523(e)–1(c)).

(3) *Property for which the election may be made*—(i) *In general.* The election may relate to all or any part of property that meets the requirements of section 2523(f)(2)(A) and (B), provided that any partial election must be made with respect to a fractional or percentage share of the property so that the elective portion reflects its proportionate share of the increase or decrease in the entire property for purposes of applying sections 2044 or 2519. Thus, if the interest of the donee spouse in a trust (or other property in which the spouse has a qualifying income interest) meets the requirements of this section, the election may be made under section 2523(f)(2)(C) with respect to a part of the trust (or other property) only if the election relates to a defined fraction or percentage of the entire trust (or other property) or specific portion thereof within the meaning of § 25.2523(e)–1(c). The fraction or percentage may be defined by formula.

(ii) *Division of trusts.* If the interest of the donee spouse in a trust meets the requirements of this section, the trust may be divided into separate trusts to reflect a partial election that has been made, if authorized under the terms of the governing instrument or otherwise permissible under local law. A trust may be divided only if the fiduciary is required, either by applicable local law or by the express or implied provisions of the governing instrument, to divide the trust according to the fair market value of the assets of the trust at the time of the division. The division of the trusts must be done on a fractional or percentage basis to reflect the partial election. However, the separate trusts do not have to be funded with a pro rata portion of each asset held by the undivided trust.

(4) *Manner and time of making election.* (i) An election under section 2523(f)(2)(C) (other than a deemed election with respect to a joint and survivor annuity as described in section 2523(f)(6)), is made on a gift tax return for the calendar year in which the interest is transferred. The return must be filed within the time prescribed by section 6075(b) (determined without regard to section 6019(a)(2)), including any extensions authorized under section 6075(b)(2) (relating to an automatic extension of time for filing a gift tax return where the donor is granted an extension of time to file the income tax return).

(ii) If the election is made on a return for the calendar year that includes the date of death of the donor, the return (as prescribed by section 6075(b)(3)) must be filed no later than the time (including extensions) for filing the estate tax return. The election, once made, is irrevocable.

(c) Qualifying income interest for life. (1) *In general.* For purposes of this section, the term qualifying income interest for life is defined as provided in section 2056(b)(7)(B)(ii) and § 20.2056(b)–7(d)(1).

(i) *Entitled for life to all the income.* The principles outlined in § 25.2523(e)–1(f) (relating to whether the spouse is entitled for life to all of the income from the entire interest or a specific portion of the entire interest) apply in determining whether the donee spouse is entitled for life to all the income from the property, regardless of whether the interest passing to the donee spouse is in trust. An income interest granted for a term of years, or a life estate subject to termination upon the occurrence of a specified event (e.g., divorce) is not a qualifying income interest for life.

(ii) *Income between last distribution date and date of spouse's death.* An income interest does not fail to constitute a qualifying income interest for life solely because income for the period between the last distribution date and the date of the donee spouse's death is not required to be distributed to the estate of the donee spouse. See § 20.2044–1 of this chapter relating to the inclusion of such undistributed income in the gross estate of the donee spouse.

(iii) *Pooled income funds.* An income interest in a pooled income fund described in section 642(c)(5) constitutes a qualifying income interest for life for purposes of this section.

(iv) *Distribution of principal for the benefit of the donee spouse.* An income interest does not fail to constitute a qualifying income interest for life solely because the trustee has a power to distribute principal to or for the benefit of the donee spouse. The fact that property distributed to a donee spouse may be transferred by the spouse to another person does not result in a failure to satisfy the requirement of section 2056(b)(7)(B)(ii)(II). However, if the governing instrument requires the donee spouse to transfer the distributed property to another person without full and adequate consideration in money or money's worth, the requirement of section 2056(b)(7)(B)(ii)(II) is not satisfied.

(2) *Immediate right to income.* In order to constitute a qualifying income interest for life, the donee spouse must be granted the immediate right to receive the income from the property. Thus, an income interest does not constitute a qualifying income interest for life if the donee spouse receives the right to trust income commencing at some time in the future, e.g., on the termination of a preceding life income interest of the donor spouse.

(3) *Annuities payable from trusts in the case of gifts made on or before October 24, 1992.* (i) In the case of gifts made on or before October 24, 1992, a donee spouse's lifetime annuity interest payable from a trust or other group of assets passing from the donor is treated as a qualifying income interest for life for purposes of section 2523(f)(2)(B). The deductible interest, for purposes of § 25.2523(a)–1(b), is the specific portion of the property that, assuming the applicable interest rate for valuing annuities at the time the annuity interest is transferred, would produce income equal to the minimum amount payable annually to the donee spouse. If, based on the applicable interest rate, the entire property from which the annuity may be satisfied is insufficient to produce income equal to the minimum annual payment, the value of the deductible interest is the entire value of the property. The value of the deductible interest may not exceed the value of the property from which the annuity is payable. If the annual payment may increase, the increased amount is not taken into account in valuing the deductible interest.

(ii) An annuity interest is not treated as a qualifying income interest for life for purposes of section 2523(f)(2)(B) if any person other than the donee spouse may receive during the donee spouse's lifetime, any distribution of the property or its income from which the annuity is payable.

(iii) To determine the applicable interest rate for valuing annuities, see sections 2512 and 7520 and the regulations under those sections.

(4) *Joint and survivor annuities.* [Reserved]

(d) Treatment of interest retained by the donor spouse. (1) *In general.* Under section 2523(f)(5)(A), if a donor spouse retains an interest in qualified terminable interest property, any subsequent transfer by the donor spouse of the retained interest in the property is not treated as a transfer for gift tax purposes. Further, the retention of the interest until the donor spouse's death does not cause the property subject to the retained interest to be includable in the gross estate of the donor spouse.

(2) *Exception.* Under section 2523(f)(5)(B), the rule contained in paragraph (d)(1) of this section does not apply to any property after the donee spouse is treated as having transferred the property under section 2519, or after the property is includable in the gross estate of the donee spouse under section 2044.

(e) Application of local law. The provisions of local law are taken into account in determining whether or not the conditions of section 2523(f)(2)(A) and (B), and the conditions of paragraph (c) of this section, are satisfied. For example, silence of a trust instrument on the frequency of payment is not regarded as a failure to satisfy the requirement that the income must be payable to the donee spouse annually or more frequently unless applicable local law permits payments less frequently to the donee spouse.

(f) Examples. The following examples illustrate the application of this section, where D, the donor, transfers property to D's spouse, S. Unless stated otherwise, it is assumed that S is not the trustee of any trust established for S's benefit:

Example (1). Life estate in residence. D transfers by gift a personal residence valued at $250,000 on the date of the gift to S and D's children, giving S the exclusive and unrestricted right to use the property (including the right to continue to occupy the property as a personal residence or rent the property and receive the income for her lifetime). After S's death, the property is to pass to D's children. Under applicable local law, S's consent is required for any sale of the property. If D elects to treat all of the transferred property as qualified terminable interest property, the deductible interest is $250,000, the value of the property for gift tax purposes.

Example (2). Power to make property productive. D transfers assets having a fair market value of $500,000 to a trust pursuant to which S is given the right exercisable annually to require distribution of all the trust income to S. No trust property may be distributed during S's lifetime to any person other than S. The assets used to fund the trust include both income producing assets and nonproductive assets. Applicable local law permits S to require that the trustee either make the trust property productive or sell the property and reinvest the proceeds in productive property within a reasonable time after the transfer. If D elects to treat the entire trust as qualified terminable interest property, the deductible interest is $500,000. If D elects to treat only 20 percent of the trust as qualified terminable interest property, the deductible interest is $100,000; i.e., 20 percent of $500,000.

Example (3). Power of distribution over fraction of trust income. The facts are the same as in Example 2 except that S is given the power exercisable annually to require distribution to S of only 50 percent of the trust income for life. The remaining trust income may be accumulated or distributed among D's children and S in the trustee's discretion. The maximum amount that D may elect to treat as qualified terminable interest property is $250,000; i.e., the value of the trust for gift tax purposes ($500,000) multiplied by the percentage of the trust in which S has a qualifying income interest for life (50 percent). If D elects to treat only 20 percent of the portion of the trust in which S has a qualifying income interest as qualified terminable interest property, the deductible interest is $50,000; i.e., 20 percent of $250,000.

Example (4). Power to distribute trust corpus to other beneficiaries. D transfers $500,000 to a trust providing that all the trust income is to be paid to D's spouse, S, during S's lifetime. The trustee is given the power to use annually $5,000 from the trust for the maintenance and support of S's minor child, C. Any such distribution does not necessarily relieve S of S's obligation to support and maintain C. S does not have a qualifying income interest for life in any portion of the trust because the gift fails to satisfy the condition in sections 2523(f)(3) and 2056(b)(7)(B)(ii)(II) that no person have a power, other than a power the exercise of which takes effect only at or after S's death, to appoint any part of the property to any person other than S. The trust would also be nondeductible under section 2523(f) if S, rather than the trustee, were given the power to appoint a portion of the principal to C. However, in the latter case, if S made a qualified disclaimer (within the meaning of section 2518) of the power to appoint to C, the trust could qualify for the marital deduction pursuant to section 2523(f), assuming that the power was personal to S and S's disclaimer terminates the power. Similarly, if C made a qualified disclaimer of the right to receive distributions from the trust, the trust would qualify under section 2523(f) assuming that C's disclaimer effectively negates the trustee's power under local law.

Example (5). Spouse's interest terminable on divorce. The facts are the same as in Example 3 except that if S and D divorce, S's interest in the trust will pass to C. S's income interest is not a qualifying income interest for life because it is terminable upon S's divorce. Therefore, no portion of the trust is deductible under section 2523(f).

Example (6). Spouse's interest in trust in the form of an annuity. Prior to October 24, 1992, D established a trust funded with income producing property valued for gift tax purposes at $800,000. The trustee is required by the trust instrument to pay $40,000 a year to S for life. Any income in excess of the annuity amount is to be accumulated in the trust and may not be distributed during S's lifetime. S's lifetime annuity interest is treated as a qualifying income interest for life. If D elects to treat the entire portion of the trust in which S has a qualifying income interest as qualified terminable interest property, the value of the deductible interest is $400,000, because that amount would yield an income to S of $40,000 a year (assuming a 10 percent interest rate applies in valuing annuities at the time of the transfer).

Example (7). Value of spouse's annuity exceeds value of trust corpus. The facts are the same as in Example 6, except that the trustee is required to pay S $100,000 a year for S's life. If D elects to treat the entire portion of the trust in which S has a qualifying income interest for life as qualified terminable interest property, the value of the deductible interest is $800,000, which is the lesser of the entire value of the property ($800,000) or the amount of property that (assuming a 10 percent interest rate) would yield an income to S of $100,000 a year ($1,000,000).

Example (8). Transfer to pooled income fund. D transfers $200,000 on June 1, 1994, to a pooled income fund (described in section 642(c)(5)) designating S as the only life income beneficiary. If D elects to treat the entire $200,000 as qualified terminable interest property, the deductible interest is $200,000.

Example (9). Retention by donor spouse of income interest in property. On October 1, 1994, D transfers property to an irrevocable trust under the terms of which trust income is to be paid to D for life, then to S for life and, on S's death, the trust corpus is to be paid to D's children. Because S does not possess an immediate right to receive trust income, S's interest does not qualify as a qualifying income interest for life under section 2523(f)(2). Further, under section 2702(a)(2) and § 25.2702–2(b), D is treated for gift tax purposes as making a gift with a value equal to the entire value of the property. If D dies in 1996 survived by S, the trust corpus will be includible in D's gross estate under section 2036. However, in computing D's estate tax liability, D's adjusted taxable gifts under section 2001(b)(1)(B) are adjusted to reflect the inclusion of the gifted property in D's gross estate. In addition, if S survives D, the trust property is eligible for treatment as qualified terminable interest property under section 2056(b)(7) in D's estate.

Example (10). Retention by donor spouse of income interest in property. On October 1, 1994, D transfers property to an irrevocable trust under the terms of which trust income is to be paid to S for life, then to D for life and, on D's death, the trust corpus is to be paid to D's children. D elects under section 2523(f) to treat the property as qualified terminable interest property. D dies in 1996, survived by S. S subsequently dies in 1998. Under § 2523(f)–1(d)(1), because D elected to treat the transfer as qualified terminable interest property, no part of the trust corpus is includible in D's gross estate because of D's retained interest in the trust corpus. On S's subsequent death in 1998, the trust corpus is includible in S's gross estate under section 2044.

Example (11). Retention by donor spouse of income interest in property. The facts are the same as in Example 10, except that S dies in 1996 survived by D, who subsequently dies in 1998. Because D made an election under section 2523(f) with respect to the trust, on S's death the trust corpus is includible in S's gross estate under section 2044. Accordingly, under section 2044(c), S is treated as the transferor of the property for estate and gift tax purposes. Upon D's subsequent death in 1998, because the property was subject to inclusion in S's gross estate under section 2044, the exclusion rule in § 25.2523(f)–1(d)(1) does not apply under § 25.2523(f)–1(d)(2). However, because S is treated as the transferor of the property, the property is not subject to inclusion in D's gross estate under section 2036 or section 2038. If the executor of S's estate made a section 2056(b)(7) election with respect to the trust, the trust is includible in D's gross estate under section 2044 upon D's later death.

[T.D. 8522, 59 FR 9660, March 1, 1994]

§ 25.2523(f)–1A Special rule applicable to community property transferred prior to January 1, 1982. [*Omitted. Ed.*]

[T.D. 6334, 23 FR 8904, Nov. 15, 1958; 25 FR 14021, Dec. 31, 1960. Redesignated and amended by T.D. 8522, 59 FR 9660, March 1, 1994]

§ 25.2523(g)–1 Special rule for charitable remainder trusts.

(a) In general. (1) With respect to gifts made after December 31, 1981, subject to section 2523(i), if the donor's spouse is the only noncharitable beneficiary (other than the donor) of a charitable remainder annuity trust or charitable remainder unitrust described in section 664 (qualified charitable remainder trust), section 2523(b) does not apply to the interest in the trust transferred to the donee spouse. Thus, the value of the annuity or unitrust interest passing to the spouse qualifies for a marital deduction under section 2523(g) and the value of the remainder interest qualifies for a charitable deduction under section 2522.

(2) A marital deduction for the value of the donee spouse's annuity or unitrust interest in a qualified charitable remainder trust to which section 2523(g) applies is allowable only under section 2523(g). Therefore, if an interest in property qualifies for a marital deduction under section 2523(g), no election may be made with respect to the property under section 2523(f).

(3) The donee spouse's interest need not be an interest for life to qualify for a marital deduction under section 2523(g). However, for purposes of section 664, an annuity or unitrust interest payable to the spouse for a term of years cannot be payable for a term that exceeds 20 years or the trust does not qualify under section 2523(g).

(4) A deduction is allowed under section 2523(g) even if the transfer to the donee spouse is conditioned on the donee spouse's payment of state death taxes, if any, attributable to the qualified charitable remainder trust.

(5) For purposes of this section, the term noncharitable beneficiary means any beneficiary of the qualified charitable remainder trust other than an organization described in section 170(c).

(b) Charitable remainder trusts where the donee spouse and the donor are not the only noncharitable beneficiaries. In the case of a charitable remainder trust where the donor and the donor's spouse are not the only noncharitable beneficiaries (for example, where the noncharitable interest is payable to the donor's spouse for life and then to another individual (other than the donor) for life), the qualification of the interest as qualified terminable interest property is determined solely under section 2523(f) and not under section 2523(g). Accordingly, if the transfer to the trust is made prior to October 24, 1992, the spousal annuity or unitrust interest may qualify under § 25.2523(f)–(1)(c)(3) as a qualifying income interest for life.

[T.D. 8522, 59 FR 9663, March 1, 1994]

§ 25.2523(h)–1 Denial of double deduction.

The value of an interest in property may not be deducted for Federal gift tax purposes more than once with respect to the same donor. For example, assume that D, a donor, transferred a life estate in a farm to D's spouse, S, with a remainder to charity and that D elects to treat the property as qualified terminable interest property. The entire value of the property is deductible under section 2523(f). No part of the value of the property qualifies for a charitable deduction under section 2522 for gift tax purposes.

[T.D. 8522, 59 FR 9663, March 1, 1994]

§ 25.2523(h)–2 Effective dates.

Except as specifically provided, in §§ 25.2523(e)–1(c)(3), 25.2523(f)–1(c)(3), and 25.2523(g)–1(b), the provisions of §§ 25.2523(e)–1(c), 25.2523(f)–1, 25.2523(g)–1, and 25.2523(h)–1 are effective with respect to gifts made after March 1, 1994. With respect to gifts made on or before such date, donors may rely on any reasonable interpretation of the statutory provisions. For these purposes, the provisions of §§ 25.2523(e)–1(c), 25.2523(f)–1, 25.2523(g)–1, and 25.2523(h)–1, (as well as project LR–211–76, 1984–1 C.B., page 598, see § 601.601(d)(2)(ii)(b) of this chapter), are considered a reasonable interpretation of the statutory provisions. In addition, the rule in the last sentence of § 25.2523(e)–1(f)(1) regarding the determination of income under applicable local law applies to trusts for taxable years ending after January 2, 2004.

[T.D. 8522, 59 FR 9663, March 1, 1994, as amended by T.D. 9102, 69 FR 21, Jan. 2, 2004]

§ 25.2523(i)–1 Disallowance of marital deduction when spouse is not a United States citizen.

(a) In general. Subject to § 20.2056A–1(c) of this chapter, section 2523(i)(1) disallows the marital deduction if the spouse of the donor is not a citizen of the United States at the time of the gift. If the spouse of the donor is a citizen of the United States at the time of the gift, the gift tax marital deduction under section 2523(a) is allowed regardless of whether the donor is a citizen or resident of the United States at the time of the gift, subject to the otherwise applicable rules of section 2523.

(b) Exception for certain joint and survivor annuities. Paragraph (a) does not apply to disallow the marital deduction with respect to any transfer resulting in the acquisition of rights by a noncitizen spouse under a joint and survivor annuity described in section 2523(f)(6).

(c) Increased annual exclusion. (1) *In general.* In the case of gifts made from a donor to the donor's spouse for which a marital deduction is not allowable under this section, if the gift otherwise qualifies for the gift tax annual exclusion under section 2503(b), the amount of the annual exclusion under section 2503(b) is $100,000 in lieu of $10,000. However, in the case of gifts made after June 29, 1989, in order for the increased annual exclusion to apply, the gift in excess of the otherwise applicable annual exclusion under section 2503(b) must be in a form that qualifies for the marital deduction but for the disallowance provision of section 2523(i)(1). See paragraph (d), Example 4, of this section.

(2) *Status of donor.* The $100,000 annual exclusion for gifts to a noncitizen spouse is available regardless of the status of the donor. Accordingly, it is immaterial whether the donor is a citizen, resident or a nonresident not a citizen of the United States, as long as the spouse of the donor is not a citizen of the United States at the time of the gift and the conditions for allowance

of the increased annual exclusion have been satisfied. See § 25.2503–2(f).

(d) Examples. The principles outlined in this section are illustrated in the following examples. Assume in each of the examples that the donee, S, is D's spouse and is not a United States citizen at the time of the gift.

Example (1). Outright transfer of present interest. In 1995, D, a United States citizen, transfers to S, outright, 100 shares of X corporation stock valued for federal gift tax purposes at $130,000. The transfer is a gift of a present interest in property under section 2503(b). Additionally, the gift qualifies for the gift tax marital deduction except for the disallowance provision of section 2523(i)(1). Accordingly, $100,000 of the $130,000 gift is excluded from the total amount of gifts made during the calendar year by D for gift tax purposes.

Example (2). Transfer of survivor benefits. In 1995, D, a United States citizen, retires from employment in the United States and elects to receive a reduced retirement annuity in order to provide S with a survivor annuity upon D's death. The transfer of rights to S in the joint and survivor annuity is a gift by D for gift tax purposes. However, under paragraph (b) of this section, the gift qualifies for the gift tax marital deduction even though S is not a United States citizen.

Example (3). Transfer of present interest in trust property. In 1995, D, a resident alien, transfers property valued at $500,000 in trust to S, who is also a resident alien. The trust instrument provides that the trust income is payable to S at least quarterly and S has a testamentary general power to appoint the trust corpus. The transfer to S qualifies for the marital deduction under section 2523 but for the provisions of section 2523(i)(1). Because S has a life income interest in the trust, S has a present interest in a portion of the trust. Accordingly, D may exclude the present value of S's income interest (up to $100,000) from D's total 1995 calendar year gifts.

Example (4). Transfer of present interest in trust property. The facts are the same as in Example 3, except that S does not have a testamentary general power to appoint the trust corpus. Instead, D's child, C, has a remainder interest in the trust. If S were a United States citizen, the transfer would qualify for the gift tax marital deduction if a qualified terminable interest property election was made under section 2523(f)(4). However, because S is not a U.S. citizen, D may not make a qualified terminable interest property election. Accordingly, the gift does not qualify for the gift tax marital deduction but for the disallowance provision of section 2523(i)(1). The $100,000 annual exclusion under section 2523(i)(2) is not available with respect to D's transfer in trust and D may not exclude the present value of S's income interest in excess of $10,000 from D's total 1995 calendar year gifts.

Example (5). Spouse becomes citizen after transfer. D, a United States citizen, transfers a residence valued at $350,000 on December 20, 1995, to D's spouse, S, a resident alien. On January 31, 1996, S becomes a naturalized United States citizen. On D's federal gift tax return for 1995, D must include $250,000 as a gift ($350,000 transfer less $100,000 exclusion). Although S becomes a citizen in January, 1996, S is not a citizen of the United States at the time the transfer is made. Therefore, no gift tax marital deduction is allowable. However, the transfer does qualify for the $100,000 annual exclusion.

[T.D. 8612, 60 FR 43552, Aug. 22, 1995]

§ 25.2523(i)–2 Treatment of spousal joint tenancy property where one spousal is not a United States citizen.

(a) In general. In the case of a joint tenancy with right of survivorship between spouses, or a tenancy by the entirety, where the donee spouse is not a United States citizen, the gift tax treatment of the creation and termination of the tenancy (regardless of whether the donor is a citizen, resident or nonresident not a citizen of the United States at such time), is governed by the principles of sections 2515 and 2515A (as such sections were in effect before their repeal by the Economic Recovery Tax Act of 1981). However, in applying these principles, the donor spouse may not elect to treat the creation of a tenancy in real property as a gift, as provided in section 2515(c) (prior to its repeal by the Economic Recovery Tax Act of 1981, Pub.L. 97–34, 95 Stat. 172).

(b) Tenancies by the entirety and joint tenancies in real property. (1) *Creation of the tenancy on or after July 14, 1988.* Under the principles of section 2515 (without regard to section 2515(c)), the creation of a tenancy by the entirety (or joint tenancy) in real property (either by one spouse alone or by both spouses), and any additions to the value of the tenancy in the form of improvements, reductions in indebtedness thereon, or otherwise, is not deemed to be a transfer of property for purposes of the gift tax, regardless of the proportion of the consideration furnished by each spouse, but only if the creation of the tenancy would otherwise be a gift to the donee spouse who is not a citizen of the United States at the time of the gift.

* * *

(3) *Miscellaneous provisions.* (i) *Tenancy by the entirety.* For purposes of this section, tenancy by the entirety includes a joint tenancy between husband and wife with right of survivorship.

(ii) *No election to treat as gift.* The regulations under section 2515 that relate to the election to treat the creation of a tenancy by the entirety as constituting a gift and the consequences of such an election upon termination of the tenancy (§§ 25.2515–2 and 25.2515–4) do not apply for purposes of section 2523(i)(3).

(4) *Examples.* The application of this section may be illustrated by the following examples:

Example (1). In 1992, A, a United States citizen, furnished $200,000 and A's spouse B, a resident alien, furnished $50,000 for the purchase and subsequent improvement of real property held by them as tenants by the entirety. The property is sold in 1998 for $300,000. A receives $225,000 and B receives $75,000 of the sales proceeds. The termination results in a gift of $15,000 by A to B, computed as follows:

$$\frac{\$\,200{,}000 \text{ (consideration furnished by A)}}{\$250{,}000 \text{ (total consideration furnished)}} * \$\,300{,}000 \text{ (proceeds of termination)} = \$240{,}000 \text{ (Proceeds of termination attributable to A.)}$$

$240,000 - $225,000 (proceeds received by A) = $15,000 gift by A to B.

Example (2). In 1986, A purchased real property for $300,000 and took title in the names of A and B, A's spouse, as joint tenants. Under section 2511 and § 25.2511–1(h)(1) of the regulations, A was treated as making a gift of one-half of the value of the property ($150,000) to B. In 1995, the real property is sold for $400,000 and B receives the entire proceeds of sale. For purposes of determining the amount of the gift on termination of the tenancy under the principles of section 2515 and the regulations thereunder, the amount treated as a gift to B on creation of the tenancy under section 2511 is treated as B's contribution towards the purchase of the property. Accordingly, the termination of the tenancy results in a gift of $200,000 from A to B determined as follows:

$$\frac{\$150{,}000 \text{ (consideration furnished by A)}}{\$300{,}000 \text{ (total consideration deemed furnished by both spouses)}} * \$400{,}000 \text{ (proceeds of termination)} = \$200{,}000 \text{ (Proceeds of termination attributable to A.)}$$

$200,000 - 0 (proceeds received by A) = $200,000 gift by A to B.

(c) Tenancies by the entirety in personal property where one spouse is not a United States citizen. (1) *In general.* In the case of the creation (either by one spouse alone or by both spouses where at least one of the spouses is not a United States citizen) of a joint interest in personal property with right of survivorship, or additions to the value thereof in the form of improvements, reductions in the indebtedness thereof, or otherwise, the retained interest of each spouse, solely for purposes of determining whether there has been a gift by the donor to the spouse who is not a citizen of the United States at the time of the gift, is treated as one-half of the value of the joint interest. See section 2523(i) and §§ 25.2523(i)–1 and 25.2503–2(f) as to certain of the tax consequences that may result upon creation and termination of the tenancy.

(2) *Exception.* The rule provided in paragraph (c)(1) of this section does not apply with respect to any joint interest in property if the fair market value of the interest in property (determined as if each spouse had a right to sever) cannot reasonably be ascertained except by reference to the life expectancy of one or both spouses. In these cases, actuarial principles may

need to be resorted to in determining the gift tax consequences of the transaction.

[T.D. 8612, 60 FR 43553, Aug. 22, 1995]

§ 25.2523(i)–3 Effective date.

The provisions of §§ 25.2523(i)–1 and 25.2523(i)–2 are effective in the case of gifts made after August 22, 1995.

[T.D. 8612, 60 FR 43554, Aug. 22, 1995]

§ 2524. Extent of Deductions

The deductions provided in sections 2522 and 2523 shall be allowed only to the extent that the gifts therein specified are included in the amount of gifts against which such deductions are applied.

Regulation

§ 25.2524–1 Extent of deductions.

Under the provisions of section 2524, the charitable deduction provided for in section 2522 and the marital deduction provided for in section 2523 are allowable only to the extent that the gifts, with respect to which those deductions are authorized, are included in the "total amount of gifts" made during the "calendar period" (as defined in § 25.2502–1(c)(1)), computed as provided in section 2503 and § 25.2503–1 (i.e., the total gifts less exclusions). The following examples (in both of which it is assumed that the donor has previously utilized his entire $30,000 specific exemption provided by section 2521, which was in effect at the time) illustrate the application of the provisions of this section:

Example (1). A donor made transfers by gift to his spouse of $5,000 cash on January 1, 1971, and $1,000 cash on April 5, 1971. The donor made no other transfers during 1971. The first $3,000 of such gifts for the calendar year is excluded under the provisions of section 2503(b) in determining the "total amount of gifts" made during the first calendar quarter of 1971. The marital deduction for the first calendar quarter of $2,500 (one-half of $5,000) otherwise allowable is limited by section 2524 to $2,000. The amount of taxable gifts is zero ($5,000–$3,000 (annual exclusion)-$2,000 (marital deduction)). For the second calendar quarter of 1971, the marital deduction is $500 (one-half of $1,000); the amount excluded under section 2503(b) is zero because the entire $3,000 annual exclusion was applied against the gift in the first calendar quarter of 1971; and the amount of taxable gifts is $500 ($1,000–$500 (marital deduction)).

Example (2). The only gifts made by a donor to his spouse during calendar year 1969 were a gift of $2,400 in May and a gift of $3,000 in August. The first $3,000 of such gifts is excluded under the provisions of section 2503(b) in determining the "total amount of gifts" made during the calendar year. The marital deduction for 1969 of $2,700 (one-half of $2,400 plus one-half $3,000) otherwise allowable is limited by section 2524 to $2,400. The amount of taxable gifts is zero ($5,400–$3,000 (annual exclusion)-$2,400 (marital deduction)).

[T.D. 6334, 23 FR 8904, Nov. 15, 1958, as amended by T.D. 7238, 37 FR 28734, Dec. 29, 1972; T.D. 7905, 48 FR 36807, Aug. 15, 1983; T.D. 7910, 48 FR 40375, Sept. 7, 1983]

Federal Generation-Skipping Tax

Code and Selected Regulations

SUBTITLE B. ESTATE AND GIFT TAXES

Chapter 13. Tax On Certain Generation-Skipping Transfers

Subchapter A. Tax Imposed

§ 2601. Tax Imposed

A tax is hereby imposed on every generation-skipping transfer (within the meaning of subchapter B).

Regulation

§ 26.2601–1 Effective dates.

(a) Transfers subject to the generation-skipping transfer tax. (1) *In general.* Except as otherwise provided in this section, the provisions of chapter 13 of the Internal Revenue Code of 1986 (Code) apply to any generation-skipping transfer (as defined in section 2611) made after October 22, 1986.

(2) *Certain transfers treated as if made after October 22, 1986.* Solely for purposes of chapter 13, an inter vivos transfer is treated as if it were made on October 23, 1986, if it was—

(i) Subject to chapter 12 (regardless of whether a tax was actually incurred or paid); and

(ii) Made after September 25, 1985, but before October 23, 1986. For purposes of this paragraph, the value of the property transferred shall be the value of the property on the date the property was transferred.

(3) *Certain trust events treated as if occurring after October 22, 1986.* For purposes of chapter 13, if an inter vivos transfer is made to a trust after September 25, 1985, but before October 23, 1986, any subsequent distribution from the trust or termination of an interest in the trust that occurred before October 23, 1986, is treated as occurring immediately after the deemed transfer on October 23, 1986. If more than one distribution or termination occurs with respect to a trust, the events are treated as if they occurred on October 23, 1986, in the same order as they occurred. See paragraph (b)(1)(iv)(B) of this section for rules determining the portion of distributions and terminations subject to tax under chapter 13. This paragraph (a)(3) does not apply to transfers to trusts not subject to chapter 13 by reason of the transition rules in paragraphs (b)(2) and (3) of this section. The provisions of this paragraph (a)(3) do not apply in determining the value of the property under chapter 13.

(4) *Example.* The following example illustrates the principle that paragraph (a)(2) of this section is not applicable to transfers under a revocable trust that became irrevocable by reason of the transferor's death after September 25, 1985, but before October 23, 1986:

Example. T created a revocable trust on September 30, 1985, that became irrevocable when T died on October 10, 1986. Although the trust terminated in favor of a grandchild of T, the transfer to the grandchild is not treated as occurring on October 23, 1986, pursuant to paragraph (a)(2) of this section because it is not an inter vivos transfer subject to chapter 12. The transfer is not subject to chapter 13 because it is in the nature of a testamentary transfer that occurred prior to October 23, 1986.

(b) Exceptions. (1) *Irrevocable trusts.* (i) *In general.* The provisions of chapter 13 do not apply to any generation-skipping transfer under a trust (as defined in section 2652(b)) that was irrevocable on September 25, 1985. The rule of the preceding sentence does not apply to a pro rata portion of any generation-skipping transfer under an irrevocable trust if additions are made to the trust after September 25, 1985. See paragraph (b)(1)(iv) of this section for rules for determining the portion of the trust that is subject to the provisions of chapter 13. Further, the rule in the first sentence of this paragraph (b)(1)(i) does not apply to a transfer of property pursuant to the exercise, release, or lapse of a general power of appointment that is treated as a taxable transfer under chapter 11 or chapter 12. The transfer is made by the person holding the power at the time the exercise, release, or lapse of the power becomes effective, and is not considered a transfer under a trust that was irrevocable on September 25, 1985. See paragraph (b)(1)(v) (B) of this section regarding the treatment of the release, exercise, or lapse of a power of appointment that will result in a constructive addition to a trust. See § 26.2652–1(a) for the definition of a transferor.

(ii) *Irrevocable trust defined.* (A) *In general.* Unless otherwise provided in either paragraph (b)(1)(ii) (B) or (C) of this section, any trust (as defined in section 2652(b)) in existence on September 25, 1985, is considered an irrevocable trust.

(B) *Property includible in the gross estate under section 2038.* For purposes of this chapter a trust is not an irrevocable trust to the extent that, on September 25, 1985, the settlor held a power with respect to such trust that would have caused the value of the trust to be included in the settlor's gross estate for Federal estate tax purposes by reason of section 2038 (without regard to powers relinquished before September 25, 1985) if the settlor had died on September 25, 1985. A trust is considered subject to a power on September 25, 1985, even though the exercise of the power was subject to the precedent giving of notice, or even though the exercise could take effect only on the expiration of a stated period, whether or not on or before September 25, 1985, notice had been given or the power had been exercised. A trust is not considered subject to a power if the power is, by its terms, exercisable only on the occurrence of an event or contingency not subject to the settlor's control (other than the death of the settlor) and if the event or contingency had not in fact taken place on September 25, 1985.

(C) *Property includible in the gross estate under section 2042.* A policy of insurance on an individual's life that is treated as a trust under section 2652(b) is not considered an irrevocable trust to the extent that, on September 25, 1985, the insured possessed any incident of ownership (as defined in § 20.2042–1(c) of this chapter, and without regard to any incidents of ownership relinquished before September 25, 1985), that would have caused the value of the trust, (i.e., the insurance proceeds) to be included in the insured's gross estate for Federal estate tax purposes by reason of section 2042, if the insured had died on September 25, 1985.

(D) *Examples.* The following examples illustrate the application of this paragraph (b)(1):

Example (1). Section 2038 applicable. On September 25, 1985, T, the settlor of a trust that was created before September 25, 1985, held a testamentary power to add new beneficiaries to the trust. T held no other powers over any portion of the trust. The testamentary power held by T would have caused the trust to be included in T's gross estate under section 2038 if T had died on September 25, 1985. Therefore, the trust is not an irrevocable trust for purposes of this section.

Example (2). Section 2038 not applicable when power held by a person other than settlor. On September 25, 1985, S, the spouse of the settlor of a trust in existence on that date, had an annual right to withdraw a portion of the principal of the trust. The trust was otherwise irrevocable on that date. Because the power was not held by the settlor of the trust, it is not a power described in section 2038. Thus, the trust is considered an irrevocable trust for purposes of this section.

Example (3). Section 2038 not applicable. In 1984, T created a trust and retained the right to expand the class of remaindermen to include any of T's afterborn grandchildren. As of September 25, 1985, all of T's grandchildren were named remaindermen of the trust. Since the exercise of T's power was dependent on there being afterborn grandchildren who were not members of the class of remaindermen, a contingency that did not exist on September 25, 1985, the trust is not considered subject to the power on September 25, 1985, and is an irrevocable trust for purposes of this section. The result is not changed even if grandchildren are born after September 25, 1985, whether or not T exercises the power to expand the class of remaindermen.

Example (4). Section 2042 applicable. On September 25, 1985, T purchased an insurance policy on T's own life and designated child, C, and grandchild, GC, as the beneficiaries. T retained the power to obtain from the insurer a loan against the surrender value of the policy. T's insurance policy is a trust (as defined in section 2652(b)) for chapter 13 purposes. The trust is not considered an irrevocable trust because, on September 25, 1985, T possessed an incident of ownership that would have caused the value of the policy to be included in T's gross estate under section 2042 if T had died on that date.

Example (5). Trust partially irrevocable. In 1984, T created a trust naming T's grandchildren as the income and remainder beneficiaries. T retained the power to revoke the trust as to one-half of the principal at any time prior to T's death. T retained no other powers over the trust principal. T did not die before September 25, 1985, and did not exercise or release the power before that date. The half of the trust not subject to T's power to revoke is an irrevocable trust for purposes of this section.

(iii) *Trust containing qualified terminable interest property.* (A) *In general.* For purposes of chapter 13, a trust described in paragraph (b)(1)(ii) of this section that holds qualified terminable interest property by reason of an election under section 2056(b)(7) or section 2523(f) (made either on, before or after September 25, 1985) is treated in the same manner as if the decedent spouse or the donor spouse (as the case may be) had made an election under section 2652(a)(3). Thus, transfers from such trusts are not subject to chapter 13, and the decedent spouse or the donor spouse (as the case may be) is treated as the transferor of such property. The rule of this paragraph (b)(1)(iii) does not apply to that portion of the trust that is subject to chapter 13 by reason of an addition to the trust occurring after September 25, 1985. See § 26.2652–2(a) for rules where an election under section 2652(a)(3) is made. See § 26.2652–2(c) for rules where a portion of a trust is subject to an election under section 2652(a)(3).

(B) *Examples.* The following examples illustrate the application of this paragraph (b)(1)(iii):

Example (1). QTIP election made after September 25, 1985. On March 28, 1985, T established a trust. The trust instrument provided that the trustee must distribute all income annually to T's spouse, S, during S's life. Upon S's death, the remainder is to be distributed to GC, the grandchild of T and S. On April 15, 1986, T elected under section 2523(f) to treat the property in the trust as qualified terminable interest property. On December 1, 1987, S died and soon thereafter the trust assets were distributed to GC. Because the trust was irrevocable on September 25, 1985, the transfer to GC is not subject to tax under chapter 13. T is treated as the transferor with respect to the transfer of the trust assets to GC in the same manner as if T had made an election under section 2652(a)(3) to reverse the effect of the section 2523(f) election for chapter 13 purposes.

Example (2). Section 2652(a)(3) election deemed to have been made. Assume the same facts as in Example 1, except the trust instrument provides that after S's death all income is to be paid annually to C, the child of T and S. Upon C's death, the remainder is to be distributed to GC. C died on October 1, 1992, and soon thereafter the trust assets are distributed to GC. Because the trust was irrevocable on September 25, 1985, the termination of C's interest is not subject to chapter 13.

(iv) *Additions to irrevocable trusts*—(A) *In general.* If an addition is made after September 25, 1985, to an irrevocable trust which is excluded from chapter 13 by reason of paragraph (b)(1) of this section, a pro rata portion of subsequent distributions from (and terminations of interests in property held in) the trust is subject to the provisions of chapter 13. If an addition is made, the trust is thereafter deemed to consist of two portions, a portion not subject to chapter 13 (the non-chapter 13 portion) and a portion subject to chapter 13 (the chapter 13 portion), each with a separate inclusion ratio (as defined in section 2642(a)).

The non-chapter 13 portion represents the value of the assets of the trust as it existed on September 25, 1985. The applicable fraction (as defined in section 2642(a)(2)) for the non-chapter 13 portion is deemed to be 1 and the inclusion ratio for such portion is 0. The chapter 13 portion of the trust represents the value of all additions made to the trust after September 25, 1985. The inclusion ratio for the chapter 13 portion is determined under section 2642. This paragraph (b)(1)(iv)(A) requires separate portions of one trust only for purposes of determining inclusion ratios. For purposes of chapter 13, a constructive addition under paragraph (b)(1)(v) of this section is treated as an addition. See paragraph (b)(4) of this section for exceptions to the additions rule of this paragraph (b)(1)(iv). See § 26.2654–1(a)(2) for rules treating additions to a trust by an individual other than the initial transferor as a separate trust for purposes of chapter 13.

(B) *Terminations of interests in and distributions from trusts.* Where a termination or distribution described in section 2612 occurs with respect to a trust to which an addition has been made, the portion of such termination or distribution allocable to the chapter 13 portion is determined by reference to the allocation fraction, as defined in paragraph (b)(1)(iv)(C) of this section. In the case of a termination described in section 2612(a) with respect to a trust, the portion of such termination that is subject to chapter 13 is the product of the allocation fraction and the value of the trust (to the extent of the terminated interest therein). In the case of a distribution described in section 2612(b) from a trust, the portion of such distribution that is subject to chapter 13 is the product of the allocation fraction and the value of the property distributed.

(C) *Allocation fraction*—(*1*) *In general.* The allocation fraction allocates appreciation and accumulated income between the chapter 13 and non-chapter 13 portions of a trust. The numerator of the allocation fraction is the amount of the addition (valued as of the date the addition is made), determined without regard to whether any part of the transfer is subject to tax under chapter 11 or chapter 12, but reduced by the amount of any Federal or state estate or gift tax imposed and subsequently paid by the recipient trust with respect to the addition. The denominator of the allocation fraction is the total value of the entire trust immediately after the addition. For purposes of this paragraph (b)(1)(iv)(C), the total value of the entire trust is the fair market value of the property held in trust (determined under the rules of section 2031), reduced by any amount attributable to or paid by the trust and attributable to the transfer to the trust that is similar to an amount that would be allowable as a deduction under section 2053 if the addition had occurred at the death of the transferor, and further reduced by the same amount that the numerator was reduced to reflect Federal or state estate or gift tax incurred by and subsequently paid by the recipient trust with respect to the addition. Where there is more than one addition to principal after September 25, 1985, the portion of the trust subject to chapter 13 after each such addition is determined pursuant to a revised fraction. In each case, the numerator of the revised fraction is the sum of the value of the chapter 13 portion of the trust immediately before the latest addition, and the amount of the latest addition. The denominator of the revised fraction is the total value of the entire trust immediately after the addition. If the transfer to the trust is a generation-skipping transfer, the numerator and denominator are reduced by the amount of the generation-skipping transfer tax, if any, that is imposed by chapter 13 on the transfer and actually recovered from the trust. The allocation fraction is rounded off to five decimal places (.00001).

(2) *Examples.* The following examples illustrate the application of paragraph (b)(1)(iv) of this section. In each of the examples, assume that the recipient trust does not pay any Federal or state transfer tax by reason of the addition.

Example (1). Post September 25, 1985, addition to trust. (i) On August 16, 1980, T established an irrevocable trust. Under the trust instrument, the trustee is required to distribute the entire income annually to T's child, C, for life, then to T's grandchild, GC, for life. Upon GC's death, the remainder is to be paid to GC's issue. On October 1, 1986, when the total value of the entire trust is $400,000, T transfers $100,000 to the trust. The allocation fraction is computed as follows:

$$\frac{\text{Value of addition}}{\text{Total value of trust}} = \frac{\$100{,}000}{\$400{,}000 + \$100{,}000} = 0.2$$

(ii) Thus, immediately after the transfer, 20 percent of the value of future generationskipping transfers under the trust will be subject to chapter 13.

Example (2). Effect of expenses. Assume the same facts as in Example 1, except immediately prior to the transfer on October 1, 1986, the fair market value of the individual assets in the trust totaled $400,000. Also, assume that the trust had accrued and unpaid debts, expenses, and taxes totaling $300,000. Assume further that the entire $300,000 represented amounts that would be deductible under section 2053 if the trust were includible in the transferor's gross estate. The numerator of the allocation fraction is $100,000 and the denominator of the allocation fraction is $200,000 (($400,000 - $300,000) + $100,000). Thus, the allocation fraction is .5 ($100,000/$200,000) and 50 percent of the value of future generation-skipping transfers will be subject to chapter 13.

Example (3). Multiple additions. (i) Assume the same facts as in Example 1, except on January 30, 1988, when the total value of the entire trust is $600,000, T transfers an additional $40,000 to the trust. Before the transfer, the value of the portion of the trust that was attributable to the prior addition was $120,000 ($600,000 * .2). The new allocation fraction is computed as follows:

$$\frac{\text{Total value of additions}}{\text{Total value of trust}} = \frac{(\$120{,}000 + \$40{,}000)}{(\$600{,}000 + \$40{,}000)} = \frac{\$160{,}000}{\$640{,}000} = 0.25$$

(ii) Thus, immediately after the transfer, 25 percent of the value of future generationskipping transfers under the trust will be subject to chapter 13.

Example (4). Allocation fraction at time of generation-skipping transfer. Assume the same facts as in Example 3, except on March 1, 1989, when the value of the trust is $800,000, C dies. A generation-skipping transfer occurs at C's death because of the termination of C's life estate. Therefore, $200,000 ($800,000 * 0.25) is subject to tax under chapter 13.

(v) *Constructive additions*—(A) *Powers of Appointment.* Except as provided in paragraph (b)(1)(v)(B) of this section, where any portion of a trust remains in the trust after the post-September 25, 1985, release, exercise, or lapse of a power of appointment over that portion of the trust, and the release, exercise, or lapse is treated to any extent as a taxable transfer under chapter 11 or chapter 12, the value of the entire portion of the trust subject to the power that was released, exercised, or lapsed is treated as if that portion had been withdrawn and immediately retransferred to the trust at the time of the release, exercise, or lapse. The creator of the power will be considered the transferor of the addition except to the extent that the release, exercise, or lapse of the power is treated as a taxable transfer under chapter 11 or chapter 12. See § 26.2652–1 for rules for determining the identity of the transferor of property for purposes of chapter 13.

(B) *Special rule for certain powers of appointment.* The release, exercise, or lapse of a power of appointment (other than a general power of appointment as defined in section 2041(b)) is not treated as an addition to a trust if—

(*1*) Such power of appointment was created in an irrevocable trust that is not subject to chapter 13 under paragraph (b)(1) of this section; and

(*2*) In the case of an exercise, the power of appointment is not exercised in a manner that may postpone or suspend the vesting, absolute ownership or power of alienation of an interest in property for a period, measured from the date of creation of the trust, extending beyond any life in being at the date of creation of the trust plus a period of 21 years plus, if necessary, a reasonable period of gestation (the perpetuities period). For purposes of this paragraph (b)(1)(v)(B)(*2*), the exercise of a power of appointment that validly postpones or suspends the vesting, absolute ownership or power of alienation of an interest in property for a term of years that will not exceed 90 years (measured from the date of creation of the trust) will not be considered an exercise that postpones or suspends vesting, absolute ownership or the power of alienation beyond the perpetuities period. If a power is exercised by creating another power, it is deemed to be exercised to whatever extent the second power may be exercised.

(C) *Constructive addition if liability is not paid out of trust principal.* Where a trust described in paragraph (b)(1) of this section is relieved of any liability properly payable out of the assets of such trust, the person or entity who actually satisfies the liability is considered to have made a constructive addition to the trust in an amount equal to the liability. The constructive addition occurs when the trust is relieved of liability (e.g., when the right of recovery is no longer enforceable). But see § 26.2652–1(a)(3) for rules involving the application of section 2207A in the case of an election under section 2652(a)(3).

(D) *Examples.* The following examples illustrate the application of this paragraph (b)(1)(v):

Example (1). Lapse of a power of appointment. On June 19, 1980, T established an irrevocable trust with a corpus of $500,000. The trust instrument provides that the trustee shall distribute the entire income from the trust annually to T's spouse, S, during S's life. At S's death, the remainder is to be distributed to T and S's grandchild, GC. T also gave S a general power of appointment over one-half of the trust assets. On December 21, 1989, when the value of the trust corpus is $1,500,000, S died without having exercised the general power of appointment. The value of one-half of the trust corpus, $750,000 ($1,500,000 * .5) is included in S's gross estate under section 2041(a) and is subject to tax under Chapter 11. Because the value of one-half of the trust corpus is subject to tax under Chapter 11 with respect to S's estate, S is treated as the transferor of that property for purposes of Chapter 13 (see section 2652(a)(1)(A)). For purposes of the generation-skipping transfer tax, the lapse of S's power of appointment is treated as if $750,000 ($1,500,000 * .5) had been distributed to S and then transferred back to the trust. Thus, S is considered to have added $750,000 ($1,500,000 * .5) to the trust at the date of S's death. Because this constructive addition occurred after September 25, 1985, 50 percent of the corpus of the trust became subject to Chapter 13 at S's death.

Example (2). Multiple actual additions. On June 19, 1980, T established an irrevocable trust with a principal of $500,000. The trust instrument provides that the trustee shall distribute the entire income from the trust annually to T's spouse, S, during S's life. At S's death, the remainder is to be distributed to GC, the grandchild of T and S. On October 1, 1985, when the trust assets were valued at $800,000, T added $200,000 to the trust. After the transfer on October 1, 1985, the allocation fraction was .2 ($200,000/$1,000,000). On December 21, 1989, when the value of the trust principal is $1,000,000, T adds $1,000,000 to the trust. After this addition, the new allocation fraction is 0.6 ($1,200,000/$2,000,000). The numerator of the fraction is the value of that portion of trust assets that were subject to chapter 13 immediately prior to the addition (by reason of the first addition), $200,000 (.2 * $1,000,000), plus the value of the second transfer, $1,000,000, which equals $1,200,000. The denominator of the fraction, $2,000,000, is the total value of the trust assets immediately after the second transfer. Thus, 60 percent of the principal of the trust becomes subject to chapter 13.

Example (3). Entire portion of trust subject to lapsed power is treated as an addition. On September 25, 1985, B possessed a general power of appointment over the assets of an irrevocable trust that had been created by T in 1980. Under the terms of the trust, B's power lapsed on July 20, 1987. For Federal gift tax purposes, B is treated as making a gift of ninety-five percent (100%–5%) of the value of the principal (see section 2514). However, because the entire trust was subject to the power of appointment, 100 percent (that portion of the trust subject to the power) of the assets of the trust are treated as a constructive addition. Thus, the entire amount of all generation-skipping transfers occurring pursuant to the trust instrument after July 20, 1987, are subject to chapter 13.

Example (4). Exercise of power of appointment in favor of another trust. On March 1, 1985, T established an irrevocable trust as defined in paragraph (b)(1)(ii) of this section. Under the terms of the trust instrument, the trustee is required to distribute the entire income annually to T's child, C, for life, then to T's grandchild, GC, for life. GC has the power to appoint any or all of the trust assets to Trust 2 which is an irrevocable trust (as defined in paragraph (b)(1)(ii) of this section) that was established on August 1, 1985. The terms of Trust 2's governing instrument provide that the trustee shall pay income to T's great grandchild, GGC, for life. Upon GGC's death, the remainder is to be paid to GGC's issue. GGC was alive on March 1, 1985, when Trust 1 was created. C died on April 1, 1986. On July 1, 1987, GC exercised the power of appointment. The exercise of GC's power does not subject future transfers from Trust 2 to tax under chapter 13 because the exercise of the power in favor of Trust 2 does not suspend the vesting, absolute ownership, or power of alienation of an interest in property for a period, measured from the date of creation of Trust 1, extending beyond the life of GGC (a beneficiary under Trust 2 who was in being at the date of creation of Trust 1) plus a period of 21 years. The result would be the same if Trust 2 had been created after the effective date of chapter 13.

Example (5). Exercise of power of appointment in favor of another trust. Assume the same facts as in Example 4, except that GGC was born on March 28, 1986. The valid exercise of GC's power in favor of Trust 2 causes the principal of Trust 1 to be subject to chapter 13, because GGC was not born until after the creation of Trust 1. Thus, such exercise may suspend the vesting, absolute ownership, or power of alienation of an interest in the trust principal for a period, measured from the date of creation of Trust 1, extending beyond the life of GGC (a beneficiary under Trust 2 who was not a life in being at the date of creation of Trust 1).

Example (6). Extension for the longer of two periods. Prior to the effective date of chapter 13, GP established an irrevocable trust under which the trust income was to be paid to GP's child, C, for life. C was given a testamentary power to appoint the remainder in further trust for the benefit of C's issue. In default of C's exercise of the power, the remainder was to pass to charity. C died on February 3, 1995, survived by a child who was alive when GP established the trust. C exercised the power in a manner that validly extends the trust in favor of C's issue until the latter of May 15, 2064 (80 years from the date the trust was created), or the death of C's child plus 21 years. C's exercise of the power is a constructive addition to the trust because the exercise may extend the trust for a period longer than the permissible periods of either the life of C's child (a life in being at the creation of the trust) plus 21 years or a term not more than 90 years measured from the creation of the trust. On the other hand, if C's exercise of the power could extend the trust based only on the life of C's child plus 21 years or only for a term of 80 years from the creation of the trust (but not the later of the two periods) then the exercise of the power would not have been a constructive addition to the trust.

Example (7). Extension for the longer of two periods. The facts are the same as in Example 6 except local law provides that the effect of C's exercise is to extend the term of the trust until May 15, 2064, whether or not C's child predeceases that date by more than 21 years. C's exercise is not a constructive addition to the trust because C exercised the power in a manner that cannot postpone or suspend vesting, absolute ownership, or power of alienation for a term of years that will exceed 90 years. The result would be the same if the effect of C's exercise is either to extend the term of the trust until 21 years after the death of C's child or to extend the term of the trust until the first to occur of May 15, 2064 or 21 years after the death of C's child.

(vi) *Appreciation and income.* Except to the extent that the provisions of paragraphs (b)(1)(iv) and (v) of this section allocate subsequent appreciation and accumulated income between the original trust and additions thereto, appreciation in the value of the trust and undistributed income added thereto are not considered an addition to the principal of a trust.

(2) *Transition rule for wills or revocable trusts executed before October 22, 1986*—(i) *In general.* The provisions of chapter 13 do not apply to any generation-skipping transfer under a will or revocable trust executed before October 22, 1986, provided that—

(A) The document in existence on October 21, 1986, is not amended at any time after October 21, 1986, in any respect which results in the creation of, or an increase in the amount of, a generation-skipping transfer;

(B) In the case of a revocable trust, no addition is made to the revocable trust after October 21, 1986, that results in the creation of, or an increase in the amount of, a generation-skipping transfer; and

(C) The decedent dies before January 1, 1987.

(ii) *Revocable trust defined.* For purposes of this section, the term revocable trust means any trust (as defined in section 2652(b)) except to the extent that, on October 22, 1986, the trust—

(A) Was an irrevocable trust described in paragraph (b)(1) of this section; or

(B) Would have been an irrevocable trust described in paragraph (b)(1) of this section had it not been created or become irrevocable after September 25, 1985, and before October 22, 1986.

(iii) *Will or revocable trust containing qualified terminable interest property.* The rules contained in paragraph (b)(1)(iii) of this section apply to any will or revocable trust within the scope of the transition rule of this paragraph (b)(2).

(iv) *Amendments to will or revocable trust.* For purposes of this paragraph (b)(2), an amendment to a will or a revocable trust in existence on October 21, 1986, is not considered to result in the creation of, or an increase in the amount of, a generation-skipping transfer where the amendment is—

(A) Basically administrative or clarifying in nature and only incidentally increases the amount transferred; or

(B) Designed to ensure that an existing bequest or transfer qualifies for the applicable marital or charitable deduction for estate, gift, or generation-skipping transfer tax purposes and only incidentally increases the amount transferred to a skip person or to a generationskipping trust.

(v) *Creation of, or increase in the amount of, a GST.* In determining whether a particular amendment to a will or revocable trust creates, or increases the amount of, a generation-skipping transfer for purposes of this paragraph (b)(2), the effect of the instrument(s) in existence on October 21, 1986, is measured against the effect of the instrument(s) in existence on the date of death of the decedent or on the date of any prior generation-skipping transfer. If the effect of an amendment cannot be immediately determined, it is deemed to create, or increase the amount of, a generation-skipping transfer until a determination can be made.

(vi) *Additions to revocable trusts.* Any addition made after October 21, 1986, but before the death of the settlor, to a revocable trust subjects all subsequent generation-skipping transfers under the trust to the provisions of chapter 13. Any addition made to a revocable trust after the death of the settlor (if the settlor dies before January 1, 1987) is treated as an addition to an irrevocable trust. See paragraph (b)(1)(v) of this section for rules involving constructive additions to trusts. See paragraph (b)(1)(v)(B) of this section for rules providing that certain transfers to trusts are not treated as additions for purposes of this section.

(vii) *Examples.* The following examples illustrate the application of paragraph (b)(2)(iv) of this section:

(A) *Facts applicable to Examples 1 through 5.* In each of Examples 1 through 5 assume that T executed a will prior to October 22, 1986, and that T dies on December 31, 1986.

Example (1). Administrative change. On November 1, 1986, T executes a codicil to T's will removing one of the co-executors named in the will. Although the codicil may have the effect of lowering administrative costs and thus increasing the amount transferred, it is considered administrative in nature and thus does not cause generation-skipping transfers under the will to be subject to chapter 13.

Example (2). Effect of amendment not immediately determinable. On November 1, 1986, T executes a codicil to T's will revoking a bequest of $100,000 to C, a non-skip person (as defined under section 2613(b)) and causing that amount to be added to a residuary trust held for a skip person. The amendment is deemed to increase the amount of a generation-skipping transfer and prevents any transfers under the will from qualifying under paragraph (b)(2)(i) of this section. If, however, C dies before T and under local law the property would have been added to the residue in any event because the bequest would have lapsed, the codicil is not considered an amendment that increases the amount of a generation-skipping transfer.

Example (3). Refund of tax paid because of amendment. T's will provided that an amount equal to the maximum allowable marital deduction would pass to T's spouse with the residue of the estate passing to a trust established for the benefit of skip persons. On October 23, 1986, the will is amended to provide that the marital share passing to T's spouse shall be the lesser of the maximum allowable marital deduction or the minimum amount that will result in no estate tax liability for T's estate. The amendment may increase the amount of a generation-skipping transfer. Therefore, any generation-skipping transfers under the will are subject to tax under chapter 13. If it becomes apparent that the amendment does not increase the amount of a generation-skipping transfer, a claim for refund may be filed with respect to any generationskipping transfer tax that was paid within the period set forth in section 6511. For example, it would become apparent that the amendment did not result in an increase in the residue if it is subsequently determined that the maximum marital deduction and the minimum amount that will result in no estate tax liability are equal in amount.

Example (4). An amendment that increases a generation-skipping transfer causes complete loss of exempt status. T's will provided for the creation of two trusts for the benefit of skip persons. On November 1, 1986, T executed a codicil to the will specifically increasing the amount of a generation-skipping transfer under the will. All transfers made pursuant to the will or either of the trusts created thereunder are precluded from qualifying under the transition rule of paragraph (b)(2)(i) of this section and are subject to tax under chapter 13.

Example (5). Corrective action effective. Assume that T in Example 4 later executes a second codicil deleting the increase to the generation-skipping transfer. Because the provision increasing a generation-skipping transfer does not become effective, it is not considered an amendment to a will in existence on October 22, 1986.

(B) *Facts applicable to Examples 6 through 8.* T created a trust on September 30, 1985, in which T retained the power to revoke the transfer at any time prior to T's death. The trust provided that, upon the death of T, the income was to be paid to T's spouse, W, for life and then to A, B, and C, the children of T's sibling, S, in equal shares for life, with one-third of the principal to be distributed per stirpes to each child's surviving issue upon the death of the child. The trustee has the power to make discretionary distributions of trust principal to T's sibling, S.

Example (6). Amendment that affects only a person who is not a skip person. A became disabled, and T modified the trust on December 1, 1986, to increase A's share of the income. Since the amendment does not result in the creation of, or increase in the amount of, a generationskipping transfer, transfers pursuant to the trust are not subject to chapter 13.

Example (7). Amendment that adds a skip person. Assume that T amends the trust to add T's grandchild, D, as an income beneficiary. The trust will be subject to the provisions of chapter 13 because the amendment creates a generationskipping transfer.

Example (8). Refund of tax paid during interim period when effect of amendment is not determinable. Assume that T amends the trust to provide that the issue of S are to take a one-fourth share of the principal per stirpes upon S's death. Because the distribution to be made upon S's death may involve skip persons, the amendment is considered an amendment that creates or increases the amount of a generationskipping transfer until a determination can be made. Accordingly, any distributions from (or terminations of interests in) such trust are subject to chapter 13 until it is determined that no skip person has been added to the trust. At that time, a claim for refund may be filed within the period set forth in section 6511 with respect to any generation-skipping transfer tax that was paid.

(3) *Transition rule in the case of mental incompetency* (i) *In general.* If an individual was under a mental disability to change the disposition of his or her property continuously from October 22, 1986, until the date of his or her death, the provisions of chapter 13 do not apply to any generation-skipping transfer—(A) Under a trust (as defined in section 2652(b)) to the extent such trust consists of property, or the proceeds of property, the value of which was included in the gross estate of the individual (other than property transferred by or on behalf of the individual during the individual's life after October 22, 1986); or

(B) Which is a direct skip (other than a direct skip from a trust) that occurs by reason of the death of the individual.

(ii) *Mental disability defined.* For purposes of this paragraph (b)(2), the term mental disability means mental incompetence to execute an instrument governing the disposition of the individual's property, whether or not there was an adjudication of incompetence and regardless of whether there has been an appointment of a guardian, fiduciary, or other person charged with either the care of the individual or the care of the individual's property.

(iii) (A) *Decedent who has not been adjudged mentally incompetent.* If there has not been a court adjudication that the decedent was mentally incompetent on or before October 22, 1986, the executor must file, with Form 706, either—

(1) A certification from a qualified physician stating that the decedent was—

(i) mentally incompetent at all times on and after October 22, 1986; and

(ii) did not regain competence to modify or revoke the terms of the trust or will prior to his or her death; or

(2) Sufficient other evidence demonstrating that the decedent was mentally incompetent at all times on

and after October 22, 1986, as well as a statement explaining why no certification is available from a physician; and

(3) Any judgement or decree relating to the decedent's incompetency that was made after October 22, 1986.

(B) Such items in paragraphs (b)(3)(iii)(A)(1), (2), and (3) of this section will be considered relevant, but not determinative, in establishing the decedent's state of competency.

(iv) *Decedent who has been adjudged mentally incompetent.* If the decedent has been adjudged mentally incompetent on or before October 22, 1986, a copy of the judgment or decree, and any modification thereof, must be filed with the Form 706.

(v) *Rule applies even if another person has power to change trust terms.* In the case of a transfer from a trust, this paragraph (b)(3) applies even though a person charged with the care of the decedent or the decedent's property has the power to revoke or modify the terms of the trust, provided that the power is not exercised after October 22, 1986, in a manner that creates, or increases the amount of, a generation-skipping transfer. See paragraph (b)(2)(iv) of this section for rules concerning amendments that create or increase the amount of a generation-skipping transfer.

(vi) *Example.* The following example illustrates the application of paragraph (b)(3)(v) of this section:

Example. T was mentally incompetent on October 22, 1986, and remained so until death in 1993. Prior to becoming incompetent, T created a revocable generation-skipping trust that was includible in T's gross estate. Prior to October 22, 1986, the appropriate court issued an order under which P, who was thereby charged with the care of T's property, had the power to modify or revoke the revocable trust. Although P exercised the power after October 22, 1986, and while T was incompetent, the power was not exercised in a manner that created, or increased the amount of, a generation-skipping transfer. Thus, the existence and exercise of P's power did not cause the trust to lose its exempt status under paragraph (b)(3) of this section. The result would be the same if the court order was issued after October 22, 1986.

(4) *Retention of trust's exempt status in the case of modifications, etc.*—(i) *In general.* This paragraph (b)(4) provides rules for determining when a modification, judicial construction, settlement agreement, or trustee action with respect to a trust that is exempt from the generationskipping transfer tax under paragraph (b)(1), (2), or (3) of this section (hereinafter referred to as an exempt trust) will not cause the trust to lose its exempt status. In general, unless specifically provided otherwise, the rules contained in this paragraph are applicable only for purposes of determining whether an exempt trust retains its exempt status for generation-skipping transfer tax purposes. Thus (unless specifically noted), the rules do not apply in determining, for example, whether the transaction results in a gift subject to gift tax, or may cause the trust to be included in the gross estate of a beneficiary, or may result in the realization of gain for purposes of section 1001.

(A) *Discretionary powers.* The distribution of trust principal from an exempt trust to a new trust or retention of trust principal in a continuing trust will not cause the new or continuing trust to be subject to the provisions of chapter 13, if—

(1) Either—

(i) The terms of the governing instrument of the exempt trust authorize distributions to the new trust or the retention of trust principal in a continuing trust, without the consent or approval of any beneficiary or court; or

(ii) at the time the exempt trust became irrevocable, state law authorized distributions to the new trust or retention of principal in the continuing trust, without the consent or approval of any beneficiary or court; and

(2) The terms of the governing instrument of the new or continuing trust do not extend the time for vesting of any beneficial interest in the trust in a manner that may postpone or suspend the vesting, absolute ownership, or power of alienation of an interest in property for a period, measured from the date the original trust became irrevocable, extending beyond any life in being at the date the original trust became irrevocable plus a period of 21 years, plus if necessary, a reasonable period of gestation. For purposes of this paragraph (b)(4)(i)(A), the exercise of a trustee's distributive power that validly postpones or suspends the vesting, absolute ownership, or power of alienation of an interest in property for a term of years that will not

exceed 90 years (measured from the date the original trust became irrevocable) will not be considered an exercise that postpones or suspends vesting, absolute ownership, or the power of alienation beyond the perpetuities period. If a distributive power is exercised by creating another power, it is deemed to be exercised to whatever extent the second power may be exercised.

(B) *Settlement.* A court-approved settlement of a bona fide issue regarding the administration of the trust or the construction of terms of the governing instrument will not cause an exempt trust to be subject to the provisions of chapter 13, if—

(*1*) The settlement is the product of arm's length negotiations; and

(*2*) The settlement is within the range of reasonable outcomes under the governing instrument and applicable state law addressing the issues resolved by the settlement. A settlement that results in a compromise between the positions of the litigating parties and reflects the parties' assessments of the relative strengths of their positions is a settlement that is within the range of reasonable outcomes.

(C) *Judicial construction.* A judicial construction of a governing instrument to resolve an ambiguity in the terms of the instrument or to correct a scrivener's error will not cause an exempt trust to be subject to the provisions of chapter 13, if—

(*1*) The judicial action involves a bona fide issue; and

(*2*) The construction is consistent with applicable state law that would be applied by the highest court of the state.

(D) *Other changes.* (*1*) A modification of the governing instrument of an exempt trust (including a trustee distribution, settlement, or construction that does not satisfy paragraph (b)(4)(i)(A), (B), or (C) of this section) by judicial reformation, or nonjudicial reformation that is valid under applicable state law, will not cause an exempt trust to be subject to the provisions of chapter 13, if the modification does not shift a beneficial interest in the trust to any beneficiary who occupies a lower generation (as defined in section 2651) than the person or persons who held the beneficial interest prior to the modification, and the modification does not extend the time for vesting of any beneficial interest in the trust beyond the period provided for in the original trust.

(*2*) For purposes of this section, a modification of an exempt trust will result in a shift in beneficial interest to a lower generation beneficiary if the modification can result in either an increase in the amount of a GST transfer or the creation of a new GST transfer. To determine whether a modification of an irrevocable trust will shift a beneficial interest in a trust to a beneficiary who occupies a lower generation, the effect of the instrument on the date of the modification is measured against the effect of the instrument in existence immediately before the modification. If the effect of the modification cannot be immediately determined, it is deemed to shift a beneficial interest in the trust to a beneficiary who occupies a lower generation (as defined in section 2651) than the person or persons who held the beneficial interest prior to the modification. A modification that is administrative in nature that only indirectly increases the amount transferred (for example, by lowering administrative costs or income taxes) will not be considered to shift a beneficial interest in the trust. In addition, administration of a trust in conformance with applicable local law that defines the term income as a unitrust amount (or permits a right to income to be satisfied by such an amount) or that permits the trustee to adjust between principal and income to fulfill the trustee's duty of impartiality between income and principal beneficiaries will not be considered to shift a beneficial interest in the trust, if applicable local law provides for a reasonable apportionment between the income and remainder beneficiaries of the total return of the trust and meets the requirements of § 1.643(b)–1 of this chapter.

(E) *Examples.* The following examples illustrate the application of this paragraph (b)(4). In each example, assume that the trust established in 1980 was irrevocable for purposes of paragraph (b)(1)(ii) of this section and that there have been no additions to any trust after September 25, 1985. The examples are as follows:

Example (1). Trustee's power to distribute principal authorized under trust instrument. In 1980, Grantor established an irrevocable trust (Trust) for the benefit of Grantor's child, A, A's spouse, and A's issue. At the time Trust was established, A had two children, B and C. A corporate fiduciary was designated as trustee. Under the terms of Trust, the trustee has the discretion to distribute all or part of the trust income to one or more of the group consisting of A, A's spouse or A's issue. The trustee is also authorized to distribute all or part of the trust principal to one or more trusts for the benefit of A, A's spouse, or A's issue under terms specified by the trustee in the trustee's discretion. Any trust established under Trust, however, must terminate 21 years after the death of the last child of A to die who was alive at the time Trust was executed. Trust will terminate on the death of A, at which time the remaining principal will be distributed to A's issue, per stirpes. In 2002, the trustee distributes part of Trust's principal to a new trust for the benefit of B and C and their issue. The new trust will terminate 21 years after the death of the survivor of B and C, at which time the trust principal will be distributed to the issue of B and C, per stirpes. The terms of the governing instrument of Trust authorize the trustee to make the distribution to a new trust without the consent or approval of any beneficiary or court. In addition, the terms of the governing instrument of the new trust do not extend the time for vesting of any beneficial interest in a manner that may postpone or suspend the vesting, absolute ownership or power of alienation of an interest in property for a period, measured from the date of creation of Trust, extending beyond any life in being at the date of creation of Trust plus a period of 21 years, plus if necessary, a reasonable period of gestation. Therefore, neither Trust nor the new trust will be subject to the provisions of chapter 13 of the Internal Revenue Code.

Example (2). Trustee's power to distribute principal pursuant to state statute. In 1980, Grantor established an irrevocable trust (Trust) for the benefit of Grantor's child, A, A's spouse, and A's issue. At the time Trust was established, A had two children, B and C. A corporate fiduciary was designated as trustee. Under the terms of Trust, the trustee has the discretion to distribute all or part of the trust income or principal to one or more of the group consisting of A, A's spouse or A's issue. Trust will terminate on the death of A, at which time, the trust principal will be distributed to A's issue, per stirpes. Under a state statute enacted after 1980 that is applicable to Trust, a trustee who has the absolute discretion under the terms of a testamentary instrument or irrevocable inter vivos trust agreement to invade the principal of a trust for the benefit of the income beneficiaries of the trust, may exercise the discretion by appointing so much or all of the principal of the trust in favor of a trustee of a trust under an instrument other than that under which the power to invade is created, or under the same instrument. The trustee may take the action either with consent of all the persons interested in the trust but without prior court approval, or with court approval, upon notice to all of the parties. The exercise of the discretion, however, must not reduce any fixed income interest of any income beneficiary of the trust and must be in favor of the beneficiaries of the trust. Under state law prior to the enactment of the state statute, the trustee did not have the authority to make distributions in trust. In 2002, the trustee distributes one-half of Trust's principal to a new trust that provides for the payment of trust income to A for life and further provides that, at A's death, one-half of the trust remainder will pass to B or B's issue and one-half of the trust will pass to C or C's issue. Because the state statute was enacted after Trust was created and requires the consent of all of the parties, the transaction constitutes a modification of Trust. However, the modification does not shift any beneficial interest in Trust to a beneficiary or beneficiaries who occupy a lower generation than the person or persons who held the beneficial interest prior to the modification. In addition, the modification does not extend the time for vesting of any beneficial interest in Trust beyond the period provided for in the original trust. The new trust will terminate at the same date provided under Trust. Therefore, neither Trust nor the new trust will be subject to the provisions of chapter 13 of the Internal Revenue Code.

Example (3). Construction of an ambiguous term in the instrument. In 1980, Grantor established an irrevocable trust for the benefit of Grantor's children, A and B, and their issue. The trust is to terminate on the death of the last to die of A and B, at which time the principal is to be distributed to their issue. However, the provision governing the termination of the trust is ambiguous regarding whether the trust principal is to be distributed per stirpes, only to the children of A and B, or per capita among the children, grandchildren, and more remote issue of A and B. In 2002, the trustee files a construction suit with the appropriate local court to resolve the ambiguity. The court issues an order construing the instrument to provide for per capita distributions to the children, grandchildren, and more remote issue of A and B living at the time the trust terminates. The court's construction resolves a bona fide issue regarding the proper interpretation of the instrument and is consistent with applicable state law as it would be interpreted by the highest court of the state. Therefore, the trust will not be subject to the provisions of chapter 13 of the Internal Revenue Code.

Example (4). Change in trust situs. In 1980, Grantor, who was domiciled in State X, executed an irrevocable trust for the benefit of Grantor's issue, naming a State X bank as trustee. Under the terms of the trust, the trust is to terminate, in all events, no later than 21 years after the death of the last to die of certain designated individuals living at the time the trust was executed. The provisions of the trust do not specify that any particular state law is to govern the administration and construction of the trust. In State X, the common law rule against perpetuities applies to trusts. In 2002, a State Y bank is named as sole trustee. The effect of changing trustees is that the situs of the trust changes to State Y, and the laws of State Y govern the administration and construction of the trust. State Y law contains no rule against perpetuities. In this case, however, in view of the terms of the trust instrument, the trust will terminate at the same time before and after the change in situs. Accordingly, the change in situs does not shift any beneficial interest in the trust to a beneficiary who occupies a lower generation (as defined in section 2651) than the person or persons who held the beneficial interest prior to the transfer. Furthermore, the change in situs does not extend the time for vesting of any beneficial interest in the trust beyond that provided for in the original trust. Therefore, the trust will not be subject to the provisions of chapter 13 of the Internal Revenue Code. If, in this example, as a result of the change in situs, State Y law governed such that the time for vesting was extended beyond the period prescribed under the terms of the original trust instrument, the trust would not retain exempt status.

Example (5). Division of a trust. In 1980, Grantor established an irrevocable trust for the benefit of his two children, A and B, and their issue. Under the terms of the trust, the trustee has the discretion to distribute income and principal to A, B, and their issue in such amounts as the trustee deems appropriate. On the death of the last to die of A and B, the trust principal is to be distributed to the living issue of A and B, per stirpes. In 2002, the appropriate local court approved the division of the trust into two equal trusts, one for the benefit of A and A's issue and one for the benefit of B and B's issue. The trust for A and A's issue provides that the trustee has the discretion to distribute trust income and principal to A and A's issue in such amounts as the trustee deems appropriate. On A's death, the trust principal is to be distributed equally to A's issue, per stirpes. If A dies with no living descendants, the principal will be added to the trust for B and B's issue. The trust for B and B's issue is identical (except for the beneficiaries), and terminates at B's death at which time the trust principal is to be distributed equally to B's issue, per stirpes. If B dies with no living descendants, principal will be added to the trust for A and A's issue. The division of the trust into two trusts does not shift any beneficial interest in the trust to a beneficiary who occupies a lower generation (as defined in section 2651) than the person or persons who held the beneficial interest prior to the division. In addition, the division does not extend the time for vesting of any beneficial interest in the trust beyond the period provided for in the original trust. Therefore, the two partitioned trusts resulting from the division will not be subject to the provisions of chapter 13 of the Internal Revenue Code.

Example (6). Merger of two trusts. In 1980, Grantor established an irrevocable trust for Grantor's child and the child's issue. In 1983, Grantor's spouse also established a separate irrevocable trust for the benefit of the same child and issue. The terms of the spouse's trust and Grantor's trust are identical. In 2002, the appropriate local court approved the merger of the two trusts into one trust to save administrative costs and enhance the management of the investments. The merger of the two trusts does not shift any beneficial interest in the trust to a beneficiary who occupies a lower generation (as defined in section 2651) than the person or persons who held the beneficial interest prior to the merger. In addition, the merger does not extend the time for vesting of any beneficial interest in the trust beyond the period provided for in the original trust. Therefore, the trust that resulted from the merger will not be subject to the provisions of chapter 13 of the Internal Revenue Code.

Example (7). Modification that does not shift an interest to a lower generation. In 1980, Grantor established an irrevocable trust for the benefit of Grantor's grandchildren, A, B, and C. The trust provides that income is to be paid to A, B, and C, in equal shares for life. The trust further provides that, upon the death of the first grandchild to die, one-third of the principal is to be distributed to that grandchild's issue, per stirpes. Upon the death of the second grandchild to die, one-half of the remaining trust principal is to be distributed to that grandchild's issue, per stirpes, and upon the death of the last grandchild to die, the remaining principal is to be distributed to that grandchild's issue, per stirpes. In 2002, A became disabled. Subsequently, the trustee, with the consent of B and C, petitioned the appropriate local court and the court approved a modification of the trust that increased A's share of trust income. The modification does not shift a beneficial interest to a lower generation beneficiary because the modification does not increase the amount of a GST transfer under the original trust or create the possibility that new GST transfers not contemplated in the original trust may be made. In this case, the modification will increase the amount payable to A who is a member of the same generation as B and C. In addition, the modification does not extend the time for vesting of any beneficial interest in the trust beyond the period provided for in the original trust. Therefore, the trust as modified will not be subject to the provisions of chapter 13 of the Internal Revenue Code. However, the modification increasing A's share of trust income is a transfer by B and C to A for Federal gift tax purposes.

Example (8). Conversion of income interest into unitrust interest. In 1980, Grantor established an irrevocable trust under the terms of which trust income is payable to A for life and, upon A's death, the remainder is to pass to A's issue, per stirpes. In 2002, the appropriate local court approves a modification to the trust that converts A's income interest into the right to receive the greater of the entire income of the trust or a fixed percentage of the trust assets valued annually (unitrust interest) to be paid each year to A for life. The modification does not result in a shift in beneficial interest to a beneficiary who occupies a lower generation (as defined in section 2651) than the person or persons who held the beneficial interest prior to the modification. In this case, the modification can only operate to increase the amount distributable to A and decrease the amount distributable to A's issue. In addition, the modification does not extend the time for vesting of any beneficial interest in the trust beyond the period provided for in the original trust. Therefore, the trust will not be subject to the provisions of chapter 13 of the Internal Revenue Code.

Example (9). Allocation of capital gain to income. In 1980, Grantor established an irrevocable trust under the terms of which trust income is payable to Grantor's child, A, for life, and upon A's death, the remainder is to pass to the A's issue, per stirpes. Under applicable state law, unless the governing instrument provides otherwise, capital gain is allocated to principal. In 2002, the trust is modified to allow the trustee to allocate capital gain to the income. The modification does not shift any beneficial interest in the trust to a beneficiary who occupies a lower generation (as defined in section 2651) than the person or persons who held the beneficial interest prior to the modification. In this case, the modification can only have the effect of increasing the amount distributable to A, and decreasing the amount distributable to A's issue. In addition, the modification does not extend the time for vesting of any beneficial interest in the trust beyond the period provided for in the original trust. Therefore, the trust will not be subject to the provisions of chapter 13 of the Internal Revenue Code.

Example (10). Administrative change to terms of a trust. In 1980, Grantor executed an irrevocable trust for the benefit of Grantor's issue, naming a bank and five other individuals as trustees. In 2002, the appropriate local court approves a modification of the trust that decreases the number of trustees which results in lower administrative costs. The modification pertains to the administration of the trust and does not shift a beneficial interest in the trust to any beneficiary who occupies a lower generation (as defined in section 2651) than the person or persons who held the beneficial interest prior to the modification. In addition, the modification does not extend the time for vesting of any beneficial interest in the trust beyond the period provided for in the original trust. Therefore, the trust will not be subject to the provisions of chapter 13 of the Internal Revenue Code.

Example (11). Conversion of income interest to unitrust interest under state statute. In 1980, Grantor, a resident of State X, established an irrevocable trust for the benefit of Grantor's child, A, and A's issue. The trust provides that trust income is payable to A for life and upon A's death the remainder is to pass to A's issue, per stirpes. In 2002, State X amends its income and principal statute to define income as a unitrust amount of 4% of the fair market value of the trust assets valued annually. For a trust established prior to 2002, the statute provides that the new definition of income will apply only if all the beneficiaries who have an interest in the trust consent to the change within two years after the effective date of the statute. The statute provides specific procedures to establish the consent of the beneficiaries. A and A's issue consent to the change in the definition of income within the time period, and in accordance with the procedures, prescribed by the state statute. The administration of the trust, in accordance with the state statute defining income to be a 4% unitrust amount, will not be considered to shift any beneficial interest in the trust. Therefore, the trust will not be subject to the provisions of chapter 13 of the Internal Revenue Code. Further, under these facts, no trust beneficiary will be treated as having made a gift for federal gift tax purposes, and neither the trust nor any trust beneficiary will be treated as having made a taxable exchange for federal income tax purposes. Similarly, the conclusions in this example would be the same if the beneficiaries' consent was not required, or, if the change in administration of the trust occurred because the situs of the trust was changed to State X from a state whose statute does not define income as a unitrust amount or if the situs was changed to such a state from State X.

Example (12). Equitable adjustments under state statute. The facts are the same as in Example 11, except that in 2002, State X amends its income and principal statute to permit the trustee to make adjustments between income and principal when the trustee invests and manages the trust assets under the state's prudent investor standard, the trust describes the amount that shall or must be distributed to a beneficiary by referring to the trust's income, and the trustee after applying the state statutory rules regarding allocation of receipts between income and principal is unable to administer the trust impartially. The provision permitting the trustees to make these adjustments is effective in 2002 for trusts created at any time. The trustee invests and manages the trust assets under the state's prudent investor standard, and pursuant to authorization in the state statute, the trustee allocates receipts between the income and principal accounts in a manner to ensure the impartial administration of the trust. The administration of the trust in accordance with the state statute will not be considered to shift any beneficial interest in the trust. Therefore, the trust will not be subject to the provisions of chapter 13 of the Internal Revenue Code. Further, under these facts, no trust beneficiary will be treated as having made a gift for federal gift tax purposes, and neither the trust nor any trust beneficiary will be treated as having made a taxable exchange for federal income tax purposes. Similarly, the conclusions in this example would be the same if the change in administration of the trust occurred because the situs of the trust was changed to State X from a state whose statute does not authorize the trustee to make adjustments between income and principal or if the situs was changed to such a state from State X.

(ii) *Effective date.* The rules in this paragraph (b)(4) are generally applicable on and after December 20, 2000. However, the rule in the last sentence of paragraph (b)(4)(i)(D)(2) of this section and Example 11 and Example 12 in paragraph (b)(4)(i)(E) of this section regarding the administration of a trust and the determination of income in conformance with applicable state law applies to trusts for taxable years ending after January 2, 2004.

(5) *Exceptions to additions rule*—(i) *In general.* Any addition to a trust made pursuant to an instrument or arrangement covered by the transition rules in paragraph (b)(1), (2) or (3) of this section is not treated as an addition for purposes of this section. Moreover, any property transferred inter vivos to a trust is not treated as an addition if the same property would have been added to the trust pursuant to an instrument covered by the transition rules in paragraph (b)(2) or (3) of this section.

(ii) *Examples.* The following examples illustrate the application of paragraph (b)(4)(i) of this section:

Example (1). Addition pursuant to terms of exempt instrument. On December 31, 1980, T created an irrevocable trust having a principal of $100,000. Under the terms of the trust, the principal was to be held for the benefit of T's grandchild, GC. Pursuant to the terms of T's will, a document entitled to relief under the transition rule of paragraph (b)(2) of this section, the residue of the estate was paid to the trust. Because the addition to the trust was paid pursuant to the terms of an instrument (T's will) that is not subject to the provisions of chapter 13 because of paragraph (b)(2) of this section, the payment to the trust is not considered an addition to the principal of the trust. Thus, distributions to or for the benefit of GC, are not subject to the provisions of chapter 13.

Example (2). Property transferred inter vivos that would have been transferred to the same trust by the transferor's will. T is the grantor of a trust that was irrevocable on September 25, 1985. T's will, which was executed before October 22, 1986, and not amended thereafter, provides that, upon T's death, the entire estate will pour over into T's trust. On October 1, 1985, T transfers $100,000 to the trust. While T's will otherwise qualifies for relief under the transition rule in paragraph (b)(2) of this section, the transition rule is not applicable unless T dies prior to January 1, 1987. Thus, if T dies after December 31, 1986, the transfer is treated as an addition to the trust for purposes of any distribution made from the trust after the transfer to the trust on October 1, 1985. If T dies before January 1, 1987, the entire trust (as well as any distributions from or terminations of interests in the trust prior to T's death) is exempt, under paragraph (b)(2) of this section, from chapter 13 because the $100,000 would have been added to the trust under a will that would have qualified under paragraph (b)(2) of this section. In either case, for any generation-skipping transfers made after the transfer to the trust on October 1, 1985, but before T's death, the $100,000 is treated as an addition to the trust and a proportionate amount of the trust is subject to chapter 13.

Example (3). Pour over to a revocable trust. T and S are the settlors of separate revocable trusts with equal values. Both trusts were established for the benefit of skip persons (as defined in section 2613). S dies on December 1, 1985, and under the provisions of S's trust, the principal pours over into T's trust. If T dies before January 1, 1987, the entire trust is excluded under paragraph (b)(2) of this section from the operation of chapter 13. If T dies after December 31, 1986, the entire trust is subject to the generation-skipping transfer tax provisions because T's trust is not a trust described in paragraph (b)(1) or (2) of this section. In the latter case, the fact that S died before January 1, 1987, is irrelevant because the principal of S's trust was added to a trust that never qualified under the transition rules of paragraph (b)(1) or (2) of this section.

Example (4). Pour over to exempt trust. Assume the same facts as in Example 3, except upon the death of S on December 1, 1985, S's trust continues as an irrevocable trust and that the principal of T's trust is to be paid over upon T's death to S's trust. Again, if T dies before January 1, 1987, S's entire trust falls within the provisions of paragraph (b)(2) of this section. However, if T dies after December 31, 1986, the pour-over is considered an addition to the trust. Therefore, S's trust is not a trust excluded under paragraph (b)(2) of this section because an addition is made to the trust.

Example (5). Lapse of a general power of appointment. S, the spouse of the settlor of an irrevocable trust that was created in 1980, had, on September 25, 1985, a general power of appointment over the trust assets. The trust provides that should S fail to exercise the power of appointment the property is to remain in the trust. On October 21, 1986, S executed a will under which S failed to exercise the power of appointment. If S dies before January 1, 1987, without having exercised the power in a manner which results in the creation of, or increase in the amount of, a generation-skipping transfer (or amended the will in a manner that results in the creation of, or increase in the amount of, a generation-skipping transfer), transfers pursuant to the trust or the will are not subject to chapter 13 because the trust is an irrevocable trust and the will qualifies under paragraph (b)(2) of this section.

Example (6). Lapse of general power of appointment held by intestate decedent. Assume the same facts as in Example 5, except on October 22, 1986, S did not have a will and that S dies after that date. Upon S's death, or upon the prior exercise or release of the power, the value of the entire trust is treated as having been distributed to S, and S is treated as having made an addition to the trust in the amount of the entire principal. Any distribution or termination pursuant to the trust occurring after S's death is subject to chapter 13. It is immaterial whether S's death occurs before January 1, 1987, since paragraph (b)(2) of this section is only applicable where a will or revocable trust was executed before October 22, 1986.

(c) Additional effective dates. Except as otherwise provided, the regulations under §§ 26.2611–1, 26.2612–1, 26.2613–1, 26.2632–1, 26.2641–1, 26.2642–1, 26.2642–2, 26.2642–3, 26.2642–4, 26.2642–5, 26.2652–1, 26.2652–2, 26.2653–1, 26.2654–1, 26.2663–1, and 26.2663–2 are effective with respect to generation-skipping transfers as defined in § 26.2611–1 made on or after December 27, 1995. However, taxpayers may, at their option, rely on these regulations in the case of generation-skipping transfers made, and trusts that became irrevocable, after December 23, 1992, and before December 27, 1995. The last four sentences in paragraph (b)(1)(i) of this section are applicable on and after November 18, 1999.

[T.D. 8644, 60 FR 66903, Dec. 27, 1995; 61 FR 29653, June 12, 1996, as amended at 61 FR 43656, Aug. 26, 1996; T.D. 8912, 65 FR 79738, Dec. 20, 2000; 66 FR 11108, Feb. 22, 2001; 66 FR 12834, Feb. 28, 2001; T.D. 9102, 69 FR 21, Jan. 2, 2004]

§ 2602. Amount of Tax

The amount of the tax imposed by section 2601 is—

(1) the taxable amount (determined under subchapter C), multiplied by

(2) the applicable rate (determined under subchapter E).

§ 2603. Liability for Tax

(a) Personal liability.

(1) Taxable distributions. In the case of a taxable distribution, the tax imposed by section 2601 shall be paid by the transferee.

(2) Taxable termination. In the case of a taxable termination or a direct skip from a trust, the tax shall be paid by the trustee.

(3) Direct skip. In the case of a direct skip (other than a direct skip from a trust), the tax shall be paid by the transferor.

(b) Source of tax. Unless otherwise directed pursuant to the governing instrument by specific reference to the tax imposed by this chapter, the tax imposed by this chapter on a generation-skipping transfer shall be charged to the property constituting such transfer.

(c) Cross reference. For provisions making estate and gift tax provisions with respect to transferee liability, liens, and related matters applicable to the tax imposed by section 2601, see section 2661.

§ 2604. [Repealed]

Subchapter B. Generation-Skipping Transfers

§ 2611. Generation-Skipping Transfer Defined

(a) In general. For purposes of this chapter, the term "generation-skipping transfer" means—

(1) a taxable distribution,

(2) a taxable termination, and

(3) a direct skip.

(b) Certain transfers excluded. The term "generation-skipping transfer" does not include—

(1) any transfer which, if made inter vivos by an individual, would not be treated as a taxable gift by reason of section 2503(e) (relating to exclusion of certain transfers for educational or medical expenses), and

(2) any transfer to the extent—

(A) the property transferred was subject to a prior tax imposed under this chapter,

(B) the transferee in the prior transfer was assigned to the same generation as (or a lower generation than) the generation assignment of the transferee in this transfer, and

(C) such transfers do not have the effect of avoiding tax under this chapter with respect to any transfer.

Regulation

§ 26.2611–1 Generation-skipping transfer defined.

A generation-skipping transfer (GST) is an event that is either a direct skip, a taxable distribution, or a taxable termination. See § 26.2612–1 for the definition of these terms. The determination as to whether an event is a GST is made by reference to the most recent transfer subject to the estate or gift tax. See § 26.2652–1(a)(2) for determining whether a transfer is subject to Federal estate or gift tax.

[T.D. 8644, 60 FR 66910, Dec. 27, 1995]

§ 2612. Taxable Termination; Taxable Distribution; Direct Skip

(a) Taxable termination.

(1) General rule. For purposes of this chapter, the term "taxable termination" means the termination (by death, lapse of time, release of power, or otherwise) of an interest in property held in a trust unless—

(A) immediately after such termination, a non-skip person has an interest in such property, or

(B) at no time after such termination may a distribution (including distributions on termination) be made from such trust to a skip person.

(2) Certain partial terminations treated as taxable. If, upon the termination of an interest in property held in trust by reason of the death of a lineal descendant of the transferor, a specified portion of the trust's assets are distributed to 1 or more skip persons (or 1 or more trusts for the exclusive benefit of such persons), such termination shall constitute a taxable termination with respect to such portion of the trust property.

(b) Taxable distribution. For purposes of this chapter, the term "taxable distribution" means any distribution from a trust to a skip person (other than a taxable termination or a direct skip).

(c) Direct skip. For purposes of this chapter—

(1) In general. The term "direct skip" means a transfer subject to a tax imposed by chapter 11 or 12 of an interest in property to a skip person.

(2) Look-thru rules not to apply. Solely for purposes of determining whether any transfer to a trust is a direct skip, the rules of section 2651(f)(2) shall not apply.

Regulation

§ 26.2612–1 Definitions.

(a) Direct skip. A direct skip is a transfer to a skip person that is subject to Federal estate or gift tax. If property is transferred to a trust, the transfer is a direct skip only if the trust is a skip person. Only one direct skip occurs when a single transfer of property skips two or more generations. See paragraph (d) of this section for the definition of skip person. See § 26.2652–1(b) for the definition of trust. See § 26.2632–1(c)(4) for the time that a direct skip occurs if the transferred property is subject to an estate tax inclusion period.

(b) Taxable termination. (1) *In general.* Except as otherwise provided in this paragraph (b), a taxable termination is a termination (occurring for any reason) of an interest in trust unless—

(i) A transfer subject to Federal estate or gift tax occurs with respect to the property held in the trust at the time of the termination;

(ii) Immediately after the termination, a person who is not a skip person has an interest in the trust; or

(iii) At no time after the termination may a distribution, other than a distribution the probability of which occurring is so remote as to be negligible (including a distribution at the termination of the trust) be made from the trust to a skip person. For this purpose, the probability that a distribution will occur is so remote as to be negligible only if it can be ascertained by actuarial standards that there is less than a 5 percent probability that the distribution will occur.

(2) *Partial termination.* If a distribution of a portion of trust property is made to a skip person by reason of a termination occurring on the death of a lineal descendant of the transferor, the termination is a taxable termination with respect to the distributed property.

(3) *Simultaneous terminations.* A simultaneous termination of two or more interests creates only one taxable termination.

(c) Taxable distribution. (1) *In general.* A taxable distribution is a distribution of income or principal from a trust to a skip person unless the distribution is a taxable termination or a direct skip. If any portion of GST tax (including penalties and interest thereon) imposed on a distributee is paid from the distributing trust, the payment is an additional taxable distribution to the distributee. For purposes of chapter 13, the additional distribution is treated as having been made on the last day of the calendar year in which the original taxable distribution is made. If Federal estate or gift tax is imposed on any individual with respect to an interest in property held by a trust, the interest in property is treated as having been distributed to the individual to the extent that the value of the interest is subject to Federal estate or gift tax. See § 26.2652–1(a)(6) Example 5, regarding the treatment of the lapse of a power of appointment as a transfer to a trust.

(2) *Look-through rule not to apply.* Solely for purposes of determining whether any transfer from a trust to another trust is a taxable distribution, the rules of section 2651(e)(2) do not apply. If the transferring trust and the recipient trust have the same transferor, see § 26.2642–4(a)(1) and (2) for rules for recomputing the applicable fraction of the recipient trust.

(d) Skip person. A skip person is—

(1) An individual assigned to a generation more than one generation below that of the transferor (determined under the rules of section 2651); or

(2) A trust if—

(i) All interests in the trust are held by skip persons; or

(ii) No person holds an interest in the trust and no distributions, other than a distribution the probability of which occurring is so remote as to be negligible (including distributions at the termination of the trust), may be made after the transfer to a person other than a skip person. For this purpose, the probability that a distribution will occur is so remote as to be negligible only if it can be ascertained by actuarial standards that there is less than a 5 percent probability that the distribution will occur.

(e) Interest in trust. (1) *In general.* An interest in trust is an interest in property held in trust as defined in section 2652(c) and these regulations. An interest in trust exists if a person—

(i) Has a present right to receive trust principal or income;

(ii) Is a permissible current recipient of trust principal or income and is not described in section 2055(a); or

(iii) Is described in section 2055(a) and the trust is a charitable remainder annuity trust or unitrust (as defined in section 664(d)) or a pooled income fund (as defined in section 642(c)(5)).

(2) *Exceptions.* (i) *Support obligations.* In general, an individual has a present right to receive trust income or principal if trust income or principal may be used to satisfy the individual's support obligations. However, an individual does not have an interest in a trust merely because a support obligation of that individual may be satisfied by a distribution that is either within the discretion of a fiduciary or pursuant to provisions of local law substantially equivalent to the Uniform Gifts (Transfers) to Minors Act.

(ii) *Certain interests disregarded.* An interest which is used primarily to postpone or avoid the GST tax is disregarded for purposes of chapter 13. An interest is considered as used primarily to postpone or avoid the GST tax if a significant purpose for the creation of the interest is to postpone or avoid the tax.

(3) *Disclaimers.* An interest does not exist to the extent it is disclaimed pursuant to a disclaimer that constitutes a qualified disclaimer under section 2518.

(f) Examples. The following examples illustrate the provisions of this section.

Example (1). Direct skip. T gratuitously conveys Blackacre to T's grandchild. Because the transfer is a transfer to a skip person of property subject to Federal gift tax, it is a direct skip.

Example (2). Direct skip of more than one generation. T gratuitously conveys Blackacre to T's great-grandchild. The transfer is a direct skip. Only one GST tax is imposed on the direct skip although two generations are skipped by the transfer.

Example (3). Withdrawal power in trust. T transfers $50,000 to a new trust providing that trust income is to be paid to T's child, C, for life and, on C's death, the trust principal is to be paid to T's descendants. Under the terms of the trust, T grants four grandchildren the right to withdraw $10,000 from the trust for a 60 day period following the transfer. Since C, who is not a skip person, has an interest in the trust, the trust is not a skip person. T's transfer to the trust is not a direct skip.

Example (4). Taxable termination. T establishes an irrevocable trust under which the income is to be paid to T's child, C, for life. On the death of C, the trust principal is to be paid to T's grandchild, GC. Since C has an interest in the trust, the trust is not a skip person and the transfer to the trust is not a direct skip. If C dies survived by GC, a taxable termination occurs at C's death because C's interest in the trust terminates and thereafter the trust property is held by a skip person who occupies a lower generation than C.

Example (5). Direct skip of property held in trust. T establishes a testamentary trust under which the income is to be paid to T's surviving spouse, S, for life and the remainder is to be paid to a grandchild of T and S. T's executor elects to treat the trust as qualified terminable interest property under section 2056(b)(7). The transfer to the trust is not a direct skip because S, a person who is not a skip person, holds a present right to receive income from the trust. Upon S's death, the trust property is included in S's gross estate under section 2044 and passes directly to a skip person. The GST occurring at that time is a direct skip because it is a transfer subject to chapter 11. The fact that the interest created by T is terminated at S's death is immaterial because S becomes the transferor at the time of the transfer subject to chapter 11.

Example (6). Taxable termination. T establishes an irrevocable trust for the benefit of T's child, C, T's grandchild, GC, and T's great grandchild, GGC. Under the terms of the trust, income and principal may be distributed to any or all of the living beneficiaries at the discretion of the trustee. Upon the death of the second beneficiary to die, the trust principal is to be paid to the survivor. C dies first. A taxable termination occurs at that time because, immediately after C's interest terminates, all interests in the trust are held by skip persons (GC and GGC).

Example (7). Taxable termination resulting from distribution. The facts are the same as in Example 6, except twenty years after C's death the trustee exercises its discretionary power and distributes the entire principal to GGC. The distribution results in a taxable termination because GC's interest in the trust terminates as a result of the distribution of the entire trust property to GGC, a skip person. The result would be the same if the trustee retained sufficient funds to pay the GST tax due by reason of the taxable termination, as well as any expenses of winding up the trust.

Example (8). Simultaneous termination of interests of more than one beneficiary. T establishes an irrevocable trust for the benefit of T's child, C, T's grandchild, GC, and T's great-grandchild, GGC. Under the terms of the trust, income and principal may be distributed to any or all of the living beneficiaries at the discretion of the trustee. Upon the death of C, the trust property is to be distributed to GGC if then living. If C is survived by both GC and GGC, both C's and GC's interests in the trust will terminate on C's death. However, because both interests will terminate at the same time and as a result of one event, only one taxable termination occurs.

Example (9). Partial taxable termination. T creates an irrevocable trust providing that trust income is to be paid to T's children, A and B, in such proportions as the trustee determines for their joint lives. On the death of the first child to die, one-half of the trust principal is to be paid to T's then living grandchildren. The balance of the trust principal is to be paid to T's grandchildren on the death of the survivor of A and B. If A predeceases B, the distribution occurring on the termination of A's interest in the trust is a taxable termination and not a taxable distribution. It is a taxable termination because the distribution is a distribution of a portion of the trust that occurs as a result of the death of A, a lineal descendant of T. It is immaterial that a portion of the trust continues and that B, a person other than a skip person, thereafter holds an interest in the trust.

Example (10). Taxable distribution. T establishes an irrevocable trust under which the trust income is payable to T's child, C, for life. When T's grandchild, GC, attains 35 years of age, GC is to receive one-half of the principal. The remaining one-half of the principal is to be distributed to GC on C's death. Assume that C survives until GC attains age 35. When the trustee distributes one-half of the principal to GC on GC's 35th birthday, the distribution is a taxable distribution because it is a distribution to a skip person and is neither a taxable termination nor a direct skip.

Example (11). Exercise of withdrawal right as taxable distribution. The facts are the same as in Example 10, except GC holds a continuing right to withdraw trust principal and after one year GC withdraws $10,000. The withdrawal by GC is not a taxable termination because the withdrawal does not terminate C's interest in the trust. The withdrawal by GC is a taxable distribution to GC.

Example (12). Interest in trust. T establishes an irrevocable trust under which the income is to be paid to T's child, C, for life. On the death of C, the trust principal is to be paid to T's grandchild, GC. Because C has a present right to receive income from the trust, C has an interest in the trust. Because GC cannot currently receive distributions from the trust, GC does not have an interest in the trust.

Example (13). Support obligation. T establishes an irrevocable trust for the benefit of T's grandchild, GC. The trustee has discretion to distribute property for GC's support without regard to the duty or ability of GC's parent, C, to support GC. Because GC is a permissible current recipient of trust property, GC has an interest in the trust. C does not have an interest in the trust because the potential use of the trust property to satisfy C's support obligation is within the discretion of a fiduciary. C would be treated as having an interest in the trust if the trustee was required to distribute trust property for GC's support.

[T.D. 8644, 60 FR 66910, Dec. 27, 1995; 61 FR 29653, June 12, 1996; T.D. 9214, 70 FR 41142, July 18, 2005]

§ 2613. Skip Person and Non-Skip Person Defined

(a) Skip person. For purposes of this chapter, the term "skip person" means—

(1) a natural person assigned to a generation which is 2 or more generations below the generation assignment of the transferor, or

(2) a trust—

(A) if all interests in such trust are held by skip persons, or

(B) if—

(i) there is no person holding an interest in such trust, and

(ii) at no time after such transfer may a distribution (including distributions on termination) be made from such trust to a nonskip person.

(b) Non-skip person. For purposes of this chapter, the term "non-skip person" means any person who is not a skip person.

Regulation

§ 26.2613–1 Skip person.

For the definition of skip person see § 26.2612–1(d).

[T.D. 8644, 60 FR 66912, Dec. 27, 1995]

Subchapter C. Taxable Amount

§ 2621. Taxable Amount in Case of Taxable Distribution

(a) In general. For purposes of this chapter, the taxable amount in the case of any taxable distribution shall be—

(1) the value of the property received by the transferee, reduced by

(2) any expense incurred by the transferee in connection with the determination, collection, or refund of the tax imposed by this chapter with respect to such distribution.

(b) Payment of GST tax treated as taxable distribution. For purposes of this chapter, if any of the tax imposed by this chapter with respect to any taxable distribution is paid out of the trust, an amount equal to the portion so paid shall be treated as a taxable distribution.

§ 2622. Taxable Amount in Case of Taxable Termination

(a) In general. For purposes of this chapter, the taxable amount in the case of a taxable termination shall be—

(1) the value of all property with respect to which the taxable termination has occurred, reduced by

(2) any deduction allowed under subsection (b).

(b) Deduction for certain expenses. For purposes of subsection (a), there shall be allowed a deduction similar to the deduction allowed by section 2053 (relating to expenses, indebtedness, and taxes) for amounts attributable to the property with respect to which the taxable termination has occurred.

§ 2623. Taxable Amount in Case of Direct Skip

For purposes of this chapter, the taxable amount in the case of a direct skip shall be the value of the property received by the transferee.

§ 2624. Valuation

(a) General rule. Except as otherwise provided in this chapter, property shall be valued as of the time of the generation-skipping transfer.

(b) Alternate valuation and special use valuation elections apply to certain direct skips. In the case of any direct skip of property which is included in the transferor's gross estate, the value of such property for purposes of this chapter shall be the same as its value for purposes of chapter 11 (determined with regard to sections 2032 and 2032A).

(c) Alternate valuation election permitted in the case of taxable terminations occurring at death. If 1 or more taxable terminations with respect to the same trust occur at the same time as and as a result of the death of an individual, an election may be made to value all of the property included in such terminations in accordance with section 2032.

(d) Reduction for consideration provided by transferee. For purposes of this chapter, the value of the property transferred shall be reduced by the amount of any consideration provided by the transferee.

Subchapter D. GST Exemption

§ 2631. GST Exemption

(a) General rule. For purposes of determining the inclusion ratio, every individual shall be allowed a GST exemption amount which may be allocated by such individual (or his executor) to any property with respect to which such individual is the transferor.

(b) Allocations irrevocable. Any allocation under subsection (a), once made, shall be irrevocable.

(c) GST Exemption Amount. For purposes of subsection (a), the GST exemption amount for any calendar year shall be equal to the basic exclusion amount under section 2010(c) for such calendar year.

§ 2632. Special Rules for Allocation of GST Exemption

(a) Time and manner of allocation.

(1) Time. Any allocation by an individual of his GST exemption under section 2631(a) may be made at any time on or before the date prescribed for filing the estate tax return for such individual's estate (determined with regard to extensions), regardless of whether such a return is required to be filed.

(2) Manner. The Secretary shall prescribe by forms or regulations the manner in which any allocation referred to in paragraph (1) is to be made.

(b) Deemed allocation to certain lifetime direct skips.

(1) In general. If any individual makes a direct skip during his lifetime, any unused portion of such individual's GST exemption shall be allocated to the property transferred to the extent necessary to make the inclusion ratio for such property zero. If the amount of the direct skip exceeds such unused portion, the entire unused portion shall be allocated to the property transferred.

(2) Unused portion. For purposes of paragraph (1), the unused portion of an individual's GST exemption is that portion of such exemption which has not previously been allocated by such individual (or treated as allocated under paragraph (1) or subsection (c)(1)).

(3) Subsection not to apply in certain cases. An individual may elect to have this subsection not apply to a transfer.

(c) Deemed allocation to certain lifetime transfers to GST trusts.

(1) In general. If any individual makes an indirect skip during such individual's lifetime, any unused portion of such individual's GST exemption shall be allocated to the property transferred to the extent necessary to make the inclusion ratio for such property zero. If the amount of the indirect skip exceeds such unused portion, the entire unused portion shall be allocated to the property transferred.

(2) Unused portion. For purposes of paragraph (1), the unused portion of an individual's GST exemption is that portion of such exemption which has not previously been—

(A) allocated by such individual,

(B) treated as allocated under subsection (b) with respect to a direct skip occurring during or before the calendar year in which the indirect skip is made, or

(C) treated as allocated under paragraph (1) with respect to a prior indirect skip.

(3) Definitions.

(A) Indirect skip. For purposes of this subsection, the term "indirect skip" means any transfer of property (other than a direct skip) subject to the tax imposed by chapter 12 made to a GST trust.

(B) GST trust. The term "GST trust" means a trust that could have a generation-skipping transfer with respect to the transferor unless—

(i) the trust instrument provides that more than 25 percent of the trust corpus must be distributed to or may be withdrawn by one or more individuals who are non-skip persons—

(I) before the date that the individual attains age 46,

(II) on or before one or more dates specified in the trust instrument that will occur before the date that such individual attains age 46, or

(III) upon the occurrence of an event that, in accordance with regulations prescribed by the Secretary, may reasonably be expected to occur before the date that such individual attains age 46,

(ii) the trust instrument provides that more than 25 percent of the trust corpus must be distributed to or may be withdrawn by one or more individuals who are non-skip persons and who are living on the date of death of another person identified in the instrument (by name or by class) who is more than 10 years older than such individuals,

(iii) the trust instrument provides that, if one or more individuals who are non-skip persons die on or before a date or event described in clause (i) or (ii), more than 25 percent of the trust corpus either must be distributed to the estate or estates of one or more of such individuals or is subject to a general power of appointment exercisable by one or more of such individuals,

(iv) the trust is a trust any portion of which would be included in the gross estate of a non-skip person (other than the transferor) if such person died immediately after the transfer,

(v) the trust is a charitable lead annuity trust (within the meaning of section 2642(e)(3)(A)) or a charitable remainder annuity trust or a charitable remainder unitrust (within the meaning of section 664(d)), or

(vi) the trust is a trust with respect to which a deduction was allowed under section 2522 for the amount of an interest in the form of the right to receive annual payments of a fixed percentage of the net fair market value of the trust property (determined yearly) and which is required to pay principal to a non-skip person if such person is alive when the yearly payments for which the deduction was allowed terminate.

For purposes of this subparagraph, the value of transferred property shall not be considered to be includible in the gross estate of a non-skip person or subject to a right of withdrawal by reason of such person holding a right to withdraw so much of such property as does not exceed the amount referred to in section 2503(b) with respect to any transferor, and it shall be assumed that powers of appointment held by non-skip persons will not be exercised.

(4) Automatic allocations to certain GST trusts. For purposes of this subsection, an indirect skip to which section 2642(f) applies shall be deemed to have been made only at the close of the estate tax inclusion period. The fair market value of such transfer shall be the fair market value of the trust property at the close of the estate tax inclusion period.

(5) Applicability and effect.

(A) In general. An individual—

(i) may elect to have this subsection not apply to—

(I) an indirect skip, or

(II) any or all transfers made by such individual to a particular trust, and

(ii) may elect to treat any trust as a GST trust for purposes of this subsection with respect to any or all transfers made by such individual to such trust.

(B) Elections.

(i) Elections with respect to indirect skips. An election under subparagraph (A)(i)(I) shall be deemed to be timely if filed on a timely filed gift tax return for the calendar year in which the transfer was made or deemed to have been made pursuant to paragraph (4) or on such later date or dates as may be prescribed by the Secretary.

(ii) Other elections. An election under clause (i)(II) or (ii) of subparagraph (A) may be made on a timely filed gift tax return for the calendar year for which the election is to become effective.

(d) Retroactive allocations.

(1) In general. If—

(A) a non-skip person has an interest or a future interest in a trust to which any transfer has been made,

(B) such person—

(i) is a lineal descendant of a grandparent of the transferor or of a grandparent of the transferor's spouse or former spouse, and

(ii) is assigned to a generation below the generation assignment of the transferor, and

(C) such person predeceases the transferor, then the transferor may make an allocation of any of such transferor's unused GST exemption to any previous transfer or transfers to the trust on a chronological basis.

(2) Special rules. If the allocation under paragraph (1) by the transferor is made on a gift tax return filed on or before the date prescribed by section 6075(b) for gifts made within the calendar year within which the non-skip person's death occurred—

(A) the value of such transfer or transfers for purposes of section 2642(a) shall be determined as if such allocation had been made on a timely filed gift tax return for each calendar year within which each transfer was made,

(B) such allocation shall be effective immediately before such death, and

(C) the amount of the transferor's unused GST exemption available to be allocated shall be determined immediately before such death.

(3) Future interest. For purposes of this subsection, a person has a future interest in a trust if the trust may permit income or corpus to be paid to such person on a date or dates in the future.

(e) Allocation of unused GST exemption.

(1) In general. Any portion of an individual's GST exemption which has not been allocated within the time prescribed by subsection (a) shall be deemed to be allocated as follows—

(A) first, to property which is the subject of a direct skip occurring at such individual's death, and

(B) second, to trusts with respect to which such individual is the transferor and from which a taxable distribution or a taxable termination might occur at or after such individual's death.

(2) Allocation within categories.

(A) In general. The allocation under paragraph (1) shall be made among the properties described in subparagraph (A) thereof and the trusts described in subparagraph (B) thereof, as the case may be, in proportion to the respective amounts (at the time of allocation) of the nonexempt portions of such properties or trusts.

(B) Nonexempt portion. For purposes of subparagraph (A), the term "nonexempt portion" means the value (at the time of allocation) of the property or trust, multiplied by the inclusion ratio with respect to such property or trust.

Regulation

§ 26.2632–1 Allocation of GST exemption.

(a) General rule. Except as otherwise provided in this section, an individual or the individual's executor may allocate the individual's $1 million GST exemption at any time from the date of the transfer through the date for filing the individual's Federal estate tax return (including any extensions for filing that have been actually granted). If no estate tax return is required to be filed, the GST exemption may be allocated at any time through the date a Federal estate tax return would be due if a return were required to be filed (including any extensions actually granted). If property is held in trust, the allocation of GST exemption is made to the entire trust rather than to specific trust assets. If a transfer is a direct skip to a trust, the allocation of GST exemption to the transferred property is also treated as an allocation of GST exemption to the trust for purposes of future GSTs with respect to the trust by the same transferor.

(b) Lifetime allocations. (1) *Automatic allocation to direct skips.* (i) *In general.* If a direct skip occurs during the transferor's lifetime, the transferor's GST exemption not previously allocated (unused GST exemption) is automatically allocated to the transferred property (but not in excess of the fair market value of the property on the date of the transfer). The transferor may prevent the automatic allocation of GST exemption by describing on a timely-filed United States Gift (and Generation-Skipping Transfer) Tax Return (Form 709) the transfer and the extent to which the automatic allocation is not to apply. In addition, a timely-filed Form 709 accompanied by payment of the GST tax (as shown on the return with respect to the direct skip) is sufficient to prevent an automatic allocation of GST exemption with respect to the transferred property. See paragraph (c)(4) of this section for special rules in the case of direct skips treated as occurring at the termination of an estate tax inclusion period.

(ii) *Time for filing Form 709.* A Form 709 is timely filed if it is filed on or before the date required for reporting the transfer if it were a taxable gift (i.e., the date prescribed by section 6075(b), including any extensions to file actually granted (the due date)). Except as provided in paragraph (b)(1)(iii) of this section, the automatic allocation of GST exemption (or the election to prevent the allocation, if made) is irrevocable after the due date. An automatic allocation of GST exemption is effective as of the date of the transfer to which it relates. Except as provided above, a Form 709 need not be filed to report an automatic allocation.

(iii) *Transitional rule.* An election to prevent an automatic allocation of GST exemption filed on or before January 26, 1996, becomes irrevocable on July 24, 1996.

(2) *Automatic allocation to indirect skips made after December 31, 2000.* (i) *In general.* An indirect skip is a transfer of property to a GST trust as defined in section 2632(c)(3)(B) provided that the transfer is subject to gift tax and does not qualify as a direct skip. In the case of an indirect skip made after December 31, 2000, to which section 2642(f) (relating to transfers subject to an estate tax inclusion period (ETIP)) does not apply, the transferor's unused GST exemption is automatically allocated to the property transferred (but not in excess of the fair market value of the property on the date of the transfer). The automatic allocation pursuant to this paragraph is effective whether or not a Form 709 is filed reporting the transfer, and is effective as of the date of the transfer to which it relates. An automatic allocation is irrevocable after the due date of the Form 709 for the calendar year in which the transfer is made. In the case of an indirect skip to which section 2642(f) does apply, the indirect skip is deemed to be made at the close of the ETIP and the GST exemption is deemed to be allocated at that time. In either case, except as otherwise provided in paragraph (b)(2)(ii) of this section, the automatic allocation of exemption applies even if an allocation of exemption is made to the indirect skip in accordance with section 2632(a).

(ii) *Prevention of automatic allocation.* Except as otherwise provided in forms or other guidance published by the Service, the transferor may prevent the automatic allocation of GST exemption with regard to an indirect skip (including indirect skips to which section 2642(f) may apply) by making an election, as provided in paragraph (b)(2)(iii) of this section. Notwithstanding paragraph (b)(2)(iii)(B) of this section, the transferor may also prevent the automatic allocation of GST exemption with regard to an indirect skip by making an affirmative allocation of GST exemption on a Form 709 filed at any time on or before the due date for timely filing (within the meaning of paragraph (b)(1)(ii) of this section) of an amount that is less than (but not equal to) the value of the property transferred as reported on that return, in accordance with the provisions of paragraph (b)(4) of this section. See paragraph (b)(4)(iii) Example 6 of this section. Any election out of the automatic allocation rules under this section has no effect on the application of the automatic allocation rules applicable after the transferor's death under section 2632(e) and paragraph (d) of this section.

(iii) *Election to have automatic allocation rules not apply.* (A) *In general.* A transferor may prevent the automatic allocation of GST exemption (elect out) with respect to any transfer or transfers constituting an indirect skip made to a trust or to one or more separate shares that are treated as separate trusts under § 26.2654–1(a)(1) (collectively referred to hereinafter as a trust). In the case of a transfer treated under section 2513 as made one-half by the transferor and one-half by the transferor's spouse, each spouse shall be treated as a separate transferor who must satisfy separately the requirements of paragraph (b)(2)(iii)(B) to elect out with respect to the transfer. A transferor may elect out with respect to—

(*1*) One or more prior-year transfers subject to section 2642(f) (regarding ETIPs) made by the transferor to a specified trust or trusts;

(*2*) One or more (or all) current-year transfers made by the transferor to a specified trust or trusts;

(*3*) One or more (or all) future transfers made by the transferor to a specified trust or trusts;

(*4*) All future transfers made by the transferor to all trusts (whether or not in existence at the time of the election out); or

(*5*) Any combination of paragraphs (b)(2)(iii)(A)(*1*) through (*4*) of this section.

(B) *Manner of making an election out.* Except as otherwise provided in forms or other guidance published by the IRS, an election out is made as described in this paragraph (b)(2)(iii)(B). To elect out, the transferor must attach a statement (election out statement) to a Form 709 filed within the time period provided in paragraph (b)(2)(iii)(C) of this section (whether or not any transfer was made in the calendar year for which the Form 709 was filed, and whether or not a Form 709 otherwise would be required to be filed for that year). See paragraph (b)(4)(iv) Example 7 of this section. The election out statement must identify the trust (except for an election out under paragraph (b)(2)(iii)(A)(*4*) of this section), and specifically must provide that the transferor is electing out of the automatic allocation of GST exemption with respect to the described transfer or transfers. Prior-year transfers that are subject to section 2642(f), and to which the election out is to apply, must be specifically described or otherwise identified in the election out statement. Further, unless the election out is made for all transfers made to the trust in the current year and/or in all future years, the current-year transfers and/or future transfers to which the election out is to apply must be specifically described or otherwise identified in the election out statement.

(C) *Time for making an election out.* To elect out, the Form 709 with the attached election out statement must be filed on or before the due date for timely filing (within the meaning of paragraph (b)(1)(ii) of this section) of the Form 709 for the calendar year in which—

(*1*) For a transfer subject to section 2642(f), the ETIP closes; or

(*2*) For all other elections out, the first transfer to be covered by the election out was made.

(D) *Effect of election out.* An election out does not affect the automatic allocation of GST exemption to any transfer not covered by the election out statement. Except for elections out for transfers described in paragraph (b)(2)(iii)(A)(*1*) of this section that are specifically described in an election out statement, an election out does not apply to any prior-year transfer to a trust, including any transfer subject to an ETIP (even if the ETIP closes after the election is made). An election out does not prevent the transferor from allocating the transferor's available GST exemption to any transfer covered by the election out, either on a timely filed Form 709 reporting the transfer or at a later date in accordance with the provisions of paragraph (b)(4) of this section. An election out with respect to future transfers remains in effect unless and until terminated. Once an election out with respect to future transfers is made, a transferor need not file a Form 709 in future years solely to prevent the automatic allocation of the GST exemption to any future transfer covered by the election out.

(E) *Termination of election out.* Except as otherwise provided in forms or other guidance published by the IRS, an election out may be terminated as described in this paragraph (b)(2)(iii)(E). Pursuant to this section, a transferor may terminate an election out made on a Form 709 for a prior year, to the extent that election out applied to future transfers or to a transfer subject to section 2642(f). To terminate an election out, the transferor must attach a statement (termination statement) to a Form 709 filed on or before the due date of the Form 709 for the calendar year in which is made the first transfer to which the election out is not to apply (whether or not any transfer was made in the calendar year for which the Form 709 was filed, and whether or not a Form 709 otherwise would be required to be filed for that year). The termination statement must identify the trust (if applicable), describe the prior election out that is being terminated, specifically provide that the prior election out is being terminated, and either describe the extent to which the prior election out is being terminated or describe any current-year transfers to which the election out is not to apply. Consequently, the automatic allocation rules contained in section 2632(c)(1) will apply to any current-year transfer described on the termination statement and, except as otherwise provided in this paragraph, to all future transfers that otherwise would have been covered by the election out. The termination of an election out does not affect any transfer, or any election out, that is not described in the termination statement. The termination of an election out will not revoke the election out for any prior-year transfer, except for a prior-year transfer subject to section 2642(f) for which the election out is revoked on a timely filed Form 709 for the calendar year in which the ETIP closes or for any prior calendar year. The termination of an election out does not preclude the transferor from making another election out in the same or any subsequent year.

(3) *Election to treat trust as a GST trust.* (i) *In general.* A transferor may elect to treat any trust as a GST trust (GST trust election), without regard to whether the trust is subject to section 2642(f), with respect to—

(A) Any current-year transfer (or any or all current-year transfers) by the electing transferor to the trust;

(B) Any selected future transfers by the electing transferor to the trust;

(C) All future transfers by the electing transferor to the trust; or

(D) Any combination of paragraphs (b)(3)(i)(A) through (C) of this section.

(ii) *Time and manner of making GST trust election.* Except as otherwise provided in forms or other guidance published by the Internal Revenue Service, a GST trust election is made as described in this paragraph (b)(3)(ii). To make a GST trust election, the transferor must attach a statement (GST trust election statement) to a Form 709 filed on or before the due date for timely filing (within the meaning of paragraph (b)(1)(ii) of this section) of the Form 709 for the calendar year in which the first transfer to be covered by the GST trust election is made (whether or not any transfer was made in the calendar year for which the Form 709 was filed, and whether or not a Form 709 otherwise would be required to be filed for that year). The GST trust election statement must identify the trust, specifically describe or otherwise clearly identify the transfers to be covered by the election, and specifically provide that the transferor is electing to have the trust treated as a GST trust with respect to the covered transfers.

(iii) *Effect of GST trust election.* Except as otherwise provided in this paragraph, a GST trust election will cause all transfers made by the electing transferor to the trust that are subject to the election to be deemed to be made to a GST trust as defined in section 2632(c)(3)(B). Thus, the electing transferor's unused GST exemption may be allocated automatically to such transfers in accordance with paragraph (b)(2) of this section. A transferor may prevent the automatic allocation of GST exemption to future transfers to the trust either by terminating the GST trust election in accordance with paragraph (b)(3)(iv) of this section (in the case of trusts that would not otherwise be treated as GST trusts) or by electing out of the automatic allocation of GST exemption in accordance with paragraph (b)(2) of this section.

(iv) *Termination of GST trust election.* Except as otherwise provided in forms or other guidance published by the Service, a GST trust election may be terminated as described in this paragraph (b)(3)(iv). A transferor may terminate a GST trust election made on a Form 709 for a prior year, to the extent that election applied to future transfers or to a transfer subject to section 2642(f). To terminate a GST trust election, the transferor must attach a statement (termination statement) to a Form 709 filed on or before the due date for timely filing (within the meaning of paragraph (b)(1)(ii) of this section) a Form 709 for the calendar year: in which is made the electing transferor's first transfer to which the GST trust election is not to apply; or that is the first calendar year for which the GST trust election is not to apply, even if no transfer is made to the trust during that year. The termination statement must identify the trust, describe the current-year transfer (if any), and provide that the prior GST trust election is terminated. Accordingly, if the trust otherwise does not satisfy the definition of a GST trust, the automatic allocation rules contained in section 2632(c)(1) will not apply to the described current-year transfer or to any future transfers made by the transferor to the trust, unless and until another election under this paragraph (b)(3) is made.

(4) *Allocation to other transfers*—(i) *In general.* An allocation of GST exemption to property transferred during the transferor's lifetime, other than in a direct skip, is made on Form 709. The allocation must clearly identify the trust to which the allocation is being made, the amount of GST exemption allocated to it, and if the allocation is late or if an inclusion ratio greater than zero is claimed, the value of the trust assets at the effective date of the allocation. See paragraph (b)(4)(ii) of this section. The allocation should also state the inclusion ratio of the trust after the allocation. Except as otherwise provided in this paragraph, an allocation of GST exemption may be made by a formula; e.g., the allocation may be expressed in terms of the amount necessary to produce an inclusion ratio of zero. However, formula allocations made with respect to charitable lead annuity trusts are not valid except to the extent they are dependent on values as finally determined for Federal estate or gift tax purposes. With respect to a timely allocation, an allocation of GST exemption becomes irrevocable after the due date of the return. Except as provided in § 26.2642–3 (relating to charitable lead annuity trusts), an allocation of GST exemption to a trust is void to the extent the amount allocated exceeds the amount necessary to obtain an inclusion ratio of zero with respect to the trust. See § 26.2642–1 for the definition of inclusion ratio. An allocation is also void if the allocation is made with respect to a trust that has no GST potential with respect to the transferor making the allocation, at the time of the allocation. For this purpose, a trust has GST potential even if the possibility of a GST is so remote as to be negligible.

(ii) *Effective date of allocation.* (A) *In general.* (1) Except as otherwise provided, an allocation of GST exemption is effective as of the date of any transfer as to which the Form 709 on which it is made is a timely filed return (a timely allocation). If more than one timely allocation is made, the earlier allocation is modified only if the later allocation clearly identifies the transfer and the nature and extent of the modification. Except as provided in paragraph (d)(1) of this section, an allocation to a trust made on a Form 709 filed after the due date for reporting a transfer to the trust (a late allocation) is effective on the date the Form 709 is filed and is deemed to precede in point of time any taxable event occurring on such date. For purposes of this paragraph (b)(4)(ii), the Form 709 is deemed filed on the date it is postmarked to the Internal Revenue Service address as directed in forms or other guidance published by the Service. See § 26.2642–2 regarding the effect of a late allocation in determining the inclusion ratio, etc. See paragraph (c)(1) of this section regarding allocation of GST exemption to property subject to an estate tax inclusion period. If it is unclear whether an allocation of GST exemption on a Form 709 is a late or a timely allocation to a trust, the allocation is effective in the following order—

(i) To any transfer to the trust disclosed on the return as to which the return is a timely return;

(ii) As a late allocation; and

(iii) To any transfer to the trust not disclosed on the return as to which the return would be a timely return.

(2) A late allocation to a trust may be made on a Form 709 that is timely filed with respect to another transfer. A late allocation is irrevocable when made.

(B) *Amount of allocation.* If other transfers exist with respect to which GST exemption could be allocated under paragraphs (b)(4)(ii)(A)(1)(ii) and (iii), any GST exemption allocated under paragraph (b)(4)(ii)(A)(1)(i) of this section is allocated in an amount equal to the value of the transferred property as reported on the Form 709. Thus, if the GST exemption allocated on the Form 709 exceeds the value of the transfers reported on that return that have generationskipping potential, the initial allocation under paragraph (b)(4)(ii)(A)(1)(i) of this section is in the amount of the value of those transfers as reported on that return. Any remaining amount of GST exemption allocated on that return is then allocated pursuant to paragraphs (b)(4)(ii)(A)(1)(ii) and (iii) of this section, notwithstanding any subsequent upward adjustment in value of the transfers reported on the return.

(iii) *Examples.* The following examples illustrate the provisions of this paragraph (b):

Example (1). Modification of allocation of GST exemption. On December 1, 2003, T transfers $100,000 to an irrevocable GST trust described in section 2632(c)(3)(B). The transfer to the trust is not a direct skip. The date prescribed for filing the gift tax return reporting the taxable gift is April 15, 2004. On February 10, 2004, T files a Form 709 on which T properly elects out of the automatic allocation rules contained in section 2632(c)(1) with respect to the transfer in accordance with paragraph (b)(2)(iii) of this section, and allocates $50,000 of GST exemption to the trust. On April 13th of the same year, T files an additional Form 709 on which T confirms the election out of the automatic allocation rules contained in section 2632(c)(1) and allocates $100,000 of GST exemption to the trust in a manner that clearly indicates the intention to modify and supersede the prior allocation with respect to the 2003 transfer. The allocation made on the April 13 return supersedes the prior allocation because it is made on a timely-filed Form 709 that clearly identifies the trust and the nature and extent of the modification of GST exemption allocation. The allocation of $100,000 of GST exemption to the trust is effective as of December 1, 2003. The result would be the same if the amended Form 709 decreased the amount of the GST exemption allocated to the trust.

Example (2). Modification of allocation of GST exemption. The facts are the same as in Example 1 except, on July 8, 2004, T files a Form 709 attempting to reduce the earlier allocation. The return filed on July 8, 2004, is not a timely filed return. The $100,000 GST exemption allocated to the trust, as amended on April 13, 2004, remains in effect because an allocation, once made, is irrevocable and may not be modified after the last date on which a timely filed Form 709 may be filed.

Example (3). Effective date of late allocation of GST exemption. On November 15, 2003, T transfers $100,000 to an irrevocable GST trust described in section 2632(c)(3)(B). The transfer to the trust is not a direct skip. The date prescribed for filing the gift tax return reporting the taxable gift is April 15, 2004. On February 10, 2004, T files a Form 709 on which T properly elects out of the automatic allocation rules contained in section 2632(c)(1) in accordance with paragraph (b)(2)(iii) of this section with respect to that transfer. On December 1, 2004, T files a Form 709 and allocates $50,000 to the trust. The allocation is effective as of December 1, 2004.

Example (4). Effective date of late allocation of GST exemption. T transfers $100,000 to an irrevocable GST trust on December 1, 2003, in a transfer that is not a direct skip. On April 15, 2004, T files a Form 709 on which T properly elects out of the automatic allocation rules contained in section 2632(c)(1) with respect to the entire transfer in accordance with paragraph (b)(2)(iii) of this section and T does not make an allocation of any GST exemption on the Form 709. On September 1, 2004, the trustee makes a taxable distribution from the trust to T's grandchild in the amount of $30,000. Immediately prior to the distribution, the value of the trust assets was $150,000. On the same date, T allocates GST exemption to the trust in the amount of $50,000. The allocation of GST exemption on the date of the transfer is treated as preceding in point of time the taxable distribution. At the time of the GST, the trust has an inclusion ratio of .6667 (1-(50,000/150,000)).

Example (5). Automatic allocation to splitgift. On December 1, 2003, T transfers $50,000 to an irrevocable GST Trust described in section 2632(c)(3)(B). The transfer to the trust is not a direct skip. On April 30, 2004, T and T's spouse, S, each files an initial gift tax return for 2003, on which they consent, pursuant to section 2513, to have the gift treated as if one-half had been made by each. In spite of being made on a late-filed gift tax return for 2003, the election under section 2513 is valid because neither spouse had filed a timely gift tax return for that year. Previously, neither T nor S filed a timely gift tax return electing out of the automatic allocation rules contained in section 2632(c)(1). As a result of the election under section 2513, which is retroactive to the date of T's transfer, T and S are each treated as the transferor of one-half of the property transferred in the indirect skip. Thus, $25,000 of T's unused GST exemption and $25,000 of S's unused GST exemption is automatically allocated to the trust. Both allocations are effective on and after the date that T made the transfer. The result would be the same if T's transfer constituted a direct skip subject to the automatic allocation rules contained in section 2632(b).

Example (6). Partial allocation of GST exemption. On December 1, 2003, T transfers $100,000 to an irrevocable GST trust described in section 2632(c)(3)(B). The transfer to the trust is not a direct skip. The date prescribed for filing the gift tax return reporting the taxable gift is April 15, 2004. On February 10, 2004, T files a Form 709 on which T allocates $40,000 of GST exemption to the trust. By filing a timely Form 709 on which a partial allocation is made of $40,000, T effectively elected out of the automatic allocation rules for the remaining value of the transfer for which T did not allocate GST exemption.

(iv) *Example.* The following example illustrates language that may be used in the statement required under paragraph (b)(2)(iii) of this section to elect out of the automatic allocation rules under various scenarios:

Example (1). On March 1, 2006, T transfers $100,000 to Trust B, a GST trust described in section 2632(c)(3)(B). Subsequently, on September 15, 2006, T transfers an additional $75,000 to Trust B. No other transfers are made to Trust B in 2006. T attaches an election out statement to a timely filed Form 709 for calendar year 2006. Except with regard to paragraph (v) of this Example 1, the election out statement identifies Trust B as required under paragraph (b)(2)(iii)(B) of this section, and contains the following alternative election statements:

(i) "T hereby elects that the automatic allocation rules will not apply to the $100,000 transferred to Trust B on March 1, 2006." The election out of the automatic allocation rules will be effective only for T's March 1, 2006, transfer and will not apply to T's $75,000 transfer made on September 15, 2006.

(ii) "T hereby elects that the automatic allocation rules will not apply to any transfers to Trust B in 2006." The election out of the automatic allocation rules will be effective for T's transfers to Trust B made on March 1, 2006, and September 15, 2006.

(iii) "T hereby elects that the automatic allocation rules will not apply to any transfers to Trust B made by T in 2006 or to any additional transfers T may make to Trust B in subsequent years." The election out of the automatic allocation rules will be effective for T's transfers to Trust B in 2006 and for all future transfers to be made by T to Trust B, unless and until T terminates the election out of the automatic allocation rules.

(iv) "T hereby elects that the automatic allocation rules will not apply to any transfers T has made or will make to Trust B in the years 2006 through 2008." The election out of the automatic allocation rules will be effective for T's transfers to Trust B in 2006 through 2008. T's transfers to Trust B after 2008 will be subject to the automatic allocation rules, unless T elects out of those rules for one or more years after 2008. T may terminate the election out of the automatic allocation rules for 2007, 2008, or both in accordance with the termination rules of paragraph (b)(2)(iii)(E) of this section. T may terminate the election out for one or more of the transfers made in 2006 only on a later but still timely filed Form 709 for calendar year 2006.

(v) "T hereby elects that the automatic allocation rules will not apply to any current or future transfer that T may make to any trust." The election out of the automatic allocation rules will be effective for all of T's transfers (current-year and future) to Trust B and to any and all other trusts (whether such trusts exist in 2006 or are created in a later year), unless and until T terminates the election out of the automatic allocation rules. T may terminate the election out with regard to one or more (or all) of the transfers covered by the election out in accordance with the termination rules of paragraph (b)(2)(iii)(E) of this section.

(c) Special rules during an estate tax inclusion period. (1) *In general.* (i) *Automatic allocations with respect to direct skips and indirect skips.* A direct skip or an indirect skip that is subject to an estate tax inclusion period (ETIP) is deemed to have been made only at the close of the ETIP. The transferor may prevent the automatic allocation of GST exemption to a direct skip or an indirect skip by electing out of the automatic allocation rules at any time prior to the due date of the Form 709 for the calendar year in which the close of the ETIP occurs (whether or not any transfer was made in the calendar year for which the Form 709 was filed, and whether or not a Form 709 otherwise would be required to be filed for that year). See paragraph (b)(2)(i) of this section regarding the automatic allocation of GST exemption to an indirect skip subject to an ETIP.

(ii) *Other allocations.* An affirmative allocation of GST exemption cannot be revoked, but becomes effective as of (and no earlier than) the date of the close of the ETIP with respect to the trust. If an allocation has not been made prior to the close of the ETIP, an allocation of exemption is effective as of the close of the ETIP during the transferor's lifetime if made by the due date for filing the Form 709 for the calendar year in which the close of the ETIP occurs (timely ETIP return). An allocation of exemption is effective in the case of the close of the ETIP by reason of the death of the transferor as provided in paragraph (d) of this section.

(iii) *Portion of trust subject to ETIP.* If any part of a trust is subject to an ETIP, the entire trust is subject to the ETIP. See § 26.2642–1(b)(2) for rules determining the inclusion ratio applicable in the case of GSTs during an ETIP.

(2) *Estate tax inclusion period defined.* (i) *In general.* An ETIP is the period during which, should death occur, the value of transferred property would be includible (other than by reason of section 2035) in the gross estate of—

(A) The transferor; or

(B) The spouse of the transferor.

(ii) *Exceptions.* (A) For purposes of paragraph (c)(2) of this section, the value of transferred property is not considered as being subject to inclusion in the gross estate of the transferor or the spouse of the transferor if the possibility that the property will be included is so remote as to be negligible. A possibility is so remote as to be negligible if it can be ascertained by actuarial standards that there is less than a 5 percent probability that the property will be included in the gross estate.

(B) For purposes of paragraph (c)(2) of this section, the value of transferred property is not considered as being subject to inclusion in the gross estate of the spouse of the transferor, if the spouse possesses with respect to any transfer to the trust, a right to withdraw no more than the greater of $5,000 or 5 percent of the trust corpus, and such withdrawal right terminates no later than 60 days after the transfer to the trust.

(C) The rules of this paragraph (c)(2) do not apply to qualified terminable interest property with respect to which the special election under § 26.2652–2 has been made.

(3) *Termination of an ETIP.* An ETIP terminates on the first to occur of—

(i) The death of the transferor;

(ii) The time at which no portion of the property is includible in the transferor's gross estate (other than by reason of section 2035) or, in the case of an individual who is a transferor solely by reason of an election under section 2513, the time at which no portion would be includible in the gross estate of the individual's spouse (other than by reason of section 2035);

(iii) The time of a GST, but only with respect to the property involved in the GST; or

(iv) In the case of an ETIP arising by reason of an interest or power held by the transferor's spouse under subsection (c)(2)(i)(B) of this section, at the first to occur of—

(A) The death of the spouse; or

(B) The time at which no portion of the property would be includible in the spouse's gross estate (other than by reason of section 2035).

(4) *Treatment of direct skips.* If property transferred to a skip person is subject to an ETIP, the direct skip is treated as occurring on the termination of the ETIP.

(5) *Examples.* The following examples illustrate the rules of this section as they apply to the termination of an ETIP during the lifetime of the transferor. In each example assume that T transfers $100,000 to an irrevocable trust:

Example (1). Allocation of GST exemption during ETIP. The trust instrument provides that trust income is to be paid to T for 9 years or until T's prior death. The trust principal is to be paid to T's grandchild on the termination of T's income interest. If T dies within the 9-year period, the value of the trust principal is includible in T's gross estate under section 2036(a). Thus, the trust is subject to an ETIP. T files a timely Form 709 reporting the transfer and allocating $100,000 of GST exemption to the trust. The allocation of GST exemption to the trust is not effective until the termination of the ETIP.

Example (2). Effect of prior allocation on termination of ETIP. The facts are the same as in Example 1, except the trustee has the power to invade trust principal on behalf of T's grandchild, GC, during the term of T's income interest. In year 4, when the value of the trust is $200,000, the trustee distributes $15,000 to GC. The distribution is a taxable distribution. The ETIP with respect to the property distributed to GC terminates at the time of the taxable distribution. See paragraph (c)(3)(iii) of this section. Solely for purposes of determining the trust's inclusion ratio with respect to the taxable distribution, the prior $100,000 allocation of GST exemption (as well as any additional allocation made on a timely ETIP return) is effective immediately prior to the taxable distribution. See § 26.2642–1(b)(2). The trust's inclusion ratio with respect to the taxable distribution is therefore .50 (1 - (100,000/200,000)).

Example (3). Split-gift transfers subject to ETIP. The trust instrument provides that trust income is to be paid to T for 9 years or until T's prior death. The trust principal is to be paid to T's grandchild on the termination of T's income interest. T files a timely Form 709 reporting the transfer. T's spouse, S, consents to have the gift treated as made one-half by S under section 2513. Because S is treated as transferring one-half of the property to T's grandchild, S becomes the transferor of one-half of the trust for purposes of chapter 13. Because the value of the trust would be includible in T's gross estate if T died immediately after the transfer, S's transfer is subject to an ETIP. If S should die prior to the termination of the trust, S's executor may allocate S's GST exemption to the trust, but only to the portion of the trust for which S is treated as the transferor. However, the allocation does not become effective until the earlier of the expiration of T's income interest or T's death.

Example (4). Transfer of retained interest as ETIP termination. The trust instrument provides that trust income is to be paid to T for 9 years or until T's prior death. The trust principal is to be paid to T's grandchild on the termination of T's income interest. Four years after the initial transfer, T transfers the income interest to T's sibling. The ETIP with respect to the trust terminates on T's transfer of the income interest because, after the transfer, the trust property would not be includible in T's gross estate (other than by reason of section 2035) if T died at that time.

Example (5). Election out of automatic allocation of GST exemption for trust subject to an ETIP. On December 1, 2003, T transfers $100,000 to Trust A, an irrevocable GST trust described in section 2632(c)(3) that is subject to an estate tax inclusion period (ETIP). T made no other gifts in 2003. The ETIP terminates on December 31, 2008. T timely files a gift tax return (Form 709) reporting the gift on April 15, 2004. On May 15, 2006, T files a Form 709 on which T properly elects out of the automatic allocation rules contained in section 2632(c)(1) with respect to the December 1, 2003, transfer to Trust A in accordance with paragraph (b)(2)(iii) of this section. Because the indirect skip is not deemed to occur until December 31, 2008, T's election out of automatic GST allocation filed on May 15, 2006, is timely, and will be effective as of December 31, 2008 (unless revoked on a Form 709 filed on or before the due date of a Form 709 for calendar year 2008).

(d) Allocations after the transferor's death. (1) *Allocation by executor.* Except as otherwise provided in this paragraph (d), an allocation of a decedent's unused GST exemption by the executor of the decedent's estate is made on the appropriate United States Estate (and Generation-Skipping Transfer) Tax Return (Form 706 or Form 706NA) filed on or before the date prescribed for filing the return by section 6075(a) (including any extensions actually granted (the due date)). An allocation of GST exemption with respect to property included in the gross estate of a decedent is effective as of the date of death. A timely allocation of GST exemption by an executor with respect to a lifetime transfer of property that is not included in the transferor's gross estate is made on a Form 709. A late allocation of GST exemption by an executor, other than an allocation that is deemed to be made under section 2632(b)(1) or (c)(1), with respect to a lifetime transfer of property is made on Form 706, Form 706NA, or Form 709 (filed on or before the due date of the transferor's estate tax return) and applies as of the date the allocation is filed. An allocation of GST exemption to a trust (whether or not funded at the time the Form 706 or Form 706NA is filed) is effective if the notice of allocation clearly identifies the trust and the amount of the decedent's GST exemption allocated to the trust. An executor may allocate the decedent's GST exemption by use of a formula. For purposes of this section, an allocation is void if the allocation is made for a trust that has no GST potential with respect to the transferor for whom the allocation is being made, as of the date of the transferor's death. For this purpose, a trust has GST potential even if the possibility of a GST is so remote as to be negligible.

(2) *Automatic allocation after death.* A decedent's unused GST exemption is automatically allocated on the due date for filing Form 706 or Form 706NA to the extent not otherwise allocated by the decedent's executor on or before that date. The automatic allocation occurs whether or not a return is actually required to be filed. Unused GST exemption is allocated pro rata (subject to the rules of § 26.2642–2(b)), on the basis of the value of the property as finally determined for purposes of chapter 11 (chapter 11 value), first to direct skips treated as occurring at the transferor's death. The balance, if any, of unused GST exemption is allocated pro rata (subject to the rules of § 26.2642–2(b)) on the basis of the chapter 11 value of the nonexempt portion of the trust property (or in the case of trusts that are not included in the gross estate, on the basis of the date of death value of the trust) to trusts with respect to which a taxable termination may occur or from which a taxable distribution may be made. The automatic allocation of GST exemption is irrevocable, and an allocation made by the executor after the automatic allocation is made is ineffective. No automatic allocation of GST exemption is made to a trust that will have a new transferor with respect to the entire trust prior to the occurrence of any GST with respect to the trust. In addition, no automatic allocation of GST exemption is made to a trust if, during the nine month period ending immediately after the death of the transferor—

(i) No GST has occurred with respect to the trust; and

(ii) At the end of such period no future GST can occur with respect to the trust.

(e) Effective dates. This section is applicable as provided in § 26.2601–1(c), with the following exceptions:

(1) Paragraphs (b)(2) and (b)(3), the third sentence of paragraph (b)(4)(i), the fourth sentence of paragraph (b)(4)(ii)(A)(1), paragraphs (b)(4)(iii) and (b)(4)(iv), and the fourth sentence of paragraph (d)(1) of this section, which will apply to elections made on or after July 13, 2004; and

(2) Paragraph (c)(1), and Example 5 of paragraph (c)(5), which will apply to elections made on or after June 29, 2005.

[T.D. 8644, 60 FR 66912, Dec. 27, 1995; 61 FR 29654, June 12, 1996; T.D. 9208, 70 FR 37260, June 29, 2005]

Subchapter E. Applicable Rate; Inclusion Ratio

§ 2641. Applicable Rate

(a) General rule. For purposes of this chapter, the term "applicable rate" means, with respect to any generation-skipping transfer, the product of—

(1) the maximum Federal estate tax rate, and

(2) the inclusion ratio with respect to the transfer.

(b) Maximum federal estate tax rate. For purposes of subsection (a), the term "maximum Federal estate tax rate" means the maximum rate imposed by section 2001 on the estates of decedents dying at the time of the taxable distribution, taxable termination, or direct skip, as the case may be.

Section 302(c) of the Tax Relief, Unemployment Insurance Reauthorization, and Job Creation Act of 2010 (P.L. 111–312) states "[i]n the case of any generation-skipping transfer made after December 31, 2009, and before January 1, 2011, the applicable rate determined under section 2641(a) of the Internal Revenue Code of 1986 shall be zero."

Regulation

§ 26.2641–1 Applicable rate of tax.

The rate of tax applicable to any GST (applicable rate) is determined by multiplying the maximum Federal estate tax rate in effect at the time of the GST by the inclusion ratio (as defined in § 26.2642–1). For this purpose, the maximum Federal estate tax rate is the maximum rate set forth under section 2001(c) (without regard to section 2001(c)(2)).

[T.D. 8644, 60 FR 66915, Dec. 27, 1995]

§ 2642. Inclusion Ratio

(a) Inclusion ratio defined. For purposes of this chapter—

(1) In general. Except as otherwise provided in this section, the inclusion ratio with respect to any property transferred in a generation-skipping transfer shall be the excess (if any) of 1 over—

(A) except as provided in subparagraph (B), the applicable fraction determined for the trust from which such transfer is made, or

(B) in the case of a direct skip, the applicable fraction determined for such skip.

(2) Applicable fraction. For purposes of paragraph (1), the applicable fraction is a fraction—

(A) the numerator of which is the amount of the GST exemption allocated to the trust (or in the case of a direct skip, allocated to the property transferred in such skip), and

(B) the denominator of which is—

(i) the value of the property transferred to the trust (or involved in the direct skip), reduced by

(ii) the sum of—

(I) any Federal estate tax or State death tax actually recovered from the trust attributable to such property, and

(II) any charitable deduction allowed under section 2055 or 2522 with respect to such property.

(3) Severing of trusts.

(A) In general. If a trust is severed in a qualified severance, the trusts resulting from such severance shall be treated as separate trusts thereafter for purposes of this chapter.

(B) Qualified severance. For purposes of subparagraph (A)—

(i) In general. The term "qualified severance" means the division of a single trust and the creation (by any means available under the governing instrument or under local law) of two or more trusts if—

(I) the single trust was divided on a fractional basis, and

(II) the terms of the new trusts, in the aggregate, provide for the same succession of interests of beneficiaries as are provided in the original trust.

(ii) Trusts with inclusion ratio greater than zero. If a trust has an inclusion ratio of greater than zero and less than 1, a severance is a qualified severance only if the single trust is divided into two trusts, one of which receives a fractional share of the total value of all trust assets equal to the applicable fraction of the single trust immediately before the severance. In such case, the trust receiving such fractional share shall have an inclusion ratio of zero and the other trust shall have an inclusion ratio of 1.

(iii) Regulations. The term "qualified severance" includes any other severance permitted under regulations prescribed by the Secretary.

(C) Timing and manner of severances. A severance pursuant to this paragraph may be made at any time. The Secretary shall prescribe by forms or regulations the manner in which the qualified severance shall be reported to the Secretary.

(b) Valuation rules, etc. Except as provided in subsection (f)—

(1) Gifts for which gift tax return filed or deemed allocation made. If the allocation of the GST exemption to any transfers of property is made on a gift tax return filed on or before the date prescribed by section 6075(b) for such transfer or is deemed to be made under section 2632 (b)(1) or (c)(1)—

(A) the value of such property for purposes of subsection (a) shall be its value as finally determined for purposes of chapter 12 (within the meaning of section 2001(f)(2)), or, in the case of an allocation deemed to have been made at the close of an estate tax inclusion period, its value at the time of the close of the estate tax inclusion period, and

(B) such allocation shall be effective on and after the date of such transfer, or, in the case of an allocation deemed to have been made at the close of an estate tax inclusion period, on and after the close of such estate tax inclusion period.

(2) Transfers and allocations at or after death.

(A) Transfers at death. If property is transferred as a result of the death of the transferor, the value of such property for purposes of subsection (a) shall be its value as finally determined for purposes of chapter 11; except that, if the requirements prescribed by the Secretary respecting allocation of post-death changes in value are not met, the value of such property shall be determined as of the time of the distribution concerned.

(B) Allocations to property transferred at death of transferor. Any allocation to property transferred as a result of the death of the transferor shall be effective on and after the date of the death of the transferor.

(3) Allocations to inter vivos transfers not made on timely filed gift tax return. If any allocation of the GST exemption to any property not transferred as a result of the death of the transferor is not made on a gift tax return filed on or before the date prescribed by section 6075(b) and is not deemed to be made under section 2632(b)(1)—

(A) the value of such property for purposes of subsection (a) shall be determined as of the time such allocation is filed with the Secretary, and

(B) such allocation shall be effective on and after the date on which such allocation is filed with the Secretary.

(4) QTIP trusts. If the value of property is included in the estate of a spouse by virtue of section 2044, and if such spouse is treated as the transferor of such property under section 2652(a), the value of such property for purposes of subsection (a) shall be its value for purposes of chapter 11 in the estate of such spouse.

(c) Treatment of certain direct skips which are nontaxable gifts.

(1) In general. In the case of a direct skip which is a nontaxable gift, the inclusion ratio shall be zero.

(2) Exception for certain transfers in trust. Paragraph (1) shall not apply to any transfer to a trust for the benefit of an individual unless—

(A) during the life of such individual, no portion of the corpus or income of the trust may be distributed to (or for the benefit of) any person other than such individual, and

(B) if the trust does not terminate before the individual dies, the assets of such trust will be includible in the gross estate of such individual.

Rules similar to the rules of section 2652(c)(3) shall apply for purposes of subparagraph (A).

(3) Nontaxable gift. For purposes of this subsection, the term "nontaxable gift" means any transfer of property to the extent such transfer is not treated as a taxable gift by reason of—

(A) section 2503(b) (taking into account the application of section 2513), or

(B) section 2503(e).

(d) Special rules where more than 1 transfer made to trust.

(1) In general. If a transfer of property is made to a trust in existence before such transfer, the applicable fraction for such trust shall be recomputed as of the time of such transfer in the manner provided in paragraph (2).

(2) Applicable fraction. In the case of any such transfer, the recomputed applicable fraction is a fraction—

(A) the numerator of which is the sum of—

(i) the amount of the GST exemption allocated to property involved in such transfer, plus

(ii) the nontax portion of such trust immediately before such transfer, and

(B) the denominator of which is the sum of—

(i) the value of the property involved in such transfer reduced by the sum of—

(I) any Federal estate tax or State death tax actually recovered from the trust attributable to such property, and

(II) any charitable deduction allowed under section 2055 or 2522 with respect to such property, and

(ii) the value of all of the property in the trust (immediately before such transfer).

(3) Nontax portion. For purposes of paragraph (2), the term "nontax portion" means the product of—

(A) the value of all of the property in the trust, and

(B) the applicable fraction in effect for such trust.

(4) Similar recomputation in case of certain late allocations. If—

(A) any allocation of the GST exemption to property transferred to a trust is not made on a timely filed gift tax return required by section 6019, and

(B) there was a previous allocation with respect to property transferred to such trust,

the applicable fraction for such trust shall be recomputed as of the time of such allocation under rules similar to the rules of paragraph (2).

(e) Special rules for charitable lead annuity trusts.

(1) In general. For purposes of determining the inclusion ratio for any charitable lead annuity trust, the applicable fraction shall be a fraction—

(A) the numerator of which is the adjusted GST exemption, and

(B) the denominator of which is the value of all of the property in such trust immediately after the termination of the charitable lead annuity.

(2) Adjusted GST exemption. For purposes of paragraph (1), the adjusted GST exemption is an amount equal to the GST exemption allocated to the trust increased by interest determined—

(A) at the interest rate used in determining the amount of the deduction under section 2055 or 2522 (as the case may be) for the charitable lead annuity, and

(B) for the actual period of the charitable lead annuity.

(3) Definitions. For purposes of this subsection—

(A) Charitable lead annuity trust. The term "charitable lead annuity trust" means any trust in which there is a charitable lead annuity.

(B) Charitable lead annuity. The term "charitable lead annuity" means any interest in the form of a guaranteed annuity with respect to which a deduction was allowed under section 2055 or 2522 (as the case may be).

(4) Coordination with subsection (d). Under regulations, appropriate adjustments shall be made in the application of subsection (d) to take into account the provisions of this subsection.

(f) Special rules for certain inter vivos transfers. Except as provided in regulations—

(1) In general. For purposes of determining the inclusion ratio, if—

(A) an individual makes an inter vivos transfer of property, and

(B) the value of such property would be includible in the gross estate of such individual under chapter 11 if such individual died immediately after making such transfer (other than by reason of section 2035),

any allocation of GST exemption to such property shall not be made before the close of the estate tax inclusion period (and the value of such property shall be determined under paragraph (2)). If such transfer is a direct skip, such skip shall be treated as occurring as of the close of the estate tax inclusion period.

(2) Valuation. In the case of any property to which paragraph (1) applies, the value of such property shall be—

(A) if such property is includible in the gross estate of the transferor (other than by reason of section 2035), its value for purposes of chapter 11, or

(B) if subparagraph (A) does not apply, its value as of the close of the estate tax inclusion period (or, if any allocation of GST exemption to such property is not made on a timely filed gift tax return for the calendar year in which such period ends, its value as of the time such allocation is filed with the Secretary).

(3) Estate tax inclusion period. For purposes of this subsection, the term "estate tax inclusion period" means any period after the transfer described in paragraph (1) during which the value of the property involved in such transfer would be includible in the gross estate of the transferor under chapter 11 if he died. Such period shall in no event extend beyond the earlier of—

(A) the date on which there is a generation-skipping transfer with respect to such property, or

(B) the date of the death of the transferor.

(4) Treatment of spouse. Except as provided in regulations, any reference in this subsection to an individual or transferor shall be treated as including a reference to the spouse of such individual or transferor.

(5) Coordination with subsection (d). Under regulations, appropriate adjustments shall be made in the application of subsection (d) to take into account the provisions of this subsection.

(g) Relief provisions.

(1) Relief from late elections.

(A) In general. The Secretary shall by regulation prescribe such circumstances and procedures under which extensions of time will be granted to make—

(i) an allocation of GST exemption described in paragraph (1) or (2) of subsection (b), and

(ii) an election under subsection (b)(3) or (c)(5) of section 2632.

Such regulations shall include procedures for requesting comparable relief with respect to transfers made before the date of the enactment of this paragraph.

(B) Basis for determinations. In determining whether to grant relief under this paragraph, the Secretary shall take into account all relevant circumstances, including evidence of intent contained in the trust instrument or instrument of transfer and such other factors as the Secretary deems relevant. For purposes of determining whether to grant relief under this paragraph, the time for making the allocation (or election) shall be treated as if not expressly prescribed by statute.

(2) Substantial compliance. An allocation of GST exemption under section 2632 that demonstrates an intent to have the lowest possible inclusion ratio with respect to a transfer or a trust shall be deemed to be an allocation of so much of the transferor's unused GST exemption as produces the lowest possible inclusion ratio. In determining whether there has been substantial compliance, all relevant circumstances shall be taken into account, including evidence of intent contained in the trust instrument or instrument of transfer and such other factors as the Secretary deems relevant.

Regulations

§ 26.2642–1 Inclusion ratio.

(a) In general. Except as otherwise provided in this section, the inclusion ratio is determined by subtracting the applicable fraction (rounded to the nearest one-thousandth (.001)) from 1. In rounding the applicable fraction to the nearest one-thousandth, any amount that is midway between one one-thousandth and another one-thousandth is rounded up to the higher of those two amounts. For generation-skipping transfer tax rules related to an ABLE account established under section 529A, see § 1.529A–4 of this chapter.

(b) Numerator of applicable fraction. (1) *In general.* Except as otherwise provided in this paragraph (b), and in §§ 26.2642–3 (providing a special rule for charitable lead annuity trusts) and 26.2642–4 (providing rules for the redetermination of the applicable fraction), the numerator of the applicable fraction is the amount of GST exemption allocated to the trust (or to the transferred property in the case of a direct skip not in trust).

(2) *GSTs occurring during an ETIP.* (i) *In general.* For purposes of determining the inclusion ratio with respect to a taxable termination or a taxable distribution that occurs during an ETIP, the numerator of the applicable fraction is the sum of—

(A) The GST exemption previously allocated to the trust (including any allocation made to the trust prior to any taxable termination or distribution) reduced (but not below zero) by the nontax amount of any prior GSTs with respect to the trust; and

(B) Any GST exemption allocated to the trust on a timely ETIP return filed after the termination of the ETIP. See § 26.2632–1(c)(5) Example 2.

(ii) *Nontax amount of a prior GST.* (1) The nontax amount of a prior GST with respect to the trust is the amount of the GST multiplied by the applicable fraction attributable to the trust at the time of the prior GST.

(2) For rules regarding the allocation of GST exemption to property during an ETIP, see § 26.2632–1(c).

(c) Denominator of applicable fraction. (1) *In general.* Except as otherwise provided in this paragraph (c) and in §§ 26.2642–3 and 26.2642–4, the denominator of the applicable fraction is the value of the property transferred to the trust (or transferred in a direct skip not in trust) (as determined under § 26.2642–2) reduced by the sum of—

(i) Any Federal estate tax and any State death tax incurred by reason of the transfer that is chargeable to the trust and is actually recovered from the trust;

(ii) The amount of any charitable deduction allowed under section 2055, 2106, or 2522 with respect to the transfer; and

(iii) In the case of a direct skip, the value of the portion of the transfer that is a nontaxable gift. See paragraph (c)(3) of this section for the definition of nontaxable gift.

(2) *Zero denominator.* If the denominator of the applicable fraction is zero, the inclusion ratio is zero.

(3) *Nontaxable gifts.* Generally, for purposes of chapter 13, a transfer is a nontaxable gift to the extent the transfer is excluded from taxable gifts by reason of section 2503(b) (after application of section 2513) or section 2503(e). However, a transfer to a trust for the benefit of an individual is not a nontaxable gift for purposes of this section unless—

(i) Trust principal or income may, during the individual's lifetime, be distributed only to or for the benefit of the individual; and

(ii) The assets of the trust will be includible in the gross estate of the individual if the individual dies before the trust terminates.

(d) Examples. The following examples illustrate the provisions of this section. See § 26.2652–2(d) Examples 2 and 3 for illustrations of the computation of the inclusion ratio where the special (reverse QTIP) election may be applicable.

Example (1). Computation of the inclusion ratio. T transfers $100,000 to a newly-created irrevocable trust providing that income is to be accumulated for 10 years. At the end of 10 years, the accumulated income is to be distributed to T's child, C, and the trust principal is to be paid to T's grandchild. T allocates $40,000 of T's GST exemption to the trust on a timely-filed gift tax return. The applicable fraction with respect to the trust is .40 ($40,000 (the amount of GST exemption allocated to the trust) over $100,000 (the value of the property transferred to the trust)). The inclusion ratio is .60 (1–.40). If the maximum Federal estate tax rate is 55 percent at the time of a GST, the rate of tax applicable to the transfer (applicable rate) will be .333 (55 percent (the maximum estate tax rate) x .60 (the inclusion ratio)).

Example (2). Gift entirely nontaxable. On December 1, 1996, T transfers $10,000 to an irrevocable trust for the benefit of T's grandchild, GC. GC possesses a right to withdraw any contributions to the trust such that the entire transfer qualifies for the annual exclusion under section 2503(b). Under the terms of the trust, the income is to be paid to GC for 10 years or until GC's prior death. Upon the expiration of GC's income interest, the trust principal is payable to GC or GC's estate. The transfer to the trust is a direct skip. T made no prior gifts to or for the benefit of GC during 1996. The entire $10,000 transfer is a nontaxable transfer. For purposes of computing the tax on the direct skip, the denominator of the applicable fraction is zero, and thus, the inclusion ratio is zero.

Example (3). Gift nontaxable in part. T transfers $12,000 to an irrevocable trust for the benefit of T's grandchild, GC. Under the terms of the trust, the income is to be paid to GC for 10 years or until GC's prior death. Upon the expiration of GC's income interest, the trust principal is payable to GC or GC's estate. Further, GC has the right to withdraw $10,000 of any contribution to the trust such that $10,000 of the transfer qualifies for the annual exclusion under section 2503(b). The amount of the nontaxable transfer is $10,000. Solely for purposes of computing the tax on the direct skip, T's transfer is divided into two portions. One portion is equal to the amount of the nontaxable transfer ($10,000) and has a zero inclusion ratio; the other portion is $2,000 ($12,000 - $10,000). With respect to the $2,000 portion, the denominator of the applicable fraction is $2,000. Assuming that T has sufficient GST exemption available, the numerator of the applicable fraction is $2,000 (unless T elects to have the automatic allocation provisions not apply). Thus, assuming T does not elect to have the automatic allocation not apply, the applicable fraction is one ($2,000/$2,000 = 1) and the inclusion ratio is zero (1 - 1 = 0).

Example (4). Gift nontaxable in part. Assume the same facts as in Example 3, except T files a timely Form 709 electing that the automatic allocation of GST exemption not apply to the $12,000 transferred in the direct skip. T's transfer is divided into two portions, a $10,000 portion with a zero inclusion ratio and a $2,000 portion with an applicable fraction of zero (0/$2,000 = 0) and an inclusion ratio of one (1 - 0 = 1).

[T.D. 8644, 60 FR 66915, Dec. 27, 1995; T.D. 9923, 85 FR 74047, Nov. 19, 2020]

§ 26.2642–2 Valuation.

(a) Lifetime transfers. (1) *In general.* For purposes of determining the denominator of the applicable fraction, the value of property transferred during life is its fair market value on the effective date of the allocation of GST exemption. In the case of a timely allocation under § 26.2632–1(b)(2)(ii), the denominator of the applicable fraction is the fair market value of the property as finally determined for purposes of chapter 12.

(2) *Special rule for late allocations during life.* If a transferor makes a late allocation of GST exemption to a trust, the value of the property transferred to the trust is the fair market value of the trust assets determined on the effective date of the allocation of GST exemption. Except as otherwise provided in this paragraph (a)(2), if a transferor makes a late allocation of GST exemption to a trust, the transferor may, solely for purposes of determining the fair market value of the trust assets, elect to treat the allocation as having been made on the first day of the month during which the late allocation is made (valuation date). An election under this paragraph (a)(2) is not effective with respect to a life insurance policy or a trust holding a life insurance policy, if the insured individual has died. An allocation subject to the election contained in this paragraph (a)(2) is not effective until it is actually filed with the Internal Revenue Service. The election is made by stating on the Form 709 on which the allocation is made—

(i) That the election is being made;

(ii) The applicable valuation date; and

(iii) The fair market value of the trust assets on the valuation date.

(b) Transfers at death. (1) *In general.* Except as provided in paragraphs (b)(2) and (3) of this section, in determining the denominator of the applicable fraction, the value of property included in the decedent's gross estate is its value for purposes of chapter 11. In the case of qualified real property with respect to which the election under section 2032A is made, the value of the property is the value determined under section 2032A provided the recapture agreement described in section 2032A(d)(2) filed with the Internal Revenue Service specifically provides for the signatories' consent to the imposition of, and personal liability for, additional GST tax in the event an additional estate tax is imposed under section 2032A(c). See § 26.2642–4(a)(4). If the recapture agreement does not contain these provisions, the value of qualified real property as to which the election under section 2032A is made is the fair market value of the property determined without regard to the provisions of section 2032A.

(2) *Special rule for pecuniary payments*—(i) *In general.* If a pecuniary payment is satisfied with cash, the denominator of the applicable fraction is the pecuniary amount. If property other than cash is used to satisfy a pecuniary payment, the denominator of the applicable fraction is the pecuniary amount only if payment must be made with property on the basis of the value of the property on—

(A) The date of distribution; or

(B) A date other than the date of distribution, but only if the pecuniary payment must be satisfied on a basis that fairly reflects net appreciation and depreciation (occurring between the valuation date and the date of distribution) in all of the assets from which the distribution could have been made.

(ii) *Other pecuniary amounts payable in kind.* The denominator of the applicable fraction with respect to any property used to satisfy any other pecuniary payment payable in kind is the date of distribution value of the property.

(3) *Special rule for residual transfers after payment of a pecuniary payment*—(i) *In general.* Except as otherwise provided in this paragraph (b)(3), the denominator of the applicable fraction with respect to a residual transfer of property after the satisfaction of a pecuniary payment is the estate tax value of the assets available to satisfy the pecuniary payment reduced, if the pecuniary payment carries appropriate interest (as defined in paragraph (b)(4) of this section), by the pecuniary amount. The denominator of the applicable fraction with respect to a residual transfer of property after the satisfaction of a pecuniary payment that does not carry appropriate interest is the estate tax value of the assets available to satisfy the pecuniary payment reduced by the present value of the pecuniary payment. For purposes of this paragraph (b)(3)(i), the present value of the pecuniary payment is determined by using—

(A) The interest rate applicable under section 7520 at the death of the transferor; and

(B) The period between the date of the transferor's death and the date the pecuniary amount is paid.

(ii) *Special rule for residual transfers after pecuniary payments payable in kind.* The denominator of the applicable fraction with respect to any residual transfer after satisfaction of a pecuniary payment payable in kind is the date of distribution value of the property distributed in satisfaction of the residual transfer, unless the pecuniary payment must be satisfied on the basis of the value of the property on—

(A) The date of distribution; or

(B) A date other than the date of distribution, but only if the pecuniary payment must be satisfied on a basis that fairly reflects net appreciation and depreciation (occurring between the valuation date and the date of distribution) in all of the assets from which the distribution could have been made.

(4) *Appropriate interest*—(i) *In general.* For purposes of this section and § 26.2654–1 (relating to certain trusts treated as separate trusts), appropriate interest means that interest must be payable from the date of death of the transferor (or from the date specified under applicable State law requiring the payment of interest) to the date of payment at a rate—

(A) At least equal to—

(*1*) The statutory rate of interest, if any, applicable to pecuniary bequests under the law of the State whose law governs the administration of the estate or trust; or

(*2*) If no such rate is indicated under applicable State law, 80 percent of the rate that is applicable under section 7520 at the death of the transferor; and

(B) Not in excess of the greater of—

(*1*) The statutory rate of interest, if any, applicable to pecuniary bequests under the law of the State whose law governs the administration of the trust; or

(*2*) 120 percent of the rate that is applicable under section 7520 at the death of the transferor.

(ii) *Pecuniary payments deemed to carry appropriate interest.* For purposes of this paragraph (b)(4), if a pecuniary payment does not carry appropriate interest, the pecuniary payment is considered to carry appropriate interest to the extent—

(A) The entire payment is made or property is irrevocably set aside to satisfy the entire pecuniary payment within 15 months of the transferor's death; or

(B) The governing instrument or applicable local law specifically requires the executor or trustee to allocate to the pecuniary payment a pro rata share of the income earned by the fund from which the pecuniary payment is to be made between the date of death of the transferor and the date of payment. For purposes of paragraph (b)(4)(ii)(A) of this section, property is irrevocably set aside if it is segregated and held in a separate account pending distribution.

(c) Examples. The following examples illustrate the provisions of this section:

Example (1). T transfers $100,000 to a newly-created irrevocable trust on December 15, 1996. The trust provides that income is to be paid to T's child for 10 years. At the end of the 10-year period, the trust principal is to be paid to T's grandchild. T does not allocate any GST exemption to the trust on the gift tax return reporting the transfer. On November 15, 1997, T files a Form 709 allocating $50,000 of GST exemption to the trust. Because the allocation was made on a late filed return, the value of the property transferred to the trust is determined on the date the allocation is filed (unless an election is made pursuant to paragraph (a)(2) of this section to value the trust property as of the first day of the month in which the allocation document is filed with the Internal Revenue Service). On November 15, 1997, the value of the trust property is $150,000. Effective as of November 15, 1997, the applicable fraction with respect to the trust is .333 ($50,000 (the amount of GST exemption allocated to the trust) over $150,000 (the value of the trust principal on the effective date of the GST exemption allocation)), and the inclusion ratio is .667 (1.0 - 333).

Example (2). The facts are the same as in Example 1, except the value of the trust property is $80,000 on November 15, 1997. The applicable fraction is .625 ($50,000 over $80,000) and the inclusion ratio is .375 (1.0 - .625).

Example (3). T transfers $100,000 to a newly-created irrevocable trust on December 15, 1996. The trust provides that income is to be paid to T's child for 10 years. At the end of the 10-year period, the trust principal is to be paid to T's grandchild. T does not allocate any GST exemption to the trust on the gift tax return reporting the transfer. On November 15, 1997, T files a Form 709 allocating $50,000 of GST exemption to the trust. T elects to value the trust principal on the first day of the month in which the allocation is made pursuant to the election provided in paragraph (a)(2) of this section. Because the late allocation is made in November, the value of the trust is determined as of November 1, 1997.

[T.D. 8644, 60 FR 66915, Dec. 27, 1995; 61 FR 29654, June 12, 1996]

§ 26.2642–3 Special rule for charitable lead annuity trusts.

(a) In general. In determining the applicable fraction with respect to a charitable lead annuity trust—

(1) The numerator is the adjusted generation-skipping transfer tax exemption (adjusted GST exemption); and

(2) The denominator is the value of all property in the trust immediately after the termination of the charitable lead annuity.

(b) Adjusted GST exemption defined. The adjusted GST exemption is the amount of GST exemption allocated to the trust increased by an amount equal to the interest that would accrue if an amount equal to the allocated GST exemption were invested at the rate used to determine the amount of the estate or gift tax charitable deduction, compounded annually, for the actual period of the charitable lead annuity. If a late allocation is made to a charitable lead annuity trust, the adjusted GST exemption is the amount of GST exemption allocated to the trust increased by the interest that would accrue if invested at such rate for the period beginning on the date of the late allocation and extending for the balance of the actual period of the charitable lead annuity. The amount of GST exemption allocated to a charitable lead annuity trust is not reduced even though it is ultimately determined that the allocation of a lesser amount of GST exemption would have resulted in an inclusion ratio of zero. For purposes of chapter 13, a charitable lead annuity trust is any trust providing an interest in the form of a guaranteed annuity described in § 25.2522(c)–3(c)(2)(vi) of this chapter for which the transferor is allowed a charitable deduction for Federal estate or gift tax purposes.

(c) Example. The following example illustrates the provisions of this section:

Example. T creates a charitable lead annuity trust for a 10-year term with the remainder payable to T's grandchild. T timely allocates an amount of GST exemption to the trust which T expects will ultimately result in a zero inclusion ratio. However, at the end of the charitable lead interest, because the property has not appreciated to the extent T anticipated, the numerator of the applicable fraction is greater than the denominator. The inclusion ratio for the trust is zero. No portion of the GST exemption allocated to the trust is restored to T or to T's estate.

[T.D. 8644, 60 FR 66917, Dec. 27, 1995]

§ 26.2642–4 Redetermination of applicable fraction.

(a) In general. The applicable fraction for a trust is redetermined whenever additional exemption is allocated to the trust or when certain changes occur with respect to the principal of the trust. Except as otherwise provided in this paragraph (a), the numerator of the redetermined applicable fraction is the sum of the amount of GST exemption currently being allocated to the trust (if any) plus the value of the nontax portion of the trust, and the denominator of the redetermined applicable fraction is the value of the trust principal immediately after the event occurs. The nontax portion of a trust is determined by multiplying the value of the trust assets, determined immediately prior to the event, by the then applicable fraction.

(1) *Multiple transfers to a single trust.* If property is added to an existing trust, the denominator of the redetermined applicable fraction is the value of the trust immediately after the addition reduced as provided in § 26.2642–1(c).

(2) *Consolidation of separate trusts.* If separate trusts created by one transferor are consolidated, a single applicable fraction for the consolidated trust is determined. The numerator of the redetermined applicable fraction is the sum of the nontax portions of each trust immediately prior to the consolidation.

(3) *Property included in transferor's gross estate.* If the value of property held in a trust created by the transferor, with respect to which an allocation was made at a time that the trust was not subject to an ETIP, is included in the transferor's gross estate, the applicable fraction is redetermined if additional GST exemption is allocated to the property. The numerator of the redetermined applicable fraction is an amount

equal to the nontax portion of the property immediately after the death of the transferor increased by the amount of GST exemption allocated by the executor of the transferor's estate to the trust. If additional GST exemption is not allocated to the trust, then, except as provided in this paragraph (a)(3), the applicable fraction immediately before death is not changed, if the trust was not subject to an ETIP at the time GST exemption was allocated to the trust. In any event, the denominator of the applicable fraction is reduced to reflect any federal or state, estate or inheritance taxes paid from the trust.

(4) *Imposition of recapture tax under section 2032A* (i) If an additional estate tax is imposed under section 2032A and if the section 2032A election was effective (under § 26.2642–2(b)) for purposes of the GST tax, the applicable fraction with respect to the property is redetermined as of the date of death of the transferor. In making the redetermination, any available GST exemption not allocated at the death of the transferor (or at a prior recapture event) is automatically allocated to the property. The denominator of the applicable fraction is the fair market value of the property at the date of the transferor's death reduced as provided in § 26.2642–1(c) and further reduced by the amount of the additional GST tax actually recovered from the trust.

(ii) The GST tax imposed with respect to any taxable termination, taxable distribution, or direct skip occurring prior to the recapture event is recomputed based on the applicable fraction as redetermined. Any additional GST tax as recomputed is due and payable on the date that is six months after the event that causes the imposition of the additional estate tax under section 2032A. The additional GST tax is remitted with Form 706-A and is reported by attaching a statement to Form 706-A showing the computation of the additional GST tax.

(iii) The applicable fraction, as redetermined under this section, is also used in determining any GST tax imposed with respect to GSTs occurring after the date of the recapture event.

(b) Examples. The following examples illustrate the principles of this section:

Example (1). Allocation of additional exemption. T transfers $200,000 to an irrevocable trust under which the income is payable to T's child, C, for life. Upon the termination of the trust, the remainder is payable to T's grandchild, GC. At a time when no ETIP exists with respect to the trust property, T makes a timely allocation of $100,000 of GST exemption, resulting in an inclusion ratio of .50. Subsequently, when the entire trust property is valued at $500,000, T allocates an additional $100,000 of T's unused GST exemption to the trust. The inclusion ratio of the trust is recomputed at that time. The numerator of the applicable fraction is $350,000 ($250,000 (the nontax portion as of the date of the allocation) plus $100,000 (the GST exemption currently being allocated)). The denominator is $500,000 (the date of allocation fair market value of the trust). The inclusion ratio is .30 (1 - .70).

Example (2). Multiple transfers to a trust, allocation both timely and late. On December 10, 1993, T transfers $10,000 to an irrevocable trust that does not satisfy the requirements of section 2642(c)(2). T makes identical transfers to the trust on December 10, 1994, 1995, 1996, and on January 15, 1997. Immediately after the transfer on January 15, 1997, the value of the trust principal is $40,000. On January 14, 1998, when the value of the trust principal is $50,000, T allocates $30,000 of GST exemption to the trust. T discloses the 1997 transfer on the Form 709 filed on January 14, 1998. Thus, T's allocation is a timely allocation with respect to the transfer in 1997, $10,000 of the allocation is effective as of the date of that transfer, and, on and after January 15, 1997, the inclusion ratio of the trust is .75 (1 - ($10,000/$40,000)). The balance of the allocation is a late allocation with respect to prior transfers to the trust and is effective as of January 14, 1998. In redetermining the inclusion ratio as of that date, the numerator of the redetermined applicable fraction is $32,500 ($12,500 (.25 * $50,000), the nontax portion of the trust on January 14, 1998) plus $20,000 (the amount of GST exemption allocated late to the trust). The denominator of the new applicable fraction is $50,000 (the value of the trust principal at the time of the late allocation).

Example (3). Excess allocation. (i) T creates an irrevocable trust for the benefit of T's child and grandchild in 1996 transferring $50,000 to the trust on the date of creation. T allocates no GST exemption to the trust on the Form 709 reporting the transfer. On July 1, 1997 (when the value of the trust property is $60,000), T transfers an additional $40,000 to the trust.

(ii) On April 15, 1998, when the value of the trust is $150,000, T files a Form 709 reporting the 1997 transfer and allocating $150,000 of GST exemption to the trust. The allocation is a timely allocation of $40,000 with respect to the 1997 transfer and is effective as of that date. Thus, the applicable fraction for the trust as of July 1, 1997 is .40 ($40,000/$100,000 ($40,000 + $60,000)).

(iii) The allocation is also a late allocation of $90,000, the amount necessary to attain a zero inclusion ratio on April 15, 1998, computed as follows: $60,000 (the nontax portion immediately prior to the allocation (.40 * $150,000)) plus $90,000 (the additional allocation necessary to produce a zero inclusion ratio based on a denominator of $150,000)/$150,000 equals one and, thus, an inclusion ratio of zero. The balance of the allocation, $20,000 ($150,000 less the timely allocation of $40,000 less the late allocation of $90,000) is void.

Example (4). Undisclosed transfer. (i) The facts are the same as in Example 3, except that on February 1, 1998 (when the value of the trust is $150,000), T transfers an additional $50,000 to the trust and the value of the entire trust corpus on April 15, 1998 is $220,000. The Form 709 filed on April 15, 1998 does not disclose the 1998 transfer. Under the rule in § 26.2632–1(b)(2)(ii), the allocation is effective first as a timely allocation to the 1997 transfer; second, as a late allocation to the trust as of April 15, 1998; and, finally as a timely allocation to the February 1, 1998 transfer. As of April 15, 1998, $55,000, a pro rata portion of the trust assets, is considered to be the property transferred to the trust on February 1, 1998 (($50,000/$200,000) * $220,000). The balance of the trust, $165,000, represents prior transfers to the trust.

(ii) As in Example 3, the allocation is a timely allocation as to the 1997 transfer (and the applicable fraction as of July 1, 1997 is .40) and a late allocation as of 1998. The amount of the late allocation is $99,000, computed as follows: (.40 * $165,000 plus $99,000)/$165,000 = one.

(iii) The balance of the allocation, $11,000 ($150,000 less the timely allocation of $40,000 less the late allocation of $99,000) is a timely allocation as of February 1, 1998. The applicable fraction with respect to the trust, as of February 1, 1998, is .355, computed as follows: $60,000 (the nontax portion of the trust immediately prior to the February 1, 1998 transfer (.40 * $150,000)) plus $11,000 (the amount of the timely allocation to the 1998 transfer)/$200,000 (the value of the trust on February 1, 1998, after the transfer on that date) = $71,000/$200,000 = .355.

(iv) The applicable fraction with respect to the trust, as of April 15, 1998, is .805 computed as follows: $78,100 (the nontax portion immediately prior to the allocation (.355 * $220,000)) plus $99,000 (the amount of the late allocation)/ $220,000 = $177,100/$220,000 = .805.

Example (5). Redetermination of inclusion ratio on ETIP termination. (i) T transfers $100,000 to an irrevocable trust. The trust instrument provides that trust income is to be paid to T for 9 years or until T's prior death. The trust principal is to be paid to T's grandchild, GC, on the termination of T's income interest. The trustee has the power to invade trust principal for the benefit of GC during the term of T's income interest. The trust is subject to an ETIP while T holds the retained income interest. T files a timely Form 709 reporting the transfer and allocates $100,000 of GST exemption to the trust. In year 4, when the value of the trust is $200,000, the trustee distributes $15,000 to GC. The distribution is a taxable distribution. Because of the existence of the ETIP, the inclusion ratio with respect to the taxable distribution is determined immediately prior to the occurrence of the GST. Thus, the inclusion ratio applicable to the year 4 GST is .50 (1 - ($100,000/ $200,000)).

(ii) In year 5, when the value of the trust is again $200,000, the trustee distributes another $15,000 to GC. Because the trust is still subject to the ETIP in year 5, the inclusion ratio with respect to the year 5 GST is again computed immediately prior to the GST. In computing the new inclusion ratio, the numerator of the applicable fraction is reduced by the nontax portion of prior GSTs occurring during the ETIP. Thus, the numerator of the applicable fraction with respect to the GST in year 5 is $92,500 ($100,000 - (.50 * $15,000)) and the inclusion ratio applicable with respect to the GST in year 5 is .537 (1 - ($92,500/$200,000) = .463). Any additional GST exemption allocated on a timely ETIP return with respect to the GST in year 5 is effective immediately prior to the transfer.

[T.D. 8644, 60 FR 66917, Dec. 27, 1995; 61 FR 29654, June 12, 1996]

§ 26.2642–5 Finality of inclusion ratio.

(a) Direct skips. The inclusion ratio applicable to a direct skip becomes final when no additional GST tax (including additional GST tax payable as a result of a cessation, etc. of qualified use under section 2032A(c)) may be assessed with respect to the direct skip.

(b) Other GSTs. With respect to taxable distributions and taxable terminations, the inclusion ratio for a trust becomes final, on the later of—

(1) The expiration of the period for assessment with respect to the first GST tax return filed using that inclusion ratio (unless the trust is subject to an election under section 2032A in which case the applicable date under this subsection is the expiration of the period of assessment of any additional GST tax due as a result of a cessation, etc. of qualified use under section 2032A); or

(2) The expiration of the period for assessment of Federal estate tax with respect to the estate of the transferor. For purposes of this paragraph (b)(2), if an estate tax return is not required to be filed, the period for assessment is determined as if a return were required to be filed and as if the return were timely filed within the period prescribed by section 6075(a).

[T.D. 8644, 60 FR 66918, Dec. 27, 1995; 61 FR 43656, Aug. 26, 1996]

§ 26.2642–6 Qualified severance.

(a) In general. If a trust is divided in a qualified severance into two or more trusts, the separate trusts resulting from the severance will be treated as separate trusts for generation-skipping transfer (GST) tax purposes and the inclusion ratio of each new resulting trust may differ from the inclusion ratio of the original trust. Because the post-severance resulting trusts are treated as separate trusts for GST tax purposes, certain actions with respect to one resulting trust will generally have no GST tax impact with respect to the other resulting trust(s). For example, GST exemption allocated to one resulting trust will not impact on the inclusion ratio of the other resulting trust(s); a GST tax election made with respect to one resulting trust will not apply to the other resulting trust(s); the occurrence of a taxable distribution or termination with regard to a particular resulting trust will not have any GST tax impact on any other trust resulting from that severance. In general, the rules in this section are applicable only for purposes of the GST tax and are not applicable in determining, for example, whether the resulting trusts may file separate income tax returns or whether the severance may result in a gift subject to gift tax, may cause any trust to be included in the gross estate of a beneficiary, or may result in a realization of gain for purposes of section 1001. See § 1.1001–1(h) of this chapter for rules relating to whether a qualified severance will constitute an exchange of property for other property differing materially either in kind or in extent.

(b) Qualified severance defined. A qualified severance is a division of a trust (other than a division described in § 26.2654–1(b)) into two or more separate trusts that meets each of the requirements in paragraph (d) of this section.

(c) Effective date of qualified severance. A qualified severance is applicable as of the date of the severance, as defined in § 26.2642–6(d)(3), and the resulting trusts are treated as separate trusts for GST tax purposes as of that date.

(d) Requirements for a qualified severance. For purposes of this section, a qualified severance must satisfy each of the following requirements:

(1) The single trust is severed pursuant to the terms of the governing instrument, or pursuant to applicable local law.

(2) The severance is effective under local law.

(3) The date of severance is either the date selected by the trustee as of which the trust assets are to be valued in order to determine the funding of the resulting trusts, or the court-imposed date of funding in the case of an order of the local court with jurisdiction over the trust ordering the trustee to fund the resulting trusts on or as of a specific date. For a date to satisfy the definition in the preceding sentence, however, the funding must be commenced immediately upon, and funding must occur within a reasonable time (but in no event more than 90 days) after, the selected valuation date.

(4) The single trust (original trust) is severed on a fractional basis, such that each new trust (resulting trust) is funded with a fraction or percentage of the original trust, and the sum of those fractions or percentages is one or one hundred percent, respectively. For this purpose, the fraction or percentage may be determined by means of a formula (for example, that fraction of the trust the numerator of which is equal to

the transferor's unused GST tax exemption, and the denominator of which is the fair market value of the original trust's assets on the date of severance). The severance of a trust based on a pecuniary amount does not satisfy this requirement. For example, the severance of a trust is not a qualified severance if the trust is divided into two trusts, with one trust to be funded with $1,500,000 and the other trust to be funded with the balance of the original trust's assets. With respect to the particular assets to be distributed to each separate trust resulting from the severance, each such trust may be funded with the appropriate fraction or percentage (pro rata portion) of each asset held by the original trust. Alternatively, the assets may be divided among the resulting trusts on a non-pro rata basis, based on the fair market value of the assets on the date of severance. However, if a resulting trust is funded on a non-pro rata basis, each asset received by a resulting trust must be valued, solely for funding purposes, by multiplying the fair market value of the asset held in the original trust as of the date of severance by the fraction or percentage of that asset received by that resulting trust. Thus, the assets must be valued without taking into account any discount or premium arising from the severance, for example, any valuation discounts that might arise because the resulting trust receives less than the entire interest held by the original trust. See paragraph (j), Example 6 of this section.

(5) The terms of the resulting trusts must provide, in the aggregate, for the same succession of interests of beneficiaries as are provided in the original trust. This requirement is satisfied if the beneficiaries of the separate resulting trusts and the interests of the beneficiaries with respect to the separate trusts, when the separate trusts are viewed collectively, are the same as the beneficiaries and their respective beneficial interests with respect to the original trust before severance. With respect to trusts from which discretionary distributions may be made to any one or more beneficiaries on a non-pro rata basis, this requirement is satisfied if—

(i) The terms of each of the resulting trusts are the same as the terms of the original trust (even though each permissible distributee of the original trust is not a beneficiary of all of the resulting trusts);

(ii) Each beneficiary's interest in the resulting trusts (collectively) equals the beneficiary's interest in the original trust, determined by the terms of the trust instrument or, if none, on a per-capita basis. For example, in the case of the severance of a discretionary trust established for the benefit of A, B, and C and their descendants with the remainder to be divided equally among those three families, this requirement is satisfied if the trust is divided into three separate trusts of equal value with one trust established for the benefit of A and A's descendants, one trust for the benefit of B and B's descendants, and one trust for the benefit of C and C's descendants;

(iii) The severance does not shift a beneficial interest in the trust to any beneficiary in a lower generation (as determined under section 2651) than the person or persons who held the beneficial interest in the original trust; and

(iv) The severance does not extend the time for the vesting of any beneficial interest in the trust beyond the period provided for in (or applicable to) the original trust.

(6) In the case of a qualified severance of a trust with an inclusion ratio as defined in § 26.2642–1 of either one or zero, each trust resulting from the severance will have an inclusion ratio equal to the inclusion ratio of the original trust.

(7)(i) In the case of a qualified severance occurring after GST tax exemption has been allocated to the trust (whether by an affirmative allocation, a deemed allocation, or an automatic allocation pursuant to the rules contained in section 2632), if the trust has an inclusion ratio as defined in § 26.2642–1 that is greater than zero and less than one, then either paragraph (d)(7)(ii) or (iii) of this section must be satisfied.

(ii) The trust is severed initially into only two resulting trusts. One resulting trust must receive that fractional share of the total value of the original trust as of the date of severance that is equal to the applicable fraction, as defined in § 26.2642–1(b) and (c), used to determine the inclusion ratio of the original trust immediately before the severance. The other resulting trust must receive that fractional share of the total value of the original trust as of the date of severance that is equal to the excess of one over the fractional share described in the preceding sentence. The trust receiving the fractional share equal to the applicable fraction shall have an inclusion ratio of zero, and the other trust shall have an inclusion ratio of one. If the applicable fraction with respect to the original trust is

.50, then, with respect to the two equal trusts resulting from the severance, the trustee may designate which of the resulting trusts will have an inclusion ratio of zero and which will have an inclusion ratio of one. Each separate trust resulting from the severance then may be further divided in accordance with the rules of this section. See paragraph (j), Example 7, of this section.

(iii) The trust is severed initially into more than two resulting trusts. One or more of the resulting trusts in the aggregate must receive that fractional share of the total value of the original trust as of the date of severance that is equal to the applicable fraction used to determine the inclusion ratio of the original trust immediately before the severance. The trust or trusts receiving such fractional share shall have an inclusion ratio of zero, and each of the other resulting trust or trusts shall have an inclusion ratio of one. (If, however, two or more of the resulting trusts each receives the fractional share of the total value of the original trust equal to the applicable fraction, the trustee may designate which of those resulting trusts will have an inclusion ratio of zero and which will have an inclusion ratio of one.) The resulting trust or trusts with an inclusion ratio of one must receive in the aggregate that fractional share of the total value of the original trust as of the date of severance that is equal to the excess of one over the fractional share described in the second sentence of this paragraph. See paragraph (j), Example 9, of this section.

(e) Reporting a qualified severance. (1) *In general.* A qualified severance is reported by filing Form 706-GS(T), "Generation-Skipping Transfer Tax Return For Terminations," (or such other form as may be provided from time to time by the Internal Revenue Service (IRS) for the purpose of reporting a qualified severance). Unless otherwise provided in the applicable form or instructions, the IRS requests that the filer write "Qualified Severance" at the top of the form and attach a Notice of Qualified Severance (Notice). The return and attached Notice should be filed by April 15th of the year immediately following the year during which the severance occurred or by the last day of the period covered by an extension of time, if an extension of time is granted, to file such form.

(2) *Information concerning the original trust.* The Notice should provide, with respect to the original trust that was severed—

(i) The name of the transferor;

(ii) The name and date of creation of the original trust;

(iii) The tax identification number of the original trust; and

(iv) The inclusion ratio before the severance.

(3) *Information concerning each new trust.* The Notice should provide, with respect to each of the resulting trusts created by the severance—

(i) The name and tax identification number of the trust;

(ii) The date of severance (within the meaning of paragraph (c) of this section);

(iii) The fraction of the total assets of the original trust received by the resulting trust;

(iv) Other details explaining the basis for the funding of the resulting trust (a fraction of the total fair market value of the assets on the date of severance, or a fraction of each asset); and

(v) The inclusion ratio.

(f) Time for making a qualified severance. (1) A qualified severance of a trust may occur at any time prior to the termination of the trust. Thus, provided that the separate resulting trusts continue in existence after the severance, a qualified severance may occur either before or after—

(i) GST tax exemption has been allocated to the trust;

(ii) A taxable event has occurred with respect to the trust; or

(iii) An addition has been made to the trust.

(2) Because a qualified severance is effective as of the date of severance, a qualified severance has no effect on a taxable termination as defined in section 2612(a) or a taxable distribution as defined in section 2612(b) that occurred prior to the date of severance. A qualified severance shall be deemed to occur before a taxable termination or a taxable distribution that occurs by reason of the qualified severance. See paragraph (j) Example 8 of this section.

(g) Trusts that were irrevocable on September 25, 1985. (1) *In general.* See § 26.2601–1(b)(4) for rules regarding severances and other actions with respect to trusts that were irrevocable on September 25, 1985.

(2) *Trusts in receipt of a post-September 25, 1985, addition.* A trust described in § 26.2601–1(b)(1)(iv)(A) that is deemed for GST tax purposes to consist of one separate share not subject to GST tax (the non-chapter 13 portion) with an inclusion ratio of zero, and one separate share subject to GST tax (the chapter 13 portion) with an inclusion ratio determined under section 2642, may be severed into two trusts in accordance with § 26.2654–1(a)(3). One resulting trust will hold the non-chapter 13 portion of the original trust (the non-chapter 13 trust) and will not be subject to GST tax, and the other resulting trust will hold the chapter 13 portion of the original trust (the chapter 13 trust) and will have the same inclusion ratio as the chapter 13 portion immediately prior to the severance. The chapter 13 trust may be further divided in a qualified severance in accordance with the rules of this section. The non-chapter 13 trust may be further divided in accordance with the rules of § 26.2601–1(b)(4).

(h) Treatment of trusts resulting from a severance that is not a qualified severance. Trusts resulting from a severance (other than a severance recognized for GST tax purposes under § 26.2654–1) that does not meet the requirements of a qualified severance under paragraph (b) of this section will be treated, after the date of severance, as separate trusts for purposes of the GST tax, provided that the trusts resulting from such severance are recognized as separate trusts under applicable state law. The post-severance treatment of the resulting trusts as separate trusts for GST tax purposes generally permits the allocation of GST tax exemption, the making of various elections permitted for GST tax purposes, and the occurrence of a taxable distribution or termination with regard to a particular resulting trust, with no GST tax impact on any other trust resulting from that severance. Each trust resulting from a severance described in this paragraph (h), however, will have the same inclusion ratio immediately after the severance as that of the original trust immediately before the severance. (See § 26.2654–1 for the inclusion ratio of each trust resulting from a severance described in that section.) Further, any trust resulting from a nonqualified severance may be severed subsequently, pursuant to a qualified severance described in this § 26.2642–6.

(i) [Reserved].

(j) Examples. The rules of this section are illustrated by the following examples:

Example (1). Succession of interests. T dies in 2006. T's will establishes a testamentary trust (Trust) providing that income is to be paid to T's sister, S, for her life. On S's death, one-half of the corpus is to be paid to T's child, C (or to C's estate if C fails to survive S), and one-half of the corpus is to be paid to T's grandchild, GC (or to GC's estate if GC fails to survive S). On the Form 706, "United States Estate (and Generation-Skipping Transfer) Tax Return," filed for T's estate, T's executor allocates all of T's available GST tax exemption to other transfers and trusts, such that Trust's inclusion ratio is 1. Subsequent to filing the Form 706 in 2007 and in accordance with applicable state law, the trustee divides Trust into two separate trusts, Trust 1 and Trust 2, with each trust receiving 50 percent of the value of the assets of the original trust as of the date of severance. Trust 1 provides that trust income is to be paid to S for life with remainder to C or C's estate, and Trust 2 provides that trust income is to be paid to S for life with remainder to GC or GC's estate. Because Trust 1 and Trust 2 provide for the same succession of interests in the aggregate as provided in the original trust, the severance constitutes a qualified severance, provided that all other requirements of section 2642(a)(3) and this section are satisfied.

Example (2). Succession of interests in discretionary trust. In 2006, T establishes Trust, an irrevocable trust providing that income may be paid from time to time in such amounts as the trustee deems advisable to any one or more members of the group consisting of T's children (A and B) and their respective descendants. In addition, the trustee may distribute corpus to any trust beneficiary in such amounts as the trustee deems advisable. On the death of the last to die of A and B, the trust is to terminate and the corpus is to be distributed in two equal shares, one share to the then-living descendants of each child, per stirpes. T elects, under section 2632(c)(5), to not have the automatic allocation rules contained in section 2632(c) apply with respect to T's transfers to Trust, and T does not otherwise allocate GST tax exemption with respect to Trust. As a result, Trust has an inclusion ratio of one. In 2008, the trustee of Trust, pursuant to applicable state law, divides Trust into two equal but separate trusts, Trust 1 and Trust 2, each of which has terms identical to the terms of Trust except for the identity of the beneficiaries. Trust 1 and Trust 2 each has an inclusion ratio of one. Trust 1 provides that income is to be paid in such amounts as the trustee deems advisable to A and A's descendants. In addition, the trustee may distribute corpus to any trust beneficiary in such amounts as the trustee deems advisable. On the death of A, Trust 1 is to terminate and the corpus is to be distributed to the then-living descendants of A, per stirpes, but, if A dies with no living descendants, the principal will be added to Trust 2. Trust 2 contains identical provisions, except that B and B's descendants are the trust beneficiaries and, if B dies with no living descendants, the principal will be added to Trust 1. Trust 1 and Trust 2 in the aggregate provide for the same beneficiaries and the same succession of interests as provided in Trust, and the severance does not shift any beneficial interest to a beneficiary who occupies a lower generation than the person or persons who held the beneficial interest in Trust. Accordingly, the severance constitutes a qualified severance, provided that all other requirements of section 2642(a)(3) and this section are satisfied.

Example (3). Severance based on actuarial value of beneficial interests. In 2004, T establishes Trust, an irrevocable trust providing that income is to be paid to T's child C during C's lifetime. Upon C's death, Trust is to terminate and the assets of Trust are to be paid to GC, C's child, if living, or, if GC is not then living, to GC's estate. T properly elects, under section 2632(c)(5), not to have the automatic allocation rules contained in section 2632(c) apply with respect to T's transfers to Trust, and T does not otherwise allocate GST tax exemption with respect to Trust. Thus, Trust has an inclusion ratio of one. In 2009, the trustee of Trust, pursuant to applicable state law, divides Trust into two separate trusts, Trust 1 for the benefit of C (and on C's death to C's estate), and Trust 2 for the benefit of GC (and on GC's death to GC's estate). The document severing Trust directs that Trust 1 is to be funded with an amount equal to the actuarial value of C's interest in Trust prior to the severance, determined under section 7520 of the Internal Revenue Code. Similarly, Trust 2 is to be funded with an amount equal to the actuarial value of GC's interest in Trust prior to the severance, determined under section 7520. Trust 1 and Trust 2 do not provide for the same succession of interests as provided under the terms of the original trust. Therefore, the severance is not a qualified severance. Furthermore, because the severance results in no non-skip person having an interest in Trust 2, Trust 2 constitutes a skip person under section 2613 and, therefore, the severance results in a taxable termination subject to GST tax.

Example (4). Severance of a trust with a 50% inclusion ratio. On September 1, 2006, T transfers $100,000 to a trust for the benefit of T's grandchild, GC. On a timely filed Form 709, "United States Gift (and Generation-Skipping Transfer) Tax Return," reporting the transfer, T allocates all of T's remaining GST tax exemption ($50,000) to the trust. As a result of the allocation, the applicable fraction with respect to the trust is .50 [$50,000 (the amount of GST tax exemption allocated to the trust) divided by $100,000 (the value of the property transferred to the trust)]. The inclusion ratio with respect to the trust is .50 [1 - .50]. In 2007, pursuant to authority granted under applicable state law, the trustee severs the trust into two trusts, Trust 1 and Trust 2, each of which is identical to the original trust and each of which receives a 50 percent fractional share of the total value of the original trust, valued as of the date of severance. Because the applicable fraction with respect to the original trust is .50 and the trust is severed into two equal trusts, the trustee may designate which resulting trust has an inclusion ratio of one, and which resulting trust has an inclusion ratio of zero. Accordingly, in the Notice of Qualified Severance reporting the severance, the trustee designates Trust 1 as having an inclusion ratio of zero, and Trust 2 as having an inclusion ratio of one. The severance constitutes a qualified severance, provided that all other requirements of section 2642(a)(3) and this section are satisfied.

Example (5). Funding of severed trusts on a non-pro rata basis. T's will establishes a testamentary trust (Trust) for the benefit of T's descendants, to be funded with T's stock in Corporation A and Corporation B, both publicly traded stocks. T dies on May 1, 2004, at which time the Corporation A stock included in T's gross estate has a fair market value of $100,000 and the stock of Corporation B included in T's gross estate has a fair market value of $200,000. On a timely filed Form 706, T's executor allocates all of T's remaining GST tax exemption ($270,000) to Trust. As a result of the allocation, the applicable fraction with respect to Trust is .90 [$270,000 (the amount of GST tax exemption allocated to the trust) divided by $300,000 (the value of the property transferred to the trust)]. The inclusion ratio with respect to Trust is .10 [1 - .90]. On August 1, 2008, in accordance with applicable local law, the trustee executes a document severing Trust into two trusts, Trust 1 and Trust 2, each of which is identical to Trust. The instrument designates August 3, 2008, as the date of severance (within the meaning of paragraph (d)(3) of this section). The terms of the instrument severing Trust provide that Trust 1 is to be funded on a non-pro rata basis with assets having a fair market value on the date of severance equal to 90% of the value of Trust's assets on that date, and Trust 2 is to be funded with assets having a fair market value on the date of severance equal to 10% of the value of Trust's assets on that date. On August 3, 2008, the value of the Trust assets totals $500,000, consisting of Corporation A stock worth $450,000 and Corporation B stock worth $50,000. On August 4, 2008, the trustee takes all action necessary to transfer all of the Corporation A stock to Trust 1 and to transfer all of the Corporation B stock to Trust 2. On August 6, 2008, the stock transfers are completed and the stock is received by the appropriate resulting trust. Accordingly, Trust 1 is funded with assets having a value equal to 90% of the value of Trust as of the date of severance, August 3, 2008, and Trust 2 is funded with assets having a value equal to 10% of the value of Trust as of the date of severance. Therefore, the severance constitutes a qualified severance, provided that all other requirements of section 2642(a)(3) and this section are satisfied. Trust 1 will have an inclusion ratio of zero and Trust 2 will have an inclusion ratio of one.

Example (6). Funding of severed trusts on a non-pro rata basis. (i) T's will establishes an irrevocable trust (Trust) for the benefit of T's descendants. As a result of the allocation of GST tax exemption, the applicable fraction with respect to Trust is .60 and Trust's inclusion ratio is .40 [1 - .60]. Pursuant to authority granted under applicable state law, on August 1, 2008, the trustee executes a document severing Trust into two trusts, Trust 1 and Trust 2, each of which is identical to Trust. The instrument of severance provides that the severance is intended to qualify as a qualified severance within the meaning of section 2642(a)(3) and designates August 3, 2008, as the date of severance (within the meaning of paragraph (d)(3) of this section). The instrument further provides that Trust 1 and Trust 2 are to be funded on a non-pro rata basis with Trust 1 funded with assets having a fair market value on the date of severance equal to 40% of the value of Trust's assets on that date and Trust 2 funded with assets having a fair market value equal to 60% of the value of Trust's assets on that date. The fair market value of the assets used to fund each trust is to be determined in compliance with the requirements of paragraph (d)(4) of this section.

(ii) On August 3, 2008, the fair market value of the Trust assets totals $4,000,000, consisting of 52% of the outstanding common stock in Company, a closely-held corporation, valued at $3,000,000 and $1,000,000 in cash and marketable securities. Trustee proposes to divide the Company stock equally between Trust 1 and Trust 2, and thus transfer 26% of the Company stock to Trust 1 and 26% of the stock to Trust 2. In addition, the appropriate amount of cash and marketable securities will be distributed to each trust. In accordance with paragraph (d)(4) of this section, for funding purposes, the interest in the Company stock distributed to each trust is valued as a pro rata portion of the value of the 52% interest in Company held by Trust before severance, without taking into account, for example, any valuation discount that might otherwise apply in valuing the noncontrolling interest distributed to each resulting trust.

(iii) Accordingly, for funding purposes, each 26% interest in Company stock distributed to Trust 1 and Trust 2 is valued at $1,500,000 (.5 * $3,000,000). Therefore, Trust 1, which is to be funded with $1,600,000 (.40 * $4,000,000), receives $100,000 in cash and marketable securities valued as of August 3, 2008, in addition to the Company stock, and Trust 2, which is to be funded with $2,400,000 (.60 * $4,000,000), receives $900,000 in cash and marketable securities in addition to the Company stock. Therefore, the severance is a qualified severance, provided that all other requirements of section 2642(a)(3) and this section are satisfied.

Example (7). Statutory qualified severance. T dies on October 1, 2004. T's will establishes a testamentary trust (Trust) to be funded with $1,000,000. Trust income is to be paid to T's child, S, for S's life. The trustee may also distribute trust corpus from time to time, in equal or unequal shares, for the benefit of any one or more members of the group consisting of S and T's three grandchildren (GC1, GC2, and GC3). On S's death, Trust is to terminate and the assets are to be divided equally among GC1, GC2, and GC3 (or their respective then-living descendants, per stirpes). On a timely filed Form 706, T's executor allocates all of T's remaining GST tax exemption ($300,000) to Trust. As a result of the allocation, the applicable fraction with respect to the trust is .30 [$300,000 (the amount of GST tax exemption allocated to the trust) divided by $1,000,000 (the value of the property transferred to the trust)]. The inclusion ratio with respect to the trust is .70 [1 - .30]. On June 1, 2007, the trustee determines that it is in the best interest of the beneficiaries to sever Trust to provide a separate trust for each of T's three grandchildren and their respective families. The trustee severs Trust into two trusts, Trust 1 and Trust 2, each with terms and beneficiaries identical to Trust and thus each providing that trust income is to be paid to S for life, trust principal may be distributed for the benefit of any or all members of the group consisting of S and T's grandchildren, and, on S's death, the trust is to terminate and the assets are to be divided equally among GC1, GC2, and GC3 (or their respective then-living descendants, per stirpes). The instrument severing Trust provides that Trust 1 is to receive 30% of Trust's assets and Trust 2 is to receive 70% of Trust's assets. Further, each such trust is to be funded with a pro rata portion of each asset held in Trust. The trustee then severs Trust 1 into three equal trusts, Trust GC1, Trust GC2, and Trust GC3. Each trust is named for a grandchild of T and provides that trust income is to be paid to S for life, trust principal may be distributed for the benefit of S and T's grandchild for whom the trust is named, and, on S's death, the trust is to terminate and the trust proceeds distributed to the respective grandchild for whom the trust is named. If that grandchild has predeceased the termination date, the trust proceeds are to be distributed to that grandchild's then-living descendants, per stirpes, or, if none, then equally to the other two trusts resulting from the severance of Trust 1. Each such resulting trust is to be funded with a pro rata portion of each Trust 1 asset. The trustee also severs Trust 2 in a similar manner, into Trust GC1(2), Trust GC2(2), and Trust GC3(2). The severance of Trust into Trust 1 and Trust 2, the severance of Trust 1 into Trust GC1, Trust GC2, Trust GC3, and the severance of Trust 2 into Trust GC1(2), Trust GC2(2) and Trust GC3(2), constitute qualified severances, provided that all other requirements of section 2642(a)(3) and this section are satisfied with respect to each severance. Trust GC1, Trust GC2, Trust GC3 will each have an inclusion ratio of zero and Trust GC1(2), Trust GC2(2), and Trust GC3(2) will each have an inclusion ratio of one.

Example (8). Qualified severance deemed to precede a taxable termination. In 2004, T establishes an inter vivos irrevocable trust (Trust) for a term of 10 years providing that Trust income is to be paid annually in equal shares to T's child C and T's grandchild GC (the child of another then-living child of T). If either C or GC dies prior to the expiration of the 10-year term, the deceased beneficiary's share of Trust's income is to be paid to that beneficiary's then-living descendants, per stirpes, for the balance of the trust term. At the expiration of the 10-year trust term, the corpus is to be distributed equally to C and GC; if either C or GC is not then living, then such decedent's share is to be distributed instead to such decedent's then-living descendants, per stirpes. T allocates T's GST tax exemption to Trust such that Trust's applicable fraction is .50 and Trust's inclusion ratio is .50 [1-.50]. In 2006, pursuant to applicable state law, the trustee severs the trust into two equal trusts, Trust 1 and Trust 2. The instrument severing Trust provides that Trust 1 is to receive 50% of the Trust assets, and Trust 2 is to receive 50% of Trust's assets. Both resulting trusts are identical to Trust, except that each has different beneficiaries: C and C's descendants are designated as the beneficiaries of Trust 1, and GC and GC's descendants are designated as the beneficiaries of Trust 2. The severance constitutes a qualified severance, provided all other requirements of section 2642(a)(3) and this section are satisfied. Because the applicable fraction with respect to Trust is .50 and Trust was severed into two equal trusts, the trustee may designate which resulting trust has an inclusion ratio of one, and which has an inclusion ratio of zero. Accordingly, in the Notice of Qualified Severance reporting the severance, the trustee designates Trust 1 as having an inclusion ratio of one, and Trust 2 as having an inclusion ratio of zero. Because Trust 2 is a skip person under section 2613, the severance of Trust resulting in the distribution of 50% of Trust's corpus to Trust 2 would constitute a taxable termination or distribution (as described in section 2612(a)) of that 50% of Trust for GST tax purposes, but for the rule that a qualified severance is deemed to precede a taxable termination that is caused by the qualified severance. Thus, no GST tax will be due with regard to the creation and funding of Trust 2 because the inclusion ratio of Trust 2 is zero.

Example (9). Regulatory qualified severance. (i) In 2004, T establishes an inter vivos irrevocable trust (Trust) providing that trust income is to be paid annually in equal shares to T's children, A and B, for 10 years. Trust provides that the trustee has discretion to make additional distributions of principal to A and B during the 10-year term without adjustments to their shares of income or the trust remainder. If either (or both) dies prior to the expiration of the 10-year term, the deceased child's share of trust income is to be paid to the child's then living descendants, per stirpes, for the balance of the trust term. At the expiration of the 10-year term, the corpus is to be distributed equally to A and B; if A and B (or either o[f] them) is not then living, then such decedent's share is to be distributed instead to such decedent's then living descendants, per stirpes. T allocates GST tax exemption to Trust such that Trust's applicable fraction is .25 and its inclusion ratio is .75.

(ii) In 2006, pursuant to applicable state law, the trustee severs the trust into three trusts: Trust 1, Trust 2, and Trust 3. The instrument severing Trust provides that Trust 1 is to receive 50% of Trust's assets, Trust 2 is to receive 25% of Trust's assets, and Trust 3 is to receive 25% of Trust's assets. All three resulting trusts are identical to Trust, except that each has different beneficiaries: A and A's issue are designated as the beneficiaries of Trust 1, and B and B's issue are designated as the beneficiaries of Trust 2 and Trust 3. The severance constitutes a qualified severance, provided that all other requirements of section 2642(a)(3) and this section are satisfied. Trust 1 will have an inclusion ratio of 1. Because both Trust 2 and Trust 3 have each received the fractional share of Trust's assets equal to Trust's applicable fraction of .25, trustee designates that Trust 2 will have an inclusion ratio of one and that Trust 3 will have an inclusion ratio of zero.

Example (10). Beneficiary's interest dependent on inclusion ratio. On August 8, 2006, T transfers $1,000,000 to Trust and timely allocates $400,000 of T's remaining GST tax exemption to Trust. As a result of the allocation, the applicable fraction with respect to Trust is .40 [$400,000 divided by $1,000,000] and Trust's inclusion ratio is .60 [1 - .40]. Trust provides that all income of Trust will be paid annually to C, T's child, for life. On C's death, the corpus is to pass in accordance with C's exercise of a testamentary limited power to appoint the corpus of Trust to C's lineal descendants. However, Trust provides that if, at the time of C's death, Trust's inclusion ratio is greater than zero, then C may also appoint that fraction of the trust corpus equal to the inclusion ratio to the creditors of C's estate. On May 3, 2008, pursuant to authority granted under applicable state law, the trustee severs Trust into two trusts. Trust 1 is funded with 40% of Trust's assets, and Trust 2 is funded with 60% of Trust's assets in accordance with the requirements of this section. Both Trust 1 and Trust 2 provide that all income of Trust will be paid annually to C during C's life. On C's death, Trust 1 corpus is to pass in accordance with C's exercise of a testamentary limited power to appoint the corpus to C's lineal descendants. Trust 2 is to pass in accordance with C's exercise of a testamentary power to appoint the corpus of Trust to C's lineal descendants and to the creditors of C's estate. The severance constitutes a qualified severance, provided that all other requirements of section 2642(a)(3) and this section are satisfied. No additional contribution or allocation of GST tax exemption is made to either Trust 1 or Trust 2 prior to C's death. Accordingly, the inclusion ratio with respect to Trust 1 is zero. The inclusion ratio with respect to Trust 2 is one until C's death, at which time C will become the transferor of Trust 2 for GST tax purposes. (Some or all of C's GST tax exemption may be allocated to Trust 2 upon C's death.)

Example (11). Date of severance. Trust is an irrevocable trust that has both skip person and non-skip person beneficiaries. Trust holds two parcels of real estate, Property A and Property B, stock in Company X, a publicly traded company, and cash. On June 16, 2008, the local court with jurisdiction over Trust issues an order, pursuant to the trustee's petition authorized under state law, severing Trust into two resulting trusts of equal value, Trust 1 and Trust 2. The court order directs that Property A will be distributed to Trust 1 and Property B will be distributed to Trust 2, and that an appropriate amount of stock and cash will be distributed to each trust such that the total value of property distributed to each trust as of the date of severance will be equal. The court order does not mandate a particular date of funding. Trustee receives notice of the court order on June 24, and selects July 16, 2008, as the date of severance. On June 26, 2008, Trustee commences the process of transferring title to Property A and Property B to the appropriate resulting trust(s), which process is completed on July 8, 2008.

Also on June 26, the Trustee hires a professional appraiser to value Property A and Property B as of the date of severance and receives the appraisal report on Friday, October 3, 2008. On Monday, October 6, 2008, Trustee commences the process of transferring to Trust 1 and Trust 2 the appropriate amount of Company X stock valued as of July 16, 2008, and that transfer (as well as the transfer of Trust's cash) is completed by October 9, 2008. Under the facts presented, the funding of Trust 1 and Trust 2 occurred within 90 days of the date of severance selected by the trustee, and within a reasonable time after the date of severance taking into account the nature of the assets involved and the need to obtain an appraisal. Accordingly, the date of severance for purposes of this section is July 16, 2008, the resulting trusts are to be funded based on the value of the original trust assets as of that date, and the severance is a qualified severance assuming that all other requirements of section 2642(a)(3) and this section are met. (However, if Trust had contained only marketable securities and cash, then in order to satisfy the reasonable time requirement, the stock transfer would have to have been commenced, and generally completed, immediately after the date of severance, and the cash distribution would have to have been made at the same time.)

Example (12). Other severance that does not meet the requirements of a qualified severance. (i) In 2004, T establishes an irrevocable inter vivos trust (Trust) providing that Trust income is to be paid to T's children, A and B, in equal shares for their joint lives. Upon the death of the first to die of A and B, all Trust income will be paid to the survivor of A and B. At the death of the survivor, the corpus is to be distributed in equal shares to T's grandchildren, W and X (with any then-deceased grandchild's share being paid in accordance with that grandchild's testamentary general power of appointment). W is A's child and X is B's child. T elects under section 2632(c)(5) not to have the automatic allocation rules contained in section 2632(c) apply with respect to T's transfers to Trust, but T allocates GST tax exemption to Trust resulting in Trust having an inclusion ratio of .30.

(ii) In 2009, the trustee of Trust, as permitted by applicable state law, divides Trust into two separate trusts, Trust 1 and Trust 2. Trust 1 provides that trust income is to be paid to A for life and, on A's death, the remainder is to be distributed to W (or pursuant to W's testamentary general power of appointment). Trust 2 provides that trust income is to be paid to B for life and, on B's death, the remainder is to be distributed to X (or pursuant to X's testamentary general power of appointment). Because Trust 1 and Trust 2 do not provide A and B with the contingent survivor income interests that were provided to A and B under the terms of Trust, Trust 1 and Trust 2 do not provide for the same succession of interests in the aggregate as provided by Trust. Therefore, the severance does not satisfy the requirements of this section and is not a qualified severance. Provided that Trust 1 and Trust 2 are recognized as separate trusts under applicable state law, Trust 1 and Trust 2 will be recognized as separate trusts for GST tax purposes pursuant to paragraph (h) of this section, prospectively from the date of the severance. However, Trust 1 and Trust 2 each have an inclusion ratio of .30 immediately after the severance, the same as the inclusion ratio of Trust prior to severance.

Example (13). Qualified severance following a non-qualified severance. Assume the same facts as in Example 12, except that, as of November 4, 2010, the trustee of Trust 1 severs Trust 1 into two trusts, Trust 3 and Trust 4, in accordance with applicable local law. The instrument severing Trust 1 provides that both resulting trusts have provisions identical to Trust 1. The terms of the instrument severing Trust 1 further provide that Trust 3 is to be funded on a pro rata basis with assets having a fair market value as of the date of severance equal to 70% of the value of Trust 1's assets on that date, and Trust 4 is to be funded with assets having a fair market value as of the date of severance equal to 30% of the value of Trust 1's assets on that date. The severance constitutes a qualified severance, provided that all other requirements of section 2642(a)(3) and this section are satisfied. Trust 3 will have an inclusion ratio of zero and Trust 4 will have an inclusion ratio of one.

(k) Effective date. (1) *In general.* Except as otherwise provided in this paragraph (k), this section applies to severances occurring on or after August 2, 2007. Paragraph (d)(7)(iii), paragraph (h), and Examples 9, 12 and 13 of paragraph (j) of this section apply to severances occurring on or after September 2, 2008.

(2) *Transition rule.* In the case of a qualified severance occurring after December 31, 2000, and before August 2, 2007, taxpayers may rely on any reasonable

interpretation of section 2642(a)(3) as long as reasonable notice concerning the qualified severance and identification of the trusts involved has been given to the IRS. For this purpose, the proposed regulations (69 FR 51967) are treated as a reasonable interpretation of the statute. For purposes of the reporting provisions of § 26.2642–6(e), notice to the IRS should be mailed by the due date of the gift tax return (including extensions granted) for gifts made during the year in which the severance occurred. If no gift tax return is filed, notice to the IRS should be mailed by April 15th of the year immediately following the year during which the severance occurred. For severances occurring between December 31, 2000, and January 1, 2007, notification should be mailed to the IRS as soon as reasonably practicable after August 2, 2007, if sufficient notice has not already been given.

[T.D. 9348, 72 FR 42294, Aug. 2, 2007; T.D. 9421, 73 FR 44650, July 31, 2008]

§ 26.2642–7 Relief under section 2642(g)(1).

(a) In general. Under section 2642(g)(1)(A) of the Internal Revenue Code (Code), the Secretary of the Treasury or her delegate (Secretary) has the authority to issue regulations describing the circumstances in which a transferor, as defined in section 2652(a) of the Code, or the executor of a transferor's estate, as defined in section 2203 of the Code, will be granted an extension of time to allocate generation-skipping transfer (GST) exemption as described in section 2642(b)(1) and (2). The Secretary also has the authority to issue regulations describing the circumstances under which a transferor or the executor of a transferor's estate will be granted an extension of time to make the elections described in section 2632(b)(3) and (c)(5) of the Code. Section 2632(b)(3) provides that an election may be made by or on behalf of a transferor not to have the transferor's GST exemption automatically allocated under section 2632(b)(1) to a direct skip, as defined in section 2612(c), made by the transferor during life. Section 2632(c)(5)(A)(i) provides that an election may be made by or on behalf of a transferor not to have the transferor's GST exemption automatically allocated under section 2632(c)(1) to an indirect skip, as defined in section 2632(c)(3)(A), or to any or all transfers made by such transferor to a particular trust. Section 2632(c)(5)(A)(ii) provides that an election may be made by or on behalf of a transferor to treat any trust as a GST trust, as defined in section 2632(c)(3)(B), for purposes of section 2632(c) with respect to any or all transfers made by that transferor to the trust. This section generally describes the factors that the Internal Revenue Service (IRS) will consider when an extension of time is sought by or on behalf of a transferor to timely allocate GST exemption or to make an election under section 2632(b)(3) or (c)(5). If the time period for an automatic six-month extension under paragraph (i)(1) of this section has passed, relief provided under this section can be requested through the IRS private letter ruling program. See paragraph (i) of this section.

(b) Effect of relief. (1) *In general.* If an extension of time to allocate GST exemption is granted under this section, the allocation of GST exemption, once made, will be considered effective as of the date of the transfer. Further, the amount of the transferor's GST exemption required to be allocated in order to produce a zero inclusion ratio solely with regard to that transfer will be the value of the property transferred for purposes of chapter 11 or chapter 12 of the Code as of the date of the transfer. If an extension of time to elect out of the automatic allocation of GST exemption under section 2632(b)(3) or (c)(5)(A)(i) is granted under this section, the election, once made, will be considered effective as of the date of and immediately prior to the transfer. If an extension of time to elect to treat any trust as a GST trust under section 2632(c)(5)(A)(ii) is granted under this section, the election, once made, will be considered effective as of the date of and immediately prior to the first (or each) transfer covered by that election. See paragraph (h) of this section with regard to preserving a taxpayer's eligibility for a refund generated by a grant of relief, if applicable.

(2) [*Reserved*]

(3) *Effect on other transfers.* Except as otherwise provided in paragraph (e)(2)(ii) of this section, an allocation of exemption or an election made pursuant to a grant of relief under this section does not reduce or eliminate any affirmative allocation or void any election made with respect to any other transfer occurring contemporaneously with or subsequent to the transfer or transfers for which relief has been granted.

(c) Limitation on relief. The amount of GST exemption that may be allocated to a transfer as the result of relief granted under this section in no event may exceed the amount of the transferor's unused GST exemption under section 2631(c) of the Code as of the date of the transfer. Thus, if, by the time of the making of the allocation or election pursuant to relief granted under this section, the GST exemption amount under section 2631(c) has increased to an amount in excess of the amount in effect for the date of the transfer, no portion of the increased amount may be applied to that earlier transfer by reason of the relief granted under this section.

(d) Basis for determination. (1) *In general.* Requests for relief under this section will be granted when and to the extent that the transferor or the executor of the transferor's estate provides evidence (including the affidavits described in paragraph (i) of this section) establishing to the satisfaction of the IRS that the transferor or the executor of the transferor's estate acted reasonably and in good faith, and that the grant of relief will not prejudice the interests of the government. Paragraphs (d)(2) and (3) of this section set forth nonexclusive lists of factors the IRS will consider in determining whether this standard of reasonableness, good faith, and lack of prejudice to the interests of the government has been met so that such relief will be granted. In making this determination, the IRS will consider those factors set forth in paragraphs (d)(2) and (3) of this section, as well as all other facts and circumstances not specifically set forth herein that are relevant to the particular situation. Paragraph (e) of this section sets forth some situations in which this standard is not met and, as a result, in which relief under this section will not be granted.

(2) *Reasonableness and good faith.* The following is a nonexclusive list of factors that will be considered in determining whether the transferor or the executor of the transferor's estate acted reasonably and in good faith for purposes of this section. Not all of these factors may be relevant in a particular situation (and those that are not relevant are not required to be addressed in the request for relief made in accordance with paragraph (i) of this section). Further, it is possible that the evidence relating to any one of these factors, in the context of all of the facts and circumstances of the particular situation, may be sufficient to persuade the IRS that the grant of relief under section 2642(g)(1) would be appropriate. However, as a general rule, no single factor (whether listed or not) will be determinative in all cases. The factors are as follows:

(i) *Intent.* The intent of the transferor to timely allocate GST exemption to a transfer or to timely make an election under section 2632(b)(3) or (c)(5), as evidenced in the trust instrument, the instrument of transfer, or other relevant documents contemporaneous with the transfer, such as Federal gift and estate tax returns and correspondence. This may include evidence of the intended GST tax status of the transfer or the trust (for example, exempt, non-exempt, or partially exempt), or more explicit evidence of intent with regard to the allocation of GST exemption or the election under section 2632(b)(3) or (c)(5).

(ii) *Intervening events.* Intervening events beyond the control of the transferor or of the executor of the transferor's estate that caused the failure to allocate GST exemption to a transfer or the failure to make an election under section 2632(b)(3) or (c)(5).

(iii) *Lack of awareness.* Lack of awareness, despite the exercise of reasonable diligence, by the transferor or the executor of the transferor's estate of the need to allocate GST exemption to the transfer, taking into account the experience of the transferor or the executor of the transferor's estate and the complexity of the GST tax issue, as the cause of the failure to allocate GST exemption to a transfer or to make an election under section 2632(b)(3) or (c)(5).

(iv) *Consistency.* Consistency by the transferor with regard to the allocation of the transferor's GST exemption to one or more trusts or skip persons. For example, the transferor's consistent pattern of allocation of GST exemption to transfers (whether or not made in consecutive years) to skip persons or to a particular trust, or the transferor's consistent pattern of electing not to have the automatic allocation of GST exemption apply to transfers (whether or not made in consecutive years), will be taken into consideration. Evidence of consistency may be less relevant if there has been a change of circumstances or a change of trust beneficiaries that otherwise would explain a deviation from prior GST exemption allocation decisions. Relief under this section will not be denied merely because a pattern of allocation or election does not exist or because the existing pattern changed at some point, whether in response to the enactment of section 2642(g) or to some other factor unrelated to either a lack of reasonableness or good faith or prejudice to the interests of the government.

(v) *Qualified tax professional.* Reasonable reliance by the transferor or the executor of the transferor's estate on the advice of a qualified tax professional retained or employed by one or both of them and either the failure of the tax professional, or, in reliance on or consistent with (or in the absence of) that tax professional's advice, the failure of the transferor or the executor, to allocate GST exemption to the transfer or to make an election described in section 2632(b)(3) or (c)(5). Reliance on a qualified tax professional will not be considered to have been reasonable if the transferor or the executor of the transferor's estate knew or should have known that the professional either—

(A) Was not competent to render advice on the GST exemption; or

(B) Was not aware of all relevant facts.

(3) *Prejudice to the interests of the government.* The following is a nonexclusive list of factors that will be considered to determine whether the interests of the government would be prejudiced for purposes of this section:

(i) *Hindsight.* An attempt to benefit from hindsight will be deemed to prejudice the interests of the government. A factor relevant to this determination is whether the grant of the requested relief would permit an economic advantage or other benefit that would not have been available if the allocation or election had been timely made. For example, there may be prejudice if a grant of the requested relief would permit an economic advantage or other benefit that results from the selection of one out of a number of alternatives (other than whether or not to make an allocation or election) that were available at the time the allocation or election could have been timely made, if hindsight makes the selected alternative more beneficial than the other alternatives. Prejudice also would exist if the transferor failed to make the allocation or election in order to wait to see (thus, with the benefit of hindsight) whether making an allocation of exemption or election would be more beneficial than not making the allocation or election. For instance, assume that a transferor funds several trusts with different property interests on the same date, and does not allocate GST exemption to any trust. Several years later, the transferor seeks relief to allocate GST exemption to the trust that enjoyed the greatest asset appreciation and thus constitutes the most effective use of the transferor's GST exemption. Relief will not be granted because the transferor attempted to benefit from hindsight and thereby acquire an economic advantage.

(ii) *Timing of the request for relief.* The timing of the request for relief will be considered in determining whether the interests of the government would be prejudiced by granting relief under this section. The interests of the government would be prejudiced if delay by the transferor or the executor of the transferor's estate in the filing of the request for relief was intended to deprive the IRS of a sufficient period of time in which to challenge any element of the transfer that is the subject of the request for relief, such as the value of the transferred property for Federal gift or estate tax purposes, the claimed identity of the transferor of the transferred property, or any other aspect of the transfer that is relevant for Federal gift or estate tax purposes. For this purpose, such intent will be presumed, but may be rebutted by evidence persuasive to the IRS of the existence of other reasons for or circumstances causing the delay.

(iii) *Intervening taxable events.* The occurrence and effect of an intervening taxable termination or taxable distribution will be considered in determining whether and to what extent the interests of the government would be prejudiced by a grant of relief under this section. The interests of the government may be prejudiced if a taxable termination or a taxable distribution occurred between the time for making a timely allocation of GST exemption or a timely election described in section 2632(b)(3) or (c)(5) and the time at which the request for relief under this section was filed. The impact of a grant of relief on (and the difficulty of adjusting) the GST tax consequences of that intervening termination or distribution will be considered in determining whether the occurrence of a taxable termination or taxable distribution constitutes prejudice.

(iv) *Closed years.* Subject to the considerations described in paragraph (d)(3)(ii) of this section, the expiration of any period of limitations on the assessment or collection of transfer taxes prior to the filing of a request for relief under this section generally is not relevant to the determination of whether the requirements for a grant of relief under this section have been met. If that period has expired, however, and if the IRS concludes that the value of the transferred asset or assets as reported on a Federal gift or estate tax return by the transferor or the executor of the transferor's estate is likely to have satisfied the definition of a gross valuation misstatement as defined in section 6662(h)(2)

(C) of the Code, the IRS will consider the purported undervaluation in determining whether a grant of relief will prejudice the interests of the government.

(e) Situations in which the standard of reasonableness, good faith, and lack of prejudice to the interests of the government has not been met. (1) *In general.* Relief under this section will not be granted if the IRS determines that the transferor or the executor of the transferor's estate has not acted reasonably and in good faith, or that the grant of relief would prejudice the interests of the government. The following situations illustrate some circumstances in which the standard of reasonableness, good faith, and lack of prejudice to the interests of the government has not been met, and as a result, in which relief under this section will not be granted.

(2) *Affirmative allocations.*

(i) In general, relief will not be granted under this section to the extent that it would decrease or revoke an affirmative (but not automatic) allocation of GST exemption under section 2632(a) or 2642(b) that was made on a Federal gift or estate tax return, regardless of whether the transfer or the allocation of exemption was made during the transferor's life or upon the transferor's death.

(ii) There are three exceptions to this general rule, as follows. No request for relief is required for either of the first two exceptions:

(A) An allocation of GST exemption is void to the extent the amount allocated exceeds the amount necessary to obtain an inclusion ratio of zero with respect to the property transferred or to the trust. This provision does not apply to charitable lead annuity trusts, nor does it apply to an allocation made to a trust subject to an estate tax inclusion period before the termination of that period. See § 26.2632–1(b)(4)(i).

(B) An allocation is void if the allocation is made with respect to a trust that, at the time of the allocation, has no GST potential with respect to the transferor making the allocation. For this purpose, a trust has GST potential even if the possibility of a GST is so remote as to be negligible. See § 26.2632–1(b)(4)(i).

(C) A late allocation of GST exemption, as described in section 2642(b)(3), to a transfer or to a trust will be deemed void upon the grant of relief under this section if—

(1) Prior to December 31, 2000, a transfer is made that is subject to GST tax or to a trust that has GST potential with respect to the transferor;

(2) A timely allocation of GST exemption was not made to the transfer or the trust, and this missed allocation was not eligible for relief prior to the enactment of section 2642(g)(1);

(3) Prior to December 31, 2000, a late allocation of GST exemption was made to the transfer or the trust;

(4) The late allocation is disclosed as part of the request for relief or during the IRS's consideration of that request; and

(5) Relief under this section is granted to make a timely allocation to the transfer or the trust described in paragraph (e)(2)(ii)(C)(1) of this section.

(3) Timing. Relief will not be granted with regard to a transfer reported on the transferor's gift tax return in the situation in which the transferor filed the request for relief shortly after the expiration of the period during which an assessment of gift tax could be made with respect to that transfer, the IRS reasonably concludes that the transferor intentionally delayed that filing for the purpose of preventing an IRS examination of the reported value of the property subject to that transfer or the claimed identity of the transferor or other fact relevant for transfer tax purposes, and the transferor is unable to produce evidence sufficient to convince the IRS that the filing delay was attributable to some other reason or purpose.

(4) Failure after being accurately informed. Relief will not be granted under this section if the decision made by the transferor or the executor of the transferor's estate (who had been accurately informed in all material respects by a qualified tax professional retained or employed by either (or both) of them with regard to the allocation of GST exemption or an election described in section 2632(b)(3) or (c)(5)) was reflected or implemented by the action or inaction that is the subject of the request for relief.

(5) Hindsight. Relief under this section will not be granted if the IRS determines that the requested relief is an attempt to benefit from hindsight by waiting to see which of multiple transfers, made at substantially the same time but consisting of different property interests, enjoyed the greatest appreciation and thus

would constitute the most effective use of the transferor's GST exemption.

(f) [Reserved]

(g) Period of limitations under section 6501. A request for relief under this section does not reopen, suspend, or extend the period of limitations on assessment or collection of any estate, gift, or GST tax under section 6501 of the Code. The IRS may request that the transferor or the transferor's executor consent, under section 6501(c)(4) and prior to the expiration of that period of limitations, to an extension of the period of limitations on assessment or collection of any or all gift and GST taxes for the transfer or transfers that are the subject of the requested relief. The transferor or the transferor's executor has the right to refuse to extend the period of limitations, or to limit any such extension to particular issues or to a particular period of time. See section 6501(c)(4)(B). Because a consent to an extension (whether or not limited) may eliminate prejudice to the interests of the government described in paragraphs (d)(3)(ii) and (e)(3) of this section, a refusal to consent to an extension is a factor that may adversely impact the availability of the requested relief.

(h) Refunds. The filing of a request for relief under section 2642(g)(1) with the IRS does not constitute a claim for refund or credit of an overpayment and no implied right to refund will arise from the filing of such a request for relief. Similarly, the filing of such a request for relief does not extend the period of limitations under section 6511 of the Code for filing a claim for refund or credit of an overpayment. If the grant of relief under section 2642(g)(1) results in the decrease of a trust's inclusion ratio or a reduction in the amount of a direct skip, and thus in a potential claim for refund or credit of an overpayment of tax, no such refund or credit will be allowed to the taxpayer or to the taxpayer's estate if the period of limitations under section 6511 for filing a claim for a refund or credit of the Federal gift, estate, or GST tax that was reduced by the granted relief has expired, unless a claim for refund or credit was filed before the expiration of that period. The taxpayer or the taxpayer's estate is responsible for preserving any potential claim for refund or credit.

(i) Procedural requirements. (1) *Automatic 6-month extension.* An automatic extension of 6 months from the due date of the gift or estate tax return, or of the Form 8939, Allocation of Increase in Basis for Property Acquired From a Decedent, of a decedent dying in calendar year 2010, (in each case, excluding extensions) is granted to file a supplemental return or Form 8939 on which the transferor or the executor of the transferor's estate may allocate GST exemption or make an election under section 2632(b)(3) or (c)(5). This extension, however, is available only if the transferor (or the executor of a transferor's estate) both timely filed the gift or estate tax return or the Form 8939 on which the GST exemption should have been allocated or the election should have been made, and, within that 6-month extension period, files a supplemental return or other supplementary filing. On the supplemental return or other filing, the taxpayer must comply with all of the requirements for allocating GST exemption under section 2632 or for making the election under section 2632(b)(3) or (c)(5) for the year the allocation or election should have been made to make a valid allocation or election. Any supplemental return filed pursuant to this paragraph must say FILED PURSUANT TO § 26.2642–7(i)(1) on the front page of the return or the Form 8939, and must be sent to the same address that a timely return or Form 8939 on which the allocation or election should have been made would have been sent, subject to address changes in future forms or instructions or guidance published in the Internal Revenue Bulletin. See § 601.601(d)(2) of this chapter. No request for a private letter ruling is required and, as a result, no user fee is required to be paid.

(2) *Private letter ruling program.* Except for the automatic 6-month extension provided in paragraph (i)(1) of this section, the relief described in this section is provided through the IRS's private letter ruling program. Requests for relief may be submitted in accordance with the applicable procedures for requests for a private letter ruling.

(3) *Affidavit and declaration of transferor or the executor of the transferor's estate.* (i) The transferor or the executor of the transferor's estate must submit a detailed affidavit describing the events that led to the failure to timely allocate GST exemption to a transfer or the failure to timely elect under section 2632(b)(3) or (c)(5), and the events that led to the discovery of the failure. In situations described in paragraph (i)(4)(vi) of this section, this affidavit also must include the additional information and statements described in that paragraph. If the transferor or the executor of

the transferor's estate relied on a tax professional for advice with respect to the allocation or election, the affidavit also must describe

(A) The scope of the engagement;

(B) The responsibilities the transferor or the executor of the transferor's estate believed the professional had assumed; and

(C) The extent to which the transferor or the executor of the transferor's estate relied on the professional.

(ii) Attached to each affidavit must be copies of any writings (including, without limitation, notes and emails) and other contemporaneous documents within the possession or control of the affiant relevant to the determination of the transferor's intent with regard to the application of GST tax to the transaction for which relief under this section is requested.

(iii) The affidavit must be accompanied by a dated declaration, signed by the transferor or the executor of the transferor's estate, that states:

Under penalties of perjury, I declare that I have examined this affidavit, including any attachments thereto, and to the best of my knowledge and belief, this affidavit, including any attachments thereto, is true, correct, and complete. In addition, under penalties of perjury, I declare that I have examined all the documents included as part of this request for relief, and that, to the best of my knowledge and belief, these documents collectively contain all the relevant facts relating to the request for relief and such facts are true, correct, and complete.

(4) *Affidavits and declarations from other parties.*

(i) The transferor or the executor of the transferor's estate must submit detailed affidavits from the individuals specified in paragraphs (i)(4)(i)(A) through (D) of this section and other individuals who have knowledge or information about the events that led to the failure to allocate GST exemption or to elect under section 2632(b)(3) or (c)(5), or to the discovery of the failure. These individuals may include individuals whose knowledge or information is not within the personal knowledge of the transferor or the executor of the transferor's estate. The individuals described in this paragraph must include—

(A) Each agent or legal representative of the transferor who participated in the consideration of, or the decision with regard to, the allocation of GST exemption or the election under section 2632(b)(3) or (c)(5), or the preparation of the return for which relief is being requested;

(B) The preparer of the relevant Federal estate or gift tax return or returns;

(C) Each individual (including an employee of the transferor or of the executor of the transferor's estate) who provided information or advice with regard to, or otherwise made a significant contribution to, the decision concerning the allocation of GST exemption, the election under section 2632(b)(3) or (c)(5), or the preparation of the relevant Federal estate and/or gift tax return or returns; and

(D) Each tax professional who advised or was consulted by the transferor or the executor of the transferor's estate with regard to the allocation of GST exemption, the election under section 2632(b)(3) or (c)(5), or the preparation of the relevant Federal estate or gift tax return or returns.

(ii) Each affidavit must describe the scope of the engagement and the responsibilities of the individual as well as the advice or service the individual provided to the transferor or the executor of the transferor's estate.

(iii) Attached to each affidavit must be a copy of each writing (including, without limitation, notes and emails) and other contemporaneous documents within the possession of the affiant relevant to the transferor's intent or the affiant's advice with regard to the application of GST tax to the transaction for which relief under this section is requested. The documents that the affiant discovers by conducting in good faith a reasonably diligent search of records in the possession of or accessible to the affiant, or subject to the affiant's control, will be sufficient to satisfy the requirements of this paragraph (i)(4)(iii). A reasonably diligent search generally would include, without limitation, a review of the records in the possession or control of the affiant or the firm at which the affiant is employed or associated relating to the transaction or tax return at issue.

(iv) The IRS may require additional affidavits from persons not set forth in paragraph (i)(4)(i) of this section as well as additional documents when additional information or documents with respect to a transfer is believed by the IRS to be required or helpful in making its determination as to whether relief under this section should be granted.

(v) Each affidavit also must include the name and current address of the affiant, and must be accompanied by a dated declaration signed by the affiant that states:

Under penalties of perjury, I declare that I have personal knowledge of the information set forth in this affidavit, including any attachments thereto. In addition, under penalties of perjury, I declare that I have examined this affidavit, including any attachments thereto, and, to the best of my knowledge and belief, the affidavit contains all the relevant facts and the attachments include copies of all relevant writings or other documents resulting from a reasonably diligent search, conducted in good faith, of all records within my possession, accessible to me, or subject to my control, relating to the allocation of GST exemption, the election under section 2632(b)(3) or (c)(5), and the preparation of the tax return at issue in the request for relief filed by or on behalf of [transferor or executor of transferor's estate], and such facts and attached documents are true, correct, and complete.

(vi) If an individual who would be required to provide an affidavit under paragraph (i)(4)(i) of this section has died or is unwilling or otherwise unable to provide the required affidavit, the affidavit required under paragraph (i)(3) of this section must include a statement to that effect, as well as a statement describing the relationship between that individual and the transferor or the executor of the transferor's estate; the information or knowledge the transferor or the executor of the transferor's estate believes that individual had about the events that led to the failure to make the allocation or the election or to the discovery of that failure; and, in cases other than the death of the individual, a detailed description of the efforts made to obtain the affidavit from the individual. The unwillingness of certain affiants to provide an affidavit, however, may be considered by the IRS in determining whether to grant the requested relief. For purposes of this paragraph (i)(4)(vi), the term unwilling refers to a person who is apparently able but refuses or otherwise fails, despite the best efforts, made in good faith, of the transferor or the transferor's executor, to provide the required affidavit. In addition, for purposes of this paragraph, the term unable refers to a permanent or potentially long-term condition such as physical or mental incapacity that prevents the person from providing the required affidavit, but not a temporary condition such as a temporary physical or mental incapacity or a person's inability due to a leave of absence, travel, or a contractual requirement such as a confidentiality agreement.

(5) Additional rules regarding relief. For purposes of relief under paragraphs (i)(1) and (2) of this section, the grant of relief in the form of an extension of time is not a determination that the taxpayer is otherwise eligible to make the election. In addition, notwithstanding the provisions of this section, an extension of time will not be granted under this section if alternative relief is provided by a statute, a regulation published in the Federal Register, or a revenue ruling, revenue procedure, notice, or announcement published in the Internal Revenue Bulletin (see § 601.601(d)(2) of this chapter).

(j) Applicability date. This section applies to requests for relief to which section 2642(g)(1) applies that are filed on or after May 6, 2024, regardless of the date of the transfer.

[T.D. 9996, 89 FR 37123, May 6, 2024]

Subchapter F. Other Definitions and Special Rules

§ 2651. Generation Assignment

(a) In general. For purposes of this chapter, the generation to which any person (other than the transferor) belongs shall be determined in accordance with the rules set forth in this section.

(b) Lineal descendants.

(1) In general. An individual who is a lineal descendant of a grandparent of the transferor shall be assigned to that generation which results from comparing the number of generations between the grandparent and such individual with the number of generations between the grandparent and the transferor.

(2) On spouse's side. An individual who is a lineal descendant of a grandparent of a spouse (or former spouse) of the transferor (other than such spouse) shall be assigned to that generation which results from comparing the number of generations between such grandparent and such individual with the number of generations between such grandparent and such spouse.

(3) Treatment of legal adoptions, etc. For purposes of this subsection—

(A) Legal adoptions. A relationship by legal adoption shall be treated as a relationship by blood.

(B) Relationships by half-blood. A relationship by the half-blood shall be treated as a relationship of the whole-blood.

(c) Marital relationship.

(1) Marriage to transferor. An individual who has been married at any time to the transferor shall be assigned to the transferor's generation.

(2) Marriage to other lineal descendants. An individual who has been married at any time to an individual described in subsection (b) shall be assigned to the generation of the individual so described.

(d) Persons who are not lineal descendants. An individual who is not assigned to a generation by reason of the foregoing provisions of this section shall be assigned to a generation on the basis of the date of such individual's birth with—

(1) an individual born not more than 12 1/2 years after the date of the birth of the transferor assigned to the transferor's generation,

(2) an individual born more than 12 1/2 years but not more than 37 1/2 years after the date of the birth of the transferor assigned to the first generation younger than the transferor, and

(3) similar rules for a new generation every 25 years.

(e) Special rule for persons with a deceased parent.

(1) In general. For purposes of determining whether any transfer is a generation-skipping transfer, if—

(A) an individual is a descendant of a parent of the transferor (or the transferor's spouse or former spouse), and

(B) such individual's parent who is a lineal descendant of the parent of the transferor (or the transferor's spouse or former spouse) is dead at the time the transfer (from which an interest of such individual is established or derived) is subject to a tax imposed by chapter 11 or 12 upon the transferor (and if there shall be more than 1 such time, then at the earliest such time), such individual shall be treated as if such individual were a member of the generation which is 1 generation below the lower of the transferor's generation or the generation assignment of the youngest living ancestor of such individual who is also a descendant of the parent of the transferor (or the transferor's spouse or former spouse), and the generation assignment of any descendant of such individual shall be adjusted accordingly.

(2) Limited application of subsection to collateral heirs. This subsection shall not apply with respect to a transfer to any individual who is not a lineal descendant of the transferor (or the transferor's spouse or former spouse) if, at the time of the transfer, such transferor has any living lineal descendant.

(f) Other special rules.

(1) Individuals assigned to more than 1 generation. Except as provided in regulations, an individual who, but for this subsection, would be assigned to more than 1 generation shall be assigned to the youngest such generation.

(2) Interests through entities. Except as provided in paragraph (3), if an estate, trust, partnership, corporation, or other entity has an interest in property, each individual having a beneficial interest in such entity shall be treated as having an interest in such property and shall be assigned to a generation under the foregoing provisions of this subsection.

(3) Treatment of certain charitable organizations and governmental entities. Any—

(A) organization described in section 511(a)(2),

(B) charitable trust described in section 511(b)(2), and

(C) governmental entity,

shall be assigned to the transferor's generation.

Regulations

§ 26.2651–1 Generation assignment.

(a) Special rule for persons with a deceased parent. (1) *In general.* This paragraph (a) applies for purposes of determining whether a transfer to or for the benefit of an individual who is a descendant of a parent of the transferor (or the transferor's spouse or former spouse) is a generation-skipping transfer. If that individual's parent, who is a lineal descendant of the parent of the transferor (or the transferor's spouse or former spouse), is deceased at the time the transfer (from which an interest of such individual is established or derived) is subject to the tax imposed on the transferor by chapter 11 or 12 of the Internal Revenue Code, the individual is treated as if that individual were a member of the generation that is one generation below the lower of—

(i) The transferor's generation; or

(ii) The generation assignment of the individual's youngest living lineal ancestor who is also a descendant of the parent of the transferor (or the transferor's spouse or former spouse).

(2) *Special rules.* (i) *Corresponding generation adjustment.* If an individual's generation assignment is adjusted with respect to a transfer in accordance with paragraph (a)(1) of this section, a corresponding adjustment with respect to that transfer is made to the generation assignment of each—

(A) Spouse or former spouse of that individual;

(B) Descendant of that individual; and

(C) Spouse or former spouse of each descendant of that individual.

(ii) *Continued application of generation assignment.* If a transfer to a trust would be a generation-skipping transfer but for paragraph (a)(1) of this section, any generation assignment determined under this paragraph (a) continues to apply in determining whether any subsequent distribution from (or termination of an interest in) the portion of the trust attributable to that transfer is a generation-skipping transfer.

(iii) *Ninety-day rule.* For purposes of paragraph (a)(1) of this section, any individual who dies no later than 90 days after a transfer occurring by reason of the death of the transferor is treated as having predeceased the transferor.

(iv) *Local law.* A living person is not treated as having predeceased the transferor solely by reason of a provision of applicable local law; e.g., an individual who disclaims is not treated as a predeceased parent solely because state law treats a disclaimant as having predeceased the transferor for purposes of determining the disposition of the disclaimed property.

(3) *Established or derived.* For purposes of section 2651(e) and paragraph (a)(1) of this section, an individual's interest is established or derived at the time the transferor is subject to transfer tax on the property. See § 26.2652–1(a) for the definition of a transferor. If the same transferor, on more than one occasion, is subject to transfer tax imposed by either chapter 11 or 12 of the Internal Revenue Code on the property so

transferred (whether the same property, reinvestments thereof, income thereon, or any or all of these), then the relevant time for determining whether paragraph (a)(1) of this section applies is the earliest time at which the transferor is subject to the tax imposed by either chapter 11 or 12 of the Internal Revenue Code. For purposes of section 2651(e) and paragraph (a)(1) of this section, the interest of a remainder beneficiary of a trust for which an election under section 2523(f) or section 2056(b)(7) (QTIP election) has been made will be deemed to have been established or derived, to the extent of the QTIP election, on the date as of which the value of the trust corpus is first subject to tax under section 2519 or section 2044. The preceding sentence does not apply to a trust, however, to the extent that an election under section 2652(a)(3) (reverse QTIP election) has been made for the trust because, to the extent of a reverse QTIP election, the spouse who established the trust will remain the transferor of the trust for generation-skipping transfer tax purposes.

(4) *Special rule in the case of additional contributions to a trust.* If a transferor referred to in paragraph (a)(1) of this section contributes additional property to a trust that existed before the application of paragraph (a)(1), then the additional property is treated as being held in a separate trust for purposes of chapter 13 of the Internal Revenue Code. The provisions of § 26.2654–1(a)(2), regarding treatment as separate trusts, apply as if different transferors had contributed to the separate portions of the single trust. Additional subsequent contributions from that transferor will be added to the new share that is treated as a separate trust.

(b) Limited application to collateral heirs. Paragraph (a) of this section does not apply in the case of a transfer to any individual who is not a lineal descendant of the transferor (or the transferor's spouse or former spouse) if the transferor has any living lineal descendant at the time of the transfer.

(c) Examples. The following examples illustrate the provisions of this section:

Example (1). T establishes an irrevocable trust, Trust, providing that trust income is to be paid to T's grandchild, GC, for 5 years. At the end of the 5-year period or on GC's prior death, Trust is to terminate and the principal is to be distributed to GC if GC is living or to GC's children if GC has died. The transfer that occurred on the creation of the trust is subject to the tax imposed by chapter 12 of the Internal Revenue Code and, at the time of the transfer, T's child, C, who is a parent of GC, is deceased. GC is treated as a member of the generation that is one generation below T's generation. As a result, GC is not a skip person and Trust is not a skip person. Therefore, the transfer to Trust is not a direct skip. Similarly, distributions to GC during the term of Trust and at the termination of Trust will not be GSTs.

Example (2). On January 1, 2004, T transfers $100,000 to an irrevocable inter vivos trust that provides T with an annuity payable for four years or until T's prior death. The annuity satisfies the definition of a qualified interest under section 2702(b). When the trust terminates, the corpus is to be paid to T's grandchild, GC. The transfer is subject to the tax imposed by chapter 12 of the Internal Revenue Code and, at the time of the transfer, T's child, C, who is a parent of GC, is living. C dies in 2006. In this case, C was alive at the time the transfer by T was subject to the tax imposed by chapter 12 of the Internal Revenue Code. Therefore, section 2651(e) and paragraph (a)(1) of this section do not apply. When the trust subsequently terminates, the distribution to GC is a taxable termination that is subject to the GST tax to the extent the trust has an inclusion ratio greater than zero. See section 2642(a).

Example (3). T dies testate in 2002, survived by T's spouse, S, their children, C1 and C2, and C1's child, GC. Under the terms of T's will, a trust is established for the benefit of S and of T and S's descendants. Under the terms of the trust, all income is payable to S during S's lifetime and the trustee may distribute trust corpus for S's health, support and maintenance. At S's death, the corpus is to be distributed, outright, to C1 and C2. If either C1 or C2 has predeceased S, the deceased child's share of the corpus is to be distributed to that child's then-living descendants, per stirpes. The executor of T's estate makes the election under section 2056(b)(7) to treat the trust property as qualified terminable interest property (QTIP) but does not make the election under section 2652(a)(3) (reverse QTIP election). In 2003, C1 dies survived by S and GC. In 2004, S dies, and the trust terminates. The full fair market value of the trust is includible in S's gross estate under section 2044 and S becomes the transferor of the trust under section 2652(a)(1)(A). GC's interest is considered established or derived at S's death, and because C1 is deceased at that time, GC is treated as a member of the generation that is one generation below the generation of the transferor, S. As a result, GC is not a skip person and the transfer to GC is not a direct skip.

Example (4). The facts are the same as in Example 3. However, the executor of T's estate makes the election under section 2652(a)(3) (reverse QTIP election) for the entire trust. Therefore, T remains the transferor because, for purposes of chapter 13 of the Internal Revenue Code, the election to be treated as qualified terminable interest property is treated as if it had not been made. In this case, GC's interest is established or derived on T's death in 2002. Because C1 was living at the time of T's death, the predeceased parent rule under section 2651(e) does not apply, even though C1 was deceased at the time the transfer from S to GC was subject to the tax under chapter 11 of the Internal Revenue Code. When the trust terminates, the distribution to GC is a taxable termination that is subject to the GST tax to the extent the trust has an inclusion ratio greater than zero. See section 2642(a).

Example (5). T establishes an irrevocable trust providing that trust income is to be paid to T's grandniece, GN, for 5 years or until GN's prior death. At the end of the 5-year period or on GN's prior death, the trust is to terminate and the principal is to be distributed to GN if living, or if GN has died, to GN's then-living descendants, per stirpes. S is a sibling of T and the parent of N. N is the parent of GN. At the time of the transfer, T has no living lineal descendant, S is living, N is deceased, and the transfer is subject to the gift tax imposed by chapter 12 of the Internal Revenue Code. GN is treated as a member of the generation that is one generation below T's generation because S, GN's youngest living lineal ancestor who is also a descendant of T's parent, is in T's generation. As a result, GN is not a skip person and the transfer to the trust is not a direct skip. In addition, distributions to GN during the term of the trust and at the termination of the trust will not be GSTs.

Example (6). On January 1, 2004, T transfers $50,000 to a great-grandniece, GGN, who is the great-grandchild of B, a brother of T. At the time of the transfer, T has no living lineal descendants and B's grandchild, GN, who is a parent of GGN and a child of B's living child, N, is deceased. GGN will be treated as a member of the generation that is one generation below the lower of T's generation or the generation assignment of GGN's youngest living lineal ancestor who is also a descendant of the parent of the transferor. In this case, N is GGN's youngest living lineal ancestor who is also a descendant of the parent of T. Because N's generation assignment is lower than T's generation, GGN will be treated as a member of the generation that is one generation below N's generation assignment (i.e., GGN will be treated as a member of her parent's generation). As a result, GGN remains a skip person and the transfer to GGN is a direct skip.

Example (7). T has a child, C. C and C's spouse, S, have a 20-year-old child, GC. C dies and S subsequently marries S2. S2 legally adopts GC. T transfers $100,000 to GC. Under section 2651(b)(1), GC is assigned to the generation that is two generations below T. However, since GC's parent, C, is deceased at the time of the transfer, GC will be treated as a member of the generation that is one generation below T. As a result, GC is not a skip person and the transfer to GC is not a direct skip.

[T.D. 9214, 70 FR 41142, July 18, 2005]

§ 26.2651–2 Individual assigned to more than 1 generation.

(a) In general. Except as provided in paragraph (b) or (c) of this section, an individual who would be assigned to more than 1 generation is assigned to the youngest of the generations to which that individual would be assigned.

(b) Exception. Notwithstanding paragraph (a) of this section, an adopted individual (as defined in this paragraph) will be treated as a member of the generation that is one generation below the adoptive parent for purposes of determining whether a transfer to the adopted individual from the adoptive parent (or the spouse or former spouse of the adoptive parent, or a lineal descendant of a grandparent of the adoptive parent) is subject to chapter 13 of the Internal Revenue Code. For purposes of this paragraph (b), an adopted individual is an individual who is—

(1) Legally adopted by the adoptive parent;

(2) A descendant of a parent of the adoptive parent (or the spouse or former spouse of the adoptive parent);

(3) Under the age of 18 at the time of the adoption; and

(4) Not adopted primarily for the purpose of avoiding GST tax. The determination of whether an adoption is primarily for GST tax-avoidance purposes is made based upon all of the facts and circumstances. The most significant factor is whether there is a bona fide parent/child relationship between the adoptive parent and the adopted individual, in which the adoptive parent has fully assumed all significant responsibilities for the care and raising of the adopted child. Other factors may include (but are not limited to), at the time of the adoption—

(i) The age of the adopted individual (for example, the younger the age of the adopted individual, or the age of the youngest of siblings who are all adopted together, the more likely the adoption will not be considered primarily for GST tax-avoidance purposes); and

(ii) The relationship between the adopted individual and the individual's parents (for example, objective evidence of the absence or incapacity of the parents may indicate that the adoption is not primarily for GST tax-avoidance purposes).

(c) Special rules. (1) *Corresponding generation adjustment.* If an individual's generation assignment is adjusted with respect to a transfer in accordance with paragraph (b) of this section, a corresponding adjustment with respect to that transfer is made to the generation assignment of each—

(i) Spouse or former spouse of that individual;

(ii) Descendant of that individual; and

(iii) Spouse or former spouse of each descendant of that individual.

(2) *Continued application of generation assignment.* If a transfer to a trust would be a generation-skipping transfer but for paragraph (b) of this section, any generation assignment determined under paragraph (b) or (c) of this section continues to apply in determining whether any subsequent distribution from (or termination of an interest in) the portion of the trust attributable to that transfer is a generation-skipping transfer.

(d) Example. The following example illustrates the provisions of this section:

Example. T has a child, C. C has a 20-year-old child, GC. T legally adopts GC and transfers $100,000 to GC. GC's generation assignment is determined by section 2651(b)(1) and GC is assigned to the generation that is two generations below T. In addition, because T has legally adopted GC, GC is generally treated as a child of T under state law. Under these circumstances, GC is an individual who is assigned to more than one generation and the exception in § 26.2651–2(b) does not apply. Thus, the special rule under section 2651(f)(1) applies and GC is assigned to the generation that is two generations below T. GC remains a skip person with respect to T and the transfer to GC is a direct skip.

[T.D. 9214, 70 FR 41143, July 18, 2005]

§ 26.2651–3 Effective dates.

(a) In general. The rules of §§ 26.2651–1 and 26.2651–2 are applicable for terminations, distributions, and transfers occurring on or after July 18, 2005.

(b) Transition rule. In the case of transfers occurring after December 31, 1997, and before July 18, 2005, taxpayers may rely on any reasonable interpretation of section 2651(e). For this purpose, these final regulations, as well as the proposed regulations issued on September 3, 2004 (69 FR 53862), are treated as a reasonable interpretation of the statute.

[T.D. 9214, 70 FR 41143, July 18, 2005]

§ 2652. Other Definitions

(a) Transferor. For purposes of this chapter—

(1) In general. Except as provided in this subsection or section 2653(a), the term "transferor" means—

(A) in the case of any property subject to the tax imposed by chapter 11, the decedent, and

(B) in the case of any property subject to the tax imposed by chapter 12, the donor. An individual shall be treated as transferring any property with respect to which such individual is the transferor.

(2) Gift-splitting by married couples. If, under section 2513, one-half of a gift is treated as made by an individual and one-half of such gift is treated as made by the spouse of such individual, such gift shall be so treated for purposes of this chapter.

(3) Special election for qualified terminable interest property. In the case of—

(A) any trust with respect to which a deduction is allowed to the decedent under section 2056 by reason of subsection (b)(7) thereof, and

(B) any trust with respect to which a deduction to the donor spouse is allowed under section 2523 by reason of subsection (f) thereof,

the estate of the decedent or the donor spouse, as the case may be, may elect to treat all of the property in such trust for purposes of this chapter as if the election to be treated as qualified terminable interest property had not been made.

(b) Trust and trustee.

(1) Trust. The term "trust" includes any arrangement (other than an estate) which, although not a trust, has substantially the same effect as a trust.

(2) Trustee. In the case of an arrangement which is not a trust but which is treated as a trust under this subsection, the term "trustee" shall mean the person in actual or constructive possession of the property subject to such arrangement.

(3) Examples. Arrangements to which this subsection applies include arrangements involving life estates and remainders, estates for years, and insurance and annuity contracts.

(c) Interest.

(1) In general. A person has an interest in property held in trust if (at the time the determination is made) such person—

(A) has a right (other than a future right) to receive income or corpus from the trust,

(B) is a permissible current recipient of income or corpus from the trust and is not described in section 2055(a), or

(C) is described in section 2055(a) and the trust is—

(i) a charitable remainder annuity trust,

(ii) a charitable remainder unitrust within the meaning of section 664, or

(iii) a pooled income fund within the meaning of section 642(c)(5).

(2) Certain interests disregarded. For purposes of paragraph (1), an interest which is used primarily to postpone or avoid any tax imposed by this chapter shall be disregarded.

(3) Certain support obligations disregarded. The fact that income or corpus of the trust may be used to satisfy an obligation of support arising under State law shall be disregarded in determining whether a person has an interest in the trust, if—

(A) such use is discretionary, or

(B) such use is pursuant to the provisions of any State law substantially equivalent to the Uniform Gifts to Minors Act.

(d) Executor. For purposes of this chapter, the term "executor" has the meaning given such term by section 2203.

Regulations

§ 26.2652–1 Transferor defined; other definitions.

(a) Transferor defined. (1) *In general.* Except as otherwise provided in paragraph (a)(3) of this section, the individual with respect to whom property was most recently subject to Federal estate or gift tax is the transferor of that property for purposes of chapter 13. An individual is treated as transferring any property with respect to which the individual is the transferor. Thus, an individual may be a transferor even though there is no transfer of property under local law at the time the Federal estate or gift tax applies. For purposes of this paragraph, a surviving spouse is the transferor of a qualified domestic trust created by the deceased spouse that is included in the surviving spouse's gross estate, provided the trust is not subject to the election described in § 26.2652–2 (reverse QTIP election). A surviving spouse is also the transferor of a qualified domestic trust created by the surviving spouse pursuant to section 2056(d)(2)(B). For generation-skipping transfer tax rules related to an ABLE account established under section 529A, see § 1.529A–4 of this chapter.

(2) *Transfers subject to Federal estate or gift tax.* For purposes of this chapter, a transfer is subject to Federal gift tax if a gift tax is imposed under section 2501(a) (without regard to exemptions, exclusions, deductions, and credits). A transfer is subject to Federal estate tax if the value of the property is includible in the decedent's gross estate as determined under section 2031 or section 2103.

(3) *Special rule for certain QTIP trusts.* Solely for purposes of chapter 13, if a transferor of qualified terminable interest property (QTIP) elects under § 26.2652–2(a) to treat the property as if the QTIP election had not been made (reverse QTIP election), the identity of the transferor of the property is determined without regard to the application of sections 2044, 2207A, and 2519.

(4) *Split-gift transfers.* In the case of a transfer with respect to which the donor's spouse makes an election under section 2513 to treat the gift as made one-half by the spouse, the electing spouse is treated as the transferor of one-half of the entire value of the property transferred by the donor, regardless of the interest the electing spouse is actually deemed to have transferred under section 2513. The donor is treated as the transferor of one-half of the value of the entire property. See § 26.2632–1(c)(5) Example 3, regarding allocation of GST exemption with respect to split-gift transfers subject to an ETIP.

(5) *Examples.* The following examples illustrate the principles of this paragraph (a):

Example (1). Identity of transferor. T transfers $100,000 to a trust for the sole benefit of T's grandchild. The transfer is subject to Federal gift tax because a gift tax is imposed under section 2501(a) (without regard to exemptions, exclusions, deductions, and credits). Thus, for purposes of chapter 13, T is the transferor of the $100,000. It is immaterial that a portion of the transfer is excluded from the total amount of T's taxable gift by reason of section 2503(b).

Example (2). Gift splitting and identity of transferor. The facts are the same as in Example 1, except T's spouse, S, consents under section 2513 to split the gift with T. For purposes of chapter 13, S and T are each treated as a transferor of $50,000 to the trust.

Example (3). Change of transferor on subsequent transfer tax event. T transfers $100,000 to a trust providing that all the net trust income is to be paid to T's spouse, S, for S's lifetime. T elects under section 2523(f) to treat the transfer as a transfer of qualified terminable interest property, and T does not make the reverse QTIP election under section 2652(a)(3). On S's death, the trust property is included in S's gross estate under section 2044. Thus, S becomes the transferor at the time of S's death.

Example (4). Effect of transfer of an interest in trust on identity of the transferor. T transfers $100,000 to a trust providing that all of the net income is to be paid to T's child, C, for C's lifetime. At C's death, the trust property is to be paid to T's grandchild. C transfers the income interest to X, an unrelated party, in a transfer that is a completed transfer for Federal gift tax purposes. Because C's transfer is a transfer of a term interest in the trust that does not affect the rights of other parties with respect to the trust property, T remains the transferor with respect to the trust.

Example (5). Effect of lapse of withdrawal right on identity of transferor. T transfers $10,000 to a new trust providing that the trust income is to be paid to T's child, C, for C's life and, on the death of C, the trust principal is to be paid to T's grandchild, GC. The trustee has discretion to distribute principal for GC's benefit during C's lifetime. C has a right to withdraw $10,000 from the trust for a 60-day period following the transfer. Thereafter, the power lapses. C does not exercise the withdrawal right. The transfer by T is subject to Federal gift tax because a gift tax is imposed under section 2501(a) (without regard to exemptions, exclusions, deductions, and credits) and, thus, T is treated as having transferred the entire $10,000 to the trust. On the lapse of the withdrawal right, C becomes a transferor to the extent C is treated as having made a completed transfer for purposes of chapter 12. Therefore, except to the extent that the amount with respect to which the power of withdrawal lapses exceeds the greater of $5,000 or 5% of the value of the trust property, T remains the transferor of the trust property for purposes of chapter 13.

Example (6). Effect of reverse QTIP election on identity of the transferor. T establishes a testamentary trust having a principal of $500,000. Under the terms of the trust, all trust income is payable to T's surviving spouse, S, during S's lifetime. T's executor makes an election to treat the trust property as qualified terminable interest property and also makes the reverse QTIP election. For purposes of chapter 13, T is the transferor with respect to the trust. On S's death, the then full fair market value of the trust is includible in S's gross estate under section 2044. However, because of the reverse QTIP election, S does not become the transferor with respect to the trust; T continues to be the transferor.

Example (7). Effect of reverse QTIP election on constructive additions. The facts are the same as in Example 6, except the inclusion of the QTIP trust in S's gross estate increased the Federal estate tax liability of S's estate by $200,000. The estate does not exercise the right of recovery from the trust granted under section 2207A. Under local law, the beneficiaries of S's residuary estate (which bears all estate taxes under the will) could compel the executor to exercise the right of recovery but do not do so. Solely for purposes of chapter 13, the beneficiaries of the residuary estate are not treated as having made an addition to the trust by reason of their failure to exercise their right of recovery. Because of the reverse QTIP election, for GST purposes, the trust property is not treated as includible in S's gross estate and, under those circumstances, no right of recovery exists.

Example (8). Effect of reverse QTIP election on constructive additions. S, the surviving spouse of T, dies testate. At the time of S's death, S was the beneficiary of a trust with respect to which T's executor made a QTIP election under section 2056(b)(7). Thus, the trust is includible in S's gross estate under section 2044. T's executor also made the reverse QTIP election with respect to the trust. S's will provides that all death taxes payable with respect to the trust are payable from S's residuary estate. Since the transferor of the property is determined without regard to section 2044 and section 2207A, S is not treated as making a constructive addition to the trust by reason of the tax apportionment clause in S's will.

Example (9). Split-gift transfers. T transfers $100,000 to an inter vivos trust that provides T with an annuity payable for ten years or until T's prior death. The annuity satisfies the definition of a qualified interest under section 2702(b). When the trust terminates, the corpus is to be paid to T's grandchild, GC. T's spouse, S, consents under section 2513 to have the gift treated as made one-half by S. Under section 2513, only the actuarial value of the gift to GC is eligible to be treated as made one-half by S. However, because S is treated as the donor of one-half of the gift to GC, S becomes the transferor of one-half of the entire trust ($50,000) for purposes of Chapter 13.

(b) Trust defined. (1) *In general.* A trust includes any arrangement (other than an estate) that has substantially the same effect as a trust. Thus, for example, arrangements involving life estates and remainders, estates for years, and insurance and annuity contracts are trusts. Generally, a transfer as to which the identity of the transferee is contingent upon the occurrence of an event is a transfer in trust; however, a transfer of property included in the transferor's gross estate, as to which the identity of the transferee is contingent upon an event that must occur within 6 months of the transferor's death, is not considered a transfer in trust solely by reason of the existence of the contingency.

(2) *Examples.* The following examples illustrate the provisions of this paragraph (b):

Example (1). Uniform gifts to minors transfers. T transfers cash to an account in the name of T's child, C, as custodian for C's child, GC (who is a minor), under a state statute substantially similar to the Uniform Gifts to Minors Act. For purposes of chapter 13, the transfer to the custodial account is treated as a transfer to a trust.

Example (2). Contingent transfers. T bequeaths $200,000 to T's child, C, provided that if C does not survive T by more than 6 months, the bequest is payable to T's grandchild, GC. C dies 4 months after T. The bequest is not a transfer in trust because the contingency that determines the recipient of the bequest must occur within 6 months of T's death. The bequest to GC is a direct skip.

Example (3). Contingent transfers. The facts are the same as in Example 2, except C must survive T by 18 months to take the bequest. The bequest is a transfer in trust for purposes of chapter 13, and the death of C is a taxable termination.

(c) Trustee defined. The trustee of a trust is the person designated as trustee under local law or, if no such person is so designated, the person in actual or constructive possession of property held in trust.

(d) Executor defined. For purposes of chapter 13, the executor is the executor or administrator of the decedent's estate. However, if no executor or administrator is appointed, qualified or acting within the United States, the executor is the fiduciary who is primarily responsible for payment of the decedent's debts and expenses. If there is no such executor, administrator or fiduciary, the executor is the person in actual or constructive possession of the largest portion of the value of the decedent's gross estate.

(e) Interest in trust. See § 26.2612–1(e) for the definition of interest in trust.

[T.D. 8644, 60 FR 66918, Dec. 27, 1995; 61 FR 29654, June 12, 1996; T.D. 8720, 62 FR 27498, May 20, 1997; T.D. 9923, 85 FR 74047, Nov. 19, 2020]

§ 26.2652–2 Special election for qualified terminable interest property.

(a) In general. If an election is made to treat property as qualified terminable interest property (QTIP) under section 2523(f) or section 2056(b)(7), the person making the election may, for purposes of chapter 13, elect to treat the property as if the QTIP election had not been made (reverse QTIP election). An election under this section is irrevocable. An election under this section is not effective unless it is made with respect to all of the property in the trust to which the QTIP election applies. See, however, § 26.2654–1(b)(1). Property that qualifies for a deduction under section 2056(b)(5) is not eligible for the election under this section.

(b) Time and manner of making election. An election under this section is made on the return on which the QTIP election is made. If a protective QTIP election is made, no election under this section is effective unless a protective reverse QTIP election is also made.

(c) Transitional rule. If a reverse QTIP election is made with respect to a trust prior to December 27, 1995, and GST exemption has been allocated to that trust, the transferor (or the transferor's executor) may elect to treat the trust as two separate trusts, one of which has a zero inclusion ratio by reason of the transferor's GST exemption previously allocated to the trust. The separate trust with the zero inclusion ratio consists of that fractional share of the value of the entire trust equal to the value of the nontax portion of the trust under § 26.2642–4(a). The reverse QTIP election is treated as applying only to the trust with the zero inclusion ratio. An election under this paragraph (c) is made by attaching a statement to a copy of the return on which the reverse QTIP election was made under section 2652(a)(3). The statement must indicate that an election is being made to treat the trust as two separate trusts and must identify the values of the two separate trusts. The statement is to be filed in the same place in which the original return was filed and must be filed before June 24, 1996. A trust subject to the election described in this paragraph is treated as a trust that was created by two transferors. See § 26.2654–1(a)(2) for special rules involving trusts with multiple transferors.

(d) Examples. The following examples illustrate the provisions of this section:

Example (1). Special (reverse QTIP) election under section 2652(a)(3). T transfers $1,000,000 to a trust providing that all trust income is to be paid to T's spouse, S, for S's lifetime. On S's death, the trust principal is payable to GC, a grandchild of S and T. T elects to treat all of the transfer as a transfer of QTIP and also makes the reverse QTIP election for all of the property. Because of the reverse QTIP election, T continues to be treated as the transferor of the property after S's death for purposes of chapter 13. A taxable termination rather than a direct skip occurs on S's death.

Example (2). Election under transition rule. In 1994, T died leaving $4 million in trust for the benefit of T's surviving spouse, S. On January 16, 1995, T's executor filed T's Form 706 on which the executor elects to treat the entire trust as qualified terminable interest property. The executor also makes a reverse QTIP election. The reverse QTIP election is effective with respect to the entire trust even though T's executor could allocate only $1 million of GST exemption to the trust. T's executor may elect to treat the trust as two separate trusts, one having a value of 25% of the value of the single trust and an inclusion ratio of zero, but only if the election is made prior to June 24, 1996. If the executor makes the transitional election, the other separate trust, having a value of 75% of the value of the single trust and an inclusion ratio of one, is not treated as subject to the reverse QTIP election.

Example (3). Denominator of the applicable fraction of QTIP trust. T bequeaths $1,500,000 to a trust in which T's surviving spouse, S, receives an income interest for life. Upon the death of S, the property is to remain in trust for the benefit of C, the child of T and S. Upon C's death, the trust is to terminate and the trust property paid to the descendants of C. The bequest qualifies for the estate tax marital deduction under section 2056(b)(7) as QTIP. The executor does not make the reverse QTIP election under section 2652(a)(3). As a result, S becomes the transferor of the trust at S's death when the value of the property in the QTIP trust is included in S's gross estate under section 2044. For purposes of computing the applicable fraction with respect to the QTIP trust upon S's death, the denominator of the fraction is reduced by any Federal estate tax (whether imposed under section 2001, 2101 or 2056A(b)) and State death tax attributable to the trust property that is actually recovered from the trust.

[T.D. 8644, 60 FR 66920, Dec. 27, 1995]

§ 2653. Taxation of Multiple Skips

(a) General rule. For purposes of this chapter, if—

(1) there is a generation-skipping transfer of any property, and

(2) immediately after such transfer such property is held in trust,

for purposes of applying this chapter (other than section 2651) to subsequent transfers from the portion of such trust attributable to such property, the trust will be treated as if the transferor of such property were assigned to the first generation above the highest generation of any person who has an interest in such trust immediately after the transfer.

(b) Trust retains inclusion ratio.

(1) In general. Except as provided in paragraph (2), the provisions of subsection (a) shall not affect the inclusion ratio determined with respect to any trust. Under regulations prescribed by the Secretary, notwithstanding the preceding sentence, proper adjustment shall be made to the inclusion ratio with respect to such trust to take into account any tax under this chapter borne by such trust which is imposed by this chapter on the transfer described in subsection (a).

(2) Special rule for pour-over trust.

(A) In general. If the generation-skipping transfer referred to in subsection (a) involves the transfer of property from 1 trust to another trust (hereinafter in this paragraph referred to as the "pour-over trust"), the inclusion ratio for the pour-over trust shall be determined by treating the nontax portion of such distribution as if it were a part of a GST exemption allocated to such trust.

(B) Nontax portion. For purposes of subparagraph (A), the nontax portion of any distribution is the amount of such distribution multiplied by the applicable fraction which applies to such distribution.

Regulation

§ 26.2653–1 Taxation of multiple skips.

(a) General rule. If property is held in trust immediately after a GST, solely for purposes of determining whether future events involve a skip person, the transferor is thereafter deemed to occupy the generation immediately above the highest generation of any person holding an interest in the trust immediately after the transfer. If no person holds an interest in the trust immediately after the GST, the transferor is treated as occupying the generation above the highest generation of any person in existence at the time of the GST who then occupies the highest generation level of any person who may subsequently hold an interest in the trust. See § 26.2612–1(e) for rules determining when a person has an interest in property held in trust.

(b) Examples. The following examples illustrate the provisions of this section:

Example (1). T transfers property to an irrevocable trust for the benefit of T's grandchild, GC, and great-grandchild, GGC. During GC's life, the trust income may be distributed to GC and GGC in the trustee's absolute discretion. At GC's death, the trust property passes to GGC. Both GC and GGC have an interest in the trust for purposes of chapter 13. The transfer by T to the trust is a direct skip, and the property is held in trust immediately after the transfer. After the direct skip, the transferor is treated as being one generation above GC, the highest generation individual having an interest in the trust. Therefore, GC is no longer a skip person and distributions to GC are not taxable distributions. However, because GGC occupies a generation that is two generations below the deemed generation of T, GGC is a skip person and distributions of trust income to GGC are taxable distributions.

Example (2). T transfers property to an irrevocable trust providing that the income is to be paid to T's child, C, for life. At C's death, the trust income is to be accumulated for 10 years and added to principal. At the end of the 10-year accumulation period, the trust income is to be paid to T's grandchild, GC, for life. Upon GC's death, the trust property is to be paid to T's great-grandchild, GGC, or to GGC's estate. A GST occurs at C's death. Immediately after C's death and during the 10-year accumulation period, no person has an interest in the trust within the meaning of section 2652(c) and § 26.2612–1(e) because no one can receive current distributions of income or principal. Immediately after C's death, T is treated as occupying the generation above the generation of GC (the trust beneficiary in existence at the time of the GST who then occupies the highest generation level of any person who may subsequently hold an interest in the trust). Thus, subsequent income distributions to GC are not taxable distributions.

[T.D. 8644, 60 FR 66920, Dec. 27, 1995]

§ 2654. Special Rules

(a) Basis adjustment.

(1) In general. Except as provided in paragraph (2), if property is transferred in a generation-skipping transfer, the basis of such property shall be increased (but not above the fair market value of such property) by an amount equal to that portion of the tax imposed by section 2601 with respect to the transfer which is attributable to the excess of the fair market value of such property over its adjusted basis immediately before the transfer. The preceding shall be applied after any basis adjustment under section 1015 with respect to the transfer.

(2) Certain transfers at death. If property is transferred in a taxable termination which occurs at the same time as and as a result of the death of an individual, the basis of such property shall be adjusted in a manner similar to the manner provided under section 1014(a); except that, if the inclusion ratio with respect to such property is less than 1, any increase or decrease in basis shall be limited by multiplying such increase or decrease (as the case may be) by the inclusion ratio.

(b) Certain trusts treated as separate trusts. For purposes of this chapter—

(1) the portions of a trust attributable to transfers from different transferors shall be treated as separate trusts, and

(2) substantially separate and independent shares of different beneficiaries in a trust shall be treated as separate trusts.

Except as provided in the preceding sentence, nothing in this chapter shall be construed as authorizing a single trust to be treated as 2 or more trusts. For purposes of this subsection, a trust shall be treated as part of an estate during any period that the trust is so treated under section 645.

(c) Disclaimers. For provisions relating to the effect of a qualified disclaimer for purposes of this chapter, see section 2518.

(d) Limitation on personal liability of trustee. A trustee shall not be personally liable for any increase in the tax imposed by section 2601 which is attributable to the fact that—

(1) section 2642(c) (relating to exemption of certain nontaxable gifts) does not apply to a transfer to the trust which was made during the life of the transferor and for which a gift tax return was not filed, or

(2) the inclusion ratio with respect to the trust is greater than the amount of such ratio as computed on the basis of the return on which was made (or was deemed made) an allocation of the GST exemption to property transferred to such trust.

The preceding sentence shall not apply if the trustee has knowledge of facts sufficient reasonably to conclude that a gift tax return was required to be filed or that the inclusion ratio was erroneous.

Regulations

§ 26.2654–1 Certain trusts treated as separate trusts.

(a) Single trust treated as separate trusts. (1) *Substantially separate and independent shares.* (i) *In general.* If a single trust consists solely of substantially separate and independent shares for different beneficiaries, the share attributable to each beneficiary (or group of beneficiaries) is treated as a separate trust for purposes of Chapter 13. The phrase "substantially separate and independent shares" generally has the same meaning as provided in § 1.663(c)–3. However, except as provided in paragraph (a)(1)(iii) of this section, a portion of a trust is not a separate share unless such share exists from and at all times after the creation of the trust. For purposes of this paragraph (a)(1), a trust is treated as created at the date of death of the grantor if the trust is includible in its entirety in the grantor's gross estate for Federal estate tax purposes. Further, except with respect to shares or trusts that are treated as separate trusts under local law, treatment of a single trust as separate trusts under this paragraph (a)(1) does not permit treatment of those portions as separate trusts for purposes of filing returns and payment of tax or for purposes of computing any other tax imposed under the Internal Revenue Code. Also, additions to, and distributions from, such trusts are allocated pro rata among the separate trusts, unless the governing instrument expressly provides otherwise. See § 26.2642–6 and paragraph (b) of this section regarding the treatment, for purposes of Chapter 13, of separate trusts resulting from the discretionary severance of a single trust.

(ii) *Certain pecuniary amounts.* For purposes of this section, if a person holds the current right to receive a mandatory (i.e., nondiscretionary and noncontingent) payment of a pecuniary amount at the death of the transferor from an inter vivos trust that is includible in the transferor's gross estate, or a testamentary trust, the pecuniary amount is a separate and independent share if—

(A) The trustee is required to pay appropriate interest (as defined in § 26.2642–2(b)(4)(i) and (ii)) to the person; and

(B) If the pecuniary amount is payable in kind on the basis of value other than the date of distribution value of the assets, the trustee is required to allocate assets to the pecuniary payment in a manner that fairly reflects net appreciation or depreciation in the value of the assets in the fund available to pay the pecuniary amount measured from the valuation date to the date of payment.

(iii) *Mandatory severances.* For purposes of this section, if the governing instrument of a trust requires the division or severance of a single trust into separate trusts upon the future occurrence of a particular event not within the discretion of the trustee or any other person, and if the trusts resulting from such a division or severance are recognized as separate trusts under applicable state law, then each resulting trust is treated as a separate trust for purposes of Chapter 13. For this purpose, the rules of paragraph (b)(1)(ii)(C) of this section apply with respect to the severance and funding of the trusts. Similarly, if the governing instrument requires the division of a single trust into separate shares under the circumstances described in this paragraph, each such share is treated as a separate trust for purposes of Chapter 13. The post-severance treatment of the resulting shares or trusts as separate trusts for GST tax purposes generally permits the allocation of GST tax exemption, the making of various elections permitted for GST tax purposes, and the occurrence of a taxable distribution or termination with regard to a particular resulting share or trust, with no GST tax impact on any other trust or share resulting from that severance. The treatment of a single trust as separate trusts under this paragraph (a)(1), however, does not permit treatment of those portions as separate trusts for purposes of filing returns and payment of tax or for purposes of computing any other tax imposed under the Internal Revenue Code, if those portions are not treated as separate trusts under local law. Also, additions to, and distributions from, such trusts are allocated pro rata among the separate trusts, unless the governing instrument expressly provides otherwise. Each separate share and each trust resulting from a mandatory division or severance described in this paragraph will have the same inclusion ratio immediately after the severance as that of the original trust immediately before the division or severance.

(2) *Multiple transferors with respect to single trust*—(i) *In general.* If there is more than one transferor with respect to a trust, the portions of the trust attributable to the different transferors are treated as separate trusts for purposes of chapter 13. Treatment of a single trust as separate trusts under this paragraph (a)(2) does not permit treatment of those portions as separate trusts for purposes of filing returns and payment of tax or for purposes of computing any other tax imposed under the Internal Revenue Code. Also, additions to, and distributions from, such trusts are allocated pro rata among the separate trusts unless otherwise expressly provided in the governing instrument.

(ii) *Addition by a transferor.* If an individual makes an addition to a trust of which the individual is not the sole transferor, the portion of the single trust attributable to each separate trust is determined by multiplying the fair market value of the single trust immediately after the contribution by a fraction. The numerator of the fraction is the value of the separate trust immediately after the contribution. The denominator of the fraction is the fair market value of all the property in the single trust immediately after the transfer.

(3) *Severance of a single trust.* A single trust treated as separate trusts under paragraphs (a)(1) or (2) of this section may be divided at any time into separate trusts to reflect that treatment. For this purpose, the rules of paragraph (b)(1)(ii)(C) of this section apply with respect to the severance and funding of the severed trusts.

(4) *Allocation of exemption*—(i) *In general.* With respect to a separate share treated as a separate trust under paragraph (a)(1) or (2) of this section, an individual's GST exemption is allocated to the separate trust. See § 26.2632–1 for rules concerning the allocation of GST exemption.

(ii) *Automatic allocation to direct skips.* If the transfer is a direct skip to a trust that occurs during the transferor's lifetime and is treated as a transfer to separate trusts under paragraphs (a)(1) or (a)(2) of this section, the transferor's GST exemption not previously allocated is automatically allocated on a pro rata basis among the separate trusts. The transferor may prevent an automatic allocation of GST exemption to a separate share of a single trust by describing on a timely-filed United States Gift (and Generation-Skipping Transfer) Tax Return (Form 709) the transfer and the extent to which the automatic allocation is not to apply to a particular share. See § 26.2632–1(b) for rules for avoiding the automatic allocation of GST exemption.

(5) *Examples.* The following examples illustrate the principles of this section (a):

Example (1). Separate shares as separate trusts. T transfers $100,000 to a trust under which income is to be paid in equal shares for 10 years to T's child, C, and T's grandchild, GC (or their respective estates). The trust does not permit distributions of principal during the term of the trust. At the end of the 10-year term, the trust principal is to be distributed to C and GC in equal shares. The shares of C and GC in the trust are separate and independent and, therefore, are treated as separate trusts. The result would not be the same if the trust permitted distributions of principal unless the distributions could only be made from a one-half separate share of the initial trust principal and the distributee's future rights with respect to the trust are correspondingly reduced. T may allocate part of T's GST exemption under section 2632(a) to the share held for the benefit of GC.

Example (2). Separate share rule inapplicable. The facts are the same as in Example 1, except the trustee holds the discretionary power to distribute the income in any proportion between C and GC during the last year of the trust. The shares of C and GC in the trust are not separate and independent shares throughout the entire term of the trust and, therefore, are not treated as separate trusts for purposes of chapter 13.

Example (3). Pecuniary payment as separate share. T creates a lifetime revocable trust providing that on T's death $500,000 is payable to T's spouse, S, with the balance of the principal to be held for the benefit of T's grandchildren. The value of the trust is includible in T's gross estate upon T's death. Under the terms of the trust, the payment to S is required to be made in cash, and under local law S is entitled to receive interest on the payment at an annual rate of 6 percent, commencing immediately upon T's death. For purposes of chapter 13, the trust is treated as created at T's death, and the $500,000 payable to S from the trust is treated as a separate share. The result would be the same if the payment to S could be satisfied using noncash assets at their value on the date of distribution. Further, the result would be the same if the decedent's probate estate poured over to the revocable trust on the decedent's death and was then distributed in accordance with the terms of the trust.

Example (4). Pecuniary payment not treated as separate share. The facts are the same as in Example 3, except the bequest to S is to be paid in noncash assets valued at their values as finally determined for Federal estate tax purposes. Neither the trust instrument nor local law requires that the assets distributed in satisfaction of the bequest fairly reflect net appreciation or depreciation in all the assets from which the bequest may be funded. S's $500,000 bequest is not treated as a separate share and the trust is treated as a single trust for purposes of chapter 13.

Example (5). Multiple transferors to single trust. A transfers $100,000 to an irrevocable generation-skipping trust; B simultaneously transfers $50,000 to the same trust. As of the time of the transfers, the single trust is treated as two trusts for purposes of chapter 13. Because A contributed 2/3 of the value of the initial corpus, 2/3 of the single trust principal is treated as a separate trust created by A. Similarly, because B contributed 1/3 of the value of the initial corpus, 1/3 of the single trust is treated as a separate trust created by B. A or B may allocate their GST exemption under section 2632(a) to the respective separate trusts.

Example (6). Additional contributions. A transfers $100,000 to an irrevocable generationskipping trust; B simultaneously transfers $50,000 to the same trust. When the value of the single trust has increased to $180,000, A contributes an additional $60,000 to the trust. At the time of the additional contribution, the portion of the single trust attributable to each grantor's separate trust must be redetermined. The portion of the single trust attributable to A's separate trust immediately after the contribution is 3/4 ((2/3 x $180,000) + $60,000)/$240,000). The portion attributable to B's separate trust after A's addition is 1/4.

Example (7). Distributions from a separate share. The facts are the same as in Example 6, except that, after A's second contribution, $50,000 is distributed to a beneficiary of the trust. Absent a provision in the trust instrument that charges the distribution against the contribution of either A or B, 3/4 of the distribution is treated as made from the separate trust of which A is the transferor and 1/4 from the separate trust of which B is the transferor.

Example (8). Subsequent mandatory division into separate trusts. T creates an irrevocable trust that provides the trustee with the discretionary power to distribute income or corpus to T's children and grandchildren. The trust provides that, when T's youngest child reaches age 21, the trust will be divided into separate shares, one share for each child of T. The income from a respective child's share will be paid to the child during the child's life, with the remainder passing on the child's death to such child's children (grandchildren of T). The separate shares that come into existence when the youngest child reaches age 21 will be recognized as of that date as separate trusts for purposes of Chapter 13. The inclusion ratio of the separate trusts will be identical to the inclusion ratio of the trust before the severance. Any allocation of GST tax exemption to the trust after T's youngest child reaches age 21 may be made to any one or more of the separate shares. The result would be the same if the trust instrument provided that the trust was to be divided into separate trusts when T's youngest child reached age 21, provided that the severance and funding of the separate trusts meets the requirements of this section.

(b) Division of a trust included in the gross estate. (1) *In general.* The severance of a trust that is included in the transferor's gross estate (or created under the transferor's will) into two or more trusts is recognized for purposes of chapter 13 if—

(i) The trust is severed pursuant to a direction in the governing instrument providing that the trust is to be divided upon the death of the transferor; or

(ii) The governing instrument does not require or otherwise direct severance but the trust is severed pursuant to discretionary authority granted either under the governing instrument or under local law; and

(A) The terms of the new trusts provide in the aggregate for the same succession of interests and beneficiaries as are provided in the original trust;

(B) The severance occurs (or a reformation proceeding, if required, is commenced) prior to the date prescribed for filing the Federal estate tax return (including extensions actually granted) for the estate of the transferor; and

(C) Either—

(*1*) The new trusts are severed on a fractional basis. If severed on a fractional basis, the separate trusts need not be funded with a pro rata portion of each asset held by the undivided trust. The trusts may be funded on a nonprorata basis provided funding is based on either the fair market value of the assets on the date of funding or in a manner that fairly reflects the net appreciation or depreciation in the value of the assets measured from the valuation date to the date of funding; or

(*2*) If the severance is required (by the terms of the governing instrument) to be made on the basis of a pecuniary amount, the pecuniary payment is satisfied in a manner that would meet the requirements of paragraph (a)(1)(ii) of this section if it were paid to an individual.

(2) *Special rule.* If a court order severing the trust has not been issued at the time the Federal estate tax return is filed, the executor must indicate on a statement attached to the return that a proceeding has been commenced to sever the trust and describe the manner in which the trust is proposed to be severed. A copy of the petition or other instrument used to commence the proceeding must also be attached to the return. If the governing instrument of a trust or local law authorizes the severance of the trust, a severance pursuant to that authorization is treated as meeting the requirement of paragraph (b)(1)(ii)(B) of this section if the executor indicates on the Federal estate tax return that separate trusts will be created (or funded) and clearly sets forth the manner in which the trust is to be severed and the separate trusts funded.

(3) *Allocation of exemption.* An individual's GST exemption under § 2632 may be allocated to the separate trusts created pursuant to this section at the discretion of the executor or trustee.

(4) *Examples.* The following examples illustrate the provisions of this section (b):

Example (1). Severance of single trust. T's will establishes a testamentary trust providing that income is to be paid to T's spouse for life. At the spouse's death, one-half of the corpus is to be paid to T's child, C, or C's estate (if C fails to survive the spouse) and one-half of the corpus is to be paid to T's grandchild, GC, or GC's estate (if GC fails to survive the spouse). If the requirements of paragraph (b) of this section are otherwise satisfied, T's executor may divide the testamentary trust equally into two separate trusts, one trust providing an income interest to spouse for life with remainder to C, and the other trust with an income interest to spouse for life with remainder to GC. Furthermore, if the requirements of paragraph (b) of this section are satisfied, the executor or trustee may further divide the trust for the benefit of GC. GST exemption may be allocated to any of the divided trusts.

Example (2). Severance of revocable trust. T creates an inter vivos revocable trust providing that, at T's death and after payment of all taxes and administration expenses, the remaining corpus will be divided into two trusts. One trust, for the benefit of T's spouse, is to be funded with the smallest amount that, if qualifying for the marital deduction, will reduce the estate tax to zero. The other trust, for the benefit of T's descendants, is to be funded with the balance of the revocable trust corpus. The trust corpus is includible in T's gross estate. Each trust is recognized as a separate trust for purposes of chapter 13.

Example (3). Formula severance. T's will establishes a testamentary marital trust (Trust) that meets the requirements of qualified terminable interest property (QTIP) if an election under section 2056(b)(7) is made. Trust provides that all trust income is to be paid to T's spouse for life. On the spouse's death, the trust corpus is to be held in further trust for the benefit of T's then-living descendants. On T's date of death in January of 2004, T's unused GST tax exemption is $1,200,000, and T's will includes $200,000 of bequests to T's grandchildren. Prior to the due date for filing the Form 706, "United States Estate (and Generation-Skipping Transfer) Tax Return," for T's estate, T's executor, pursuant to applicable state law, divides Trust into two separate trusts, Trust 1 and Trust 2. Trust 1 is to be funded with that fraction of the Trust assets, the numerator of which is $1,000,000, and the denominator of which is the value of the Trust assets as finally determined for federal estate tax purposes. Trust 2 is to be funded with that fraction of the Trust assets, the numerator of which is the excess of the Trust assets over $1,000,000, and the denominator of which is the value of the Trust assets as finally determined for federal estate tax purposes. On the Form 706 filed for the estate, T's executor makes a QTIP election under section 2056(b)(7) with respect to Trust 1 and Trust 2 and a "reverse" QTIP election under section 2652(a)(3) with respect to Trust 1. Further, T's executor allocates $200,000 of T's available GST tax exemption to the bequests to T's grandchildren, and the balance of T's exemption ($1,000,000) to Trust 1. If the requirements of paragraph (b) of this section are otherwise satisfied, Trust 1 and Trust 2 are recognized as separate trusts for GST tax purposes. Accordingly, the "reverse" QTIP election and allocation of GST tax exemption with respect to Trust 1 are recognized and effective for generation-skipping transfer tax purposes.

(c) Cross reference. For rules applicable to the qualified severance of trusts (whether or not includible in the transferor's gross estate), see § 26.2642–6.

(d) Effective date. Paragraph (a)(1)(i), paragraph (a)(1)(iii), and Example 8 of paragraph (a)(5) apply to severances occurring on or after September 2, 2008.

[T.D. 8644, 60 FR 66921, Dec. 27, 1995; 61 FR 29654, June 12, 1996; 61 FR 43656, Aug. 26, 1996; T.D. 9348, 72 FR 42297, Aug. 2, 2007; T.D. 9421, 73 FR 44652, July 31, 2008]

Proposed § 26.2654–1 (REG–128843–05, Sept. 10, 2007) Certain trusts treated as separate trusts.

Section 26.2654–1 is amended as follows:

1. Paragraph (a)(1)(i) is revised.

2. A new paragraph (a)(1)(iii) is added.

3. In paragraph (a)(5), Example 8 is revised.

The additions and revisions read as follows:

(a) Single trust treated as separate trusts. (1) *Substantially separate and independent shares.* (i) *In general.* If a single trust consists solely of substantially separate and independent shares for different beneficiaries, the share attributable to each beneficiary (or group of beneficiaries) is treated as a separate trust for purposes of chapter 13. The phrase "substantially separate and independent shares" generally has the same meaning as provided in § 1.663(c)–3 of this chapter. However, except as provided in paragraph (a)(1)(iii) of this section, a portion of a trust is not a separate share unless such share exists from and at all times after the creation of the trust. For purposes of this paragraph (a)(1), a trust is treated as created at the date of death of the grantor if the trust is includible in its entirety in the grantor's gross estate for Federal estate tax purposes. Further, treatment of a single trust as separate trusts under this paragraph (a)(1) does not permit treatment of those portions as separate trusts for purposes of filing returns and payment of tax or for purposes of computing any other tax imposed under the Internal Revenue Code. Also, additions to, and distributions from, such trusts are allocated pro rata among the separate trusts, unless the governing instrument expressly provides otherwise. See § 26.2642–6 and paragraph (b) of this section regarding the treatment, for purposes of chapter 13, of separate trusts resulting from the actual severance of a single trust.

* * *

(iii) *Mandatory severances.* For purposes of this section, if the governing instrument of a trust requires the division or severance of a single trust into separate trusts upon the future occurrence of a particular event not within the discretion of the trustee or any other person, and if the trusts resulting from such a division or severance are recognized as separate trusts under applicable state law, then each resulting trust is treated as a separate trust for purposes of chapter 13. For this purpose, the rules of paragraph (b)(1)(ii)(C) of this section apply with respect to the severance and funding of the trusts. Similarly, if the governing instrument requires the division of a single trust into separate shares under the circumstances described in this paragraph, each such resulting share is treated as a separate trust for purposes of chapter 13. The post-severance treatment of the resulting trusts or shares as separate trusts for GST tax purposes generally permits the allocation of GST tax exemption, the making of various elections permitted for GST tax purposes, and the occurrence of a taxable distribution or termination with regard to a particular resulting trust or share, with no GST tax impact on any other trust or share resulting from that severance. The treatment of a single trust as separate trusts under this paragraph (a)(1), however, does not permit treatment of those portions as separate trusts for purposes of filing returns and payment of tax or for purposes of computing any other tax imposed under the Internal Revenue Code. Also, additions to, and distributions from, such trusts are allocated pro rata among the separate trusts, unless the governing instrument expressly provides otherwise. Each separate share and each trust resulting from a mandatory division or severance described in this paragraph will have the same inclusion ratio immediately after the severance as that of the original trust immediately before the division or severance.

* * *

(5) * * *

Example 8. Subsequent mandatory division into separate trusts. T creates an irrevocable trust that provides the trustee with the discretionary power to distribute income or corpus to T's children and grandchildren. The trust provides that, when T's youngest child reaches age 21, the trust will be divided into separate shares, one share for each child of T. The income from a respective child's share will be paid to the child during the child's life, with the remainder passing on the child's death to such child's children (grandchildren of T). The separate shares that come into existence when the youngest child reaches age 21 will be recognized as of that date as separate trusts for purposes of Chapter 13. Any allocation of GST tax exemption to the trust after T's youngest child reaches age 21 may be made to any one or more of the separate shares. The result would be the same if the trust instrument provided that the trust was to be divided into separate trusts when T's youngest child reached age 21, provided that the severance and funding of the separate trusts meets the requirements of this section.

* * *

Subchapter G. Administration

§ 2661. Administration

Insofar as applicable and not inconsistent with the provisions of this chapter—

(1) except as provided in paragraph (2), all provisions of subtitle F (including penalties) applicable to the gift tax, to chapter 12, or to section 2501, are hereby made applicable in respect of the generation-skipping transfer tax, this chapter, or section 2601, as the case may be, and

(2) in the case of a generation-skipping transfer occurring at the same time as and as a result of the death of an individual, all provisions of subtitle F (including penalties) applicable to the estate tax, to chapter 11, or to section 2001 are hereby made applicable in respect of the generation-skipping transfer tax, this chapter, or section 2601 (as the case may be).

§ 2662. Return Requirements

(a) In general. The Secretary shall prescribe by regulations the person who is required to make the return with respect to the tax imposed by this chapter and the time by which any such return must be filed. To the extent practicable, such regulations shall provide that—

(1) the person who is required to make such return shall be the person liable under section 2603(a) for payment of such tax, and

(2) the return shall be filed—

(A) in the case of a direct skip (other than from a trust), on or before the date on which an estate or gift tax return is required to be filed with respect to the transfer, and

(B) in all other cases, on or before the 15th day of the 4th month after the close of the taxable year of the person required to make such return in which such transfer occurs.

(b) Information returns. The Secretary may by regulations require a return to be filed containing such information as he determines to be necessary for purposes of this chapter.

Regulation

§ 26.2662–1 Generation-skipping transfer tax return requirements.

(a) In general. Chapter 13 imposes a tax on generation-skipping transfers (as defined in section 2611). The requirements relating to the return of tax depend on the type of generationskipping transfer involved. This section contains rules for filing the required tax return. Paragraph (c)(2) of this section provides special rules concerning the return requirements for generationskipping transfers pursuant to certain trust arrangements (as defined in paragraph (c)(2)(ii) of this section), such as life insurance policies and annuities.

(b) Form of return. (1) *Taxable distributions.* Form 706GS(D) must be filed in accordance with its instructions for any taxable distribution (as defined in section 2612(b)). The trust involved in a transfer described in the preceding sentence must file Form 706GS(D-1) in accordance with its instructions. A copy of Form 706GS(D-1) shall be sent to each distributee.

(2) *Taxable terminations.* Form 706GS(T) must be filed in accordance with its instructions for any taxable termination (as defined in section 2612(a)).

(3) *Direct skip.* (i) *Inter vivos direct skips.* Form 709 must be filed in accordance with its instructions for any direct skip (as defined in section 2612(c)) that is subject to chapter 12 and occurs during the life of the transferor.

(ii) *Direct skips occurring at death.* (A) *In general.* Form 706 or Form 706NA must be filed in accordance with its instructions for any direct skips (as defined in section 2612(c)) that are subject to chapter 11 and occur at the death of the decedent.

(B) *Direct skips payable from a trust.* Schedule R-1 of Form 706 must be filed in accordance with its instructions for any direct skip from a trust if such direct skip is subject to chapter 11. See paragraph (c)(2) of this section for special rules relating to the person liable for tax and required to make the return under certain circumstances.

(c) Person liable for tax and required to make return. (1) *In general.* Except as otherwise provided in this section, the following person is liable for the tax imposed by section 2601 and must make the required tax return—

(i) The transferee in a taxable distribution (as defined in section 2612(b));

(ii) The trustee in the case of a taxable termination (as defined in section 2612(a));

(iii) The transferor (as defined in section 2652(a)(1)(B)) in the case of an inter vivos direct skip (as defined in section 2612(c));

(iv) The trustee in the case of a direct skip from a trust or with respect to property that continues to be held in trust; or

(v) The executor in the case of a direct skip (other than a direct skip described in paragraph (c)(1)(iv) of this section) if the transfer is subject to chapter 11. See paragraph (c)(2) of this section for special rules relating to direct skips to or from certain trust arrangements (as defined in paragraph (c)(2)(ii) of this section).

(2) *Special rule for direct skips occurring at death with respect to property held in trust arrangements.* (i) *In general.* In the case of certain property held in a trust arrangement (as defined in paragraph (c)(2)(ii) of this section) at the date of death of the transferor, the person who is required to make the return and who is liable for the tax imposed by chapter 13 is determined under paragraphs (c)(2)(iii) and (iv) of this section.

(ii) *Trust arrangement defined.* For purposes of this section, the term trust arrangement includes any arrangement (other than an estate) which, although not an explicit trust, has the same effect as an explicit trust. For purposes of this section, the term "explicit trust" means a trust described in § 301.7701–4(a).

(iii) *Executor's liability in the case of transfers with respect to decedents dying on or after June 24, 1996 if the transfer is less than $250,000.* In the case of a direct skip occurring at death, the executor of the decedent's estate is liable for the tax imposed on that direct skip by chapter 13 and is required to file Form 706 or Form 706NA (and not Schedule R-1 of Form 706) if, at the date of the decedent's death—

(A) The property involved in the direct skip is held in a trust arrangement; and

(B) The total value of the property involved in direct skips with respect to the trustee of that trust arrangement is less than $250,000.

(iv) *Executor's liability in the case of transfers with respect to decedents dying prior to June 24, 1996 if the transfer is less than $100,000.* In the case of a direct skip occurring at death with respect to a decedent dying prior to June 24, 1996, the rule in paragraph (c)(2)(iii) of this section that imposes liability upon the executor applies only if the property involved in the direct skip with respect to the trustee of the trust arrangement, in the aggregate, is less than $100,000.

(v) *Executor's right of recovery.* In cases where the rules of paragraphs (c)(2)(iii) and (iv) of this section impose liability for the generation-skipping transfer tax on the executor, the executor is entitled to recover from the trustee (if the property continues to be held in trust) or from the recipient of the property (in the case of a transfer from a trust), the generation-skipping transfer tax attributable to the transfer.

(vi) *Examples.* The following examples illustrate the application of this paragraph (c)(2) with respect to decedents dying on or after June 24, 1996:

Example (1). Insurance proceeds less than $250,000. On August 1, 1997, T, the insured under an insurance policy, died. The proceeds ($200,000) were includible in T's gross estate for Federal estate tax purposes. T's grandchild, GC, was named the sole beneficiary of the policy. The insurance policy is treated as a trust under section 2652(b)(1), and the payment of the proceeds to GC is a transfer from a trust for purposes of chapter 13. Therefore, the payment of the proceeds to GC is a direct skip. Since the proceeds from the policy ($200,000) are less than $250,000, the executor is liable for the tax imposed by chapter 13 and is required to file Form 706.

Example (2). Aggregate insurance proceeds of $250,000 or more. Assume the same facts as in Example 1, except T is the insured under two insurance policies issued by the same insurance company. The proceeds ($150,000) from each policy are includible in T's gross estate for Federal estate tax purposes. T's grandchild, GC1, was named the sole beneficiary of Policy 1, and T's other grandchild, GC2, was named the sole beneficiary of Policy 2. GC1 and GC2 are skip persons (as defined in section 2613). Therefore, the payments of the proceeds are direct skips. Since the total value of the policies ($300,000) exceeds $250,000, the insurance company is liable for the tax imposed by chapter 13 and is required to file Schedule R-1 of Form 706.

Example (3). Insurance proceeds of $250,000 or more held by insurance company. On August 1, 1997, T, the insured under an insurance policy, dies. The policy provides that the insurance company shall make monthly payments of $750 to GC, T's grandchild, for life with the remainder payable to T's great grandchild, GGC. The face value of the policy is $300,000. Since the proceeds continue to be held by the insurance company (the trustee), the proceeds are treated as if they were transferred to a trust for purposes of chapter 13. The trust is a skip person (as defined in section 2613(a)(2)) and the transfer is a direct skip. Since the total value of the policy ($300,000) exceeds $250,000, the insurance company is liable for the tax imposed by chapter 13 and is required to file Schedule R-1 of Form 706.

Example (4). Insurance proceeds less than $250,000 held by insurance company. Assume the same facts as in Example 3, except the policy provides that the insurance company shall make monthly payments of $500 to GC and that the face value of the policy is $200,000. The transfer is a transfer to a trust for purposes of chapter 13. However, since the total value of the policy ($200,000) is less than $250,000, the executor is liable for the tax imposed by chapter 13 and is required to file Form 706.

Example (5). On August 1, 1997, A, the insured under a life insurance policy, dies. The insurance proceeds on A's life that are payable under policies issued by Company X are in the aggregate amount of $200,000 and are includible in A's gross estate. Because the proceeds are includible in A's gross estate, the generationskipping transfer that occurs upon A's death, if any, will be a direct skip rather than a taxable distribution or a taxable termination. Accordingly, because the aggregate amount of insurance proceeds with respect to Company X is less than $250,000, Company X may pay the proceeds without regard to whether the beneficiary is a skip person in relation to the decedent-transferor.

(3) *Limitation on personal liability of trustee.* Except as provided in paragraph (c)(3)(iii) of this section, a trustee is not personally liable for any increases in the tax imposed by section 2601 which is attributable to the fact that—

(i) A transfer is made to the trust during the life of the transferor for which a gift tax return is not filed; or

(ii) The inclusion ratio with respect to the trust, determined by reference to the transferor's gift tax return, is erroneous, the actual inclusion ratio being greater than the reported inclusion ratio.

(iii) This paragraph (c)(3) does not apply if the trustee has or is deemed to have knowledge of facts sufficient to reasonably conclude that a gift tax return was required to be filed or that the inclusion ratio is erroneous. A trustee is deemed to have knowledge of such facts if the trustee's agent, employee, partner, or co-trustee has knowledge of such facts.

(4) *Exceptions*—(i) *Legal or mental incapacity.* If a distributee is legally or mentally incapable of making a return, the return may be made for the distributee by the distributee's guardian or, if no guardian has been appointed, by a person charged with the care of the distributee's person or property.

(ii) *Returns made by fiduciaries.* See section 6012(b) for a fiduciary's responsibilities regarding the returns of decedents, returns of persons under a disability, returns of estates and trusts, and returns made by joint fiduciaries.

(d) Time and manner of filing return. (1) *In general.* Forms 706, 706NA, 706GS(D), 706GS(D-1), 706GS(T), 709, and Schedule R-1 of Form 706 must be filed with the Internal Revenue Service office with which an estate or gift tax return of the transferor must be filed. The return shall be filed—

(i) *Direct skip.* In the case of a direct skip, on or before the date on which an estate or gift tax return is required to be filed with respect to the transfer (see section 6075(b)(3)); and

(ii) *Other transfers.* In all other cases, on or before the 15th day of the 4th month after the close of the calendar year in which such transfer occurs. See paragraph (d)(2) of this section for an exception to this rule when an election is made under section 2624(c) to value property included in certain taxable terminations in accordance with section 2032.

(2) *Exception for alternative valuation of taxable termination.* In the case of a taxable termination with respect to which an election is made under section 2624(c) to value property in accordance with section 2032, a Form 706GS(T) must be filed on or before the 15th day of the 4th month after the close of the calendar year in which the taxable termination occurred, or on or before the 10th month following the month in which the death that resulted in the taxable termination occurred, whichever is later.

(e) Place for filing returns. See section 6091 for the place for filing any return, declaration, statement, or other document, or copies thereof, required by chapter 13.

(f) Lien on property. The liens imposed under sections 6324, 6324A, and 6324B are applicable with respect to the tax imposed under chapter 13. Thus, a lien under section 6324 is imposed in the amount of the tax imposed by section 2601 on all property transferred in a generation-skipping transfer until the tax is fully paid or becomes uncollectible by reason of lapse of time. The lien attaches at the time of the generation-skipping transfer and is in addition to the lien for taxes under section 6321.

[T.D. 8644, 60 FR 66923, Dec. 27, 1995; 61 FR 29654, June 12, 1996]

§ 2663. Regulations

The Secretary shall prescribe such regulations as may be necessary or appropriate to carry out the purposes of this chapter, including—

(1) such regulations as may be necessary to coordinate the provisions of this chapter with the recapture tax imposed under section 2032A(c),

(2) regulations (consistent with the principles of chapters 11 and 12) providing for the application of this chapter in the case of transferors who are nonresidents not citizens of the United States, and

(3) regulations providing for such adjustments as may be necessary to the application of this chapter in the case of any arrangement which, although not a trust, is treated as a trust under section 2652(b).

Regulations

§ 26.2663–1 Recapture tax under section 2032A.

See § 26.2642–4(a)(4) for rules relating to the recomputation of the applicable fraction and the imposition of additional GST tax, if additional estate tax is imposed under section 2032A.

[T.D. 8644, 60 FR 66924, Dec. 27, 1995]

§ 26.2663–2 Application of chapter 13 to transfers by nonresidents not citizens of the United States.

(a) In general. This section provides rules for applying chapter 13 of the Internal Revenue Code to transfers by a transferor who is a nonresident not a citizen of the United States (NRA transferor). For purposes of this section, an individual is a resident or citizen of the United States if that individual is a resident or citizen of the United States under the rules of chapter 11 or 12 of the Internal Revenue Code, as the case may be. Every NRA transferor is allowed a GST exemption of $1,000,000. See § 26.2632–1 regarding the allocation of the exemption.

(b) Transfers subject to chapter 13. (1) *Direct skips.* A transfer by a NRA transferor is a direct skip subject to chapter 13 only to the extent that the transfer is subject to the Federal estate or gift tax within the meaning of § 26.2652–1(a)(2). See § 26.2612–1(a) for the definition of direct skip.

(2) *Taxable distributions and taxable terminations.* Chapter 13 applies to a taxable distribution or a taxable termination to the extent that the initial transfer of property to the trust by a NRA transferor, whether during life or at death, was subject to the Federal estate or gift tax within the meaning of § 26.2652–1(a)(2). See § 26.2612–1(b) for the definition of a taxable termination and § 26.2612–1(c) for the definition of a taxable distribution.

(c) Trusts funded in part with property subject to chapter 13 and in part with property not subject to chapter 13. (1) *In general.* If a single trust created by a NRA transferor is in part subject to chapter 13 under the rules of paragraph (b) of this section and in part not subject to chapter 13, the applicable fraction with respect to the trust is determined as of the date of the transfer, except as provided in paragraph (c)(3) of this section.

(i) *Numerator of applicable fraction.* The numerator of the applicable fraction is the sum of the amount of GST exemption allocated to the trust (if any) plus the value of the nontax portion of the trust.

(ii) *Denominator of applicable fraction.* The denominator of the applicable fraction is the value of the property transferred to the trust reduced as provided in § 26.2642–1(c).

(2) *Nontax portion of the trust.* The nontax portion of a trust is a fraction, the numerator of which is the value of property not subject to chapter 13 determined as of the date of the initial completed transfer to the trust, and the denominator of which is the value of the entire trust. For example, T, a NRA transferor, transfers property that has a value of $1,000 to a generation-skipping trust. Of the property transferred to the trust, property having a value of $200 is subject to chapter 13 and property having a value of $800 is not subject to chapter 13. The nontax portion is .8 ($800 (the value of the property not subject to chapter 13) over $1,000 (the total value of the property transferred to the trust)).

(3) *Special rule with respect to the estate tax inclusion period.* For purposes of this section, the provisions of § 26.2632–1(c), providing rules applicable in the case of an estate tax inclusion period (ETIP), apply only if the property transferred by the NRA transferor is subsequently included in the transferor's gross estate. If the property is not subsequently included in the gross estate, then the nontax portion of the trust and the applicable fraction are determined as of the date of the initial transfer. If the property is subsequently included in the gross estate, then the nontax portion and the applicable fraction are determined as of the date of death.

(d) Examples. The following examples illustrate the provisions of this section. In each example T, a NRA, is the transferor; C is T's child; and GC is C's child and a grandchild of T:

Example (1). Direct transfer to skip person. T transfers property to GC in a transfer that is subject to Federal gift tax under chapter 12 within the meaning of § 26.2652–1(a)(2). At the time of the transfer, C and GC are NRAs. T's transfer is subject to chapter 13 because the transfer is subject to gift tax under chapter 12.

Example (2). Transfers of both U.S. and foreign situs property. (i) T's will established a testamentary trust for the benefit of C and GC. The trust was funded with stock in a publicly traded U.S. corporation having a value on the date of T's death of $100,000, and property not situated in the United States (and therefore not subject to estate tax) having a value on the date of T's death of $400,000.

(ii) On a timely filed estate tax return (Form 706NA), the executor of T's estate allocates $50,000 of GST exemption under section 2632(a) to the trust. The numerator of the applicable fraction is $450,000, the sum of $50,000 (the amount of exemption allocated to the trust) plus $400,000 (the value of the nontax portion of the trust (4/5 * $500,000)). The denominator is $500,000. Hence, the applicable fraction with respect to the trust is .9 ($450,000/ $500,000), and the inclusion ratio is .1 (1 - 9/10).

Example (3). Inter vivos transfer of U.S. and foreign situs property to a trust and a timely allocation of GST exemption. T establishes a trust providing that trust income is payable to T's child for life and the remainder is to be paid to T's grandchild. T transfers property to the trust that has a value of $100,000 and is subject to chapter 13. T also transfers property to the trust that has a value of $300,000 but is not subject to chapter 13. T allocates $100,000 of exemption to the trust on a timely filed United States Gift (and Generation-Skipping Transfer) Tax Return (Form 709). The applicable fraction with respect to the trust is 1, determined as follows: $300,000 (the value of the nontax portion of the trust) plus $100,000 (the exemption allocated to the trust)/ $400,000 (the total value of the property transferred to the trust).

Example (4). Inter vivos transfer of U.S. and foreign situs property to a trust and a late allocation of GST exemption. (i) In 1996, T transfers $500,000 of property to an inter vivos trust the terms of which provide that income is payable to C, for life, with the remainder to GC. The property transferred to the trust consists of property subject to chapter 13 that has a value of $400,000 on the date of the transfer and property not subject to chapter 13 that has a value of $100,000. T does not allocate GST exemption to the trust. On the transfer date, the nontax portion of the trust is .2 ($100,000/$500,000) and the applicable fraction is also .2 determined as follows: $100,000 (the value of the nontax portion of the trust)/$500,000 (the value of the property transferred to the trust).

(ii) In 1999, when the value of the trust is $800,000, T allocates $100,000 of GST exemption to the trust. The applicable fraction of the trust must be recomputed. The numerator of the applicable fraction is $260,000 ($100,000 (the amount of GST exemption allocated to the trust)) plus $160,000 (the value of the nontax portion of the trust as of the date of allocation

(.2 * $800,000)). The denominator of the applicable fraction is $800,000. Accordingly, the applicable fraction with respect to the trust after the allocation is .325 ($260,000/$800,000) and the inclusion ratio is .675 (1 - .325).

Example (5). Taxable termination. The facts are the same as in Example 4 except that, in 2006, when the value of the property is $1,200,000, C dies and the trust corpus is distributed to GC. The termination is a taxable termination. If no further GST exemption has been allocated to the trust, the applicable fraction remains .325 and the inclusion ratio remains .675.

Example (6). Estate Tax Inclusion Period. (i) T transferred property to an inter vivos trust the terms of which provided T with an annuity payable for 10 years or until T's prior death. The annuity satisfies the definition of a qualified interest under section 2702(b). The trust also provided that, at the end of the trust term, the remainder will pass to GC or GC's estate. The property transferred to the trust consisted of property subject to chapter 13 that has a value of $100,000 and property not subject to chapter 13 that has a value of $400,000. T allocated $100,000 of GST exemption to the trust. If T dies within the 10 year period, the value of the trust principal will be subject to inclusion in T's gross estate to the extent provided in sections 2103 and 2104(b). Accordingly, the ETIP rule under paragraph (c)(3) of this section applies.

(ii) In year 6 of the trust term, T died. At T's death, the trust corpus had a value of $800,000, and $500,000 was includible in T's gross estate as provided in sections 2103 and 2104(b). Thus, $500,000 of the trust corpus is subject to chapter 13 and $300,000 is not subject to chapter 13. The $100,000 GST exemption allocation is effective as of T's date of death. Also, the nontax portion of the trust and the applicable fraction are determined as of T's date of death. In this case, the nontax portion of the trust is .375, determined as follows: $300,000 (the value of the trust not subject to chapter 13)/$800,000 (the value of the trust). The numerator of the applicable fraction is $400,000, determined as follows: $100,000 (GST exemption previously allocated to the trust) plus $300,000 (the value of the nontax portion of the trust). The denominator of the applicable fraction is $800,000. Thus, the applicable fraction with respect to the trust is .50, unless additional exemption is allocated to the trust by T's executor or the automatic allocation rules of § 26.2632–1(d)(2) apply.

Example (7). The facts are the same as in Example 6 except that T survives the termination date of T's retained annuity and the trust corpus is distributed to GC. Since the trust was not included in T's gross estate, the ETIP rules do not apply. Accordingly, the nontax portion of the trust and the applicable fraction are determined as of the date of the transfer to the trust. The nontax portion of the trust is .80 ($400,000/$500,000). The numerator of the applicable fraction is $500,000 determined as follows: $100,000 (GST exemption allocated to the trust) plus $400,000 (the value of the nontax portion of the trust). Accordingly, the applicable fraction is 1, and the inclusion ratio is zero.

(e) Transitional rule for allocations for transfers made before December 27, 1995. * * *

[T.D. 8644, 60 FR 66924, Dec. 27, 1995; 61 FR 29654, June 12, 1996]

Under § 301(a) of the Tax Relief, Unemployment Insurance Reauthorization, and Job Creation Act of 2010 (P.L. 111–312) § 2210 was eliminated from the Code. However, § 301(c) of the Act provides "[n]otwithstanding sub-section (a), in the case of an estate of a decedent dying after December 31, 2009, and before January 1, 2011, the executor (within the meaning of section 2203 of the Internal Revenue Code of 1986) may elect to apply such Code as though the amendments made by subsection (a) do not apply with respect to chapter 11 of such Code and with respect to property acquired or passing from such decedent . . . ." Therefore, § 2664 is included for those estates where the executor makes such election.

§ 2664. Termination

This chapter shall not apply to generation-skipping transfers after December 31, 2009.

Special Valuation Rules

Code and Selected Regulations

SUBTITLE B. ESTATE AND GIFT TAXES

Chapter 14. Special Valuation Rules

§ 2701. Special Valuation Rules in Case of Transfers of Certain Interests in Corporations or Partnerships

(a) Valuation rules.

(1) In general. Solely for purposes of determining whether a transfer of an interest in a corporation or partnership to (or for the benefit of) a member of the transferor's family is a gift (and the value of such transfer), the value of any right—

(A) which is described in subparagraph (A) or (B) of subsection (b)(1), and

(B) which is with respect to any applicable retained interest that is held by the transferor or an applicable family member immediately after the transfer,

shall be determined under paragraph (3). This paragraph shall not apply to the transfer of any interest for which market quotations are readily available (as of the date of transfer) on an established securities market.

(2) Exceptions for marketable retained interests, etc. Paragraph (1) shall not apply to any right with respect to an applicable retained interest if—

(A) market quotations are readily available (as of the date of the transfer) for such interest on an established securities market,

(B) such interest is of the same class as the transferred interest, or

(C) such interest is proportionally the same as the transferred interest, without regard to nonlapsing differences in voting power (or, for a partnership, nonlapsing differences with respect to management and limitations on liability).

Subparagraph (C) shall not apply to any interest in a partnership if the transferor or an applicable family member has the right to alter the liability of the transferee of the transferred property. Except as provided by the Secretary, any difference described in subparagraph (C) which lapses by reason of any Federal or State law shall be treated as a nonlapsing difference for purposes of such subparagraph.

(3) Valuation of rights to which paragraph (1) applies.

(A) In general. The value of any right described in paragraph (1), other than a distribution right which consists of a right to receive a qualified payment, shall be treated as being zero.

(B) Valuation of certain qualified payments. If—

(i) any applicable retained interest confers a distribution right which consists of the right to a qualified payment, and

(ii) there are 1 or more liquidation, put, call, or conversion rights with respect to such interest,

the value of all such rights shall be determined as if each liquidation, put, call, or conversion right were exercised in the manner resulting in the lowest value being determined for all such rights.

(C) Valuation of qualified payments where no liquidation, etc. rights. In the case of an applicable retained interest which is described in subparagraph (B)(i) but not subparagraph (B)(ii), the value of the distribution right shall be determined without regard to this section.

(4) Minimum valuation of junior equity.

(A) In general. In the case of a transfer described in paragraph (1) of a junior equity interest in a corporation or partnership, such interest shall in no event be valued at an amount less than the value which would be determined if the total value of all of the junior equity interests in the entity were equal to 10 percent of the sum of—

(i) the total value of all of the equity interests in such entity, plus

(ii) the total amount of indebtedness of such entity to the transferor (or an applicable family member).

(B) Definitions. For purposes of this paragraph—

(i) Junior equity interest. The term "junior equity interest" means common stock or, in the case of a partnership, any partnership interest under which the rights as to income and capital (or, to the extent provided in regulations, the rights as to either income or capital) are junior to the rights of all other classes of equity interests.

(ii) Equity interest. The term "equity interest" means stock or any interest as a partner, as the case may be.

(b) Applicable retained interests. For purposes of this section—

(1) In general. The term "applicable retained interest" means any interest in an entity with respect to which there is—

(A) a distribution right, but only if, immediately before the transfer described in subsection (a)(1), the transferor and applicable family members hold (after application of subsection (e)(3)) control of the entity, or

(B) a liquidation, put, call, or conversion right.

(2) Control. For purposes of paragraph (1)—

(A) Corporations. In the case of a corporation, the term "control" means the holding of at least 50 percent (by vote or value) of the stock of the corporation.

(B) Partnerships. In the case of a partnership, the term "control" means—

(i) the holding of at least 50 percent of the capital or profits interests in the partnership, or

(ii) in the case of a limited partnership, the holding of any interest as a general partner.

(C) Applicable family member. For purposes of this subsection, the term "applicable family member" includes any lineal descendant of any parent of the transferor or the transferor's spouse.

(c) Distribution and other rights; qualified payments. For purposes of this section—

(1) Distribution right.

(A) In general. The term "distribution right" means—

(i) a right to distributions from a corporation with respect to its stock, and

(ii) a right to distributions from a partnership with respect to a partner's interest in the partnership.

(B) Exceptions. The term "distribution right" does not include—

(i) a right to distributions with respect to any interest which is junior to the rights of the transferred interest,

(ii) any liquidation, put, call, or conversion right, or

(iii) any right to receive any guaranteed payment described in section 707(c) of a fixed amount.

(2) Liquidation, etc. rights.

(A) In general. The term "liquidation, put, call, or conversion right" means any liquidation, put, call, or conversion right, or any similar right, the exercise or nonexercise of which affects the value of the transferred interest.

(B) Exception for fixed rights.

(i) In general. The term "liquidation, put, call, or conversion right" does not include any right which must be exercised at a specific time and at a specific amount.

(ii) Treatment of certain rights. If a right is assumed to be exercised in a particular manner under subsection (a)(3)(B), such right shall be treated as so exercised for purposes of clause (i).

(C) Exception for certain rights to convert. The term "liquidation, put, call, or conversion right" does not include any right which—

(i) is a right to convert into a fixed number (or a fixed percentage) of shares of the same class of stock in a corporation as the transferred stock in such corporation under subsection (a)(1) (or stock which would be of the same class but for nonlapsing differences in voting power),

(ii) is nonlapsing,

(iii) is subject to proportionate adjustments for splits, combinations, reclassifications, and similar changes in the capital stock, and

(iv) is subject to adjustments similar to the adjustments under subsection (d) for accumulated but unpaid distributions.

A rule similar to the rule of the preceding sentence shall apply for partnerships.

(3) Qualified payment.

(A) In general. Except as otherwise provided in this paragraph, the term "qualified payment" means any dividend payable on a periodic basis under any cumulative preferred stock (or a comparable payment under any partnership interest) to the extent that such dividend (or comparable payment) is determined at a fixed rate.

(B) Treatment of variable rate payments. For purposes of subparagraph (A), a payment shall be treated as fixed as to rate if such payment is determined at a rate which bears a fixed relationship to a specified market interest rate.

(C) Elections.

(i) In general. Payments under any interest held by a transferor which (without regard to this subparagraph) are qualified payments shall be treated as qualified payments unless the transferor elects not to treat such payments as qualified payments. Payments described in the preceding sentence which are held by an applicable family member shall be treated as qualified payments only if such member elects to treat such payments as qualified payments.

(ii) Election to have interest treated as qualified payment. A transferor or applicable family member holding any distribution right which (without regard to this subparagraph) is not a qualified payment may elect to treat such right as a qualified payment, to be paid in the amounts and at the times specified in such election. The preceding sentence shall apply only to the extent that the amounts and times so specified are not inconsistent with the underlying legal instrument giving rise to such right.

(iii) Elections irrevocable. Any election under this subparagraph with respect to an interest shall, once made, be irrevocable.

(d) Transfer tax treatment of cumulative but unpaid distributions.

(1) In general. If a taxable event occurs with respect to any distribution right to which subsection (a)(3)(B) or (C) applied, the following shall be increased by the amount determined under paragraph (2):

(A) The taxable estate of the transferor in the case of a taxable event described in paragraph (3)(A)(i).

(B) The taxable gifts of the transferor for the calendar year in which the taxable event occurs in the case of a taxable event described in paragraph (3)(A)(ii) or (iii).

(2) Amount of increase.

(A) In general. The amount of the increase determined under this paragraph shall be the excess (if any) of—

(i) the value of the qualified payments payable during the period beginning on the date of the transfer under subsection (a)(1) and ending on the date of the taxable event determined as if—

(I) all such payments were paid on the date payment was due, and

(II) all such payments were reinvested by the transferor as of the date of payment at a yield equal to the discount rate used in determining the value of the applicable retained interest described in subsection (a)(1), over

(ii) the value of such payments paid during such period computed under clause (i) on the basis of the time when such payments were actually paid.

(B) Limitation on amount of increase.

(i) In general. The amount of the increase under subparagraph (A) shall not exceed the applicable percentage of the excess (if any) of—

(I) the value (determined as of the date of the taxable event) of all equity interests in the entity which are junior to the applicable retained interest, over

(II) the value of such interests (determined as of the date of the transfer to which subsection (a)(1) applied).

(ii) Applicable percentage. For purposes of clause (i), the applicable percentage is the percentage determined by dividing—

(I) the number of shares in the corporation held (as of the date of the taxable event) by the transferor which are applicable retained interests of the same class, by

(II) the total number of shares in such corporation (as of such date) which are of the same class as the class described in subclause (I).

A similar percentage shall be determined in the case of interests in a partnership.

(iii) Definition. For purposes of this subparagraph, the term "equity interest" has the meaning given such term by subsection (a)(4)(B).

(C) Grace period. For purposes of subparagraph (A), any payment of any distribution during the 4-year period beginning on its due date shall be treated as having been made on such due date.

(3) Taxable events. For purposes of this subsection—

(A) In general. The term "taxable event" means any of the following:

(i) The death of the transferor if the applicable retained interest conferring the distribution right is includible in the estate of the transferor.

(ii) The transfer of such applicable retained interest.

(iii) At the election of the taxpayer, the payment of any qualified payment after the period described in paragraph (2)(C), but only with respect to such payment.

(B) Exception where spouse is transferee.

(i) Deathtime transfers. Subparagraph (A)(i) shall not apply to any interest includible in the gross estate of the transferor if a deduction with respect to such interest is allowable under section 2056 or 2106(a)(3).

(ii) Lifetime transfers. A transfer to the spouse of the transferor shall not be treated as a taxable event under subparagraph (A)(ii) if such transfer does not result in a taxable gift by reason of—

(I) any deduction allowed under section 2523, or the exclusion under section 2503(b), or

(II) consideration for the transfer provided by the spouse.

(iii) Spouse succeeds to treatment of transferor. If an event is not treated as a taxable event by reason of this subparagraph, the transferee spouse or surviving spouse (as the case may be) shall be treated in the same manner as the transferor in applying this subsection with respect to the interest involved.

(4) Special rules for applicable family members.

(A) Family member treated in same manner as transferor. For purposes of this subsection, an applicable family member shall be treated in the same manner as the transferor with respect to any distribution right retained by such family member to which subsection (a)(3)(B) or (C) applied.

(B) Transfer to applicable family member. In the case of a taxable event described in paragraph (3)(A)(ii) involving the transfer of an applicable retained interest to an applicable family member (other than the spouse of the transferor), the applicable family member shall be treated in the same manner as the transferor in applying this subsection to distributions accumulating with respect to such interest after such taxable event.

(C) Transfer to transferors. In the case of a taxable event described in paragraph (3)(A)(ii) involving a transfer of an applicable retained interest from an applicable family member to a transferor, this subsection shall continue to apply to the transferor during any period the transferor holds such interest.

(5) Transfer to include termination. For purposes of this subsection, any termination of an interest shall be treated as a transfer.

(e) Other definitions and rules. For purposes of this section—

(1) Member of the family. The term "member of the family" means, with respect to any transferor—

(A) the transferor's spouse,

(B) a lineal descendant of the transferor or the transferor's spouse, and

(C) the spouse of any such descendant.

(2) Applicable family member. The term "applicable family member" means, with respect to any transferor—

(A) the transferor's spouse,

(B) an ancestor of the transferor or the transferor's spouse, and

(C) the spouse of any such ancestor.

(3) Attribution of indirect holdings and transfers. An individual shall be treated as holding any interest to the extent such interest is held indirectly by such individual through a corporation, partnership, trust, or other entity. If any individual is treated as holding any interest by reason of the preceding sentence, any transfer which results in such interest being treated as no longer held by such individual shall be treated as a transfer of such interest.

(4) Effect of adoption. A relationship by legal adoption shall be treated as a relationship by blood.

(5) Certain changes treated as transfers. Except as provided in regulations, a contribution to capital or a redemption, recapitalization, or other change in the capital structure of a corporation or partnership shall be treated as a transfer of an interest in such entity to which this section applies if the taxpayer or an applicable family member—

(A) receives an applicable retained interest in such entity pursuant to such transaction, or

(B) under regulations, otherwise holds, immediately after such transaction, an applicable retained interest in such entity.

This paragraph shall not apply to any transaction (other than a contribution to capital) if the interests in the entity held by the transferor, applicable family members, and members of the transferor's family before and after the transaction are substantially identical.

(6) Adjustments. Under regulations prescribed by the Secretary, if there is any subsequent transfer, or inclusion in the gross estate, of any applicable retained interest which was valued under the rules of subsection (a), appropriate adjustments shall be made for purposes of chapter 11, 12, or 13 to reflect the increase in the amount of any prior taxable gift made by the transferor or decedent by reason of such valuation or to reflect the application of subsection (d).

(7) Treatment as separate interests. The Secretary may by regulation provide that any applicable retained interest shall be treated as 2 or more separate interests for purposes of this section.

Regulations

§ 25.2701–0 Table of contents. [*Omitted. Ed.*]

[T.D. 8395, 57 FR 4255, Feb. 4, 1992; T.D. 8536, 59 FR 23154, May 5, 1994]

§ 25.2701–1 Special valuation rules in the case of transfers of certain interests in corporations and partnerships.

(a) In general. (1) *Scope of section 2701.* Section 2701 provides special valuation rules to determine the amount of the gift when an individual transfers an equity interest in a corporation or partnership to a member of the individual's family. For section 2701 to apply, the transferor or an applicable family member (as defined in paragraph (d)(2) of this section) must, immediately after the transfer, hold an applicable retained interest (a type of equity interest defined in § 25.2701–2(b)(1)). If certain subsequent payments with respect to the applicable retained interest do not conform to the assumptions used in valuing the interest at the time of the initial transfer, § 25.2701–4 provides a special rule to increase the individual's later taxable gifts or taxable estate. Section 25.2701–5 provides an adjustment to mitigate the effects of double taxation when an applicable retained interest is subsequently transferred.

(2) *Effect of section 2701.* If section 2701 applies to a transfer, the amount of the transferor's gift, if any, is determined using a subtraction method of valuation (described in § 25.2701–3). Under this method, the amount of the gift is determined by subtracting the value of any family-held applicable retained interests and other non-transferred equity interests from the aggregate value of family-held interests in the corporation or partnership (the "entity"). Generally, in determining

the value of any applicable retained interest held by the transferor or an applicable family member—

(i) Any put, call, or conversion right, any right to compel liquidation, or any similar right is valued at zero if the right is an "extraordinary payment right" (as defined in § 25.2701–2(b)(2));

(ii) Any distribution right in a controlled entity (e.g., a right to receive dividends) is valued at zero unless the right is a "qualified payment right" (as defined in § 25.2701–2(b)(6)); and

(iii) Any other right (including a qualified payment right) is valued as if any right valued at zero did not exist but otherwise without regard to section 2701.

(3) *Example.* The following example illustrates rules of this paragraph (a).

Example. A, an individual, holds all the outstanding stock of S Corporation. A exchanges A's shares in S for 100 shares of 10-percent cumulative preferred stock and 100 shares of voting common stock. A transfers the common stock to A's child. Section 2701 applies to the transfer because A has transferred an equity interest (the common stock) to a member of A's family, and immediately thereafter holds an applicable retained interest (the preferred stock). A's preferred stock is valued under the rules of section 2701. A's gift is determined under the subtraction method by subtracting the value of A's preferred stock from the value of A's interest in S immediately prior to the transfer.

(b) Transfers and other triggering events. (1) *Completed transfers.* Section 2701 applies to determine the existence and amount of any gift, whether or not the transfer would otherwise be a taxable gift under chapter 12 of the Internal Revenue Code. For example, section 2701 applies to a transfer that would not otherwise be a gift under chapter 12 because it was a transfer for full and adequate consideration.

(2) *Transactions treated as transfers.* (i) *In general.* Except as provided in paragraph (b)(3) of this section, for purposes of section 2701, transfer includes the following transactions:

(A) A contribution to the capital of a new or existing entity;

(B) A redemption, recapitalization, or other change in the capital structure of an entity (a "capital structure transaction"), if—

(1) The transferor or an applicable family member receives an applicable retained interest in the capital structure transaction;

(2) The transferor or an applicable family member holding an applicable retained interest before the capital structure transaction surrenders an equity interest that is junior to the applicable retained interest (a "subordinate interest") and receives property other than an applicable retained interest; or

(3) The transferor or an applicable family member holding an applicable retained interest before the capital structure transaction surrenders an equity interest in the entity (other than a subordinate interest) and the fair market value of the applicable retained interest is increased; or

(C) The termination of an indirect holding in an entity (as defined in § 25.2701–6) (or a contribution to capital by an entity to the extent an individual indirectly holds an interest in the entity), if—

(1) The property is held in a trust as to which the indirect holder is treated as the owner under subchapter J of chapter 1 of the Internal Revenue Code; or

(2) If the termination (or contribution) is not treated as a transfer under paragraph (b)(2)(i)(C)(1) of this section, to the extent the value of the indirectly-held interest would have been included in the value of the indirect holder's gross estate for Federal estate tax purposes if the indirect holder died immediately prior to the termination.

(ii) *Multiple attribution.* For purposes of paragraph (b)(2)(i)(C) of this section, if the transfer of an indirect holding in property is treated as a transfer with respect to more than one indirect holder, the transfer is attributed in the following order:

(A) First, to the indirect holder(s) who transferred the interest to the entity (without regard to section 2513);

(B) Second, to the indirect holder(s) possessing a presently exercisable power to designate the person who shall possess or enjoy the property;

(C) Third, to the indirect holder(s) presently entitled to receive the income from the interest;

(D) Fourth, to the indirect holder(s) specifically entitled to receive the interest at a future date; and

(E) Last, to any other indirect holder(s) proportionally.

(3) *Excluded transactions.* For purposes of section 2701, a transfer does not include the following transactions:

(i) A capital structure transaction, if the transferor, each applicable family member, and each member of the transferor's family holds substantially the same interest after the transaction as that individual held before the transaction. For this purpose, common stock with non-lapsing voting rights and nonvoting common stock are interests that are substantially the same;

(ii) A shift of rights occurring upon the execution of a qualified disclaimer described in section 2518; and

(iii) A shift of rights occurring upon the release, exercise, or lapse of a power of appointment other than a general power of appointment described in section 2514, except to the extent the release, exercise, or lapse would otherwise be a transfer under chapter 12.

(c) Circumstances in which section 2701 does not apply. To the extent provided, section 2701 does not apply in the following cases:

(1) *Marketable transferred interests.* Section 2701 does not apply if there are readily available market quotations on an established securities market for the value of the transferred interests.

(2) *Marketable retained interests.* Section 25.2701–2 does not apply to any applicable retained interest if there are readily available market quotations on an established securities market for the value of the applicable retained interests.

(3) *Interests of the same class.* Section 2701 does not apply if the retained interest is of the same class of equity as the transferred interest or if the retained interest is of a class that is pro-portional to the class of the transferred interest. A class is the same class as (or is proportional to the class of) the transferred interest if the rights are identical (or proportional) to the rights of the transferred interest, except for non-lapsing differences in voting rights (or, for a partnership, non-lapsing differences with respect to management and limitations on liability). For purposes of this section, non-lapsing provisions necessary to comply with partnership allocation requirements of the Internal Revenue Code (e.g., section 704(b)) are non-lapsing differences with respect to limitations on liability. A right that lapses by reason of Federal or State law is treated as a nonlapsing right unless the Secretary determines, by regulation or by published revenue ruling, that it is necessary to treat such a right as a lapsing right to accomplish the purposes of section 2701. An interest in a partnership is not an interest in the same class as the transferred interest if the transferor or applicable family members have the right to alter the liability of the transferee.

(4) *Proportionate transfers.* Section 2701 does not apply to a transfer by an individual to a member of the individual's family of equity interests to the extent the transfer by that individual results in a proportionate reduction of each class of equity interest held by the individual and all applicable family members in the aggregate immediately before the transfer. Thus, for example, section 2701 does not apply if P owns 50 percent of each class of equity interest in a corporation and transfers a portion of each class to P's child in a manner that reduces each interest held by P and any applicable family members, in the aggregate, by 10 percent even if the transfer does not proportionately reduce P's interest in each class. See § 25.2701–6 regarding indirect holding of interests.

(d) Family definitions. (1) *Member of the family.* A member of the family is, with respect to any transferor—

(i) The transferor's spouse;

(ii) Any lineal descendant of the transferor or the transferor's spouse; and

(iii) The spouse of any such lineal descendant.

(2) *Applicable family member.* An applicable family member is, with respect to any transferor—

(i) The transferor's spouse;

(ii) Any ancestor of the transferor or the transferor's spouse; and

(iii) The spouse of any such ancestor.

(3) *Relationship by adoption.* For purposes of section 2701, any relationship by legal adoption is the same as a relationship by blood.

(e) Examples. The following examples illustrate provisions of this section:

Example (1). P, an individual, holds all the outstanding stock of X Corporation. Assume the fair market value of P's interest in X immediately prior to the transfer is $1.5 million. X is recapitalized so that P holds 1,000 shares of $1,000 par value preferred stock bearing an annual cumulative dividend of $100 per share (the aggregate fair market value of which is assumed to be $1 million) and 1,000 shares of voting common stock. P transfers the common stock to P's child. Section 2701 applies to the transfer because P has transferred an equity interest (the common stock) to a member of P's family and immediately thereafter holds an applicable retained interest (the preferred stock). P's right to receive annual cumulative dividends is a qualified payment right and is valued for purposes of section 2701 at its fair market value of $1,000,000. The amount of P's gift, determined using the subtraction method of § 25.2701–3, is $500,000 ($1,500,000 minus $1,000,000).

Example (2). The facts are the same as in Example 1, except that the preferred dividend right is noncumulative. Under § 25.2701–2, P's preferred dividend right is valued at zero because it is a distribution right in a controlled entity, but is not a qualified payment right. All of P's other rights in the preferred stock are valued as if P's dividend right does not exist but otherwise without regard to section 2701. The amount of P's gift, determined using the subtraction method, is $1,500,000 ($1,500,000 minus $0). P may elect, however, to treat the dividend right as a qualified payment right as provided in § 25.2701–2(c)(2).

[T.D. 8395, 57 FR 4255, Feb. 4, 1992; T.D. 8395, 57 FR 11264, April 2, 1992; T.D. 8536, 59 FR 23154, May 5, 1994]

§ 25.2701–2 Special valuation rules for applicable retained interests.

(a) In general. In determining the amount of a gift under § 25.2701–3, the value of any applicable retained interest (as defined in paragraph (b)(1) of this section) held by the transferor or by an applicable family member is determined using the rules of chapter 12, with the modifications prescribed by this section. See § 25.2701–6 regarding the indirect holding of interests.

(1) *Valuing an extraordinary payment right.* Any extraordinary payment right (as defined in paragraph (b)(2) of this section) is valued at zero.

(2) *Valuing a distribution right.* Any distribution right (as defined in paragraph (b)(3) of this section) in a controlled entity is valued at zero, unless it is a qualified payment right (as defined in paragraph (b)(6) of this section). Controlled entity is defined in paragraph (b)(5) of this section.

(3) *Special rule for valuing a qualified payment right held in conjunction with an extraordinary payment right.* If an applicable retained interest confers a qualified payment right and one or more extraordinary payment rights, the value of all these rights is determined by assuming that each extraordinary payment right is exercised in a manner that results in the lowest total value being determined for all the rights, using a consistent set of assumptions and giving due regard to the entity's net worth, prospective earning power, and other relevant factors (the "lower of" valuation rule). See §§ 20.2031–2(f) and 20.2031–3 for rules relating to the valuation of business interests generally.

(4) *Valuing other rights.* Any other right (including a qualified payment right not subject to the prior paragraph) is valued as if any right valued at zero does not exist and as if any right valued under the lower of rule is exercised in a manner consistent with the assumptions of that rule but otherwise without regard to section 2701. Thus, if an applicable retained interest carries no rights that are valued at zero or under the lower of rule, the value of the interest for purposes of section 2701 is its fair market value.

(5) *Example.* The following example illustrates rules of this paragraph (a).

Example. P, an individual, holds all 1,000 shares of X Corporation's $1,000 par value preferred stock bearing an annual cumulative dividend of $100 per share and holds all 1,000 shares of X's voting common stock. P has the right to put all the preferred stock to X at any time for $900,000. P transfers the common stock to P's child and immediately thereafter holds the preferred stock. Assume that at the time of the transfer, the fair market value of X is $1,500,000, and the fair market value of P's annual cumulative dividend right is $1,000,000. Because the preferred stock confers both an extraordinary payment right (the put right) and a qualified payment right (i.e., the right to receive cumulative dividends), the lower of rule applies and the value of these rights is determined as if the put right will be exercised in a manner that results in the lowest total value being determined for the rights (in this case, by assuming that the put will be exercised immediately). The value of P's preferred stock is $900,000 (the lower of $1,000,000 or $900,000). The amount of the gift is $600,000 ($1,500,000 minus $900,000).

(b) Definitions. (1) *Applicable retained interest.* An applicable retained interest is any equity interest in a corporation or partnership with respect to which there is either—

(i) An extraordinary payment right (as defined in paragraph (b)(2) of this section), or

(ii) In the case of a controlled entity (as defined in paragraph (b)(5) of this section), a distribution right (as defined in paragraph (b)(3) of this section).

(2) *Extraordinary payment right.* Except as provided in paragraph (b)(4) of this section, an extraordinary payment right is any put, call, or conversion right, any right to compel liquidation, or any similar right, the exercise or nonexercise of which affects the value of the transferred interest. A call right includes any warrant, option, or other right to acquire one or more equity interests.

(3) *Distribution right.* A distribution right is the right to receive distributions with respect to an equity interest. A distribution right does not include—

(i) Any right to receive distributions with respect to an interest that is of the same class as, or a class that is subordinate to, the transferred interest;

(ii) Any extraordinary payment right; or (iii) Any right described in paragraph (b)(4) of this section.

(4) *Rights that are not extraordinary payment rights or distribution rights.* Mandatory payment rights, liquidation participation rights, rights to guaranteed payments of a fixed amount under section 707(c), and non-lapsing conversion rights are neither extraordinary payment rights nor distribution rights.

(i) *Mandatory payment right.* A mandatory payment right is a right to receive a payment required to be made at a specific time for a specific amount. For example, a mandatory redemption right in preferred stock requiring that the stock be redeemed at its fixed par value on a date certain is a mandatory payment right and therefore not an extraordinary payment right or a distribution right. A right to receive a specific amount on the death of the holder is a mandatory payment right.

(ii) *Liquidation participation rights.* A liquidation participation right is a right to participate in a liquidating distribution. If the transferor, members of the transferor's family, or applicable family members have the ability to compel liquidation, the liquidation participation right is valued as if the ability to compel liquidation—

(A) Did not exist, or

(B) If the lower of rule applies, is exercised in a manner that is consistent with that rule.

(iii) *Right to a guaranteed payment of a fixed amount under section 707(c).* The right to a guaranteed payment of a fixed amount under section 707(c) is the right to a guaranteed payment (within the meaning of section 707(c)) the amount of which is determined at a fixed rate (including a rate that bears a fixed relationship to a specified market interest rate). A payment that is contingent as to time or amount is not a guaranteed payment of a fixed amount.

(iv) *Non-lapsing conversion right*—(A) *Corporations.* A non-lapsing conversion right, in the case of a corporation, is a non-lapsing right to convert an equity interest in a corporation into a fixed number or a fixed percentage of shares of the same class as the transferred interest (or into an interest that would be of the same class but for non-lapsing differences in voting rights), that is subject to proportionate adjustments for changes in the equity ownership of the corporation and to adjustments similar to those provided in section 2701(d) for unpaid payments.

(B) *Partnerships.* A non-lapsing conversion right, in the case of a partnership, is a nonlapsing right to convert an equity interest in a partnership into a specified interest (other than an interest represented by a fixed dollar amount) of the same class as the transferred interest (or into an interest that would be of the same class but for non-lapsing differences in management rights or limitations on liability) that is subject to proportionate adjustments for changes in the equity ownership of the partnership and to adjustments similar to those provided in section 2701(d) for unpaid payments.

(C) *Proportionate adjustments in equity ownership.* For purposes of this paragraph (b)(4), an equity interest is subject to proportionate adjustments for changes in equity ownership if, in the case of a corporation, proportionate adjustments are required to be made for splits, combinations, reclassifications, and similar changes in capital stock, or, in the case of a partnership, the equity interest is protected from dilution resulting from changes in the partnership structure.

(D) *Adjustments for unpaid payments.* For purposes of this paragraph (b)(4), an equity interest is subject to adjustments similar to those provided in section 2701(d) if it provides for—

(1) Cumulative payments;

(2) Compounding of any unpaid payments at the rate specified in § 25.2701–4(c)(2); and

(3) Adjustment of the number or percentage of shares or the size of the interest into which it is convertible to take account of accumulated but unpaid payments.

(5) *Controlled entity*—(i) *In general.* For purposes of section 2701, a controlled entity is a corporation or partnership controlled, immediately before a transfer, by the transferor, applicable family members, and any lineal descendants of the parents of the transferor or the transferor's spouse. See § 25.2701–6 regarding indirect holding of interests.

(ii) *Corporations*—(A) *In general.* In the case of a corporation, control means the holding of at least 50 percent of the total voting power or total fair market value of the equity interests in the corporation.

(B) *Voting rights.* Equity interests that carry no right to vote other than on liquidation, merger, or a similar event are not considered to have voting rights for purposes of this paragraph (b)(5)(ii). Generally, a voting right is considered held by an individual to the extent that the individual, either alone or in conjunction with any other person, is entitled to exercise (or direct the exercise of) the right. However, if an equity interest carrying voting rights is held in a fiduciary capacity, the voting rights are not considered held by the fiduciary, but instead are considered held by each beneficial owner of the interest and by each individual who is a permissible recipient of the income from the interest. A voting right does not include a right to vote that is subject to a contingency that has not occurred, other than a contingency that is within the control of the individual holding the right.

(iii) *Partnerships.* In the case of any partnership, control means the holding of at least 50 percent of either the capital interest or the profits interest in the partnership. Any right to a guaranteed payment under section 707(c) of a fixed amount is disregarded in making this determination. In addition, in the case of a limited partnership, control means the holding of any equity interest as a general partner. See § 25.2701–2(b)(4)(iii) for the definition of a right to a guaranteed payment of a fixed amount under section 707(c).

(6) *Qualified payment right*—(i) *In general.* A qualified payment right is a right to receive qualified payments. A qualified payment is a distribution that is—

(A) A dividend payable on a periodic basis (at least annually) under any cumulative preferred stock, to the extent such dividend is determined at a fixed rate;

(B) Any other cumulative distribution payable on a periodic basis (at least annually) with respect to an equity interest, to the extent determined at a fixed rate or as a fixed amount; or

(C) Any distribution right for which an election has been made pursuant to paragraph (c)(2) of this section.

(ii) *Fixed rate.* For purposes of this section, a payment rate that bears a fixed relationship to a specified market interest rate is a payment determined at a fixed rate.

(c) Qualified payment elections. (1) *Election to treat a qualified payment right as other than a qualified payment right.* Any transferor holding a qualified payment right may elect to treat all rights held by the transferor of the same class as rights that are not qualified payment rights. An election may be a partial election, in which case the election must be exercised with respect to a consistent portion of each payment right in the class as to which the election has been made.

(2) *Election to treat other distribution rights as qualified payment rights.* Any individual may elect to treat a distribution right held by that individual in a controlled entity as a qualified payment right. An election may be a partial election, in which case the election must be exercised with respect to a consistent portion of each payment right in the class as to which the election has been made. An election under this paragraph (c)(2) will not cause the value of the applicable retained interest conferring the distribution

right to exceed the fair market value of the applicable retained interest (determined without regard to section 2701). The election is effective only to the extent—

(i) Specified in the election, and

(ii) That the payments elected are permissible under the legal instrument giving rise to the right and are consistent with the legal right of the entity to make the payment.

(3) *Elections irrevocable.* Any election under paragraph (c)(1) or (c)(2) of this section is revocable only with the consent of the Commissioner.

(4) *Treatment of certain payments to applicable family members.* Any payment right described in paragraph (b)(6) of this section held by an applicable family member is treated as a payment right that is not a qualified payment right unless the applicable family member elects (pursuant to paragraph (c)(2) of this section) to treat the payment right as a qualified payment right. An election may be a partial election, in which case the election must be exercised with respect to a consistent portion of each payment right in the class as to which the election has been made.

(5) *Time and manner of elections.* Any election under paragraph (c)(1) or (c)(2) of this section is made by attaching a statement to the Form 709, Federal Gift Tax Return, filed by the transferor on which the transfer is reported. An election filed after the time of the filing of the Form 709 reporting the transfer is not a valid election. An election filed as of April 6, 1992, for transfers made prior to its publication is effective. The statement must—

(i) Set forth the name, address, and taxpayer identification number of the electing individual and of the transferor, if different;

(ii) If the electing individual is not the transferor filing the return, state the relationship between the individual and the transferor;

(iii) Specifically identify the transfer disclosed on the return to which the election applies;

(iv) Describe in detail the distribution right to which the election applies;

(v) State the provision of the regulation under which the election is being made; and

(vi) If the election is being made under paragraph (c)(2) of this section—

(A) State the amounts that the election assumes will be paid, and the times that the election assumes the payments will be made;

(B) Contain a statement, signed by the electing individual, in which the electing individual agrees that—

(*1*) If payments are not made as provided in the election, the individual's subsequent taxable gifts or taxable estate will, upon the occurrence of a taxable event (as defined in § 25.2701–4(b)), be increased by an amount determined under § 25.2701–4(c), and

(*2*) The individual will be personally liable for any increase in tax attributable thereto.

(d) Examples. The following examples illustrate provisions of this section:

Example (1). On March 30, 1991, P transfers non-voting common stock of X Corporation to P's child, while retaining $100 par value voting preferred stock bearing a cumulative annual dividend of $10. Immediately before the transfer, P held 100 percent of the stock. Because X is a controlled entity (within the meaning of paragraph (b)(5) of this section), P's dividend right is a distribution right that is subject to section 2701. See § 25.2701–2(b)(3). Because the distribution right is an annual cumulative dividend, it is a qualified payment right. See § 25.2701–2(b)(6).

Example (2). The facts are the same as in Example 1, except that the dividend right is non-cumulative. P's dividend right is a distribution right in a controlled entity, but is not a qualified payment right because the dividend is non-cumulative. Therefore, the non-cumulative dividend right is valued at zero under § 25.2701–2(a)(2). If the corporation were not a controlled entity, P's dividend right would be valued without regard to section 2701.

Example (3). The facts are the same as in Example 1. Because P holds sufficient voting power to compel liquidation of X, P's right to participate in liquidation is an extraordinary payment right under paragraph (b)(2) of this section. Because P holds an extraordinary payment right in conjunction with a qualified payment right (the right to receive cumulative dividends), the lower of rule applies.

Example (4). The facts are the same as in Example 1, except that immediately before the transfer, P, applicable family members of P, and members of P's family, hold 60 percent of the voting rights in X. Assume that 80 percent of the vote is required to compel liquidation of any interest in X. P's right to participate in liquidation is not an extraordinary payment right under paragraph (b)(2) of this section, because P and P's family cannot compel liquidation of X. P's preferred stock is an applicable retained interest that carries no rights that are valued under the special valuation rules of section 2701. Thus, in applying the valuation method of § 25.2701–3, the value of P's preferred stock is its fair market value determined without regard to section 2701.

Example (5). L holds 10-percent noncumulative preferred stock and common stock in a corporation that is a controlled entity. L transfers the common stock to L's child. L holds no extraordinary payment rights with respect to the preferred stock. L elects under paragraph (c)(2) of this section to treat the noncumulative dividend right as a qualified payment right consisting of the right to receive a cumulative annual dividend of 5 percent. Under § 25.2701–2(c)(2), the value of the distribution right pursuant to the election is the lesser of—

(A) The fair market value of the right to receive a cumulative 5-percent dividend from the corporation, giving due regard to the corporation's net worth, prospective earning power, and dividend-paying capacity; or

(B) The value of the distribution right determined without regard to section 2701 and without regard to the terms of the qualified payment election.

[T.D. 8395, 57 FR 4257, Feb. 4, 1992]

§ 25.2701–3 Determination of amount of gift.

(a) Overview. (1) *In general.* The amount of the gift resulting from any transfer to which section 2701 applies is determined by a subtraction method of valuation. Under this method, the amount of the transfer is determined by subtracting the values of all family-held senior equity interests from the fair market value of all family-held interests in the entity determined immediately before the transfer. The values of the senior equity interests held by the transferor and applicable family members generally are determined under section 2701. Other family-held senior equity interests are valued at their fair market value. The balance is then appropriately allocated among the transferred interests and other family-held subordinate equity interests. Finally, certain discounts and other appropriate reductions are provided, but only to the extent permitted by this section.

(2) *Definitions.* The following definitions apply for purposes of this section.

(i) *Family-held.* Family-held means held (directly or indirectly) by an individual described in § 25.2701–2(b)(5)(i).

(ii) *Senior equity interest.* Senior equity interest means an equity interest in the entity that carries a right to distributions of income or capital that is preferred as to the rights of the transferred interest.

(iii) *Subordinate equity interest.* Subordinate equity interest means an equity interest in the entity as to which an applicable retained interest is a senior equity interest.

(b) Valuation methodology. The following methodology is used to determine the amount of the gift when section 2701 applies.

(1) *Step 1—Valuation of family-held interest*—(i) *In general.* Except as provided in paragraph (b)(1)(ii) of this section determine the fair market value of all family-held equity interests in the entity immediately after the transfer. The fair market value is determined by assuming that the interests are held by one individual, using a consistent set of assumptions.

(ii) *Special rule for contributions to capital.* In the case of a contribution to capital, determine the fair market value of the contribution.

(2) *Step 2—Subtract the value of senior equity interests.* (i) *In general.* If the amount determined in Step 1 of paragraph (b)(1) of this section is not determined under the special rule for contributions to capital, from that value subtract the following amounts:

(A) An amount equal to the sum of the fair market value of all family-held senior equity interests, (other than applicable retained interests held by the transferor or applicable family members) and the fair market value of any family-held equity interests of the same class or a subordinate class to the transferred interests held by persons other than the transferor, members of the transferor's family, and applicable family members of the transferor. The fair market value of an interest is its pro rata share of the fair market value of all family-held senior equity interests of the same class (determined, immediately after the transfer, as is all family-held senior equity interests were held by one individual); and

(B) The value of all applicable retained interests held by the transferor or applicable family members (other than an interest received as consideration for the transfer) determined under § 25.2701–2, taking into account the adjustment described in paragraph (b)(5) of this section.

(ii) *Special rule for contributions to capital.* If the value determined in Step 1 of paragraph (b)(1) of this section is determined under the special rule for contributions to capital, subtract the value of any applicable retained interest received in exchange for the contribution to capital determined under § 25.2701–2.

(3) *Step 3—Allocate the remaining value among the transferred interests and other family-held subordinate equity interests.* The value remaining after Step 2 is allocated among the transferred interests and other subordinate equity interests held by the transferor, applicable family members, and members of the transferor's family. If more than one class of family-held subordinate equity interest exists, the value remaining after Step 2 is allocated, beginning with the most senior class of subordinate equity interest, in the manner that would most fairly approximate their value if all rights valued under section 2701 at zero did not exist (or would be exercised in a manner consistent with the assumptions of the rule of § 25.2702–2(a)(4), if applicable). If there is no clearly appropriate method of allocating the remaining value pursuant to the preceding sentence, the remaining value (or the portion remaining after any partial allocation pursuant to the preceding sentence) is allocated to the interests in proportion to their fair market values determined without regard to section 2701.

(4) *Step 4—Determine the amount of the gift*—(i) *In general.* The amount allocated to the transferred interests in Step 3 is reduced by the amounts determined under this paragraph (b)(4).

(ii) *Reduction for minority or similar discounts.* Except as provided in § 25.2701–3(c), if the value of the transferred interest (determined without regard to section 2701) would be determined after application of a minority or similar discount with respect to the transferred interest, the amount of the gift determined under section 2701 is reduced by the excess, if any, of—

(A) A pro rata portion of the fair market value of the family-held interests of the same class (determined as if all voting rights conferred by family-held equity interests were held by one person who had no interest in the entity other than the family-held interests of the same class, but otherwise without regard to section 2701), over

(B) The value of the transferred interest (without regard to section 2701).

(iii) *Adjustment for transfers with a retained interest.* If the value of the transferor's gift (determined without regard to section 2701) would be reduced under section 2702 to reflect the value of a retained interest, the value determined under section 2701 is reduced by the same amount.

(iv) *Reduction for consideration.* The amount of the transfer (determined under section 2701) is reduced by the amount of consideration in money or money's worth received by the transferor, but not in excess of the amount of the gift (determined without regard to section 2701). The value of consideration received by the transferor in the form of an applicable retained interest in the entity is determined under section 2701 except that, in the case of a contribution to capital, the Step 4 value of such an interest is zero.

(5) *Adjustment in Step 2*—(i) *In general.* For purposes of paragraph (b)(2) of this section, if the percentage of any class of applicable retained interest held by the transferor and by applicable family members (including any interest received as consideration for the transfer) exceeds the family interest percentage, the excess is treated as a family-held interest that is not held by the transferor or an applicable family member.

(ii) *Family interest percentage.* The family interest percentage is the highest ownership percentage (determined on the basis of relative fair market values) of family-held interests in—

(A) Any class of subordinate equity interest; or

(B) All subordinate equity interests, valued in the aggregate.

(c) Minimum value rule. (1) *In general.* If section 2701 applies to the transfer of an interest in an entity, the value of a junior equity interest is not less than its pro-rata portion of 10 percent of the sum of—

(i) The total value of all equity interests in the entity, and

(ii) The total amount of any indebtedness of the entity owed to the transferor and applicable family members.

(2) *Junior equity interest.* For purposes of paragraph (c)(1) of this section, junior equity interest means common stock or, in the case of a partnership, any partnership interest under which the rights to income and capital are junior to the rights of all other classes of partnership interests. Common stock means the class or classes of stock that, under the facts and circumstances, are entitled to share in the reasonably anticipated residual growth in the entity.

(3) *Indebtedness*—(i) *In general.* For purposes of paragraph (c)(1) of this section, indebtedness owed to the transferor (or an applicable family member) does not include—

(A) Short-term indebtedness incurred with respect to the current conduct of the entity's trade or business (such as amounts payable for current services);

(B) Indebtedness owed to a third party solely because it is guaranteed by the transferor or an applicable family member; or

(C) Amounts permanently set aside in a qualified deferred compensation arrangement, to the extent the amounts are unavailable for use by the entity.

(ii) *Leases.* A lease of property is not indebtedness, without regard to the length of the lease term, if the lease payments represent full and adequate consideration for use of the property. Lease payments are considered full and adequate consideration if a good faith effort is made to determine the fair rental value under the lease and the terms of the lease conform to the value so determined. Arrearages with respect to a lease are indebtedness.

(d) Examples. The application of the subtraction method described in this section is illustrated by the following Examples:

Example (1). Corporation X has outstanding 1,000 shares of $1,000 par value voting preferred stock, each share of which carries a cumulative annual dividend of 8 percent and a right to put the stock to X for its par value at any time. In addition, there are outstanding 1,000 shares of non-voting common stock. A holds 600 shares of the preferred stock and 750 shares of the common stock. The balance of the preferred and common stock is held by B, a person unrelated to A. Because the preferred stock confers both a qualified payment right and an extraordinary payment right, A's rights are valued under the "lower of" rule of § 25.2701–2(a)(3). Assume that A's rights in the preferred stock are valued at $800 per share under the "lower of" rule (taking account of A's voting rights). A transfers all of A's common stock to A's child. The method for determining the amount of A's gift is as follows—

Step 1: Assume the fair market value of all the family-held interests in X, taking account of A's control of the corporation, is determined to be $1 million.

Step 2: From the amount determined under Step 1, subtract $480,000 (600 shares x $800 (the section 2701 value of A's preferred stock, computed under the "lower of" rule of § 25.2701–2(a)(3)).

Step 3: The result of Step 2 is a balance of $520,000. This amount is fully allocated to the 750 shares of family-held common stock.

Step 4: Because no consideration was furnished for the transfer, the adjustment under Step 4 is limited to the amount of any appropriate minority or similar discount. Before the application of Step 4 the amount of A's gift is $520,000.

Example (2). The facts are the same as in Example 1, except that prior to the transfer A holds only 50 percent of the common stock and B holds the remaining 50 percent. Assume that the fair market value of A's 600 shares of preferred stock is $600,000.

Step 1: Assume that the result of this step (determining the value of the family-held interest) is $980,000.

Step 2: From the amount determined under Step 1, subtract $500,000 ($400,000, the value of 500 shares of A's preferred stock determined under section 2701 plus $100,000, the fair market value of A's other 100 shares of preferred stock determined without regard to section 2701 pursuant to the valuation adjustment determined under paragraph (b)(5) of this section). The adjustment in step 2 applies in this example because A's percentage ownership of the preferred stock (60 percent) exceeds the family interest percentage of the common stock (50 percent). Therefore, 100 shares of

A's preferred stock are valued at fair market value, or $100,000 (100 x $1,000). The balance of A's preferred stock is valued under section 2701 at $400,000 (500 shares x $800). The value of A's preferred stock for purposes of section 2701 equals $500,000 ($100,000 plus $400,000).

Step 3: The result of Step 2 is $480,000 ($980,000 minus $500,000) which is allocated to the family-held common stock. Because A transferred all of the family-held subordinate equity interests, all of the value determined under Step 2 is allocated to the transferred shares.

Step 4: The adjustment under Step 4 is the same as in Example 1. Thus, the amount of the gift is $480,000.

Example (3). Corporation X has outstanding 1,000 shares of $1,000 par value non-voting preferred stock, each share of which carries a cumulative annual dividend of 8 percent and a right to put the stock to X for its par value at any time. In addition, there are outstanding 1,000 shares of voting common stock. A holds 600 shares of the preferred stock and 750 shares of the common stock. The balance of the preferred and common stock is held by B, a person unrelated to A. Assume further that steps one through three, as in Example 1, result in $520,000 being allocated to the family-held common stock and that A transfers only 75 shares of A's common stock. The transfer fragments A's voting interest. Under Step 4, an adjustment is appropriate to reflect the fragmentation of A's voting rights. The amount of the adjustment is the difference between 10 percent (75/750) of the fair market value of A's common shares and the fair market value of the transferred shares, each determined as if the holder thereof had no other interest in the corporation.

Example (4). On December 31, 1990, the capital structure of Y corporation consists of 1,000 shares of voting common stock held three-fourths by A and one-fourth by A's child, B. On January 15, 1991, A transfers 250 shares of common stock to Y in exchange for 300 shares of nonvoting, noncumulative 8% preferred stock with a section 2701 value of zero. Assume that the fair market value of Y is $1,000,000 at the time of the exchange and that the exchange by A is for full and adequate consideration in moneys' worth. However, for purposes of section 2701, if a subordinate equity interest is transferred in exchange for an applicable retained interest, consideration in the exchange is determined with reference to the section 2701 value of the senior interest. Thus, A is treated as transferring the common stock to the corporation for no consideration. Immediately after the transfer, B is treated as holding one-third (250/750) of the common stock and A is treated as holding two-thirds (500/750). The amount of the gift is determined as follows:

Step 1. Because Y is held exclusively by A and B, the Step 1 value is $1,000,000.

Step 2. The result of Step 2 is $1,000,000 ($1,000,000 - 0).

Step 3. The amount allocated to the transferred common stock is $250,000 (250/1,000 * $1,000,000). That amount is further allocated in proportion to the respective holdings of A and B in the common stock ($166,667 and $83,333, respectively).

Step 4. There is no Step 4 adjustment because the section 2701 value of the consideration received by A was zero and no minority discount would have been involved in the exchange. Thus, the amount of the gift is $83,333. If the section 2701 value of the applicable retained interested were $100,000, the Step 4 adjustment would have been a $33,333 reduction for consideration received ((250/750) * $100,000).

Example (5). The facts are the same as in Example 4, except that on January 6, 1992, when the fair market value of Y is still $1,000,000, A transfers A's remaining 500 shares of common stock to Y in exchange for 2500 shares of preferred stock. The second transfer is also for full and adequate consideration in money or money's worth. The result of Step 2 is the same—$1,000,000.

Step 3. The amount allocated to the transferred common stock is $666,667 (500/750 * $1,000,000). Since A holds no common stock immediately after the transfer, A is treated as transferring the entire interest to the other shareholder (B). Thus, $666,667 is fully allocated to the shares held by B.

Step 4. There is no Step 4 adjustment because the section 2701 value of the consideration received by A was zero and no minority discount would have been involved in the exchange. Thus, the amount of the gift is $666,667.

[T.D. 8395, 57 FR 4259, Feb. 4, 1992; T.D. 8395, 57 FR 11265, April 2, 1992]

§ 25.2701–4 Accumulated qualified payments.

(a) In general. If a taxable event occurs with respect to any applicable retained interest conferring a distribution right that was previously valued as a qualified payment right (a "qualified payment interest"), the taxable estate or taxable gifts of the individual holding the interest are increased by the amount determined under paragraph (c) of this section.

(b) Taxable event. (1) *In general.* Except as otherwise provided in this section, taxable event means the transfer of a qualified payment interest, either during life or at death, by the individual in whose hands the interest was originally valued under section 2701 (the "interest holder") or by any individual treated pursuant to paragraph (b)(3) of this section in the same manner as the interest holder. Except as provided in paragraph (a)(2) of this section, any termination of an individual's rights with respect to a qualified payment interest is a taxable event. Thus, for example, if an individual is treated as indirectly holding a qualified payment interest held by a trust, a taxable event occurs on the earlier of—

(i) The termination of the individual's interest in the trust (whether by death or otherwise), or

(ii) The termination of the trust's interest in the qualified payment interest (whether by disposition or otherwise).

(2) *Exception.* If, at the time of a termination of an individual's rights with respect to a qualified payment interest, the value of the property would be includible in the individual's gross estate for Federal estate tax purposes if the individual died immediately after the termination, a taxable transfer does not occur until the earlier of—

(i) The time the property would no longer be includible in the individual's gross estate (other than by reason of section 2035), or

(ii) The death of the individual.

(3) *Individual treated as interest holder.* (i) *In general.* If a taxable event involves the transfer of a qualified payment interest by the interest holder (or an individual treated as the interest holder) to an applicable family member of the individual who made the transfer to which section 2701 applied (other than the spouse of the individual transferring the qualified payment interest), the transferee applicable family member is treated in the same manner as the interest holder with respect to late or unpaid qualified payments first due after the taxable event. Thus, for example, if an interest holder transfers during life a qualified payment interest to an applicable family member, that transfer is a taxable event with respect to the interest holder whose taxable gifts are increased for the year of the transfer as provided in paragraph (c) of this section. The transferee is treated thereafter in the same manner as the interest holder with respect to late or unpaid qualified payments first due after the taxable event.

(ii) *Transfers to spouse.* (A) *In general.* If an interest holder (or an individual treated as the interest holder) transfers a qualified payment interest, the transfer is not a taxable event to the extent a marital deduction is allowed with respect to the transfer under sections 2056, 2106(a)(3), or 2523 or, in the case of a transfer during the individual's lifetime, to the extent the spouse furnishes consideration for the transfer. If this exception applies, the transferee spouse is treated as if he or she were the holder of the interest from the date the transferor spouse acquired the interest. If the deduction for a transfer to a spouse is allowable under section 2056(b)(8) or 2523(g) (relating to charitable remainder trusts), the transferee spouse is treated as the holder of the entire interest passing to the trust.

(B) *Marital bequests.* If the selection of property with which a marital bequest is funded is discretionary, a transfer of a qualified payment interest will not be considered a transfer to the surviving spouse unless—

(*1*) The marital bequest is funded with the qualified payment interest before the due date for filing the decedent's Federal estate tax return (including extensions actually granted) (the "due date"), or

(*2*) The executor—

(*i*) Files a statement with the return indicating the extent to which the marital bequest will be funded with the qualified payment interest, and

(*ii*) Before the date that is one year prior to the expiration of the period of limitations on assessment of the Federal estate tax, notifies the District Director having jurisdiction over the return of the extent to which the bequest was funded with the qualified payment interest (or the extent to which the qualified payment interest has been permanently set aside for that purpose).

(C) *Purchase by the surviving spouse.* For purposes of this section, the purchase (before the date prescribed for filing the decedent's estate tax return, including extensions actually granted) by the surviving spouse (or a trust described in section 2056(b)(7)) of a qualified payment interest held (directly or indirectly) by the decedent immediately before death is considered a transfer with respect to which a deduction is allowable under section 2056 or section 2106(a)(3), but only to the extent that the deduction is allowed to the estate. For example, assume that A bequeaths $50,000 to A's surviving spouse, B, in a manner that qualifies for deduction under section 2056, and that subsequent to A's death B purchases a qualified payment interest from A's estate for $200,000, its fair market value. The economic effect of the transaction is the equivalent of a bequest by A to B of the qualified payment interest, one-fourth of which qualifies for the marital deduction. Therefore, for purposes of this section, one-fourth of the qualified payment interest purchased by B ($50,000 / $200,000) is considered a transfer of an interest with respect to which a deduction is allowed under 2056. If the purchase by the surviving spouse is not made before the due date of the decedent's return, the purchase of the qualified payment interest will not be considered a bequest for which a marital deduction is allowed unless the executor—

(1) Files a statement with the return indicating the qualified payment interests to be purchased by the surviving spouse (or a trust described in section 2056(b)(7)), and

(2) Before the date that is one year prior to the expiration of the period of limitations on assessment of the Federal estate tax, notifies the District Director having jurisdiction over the return that the purchase of the qualified payment interest has been made (or that the funds necessary to purchase the qualified payment interest have been permanently set aside for that purpose).

(c) Amount of increase. (1) *In general.* Except as limited by paragraph (c)(6) of this section, the amount of the increase to an individual's taxable estate or taxable gifts is the excess, if any, of—

(i) The sum of—

(A) The amount of qualified payments payable during the period beginning on the date of the transfer to which section 2701 applied (or, in the case of an individual treated as the interest holder, on the date the interest of the prior interest holder terminated) and ending on the date of the taxable event; and

(B) The earnings on those payments, determined hypothetically as if each payment were paid on its due date and reinvested as of that date at a yield equal to the appropriate discount rate (as defined below); over

(ii) The sum of—

(A) The amount of the qualified payments actually paid during the same period;

(B) The earnings on those payments, determined hypothetically as if each payment were reinvested as of the date actually paid at a yield equal to the appropriate discount rate; and

(C) To the extent required to prevent double inclusion, by an amount equal to the sum of—

(1) The portion of the fair market value of the qualified payment interest solely attributable to any right to receive unpaid qualified payments determined as of the date of the taxable event;

(2) The fair market value of any equity interest in the entity received by the individual in lieu of qualified payments and held by the individual at the taxable event, and

(3) The amount by which the individual's aggregate taxable gifts were increased by reason of the failure of the individual to enforce the right to receive qualified payments.

(2) *Due date of qualified payments.* With respect to any qualified payment, the "due date" is that date specified in the governing instrument as the date on which payment is to be made. If no date is specified in the governing instrument, the due date is the last day of each calendar year.

(3) *Appropriate discount rate.* The appropriate discount rate is the discount rate that was applied in determining the value of the qualified payment right at the time of the transfer to which section 2701 applied.

(4) *Application of payments.* For purposes of this section, any payment of an unpaid qualified payment is applied in satisfaction of unpaid qualified payments beginning with the earliest unpaid qualified payment. Any payment in excess of the total of all unpaid qualified payments is treated as a prepayment of future qualified payments.

(5) *Payment.* For purposes of this paragraph (c), the transfer of a debt obligation bearing compound interest from the due date of the payment at a rate not less than the appropriate discount rate is a qualified payment if the term of the obligation (including extensions) does not exceed four years from the date issued. A payment in the form of an equity interest in the entity is not a qualified payment. Any payment of a qualified payment made (or treated as made) either before or during the four-year period beginning on the due date of the payment but before the date of the taxable event is treated as having been made on the due date.

(6) *Limitation*—(i) *In general.* The amount of the increase to an individual's taxable estate or taxable gifts is limited to the applicable percentage of the excess, if any, of—

(A) The sum of—

(*1*) The fair market value of all outstanding equity interests in the entity that are subordinate to the applicable retained interest, determined as of the date of the taxable event without regard to any accrued liability attributable to unpaid qualified payments; and

(*2*) Any amounts expended by the entity to redeem or otherwise acquire any such subordinate interest during the period beginning on the date of the transfer to which section 2701 applied (or, in the case of an individual treated as an interest holder, on the date the interest of the prior interest holder terminated) and ending on the date of the taxable event (reduced by any amounts received on the resale or issuance of any such subordinate interest during the same period); over

(B) The fair market value of all outstanding equity interests in the entity that are subordinate to the applicable retained interest, determined as of the date of the transfer to which section 2701 applied (or, in the case of an individual treated as an interest holder, on the date the interest of the prior interest holder terminated).

(ii) *Computation of limitation.* For purposes of computing the limitation applicable under this paragraph (c)(6), the aggregate fair market value of the subordinate interests in the entity are determined without regard to § 25.2701–3(c).

(iii) *Applicable percentage.* The applicable percentage is determined by dividing the number of shares or units of the applicable retained interest held by the interest holder (or an individual treated as the interest holder) on the date of the taxable event by the total number of such shares or units outstanding on the same date. If an individual holds applicable retained interests in two or more classes of interests, the applicable percentage is equal to the largest applicable percentage determined with respect to any class. For example, if T retains 40 percent of the class A preferred and 60 percent of the class B preferred in a corporation, the applicable percentage with respect to T's holdings is 60 percent.

(d) Taxpayer election. (1) *In general.* An interest holder (or individual treated as an interest holder) may elect to treat as a taxable event the payment of an unpaid qualified payment occurring more than four years after its due date. Under this election, the increase under paragraph (c) of this section is determined only with respect to that payment and all previous payments for which an election was available but not made. Payments for which an election applies are treated as having been paid on their due dates for purposes of subsequent taxable events. The election is revocable only with the consent of the Commissioner.

(2) *Limitation not applicable.* If a taxable event occurs by reason of an election described in paragraph (d)(1) of this section, the limitation described in paragraph (c)(6) of this section does not apply.

(3) *Time and manner of election*—(i) *Timely-filed returns.* The election may be made by attaching a statement to a Form 709, Federal Gift Tax Return, filed by the recipient of the qualified payment on a timely basis for the year in which the qualified payment is received. In that case, the taxable event is deemed to occur on the date the qualified payment is received.

(ii) *Election on late returns.* The election may be made by attaching a statement to a Form 709, Federal Gift Tax Return, filed by the recipient of the qualified payment other than on a timely basis for the year in which the qualified payment is received. In that case, the taxable event is deemed to occur on the first day of the month immediately preceding the month in which the return is filed. If an election, other than an election on a timely return, is made after the death of the interest holder, the taxable event with respect to the decedent is deemed to occur on the later of—

(A) The date of the recipient's death, or

(B) The first day of the month immediately preceding the month in which the return is filed.

(iii) *Requirements of statement.* The statement must—

(A) Provide the name, address, and taxpayer identification number of the electing individual and the interest holder, if different;

(B) Indicate that a taxable event election is being made under paragraph (d) of this section;

(C) Disclose the nature of the qualified payment right to which the election applies, including the due dates of the payments, the dates the payments were made, and the amounts of the payments;

(D) State the name of the transferor, the date of the transfer to which section 2701 applied, and the discount rate used in valuing the qualified payment right; and

(E) State the resulting amount of increase in taxable gifts.

(4) *Example.* The following example illustrates the rules of this paragraph (d).

Example. A holds cumulative preferred stock that A retained in a transfer to which section 2701 applied. No dividends were paid in years 1 through 5 following the transfer. In year 6, A received a qualified payment that, pursuant to paragraph (c)(3) of this section, is considered to be in satisfaction of the unpaid qualified payment for year 1. No election was made to treat that payment as a taxable event. In year 7, A receives a qualified payment that, pursuant to paragraph (c)(4) of this section, is considered to be in satisfaction of the unpaid qualified payment for year 2. A elects to treat the payment in year 7 as a taxable event. The election increases A's taxable gifts in year 7 by the amount computed under paragraph (c) of this section with respect to the payments due in both year l and year 2. For purposes of any future taxable events, the payments with respect to years 1 and 2 are treated as having been made on their due dates.

[T.D. 8395, 57 FR 4261, Feb. 4, 1992]

§ 25.2701–5 Adjustments to mitigate double taxation.

(a) Reduction of transfer tax base. (1) *In general.* This section provides rules under which an individual (the initial transferor) making a transfer subject to section 2701 (the initial transfer) is entitled to reduce his or her taxable gifts or adjusted taxable gifts (the reduction). The amount of the reduction is determined under paragraph (b) of this section. See paragraph (e) of this section if section 2513 (split gifts) applied to the initial transfer.

(2) *Federal gift tax modification.* If, during the lifetime of the initial transferor, the holder of a section 2701 interest (as defined in paragraph (a)(4) of this section) transfers the interest to or for the benefit of an individual other than the initial transferor or an applicable family member of the initial transferor in a transfer subject to Federal estate or gift tax, the initial transferor may reduce the amount on which the initial transferor's tentative tax is computed under section 2502(a). The reduction is first applied on any gift tax return required to be filed for the calendar year in which the section 2701 interest is transferred; any excess reduction is carried forward and applied in each succeeding calendar year until the reduction is exhausted. The amount of the reduction that is used in a calendar year is the amount of the initial transferor's taxable gifts for that year. Any excess reduction remaining at the death of the initial transferor may be applied by the executor of the initial transferor's estate as provided under paragraph (a)(3) of this section. See paragraph (a)(4) of this section for the definition of a section 2701 interest. See § 25.2701–6 for rules relating to indirect ownership of equity interests transferred to trusts and other entities.

(3) *Federal estate tax modification.* Except as otherwise provided in this paragraph (a)(3), in determining the Federal estate tax with respect to an initial transferor, the executor of the initial transferor's estate may reduce the amount on which the decedent's tentative tax is computed under section 2001(b) (or section 2101(b)) by the amount of the reduction (including any excess reduction carried forward under paragraph (a)(2) of this section). The amount of the reduction under this paragraph (a)(3) is limited to the amount that results in zero Federal estate tax with respect to the estate of the initial transferor.

(4) *Section 2701 interest.* A section 2701 interest is an applicable retained interest that was valued using the special valuation rules of section 2701 at the time of the initial transfer. However, an interest is a section 2701 interest only to the extent the transfer of that interest effectively reduces the aggregate ownership

of such class of interest by the initial transferor and applicable family members of the initial transferor below that held by such persons at the time of the initial transfer (or the remaining portion thereof).

(b) Amount of reduction. Except as otherwise provided in paragraphs (c)(3)(iv) (pertaining to transfers of partial interests) and (e) (pertaining to initial split gifts) of this section, the amount of the reduction is the lesser of—

(1) The amount by which the initial transferor's taxable gifts were increased as a result of the application of section 2701 to the initial transfer; or

(2) The amount (determined under paragraph (c) of this section) duplicated in the transfer tax base at the time of the transfer of the section 2701 interest (the duplicated amount).

(c) Duplicated amount. (1) *In general.* The duplicated amount is the amount by which the transfer tax value of the section 2701 interest at the time of the subsequent transfer exceeds the value of that interest determined under section 2701 at the time of the initial transfer. If, at the time of the initial transfer, the amount allocated to the transferred interest under § 25.2701–3(b)(3) (Step 3 of the valuation methodology) is less than the entire amount available for allocation at that time, the duplicated amount is a fraction of the amount described in the preceding sentence. The numerator of the fraction is the amount allocated to the transferred interest at the time of the initial transfer (pursuant to § 25.2701–3(b)(3)) and the denominator of the fraction is the amount available for allocation at the time of the initial transfer (determined after application of § 25.2701–3(b)(2)).

(2) *Transfer tax value*—(i) *In general.* Except as provided in paragraph (c)(3) of this section, for purposes of paragraph (c)(1) of this section the transfer tax value of a section 2701 interest is the value of that interest as finally determined for Federal transfer tax purposes under chapter 11 or chapter 12, as the case may be (including the right to receive any distributions thereon (other than qualified payments)), reduced by the amount of any deduction allowed with respect to the section 2701 interest to the extent that the deduction would not have been allowed if the section 2701 interest were not included in the transferor's total amount of gifts for the calendar year or the transferor's gross estate, as the case may be. Rules similar to the rules of section 691(c)(2)(C) are applicable to determine the extent that a deduction would not be allowed if the section 2701 interest were not so included.

(3) *Special transfer tax value rules*—(i) *Transfers for consideration.* Except as provided in paragraph (c)(3)(iii) of this section, if, during the life of the initial transferor, a section 2701 interest is transferred to or for the benefit of an individual other than the initial transferor or an applicable family member of the initial transferor for consideration in money or money's worth, or in a transfer that is treated as a transfer for consideration in money or money's worth, the transfer of the section 2701 interest is deemed to occur at the death of the initial transferor. In this case, the estate of the initial transferor is entitled to a reduction in the same manner as if the initial transferor's gross estate included a section 2701 interest having a chapter 11 value equal to the amount of consideration in money or money's worth received in the exchange (determined as of the time of the exchange).

(ii) *Interests held by applicable family members at date of initial transferor's death.* If a section 2701 interest in existence on the date of the initial transferor's death is held by an applicable family member and, therefore, is not included in the gross estate of the initial transferor, the section 2701 interest is deemed to be transferred at the death of the initial transferor to or for the benefit of an individual other than the initial transferor or an applicable family member of the initial transferor. In this case, the transfer tax value of that interest is the value that the executor of the initial transferor's estate can demonstrate would be determined under chapter 12 if the interest were transferred immediately prior to the death of the initial transferor.

(iii) *Nonrecognition transactions.* If an individual exchanges a section 2701 interest in a nonrecognition transaction (within the meaning of section 7701(a)(45)), the exchange is not treated as a transfer of a section 2701 interest and the transfer tax value of that interest is determined as if the interest received in exchange is the section 2701 interest.

(iv) *Transfer of less than the entire section 2701 interest.* If a transfer is a transfer of less than the entire section 2701 interest, the amount of the reduction under paragraph (a)(2) or (a)(3) of this section is reduced proportionately.

(v) *Multiple classes of section 2701 interest.* For purposes of paragraph (b) of this section, if more than one class of section 2701 interest exists, the amount of the reduction is determined separately with respect to each such class.

(vi) *Multiple initial transfers.* If an initial transferor has made more than one initial transfer, the amount of the reduction with respect to any section 2701 interest is the sum of the reductions computed under paragraph (b) of this section with respect to each such initial transfer.

(d) Examples. The following examples illustrate the provisions of paragraphs (a) through (c) of this section.

Facts. (1) *In general.* (i) P, an individual, holds 1,500 shares of $1,000 par value preferred stock of X corporation (bearing an annual noncumulative dividend of $100 per share that may be put to X at any time for par value) and 1,000 shares of voting common stock of X. There is no other outstanding common stock of X.

(ii) On January 15, 1991, when the aggregate fair market value of the preferred stock is $1,500,000 and the aggregate fair market value of the common stock is $500,000, P transfers common stock to P's child. The fair market value of P's interest in X (common and preferred) immediately prior to the transfer is $2,000,000, and the section 2701 value of the preferred stock (the section 2701 interest) is zero. Neither P nor P's spouse, S, made gifts prior to 1991.

(2) *Additional facts applicable to Examples 1 through 3.* P's transfer consists of all 1,000 shares of P's common stock. With respect to the initial transfer, the amount remaining after Step 2 of the subtraction method of § 25.2701–3 is $2,000,000 ($2,000,000 minus zero), all of which is allocated to the transferred stock. P's aggregate taxable gifts for 1991 (including the section 2701 transfer) equal $2,500,000.

(3) *Additional facts applicable to Examples 4 and 5.* P's initial transfer consists of one-half of P's common stock. With respect to the initial transfer in this case, only $1,000,000 (one-half of the amount remaining after Step 2 of the subtraction method of § 25.2701–3) is allocated to the transferred stock. P's aggregate taxable gifts for 1991 (the section 2701 transfer and P's other transfers) equal $2,500,000.

Example (1). Inter vivos transfer of entire section 2701 interest. (i) On October 1, 1994, at a time when the value of P's preferred stock is $1,400,000, P transfers all of the preferred stock to P's child. In computing P's 1994 gift tax, P, as the initial transferor, is entitled to reduce the amount on which P's tentative tax is computed under section 2502(a) by $1,400,000.

(ii) The amount of the reduction computed under paragraph (b) of this section is the lesser of $1,500,000 (the amount by which the initial transferor's taxable gifts were increased as a result of the application of section 2701 to the initial transfer) or $1,400,000 (the duplicated amount). The duplicated amount is 100 percent (the portion of the section 2701 interest subsequently transferred) times $1,400,000 (the amount by which the gift tax value of the preferred stock ($1,400,000 at the time of the subsequent transfer) exceeds zero (the section 2701 value of the preferred stock at the time of the initial transfer)).

(iii) The result would be the same if the preferred stock had been held by P's parent, GM, and GM had, on October 1, 1994, transferred the preferred stock to or for the benefit of an individual other than P or an applicable family member of P. In that case, in computing the tax on P's 1994 and subsequent transfers, P would be entitled to reduce the amount on which P's tentative tax is computed under section 2502(a) by $1,400,000. If the value of P's 1994 gifts is less than $1,400,000, P is entitled to claim the excess adjustment in computing the tax with respect to P's subsequent transfers.

Example (2). Transfer of section 2701 interest at death of initial transferor. (i) P continues to hold the preferred stock until P's death. The chapter 11 value of the preferred stock at the date of P's death is the same as the fair market value of the preferred stock at the time of the initial transfer. In computing the Federal estate tax with respect to P's estate, P's executor is entitled to a reduction of $1,500,000 under paragraph (a)(3) of this section.

(ii) The result would be the same if P had sold the preferred stock to any individual other than an applicable family member at a time when the value of the preferred stock was $1,500,000. In that case, the amount of the reduction is computed as if the preferred stock were included in P's gross estate at a fair market value equal to the sales price. If the value of P's taxable estate is less than $1,500,000, the amount of the adjustment available to P's executor is limited to the actual value of P's taxable estate.

(iii) The result would also be the same if the preferred stock had been held by P's parent, GM, and at the time of P's death, GM had not transferred the preferred stock.

Example (3). Transfer of after-acquired preferred stock. On September 1, 1992, P purchases 100 shares of X preferred stock from an unrelated party. On October 1, 1994, P transfers 100 shares of X preferred stock to P's child. In computing P's 1994 gift tax, P is not entitled to reduce the amount on which P's tentative tax is computed under section 2502(a) because the 1994 transfer does not reduce P's preferred stock holding below that held at the time of the initial transfer. See paragraph (a)(4) of this section.

Example (4). Inter vivos transfer of entire section 2701 interest. (i) On October 1, 1994, at a time when the value of P's preferred stock is $1,400,000, P transfers all of the preferred stock to P's child. In computing P's 1994 gift tax, P, as the initial transferor, is entitled to reduce the amount on which P's tentative tax is computed under section 2502(a) by $700,000.

(ii) The amount of the reduction computed under paragraph (b) of this section is the lesser of $750,000 (($1,500,000 x .5 ($1,000,000 over $2,000,000)) the amount by which the initial transferor's taxable gifts were increased as a result of the application of section 2701 to the initial transfer) or $700,000 (($1,400,000 * .5) the duplicated amount). The duplicated amount is 100 percent (the portion of the section 2701 interest subsequently transferred) times $700,000; e.g., one-half (the fraction representing the portion of the common stock transferred in the initial transfer ($1,000,000/$2,000,000)) of the amount by which the gift tax value of the preferred stock at the time of the subsequent transfer ($1,400,000) exceeds zero (the section 2701 value of the preferred stock at the time of the initial transfer).

Example (5). Subsequent transfer of less than the entire section 2701 interest. On October 1, 1994, at a time when the value of P's preferred stock is $1,400,000, P transfers only 250 of P's 1,000 shares of preferred stock to P's child. In this case, the amount of the reduction computed under paragraph (b) is $175,000 (one-fourth (250/1,000) of the amount of the reduction available if P had transferred all 1,000 shares of preferred stock).

(e) Computation of reduction if initial transfer is split under section 2513. (1) *In general.* If section 2513 applies to the initial transfer (a split initial transfer), the special rules of this paragraph (e) apply.

(2) *Transfers during joint lives.* If there is a split initial transfer and the corresponding section 2701 interest is transferred during the joint lives of the donor and the consenting spouse, for purposes of determining the reduction under paragraph (a)(2) of this section each spouse is treated as if the spouse was the initial transferor of one-half of the split initial transfer.

(3) *Transfers at or after death of either spouse.* (i) *In general.* If there is a split initial transfer and the corresponding section 2701 interest is transferred at or after the death of the first spouse to die, the reduction under paragraph (a)(2) or (a)(3) of this section is determined as if the donor spouse was the initial transferor of the entire initial transfer.

(ii) *Death of donor spouse.* Except as provided in paragraph (e)(3)(iv) of this section, the executor of the estate of the donor spouse in a split initial transfer is entitled to compute the reduction as if the donor spouse was the initial transferor of the section 2701 interest otherwise attributable to the consenting spouse. In this case, if the consenting spouse survives the donor spouse—

(A) The consenting spouse's aggregate sum of taxable gifts used in computing each tentative tax under section 2502(a) (and, therefore, adjusted taxable gifts under section 2001(b)(1)(B) (or section 2101(b)(1)(B)) and the tax payable on the consenting spouse's prior taxable gifts under section 2001(b)(2) (or section 2101(b)(2))) is reduced to eliminate the remaining effect of the section 2701 interest; and

(B) Except with respect to any excess reduction carried forward under paragraph (a)(2) of this section, the consenting spouse ceases to be treated as the initial transferor of the section 2701 interest.

(iii) *Death of consenting spouse.* If the consenting spouse predeceases the donor spouse, except for any excess reduction carried forward under paragraph (a)(2) of this section, the reduction with respect to any section 2701 interest in the split initial transfer is not available to the estate of the consenting spouse (regardless of whether the interest is included in the consenting spouse's gross estate). Similarly, if the consenting spouse predeceases the donor spouse, no reduction is available to the consenting spouse's adjusted taxable gifts under section 2001(b)(1)(B) (or section 2101(b)(1)(B)) or to the consenting spouse's gift tax payable under section 2001(b)(2) (or section 2101(b)(2)). See paragraph (a)(2) of this section for rules involving transfers by an applicable family member during the life of the initial transferor.

(iv) *Additional limitation on reduction.* If the donor spouse (or the estate of the donor spouse) is treated under this paragraph (e) as the initial transferor of the section 2701 interest otherwise attributable to the consenting spouse, the amount of additional reduction determined under paragraph (b) of this section is the amount determined under that paragraph with respect to the consenting spouse. If a reduction was previously available to the consenting spouse under this paragraph (e), the amount determined under this paragraph (e)(3)(iv) with respect to the consenting spouse is determined as if the consenting spouse's taxable gifts in the split initial transfer had been increased only by that portion of the increase that corresponds to the remaining portion of the section 2701 interest. The amount of the additional reduction (i.e., the amount determined with respect to the consenting spouse) is limited to the amount that results in a reduction in the donor spouse's Federal transfer tax no greater than the amount of the increase in the consenting spouse's gift tax incurred by reason of the section 2701 interest (or the remaining portion thereof).

(f) Examples. The following examples illustrate the provisions of paragraph (e) of this section. The examples assume the facts set out in this paragraph (f).

Facts. (1) In each example assume that P, an individual, holds 1,500 shares of $1,000 par value preferred stock of X corporation (bearing an annual noncumulative dividend of $100 per share that may be put to X at any time for par value) and 1,000 shares of voting common stock of X. There is no other outstanding stock of X. The annual exclusion under section 2503 is not allowable with respect to any gift.

(2) On January 15, 1991, when the aggregate fair market value of the preferred stock is $1,500,000 and the aggregate fair market value of the common stock is $500,000, P transfers all 1,000 shares of the common stock to P's child. Section 2701 applies to the initial transfer because P transferred an equity interest (the common stock) to a member of P's family and immediately thereafter held an applicable retained interest (the preferred stock). The fair market value of P's interest in X immediately prior to the transfer is $2,000,000 and the section 2701 value of the preferred stock (the section 2701 interest) is zero. With respect to the initial transfer, the amount remaining after Step 2 of the subtraction method of § 25.2701–3 was $2,000,000 ($2,000,000 minus zero), all of which is allocated to the transferred stock. P had made no gifts prior to 1991. The sum of P's aggregate taxable gifts for the calendar year 1991 (including the section 2701 transfer) is $2,500,000. P's spouse, S, made no gifts prior to 1991.

(3) P and S elected pursuant to section 2513 to treat one-half of their 1991 gifts as having been made by each spouse. Without the application of section 2701, P and S's aggregate gifts would have been $500,000 and each spouse would have paid no gift tax because of the application of the unified credit under section 2505. However, because of the application of section 2701, both P and S are each treated as the initial transferor of aggregate taxable gifts in the amount of $1,250,000 and, after the application of the unified credit under section 2505, each paid $255,500 in gift tax with respect to their 1991 transfers. On October 1, 1994, at a time when the value of the preferred stock is the same as at the time of the initial transfer, P transfers the preferred stock (the section 2701 interest) to P's child.

Example (1). Inter vivos transfer of entire section 2701 interest. P transfers all of the preferred stock to P's child. P and S are each entitled to a reduction of $750,000 in computing their 1994 gift tax. P is entitled to the reduction because P subsequently transferred the one-half share of the section 2701 interest as to which P was the initial transferor to an individual who was not an applicable family member of P. S is entitled to the reduction because P, an applicable family member with respect to S, transferred the one-half share of the section 2701 interest as to which S was the initial transferor to an individual other than S or an applicable family member of S. S may claim the reduction against S's 1994 gifts. If S's 1994 taxable gifts are less than $750,000, S may claim the remaining amount of the reduction against S's next succeeding lifetime transfers.

Example (2). Inter vivos transfer of portion of section 2701 interest. P transfers one-fourth of the preferred stock to P's child. In this case, P and S are each entitled to a reduction of $187,500, the corresponding portion of the reduction otherwise available to each spouse (one-fourth of $750,000).

Example (3). Transfer at death of donor spouse. P, the donor spouse in the section 2513 election, dies on October 1, 1994, while holding all of the preferred stock. The executor of P's estate is entitled to a reduction in the computation of the tentative tax under section 2001(b). Since no reduction had been previously available with respect to the section 2701 interest, P's estate is entitled to a full reduction of $750,000 with respect to the one-half share of the preferred stock as to which P was the initial transferor. In addition, P's estate is entitled to an additional reduction of up to $750,000 for the remaining section 2701 interest as to which S was the initial transferor. The reduction for the consenting spouse's remaining section 2701 interest is limited to that amount that will produce a tax saving in P's Federal estate tax of $255,500, the amount of gift tax incurred by S by reason of the application of section 2701 to the split initial transfer.

Example (4). Transfer after death of donor spouse. The facts are the same as in Example 3, except that S acquires the preferred stock from P's estate and subsequently transfers the preferred stock to S's child. S is not entitled to a reduction because S ceased to be an initial transferor upon P's death (and S's prior taxable gifts were automatically adjusted at that time to the level that would have existed had the split initial transfer not been subject to section 2701).

Example (5). Death of donor spouse after inter vivos transfer. (i) P transfers one-fourth of the preferred stock to P's child. In this case, P and S are each entitled to a reduction of $187,500, the corresponding portion of the reduction otherwise available to each spouse (one-fourth of $750,000). S may claim the reduction against S's 1994 or subsequent transfers. P dies on November 1, 1994.

(ii) P's executor is entitled to include, in computing the reduction available to P's estate, the remaining reduction to which P is entitled and an additional amount of up to $562,500 ($750,000 minus $187,500, the amount of the remaining reduction attributable to the consenting spouse determined immediately prior to P's death). The amount of additional reduction available to P's estate cannot exceed the amount that will reduce P's estate tax by $178,625, the amount that S's 1991 gift tax would have been increased if the application of section 2701 had increased S's taxable gifts by only $562,500 ($750,000 $187,500).

(g) Double taxation otherwise avoided. No reduction is available under this section if—

(1) Double taxation is otherwise avoided in the computation of the estate tax under section 2001 (or section 2101); or

(2) A reduction was previously taken under the provisions of section 2701(e)(6) with respect to the same section 2701 interest and the same initial transfer.

(h) Effective date. This section is effective for transfers of section 2701 interests after May 4, 1994. If the transfer of a section 2701 interest occurred on or before May 4, 1994, the initial transferor may rely on either this section, project PS–30–91 (1991–2 C.B. 1118, and 1992–1 C.B. 1239 (see § 601.601(d)(2)(ii)(b) of this chapter)) or any other reasonable interpretation of the statute.

[T.D. 8536, 59 FR 23154, May 5, 1994]

§ 25.2701–6 Indirect holding of interests.

(a) In general. (1) *Attribution to individuals.* For purposes of section 2701, an individual is treated as holding an equity interest to the extent the interest is held indirectly through a corporation, partnership, estate, trust, or other entity. If an equity interest is treated as held by a particular individual in more than one capacity, the interest is treated as held by the individual in the manner that attributes the largest total ownership of the equity interest. An equity interest held by a lower-tier entity is attributed to higher-tier entities in accordance with the rules of this section. For example, if an individual is a 50-percent beneficiary of a trust that holds 50 percent of the preferred stock of a corporation, 25 percent of the preferred stock is considered held by the individual under these rules.

(2) *Corporations.* A person is considered to hold an equity interest held by or for a corporation in the proportion that the fair market value of the stock the person holds bears to the fair market value of all the stock in the corporation (determined as if each class

of stock were held separately by one individual). This paragraph applies to any entity classified as a corporation or as an association taxable as a corporation for federal income tax purposes.

(3) *Partnerships.* A person is considered to hold an equity interest held by or for a partnership in the proportion that the fair market value of the larger of the person's profits interest or capital interest in the partnership bears to the total fair market value of the corresponding profits interests or capital interests in the partnership, as the case may be (determined as if each class were held by one individual). This paragraph applies to any entity classified as a partnership for federal income tax purposes.

(4) *Estates, trusts and other entities.* (i) *In general.* A person is considered to hold an equity interest held by or for an estate or trust to the extent the person's beneficial interest therein may be satisfied by the equity interest held by the estate or trust, or the income or proceeds thereof, assuming the maximum exercise of discretion in favor of the person. A beneficiary of an estate or trust who cannot receive any distribution with respect to an equity interest held by the estate or trust, including the income therefrom or the proceeds from the disposition thereof, is not considered the holder of the equity interest. Thus, if stock held by a decedent's estate has been specifically bequeathed to one beneficiary and the residue of the estate has been bequeathed to other beneficiaries, the stock is considered held only by the beneficiary to whom it was specifically bequeathed. However, any person who may receive distributions from a trust is considered to hold an equity interest held by the trust if the distributions may be made from current or accumulated income from or the proceeds from the disposition of the equity interest, even though under the terms of the trust the interest can never be distributed to that person. This paragraph applies to any entity that is not classified as a corporation, an association taxable as a corporation, or a partnership for federal income tax purposes.

(ii) *Special rules.* (A) Property is held by a decedent's estate if the property is subject to claims against the estate and expenses of administration.

(B) A person holds a beneficial interest in a trust or an estate so long as the person may receive distributions from the trust or the estate other than payments for full and adequate consideration.

(C) An individual holds an equity interest held by or for a trust if the individual is considered an owner of the trust (a "grantor trust") under subpart E, part 1, subchapter J of the Internal Revenue Code (relating to grantors and others treated as substantial owners). However, if an individual is treated as the owner of only a fractional share of a grantor trust because there are multiple grantors, the individual holds each equity interest held by the trust, except to the extent that the fair market value of the interest exceeds the fair market value of the fractional share.

(5) *Multiple attribution.* (i) *Applicable retained interests.* If this section attributes an applicable retained interest to more than one individual in a class consisting of the transferor and one or more applicable family members, the interest is attributed within that class in the following order—

(A) If the interest is held in a grantor trust, to the individual treated as the holder thereof;

(B) To the transferor;

(C) To the transferor's spouse; or

(D) To each applicable family member on a pro rata basis.

(ii) *Subordinate equity interests.* If this section attributes a subordinate equity interest to more than one individual in a class consisting of the transferor, applicable family members, and members of the transferor's family, the interest is attributed within that class in the following order—

(A) To the transferee;

(B) To each member of the transferor's family on a pro rata basis;

(C) If the interest is held in a grantor trust, to the individual treated as the holder thereof;

(D) To the transferor;

(E) To the transferor's spouse; or

(F) To each applicable family member on a pro rata basis.

(b) Examples. The following examples illustrate the provisions of this section:

Example (1). A, an individual, holds 25 percent by value of each class of stock of Y Corporation. Persons unrelated to A hold the remaining stock. Y holds 50 percent of the stock of Corporation X. Under paragraph (a)(2) of this section, Y's interests in X are attributed proportionately to the shareholders of Y. Accordingly, A is considered to hold a 12.5 percent (25 percent * 50 percent) interest in X.

Example (2). Z Bank's authorized capital consists of 100 shares of common stock and 100 shares of preferred stock. A holds 60 shares of each (common and preferred) and A's child, B, holds 40 shares of common stock. Z holds the balance of its own preferred stock, 30 shares as part of a common trust fund it maintains and 10 shares permanently set aside to satisfy a deferred obligation. For purposes of section 2701, A holds 60 shares of common stock and 66 shares of preferred stock in Z, 60 shares of each class directly and 6 shares of preferred stock indirectly (60 percent of the 10 shares set aside to fund the deferred obligation).

Example (3). An irrevocable trust holds a 10-percent general partnership interest in Partnership Q. One-half of the trust income is required to be distributed to O Charity. The other one-half of the income is to be distributed to D during D's life and thereafter to E for such time as E survives D. D holds one-half of the trust's interest in Q by reason of D's present right to receive one-half of the trust's income, and E holds one-half of the trust's interest in Q by reason of E's future right to receive one-half of the trust's income. Nevertheless, no family member is treated as holding more than one-half of the trust's interest in Q because at no time will either D or E actually hold, in the aggregate, any right with respect to income or corpus greater than one-half.

Example (4). An irrevocable trust holds a 10-percent general partnership interest in partnership M. One-half of the trust income is to be paid to D for D's life. The remaining income may, in the trustee's discretion, be accumulated or paid to or for the benefit of a class that includes D's child F, in such amounts as the trustee determines. On the death of the survivor of D and F, the trust corpus is required to be distributed to O Charity. The trust's interest in M is held by the trust's beneficiaries to the extent that present and future income or corpus may be distributed to them. Accordingly, D holds one-half of the trust's interest in M because D is entitled to receive one-half of the trust income currently. F holds the entire value of the interest because F is a member of the class eligible to receive the entire trust income for such time as F survives D. See paragraph (a)(5) of this section for rules applicable in the case of multiple attribution.

Example (5). The facts are the same as in Example 4, except that all the income is required to be paid to O Charity for the trust's initial year. The result is the same as in Example 4.

[T.D. 8395, 57 FR 4263, Feb. 4, 1992]

§ 25.2701–7 Separate interests.

The Secretary may, by regulation, revenue ruling, notice, or other document of general application, prescribe rules under which an applicable retained interest is treated as two or more separate interests for purposes of section 2701. In addition, the Commissioner may, by ruling issued to a taxpayer upon request, treat any applicable retained interest as two or more separate interests as may be necessary and appropriate to carry out the purposes of section 2701.

[T.D. 8395, 57 FR 4264, Feb. 4, 1992]

§ 25.2701–8 Effective dates.

Sections 25.2701–1 through 25.2701–4 and §§ 25.2701–6 and 25.2701–7 are effective as of January 28, 1992. For transfers made prior to January 28, 1992, taxpayers may rely on any reasonable interpretation of the statutory provisions. For these purposes, the provisions of the proposed regulations and the final regulations are considered a reasonable interpretation of the statutory provisions.

[T.D. 8395, 57 FR 4264, Feb. 4, 1992]

§ 2702. Special Valuation Rules in Case of Transfers of Interests in Trusts

(a) Valuation rules.

(1) In general. Solely for purposes of determining whether a transfer of an interest in trust to (or for the benefit of) a member of the transferor's family is a gift (and the value of such transfer), the value of any interest in such trust retained by the transferor or any applicable family member (as defined in section 2701(e)(2)) shall be determined as provided in paragraph (2).

(2) Valuation of retained interests.

(A) In general. The value of any retained interest which is not a qualified interest shall be treated as being zero.

(B) Valuation of qualified interest. The value of any retained interest which is a qualified interest shall be determined under section 7520.

(3) Exceptions.

(A) In general. This subsection shall not apply to any transfer—

(i) if such transfer is an incomplete gift,

(ii) if such transfer involves the transfer of an interest in trust all the property in which consists of a residence to be used as a personal residence by persons holding term interests in such trust, or

(iii) to the extent that regulations provide that such transfer is not inconsistent with the purposes of this section.

(B) Incomplete gift. For purposes of subparagraph (A), the term "incomplete gift" means any transfer which would not be treated as a gift whether or not consideration was received for such transfer.

(b) Qualified interest. For purposes of this section, the term "qualified interest" means—

(1) any interest which consists of the right to receive fixed amounts payable not less frequently than annually,

(2) any interest which consists of the right to receive amounts which are payable not less frequently than annually and are a fixed percentage of the fair market value of the property in the trust (determined annually), and

(3) any noncontingent remainder interest if all of the other interests in the trust consist of interests described in paragraph (1) or (2).

(c) Certain property treated as held in trust. For purposes of this section—

(1) In general. The transfer of an interest in property with respect to which there is 1 or more term interests shall be treated as a transfer of an interest in a trust.

(2) Joint purchases. If 2 or more members of the same family acquire interests in any property described in paragraph (1) in the same transaction (or a series of related transactions), the person (or persons) acquiring the term interests in such property shall be treated as having acquired the entire property and then transferred to the other persons the interests acquired by such other persons in the transaction (or series of transactions). Such transfer shall be treated as made in exchange for the consideration (if any) provided by such other persons for the acquisition of their interests in such property.

(3) Term interest. The term "term interest" means—

(A) a life interest in property, or

(B) an interest in property for a term of years.

(4) Valuation rule for certain term interests. If the nonexercise of rights under a term interest in tangible property would not have a substantial effect on the valuation of the remainder interest in such property—

(A) subparagraph (A) of subsection (a)(2) shall not apply to such term interest, and

(B) the value of such term interest for purposes of applying subsection (a)(1) shall be the amount which the holder of the term interest establishes as the amount for which such interest could be sold to an unrelated third party.

(d) Treatment of transfers of interests in portion of trust. In the case of a transfer of an income or remainder interest with respect to a specified portion of the property in a trust, only such portion shall be taken into account in applying this section to such transfer.

(e) Member of the family. For purposes of this section, the term "member of the family" shall have the meaning given such term by section 2704(c)(2).

Regulations

§ 25.2702–0 Table of contents. [*Omitted. Ed.*]

[T.D. 8395, 57 FR 4264, Feb. 4, 1992; T.D. 9181, 70 FR 9223, Feb. 25, 2005]

§ 25.2702–1 Special valuation rules in the case of transfers of interests in trust.

(a) Scope of section 2702. Section 2702 provides special rules to determine the amount of the gift when an individual makes a transfer in trust to (or for the benefit of) a member of the individual's family and the individual or an applicable family member retains an interest in the trust. Section 25.2702–4 treats certain transfers of property as transfers in trust. Certain transfers, including transfers to a personal residence trust, are not subject to section 2702. See paragraph (c) of this section. Member of the family is defined in § 25.2702–2(a)(1). Applicable family member is defined in § 25.2701–1(d)(2).

(b) Effect of section 2702. If section 2702 applies to a transfer, the value of any interest in the trust retained by the transferor or any applicable family member is determined under § 25.2702–2(b). The amount of the gift, if any, is then determined by subtracting the value of the interests retained by the transferor or any applicable family member from the value of the transferred property. If the retained interest is not a qualified interest (as defined in § 25.2702–3), the retained interest is generally valued at zero, and the amount of the gift is the entire value of the property.

(c) Exceptions to section 2702. Section 2702 does not apply to the following transfers.

(1) *Incomplete gift.* A transfer no portion of which would be treated as a completed gift without regard to any consideration received by the transferor. If a transfer is wholly incomplete as to an undivided fractional share of the property transferred (without regard to any consideration received by the transferor), for purposes of this paragraph the transfer is treated as incomplete as to that share.

(2) *Personal residence trust.* A transfer in trust that meets the requirements of § 25.2702–5.

(3) *Charitable remainder trust.* (i) For transfers made on or after May 19, 1997, a transfer to a pooled income fund described in section 642(c)(5); a transfer to a charitable remainder annuity trust described in section 664(d)(1); a transfer to a charitable remainder unitrust described in section 664(d)(2) if under the terms of the governing instrument the unitrust amount can be computed only under section 664(d)(2)(A); and a transfer to a charitable remainder unitrust if under the terms of the governing instrument the unitrust amount can be computed under section 664(d)(2) and (3) and either there are only two consecutive noncharitable beneficial interests and the transferor holds the second of the two interests, or the only permissible recipients of the unitrust amount are the transferor, the transferor's U.S. citizen spouse, or both the transferor and the transferor's U.S. citizen spouse.

(ii) For transfers made before May 19, 1997, a transfer in trust if the remainder interest in the trust qualifies for a deduction under section 2522.

(4) *Pooled income fund.* A transfer of property to a pooled income fund (as defined in section 642(c)(5)).

(5) *Charitable lead trust.* A transfer in trust if the only interest in the trust, other than the remainder interest or a qualified annuity or unitrust interest, is an interest that qualifies for deduction under section 2522.

(6) *Certain assignments of remainder interests.* The assignment of a remainder interest if the only retained interest of the transferor or an applicable family member is as the permissible recipient of distributions of income in the sole discretion of an independent trustee (as defined in section 674(c)).

(7) *Certain property settlements.* A transfer in trust if the transfer of an interest to a spouse is deemed to be for full and adequate consideration by reason of section 2516 (relating to certain property settlements) and

the remaining interests in the trust are retained by the other spouse.

(8) *Transfer or assignment to a Qualified Domestic Trust.* A transfer or assignment (as described in section 2056(d)(2)(B)) by a noncitizen surviving spouse of property to a Qualified Domestic Trust under the circumstances described in § 20.2056A–4(b) of this chapter, where the surviving spouse retains an interest in the transferred property that is not a qualified interest and the transfer is not described in sections 2702(a)(3)(A)(ii) or 2702(c)(4).

[T.D. 8395, 57 FR 4265, Feb. 4, 1992; T.D. 8612, 60 FR 43554, Aug. 22, 1995; T.D. 8791, 63 FR 68194, Dec. 10, 1998]

§ 25.2702–2 Definitions and valuation rules.

(a) Definitions. The following definitions apply for purposes of section 2702 and the regulations thereunder.

(1) *Member of the family.* With respect to any individual, member of the family means the individual's spouse, any ancestor or lineal descendant of the individual or the individual's spouse, any brother or sister of the individual, and any spouse of the foregoing.

(2) *Transfer in trust.* A transfer in trust includes a transfer to a new or existing trust and an assignment of an interest in an existing trust. Transfer in trust does not include—

(i) The exercise, release or lapse of a power of appointment over trust property that is not a transfer under chapter 12; or

(ii) The execution of a qualified disclaimer (as defined in section 2518).

(3) *Retained.* Retained means held by the same individual both before and after the transfer in trust. In the case of the creation of a term interest, any interest in the property held by the transferor immediately after the transfer is treated as held both before and after the transfer.

(4) *Interest.* An interest in trust includes a power with respect to a trust if the existence of the power would cause any portion of a transfer to be treated as an incomplete gift under chapter 12.

(5) *Holder.* The holder is the person to whom the annuity or unitrust interest is payable during the fixed term of that interest. References to holder shall also include the estate of that person.

(6) *Qualified interest.* Qualified interest means a qualified annuity interest, a qualified unitrust interest, or a qualified remainder interest. If a transferor retains a power to revoke a qualified annuity interest or qualified unitrust interest of the transferor's spouse, then the revocable qualified annuity or unitrust interest of the transferor's spouse is treated as a retained qualified interest of the transferor. In order for the transferor to be treated as having retained a qualified interest under the preceding sentence, the interest of the transferor's spouse (the successor holder) must be an interest that meets the requirements of a qualified annuity interest in accordance with § 25.2702–3(b) and (d), or a qualified unitrust interest in accordance with § 25.2702–3(c) and (d), but for the transferor's retained power to revoke the interest.

(7) *Qualified annuity interest.* Qualified annuity interest means an interest that meets all the requirements of § 25.2702–3(b) and (d).

(8) *Qualified unitrust interest.* Qualified unitrust interest means an interest that meets all the requirements of § 25.2702–3(c) and (d).

(9) *Qualified remainder interest.* Qualified remainder interest means an interest that meets all the requirements of § 25.2702–3(f).

(10) *Governing instrument.* Governing instrument means the instrument or instruments creating and governing the operation of the trust arrangement.

(b) Valuation of retained interests. (1) *In general.* Except as provided in paragraphs (b)(2) and (c) of this section, the value of any interest retained by the transferor or an applicable family member is zero.

(2) *Qualified interest.* The value of a qualified annuity interest and a qualified remainder interest following a qualified annuity interest are determined under section 7520. The value of a qualified unitrust interest and a qualified remainder interest following a qualified unitrust interest are determined as if they were interests described in section 664.

(c) Valuation of a term interest in certain tangible property. (1) *In general.* If section 2702 applies to a transfer in trust of tangible property described in paragraph (c)(2) of this section ("tangible property"), the value of a retained term interest (other than a qualified interest) is not determined under section 7520 but is the amount the transferor establishes as the amount a willing buyer would pay a willing seller for the interest, each having reasonable knowledge of the relevant facts and neither being under any compulsion to buy or sell. If the transferor cannot reasonably establish the value of the term interest pursuant to this paragraph (c)(1), the interest is valued at zero.

(2) *Tangible property subject to rule.* (i) *In general.* Except as provided in paragraph (c)(2)(ii) of this section, paragraph (c)(1) of this section applies only to tangible property—

(A) For which no deduction for depreciation or depletion would be allowable if the property were used in a trade or business or held for the production of income; and

(B) As to which the failure to exercise any rights under the term interest would not increase the value of the property passing at the end of the term interest.

(ii) *Exception for de minimis amounts of depreciable property.* In determining whether property meets the requirements of this paragraph (c)(2) at the time of the transfer in trust, improvements that would otherwise cause the property not to qualify are ignored if the fair market value of the improvements, in the aggregate, do not exceed 5 percent of the fair market value of the entire property.

(3) *Evidence of value of property.* The best evidence of the value of any term interest to which this paragraph (c) applies is actual sales or rentals that are comparable both as to the nature and character of the property and the duration of the term interest. Little weight is accorded appraisals in the absence of such evidence. Amounts determined under section 7520 are not evidence of what a willing buyer would pay a willing seller for the interest.

(4) *Conversion of property*—(i) *In general.* Except as provided in paragraph (c)(4)(iii) of this section, if a term interest in property is valued under paragraph (c)(1) of this section, and during the term the property is converted into property a term interest in which would not qualify for valuation under paragraph (c)(1) of this section, the conversion is treated as a transfer for no consideration for purposes of chapter 12 of the value of the unexpired portion of the term interest.

(ii) *Value of unexpired portion of term interest.* For purposes of paragraph (c)(4)(i) of this section, the value of the unexpired portion of a term interest is the amount that bears the same relation to the value of the term interest as of the date of conversion (determined under section 7520 using the rate in effect under section 7520 on the date of the original transfer and the fair market value of the property as of the date of the original transfer) as the value of the term interest as of the date of the original transfer (determined under paragraph (c)(1) of this section) bears to the value of the term interest as of the date of the original transfer (determined under section 7520).

(iii) *Conversion to qualified annuity interest.* The conversion of tangible property previously valued under paragraph (c)(1) of this section into property a term interest in which would not qualify for valuation under paragraph (c)(1) of this section is not a transfer of the value of the unexpired portion of the term interest if the interest thereafter meets the requirements of a qualified annuity interest. The rules of § 25.2702–5(d)(8) (including governing instrument requirements) apply for purposes of determining the amount of the annuity payment required to be made and the determination of whether the interest meets the requirements of a qualified annuity interest.

(5) *Additions or improvements to property*—(i) *Additions or improvements substantially affecting nature of property.* If an addition or improvement is made to property a term interest in which was valued under paragraph (c)(1) of this section, and the addition or improvement affects the nature of the property to such an extent that the property would not be treated as property meeting the requirements of paragraph (c)(2) of this section if the property had included the addition or improvement at the time it was transferred, the entire property is deemed, for purposes of paragraph (c)(4) of this section, to convert (effective as of the date the addition or improvement is commenced) into property a term interest in which would not qualify for valuation under paragraph (c)(1) of this section.

(ii) *Other additions or improvements.* If an addition or improvement is made to property, a term interest in which was valued under paragraph (c)(1) of this section, and the addition or improvement does not affect the nature of the property to such an extent that the property would not be treated as property meeting the requirements of paragraph (c)(2) of this section if the property had included the addition or improvement at the time it was transferred, the addition or improvement is treated as an additional transfer (effective as of the date the addition or improvement is commenced) subject to § 25.2702–2(b)(1).

(d) Examples. (1) The following examples illustrate the rules of § 25.2702–1 and § 25.2702–2. Each example assumes that all applicable requirements of those sections not specifically described in the example are met.

Example (1). A transfers property to an irrevocable trust, retaining the right to receive the income of the trust for 10 years. On the expiration of the 10-year term, the trust is to terminate and the trust corpus is to be paid to A's child. However, if A dies during the 10-year term, the entire trust corpus is to be paid to A's estate. Each retained interest is valued at zero because it is not a qualified interest. Thus, the amount of A's gift is the fair market value of the property transferred to the trust.

Example (2). A transfers property to an irrevocable trust, retaining a 10-year annuity interest that meets the requirements set forth in § 25.2702–3 for a qualified annuity interest. Upon expiration of the 10-year term, the trust is to terminate and the trust corpus is to be paid to A's child. The amount of A's gift is the fair market value of the property transferred to the trust less the value of the retained qualified annuity interest determined under section 7520.

Example (3). D transfers property to an irrevocable trust under which the income is payable to D's spouse for life. Upon the death of D's spouse, the trust is to terminate and the trust corpus is to be paid to D's child. D retains no interest in the trust. Although the spouse is an applicable family member of D under section 2702, the spouse has not retained an interest in the trust because the spouse did not hold the interest both before and after the transfer. Section 2702 does not apply because neither the transferor nor an applicable family member has retained an interest in the trust. The result is the same whether or not D elects to treat the transfer as a transfer of qualified terminable interest property under section 2056(b)(7).

Example (4). A transfers property to an irrevocable trust, under which the income is to be paid to A for life. Upon termination of the trust, the trust corpus is to be distributed to A's child. A also retains certain powers over principal that cause the transfer to be wholly incomplete for federal gift tax purposes. Section 2702 does not apply because no portion of the transfer would be treated as a completed gift.

Example (5). The facts are the same as in Example 4, except that the trust is divided into separate fractional shares and A's retained powers apply to only one of the shares. Section 2702 applies except with respect to the share of the trust as to which A's retained powers cause the transfer to be an incomplete gift.

(2) The following facts apply for Examples 6 through 8 (examples illustrating § 25.2702–2(c)—tangible property exception):

Facts. A transfers a painting having a fair market value of $2,000,000 to A's child, B, retaining the use of the painting for 10 years. The painting does not possess an ascertainable useful life. Assume that the painting would not be depreciable if it were used in a trade or business or held for the production of income. Assume that the value of A's term interest, determined under section 7520, is $1,220,000, and that A establishes that a willing buyer of A's interest would pay $500,000 for the interest.

Example (6). A's term interest is not a qualified interest under § 25.2702–3. However, because of the nature of the property, A's failure to exercise A's rights with regard to the painting would not be expected to cause the value of the painting to be higher than it would otherwise be at the time it passes to B. Accordingly, A's interest is valued under § 25.2702–2(c)(1) at $500,000. The amount of A's gift is $1,500,000, the difference between the fair market value of the painting and the amount determined under § 25.2702–2(c)(1).

Example (7). Assume that the only evidence produced by A to establish the value of A's 10-year term interest is the amount paid by a museum for the right to use a comparable painting for 1 year. A asserts that the value of the 10-year term is 10 times the value of the 1-year term. A has not established the value of the 10-year term interest because a series of short-term rentals the aggregate duration of which equals the duration of the actual term interest does not establish what a willing buyer would pay a willing seller for the 10-year term interest. However, the value of the 10-year term interest is not less than the value of the 1-year term because it can be assumed that a willing buyer would pay no less for a 10-year term interest than a 1-year term interest.

Example (8). Assume that after 24 months A and B sell the painting for $2,000,000 and invest the proceeds in a portfolio of securities. A continues to hold an income interest in the securities for the duration of the 10-year term. Under § 25.2702–2(c)(4) the conversion of the painting into a type of property a term interest in which would not qualify for valuation under § 25.2702–2(c)(1) is treated as a transfer by A of the value of the unexpired portion of A's original term interest, unless the property is thereafter held in a trust meeting the requirements of a qualified annuity interest. Assume that the value of A's remaining term interest in $2,000,000 (determined under section 7520 using the section 7520 rate in effect on the date of the original transfer) is $1,060,000. The value of the unexpired portion of A's interest is $434,426, the amount that bears the same relation to $1,060,000 as $500,000 (the value of A's interest as of the date of the original transfer determined under paragraph (c)(1) of this section) bears to $1,220,000 (the value of A's interest as of the date of the original transfer determined under section 7520).

[T.D. 8395, 57 FR 4265, Feb. 4, 1992; T.D. 9181, 70 FR 9223, Feb. 25, 2005]

§ 25.2702–3 Qualified interests.

(a) In general. This section provides rules for determining if an interest is a qualified annuity interest, a qualified unitrust interest, or a qualified remainder interest.

(b) Special rules for qualified annuity interests. An interest is a qualified annuity interest only if it meets the requirements of this paragraph and paragraph (d) of this section.

(1) *Payment of annuity amount.* (i) *In general.* A qualified annuity interest is an irrevocable right to receive a fixed amount. The annuity amount must be payable to (or for the benefit of) the holder of the annuity interest at least annually. A right of withdrawal, whether or not cumulative, is not a qualified annuity interest. Issuance of a note, other debt instrument, option, or other similar financial arrangement, directly or indirectly, in satisfaction of the annuity amount does not constitute payment of the annuity amount.

(ii) *Fixed amount.* A fixed amount means—

(A) A stated dollar amount payable periodically, but not less frequently than annually, but only to the extent the amount does not exceed 120 percent of the stated dollar amount payable in the preceding year; or

(B) A fixed fraction or percentage of the initial fair market value of the property transferred to the trust, as finally determined for federal tax purposes, payable periodically but not less frequently than annually, but only to the extent the fraction or percentage does not exceed 120 percent of the fixed fraction or percentage payable in the preceding year.

(iii) *Income in excess of the annuity amount.* An annuity interest does not fail to be a qualified annuity interest merely because the trust permits income in excess of the amount required to pay the annuity amount to be paid to or for the benefit of the holder of the qualified annuity interest. Nevertheless, the right to receive the excess income is not a qualified interest and is not taken into account in valuing the qualified annuity interest.

(2) *Incorrect valuations of trust property.* If the annuity is stated in terms of a fraction or percentage of the initial fair market value of the trust property, the governing instrument must contain provisions meeting the requirements of § 1.664–2(a)(1)(iii) of this chapter (relating to adjustments for any incorrect determination of the fair market value of the property in the trust).

(3) *Period for payment of annuity amount.* The annuity amount may be payable based on either the anniversary date of the creation of the trust or the taxable year of the trust. In either situation, the annuity amount may be paid annually or more frequently, such as semi-annually, quarterly, or monthly. If the payment is made based on the anniversary date, proration of the annuity amount is required only if the last period during which the annuity is payable to the grantor is a period of less than 12 months. If the payment is made based on the taxable year, proration of the annuity amount is required for each short taxable year of the trust during the grantor's term. The prorated amount is the annual annuity amount multiplied by a fraction, the numerator of which is the number of days in the short period and the denominator of which is 365 (366 if February 29 is a day included in the numerator).

(4) *Payment of the annuity amount in certain circumstances.* An annuity amount payable based on the

anniversary date of the creation of the trust must be paid no later than 105 days after the anniversary date. An annuity amount payable based on the taxable year of the trust may be paid after the close of the taxable year, provided the payment is made no later than the date by which the trustee is required to file the Federal income tax return of the trust for the taxable year (without regard to extensions). If the trustee reports for the taxable year pursuant to § 1.671–4(b) of this chapter, the annuity payment must be made no later than the date by which the trustee would have been required to file the Federal income tax return of the trust for the taxable year (without regard to extensions) had the trustee reported pursuant to § 1.671–4(a) of this chapter.

(5) *Additional contributions prohibited.* The governing instrument must prohibit additional contributions to the trust.

(c) Special rules for qualified unitrust interests. An interest is a qualified unitrust interest only if it meets the requirements of this paragraph and paragraph (d) of this section.

(1) *Payment of unitrust amount.* (i) *In general.* A qualified unitrust interest is an irrevocable right to receive payment periodically, but not less frequently than annually, of a fixed percentage of the net fair market value of the trust assets, determined annually. For rules relating to computation of the net fair market value of the trust assets see § 25.2522(c)–3(c)(2)(vii). The unitrust amount must be payable to (or for the benefit of) the holder of the unitrust interest at least annually. A right of withdrawal, whether or not cumulative, is not a qualified unitrust interest. Issuance of a note, other debt instrument, option, or other similar financial arrangement, directly or indirectly, in satisfaction of the unitrust amount does not constitute payment of the unitrust amount.

(ii) *Fixed percentage.* A fixed percentage is a fraction or percentage of the net fair market value of the trust assets, determined annually, payable periodically but not less frequently than annually, but only to the extent the fraction or percentage does not exceed 120 percent of the fixed fraction or percentage payable in the preceding year.

(iii) *Income in excess of unitrust amount.* A unitrust interest does not fail to be a qualified unitrust interest merely because the trust permits income in excess of the amount required to pay the unitrust amount to be paid to or for the benefit of the holder of the qualified unitrust interest. Nevertheless, the right to receive the excess income is not a qualified interest and is not taken into account in valuing the qualified unitrust interest.

(2) *Incorrect valuations of trust property.* The governing instrument must contain provisions meeting the requirements of § 1.664–3(a)(1)(iii) of this chapter (relating to the incorrect determination of the fair market value of the property in the trust).

(3) *Period for payment of unitrust amount.* The unitrust amount may be payable based on either the anniversary date of the creation of the trust or the taxable year of the trust. In either situation, the unitrust amount may be paid annually or more frequently, such as semi-annually, quarterly, or monthly. If the payment is made based on the anniversary date, proration of the unitrust amount is required only if the last period during which the annuity is payable to the grantor is a period of less than 12 months. If the payment is made based on the taxable year, proration of the unitrust amount is required for each short taxable year of the trust during the grantor's term. The prorated amount is the annual unitrust amount multiplied by a fraction, the numerator of which is the number of days in the short period and the denominator of which is 365 (366 if February 29 is a day included in the numerator).

(4) *Payment of the unitrust amount in certain circumstances.* A unitrust amount payable based on the anniversary date of the creation of the trust must be paid no later than 105 days after the anniversary date. A unitrust amount payable based on the taxable year of the trust may be paid after the close of the taxable year, provided the payment is made no later than the date by which the trustee is required to file the Federal income tax return of the trust for the taxable year (without regard to extensions). If the trustee reports for the taxable year pursuant to § 1.671–4(b) of this chapter, the unitrust payment must be made no later than the date by which the trustee would have been required to file the Federal income tax return of the trust for the taxable year (without regard to extensions) had the trustee reported pursuant to § 1.671–4(a) of this chapter.

(d) Requirements applicable to qualified annuity interests and qualified unitrust interests. (1) *In general.* To be a qualified annuity or unitrust interest, an interest must be a qualified annuity interest in every respect or a qualified unitrust interest in every respect. For example, if the interest consists of the right to receive each year a payment equal to the lesser of a fixed amount of the initial trust assets or a fixed percentage of the annual value of the trust assets, the interest is not a qualified interest. If, however, the interest consists of the right to receive each year a payment equal to the greater of a stated dollar amount or a fixed percentage of the initial trust assets or a fixed percentage of the annual value of the trust assets, the interest is a qualified interest that is valued at the greater of the two values. To be a qualified interest, the interest must meet the definition of and function exclusively as a qualified interest from the creation of the trust.

(2) *Contingencies.* A holder's qualified interest must be payable in any event to or for the benefit of the holder for the fixed term of that interest. Thus, payment of the interest cannot be subject to any contingency other than either the survival of the holder until the commencement, or throughout the term, of that holder's interest, or, in the case of a revocable interest described in § 25.2702–2(a)(6), the transferor's right to revoke the qualified interest of that transferor's spouse.

(3) *Amounts payable to other persons.* The governing instrument must prohibit distributions from the trust to or for the benefit of any person other than the holder of the qualified annuity or unitrust interest during the term of the qualified interest.

(4) *Term of the annuity or unitrust interest.* The governing instrument must fix the term of the annuity or unitrust and the term of the interest must be fixed and ascertainable at the creation of the trust. The term must be for the life of the holder, for a specified term of years, or for the shorter (but not the longer) of those periods. Successive term interests for the benefit of the same individual are treated as the same term interest.

(5) *Commutation.* The governing instrument must prohibit commutation (prepayment) of the interest of the holder.

(6) *Use of debt obligations to satisfy the annuity or unitrust payment obligation*—(i) *In general.* In the case of a trust created on or after September 20, 1999, the trust instrument must prohibit the trustee from issuing a note, other debt instrument, option, or other similar financial arrangement in satisfaction of the annuity or unitrust payment obligation.

(ii) *Special rule in the case of a trust created prior to September 20, 1999.* In the case of a trust created prior to September 20, 1999, the interest will be treated as a qualified interest under section 2702(b) if—

(A) Notes, other debt instruments, options, or similar financial arrangements are not issued after September 20, 1999, to satisfy the annuity or unitrust payment obligation; and

(B) Any notes or any other debt instruments that were issued to satisfy the annual payment obligation on or prior to September 20, 1999, are paid in full by December 31, 1999, and any option or similar financial arrangement issued to satisfy the annual payment obligation is terminated by December 31, 1999, such that the grantor receives cash or other trust assets in satisfaction of the payment obligation. For purposes of the preceding sentence, an option will be considered terminated only if the grantor receives cash or other trust assets equal in value to the greater of the required annuity or unitrust payment plus interest computed under section 7520 of the Internal Revenue Code, or the fair market value of the option.

(e) Examples. The following examples illustrate the rules of paragraphs (b), (c), and (d) of this section. Each example assumes that all applicable requirements for a qualified interest are met unless otherwise specifically stated.

Example (1). A transfers property to an irrevocable trust, retaining the right to receive the greater of $10,000 or the trust income in each year for a term of 10-years. Upon expiration of the 10-year term, the trust is to terminate and the entire trust corpus is to be paid to A's child, provided that if A dies within the 10-year term the trust corpus is to be paid to A's estate. A's annual payment right is a qualified annuity interest to the extent of the right to receive $10,000 per year for 10 years or until A's prior death, and is valued under section 7520 without regard to the right to receive any income in excess of $10,000 per year. The contingent reversion is valued at zero. The amount of A's gift is the fair market value of the property transferred to the trust less the value of the qualified annuity interest.

Example (2). U transfers property to an irrevocable trust, retaining the right to receive $10,000 in each of years 1 through 3, $12,000 in each of years 4 through 6, and $15,000 in each of years 7 through 10. The interest is a qualified annuity interest to the extent of U's right to receive $10,000 per year in years 1 through 3, $12,000 in years 4 through 6, $14,400 in year 7, and $15,000 in years 8 through 10, because those amounts represent the lower of the amount actually payable each year or an amount that does not exceed 120 percent of the stated dollar amount for the preceding year.

Example (3). S transfers property to an irrevocable trust, retaining the right to receive $50,000 in each of years 1 through 3 and $10,000 in each of years 4 through 10. S's entire retained interest is a qualified annuity interest.

Example (4). R transfers property to an irrevocable trust retaining the right to receive annually an amount equal to the lesser of 8 percent of the initial fair market value of the trust property or the trust income for the year. R's annual payment right is not a qualified annuity interest to any extent because R does not have the irrevocable right to receive a fixed amount for each year of the term.

Example (5). A transfers property to an irrevocable trust, retaining the right to receive 5 percent of the net fair market value of the trust property, valued annually, for 10 years. If A dies within the 10-year term, the unitrust amount is to be paid to A's estate for the balance of the term. The interest of A (and A's estate) to receive the unitrust amount for the specified term of 10 years in all events is a qualified unitrust interest for a term of 10 years.

Example (6). The facts are the same as in Example 5, except that if A dies within the 10-year term the unitrust amount will be paid to A's estate for an additional 35 years. As in Example 5, the interest of A (and A's estate) to receive the unitrust amount for a specified term of 10 years in all events is a qualified unitrust interest for a term of 10 years. However, the right of A's estate to continue to receive the unitrust amount after the expiration of the 10-year term if A dies within that 10-year period is not fixed and ascertainable at the creation of the interest and is not a qualified unitrust interest.

Example (7). B transfers property to an irrevocable trust retaining the right to receive annually an amount equal to 8 percent of the initial fair market value of the trust property for 10 years. Upon expiration of the 10-year term, the trust is to terminate and the entire trust corpus is to be paid to B's child. The governing instrument provides that income in excess of the annuity amount may be paid to B's child in the trustee's discretion. B's interest is not a qualified annuity interest to any extent because a person other than the individual holding the term interest may receive distributions from the trust during the term.

Example (8). A transfers property to an irrevocable trust, retaining the right to receive an annuity equal to 6 percent of the initial net fair market value of the trust property for 10 years, or until A's prior death. At the expiration of the 10-year term, or on A's death prior to the expiration of the 10-year term, the annuity is to be paid to B, A's spouse, if then living, for 10 years or until B's prior death. A retains an inter vivos and testamentary power to revoke B's interest during the initial 10-year term. If not exercised by A during the initial 10-year term (whether during A's life or on A's death), A's right to revoke B's interest will lapse upon either A's death during the 10-year term, or the expiration of A's 10-year term (assuming A survives the term). Upon expiration of B's interest (or on the expiration of A's interest if A revokes B's interest or if B predeceases A), the trust terminates and the trust corpus is payable to A's child. Because A has made a completed gift of the remainder interest, the transfer of property to the trust is not incomplete as to all interests in the property and section 2702 applies. A's annuity interest (A's right to receive the annuity for 10 years, or until A's prior death) is a retained interest that is a qualified annuity interest under paragraphs (b) and (d) of this section. In addition, because A has retained the power to revoke B's interest, B's interest is treated as an interest retained by A for purposes of section 2702. B's successive annuity interest otherwise satisfies the requirements for a qualified interest contained in paragraph (d) of this section, but for A's power to revoke. The term of B's interest is specified in the governing instrument and is fixed and ascertainable at the creation of the trust, and B's right to receive the annuity is contingent only on B's survival, and A's power to revoke. Following the expiration of A's interest, the annuity is to be paid for a 10-year term or for B's (the successor holder's) life, whichever is shorter. Accordingly, A is treated as retaining B's revocable qualified annuity interest pursuant to § 25.2702–2(a)(6). Because both A's interest and B's interest are treated as qualified interests retained by A, the value of the gift is the value of the property transferred to the trust less the value of both A's qualified interest and B's qualified interest (subject to A's power to revoke), each valued as a single-life annuity. If A survives the 10-year term without having revoked B's interest, then A's power to revoke lapses and A will make a completed gift to B at that time. Further, if A revokes B's interest prior to the commencement of that interest, A is treated as making an additional completed gift at that time to A's child. In either case, the amount of the gift would be the present value of B's interest determined under section 7520 and the applicable regulations, as of the date the revocation power lapses or the interest is revoked. See § 25.2511–2(f).

Example (9). (i) A transfers property to an irrevocable trust, retaining the right to receive 6 percent of the initial net fair market value of the trust property for 10 years, or until A's prior death. If A survives the 10-year term, the trust terminates and the trust corpus is payable to A's child. If A dies prior to the expiration of the 10-year term, the annuity is payable to B, A's spouse, if then living, for the balance of the 10-year term, or until B's prior death. A retains the right to revoke B's interest. Upon expiration of B's interest (or upon A's death if A revokes B's interest or if B predeceases A), the trust terminates and the trust corpus is payable to A's child. As is the case in Example 8, A's retained annuity interest (A's right to receive the annuity for 10 years, or until A's prior death) is a qualified annuity interest under paragraphs (b) and (d) of this section. However, B's interest does not meet the requirements of paragraph (d) of this section. The term of B's annuity is not fixed and ascertainable at the creation of the trust, because it is not payable for the life of B, a specified term of years, or for the shorter of those periods. Rather, B's annuity is payable for an unspecified period that will depend upon the number of years left in the original term after A's death. Further, B's annuity is payable only if A dies prior to the expiration of the 10-year term. Thus, payment of B's annuity is not dependent solely on B's survival, but rather is dependent on A's failure to survive.

(ii) Accordingly, the amount of the gift is the fair market value of the property transferred to the trust reduced by the value of A's qualified interest (A's right to receive the stated annuity for 10 years or until A's prior death). B's interest is not a qualified interest and is thus valued at zero under section 2702.

(f) Qualified remainder interest. (1) *Requirements.* An interest is a qualified remainder interest only if it meets all of the following requirements:

(i) It is a qualified remainder interest in every respect.

(ii) It meets the definition of and functions exclusively as a qualified interest from the creation of the interest.

(iii) It is non-contingent. For this purpose, an interest is non-contingent only if it is payable to the beneficiary or the beneficiary's estate in all events.

(iv) All interests in the trust, other than noncontingent remainder interests, are qualified annuity interests or qualified unitrust interests. Thus, an interest is a qualified remainder interest only if the governing instrument does not permit payment of income in excess of the annuity or unitrust amount to the holder of the qualified annuity or unitrust interest.

(2) *Remainder interest.* Remainder interest is the right to receive all or a fractional share of the trust property on termination of all or a fractional share of the trust. Remainder interest includes a reversion. A transferor's right to receive an amount that is a stated or pecuniary amount is not a remainder interest. Thus, the right to receive the original value of the trust corpus (or a fractional share) is not a remainder interest.

(3) *Examples.* The following examples illustrate rules of this paragraph (f). Each example assumes that all applicable requirements of a qualified interest are met unless otherwise specifically stated.

Example (1). A transfers property to an irrevocable trust. The income of the trust is payable to A's child for life. On the death of A's child, the trust is to terminate and the trust corpus is to be paid to A. A's remainder interest is not a qualified remainder interest because the interest of A's child is neither a qualified annuity interest nor a qualified unitrust interest.

Example (2). The facts are the same as in Example 1, except that A's child has the right to receive the greater of the income of the trust or $10,000 per year. A's remainder interest is not a qualified remainder interest because the right of A's child to receive income in excess of the annuity amount is not a qualified interest.

Example (3). A transfers property to an irrevocable trust. The trust provides a qualified annuity interest to A's child for 12 years. An amount equal to the initial value of the trust corpus is to be paid to A at the end of that period and the balance is to be paid to A's grandchild. A's interest is not a qualified remainder interest because the amount A is to receive is not a fractional share of the trust property.

Example (4). U transfers property to an irrevocable trust. The trust provides a qualified unitrust interest to U's child for 15 years, at which time the trust terminates and the trust corpus is paid to U or, if U is not then living, to U's child. Because U's remainder interest is contingent, it is not a qualified remainder interest.

[T.D. 8395, 57 FR 4267, Feb. 9, 1992; T.D. 8536, 59 FR 23157, May 5, 1994; T.D. 8633, 60 FR 66090, Dec. 21, 1995; T.D. 8899, 65 FR 53588, Sept. 5, 2000; 65 FR 70792, Nov. 28, 2000; T.D. 9181, 70 FR 9224, Feb. 25, 2005]

§ 25.2702–4 Certain property treated as held in trust.

(a) In general. For purposes of section 2702, a transfer of an interest in property with respect to which there are one or more term interests is treated as a transfer in trust. A term interest is one of a series of successive (as contrasted with concurrent) interests. Thus, a life interest in property or an interest in property for a term of years is a term interest. However, a term interest does not include a fee interest in property merely because it is held as a tenant in common, a tenant by the entireties, or a joint tenant with right of survivorship.

(b) Leases. A leasehold interest in property is not a term interest to the extent the lease is for full and adequate consideration (without regard to section 2702). A lease will be considered for full and adequate consideration if, under all the facts and circumstances as of the time the lease is entered into or extended, a good faith effort is made to determine the fair rental value of the property and the terms of the lease conform to the value so determined.

(c) Joint purchases. Solely for purposes of section 2702, if an individual acquires a term interest in property and, in the same transaction or series of transactions, one or more members of the individual's family acquire an interest in the same property, the individual acquiring the term interest is treated as acquiring the entire property so acquired, and transferring to each of those family members the interests acquired by that family member in exchange for any consideration paid by that family member. For purposes of this paragraph (c), the amount of the individual's gift will not exceed the amount of consideration furnished by that individual for all interests in the property.

(d) Examples. The following examples illustrate rules of this section:

Example (1). A purchases a 20-year term interest in an apartment building and A's child purchases the remainder interest in the property. A and A's child each provide the portion of the purchase price equal to the value of their respective interests in the property determined under section 7520. Solely for purposes of section 2702, A is treated as acquiring the entire property and transferring the remainder interest to A's child in exchange for the portion of the purchase price provided by A's child. In determining the amount of A's gift, A's retained interest is valued at zero because it is not a qualified interest.

Example (2). K holds rental real estate valued at $100,000. K sells a remainder interest in the property to K's child, retaining the right to receive the income from the property for 20 years. Assume the purchase price paid by K's child for the remainder interest is equal to the value of the interest determined under section 7520. K's retained interest is not a qualified interest and is therefore valued at zero. K has made a gift in the amount of $100,000 less the consideration received from K's child.

Example (3). G and G's child each acquire a 50 percent undivided interest as tenants in common in an office building. The interests of G and G's child are not term interests to which section 2702 applies.

Example (4). B purchases a life estate in property from R, B's grandparent, for $100 and B's child purchases the remainder interest for $50. Assume that the value of the property is $300, the value of the life estate determined under section 7520 is $250 and the value of the remainder interest is $50. B is treated as acquiring the entire property and transferring the remainder interest to B's child. However, the amount of

B's gift is $100, the amount of consideration ($100) furnished by B for B's interest.

Example (5). H and W enter into a written agreement relative to their marital and property rights that requires W to transfer property to an irrevocable trust, the terms of which provide that the income of the trust will be paid to H for 10 years. On the expiration of the 10-year term, the trust is to terminate and the trust corpus is to be paid to W. H and W divorce within two years after the agreement is entered into. Pursuant to section 2516, the transfer to H would otherwise be deemed to be for full and adequate consideration. Section 2702 does not apply to the acquisition of the term interest by H because no member of H's family acquired an interest in the property in the same transaction or series of transactions. The result would not be the same if, on the termination of H's interest in the trust, the trust corpus were distributable to the children of H and W rather than W.

[T.D. 8395, 57 FR 4269, Feb. 4, 1992]

§ 25.2702–5 Personal residence trusts.

(a)(1) *In general.* Section 2702 does not apply to a transfer in trust meeting the requirements of this section. A transfer in trust meets the requirements of this section only if the trust is a personal residence trust (as defined in paragraph (b) of this section). A trust meeting the requirements of a qualified personal residence trust (as defined in paragraph (c) of this section) is treated as a personal residence trust. A trust of which the term holder is the grantor that otherwise meets the requirements of a personal residence trust (or a qualified personal residence trust) is not a personal residence trust (or a qualified personal residence trust) if, at the time of transfer, the term holder of the trust already holds term interests in two trusts that are personal residence trusts (or qualified personal residence trusts) of which the term holder was the grantor. For this purpose, trusts holding fractional interests in the same residence are treated as one trust.

(2) *Modification of trust.* A trust that does not comply with one or more of the regulatory requirements under paragraph (b) or (c) of this section will, nonetheless, be treated as satisfying these requirements if the trust is modified, by judicial reformation (or nonjudicial reformation if effective under state law), to comply with the requirements. In the case of a trust created after December 31, 1996, the reformation must be commenced within 90 days after the due date (including extensions) for the filing of the gift tax return reporting the transfer of the residence under section 6075 and must be completed within a reasonable time after commencement. If the reformation is not completed by the due date (including extensions) for filing the gift tax return, the grantor or grantor's spouse must attach a statement to the gift tax return stating that the reformation has been commenced or will be commenced within the 90-day period. In the case of a trust created before January 1, 1997, the reformation must be commenced within 90 days after December 23, 1997 and must be completed within a reasonable time after commencement.

(b) Personal residence trust. (1) *In general.* A personal residence trust is a trust the governing instrument of which prohibits the trust from holding, for the original duration of the term interest, any asset other than one residence to be used or held for use as a personal residence of the term holder and qualified proceeds (as defined in paragraph (b)(3) of this section). A residence is held for use as a personal residence of the term holder so long as the residence is not occupied by any other person (other than the spouse or a dependent of the term holder) and is available at all times for use by the term holder as a personal residence. A trust does not meet the requirements of this section if, during the original duration of the term interest, the residence may be sold or otherwise transferred by the trust or may be used for a purpose other than as a personal residence of the term holder. In addition, the trust does not meet the requirements of this section unless the governing instrument prohibits the trust from selling or transferring the residence, directly or indirectly, to the grantor, the grantor's spouse, or an entity controlled by the grantor or the grantor's spouse, at any time after the original duration of the term interest during which the trust is a grantor trust. For purposes of the preceding sentence, a sale or transfer to another grantor trust of the grantor or the grantor's spouse is considered a sale or transfer to the grantor or the grantor's spouse; however, a distribution (for no consideration) upon or after the expiration of the original duration of the term interest to another grantor trust of the grantor or the grantor's spouse pursuant to the express terms of the trust will not be considered a sale or transfer to the grantor or the grantor's spouse if such other grantor trust prohibits the sale or transfer of the property to the grantor, the grantor's spouse, or an entity controlled by the grantor or the grantor's spouse. In the event the grantor dies prior to the expiration of the original duration of the term interest, this paragraph (b)(1) does not apply to the distribution (for no consideration) of the residence to any person (including the grantor's estate) pursuant to the express terms of the trust or pursuant to the exercise of a power retained by the grantor under the terms of the trust. Further, this paragraph (b)(1) does not apply to any outright distribution (for no consideration) of the residence to the grantor's spouse after the expiration of the original duration of the term interest pursuant to the express terms of the trust. For purposes of this paragraph (b)(1), a grantor trust is a trust treated as owned in whole or in part by the grantor or the grantor's spouse pursuant to sections 671 through 678, and control is defined in § 25.2701–2(b)(5)(ii) and (iii). Expenses of the trust whether or not attributable to trust principal may be paid directly by the term holder of the trust.

(2) *Personal residence.* (i) *In general.* For purposes of this paragraph (b), a personal residence of a term holder is either—

(A) The principal residence of the term holder (within the meaning of section 1034);

(B) One other residence of the term holder (within the meaning of section 280A(d)(1) but without regard to section 280A(d)(2)); or

(C) An undivided fractional interest in either.

(ii) *Additional property.* A personal residence may include appurtenant structures used by the term holder for residential purposes and adjacent land not in excess of that which is reasonably appropriate for residential purposes (taking into account the residence's size and location). The fact that a residence is subject to a mortgage does not affect its status as a personal residence. The term personal residence does not include any personal property (e.g., household furnishings).

(iii) *Use of residence.* A residence is a personal residence only if its primary use is as a residence of the term holder when occupied by the term holder. The principal residence of the term holder will not fail to meet the requirements of the preceding sentence merely because a portion of the residence is used in an activity meeting the requirements of section 280A(c)(1) or (4) (relating to deductibility of expenses related to certain uses), provided that such use is secondary to use of the residence as a residence. A residence is not used primarily as a residence if it is used to provide transient lodging and substantial services are provided in connection with the provision of lodging (e.g. a hotel or a bed and breakfast). A residence is not a personal residence if, during any period not occupied by the term holder, its primary use is other than as a residence.

(iv) *Interests of spouses in the same residence.* If spouses hold interests in the same residence (including community property interests), the spouses may transfer their interests in the residence (or a fractional portion of their interests in the residence) to the same personal residence trust, provided that the governing instrument prohibits any person other than one of the spouses from holding a term interest in the trust concurrently with the other spouse.

(3) *Qualified proceeds.* Qualified proceeds means the proceeds payable as a result of damage to, or destruction or involuntary conversion (within the meaning of section 1033) of, the residence held by a personal residence trust, provided that the governing instrument requires that the proceeds (including any income thereon) be reinvested in a personal residence within two years from the date on which the proceeds are received.

(c) Qualified personal residence trust. (1) *In general.* A qualified personal residence trust is a trust meeting all the requirements of this paragraph (c). These requirements must be met by provisions in the governing instrument, and these governing instrument provisions must by their terms continue in effect during the existence of any term interest in the trust.

(2) *Personal residence.* (i) *In general.* For purposes of this paragraph (c), a personal residence of a term holder is either—

(A) The principal residence of the term holder (within the meaning of section 1034);

(B) One other residence of the term holder (within the meaning of section 280A(d)(1) but without regard to section 280A(d)(2)); or

(C) An undivided fractional interest in either.

(ii) *Additional property.* A personal residence may include appurtenant structures used by the term holder for residential purposes and adjacent land not in excess of that which is reasonably appropriate for residential purposes (taking into account the residence's size and location). The fact that a residence is subject to a mortgage does not affect its status as a personal residence. The term personal residence does not include any personal property (e.g., household furnishings).

(iii) *Use of residence.* A residence is a personal residence only if its primary use is as a residence of the term holder when occupied by the term holder. The principal residence of the term holder will not fail to meet the requirements of the preceding sentence merely because a portion of the residence is used in an activity meeting the requirements of section 280A(c)(1) or (4) (relating to deductibility of expenses related to certain uses), provided that such use is secondary to use of the residence as a residence. A residence is not used primarily as a residence if it is used to provide transient lodging and substantial services are provided in connection with the provision of lodging (e.g., a hotel or a bed and breakfast). A residence is not a personal residence if, during any period not occupied by the term holder, its primary use is other than as a residence. A residence is not a personal residence if, during any period not occupied by the term holder, its primary use is other than as a residence.

(iv) *Interests of spouses in the same residence.* If spouses hold interests in the same residence (including community property interests), the spouses may transfer their interests in the residence (or a fractional portion of their interests in the residence) to the same qualified personal residence trust, provided that the governing instrument prohibits any person other than one of the spouses from holding a term interest in the trust concurrently with the other spouse.

(3) *Income of the trust.* The governing instrument must require that any income of the trust be distributed to the term holder not less frequently than annually.

(4) *Distributions from the trust to other persons.* The governing instrument must prohibit distributions of corpus to any beneficiary other than the transferor prior to the expiration of the retained term interest.

(5) *Assets of the trust.* (i) *In general.* Except as otherwise provided in paragraphs (c)(5)(ii) and (c)(8) of this section, the governing instrument must prohibit the trust from holding, for the entire term of the trust, any asset other than one residence to be used or held for use (within the meaning of paragraph (c)(7)(i) of this section) as a personal residence of the term holder (the "residence").

(ii) *Assets other than personal residence.* Except as otherwise provided, the governing instrument may permit a qualified personal residence trust to hold the following assets (in addition to the residence) in the amounts and in the manner described in this paragraph (c)(5)(ii):

(A) *Additions of cash for payment of expenses, etc. (1) Additions.* The governing instrument may permit additions of cash to the trust, and may permit the trust to hold additions of cash in a separate account, in an amount which, when added to the cash already held in the account for such purposes, does not exceed the amount required:

(i) For payment of trust expenses (including mortgage payments) already incurred or reasonably expected to be paid by the trust within six months from the date the addition is made;

(ii) For improvements to the residence to be paid by the trust within six months from the date the addition is made; and

(iii) For purchase by the trust of the initial residence, within three months of the date the trust is created, provided that no addition may be made for this purpose, and the trust may not hold any such addition, unless the trustee has previously entered into a contract to purchase that residence; and

(iv) For purchase by the trust of a residence to replace another residence, within three months of the date the addition is made, provided that no addition may be made for this purpose, and the trust may not hold any such addition, unless the trustee has previously entered into a contract to purchase that residence.

(2) Distributions of excess cash. If the governing instrument permits additions of cash to the trust pursuant to paragraph (c)(5)(ii)(A)(1) of this section, the governing instrument must require that the trustee determine, not less frequently than quarterly, the amounts held by the trust for payment of expenses in excess of the amounts permitted by that paragraph and must require that those amounts be distributed immediately thereafter to the term holder. In addition, the governing instrument must require, upon termination of the term holder's interest in the trust, any amounts held by the trust for the purposes permitted by para-

graph (c)(5)(ii)(A)(1) of this section that are not used to pay trust expenses due and payable on the date of termination (including expenses directly related to termination) be distributed outright to the term holder within 30 days of termination.

(B) *Improvements.* The governing instrument may permit improvements to the residence to be added to the trust and may permit the trust to hold such improvements, provided that the residence, as improved, meets the requirements of a personal residence.

(C) *Sale proceeds.* The governing instrument may permit the sale of the residence (except as set forth in paragraph (c)(9) of this section) and may permit the trust to hold proceeds from the sale of the residence, in a separate account.

(D) *Insurance and insurance proceeds.* The governing instrument may permit the trust to hold one or more policies of insurance on the residence. In addition, the governing instrument may permit the trust to hold, in a separate account, proceeds of insurance payable to the trust as a result of damage to or destruction of the residence. For purposes of this paragraph, amounts (other than insurance proceeds payable to the trust as a result of damage to or destruction of the residence) received as a result of the involuntary conversion (within the meaning of section 1033) of the residence are treated as proceeds of insurance.

(6) *Commutation.* The governing instrument must prohibit commutation (prepayment) of the term holder's interest.

(7) *Cessation of use as a personal residence.* (i) *In general.* The governing instrument must provide that a trust ceases to be a qualified personal residence trust if the residence ceases to be used or held for use as a personal residence of the term holder. A residence is held for use as a personal residence of the term holder so long as the residence is not occupied by any other person (other than the spouse or a dependent of the term holder) and is available at all times for use by the term holder as a personal residence. See § 25.2702–5(c)(8) for rules governing disposition of assets of a trust as to which the trust has ceased to be a qualified personal residence trust.

(ii) *Sale of personal residence.* The governing instrument must provide that the trust ceases to be a qualified personal residence trust upon sale of the residence if the governing instrument does not permit the trust to hold proceeds of sale of the residence pursuant to paragraph (c)(5)(ii)(C) of this section. If the governing instrument permits the trust to hold proceeds of sale pursuant to that paragraph, the governing instrument must provide that the trust ceases to be a qualified personal residence trust with respect to all proceeds of sale held by the trust not later than the earlier of—

(A) The date that is two years after the date of sale;

(B) The termination of the term holder's interest in the trust; or

(C) The date on which a new residence is acquired by the trust.

(iii) *Damage to or destruction of personal residence.* (A) *In general.* The governing instrument must provide that, if damage or destruction renders the residence unusable as a residence, the trust ceases to be a qualified personal residence trust on the date that is two years after the date of damage or destruction (or the date of termination of the term holder's interest in the trust, if earlier) unless, prior to such date—

(1) Replacement of or repairs to the residence are completed; or

(2) A new residence is acquired by the trust.

(B) *Insurance proceeds.* For purposes of this paragraph (C)(7)(iii), if the governing instrument permits the trust to hold proceeds of insurance received as a result of damage to or destruction of the residence pursuant to paragraph (c)(5)(ii)(D) of this section, the governing instrument must contain provisions similar to those required by paragraph (c)(7)(ii) of this section.

(8) *Disposition of trust assets on cessation as personal residence trust.* (i) *In general.* The governing instrument must provide that, within 30 days after the date on which the trust has ceased to be a qualified personal residence trust with respect to certain assets, either—

(A) The assets be distributed outright to the term holder;

(B) The assets be converted to and held for the balance of the term holder's term in a separate share of the trust meeting the requirements of a qualified annuity interest; or

(C) In the trustee's sole discretion, the trustee may elect to comply with either paragraph (c)(8)(i)(A) or (B) of this section pursuant to their terms.

(ii) *Requirements for conversion to a qualified annuity interest*—(A) *Governing instrument requirements.* For assets subject to this paragraph (c)(8) to be converted to and held as a qualified annuity interest, the governing instrument must contain all provisions required by § 25.2702–3 with respect to a qualified annuity interest.

(B) *Effective date of annuity.* The governing instrument must provide that the right of the term holder to receive the annuity amount begins on the date of sale of the residence, the date of damage to or destruction of the residence, or the date on which the residence ceases to be used or held for use as a personal residence, as the case may be ("the cessation date"). Notwithstanding the preceding sentence, the governing instrument may provide that the trustee may defer payment of any annuity amount otherwise payable after the cessation date until the date that is 30 days after the assets are converted to a qualified annuity interest under paragraph (c)(8)(i)(B) of this section ("the conversion date"); provided that any deferred payment must bear interest from the cessation date at a rate not less than the section 7520 rate in effect on the cessation date. The governing instrument may permit the trustee to reduce aggregate deferred annuity payments by the amount of income actually distributed by the trust to the term holder during the deferral period.

(C) *Determination of annuity amount. (1) In general.* The governing instrument must require that the annuity amount be no less than the amount determined under this paragraph (C).

(2) Entire trust ceases to be a qualified personal residence trust. If, on the conversion date, the assets of the trust do not include a residence used or held for use as a personal residence, the annuity may not be less than an amount determined by dividing the lesser of the value of all interests retained by the term holder (as of the date of the original transfer or transfers) or the value of all the trust assets (as of the conversion date) by an annuity factor determined—

(i) For the original term of the term holder's interest; and

(ii) At the rate used in valuing the retained interest at the time of the original transfer.

(3) Portion of trust continues as qualified personal residence trust. If, on the conversion date, the assets of the trust include a residence used or held for use as a personal residence, the annuity must not be less than the amount determined under paragraph (c)(8)(ii)(C)(2) of this section multiplied by a fraction. The numerator of the fraction is the excess of the fair market value of the trust assets on the conversion date over the fair market value of the assets as to which the trust continues as a qualified personal residence trust, and the denominator of the fraction is the fair market value of the trust assets on the conversion date.

(9) *Sale of residence to grantor, grantor's spouse, or entity controlled by grantor or grantor's spouse.* The governing instrument must prohibit the trust from selling or transferring the residence, directly or indirectly, to the grantor, the grantor's spouse, or an entity controlled by the grantor or the grantor's spouse during the retained term interest of the trust, or at any time after the retained term interest that the trust is a grantor trust. For purposes of the preceding sentence, a sale or transfer to another grantor trust of the grantor or the grantor's spouse is considered a sale or transfer to the grantor or the grantor's spouse; however, a distribution (for no consideration) upon or after the expiration of the retained term interest to another grantor trust of the grantor or the grantor's spouse pursuant to the express terms of the trust will not be considered a sale or transfer to the grantor or the grantor's spouse if such other grantor trust prohibits the sale or transfer of the property to the grantor, the grantor's spouse, or an entity controlled by the grantor or the grantor's spouse. In the event the grantor dies prior to the expiration of the retained term interest, this paragraph (c)(9) does not apply to the distribution (for no consideration) of the residence to any person (including the grantor's estate) pursuant to the express terms of the trust or pursuant to the exercise of a power retained by the grantor under the terms of the trust. Further, this paragraph (c)(9) does not apply to an outright distribution (for no consideration) of the residence to the grantor's spouse after the expiration of the retained trust term pursuant to the express terms of the trust. For purposes of this paragraph (c)(9), a grantor trust is a trust treated as owned in whole or in part by the grantor or the grant-

or's spouse pursuant to sections 671 through 678, and control is defined in § 25.2701–2(b)(5)(ii) and (iii).

(d) Examples. The following examples illustrate rules of this section. Each example assumes that all applicable requirements of a personal residence trust (or qualified personal residence trust) are met unless otherwise stated.

Example (1). C maintains C's principal place of business in one room of C's principal residence. The room meets the requirements of section 280A(c)(1) for deductibility of expenses related to such use. The residence is a personal residence.

Example (2). L owns a vacation condominium that L rents out for six months of the year, but which is treated as L's residence under section 280A(d)(1) because L occupies it for at least 18 days per year. L provides no substantial services in connection with the rental of the condominium. L transfers the condominium to an irrevocable trust, the terms of which meet the requirements of a qualified personal residence trust. L retains the right to use the condominium during L's lifetime. The trust is a qualified personal residence trust.

Example (3). W owns a 200-acre farm. The farm includes a house, barns, equipment buildings, a silo, and enclosures for confinement of farm animals. W transfers the farm to an irrevocable trust, retaining the use of the farm for 20 years, with the remainder to W's child. The trust is not a personal residence trust because the farm includes assets not meeting the requirements of a personal residence.

Example (4). A transfers A's principal residence to an irrevocable trust, retaining the right to use the residence for a 20-year term. The governing instrument of the trust does not prohibit the trust from holding personal property. The trust is not a qualified personal residence trust.

Example (5). T transfers a personal residence to a trust that meets the requirements of a qualified personal residence trust, retaining a term interest in the trust for 10 years. During the period of T's retained term interest, T is forced for health reasons to move to a nursing home. T's spouse continues to occupy the residence. If the residence is available at all times for T's use as a residence during the term (without regard to T's ability to actually use the residence), the residence continues to be held for T's use and the trust does not cease to be a qualified personal residence trust. The residence would cease to be held for use as a personal residence of T if the trustee rented the residence to an unrelated party, because the residence would no longer be available for T's use at all times.

Example (6). T transfers T's personal residence to a trust that meets the requirements of a qualified personal residence trust, retaining the right to use the residence for 12 years. On the date the residence is transferred to the trust, the fair market value of the residence is $100,000. After 6 years, the trustee sells the residence, receiving net proceeds of $250,000, and invests the proceeds of sale in common stock. After an additional eighteen months, the common stock has paid $15,000 in dividends and has a fair market value of $260,000. On that date, the trustee purchases a new residence for $200,000. On the purchase of the new residence, the trust ceases to be a qualified personal residence trust with respect to any amount not reinvested in the new residence. The governing instrument of the trust provides that the trustee, in the trustee's sole discretion, may elect either to distribute the excess proceeds or to convert the proceeds into a qualified annuity interest. The trustee elects the latter option. The amount of the annuity is the amount of the annuity that would be payable if no portion of the sale proceeds had been reinvested in a personal residence multiplied by a fraction. The numerator of the fraction is $60,000 (the amount remaining after reinvestment) and the denominator of the fraction is $260,000 (the fair market value of the trust assets on the conversion date). The obligation to pay the annuity commences on the date of sale, but payment of the annuity that otherwise would have been payable during the period between the date of sale and the date on which the trust ceased to be a qualified personal residence trust with respect to the excess proceeds may be deferred until 30 days after the date on which the new residence is purchased. Any amount deferred must bear compound interest from the date the annuity is payable at the section 7520 rate in effect on the date of sale. The $15,000 of income distributed to the term holder during that period may be used to reduce the annuity amount payable with respect to that period if the governing instrument so provides and thus reduce the amount on which compound interest is computed.

[T.D. 8395, 57 FR 4269, Feb. 4, 1992; T.D. 8395, 57 FR 11265, April 2, 1992; T.D. 8743, 62 FR 66988, Dec. 23, 1997]

§ 25.2702–6 Reduction in taxable gifts.

(a) Transfers of retained interests in trust. (1) *Inter vivos transfers.* If an individual subsequently transfers by gift an interest in trust previously valued (when held by that individual) under § 25.2702–2 (b)(1) or (c), the individual is entitled to a reduction in aggregate taxable gifts. The amount of the reduction is determined under paragraph (b) of this section. Thus, for example, if an individual transferred property to an irrevocable trust, retaining an interest in the trust that was valued at zero under § 25.2702–2(b)(1), and the individual later transfers the retained interest by gift, the individual is entitled to a reduction in aggregate taxable gifts on the subsequent transfer. For purposes of this section, aggregate taxable gifts means the aggregate sum of the individual's taxable gifts for the calendar year determined under section 2502(a)(1).

(2) *Testamentary transfers.* If either—

(i) A term interest in trust is included in an individual's gross estate solely by reason of section 2033, or

(ii) A remainder interest in trust is included in an individual's gross estate, and the interest was previously valued (when held by that individual) under § 25.2702–2(b)(1) or (c), the individual's estate is entitled to a reduction in the individual's adjusted taxable gifts in computing the Federal estate tax payable under section 2001. The amount of the reduction is determined under paragraph (b) of this section.

(3) *Gift splitting on subsequent transfer.* If an individual who is entitled to a reduction in aggregate taxable gifts (or adjusted taxable gifts) subsequently transfers the interest in a transfer treated as made one-half by the individual's spouse under section 2513, the individual may assign one-half of the amount of the reduction to the consenting spouse. The assignment must be attached to the Form 709 on which the consenting spouse reports the split gift.

(b) Amount of reduction. (1) *In general.* The amount of the reduction in aggregate taxable gifts (or adjusted taxable gifts) is the lesser of—

(i) The increase in the individual's taxable gifts resulting from the interest being valued at the time of the initial transfer under § 25.2702–2(b)(1) or (c); or

(ii) The increase in the individual's taxable gifts (or gross estate) resulting from the subsequent transfer of the interest.

(2) *Treatment of annual exclusion.* For purposes of determining the amount under paragraph (b)(1)(ii) of this section, the exclusion under section 2503(b) applies first to transfers in that year other than the transfer of the interest previously valued under § 25.2702–2(b)(1) or (c).

(3) *Overlap with section 2001.* Notwithstanding paragraph (b)(1) of this section, the amount of the reduction is reduced to the extent section 2001 would apply to reduce the amount of an individual's adjusted taxable gifts with respect to the same interest to which paragraph (b)(1) of this section would otherwise apply.

(c) Examples. The rules of this section are illustrated by the following examples. The following facts apply for Examples 1–4:

Facts. In 1992, X transferred property to an irrevocable trust retaining the right to receive the trust income for life. On the death of X, the trust is to terminate and the trust corpus is to be paid to X's child, C. X's income interest had a value under section 7520 of $40,000 at the time of the transfer; however, because X's retained interest was not a qualified interest, it was valued at zero under § 25.2702–2(b)(1) for purposes of determining the amount of X's gift. X's taxable gifts in 1992 were therefore increased by $40,000. In 1993, X transfers the income interest to C for no consideration.

Example (1). Assume that the value under section 7520 of the income interest on the subsequent transfer to C is $30,000. If X makes no other gifts to C in 1993, X is entitled to a reduction in aggregate taxable gifts of $20,000, the lesser of the amount by which X's taxable gifts were increased as a result of the income interest being valued at zero on the initial transfer ($40,000) or the amount by which X's taxable gifts are increased as a result of the subsequent transfer of the income interest ($30,000 minus $10,000 annual exclusion).

Example (2). Assume that in 1993, 4 months after X transferred the income interest to C, X transferred $5,000 cash to C. In determining the increase in taxable gifts occurring on the subsequent transfer, the annual exclusion under section 2503(b) is first applied to the cash gift. X is entitled to a reduction in aggregate taxable gifts of $25,000, the lesser of the amount by which X's taxable gifts were increased as a result of the income interest being valued at zero on the initial transfer ($40,000) or the amount by which X's taxable gifts are increased as a result of the subsequent transfer of the income interest ($25,000 (($30,000 + $5,000) - $10,000 annual exclusion).

Example (3). Assume that the value under section 7520 of the income interest on the subsequent transfer to C is $55,000. X is entitled to reduce aggregate taxable gifts by $40,000, the lesser of the amount by which X's taxable gifts were increased as a result of the income interest being valued at zero on the initial transfer ($40,000) or the amount by which X's taxable gifts are increased as a result of the subsequent transfer of the income interest ($55,000 minus $10,000 annual exclusion = $45,000).

Example (4). Assume that X and X's spouse, S, split the subsequent gift to C. X is entitled to assign one-half the reduction to S. If the assignment is made, each is entitled to reduce aggregate taxable gifts by $17,500, the lesser of their portion of the increase in taxable gifts on the initial transfer by reason of the application of section 2702 ($20,000) and their portion of the increase in taxable gifts on the subsequent transfer of the retained interest ($27,500-$10,000 annual exclusion).

Example (5). In 1992, A transfers property to an irrevocable trust, retaining the right to receive the trust income for 10 years. On the expiration of the 10-year term, the trust is to terminate and the trust corpus is to be paid to A's child, B. Assume that A's term interest has a value under section 7520 of $20,000 at the time of the transfer; however, because A's retained interest was not a qualified interest, it was valued at zero under § 25.2702–2(b)(1) for purposes of determining the amount of A's gift. Assume also that A and A's spouse, S, split the gift of the remainder interest under section 2513. In 1993, A transfers A's term interest to D, A's other child, for no consideration. A is entitled to reduce A's aggregate taxable gifts on the transfer. Assume that A and S also split the subsequent gift to D, and that A dies one month after making the subsequent transfer of the term interest and S dies six months later. The gift of the term interest is included in A's gross estate under section 2035(d)(2). To the extent S's taxable gifts are reduced pursuant to section 2001(e), S is entitled to no reduction in aggregate or adjusted taxable gifts under this section.

Example (6). T transfers property to an irrevocable trust retaining the power to direct the distribution of trust income for 10 years among T's descendants in whatever shares T deems appropriate. On the expiration of the 10-year period, the trust corpus is to be paid in equal shares to T's children. T's transfer of the remainder interest is a completed gift. Because T's retained interest is not a qualified interest, it is valued at zero under § 25.2702–2(b)(1) and the amount of T's gift is the fair market value of the property transferred to the trust. The distribution of income each year is not a transfer of a retained interest in trust. Therefore, T is not entitled to reduce aggregate taxable gifts as a result of the distributions of income from the trust.

Example (7). The facts are the same as in Example 6, except that after 3 years T exercises the right to direct the distribution of trust income by assigning the right to the income for the balance of the term to T's child, C. The exercise is a transfer of a retained interest in trust for purposes of this section. T is entitled to reduce aggregate taxable gifts by the lesser of the increase in taxable gifts resulting from the application of section 2702 to the initial transfer or the increase in taxable gifts resulting from the transfer of the retained interest in trust.

Example (8). In 1992, V purchases an income interest for 10 years in property in the same transaction or series of transactions in which G, V's child, purchases the remainder interest in the same property. V dies in 1997 still holding the term interest, the value of which is includible in V's gross estate under section 2033. V's estate would be entitled to a reduction in adjusted taxable gifts in the amount determined under paragraph (b) of this section.

[T.D. 8395, 57 FR 4272, Feb. 4, 1992]

§ 25.2702–7 Effective dates.

Except as provided in this section, §§ 25.2702–1 through 25.2702–6 apply as of January 28, 1992. With respect to transfers to which section 2702 applied made prior to January 28, 1992, taxpayers may rely on any reasonable interpretation of the statutory provisions. For these purposes, the provisions of the proposed regulations and the final regulations are considered a reasonable interpretation of the statutory provisions. The fourth through eighth sentences of § 25.2702–5(b)(1) and § 25.2702–5(c)(9) apply with respect to trusts created after May 16, 1996. Section

25.2702–2(a)(5), the second and third sentences of § 25.2702–2(a)(6), § 25.2702–3(d)(2), the first two sentences of § 25.2702–3(d)(4), the last sentence of § 25.2702–3(e), Example 5, the last two sentences of § 25.2702–3(e), Example 6, and § 25.2702–3(e), Examples 8 and 9, apply for trusts created on or after July 26, 2004. However, the Internal Revenue Service will not challenge any prior application of the changes to Examples 5 and 6 in § 25.2702–3(e).

[T.D. 8395, 57 FR 4273, Feb. 4, 1992; T.D. 8743, 62 FR 66989, Dec. 23, 1997; T.D. 9181, 70 FR 9224, Feb. 25, 2005]

§ 2703. Certain Rights and Restrictions Disregarded

(a) General rule. For purposes of this subtitle, the value of any property shall be determined without regard to—

(1) any option, agreement, or other right to acquire or use the property at a price less than the fair market value of the property (without regard to such option, agreement, or right), or

(2) any restriction on the right to sell or use such property.

(b) Exceptions. Subsection (a) shall not apply to any option, agreement, right, or restriction which meets each of the following requirements:

(1) It is a bona fide business arrangement.

(2) It is not a device to transfer such property to members of the decedent's family for less than full and adequate consideration in money or money's worth.

(3) Its terms are comparable to similar arrangements entered into by persons in an arms' length transaction.

Regulations

§ 25.2703–1 Property subject to restrictive arrangements.

(a) Disregard of rights or restrictions. (1) *In general.* For purposes of subtitle B (relating to estate, gift, and generation-skipping transfer taxes), the value of any property is determined without regard to any right or restriction relating to the property.

(2) *Right or restriction.* For purposes of this section, right or restriction means—

(i) Any option, agreement, or other right to acquire or use the property at a price less than fair market value (determined without regard to the option, agreement, or right); or

(ii) Any restriction on the right to sell or use the property.

(3) *Agreements, etc. containing rights or restrictions.* A right or restriction may be contained in a partnership agreement, articles of incorporation, corporate bylaws, a shareholders' agreement, or any other agreement. A right or restriction may be implicit in the capital structure of an entity.

(4) *Qualified easements.* A perpetual restriction on the use of real property that qualified for a charitable deduction under either section 2522(d) or section 2055(f) of the Internal Revenue Code is not treated as a right or restriction.

(b) Exceptions. (1) *In general.* This section does not apply to any right or restriction satisfying the following three requirements—

(i) The right or restriction is a bona fide business arrangement;

(ii) The right or restriction is not a device to transfer property to the natural objects of the transferor's bounty for less than full and adequate consideration in money or money's worth; and

(iii) At the time the right or restriction is created, the terms of the right or restriction are comparable to similar arrangements entered into by persons in an arm's length transaction.

(2) *Separate requirements.* Each of the three requirements described in paragraph (b)(1) of this section must be independently satisfied for a right or re-

striction to meet this exception. Thus, for example, the mere showing that a right or restriction is a bona fide business arrangement is not sufficient to establish that the right or restriction is not a device to transfer property for less than full and adequate consideration.

(3) *Exception for certain rights or restrictions.* A right or restriction is considered to meet each of the three requirements described in paragraph (b)(1) of this section if more than 50 percent by value of the property subject to the right or restriction is owned directly or indirectly (within the meaning of § 25.2701–6) by individuals who are not members of the transferor's family. In order to meet this exception, the property owned by those individuals must be subject to the right or restriction to the same extent as the property owned by the transferor. For purposes of this section, members of the transferor's family include the persons described in § 25.2701–2(b)(5) and any other individual who is a natural object of the transferor's bounty. Any property held by a member of the transferor's family under the rules of § 25.2701–6 (without regard to § 25.2701–6(a)(5)) is treated as held only by a member of the transferor's family.

(4) *Similar arrangement.* (i) *In general.* A right or restriction is treated as comparable to similar arrangements entered into by persons in an arm's length transaction if the right or restriction is one that could have been obtained in a fair bargain among unrelated parties in the same business dealing with each other at arm's length. A right or restriction is considered a fair bargain among unrelated parties in the same business if it conforms with the general practice of unrelated parties under negotiated agreements in the same business. This determination generally will entail consideration of such factors as the expected term of the agreement, the current fair market value of the property, anticipated changes in value during the term of the arrangement, and the adequacy of any consideration given in exchange for the rights granted.

(ii) *Evidence of general business practice.* Evidence of general business practice is not met by showing isolated comparables. If more than one valuation method is commonly used in a business, a right or restriction does not fail to evidence general business practice merely because it uses only one of the recognized methods. It is not necessary that the terms of a right or restriction parallel the terms of any particular agreement. If comparables are difficult to find because the business is unique, comparables from similar businesses may be used.

(5) *Multiple rights or restrictions.* If property is subject to more than one right or restriction described in paragraph (a)(2) of this section, the failure of a right or restriction to satisfy the requirements of paragraph (b)(1) of this section does not cause any other right or restriction to fail to satisfy those requirements if the right or restriction otherwise meets those requirements. Whether separate provisions are separate rights or restrictions, or are integral parts of a single right or restriction, depends on all the facts and circumstances.

(c) Substantial modification of a right or restriction. (1) *In general.* A right or restriction that is substantially modified is treated as a right or restriction created on the date of the modification. Any discretionary modification of a right or restriction, whether or not authorized by the terms of the agreement, that results in other than a de minimis change to the quality, value, or timing of the rights of any party with respect to property that is subject to the right or restriction is a substantial modification. If the terms of the right or restriction require periodic updating, the failure to update is presumed to substantially modify the right or restriction unless it can be shown that updating would not have resulted in a substantial modification. The addition of any family member as a party to a right or restriction (including by reason of a transfer of property that subjects the transferee family member to a right or restriction with respect to the transferred property) is considered a substantial modification unless the addition is mandatory under the terms of the right or restriction or the added family member is assigned to a generation (determined under the rules of section 2651 of the Internal Revenue Code) no lower than the lowest generation occupied by individuals already party to the right or restriction).

(2) *Exceptions.* A substantial modification does not include—

(i) A modification required by the terms of a right or restriction;

(ii) A discretionary modification of an agreement conferring a right or restriction if the modification does not change the right or restriction;

(iii) A modification of a capitalization rate used with respect to a right or restriction if the rate is modified in a manner that bears a fixed relationship to a specified market interest rate; and

(iv) A modification that results in an option price that more closely approximates fair market value.

(d) Examples. The following examples illustrate the provisions of this section:

Example (1). T dies in 1992 owning title to Blackacre. In 1991, T and T's child entered into a lease with respect to Blackacre. At the time the lease was entered into, the terms of the lease were not comparable to leases of similar property entered into among unrelated parties. The lease is a restriction on the use of the property that is disregarded in valuing the property for Federal estate tax purposes.

Example (2). T and T's child, C, each own 50 percent of the outstanding stock of X corporation. T and C enter into an agreement in 1987 providing for the disposition of stock held by the first to die at the time of death. The agreement also provides certain restrictions with respect to lifetime transfers. In 1992, as permitted (but not required) under the agreement, T transfers one-half of T's stock to T's spouse, S. S becomes a party to the agreement between T and C by reason of the transfer. The transfer is the addition of a family member to the right or restriction. However, it is not a substantial modification of the right or restriction because the added family member would be assigned to a generation under section 2651 of the Internal Revenue Code no lower than the generation occupied by C.

Example (3). The facts are the same as in Example 2. In 1993, the agreement is amended to reflect a change in the company's name and a change of address for the company's registered agent. These changes are not a substantial modification of the agreement conferring the right or restriction because the right or restriction has not changed.

[T.D. 8395, 57 FR 4273, Feb. 4, 1992]

§ 25.2703–2 Effective date.

Section 25.2703–1 applies to any right or restriction created or substantially modified after October 8, 1990, and is effective as of January 28, 1992. With respect to transfers occurring prior to January 28, 1992, and for purposes of determining whether an event occurring prior to January 28, 1992 constitutes a substantial modification, taxpayers may rely on any reasonable interpretation of the statutory provisions. For these purposes, the provisions of the proposed regulations and the final regulations are considered a reasonable interpretation of the statutory provisions.

[T.D. 8395, 57 FR 4274, Feb. 4, 1992]

§ 2704. Treatment of Certain Lapsing Rights and Restrictions

(a) Treatment of lapsed voting or liquidation rights.

(1) In general. For purposes of this subtitle, if—

(A) there is a lapse of any voting or liquidation right in a corporation or partnership, and

(B) the individual holding such right immediately before the lapse and members of such individual's family hold, both before and after the lapse, control of the entity,

such lapse shall be treated as a transfer by such individual by gift, or a transfer which is includible in the gross estate of the decedent, whichever is applicable, in the amount determined under paragraph (2).

(2) Amount of transfer. For purposes of paragraph (1), the amount determined under this paragraph is the excess (if any) of—

(A) the value of all interests in the entity held by the individual described in paragraph (1) immediately before the lapse (determined as if the voting and liquidation rights were nonlapsing), over

(B) the value of such interests immediately after the lapse.

(3) Similar rights. The Secretary may by regulations apply this subsection to rights similar to voting and liquidation rights.

(b) Certain restrictions on liquidation disregarded.

(1) In general. For purposes of this subtitle, if—

(A) there is a transfer of an interest in a corporation or partnership to (or for the benefit of) a member of the transferor's family, and

(B) the transferor and members of the transferor's family hold, immediately before the transfer, control of the entity,

any applicable restriction shall be disregarded in determining the value of the transferred interest.

(2) Applicable restriction. For purposes of this subsection, the term "applicable restriction" means any restriction—

(A) which effectively limits the ability of the corporation or partnership to liquidate, and

(B) with respect to which either of the following applies:

(i) The restriction lapses, in whole or in part, after the transfer referred to in paragraph (1).

(ii) The transferor or any member of the transferor's family, either alone or collectively, has the right after such transfer to remove, in whole or in part, the restriction.

(3) Exceptions. The term "applicable restriction" shall not include—

(A) any commercially reasonable restriction which arises as part of any financing by the corporation or partnership with a person who is not related to the transferor or transferee, or a member of the family of either, or

(B) any restriction imposed, or required to be imposed, by any Federal or State law.

(4) Other restrictions. The Secretary may by regulations provide that other restrictions shall be disregarded in determining the value of the transfer of any interest in a corporation or partnership to a member of the transferor's family if such restriction has the effect of reducing the value of the transferred interest for purposes of this subtitle but does not ultimately reduce the value of such interest to the transferee.

(c) Definitions and special rules. For purposes of this section—

(1) Control. The term "control" has the meaning given such term by section 2701(b)(2).

(2) Member of the family. The term "member of the family" means, with respect to any individual—

(A) such individual's spouse,

(B) any ancestor or lineal descendant of such individual or such individual's spouse,

(C) any brother or sister of the individual, and

(D) any spouse of any individual described in subparagraph (B) or (C).

(3) Attribution. The rule of section 2701(e)(3) shall apply for purposes of determining the interests held by any individual.

Regulations

§ 25.2704–1 Lapse of certain rights.

(a) Lapse treated as transfer. (1) *In general.* The lapse of a voting right or a liquidation right in a corporation or partnership (an "entity") is a transfer by the individual directly or indirectly holding the right immediately prior to its lapse (the "holder") to the extent provided in paragraphs (b) and (c) of this section. This section applies only if the entity is controlled by the holder and members of the holder's family immediately before and after the lapse. The amount of the transfer is determined under paragraph (d) of this section. If the lapse of a voting right or a liquidation right occurs during the holder's lifetime, the lapse is a transfer by gift. If the lapse occurs at the holder's death, the lapse is a transfer includible in the holder's gross estate.

(2) *Definitions.* The following definitions apply for purposes of this section.

(i) *Control.* Control has the meaning given it in § 25.2701–2(b)(5).

(ii) *Member of the family.* Member of the family has the meaning given it in § 25.2702–2(a)(1).

(iii) *Directly or indirectly held.* An interest is directly or indirectly held only to the extent the value of the interest would have been includible in the gross estate of the individual if the individual had died immediately prior to the lapse.

(iv) *Voting right.* Voting right means a right to vote with respect to any matter of the entity. In the case of a partnership, the right of a general partner to participate in partnership management is a voting right. The right to compel the entity to acquire all or a portion of the holder's equity interest in the entity by reason of aggregate voting power is treated as a liquidation right and is not treated as a voting right.

(v) *Liquidation right.* Liquidation right means a right or ability to compel the entity to acquire all or a portion of the holder's equity interest in the entity, including by reason of aggregate voting power, whether or not its exercise would result in the complete liquidation of the entity.

(vi) *Subordinate.* Subordinate has the meaning given it in § 25.2701–3(a)(2)(iii).

(3) *Certain temporary lapses.* If a lapsed right may be restored only upon the occurrence of a future event not within the control of the holder or members of the holder's family, the lapse is deemed to occur at the time the lapse becomes permanent with respect to the holder, i.e. either by a transfer of the interest or otherwise.

(4) *Source of right or lapse.* A voting right or a liquidation right may be conferred by and may lapse by reason of a State law, the corporate charter or bylaws, an agreement, or other means.

(b) Lapse of voting right. A lapse of a voting right occurs at the time a presently exercisable voting right is restricted or eliminated.

(c) Lapse of liquidation right. (1) *In general.* A lapse of a liquidation right occurs at the time a presently exercisable liquidation right is restricted or eliminated. Except as otherwise provided, a transfer of an interest that results in the lapse of a liquidation right is not subject to this section if the rights with respect to the transferred interest are not restricted or eliminated. However, a transfer that results in the elimination of the transferor's right or ability to compel the entity to acquire an interest retained by the transferor that is subordinate to the transferred interest is a lapse of a liquidation right with respect to the subordinate interest.

(2) *Exceptions.* Section 2704(a) does not apply to the lapse of a liquidation right under the following circumstances.

(i) *Family cannot obtain liquidation value.* (A) *In general.* Section 2704(a) does not apply to the lapse of a liquidation right to the extent the holder (or the holder's estate) and members of the holder's family cannot immediately after the lapse liquidate an interest that the holder held directly or indirectly and could have liquidated prior to the lapse.

(B) *Ability to liquidate.* Whether an interest can be liquidated immediately after the lapse is determined under the State law generally applicable to the entity, as modified by the governing instruments of the entity, but without regard to any restriction described in section 2704(b). Thus, if, after any restriction described in section 2704(b) is disregarded, the remaining requirements for liquidation under the governing instruments are less restrictive than the State law that would apply in the absence of the governing instruments, the ability to liquidate is determined by reference to the governing instruments.

(ii) *Rights valued under section 2701.* Section 2704(a) does not apply to the lapse of a liquidation right previously valued under section 2701 to the extent necessary to prevent double taxation (taking into account any adjustment available under § 25.2701–5).

(iii) *Certain changes in State law.* Section 2704(a) does not apply to the lapse of a liquidation right that occurs solely by reason of a change in State law. For purposes of this paragraph, a change in the governing instrument of an entity is not a change in State law.

(d) Amount of transfer. The amount of the transfer is the excess, if any, of—

(1) The value of all interests in the entity owned by the holder immediately before the lapse (determined immediately after the lapse as if the lapsed right was nonlapsing); over

(2) The value of the interests described in the preceding paragraph immediately after the lapse (determined as if all such interests were held by one individual).

(e) Application to similar rights. [Reserved]

(f) Examples. The following examples illustrate the provisions of this section:

Example (1). Prior to D's death, D owned all the preferred stock of Corporation Y and D's children owned all the common stock. At that time, the preferred stock had 60 percent of the total voting power and the common stock had 40 percent. Under the corporate by-laws, the voting rights of the preferred stock terminated on D's death. The value of D's interest immediately prior to D's death (determined as if the voting rights were nonlapsing) was $100X. The value of that interest immediately after death would have been $90X if the voting rights had been nonlapsing. The decrease in value reflects the loss in value resulting from the death of D (whose involvement in Y was a key factor in Y's profitability). Section 2704(a) applies to the lapse of voting rights on D's death. D's gross estate includes an amount equal to the excess, if any, of $90X over the fair market value of the preferred stock determined after the lapse of the voting rights.

Example (2). Prior to D's death, D owned all the preferred stock of Corporation Y. The preferred stock and the common stock each carried 50 percent of the total voting power of Y. D's children owned 40 percent of the common stock and unrelated parties own the remaining 60 percent. Under the corporate by-laws, the voting rights of the preferred stock terminate on D's death. Section 2704(a) does not apply to the lapse of D's voting rights because members of D's family do not control Y after the lapse.

Example (3). The by-laws of Corporation Y provide that the voting rights of any transferred shares of the single outstanding class of stock are reduced to ½ vote per share after the transfer but are fully restored to the transferred shares after 5 years. D owned 60 percent of the shares prior to death and members of D's family owned the balance. On D's death, D's shares pass to D's children and the voting rights are reduced pursuant to the by-laws. Section 2704(a) applies to the lapse of D's voting rights. D's gross estate includes an amount equal to the excess, if any, of the fair market value of D's stock (determined immediately after D's death as though the voting rights had not been reduced and would not be reduced) over the stock's fair market value immediately after D's death.

Example (4). D owns 84 percent of the single outstanding class of stock of Corporation Y. The by-laws require at least 70 percent of the vote to liquidate Y. D gives one-half of D's stock in equal shares to D's three children (14 percent to each). Section 2704(a) does not apply to the loss of D's ability to liquidate Y, because the voting rights with respect to the corporation are not restricted or eliminated by reason of the transfer.

Example (5). D and D's two children, A and B, are partners in Partnership X. Each has a 3 1/3 percent general partnership interest and a 30 percent limited partnership interest. Under State law, a general partner has the right to participate in partnership management. The partnership agreement provides that when a general partner withdraws or dies, X must redeem the general partnership interest for its liquidation value. Also, under the agreement any general partner can liquidate the partnership. A limited partner cannot liquidate the partnership and a limited partner's capital interest will be returned only when the partnership is liquidated. A deceased limited partner's interest continues as a limited partnership interest. D dies, leaving his limited partnership interest to D's spouse. Because of a general partner's right to dissolve the partnership, a limited partnership interest has a greater fair market value when held in conjunction with a general partnership interest than when held alone. Section 2704(a) applies to the lapse of D's liquidation right because after the lapse, members of D's family could liquidate D's limited partnership interest. D's gross estate includes an amount equal to the excess of the value of all D's interests in X immediately before D's death (determined immediately after D's death but as though the liquidation right had not lapsed and would not lapse) over the fair market value of all D's interests in X immediately after D's death.

Example (6). The facts are the same as in Example 5, except that under the partnership agreement D is the only general partner who holds a unilateral liquidation right. Assume further that the partnership agreement contains a restriction described in section 2704(b) that prevents D's family members from liquidating D's limited partnership interest immediately after D's death. Under State law, in the absence of the restriction in the partnership agreement, D's family members could liquidate the partnership. The restriction on the family's ability to liquidate is disregarded and the amount of D's gross estate is increased by reason of the lapse of D's liquidation right.

Example (7). D owns all the stock of Corporation X, consisting of 100 shares of non-voting preferred stock and 100 shares of voting common stock. Under the by-laws, X can only be liquidated with the consent of at least 80 percent of the voting shares. D transfers 30 shares of common stock to D's child. The transfer is not a lapse of a liquidation right with respect to the common stock because the voting rights that enabled D to liquidate prior to the transfer are not restricted or eliminated. The transfer is not a lapse of a liquidation right with respect to the retained preferred stock because the preferred stock is not subordinate to the transferred common stock.

Example (8). D owns all of the single class of stock of Corporation Y. D recapitalizes Y, exchanging D's common stock for voting common stock and non-voting, non-cumulative preferred stock. The preferred stock carries a right to put the stock for its par value at any time during the next 10 years. D transfers the common stock to D's grandchild in a transfer subject to section 2701. In determining the amount of D's gift under section 2701, D's retained put right is valued at zero. D's child, C, owns the preferred stock when the put right lapses. Section 2704(a) applies to the lapse, without regard to the application of section 2701, because the put right was not valued under section 2701 in the hands of C.

Example (9). A and A's two children are equal general and limited partners in Partnership Y. Under the partnership agreement, each general partner has a right to liquidate the partnership at any time. Under State law that would apply in the absence of contrary provisions in the partnership agreement, the death or incompetency of a general partner terminates the partnership. However, the partnership agreement provides that the partnership does not terminate on the incompetence or death of a general partner, but that an incompetent partner cannot exercise rights as a general partner during any period of incompetency. A partner's full rights as general partner are restored if the partner regains competency. A becomes incompetent. The lapse of A's voting right on becoming incompetent is not subject to section 2704(a) because it may be restored to A in the future. However, if A dies while incompetent, a lapse subject to section 2704(a) is deemed to occur at that time because the lapsed right cannot thereafter be restored to A.

[T.D. 8395, 57 FR 4274, Feb. 4, 1992]

§ 25.2704–2 Transfers subject to applicable restrictions.

(a) In general. If an interest in a corporation or partnership (an "entity") is transferred to or for the benefit of a member of the transferor's family, any applicable restriction is disregarded in valuing the transferred interest. This section applies only if the transferor and members of the transferor's family control the entity immediately before the transfer. For the definition of control, see § 25.2701–2(b)(5). For the definition of member of the family, see § 25.2702–2(a)(1).

(b) Applicable restriction defined. An applicable restriction is a limitation on the ability to liquidate the entity (in whole or in part) that is more restrictive than the limitations that would apply under the State law generally applicable to the entity in the absence of the restriction. A restriction is an applicable restriction only to the extent that either the restriction by its terms will lapse at any time after the transfer, or the transferor (or the transferor's estate) and any members of the transferor's family can remove the restriction immediately after the transfer. Ability to remove the restriction is determined by reference to the State law that would apply but for a more restrictive rule in the governing instruments of the entity. See § 25.2704–1(c)(1)(B) for a discussion of the term "State law." An applicable restriction does not include a commercially reasonable restriction on liquidation imposed by an unrelated person providing capital to the entity for the entity's trade or business operations whether in the form of debt or equity. An unrelated person is any person whose relationship to the transferor, the transferee, or any member of the family of either is not described in section 267(b) of the Internal Revenue Code, provided that for purposes of this section the term "fiduciary of a trust" as used in section 267(b) does not include a bank as defined in section 581 of the Internal Revenue Code. A restriction imposed or required to be imposed by Federal or State law is not an applicable restriction. An option, right to use property, or agreement that is subject to section 2703 is not an applicable restriction.

(c) Effect of disregarding an applicable restriction. If an applicable restriction is disregarded under this section, the transferred interest is valued as if the restriction does not exist and as if the rights of the transferor are determined under the State law that would apply but for the restriction. For example, an applicable restriction with respect to preferred stock will be disregarded in determining the amount of a transfer of common stock under section 2701.

(d) Examples. The following examples illustrate the provisions of this section:

Example (1). D owns a 76 percent interest and each of D's children, A and B, owns a 12 percent interest in General Partnership X. The partnership agreement requires the consent of all the partners to liquidate the partnership. Under the State law that would apply in the absence of the restriction in the partnership agreement, the consent of partners owning 70 percent of the total partnership interests would be required to liquidate X. On D's death, D's partnership interest passes to D's child, C. The requirement that all the partners consent to liquidation is an applicable restriction. Because A, B and C (all members of D's family), acting together after the transfer, can remove the restriction on liquidation, D's interest is valued without regard to the restriction; i.e., as though D's interest is sufficient to liquidate the partnership.

Example (2). D owns all the preferred stock in Corporation X. The preferred stock carries a right to liquidate X that cannot be exercised until 1999. D's children, A and B, own all the common stock of X. The common stock is the only voting stock. In 1994, D transfers the preferred stock to D's child, A. The restriction on D's right to liquidate is an applicable restriction that is disregarded. Therefore, the preferred stock is valued as though the right to liquidate were presently exercisable.

Example (3). D owns 60 percent of the stock of Corporation X. The corporate by-laws provide that the corporation cannot be liquidated for 10 years after which time liquidation requires approval by 60 percent of the voting interests. In the absence of the provision in the by-laws, State law would require approval by 80 percent of the voting interests to liquidate X. D transfers the stock to a trust for the benefit of D's child, A, during the 10-year period. The 10-year restriction is an applicable restriction and is disregarded. Therefore, the value of the stock is determined as if the transferred block could currently liquidate X.

Example (4). D and D's children, A and B, are partners in Limited Partnership Y. Each has a 3.33 percent general partnership interest and a 30 percent limited partnership interest. Any general partner has the right to liquidate the partnership at any time. As part of a loan agreement with a lender who is related to D, each of the partners agree that the partnership may not be liquidated without the lender's consent while any portion of the loan remains outstanding. During the term of the loan agreement, D transfers one-half of both D's partnership interests to each of A and B. Because the lender is a related party, the requirement that the lender consent to liquidation is an applicable restriction and the transfers of D's interests are valued as if such consent were not required.

Example (5). D owns 60 percent of the preferred and 70 percent of the common stock in Corporation X. The remaining stock is owned by individuals unrelated to D. The preferred stock carries a put right that cannot be exercised until 1999. In 1995, D transfers the common stock to D's child in a transfer that is subject to section 2701. The restriction on D's right to liquidate is an applicable restriction that is disregarded in determining the amount of the gift under section 2701.

[T.D. 8395, 57 FR 4276, Feb. 4, 1992; T.D. 8395, 57 FR 11265, April 2, 1992]

§ 25.2704–3 Effective date.

Section 25.2704–1 applies to lapses occurring after January 28, 1992, of rights created after October 8, 1990. Section 25.2704–2 applies to transfers occurring after January 28, 1992, of property subject to applicable restrictions created after October 8, 1990. In determining whether a voting right or a liquidation right has lapsed prior to that date, and for purposes of determining whether the lapse is subject to section 2704(a), taxpayers may rely on any reasonable interpretation of the statutory provisions. For transfers of interests occurring before January 28, 1992, taxpayers may rely on any reasonable interpretation of the statutory provisions in determining whether a restriction is an applicable restriction that must be disregarded in determining the value of the transferred interest. For these purposes, the provisions of the proposed regulations and the final regulations are considered a reasonable interpretation of the statutory provisions.

[T.D. 8395, 57 FR 4277, Feb. 4, 1992; T.D. 8395, 57 FR 11265, April 2, 1992]

Chapter 15. Gifts and Bequests from Expatriates

§ 2801. Imposition of Tax

(a) In general. If, during any calendar year, any United States citizen or resident receives any covered gift or bequest, there is hereby imposed a tax equal to the product of—

(1) the highest rate of tax specified in the table contained in section 2001(c) as in effect on the date of such receipt, and

(2) the value of such covered gift or bequest.

(b) Tax to be paid by recipient. The tax imposed by subsection (a) on any covered gift or bequest shall be paid by the person receiving such gift or bequest.

(c) Exception for certain gifts. Subsection (a) shall apply only to the extent that the value of covered gifts and bequests received by any person during the calendar year exceeds the dollar amount in effect under section 2503(b) for such calendar year.*

(d) Tax reduced by foreign gift or estate tax. The tax imposed by subsection (a) on any covered gift or bequest shall be reduced by the amount of any gift or estate tax paid to a foreign country with respect to such covered gift or bequest.

(e) Covered gift or bequest.

(1) In general. For purposes of this chapter, the term "covered gift or bequest" means—

(A) any property acquired by gift directly or indirectly from an individual who, at the time of such acquisition, is a covered expatriate, and

(B) any property acquired directly or indirectly by reason of the death of an individual who, immediately before such death, was a covered expatriate.

(2) Exceptions for transfers otherwise subject to estate or gift tax. Such term shall not include

(A) any property shown on a timely filed return of tax imposed by chapter 12 which is a taxable gift by the covered expatriate, and

(B) any property included in the gross estate of the covered expatriate for purposes of chapter 11 and shown on a timely filed return of tax imposed by chapter 11 of the estate of the covered expatriate.

(3) Exceptions for transfers to spouse or charity. Such term shall not include any property with respect to which a deduction would be allowed under section 2055, 2056, 2522, or 2523, whichever is appropriate, if the decedent or donor were a United States person.

(4) Transfers in trust.

(A) Domestic trusts. In the case of a covered gift or bequest made to a domestic trust—

(i) subsection (a) shall apply in the same manner as if such trust were a United States citizen, and

(ii) the tax imposed by subsection (a) on such gift or bequest shall be paid by such trust.

(B) Foreign trusts.

* Rev. Proc. 2025–32 provides that "[t]he tax imposed under § 2801 on the receipt of covered gifts or covered bequests from a covered expatriate shall apply only to the extent that the value of covered gifts and covered bequests received during calendar year 2026 exceeds $19,000." *Ed.*

(i) In general. In the case of a covered gift or bequest made to a foreign trust, subsection (a) shall apply to any distribution attributable to such gift or bequest from such trust (whether from income or corpus) to a United States citizen or resident in the same manner as if such distribution were a covered gift or bequest.

(ii) Deduction for tax paid by recipient. There shall be allowed as a deduction under section 164 the amount of tax imposed by this section which is paid or accrued by a United States citizen or resident by reason of a distribution from a foreign trust, but only to the extent such tax is imposed on the portion of such distribution which is included in the gross income of such citizen or resident.

(iii) Election to be treated as domestic trust. Solely for purposes of this section, a foreign trust may elect to be treated as a domestic trust. Such an election may be revoked with the consent of the Secretary.

(f) Covered expatriate. For purposes of this section, the term "covered expatriate" has the meaning given to such term by section 877A(g)(1).

Regulations

§ 28.2801–0 Table of contents. [*Omitted. Ed.*]

[T.D. 10027, 90 FR 3376, Jan. 14, 2025]

§ 28.2801–1 Tax on certain gifts and bequests from covered expatriates.

(a) In general. Section 2801 of the Internal Revenue Code (Code) imposes a tax (section 2801 tax) on covered gifts and covered bequests, including distributions attributable to covered gifts and covered bequests from non-electing foreign trusts, received by a U.S. citizen or resident from a covered expatriate during a calendar year. Domestic trusts, as well as electing foreign trusts, are subject to tax under section 2801 in the same manner as if the trusts were U.S. citizens. *See* section 2801(e)(4)(A)(i) and (B)(iii). Accordingly, the section 2801 tax is paid by the U.S. citizen or resident, domestic trust, or electing foreign trust that receives the covered gift or covered bequest, including distributions attributable to covered gifts and covered bequests from non-electing foreign trusts. For purposes of the regulations in this part 28 (26 CFR part 28), references to U.S. citizens are considered to include domestic trusts and electing foreign trusts.

(b) Applicability date. This section applies to covered gifts or covered bequests received on or after January 1, 2025.

[T.D. 10027, 90 FR 3376, Jan. 14, 2025]

§ 28.2801–2 Definitions.

(a) Overview. This section provides definitions of terms applicable solely for purposes of section 2801 of the Code and the regulations in this part 28.

(b) U.S. citizen or resident. A U.S. citizen or resident is an individual who is a citizen or resident of the United States for purposes of chapter 11 or 12 of subtitle B, as the case may be, at the time of receipt of the covered gift or covered bequest. Furthermore, references to a U.S. citizen also include a domestic trust, as well as an electing foreign trust. See § 28.2801–1(a).

(c) Domestic trust. The term domestic trust means a trust defined in section 7701(a)(30)(E) of the Code. References to a domestic trust include an electing foreign trust.

(d) Foreign trust (1) *In general.* The term foreign trust means a trust defined in section 7701(a)(31)(B).

(2) *Electing foreign trust.* The term electing foreign trust means a foreign trust that has in effect a valid election to be treated as a domestic trust for purposes of section 2801. *See* § 28.2801–5(d).

(3) *Non-electing foreign trust.* The term non-electing foreign trust means any foreign trust other than an electing foreign trust described in paragraph (d)(2) of this section.

(e) U.S. recipient. The term U.S. recipient means a U.S. citizen or resident, a domestic trust, or an electing foreign trust that receives a covered gift or covered bequest, whether directly or indirectly, during the calendar year. The term U.S. recipient includes a U.S. citizen or resident receiving a distribution from a non-electing foreign trust if the distribution is attributable (in whole or in part) to one or more covered gifts or covered bequests received by the non-electing foreign trust. *See* § 28.2801–5(c) to determine the amount of a distribution attributable to covered gifts and covered bequests. This term also includes the U.S. citizen or resident shareholders, partners, or other interest-holders, as the case may be (if any), of a business entity that receives a covered gift or covered bequest.

(f) Covered bequest. The term covered bequest means any property acquired by a recipient on or after June 17, 2008, directly or indirectly by reason of the death of a covered expatriate, regardless of the situs of the property and of whether such property was acquired by the covered expatriate before or after expatriation from the United States, but only to the extent the property would have been included in the covered expatriate's gross estate for Federal estate tax purposes if the covered expatriate had been a U.S. citizen immediately before death. See paragraph (i) of this section for guidance in determining when property is acquired indirectly for purposes of this paragraph (f). The term covered bequest also includes any other property that would have been included in the covered expatriate's gross estate for Federal estate tax purposes (for example, under section 2035 of the Code) if the covered expatriate had been a U.S. citizen immediately before death, as well as distributions made by reason of the death of a covered expatriate from a non-electing foreign trust to the extent the distributions are attributable to covered gifts and covered bequests made to the non-electing foreign trust on or after June 17, 2008. *See* § 28.2801–3 for additional rules and exceptions applicable to the term covered bequest.

(g) Covered gift. The term covered gift means any property acquired by a recipient on or after June 17, 2008, by gift directly or indirectly from an individual who is a covered expatriate at the time the property is received by the recipient, regardless of the situs of such property and of whether such property was acquired by the covered expatriate before or after expatriation from the United States. See paragraph (i) of this section for guidance in determining when property is acquired indirectly for purposes of this paragraph (g). The term covered gift also includes distributions made, other than by reason of the death of a covered expatriate, from a non-electing foreign trust to the extent the distributions are attributable to covered gifts and covered bequests made to the non-electing foreign trust on or after June 17, 2008. *See* § 28.2801–3 for additional rules and exceptions applicable to the term covered gift.

(h) Expatriate and covered expatriate. The term expatriate has the same meaning for purposes of section 2801 as that term has in section 877A(g)(2) of the Code. The term covered expatriate has the same meaning for purposes of section 2801 as that term has in section 877A(g)(1). The determination of whether an individual is a covered expatriate is made as of the expatriation date as defined in section 877A(g)(3), and if an expatriate meets the definition of a covered expatriate, the expatriate is a covered expatriate for purposes of section 2801 at all times after the expatriation date. However, an expatriate is not treated as a covered expatriate for purposes of section 2801 during any period beginning after the expatriation date during which such individual is subject to United States estate or gift tax (chapter 11 or chapter 12 of subtitle B) as a U.S. citizen or resident. *See* section 877A(g)(1)(C). An individual's status as a covered expatriate will be determined as of the date of the most recent expatriation, if there has been more than one.

(i) Indirect acquisition of property. For purposes of paragraphs (f) and (g) of this section, an indirect acquisition of property means the receipt of an interest in property, gratuitously passed from or conferred by the covered expatriate, by or on behalf of the recipient through another person, or by a trust or entity in which the recipient has an interest, regardless of the means or device employed. Such an indirect acquisition includes but is not limited to

(1) Property acquired by a recipient through a transfer to a corporation or other entity other than a trust or estate, to the extent of the ownership interest of the recipient in that corporation or other entity;

(2) Money paid or property distributed by a covered expatriate, or distributed from a non-electing foreign trust that received a covered gift or covered bequest, in satisfaction of a debt or liability of the recipient, regardless of the payee of that payment or distribution;

(3) Property acquired by or on behalf of a recipient pursuant to the exercise, release, or lapse (without regard to the exception in section 2041(b)(2) or 2514(e) of the Code) of a non-covered expatriate's power of appointment granted by a covered expatriate over property not in trust, unless the property previously was subjected to section 2801 tax upon the grant of

the power or the covered expatriate had no more than a non-general power of appointment over that property; and

(4) Property acquired through or from any person not subject to the section 2801 tax that is, in substance, a covered gift or covered bequest from a covered expatriate.

(j) Power of appointment. The term power of appointment refers to both a general and non-general power of appointment, except as expressly limited to one or the other in a particular provision of the regulations in this part 28. The term general power of appointment has the same meaning as in sections 2041(b)(1) and 2514(c). The term non-general power of appointment means any power of appointment that is not a general power of appointment. For purposes of section 2801, the term power of appointment is defined without regard to the exception in section 2041(b)(2) or 2514(e).

(k) Section 2801 tax. The term section 2801 tax has the meaning provided in § 28.2801–1(a).

(*l*) Section 2801(c) amount. The term section 2801(c) amount is the dollar amount of the per-donee gift tax exclusion in effect under section 2503(b) for that calendar year.

(m) Statutory references (1) *Code.* The term Code means the Internal Revenue Code.

(2) *Subtitle B.* The term subtitle B means subtitle B of the Code.

(n) Applicability date. This section applies to covered gifts or covered bequests received on or after January 1, 2025.

[T.D. 10027, 90 FR 3376, Jan. 14, 2025]

§ 28.2801–3 Rules and exceptions applicable to covered gifts and covered bequests.

(a) Covered gift. Subject to the provisions of paragraphs (c) through (e) of this section, the term gift as used in the definition of covered gift in § 28.2801–2(g) has the same meaning as in chapter 12 of subtitle B, but without regard to the exceptions in section 2501(a)(2), (4), and (5) of the Code, the per-donee exclusion under section 2503(b) of the Code for certain transfers of a present interest, the exclusion under section 2503(e) for certain educational or medical expenses, and the waiver of certain pension rights under section 2503(f).

(b) Covered bequest. Subject to the provisions of paragraphs (c) through (e) of this section, property acquired by reason of the death of a covered expatriate (one of the types of transfers defined as a covered bequest in § 28.2801–2(f)) includes any property that would have been includible in the gross estate of the covered expatriate under chapter 11 of subtitle B if the covered expatriate had been a U.S. citizen at the time of death. Therefore, property acquired by reason of a covered expatriate's death includes, without limitation, property or an interest in property acquired by reason of a covered expatriate's death

(1) By bequest, devise, trust provision, beneficiary designation, or other contractual arrangement, or by operation of law, to the extent the property would have been includible in the covered expatriate's gross estate if the covered expatriate had been a U.S. citizen at death;

(2) That was transferred by the covered expatriate during life, either before or after expatriation, and that would have been includible in the covered expatriate's gross estate under section 2036, 2037, or 2038 of the Code had the covered expatriate been a U.S. citizen at death;

(3) That was received for the benefit of a covered expatriate from such covered expatriate's spouse, or predeceased spouse, for which a valid qualified terminable interest property (QTIP) election was made on such spouse's, or predeceased spouse's, Form 709, United States Gift (and Generation-Skipping Transfer) Tax Return, Form 709-NA, United States Gift (and Generation-Skipping Transfer) Tax Return of Nonresident Not a Citizen of the United States, Form 706, United States Estate (and Generation-Skipping Transfer) Tax Return, or Form 706-NA, United States Estate (and Generation-Skipping Transfer) Tax Return, Estate of nonresident not a citizen of the United States, which would have been includible in the covered expatriate's gross estate under section 2044 of the Code if the covered expatriate had been a U.S. citizen at death; or

(4) That otherwise passed from the covered expatriate by reason of his or her death, such as

(i) Property held by the covered expatriate and another person as joint tenants with right of survivorship or as tenants by the entirety, but only to the extent such property would have been includible in the covered expatriate's gross estate under section 2040 of the Code if the covered expatriate had been a U.S. citizen at death;

(ii) Any annuity or other payment that would have been includible in the covered expatriate's gross estate if the covered expatriate had been a U.S. citizen at death;

(iii) Property subject to a general power of appointment held by the covered expatriate at death that would have been includible in the covered expatriate's gross estate under section 2041 if the covered expatriate had been a U.S. citizen at death; or

(iv) Life insurance proceeds payable upon the covered expatriate's death that would have been includible in the covered expatriate's gross estate under section 2042 of the Code if the covered expatriate had been a U.S. citizen at death.

(c) Exceptions to covered gift and covered bequest. Notwithstanding the definitions of covered gift and covered bequest in § 28.2801–2(f) and (g), respectively, as further described in paragraphs (a) and (b) of this section, the terms covered gift and covered bequest do not include property described in paragraphs (c)(1) through (6) of this section.

(1) *Reported taxable gifts.* Property transferred as a taxable gift under section 2503(a) that is reported on the donor's timely filed Form 709 or Form 709-NA is not a covered gift. However, property excluded from the definition of a taxable gift, such as a present interest not in excess of the annual exclusion amount under section 2503(b), is not excluded from the definition of a covered gift under this paragraph (c)(1) even if reported on the donor's Form 709 or Form 709-NA.

(2) *Property reported as subject to estate tax.* Property that is includible in the gross estate of the covered expatriate and is reported on a timely filed Form 706, Form 706-NA, or Form 706-QDT, U.S. Estate Tax Return for Qualified Domestic Trusts, or any successor form, is not a covered bequest. Thus, if the covered expatriate's gross estate is not of sufficient value to require the filing of a Form 706-NA, for example, and no Form 706-NA is timely filed, the property passing from that covered expatriate is not excluded from the definition of a covered bequest under the rule of this paragraph (c)(2). Further, this exclusion does not apply to the property not reported on such a form, whether or not subject to United States estate tax (that is, non-U.S. situs property that passes to U.S. citizens or residents).

(3) *Covered bequest previously subject to section 2801 tax as a covered gift.* If a covered bequest from a covered expatriate previously constituted a covered gift from that covered expatriate (for example, because of a retained power or right described in section 2036), the property is a covered bequest only to the extent that the value of the covered bequest exceeds the value of the covered gift that was subject to section 2801.

(4) *Transfers to charity.* A gift to a donee described in section 2522(b) of the Code or a bequest to a beneficiary described in section 2055(a) of the Code is not a covered gift or covered bequest to the extent a charitable deduction under section 2522 or 2055 would have been allowed if the covered expatriate had been a U.S. citizen at the time of the transfer.

(5) *Transfers to spouse.* Property transferred from a covered expatriate to the covered expatriate's spouse generally is not a covered gift or covered bequest to the extent a marital deduction under section 2523 or 2056 of the Code would have been allowed if the covered expatriate had been a U.S. citizen at the time of the transfer. To the extent that a gift or bequest of property to a trust (or to a separate share of the trust) would qualify for the marital deduction, the property transferred in the gift or bequest is not a covered gift or covered bequest. To the extent the gift or bequest of property to the trust (or to a separate share of the trust) would not qualify for the marital deduction, the property transferred in the gift or bequest is a covered gift or covered bequest to the trust, and in the case of a non-electing foreign trust, distributions attributable to such gift or bequest will subject the U.S. citizen or resident spouse receiving such distributions to the section 2801 tax. *See* §§ 28.2801–4(a)(3) and 28.2801–5(a). For qualified terminable interest property (QTIP) described in section 2056(b)(7) and for property in a qualified domestic trust (QDOT) described in section 2056A of the Code, a valid QTIP and/or QDOT election must be made by the covered expatriate or covered expatriate's estate in order for the gift or bequest of such property to qualify for the marital exclusion

under section 2801(e)(3), and, thus not be a covered gift or covered bequest under this paragraph (c)(5). Such an election can be made only with respect to the transfer of property subject to gift or estate tax under section 2511(a) or 2103 of the Code. Furthermore, to exclude from covered bequests property in a QDOT for the benefit of a covered expatriate, funded pursuant to a bequest by the covered expatriate's predeceased spouse who also was a covered expatriate, a valid QDOT election must have been made in the predeceased covered expatriate's estate.

(6) *Qualified disclaimers*. Property transferred pursuant to a covered expatriate's qualified disclaimer, as defined in section 2518(b) of the Code, is not a covered gift or covered bequest from that covered expatriate.

(d) Covered gifts and covered bequests made in trust. For transfers of property to a trust that are covered gifts or covered bequests as described in §§ 28.2801–2 and 28.2801–3, the property is treated as a covered gift or covered bequest to the trust without regard to the beneficial interests in the trust or whether any person has a general power of appointment or a power of withdrawal over trust property. Accordingly, the rules in section 2801(e)(4) and § 28.2801–4(a) apply to determine liability for payment of the section 2801 tax. The U.S. recipient of a covered gift or a covered bequest made to a domestic trust or to an electing foreign trust is the domestic or electing foreign trust, and the U.S. recipient of a covered gift or a covered bequest made to a non-electing foreign trust is each U.S. citizen or resident receiving a distribution from the non-electing foreign trust (without regard to whether that distribution is or is not pursuant to the exercise or release of a general power of appointment). *See* § 28.2801–2(e) for the definition of a U.S. recipient.

(e) Powers of appointment (1) *Covered expatriate as holder of power*. The exercise or release of a general power of appointment held by a covered expatriate over property, whether or not in trust (even if that covered expatriate was a U.S. citizen or resident when the general power of appointment was granted), for the benefit of a U.S. citizen or resident is a covered gift or covered bequest. For this purpose, the lapse of a general power of appointment held by a covered expatriate is treated as a release to the extent provided in sections 2041(b)(2) and 2514(e) of the Code. Furthermore, the exercise of a power of appointment by a covered expatriate that creates another power of appointment as described in section 2041(a)(3) or 2514(d) for the benefit of a U.S. citizen or resident is a covered gift or a covered bequest.

(2) *Covered expatriate as grantor of power*. The grant by a covered expatriate to an individual who is a U.S. citizen or resident of a general power of appointment over property not held in trust is a covered gift or covered bequest to the powerholder. For the rule applying to the grant by a covered expatriate of a general power of appointment over property in trust, see paragraph (d) of this section.

(f) Examples. The provisions of this section are illustrated by the following examples:

(1) Example 1: Transfer to spouse. In Year 1, CE, a covered expatriate domiciled in Country F, a foreign country with which the United States does not have a gift tax treaty, gives $300,000 cash to his wife, W, a U.S. resident and citizen of Country F. Under paragraph (c)(5) of this section, the $100,000 exclusion for a noncitizen spouse, as indexed for inflation in Year 1, is excluded from the definition of a covered gift under section 2801 because only that amount of the transfer would have qualified for the gift tax marital deduction if CE had been a U.S. citizen at the time of the gift. *See* sections 2801(e)(3), 2523(i), and 2503(b). The remaining amount ($300,000, less the $100,000 exclusion for a noncitizen spouse, as indexed for inflation) is a covered gift from CE to W. W must timely file Form 708, United States Return of Tax for Gifts and Bequests Received from Covered Expatriates, and timely pay the tax. See §§ 28.6011–1(a), 28.6071–1(a), and 28.6151–1(a). W also must report the transfer on Form 3520, Annual Return to Report Transactions With Foreign Trusts and Receipt of Certain Foreign Gifts,and any other required form. *See* § 28.2801–6(c)(1).

(2) Example 2: Reporting property as subject to estate tax (i) Year 1. CE, a covered expatriate domiciled in Country F, a foreign country with which the United States does not have an estate tax treaty, owns a condominium in the United States with son, S, a U.S. citizen. CE and S each contributed their actuarial share of the purchase price when purchasing the condominium and own it as joint tenants with rights of survivorship. On December 14, Year 1, CE dies. At the time of CE's death, the fair market value of CE's share of the con-

dominium, $250,000, is included in CE's gross estate under sections 2040 and 2103.

(ii) Year 2. On September 14 of the following calendar year, Year 2, the executor of CE's estate timely files a Form 4768, Application for Extension of Time to File a Return and/or Pay U.S. Estate (and Generation-Skipping Transfer) Taxes, requesting a 6-month extension of time to file Form 706-NA, and a 1-year extension of time to pay the estate tax. The Internal Revenue Service grants both extensions, but CE's executor fails to file the Form 706-NA until after March 14 of Year 3.

(iii) Analysis. S learns that the executor of CE's estate did not timely file Form 706-NA. CE's estate remains liable for estate tax on CE's interest in the condominium. In addition, because CE is a covered expatriate and CE's estate failed to timely file the tax return reporting the transaction, S received a covered bequest as defined in § 28.2801–2(f) and paragraph (b) of this section and must timely file Form 708 and pay the section 2801 tax. See §§ 28.6011–1(a), 28.6071–1(a), and 28.6151–1(a). S also must file Form 3520 to report a large gift or bequest from a foreign person and any other required form. *See* § 28.2801–6(c)(1).

(3) Example 3: Covered gift in trust with grant of general power of appointment over trust property (i) *Facts*. On October 20, Year 1, CE, a covered expatriate domiciled in Country F, a foreign country with which the United States does not have a gift tax treaty, transfers $500,000 in cash from an account in Country F to an irrevocable foreign trust created on that same date. The foreign trust does not elect to be treated as a domestic trust for purposes of section 2801. Under section 2511(a), no gift tax is imposed on the transfer and thus, CE is not required to file a U.S. gift tax return. Under the terms of the foreign trust, A, CE's child and a U.S. resident, and Q, A's child and a U.S. citizen, may receive discretionary distributions of income and principal during life. At A's death, the assets remaining in the foreign trust will be distributed to B, CE's other U.S. resident child, or if B is not living at the time of A's death, then to CE's then-living issue, per stirpes. The terms of the foreign trust also allow A to appoint trust principal and/or income to A, A's estate, A's creditors, the creditors of A's estate, or A's issue at any time. On March 5, Year 2, A exercises this power to appoint and causes the trustee to distribute $100,000 to Q.

(ii) *Effects on Q*. On October 20, Year 1, the irrevocable, non-electing foreign trust receives a covered gift for purposes of section 2801, but no section 2801 tax is imposed at that time. On March 5, Year 2, when Q receives $100,000 from the irrevocable foreign trust pursuant to the exercise of A's power of appointment, Q receives a distribution attributable to a covered gift and section 2801 tax is imposed on Q. *See* § 28.2801–4(d)(5). Q must timely file Form 708 to report the covered gift from a foreign person (specifically, from CE). *See* section 6039F(a) and §§ 28.6011–1(a), 28.6071–1(a), and 28.6151–1(a). Furthermore, because the $100,000 is being distributed from a foreign trust, Q must report the gift on a Form 3520 as a distribution from a foreign trust. *See* § 28.2801–6(c)(2).

(iii) *Effects on A*. Although A has no section 2801 reporting requirement, under section 2501, A makes a taxable gift to Q of $100,000 when A exercises the general power of appointment for Q's benefit. *See* section 2514(b). Accordingly, A must report A's $100,000 gift to Q on a timely filed Form 709. *See* section 6019. Because A is considered the transferor of the $100,000 for gift and GST tax purposes, the distribution to Q is not a generation-skipping transfer under chapter 13. *See* § 26.2652–1(a)(1) of this chapter.

(4) Example 4: Lapse of power of appointment held by covered expatriate. A, a U.S. citizen, creates an irrevocable domestic trust for the benefit of A's issue, CE, and CE's children. CE is a covered expatriate, but CE's children are U.S. citizens. CE has the right to withdraw $5,000 in each year in which A makes a contribution to the trust, but the withdrawal right lapses 30 days after the date of the contribution. In Year 1, A funds the trust, but CE fails to exercise CE's right to withdraw $5,000 within 30 days of the contribution. The $5,000 lapse is not considered to be a release of the power by CE, so it is neither a gift for U.S. gift tax purposes, nor a covered gift for purposes of section 2801 under paragraph (e)(1) of this section.

(5) Example 5: Property subject to section 2801 tax as a covered gift and as a covered bequest. F, a CE, transfers an income interest in property to A, a U.S. citizen, while retaining the remainder interest. F was not required to, and did not, file a gift tax return. Upon F's death, A receives full title to the property. The initial transfer of the income interest was a covered gift valued at $1,000,000, upon which A paid the section 2801 tax. The value of the property at F's death

is $4,500,000. Because the full value of the property would have been included in F's gross estate if F had died as a U.S. citizen, there is a covered bequest at F's death. The covered bequest is subject to section 2801 tax on the excess of the value of the covered bequest over the value of the covered gift ($4,500,000 minus $1,000,000), or $3,500,000.

(g) Applicability date. This section applies to covered gifts or covered bequests received on or after January 1, 2025.

[T.D. 10027, 90 FR 3376, Jan. 14, 2025]

§ 28.2801–4 Liability for and payment of tax on covered gifts and covered bequests; computation of tax. [*Omitted. Ed.*]

[T.D. 10027, 90 FR 3376, Jan. 14, 2025]

§ 28.2801–5 Foreign trusts. [*Omitted. Ed.*]

[T.D. 10027, 90 FR 3376, Jan. 14, 2025]

§ 28.2801–6 Special rules and cross-references. [*Omitted. Ed.*]

[T.D. 10027, 90 FR 3376, Jan. 14, 2025]

§ 28.2801–7 Determining responsibility under section 2801. [*Omitted. Ed.*]

[T.D. 10027, 90 FR 3376, Jan. 14, 2025]

Procedure and Administration

Code and Regulations
Selected and Edited

SUBTITLE F. PROCEDURE AND ADMINISTRATION

Chapter 61. Information and Returns

Subchapter A. Returns and Records

Part I. Returns, Statements, and Special Returns

Part II. Tax Returns or Statements

Part III. Information Returns

* * *

Part V. Time for Filing Returns and Other Documents

Part VI. Extension of Time for Filing Returns

Part I. Records, Statements, and Special Returns

§ 6001. Notice or Regulations Requiring Records, Statements, and Special Returns

Every person liable for any tax imposed by this title, or for the collection thereof, shall keep such records, render such statements, make such returns, and comply with such rules and regulations as the Secretary may from time to time prescribe. Whenever in the judgment of the Secretary it is necessary, he may require any person, by notice served upon such person or by regulations, to make such returns, render such statements, or keep such records, as the Secretary deems sufficient to show whether or not such person is liable for tax under this title. The only records which an employer shall be required to keep under this section in connection with charged tips shall be charge receipts, records necessary to comply with section 6053(c), and copies of statements furnished by employees under section 6053(a).

Regulations

§ 20.6001–1 Persons required to keep records and render statements.

(a) It is the duty of the executor to keep such complete and detailed records of the affairs of the estate for which he acts as will enable the district director to determine accurately the amount of the estate tax liability. All documents and vouchers used in preparing the estate tax return (§ 20.6018–1) shall be retained by the executor so as to be available for inspection whenever required.

(b) In addition to filing an estate tax return (see § 20.6018–1) and, if applicable, a preliminary notice (see § 20.6036–1), the executor shall furnish such supplemental data as may be necessary to establish the correct estate tax. It is therefore the duty of the executor (1) to furnish, upon request, copies of any documents in his possession (or on file in any court having jurisdiction over the estate) relating to the estate, appraisal lists of any items included in the gross estate, copies of balance sheets or other financial statements obtainable by him relating to the value of stock, and any other information obtainable by him that may be found necessary in the determination of the tax, and (2) to render any written statement, containing a declaration that it is made under penalties of perjury, of facts within his knowledge which the district director may require for the purpose of determining whether a tax liability exists and, if so, the extent thereof. Failure to comply with such a request will render the executor liable to penalties (see section 7269), and proceedings may be instituted in the proper court of the United States to secure compliance therewith (see section 7604).

(c) Persons having possession or control of any records or documents containing or supposed to contain any information concerning the estate, or having knowledge of or information about any fact or facts which have a material bearing upon the liability, or the extent of liability, of the estate for the estate tax, shall, upon request of the district director, make disclosure thereof. Failure on the part of any person to comply with such request will render him liable to penalties (section 7269), and compliance with the request may be enforced in the proper court of the United States (section 7604).

(d) Upon notification from the Internal Revenue Service, a corporation (organized or created in the United States) or its transfer agent is required to furnish the following information pertaining to stocks or bonds registered in the name of a nonresident decedent (regardless of citizenship): (1) The name of the decedent as registered; (2) the date of the decedent's death; (3) the decedent's residence and his place of death; (4) the names and addresses of executors, attorneys, or other representatives of the estate, within and without the United States; and (5) a description of the securities, the number of shares or bonds and the par values thereof.

[T.D. 6296, 23 FR 4529, June 24, 1958, as amended by T.D. 7238, 37 FR 28720, Dec. 29, 1972]

§ 25.6001–1 Records required to be kept.

(a) In general. Every person subject to taxation under chapter 12 of the Internal Revenue Code of 1954 shall for the purpose of determining the total amount of his gifts, keep such permanent books of account or records as are necessary to establish the amount of his total gifts (limited as provided by section 2503(b)), together with the deductions allowable in determining the amount of his taxable gifts, and the other information required to be shown in a gift tax return. All documents and vouchers used in preparing the gift tax return (see § 25.6019–1) shall be retained by the donor so as to be available for inspection whenever required.

(b) Supplemental data. In order that the Internal Revenue Service may determine the correct tax the donor shall furnish such supplemental data as may be deemed necessary by the Internal Revenue Service. It is, therefore, the duty of the donor to furnish, upon request, copies of all documents relating to his gift or gifts, appraisal lists of any items included in the total amount of gifts, copies of balance sheets or other financial statements obtainable by him relating to the value of stock constituting the gift, and any other information obtainable by him that may be necessary in the determination of the tax. See section 2512 and the regulations issued thereunder. For every policy of life insurance listed on the return, the donor must procure a statement from the insurance company on Form 712 and file it with the internal revenue officer with whom the return is filed. If specifically requested by an internal revenue officer, the insurance company shall file this statement direct with the internal revenue officer.

[T.D. 6334, 23 FR 8904, Nov. 15, 1958, as amended by T.D. 7012, 34 FR 7691, May 15, 1969; T.D. 7517, 42 FR 58935, Nov. 14, 1977]

§ 28.6001–1 Records required to be kept.

(a) In general. Every U.S. recipient (as defined in § 28.2801–2(e)) subject to taxation under chapter 15 of subtitle B must keep, for the purpose of determining the total amount of covered gifts and covered bequests, such permanent books of account or records as are necessary to establish the amount of that person's aggregate covered gifts and covered bequests, and the other information required to be shown on Form 708, United States Return of Tax for Gifts and Bequests Received from Covered Expatriates, or any successor form. All documents and vouchers used in preparing Form 708 must be retained by the person required to file the return so as to be available for inspection so long as the contents thereof may become material in the administration of any internal revenue law.

(b) Supplemental information. The U.S. recipient, as defined in § 28.2801–2(e), must furnish such supplemental information as may be deemed necessary by the Internal Revenue Service (IRS) to allow the IRS to determine the correct amount of tax. Therefore, the U.S. recipient must furnish, upon request, copies of all documents relating to the covered gift or covered bequest, appraisals of any items included in the aggregate amount of covered gifts and covered bequests, copies of balance sheets and other financial statements obtainable by that person relating to the value of stock or other property constituting the covered gift or covered bequest, and any other information obtainable by that person that may be necessary in the determination of the tax. See section 2801 of the Code and the corresponding regulations. For every policy of life insurance listed on the return, the U.S. recipient must procure a statement from the insurance company on Form 712, Life Insurance Statement, or any successor form, and file it with the IRS office where the return is filed. If specifically requested by the IRS, the insurance company must file this statement directly with the IRS.

(c) Applicability date. This section applies on and after January 14, 2025.

[T.D. 10027, 90 FR 3376, Jan. 14, 2025]

Part II. Tax Returns or Statements

Subpart A. General Requirements

§ 6011. General Requirement of Return, Statement, or List

(a) General rule. When required by regulations prescribed by the Secretary any person made liable for any tax imposed by this title, or with respect to the collection thereof, shall make a return or statement according to the forms and regulations prescribed by the Secretary. Every person required to make a return or statement shall include therein the information required by such forms or regulations.

(b) Identification of taxpayer. The Secretary is authorized to require such information with respect to persons subject to the taxes imposed by chapter 21 or chapter 24 as is necessary or helpful in securing proper identification of such persons.

* * *

(e) Regulations requiring returns on magnetic media, etc.

(1) In general. The Secretary shall prescribe regulations providing standards for determining which returns must be filed on magnetic media or in other machine-readable form. The Secretary may not require returns of any tax imposed by subtitle A on individuals, estates, and trusts to be other than on paper forms supplied by the Secretary.

* * *

(h) Income, estate, and gift taxes. For requirement that returns of income, estate, and gift taxes be made whether or not there is tax liability, see subparts B and C.

Regulations

§ 1.6011–9 Syndicated conservation easement listed transactions.

(a) Identification as listed transaction. Transactions that are the same as, or substantially similar to, a transaction described in paragraph (b) of this section are identified as listed transactions for purposes of § 1.6011–4(b)(2).

(b) Syndicated conservation easement transaction. The term syndicated conservation easement transaction means a transaction in which the following steps occur (regardless of the order in which they occur)

(1) A taxpayer receives promotional materials that offer investors in a pass-through entity the possibility of being allocated a charitable contribution deduction the amount of which equals or exceeds an amount that is two and one-half times the amount of the taxpayer's investment, as determined in paragraph (d)(4) of this section, in the pass-through entity, as determined under paragraph (d) of this section (2.5 times rule);

(2) The taxpayer acquires an interest, directly or indirectly through one or more tiers of pass-through entities, in the pass-through entity that owns or acquires real property (that is, becomes an investor in the entity);

(3) The pass-through entity that owns the real property contributes an easement on such real property, which it treats as a conservation easement, to a quali-

fied organization and allocates, directly or through one or more tiers of pass-through entities, a charitable contribution deduction to the taxpayer; and

(4) The taxpayer claims a charitable contribution deduction with respect to the contribution of the real property interest on the taxpayer's Federal income tax return.

(c) Definitions. The following definitions apply for purposes of this section:

(1) *Charitable contribution deduction.* The term charitable contribution deduction means a deduction under section 170 of the Internal Revenue Code (Code), which includes a deduction arising from a qualified conservation contribution as defined in section 170(h)(1) of the Code.

(2) *Conservation easement.* The term conservation easement means a restriction (granted in perpetuity) on the use which may be made of the real property, within the meaning of section 170(h)(2)(C) of the Code, exclusively for conservation purposes, within the meaning of section 170(h)(1)(C) and (h)(4) of the Code.

(3) *Pass-through entity.* The term pass-through entity means a partnership, S corporation, or trust (other than a grantor trust within the meaning of subchapter J of chapter 1 of the Code).

(4) *Promotional materials.* The term promotional materials includes materials described in § 301.6112–1(b)(3)(iii)(B) of this chapter and any other written or oral communication regarding the transaction provided to investors, such as marketing materials, appraisals (including preliminary appraisals, draft appraisals, and the appraisal that is attached to the taxpayer's return), websites, transactional documents such as deeds of conveyance, private placement memoranda, tax opinions, operating agreements, subscription agreements, statements of the anticipated value of the conservation easement, and statements of the anticipated amount of the charitable contribution deduction.

(5) *Qualified organization.* The term qualified organization means an organization described in section 170(h)(3) of the Code.

(6) *Real property.* The term real property includes all land, structures, and buildings, including a certified historic structure defined in section 170(h)(4)(C) of the Code.

(7) *Substantially similar.* The term substantially similar is defined in § 1.6011–4(c)(4). For example, transactions that meet the elements of paragraph (b) of this section, except that the pass-through entity contributes a fee simple interest in real property or a real property interest described in section 170(h)(2)(A) or (B) of the Code rather than a conservation easement, are substantially similar to the listed transaction identified in this section.

(d) Application of the 2.5 times rule (1) *Bright-line rule.* Transactions for which the promotional materials offer the taxpayer the possibility of being allocated a charitable contribution deduction of only an amount less than 2.5 times the taxpayer's investment and for which the taxpayer is actually allocated a charitable contribution deduction of an amount less than 2.5 times the taxpayer's investment (so that the rebuttable presumption in paragraph (d)(3) of this section does not apply) are generally not considered substantially similar to the listed transaction identified in this section. However, if a pass-through entity engages in a series of transactions with a principal purpose of avoiding the application of the bright-line rule in this paragraph (d)(1), the series of transactions may be disregarded or the arrangement may be recharacterized in accordance with its substance. Whether a series of transactions has a principal purpose of avoiding the application of this bright-line rule is determined based on all the facts and circumstances.

(2) *Multiple suggested contribution amounts.* If the promotional materials suggest or imply a range of possible charitable contribution deduction amounts that may be allocated to the taxpayer, the highest suggested or implied contribution amount determines whether the 2.5 times rule in this paragraph (d) is met. In addition, if one piece of promotional materials (for example, an appraisal or oral statement) states a higher charitable contribution deduction amount than stated by other promotional materials, then the highest stated charitable contribution deduction amount determines whether the 2.5 times rule is met.

(3) *Rebuttable presumption.* The 2.5 times rule in this paragraph (d) is deemed to be met if the pass-through entity donates a real property interest within three years following the taxpayer's investment in the pass-through entity, the pass-through entity allocates a charitable contribution deduction to the taxpayer the amount of which equals or exceeds two and one-half

times the amount of the taxpayer's investment, and the taxpayer claims a charitable contribution deduction the amount of which equals or exceeds two and one-half times the amount of the taxpayer's investment. This presumption may be rebutted if the taxpayer establishes to the satisfaction of the Commissioner that none of the promotional materials contained a suggestion or implication that investors might be allocated a charitable contribution deduction that equals or exceeds an amount that is two and one-half times the amount of their investment in the pass-through entity.

(4) *Determining the amount of the taxpayer's investment in the pass-through entity* (i) *In general.* A taxpayer may determine the amount of the taxpayer's investment in the pass-through entity for purposes of paragraph (b) of this section using either the anti-stuffing method in paragraph (d)(4)(ii) of this section or, for contributions made after December 29, 2022, the relevant basis method in paragraph (d)(4)(iii) of this section. No other methods may be used.

(ii) *Anti-stuffing method.* Under the anti-stuffing method, the amount of a taxpayer's investment in the pass-through entity is the portion of the cash or fair market value of the assets the taxpayer uses to acquire its interest in the pass-through entity that is attributable to the real property on which a conservation easement is placed (or the portion thereof, if an easement is placed on a portion of the real property) that gives rise to the charitable contribution described in paragraph (b)(3) of this section. For example, if a portion of the taxpayer's cost of acquiring the taxpayer's interest in the pass-through entity is attributable to property held directly or indirectly by the pass-through entity other than the real property on which a conservation easement is placed as described in paragraph (b)(3) of this section (such other property may include other real property, cash, cash equivalents, digital assets, marketable securities, or other tangible or intangible assets), that portion of the taxpayer's acquisition cost is not considered part of the taxpayer's investment for purposes of this section because it is not attributable to the portion of the real property on which a conservation easement is placed as described in paragraph (b)(3) of this section. For purposes of this paragraph (d)(4)(ii), assets retained to pay for costs related to the operation and maintenance of the real property on which the conservation easement is placed, including costs that may be incurred in future years, are not attributable to the real property on which a conservation easement is placed as described in paragraph (b)(3) of this section. In the case of a substantially similar transaction described in paragraph (c)(7) of this section, the rules in this paragraph (d)(4)(ii) apply except that the relevant real property that gives rise to the charitable contribution deduction described in paragraph (b)(3) of this section is the real property donated.

(iii) *Relevant basis method.* For contributions made after December 29, 2022, taxpayers may use their relevant basis, as determined in accordance with section 170(h)(7)(B) of the Code and § 1.170A–14(k), as the amount of their investment for purposes of paragraph (b) of this section.

(5) *Examples.* For the examples in this paragraph (d)(5), assume that the partnerships are respected for Federal tax purposes, and that the partnership allocations comply with the rules of subchapter K of chapter 1 of the Code.

(i) *Example 1* (A) *Facts.* Individual A purchased an interest in P, a partnership that owns real property with a fair market value of $500,000 and marketable securities with a fair market value of $500,000. A is one of four equal investors in P, each of whom purchased its interest in P for $250,000 of cash. With respect to an investor's $250,000 payment for its interest in P, the promotional materials stated that P expected to allocate a $500,000 charitable contribution deduction to the investor (that is, a charitable contribution deduction that is two times the amount an investor paid for its interest in P). After all four investors have purchased their interests in P, P donates a conservation easement on all of its real property to a qualified organization as defined in section 170(h)(3) of the Code and reports a $2,000,000 charitable contribution on its Form 1065, U.S. Return of Partnership Income, based on P obtaining an appraisal indicating that the value of the conservation easement is $2,000,000. The Schedule K-1 (Form 1065) that P furnishes to A indicates that P allocated a charitable contribution deduction to A for the taxable year. A claims a charitable contribution deduction with respect to the charitable contribution on A's Federal income tax return.

(B) *Analysis.* A's cost of acquiring its interest in P is $250,000. The real property on which a conservation easement was placed and that gave rise to the charitable contribution deduction described in paragraph (b)(3) of this section was P's property valued at $500,000. P's only other asset was marketable securities worth $500,000. Accordingly, half of A's share of the value of the assets held by P was attributable to the real property on which P placed a conservation easement and that gave rise to the charitable contribution deduction described in paragraph (b)(3) of this section. Therefore, under paragraph (d)(4)(i) of this section, for purposes of paragraph (b) of this section, the amount of A's investment in P is $125,000 (that is, half of A's $250,000 acquisition cost, which is the portion of A's acquisition cost that is attributable to the real property on which P placed a conservation easement and that gave rise to the charitable contribution deduction described in paragraph (b)(3) of this section). Because A's investment for purposes of the 2.5 times rule is $125,000 and A's expected charitable contribution deduction, based on the promotional materials, is $500,000 (that is, an expected deduction that is four times A's investment), the 2.5 times rule of paragraph (b)(1) of this section is met. The transaction also meets the other elements of a syndicated conservation easement within the meaning of paragraph (b) of this section and therefore is a listed transaction for purposes of § 1.6011–4(b)(2).

(ii) *Example 2* (A) *Facts*. Individual B acquires a ten percent interest in InvestCo, a partnership, by making a $250,000 cash contribution. Immediately after B's acquisition, InvestCo's only asset is $2,500,000 of cash. The promotional materials state that InvestCo expects to allocate a $500,000 charitable contribution deduction to B with respect to B's partnership interest. InvestCo pays $600,000 to purchase marketable securities. InvestCo also purchases an interest in another partnership, PropCo, for $1,900,000 from one of PropCo's partners. At the same time as the purchase, InvestCo also contributes $100,000 of its marketable securities to PropCo. Immediately after InvestCo's purchase and contribution, PropCo's only assets are real property worth $2,400,000 and the marketable securities worth $100,000. PropCo donates its entire interest in the real property (a fee simple interest) to a qualified organization as defined in section 170(h)(3) of the Code and reports a $6,250,000 charitable contribution on its Form 1065, U.S. Return of Partnership Income, based on PropCo obtaining an appraisal indicating that the value of the real property is $6,250,000. PropCo allocates a portion of the charitable contribution deduction to InvestCo. The Schedule K-1 (Form 1065) that InvestCo furnishes to B indicates that InvestCo allocated a charitable contribution deduction to B for the taxable year. B claims a charitable contribution deduction with respect to the contribution on B's Federal income tax return.

(B) *Analysis*. Immediately after InvestCo's acquisition of its interest in PropCo, InvestCo's only assets were its interest in PropCo and $500,000 in marketable securities. Accordingly, eighty percent of InvestCo's funds ($2,000,000/$2,500,000) were used to acquire its interest in PropCo. B's investment in InvestCo is $250,000; therefore, eighty percent of that amount, $200,000, is attributable to InvestCo's interest in PropCo. Immediately after InvestCo's acquisition of its interest in PropCo, PropCo had real property worth $2,400,000 and marketable securities worth $100,000. As such, ninety-six percent ($2,400,000/$2,500,000) of PropCo's assets were the real property that was subsequently donated. Therefore, under paragraph (d)(4)(i) of this section, for purposes of paragraph (b) of this section, the amount of B's investment in InvestCo that is attributable to the donated real property that gave rise to the charitable contribution deduction described in paragraph (b)(3) of this section is $200,000 multiplied by ninety-six percent, or $192,000. Because B's investment for purposes of the 2.5 times rule is $192,000 and B's expected charitable contribution deduction, based on the promotional materials, is $500,000 (that is, an expected deduction that is at least 2.5 times B's investment), the 2.5 times rule of paragraph (b)(1) of this section is met. The transaction also meets the other elements of a syndicated conservation easement within the meaning of paragraph (b) of this section, except that PropCo contributed a fee simple interest in real property rather than a conservation easement. Under paragraph (c)(7) of this section, the transaction is substantially similar to the listed transaction described in paragraph (b) of this section and, therefore, under paragraph (a) of this section, the transaction in this example is a listed transaction for purposes of § 1.6011–4(b)(2).

(e) Participation in a syndicated conservation easement transaction (1) *In general*. Whether a taxpayer has participated in a syndicated conservation easement transaction described in paragraph (b) of this section is determined under § 1.6011–4(c)(3)(i)(A).

(2) *Class of participants*. For purposes of § 1.6011–4(c)(3)(i)(A), participants in a transaction that is the same as, or substantially similar to, a syndicated conservation easement transaction described in paragraph (b) of this section include

(i) An owner of a pass-through entity;

(ii) A pass-through entity; and

(iii) Any other taxpayer whose Federal income tax return reflects tax consequences or a tax strategy arising from a transaction that is the same as, or substantially similar to, the transaction described in paragraph (b) of this section.

(3) *Exclusion*. A qualified organization to which the conservation easement is donated is not treated as a participant under § 1.6011–4(c)(3)(i)(A) in a syndicated conservation easement transaction described in paragraph (b) of this section.

(f) Application of section 4965. A qualified organization to which the real property interest is donated is not treated under section 4965 of the Code as a party to the transaction described in paragraph (b) of this section.

(g) Disclosures under Notice 2017–10. A taxpayer who disclosed their participation in a transaction pursuant to Notice 2017–10 and in accordance with § 1.6011–4 before October 8, 2024, is treated as having made the disclosure required under this section and § 1.6011–4, for the years covered by that disclosure, as of the date of the disclosure under Notice 2017–10.

(h) Applicability date (1) *In general*. This section's identification of transactions that are the same as, or substantially similar to, the transactions described in paragraph (b) of this section as listed transactions for purposes of § 1.6011–4(b)(2) and sections 6111 and 6112 of the Code is effective October 8, 2024.

(2) *Applicability date for material advisors*. Notwithstanding § 301.6111–3(b)(4)(i) and (iii) of this chapter, material advisors are required to disclose only if they have made a tax statement on or after October 8, 2018.

[T.D. 10007, 89 FR 81355, Oct. 8, 2024]

Proposed § 1.6011–15 (REG–108761–22, March 25, 2024) Charitable Remainder Annuity Trust Listed Transaction.

(a) In general. Transactions that are the same as, or substantially similar to, a transaction described in paragraph (b) of this section are identified as listed transactions for purposes of § 1.6011–4(b)(2).

(b) Charitable remainder annuity trusts. A transaction is described in this paragraph (b) if:

(1) The grantor creates a trust purporting to qualify as a charitable remainder annuity trust under section 664(d)(1) of the Internal Revenue Code (Code);

(2) The grantor funds the trust with property having a fair market value in excess of its basis (contributed property);

(3) The trustee sells the contributed property;

(4) The trustee uses some or all of the proceeds from the sale of the contributed property to purchase an annuity; and

(5) On a Federal income tax return, the beneficiary of the trust treats the annuity amount payable from the trust as if it were, in whole or in part, an annuity payment subject to section 72 of the Code, instead of as carrying out to the beneficiary amounts in the ordinary income and capital gain tiers of the trust in accordance with section 664(b).

(c) Participation (1) In general. A taxpayer has participated in a transaction identified as a listed transaction in paragraph (a) of this section if the taxpayer's tax return reflects tax consequences or a tax strategy described in this section as provided under § 1.6011–4(c)(3)(i)(A). These tax consequences include those tax consequences that would affect any gift tax return, whether or not such gift tax return was filed. See § 25.6011–4 of this chapter.

(2) Treatment of charitable remainderman. An organization described in section 170(c) of the Code that the purported Charitable Remainder Annuity Trust designates as a recipient of the remainder interest described in section 664(d)(1) is not treated as a participant under § 1.6011–4(c)(3)(i)(A) in the transaction described in this section solely by reason of its status as a recipient of the remainder interest described in section 664(d)(1).

(d) Treatment of charitable remainderman under section 4965. A tax-exempt entity (as defined in section 4965 of the Code) that is an organization described in section 170(c) and that the purported Charitable Remainder Annuity Trust designates as a recipient of the remainder interest described in section 664(d)(1) is not treated as a party to the transaction described in this section for purposes of section 4965 solely by reason of its status as a recipient of the remainder interest described in section 664(d)(1).

(e) Applicability date. This section's identification of transactions that are the same as, or substantially similar to, the transaction described in paragraph (b) of this section as listed transactions for purposes of § 1.6011–4(b)(2) is effective on [date of publication of final regulations in the Federal Register].

Subpart B. Income Tax Returns

§ 6012. Persons Required to Make Returns of Income

(a) General rule. Returns with respect to income taxes under subtitle A shall be made by the following:

* * *

(3) Every estate the gross income of which for the taxable year is $600 or more;

(4) Every trust having for the taxable year any taxable income, or having gross income of $600 or over, regardless of the amount of taxable income;

(5) Every estate or trust of which any beneficiary is a nonresident alien;

* * *

(8) Every estate of an individual under chapter 7 or 11 of title 11 of the United States Code (relating to bankruptcy) the gross income of which for the taxable year is not less than the sum of the exemption amount plus the basic standard deduction under section 63(c)(2)(C);

* * *

(b) Returns made by fiduciaries and receivers.

(1) Returns of decedents. If an individual is deceased, the return of such individual required under subsection (a) shall be made by his executor, administrator, or other person charged with the property of such decedent.

(2) Persons under a disability. If an individual is unable to make a return required under subsection (a), the return of such individual shall be made by a duly authorized agent, his committee, guardian, fiduciary or other person charged with the care of the person or property of such individual. The preceding sentence shall not apply in the case of a receiver appointed by authority of law in possession of only a part of the property of an individual.

* * *

(4) Returns of estates and trusts. Returns of an estate, a trust, or an estate of an individual under chapter 7 or 11 of title 11 of the United States Code shall be made by the fiduciary thereof.

(5) Joint fiduciaries. Under such regulations as the Secretary may prescribe, a return made by one of two or more joint fiduciaries shall be sufficient compliance with the requirements of this section. A return made pursuant to this paragraph shall contain a statement that the fiduciary has sufficient knowledge of the affairs of the person for whom the return is made to enable him to make the return, and that the return is, to the best of his knowledge and belief, true and correct.

* * *

§ 6013. Joint Returns of Income Tax by Husband and Wife

(a) Joint returns. A husband and wife may make a single return jointly of income taxes under subtitle A, even though one of the spouses has neither gross income nor deductions, except as provided below:

* * *

(2) no joint return shall be made if the husband and wife have different taxable years; except that if such taxable years begin on the same day and end on different days because of the death of either or both, then the joint return may be made with respect to the taxable year of each. The above exception shall not apply if the surviving spouse remarries before the close of his taxable year, nor if the taxable year of either spouse is a fractional part of a year under section 443(a)(1);

(3) in the case of death of one spouse or both spouses the joint return with respect to the decedent may be made only by his executor or administrator; except that in the case of the death of one spouse the joint return may be made by the surviving spouse with respect to both himself and the decedent if no return for the taxable year has been made by the decedent, no executor or administrator has been appointed, and no executor or administrator is appointed before the last day prescribed by law for filing the return of the surviving spouse. If an executor or administrator of the decedent is appointed after the making of the joint return by the surviving spouse, the executor or administrator may disaffirm such joint return by making, within 1 year after the last day prescribed by law for filing the return of the surviving spouse, a separate return for the taxable year of the decedent with respect to which the joint return was made, in which case the return made by the survivor shall constitute his separate return.

* * *

Subpart C. Estate and Gift Tax Returns

§ 6018. Estate Tax Returns

(a) Returns by Executor.

(1) Citizens or residents. In all cases where the gross estate at the death of a citizen or resident exceeds the basic exclusion amount in effect under section 2010(c) for the calendar year which includes the date of death, the executor shall make a return with respect to the estate tax imposed by subtitle B.

(2) Nonresidents not citizens of the United States. In the case of the estate of every nonresident not a citizen of the United States if that part of the gross estate which is situated in the United States exceeds $60,000, the executor shall make a return with respect to the estate tax imposed by subtitle B.

(3) Adjustment for certain gifts. The amount applicable under paragraph (1) and the amount set forth in paragraph (2) shall each be reduced (but not below zero) by the sum of—

(A) the amount of the adjusted taxable gifts (within the meaning of section 2001(b)) made by the decedent after December 31, 1976, plus

(B) the aggregate amount allowed as a specific exemption under section 2521 (as in effect before its repeal by the Tax Reform Act of 1976) with respect to gifts made by the decedent after September 8, 1976.

(b) Returns by Beneficiaries. If the executor is unable to make a complete return as to any part of the gross estate of the decedent, he shall include in his return a description of such part and the name of every person holding a legal or beneficial interest therein. Upon notice from the Secretary such person shall in like manner make a return as to such part of the gross estate.

§ 6019. Gift Tax Returns

Any individual who in any calendar year makes any transfer by gift other than

(1) a transfer which under subsection (b) or (e) of section 2503 is not to be included in the total amount of gifts for such year,

(2) a transfer of an interest with respect to which a deduction is allowed under section 2523, or

(3) a transfer with respect to which a deduction is allowed under section 2522 but only if—

(A)

(i) such transfer is of the donor's entire interest in the property transferred, and

(ii) no other interest in such property is or has been transferred (for less than adequate and full consideration in money or money's worth) from the donor to a person, or for a use, not described in subsection (a) or (b) of section 2522, or

(B) such transfer is described in section 2522(d),

shall make a return for such year with respect to the gift tax imposed by subtitle B.

Regulation

§ 25.6019–3 Contents of return.

* * *

(b) Disclosure of transfers coming within provisions of section 2516. Section 2516 provides that certain transfers of property pursuant to written property settlements between husband and wife are deemed to be transfers for full and adequate consideration in money or money's worth if divorce occurs within 2 years. In any case where a husband and wife enter into a written agreement of the type contemplated by section 2516 and the final decree of divorce is not granted on or before the due date for the filing of a gift tax return for the calendar year (or calendar quarter with respect to periods beginning after December 31, 1970, and ending before January 1, 1982) in which the agreement became effective (see § 25.6075–1), then, except to the extent § 25.6019–1 provides otherwise, the transfer must be disclosed by the transferor upon a gift tax return filed for the calendar year (or calendar quarter) in which the agreement becomes effective, and a copy of the agreement must be attached to the return. In addition, a certified copy of the final divorce decree shall be furnished the internal revenue officer with whom the return was filed not later than 60 days after the divorce is granted. Pending receipt of evidence that the final decree of divorce has been granted (but in no event for a period of more than 2 years from the effective date of the agreement), the transfer will tentatively be treated as made for a full and adequate consideration in money or money's worth.

[T.D. 6334, 23 FR 8904, Nov. 15, 1958, as amended by T.D. 7012, 34 FR 7691, May 15, 1969; T.D. 7238, 37 FR 28736, Dec. 29, 1972; T.D. 8522, 59 FR 9664, March 1, 1994]

Part III. Information Returns

Subpart A. Information Concerning Persons Subject to Special Provisions

§ 6034. Returns by Certain Trusts

(a) Split-interest trusts. Every trust described in section 4947(a)(2) shall furnish such information with respect to the taxable year as the Secretary may by forms or regulations require.

(b) Trusts claiming certain charitable deductions.

(1) In general. Every trust not required to file a return under subsection (a) but claiming a deduction under section 642(c) for the taxable year shall furnish such information with respect to such taxable year as the Secretary may by forms or regulations prescribe, including—

(A) the amount of the deduction taken under section 642(c) within such year,

(B) the amount paid out within such year which represents amounts for which deductions under section 642(c) have been taken in prior years,

(C) the amount for which such deductions have been taken in prior years but which has not been paid out at the beginning of such year,

(D) the amount paid out of principal in the current and prior years for the purposes described in section 642(c),

(E) the total income of the trust within such year and the expenses attributable thereto, and

(F) a balance sheet showing the assets, liabilities, and net worth of the trust as of the beginning of such year.

(2) Exceptions. Paragraph (1) shall not apply to a trust for any taxable year if—

(A) all the net income for such year, determined under the applicable principles of the law of trusts, is required to be distributed currently to the beneficiaries, or

(B) the trust is described in section 4947(a)(1).

§ 6034A. Information to Beneficiaries of Estates and Trusts

(a) General rule. The fiduciary of any estate or trust required to file a return under section 6012(a) for any taxable year shall, on or before the date on which such return was required to be filed, furnish to each beneficiary (or nominee thereof)—

(1) who receives a distribution from such estate or trust with respect to such taxable year, or

(2) to whom any item with respect to such taxable year is allocated,

a statement containing such information required to be shown on such return as the Secretary may prescribe.

(b) Nominee reporting. Any person who holds an interest in an estate or trust as a nominee for another person—

(1) shall furnish to the estate or trust, in the manner prescribed by the Secretary, the name and address of such other person, and any other information for the taxable year as the Secretary may by form and regulations prescribe, and

(2) shall furnish in the manner prescribed by the Secretary to such other person the information provided by the estate or trust under subsection (a).

(c) Beneficiary's return must be consistent with estate or trust return or secretary notified of inconsistency.

(1) In general. A beneficiary of any estate or trust to which subsection (a) applies shall, on such beneficiary's return, treat any reported item in a manner which is consistent with the treatment of such item on the applicable entity's return.

(2) Notification of inconsistent treatment.

(A) In general. In the case of any reported item, if—

(i) (I) the applicable entity has filed a return but the beneficiary's treatment on such beneficiary's return is (or may be) inconsistent with the treatment of the item on the applicable entity's return, or

(II) the applicable entity has not filed a return, and

(ii) the beneficiary files with the Secretary a statement identifying the inconsistency,

paragraph (1) shall not apply to such item.

(B) Beneficiary receiving incorrect information. A beneficiary shall be treated as having complied with clause (ii) of subparagraph (A) with respect to a reported item if the beneficiary—

(i) demonstrates to the satisfaction of the Secretary that the treatment of the reported item on the beneficiary's return is consistent with the treatment of the item on the statement furnished under subsection (a) to the beneficiary by the applicable entity, and

(ii) elects to have this paragraph apply with respect to that item.

(3) Effect of failure to notify. In any case—

(A) described in subparagraph (A)(i)(I) of paragraph (2), and

(B) in which the beneficiary does not comply with subparagraph (A)(ii) of paragraph (2),

any adjustment required to make the treatment of the items by such beneficiary consistent with the treatment of the items on the applicable entity's return shall be treated as arising out of mathematical or clerical errors and assessed according to section 6213(b)(1). Paragraph (2) of section 6213(b) shall not apply to any assessment referred to in the preceding sentence.

(4) Definitions. For purposes of this subsection—

(A) Reported item. The term "reported item" means any item for which information is required to be furnished under subsection (a).

(B) Applicable entity. The term "applicable entity" means the estate or trust of which the taxpayer is the beneficiary.

(5) Addition to tax for failure to comply with section. For addition to tax in the case of a beneficiary's negligence in connection with, or disregard of, the requirements of this section, see part II of subchapter A of chapter 68.

§ 6035. Basis Information to Persons Acquiring Property from Decedent

(a) Information with respect to property acquired from decedents.

(1) In general. The executor of any estate required to file a return under section 6018(a) shall furnish to the Secretary and to each person acquiring any interest in property included in the decedent's gross estate for Federal estate tax purposes a statement identifying the value of each interest in such property as reported on such return and such other information with respect to such interest as the Secretary may prescribe.

(2) Statements by beneficiaries. Each person required to file a return under section 6018(b) shall furnish to the Secretary and to each other person who holds a legal or beneficial interest in the property to which such return relates a statement identifying the information described in paragraph (1).

(3) Time for furnishing statement.

(A) In general. Each statement required to be furnished under paragraph (1) or (2) shall be furnished at such time as the Secretary may prescribe, but in no case at a time later than the earlier of—

(i) the date which is 30 days after the date on which the return under section 6018 was required to be filed (including extensions, if any), or

(ii) the date which is 30 days after the date such return is filed.

(B) Adjustments. In any case in which there is an adjustment to the information required to be included on a statement filed under paragraph (1) or (2) after such statement has been filed, a supplemental statement under such paragraph shall be filed not later than the date which is 30 days after such adjustment is made.

(b) Regulations. The Secretary shall prescribe such regulations as necessary to carry out this section, including regulations relating to—

(1) the application of this section to property with regard to which no estate tax return is required to be filed, and

(2) situations in which the surviving joint tenant or other recipient may have better information than the executor regarding the basis or fair market value of the property.

Regulations

§ 1.6035–0 Table of contents. [*Omitted. Ed.*]

[T.D. 9991, Sept. 16, 2024]

§ 1.6035–1 Basis information to persons acquiring property from decedent.

(a) Overview. This section implements the reporting requirements under section 6035 of the Internal Revenue Code (Code) applicable to executors and certain trustees. In general, the reporting requirements of this section require providing information to the IRS on the identity of persons acquiring property from a decedent and providing basis information to persons acquiring that property from the decedent. Basis information is needed by certain persons acquiring property from a decedent in order to comply with the consistent basis requirement of section 1014(f) of the Code. See § 1.1014–10 for rules applicable to the consistent basis requirement.

(b) Applicability of section 6035 reporting requirements (1) *In general.* The reporting requirements under section 6035 of the Code apply only in the case of an estate in which the executor is required to file an estate tax return under section 6018 of the Code (determined without regard to § 20.2010–2(a)(1) of this chapter) (required estate tax return) and the executor files that return after July 31, 2015. The requirements do not apply in the case of an estate whose required estate tax return is filed on or before July 31, 2015, even if the due date of the return is after July 31, 2015, or if one or more supplements to that return are filed with the IRS after July 31, 2015. Whether an estate tax return is a required estate tax return depends on the relevant factors identified in section 6018 and the corresponding regulations, including the date of death value of property includible in the decedent's gross estate, the amount of adjusted taxable gifts, and the applicable filing threshold. An election under section 2032 or 2032A of the Code to determine the value of the gross estate in accordance with those respective provisions is not relevant to whether an executor is required to file an estate tax return under section 6018. If an estate tax return is not required to be filed under section 6018 based on the relevant factors identified in section 6018, then an estate tax return filed for another purpose (such as to make a portability election under section 2010(c)(5) of the Code, an allocation or election under section 2632 of the Code with regard to a decedent's generation-skipping transfer tax exemption, or a protective filing to avoid a penalty or satisfy a State law requirement) is not a required estate tax return for purposes of this section.

(2) *Executor(s) subject to section 6035 reporting requirements.* For purposes of this section, the term executor has the same meaning as in section 2203 of

the Code, as expanded to include all persons required under section 6018(b) to file an estate tax return. Thus, more than one person may be subject to the reporting requirements for the same decedent's estate. If one executor is unable to file a complete estate tax return (for example, if the executor has insufficient information about property in the decedent's gross estate that is not in the possession of that executor), each person required to file a return is subject to the reporting requirements of this section only with regard to the property reported (or required to be reported) on the estate tax return required to be filed by that person. Similarly, if no executor is appointed by a court, each person in actual or constructive possession of any property of the decedent is an executor for purposes of this section and is subject to the reporting requirements of this section, but only with regard to the property reported or required to be reported on the estate tax return required to be filed by that executor under section 6018(b).

(3) *Examples*. The following examples, in which the decedent D was a United States citizen at the time of the decedent's death, illustrates the application of this paragraph (b).

(i) *Example 1* Executor required to file a return under section 6018. The value at death of property includible in D's gross estate exceeds the basic exclusion amount in effect for the year of D's death under section 2010(c). On the timely-filed estate tax return, D's executor makes a valid alternate valuation election under section 2032 to value the property of D's gross estate as of a date subsequent to the date of death. As a result, the value of property includible in D's gross estate is decreased to a value that is less than the basic exclusion amount in effect for the year of D's death. Because D's executor is required to file an estate tax return under section 6018, D's executor also is subject to the reporting requirements of section 6035. This is true even though no estate tax liability was incurred, and the requirements of section 1014(f) do not apply to any property includible in D's gross estate. See § 1.1014–10(c)(1).

(ii) *Example 2* Executor not required to file a return under section 6018. The value at death of property includible in D's gross estate does not exceed the basic exclusion amount in effect for the year of D's death under section 2010(c) of the Code. In accordance with the terms of D's will, D's executor distributes D's entire estate to D's only child. D's executor files an estate tax return solely for the purpose of making a portability election under section 2010(c)(5). Because D's executor is not required to file an estate tax return under section 6018, D's executor is not subject to the reporting requirements of section 6035.

(iii) *Example 3* No executor appointed. The value at death of property includible in D's gross estate exceeds the basic exclusion amount in effect for the year of D's death under section 2010(c) and consists entirely of D's interests in Property A and Property B that D owned with Nephew A and Nephew B, respectively, as joint tenants with rights of survivorship. Pursuant to local law, Nephew A becomes the sole owner of Property A and Nephew B becomes the sole owner of Property B upon D's death. No executor or administrator is appointed, qualified, or acting within the United States for D's estate on the due date of D's estate tax return. Because Nephew A has actual or constructive possession of Property A, Nephew A is an executor described in paragraph (b)(2) of this section with regard to D's interest in Property A. Because Nephew A is required to file an estate tax return under section 6018 with regard to D's interest in Property A, Nephew A also is subject to the reporting requirements of section 6035 with respect to Property A. Similarly, because Nephew B has actual or constructive possession of Property B on the due date of D's estate tax return, Nephew B is an executor described in paragraph (b)(2) of this section with regard to D's interest in Property B. Because Nephew B is required to file an estate tax return under section 6018 with regard to D's interest in Property B, Nephew B also is subject to the reporting requirements of section 6035 with respect to Property B.

(iv) *Example 4* Executor unable to make a complete return. The value at death of property includible in D's gross estate exceeds the basic exclusion amount in effect for the year of D's death under section 2010(c). E is appointed the executor of D's estate. During the administration of D's estate, E discovers that D has made transfers each year for the past ten years to T as trustee of Trust. E contacts T, but T refuses to provide E with any information regarding Trust. E timely files D's estate tax return reporting the value of all of the property in D's gross estate except Trust. Pursuant to § 20.6018–2 of this chapter, E includes with the return a statement that gives T's name and contact information and the date and amount of each transfer from D to T as trustee of Trust, which is all the information E has about Trust. The IRS provides notice to T of T's obligation to make D's estate return as to Trust. Because E is required to file an estate tax return under section 6018, E is subject to the reporting requirements of section 6035 as to the property reported on the estate tax return filed by E. Because T is required to file an estate tax return under section 6018, T is subject to the reporting requirements of section 6035 as to Trust.

(c) Required Information Return and Statement(s) (1) *Required Information Return.* An executor required to file an estate tax return under section 6018 must file with the IRS an Information Return by the date required under paragraph (c)(3) of this section. The term Information Return refers to the Form 8971, Information Regarding Beneficiaries Acquiring Property from a Decedent, and all required attachments. Required attachments include a copy of each Statement described in paragraph (c)(2) of this section (if any) required to be furnished to a beneficiary who acquires property within the meaning of paragraph (c)(4) of this section on or before the due date of the estate tax return or, if earlier, the date on which the estate tax return is filed with the IRS. Required attachments also include a copy of each Statement (if any) furnished pursuant to paragraph (c)(5) of this section before the filing of the Information Return. The term Information Return also refers to any successor form or procedure designated by the IRS for this purpose. The Information Return must identify each beneficiary who has acquired or will acquire property subject to reporting (under paragraph (e) of this section), as well as other information prescribed by the Information Return and the instructions for that form. For the duty to supplement the Information Return in the event such property is acquired by a beneficiary after the filing of the estate tax return, see paragraph (c)(3)(ii) of this section. For the duty to supplement the Information Return in the event of a change to the information required to be reported, see paragraph (d) of this section.

(2) *Required Statement(s).* An executor required to file an estate tax return under section 6018 also must furnish a Statement to each beneficiary who acquires property subject to reporting under paragraph (e) of this section. For purposes of this section, the term Statement refers to the payee statement described as Schedule A of the Information Return to be furnished to a beneficiary, or any successor form, schedule, or procedure designated by the IRS for this purpose. The Statement furnished to a beneficiary must identify that beneficiary's acquired property and its value and other information prescribed by the Statement and the instructions for that form. For each property reported on a Statement, the value the executor reports on that Statement is the value of the property as reported on the estate tax return filed with the IRS. Generally, this is the value of the property on the date of the decedent's death, except in the case of an election in which the value is determined under section 2032 or 2032A, in which case it is the value determined under the applicable provision. If different interests in the same property pass from the decedent to one or more income beneficiaries or life tenants and remaindermen, the value to be reported is the value of the entire property and each recipient will be responsible for identifying his or her respective share of uniform basis. For the duty to supplement the Statement in the event of a change to the information required to be reported, including a change in the identified value of property reported on a Statement, see paragraph (d) of this section.

(3) *Due dates* (i) *General rule.* Except as provided in paragraphs (c)(3)(ii) and (iii) of this section and in § 1.6035–2, the executor must file the Information Return with the IRS on or before the due date specified in this paragraph (c)(3)(i). In addition, each Statement, a copy of which is required to be attached to the Information Return, must be furnished to the named beneficiary on or before this same due date. The Information Return must be filed, and each such Statement (if any) must be furnished to its named beneficiary, on or before the earlier of—

(A) The date that is 30 days after the due date of the estate tax return required under section 6018 (including extensions, if any); or

(B) The date that is 30 days after the date on which that estate tax return is filed with the IRS.

(ii) *Due date and applicable rules if property is acquired subsequently by beneficiary.* If a beneficiary acquires property subject to reporting after the due date of the estate tax return (or the earlier filing of the Information Return), the executor must furnish a Statement to that beneficiary with regard to that acquired property on or before January 31 of the year following the beneficiary's acquisition of that property. By that same January 31, the executor also must attach a copy of the Statement to a supplement to the Information Return (a supplemental Information Return) and must file the supplemental Information Return with the IRS. The supplemental Information Return must include a copy of each Statement required to be furnished for that year pursuant to this paragraph (c)(3)(ii), as well as a copy of each Statement (if any) furnished in accordance with paragraph (c)(5) of this section that has not already been filed with the IRS as an attachment to the Information Return or a supplement to the Information Return. The requirements of this paragraph (c)(3)(ii) do not apply if the property already has been reported on a Statement furnished pursuant to paragraph (c)(5) of this section. See this paragraph (c)(3) and paragraph (d)(4) of this section for the due date of other required supplements to this reporting.

(iii) *Transition rule.* If the due date of an estate tax return required to be filed by section 6018 is on or before July 31, 2015, but the executor does not file the estate tax return with the IRS until after July 31, 2015, then the Information Return and all required Statements are due on or before the date that is 30 days after the date on which the estate tax return is filed, except as provided in § 1.6035–2.

(4) *Acquiring an interest in property.* For purposes of this section, the term acquired property refers to property subject to reporting under paragraph (e) of this section that a beneficiary acquires. A beneficiary acquires such property when, under local law, title vests in the beneficiary or when the beneficiary otherwise has sufficient control over or connection with the property that the beneficiary is able to take action related to the property for which basis is relevant for Federal income tax purposes (such as, for example, to sell or depreciate the property). In many cases, a beneficiary's acquisition of property occurs upon an executor's or trustee's distribution of the property. For property passing by contract or by operation of law, the beneficiary's acquisition of that property generally occurs automatically upon the death of the decedent.

(5) *Option to furnish Statement(s) prior to the acquisition of property by a beneficiary.* An executor may satisfy the requirement in paragraph (c)(2) of this section to furnish a Statement to a beneficiary by furnishing the Statement to the beneficiary prior to the beneficiary's acquisition of the property subject to reporting under paragraph (e) of this section, provided that the executor has reason to believe that the beneficiary will acquire that property. The Statement furnished to such a beneficiary must identify the property the beneficiary is expected to acquire as well as the value of that property and other information prescribed by the Statement and the instructions for that form (and must include information relating to other property actually acquired by such beneficiary as may be required under paragraph (c)(2) of this section). If, after satisfying the requirements of this paragraph (c)(5), the property is acquired by a different beneficiary, the executor must update the beneficiary information in the Information Return and furnish a Statement to that beneficiary pursuant to the duty to supplement to report a change in beneficiary information as described in paragraph (d)(2)(i) of this section. The executor additionally is subject to the duty to supplement to report other changes to the information required to be reported as identified in paragraph (d) of this section.

(6) *Example.* The following example illustrates the application of this paragraph (c).

(i) The decedent D was a United States citizen at the time of D's death and the executor of D's estate E is required to file an estate tax return under section 6018. The terms of D's will provide for D's entire estate to be distributed to a marital trust. Prior to timely filing the estate tax return for D's estate, E funded the marital trust with a portion of the property, the value of which is included in D's gross estate. Under paragraph (c)(4) of this section, the marital trust has acquired this property upon the funding of the trust by E. Under paragraphs (c)(1) and (c)(3)(i) of this section, within 30 days of filing the estate tax return, E must file with the IRS the Information Return identifying the marital trust as the beneficiary (as well as other information prescribed by the Information Return or instructions) and must include with the Information Return all required attachments. Under paragraphs (c)(2) and (c)(3)(i) of this section, by the same date, E must furnish to the marital trust the Statement identifying the portion of the property distributed to the marital trust and its estate tax value (as well as any other information prescribed by the Statement or instructions). A copy of the Statement is a required attachment to be included with the Information Return. Pursuant to paragraph (c)(5) of this section, E may choose to expand the property identified on the Statement to also include the property the marital trust is expected to acquire subsequently. If E so chooses, the Statement to be furnished to the marital trust will identify all such property and its value at the date of death and, except in the case of any changes to the information required to be reported, no further Statement will be required at the time of the completion of the funding of the trust.

(ii) However, if E chooses not to expand the reporting to property not yet acquired by the marital trust, then, once the marital trust has acquired additional property, E is subject to further reporting. Under paragraph (c)(3)(ii) of this section, in each year that E distributes additional property to the marital trust, E must furnish, by January 31 of the following year, a Statement to the marital trust identifying all of the property the marital trust has acquired from D's estate that year and the property's estate tax value (as well as any other information prescribed by the Statement or instructions). By the same date, E must file with the IRS a supplemental Information Return and attach a copy of that Statement as well as any other required attachments.

(d) Duty to supplement (1) *Duty to supplement to report changes to the information reported on the Information Return or Statement(s).* An executor to whom the reporting requirements of this section apply must file a supplemental Information Return with the IRS and furnish a Statement or supplemental Statement to each affected beneficiary if a change to the information required to be reported on the Information Return or Statement (or supplement to either) causes the information as reported to be incorrect or incomplete. The executor must file the supplemental Information Return with the IRS, including copies of each Statement or supplemental Statement furnished to affected beneficiaries, and must furnish a Statement or supplemental Statement to each affected beneficiary, by the due date described in paragraph (d)(4) of this section.

(2) *Changes requiring supplement.* This paragraph (d)(2) provides a nonexhaustive list of changes that require supplemental reporting under paragraph (d)(1) of this section.

(i) *Change in beneficiary information.* The receipt, discovery, or acquisition by the executor of information that changes the beneficiary to whom property is to be distributed (pursuant to a death, disclaimer, bankruptcy, or otherwise), or corrects or completes other beneficiary information originally reported, will give rise to a duty to supplement.

(ii) *Change in the identified value of property.* The supplementing of an estate tax return to report a corrected estate tax value of property that was previously reported on an estate tax return and a Statement will give rise to a duty to supplement. In addition, a final determination of value of property for Federal estate tax purposes (within the meaning of § 1.1014–10(b)(1)) that differs from the value provided on a Statement or supplement to a Statement will give rise to a duty to supplement.

(iii) *Change or addition of property subject to reporting.* The supplementing of an estate tax return to report the estate tax value of property subject to reporting under paragraph (e) of this section, if that property and/or its value previously was not reported on an estate tax return or supplement to the estate tax return, will give rise to a duty to supplement. A duty to supplement also will arise if such property or its value that previously was not reported on an estate tax return or supplement to the estate tax return is included in the decedent's gross estate pursuant to an examination by the IRS or otherwise.

(iv) *Change in property to be acquired by beneficiary.* A duty to supplement will arise if an executor furnishes a Statement to a beneficiary prior to the beneficiary's acquisition of property pursuant to paragraph (c)(5) of this section and the beneficiary ultimately acquires property different from the property identified on that Statement. A beneficiary's acquisition of different property may occur for any reason, including an executor's receipt of different property in a transaction in which the basis of the new property received by the executor is determined, in whole or in part, by reference to the final value of property acquired from or as a result of the death of the decedent (for example, as the result of a like-kind exchange under section 1031 or an involuntary conversion).

(3) *Exceptions; no duty to supplement despite certain changes.* Notwithstanding paragraph (d)(2) of this section, no supplemental reporting under this section is required for:

(i) Inconsequential errors or omissions within the meaning of § 301.6722–1(b) of this chapter;

(ii) Changes resulting from an event that triggers an additional estate tax under section 2032A, including changes in value in the event of a beneficiary election under section 1016(c) of the Code;

(iii) Adjustments to the basis of property pursuant to sections of the Code otherthan section 1014(f); and

(iv) Any other change that is identified as requiring no supplemental reporting under this section in published guidance in the Federal Register or in the Internal Revenue Bulletin (see § 601.601(d)(2)(ii)(b) of this chapter).

(4) *Due date of supplemental reporting*. The supplemental reporting required by this paragraph (d) must be filed with the IRS and furnished to each affected beneficiary on or before 30 days after the date on which information becomes available to the executor from which the executor can conclude that a change to the information provided on the Information Return or Statement (or supplement to either) requires supplemental reporting. For changes occurring as a result of supplementing the estate tax return, the date on which the information becomes available to the executor is deemed to be the filing date of the supplemental information. Therefore, for changes occurring as a result of supplementing the estate tax return, the due date of the supplemental reporting required by this paragraph (d) is 30 days after thc filing date of the supplemental information. For changes occurring as a result of a determination of final value, the date on which the information becomes available to the executor is deemed to be the date a value becomes the final value under § 1.1014–10(b)(1). Therefore, for changes occurring as a result of a determination of final value, the due date of the supplemental reporting required by this paragraph (d) is 30 days after the date a value becomes the final value under § 1.1014–10(b)(1). However, with regard to property that has not been acquired by a beneficiary on or before the due date described in this paragraph (d)(4) and for which a Statement was not provided to the beneficiary pursuant to paragraph (c)(5) of this section, the due date may be delayed until the due date described in paragraph (c)(3)(ii) of this section.

(5) *Duration of duty to supplement*. An executor's duty to supplement as described in this section continues to apply until a final determination of value for Federal estate tax purposes (a final value within the meaning of § 1.1014–10(b)(1)) is determined for all property subject to reporting (under paragraph (e) of this section) or, if later, until such property has been acquired by a beneficiary. Therefore, the executor's final supplemental reporting is the reporting to the IRS and the furnishing of Statements to beneficiaries with regard to the last to occur of these two events, assuming that either event would create a change requiring supplemental reporting.

(6) *Examples*. The following examples illustrate the application of this paragraph (d). In each case, the decedent D was a U.S. citizen and D's executor E was required under section 6018 to file an estate tax return.

(i) *Example 1* Change in identified value of property. D's estate includes stock in a closely-held corporation. E distributes the stock to a beneficiary B of the estate before the due date of the estate tax return. D's executor reports the value of the stock at $14 million on D's estate tax return and on the Statement furnished to B. On examination of D's estate tax return, the IRS adjusts the value of the closely-held stock to $18 million. A court subsequently determines that the fair market value of the closely-held stock for Federal estate tax purposes is $17 million and the court's decision becomes final on June 15th. On or before July 15th of the same year, E must furnish a supplemental Statement to B showing the final value of $17 million for the closely-held stock, and must attach a copy of that supplemental Statement to a supplemental Information Return and file it with the IRS.

(ii) *Example 2* Duration of the duty to supplement. D's gross estate includes stock in closely-held corporation X, stock in closely-held corporation Y, and cash. D's will directs E to distribute 50% of the value of D's estate to A and 50% to B in any manner to which A and B agree. A and B agree that A will take the stock in corporation X and B will take stock in corporation Y and they will divide the cash in such amounts as to cause each to take an equal share of the value D's estate. E timely files D's estate tax return and furnishes a Statement to A and to B pursuant to paragraph (c)(5) of this section. The IRS accepts the return as filed and the period of limitations on assessment of estate tax expires. Thereafter, A and B agree to revise their agreement. E distributes the stock in corporation X to B and the stock in corporation Y to A in accordance with a revised agreement between A and B. E's final supplemental reporting is the filing of a supplemental

Information Return and furnishing of a supplemental Statement to A describing the shares and value of stock distributed to A and a supplemental Statement to B describing the shares and value of stock distributed to B.

(e) Property for which reporting is required (1) *In general.* Except for excepted property subject to only limited reporting as described in paragraph (f) of this section, the property subject to reporting under this section is included property and any other property the basis of which is determined, in whole or in part, by reference to the basis of the included property (for example, property acquired in a like-kind exchange or an involuntary conversion). For purposes of this section, included property is property the value of which is included in the value of the decedent's gross estate as defined in section 2031 or 2103. Generally, included property refers to property whose value is reported on an estate tax return, but it also refers to property whose value otherwise is included in the total value of the gross estate (for example, during examination by the IRS). Thus, included property includes property that qualified, in whole or in part, for an estate tax marital deduction under section 2056, 2056A, or 2106(a)(3) or for an estate tax charitable deduction under section 2055 or 2106(a)(2). It further includes property included in the decedent's gross estate that is distributed to a surviving spouse in satisfaction of that surviving spouse's interest in community property not included in the gross estate that the executor has distributed to a non-spouse pursuant to State law properly applied. However, included property does not include property whose value is not reported on an estate tax return and whose value is not otherwise included in the value of the decedent's gross estate, such as the property of a deceased nonresident noncitizen that is not subject to United States estate tax, and the surviving spouse's share of community property described in section 1014(b)(6).

(2) *Examples.* The following examples illustrate the application of this paragraph (e). In each case, the decedent D was a U.S. citizen and D's executor E was required under section 6018 to file an estate tax return.

(i) *Example 1* Included property. Pursuant to the terms of D's will, a trust is established and funded with property, the value of which is includible in D's gross estate under section 2031. The trust is a charitable remainder annuity trust described in section 664(d)(1). The terms of the trust provide that, in each taxable year during the lifetime of D's surviving spouse S, the trustee must pay to S an annuity of 5% of the initial net fair market value of all property passing to the trust as finally determined for Federal estate tax purposes. Upon the death of S, the trustee must distribute all of the then-principal and income of the trust to organizations described in sections 170(c), 2055(a) and 2522(a) as the trustee selects, in the trustee's sole discretion. The property used to fund the trust is included property and is subject to the reporting requirements of this section. This is true whether or not the requirements of section 1014(f) apply to the property transferred to the trust. See § 1.1014–10(d)(4).

(ii) *Example 2* Property the basis of which is determined by reference to the basis of included property. D's gross estate includes the value of Property A. Before the due date for filing the estate tax return, E exchanges Property A for Property B in a like-kind exchange pursuant to section 1031, for which D's estate recognizes no gain or loss. Property B is property subject to reporting as prescribed in this section. With respect to Property B, the value E reports on the Statement is the value reported for Property A on the estate tax return filed with the IRS.

(f) Excepted property requiring only limited reporting (1) *Excepted property.* Certain included property that is described in paragraph (f)(2) of this section (excepted property) is subject to more limited reporting than the reporting required under paragraph (c) of this section. The requirement to file an Information Return with the IRS as described in paragraph (c)(1) of this section remains the same even if all property subject to reporting under paragraph (e) of this section is excepted property. However, the executor is not required to identify or provide any other information for excepted property on the Information Return, and the executor is not required to furnish a Statement to the beneficiary with regard to that property. Instead, the executor is required only to report on the Information Return, in accordance with the instructions for that form, that some or all of the property subject to reporting is excepted property described in this paragraph (f). Further, the executor is not required to identify or provide any other information for excepted property on any Statement furnished to a beneficiary and, if this property is the only property that a beneficiary has acquired, an executor is not required to furnish a Statement to that beneficiary.

(2) *List of excepted property.* Excepted property includes

(i) United States dollars (as defined in paragraph (f)(3) of this section).

(ii) United States dollar-denominated demand deposits.

(iii) Certificates of deposit denominated in United States dollars.

(iv) Cash collateral denominated in United States dollars held by a third party to secure a liability (such as a deposit of purchase money or a security deposit).

(v) Shares of a registered investment company priced in United States dollars that is a money market fund under Rule 2a–7 under the Investment Company Act of 1940 (17 CFR 270.2a).

(vi) Life insurance proceeds on the life of the decedent payable in a lump sum in United States dollars.

(vii) Federal, State, and local tax refunds and other refunds payable in United States dollars.

(viii) Notes that are forgiven in full by the decedent upon the decedent's death, whether or not denominated in United States dollars.

(ix) Household and personal effects for which an appraisal is not required under § 20.2031–6(b) of this chapter.

(x) Property that, prior to distribution from the estate or the decedent's revocable trust, is completely sold, exchanged, or otherwise disposed of in one or more transactions that are recognition events for Federal income tax purposes (whether or not resulting in a gain or loss, and whether or not any gain is capital or ordinary). Such property includes, but is not limited to

(A) Property distributed in satisfaction of a pecuniary bequest on which the estate recognizes any gain or loss pursuant to § 1.661(a)–2(f);

(B) Property for which an election under section 643(e)(3) has been made for the estate to recognize any gain or loss;

(C) Interests in a business entity that are redeemed for United States dollars prior to being distributed to the beneficiary;

(D) Property disposed of in a transaction described in section 267(a) and (b)(13); and

(E) Property subject to the mark to market accounting method at the time of distribution from the estate or from the decedent's revocable trust.

(xi) Other property having an initial basis that is not in any way determined with regard to or derived from the property's fair market value for Federal estate tax purposes. For purposes of this section, such property includes but is not limited to

(A) Annuity contracts subject to section 72 and amounts received as an annuity subject to section 72;

(B) An interest in property that consists entirely of the right to receive an item of income in respect of a decedent as defined in section 691;

(C) Amounts received under installment obligations arising from a transaction for which the installment method for determining gain under section 453 applies;

(D) Appreciated property described in section 1014(e) that is acquired by the decedent within 1 year of death;

(E) Stock of a passive foreign investment company subject to section 1296(i), but only if the basis of such stock is the adjusted basis in the hands of the decedent immediately before the decedent's death; and

(F) Interests in and distributions from retirement plans and deferred compensation plans, including individual retirement arrangements as defined in sections 408 and 408A, that are expressed entirely in United States dollars.

(xii) Bonds to the extent that they are redeemed by the issuer for United States dollars prior to being distributed to a beneficiary so that any resulting gain or loss is recognized by the estate.

(xiii) Property included in the gross estate of a beneficiary who died before the due date of the Information Return.

(xiv) Any other property that is identified as excepted property in published guidance in the Federal Register or in the Internal Revenue Bulletin (see § 601.601(d)(2)(ii)(b) of this chapter).

(3) *United States dollars defined.* For purposes of this paragraph (f), the term United States dollars

means the official currency of the United States. The term United States dollars includes physical bills and coins for which the value of each bill or coin is equivalent to the face amount of that bill or coin. This definition does not include other physical United States bills or coins with numismatic value because these bills or coins typically do not have a value equal to their face value.

(4) *Examples*. The following examples illustrate the application of this paragraph (f). In each case, the decedent D was a U.S. citizen and D's executor E is required under section 6018 to file an estate tax return.

(i) *Example 1* Reporting household and personal effects. Included in D's gross estate are D's household and personal effects. The only item included in D's household and personal effects with a value in excess of $3,000 is a painting. E attaches to D's estate tax return an appraisal of the painting prepared in accordance with § 20.2031–6(b) of this chapter and a room-by-room itemization of D's other household and personal effects prepared in accordance with § 20.2031–6(a) of this chapter. E must furnish to the beneficiary of the painting the Statement required by paragraph (c)(2) of this section. E is not required to report on a Statement furnished to any beneficiary any information about D's other household and personal effects. If a beneficiary of D's household effects, other than the beneficiary of the painting, has acquired no other property, E is not required to furnish a Statement to that beneficiary. E is required to file the Information Return required by section (c)(1) of this section and attach to that Information Return a copy of the Statement furnished to the beneficiary of the painting. E must disclose on the Information Return that some or all of the property included in D's gross estate is excepted property described in this paragraph (f).

(ii) *Example 2* Reporting if property is disposed of in taxable transaction. Included in D's estate are shares in X, a publicly traded company. Shortly after D's death but prior to the filing of the estate tax return for D's estate, X is acquired by T, also a publicly traded company. In exchange for the shares in X, the estate receives shares in T and cash in a fully taxable transaction. E is required to report on the Information Return required by paragraph (c)(1) of this section that some or all of the property included in D's gross estate is excepted property described in this paragraph (f). E is not required to furnish a Statement to any recipient with respect to the cash, X stock, or T stock.

(iii) *Example 3* Reporting if estate is liquidated prior to distribution. Property A is the only property in D's estate. Prior to filing the estate tax return for D's estate, E sells Property A for $15,000,000. D's estate recognizes gain on the sale of Property A for income tax purposes. E distributes the $15,000,000 among the beneficiaries of D's estate. E must file the Information Return required by paragraph (c)(1) of this section even though all of the property included in D's gross estate is excepted property within the meaning of this paragraph (f). E is not required to furnish to the beneficiaries of D's estate a Statement with regard to Property A, and therefore is not required to attach a copy of any Statement to the Information Return. E is required to file an Information Return with the IRS indicating that all of the property included in D's gross estate is excepted property described in this paragraph (f), and must provide other information as required by the Information Return and the instructions.

(g) Beneficiaries (1) *In general*. Each person who acquires (or will acquire) property from a decedent or by reason of the decedent's death that is subject to the reporting described in paragraph (e) of this section is a beneficiary for purposes of this section and thus is a person to be listed on the Information Return and, except with respect to excepted property (described in paragraph (f) of this section), is a person to whom the executor must furnish a required Statement. Thus, a beneficiary may be:

(i) An individual, including one who is both the executor and a beneficiary, who acquires (or will acquire) property subject to reporting not in trust;

(ii) The estate of a deceased individual who survived the decedent if such individual or estate acquires (or will acquire) property subject to reporting not in trust;

(iii) A trust, whether foreign or domestic, including without limitation a grantor retained annuity trust, charitable remainder trust, and charitable lead trust (each referred to in this section as beneficiary trusts); or

(iv) An entity other than a trust, including without limitation a business entity or an organization described in section 501(c).

(2) *Required Statement to beneficiary trust*—(i) In general. If a beneficiary trust is the beneficiary to be identified on the Information Return pursuant to paragraph (g)(1) of this section, the executor must furnish the Statement described in paragraph (c)(2) of this section to the trustee rather than to the beneficiaries of the trust. However, if the executor reasonably believes that it is unlikely that the beneficiary trust will depreciate, sell, or otherwise dispose of the property subject to reporting in a recognition event for income tax purposes but instead will distribute the property in kind to the trust beneficiaries, the executor instead may furnish the Statement described in paragraph (c)(2) of this section to each of the trust beneficiaries, with copies of the Statements to the trustee. For this purpose, the trust beneficiaries include all potential current income beneficiaries and each remainderman who would have had a current interest in the trust if one or more of the income beneficiaries had died immediately after the decedent. For purposes of determining the due date of such Statements, each trust beneficiary will be deemed to have acquired the trust property when the trust acquired that property.

(ii) Beneficiary trust not yet established. If, by the date required for filing the Information Return with the IRS, a beneficiary trust does not have at least one trustee and a tax identification number, an executor must report on the Information Return that the beneficiary trust has not yet been established in accordance with the instructions. Once the beneficiary trust has been established and the trust information becomes available to the executor, the executor must supplement the required reporting as described in paragraph (d) of this section to update the beneficiary information on the Information Return and Statement.

(3) Required Statement to the holder of a split interest in property, not in trust. The beneficiary of a life estate not in trust, and thus the beneficiary to whom the executor is to furnish any required Statement, is the life tenant. Similarly, the beneficiary of a remainder interest not in trust is each remainderman identified as if the life tenant were to die immediately after the decedent. For purposes of determining the due date of the Statements reporting these interests under paragraph (c)(3) of this section, each beneficiary will be deemed to have acquired the property subject to reporting on the date of the decedent's death. The beneficiary of a contingent interest, not in trust, is a beneficiary only if the contingency occurs before the end of the period during which the executor has an obligation to supplement the reporting as provided in paragraph (d)(5) of this section. If the contingency occurs during this period, the executor must update the beneficiary information on the Information Return and furnish a Statement to that beneficiary pursuant to the executor's duty to supplement to report a change in beneficiary information as described in paragraph (d) of this section. Usufruct interests are treated in the same manner.

(4) Reporting for a missing beneficiary. If the executor is unable to locate a beneficiary by the date required for filing the Information Return with the IRS, the executor must report on the Information Return the failure to locate the beneficiary and the efforts the executor has made to locate the beneficiary. The executor must supplement the Information Return and must furnish the required Statement, as provided in paragraph (d) of this section, to report the subsequent location of the beneficiary or, if the beneficiary is not located, to report the distribution of the property subject to reporting to a different beneficiary.

(h) Reporting requirements applicable to trustees (1) *Circumstances under which trustees of beneficiary trusts and other trusts are subject to reporting.* Trustees of beneficiary trusts making a distribution of property that was reported on a Statement furnished to those trustees, or of any other property the basis of which is determined, in whole or in part, by reference to the basis of property subject to reporting under paragraph (e) of this section, are subject to the reporting requirements described in paragraph (h)(2) of this section and the supplemental reporting requirements described in paragraph (d) of this section (to the extent applicable) with respect to such property. In addition, trustees of trusts that receive a distribution of such property, whether from a beneficiary trust or from any other trust that has received such property, either directly or indirectly, also are subject to these reporting requirements when making a distribution of that property. This reporting obligation imposed on trustees continues to apply for each subsequent transfer or distribution until the property is distributed to a beneficiary not in trust. However, no trustee of a beneficiary trust or of a subsequent recipient trust is subject to the reporting requirements described in paragraph (h)(2) of this section for a disposition of property in a transaction that is a recognition event for income tax purposes (whether or not resulting in a gain or loss) that results in the entire property having a basis that no longer is related, in whole or in part, to the property's final value or, if applicable, reported value (within the meaning of § 1.1014–10(b)(1) or (2), respectively).

(2) *Required reporting.* On or before January 31 of the calendar year immediately following the year during which occurs a distribution of property subject to reporting under this paragraph (h), the trustee making the distribution must file an Information Return in accordance with the instructions for that form and must furnish a Statement to each recipient of the distribution. For purposes of this section, each recipient is a beneficiary.

(3) *Example.* The following example illustrates the application of this paragraph (h). Decedent D was a U.S. citizen and D's executor E was required under section 6018 to file an estate tax return. Pursuant to the will of D, E distributed 100 shares of publicly traded stock in Company X to a trust (Children's Trust) for the benefit of D's two children A and B and their respective issue. E provided a Statement to the trustee of Children's Trust in accordance with the requirements of paragraph (c)(2) of this section. Shortly thereafter, pursuant to the terms of Children's Trust, Children's Trust terminates with the 100 shares of Company X stock being distributed in equal shares between Trust A, for the benefit of A and A's issue, and Trust B, for the benefit of B and B's issue. Pursuant to paragraph (h)(2) of this section, the trustee of Children's Trust files an Information Return with the IRS and furnishes a Statement to the trustees of Trust A and Trust B. Several years later, the trustee of Trust A distributes its 50 shares of Company X stock to C, the only child of A. Pursuant to this paragraph (h), the trustee of Trust A files an Information Return with the IRS and furnishes a Statement to C. Shortly thereafter, C gives the 50 shares of Company X stock, outright, to C's nephew N. C has no obligation to file an Information Return with the IRS or furnish a Statement to N to report the distribution of the 50 shares of Company X stock to N.

(i) Penalties. For the penalties applicable to the filing of Information Returns and the furnishing of Statements required by this section, including waivers for reasonable cause, see sections 6721 through 6724 and the regulations in part 301 under sections 6721 through 6724.

(j) Applicability date. This section applies to executors of the estate of a decedent who are required to file a Federal estate tax return under section 6018 if that return is filed after September 17, 2024, and to trustees receiving certain property included in the gross estate of such a decedent.

[T.D. 9991, Sept. 16, 2024]

§ 1.6035–2 Transitional relief.

(a) Statements due before June 30, 2016. Executors and other persons required to file or furnish a statement under section 6035(a)(1) or (2) after July 31, 2015 and before June 30, 2016, need not have done so until June 30, 2016.

(b) Applicability Date. This section is applicable to executors and other persons who file a return required by section 6018(a) or (b) after July 31, 2015

[T.D. 6364, Feb. 13, 1959; amend T.D. 7322, Aug. 23, 1974; T.D. 8082, June 3, 1985; T.D. 9797, Dec. 1, 2016]

§ 6036. Notice of Qualification as Executor or Receiver

Every receiver, trustee in a case under title 11 of the United States Code, assignee for benefit of creditors, or other like fiduciary, and every executor (as defined in section 2203), shall give notice of his qualification as such to the Secretary in such manner and at such time as may be required by regulations of the Secretary. The Secretary may by regulation provide such exemptions from the requirements of this section as the Secretary deems proper.

Regulation

§ 20.6036–2 Notice of qualification as executor of estate of decedent dying after 1970.

In the case of the estate of a decedent dying after December 31, 1970, no special notice of qualification as executor of an estate is required to be filed. The requirement of section 6036 for notification of qualification as executor of an estate shall be satisfied by the filing of the estate tax return required by section 6018 and the regulations thereunder.

[T.D. 7238, 37 FR 28721, Dec. 29, 1972]

Subpart B. Information Concerning Transactions With Other Persons

§ 6050Y. Returns Relating to Certain Life Insurance Contract Transactions

(a) Requirements of reporting of certain payments.

(1) In general. Every person who acquires a life insurance contract or any interest in a life insurance contract in a reportable policy sale during any taxable year shall make a return for such taxable year (at such time and in such manner as the Secretary shall prescribe) setting forth

(A) the name, address, and TIN of such person,

(B) the name, address, and TIN of each recipient of payment in the reportable policy sale,

(C) the date of such sale,

(D) the name of the issuer of the life insurance contract sold and the policy number of such contract, and

(E) the amount of each payment.

(2) Statement to be furnished to persons with respect to whom information is required. Every person required to make a return under this subsection shall furnish to each person whose name is required to be set forth in such return a written statement showing

(A) the name, address, and phone number of the information contact of the person required to make such return, and

(B) the information required to be shown on such return with respect to such person, except that in the case of an issuer of a life insurance contract, such statement is not required to include the information specified in paragraph (1)(E).

(b) Requirement of reporting of seller's basis in life insurance contracts.

(1) In general. Upon receipt of the statement required under subsection (a)(2) or upon notice of a transfer of a life insurance contract to a foreign person, each issuer of a life insurance contract shall make a return (at such time and in such manner as the Secretary shall prescribe) setting forth

(A) the name, address, and TIN of the seller who transfers any interest in such contract in such sale,

(B) the investment in the contract (as defined in section 72(e)(6)) with respect to such seller, and

(C) the policy number of such contract.

(2) Statement to be furnished to persons with respect to whom information is required. Every person required to make a return under this subsection shall furnish to each person whose name is required to be set forth in such return a written statement showing

(A) the name, address, and phone number of the information contact of the person required to make such return, and

(B) the information required to be shown on such return with respect to each seller whose name is required to be set forth in such return.

(c) Requirement of reporting with respect to reportable death benefits.

(1) In general. Every person who makes a payment of reportable death benefits during any taxable year shall make a return for such taxable year (at such time and in such manner as the Secretary shall prescribe) setting forth

(A) the name, address, and TIN of the person making such payment,

(B) the name, address, and TIN of each recipient of such payment,

(C) the date of each such payment,

(D) the gross amount of each such payment, and

(E) such person's estimate of the investment in the contract (as defined in section 72(e)(6)) with respect to the buyer.

(2) Statement to be furnished to persons with respect to whom information is required. Every person required to make a return under this subsection shall furnish to each person whose name is required to be set forth in such return a written statement showing

(A) the name, address, and phone number of the information contact of the person required to make such return, and

(B) the information required to be shown on such return with respect to each recipient of payment whose name is required to be set forth in such return.

(d) Definitions. For purposes of this section:

(1) Payment. The term "payment" means, with respect to any reportable policy sale, the amount of cash and the fair market value of any consideration transferred in the sale.

(2) Reportable policy sale. The term "reportable policy sale" has the meaning given such term in section 101(a)(3)(B).

(3) Issuer. The term "issuer" means any life insurance company that bears the risk with respect to a life insurance contract on the date any return or statement is required to be made under this section.

(4) Reportable death benefits. The term "reportable death benefits" means amounts paid by reason of the death of the insured under a life insurance contract that has been transferred in a reportable policy sale.

Part V. Time for Filing Returns and Other Documents

§ 6071. Time for Filing Returns and Other Documents

(a) General rule. When not otherwise provided for by this title, the Secretary shall by regulations prescribe the time for filing any return, statement, or other document required by this title or by regulations.

* * *

§ 6072. Time for Filing Income Tax Returns

(a) General rule. In the case of returns under section 6012, 6013, or 6017 (relating to income tax under subtitle A), returns made on the basis of the calendar year shall be filed on or before the 15th day of April following the close of the calendar year and returns made on the basis of a fiscal year shall be filed on or before the 15th day of the fourth month following the close of the fiscal year, except as otherwise provided in the following subsections of this section.

* * *

§ 6075. Time for Filing Estate and Gift Tax Returns

(a) Estate tax returns. Returns made under section 6018(a) (relating to estate taxes) shall be filed within 9 months after the date of the decedent's death.

(b) Gift tax returns.

(1) General rule. Returns made under section 6019 (relating to gift taxes) shall be filed on or before the 15th day of April following the close of the calendar year.

(2) Extension where taxpayer granted extension for filing income tax return. Any extension of time granted the taxpayer for filing the return of income taxes imposed by subtitle A for any taxable year which is a calendar year shall be deemed to be also an extension of time granted the taxpayer for filing the return under section 6019 for such calendar year.

(3) Coordination with due date for estate tax return. Notwithstanding paragraphs (1) and (2), the time for filing the return made under section 6019 for the calendar year which includes the date of death of the donor shall not be later than the time (including extensions) for filing the return made under section 6018 (relating to estate tax returns) with respect to such donor.

Part VI. Extension of Time for Filing Returns

§ 6081. Extension of Time for Filing Returns

(a) General rule. The Secretary may grant a reasonable extension of time for filing any return, declaration, statement, or other document required by this title or by regulations. Except in the case of taxpayers who are abroad, no such extension shall be for more than 6 months.

* * *

Regulations

§ 1.6081–6 Automatic extension of time to file estate or trust income tax return.

(a) In general. (1) Except as provided in paragraph (a)(2) of this section, any estate, including but not limited to an estate defined in section 2031, or trust required to file an income tax return on Form 1041, "U.S. Income Tax Return for Estates and Trusts," will be allowed an automatic five and one-half month extension of time to file the return after the date prescribed for filing the return if the estate or trust files an application under this section in accordance with paragraph (b) of this section. No additional extension will be allowed pursuant to § 1.6081–1(b) beyond the automatic five and one-half month extension provided by this section.

(2) A bankruptcy estate that is created when an individual debtor files a petition under either chapter 7 or chapter 11 of title 11 of the U.S. Code that is required to file an income tax return on Form 1041, "U.S. Income Tax Return for Estates and Trusts," and an estate or trust required to file an income tax return on Form 1041-N, "U.S. Income Tax Return for Electing Alaska Native Settlement," or Form 1041-QFT, "U.S. Income Tax Return for Qualified Funeral Trusts" for any taxable year will be allowed an automatic 6–month extension of time to file the return after the date prescribed

for filing the return if the estate files an application under this section in accordance with paragraph (b) of this section.

(b) Requirements. To satisfy this paragraph (b), an estate or trust must—

(1) Submit a complete application on Form 7004, "Application for Automatic Extension of Time to File Certain Business Income Tax, Information, and Other Returns," or in any other manner prescribed by the Commissioner;

(2) File the application on or before the date prescribed for filing the return with the Internal Revenue Service office designated in the application's instructions; and

(3) Show the amount properly estimated as tax for the estate or trust for the taxable year.

(c) No extension of time for the payment of tax. An automatic extension of time for filing a return granted under paragraph (a) of this section will not extend the time for payment of any tax due on such return.

(d) Effect of extension on beneficiary. An automatic extension of time to file an estate or trust income tax return under this section will not extend the time for filing the income tax return of a beneficiary of the estate or trust or the time for the payment of any tax due on the beneficiary's income tax return.

(e) Termination of automatic extension. The Commissioner may terminate an automatic extension at any time by mailing to the estate or trust a notice of termination at least 10 days prior to the termination date designated in such notice. The Commissioner must mail the notice of termination to the address shown on the Form 7004 or to the estate or trust's last known address. For further guidance regarding the definition of last known address, see § 301.6212–2 of this chapter.

(f) Penalties. See section 6651 for failure to file an estate or trust income tax return or failure to pay the amount shown as tax on the return.

(g) Applicability date. This section applies to applications for an automatic extension of time to file an estate or trust income tax return on or after January 30, 2020. Section 1.6081–6T (as contained in 26 CFR part 1, revised April 2019) applies to applications for an automatic extension of time to file a return before January 30, 2020.

[T.D. 9531, 76 FR 36999, June 24, 2011; T.D. 9821, 82 FR 33447, July 20, 2017; T.D. 9892, 85 FR 5326, Jan. 30, 2020]

§ 20.6081–1 Extension of time for filing the return.

(a) Procedures for requesting an extension of time for filing the return. A request for an extension of time to file the return required by section 6018 must be made by filing Form 4768, "Application for Extension of Time To File a Return and/or Pay U.S. Estate (and Generation-Skipping Transfer) Taxes." Form 4768 must be filed with the Internal Revenue Service office designated in the application's instructions (except as provided in § 301.6091–1(b) of this chapter for hand-carried documents). Form 4768 must include an estimate of the amounts of estate and generation-skipping transfer tax liabilities with respect to the estate.

(b) Automatic extension. An estate will be allowed an automatic 6-month extension of time beyond the date prescribed in section 6075(a) to file Form 706, "United States Estate (and Generation-Skipping Transfer) Tax Return," if Form 4768 is filed on or before the due date for filing Form 706 and in accordance with the procedures under paragraph (a) of this section.

(c) Extension for good cause shown. In its discretion, the Internal Revenue Service may, upon the showing of good and sufficient cause, grant an extension of time to file the return required by section 6018 in certain situations. Such an extension may be granted to an estate that did not request an automatic extension of time to file Form 706 prior to the due date under paragraph (b) of this section, to an estate or person that is required to file forms other than Form 706, or to an executor who is abroad and is requesting an additional extension of time to file Form 706 beyond the 6-month automatic extension. Unless the executor is abroad, the extension of time may not be for more than 6 months beyond the filing date prescribed in section 6075(a). To obtain such an extension, Form 4768 must be filed in accordance with the procedures under paragraph (a) of this section and must contain a detailed explanation of why it is impossible or impractical to file a reasonably complete return by the due date. Form 4768 should be filed sufficiently early to permit the Internal Revenue Service time to consider the matter and reply before what otherwise would be the due date of the return. Failure to file Form 4768 before that due date may indicate negligence and constitute sufficient cause for denial of the extension. If an estate did not request an automatic extension of time to file Form 706 under paragraph (b) of this section, Form 4768 must also contain an explanation showing good cause for not requesting the automatic extension.

(d) Filing the return. A return as complete as possible must be filed before the expiration of the extension period. The return thus filed will be the return required by section 6018(a), and any tax shown on the return will be the amount determined by the executor as the tax referred to in section 6161(a)(2), or the amount shown as the tax by the taxpayer upon the taxpayer's return referred to in section 6211(a)(1)(A). The return cannot be amended after the expiration of the extension period although supplemental information may subsequently be filed that may result in a finally determined tax different from the amount shown as the tax on the return.

(e) Payment of the tax. An extension of time for filing a return does not operate to extend the time for payment of the tax. See s 20.6151–1 for the time for payment of the tax, and §§ 20.6161–1 and 20.6163–1 for extensions of time for payment of the tax. If an extension of time to file a return is obtained, but no extension of time for payment of the tax is granted, interest will be due on the tax not paid by the due date and the estate will be subject to all applicable late payment penalties.

(f) Effective date. This section applies to estates of decedents dying after August 16, 1954, except for paragraph (b) of this section which applies to estate tax returns due after July 25, 2001.

[T.D. 6296, 23 FR 4529, June 24, 1958, as amended by T.D. 6711, 29 FR 3656, March 24, 1964; T.D. 7238, 37 FR 28722, Dec. 29, 1972; T.D. 7710, 45 FR 50745, July 31, 1980; T.D. 8957, 66 FR 38546, July 25, 2001]

§ 25.6081–1 Automatic extension of time for filing gift tax returns.

(a) In general. Under section 6075(b)(2), an automatic six-month extension of time granted to a donor to file the donor's return of income under § 1.6081–4 of this chapter shall be deemed also to be a six-month extension of time granted to file a return on Form 709, "United States Gift (and Generation-Skipping Transfer) Tax Return." If a donor does not obtain an extension of time to file the donor's return of income under § 1.6081–4 of this chapter, the donor will be allowed an automatic 6-month extension of time to file Form 709 after the date prescribed for filing if the donor files an application under this section in accordance with paragraph (b) of this section. In the case of an individual described in § 1 6081–5(a)(5) or (6) of this chapter, the automatic 6-month extension of time to file Form 709 will run concurrently with the extension of time to file granted pursuant to § 1.6081–5 of this chapter.

(b) Requirements. To satisfy this paragraph (b), a donor must—

(1) Submit a complete application on Form 8892, "Payment of Gift/GST Tax and/or Application for Extension of Time To File Form 709," or in any other manner prescribed by the Commissioner;

(2) File the application on or before the later of—

(i) The date prescribed for filing the return; or

(ii) The expiration of any extension of time to file granted pursuant to § 1.6081–5 of this chapter; and

(3) File the application with the Internal Revenue Service office designated in the application's instructions.

(c) No extension of time for the payment of tax. An automatic extension of time for filing a return granted under paragraph (a) of this section will not extend the time for payment of any tax due on such return.

(d) Termination of automatic extension. The Commissioner may terminate an extension at any time by mailing to the donor a notice of termination at least 10 days prior to the termination date designated in such notice. The Commissioner must mail the notice of termination to the address shown on the Form 8892, or to the donor's last known address. For further guidance regarding the definition of last known address, see § 301.6212–2 of this chapter.

(e) Penalties. See section 6651 for failure to file a gift tax return or failure to pay the amount shown as tax on the return.

(f) Effective/applicability dates. This section is applicable for applications for an extension of time to file Form 709 filed after July 1, 2008.

[T.D. 9407, 73 FR 37368, July 1, 2008]

§ 26.6081–1 Automatic extension of time for filing generation-skipping transfer tax returns.

(a) In general. A skip person distributee required to file a return on Form 706-GS(D), "Generation-Skipping Transfer Tax Return for Distributions," or a trustee required to file a return on Form 706-GS(T), "Generation-Skipping Transfer Tax Return for Terminations," will be allowed an automatic 6-month extension of time to file the return after the date prescribed for filing if the skip person distributee or trustee files an application under this section in accordance with paragraph (b) of this section.

(b) Requirements. To satisfy this paragraph (b), a skip person distributee or trustee must—

(1) Submit a complete application on Form 7004, "Application for Automatic Extension of Time to File Certain Business Income Tax, Information, and Other Returns," or in any other manner prescribed by the Commissioner;

(2) File the application on or before the date prescribed for filing the return with the Internal Revenue Service office designated in the application's instructions; and

(3) Remit the amount of the properly estimated unpaid tax liability on or before the date prescribed for payment.

(c) No extension of time for the payment of tax. An automatic extension of time for filing a return granted under paragraph (a) of this section will not extend the time for payment of any tax due on such return.

(d) Termination of automatic extension. The Commissioner may terminate an automatic extension at any time by mailing to the skip person distributee or trustee a notice of termination at least 10 days prior to the termination date designated in such notice. The Commissioner must mail the notice of termination to the address shown on the Form 7004 or to the skip person distributee or trustee's last known address. For further guidance regarding the definition of last known address, see § 301.6212–2 of this chapter.

(e) Penalties. See section 6651 for failure to file a generation-skipping transfer tax return or failure to pay the amount shown as tax on the return.

(f) Effective/applicability dates. This section is applicable for applications for an automatic extension of time to file a generation-skipping transfer tax return filed after July 1, 2008.

[T.D. 9407, 73 FR 37369, July 1, 2008]

§ 28.6081–1 Extension of time for filing returns reporting gifts and bequests from covered expatriates.

(a) In general. A U.S. recipient as defined in § 28.2801–2(e) may request an extension of time to file a Form 708, United States Return of Tax for Gifts and Bequests Received from Covered Expatriates, by filing an appropriate form for extension as specified by guidance or instructions. A U.S. recipient must include on the form for extension an estimate of the amount of section 2801 tax liability and must file the form for extension with the Internal Revenue Service in the manner designated in the instructions issued with respect to such form.

(b) Automatic extension. A U.S. recipient as defined in § 28.2801–2(e) will be allowed an automatic six-month extension of time beyond the date prescribed in § 28.6071–1 to file Form 708 if the form for extension is filed on or before the due date for filing Form 708 in accordance with the procedures under paragraph (a) of this section.

(c) No extension of time for the payment of tax. An automatic extension of time for filing a return granted under paragraph (b) of this section will not extend the time for payment of any tax due with such return.

(d) Penalties. See section 6651 of the Code regarding penalties for failure to file the required tax return or failure to pay the amount shown as tax on the return.

(e) Applicability date. This section applies on and after January 14, 2025.

[T.D. 10027, 90 FR 3376, Jan. 14, 2025]

Chapter 62. Time and Place for Paying Tax

Subchapter A. Place and Due Date for Payment of Tax

Subchapter B. Extensions of Time for Payment

Subchapter A. Place and Due Date for Payment of Tax

§ 6151. Time and Place for Paying Tax Shown on Returns

(a) General rule. Except as otherwise provided in this subchapter, when a return of tax is required under this title or regulations, the person required to make such return shall, without assessment or notice and demand from the Secretary, pay such tax to the internal revenue officer with whom the return is filed, and shall pay such tax at the time and place fixed for filing the return (determined without regard to any extension of time for filing the return).

* * *

(c) Date fixed for payment of tax. In any case in which a tax is required to be paid on or before a certain date, or within a certain period, any reference in this title to the date fixed for payment of such tax shall be deemed a reference to the last day fixed for such payment (determined without regard to any extension of time for paying the tax).

Regulations

§ 20.6151–1 Time and place for paying tax shown on the return.

(a) General rule. The tax shown on the estate tax return is to be paid at the time and place fixed for filing the return (determined without regard to any extension of time for filing the return). For provisions relating to the time and place for filing the return, see §§ 20.6075–1 and 20.6091–1. For the duty of the executor to pay the tax, see § 20.2002–1.

(b) Extension of time for paying—(1) *In general.* For general provisions relating to extension of time for paying the tax, see § 20.6161–1.

(2) *Reversionary or remainder interests.* For provisions relating to extension of time for payment of estate tax on the value of a reversionary or remainder interest in property, see § 20.6163–1.

(3) *Interest in a closely held business.* For provisions relating to payment in installments of the estate tax attributable to inclusion in the gross estate of an interest in a closely held business, see §§ 20.6166–1 through 20.6166–4.

(c) Payment with obligations of the United States. Treasury bonds of certain issues which were owned by the decedent at the time of his death or which were treated as part of his gross estate under the rules contained in § 306.28 of Treasury Department Circular No. 300, Revised (31 CFR part 306), may be redeemed at par plus accrued interest for the purpose of payment of the estate tax, as provided in said section. Whether bonds of particular issues may be redeemed for this purpose will depend on the terms of the offering circulars cited on the face of the bonds. A current list of eligible issues may be obtained from any Federal reserve bank or branch, or from the Bureau of Public Debt, Washington, DC. See section 6312 and §§ 301.6312–1 and 301.6312–2 of this chapter (Regulations on Procedure and Administration) for provisions relating to the payment of taxes with United States Treasury obligations.

(d) Receipt for payment. For provisions relating to duplicate receipts for payment of the tax, see § 20.6314–1.

[T.D. 6296, 23 FR 4529, June 24, 1958, as amended by T.D. 6522, 25 FR 13885, Dec. 29, 1960]

§ 25.6151–1 Time and place for paying tax shown on return.

The tax shown on the gift tax return is to be paid by the donor at the time and place fixed for filing the return (determined without regard to any extension of time for filing the return), unless the time for paying the tax is extended in accordance with the provisions of section 6161. However, for provisions relating to certain cases in which the time for paying the gift tax is postponed by reason of an individual serving in, or in support of, the Armed Forces of the United States in a combat zone, see section 7508. For provisions relating to the time and place for filing the return, see §§ 25.6075–1 and 25.6091–1.

[T.D. 6334, 23 FR 8904, Nov. 15, 1958]

§ 28.6151–1 Time and place for paying tax shown on returns.

(a) In general. The section 2801 tax shown on the return must be paid at the time prescribed in § 28.6071–1 for filing the return, and in the manner prescribed in § 28.6091–1 for filing the return.

(b) Applicability date. This section applies to covered gifts or covered bequests received on or after January 1, 2025.

[T.D. 10027, 90 FR 3376, Jan. 14, 2025]

Subchapter B. Extensions of Time for Payment

§ 6161. Extension of Time for Paying Tax

(a) Amount determined by taxpayer on return.

(1) General rule. The Secretary, except as otherwise provided in this title, may extend the time for payment of the amount of the tax shown, or required to be shown, on any return or declaration required under authority of this title (or any installment thereof), for a reasonable period not to exceed 6 months (12 months in the case of estate tax) from the date fixed for payment thereof. Such extension may exceed 6 months in the case of a taxpayer who is abroad.

(2) Estate tax. The Secretary may, for reasonable cause, extend the time for payment of—

(A) any part of the amount determined by the executor as the tax imposed by chapter 11, or

(B) any part of any installment under section 6166 (including any part of a deficiency prorated to any installment under such section), for a reasonable period not in excess of 10 years from the date prescribed by section 6151(a) for payment of the tax (or, in the case of an amount referred to in subparagraph (B), if later, not beyond the date which is 12 months after the due date for the last installment).

(b) Amount determined as deficiency.

(1) Income, gift, and certain other taxes. Under regulations prescribed by the Secretary, the Secretary may extend the time for the payment of the amount determined as a deficiency of a tax imposed by chapter 1, 12, 41, 42, 43, or 44 for a period not to exceed 18 months from the date fixed for the payment of the deficiency, and in exceptional cases, for a further period not to exceed 12 months. An extension under this paragraph may be granted only where it is shown to the satisfaction of the Secretary that payment of a deficiency upon the date fixed for the payment thereof will result in undue hardship to the taxpayer in the case of a tax imposed by chapter 1, 41, 42, 43, or 44, or to the donor in the case of a tax imposed by chapter 12.

(2) Estate tax. Under regulations prescribed by the Secretary, the Secretary may, for reasonable cause, extend the time for the payment of any deficiency of a tax imposed by chapter 11 for a reasonable period not to exceed 4 years from the date otherwise fixed for the payment of the deficiency.

(3) No extension for certain deficiencies. No extension shall be granted under this subsection for any deficiency if the deficiency is due to negligence, to intentional disregard of rules and regulations, or to fraud with intent to evade tax.

* * *

(d) Cross references.

(1) Period of limitation. For extension of the period of limitation in case of an extension under subsection (a)(2) or subsection (b)(2), see section 6503(d).

(2) Security. For authority of the Secretary to require security in case of an extension under subsection (a)(2) or subsection (b), see section 6165.

* * *

§ 6163. Extension of Time for Payment of Estate Tax on Value of Reversionary or Remainder Interest in Property

(a) Extension permitted. If the value of a reversionary or remainder interest in property is included under chapter 11 in the value of the gross estate, the payment of the part of the tax under chapter 11 attributable to such interest may, at the election of the executor, be postponed until 6 months after the termination of the precedent interest or interests in the property, under such regulations as the Secretary may prescribe.

(b) Extension for reasonable cause. At the expiration of the period of postponement provided for in subsection (a), the Secretary may, for reasonable cause, extend the time for payment for a reasonable period or periods not in excess of 3 years from the expiration of the period of postponement provided in subsection (a).

(c) Cross reference. For authority of the Secretary to require security in the case of an extension under this section, see section 6165.

§ 6166. Extension of Time for Payment of Estate Tax Where Estate Consists Largely of Interest in Closely Held Business

(a) 5-year deferral; 10-year installment payment.

(1) In general. If the value of an interest in a closely held business which is included in determining the gross estate of a decedent who was (at the date of his death) a citizen or resident of the United States exceeds 35 percent of the adjusted gross estate, the executor may elect to pay part or all of the tax imposed by section 2001 in 2 or more (but not exceeding 10) equal installments.

(2) Limitation. The maximum amount of tax which may be paid in installments under this subsection shall be an amount which bears the same ratio to the tax imposed by section 2001 (reduced by the credits against such tax) as—

(A) the closely held business amount, bears to

(B) the amount of the adjusted gross estate.

(3) Date for payment of installments. If an election is made under paragraph (1), the first installment shall be paid on or before the date selected by the executor which is not more than 5 years after the date prescribed by section 6151(a) for payment of the tax, and each succeeding installment shall be paid on or before the date which is 1 year after the date prescribed by this paragraph for payment of the preceding installment.

(b) Definitions and special rules.

(1) Interest in closely held business. For purposes of this section, the term "interest in a closely held business" means—

(A) an interest as a proprietor in a trade or business carried on as a proprietorship;

(B) an interest as a partner in a partnership carrying on a trade or business, if—

(i) 20 percent or more of the total capital interest in such partnership is included in determining the gross estate of the decedent, or

(ii) such partnership had 45 or fewer partners; or

(C) stock in a corporation carrying on a trade or business if—

(i) 20 percent or more in value of the voting stock of such corporation is included in determining the gross estate of the decedent, or

(ii) such corporation had 45 or fewer shareholders.

(2) Rules for applying paragraph (1). For purposes of paragraph (1)—

(A) Time for testing. Determinations shall be made as of the time immediately before the decedent's death.

(B) Certain interests held by husband and wife. Stock or a partnership interest which—

(i) is community property of a husband and wife (or the income from which is community income) under the applicable community property law of a State, or

(ii) is held by a husband and wife as joint tenants, tenants by the entirety, or tenants in common,

shall be treated as owned by one shareholder or one partner, as the case may be.

(C) Indirect ownership. Property owned, directly or indirectly, by or for a corporation, partnership, estate, or trust shall be considered as being owned proportionately by or for its shareholders, partners, or beneficiaries. For purposes of the preceding sentence, a person shall be treated as a beneficiary of any trust only if such person has a present interest in the trust.

(D) Certain interests held by members of decedent's family. All stock and all partnership interests held by the decedent or by any member of his family (within the meaning of section 267(c)(4)) shall be treated as owned by the decedent.

(3) Farmhouses and certain other structures taken into account. For purposes of the 35-percent requirement of subsection (a)(1), an interest in a closely held business which is the business of farming includes an interest in residential buildings and related improvements on the farm which are occupied on a regular basis by the owner or lessee of the farm or by persons employed by such owner or lessee for purposes of operating or maintaining the farm.

(4) Value. For purposes of this section, value shall be value determined for purposes of chapter 11 (relating to estate tax).

(5) Closely held business amount. For purposes of this section, the term "closely held business amount" means the value of the interest in a closely held business which qualifies under subsection (a)(1).

(6) Adjusted gross estate. For purposes of this section, the term, "adjusted gross estate" means the value of the gross estate reduced by the sum of the amounts allowable as a deduction under section 2053 or 2054. Such sum shall be determined on the basis of the facts and circumstances in existence on the date (including extensions) for filing the return of tax imposed by section 2001 (or, if earlier, the date on which such return is filed).

(7) Partnership interests and stock which is not readily tradable.

(A) In general. If the executor elects the benefits of this paragraph (at such time and in such manner as the Secretary shall by regulations prescribe), then—

(i) for purposes of paragraph (1)(B)(i) or (1)(C)(i) (whichever is appropriate) and for purposes of subsection (c), any capital interest in a partnership and any nonreadily-tradable stock which (after the application of paragraph (2)) is treated as owned by the decedent shall be treated as included in determining the value of the decedent's gross estate,

(ii) the executor shall be treated as having selected under subsection (a)(3) the date prescribed by section 6151(a), and

(iii) for purposes of applying section 6601(j), the 2-percent portion (as defined in such section) shall be treated as being zero.

(B) Non-readily-tradable stock defined. For purposes of this paragraph, the term "non-readily-tradable stock" means stock for which, at the time of the decedent's death, there was no market on a stock exchange or in an over-the-counter market.

(8) Stock in holding company treated as business company stock in certain cases.

(A) In general. If the executor elects the benefits of this paragraph, then—

(i) Holding company stock treated as business company stock. For purposes of this section, the portion of the stock of any holding company which represents direct ownership (or indirect ownership through 1 or more other holding companies) by such company in a business company shall be deemed to be stock in such business company.

(ii) 5-year deferral for principal not to apply. The executor shall be treated as having selected under subsection (a)(3) the date prescribed by section 6151(a).

(iii) 2-percent interest rate not to apply. For purposes of applying section 6601(j), the 2-percent portion (as defined in such section) shall be treated as being zero.

(B) All stock must be non-readily-tradable stock.

(i) In general. No stock shall be taken into account for purposes of applying this paragraph unless it is non-readily-tradable stock (within the meaning of paragraph (7)(B)).

(ii) Special application where only holding company stock is non-readily-tradable stock. If the requirements of clause (i) are not met, but all of the stock of each holding company taken into account is non-readily-tradable, then this paragraph shall apply, but subsection (a)(1) shall be applied by substituting "5" for "10".

(C) Application of voting stock requirement of paragraph (1)(C)(i). For purposes of clause (i) of paragraph (1)(C), the deemed stock resulting from the application of subparagraph (A) shall be treated as voting stock to the extent that voting stock in the holding company owns directly (or through the voting stock of 1 or more other holding companies) voting stock in the business company.

(D) Definitions. For purposes of this paragraph—

(i) Holding company. The term "holding company" means any corporation holding stock in another corporation.

(ii) Business company. The term "business company" means any corporation carrying on a trade or business.

(9) Deferral not available for passive assets.

(A) In general. For purposes of subsection (a)(1) and determining the closely held business amount (but not for purposes of subsection (g)), the value of any interest in a closely held business shall not include the value of that portion of such interest which is attributable to passive assets held by the business.

(B) Passive asset defined. For purposes of this paragraph—

(i) In general. The term "passive asset" means any asset other than an asset used in carrying on a trade or business.

(ii) Stock treated as passive asset. The term "passive asset" includes any stock in another corporation unless—

(I) such stock is treated as held by the decedent by reason of an election under paragraph (8), and

(II) such stock qualified under subsection (a)(1).

(iii) Exception for active corporations. If—

(I) a corporation owns 20 percent or more in value of the voting stock of another corporation, or such other corporation has 45 or fewer shareholders, and

(II) 80 percent or more of the value of the assets of each such corporation is attributable to assets used in carrying on a trade or business, then such corporations shall be treated as 1 corporation for purposes of clause (ii). For purposes of applying subclause (II) to the corporation holding the stock of the other corporation, such stock shall not be taken into account.

(10) Stock in qualifying lending and finance business treated as stock in an active trade or business company.

(A) In general. If the executor elects the benefits of this paragraph, then—

(i) Stock in qualifying lending and finance business treated as stock in an active trade or business company. For purposes of this section, any asset used in a qualifying lending and finance business shall be treated as an asset which is used in carrying on a trade or business.

(ii) 5-year deferral for principal not to apply. The executor shall be treated as having selected under subsection (a)(3) the date prescribed by section 6151(a).

(iii) 5 equal installments allowed. For purposes of applying subsection (a)(1), "5" shall be substituted for "10".

(B) Definitions. For purposes of this paragraph—

(i) Qualifying lending and finance business. The term "qualifying lending and finance business" means a lending and finance business, if—

(I) based on all the facts and circumstances immediately before the date of the decedent's death, there was substantial activity with respect to the lending and finance business, or

(II) during at least 3 of the 5 taxable years ending before the date of the decedent's death, such business had at least 1 full-time employee substantially all of whose services were the active management of such business, 10 full-time, nonowner employees substantially all of whose services were directly related to such business, and $5,000,000 in gross receipts from activities described in clause (ii).

(ii) Lending and finance business. The term "lending and finance business" means a trade or business of—

(I) making loans,

(II) purchasing or discounting accounts receivable, notes, or installment obligations,

(III) engaging in rental and leasing of real and tangible personal property, including entering into leases and purchasing, servicing, and disposing of leases and leased assets,

(IV) rendering services or making facilities available in the ordinary course of a lending or finance business, and

(V) rendering services or making facilities available in connection with activities described in subclauses (I) through (IV) carried on by the corporation rendering services or making facilities available, or another corporation which is a member of the same affiliated group (as defined in section 1504 without regard to section 1504(b)(3)).

(iii) Limitation. The term "qualifying lending and finance business" shall not include any interest in an entity, if the stock or debt of such entity or a controlled group (as defined in section 267(f)(1)) of which such entity was a member was readily tradable on an established securities market or secondary market (as defined by the Secretary) at any time within 3 years before the date of the decedent's death.

(c) Special rule for interests in 2 or more closely held businesses. For purposes of this section, interests in 2 or more closely held businesses, with respect to each of which there is included in determining the value of the decedent's gross estate 20 percent or more of the total value of each such business, shall be treated as an interest in a single closely held business. For purposes of the 20-percent requirement of the preceding sentence, an interest in a closely held business which represents the surviving spouse's interest in property held by the decedent and the surviving spouse as community property or as joint tenants, tenants by the entirety, or tenants in common shall be treated as having been included in determining the value of the decedent's gross estate.

(d) Election. Any election under subsection (a) shall be made not later than the time prescribed by section 6075(a) for filing the return of tax imposed by section 2001 (including extensions thereof), and shall be made in such manner as the Secretary shall by regulations prescribe. If an election under subsection (a) is made, the provisions of this subtitle shall apply as though the Secretary were extending the time for payment of the tax.

(e) Proration of deficiency to installments. If an election is made under subsection (a) to pay any part of the tax imposed by section 2001 in installments and a deficiency has been assessed, the deficiency shall (subject to the limitation provided by subsection (a)(2)) be prorated to the installments payable under subsection (a). The part of the deficiency so prorated to any installment the date for payment of which has not arrived shall be collected at the same time as, and as a part of, such installment. The part of the deficiency so prorated to any installment the date for payment of which has arrived shall be paid upon notice and demand from the Secretary. This subsection shall not apply if the deficiency is due to negligence, to intentional disregard of rules and regulations, or to fraud with intent to evade tax.

(f) Time for payment of interest. If the time for payment of any amount of tax has been extended under this section—

(1) Interest for first 5 years. Interest payable under section 6601 of any unpaid portion of such amount attributable to the first 5 years after the date prescribed by section 6151(a) for payment of the tax shall be paid annually.

(2) Interest for periods after first 5 years. Interest payable under section 6601 on any unpaid portion of such amount attributable to any period after the 5-year period referred to in paragraph (1) shall be paid annually at the same time as, and as a part of, each installment payment of the tax.

(3) Interest in the case of certain deficiencies. In the case of a deficiency to which subsection (e) applies which is assessed after the close of the 5-year period referred to in paragraph (1), interest attributable to such 5-year period, and interest assigned under paragraph (2) to any installment the date for payment of which has arrived on or before the date of the assessment of the deficiency, shall be paid upon notice and demand from the Secretary.

(4) Selection of shorter period. If the executor has selected a period shorter than 5 years under subsection (a)(3), such shorter period shall be substituted for 5 years in paragraphs (1), (2), and (3) of this subsection.

(g) Acceleration of payment.

(1) Disposition of interest; withdrawal of funds from business.

(A) If—

(i) **(I)** any portion of an interest in a closely held business which qualifies under subsection (a)(1) is distributed, sold, exchanged, or otherwise disposed of, or

(II) money and other property attributable to such an interest is withdrawn from such trade or business, and

(ii) the aggregate of such distributions, sales, exchanges, or other dispositions and withdrawals equals or exceeds 50 percent of the value of such interest,

then the extension of time for payment of tax provided in subsection (a) shall cease to apply, and the unpaid portion of the tax payable in installments shall be paid upon notice and demand from the Secretary.

(B) In the case of a distribution in redemption of stock to which section 303 (or so much of section 304 as relates to section 303) applies—

(i) the redemption of such stock, and the withdrawal of money and other property distributed in such redemption, shall not be treated as a distribution or withdrawal for purposes of subparagraph (A), and

(ii) for purposes of subparagraph (A), the value of the interest in the closely held business shall be considered to be such value reduced by the value of the stock redeemed.

This subparagraph shall apply only if, on or before the date prescribed by subsection (a)(3) for the payment of the first installment which becomes due after the date of the distribution (or, if earlier, on or before the day which is 1 year after the date of the distribution), there is paid an amount of the tax imposed by section 2001 not less than the amount of money and other property distributed.

(C) Subparagraph (A)(i) does not apply to an exchange of stock pursuant to a plan of reorganization described in subparagraph (D), (E), or (F) of section 368(a)(1) nor to an exchange to which section 355 (or so much of section 356 as relates to section 355) applies; but any stock received in such an exchange shall be treated for purposes of subparagraph (A)(i) as an interest qualifying under subsection (a)(1).

(D) Subparagraph (A)(i) does not apply to a transfer of property of the decedent to a person entitled by reason of the decedent's death to receive such property under the decedent's will, the applicable law of descent and distribution, or a trust created by the decedent. A similar rule shall apply in the case of a series of subsequent transfers of the property by reason of death so long as each transfer is to a member of the family (within the meaning of section 267(c)(4)) of the transferor in such transfer.

(E) Changes in interest in holding company. If any stock in a holding company is treated as stock in a business company by reason of subsection (b)(8)(A)—

(i) any disposition of any interest in such stock in such holding company which was included in determining the gross estate of the decedent, or

(ii) any withdrawal of any money or other property from such holding company attributable to any interest included in determining the gross estate of the decedent,

shall be treated for purposes of subparagraph (a) as a disposition of (or a withdrawal with respect to) the stock qualifying under subsection (a)(1).

(F) Changes in interest in business company. If any stock in a holding company is treated as stock in a business company by reason of subsection (b)(8)(A)—

(i) any disposition of any interest in such stock in the business company by such holding company, or

(ii) any withdrawal of any money or other property from such business company attributable to such stock by such holding company owning such stock,

shall be treated for purposes of subparagraph (a) as a disposition of (or a withdrawal with respect to) the stock qualifying under subsection (a)(1).

(2) Undistributed income of estate.

(A) If an election is made under this section and the estate has undistributed net income for any taxable year ending on or after the due date for the first installment, the executor shall, on or before the date prescribed by law for filing the income tax return for such taxable year (including extensions thereof), pay an amount equal to such undistributed net income in liquidation of the unpaid portion of the tax payable in installments.

(B) For purposes of subparagraph (A), the undistributed net income of the estate for any taxable year is the amount by which the distributable net income of the estate for such taxable year (as defined in section 643) exceeds the sum of—

(i) the amounts for such taxable year specified in paragraphs (1) and (2) of section 661(a) (relating to deductions for distributions, etc.);

(ii) the amount of tax imposed for the taxable year on the estate under chapter 1; and

(iii) the amount of the tax imposed by section 2001 (including interest) paid by the executor during the taxable year (other than any amount paid pursuant to this paragraph).

(C) For purposes of this paragraph, if any stock in a corporation is treated as stock in another corporation by reason of subsection (b)(8)(A), any dividends paid by such other corporation to the corporation shall be treated as paid to the estate of the decedent to the extent attributable to the stock qualifying under subsection (a)(1).

(3) Failure to make payment of principal or interest.

(A) In general. Except as provided in subparagraph (B), if any payment of principal or interest under this section is not paid on or before the date fixed for its payment by this section (including any extension of time), the unpaid portion of the tax payable in installments shall be paid upon notice and demand from the Secretary.

(B) Payment within 6 months. If any payment of principal or interest under this section is not paid on or before the date determined under subparagraph (A) but is paid within 6 months of such date—

(i) the provisions of subparagraph (A) shall not apply with respect to such payment,

(ii) the provisions of section 6601(j) shall not apply with respect to the determination of interest on such payment, and

(iii) there is imposed a penalty in an amount equal to the product of—

(I) 5 percent of the amount of such payment, multiplied by

(II) the number of months (or fractions thereof) after such date and before payment is made.

The penalty imposed under clause (iii) shall be treated in the same manner as a penalty imposed under subchapter B of chapter 68.

(h) Election in case of certain deficiencies.

(1) In general. If—

(A) a deficiency in the tax imposed by section 2001 is assessed,

(B) the estate qualifies under subsection (a)(1), and

(C) the executor has not made an election under subsection (a),

the executor may elect to pay the deficiency in installments. This subsection shall not apply if the deficiency is due to negligence, to intentional disregard of rules and regulations, or to fraud with intent to evade tax.

(2) Time of election. An election under this subsection shall be made not later than 60 days after issuance of notice and demand by the Secretary for the payment of the deficiency, and shall be made in such manner as the Secretary shall by regulations prescribe.

(3) Effect of election on payment. If an election is made under this subsection, the deficiency shall (subject to the limitation provided by subsection (a)(2)) be prorated to the installments which would have been due if an election had been timely made under subsection (a) at the time the estate tax return was filed. The part of the deficiency so prorated to any installment the date for payment of which would have arrived shall be paid at the time of the making of the election under this subsection. The portion of the deficiency so prorated to installments the date for payment of which would not have so arrived shall be paid at the time such installments would have been due if such an election had been made.

(i) Special rule for certain direct skips. To the extent that an interest in a closely held business is the subject of a direct skip (within the meaning of section 2612(c)) occurring at the same time as and as a result of the decedent's death, then for purposes of this section any tax imposed by section 2601 on the transfer of such interest shall be treated as if it were additional tax imposed by section 2001.

(j) Regulations. The Secretary shall prescribe such regulations as may be necessary to the application of this section.

(k) Cross references.

(1) Security. For authority of the Secretary to require security in the case of an extension under this section, see section 6165.

(2) Lien. For special lien (in lieu of bond) in the case of an extension under this section, see section 6324A.

(3) Period of limitation. For extension of the period of limitation in the case of an extension under this section, see section 6503(d).

(4) Interest. For provisions relating to interest on tax payable in installments under this section, see subsection (j) of section 6601.

(5) Transfers within 3 years of death. For special rule for qualifying an estate under this section where property has been transferred within 3 years of decedent's death, see section 2035(d)(4).

Chapter 63. Assessment

Subchapter B. Deficiency Procedures in the Case of Income, Estate, Gift, and Certain Excise Taxes

§ 6211. Definition of a Deficiency

(a) In general. For purposes of this title in the case of income, estate, and gift taxes imposed by subtitles A and B and excise taxes imposed by chapters 41, 42, 43, and 44 the term "deficiency" means the amount by which the tax imposed by subtitle A or B, or chapter 41, 42, 43, or 44 exceeds the excess of—

(1) the sum of

(A) the amount shown as the tax by the taxpayer upon his return, if a return was made by the taxpayer and an amount was shown as the tax by the taxpayer thereon, plus

(B) the amounts previously assessed (or collected without assessment) as a deficiency, over—

(2) the amount of rebates, as defined in subsection (b)(2), made.

* * *

§ 6212. Notice of Deficiency

(a) In general. If the Secretary determines that there is a deficiency in respect of any tax imposed by subtitles A or B or chapter 41, 42, 43, or 44, he is authorized to send notice of such deficiency to the taxpayer by certified mail or registered mail. Such notice shall include a notice to the taxpayer of the taxpayer's right to contact a local office of the taxpayer advocate and the location and phone number of the appropriate office.

(b) Address for notice of deficiency.

(1) Income and gift taxes and certain excise taxes. In the absence of notice to the Secretary under section 6903 of the existence of a fiduciary relationship, notice of a deficiency in respect of a tax imposed by subtitle A, chapter 12, chapter 41, chapter 42, chapter 43, or chapter 44, if mailed to the taxpayer at his last known address, shall be sufficient for purposes of subtitle A, chapter 12, chapter 41, chapter 42, chapter 43, chapter 44, and this chapter even if such taxpayer is deceased, or is under a legal disability, or, in the case of a corporation, has terminated its existence.

* * *

(3) Estate tax. In the absence of notice to the Secretary under section 6903 of the existence of a fiduciary relationship, notice of a deficiency in respect of a tax imposed by chapter 11, if addressed in the name of the decedent or other person subject to liability and mailed to his last known address, shall be sufficient for purposes of chapter 11 and of this chapter.

(c) Further deficiency letters restricted.

(1) General rule. If the Secretary has mailed to the taxpayer a notice of deficiency as provided in subsection (a), and the taxpayer files a petition with the Tax Court within the time prescribed in section 6213(a), the Secretary shall have no right to determine any additional deficiency of income tax for the same taxable year, of gift tax for the same calendar year, of estate tax in respect of the taxable estate of the same decedent, of chapter 41 tax for the same taxable year, of chapter 43 tax for the same taxable year, of chapter 44 tax for the same taxable year, of section 4940 tax for the same taxable year, or of chapter 42 tax (other than under section 4940) with respect to any act (or failure to act) to which such petition relates, except in the case of fraud, and except as provided in section 6214(a) (relating to assertion of greater deficiencies before the Tax Court), in section 6213(b)(1) (relating to mathematical or clerical errors), in section 6851 or 6852 (relating to termination assessments), or in section 6861(c) (relating to the making of jeopardy assessments).

* * *

(d) Authority to rescind notice of deficiency with taxpayer's consent. The Secretary may, with the consent of the taxpayer, rescind any notice of deficiency mailed to the taxpayer. Any notice so rescinded shall not be treated as a notice of deficiency for purposes of subsection (c)(1) (relating to further deficiency letters restricted), section 6213(a) (relating to restrictions applicable to deficiencies; petition to Tax Court), and section 6512(a) (relating to limitations in case of petition to Tax Court), and the taxpayer shall have no right to file a petition with the Tax Court based on such notice. Nothing in this subsection shall affect any suspension of the running of any period of limitations during any period during which the rescinded notice was outstanding.

§ 6213. Restrictions Applicable to Deficiencies; Petition to Tax Court

(a) Time for filing petition and restriction on assessment. Within 90 days, or 150 days if the notice is addressed to a person outside the United States, after the notice of deficiency authorized in section 6212 is mailed (not counting Saturday, Sunday, or a legal holiday in the District of Columbia as the last day), the taxpayer may file a petition with the Tax Court for a redetermination of the deficiency. Except as otherwise provided in section 6851, 6852 or 6861, no assessment of a deficiency in respect of any tax imposed by subtitle A, or B, chapter 41, 42, 43, or 44 and no levy or proceeding in court for its collection shall be made, begun, or prosecuted until such notice has been mailed to the taxpayer, nor until the expiration of such 90-day or 150-day period, as the case may be, nor, if a petition has been filed with the Tax Court, until the decision of the Tax Court has become final. Notwithstanding the provisions of section 7421(a), the making of such assessment or the beginning of such proceeding or levy during the time such prohibition is in force may be enjoined by a proceeding in the proper court, including the Tax Court, and a refund may be ordered by such court of any amount collected within the period during which the Secretary is prohibited from collecting by levy or through a proceeding in court under the provisions of this subsection. The Tax Court shall have no jurisdiction to enjoin any action or proceeding or order any refund under this subsection unless a timely petition for a redetermination of the deficiency has been filed and then only in respect of the deficiency that is the subject of such petition. Any petition filed with the Tax Court on or before the last date specified for filing such petition by the Secretary in the notice of deficiency shall be treated as timely filed.

* * *

Chapter 64. Collection

Subchapter C. Lien for Taxes

Part II. Liens

§ 6324. Special Liens for Estate and Gift Taxes

(a) Liens for estate tax. Except as otherwise provided in subsection (c)—

(1) Upon gross estate. Unless the estate tax imposed by chapter 11 is sooner paid in full, or becomes unenforceable by reason of lapse of time, it shall be a lien upon the gross estate of the decedent for 10 years from the date of death, except that such part of the gross estate as is used for the payment of charges against the estate and expenses of its administration, allowed by any court having jurisdiction thereof, shall be divested of such lien.

(2) Liability of transferees and others. If the estate tax imposed by chapter 11 is not paid when due, then the spouse, transferee, trustee (except the trustee of an employees' trust which meets the requirements of section 401(a)), surviving tenant, person in possession of the property by reason of the exercise, nonexercise, or release of a power of appointment, or beneficiary, who receives, or has on the date of the decedent's death, property included in the gross estate under sections 2034 to 2042, inclusive, to the extent of the value, at the time of the decedent's death, of such property, shall be personally liable for such tax. Any part of such property transferred by (or transferred by a transferee of) such spouse, transferee, trustee, surviving tenant, person in possession, or beneficiary, to a purchaser or holder of a security interest shall be divested of the lien provided in paragraph (1) and a like lien shall then attach to all the property of such spouse, transferee, trustee, surviving tenant, person in possession, or beneficiary, or transferee of any such person, except any part transferred to a purchaser or a holder of a security interest.

(3) Continuance after discharge of fiduciary. The provisions of section 2204 (relating to discharge of fiduciary from personal liability) shall not operate as a release of any part of the gross estate from the lien for any deficiency that may thereafter be determined to be due, unless such part of the gross estate (or any interest therein) has been transferred to a purchaser or a holder of a security interest, in which case such part (or such interest) shall not be subject to a lien or to any claim or demand for any such deficiency, but the lien shall attach to the consideration received from such purchaser or holder of a security interest, by the heirs, legatees, devisees, or distributees.

(b) Lien for gift tax. Except as otherwise provided in subsection (c), unless the gift tax imposed by chapter 12 is sooner paid in full or becomes unenforceable by reason of lapse of time, such tax shall be a lien upon all gifts made during the period for which the return was filed, for 10 years from the date the gifts are made. If the tax is not paid when due, the donee of any gift shall be personally liable for such tax to the extent of the value of such gift. Any part of the property comprised in the gift transferred by the donee (or by a transferee of the donee) to a purchaser or holder of a security interest shall be divested of the lien imposed by this subsection and such lien, to the extent of the value of such gift, shall attach to all the property (including after-acquired property) of the donee (or the transferee) except any part transferred to a purchaser or holder of a security interest.

(c) Exceptions.

(1) The lien imposed by subsection (a) or (b) shall not be valid as against a mechanic's lienor and, subject to the conditions provided by section 6323(b) (relating to protection for certain interests even though noticed filed), shall not be valid with respect to any lien or interest described in section 6323(b).

(2) If a lien imposed by subsection (a) or (b) is not valid as against a lien or security interest, the priority of such lien or security interest shall extend to any item described in section 6323(e) (relating to priority of interest and expenses) to the extent that, under local law, such item has the same priority as the lien or security interest to which it relates.

§ 6324A. Special Lien for Estate Tax Deferred under Section 6166

(a) General rule. In the case of any estate with respect to which an election has been made under section 6166, if the executor makes an election under this section (at such time and in such manner as the Secretary shall by regulations prescribe) and files the agreement referred to in subsection (c), the deferred amount (plus any interest, additional amount, addition to tax, assessable penalty, and costs attributable to the deferred amount) shall be a lien in favor of the United States on the section 6166 lien property.

(b) Section 6166 lien property.

(1) In general. For purposes of this section, the term "section 6166 lien property" means interests in real and other property to the extent such interests—

(A) can be expected to survive the deferral period, and

(B) are designated in the agreement referred to in subsection (c).

(2) Maximum value of required property. The maximum value of the property which the Secretary may require as section 6166 lien property with respect to any estate shall be a value which is not greater than the sum of—

(A) the deferred amount, and

(B) the required interest amount.

For purposes of the preceding sentence, the value of any property shall be determined as of the date prescribed by section 6151(a) for payment of the tax imposed by chapter 11 and shall be determined by taking into account any encumbrance such as a lien under section 6324B.

(3) Partial substitution of bond for lien. If the value required as section 6166 lien property pursuant to paragraph (2) exceeds the value of the interests in property covered by the agreement referred to in subsection (c), the Secretary may accept bond in an amount equal to such excess conditioned on the payment of the amount extended in accordance with the terms of such extension.

(c) Agreement. The agreement referred to in this subsection is a written agreement signed by each person in being who has an interest (whether or not in possession) in any property designated in such agreement—

(1) consenting to the creation of the lien under this section with respect to such property, and

(2) designating a responsible person who shall be the agent for the beneficiaries of the estate and for the persons who have consented to the creation of the lien in dealings with the Secretary on matters arising under section 6166 or this section.

(d) Special rules.

(1) Requirement that lien be filed. The lien imposed by this section shall not be valid as against any purchaser, holder of a security interest, mechanic's lien, or judgment lien creditor until notice thereof which meets the requirements of section 6323(f) has been filed by the Secretary. Such notice shall not be required to be refiled.

(2) Period of lien. The lien imposed by this section shall arise at the time the executor is discharged from liability under section 2204 (or, if earlier, at the time notice is filed pursuant to paragraph (1)) and shall continue until the liability for the deferred amount is satisfied or becomes unenforceable by reason of lapse of time.

(3) Priorities. Even though notice of a lien imposed by this section has been filed as provided in paragraph (1), such lien shall not be valid—

(A) Real property tax and special assessment liens. To the extent provided in section 6323(b)(6).

(B) Real property subject to a mechanic's lien for repairs and improvements. In the case of any real property subject to a lien for repair or improvement, as against a mechanic's lienor.

(C) Real property construction or improvement financing agreement. As against any security interest set forth in paragraph (3) of section 6323(c) (whether such security interest came into existence before or after tax lien filing).

Subparagraphs (B) and (C) shall not apply to any security interest which came into existence after the date on which the Secretary filed notice (in a manner similar to notice filed under section 6323(f)) that payment of the deferred amount has been accelerated under section 6166(g).

(4) Lien to be in lieu of section 6324 lien. If there is a lien under this section on any property with respect to any estate, there shall not be any lien under section 6324 on such property with respect to the same estate.

(5) Additional lien property required in certain cases. If at any time the value of the property covered by the agreement is less than the unpaid portion of the deferred amount and the required interest amount, the Secretary may require the addition of property to the agreement (but he may not require under this paragraph that the value of the property covered by the agreement exceed such unpaid portion). If property having the required value is not added to the property covered by the agreement (or if other security equal to the required value is not furnished) within 90 days after notice and demand therefor by the Secretary, the failure to comply with the preceding sentence shall be treated as an act accelerating payment of the installments under section 6166(g).

(6) Lien to be in lieu of bond. The Secretary may not require under section 6165 the furnishing of any bond for the payment of any tax to which an agreement which meets the requirements of subsection (c) applies.

(e) Definitions. For purposes of this section—

(1) Deferred amount. The term "deferred amount" means the aggregate amount deferred under section 6166 (determined as of the date prescribed by section 6151(a) for payment of the tax imposed by chapter 11).

(2) Required interest amount. The term "required interest amount" means the aggregate amount of interest which will be payable over the first 4 years of the deferral period with respect to the deferred amount (determined as of the date prescribed by section 6151(a) for the payment of the tax imposed by chapter 11).

(3) Deferral period. The term "deferral period" means the period for which the payment of tax is deferred pursuant to the election under section 6166.

(4) Application of definitions in case of deficiencies. In the case of a deficiency, a separate deferred amount, required interest amount, and deferral period shall be determined as of the due date of the first installment after the deficiency is prorated to installments under section 6166.

§ 6324B. Special Lien for Additional Estate Tax Attributable to Farm, Etc., Valuation

(a) General rule. In the case of any interest in qualified real property (within the meaning of section 2032A(b)), an amount equal to the adjusted tax difference attributable to such interest (within the meaning of section 2032A(c)(2)(B)) shall be a lien in favor of the United States on the property in which such interest exists.

(b) Period of lien. The lien imposed by this section shall arise at the time an election is filed under section 2032A and shall continue with respect to any interest in the qualified real property—

(1) until the liability for tax under subsection (c) of section 2032A with respect to such interest has been satisfied or has become unenforceable by reason of lapse of time, or

(2) until it is established to the satisfaction of the Secretary that no further tax liability may arise under section 2032A(c) with respect to such interest.

(c) Certain rules and definitions made applicable.

(1) In general. The rule set forth in paragraphs (1), (3), and (4) of section 6324A(d) shall apply with respect to the lien imposed by this section as if it were a lien imposed by section 6324A.

(2) Qualified real property. For purposes of this section, the term "qualified real property" includes qualified replacement property (within the meaning of section 2032A(h)(3)(B)) and qualified exchange property (within the meaning of section 2032A(i)(3)).

(d) Substitution of security for lien. To the extent provided in regulations prescribed by the Secretary, the furnishing of security may be substituted for the lien imposed by this section.

Chapter 66. Limitations

Subchapter A. Limitations on Assessment and Collection

§ 6501. Limitations on Assessment and Collection

(a) General rule. Except as otherwise provided in this section, the amount of any tax imposed by this title shall be assessed within 3 years after the return was filed (whether or not such return was filed on or after the date prescribed) or, if the tax is payable by stamp, at any time after such tax became due and before the expiration of 3 years after the date on which any part of such tax was paid, and no proceeding in court without assessment for the collection of such tax shall be begun after the expiration of such period. For purposes of this chapter, the term "return" means the return required to be filed by the taxpayer (and does not include a return of any person from whom the taxpayer has received an item of income, gain, loss, deduction, or credit).

(b) Time return deemed filed.

(1) Early return. For purposes of this section, a return of tax imposed by this title, except tax imposed by chapter 3, 4, 21, or 24, filed before the last day prescribed by law or by regulations promulgated pursuant to law for the filing thereof, shall be considered as filed on such last day.

(2) Return of certain employment and withholding taxes. For purposes of this section, if a return of tax imposed by chapter 3, 4, 21, or 24 for any period ending with or within a calendar year is filed before April 15 of the succeeding calendar year, such return shall be considered filed on April 15 of such calendar year.

(3) Return executed by Secretary. Notwithstanding the provisions of paragraph (2) of section 6020(b), the execution of a return by the Secretary pursuant to the authority conferred by such section shall not start the running of the period of limitations on assessment and collection.

(4) Return of excise taxes. For purposes of this section, the filing of a return for a specified period on which an entry has been made with respect to a tax imposed under a provision of subtitle D (including a return on which an entry has been made showing no liability for such tax for such period) shall constitute the filing of a return of all amounts of such tax which, if properly paid, would be required to be reported on such return for such period.

(c) Exceptions.

(1) False return. In the case of a false or fraudulent return with the intent to evade tax, the tax may be assessed, or a proceeding in court for collection of such tax may be begun without assessment, at any time.

(2) Willful attempt to evade tax. In case of a willful attempt in any manner to defeat or evade tax imposed by this title (other than tax imposed by subtitle A or B), the tax may be assessed, or a proceeding in court for the collection of such tax may be begun without assessment, at any time.

(3) No return. In the case of failure to file a return, the tax may be assessed, or a proceeding in court for the collection of such tax may be begun without assessment, at any time.

(4) Extension by agreement.

(A) In general. Where, before the expiration of the time prescribed for the assessment of any tax imposed by this title, except the estate tax provided in chapter 11, both the Secretary and the taxpayer have consented in writing to its assessment after such time, the tax may be assessed at any time prior to the expiration of the period agreed upon. The period so agreed upon may be extended by subsequent agreements in writing made before the expiration of the period previously agreed upon.

(B) Notice to taxpayer of right to refuse or limit extension. The Secretary shall notify the taxpayer of the taxpayer's right to refuse to extend the period of limitations, or to limit such extension to particular issues or to a particular period of time, on each occasion when the taxpayer is requested to provide such consent.

(5) Tax resulting from changes in certain income tax or estate tax credits. For special rules applicable in cases where the adjustment of certain taxes allowed as a credit against income taxes or estate taxes results in additional tax, see section 905(c) (relating to the foreign tax credit for income tax purposes) and section 2016 (relating to taxes of foreign countries, States, etc., claimed as credit against estate taxes).

* * *

(7) Special rule for certain amended returns. Where, within the 60-day period ending on the day on which the time prescribed in this section for the assessment of any tax imposed by subtitle A for any taxable year would otherwise expire, the Secretary receives a written document signed by the taxpayer showing that the taxpayer owes an additional amount of such tax for such taxable year, the period for the assessment of such additional amount shall not expire before the day 60 days after the day on which the Secretary receives such document.

(8) Failure to notify Secretary of certain foreign transfers. In the case of any information which is required to be reported to the Secretary under section 6038, 6038A, 6038B, 6046, 6046A, or 6048, the time for assessment of any tax imposed by this title with respect to any event or period to which such information relates shall not expire before the date which is 3 years after the date on which the Secretary is furnished the information required to be reported under such section.

(9) Gift tax on certain gifts not shown on return. If any gift of property the value of which (or any increase in taxable gifts required under section 2701(d) which) is required to be shown on a return of tax imposed by chapter 12 (without regard to section 2503(b)), and is not shown on such return, any tax imposed by chapter 12 on such gift may be assessed, or a proceeding in court for the collection of such tax may be begun without assessment, at any time. The preceding sentence shall not apply to any item which is disclosed in such return, or in a statement attached to the return, in a manner adequate to apprise the Secretary of the nature of such item.

(10) Listed transactions. If a taxpayer fails to include on any return or statement for any taxable year any information with respect to a listed transaction (as defined in section 6707A(c)(2)) which is required under section 6011 to be included with such return or statement, the time for assessment of any tax imposed by this title with respect to such transaction shall not expire before the date which is 1 year after the earlier of—

(A) the date on which the Secretary is furnished the information so required, or

(B) the date that a material advisor meets the requirements of section 6112 with respect to a request by the Secretary under section 6112(b) relating to such transaction with respect to such taxpayer.

* * *

(d) Request for prompt assessment. Except as otherwise provided in subsection (c), (e), or (f), in the case of any tax (other than the tax imposed by chapter 11 of subtitle B, relating to estate taxes) for which return is required in the case of a decedent, or by his estate during the period of administration, or by a corporation, the tax shall be assessed, and any proceeding in court without assessment for the collection of such tax shall be begun, within 18 months after written request therefor (filed after the return is made and filed in such manner and such form as may be prescribed by regulations of the Secretary) by the executor, administrator, or other fiduciary representing the estate of such decedent, or by the corporation, but not after the expiration of 3 years after the return was filed. This subsection shall not apply in the case of a corporation unless—

(1)(A) such written request notifies the Secretary that the corporation contemplates dissolution at or before the expiration of such 18-month period, (B) the dissolution is in good faith begun before the expiration of such 18-month period, and (C) the dissolution is completed;

(2)(A) such written request notifies the Secretary that a dissolution has in good faith been begun, and (B) the dissolution is completed; or

(3) a dissolution has been completed at the time such written request is made.

(e) Substantial omission of items. Except as otherwise provided in subsection (c)—

(1) Income taxes. In the case of any tax imposed by subtitle A—

(A) General rule. If the taxpayer omits from gross income an amount properly includible therein and

(i) such amount is in excess of 25 percent of the amount of gross income stated in the return, or

(ii) such amount

(I) is attributable to one or more assets with respect to which information is required to be reported under section 6038D (or would be so required if such section were applied without regard to the dollar threshold specified in subsection (a) thereof and without regard to any exceptions provided pursuant to subsection (h)(1) thereof), and

(II) is in excess of $5,000,

the tax may be assessed, or a proceeding in court for collection of such tax may be begun without assessment, at any time within 6 years after the return was filed.

(B) Determination of gross income. For purposes of subparagraph (A)

(i) In the case of a trade or business, the term "gross income" means the total of the amounts received or accrued from the sale of goods or services (if such amounts are required to be shown on the return) prior to diminution by the cost of such sales or services;

(ii) An understatement of gross income by reason of an overstatement of unrecovered cost or other basis is an omission from gross income; and

(iii) In determining the amount omitted from gross income (other than in the case of an overstatement of unrecovered cost or other basis), there shall not be taken into account any amount which is omitted from gross income stated in the return if such amount is disclosed in the return, or in a statement attached to the return, in a manner adequate to apprise the Secretary of the nature and amount of such item.

(C) Constructive dividends. If the taxpayer omits from gross income an amount properly includible therein under section 951(a), the tax may be assessed, or a proceeding in court for the collection of such tax may be done without assessing, at any time within 6 years after the return was filed.

(2) Estate and gift taxes. In the case of a return of estate tax under chapter 11 or a return of gift tax under chapter 12, if the taxpayer omits from the gross estate or from the total amount of the gifts made during the period for which the return was filed items includible in such gross estate or such total gifts, as the case may be, as exceed in amount 25 percent of the gross estate stated in the return or the total amount of gifts stated in the return, the tax may be assessed, or a proceeding in court for the collection of such tax may be begun without assessment, at any time within 6 years after the return was filed. In determining the items omitted from the gross estate or the total gifts, there shall not be taken into account any item which is omitted from the gross estate or from the total gifts stated in the return if such item is disclosed in the return, or in a statement attached to the return, in a manner adequate to apprise the Secretary of the nature and amount of such item.

* * *

Regulation

§ 301.6501(c)–1 Exceptions to general period of limitations on assessment and collection.

(a) False return. In the case of a false or fraudulent return with intent to evade any tax, the tax may be assessed, or a proceeding in court for the collection of such tax may be begun without assessment, at any time after such false or fraudulent return is filed.

(b) Willful attempt to evade tax. In the case of a willful attempt in any manner to defeat or evade any tax imposed by the Code (other than a tax imposed by subtitle A or B, relating to income, estate, or gift taxes), the tax may be assessed, or a proceeding in court for the collection of such tax may be begun without assessment, at any time.

(c) No return. In the case of a failure to file a return, the tax may be assessed, or a proceeding in court for the collection of such tax may be begun without assessment, at any time after the date prescribed for filing the return. For special rules relating to filing a return for chapter 42 and similar taxes, see §§ 301.6501(n)–1, 301.6501(n)–2, and 301.6501(n)–3.

(d) Extension by agreement. The time prescribed by section 6501 for the assessment of any tax (other than the estate tax imposed by chapter 11 of the Code) may, prior to the expiration of such time, be extended for any period of time agreed upon in writing by the taxpayer and the district director or an assistant regional commissioner. The extension shall become effective when the agreement has been executed by both parties. The period agreed upon may be extended by subsequent agreements in writing made before the expiration of the period previously agreed upon.

(e) Gifts subject to chapter 14 of the Internal Revenue Code not adequately disclosed on the return. (1) *In general.* If any transfer of property subject to the special valuation rules of section 2701 or section 2702, or if the occurrence of any taxable event described in section § 25.2701–4 of this chapter, is not adequately shown on a return of tax imposed by chapter 12 of subtitle B of the Internal Revenue Code (without regard to section 2503(b)), any tax imposed by chapter 12 of subtitle B of the Code on the transfer or resulting from the taxable event may be assessed, or a proceeding in court for the collection of the appropriate tax may be begun without assessment, at any time.

(2) *Adequately shown.* A transfer of property valued under the rules of section 2701 or section 2702 or any taxable event described in § 25.2701–4 of this chapter will be considered adequately shown on a return of tax imposed by chapter 12 of subtitle B of the Internal Revenue Code only if, with respect to the entire transaction or series of transactions (including any transaction that affected the transferred interest) of which the transfer (or taxable event) was a part, the return provides:

(i) A description of the transactions, including a description of transferred and retained interests and the method (or methods) used to value each;

(ii) The identity of, and relationship between, the transferor, transferee, all other persons participating in the transactions, and all parties related to the transferor holding an equity interest in any entity involved in the transaction; and

(iii) A detailed description (including all actuarial factors and discount rates used) of the method used to determine the amount of the gift arising from the transfer (or taxable event), including, in the case of an equity interest that is not actively traded, the financial and other data used in determining value. Financial data should generally include balance sheets and statements of net earnings, operating results, and dividends paid for each of the 5 years immediately before the valuation date.

(3) *Effective date.* The provisions of this paragraph (e) are effective as of January 28, 1992. In determining whether a transfer or taxable event is adequately shown on a gift tax return filed prior to that date, taxpayers may rely on any reasonable interpretation of the statutory provisions. For these purposes, the provisions of the proposed regulations and the final regulations are considered a reasonable interpretation of the statutory provisions.

(f) Gifts made after December 31, 1996, not adequately disclosed on the return. (1) *In general.* If a transfer of property, other than a transfer described in paragraph (e) of this section, is not adequately disclosed on a gift tax return (Form 709, "United States Gift (and Generation-Skipping Transfer) Tax Return"), or in a statement attached to the return, filed for the calendar period in which the transfer occurs, then any gift tax imposed by chapter 12 of subtitle B of the Internal Revenue Code on the transfer may be assessed, or a proceeding in court for the collection of the appropriate tax may be begun without assessment, at any time.

(2) *Adequate disclosure of transfers of property reported as gifts.* A transfer will be adequately disclosed on the return only if it is reported in a manner adequate to apprise the Internal Revenue Service of the nature of the gift and the basis for the value so reported. Transfers reported on the gift tax return as transfers of property by gift will be considered adequately disclosed under this paragraph (f)(2) if the return (or a statement attached to the return) provides the following information—

(i) A description of the transferred property and any consideration received by the transferor;

(ii) The identity of, and relationship between, the transferor and each transferee;

(iii) If the property is transferred in trust, the trust's tax identification number and a brief description of the terms of the trust, or in lieu of a brief description of the trust terms, a copy of the trust instrument;

(iv) Except as provided in § 301.6501–1(f)(3), a detailed description of the method used to determine the fair market value of property transferred, including any financial data (for example, balance sheets, etc. with explanations of any adjustments) that were utilized in determining the value of the interest, any restrictions on the transferred property that were considered in determining the fair market value of the property, and a description of any discounts, such as discounts for blockage, minority or fractional interests, and lack of marketability, claimed in valuing the property. In the case of a transfer of an interest that is actively traded on an established exchange, such as the New York Stock Exchange, the American Stock Exchange, the NASDAQ National Market, or a regional exchange in which quotations are published on a daily basis, including recognized foreign exchanges, recitation of the exchange where the interest is listed, the CUSIP number of the security, and the mean between the highest and lowest quoted selling prices on the applicable valuation date will satisfy all of the requirements of this paragraph (f)(2)(iv). In the case of the transfer of an interest in an entity (for example, a corporation or partnership) that is not actively traded, a description must be provided of any discount claimed in valuing the interests in the entity or any assets owned by such entity. In addition, if the value of the entity or of the interests in the entity is properly determined based on the net value of the assets held by the entity, a statement must be provided regarding the fair market value of 100 percent of the entity (determined without regard to any discounts in valuing the entity or any assets owned by the entity), the pro rata portion of the entity subject to the transfer, and the fair market value of the transferred interest as reported on the return. If 100 percent of the value of the entity is not disclosed, the taxpayer bears the burden of demonstrating that the fair market value of the entity is properly determined by a method other than a method based on the net value of the assets held by the entity. If the entity that is the subject of the transfer owns an interest in another non-actively traded entity (either directly or through ownership of an entity), the information required in this paragraph (f)(2)(iv) must be provided for each entity if the information is relevant and material in determining the value of the interest; and

(v) A statement describing any position taken that is contrary to any proposed, temporary or final Treasury regulations or revenue rulings published at the time of the transfer (see § 601.601(d)(2) of this chapter).

(3) *Submission of appraisals in lieu of the information required under paragraph (f)(2)(iv) of this section.* The requirements of paragraph (f)(2)(iv) of this section will be satisfied if the donor submits an appraisal of the transferred property that meets the following requirements—

(i) The appraisal is prepared by an appraiser who satisfies all of the following requirements:

(A) The appraiser is an individual who holds himself or herself out to the public as an appraiser or performs appraisals on a regular basis.

(B) Because of the appraiser's qualifications, as described in the appraisal that details the appraiser's background, experience, education, and membership, if any, in professional appraisal associations, the appraiser is qualified to make appraisals of the type of property being valued.

(C) The appraiser is not the donor or the donee of the property or a member of the family of the donor or donee, as defined in section 2032A(e)(2), or any person employed by the donor, the donee, or a member of the family of either; and

(ii) The appraisal contains all of the following:

(A) The date of the transfer, the date on which the transferred property was appraised, and the purpose of the appraisal.

(B) A description of the property.

(C) A description of the appraisal process employed.

(D) A description of the assumptions, hypothetical conditions, and any limiting conditions and restrictions on the transferred property that affect the analyses, opinions, and conclusions.

(E) The information considered in determining the appraised value, including in the case of an ownership interest in a business, all financial data that was used in determining the value of the interest that is sufficiently detailed so that another person can replicate the process and arrive at the appraised value.

(F) The appraisal procedures followed, and the reasoning that supports the analyses, opinions, and conclusions.

(G) The valuation method utilized, the rationale for the valuation method, and the procedure used in determining the fair market value of the asset transferred.

(H) The specific basis for the valuation, such as specific comparable sales or transactions, sales of similar interests, asset-based approaches, merger-acquisition transactions, etc.

(4) *Adequate disclosure of non-gift completed transfers or transactions.* Completed transfers to members of the transferor's family, as defined in section 2032A(e)(2), that are made in the ordinary course of operating a business are deemed to be adequately disclosed under paragraph (f)(2) of this section, even if the transfer is not reported on a gift tax return, provided the transfer is properly reported by all parties for income tax purposes. For example, in the case of salary paid to a family member employed in a family owned business, the transfer will be treated as adequately disclosed for gift tax purposes if the item is properly reported by the business and the family member on their income tax returns. For purposes of this paragraph (f)(4), any other completed transfer that is reported, in its entirety, as not constituting a transfer by gift will be considered adequately disclosed under paragraph (f)(2) of this section only if the following information is provided on, or attached to, the return—

(i) The information required for adequate disclosure under paragraphs (f)(2)(i), (ii), (iii) and (v) of this section; and

(ii) An explanation as to why the transfer is not a transfer by gift under chapter 12 of the Internal Revenue Code.

(5) *Adequate disclosure of incomplete transfers.* Adequate disclosure of a transfer that is reported as a completed gift on the gift tax return will commence the running of the period of limitations for assessment of gift tax on the transfer, even if the transfer is ultimately determined to be an incomplete gift for purposes of § 25.2511–2 of this chapter. For example, if an incomplete gift is reported as a completed gift on the gift tax return and is adequately disclosed, the period for assessment of the gift tax will begin to run when the return is filed, as determined under section 6501(b). Further, once the period of assessment for gift tax expires, the transfer will be subject to inclusion in the donor's gross estate for estate tax purposes only to the extent that a completed gift would be so included. On the other hand, if the transfer is reported as an incomplete gift whether or not adequately disclosed, the period for assessing a gift tax with respect to the transfer will not commence to run even if the transfer is ultimately determined to be a completed gift. In that situation, the gift tax with respect to the transfer may be assessed at any time, up until three years after the donor files a return reporting the transfer as a completed gift with adequate disclosure.

(6) *Treatment of split gifts.* If a husband and wife elect under section 2513 to treat a gift made to a third party as made one-half by each spouse, the requirements of this paragraph (f) will be satisfied with respect to the gift deemed made by the consenting spouse if the return filed by the donor spouse (the spouse that transferred the property) satisfies the requirements of this paragraph (f) with respect to that gift.

(7) *Examples.* The following examples illustrate the rules of this paragraph (f):

Example (1). (i) *Facts.* In 2001, A transfers 100 shares of common stock of XYZ Corporation to A's child. The common stock of XYZ Corporation is actively traded on a major stock exchange. For gift tax purposes, the fair market value of one share of XYZ common stock on the date of the transfer, determined in accordance with § 25.2512–2(b) of this chapter (based on the mean between the highest and lowest quoted selling prices), is $150.00. On A's Federal gift tax return, Form 709, for the 2001 calendar year, A reports the gift to A's child of 100 shares of common stock of XYZ Corporation with a value for gift tax purposes of $15,000. A specifies the date of the transfer, recites that the stock is publicly traded, identifies the stock exchange on which the stock is traded, lists the stock's CUSIP number, and lists the mean between the highest and lowest quoted selling prices for the date of transfer.

(ii) *Application of the adequate disclosure standard.* A has adequately disclosed the transfer. Therefore, the period of assessment for the transfer under section 6501 will run from the time the return is filed (as determined under section 6501(b)).

Example (2). (i) *Facts.* On December 30, 2001, A transfers closely-held stock to B, A's child. A determined that the value of the transferred stock, on December 30, 2001, was $9,000. A made no other transfers to B, or any other donee, during 2001. On A's Federal gift tax return, Form 709, for the 2001 calendar year, A provides the information required under paragraph (f)(2) of this section such that the transfer is adequately disclosed. A claims an annual exclusion under section 2503(b) for the transfer.

(ii) *Application of the adequate disclosure standard.* Because the transfer is adequately disclosed under paragraph (f)(2) of this section, the period of assessment for the transfer will expire as prescribed by section 6501(b), notwithstanding that if A's valuation of the closely-held stock was correct, A was not required to file a gift tax return reporting the transfer under section 6019. After the period of assessment has expired on the transfer, the Internal Revenue Service is precluded from redetermining the amount of the gift for purposes of assessing gift tax or for purposes of determining the estate tax liability. Therefore, the amount of the gift as reported on A's 2001 Federal gift tax return may not be redetermined for purposes of determining A's prior taxable gifts (for gift tax purposes) or A's adjusted taxable gifts (for estate tax purposes).

Example (3). (i) *Facts.* A owns 100 percent of the common stock of X, a closely-held corporation. X does not hold an interest in any other entity that is not actively traded. In 2001, A transfers 20 percent of the X stock to B and C, A's children, in a transfer that is not subject to the special valuation rules of section 2701. The transfer is made outright with no restrictions on ownership rights, including voting rights and the right to transfer the stock. Based on generally applicable valuation principles, the value of X would be determined based on the net value of the assets owned by X. The reported value of the transferred stock incorporates the use of minority discounts and lack of marketability discounts. No other discounts were used in arriving at the fair market value of the transferred stock or any assets owned by X. On A's Federal gift tax return, Form 709, for the 2001 calendar year, A provides the information required under paragraph (f)(2) of this section including a statement reporting the fair market value of 100 percent of X (before taking into account any discounts), the pro rata portion of X subject to the transfer, and the reported value of the transfer. A also attaches a statement regarding the determination of value that includes a discussion of the discounts claimed and how the discounts were determined.

(ii) *Application of the adequate disclosure standard.* A has provided sufficient information such that the transfer will be considered adequately disclosed and the period of assessment for the transfer under section 6501 will run from the time the return is filed (as determined under section 6501(b)).

Example (4). (i) *Facts.* A owns a 70 percent limited partnership interest in PS. PS owns 40 percent of the stock in X, a closely-held corporation. The assets of X include a 50 percent general partnership interest in PB. PB owns an interest in commercial real property. None of the entities (PS, X, or PB) is actively traded and, based on generally applicable valuation principles, the value of each entity would be determined based on the net value of the assets owned by each entity. In 2001, A transfers a 25 percent limited partnership interest in PS to B, A's child. On the Federal gift tax return, Form 709, for the 2001 calendar year, A reports the transfer of the 25 percent limited partnership interest in PS and that the fair market value of 100 percent of PS is $y and that the value of 25 percent of PS is $z, reflecting marketability and minority discounts with respect to the 25 percent interest. However, A does not disclose that PS owns 40 percent of X, and that X owns 50 percent of PB and that, in arriving at the $y fair market value of 100 percent of PS, discounts were claimed in valuing PS's interest in X, X's interest in PB, and PB's interest in the commercial real property.

(ii) *Application of the adequate disclosure standard.* The information on the lower tiered entities is relevant and material in determining the value of the transferred interest in PS. Accordingly, because A has failed to comply with requirements of paragraph (f)(2)(iv) of this section regarding PS's interest in X, X's interest in PB, and PB's interest in the commercial real property, the transfer will not be considered adequately disclosed and the period of assessment for the transfer under section 6501 will remain open indefinitely.

Example (5). The facts are the same as in Example 4 except that A submits, with the Federal tax return, an appraisal of the 25 percent limited partnership interest in PS that satisfies the requirements of paragraph (f)(3) of this section in lieu of the information required in paragraph (f)(2)(iv) of this section. Assuming the other requirements of paragraph (f)(2) of this section are satisfied, the transfer is considered adequately disclosed and the period for assessment for the transfer under section 6501 will run from the time the return is filed (as determined under section 6501(b) of this chapter).

Example (6). A owns 100 percent of the stock of X Corporation, a company actively engaged in a manufacturing business. B, A's child, is an employee of X and receives an annual salary paid in the ordinary course of operating X Corporation. B reports the annual salary as income on B's income tax returns. In 2001, A transfers property to family members and files a Federal gift tax return reporting the transfers. However, A does not disclose the 2001 salary payments made to B. Because the salary payments were reported as income on B's income tax return, the salary payments are deemed to be adequately disclosed. The transfer of property to family members, other than the salary payments to B, reported on the gift tax return must satisfy the adequate disclosure requirements under paragraph (f)(2) of this section in order for the period of assessment under section 6501 to commence to run with respect to those transfers.

(8) *Effective date.* This paragraph (f) is applicable to gifts made after December 31, 1996, for which the gift tax return for such calendar year is filed after December 3, 1999.

* * *

[32 FR 15241, Nov. 3, 1967; T.D. 7838, 47 FR 44250, Oct. 7, 1982; T.D. 8395, 57 FR 4277, Feb. 4, 1992; T.D. 8845, 64 FR 67771, Dec. 3, 1999; 65 FR 1059, Jan. 7, 2000; T.D. 9718, 80 FR 16976, March 31, 2015; 80 FR 23444, April 28, 2015]

§ 6502. Collection after Assessment

(a) Length of period. Where the assessment of any tax imposed by this title has been made within the period of limitation properly applicable thereto, such tax may be collected by levy or by a proceeding in court, but only if the levy is made or the proceeding begun—

(1) within 10 years after the assessment of the tax, or

(2) if—

(A) there is an installment agreement between the taxpayer and the Secretary, prior to the date which is 90 days after the expiration of any period for collection agreed upon in writing by the Secretary and the taxpayer at the time the installment agreement was entered into; or

(B) there is a release of levy under section 6343 after such 10-year period, prior to the expiration of any period for collection agreed upon in writing by the Secretary and the taxpayer before such release.

If a timely proceeding in court for the collection of a tax is commenced, the period during which such tax may be collected by levy shall be extended and shall not expire until the liability for the tax (or a judgment against the taxpayer arising from such liability) is satisfied or becomes unenforceable.

(b) Date when levy is considered made. The date on which a levy on property or rights to property is made shall be the date on which the notice of seizure provided in section 6335(a) is given.

§ 6503. Suspension of Running of Period of Limitation

(a) Issuance of statutory notice of deficiency.

(1) General rule. The running of the period of limitations provided in section 6501 or 6502 on the making of assessments or the collection by levy or a proceeding in court, in respect of any deficiency as defined in section 6211 (relating to income, estate, gift and certain excise taxes), shall (after the mailing of a notice under section 6212(a)) be suspended for the period during which the Secretary is prohibited from making the assessment or from collecting by levy or a proceeding in court (and in any event, if a proceeding in respect of the deficiency is placed on the docket of the Tax Court, until the decision of the Tax Court becomes final), and for 60 days thereafter.

* * *

(d) Extensions of time for payment of estate tax. The running of the period of limitations for collection of any tax imposed by chapter 11 shall be suspended for the period of any extension of time for payment granted under the provisions of section 6161(a)(2) or (b)(2) or under the provisions of section 6163 or 6166.

(e) Extensions of time for payment of tax attributable to recoveries of foreign expropriation losses. The running of the period of limitations for collection of the tax attributable to a recovery of a foreign expropriation loss (within the meaning of section 6167(f)) shall be suspended for the period of any extension of time for payment under subsection (a) or (b) of section 6167.

* * *

(k) Cross references.

For suspension in case of—

(1) Deficiency dividends of a personal holding company, see section 547(f).

(2) Receiverships, see subchapter B of chapter 70.

(3) Claims against transferees and fiduciaries, see chapter 71.

(4) Tax return preparers, see section 6694(c)(3).

(5) Deficiency dividends in the case of a regulated investment company or a real estate investment trust, see section 860(h).

Subchapter B. Limitations on Credit or Refund

§ 6511. Limitations on Credit or Refund

(a) Period of limitation on filing claim. Claim for credit or refund of an overpayment of any tax imposed by this title in respect of which tax the taxpayer is required to file a return shall be filed by the taxpayer within 3 years from the time the return was filed or 2 years from the time the tax was paid, whichever of such periods expires the later, or if no return was filed by the taxpayer, within 2 years from the time the tax was paid. Claim for credit or refund of an overpayment of any tax imposed by this title which is required to be paid by means of a stamp shall be filed by the taxpayer within 3 years from the time the tax was paid.

(b) Limitation on allowance of credits and refunds.

(1) Filing of claim within prescribed period. No credit or refund shall be allowed or made after the expiration of the period of limitation prescribed in subsection (a) for the filing of a claim for credit or refund, unless a claim for credit or refund is filed by the taxpayer within such period.

(2) Limit on amount of credit or refund.

(A) Limit where claim filed within 3-year period. If the claim was filed by the taxpayer during the 3-year period prescribed in subsection (a), the amount of the credit or refund shall not exceed the portion of the tax paid within the period, immediately preceding the filing of the claim, equal to 3 years plus the period of any extension of time for filing the return. If the tax was required to be paid by means of a stamp, the amount of the credit or refund shall not exceed the portion of the tax paid within the 3 years immediately preceding the filing of the claim.

(B) Limit where claim not filed within 3-year period. If the claim was not filed within such 3-year period, the amount of the credit or refund shall not exceed the portion of the tax paid during the 2 years immediately preceding the filing of the claim.

(C) Limit if no claim filed. If no claim was filed, the credit or refund shall not exceed the amount which would be allowable under subparagraph (A) or (B), as the case may be, if claim was filed on the date the credit or refund is allowed.

(c) Special rules applicable in case of extension of time by agreement. If an agreement under the provisions of section 6501(c)(4) extending the period for assessment of a tax imposed by this title is made within the period prescribed in subsection (a) for the filing of a claim for credit or refund—

(1) Time for filing claim. The period for filing claim for credit or refund or for making credit or refund if no claim is filed, provided in subsections (a) and (b)(1), shall not expire prior to 6 months after the expiration of the period within which an assessment may be made pursuant to the agreement or any extension thereof under section 6501(c)(4).

(2) Limit on amount. If a claim is filed, or a credit or refund is allowed when no claim was filed, after the execution of the agreement and within 6 months after the expiration of the period within which an assessment may be made pursuant to the agreement or any extension thereof, the amount of the credit or refund shall not exceed the portion of the tax paid after the execution of the agreement and before the filing of the claim or the making of the credit or refund, as the case may be, plus the portion of the tax paid within the period which would be applicable under subsection (b)(2) if a claim had been filed on the date the agreement was executed.

(3) Claims not subject to special rule. This subsection shall not apply in the case of a claim filed, or credit or refund allowed if no claim is filed, either—

(A) prior to the execution of the agreement or

(B) more than 6 months after the expiration of the period within which an assessment may be made pursuant to the agreement or any extension thereof.

* * *

§ 6514. Credits or Refunds after Period of Limitation

(a) Credits or refunds after period of limitation. A refund of any portion of an internal revenue tax shall be considered erroneous and a credit of any such portion shall be considered void—

(1) Expiration of period for filing claim. If made after the expiration of the period of limitation for filing claim therefor, unless within such period claim was filed; or

(2) Disallowance of claim and expiration of period for filing suit. In the case of a claim filed within the proper time and disallowed by the Secretary, if the credit or refund was made after the expiration of the period of limitation for filing suit, unless within such period suit was begun by the taxpayer.

(3) Recovery of erroneous refunds. For procedure by the United States to recover erroneous refunds, see sections 6532(b) and 7405.

(b) Credit after period of limitation. Any credit against a liability in respect of any taxable year shall be void if any payment in respect of such liability would be considered an overpayment under section 6401(a).

Chapter 67. Interest

Subchapter A. Interest on Underpayments

§ 6601. Interest on Underpayment, Nonpayment, or Extensions of Time for Payment, of Tax

(a) General rule. If any amount of tax imposed by this title (whether required to be shown on a return, or to be paid by stamp or by some other method) is not paid on or before the last date prescribed for payment, interest on such amount at the underpayment rate established under section 6621 shall be paid for the period from such last date to the date paid.

(b) Last date prescribed for payment. For purposes of this section, the last date prescribed for payment of the tax shall be determined under chapter 62 with the application of the following rules:

(1) Extensions of time disregarded. The last date prescribed for payment shall be determined without regard to any extension of time for payment or any installment agreement entered into under section 6159.

(2) Jeopardy. The last date prescribed for payment shall be determined without regard to any notice and demand for payment issued, by reason of jeopardy (as provided in chapter 70), prior to the last date otherwise prescribed for such payment.

* * *

(4) Last date for payment not otherwise prescribed. In the case of taxes payable by stamp and in all other cases in which the last date for payment is not otherwise prescribed, the last date for payment shall be deemed to be the date the liability for tax arises (and in no event shall be later than the date notice and demand for the tax is made by the Secretary).

(c) Suspension of interest in certain income, estate, gift, and certain excise tax cases. In the case of a deficiency as defined in section 6211 (relating to income, estate, gift and certain excise taxes), if a waiver of restrictions under section 6213(d) on the assessment of such deficiency has been filed, and if notice and demand by the Secretary for payment of such deficiency is not made within 30 days after the filing of such waiver, interest shall not be imposed on such deficiency for the period beginning immediately after such 30th day and ending with the date of notice and demand and interest shall not be imposed during such period on any interest with respect to such deficiency for any prior period.

* * *

(g) Limitation on assessment and collection. Interest prescribed under this section on any tax may be assessed and collected at any time during the period within which the tax to which such interest relates may be collected.

* * *

(j) 2-percent rate on certain portion of estate tax extended under section 6166.

(1) In general. If the time for payment of an amount of tax imposed by chapter 11 is extended as provided in section 6166, then in lieu of the annual rate provided by subsection (a)—

(A) the interest on the 2-percent portion of such amount shall be paid at the rate of 2 percent, and

(B) interest on so much of such amount as exceeds the 2-percent portion shall be paid at a rate equal to 45 percent of the annual rate provided by subsection (a).

For purposes of this subsection, the amount of any deficiency which is prorated to installments payable under section 6166 shall be treated as an amount of tax payable in installments under such section.

(2) 2-percent portion. For purposes of this subsection, the term "2-percent portion" means the lesser of—

(A) (i) the amount of the tentative tax which would be determined under the rate schedule set forth in section 2001(c) if the amount with respect to which such tentative tax is to be computed were the sum of $1,000,000 and the applicable exclusion amount in effect under section 2010(c), reduced by

(ii) the applicable credit amount in effect under section 2010(c), or

(B) the amount of the tax imposed by chapter 11 which is extended as provided in section 6166.

(3) Inflation adjustment. In the case of estates of decedents dying in a calendar year after 1998, the $1,000,000 amount contained in paragraph (2)(A) shall be increased by an amount equal to—

(A) $1,000,000, multiplied by

(B) the cost-of-living adjustment determined under section 1(f)(3) for such calendar year by substituting "calendar year 1997" for "calendar year 2016" in subparagraph (A)(ii) thereof.

If any amount as adjusted under the preceding sentence is not a multiple of $10,000, such amount shall be rounded to the next lowest multiple of $10,000.*

(4) Treatment of payments. If the amount of tax imposed by chapter 11 which is extended as provided in section 6166 exceeds the 2-percent portion, any payment of a portion of such amount shall, for purposes of computing interest for periods after such payment, be treated as reducing the 2-percent portion by an amount which bears the same ratio to the amount of such payment as the amount of the 2-percent portion (determined without regard to this paragraph) bears to the amount of the tax which is extended as provided in section 6166.

(k) No interest on certain adjustments. For provisions prohibiting interest on certain adjustments in tax, see section 6205(a).

Subchapter C. Determination of Interest Rate; Compounding of Interest

§ 6621. Determination of Rate of Interest

(a) General rule.

(1) Overpayment rate. The overpayment rate established under this section shall be the sum of—

(A) the Federal short-term rate determined under subsection (b), plus

(B) 3 percentage points (2 percentage points in the case of a corporation).

To the extent that an overpayment of tax by a corporation for any taxable period (as defined in subsection (c)(3), applied by substituting "overpayment" for "underpayment") exceeds $10,000, subparagraph (B) shall be applied by substituting "0.5 percentage point" for "2 percentage points".

(2) Underpayment rate. The underpayment rate established under this section shall be the sum of—

(A) the Federal short-term rate determined under subsection (b), plus

* Rev. Proc. 2025–32 provides that "[f]or an estate of a decedent dying in calendar year 2026, the dollar amount used to determine the '2-percent portion' (for purposes of calculating interest under § 6601(j)) of the estate tax extended as provided in § 6166 is $1,940,000." *Ed.*

(B) 3 percentage points.

(b) Federal short-term rate. For purposes of this section—

(1) General rule. The Secretary shall determine the Federal short-term rate for the first month in each calendar quarter.

(2) Period during which rate applies.

(A) In general. Except as provided in subparagraph (B), the Federal short-term rate determined under paragraph (1) for any month shall apply during the first calendar quarter beginning after such month.

(B) Special rule for individual estimated tax. In determining the addition to tax under section 6654 for failure to pay estimated tax for any taxable year, the Federal short-term rate which applies during the 3rd month following such taxable year shall also apply during the first 15 days of the 4th month following such taxable year.

(3) Federal short-term rate. The Federal short-term rate for any month shall be the Federal short-term rate determined during such month by the Secretary in accordance with section 1274(d). Any such rate shall be rounded to the nearest full percent (or, if a multiple of ½ of 1 percent, such rate shall be increased to the next highest full percent).

* * *

(d) Elimination of interest on overlapping periods of tax overpayments and underpayments. To the extent that, for any period, interest is payable under subchapter A and allowable under subchapter B on equivalent underpayments and overpayments by the same taxpayer of tax imposed by this title, the net rate of interest under this section on such amounts shall be zero for such period.

Chapter 68. Additions to the Tax, Additional Amounts, and Assessable Penalties

Subchapter A. Additions to the Tax and Additional Amounts

Subchapter B. Assessable Penalties

Subchapter A. Additions to the Tax and Additional Amounts

Part I. General Provisions

§ 6651. Failure to File Tax Return or to Pay Tax

(a) Addition to the tax. In case of failure—

(1) to file any return required under authority of subchapter A of chapter 61 (other than part III thereof), subchapter A of chapter 51 (relating to distilled spirits, wines, and beer), or of subchapter A of chapter 52 (relating to tobacco, cigars, cigarettes, and cigarette papers and tubes), or of subchapter A of chapter 53 (relating to machine guns and certain other firearms), on the date prescribed therefor (determined with regard to any extension of time for filing), unless it is shown that such failure is due to reasonable cause and not due to willful neglect, there shall be added to the amount required to be shown as tax on such return 5 percent of the amount of such tax if the failure is for not more than 1 month, with an additional 5 percent for each additional month or fraction thereof during which such failure continues, not exceeding 25 percent in the aggregate;

(2) to pay the amount shown as tax on any return specified in paragraph (1) on or before the date prescribed for payment of such tax (determined with regard to any extension of time for payment), unless it is shown that such failure is due to reasonable cause and not due to willful neglect, there shall be added to the amount shown as tax on such return 0.5 percent of the amount of such tax if the failure is for not more than 1 month, with an additional 0.5 percent for each additional month or fraction thereof during which such failure continues, not exceeding 25 percent in the aggregate; or

(3) to pay any amount in respect of any tax required to be shown on a return specified in paragraph (1) which is not so shown (including an assessment made pursuant to section 6213(b)) within 21 calendar days from the date of notice and demand therefor (10 business days if the amount for which such notice and demand is made equals or exceeds $100,000), unless it is shown that such failure is due to reasonable cause and not due to willful neglect, there shall be added to the amount of tax stated in such notice and demand 0.5 percent of the amount of such tax if the failure is for not more than 1 month, with an additional 0.5 percent for each additional month or fraction thereof during which such failure continues, not exceeding 25 percent in the aggregate.

In the case of a failure to file a return of tax imposed by chapter 1 within 60 days of the date prescribed for filing of such return (determined with regard to any extensions of time for filing), unless it is shown that such failure is due to reasonable cause and not due to willful neglect, the addition to tax under paragraph (1) shall not be less than the lesser of $435 or 100 percent of the amount required to be shown as tax on such return.*

(b) Penalty imposed on net amount due. For purposes of—

(1) subsection (a)(1), the amount of tax required to be shown on the return shall be reduced by the amount of any part of the tax which is paid on or before the date prescribed for payment of the tax and by the amount of any credit against the tax which may be claimed on the return,

(2) subsection (a)(2), the amount of tax shown on the return shall, for purposes of computing the addition for any month, be reduced by the amount of any part of the tax which is paid on or before the beginning of such month and by the amount of any credit against the tax which may be claimed on the return, and

(3) subsection (a)(3), the amount of tax stated in the notice and demand shall, for the purpose of computing the addition for any month, be reduced by the amount of any part of the tax which is paid before the beginning of such month.

(c) Limitations and special rule.

(1) Additions under more than one paragraph. With respect to any return, the amount of the addition under paragraph (1) of subsection (a) shall be reduced by the amount of the addition under paragraph (2) of subsection (a) for any month (or fraction thereof) to which an addition to tax applies under both paragraphs (1) and (2). In any case described in the last sentence of subsection (a), the amount of the addition under paragraph (1) of subsection (a) shall not be reduced under the preceding sentence below the amount provided in such last sentence.

(2) Amount of tax shown more than amount required to be shown. If the amount required to be shown as tax on a return is less than the amount shown as tax on such return, subsections (a)(2) and (b)(2) shall be applied by substituting such lower amount.

(d) Increase in penalty for failure to pay tax in certain cases.

(1) In general. In the case of each month (or fraction thereof) beginning after the day described in paragraph (2) of this subsection, paragraphs (2) and (3) of subsection (a) shall be applied by substituting "1 percent" for "0.5 percent" each place it appears.

(2) Description. For purposes of paragraph (1), the day described in this paragraph is the earlier of—

(A) the day 10 days after the date on which notice is given under section 6331(d), or

* Rev. Proc. 2025–32 provides that "[i]n the case of any return required to be filed in 2027, the amount of the addition to tax under § 6651(a) for failure to file an income tax return within 60 days of the due date of such return (determined with regard to any extensions of time for filing) will not be less than the lesser of $535 or 100 percent of the amount required to be shown as tax on such return." *Ed.*

(B) the day on which notice and demand for immediate payment is given under the last sentence of section 6331(a).

* * *

(f) Increase in penalty for fraudulent failure to file. If any failure to file any return is fraudulent, paragraph (1) of subsection (a) shall be applied—

(1) by substituting "15 percent" for "5 percent" each place it appears, and

(2) by substituting "75 percent" for "25 percent".

* * *

(h) Limitation on penalty on individual's failure to pay for months during period of installment agreement. In the case of an individual who files a return of tax on or before the due date for the return (including extensions), paragraphs (2) and (3) of subsection (a) shall each be applied by substituting "0.25" for "0.5" each place it appears for purposes of determining the addition to the tax for any month during which an installment agreement under section 6159 is in effect for the payment of such tax.

* * *

(j) Adjustment for inflation.

(1) In general. In the case of any return required to be filed in a calendar year beginning after 2020, the $435 dollar amount under subsection (a) shall be increased by an amount equal to such dollar amount multiplied by the cost-of-living adjustment determined under section 1(f)(3) for the calendar year determined by substituting "calendar year 2019" for "calendar year 2016" in subparagraph (A)(ii) thereof.

(2) Rounding. If any amount adjusted under paragraph (1) is not a multiple of $5, such amount shall be rounded to the next lowest multiple of $5.

Part II. Accuracy-Related and Fraud Penalties

§ 6662. Imposition of Accuracy-Related Penalty on Underpayments

(a) Imposition of penalty. If this section applies to any portion of an underpayment of tax required to be shown on a return, there shall be added to the tax an amount equal to 20 percent of the portion of the underpayment to which this section applies.

(b) Portion of underpayment to which section applies. This section shall apply to the portion of any underpayment which is attributable to 1 or more of the following:

(1) Negligence or disregard of rules or regulations.

(2) Any substantial understatement of income tax.

(3) Any substantial valuation misstatement under chapter 1.

* * *

(5) Any substantial estate or gift tax valuation understatement.

(6) Any disallowance of claimed tax benefits by reason of a transaction lacking economic substance (within the meaning of section 7701(*o*)) or failing to meet the requirements of any similar rule of law.

* * *

(8) Any inconsistent estate basis.

(9) Any overstatement of the deduction provided in section 170(p).

This section shall not apply to any portion of an underpayment on which a penalty is imposed under section 6663. Except as provided in paragraph (1) or (2)(B) of section 6662A(e), this section shall not apply to the portion of any underpayment which is attributable to a reportable transaction understatement on which a penalty is imposed under section 6662A.

(c) Negligence. For purposes of this section, the term "negligence" includes any failure to make a reasonable attempt to comply with the provisions of this title, and the term "disregard" includes any careless, reckless, or intentional disregard.

(d) Substantial understatement of income tax.

(1) Substantial understatement.

(A) In general. For purposes of this section, there is a substantial understatement of income tax for any taxable year if the amount of the understatement for the taxable year exceeds the greater of—

(i) 10 percent of the tax required to be shown on the return for the taxable year, or

(ii) $5,000.

* * *

(2) Understatement.

(A) In general. For purposes of paragraph (1), the term "understatement" means the excess of—

(i) the amount of the tax required to be shown on the return for the taxable year, over

(ii) the amount of the tax imposed which is shown on the return, reduced by any rebate (within the meaning of section 6211(b)(2)).

The excess under the preceding sentence shall be determined without regard to items to which section 6662A applies.

(B) Reduction for understatement due to position of taxpayer or disclosed item. The amount of the understatement under subparagraph (A) shall be reduced by that portion of the understatement which is attributable to—

(i) the tax treatment of any item by the taxpayer if there is or was substantial authority for such treatment, or

(ii) any item if—

(I) the relevant facts affecting the item's tax treatment are adequately disclosed in the return or in a statement attached to the return, and

(II) there is a reasonable basis for the tax treatment of such item by the taxpayer.

For purposes of clause (ii)(II), in no event shall a corporation be treated as having a reasonable basis for its tax treatment of an item attributable to a multiple-party financing transaction if such treatment does not clearly reflect the income of the corporation.

* * *

(e) Substantial valuation misstatement under chapter 1.

(1) In general. For purposes of this section, there is a substantial valuation misstatement under chapter 1 if—

(A) the value of any property (or the adjusted basis of any property) claimed on any return of tax imposed by chapter 1 is 150 percent or more of the amount determined to be the correct amount of such valuation or adjusted basis (as the case may be), or

(B) (i) the price for any property or services (or for the use of property) claimed on any such return in connection with any transaction between persons described in section 482 is 200 percent or more (or 50 percent or less) of the amount determined under section 482 to be the correct amount of such price, or

(ii) the net section 482 transfer price adjustment for the taxable year exceeds the lesser of $5,000,000 or 10 percent of the taxpayer's gross receipts.

(2) Limitation. No penalty shall be imposed by reason of subsection (b)(3) unless the portion of the underpayment for the taxable year attributable to substantial valuation misstatements under chapter 1 exceeds $5,000 ($10,000 in the case of a corporation other than an S corporation or a personal holding company (as defined in section 542)).

* * *

(g) Substantial estate or gift tax valuation understatement.

(1) In general. For purposes of this section, there is a substantial estate or gift tax valuation understatement if the value of any property claimed on any return of tax imposed by subtitle B is 65 percent or less of the amount determined to be the correct amount of such valuation.

(2) Limitation. No penalty shall be imposed by reason of subsection (b)(5) unless the portion of the underpayment attributable to substantial estate or gift tax valuation understatements for the taxable period (or, in the case of the tax imposed by chapter 11, with respect to the estate of the decedent) exceeds $5,000.

(h) Increase in penalty in case of gross valuation misstatements.

(1) In general. To the extent that a portion of the underpayment to which this section applies is attributable to one or more gross valuation misstatements, subsection (a) shall be applied with respect to such portion by substituting "40 percent" for "20 percent".

(2) Gross valuation misstatements. The term "gross valuation misstatements" means—

(A) any substantial valuation misstatement under chapter 1 as determined under subsection (e) by substituting—

(i) in paragraph (1)(A), "200 percent" for "150 percent",

(ii) in paragraph (1)(B)(i)—

(I) "400 percent" for "200 percent", and

(II) "25 percent" for "50 percent", and

(iii) in paragraph (1)(B)(ii)—

(I) "$20,000,000" for "$5,000,000", and

(II) "20 percent" for "10 percent".

* * *

(C) any substantial estate or gift tax valuation understatement as determined under subsection (g) by substituting "40 percent" for "65 percent".

(i) Increase in Penalty in Case of Nondisclosed Noneconomic Substance Transactions.

(1) In general. In the case of any portion of an underpayment which is attributable to one or more nondisclosed noneconomic substance transactions, subsection (a) shall be applied with respect to such portion by substituting "40 percent" for "20 percent".

(2) Nondisclosed noneconomic substance transactions. For purposes of this subsection, the term "nondisclosed noneconomic substance transaction" means any portion of a transaction described in subsection (b)(6) with respect to which the relevant facts affecting the tax treatment are not adequately disclosed in the return nor in a statement attached to the return.

(3) Special rule for amended returns. In no event shall any amendment or supplement to a return of tax be taken into account for purposes of this subsection if the amendment or supplement is filed after the earlier of the date the taxpayer is first contacted by the Secretary regarding the examination of the return or such other date as is specified by the Secretary.

* * *

(k) Inconsistent Estate Basis Reporting. For purposes of this section, the term "inconsistent estate basis" means any portion of an underpayment attributable to the failure to comply with section 1014(f).

(*l*) Increase in Penalty in Case of Overstatement of Qualified Charitable Contributions. In the case of any portion of an underpayment which is attributable to one or more overstatements of the deduction provided in section 170(p), subsection (a) shall be applied with respect to such portion by substituting "50 percent" for "20 percent".

Regulation

§ 1.6662–9 Inconsistent estate basis reporting.

(a) In general. Section 6662(a) and (b)(8) impose an accuracy-related penalty on the portion of any underpayment of tax required to be shown on an income tax return that is attributable to an inconsistent estate basis.

(b) Inconsistent estate basis (1) *In general.* There is an inconsistent estate basis in property under section 6662(k) to the extent that a taxpayer claims a basis that was determined by using an initial basis as defined in § 1.1014–10(a)(2) that exceeds the property's final value as determined under § 1.1014–10(b)(1). The property to which this section applies is the property described in § 1.1014–10(c)(1).

(2) *Example.* The following example illustrates the provisions of paragraph (b)(1) of this section. In year 1, taxpayer (T), a citizen of the United States, inherited a house, property described in § 1.1014–10(c)(1) and not described in § 1.1014–10(c)(2). The final value and thus initial basis of the house as determined under § 1.1014–10(b) was $300,000. In year 5, T spent $85,000 on an addition to the house, which is added to T's initial basis in the house under section 1016(a). In year 11, T sold the house to an unrelated third party for $650,000. On T's return, T claims an initial basis of $400,000 and the $85,000 spent on the addition to the house, for a total claimed basis of $485,000. T's claimed initial basis exceeds the allowable basis by $100,000. Because this amount is due to T claiming an initial basis as defined in § 1.1014–10(a)(2) that exceeds the property's final value as determined under § 1.1014–10(b), T is liable for the 20% accuracy-related penalty for the portion of any underpayment that is attributable to the reporting of an inconsistent basis.

(c) Applicability date. This section applies to property described in § 1.1014–10(c)(1) that is reported on an estate tax return required under section 6018 that is filed after September 17, 2024.

[T.D. 9991, 89 FR 76386, Sept. 17, 2024]

Subchapter B. Assessable Penalties

Part I. General Provisions

§ 6702. Frivolous Tax Submissions

(a) Civil penalty for frivolous tax returns. A person shall pay a penalty of $5,000 if—

(1) Such person files what purports to be a return of a tax imposed by this title but which—

(A) does not contain information on which the substantial correctness of the self-assessment may be judged, or

(B) contains information that on its face indicates that the self-assessment is substantially incorrect, and

(2) the conduct referred to in paragraph (1)—

(A) is based on a position which the Secretary has identified as frivolous under subsection (c), or

(B) reflects a desire to delay or impede the administration of Federal tax laws.

(b) Civil penalty for specified frivolous submissions.

* * *

(3) Opportunity to withdraw submission. If the Secretary provides a person with notice that a submission is a specified frivolous submission and such person withdraws such submission within 30 days after such notice, the penalty imposed under paragraph (1) shall not apply with respect to such submission.

(c) Listing of frivolous positions. The Secretary shall prescribe (and periodically revise) a list of positions which the Secretary has identified as being frivolous for purposes of this subsection. The Secretary shall not include in such list any position that the Secretary determines meets the requirement of section 6662(d)(2)(B)(ii)(II).

(d) Reduction of penalty. The Secretary may reduce the amount of any penalty imposed under this section if the Secretary determines that such reduction would promote compliance with and administration of the Federal tax laws.

(e) Penalties in addition to other penalties. The penalties imposed by this section shall be in addition to any other penalty provided by law.

* * *

Chapter 70. Jeopardy, Receiverships, Etc.

Subchapter A. Jeopardy

Subchapter B. Receiverships, Etc.

Subchapter A. Jeopardy

Part II. Jeopardy Assessments

§ 6861. Jeopardy Assessments of Income, Estate, Gift, And Certain Excise Taxes

(a) Authority for making. If the Secretary believes that the assessment or collection of a deficiency, as defined in section 6211, will be jeopardized by delay, he shall, notwithstanding the provisions of section 6213(a), immediately assess such deficiency (together with all interest, additional amounts, and additions to the tax provided for by law), and notice and demand shall be made by the Secretary for the payment thereof.

(b) Deficiency letters. If the jeopardy assessment is made before any notice in respect of the tax to which the jeopardy assessment relates has been mailed under section 6212(a), then the Secretary shall mail a notice under such subsection within 60 days after the making of the assessment.

(c) Amount assessable before decision of Tax Court. The jeopardy assessment may be made in respect of a deficiency greater or less than that notice of which has been mailed to the taxpayer, despite the provisions of section 6212(c) prohibiting the determination of additional deficiencies, and whether or not the taxpayer has theretofore filed a petition with the Tax Court. The Secretary may, at any time before the decision of the Tax Court is rendered, abate such assessment, or any unpaid portion thereof, to the extent that he believes the assessment to be excessive in amount. The Secretary shall notify the Tax Court of the amount of such assessment, or abatement, if the petition is filed with the Tax Court before the making of the assessment or is subsequently filed, and the Tax Court shall have jurisdiction to redetermine the entire amount of the deficiency and of all amounts assessed at the same time in connection therewith.

(d) Amount assessable after decision of Tax Court. If the jeopardy assessment is made after the decision of the Tax Court is rendered, such assessment may be made only in respect of the deficiency determined by the Tax Court in its decision.

(e) Expiration of right to assess. A jeopardy assessment may not be made after the decision of the Tax Court has become final or after the taxpayer has filed a petition for review of the decision of the Tax Court.

(f) Collection of unpaid amounts. When the petition has been filed with the Tax Court and when the amount which should have been assessed has been determined by a decision of the Tax Court which has become final, then any unpaid portion, the collection of which has been stayed by bond as provided in section 6863(b) shall be collected as part of the tax upon notice and demand from the Secretary, and any remaining portion of the assessment shall be abated. If the amount already collected exceeds the amount determined as the amount which should have been assessed, such excess shall be credited or refunded to the taxpayer as provided in section 6402, without the filing of claim therefor. If the amount determined as the amount which should have been assessed is greater than the amount actually assessed, then the difference shall be assessed and shall be collected as part of the tax upon notice and demand from the Secretary.

(g) Abatement if jeopardy does not exist. The Secretary may abate the jeopardy assessment if he finds that jeopardy does not exist. Such abatement may not be made after a decision of the Tax Court in respect of the deficiency has been rendered or, if no petition is filed with the Tax Court, after the expiration of the period for filing such petition. The period of limitation on the making of assessments and levy or a proceeding in court for collection, in respect of any deficiency, shall be determined as if the jeopardy assessment so abated had not been made, except that the running of such period shall in any event be suspended for the period from the date of such jeopardy assessment until the expiration of the 10th day after the day on which such jeopardy assessment is abated.

(h) Cross references.

(1) For the effect of the furnishing of security for payment, see section 6863.

(2) For provision permitting immediate levy in case of jeopardy, see section 6331(a).

Subchapter B. Receiverships, Etc.

§ 6871. Claims for Income, Estate, Gift, and Certain Excise Taxes in Receivership Proceedings, Etc.

(a) Immediate assessment in receivership proceedings. On the appointment of a receiver for the taxpayer in any receivership proceeding before any court of the United States or of any State or of the District of Columbia, any deficiency (together with all interest, additional amounts, and additions to the tax provided by law) determined by the Secretary in respect of a tax imposed by subtitle A or B or by chapter 41, 42, 43, or 44 on such taxpayer may, despite the restrictions imposed by section 6213(a) on assessments, be immediately assessed if such deficiency has not theretofore been assessed in accordance with law.

(b) Immediate assessment with respect to certain Title 11 cases. Any deficiency (together with all interest, additional amounts, and additions to the tax provided by law) determined by the Secretary in respect of a tax imposed by subtitle A or B or by chapter 41, 42, 43, or 44 on—

(1) the debtor's estate in a case under title 11 of the United States Code, or

(2) the debtor, but only if liability for such tax has become res judicata pursuant to a determination in a case under title 11 of the United States Code, may, despite the restrictions imposed by section 6213(a) on assessments, be immediately assessed if such deficiency has not theretofore been assessed in accordance with law.

(c) Claim filed despite pendency of Tax Court proceedings. In the case of a tax imposed by subtitle A or B or by chapter 41, 42, 43, or 44—

(1) claims for the deficiency and for interest, additional amounts, and additions to the tax may be presented, for adjudication in accordance with law, to the court before which the receivership proceeding (or the case under title 11 of the United States Code) is pending, despite the pendency of proceedings for the redetermination of the deficiency pursuant to a petition to the Tax Court; but

(2) in the case of a receivership proceeding, no petition for any such redetermination shall be filed with the Tax Court after the appointment of the receiver.

Chapter 71. Transferees and Fiduciaries

§ 6901. Transferred Assets

(a) Method of collection. The amounts of the following liabilities shall, except as hereinafter in this section provided, be assessed, paid, and collected in the same manner and subject to the same provisions and limitations as in the case of the taxes with respect to which the liabilities were incurred:

(1) Income, estate, and gift taxes.

(A) Transferees. The liability, at law or in equity, of a transferee of property—

(i) of a taxpayer in the case of a tax imposed by subtitle A (relating to income taxes),

(ii) of a decedent in the case of a tax imposed by chapter 11 (relating to estate taxes), or

(iii) of a donor in the case of a tax imposed by chapter 12 (relating to gift taxes), in respect of the tax imposed by subtitle A or B.

(B) Fiduciaries. The liability of a fiduciary under section 3713(b) of title 31, United States Code, in respect of the payment of any tax described in subparagraph (A) from the estate of the taxpayer, the decedent, or the donor, as the case may be.

(2) Other taxes. The liability, at law or in equity of a transferee of property of any person liable in respect of any tax imposed by this title (other than a tax imposed by subtitle A or B), but only if such liability arises on the liquidation of a partnership or corporation, or on a reorganization within the meaning of section 368(a).

(b) Liability. Any liability referred to in subsection (a) may be either as to the amount of tax shown on a return or as to any deficiency or underpayment of any tax.

(c) Period of limitations. The period of limitations for assessment of any such liability of a transferee or a fiduciary shall be as follows:

(1) Initial transferee. In the case of the liability of an initial transferee, within 1 year after the expiration of the period of limitation for assessment against the transferor;

(2) Transferee of transferee. In the case of the liability of a transferee of a transferee, within 1 year after the expiration of the period of limitation for assessment against the preceding transferee, but not more than

3 years after the expiration of the period of limitation for assessment against the initial transferor; except that if, before the expiration of the period of limitation for the assessment of the liability of the transferee, a court proceeding for the collection of the tax or liability in respect thereof has been begun against the initial transferor or the last preceding transferee, respectively, then the period of limitation for assessment of the liability of the transferee shall expire 1 year after the return of execution in the court proceeding.

(3) Fiduciary. In the case of the liability of a fiduciary, not later than 1 year after the liability arises or not later than the expiration of the period for collection of the tax in respect of which such liability arises, whichever is the later.

(d) Extension by agreement.

(1) Extension of time for assessment. If before the expiration of the time prescribed in subsection (c) for the assessment of the liability, the Secretary and the transferee or fiduciary have both consented in writing to its assessment after such time, the liability may be assessed at any time prior to the expiration of the period agreed upon. The period so agreed upon may be extended by subsequent agreements in writing made before the expiration of the period previously agreed upon. For the purpose of determining the period of limitation on credit or refund to the transferee or fiduciary of overpayments of tax made by such transferee or fiduciary or overpayments of tax made by the transferor of which the transferee or fiduciary is legally entitled to credit or refund, such agreement and any extension thereof shall be deemed an agreement and extension thereof referred to in section 6511(c).

(2) Extension of time for credit or refund. If the agreement is executed after the expiration of the period of limitation for assessment against the taxpayer with reference to whom the liability of such transferee or fiduciary rises, then in applying the limitations under section 6511(c) on the amount of the credit or refund, the periods specified in section 6511(b)(2) shall be increased by the period from the date of such expiration to the date of the agreement.

(e) Period for assessment against transferor. For purposes of this section, if any person is deceased, or is a corporation which has terminated its existence, the period of limitation for assessment against such person shall be the period that would be in effect had death or termination of existence not occurred.

(f) Suspension of running of period of limitations. The running of the period of limitations upon the assessment of the liability of a transferee or fiduciary shall, after the mailing to the transferee or fiduciary of the notice provided for in section 6212 (relating to income, estate, and gift taxes), be suspended for the period during which the Secretary is prohibited from making the assessment in respect of the liability of the transferee or fiduciary (and in any event, if a proceeding in respect of the liability is placed on the docket of the Tax Court, until the decision of the Tax Court becomes final), and for 60 days thereafter.

(g) Address for notice of liability. In the absence of notice to the Secretary under section 6903 of the existence of a fiduciary relationship, any notice of liability enforceable under this section required to be mailed to such person, shall, if mailed to the person subject to the liability at his last known address, be sufficient for purposes of this title, even if such person is deceased, or is under a legal disability, or, in the case of a corporation, has terminated its existence.

(h) Definition of transferee. As used in this section, the term "transferee" includes donee, heir, legatee, devisee, and distributee, and with respect to estate taxes, also includes any person who, under section 6324(a)(2), is personally liable for any part of such tax.

(i) Extension of time. For extensions of time by reason of armed service in a combat zone, see section 7508.

§ 6902. Provisions of Special Application to Transferees

(a) Burden of proof. In proceedings before the Tax Court the burden of proof shall be upon the Secretary to show that a petitioner is liable as a transferee of property of a taxpayer, but not to show that the taxpayer was liable for the tax.

(b) Evidence. Upon application to the Tax Court, a transferee of property of a taxpayer shall be entitled, under rules prescribed by the Tax Court, to a preliminary examination of books, papers, documents, correspondence, and other evidence of the taxpayer or a preceding transferee of the taxpayer's property, if the transferee making the application is a petitioner before the Tax Court for the redetermination of his liability in respect of the tax (including interest, additional amounts, and additions to the tax provided by law) imposed upon the taxpayer. Upon such application, the Tax Court may require by subpoena, ordered by the Tax Court or any division thereof and signed by a judge, the production of all such books, papers, documents, correspondence, and other evidence within the United States the production of which, in the opinion of the Tax Court or division thereof, is necessary to enable the transferee to ascertain the liability of the taxpayer or preceding transferee and will not result in undue hardship to the taxpayer or preceding transferee. Such examination shall be had at such time and place as may be designated in the subpoena.

§ 6903. Notice of Fiduciary Relationship

(a) Rights and obligations of fiduciary. Upon notice to the Secretary that any person is acting for another person in a fiduciary capacity, such fiduciary shall assume the powers, rights, duties, and privileges of such other person in respect of a tax imposed by this title (except as otherwise specifically provided and except that the tax shall be collected from the estate of such other person), until notice is given that the fiduciary capacity has terminated.

(b) Manner of notice. Notice under this section shall be given in accordance with regulations prescribed by the Secretary.

§ 6904. Prohibition of Injunctions

For prohibition of suits to restrain enforcement of liability of transferee, or fiduciary, see section 7421(b).

§ 6905. Discharge of Executor from Personal Liability for Decedent's Income and Gift Taxes

(a) Discharge of liability. In the case of liability of a decedent for taxes imposed by subtitle A or by chapter 12, if the executor makes written application (filed after the return with respect to such taxes is made and filed in such manner and such form as may be prescribed by regulations of the Secretary) for release from personal liability for such taxes, the Secretary may notify the executor of the amount of such taxes. The executor, upon payment of the amount of which he is notified, or 9 months after receipt of the application if no notification is made by the Secretary before such date, shall be discharged from personal liability for any deficiency in such tax thereafter found to be due and shall be entitled to a receipt or writing showing such discharge.

(b) Definition of executor. For purposes of this section, the term "executor" means the executor or administrator of the decedent appointed, qualified, and acting within the United States.

(c) Cross reference. For discharge of executor from personal liability for taxes imposed under chapter 11, see section 2204.

Chapter 75. Crimes, Other Offenses, and Forfeitures

Subchapter A. Crimes

Part I. General Provisions

§ 7201. Attempt to Evade or Defeat Tax

Any person who willfully attempts in any manner to evade or defeat any tax imposed by this title or the payment thereof shall, in addition to other penalties provided by law, be guilty of a felony and, upon conviction thereof, shall be fined not more than $100,000 ($500,000 in the case of a corporation), or imprisoned not more than 5 years, or both, together with the costs of prosecution.

§ 7203. Willful Failure to File Return, Supply Information, or Pay Tax

Any person required under this title to pay any estimated tax or tax, or required by this title or by regulations made under authority thereof to make a return, keep any records, or supply any information, who willfully fails to pay such estimated tax or tax, make such return, keep such records, or supply such information, at the time or times required by law or regulations, shall, in addition to other penalties provided by law, be guilty of a misdemeanor and, upon conviction thereof, shall be fined not more than $25,000 ($100,000 in the case of a corporation), or imprisoned not more than 1 year, or both, together with the costs of prosecution. In the case of any person with respect to whom there is a failure to pay any estimated tax, this section shall not apply to such person with respect to such failure if there is no addition to tax under section 6654 or 6655 with respect to such failure. In the case of a willful violation of any provision of section 6050I, the first sentence of this section shall be applied by substituting "felony" for "misdemeanor" and "5 years" for "1 year".

Chapter 76. Judicial Proceedings

Subchapter A. Civil Actions by the United States

§ 7404. Authority to Bring Civil Action for Estate Taxes

If the estate tax imposed by chapter 11 is not paid on or before the due date thereof, the Secretary shall proceed to collect the tax under the provisions of general law; or appropriate proceedings in the name of the United States may be commenced in any court of the United States having jurisdiction to subject the property of the decedent to be sold under the judgment or decree of the court. From the proceeds of such sale the amount of the tax, together with the costs and expenses of every description to be allowed by the court, shall be first paid, and the balance shall be deposited according to the order of the court, to be paid under its direction to the person entitled thereto. This section insofar as it applies to the collection of a deficiency shall be subject to the provisions of sections 6213 and 6601.

Subchapter C. The Tax Court

Part II. Procedure

§ 7453. Rules of Practice, Procedure, and Evidence

Except in the case of proceedings conducted under section 7436(c) or 7463, the proceedings of the Tax Court and its divisions shall be conducted in accordance with such rules of practice and procedure (other than rules of evidence) as the Tax Court may prescribe and in accordance with the Federal Rules of Evidence.

Part IV. Declaratory Judgments

§ 7477. Declaratory Judgments Relating to Value Of Certain Gifts

(a) Creation of remedy. In a case of an actual controversy involving a determination by the Secretary of the value of any gift shown on the return of tax imposed by chapter 12 or disclosed on such return or in any statement attached to such return, upon the filing of an appropriate pleading, the Tax Court may make a declaration of the value of such gift. Any such declaration shall have the force and effect of a decision of the Tax Court and shall be reviewable as such.

(b) Limitations.

(1) Petitioner. A pleading may be filed under this section only by the donor.

(2) Exhaustion of administrative remedies. The court shall not issue a declaratory judgment or decree under this section in any proceeding unless it determines that the petitioner has exhausted all available administrative remedies within the Internal Revenue Service.

(3) Time for bringing action. If the Secretary sends by certified or registered mail notice of his determination as described in subsection (a) to the petitioner, no proceeding may be initiated under this section unless the pleading is filed before the 91st day after the date of such mailing.

§ 7479. Declaratory Judgments Relating to Eligibility of Estate with Respect to Installment Payments under Section 6166

(a) Creation of remedy. In a case of actual controversy involving a determination by the Secretary of (or a failure by the Secretary to make a determination with respect to)—

(1) whether an election may be made under section 6166 (relating to extension of time for payment of estate tax where estate consists largely of interest in closely held business) with respect to an estate (or with respect to any property included therein), or

(2) whether the extension of time for payment of tax provided in section 6166(a) has ceased to apply with respect to an estate (or with respect to any property included therein), upon the filing of an appropriate pleading, the Tax Court may make a declaration with respect to whether such election may be made or whether such extension has ceased to apply. Any such declaration shall have the force and effect of a decision of the Tax Court and shall be reviewable as such.

(b) Limitations.

(1) Petitioner. A pleading may be filed under this section, with respect to any estate, only—

(A) by the executor of such estate, or

(B) by any person who has assumed an obligation to make payments under section 6166 with respect to such estate (but only if each other such person is joined as a party).

(2) Exhaustion of administrative remedies. The court shall not issue a declaratory judgment or decree under this section in any proceeding unless it determines that the petitioner has exhausted all available administrative remedies within the Internal Revenue Service. A petitioner shall be deemed to have exhausted its administrative remedies with respect to a failure of the Secretary to make a determination at the expiration of 180 days after the date on which the request for such determination was made if the petitioner has taken, in a timely manner, all reasonable steps to secure such determination.

(3) Time for bringing action. If the Secretary sends by certified or registered mail notice of his determination as described in subsection (a) to the petitioner, no proceeding may be initiated under this section unless the pleading is filed before the 91st day after the date of such mailing.

(c) Extension of time to file refund suit. The 2-year period in section 6532(a)(1) for filing suit for refund after disallowance of a claim shall be suspended during the 90-day period after the mailing of the notice referred to in subsection (b)(3) and, if a pleading has been filed with the Tax Court under this section, until the decision of the Tax Court has become final.

Subchapter E. Burden of Proof

§ 7491. Burden of Proof

(a) Burden shifts where taxpayer produces credible evidence.

(1) General rule. If, in any court proceeding, a taxpayer introduces credible evidence with respect to any factual issue relevant to ascertaining the liability of the taxpayer for any tax imposed by subtitle A or B, the Secretary shall have the burden of proof with respect to such issue.

(2) Limitations. Paragraph (1) shall apply with respect to an issue only if

(A) the taxpayer has complied with the requirements under this title to substantiate any item;

(B) the taxpayer has maintained all records required under this title and has cooperated with reasonable requests by the Secretary for witnesses, information, documents, meetings, and interviews; and

(C) in the case of a partnership, corporation, or trust, the taxpayer is described in section 7430(c)(4)(A)(ii).

Subparagraph (C) shall not apply to any qualified revocable trust (as defined in section 645(b)(1)) with respect to liability for tax for any taxable year ending after the date of the decedent's death and before the applicable date (as defined in section 645(b)(2)).

(3) Coordination. Paragraph (1) shall not apply to any issue if any other provision of this title provides for a specific burden of proof with respect to such issue.

(b) Use of statistical information on unrelated taxpayers. In the case of an individual taxpayer, the Secretary shall have the burden of proof in any court proceeding with respect to any item of income which was reconstructed by the Secretary solely through the use of statistical information on unrelated taxpayers.

(c) Penalties. Notwithstanding any other provision of this title, the Secretary shall have the burden of production in any court proceeding with respect to the liability of any individual for any penalty, addition to tax, or additional amount imposed by this title.

Chapter 77. Miscellaneous Provisions

§ 7517. Furnishing on Request of Statement Explaining Estate or Gift Valuation

(a) General rule. If the Secretary makes a determination or a proposed determination of the value of an item of property for purposes of the tax imposed under chapter 11, 12, or 13, he shall furnish, on the written request of the executor, donor, or the person required to make the return of the tax imposed by chapter 13 (as the case may be), to such executor, donor, or person a written statement containing the material required by subsection (b). Such statement shall be furnished not later than 45 days after the later of the date of such request or the date of such determination or proposed determination.

(b) Contents of statement. A statement required to be furnished under subsection (a) with respect to the value of an item of property shall—

(1) explain the basis on which the valuation was determined or proposed,

(2) set forth any computation used in arriving at such value, and

(3) contain a copy of any expert appraisal made by or for the Secretary.

(c) Effect of statement. Except to the extent otherwise provided by law, the value determined or proposed by the Secretary with respect to which a statement is furnished under this section, and the method used in arriving at such value, shall not be binding on the Secretary.

§ 7520. Valuation Tables

(a) General rule. For purposes of this title, the value of any annuity, any interest for life or a term of years, or any remainder or reversionary interest shall be determined—

(1) under tables prescribed by the Secretary, and

(2) by using an interest rate (rounded to the nearest 2/10ths of 1 percent) equal to 120 percent of the Federal midterm rate in effect under section 1274(d)(1) for the month in which the valuation date falls. If an income, estate, or gift tax charitable contribution is allowable for any part of the property transferred, the taxpayer may elect to use such Federal midterm rate for either of the 2 months preceding the month in which the valuation date falls for purposes of paragraph (2). In the case of transfers of more than 1 interest in the same property with respect to which the taxpayer may use the same rate under paragraph (2), the taxpayer shall use the same rate with respect to each such interest.

(b) Section not to apply for certain purposes. This section shall not apply for purposes of part I of subchapter D of chapter 1 or any other provision specified in regulations.

(c) Tables.

(1) In general. The tables prescribed by the Secretary for purposes of subsection (a) shall contain valuation factors for a series of interest rate categories.

(2) Revision for recent mortality charges. The Secretary shall revise the initial tables prescribed for purposes of subsection (a) to take into account the most recent mortality experience available as of the time of such revision. Such tables shall be revised not less frequently than once each 10 years to take into account the most recent mortality experience available as of the time of the revision.

(d) Valuation date. For purposes of this section, the term "valuation date" means the date as of which the valuation is made.

(e) Tables to include formulas. For purposes of this section, the term "tables" includes formulas.

Regulations

§ 1.7520–1 Valuation of annuities, unitrust interests, interests for life or terms of years, and remainder or reversionary interests.

(a) General actuarial valuations. (1) Except as otherwise provided in this section and in § 1.7520–3 (relating to exceptions to the use of prescribed tables under certain circumstances), in the case of certain transactions after April 30, 1989, subject to income tax, the fair market value of annuities, interests for life or a term of years (including unitrust interests), and remainder or reversionary interests is their present value determined under this section. See § 20.2031–7(d) of this chapter (and, for periods prior to June 1, 2023, §§ 20.2031–7(d)(3) and 20.2031–7A of this chapter) for the computation of the value of annuities, interests for life or a term of years, and remainder or reversionary interests other than interests described in paragraphs (a)(2) and (3) of this section.

(2) For a transfer to a pooled income fund, see § 1.642(c)–6(e) (or, for periods prior to June 1, 2023, § 1.642(c)–6A) with respect to the valuation of the remainder interest.

(3) For a transfer to a charitable remainder annuity trust after April 30, 1989, see § 1.664–2 with respect to the valuation of the remainder interest. See § 1.664–4 with respect to the valuation of the remainder interest in property transferred to a charitable remainder unitrust.

(b) Components of valuation. (1) *Interest rate component.* (i) *Section 7520 Interest rate.* The section 7520 interest rate is the rate of return, rounded to the nearest two-tenths of one percent, that is equal to 120 percent of the applicable Federal mid-term rate, compounded annually, for purposes of section 1274(d)(1), for the month in which the valuation date falls. In rounding the rate to the nearest two-tenths of a percent, any rate that is midway between one two-tenths of a percent and another is rounded up to the higher of those two rates. For example, if 120 percent of the applicable Federal midterm rate is 10.30, the section 7520 interest rate component is 10.4. The section 7520 interest rate is published monthly by the Internal Revenue Service in the Internal Revenue Bulletin (see § 601.601(d)(2)(ii)(b) of this chapter).

(ii) *Valuation date.* Except as provided in § 1.7520–2, the valuation date is the date on which the transaction takes place.

(2) *Mortality component.* The mortality component reflects the mortality data in the most recently available decennial mortality report based on the United States census. As the appropriate new decennial mortality report becomes available after each decennial census, the Treasury Department and the IRS will revise the mortality component described in this section and will update the appropriate regulations to adopt the revised mortality component tables. For transactions with valuation dates on or after June 1, 2023, the mortality component table (Table 2010CM) is in § 20.2031–7(d)(7)(ii) of this chapter, is referenced by IRS Publication 1457, Actuarial Valuations Version 4A, and can be found on the IRS website at *https://www.irs.gov/retirement-plans/actuarial-tables* (or a corresponding URL as may be updated from time to time). See § 20.2031–7A of this chapter for mortality component tables applicable to transactions for which the valuation date falls before June 1, 2023.

(c) Actuarial factors. The present value on the valuation date of an annuity, an interest for life or a term of years, and a remainder or reversionary interest is computed by using the section 7520 interest rate component that is described in paragraph (b)(1) of this section and the mortality component that is described in paragraph (b)(2) of this section. Actuarial factors for determining these present values may be calculated by taxpayers using the actuarial formulas in § 20.2031–7(d)(2) of this chapter but, for the convenience of taxpayers, are included in tables that are referenced and explained by publications of the Internal Revenue Service. If a factor for a particular situation is required in order to value an interest, that factor may be calculated by taxpayers using the actuarial formulas in § 20.2031–7(d)(2) of this chapter or the taxpayer may request a ruling to obtain the factor from the Internal Revenue Service. The request for a ruling must be accompanied by a recitation of the facts, including the date of birth for each measuring life and copies of relevant instruments. A request for a ruling must comply with the instructions for requesting a ruling published periodically in the Internal Revenue Bulletin (see Rev. Proc. 2023–1, 2023–1 I.R.B. 1, or successor revenue procedure(s), and §§ 601.201 and 601.601(d)(2)(ii)(b) of this chapter) and must include payment of the required user fee.

(d) IRS publications referencing and explaining actuarial tables with rates from 0.2 to 20 percent, inclusive, at intervals of two-tenths of one percent, for valuation dates on or after June 1, 2023. The publications listed in paragraphs (d)(1) through (3) of this section will be available within a reasonable time after June 1, 2023. The underlying actuarial tables referenced and explained by these publications currently are available, at no charge, electronically via the IRS website at *https://www.irs.gov/retirement-plans/actuarial-tables*:

(1) *IRS Publication 1457, Actuarial Valuations Version 4A (2023).* This publication references tables of valuation factors and provides examples that show how to compute other valuation factors, for determining the present value of annuities, interests for life or a term of years, and remainder or reversionary interests, measured by one or two lives. These factors may also be used in the valuation of interests in a charitable remainder annuity trust as defined in § 1.664–2 and a pooled income fund as defined in § 1.642(c)–5. This publication references and explains Table S (single life remainder factors), Table R(2) (two-life last-to-die remainder factors), Table B (actuarial factors used in determining the present value of an interest for a term of years), Table H (commutation factors), Table J (term certain annuity beginning-of-interval adjustment factors), and Table K (annuity end-of-interval adjustment factors). *See* earlier versions of the publication, § 1.642(c)–6A, or § 20.2031–7A of this chapter for Table S applicable to valuation dates before June 1, 2023. Earlier versions of the publication also contain earlier versions of Tables H and R(2). Tables B, J, and K also can be found in § 20.2031–7(d)(6) of this chapter, but only for interest rates from 4.2 to 14 percent, inclusive.

(2) *IRS Publication 1458, Actuarial Valuations Version 4B (2023).* This publication references and explains term certain tables and tables of one and two life valuation factors for determining the present value of remainder interests in a charitable remainder unitrust as defined in § 1.664–3. This publication references Table U(1) (unitrust single life remainder factors), Table U(2) (unitrust two-life last-to-die remainder factors), Table D (actuarial factors used in determining the present value of a remainder interest postponed for a term of years), Table F (adjustment payout rate factors), and Table Z (unitrust commutation factors). See earlier versions of the publication or § 1.664–4A for Table U(1) applicable to valuation dates before June 1, 2023. Earlier versions of the publication also contain earlier versions of Tables U(2) and Z. Table D also can be found in § 1.664–4(e)(6)(iii), but only for adjusted payout rates from 4.2 to 14 percent, inclusive. Table F also can be found in § 1.664–4(e)(6)(iii), but only for interest rates from 4.2 to 14 percent, inclusive.

(3) *IRS Publication 1459, Actuarial Valuations Version 4C (2023).* This publication references and explains Table C, which provides factors for making adjustments to the standard remainder factor for valuing gifts of depreciable property. See § 1.170A–12.

(4) The publications identified in paragraphs (d)(1) through (3) of this section also reference Table 2010CM, the mortality component table.

(e) Use of approximation methods for obtaining factors when the required valuation rate falls between two listed rates. For certain cases, this part and IRS publications provide approximation methods (for example, interpolation) for obtaining factors when the required valuation rate falls between two listed rates (such as in the case of a pooled income fund's rate of return or a unitrust's adjusted payout rate). In general, exact methods of obtaining the applicable factors are allowed, such as through software using the applicable interest rate and the proper actuarial formula, provided such direct methods are applied consistently in valuing all interests in the same property. The actuarial formula in § 20.2031–7(d)(2)(ii)(B) of this chapter is used to determine the remainder factor for pooled income funds and the actuarial formula in § 1.664–4(e)(5)(i) is used to determine the remainder factor for unitrusts. The approximation method provided in this part, computed to at minimum the same number of decimal places as provided in this part, must be used if more exact methods are not available.

(f) Applicability date. This section applies on and after June 1, 2023.

[T.D. 8540, 59 FR 30149, June 10, 1994; T.D. 8819, 64 FR 23210, 23229, April 30, 1999; T.D. 8886, 65 FR 36928, 36943, June 12, 2000; T.D. 9448, 74 FR

21483, May 7, 2009; T.D. 9540, 76 FR 49611, Aug. 10, 2011; T.D. 9974, 88 FR 37438, June 7, 2023]

§ 1.7520–2 Valuation of charitable interests.

(a) In general. (1) *Valuation.* Except as otherwise provided in this section and in § 1.7520–3 (relating to exceptions to the use of prescribed tables under certain circumstances), the fair market value of annuities, interests for life or for a term of years, remainders, and reversions for which an income tax charitable deduction is allowable is the present value of such interests determined under § 1.7520–1.

(2) *Prior-month election rule.* If any part of the property interest transferred qualifies for an income tax charitable deduction under section 170(c), the taxpayer may elect (under paragraph (b) of this section) to compute the present value of the interest transferred by use of the section 7520 interest rate for the month during which the interest is transferred or the section 7520 interest rate component for either of the 2 months preceding the month during which the interest is transferred. Paragraph (b) of this section explains how a prior-month election is made. The interest rate for the month so elected is the applicable section 7520 interest rate. If the actuarial factor for either or both of the 2 months preceding the month during which the interest is transferred is based on a mortality experience that is different from the mortality experience at the date of the transfer and if the taxpayer elects to use the section 7520 rate for a prior month with the different mortality experience, the taxpayer must use the actuarial factor derived from the mortality experience in effect during the month of the section 7520 rate elected. All actuarial computations relating to the transfer must be made by applying the interest rate component and the mortality component of the month elected by the taxpayer.

(3) *Transfers of more than one interest in the same property.* If a taxpayer transfers more than one interest in the same property at the same time, for purposes of valuing the transferred interests, the taxpayer must use the same interest rate and mortality component for each interest in the property transferred. If more than one interest in the same property is transferred in two or more separate transfers at different times, the value of each interest is determined by the use of the interest rate component and mortality component in effect during the month of the transfer of that interest or, if applicable under paragraph (a)(2) of this section, either of the two months preceding the month of the transfer.

(4) *Information required with tax return.* The following information must be attached to the income tax return (or to the amended return) if the taxpayer claims a charitable deduction for the present value of a temporary or remainder interest in property—

(i) A complete description of the interest that is transferred, including a copy of the instrument of transfer;

(ii) The valuation date of the transfer;

(iii) The names and identification numbers of the beneficiaries of the transferred interest;

(iv) The names and birthdates of any measuring lives, a description of any relevant terminal illness condition of any measuring life, and (if applicable) an explanation of how any terminal illness condition was taken into account in valuing the interest; and

(v) A computation of the deduction showing the applicable section 7520 interest rate that is used to value the transferred interest.

(5) *Place for filing returns.* See section 6091 of the Internal Revenue Code and the regulations thereunder for the place for filing the return or other document required by this section.

(b) Election of interest rate component. (1) *Time for making election.* A taxpayer makes a prior-month election under paragraph (a)(2) of this section by attaching the information described in paragraph (b)(2) of this section to the taxpayer's income tax return or to an amended return for that year that is filed within 24 months after the later of the date the original return for the year was filed or the due date for filing the return.

(2) *Manner of making election.* A statement that the prior-month election under section 7520(a) of the Internal Revenue Code is being made and that identifies the elected month must be attached to the income tax return (or to the amended return).

(3) *Revocability.* The prior-month election may be revoked by filing an amended return within 24 months after the later of the date the original return of tax for the year was filed or the due date for filing the return. The revocation must be filed in the place referred to in paragraph (a)(5) of this section.

(c) Effective dates. Paragraph (a) of this section is effective as of May 1, 1989. Paragraph (b) of this section is effective for elections made after June 10, 1994.

[T.D. 8540, 59 FR 30149, June 10, 1994]

§ 1.7520–3 Limitation on the application of section 7520.

(a) Internal Revenue Code sections to which section 7520 does not apply. Section 7520 of the Internal Revenue Code does not apply for purposes of—

(1) Part I, subchapter D of subtitle A (section 401 et. seq.), relating to the income tax treatment of certain qualified plans. (However, section 7520 does apply to the estate and gift tax treatment of certain qualified plans and for purposes of determining excess accumulations under section 4980A);

(2) Sections 72 and 101(b), relating to the income taxation of life insurance, endowment, and annuity contracts, unless otherwise provided for in the regulations under sections 72, 101, and 1011 (see, particularly, §§ 1.101–2(e)(1)(iii)(b)(2), and 1.1011–2(c), Example 8);

(3) Sections 83 and 451, unless otherwise provided for in the regulations under those sections;

(4) Section 457, relating to the valuation of deferred compensation, unless otherwise provided for in the regulations under section 457;

(5) Sections 3121(v) and 3306(r), relating to the valuation of deferred amounts, unless otherwise provided for in the regulations under those sections;

(6) Section 6058, relating to valuation statements evidencing compliance with qualified plan requirements, unless otherwise provided for in the regulations under section 6058;

(7) Section 7872, relating to income and gift taxation of interest-free loans and loans with below-market interest rates, unless otherwise provided for in the regulations under section 7872; or

(8) Section 2702(a)(2)(A), relating to the value of a nonqualified retained interest upon a transfer of an interest in trust to or for the benefit of a member of the transferor's family; and

(9) Any other sections of the Internal Revenue Code to the extent provided by the Internal Revenue Service in revenue rulings or revenue procedures. (See §§ 601.201 and 601.601 of this chapter).

(b) Other limitations on the application of section 7520. (1) *In general.* (i) *Ordinary beneficial interests.* For purposes of this section:

(A) An ordinary annuity interest is the right to receive a fixed dollar amount at the end of each year during one or more measuring lives or for some other defined period. A standard section 7520 annuity factor for an ordinary annuity interest represents the present worth of the right to receive $1.00 per year for a defined period, using the interest rate prescribed under section 7520 for the appropriate month. If an annuity interest is payable more often than annually or is payable at the beginning of each period, a special adjustment must be made in any computation with a standard section 7520 annuity factor.

(B) An ordinary income interest is the right to receive the income from, or the use of, property during one or more measuring lives or for some other defined period. A standard section 7520 income factor for an ordinary income interest represents the present worth of the right to receive the use of $1.00 for a defined period, using the interest rate prescribed under section 7520 for the appropriate month.

(C) An ordinary remainder or reversionary interest is the right to receive an interest in property at the end of one or more measuring lives or some other defined period. A standard section 7520 remainder factor for an ordinary remainder or reversionary interest represents the present worth of the right to receive $1.00 at the end of a defined period, using the interest rate prescribed under section 7520 for the appropriate month.

(ii) *Certain restricted beneficial interests.* A restricted beneficial interest is an annuity, income, remainder, or reversionary interest that is subject to a contingency, power, or other restriction, whether the restriction is provided for by the terms of the trust, will, or other governing instrument or is caused by other circumstances. In general, a standard section 7520 annuity, income, or remainder factor may not be used to value a restricted beneficial interest. However, a special section 7520 annuity, income, or remainder factor may be used to value a restricted beneficial interest under some circumstances. See paragraph (b)(4) Example 2 of this section, which illustrates a situation where a special section 7520 actuarial factor is needed to take into account the shorter life expectancy of the terminally ill measuring life. See § 1.7520–1(c) for requesting a special factor from the Internal Revenue Service.

(iii) *Other beneficial interests.* If, under the provisions of this paragraph (b), the interest rate and mortality components prescribed under section 7520 are not applicable in determining the value of any annuity, income, remainder, or reversionary interest, the actual fair market value of the interest (determined without regard to section 7520) is based on all of the facts and circumstances if and to the extent permitted by the Internal Revenue Code provision applicable to the property interest.

(2) *Provisions of governing instrument and other limitations on source of payment.* (i) *Annuities.* A standard section 7520 annuity factor may not be used to determine the present value of an annuity for a specified term of years or the life of one or more individuals unless the effect of the trust, will, or other governing instrument is to ensure that the annuity will be paid for the entire defined period. In the case of an annuity payable from a trust or other limited fund, the annuity is not considered payable for the entire defined period if, considering the applicable section 7520 interest rate at the valuation date of the transfer, the annuity is expected to exhaust the fund before the last possible annuity payment is made in full. For this purpose, it must be assumed that it is possible for each measuring life to survive until age 110. For example, for a fixed annuity payable annually at the end of each year, if the amount of the annuity payment (expressed as a percentage of the initial corpus) is less than or equal to the applicable section 7520 interest rate at the date of the transfer, the corpus is assumed to be sufficient to make all payments. If the percentage exceeds the applicable section 7520 interest rate and the annuity is for a definite term of years, multiply the annual annuity amount by the Table B term certain annuity factor, as described in § 1.7520–1(c)(1), for the number of years of the defined period. If the percentage exceeds the applicable section 7520 interest rate and the annuity is payable for the life of one or more individuals, multiply the annual annuity amount by the Table B annuity factor for 110 years minus the age of the youngest individual. If the result exceeds the limited fund, the annuity may exhaust the fund, and it will be necessary to calculate a special section 7520 annuity factor that takes into account the exhaustion of the trust or fund. This computation would be modified, if appropriate, to take into account annuities with different payment terms. See § 25.7520–3(b)(2)(v) Example 5 of this chapter, which provides an illustration involving an annuity trust that is subject to exhaustion.

(ii) *Income and similar interests.* (A) *Beneficial enjoyment.* A standard section 7520 income factor for an ordinary income interest may not be used to determine the present value of an income or similar interest in trust for a term of years or for the life of one or more individuals unless the effect of the trust, will, or other governing instrument is to provide the income beneficiary with that degree of beneficial enjoyment of the property during the term of the income interest that the principles of the law of trusts accord to a person who is unqualifiedly designated as the income beneficiary of a trust for a similar period of time. This degree of beneficial enjoyment is provided only if it was the transferor's intent, as manifested by the provisions of the governing instrument and the surrounding circumstances, that the trust provide an income interest for the income beneficiary during the specified period of time that is consistent with the value of the trust corpus and with its preservation. In determining whether a trust arrangement evidences that intention, the treatment required or permitted with respect to individual items must be considered in relation to the entire system provided for in the administration of the subject trust. Similarly, in determining the present value of the right to use tangible property (whether or not in trust) for one or more measuring lives or for some other specified period of time, the interest rate component prescribed under section 7520 and § 1.7520–1 may not be used unless, during the specified period, the effect of the trust, will or other governing instrument is to provide the beneficiary with that degree of use, possession, and enjoyment of the property during the term of interest that applicable state law accords to a person who is unqualifiedly designated as a life tenant or term holder for a similar period of time.

(B) *Diversions of income and corpus.* A standard section 7520 income factor for an ordinary income interest may not be used to value an income interest or similar interest in property for a term of years or for one or more measuring lives if—

(*1*) The trust, will, or other governing instrument requires or permits the beneficiary's income or other enjoyment to be withheld, diverted, or accumulated for another person's benefit without the consent of the income beneficiary; or

(2) The governing instrument requires or permits trust corpus to be withdrawn from the trust for another person's benefit during the income beneficiary's term of enjoyment without the consent of and accountability to the income beneficiary for such diversion.

(iii) *Remainder and reversionary interests.* A standard section 7520 remainder interest factor for an ordinary remainder or reversionary interest may not be used to determine the present value of a remainder or reversionary interest (whether in trust or otherwise) unless, consistent with the preservation and protection that the law of trusts would provide for a person who is unqualifiedly designated as the remainder beneficiary of a trust for a similar duration, the effect of the administrative and dispositive provisions for the interest or interests that precede the remainder or reversionary interest is to assure that the property will be adequately preserved and protected (e.g., from erosion, invasion, depletion, or damage) until the remainder or reversionary interest takes effect in possession and enjoyment. This degree of preservation and protection is provided only if it was the transferor's intent, as manifested by the provisions of the arrangement and the surrounding circumstances, that the entire disposition provide the remainder or reversionary beneficiary with an undiminished interest in the property transferred at the time of the termination of the prior interest.

(iv) *Pooled income fund interests.* In general, pooled income funds are created and administered to achieve a special rate of return. A beneficial interest in a pooled income fund is not ordinarily valued using a standard section 7520 income or remainder interest factor. The present value of a beneficial interest in a pooled income fund is determined according to rules and special remainder factors prescribed in § 1.642(c)–6 and, when applicable, the rules set forth in paragraph (b)(3) of this section, if the individual who is the measuring life is terminally ill at the time of the transfer.

(3) *Mortality component.* The mortality component prescribed under section 7520 may not be used to determine the present value of an annuity, income interest, remainder interest, or reversionary interest if an individual who is a measuring life is terminally ill at the time of the transaction. For purposes of this paragraph (b)(3), an individual who is known to have an incurable illness or other deteriorating physical condition is considered terminally ill if there is at least a 50 percent probability that the individual will die within 1 year. However, if the individual survives for eighteen months or longer after the date of the transaction, that individual shall be presumed to have not been terminally ill at the time of the transaction unless the contrary is established by clear and convincing evidence.

(4) *Examples.* The provisions of this paragraph (b) are illustrated by the following examples:

Example (1). Annuity funded with unproductive property. The taxpayer transfers corporation stock worth $1,000,000 to a trust. The trust provides for a 6 percent ($60,000 per year) annuity in cash or other property to be paid to a charitable organization for 25 years and for the remainder to be distributed to the donor's child. The trust specifically authorizes, but does not require, the trustee to retain the shares of stock. The section 7520 interest rate for the month of the transfer is 8.2 percent. The corporation has paid no dividends on this stock during the past 5 years, and there is no indication that this policy will change in the near future. Under applicable state law, the corporation is considered to be a sound investment that satisfies fiduciary standards. Therefore, the trust's sole investment in this corporation is not expected to adversely affect the interest of either the annuitant or the remainder beneficiary. Considering the 6 percent annuity payout rate and the 8.2 percent section 7520 interest rate, the trust corpus is considered sufficient to pay this annuity for the entire 25-year term of the trust, or even indefinitely. Although it appears that neither beneficiary would be able to compel the trustee to make the trust corpus produce investment income, the annuity interest in this case is considered to be an ordinary annuity interest, and the standard section 7520 annuity factor may be used to determine the present value of the annuity. In this case, the section 7520 annuity factor would represent the right to receive $1.00 per year for a term of 25 years.

Example (2). Terminal illness. The taxpayer transfers property worth $1,000,000 to a charitable remainder unitrust described in section 664(d)(2) and § 1.664–3. The trust provides for a fixed-percentage 7 percent unitrust benefit (each annual payment is equal to 7 percent of the trust assets as valued at the beginning of each year) to be paid quarterly to an individual beneficiary for life and for the remainder to be distributed to a charitable organization. At the time the trust is created, the individual beneficiary is age 60 and has been diagnosed with an incurable illness and there is at least a 50 percent probability of the individual dying within 1 year. Assuming the presumption in paragraph (b)(3) of this section does not apply, because there is at least a 50 percent probability that this beneficiary will die within 1 year, the standard section 7520 unitrust remainder factor for a person age 60 from the valuation tables may not be used to determine the present value of the charitable remainder interest. Instead, a special unitrust remainder factor must be computed that is based on the section 7520 interest rate and that takes into account the projection of the individual beneficiary's actual life expectancy.

(5) *Additional limitations.* Section 7520 does not apply to the extent as may otherwise be provided by the Commissioner.

(c) Effective date. Section 1.7520–3(a) is effective as of May 1, 1989. The provisions of paragraph (b) of this section are effective with respect to transactions after December 13, 1995.

[T.D. 8540, 59 FR 30150, June 10, 1994; T.D. 8630, 60 FR 63915, Dec. 13, 1995; 61 FR 7992, March 1, 1996]

§ 1.7520–4 Transitional rules.

(a) Reliance. If the valuation date is after April 30, 1989, and before June 10, 1994, a taxpayer can rely on Notice 89–24, 1989–1 C.B. 660, or Notice 89–60, 1989–1 C.B. 700 (See § 601.601(d)(2)(ii)(b) of this chapter), in valuing the transferred interest.

(b) Effective date. This section is effective as of May 1, 1989.

[T.D. 8540, 59 FR 30150, June 10, 1994]

§ 20.7520–1 Valuation of annuities, unitrust interests, interests for life or terms of years, and remainder or reversionary interests.

(a) General actuarial valuations. (1) Except as otherwise provided in this section and in § 20.7520–3 (relating to exceptions to the use of prescribed tables under certain circumstances), in the case of estates of decedents with valuation dates after April 30, 1989, the fair market value of annuities, interests for life or a term of years (including unitrust interests), and remainder or reversionary interests is their present value determined under this section. See § 20.2031–7(d) (and, for periods prior to June 1, 2023, § 20.2031–7A) for the computation of the value of annuities, interests for life or a term of years, and remainder or reversionary interests, other than interests described in paragraphs (a)(2) and (3) of this section.

(2) For a transfer to a pooled income fund, see § 1.642(c)–6(e) of this chapter (or, for periods prior to June 1, 2023, § 1.642(c)–6A of this chapter) with respect to the valuation of the remainder interest.

(3) In the case of a transfer to a charitable remainder annuity trust with a valuation date after April 30, 1989, see § 1.664–2 of this chapter with respect to the valuation of the remainder interest. See § 1.664–4 of this chapter with respect to the valuation of the remainder interest in property transferred to a charitable remainder unitrust.

(b) Components of valuation. (1) *Interest rate component* (i) *Section 7520 Interest rate.* The section 7520 interest rate is the rate of return, rounded to the nearest two-tenths of one percent, that is equal to 120 percent of the applicable Federal mid-term rate, compounded annually, for purposes of section 1274(d)(1), for the month in which the valuation date falls. In rounding the rate to the nearest two-tenths of a percent, any rate that is midway between one two-tenths of a percent and another is rounded up to the higher of those two rates. For example, if 120 percent of the applicable Federal mid-term rate is 10.30, the section 7520 interest rate component is 10.4. The section 7520 interest rate is published monthly by the Internal Revenue Service in the Internal Revenue Bulletin (See § 601.601(d)(2)(ii)(b) of this chapter).

(ii) *Valuation date.* Generally, the valuation date is the date on which the transfer takes place. For estate tax purposes, the valuation date is the date of the decedent's death, unless the executor elects the alternate valuation date in accordance with section 2032, in which event, and under the limitations prescribed in section 2032 and the regulations thereunder, the valuation date is the alternate valuation date. For special rules in the case of charitable transfers, see § 20.7520–2.

(2) *Mortality component.* The mortality component reflects the mortality data in the most recently available decennial mortality report based on the United States census. As the appropriate new decennial mortality

report becomes available after each decennial census, the Treasury Department and the IRS will revise the mortality component described in this section and will update the regulations to adopt the revised mortality component tables. For decedents' estates with valuation dates on or after June 1, 2023, the mortality component table (Table 2010CM) is in § 20.2031–7(d)(7)(ii) and is referenced by IRS Publication 1457, Actuarial Valuations Version 4A, and can be found on the IRS website at https://www.irs.gov/retirement-plans/actuarial-tables (or a corresponding URL as may be updated from time to time). See § 20.2031–7A for mortality component tables applicable to decedents' estates with valuation dates before June 1, 2023.

(c) Actuarial factors. The present value on the valuation date of an annuity, an interest for life or a term of years, and a remainder or reversionary interest is computed by using the section 7520 interest rate component that is described in paragraph (b)(1) of this section and the mortality component that is described in paragraph (b)(2) of this section. Actuarial factors for determining these present values may be calculated by using the formulas in § 20.2031–7(d)(2). For the convenience of taxpayers, the IRS has computed actuarial factors and displayed them on tables that are referenced and explained by publications of the Internal Revenue Service. If a special factor is required in order to value an interest, the special factor may be calculated by the taxpayer using the actuarial formulas in § 20.2031–7(d)(2) or the taxpayer may request a ruling to obtain the factor from the Internal Revenue Service. The request for a ruling must be accompanied by a recitation of the facts, including the date of birth for each measuring life and copies of relevant instruments. A request for a ruling must comply with the instructions for requesting a ruling published periodically in the Internal Revenue Bulletin (see Rev. Proc. 2023–1, 2023–1 I.R.B. 1, or successor revenue procedures, and §§ 601.201 and 601.601(d)(2)(ii)(b) of this chapter) and must include payment of the required user fee.

(d) IRS publications referencing and explaining actuarial tables with rates from 0.2 to 20 percent, inclusive, at intervals of two-tenths of one percent, for valuation dates on and after June 1, 2023. The publications listed in paragraphs (d)(1) through (3) of this section will be available within a reasonable time after June 1, 2023. The underlying actuarial tables referenced and explained by these publications currently are available, at no charge, electronically via the IRS website at *https://www.irs.gov/retirement-plans/actuarial-tables*:

(1) *IRS Publication 1457, Actuarial Valuations Version 4A (2023)*. This publication references tables of valuation factors and provides examples that show how to compute other valuation factors, for determining the present value of annuities, interests for life or a term of years, and remainder or reversionary interests, measured by one or two lives. These factors also may be used in the valuation of interests in a charitable remainder annuity trust as defined in § 1.664–2 of this chapter and a pooled income fund as defined in § 1.642(c)–5 of this chapter. This publication references and explains Tables S (single life remainder factors), R(2) (two-life last-to-die remainder factors), B (actuarial factors used in determining the present value of an interest for a term of years), H (commutation factors), J (term certain annuity beginning-of-interval adjustment factors), and K (annuity end-of-interval adjustment factors). See earlier versions of the publication, § 1.642(c)–6A of this chapter, or § 20.2031–7A for Table S applicable to valuation dates before June 1, 2023. See earlier versions of the publication for Table R(2) applicable to valuation dates before June 1, 2023. Earlier versions of the publication also contain earlier versions of Tables H and R(2). Tables B, J, and K also can be found in § 20.2031–7(d)(6), but only for interest rates from 4.2 to 14 percent, inclusive.

(2) *IRS Publication 1458, Actuarial Valuations Version 4B (2023)*. This publication references and explains term certain tables and tables of one and two life valuation factors for determining the present value of remainder interests in a charitable remainder unitrust as defined in § 1.664–3 of this chapter. This publication references Tables U(1) (unitrust single life remainder factors), U(2) (unitrust two-life last-to-die remainder factors), D (actuarial factors used in determining the present value of a remainder interest postponed for a term of years), F (adjustment payout rate factors), and Z (unitrust commutation factors). See earlier versions of the publication or § 1.664–4A of this chapter for Table U(1) applicable to valuation dates before June 1, 2023. Earlier versions of the publication also contain earlier versions of Tables U(2) and Z. Table D also can be found in § 1.664–4(e)(6)(iii) of this chapter, but only for adjusted payout rates from 4.2 to 14 percent,

inclusive. Table F also can be found in § 1.664–4(e)(6)(iii) of this chapter, but only for interest rates from 4.2 to 14 percent, inclusive.

(3) *IRS Publication 1459, Actuarial Valuations Version 4C (2023).* This publication references and explains Table C, which provides factors for making adjustments to the standard remainder factor for valuing gifts of depreciable property. See § 1.170A–12 of this chapter.

(4) The publications identified in paragraphs (d)(1) through (3) of this section also reference Table 2010CM, the mortality component table.

(e) Use of approximation methods for obtaining factors when the required valuation rate falls between two listed rates. For certain cases, this part and IRS publications provide approximation methods (for example, interpolation) for obtaining factors when the required valuation rate falls between two listed rates (such as in the case of a pooled income fund's rate of return or a unitrust's adjusted payout rate). In general, exact methods of obtaining the applicable factors are allowed, such as through software using the actual rate of return and the proper actuarial formulas used for the published factors at the listed rates, provided such direct methods are applied consistently in valuing all interests in the same property. The actuarial formula in § 20.2031–7(d)(2)(ii)(B) is used to determine the remainder factor for pooled income funds and the actuarial formula in § 1.664–4(e)(5)(i) of this chapter is used to determine the remainder factor for unitrusts. When using either an exact method or the approximation method, the resulting actuarial factor must be expressed with at least the same number of decimal places as that used in this part. The approximation method provided in this part must be used if more exact methods are not available.

(f) Applicability date. This section applies on and after June 1, 2023.

[T.D. 8540, 59 FR 30170, June 10, 1994; T.D. 8819, 64 FR 23223, 23229, April 30, 1999; T.D. 8886, 65 FR 36939, June 12, 2000; T.D. 9448, 74 FR 21511, May 7, 2009; T.D. 9540, 76 FR 49638, Aug. 10, 2011; T.D. 9974, 88 FR 37450, June 7, 2023]

§ 20.7520–2 Valuation of charitable interests.

(a) In general. (1) *Valuation.* Except as otherwise provided in this section and in § 20.7520–3 (relating to exceptions to the use of prescribed tables under certain circumstances), the fair market value of annuities, interests for life or for a term of years, remainders, and reversions for which an estate tax charitable deduction is allowable is the present value of such interests determined under § 20.7520–1.

(2) *Prior-month election rule.* If any part of the property interest transferred qualifies for an estate tax charitable deduction under section 2055 or 2106, the executor may compute the present value of the transferred interest by use of the section 7520 interest rate for the month during which the interest is transferred or the section 7520 interest rate for either of the 2 months preceding the month during which the interest is transferred. Paragraph (b) of this section explains how a prior-month election is made. The interest rate for the month so elected is the applicable section 7520 interest rate. If the executor elects the alternate valuation date under section 2032 and also elects to use the section 7520 interest rate for either of the 2 months preceding the month in which the interest is transferred, the month so elected (either of the 2 months preceding the month in which the alternate valuation date falls) is the valuation date. If the actuarial factor for either or both of the 2 months preceding the month during which the interest is transferred is based on a mortality experience that is different from the mortality experience at the date of the transfer and if the executor elects to use the section 7520 rate for a prior month with the different mortality experience, the executor must use the actuarial factor derived from the mortality experience in effect during the month of the section 7520 rate elected. All actuarial computations relating to the transfer must be made by applying the interest rate component and the mortality component of the month elected by the executor.

(3) *Transfers of more than one interest in the same property.* If a decedent's estate includes the transfer of more than one interest in the same property, the executor must, for purposes of valuing the transferred interests, use the same interest rate and mortality components for each interest in the property transferred.

(4) *Information required with tax return.* The following information must be attached to the estate tax return (or be filed subsequently as supplemental information to the return) if the estate claims a charitable deduction for the present value of a temporary or remainder interest in property—

(i) A complete description of the interest that is transferred, including a copy of the instrument of transfer;

(ii) The valuation date of the transfer;

(iii) The names and identification numbers of the beneficiaries of the transferred interest;

(iv) The names and birthdates of any measuring lives, a description of any relevant terminal illness condition of any measuring life, and (if applicable) an explanation of how any terminal illness condition was taken into account in valuing the interest; and

(v) A computation of the deduction showing the applicable section 7520 interest rate that is used to value the transferred interest.

(5) *Place for filing returns.* See section 6091 of the Internal Revenue Code and the regulations thereunder for the place for filing the return or other document required by this section.

(b) Election of interest rate component. (1) *Time for making election.* An executor makes a prior-month election under paragraph (a)(2) of this section by attaching the information described in paragraph (b)(2) of this section to the decedent's estate tax return or by filing a supplemental statement of the election information within 24 months after the later of the date the original estate tax return was filed or the due date for filing the return.

(2) *Manner of making election.* A statement that the prior-month election under section 7520(a) of the Internal Revenue Code is being made and that identifies the elected month must be attached to the estate tax return (or by subsequently filing the statement as supplemental information to the return).

(3) *Revocability.* The prior-month election may be revoked by filing a statement of supplemental information within 24 months after the later of the date the original return of tax for the decedent's estate was filed or the due date for filing the return. The revocation must be filed in the place referred to in paragraph (a)(5) of this section.

(c) Effective dates. Paragraph (a) of this section is effective as of May 1, 1989. Paragraph (b) of this section is effective for elections made after June 10, 1994.

[T.D. 8540, 59 FR 30171, June 10, 1994]

§ 20.7520–3 Limitation on the application of section 7520.

(a) Internal Revenue Code sections to which section 7520 does not apply. Section 7520 of the Internal Revenue Code does not apply for purposes of:

(1) Part I, subchapter D of subtitle A (section 401 et. seq.), relating to the income tax treatment of certain qualified plans. (However, section 7520 does apply to the estate and gift tax treatment of certain qualified plans and for purposes of determining excess accumulations under section 4980A);

(2) Sections 72 and 101(b), relating to the income taxation of life insurance, endowment, and annuity contracts, unless otherwise provided for in the regulations under sections 72, 101, and 1011 (see, particularly, §§ 1.101–2(e)(1)(iii)(b)(2), and 1.1011–2(c), Example 8);

(3) Sections 83 and 451, unless otherwise provided for in the regulations under those sections;

(4) Section 457, relating to the valuation of deferred compensation, unless otherwise provided for in the regulations under section 457;

(5) Sections 3121(v) and 3306(r), relating to the valuation of deferred amounts, unless otherwise provided for in the regulations under those sections;

(6) Section 6058, relating to valuation statements evidencing compliance with qualified plan requirements, unless otherwise provided for in the regulations under section 6058;

(7) Section 7872, relating to income and gift taxation of interest-free loans and loans with below-market interest rates, unless otherwise provided for in the regulations under section 7872; or

(8) Section 2702(a)(2)(A), relating to the value of a nonqualified retained interest upon a transfer of an interest in trust to or for the benefit of a member of the transferor's family; and

(9) Any other sections of the Internal Revenue Code to the extent provided by the Internal Revenue Service in revenue rulings or revenue procedures. (See §§ 601.201 and 601.601 of this chapter).

(b) Other limitations on the application of section 7520. (1) *In general.* (i) *Ordinary beneficial interests.* For purposes of this section:

(A) An ordinary annuity interest is the right to receive a fixed dollar amount at the end of each year during one or more measuring lives or for some other defined period. A standard section 7520 annuity factor for an ordinary annuity interest represents the present worth of the right to receive $1.00 per year for a defined period, using the interest rate prescribed under section 7520 for the appropriate month. If an annuity interest is payable more often than annually or is payable at the beginning of each period, a special adjustment must be made in any computation with a standard section 7520 annuity factor.

(B) An ordinary income interest is the right to receive the income from or the use of property during one or more measuring lives or for some other defined period. A standard section 7520 income factor for an ordinary income interest represents the present worth of the right to receive the use of $1.00 for a defined period, using the interest rate prescribed under section 7520 for the appropriate month.

(C) An ordinary remainder or reversionary interest is the right to receive an interest in property at the end of one or more measuring lives or some other defined period. A standard section 7520 remainder factor for an ordinary remainder or reversionary interest represents the present worth of the right to receive $1.00 at the end of a defined period, using the interest rate prescribed under section 7520 for the appropriate month.

(ii) *Certain restricted beneficial interests.* A restricted beneficial interest is an annuity, income, remainder, or reversionary interest that is subject to any contingency, power, or other restriction, whether the restriction is provided for by the terms of the trust, will, or other governing instrument or is caused by other circumstances. In general, a standard section 7520 annuity, income, or remainder factor may not be used to value a restricted beneficial interest. However, a special section 7520 annuity, income, or remainder factor may be used to value a restricted beneficial interest under some circumstances. See paragraphs (b)(2)(v) Example 4 and (b)(4) Example 1 of this section, which illustrate situations where special section 7520 actuarial factors are needed to take into account limitations on beneficial interests. See § 20.7520–1(c) for requesting a special factor from the Internal Revenue Service.

(iii) *Other beneficial interests.* If, under the provisions of this paragraph (b), the interest rate and mortality components prescribed under section 7520 are not applicable in determining the value of any annuity, income, remainder, or reversionary interest, the actual fair market value of the interest (determined without regard to section 7520) is based on all of the facts and circumstances if and to the extent permitted by the Internal Revenue Code provision applicable to the property interest.

(2) *Provisions of governing instrument and other limitations on source of payment.* (i) *Annuities.* A standard section 7520 annuity factor may not be used to determine the present value of an annuity for a specified term of years or the life of one or more individuals unless the effect of the trust, will, or other governing instrument is to ensure that the annuity will be paid for the entire defined period. In the case of an annuity payable from a trust or other limited fund, the annuity is not considered payable for the entire defined period if, considering the applicable section 7520 interest rate at the valuation date of the transfer, the annuity is expected to exhaust the fund before the last possible annuity payment is made in full. For this purpose, it must be assumed that it is possible for each measuring life to survive until age 110. For example, for a fixed annuity payable annually at the end of each year, if the amount of the annuity payment (expressed as a percentage of the initial corpus) is less than or equal to the applicable section 7520 interest rate at the date of the transfer, the corpus is assumed to be sufficient to make all payments. If the percentage exceeds the applicable section 7520 interest rate and the annuity is for a definite term of years, multiply the annual annuity amount by the Table B term certain annuity factor, as described in § 20.7520–1(c)(1), for the number of years of the defined period. If the percentage exceeds the applicable section 7520 interest rate and the annuity is payable for the life of one or more individuals, multiply the annual annuity amount by the Table B annuity factor for 110 years minus the age of the youngest individual. If the result exceeds the limited fund, the annuity may exhaust the fund, and it will be necessary to calculate a special section 7520 annuity factor that takes into account the exhaustion of the trust or fund. This computation would be modified, if appropriate, to take into account annuities with different payment terms. See § 25.7520–3(b)(2)(v) Example 5 of this chapter, which

provides an illustration involving an annuity trust that is subject to exhaustion.

(ii) *Income and similar interests.* (A) *Beneficial enjoyment.* A standard section 7520 income factor for an ordinary income interest may not be used to determine the present value of an income or similar interest in trust for a term of years, or for the life of one or more individuals, unless the effect of the trust, will, or other governing instrument is to provide the income beneficiary with that degree of beneficial enjoyment of the property during the term of the income interest that the principles of the law of trusts accord to a person who is unqualifiedly designated as the income beneficiary of a trust for a similar period of time. This degree of beneficial enjoyment is provided only if it was the transferor's intent, as manifested by the provisions of the governing instrument and the surrounding circumstances, that the trust provide an income interest for the income beneficiary during the specified period of time that is consistent with the value of the trust corpus and with its preservation. In determining whether a trust arrangement evidences that intention, the treatment required or permitted with respect to individual items must be considered in relation to the entire system provided for in the administration of the subject trust. Similarly, in determining the present value of the right to use tangible property (whether or not in trust) for one or more measuring lives or for some other specified period of time, the interest rate component prescribed under section 7520 and § 1.7520–1 of this chapter may not be used unless, during the specified period, the effect of the trust, will or other governing instrument is to provide the beneficiary with that degree of use, possession, and enjoyment of the property during the term of interest that applicable state law accords to a person who is unqualifiedly designated as a life tenant or term holder for a similar period of time.

(B) *Diversions of income and corpus.* A standard section 7520 income factor for an ordinary income interest may not be used to value an income interest or similar interest in property for a term of years, or for one or more measuring lives, if—

(*1*) The trust, will, or other governing instrument requires or permits the beneficiary's income or other enjoyment to be withheld, diverted, or accumulated for another person's benefit without the consent of the income beneficiary; or

(*2*) The governing instrument requires or permits trust corpus to be withdrawn from the trust for another person's benefit without the consent of the income beneficiary during the income beneficiary's term of enjoyment and without accountability to the income beneficiary for such diversion.

(iii) *Remainder and reversionary interests.* A standard section 7520 remainder interest factor for an ordinary remainder or reversionary interest may not be used to determine the present value of a remainder or reversionary interest (whether in trust or otherwise) unless, consistent with the preservation and protection that the law of trusts would provide for a person who is unqualifiedly designated as the remainder beneficiary of a trust for a similar duration, the effect of the administrative and dispositive provisions for the interest or interests that precede the remainder or reversionary interest is to assure that the property will be adequately preserved and protected (e.g., from erosion, invasion, depletion, or damage) until the remainder or reversionary interest takes effect in possession and enjoyment. This degree of preservation and protection is provided only if it was the transferor's intent, as manifested by the provisions of the arrangement and the surrounding circumstances, that the entire disposition provide the remainder or reversionary beneficiary with an undiminished interest in the property transferred at the time of the termination of the prior interest.

(iv) *Pooled income fund interests.* In general, pooled income funds are created and administered to achieve a special rate of return. A beneficial interest in a pooled income fund is not ordinarily valued using a standard section 7520 income or remainder interest factor. The present value of a beneficial interest in a pooled income fund is determined according to rules and special remainder factors prescribed in § 1.642(c)–6 of this chapter and, when applicable, the rules set forth under paragraph (b)(3) of this section if the individual who is the measuring life is terminally ill at the time of the transfer.

(v) *Examples.* The provisions of this paragraph (b)(2) are illustrated by the following examples:

Example (1). Unproductive property. A died, survived by B and C. B died two years after A. A's will provided for a bequest of corporation stock in trust under the terms of which all of the trust income was paid to B for life. After the death of B, the trust terminated and the trust property was distributed to C. The trust specifically authorized, but did not require, the trustee to retain the shares of stock. The corporation paid no dividends on this stock during the 5 years before A's death and the 2 years before B's death. There was no indication that this policy would change after A's death. Under applicable state law, the corporation is considered to be a sound investment that satisfies fiduciary standards. The facts and circumstances, including applicable state law, indicate that B did not have the legal right to compel the trustee to make the trust corpus productive in conformity with the requirements for a lifetime trust income interest under applicable local law. Therefore, B's life income interest in this case is considered nonproductive. Consequently, B's income interest may not be valued actuarially under this section.

Example (2). Beneficiary's right to make trust productive. The facts are the same as in Example 1, except that the trustee is not specifically authorized to retain the shares of stock. Further, the terms of the trust specifically provide that B, the life income beneficiary, may require the trustee to make the trust corpus productive consistent with income yield standards for trusts under applicable state law. Under that law, the minimum rate of income that a productive trust may produce is substantially below the section 7520 interest rate for the month of A's death. In this case, because B has the right to compel the trustee to make the trust productive for purposes of applicable local law during the beneficiary's lifetime, the income interest is considered an ordinary income interest for purposes of this paragraph, and the standard section 7520 life income interest factor may be used to determine the present value of B's income interest.

Example (3). Discretionary invasion of corpus. The decedent, A, transferred property to a trust under the terms of which all of the trust income is to be paid to A's child for life and the remainder of the trust is to be distributed to a grandchild. The trust authorizes the trustee without restriction to distribute corpus to A's surviving spouse for the spouse's comfort and happiness. In this case, because the trustee's power to invade trust corpus is unrestricted, the exercise of the power could result in the termination of the income interest at any time. Consequently, the income interest is not considered an ordinary income interest for purposes of this paragraph, and may not be valued actuarially under this section.

Example (4). Limited invasion of corpus. The decedent, A, bequeathed property to a trust under the terms of which all of the trust income is to be paid to A's child for life and the remainder is to be distributed to A's grandchild. The trust authorizes the child to withdraw up to $5,000 per year from the trust corpus. In this case, the child's power to invade trust corpus is limited to an ascertainable amount each year. Annual invasions of any amount would be expected to progressively diminish the property from which the child's income is paid. Consequently, the income interest is not considered an ordinary income interest for purposes of this paragraph, and the standard section 7520 income interest factor may not be used to determine the present value of the income interest. Nevertheless, the present value of the child's income interest is ascertainable by making a special actuarial calculation that would take into account not only the initial value of the trust corpus, the section 7520 interest rate for the month of the transfer, and the mortality component for the child's age, but also the assumption that the trust corpus will decline at the rate of $5,000 each year during the child's lifetime. The child's right to receive an amount not in excess of $5,000 per year may be separately valued in this instance and, assuming the trust corpus would not exhaust before the child would attain age 110, would be considered an ordinary annuity interest.

Example (5). Power to consume. The decedent, A, devised a life estate in 3 parcels of real estate to A's surviving spouse with the remainder to a child, or, if the child doesn't survive, to the child's estate. A also conferred upon the spouse an unrestricted power to consume the property, which includes the right to sell part or all of the property and to use the proceeds for the spouse's support, comfort, happiness, and other purposes. Any portion of the property or its sale proceeds remaining at the death of the surviving spouse is to vest by operation of law in the child at that time. The child predeceased the surviving spouse. In this case, the surviving spouse's power to consume the corpus is unrestricted, and the exercise of the power could entirely exhaust the remainder interest during the life of the spouse. Consequently, the remainder interest that is includible in the child's estate is not considered an ordinary remainder interest for purposes of this paragraph and may not be valued actuarially under this section.

(3) *Mortality component*—(i) *Terminal illness.* Except as provided in paragraph (b)(3)(ii) of this section, the mortality component prescribed under section 7520 may not be used to determine the present value of an annuity, income interest, remainder interest, or reversionary interest if an individual who is a measuring life is terminally ill at the time of the decedent's death. For purposes of this paragraph (b)(3), an individual who is known to have an incurable illness or other deteriorating physical condition is considered terminally ill if there is at least a 50 percent probability that the individual will die within 1 year. However, if the individual survives for eighteen months or longer after the date of the decedent's death, that individual shall be presumed to have not been terminally ill at the date of death unless the contrary is established by clear and convincing evidence.

(ii) *Terminal illness exceptions.* In the case of the allowance of the credit for tax on a prior transfer under section 2013, if a final determination of the federal estate tax liability of the transferor's estate has been made under circumstances that required valuation of the life interest received by the transferee, the value of the property transferred, for purposes of the credit allowable to the transferee's estate, shall be the value determined previously in the transferor's estate. Otherwise, for purposes of section 2013, the provisions of paragraph (b)(3)(i) of this section shall govern in valuing the property transferred. The value of a decedent's reversionary interest under sections 2037(b) and 2042(2) shall be determined without regard to the physical condition, immediately before the decedent's death, of the individual who is the measuring life.

(iii) *Death resulting from common accidents.* The mortality component prescribed under section 7520 may not be used to determine the present value of an annuity, income interest, remainder interest, or reversionary interest if the decedent, and the individual who is the measuring life, die as a result of a common accident or other occurrence.

(4) *Examples.* The provisions of paragraph (b)(3) of this section are illustrated by the following examples:

Example (1). Terminal illness. The decedent bequeaths $1,000,000 to a trust under the terms of which the trustee is to pay $103,000 per year to a charitable organization during the life of the decedent's child. Upon the death of the child, the remainder in the trust is to be distributed to the decedent's grandchild. The child, who is age 60, has been diagnosed with an incurable illness, and there is at least a 50 percent probability of the child dying within 1 year. Assuming the presumption provided for in paragraph (b)(3)(i) of this section does not apply, the standard life annuity factor for a person age 60 may not be used to determine the present value of the charitable organization's annuity interest because there is at least a 50 percent probability that the child, who is the measuring life, will die within 1 year. Instead, a special section 7520 annuity factor must be computed that takes into account the projection of the child's actual life expectancy.

Example (2). Deaths resulting from common accidents, etc. The decedent's will establishes a trust to pay income to the decedent's surviving spouse for life. The will provides that, upon the spouse's death or, if the spouse fails to survive the decedent, upon the decedent's death the trust property is to pass to the decedent's children. The decedent and the decedent's spouse die simultaneously in an accident under circumstances in which it was impossible to determine who survived the other. Even if the terms of the will and applicable state law presume that the decedent died first with the result that the property interest is considered to have passed in trust for the benefit of the spouse for life, after which the remainder is to be distributed to the decedent's children, the spouse's life income interest may not be valued by use of the mortality component described under section 7520. The result would be the same even if it was established that the spouse survived the decedent.

(5) *Additional limitations.* Section 7520 does not apply to the extent as may otherwise be provided by the Commissioner.

(c) Effective date. Section § 20.7520–3(a) is effective as of May 1, 1989. The provisions of paragraph (b) of this section are effective with respect to estates of decedents dying after December 13, 1995.

[T.D. 8540, 59 FR 30172, June 10, 1994; T.D. 8630, 60 FR 63916, Dec. 13, 1995; 61 FR 7992, March 1, 1996]

§ 20.7520–4 Transitional rules.

(a) Reliance. If the valuation date is after April 30, 1989, and before June 10, 1994, an executor can rely on Notice 89–24, 1989–1 C.B. 660, or Notice 89–60, 1989–1 C.B. 700 (See § 601.601(d)(2)(ii)(b) of this chapter), in valuing the transferred interest.

(b) Effective date. This section is effective as of May 1, 1989.

[T.D. 8540, 59 FR 30172, June 10, 1994]

§ 25.7520–1 Valuation of annuities, unitrust interests, interests for life or terms of years, and remainder or reversionary interests.

(a) General actuarial valuations. (1) Except as otherwise provided in this section and in § 25.7520–3(b) (relating to exceptions to the use of prescribed tables under certain circumstances), in the case of certain gifts after April 30, 1989, the fair market value of annuities, interests for life or a term of years (including unitrust interests), and remainder or reversionary interests is their present value determined under this section. See § 20.2031–7(d) of this chapter (and, for periods prior to June 1, 2023, §§ 20.2031–7(d)(3) and 20.2031–7A of this chapter) for the computation of the value of annuities, interests for life or a term of years, and remainder or reversionary interests, other than interests described in paragraphs (a)(2) and (3) of this section.

(2) In the case of a gift to a pooled income fund on or after June 1, 2023, see § 1.642(c)–6(e) of this chapter (or, for periods prior to June 1, 2023, § 1.642(c)–6A of this chapter) with respect to the valuation of the remainder interest.

(3) In the case of a gift to a beneficiary of a charitable remainder annuity trust after April 30, 1989, see § 1.664–2 of this chapter with respect to the valuation of the remainder interest. See § 1.664–4 of this chapter (Income Tax Regulations) with respect to the valuation of the remainder interest in property transferred to a charitable remainder unitrust.

(b) Components of valuation. (1) *Interest rate component* (i) Section 7520 Interest rate. The section 7520 interest rate is the rate of return, rounded to the nearest two-tenths of one percent, that is equal to 120 percent of the applicable Federal mid-term rate, compounded annually, for purposes of section 1274(d)(1), for the month in which the valuation date falls. In rounding the rate to the nearest two-tenths of a percent, any rate that is midway between one two-tenths of a percent and another is rounded up to the higher of those two rates. For example, if 120 percent of the applicable Federal mid-term rate is 10.30, the section 7520 interest rate component is 10.4. The section 7520 interest rate is published monthly by the Internal Revenue Service in the Internal Revenue Bulletin (See § 601.601(d)(2)(ii)(b) of this chapter).

(ii) *Valuation date.* Generally, the valuation date is the date on which the gift is made. For gift tax purposes, the valuation date is the date on which the gift is complete under § 25.2511–2. For special rules in the case of charitable transfers, see § 25.7520–2.

(2) *Mortality component.* The mortality component reflects the mortality data most recently available from the United States census. As the appropriate new mortality report becomes available after each decennial census, the Treasury Department and the IRS will revise the mortality component described in this section and will update the appropriate regulations to adopt the revised mortality component tables. For gifts with valuation dates on or after June 1, 2023, the mortality component table (Table 2010CM) is in § 20.2031–7(d)(7)(ii) of this chapter, and is referenced by IRS Publication 1457, Actuarial Valuations Version 4A, and can be found on the IRS website at https://www.irs.gov/retirement-plans/actuarial-tables (or a corresponding URL as may be updated from time to time). See § 20.2031–7A of this chapter for mortality component tables applicable to gifts for which the valuation date falls before June 1, 2023.

(c) Actuarial factors. The present value on the valuation date of an annuity, an interest for life or a term of years, and a remainder or reversionary interest is computed by using the section 7520 interest rate component that is described in paragraph (b)(1) of this section and the mortality component that is described in paragraph (b)(2) of this section. Actuarial factors for determining these present values may be calculated using the formulas in § 20.2031–7(d)(2) of this chapter. For the convenience of taxpayers, the IRS has computed actuarial factors and displayed them on tables that are referenced and explained by publications of the Internal Revenue Service. If a particular factor is required in order to value an interest, that factor may be calculated by the taxpayer using the actuarial formulas in § 20.2031–7(d)(2) of this chapter or the taxpayer may request a ruling to obtain the factor from the Internal Revenue Service. The request for a ruling must be accompanied by a recitation of the facts, including the date of birth for each measuring life and copies of relevant instruments. A request for a ruling must comply with the instructions for requesting a ruling published periodically in the Internal Revenue Bulletin (see Rev. Proc. 2023–1, 2023–1 I.R.B. 1, or successor revenue procedures, and §§ 601.201 and 601.601(d)(2)(ii)(b) of this chapter) and must include payment of the required user fee.

(d) IRS publications referencing and explaining actuarial tables with rates from 0.2 to 20 percent, inclusive, at intervals of two-tenths of one percent, for valuation dates on or after June 1, 2023. The publications listed in paragraphs (d)(1) through (3) of this section will be available within a reasonable time after June 1, 2023. The underlying actuarial tables referenced and explained by these publications currently are available, at no charge, electronically via the IRS website at https://www.irs.gov/retirement-plans/actuarial-tables:

(1) *IRS Publication 1457, Actuarial Valuations Version 4A (2023).* This publication references tables of valuation factors and provides examples that show how to compute other valuation factors, for determining the present value of annuities, interests for life or a term of years, and remainder or reversionary interests, measured by one or two lives. These factors may also be used in the valuation of interests in a charitable remainder annuity trust as defined in § 1.664–2 of this chapter and a pooled income fund as defined in § 1.642(c)–5 of this chapter. This publication references and explains Tables S (single life remainder factors), R(2) (two-life last-to-die remainder factors), B (actuarial factors used in determining the present value of an interest for a term of years), H (commutation factors), J (term certain annuity beginning-of-interval adjustment factors), and K (annuity end-of-interval adjustment factors). See earlier versions of the publication, § 1.642(c)–6A of this chapter, or § 20.2031–7A of this chapter for Table S applicable to valuation dates before June 1, 2023. Earlier versions of the publication also contain earlier versions of Tables H and R(2). Tables B, J, and K also can be found in § 20.2031–7(d)(6) of this chapter, but only for interest rates from 4.2 to 14 percent, inclusive.

(2) *IRS Publication 1458, Actuarial Valuations Version 4B (2023).* This publication references and explains term certain tables and tables of one and two life valuation factors for determining the present value of remainder interests in a charitable remainder unitrust as defined in § 1.664–3 of this chapter. This publication references Tables U(1) (unitrust single life remainder factors), U(2) (unitrust two-life last-to-die remainder factors), D (actuarial factors used in determining the present value of a remainder interest postponed for a term of years), F (adjustment payout rate factors), and Z (unitrust commutation factors). See earlier versions of the publication or § 1.664–4A of this chapter for Table U(1) applicable to valuation dates before June 1, 2023. Earlier versions of the publication also contain earlier versions of Tables U(2) and Z. Table D also can be found in § 1.664–4(e)(6)(iii) of this chapter, but only for adjusted payout rates from 4.2 to 14 percent, inclusive. Table F also can be found in § 1.664–4(e)(6)(iii) of this chapter, but only for interest rates from 4.2 to 14 percent, inclusive.

(3) *IRS Publication 1459, Actuarial Valuations Version 4C (2023).* This publication references and explains Table C, which provides factors for making adjustments to the standard remainder factor for valuing gifts of depreciable property. See § 1.170A–12 of this chapter.

(4) The publications identified in paragraphs (d)(1) through (3) of this section also reference Table 2010CM, the mortality component table.

(e) Use of approximation methods for obtaining factors when the required valuation rate falls between two listed rates. For certain cases, this part and IRS publications provide approximation methods (for example, interpolation) for obtaining factors when the required valuation rate falls between two listed rates (such as in the case of a pooled income fund's rate of return or a unitrust's adjusted payout rate). In general, exact methods of obtaining the applicable factors are allowed, such as through software using the actual rate of return and the proper actuarial formula, provided such direct methods are applied consistently in valuing all interests in the same property. The actuarial formula in § 20.2031–7(d)(2)(ii)(B) of this chapter is used to determine the remainder factor for pooled income funds and the actuarial formula in § 1.664–4(e)(5)(i) of this chapter is used to determine the remainder factor for unitrusts. When using either an exact method or the approximation method, at least the same number of decimal places as that used in this part must be used for the resulting actuarial factor. The approximation method provided in this part must be used if more exact methods are not available.

(f) Applicability date. This section applies on and after June 1, 2023.

[T.D. 8540, 59 FR 30177, June 10, 1994; T.D. 8819, 64 FR 23227, 23229, April 30, 1999; 64 FR 33196, June 22, 1999; T.D. 8886, 65 FR 36942, 36943, June 12, 2000; T.D. 9448, 74 FR 21516, May 7, 2009; T.D. 9540, 76 FR 49642, Aug. 10, 2011; T.D. 9974, 88 FR 37462, June 7, 2023]

§ 25.7520–2 Valuation of charitable interests.

(a) In general. (1) *Valuation.* Except as otherwise provided in this section and in § 25.7520–3 (relating to exceptions to the use of prescribed tables under certain circumstances), the fair market value of annuities, interests for life or for a term for years, remainders, and reversions for which a gift tax charitable deduction is allowable is the present value of such interests determined under § 25.7520–1.

(2) *Prior-month election rule.* If any part of the property interest transferred qualifies for a gift tax charitable deduction under section 2522, the donor may elect to compute the present value of the interest transferred by use of the section 7520 interest rate for the month during which the gift is made or the section 7520 interest rate for either of the 2 months preceding the month during which the gift is made. Paragraph (b) of this section explains how a prior-month election is made. The interest rate for the month so elected is the applicable section 7520 interest rate. If the actuarial factor for either or both of the 2 months preceding the month during which the gift is made is based on a mortality experience that is different from the mortality experience at the date of the gift and if the donor elects to use the section 7520 rate for a prior month with the different mortality experience, the donor must use the actuarial factor derived from the mortality experience in effect during the month of the section 7520 rate elected. All actuarial computations relating to the gift must be made by applying the interest rate component and the mortality component of the month elected by the donor.

(3) *Gifts of more than one interest in the same property.* If a donor makes a gift of more than one interest in the same property at the same time, the donor must, for purposes of valuing the gifts, use the same interest rate and mortality components for the gift of each interest in the property. If the donor has made gifts of more than one interest in the same property at different times, the donor must determine the value of the gift by the use of the interest rate component and mortality component in effect during the month of that gift or, if applicable under paragraph (a)(2) of this section, either of the two months preceding the month of the gift.

(4) *Information required with tax return.* The following information must be attached to the gift tax return (or to the amended return) if the donor claims a charitable deduction for the present value of a temporary or remainder interest in property—

(i) A complete description of the interest that is transferred, including a copy of the instrument of transfer;

(ii) The valuation date of the transfer;

(iii) The names and identification numbers of the beneficiaries of the transferred interest;

(iv) The names and birthdates of any measuring lives, a description of any relevant terminal illness condition of any measuring life, and (if applicable) an explanation of how any terminal illness condition was taken into account in valuing the interest; and

(v) A computation of the deduction showing the applicable section 7520 interest rate that is used to value the transferred interest.

(5) *Place for filing returns.* See section 6091 of the Internal Revenue Code and the regulations thereunder for the place for filing the return or other document required by this section.

(b) Election of interest rate component. (1) *Time for making election.* A taxpayer makes a prior-month election under paragraph (a)(2) of this section by attaching the information described in paragraph (b)(2) of this section to the donor's gift tax return or to an amended return for that year that is filed within 24 months after the later of the date the original return for the year was filed or the due date for filing the return.

(2) *Manner of making election.* A statement that the prior-month election under section 7520(a) of the Internal Revenue Code is being made and that identi-

fies the elected month must be attached to the gift tax return (or to the amended return).

(3) *Revocability.* The prior-month election may be revoked by filing an amended return within 24 months after the later of the date the original return of tax for that year was filed or the due date for filing the return. The revocation must be filed in the place referred to in paragraph (a)(5) of this section.

(c) Effective dates. Paragraph (a) of this section is effective as of May 1, 1989. Paragraph (b) of this section is effective for elections made after June 10, 1994.

[T.D. 8540, 59 FR 30178, June 10, 1994]

§ 25.7520–3 Limitation on the application of section 7520.

(a) Internal Revenue Code sections to which section 7520 does not apply. Section 7520 of the Internal Revenue Code does not apply for purposes of—

(1) Part I, subchapter D of subtitle A (section 401 et. seq.), relating to the income tax treatment of certain qualified plans. (However, section 7520 does apply to the estate and gift tax treatment of certain qualified plans and for purposes of determining excess accumulations under section 4980A);

(2) Sections 72 and 101(b), relating to the income taxation of life insurance, endowment, and annuity contracts, unless otherwise provided for in the regulations under sections 72, 101, and 1011 (see, particularly, §§ 1.101–2(e)(1)(iii)(b)(2), and 1.1011–2(c), Example 8);

(3) Sections 83 and 451, unless otherwise provided for in the regulations under those sections;

(4) Section 457, relating to the valuation of deferred compensation, unless otherwise provided for in the regulations under section 457;

(5) Sections 3121(v) and 3306(r), relating to the valuation of deferred amounts, unless otherwise provided for in the regulations under those sections;

(6) Section 6058, relating to valuation statements evidencing compliance with qualified plan requirements, unless otherwise provided for in the regulations under section 6058;

(7) Section 7872, relating to income and gift taxation of interest-free loans and loans with below-market interest rates, unless otherwise provided for in the regulations under section 7872; or

(8) Section 2702(a)(2)(A), relating to the value of a nonqualified retained interest upon a transfer of an interest in trust to or for the benefit of a member of the transferor's family; and

(9) Any other section of the Internal Revenue Code to the extent provided by the Internal Revenue Service in revenue rulings or revenue procedures. (See §§ 601.201 and 601.601 of this chapter).

(b) Other limitations on the application of section 7520. (1) *In general.* (i) *Ordinary beneficial interests.* For purposes of this section:

(A) An ordinary annuity interest is the right to receive a fixed dollar amount at the end of each year during one or more measuring lives or for some other defined period. A standard section 7520 annuity factor for an ordinary annuity interest represents the present worth of the right to receive $1.00 per year for a defined period, using the interest rate prescribed under section 7520 for the appropriate month. If an annuity interest is payable more often than annually or is payable at the beginning of each period, a special adjustment must be made in any computation with a standard section 7520 annuity factor.

(B) An ordinary income interest is the right to receive the income from or the use of property during one or more measuring lives or for some other defined period. A standard section 7520 income factor for an ordinary income interest represents the present worth of the right to receive the use of $1.00 for a defined period, using the interest rate prescribed under section 7520 for the appropriate month. However, in the case of certain gifts made after October 8, 1990, if the donor does not retain a qualified annuity, unitrust, or reversionary interest, the value of any interest retained by the donor is considered to be zero if the remainder beneficiary is a member of the donor's family. See § 25.2702–2.

(C) An ordinary remainder or reversionary interest is the right to receive an interest in property at the end of one or more measuring lives or some other defined period. A standard section 7520 remainder factor for an ordinary remainder or reversionary interest represents the present worth of the right to receive $1.00 at the end of a defined period, using the interest rate prescribed under section 7520 for the appropriate month.

(ii) *Certain restricted beneficial interests.* A restricted beneficial interest is an annuity, income, remainder, or reversionary interest that is subject to any contingency, power, or other restriction, whether the restriction is provided for by the terms of the trust, will, or other governing instrument or is caused by other circumstances. In general, a standard section 7520 annuity, income, or remainder factor may not be used to value a restricted beneficial interest. However, a special section 7520 annuity, income, or remainder factor may be used to value a restricted beneficial interest under some circumstances. See paragraphs (b)(2)(v) Example 5 and (b)(4) of this section, which illustrate situations in which special section 7520 actuarial factors are needed to take into account limitations on beneficial interests. See § 25.7520–1(c) for requesting a special factor from the Internal Revenue Service.

(iii) *Other beneficial interests.* If, under the provisions of this paragraph (b), the interest rate and mortality components prescribed under section 7520 are not applicable in determining the value of any annuity, income, remainder, or reversionary interest, the actual fair market value of the interest (determined without regard to section 7520) is based on all of the facts and circumstances if and to the extent permitted by the Internal Revenue Code provision applicable to the property interest.

(2) *Provisions of governing instrument and other limitations on source of payment*—(i) *Annuities.* A standard section 7520 annuity factor may not be used to determine the present value of an annuity for a specified term of years or the life of one or more individuals unless the effect of the trust, will, or other governing instrument is to ensure that the annuity will be paid for the entire defined period. In the case of an annuity payable from a trust or other limited fund, the annuity is not considered payable for the entire defined period if, considering the applicable section 7520 interest rate on the valuation date of the transfer, the annuity is expected to exhaust the fund before the last possible annuity payment is made in full. For this purpose, it must be assumed that it is possible for each measuring life to survive until age 110. For example, for a fixed annuity payable annually at the end of each year, if the amount of the annuity payment (expressed as a percentage of the initial corpus) is less than or equal to the applicable section 7520 interest rate at the date of the transfer, the corpus is assumed to be sufficient to make all payments. If the percentage exceeds the applicable section 7520 interest rate and the annuity is for a definite term of years, multiply the annual annuity amount by the Table B term certain annuity factor, as described in § 25.7520–1(c)(1), for the number of years of the defined period. If the percentage exceeds the applicable section 7520 interest rate and the annuity is payable for the life of one or more individuals, multiply the annual annuity amount by the Table B annuity factor for 110 years minus the age of the youngest individual. If the result exceeds the limited fund, the annuity may exhaust the fund, and it will be necessary to calculate a special section 7520 annuity factor that takes into account the exhaustion of the trust or fund. This computation would be modified, if appropriate, to take into account annuities with different payment terms.

(ii) *Income and similar interests.* (A) *Beneficial enjoyment.* A standard section 7520 income factor for an ordinary income interest is not to be used to determine the present value of an income or similar interest in trust for a term of years or for the life of one or more individuals unless the effect of the trust, will, or other governing instrument is to provide the income beneficiary with that degree of beneficial enjoyment of the property during the term of the income interest that the principles of the law of trusts accord to a person who is unqualifiedly designated as the income beneficiary of a trust for a similar period of time. This degree of beneficial enjoyment is provided only if it was the transferor's intent, as manifested by the provisions of the governing instrument and the surrounding circumstances, that the trust provide an income interest for the income beneficiary during the specified period of time that is consistent with the value of the trust corpus and with its preservation. In determining whether a trust arrangement evidences that intention, the treatment required or permitted with respect to individual items must be considered in relation to the entire system provided for in the administration of the subject trust. Similarly, in determining the present value of the right to use tangible property (whether or not in trust) for one or more measuring lives or for some other specified period of time, the interest rate component prescribed under section 7520 and § 1.7520–1 of this chapter may not be used unless, during the specified period, the effect of the trust, will or other governing instrument is to provide the beneficiary with that degree of use, possession, and enjoyment of the property during the term of interest that applicable state law accords to a person who is unqualifiedly designated as a life tenant or term holder for a similar period of time.

(B) *Diversions of income and corpus.* A standard section 7520 income factor for an ordinary income interest may not be used to value an income interest or similar interest in property for a term of years, or for one or more measuring lives, if—

(1) The trust, will, or other governing instrument requires or permits the beneficiary's income or other enjoyment to be withheld, diverted, or accumulated for another person's benefit without the consent of the income beneficiary; or

(2) The governing instrument requires or permits trust corpus to be withdrawn from the trust for another person's benefit without the consent of the income beneficiary during the income beneficiary's term of enjoyment and without accountability to the income beneficiary for such diversion.

(iii) *Remainder and reversionary interests.* A standard section 7520 remainder interest factor for an ordinary remainder or reversionary interest may not be used to determine the present value of a remainder or reversionary interest (whether in trust or otherwise) unless, consistent with the preservation and protection that the law of trusts would provide for a person who is unqualifiedly designated as the remainder beneficiary of a trust for a similar duration, the effect of the administrative and dispositive provisions for the interest or interests that precede the remainder or reversionary interest is to assure that the property will be adequately preserved and protected (e.g., from erosion, invasion, depletion, or damage) until the remainder or reversionary interest takes effect in possession and enjoyment. This degree of preservation and protection is provided only if it was the transferor's intent, as manifested by the provisions of the arrangement and the surrounding circumstances, that the entire disposition provide the remainder or reversionary beneficiary with an undiminished interest in the property transferred at the time of the termination of the prior interest.

(iv) *Pooled income fund interests.* In general, pooled income funds are created and administered to achieve a special rate of return. A beneficial interest in a pooled income fund is not ordinarily valued using a standard section 7520 income or remainder interest factor. The present value of a beneficial interest in a pooled income fund is determined according to rules and special remainder factors prescribed in § 1.642(c)–6 of this chapter and, when applicable, the rules set forth under paragraph (b)(3) of this section if the individual who is the measuring life is terminally ill at the time of the transfer.

(v) *Annuity payable from a trust or other limited fund.* The present value of an annuity interest (the subject annuity) payable from a trust or other limited fund (the fund) must be determined by taking into account the possibility of exhaustion of the fund. Thus, the present value of any such annuity that will exhaust the fund (and of any other interest dependent on the present value of such an annuity) is determined by using actuarial factors, under the applicable section 7520 mortality and interest rate assumptions, reflecting the term certain period to the exhaustion of the fund. Because it is assumed under the prescribed mortality component, Table 2010CM, that any measuring life may survive past age 109 and until just before age 110, any life annuity could require payments in the person's 110th year. To determine whether a subject annuity that is payable as a level amount paid annually at the end of each year for a life, will exhaust the fund, the annuitant's age must be subtracted from 110 to determine the longest possible duration of the annuity (maximum number of years) under the prescribed mortality table. If the present value of an annuity for the same level payments, payable for a term certain equal to that maximum number of years, is greater than the value of the fund, the annuity is determined to exhaust the fund before the end of that maximum number of years (under the prescribed assumptions), and the present value of the subject annuity is determined on the basis of life annuity factors limited by the period to exhaustion. The period to exhaustion is the shortest period for which the present value of that same annuity payable for a term certain is greater than or equal to the value of the fund, under the prescribed section 7520 interest rate. If the subject annuity is for life (or for a period depending in part on life) and the period to exhaustion is shorter than the longest possible life period, the present value of the subject annuity is determined as the present value of an annuity for the shorter of life or a term of years limited by the period to exhaustion, and the actuarial commutation factors may be used in determining the present value.

The actuarial commutation factors can be computed directly by using the formulas in § 25.2512–5(d)(2)(v)(A)(1), the section 7520 rate, and Table 2010CM as set forth in § 20.2031–7(d)(7)(ii) of this chapter. For the convenience of taxpayers, actuarial commutation factors have been computed by the IRS and appear in Table H. The appropriate annuity factors for an annuity payable for a term of years certain is computed by subtracting from 1.000000 the factor for an ordinary remainder interest following the same term certain that is determined under the formula in § 20.2031–7(d)(2)(ii)(A) of this chapter and then dividing the result by the applicable section 7520 interest rate expressed to at least four decimal places. For the convenience of taxpayers, actuarial factors have been computed by the IRS and appear in the "Annuity" column of Table B. Tables B and H can be found on the IRS website at *https://www.irs.gov/retirement-plans/actuarial-tables* (or a corresponding URL as may be updated from time to time). For an annuity payable for the longer of a life (or lives) or a term of years, the year of the last possible annuity payment is determined based on the later of the end of the term period or the year the youngest measuring life would reach age 110. For an annuity payable for the shorter of a life (or lives) or a term of years, the year of the last possible payment is determined based on the earlier of the end of the term period or the year the youngest measuring life would reach age 110. After determining the point of exhaustion of funds, the approximation method for determining the present value of annuity payments for a life or lives so limited by exhaustion illustrated in the example in paragraph (b)(2)(vi)(E) of this section is to be used if a more exact method (for example, computing the year-by-year present value of each payment until the fund is exhausted) is not used. The selected method must be applied consistently in valuing all interests in the same property.

(vi) *Examples*. The provisions of this paragraph (b)(2) are illustrated by the following examples:

(A) *Example 1*. Unproductive property. The donor transfers corporation stock to a trust under the terms of which all of the trust income is payable to A for life. Considering the applicable federal rate under section 7520 and the appropriate life estate factor for a person A's age, the value of A's income interest, if valued under this section, would be $10,000. After A's death, the trust is to terminate and the trust property is to be distributed to B. The trust specifically authorizes, but does not require, the trustee to retain the shares of stock. The corporation has paid no dividends on this stock during the past 5 years, and there is no indication that this policy will change in the near future. Under applicable state law, the corporation is considered to be a sound investment that satisfies fiduciary standards. The facts and circumstances, including applicable state law, indicate that the income beneficiary would not have the legal right to compel the trustee to make the trust corpus productive in conformity with the requirements for a lifetime trust income interest under applicable local law. Therefore, the life income interest in this case is considered nonproductive. Consequently, A's income interest may not be valued actuarially under this section.

(B) *Example 2*. Beneficiary's right to make trust productive. The facts are the same as in paragraph (b)(2)(vi)(A) of this section (Example 1), except that the trustee is not specifically authorized to retain the shares of corporation stock. Further, the terms of the trust specifically provide that the life income beneficiary may require the trustee to make the trust corpus productive consistent with income yield standards for trusts under applicable state law. Under that law, the minimum rate of income that a productive trust may produce is substantially below the section 7520 interest rate on the valuation date. In this case, because A, the income beneficiary, has the right to compel the trustee to make the trust productive for purposes of applicable local law during A's lifetime, the income interest is considered an ordinary income interest for purposes of this paragraph (b)(2)(vi)(B), and the standard section 7520 life income factor may be used to determine the value of A's income interest. However, in the case of gifts made after October 8, 1990, if the donor was the life income beneficiary, the value of the income interest would be considered to be zero in this situation. See § 25.2702–2.

(C) *Example 3*. Annuity trust funded with unproductive property. The donor, who is age 60, transfers corporation stock worth $1,000,000 to a trust. The trust will pay a 6 percent ($60,000 per year) annuity in cash or other property to the donor for 10 years or until the donor's prior death. Upon the termination of the trust, the trust property is to be distributed to the donor's child. The section 7520 rate for the month of the transfer is 8.2 percent. The corporation has paid no dividends on the stock during the past 5 years, and there is no indication that this policy will change in the near future. Under applicable state law, the corporation is considered to be a sound investment that satisfies fiduciary standards. Therefore, the trust's sole investment in this corporation is not expected to adversely affect the interest of either the annuity beneficiary or the remainder beneficiary. Considering the 6 percent annuity payout rate and the 8.2 percent section 7520 interest rate, the trust corpus is considered sufficient to pay this annuity for the entire 10-year term of the trust, or even indefinitely. The trust specifically authorizes, but does not require, the trustee to retain the shares of stock. Although it appears that neither beneficiary would be able to compel the trustee to make the trust corpus produce investment income, the annuity interest in this case is considered to be an ordinary annuity interest, and a section 7520 annuity factor may be used to determine the present value of the annuity. In this case, the section 7520 annuity factor would represent the right to receive $1.00 per year for a term of 10 years or the prior death of a person age 60.

(D) *Example 4*. Unitrust funded with unproductive property. The facts are the same as in paragraph (b)(2)(vi)(C) of this section (Example 3), except that the donor has retained a unitrust interest equal to 7 percent of the value of the trust property, valued as of the beginning of each year. Although the trust corpus is non-income-producing, the present value of the donor's retained unitrust interest may be determined by using the section 7520 unitrust factor for a term of years or a prior death.

(E) *Example 5*. Annuity exhausting a trust or other limited fund. (1) The donor, who is age 60 and in normal health, transfers property worth $1,000,000 to a trust created for this purpose on or after June 1, 2023. The trust will pay a 10 percent ($100,000 per year) annuity to a charitable organization for the life of the donor, payable annually at the end of each year, and the remainder then will be distributed to the donor's child. The trust has no other beneficial interests payable before the end of the annuity. The section 7520 rate for the month of the transfer is 4.4 percent. Under section 7520(a)(2) of the Code, the donor has elected to use the section 7520 rate for the month of transfer. For purposes of this example, the relevant factors from Tables B and H(4.4) are:

Factors from Table B			
Annuity, Income, and Remainder Interests for a Term Certain			
Interest at 4.4 Percent			
Years	Annuity	Income Interest	Remainder
13	9.7423	0.428661	0.571339
14	10.2896	0.452741	0.547259
50	20.0878	0.883862	0.116138
Factors from Table H(4.4)			
Commutation Factors—Based on Table 2010CM			
Interest at 4.4 Percent			
Age (x)	D_x	N_x-factor	M_x-factor
60	6,694.636	90,259.34	2,723.225
73	3,151.228	29,432.25	1,856.209
74	2,941.075	26,452.50	1,777.165

(2) First, it is necessary to determine whether the annuity may exhaust the corpus before all planned annuity payments are made. This determination is made by using values from Table B as illustrated in Figure 1 to this paragraph (b)(2)(vi)(E)(2).

Figure 1 to paragraph (b)(2)(v)(E)(2) – Illustration of determining present value of term certain annuity

A. Highest age possible under mortality table	110
B. Less: age of the measuring life at date of transfer	- 60
C. Difference: number of years annuity obligation may continue	50
D. Annual annuity payment	$100,000
E. Table B annuity factor for 50 years at 4.4 percent	20.0878
F. Present value of term certain annuity: D x E	$2,008,780

(3) Because the present value of an annuity for a term of 50 years exceeds the corpus, the annuity may exhaust the trust before all payments are made. Consequently, the annuity must be valued as an annuity payable for a term of years or until the prior death of the annuitant, with the term of years determined by the number of years to exhaustion of the fund, assuming earnings at the section 7520 rate of 4.4 percent.

(4) If an annuity of $100,000 payable at the end of each year for a period had an annuity factor of 10.0, it would have a present value exactly equal to the principal available to pay the annuity over the term. The annuity factor for 13 years at 4.4 percent in Table B is 9.7423, so the present value of an annuity of $100,000 at 4.4 percent, payable at the end of each year for 13 years certain, is $100,000 times 9.7423 or $974,230. The annuity factor for 14 years at 4.4 percent is 10.2896, so the present value of an annual annuity of $100,000 per year at 4.4 percent for 14 years certain is $100,000 times 10.2896, or $1,028,960. Therefore, 14 years is the shortest term for which a term certain annuity of $100,000 per year is greater than the fund of $1,000,000. Thus, it is determined, under the prescribed assumptions, that the $1,000,000 initial transfer will be sufficient to make 13 annual payments of $100,000, but not to make the entire 14th payment. Subtracting the present value of the 13-year term certain annuity, $974,230, from the fund of $1,000,000 leaves a remainder of $25,770. Of the initial transfer amount, $25,770 is not needed to make payments for 13 years, so this amount, as accumulated for 14 years, will be available for the final payment. The 14-year accumulation factor at 4.4 percent is 1.827288 ((1 + 0.044)14 = 1.827288), so the amount available in 14 years is $25,770 times 1.827288 or $47,089.21. Therefore, for purposes of this present value determination, the subject annuity is treated as being composed of two distinct annuity components. The two annuity components taken together must equal the total annual amount of $100,000. The annual amount of the first annuity component is the exact amount that the trust will have available for the final payment, $47,089.21. The annual amount of the second annuity component then must be $100,000 minus $47,089.21, or $52,910.79. Under the section 7520 assumptions, the initial corpus will be able to make payments of $52,910.79 per year for 13 years, as well as payments of $47,089.21 per year for 14 years. The present value of the subject annuity is computed by adding together the present values of two separate component annuities payable for the shorter of a life or a term.

(5) The actuarial factor for determining the value of the annuity of $52,910.79 per year payable for 13 years or until the prior death of a person aged 60 is derived by the use of factors involving one life and a term of years, derived from Table H. The factor is determined as illustrated in Figure 2 to this paragraph (b)(2)(vi)(E)(5).

Figure 2 to paragraph (b)(2)(v)(E)(5) – Illustration of determining annuity factor for shorter of life or 13 years

G. Initial age	60
H. Plus: Term of years	+ 13
I. Sum (Terminal age)	73
J. $\overset{o}{N}_x$ factor, Table H(4.4), age 60	90,259.34
K. Less: $\overset{o}{N}_x$ factor, Table H(4.4), age 73	- 29,432.25
L. Difference	60,827.09
M. D_x factor, Table H(4.4), age 60	6,694.64
N. Required Annuity Factor: L / M	9.0859

(6) The actuarial factor for determining the value of the annuity $47,089.21 per year payable for 14 years or until the prior death of a person aged 60 is derived by the use of factors involving one life and a term of years, derived from Table H. The factor is determined as illustrated in Figure 3 to this paragraph (b)(2)(vi)(E)(6).

Figure 3 to paragraph (b)(2)(v)(E)(6) – Illustration of determining annuity factor for shorter of life or 14 years

O. Initial age	60
P. Plus: Term of years	+ 14
Q. Sum (Terminal age)	74
R. $\overset{o}{N}_x$ factor, Table H(2.8), age 60	90,259.34
S. Less: $\overset{o}{N}_x$ factor, Table H(2.8), age 74	- 26,452.50
T. Difference	63,806.84
U. D_x factor, Table H(2.8), age 60	6,694.64
V. Required Annuity Factor: T / U	9.5310

(7) Based on the calculations of paragraph (b)(2)(vi)(E)(5) of this section, the present value of an annuity of $52,910.79 per year payable for 13 years or until the prior death of a person aged 60 is $480,742.15 ($52,910.79 x 9.0859). Based on the calculations of paragraph (b)(2)(vi)(E)(6) of this section, the present value of an annuity of $47,089.21 per year payable for 14 years or until the prior death of a person aged 60 is $448,807.26 ($47,089.21 x 9.5310). Thus, the present value of the charitable annuity interest is the sum of the two component annuities, $929,549.41 ($480,742.15 + $448,807.26).

(3) *Mortality component.* The mortality component prescribed under section 7520 may not be used to determine the present value of an annuity, income interest, remainder interest, or reversionary interest if an individual who is a measuring life dies or is terminally ill at the time the gift is completed. For purposes of this paragraph (b)(3), an individual who is known to have an incurable illness or other deteriorating physical condition is considered terminally ill if there is at least a 50 percent probability that the individual will die within 1 year. However, if the individual survives for eighteen months or longer after the date the gift is completed, that individual shall be presumed to have not been terminally ill at the date the gift was completed unless the contrary is established by clear and convincing evidence.

(4) *Example—terminal illness* (i) Sample factors from actuarial Table S. The provisions of paragraph

(b)(3) of this section are illustrated by the example in paragraph (b)(4)(ii) of this section. The appropriate annuity factor for an annuity payable for the life of one individual is computed by subtracting from 1.00000 the factor for an ordinary remainder interest following the life of the same individual that is determined under the formula in § 20.2031–7(d)(2)(ii)(B) of this chapter and then dividing the result by the applicable section 7520 interest rate expressed to at least four decimal places. For the convenience of taxpayers, actuarial factors have been computed by the IRS and appear in the "Annuity" column of Table S. Table S can be found on the IRS website at *https://www.irs.gov/retirement-plans/actuarial-tables*. For purposes of the example in paragraph (b)(4)(ii) of this section, the relevant factor from Table S is:

Factors from Table S—Based on Table 2010CM			
Interest at 4.4 Percent			
Age	Annuity	Life Estate	Remainder
75	8.6473	0.38048	0.61952

(ii) *Example of donor with terminal illness*. The donor transfers property worth $1,000,000 to a child on or after June 1, 2023, in exchange for the child's promise to pay the donor $80,000 per year for the donor's life, payable annually at the end of each period. The section 7520 interest rate for the month of the transfer is 4.4 percent. The donor is age 75 but has been diagnosed with an incurable illness and has at least a 50 percent probability of dying within 1 year. Under Table S, the annuity factor at 4.4 percent for a person age 75 in normal health is 8.6473. Thus, if the donor were not terminally ill, the present value of the annuity would be $691,784 ($80,000 x 8.6473). Assuming the presumption provided in paragraph (b)(3) of this section does not apply, because there is at least a 50 percent probability that the donor will die within 1 year, the standard section 7520 annuity factor may not be used to determine the present value of the donor's annuity interest. Instead, a special section 7520 annuity factor must be computed that takes into account the projection of the donor's actual life expectancy.

(5) Additional limitations. Section 7520 does not apply to the extent as may otherwise be provided by the Commissioner.

(c) Applicability dates. Paragraph (a) of this section is applicable as of May 1, 1989. The provisions of paragraph (b) of this section, except paragraphs (b)(2)(v), (b)(2)(vi)(E), and (b)(4) of this section, are applicable to gifts made after December 13, 1995. Paragraphs (b)(2)(v), (b)(2)(vi)(E), and (b)(4) of this section are applicable to gifts made on or after June 1, 2023.

[T.D. 8540, 59 FR 30178, June 10, 1994; T.D. 8630, 60 FR 63919, Dec. 13, 1995; 61 FR 7992, March 1, 1996; T.D. 8819, 64 FR 23228, April 30, 1999; T.D. 8886, 65 FR 36943, June 12, 2000; T.D. 9448, 74 FR 21517, May 7, 2009; T.D. 9540, 76 FR 49642, Aug. 10, 2011; T.D. 9974, 88 FR 37463, June 7, 2023]

§ 25.7520–4 Transitional rules.

(a) Reliance. If the valuation date is after April 30, 1989, and before June 10, 994, a donor can rely on Notice 89–24, 1989–1 C.B. 660, or Notice 89–60, 1989–1 C.B. 700 (See § 601.601(d)(2)(ii)(b) of this chapter), in valuing the transferred interest.

(b) Transfers in 1989. If a donor transferred an interest in property by gift after December 31, 1988, and before May 1, 1989, retaining an interest in the same property and, after April 30, 1989, and before January 1, 1990, transferred the retained interest in the property, the donor may, at the donor's option, value the transfer of the retained interest under either § 25.2512–5(d) or § 25.2512–5A(d).

(c) Effective date. This section is effective as of May 1, 1989.

[T.D. 8540, 59 FR 30179, June 10, 1994]

Chapter 79. Definitions

§ 7701. Definitions

(a) When used in this title, where not otherwise distinctly expressed or manifestly incompatible with the intent thereof—

(1) Person. The term "person" shall be construed to mean and include an individual, a trust, estate, partnership, association, company or corporation.

* * *

(3) Corporation. The term "corporation" includes associations, joint-stock companies, and insurance companies.

* * *

(6) Fiduciary. The term "fiduciary" means a guardian, trustee, executor, administrator, receiver, conservator, or any person acting in any fiduciary capacity for any person.

* * *

(9) United States. The term "United States" when used in a geographical sense includes only the States and the District of Columbia.

(10) State. The term "State" shall be construed to include the District of Columbia, where such construction is necessary to carry out provisions of this title.

(11) Secretary of the Treasury and Secretary.

(A) Secretary of the Treasury. The term "Secretary of the Treasury" means the Secretary of the Treasury, personally, and shall not include any delegate of his.

(B) Secretary. The term "Secretary" means the Secretary of the Treasury or his delegate.

* * *

(13) Commissioner. The term "Commissioner" means the Commissioner of Internal Revenue.

(14) Taxpayer. The term "taxpayer" means any person subject to any internal revenue tax.

* * *

[As stated in P.L. 115–97 (popularly known as the "Tax Cuts and Jobs Act") § 11051(c), § 7701(a)(17) as follows is effective for divorce or separation instrument executed before 2019. *Ed.*]

(17) Husband and wife. As used in sections 682 and 2516, if the husband and wife therein referred to are divorced, wherever appropriate to the meaning of such sections, the term "wife" shall be read "former wife" and the term "husband" shall be read "former husband"; and, if the payments described in such sections are made by or on behalf of the wife or former wife to the husband or former husband instead of vice versa, wherever appropriate to the meaning of such sections, the term "husband" shall be read "wife" and the term "wife" shall be read "husband."

[As stated in P.L. 115–97 (popularly known as the "Tax Cuts and Jobs Act") § 11051(c), § 7701(a)(17) as follows is effective for divorce or separation instrument executed after 12/31/2018. *Ed.*]

(17) Husband and wife. As used in section 2516, if the husband and wife therein referred to are divorced, wherever appropriate to the meaning of such section, the term "wife" shall be read "former wife" and the term "husband" shall be read "former husband"; and, if the payments described in such section are made by or on behalf of the wife or former wife to the husband or former husband instead of vice versa, wherever appropriate to the meaning of such section, the term "husband" shall be read "wife" and the term "wife" shall be read "husband."

* * *

(23) Taxable year. The term "taxable year" means the calendar year, or the fiscal year ending during such calendar year, upon the basis of which the taxable income is computed under subtitle A. "Taxable year" means, in the case of a return made for a fractional part of a year under the provisions of subtitle A or under regulations prescribed by the Secretary, the period for which such return is made.

(24) Fiscal year. The term "fiscal year" means an accounting period of 12 months ending on the last day of any month other than December.

* * *

(26) Trade or business. The term "trade or business" includes the performance of the functions of a public office.

* * *

(30) United States person. The term "United States person" means—

(A) a citizen or resident of the United States,

(B) a domestic partnership,

(C) a domestic corporation,

(D) any estate (other than a foreign estate, within the meaning of paragraph (31)), and

(E) any trust if—

(i) a court within the United States is able to exercise primary supervision over the administration of the trust, and

(ii) one or more United States persons have the authority to control all substantial decisions of the trust.

(31) Foreign estate or trust.

(A) Foreign estate. The term "foreign estate" means an estate the income of which, from sources without the United States which is not effectively connected with the conduct of a trade or business within the United States, is not includible in gross income under subtitle A.

(B) Foreign trust. The term "foreign trust" means any trust other than a trust described in subparagraph (E) of paragraph (30).

* * *

(42) Substituted basis property. The term "substituted basis property" means property which is—

(A) transferred basis property, or

(B) exchanged basis property.

(43) Transferred basis property. The term "transferred basis property" means property having a basis determined under any provision of subtitle A (or under any corresponding provision of prior income tax law) providing that the basis shall be determined in whole or in part by reference to the basis in the hands of the donor, grantor, or other transferor.

(44) Exchanged basis property. The term "exchanged basis property" means property having a basis determined under any provision of subtitle A (or under any corresponding provision of prior income tax law) providing that the basis shall be determined in whole or in part by reference to other property held at any time by the person for whom the basis is to be determined.

(45) Nonrecognition transaction. The term "nonrecognition transaction" means any disposition of property in a transaction in which gain or loss is not recognized in whole or in part for purposes of subtitle A.

* * *

(50) Termination of United States citizenship.

(A) In general. An individual shall not cease to be treated as a United States citizen before the date on which the individual's citizenship is treated as relinquished under section 877A(g)(4).

(B) Dual citizens. Under regulations prescribed by the Secretary, subparagraph (A) shall not apply to an individual who became at birth a citizen of the United States and a citizen of another country.

(b) Definition of resident alien and nonresident alien.

(1) In general. For purposes of this title (other than subtitle B)—

(A) Resident alien. An alien individual shall be treated as a resident of the United States with respect to any calendar year if (and only if) such individual meets the requirements of clause (i), (ii), or (iii):

(i) Lawfully admitted for permanent residence. Such individual is a lawful permanent resident of the United States at any time during such calendar year.

(ii) Substantial presence test. Such individual meets the substantial presence test of paragraph (3).

(iii) First year election. Such individual makes the election provided in paragraph (4).

(B) Nonresident alien. An individual is a nonresident alien if such individual is neither a citizen of the United States nor a resident of the United States (within the meaning of subparagraph (A)).

* * *

(6) Lawful permanent resident. For purposes of this subsection, an individual is a lawful permanent resident of the United States at any time if

(A) such individual has the status of having been lawfully accorded the privilege of residing permanently in the United States as an immigrant in accordance with the immigration laws, and

(B) such status has not been revoked (and has not been administratively or judicially determined to have been abandoned).

An individual shall cease to be treated as a lawful permanent resident of the United States if such individual commences to be treated as a resident of a foreign country under the provisions of a tax treaty between the United States and the foreign country, does not waive the benefits of such treaty applicable to residents of the foreign country, and notifies the Secretary of the commencement of such treatment.

(c) Includes and including. The terms "includes" and "including" when used in a definition contained in this title shall not be deemed to exclude other things otherwise within the meaning of the term defined.

* * *

Regulations

§ 301.7701–2 Business entities; definitions.

(a) Business entities. For purposes of this section and § 301.7701–3, a business entity is any entity recognized for federal tax purposes (including an entity with a single owner that may be disregarded as an entity separate from its owner under § 301.7701–3) that is not properly classified as a trust under § 301.7701–4 or otherwise subject to special treatment under the Internal Revenue Code. A business entity with two or more members is classified for federal tax purposes as either a corporation or a partnership. A business entity with only one owner is classified as a corporation or is disregarded; if the entity is disregarded, its activities are treated in the same manner as a sole proprietorship, branch, or division of the owner. But see paragraphs (c)(2)(iii) through (vi) of this section for special rules that apply to an eligible entity that is otherwise disregarded as an entity separate from its owner.

* * *

[32 FR 15241, Nov. 3, 1967, as amended by T.D. 7515, 42 FR 55612, Oct. 18, 1977; T.D. 7889, 48 FR 18805, April 26, 1983; T.D. 8475, 58 FR 28502, May 14, 1993; T.D. 8697, 61 FR 66589, Dec. 18, 1996; T.D. 8844, 64 FR 66583, Nov. 29, 1999; T.D. 9012, 67 FR 49864, Aug. 1, 2002; T.D. 9093, 68 FR 60298, Oct. 22, 2003; T.D. 9153, 69 FR 49810, Aug. 12, 2004; T.D. 9183, 70 FR 9221, Feb. 25, 2005; T.D. 9197, 70 FR 19698, April 14, 2005; T.D. 9235, 70 FR 74658, Dec. 16, 2005; T.D. 9246, 71 FR 4817, Jan. 30, 2006; T.D. 9356, 72 FR 45893, Aug. 16, 2007; T.D. 9388, 73 FR 15065, March 21, 2008; T.D. 8697, 73 FR 18442, April 4, 2008; T.D. 9388, 73 FR 21415, April 21, 2008; T.D. 9433, 73 FR 72346, Nov. 28, 2008; T.D. 9462, 74 FR 46904, Sept. 14, 2009; T.D. 9553, 76 FR 66182, Oct. 26, 2011; T.D. 9554, 76 FR 67365, Nov. 1, 2011; T.D. 9596, 77 FR 37807, June 25, 2012; T.D. 9655, 79 FR 8601, Feb. 12, 2014; T.D. 9670, 79 FR 36206, June 26, 2014; T.D. 9766 81 FR 26694, May 4, 2016; T.D. 9796, 81 FR 89851, Dec. 13, 2016; T.D. 9869, 84 FR 31479, July 2, 2019]

§ 301.7701–4 Trusts.

(a) Ordinary trusts. In general, the term “trust” as used in the Internal Revenue Code refers to an arrangement created either by a will or by an inter vivos declaration whereby trustees take title to property for the purpose of protecting or conserving it for the beneficiaries under the ordinary rules applied in chancery or probate courts. Usually the beneficiaries of such a trust do no more than accept the benefits thereof and are not the voluntary planners or creators of the trust arrangement. However, the beneficiaries of such a trust may be the persons who create it and it will be recognized as a trust under the Internal Revenue Code if it was created for the purpose of protecting or conserving the trust property for beneficiaries who stand in the same relation to the trust as they would if the trust had been created by others for them. Generally speaking, an arrangement will be treated as a trust under the Internal Revenue Code if it can be shown that the purpose of the arrangement is to vest in trustees responsibility for the protection and conservation of property for beneficiaries who cannot share in the discharge of this responsibility and, therefore, are not associates in a joint enterprise for the conduct of business for profit.

(b) Business trusts. There are other arrangements which are known as trusts because the legal title to property is conveyed to trustees for the benefit of beneficiaries, but which are not classified as trusts for purposes of the Internal Revenue Code because they are not simply arrangements to protect or conserve the property for the beneficiaries. These trusts, which are often known as business or commercial trusts, generally are created by the beneficiaries simply as a device to carry on a profit-making business which normally would have been carried on through business organizations that are classified as corporations or partnerships under the Internal Revenue Code. However, the fact that the corpus of the trust is not supplied by the beneficiaries is not sufficient reason in itself for classifying the arrangement as an ordinary trust rather than as an association or partnership. The fact that any organization is technically cast in the trust form, by conveying title to property to trustees for the benefit of persons designated as beneficiaries, will not change the real character of the organization if the organization is more properly classified as a business entity under § 301.7701–2.

* * *

[32 FR 15241, Nov. 3, 1967; T.D. 8080, 51 FR 9952, March 24, 1986; T.D. 8668, 61 FR 19191, May 1, 1996; T.D. 8697, 61 FR 66592, Dec. 18, 1996; T.D. 9961, 87 FR 182, Jan. 4, 2022]

§ 301.7701–7 Trusts—domestic and foreign.

(a) In general. (1) A trust is a United States person if—

(i) A court within the United States is able to exercise primary supervision over the administration of the trust (court test); and

(ii) One or more United States persons have the authority to control all substantial decisions of the trust (control test).

(2) A trust is a United States person for purposes of the Internal Revenue Code (Code) on any day that the trust meets both the court test and the control test. For purposes of the regulations in this chapter, the term domestic trust means a trust that is a United States per-

son. The term foreign trust means any trust other than a domestic trust.

(3) Except as otherwise provided in part I, subchapter J, chapter 1 of the Code, the taxable income of a foreign trust is computed in the same manner as the taxable income of a nonresident alien individual who is not present in the United States at any time. Section 641(b). Section 7701(b) is not applicable to trusts because it only applies to individuals. In addition, a foreign trust is not considered to be present in the United States at any time for purposes of section 871(a)(2), which deals with capital gains of nonresident aliens present in the United States for 183 days or more.

(b) Applicable law. The terms of the trust instrument and applicable law must be applied to determine whether the court test and the control test are met.

(c) The court test. (1) *Safe harbor.* A trust satisfies the court test if—

(i) The trust instrument does not direct that the trust be administered outside of the United States;

(ii) The trust in fact is administered exclusively in the United States; and

(iii) The trust is not subject to an automatic migration provision described in paragraph (c)(4)(ii) of this section.

(2) *Example.* The following example illustrates the rule of paragraph (c)(1) of this section:

Example. A creates a trust for the equal benefit of A's two children, B and C. The trust instrument provides that DC, a State Y corporation, is the trustee of the trust. State Y is a state within the United States. DC administers the trust exclusively in State Y and the trust instrument is silent as to where the trust is to be administered. The trust is not subject to an automatic migration provision described in paragraph (c)(4)(ii) of this section. The trust satisfies the safe harbor of paragraph (c)(1) of this section and the court test.

(3) *Definitions.* The following definitions apply for purposes of this section:

(i) *Court.* The term court includes any federal, state, or local court.

(ii) *The United States.* The term the United States is used in this section in a geographical sense. Thus, for purposes of the court test, the United States includes only the States and the District of Columbia. See section 7701(a)(9). Accordingly, a court within a territory or possession of the United States or within a foreign country is not a court within the United States.

(iii) *Is able to exercise.* The term is able to exercise means that a court has or would have the authority under applicable law to render orders or judgments resolving issues concerning administration of the trust.

(iv) *Primary supervision.* The term primary supervision means that a court has or would have the authority to determine substantially all issues regarding the administration of the entire trust. A court may have primary supervision under this paragraph (c)(3)(iv) notwithstanding the fact that another court has jurisdiction over a trustee, a beneficiary, or trust property.

(v) *Administration.* The term administration of the trust means the carrying out of the duties imposed by the terms of the trust instrument and applicable law, including maintaining the books and records of the trust, filing tax returns, managing and investing the assets of the trust, defending the trust from suits by creditors, and determining the amount and timing of distributions.

(4) *Situations that cause a trust to satisfy or fail to satisfy the court test.* (i) Except as provided in paragraph (c)(4)(ii) of this section, paragraphs (c)(4)(i)(A) through (D) of this section set forth some specific situations in which a trust satisfies the court test. The four situations described are not intended to be an exclusive list.

(A) *Uniform Probate Code.* A trust meets the court test if the trust is registered by an authorized fiduciary or fiduciaries of the trust in a court within the United States pursuant to a state statute that has provisions substantially similar to Article VII, Trust Administration, of the Uniform Probate Code, 8 Uniform Laws Annotated 1 (West Supp. 1998), available from the National Conference of Commissioners on Uniform State Laws, 676 North St. Clair Street, Suite 1700, Chicago, Illinois 60611.

(B) *Testamentary trust.* In the case of a trust created pursuant to the terms of a will probated within the United States (other than an ancillary probate), if all fiduciaries of the trust have been qualified as trustees of the trust by a court within the United States, the trust meets the court test.

(C) *Inter vivos trust.* In the case of a trust other than a testamentary trust, if the fiduciaries and/or beneficiaries take steps with a court within the United States that cause the administration of the trust to be subject to the primary supervision of the court, the trust meets the court test.

(D) *A United States court and a foreign court are able to exercise primary supervision over the administration of the trust.* If both a United States court and a foreign court are able to exercise primary supervision over the administration of the trust, the trust meets the court test.

(ii) *Automatic migration provisions.* Notwithstanding any other provision in this section, a court within the United States is not considered to have primary supervision over the administration of the trust if the trust instrument provides that a United States court's attempt to assert jurisdiction or otherwise supervise the administration of the trust directly or indirectly would cause the trust to migrate from the United States. However, this paragraph (c)(4)(ii) will not apply if the trust instrument provides that the trust will migrate from the United States only in the case of foreign invasion of the United States or widespread confiscation or nationalization of property in the United States.

(5) *Examples.* The following examples illustrate the rules of this paragraph (c):

Example (1). A, a United States citizen, creates a trust for the equal benefit of A's two children, both of whom are United States citizens. The trust instrument provides that DC, a domestic corporation, is to act as trustee of the trust and that the trust is to be administered in Country X, a foreign country. DC maintains a branch office in Country X with personnel authorized to act as trustees in Country X. The trust instrument provides that the law of State Y, a state within the United States, is to govern the interpretation of the trust. Under the law of Country X, a court within Country X is able to exercise primary supervision over the administration of the trust. Pursuant to the trust instrument, the Country X court applies the law of State Y to the trust. Under the terms of the trust instrument the trust is administered in Country X. No court within the United States is able to exercise primary supervision over the administration of the trust. The trust fails to satisfy the court test and therefore is a foreign trust.

Example (2). A, a United States citizen, creates a trust for A's own benefit and the benefit of A's spouse, B, a United States citizen. The trust instrument provides that the trust is to be administered in State Y, a state within the United States, by DC, a State Y corporation. The trust instrument further provides that in the event that a creditor sues the trustee in a United States court, the trust will automatically migrate from State Y to Country Z, a foreign country, so that no United States court will have jurisdiction over the trust. A court within the United States is not able to exercise primary supervision over the administration of the trust because the United States court's jurisdiction over the administration of the trust is automatically terminated in the event the court attempts to assert jurisdiction. Therefore, the trust fails to satisfy the court test from the time of its creation and is a foreign trust.

(d) Control test. (1) *Definitions.* (i) *United States person.* The term United States person means a United States person within the meaning of section 7701(a)(30). For example, a domestic corporation is a United States person, regardless of whether its shareholders are United States persons.

(ii) *Substantial decisions.* The term substantial decisions means those decisions that persons are authorized or required to make under the terms of the trust instrument and applicable law and that are not ministerial. Decisions that are ministerial include decisions regarding details such as the bookkeeping, the collection of rents, and the execution of investment decisions. Substantial decisions include, but are not limited to, decisions concerning—

(A) Whether and when to distribute income or corpus;

(B) The amount of any distributions;

(C) The selection of a beneficiary;

(D) Whether a receipt is allocable to income or principal;

(E) Whether to terminate the trust;

(F) Whether to compromise, arbitrate, or abandon claims of the trust;

(G) Whether to sue on behalf of the trust or to defend suits against the trust;

(H) Whether to remove, add, or replace a trustee;

(I) Whether to appoint a successor trustee to succeed a trustee who has died, resigned, or otherwise ceased to act as a trustee, even if the power to make such a decision is not accompanied by an unrestricted power to remove a trustee, unless the power to make such a decision is limited such that it cannot be exercised in a manner that would change the trust's residency from foreign to domestic, or vice versa; and

(J) Investment decisions; however, if a United States person under section 7701(a)(30) hires an investment advisor for the trust, investment decisions made by the investment advisor will be considered substantial decisions controlled by the United States person if the United States person can terminate the investment advisor's power to make investment decisions at will.

(iii) *Control.* The term control means having the power, by vote or otherwise, to make all of the substantial decisions of the trust, with no other person having the power to veto any of the substantial decisions. To determine whether United States persons have control, it is necessary to consider all persons who have authority to make a substantial decision of the trust, not only the trust fiduciaries.

(iv) *Safe harbor for certain employee benefit trusts and investment trusts.* Notwithstanding the provisions of this paragraph (d), the trusts listed in this paragraph (d)(1)(iv) are deemed to satisfy the control test set forth in paragraph (a)(1)(ii) of this section, provided that United States trustees control all of the substantial decisions made by the trustees of the trust—

(A) A qualified trust described in section 401(a);

(B) A trust described in section 457(g);

(C) A trust that is an individual retirement account described in section 408(a);

(D) A trust that is an individual retirement account described in section 408(k) or 408(p);

(E) A trust that is a Roth IRA described in section 408A;

(F) A trust that is an education individual retirement account described in section 530;

(G) A trust that is a voluntary employees' beneficiary association described in section 501(c)(9);

(H) A group trust described in Rev. Rul. 81–100 (1981–1 C.B. 326) (See § 601.601(d)(2) of this chapter);

(I) An investment trust classified as a trust under § 301.7701–4(c), provided that the following conditions are satisfied—

(1) All trustees are United States persons and at least one of the trustees is a bank, as defined in section 581, or a United States Government-owned agency or United States Government-sponsored enterprise;

(2) All sponsors (persons who exchange investment assets for beneficial interests with a view to selling the beneficial interests) are United States persons; and

(3) The beneficial interests are widely offered for sale primarily in the United States to United States persons;

(J) Such additional categories of trusts as the Commissioner may designate in revenue procedures, notices, or other guidance published in the Internal Revenue Bulletin (see § 601.601(d)(2)(ii)(b)).

(v) *Examples.* The following examples illustrate the rules of paragraph (d)(1) of this section:

Example (1). Trust is a testamentary trust with three fiduciaries, A, B, and C. A and B are United States citizens, and C is a nonresident alien. No persons except the fiduciaries have authority to make any decisions of the trust. The trust instrument provides that no substantial decisions of the trust can be made unless there is unanimity among the fiduciaries. The control test is not satisfied because United States persons do not control all the substantial decisions of the trust. No substantial decisions can be made without C's agreement.

Example (2). Assume the same facts as in Example 1, except that the trust instrument provides that all substantial decisions of the trust are to be decided by a majority vote among the fiduciaries. The control test is satisfied because a majority of the fiduciaries are United States persons and therefore United States persons control all the substantial decisions of the trust.

Example (3). Assume the same facts as in Example 2, except that the trust instrument directs that C is to make all of the trust's investment decisions, but that A and B may veto C's investment decisions. A and B cannot act to make the investment decisions on their own. The control test is not satisfied because the United States persons, A and B, do not have the power to make all of the substantial decisions of the trust.

Example (4). Assume the same facts as in Example 3, except A and B may accept or veto C's investment decisions and can make investments that C has not recommended. The control test is satisfied because the United States persons control all substantial decisions of the trust.

Example (5). X, a foreign corporation, conducts business in the United States through various branch operations. X has United States employees and has established a trust as part of a qualified employee benefit plan under section 401(a) for these employees. The trust is established under the laws of State A, and the trustee of the trust is B, a United States bank governed by the laws of State A. B holds legal title to the trust assets for the benefit of the trust beneficiaries. A plan committee makes decisions with respect to the plan and the trust. The plan committee can direct B's actions with regard to those decisions and under the governing documents B is not liable for those decisions. Members of the plan committee consist of United States persons and nonresident aliens, but nonresident aliens make up a majority of the plan committee. Decisions of the plan committee are made by majority vote. In addition, X retains the power to terminate the trust and to replace the United States trustee or to appoint additional trustees. This trust is deemed to satisfy the control test under paragraph (d)(1)(iv) of this section because B, a United States person, is the trust's only trustee. Any powers held by the plan committee or X are not considered under the safe harbor of paragraph (d)(1)(iv) of this section. In the event that X appoints additional trustees including foreign trustees, any powers held by such trustees must be considered in determining whether United States trustees control all substantial decisions made by the trustees of the trust.

(2) *Replacement of any person who had authority to make a substantial decision of the trust.* (i) *Replacement within 12 months.* In the event of an inadvertent change in any person that has the power to make a substantial decision of the trust that would cause the domestic or foreign residency of the trust to change, the trust is allowed 12 months from the date of the change to make necessary changes either with respect to the persons who control the substantial decisions or with respect to the residence of such persons to avoid a change in the trust's residency. For purposes of this section, an inadvertent change means the death, incapacity, resignation, change in residency or other change with respect to a person that has a power to make a substantial decision of the trust that would cause a change to the residency of the trust but that was not intended to change the residency of the trust. If the necessary change is made within 12 months, the trust is treated as retaining its pre-change residency during the 12-month period. If the necessary change is not made within 12 months, the trust's residency changes as of the date of the inadvertent change.

(ii) *Request for extension of time.* If reasonable actions have been taken to make the necessary change to prevent a change in trust residency, but due to circumstances beyond the trust's control the trust is unable to make the modification within 12 months, the trust may provide a written statement to the district director having jurisdiction over the trust's return setting forth the reasons for failing to make the necessary change within the required time period. If the district director determines that the failure was due to reasonable cause, the district director may grant the trust an extension of time to make the necessary change. Whether an extension of time is granted is in the sole discretion of the district director and, if granted, may contain such terms with respect to assessment as may be necessary to ensure that the correct amount of tax will be collected from the trust, its owners, and its beneficiaries. If the district director does not grant an extension, the trust's residency changes as of the date of the inadvertent change.

(iii) *Examples.* The following examples illustrate the rules of paragraphs (d)(2)(i) and (ii) of this section:

Example (1). A trust that satisfies the court test has three fiduciaries, A, B, and C. A and B are United States citizens and C is a nonresident alien. All decisions of the trust are made by majority vote of the fiduciaries. The trust instrument provides that upon the death or resignation of any of the fiduciaries, D, is the successor fiduciary. A dies and D automatically becomes a fiduciary of the trust. When D becomes a fiduciary of the trust, D is a nonresident alien. Two months after A dies, B replaces D with E, a United States person. Because D was replaced with E within 12 months after the date of A's death, during the period after A's death and before E begins to serve, the trust satisfies the control test and remains a domestic trust.

Example (2). Assume the same facts as in Example 1 except that at the end of the 12-month period after A's death, D has not been replaced and remains a fiduciary of the trust. The trust becomes a foreign trust on the date A died unless the district director grants an extension of the time period to make the necessary change.

(3) *Automatic migration provisions.* Notwithstanding any other provision in this section, United States persons are not considered to control all substantial decisions of the trust if an attempt by any governmental agency or creditor to collect information from or assert a claim against the trust would cause one or more substantial decisions of the trust to no longer be controlled by United States persons.

(4) *Examples.* The following examples illustrate the rules of this paragraph (d):

Example (1). A, a nonresident alien individual, is the grantor and, during A's lifetime, the sole beneficiary of a trust that qualifies as an individual retirement account (IRA). A has the exclusive power to make decisions regarding withdrawals from the IRA and to direct its investments. The IRA's sole trustee is a United States person within the meaning of section 7701(a)(30). The control test is satisfied with respect to this trust because the special rule of paragraph (d)(1)(iv) of this section applies.

Example (2). A, a nonresident alien individual, is the grantor of a trust and has the power to revoke the trust, in whole or in part, and revest assets in A. A is treated as the owner of the trust under sections 672(f) and 676. A is not a fiduciary of the trust. The trust has one trustee, B, a United States person, and the trust has one beneficiary, C. B has the discretion to distribute corpus or income to C. In this case, decisions exercisable by A to have trust assets distributed to A are substantial decisions. Therefore, the trust is a foreign trust because B does not control all substantial decisions of the trust.

Example (3). A trust, Trust T, has two fiduciaries, A and B. Both A and B are United States persons. A and B hire C, an investment advisor who is a foreign person, and may terminate C's employment at will. The investment advisor makes the investment decisions for the trust. A and B control all other decisions of the trust. Although C has the power to make investment decisions, A and B are treated as controlling these decisions. Therefore, the control test is satisfied.

Example (4). G, a United States citizen, creates a trust. The trust provides for income to A and B for life, remainder to A's and B's descendants. A is a nonresident alien and B is a United States person. The trustee of the trust is a United States person. The trust instrument authorizes A to replace the trustee. The power to replace the trustee is a substantial decision. Because A, a nonresident alien, controls a substantial decision, the control test is not satisfied.

(e) Effective date. (1) *General rule.* Except for the election to remain a domestic trust provided in paragraph (f) of this section and except as provided in paragraph (e)(3) of this section, this section is applicable to trusts for taxable years ending after February 2, 1999. This section may be relied on by trusts for taxable years beginning after December 31, 1996, and also may be relied on by trusts whose trustees have elected to apply sections 7701(a)(30) and (31) to the trusts for taxable years ending after August 20, 1996, under section 1907(a)(3)(B) of the Small Business Job Protection Act of 1996, (the SBJP Act) Public Law 104–188, 110 Stat. 1755 (26 U.S.C. 7701 note).

(2) *Trusts created after August 19, 1996.* If a trust is created after August 19, 1996, and before April 5, 1999, and the trust satisfies the control test set forth in the regulations project REG–251703–96 published under section 7701(a)(30) and (31) (1997–1 C.B. 795) (See § 601.601(d)(2) of this chapter), but does not satisfy the control test set forth in paragraph (d) of this section, the trust may be modified to satisfy the control test of paragraph (d) by December 31, 1999. If the modification is completed by December 31, 1999, the trust will be treated as satisfying the control test of paragraph (d) for taxable years beginning after December 31, 1996, (and for taxable years ending after August 20, 1996, if the election under section 1907(a)(3)(B) of the SBJP Act has been made for the trust).

(3) *Effective date of safe harbor for certain employee benefit trusts and investment trusts.* Paragraphs (d)(1)(iv) and (v) Examples 1 and 5 of this section apply to trusts for taxable years ending on or after August 9, 2001. Paragraphs (d)(1)(iv) and (v) Examples 1 and 5 of this section may be relied on by trusts for

taxable years beginning after December 31, 1996, and also may be relied on by trusts whose trustees have elected to apply sections 7701(a)(30) and (31) to the trusts for taxable years ending after August 20, 1996, under section 1907(a)(3)(B) of the SBJP Act.

(f) Election to remain a domestic trust. (1) *Trusts eligible to make the election to remain domestic.* A trust that was in existence on August 20, 1996, and that was treated as a domestic trust on August 19, 1996, as provided in paragraph (f)(2) of this section, may elect to continue treatment as a domestic trust notwithstanding section 7701(a)(30)(E). This election is not available to a trust that was wholly-owned by its grantor under subpart E, part I, subchapter J, chapter 1, of the Code on August 20, 1996. The election is available to a trust if only a portion of the trust was treated as owned by the grantor under subpart E on August 20, 1996. If a partially-owned grantor trust makes the election, the election is effective for the entire trust. Also, a trust may not make the election if the trust has made an election pursuant to section 1907(a)(3)(B) of the SBJP Act to apply the new trust criteria to the first taxable year of the trust ending after August 20, 1996, because that election, once made, is irrevocable.

(2) *Determining whether a trust was treated as a domestic trust on August 19, 1996.* (i) *Trusts filing Form 1041 for the taxable year that includes August 19, 1996.* For purposes of the election, a trust is considered to have been treated as a domestic trust on August 19, 1996, if: the trustee filed a Form 1041, "U.S. Income Tax Return for Estates and Trusts," for the trust for the period that includes August 19, 1996 (and did not file a Form 1040NR, "U.S. Nonresident Alien Income Tax Return," for that year); and the trust had a reasonable basis (within the meaning of section 6662) under section 7701(a)(30) prior to amendment by the SBJP Act (prior law) for reporting as a domestic trust for that period.

(ii) *Trusts not filing a Form 1041.* Some domestic trusts are not required to file Form 1041. For example, certain group trusts described in Rev. Rul. 81–100 (1981–1 C.B. 326) (See § 601.601(d)(2) of this chapter) consisting of trusts that are parts of qualified retirement plans and individual retirement accounts are not required to file Form 1041. Also, a domestic trust whose gross income for the taxable year is less than the amount required for filing an income tax return and that has no taxable income is not required to file a Form 1041. Section 6012(a)(4). For purposes of the election, a trust that filed neither a Form 1041 nor a Form 1040NR for the period that includes August 19, 1996, will be considered to have been treated as a domestic trust on August 19, 1996, if the trust had a reasonable basis (within the meaning of section 6662) under prior law for being treated as a domestic trust for that period and for filing neither a Form 1041 nor a Form 1040NR for that period.

(3) *Procedure for making the election to remain domestic.* (i) *Required Statement.* To make the election, a statement must be filed with the Internal Revenue Service in the manner and time described in this section. The statement must be entitled "Election to Remain a Domestic Trust under Section 1161 of the Taxpayer Relief Act of 1997," be signed under penalties of perjury by at least one trustee of the trust, and contain the following information—

(A) A statement that the trust is electing to continue to be treated as a domestic trust under section 1161 of the Taxpayer Relief Act of 1997;

(B) A statement that the trustee had a reasonable basis (within the meaning of section 6662) under prior law for treating the trust as a domestic trust on August 19, 1996. (The trustee need not explain the reasonable basis on the election statement.);

(C) A statement either that the trust filed a Form 1041 treating the trust as a domestic trust for the period that includes August 19, 1996, (and that the trust did not file a Form 1040NR for that period), or that the trust was not required to file a Form 1041 or a Form 1040NR for the period that includes August 19, 1996, with an accompanying brief explanation as to why a Form 1041 was not required to be filed; and

(D) The name, address, and employer identification number of the trust.

(ii) *Filing the required statement with the Internal Revenue Service.* (A) Except as provided in paragraphs (f)(3)(ii)(E) through (G) of this section, the trust must attach the statement to a Form 1041. The statement may be attached to either the Form 1041 that is filed for the first taxable year of the trust beginning after December 31, 1996 (1997 taxable year), or to the Form 1041 filed for the first taxable year of the trust beginning after December 31, 1997 (1998 taxable year). The statement, however, must be filed no later than the due date for filing a Form 1041 for the 1998 taxable year, plus extensions. The election will be effective for the 1997 taxable year, and thereafter, until revoked or terminated. If the trust filed a Form 1041 for the 1997 taxable year without the statement attached, the statement should be attached to the Form 1041 filed for the 1998 taxable year.

(B) If the trust has insufficient gross income and no taxable income for its 1997 or 1998 taxable year, or both, and therefore is not required to file a Form 1041 for either or both years, the trust must make the election by filing a Form 1041 for either the 1997 or 1998 taxable year with the statement attached (even though not otherwise required to file a Form 1041 for that year). The trust should only provide on the Form 1041 the trust's name, name and title of fiduciary, address, employer identification number, date created, and type of entity. The statement must be attached to a Form 1041 that is filed no later than October 15, 1999.

(C) If the trust files a Form 1040NR for the 1997 taxable year based on application of new section 7701(a)(30)(E) to the trust, and satisfies paragraph (f)(1) of this section, in order for the trust to make the election the trust must file an amended Form 1040NR return for the 1997 taxable year. The trust must note on the amended Form 1040NR that it is making an election under section 1161 of the Taxpayer Relief Act of 1997. The trust must attach to the amended Form 1040NR the statement required by paragraph (f)(3)(i) of this section and a completed Form 1041 for the 1997 taxable year. The items of income, deduction and credit of the trust must be excluded from the amended Form 1040NR and reported on the Form 1041. The amended Form 1040NR for the 1997 taxable year, with the statement and the Form 1041 attached, must be filed with the Philadelphia Service Center no later than the due date, plus extensions, for filing a Form 1041 for the 1998 taxable year.

(D) If a trust has made estimated tax payments as a foreign trust based on application of section 7701(a)(30)(E) to the trust, but has not yet filed a Form 1040NR for the 1997 taxable year, when the trust files its Form 1041 for the 1997 taxable year it must note on its Form 1041 that it made estimated tax payments based on treatment as a foreign trust. The Form 1041 must be filed with the Philadelphia Service Center (and not with the service center where the trust ordinarily would file its Form 1041).

(E) If a trust forms part of a qualified stock bonus, pension, or profit sharing plan, the election provided by this paragraph (f) must be made by attaching the statement to the plan's annual return required under section 6058 (information return) for the first plan year beginning after December 31, 1996, or to the plan's information return for the first plan year beginning after December 31, 1997. The statement must be attached to the plan's information return that is filed no later than the due date for filing the plan's information return for the first plan year beginning after December 31, 1997, plus extensions. The election will be effective for the first plan year beginning after December 31, 1996, and thereafter, until revoked or terminated.

(F) Any other type of trust that is not required to file a Form 1041 for the taxable year, but that is required to file an information return (for example, Form 5227) for the 1997 or 1998 taxable year must attach the statement to the trust's information return for the 1997 or 1998 taxable year. However, the statement must be attached to an information return that is filed no later than the due date for filing the trust's information return for the 1998 taxable year, plus extensions. The election will be effective for the 1997 taxable year, and thereafter, until revoked or terminated.

(G) A group trust described in Rev. Rul. 81–100 consisting of trusts that are parts of qualified retirement plans and individual retirement accounts (and any other trust that is not described above and that is not required to file a Form 1041 or an information return) need not attach the statement to any return and should file the statement with the Philadelphia Service Center. The trust must make the election provided by this paragraph (f) by filing the statement by October 15, 1999. The election will be effective for the 1997 taxable year, and thereafter, until revoked or terminated.

(iii) *Failure to file the statement in the required manner and time.* If a trust fails to file the statement in the manner or time provided in paragraphs (f)(3)(i) and (ii) of this section, the trustee may provide a written statement to the district director having jurisdiction over the trust setting forth the reasons for failing to file the statement in the required manner or time. If the district director determines that the failure to file the statement in the required manner or time was due to reasonable cause, the district director may grant the trust an extension of time to file the statement. Whether an extension of time is granted shall be in the sole discretion of the district director. However, the relief provided by this paragraph (f)(3)(iii) is not ordinarily available if the statute of limitations for the trust's 1997 taxable year has expired. Additionally, if the district director grants an extension of time, it may contain terms with respect to assessment as may be necessary to ensure that the correct amount of tax will be collected from the trust, its owners, and its beneficiaries.

(4) *Revocation or termination of the election.* (i) *Revocation of election.* The election provided by this paragraph (f) to be treated as a domestic trust may only be revoked with the consent of the Commissioner. See sections 684, 6048, and 6677 for the federal tax consequences and reporting requirements related to the change in trust residence.

(ii) *Termination of the election.* An election under this paragraph (f) to remain a domestic trust terminates if changes are made to the trust subsequent to the effective date of the election that result in the trust no longer having any reasonable basis (within the meaning of section 6662) for being treated as a domestic trust under section 7701(a)(30) prior to its amendment by the SBJP Act. The termination of the election will result in the trust changing its residency from a domestic trust to a foreign trust on the effective date of the termination of the election. See sections 684, 6048, and 6677 for the federal tax consequences and reporting requirements related to the change in trust residence.

(5) *Effective date.* This paragraph (f) is applicable beginning on February 2, 1999.

[T.D. 8813, 64 FR 4970, Feb. 2, 1999; T.D. 8962, 66 FR 41779, Aug. 9, 2001]

§ 7703. Determination of Marital Status

(a) General rule. For purposes of part V of subchapter B of chapter 1 and those provisions of this title which refer to this subsection—

(1) the determination of whether an individual is married shall be made as of the close of his taxable year; except that if his spouse dies during his taxable year such determination shall be made as of the time of such death; and

(2) an individual legally separated from his spouse under a decree of divorce or of separate maintenance shall not be considered as married.

(b) Certain married individuals living apart. For purposes of those provisions of this title which refer to this subsection, if—

(1) an individual who is married (within the meaning of subsection (a)) and who files a separate return maintains as his home a household which constitutes for more than one-half of the taxable year the principal place of abode of a child (within the meaning of section 152(f)(1)) with respect to whom such individual is entitled to a deduction for the taxable year under section 151 (or would be so entitled but for section 152(e)),

(2) such individual furnishes over one-half of the cost of maintaining such household during the taxable year, and

(3) during the last 6 months of the taxable year, such individual's spouse is not a member of such household, such individual shall not be considered as married.

Chapter 80. General Rules

Subchapter A. Application of Internal Revenue Laws

§ 7801. Authority of Department of the Treasury

(a) Powers and duties of Secretary.

(1) In general. Except as otherwise expressly provided by law, the administration and enforcement of this title shall be performed by or under the supervision of the Secretary of the Treasury.

(2) Administration and enforcement of certain provisions by Attorney General.

(A) In general. The administration and enforcement of the following provisions of this title shall be performed by or under the supervision of the Attorney General; and the term "Secretary" or "Secretary of the Treasury" shall, when applied to those provisions, mean the Attorney General; and the term "internal revenue officer" shall, when applied to those provisions, mean any officer of the Bureau of Alcohol, Tobacco, Firearms, and Explosives so designated by the Attorney General:

(i) Chapter 53.

(ii) Chapters 61 through 80, to the extent such chapters relate to the enforcement and administration of the provisions referred to in clause (i).

(B) Use of existing rulings and interpretations. Nothing in the Homeland Security Act of 2002 alters or repeals the rulings and interpretations of the Bureau of Alcohol, Tobacco, and Firearms in effect on the effective date of such Act, which concerns the provisions of this title referred to in subparagraph (A). The Attorney General shall consult with the Secretary to achieve uniformity and consistency in administering provisions under chapter 53 of title 26, United States Code.

(b) [Repealed.]

(c) Functions of Department of Justice unaffected. Nothing in this section or section 301(f) of title 31 shall be considered to affect the duties, powers, or functions imposed upon, or vested in, the Department of Justice, or any officer thereof, by law existing on May 10, 1934.

§ 7805. Rules and Regulations

(a) Authorization. Except where such authority is expressly given by this title to any person other than an officer or employee of the Treasury Department, the Secretary shall prescribe all needful rules and regulations for the enforcement of this title, including all rules and regulations as may be necessary by reason of any alteration of law in relation to internal revenue.

(b) Retroactivity of regulations.

(1) In general. Except as otherwise provided in this subsection, no temporary, proposed, or final regulation relating to the internal revenue laws shall apply to any taxable period ending before the earliest of the following dates:

(A) The date on which such regulation is filed with the Federal Register.

(B) In the case of any final regulation, the date on which any proposed or temporary regulation to which such final regulation relates was filed with the Federal Register.

(C) The date on which any notice substantially describing the expected contents of any temporary, proposed, or final regulation is issued to the public.

(2) Exception for promptly issued regulations. Paragraph (1) shall not apply to regulations filed or issued within 18 months of the date of the enactment of the statutory provision to which the regulation relates.

(3) Prevention of abuse. The Secretary may provide that any regulation may take effect or apply retroactively to prevent abuse.

(4) Correction of procedural defects. The Secretary may provide that any regulation may apply retroactively to correct a procedural defect in the issuance of any prior regulation.

(5) Internal regulations. The limitation of paragraph (1) shall not apply to any regulation relating to internal Treasury Department policies, practices, or procedures.

(6) Congressional authorization. The limitation of paragraph (1) may be superseded by a legislative grant from Congress authorizing the Secretary to prescribe the effective date with respect to any regulation.

(7) Election to apply retroactively. The Secretary may provide for any taxpayer to elect to apply any regulation before the dates specified in paragraph (1).

(8) Application to rulings. The Secretary may prescribe the extent, if any, to which any ruling (including any judicial decision or any administrative determination other than by regulation) relating to the internal revenue laws shall be applied without retroactive effect.

(c) Preparation and distribution of regulations, forms, stamps, and other matters. The Secretary shall prepare and distribute all the instructions, regulations, directions, forms, blanks, stamps, and other matters pertaining to the assessment and collection of internal revenue.

(d) Manner of making elections prescribed by Secretary. Except to the extent otherwise provided by this title, any election under this title shall be made at such time and in such manner as the Secretary shall prescribe.

(e) Temporary regulations.

(1) Issuance. Any temporary regulation issued by the Secretary shall also be issued as a proposed regulation.

(2) 3-year duration. Any temporary regulation shall expire within 3 years after the date of issuance of such regulation.

* * *

Subchapter C. Provisions Affecting More than One Subtitle

§ 7872. Treatment of Loans with Below-Market Interest Rates

(a) Treatment of gift loans and demand loans.

(1) In general. For purposes of this title, in the case of any below-market loan to which this section applies and which is a gift loan or a demand loan, the forgone interest shall be treated as—

(A) transferred from the lender to the borrower, and

(B) retransferred by the borrower to the lender as interest.

(2) Time when transfers made. Except as otherwise provided in regulations prescribed by the Secretary, any forgone interest attributable to periods during any calendar year shall be treated as transferred (and retransferred) under paragraph (1) on the last day of such calendar year.

(b) Treatment of other below-market loans.

(1) In general. For purposes of this title, in the case of any below-market loan to which this section applies and to which subsection (a)(1) does not apply, the lender shall be treated as having transferred on the date the loan was made (or, if later, on the first day on which this section applies to such loan), and the borrower shall be treated as having received on such date, cash in an amount equal to the excess of—

(A) the amount loaned, over

(B) the present value of all payments which are required to be made under the terms of the loan.

(2) Obligation treated as having original issue discount. For purposes of this title—

(A) In general. Any below-market loan to which paragraph (1) applies shall be treated as having original issue discount in an amount equal to the excess described in paragraph (1).

(B) Amount in addition to other original issue discount. Any original issue discount which a loan is treated as having by reason of subparagraph (A) shall be in addition to any other original issue discount on such loan (determined without regard to subparagraph (A)).

(c) Below-market loans to which section applies.

(1) In general. Except as otherwise provided in this subsection and subsection (g), this section shall apply to—

(A) Gifts. Any below-market loan which is a gift loan.

(B) Compensation-related loans. Any below-market loan directly or indirectly between—

(i) an employer and an employee, or

(ii) an independent contractor and a person for whom such independent contractor provides services.

(C) Corporation-shareholder loans. Any below-market loan directly or indirectly between a corporation and any shareholder of such corporation.

(D) Tax avoidance loans. Any below-market loan 1 of the principal purposes of the interest arrangements of which is the avoidance of any Federal tax.

(E) Other below-market loans. To the extent provided in regulations, any below-market loan which is not described in subparagraph (A), (B), (C), or (F) if the interest arrangements of such loan have a significant effect on any Federal tax liability of the lender or the borrower.

(F) Loans to qualified continuing care facilities. Any loan to any qualified continuing care facility pursuant to a continuing care contract.

(2) $10,000 de minimis exception for gift loans between individuals.

(A) In general. In the case of any gift loan directly between individuals, this section shall not apply to any day on which the aggregate outstanding amount of loans between such individuals does not exceed $10,000.

(B) De minimis exception not to apply to loans attributable to acquisition of income-producing assets. Subparagraph (A) shall not apply to any gift loan directly attributable to the purchase or carrying of income-producing assets.

(C) Cross reference. For limitation on amount treated as interest where loans do not exceed $100,000, see subsection (d)(1).

(3) $10,000 de minimis exception for compensation-related and corporate-shareholder loans.

(A) In general. In the case of any loan described in subparagraph (B) or (C) of paragraph (1), this section shall not apply to any day on which the aggregate outstanding amount of loans between the borrower and lender does not exceed $10,000.

(B) Exception not to apply where 1 of principal purposes is tax avoidance. Subparagraph (A) shall not apply to any loan the interest arrangements of which have as 1 of their principal purposes the avoidance of any Federal tax.

(d) Special rules for gift loans.

(1) Limitation on interest accrual for purposes of income taxes where loans do not exceed $100,000.

(A) In general. For purposes of subtitle A, in the case of a gift loan directly between individuals, the amount treated as retransferred by the borrower to the lender as of the close of any year shall not exceed the borrower's net investment income for such year.

(B) Limitation not to apply where 1 of principal purposes is tax avoidance. Subparagraph (A) shall not apply to any loan the interest arrangements of which have as 1 of their principal purposes the avoidance of any Federal tax.

(C) Special rule where more than 1 gift loan outstanding. For purposes of subparagraph (A), in any case in which a borrower has outstanding more than 1 gift loan, the net investment income of such borrower shall be allocated among such loans in proportion to the respective amounts which would be treated as retransferred by the borrower without regard to this paragraph.

(D) Limitation not to apply where aggregate amount of loans exceed $100,000. This paragraph shall not apply to any loan made by a lender to a borrower for any day on which the aggregate outstanding amount of loans between the borrower and lender exceeds $100,000.

(E) Net investment income. For purposes of this paragraph—

(i) In general. The term "net investment income" has the meaning given such term by section 163(d)(4).

(ii) De minimis rule. If the net investment income of any borrower for any year does not exceed $1,000, the net investment income of such borrower for such year shall be treated as zero.

(iii) Additional amounts treated as interest. In determining the net investment income of a person for any year, any amount which would be included in the gross income of such person for such year by reason of section 1272 if such section applied to all deferred payment obligations shall be treated as interest received by such person for such year.

(iv) Deferred payment obligations. The term "deferred payment obligation" includes any market discount bond, short-term obligation, United States savings bond, annuity, or similar obligation.

(2) Special rule for gift tax. In the case of any gift loan which is a term loan, subsection (b)(1) (and not subsection (a)) shall apply for purposes of chapter 12.

(e) Definitions of below-market loan and forgone interest. For purposes of this section—

(1) Below-market loan. The term "below-market loan" means any loan if—

(A) in the case of a demand loan, interest is payable on the loan at a rate less than the applicable Federal rate, or

(B) in the case of a term loan, the amount loaned exceeds the present value of all payments due under the loan.

(2) Forgone interest. The term "forgone interest" means, with respect to any period during which the loan is outstanding, the excess of—

(A) the amount of interest which would have been payable on the loan for the period if interest accrued on the loan at the applicable Federal rate and were payable annually on the day referred to in subsection (a)(2), over

(B) any interest payable on the loan properly allocable to such period.

(f) Other definitions and special rules. For purposes of this section—

(1) Present value. The present value of any payment shall be determined in the manner provided by regulations prescribed by the Secretary—

(A) as of the date of the loan, and

(B) by using a discount rate equal to the applicable Federal rate.

(2) Applicable Federal rate.

(A) Term loans. In the case of any term loan, the applicable Federal rate shall be the applicable Federal rate in effect under section 1274(d) (as of the day on which the loan was made), compounded semiannually.

(B) Demand loans. In the case of a demand loan, the applicable Federal rate shall be the Federal short-term rate in effect under section 1274(d) for the period for which the amount of forgone interest is being determined, compounded semiannually.

(3) Gift loan. The term "gift loan" means any below-market loan where the forgoing of interest is in the nature of a gift.

(4) Amount loaned. The term "amount loaned" means the amount received by the borrower.

(5) Demand loan. The term "demand loan" means any loan which is payable in full at any time on the demand of the lender. Such term also includes (for purposes other than determining the applicable Federal rate under paragraph (2)) any loan if the benefits of the interest arrangements of such loan are not transferable and are conditioned on the future performance of substantial services by an individual. To the extent provided in regulations, such term also includes any loan with an indefinite maturity.

(6) Term loan. The term "term loan" means any loan which is not a demand loan.

(7) Husband and wife treated as 1 person. A husband and wife shall be treated as 1 person.

(8) Loans to which section 483, 643(i), or 1274 applies. This section shall not apply to any loan to which section 483, 643(i), or 1274 applies.

(9) No withholding. No amount shall be withheld under chapter 24 with respect to—

(A) any amount treated as transferred or retransferred under subsection (a), and

(B) any amount treated as received under subsection (b).

(10) Special rule for term loans. If this section applies to any term loan on any day, this section shall continue to apply to such loan notwithstanding paragraphs (2) and (3) of subsection (c). In the case of a gift loan, the preceding sentence shall only apply for purposes of chapter 12.

(11) Time for determining rate applicable to employee relocation loans.

(A) In general. In the case of any term loan made by an employer to an employee the proceeds of which are used by the employee to purchase a principal residence (within the meaning of section 121), the determination of the applicable Federal rate shall be made as of the date the written contract to purchase such residence was entered into.

(B) Paragraph only to apply to cases to which section 217 applies. Subparagraph (A) shall only apply to the purchase of a principal residence in connection with the commencement of work by an employee or a change in the principal place of work of an employee to which section 217 applies.

* * *

(i) Regulations.

(1) In general. The Secretary shall prescribe such regulations as may be necessary or appropriate to carry out the purposes of this section, including—

(A) regulations providing that where, by reason of varying rates of interest, conditional interest payments, waivers of interest, disposition of the lender's or borrower's interest in the loan, or other circumstances, the provisions of this section do not carry out the purposes of this section, adjustments to the provisions of this section will be made to the extent necessary to carry out the purposes of this section,

(B) regulations for the purpose of assuring that the positions of the borrower and lender are consistent as to the application (or nonapplication) of this section, and

(C) regulations exempting from the application of this section any class of transactions the interest arrangements of which have no significant effect on any Federal tax liability of the lender or the borrower.

(2) Estate tax coordination. Under regulations prescribed by the Secretary, any loan which is made with donative intent and which is a term loan shall be taken into account for purposes of chapter 11 in a manner consistent with the provisions of subsection (b).

Regulations

Proposed § 1.7872–1 (LR–165–84, Aug. 20, 1985) Introduction.

(a) Statement of purpose. Section 7872 generally treats certain loans in which the interest rate charged is less than the applicable Federal rate as economically equivalent to loans bearing interest at the applicable Federal rate, coupled with a payment by the lender to the borrower sufficient to fund all or part of the payment of interest by the borrower. Such loans are referred to as "below-market loans." See § 1.7872–3 for detailed definitions of below-market loans and the determination of the applicable Federal rate. Accordingly, section 7872 recharacterizes a below-market loan as two transactions:

(1) An arm's-length transaction in which the lender makes a loan to the borrower in exchange for a note requiring the payment of interest at the applicable Federal rate; and

(2) A transfer of funds by the lender to the borrower ("imputed transfer"). The timing and the characterization of the amount of the imputed transfer by the lender to the borrower are determined in accordance with the substance of the transaction. The timing and the amount of the imputed interest payment (the excess of the amount of interest required to be paid using the applicable Federal rate, over the amount of interest required to be paid according to the loan agreement) by the borrower to the lender depend on the character of the imputed transfer by the lender to the borrower and whether the loan is a term loan or a demand loan. If the imputed transfer by the lender is characterized as a gift, the provisions of chapter 12 of the Internal Revenue Code, relating to gift tax, also apply. All imputed transfers under section 7872 (e.g., interest, compensation, gift) are characterized in accordance with the substance of the transaction, and, except as otherwise provided in the regulations under section 7872, are treated as so characterized for all purposes of the Code. For example, for purposes of section 170, an interest-free loan to a charity referred to in section 170 for which interest is imputed under section 7872, is treated as an interest bearing loan coupled with periodic gifts to the charity in the amount of the imputed transfer, for purposes of section 170. In addition, all applicable information and reporting requirements (e.g., reporting on Form W-2 and Form 1099) must be satisfied.

Proposed § 20.7872–1 (LR–165–84, Aug. 20, 1985) Certain below-market loans.

For purposes of chapter 11 of the Internal Revenue Code, relating to estate tax, a gift term loan (within the meaning of § 1.7872–4(B)) that is made after June 6, 1984, shall be valued at the lesser of:

(a) The unpaid stated principal, plus accrued interest; or

(b) The sum of the present value of all payments due under the note (including accrual interest), using the applicable Federal rate for loans of a term equal to the remaining term of the loan in effect at the date of death.

No discount is allowed based on evidence that the loan is uncollectible unless the facts concerning collectibility of the loan have changed significantly since the time the loan was made. This section applies with respect to any term loan made with donative intent after June 6, 1984, regardless of the interest rate under the loan agreement, and regardless of whether that interest rate exceeds the applicable Federal rate in effect on the day on which the loan was made.

Proposed § 25.7872–1 (LR–165–84, Aug. 20, 1985) Certain below-market loans.

For purposes of chapter 12 of the Internal Revenue Code, relating to gift tax, if a taxpayer makes a gift loan (within the meaning of § 1.7872–4(B)) that is a term loan (within the meaning of § 1.7872–10(A)(2)) and that is made after June 6, 1984, the excess of the amount loaned over the present value of all payments which are required to be made under the terms of the loan agreement shall be treated as a gift from the lender to the borrower on the date the loan is made. If a taxpayer makes a gift loan that is a demand loan (within the meaning of § 1.7872–10(A)(1)) and that is outstanding during any calendar period after June 6, 1984, and not repaid before September 17, 1984, the amount of foregone interest (within the meaning of section 7872(e)(2)) attributable to that calendar period shall be treated as a gift from the lender to the borrower. The de minimis exception described in section 7872(c)(2) applies to the gift tax treatment of a gift loan. In the case of a term gift loan, however, once section 7872 applies to the loan, the de minimis exception will not apply to the loan at some later date regardless of whether the aggregate outstanding amount of loans does not continue to exceed the limitation amount. For a detailed analysis of section 7872, see the income tax regulations under section 7872, § 1.7872–1 through § 1.7872–14.

Proposed § 1.7872–2 (LR–165–84, Aug. 20, 1985) Definition of loan.

(a) In general.

(1) *"Loan" interpreted broadly*. For purposes of section 7872, the term "loan" includes generally any extension of credit (including, for example, a purchase money mortgage) and any transaction under which the owner of money permits another person to use the money for a period of time after which the money is to be transferred to the owner or applied according to an express or implied agreement with the owner. The term "loan" is interpreted broadly to implement the anti-abuse intent of the statute. An integrated series of transactions which is the equivalent of a loan is treated as a loan. A payment for property, goods, or services under a contract, however, is not a loan merely because one of the payor's remedies for breach of the contract is recovery of the payment. Similarly, a bona fide prepayment made in a manner consistent with normal commercial practices for services, property, or the use of property, generally, is not a loan; see section 461 and the regulations thereunder for the treatment of certain prepaid expenses and for the special rules of sections 461(h) and (i). However, a taxpayer's characterization of a transaction as a prepayment or as a loan is not conclusive. Transactions will be characterized for tax purposes according to their economic substance, rather than the terms used to describe them. Thus, for example, receipt by a partner from a partnership of money is treated as a loan if it is so characterized under § 1.731–1(c)(2).

(2) *Limitations on applicability of section 7872.*

(i) *In general*. Section 7872 applies only to certain below-market loans (as defined in section 7872(e)(1)). Section 1.7872–4 lists the categories of below-market loans to which section 7872 generally applies. Certain below market loans within these categories, however, are exempt from the provisions of section 7872. See § 1.7872–5 for specific exemptions from the rules.

(ii) *Loans to which section 483 or 1274 applies*. Generally, section 7872 does not apply to any loan which is given in consideration for the sale or exchange of property (within the meaning of section 1274(c)(1)) or paid on account of the sale or exchange of property (within the meaning of section 483(c)(1)), even if the rules of those sections do not apply by reason of exceptions or safe harbor provisions. Any transaction, however, which otherwise is described in section 7872(c)(1)(A), (B), or (C), and is—

(A) A debt instrument that is issued in exchange for property and that is payable on demand.

(B) A debt instrument described in section 1273(b)(3), or

(C) A debt instrument described in section 1275(b), unless the transaction is described in § 1.7872–5(b)(1). is not subject to sections 483 and 1274 and is subject to section 7872.

(iii) *Relation to section 482*. If a below-market loan subject to section 7872 would also be subject to section 482 if the Commissioner chose to apply section 482 to the loan transaction, then section 7872 will be applied first. If the Commissioner chooses to apply section 482, then the loan transaction is subject to section 482 in addition to section 7872.

(3) *Loan proceeds transferred over time.* In general, each extension or credit or transfer of money by a lender to a borrower is treated as a separate loan. Accordingly, if the loan agreement provides that the lender will transfer the loan proceeds to the borrower in installments, each installment payment is treated as a separate loan. Similarly, in the case of a loan in which the transfer of the loan proceeds to the borrower is subject to a draw-down restriction, each draw-down of loan proceeds is treated as a separate loan.

(b) Examples of transactions treated as loans.

(1) *Refundable deposits.*

(i) *In general.* If an amount is treated for Federal tax purposes as a deposit rather than as a prepayment or an advance payment, the amount is treated as a loan for purposes of section 7872.

(ii) *Partially refundable deposits.* If an amount is treated for Federal tax purposes as a deposit rather than as a prepayment or an advance payment and the amount is refundable only for a certain period of time or is only partially refundable, then the deposit is treated as a loan only to the extent that it is refundable and only for the period of time that it is refundable.

(iii) *Exception.* Paragraph (b)(1)(i) of this section does not apply if the deposit is custodial in nature or is held in trust for the benefit of the transferor. The deposit is treated as custodial in nature if the transferee is not entitled to the beneficial enjoyment of the amount deposited including interest thereon (except as security for an obligation of the transferor). Thus, if an amount is placed in escrow to secure a contractual obligation of the transferor, and the escrow agreement provides that all interest earned is paid to the transferor and that the transferee has no rights to or interest in the escrowed amount unless and until the transferor defaults on the obligation, then, in the absence of any facts which indicate that the transaction was entered into for tax avoidance purposes, the deposit is not a loan.

(2) *Permitting agent or intermediary to retain funds.* An agreement under which an agent or intermediary is permitted to retain possession of money for a period of time before transferring the money to his or her principal is treated as a loan for purposes of section 7872. For example, a taxpayer who enters into an agreement with a broker under which the broker may retain possession of the proceeds from the sale of the taxpayer's property (e.g., securities issued by the taxpayer) for a period of time and uses or invests those funds (other than for the taxpayer's account) is treated as making a loan to the broker for the period of time that the broker retains possession of the proceeds.

(3) *Advances.* An advance of money to an employee, salesman, or other similar person to defray anticipated expenditures is not treated as a loan for purposes of section 7872 if the amount of money advanced is reasonably calculated not to exceed the anticipated expenditures and if the advance of money is made on a day within a reasonable period of time of the day that the anticipated expenditure will be incurred. An advance or draw of money against a partner's distributive share of income which is treated in the manner described in § 1.731–1(a)(1)(ii) is not a loan for purposes of section 7872.

Proposed § 1.7872–3 (LR–165–84, Aug. 20, 1985) Definition of below-market loans.

(a) In general. Section 7872 does not impute interest on loans which require the payment of interest at the applicable Federal rate. This section defines the applicable Federal rate and provides rules for determining whether an interest-bearing loan provides sufficient stated interest to avoid classification as a below-market loan. The term "below-market loan" means any loan if—

(1) In the case of a demand loan, interest is payable at a rate less than the applicable Federal rate; or

(2) In the case of a term loan, the amount loaned exceeds the present value of all payments due under the loan, determined as of the day the loan is made, using a discount rate equal to the applicable Federal rate in effect on the day the loan is made. Sections 1.7872–13 and 1.7872–14 contain the computations necessary for determining the amount of imputed interest on a below-market loan which is subject to section 7872.

Proposed § 1.7872–4 (LR–165–84, Aug. 20, 1985) Types of below-market loans.

(a) In general. Section 7872 applies only to certain categories of below-market loans. These categories are gift loans, compensation-related loans, corporation-shareholder loans, tax avoidance loans, and certain other loans classified in the regulations under section 7872 as significant tax effect loans (i.e., loans whose interest arrangements have a significant effect on any Federal tax liability of the lender or the borrower.)

(b) Gift loans. (1) *In general.* The term "gift loan" means any below-market loan in which the foregoing of interest is in the nature of a gift within the meaning of Chapter 12 of the Internal Revenue Code (whether or not the lender is a natural person).

(2) *Cross reference.* See § 1.7872–8 for special rules limiting the application of section 7872 to gift loans. See paragraph (g) of this section for rules with respect to below-market loans which are indirectly gift loans.

§ 1.7872–5 Exempted loans.

(a) In general. (1) *General rule.* Except as provided in paragraph (a)(2) of this section, notwithstanding any other provision of section 7872 and the regulations under that section, section 7872 does not apply to the loans listed in paragraph (b) of this section because the interest arrangements do not have a significant effect on the Federal tax liability of the borrower or the lender.

(2) *No exemption for tax avoidance loans.* If a taxpayer structures a transaction to be a loan described in paragraph (b) of this section and one of the principal purposes of so structuring the transaction is the avoidance of Federal tax, then the transaction will be recharacterized as a tax avoidance loan as defined in section 7872(c)(1)(D).

(b) List of exemptions. Except as provided in paragraph (a) of this section, the following transactions are exempt from section 7872:

(1) to (15) [*Reserved*]. For further guidance, see § 1.7872–5T(b)(1) through (15).

(16) An exchange facilitator loan (within the meaning of § 1.468B–6(c)(1)) if the amount of the exchange funds (as defined in § 1.468B–6(b)(2)) treated as loaned does not exceed $2,000,000 and the duration of the loan is 6 months or less. The Commissioner may increase this $2,000,000 loan exemption amount in published guidance of general applicability, see § 601.601(d)(2) of this chapter.

(c) [Reserved]. For further guidance, see § 1.7872–5T(c).

(d) Effective/applicability date. This section applies to exchange facilitator loans issued on or after October 8, 2008.

[T.D. 9413, 73 FR 39622, July 10, 2008]

§ 1.7872–5T Exempted loans (temporary). [*Omitted. Ed.*]

[T.D. 8045, 50 FR 33520, Aug. 20, 1985; T.D. 8093, 51 FR 25033, July 10, 1986; 51 FR 28553, Aug. 8, 1986; T.D. 8204, 53 FR 18282, May 23, 1988]

Proposed § 1.7872–6 (LR–165–84, Aug. 20, 1985) Timing and amount of transfers in connection with gift loans and demand loans. [*Omitted. Ed.*]

Proposed § 1.7872–7 (LR–165–84, Aug. 20, 1985) Timing and amount of transfers in connection with below-market term loans. [*Omitted. Ed.*]

Proposed § 1.7872–8 (LR–165–84, Aug. 20, 1985) Special rules for gift loans directly between natural persons.

(a) Special rules for gift loans directly between natural persons. (1) *In general.* Section 7872 (c)(2) and (d) apply special rules to gift loans directly between natural persons if the aggregate outstanding amount of loans (as determined in paragraph (b)(2) of this section) between those natural persons does not exceed specified limitations.

(2) *Loans directly between natural persons.* (i) For purposes of this section, a loan is made directly between natural persons only if both the lender and borrower are natural persons. For this purpose, a loan by a natural person lender to the guardian (or custodian, in the case of a gift made pursuant to the Uniform Gift to Minors Act) of a natural person is treated as a loan directly between natural persons. If, however, a parent lends money to a trust of which the child is the sole beneficiary, the loan is not treated as directly between natural persons for purposes of this section.

(ii) A gift loan which results from restructuring an indirect loan as two or more loans (as described in § 1.7872–4(G)) and in which natural persons are deemed to be the lender and the borrower is treated as a loan directly between natural persons. Thus, for example, if an employer makes a below-market loan to an employee's child, the loan is restructured as one loan from the employer to the employee, and a second loan from the employee to his child. The deemed gift loan between the employee and the employee's child is treated as directly between natural persons.

(b) De minimis exception. (1) *In general.* Except as otherwise provided in paragraph (b)(3) of this section or in § 1.7872–7(A) (with respect to the gift tax consequences of a gift term loan to which the provisions of section 7872 have already been applied), in the case of any gift loan directly between natural persons, the provisions of section 7872 do not apply to any loan outstanding on any day on which the aggregate outstanding amount of loans between the lender and borrower does not exceed $10,000. The de minimis rule of this paragraph (b)(1) applies with respect to a gift loan even though that loan could also be characterized as a tax avoidance loan within the meaning of section 7872(c)(1)(D) and § 1.7872–4(E).

(2) *Aggregate outstanding amount of loans.* The aggregate outstanding amount of loans between natural persons is the sum of the principal amounts of outstanding loans directly between the individuals, regardless of the character of the loans, regardless of the interest rate charged on the loans, and regardless of the date on which the loans were made. For this purpose, the principal amount of a loan which is also subject to section 1272 (without applying the limitation of section 1273(a)(3)) is the "adjusted issue price" as that term is defined in section 1272(a)(4). See § 1.7872–7(A)(3)(I) for the determination of the issue price of a loan which is also subject to section 1272.

(3) *Loans attributable to acquisition or carrying of income-producing assets.* The de minimis exception described in paragraph (b)(1) of this section does not apply to any gift loan directly attributable to the purchase or carrying of income-producing assets. A gift loan is directly attributable to the purchase or carrying of income-producing assets, for example, if the loan proceeds are directly traceable to the purchase of the income-producing assets, the assets are used as collateral for the loan, or there is direct evidence that the loan was made to avoid disposition of the assets.

(4) *Income-producing assets.* For purposes of this paragraph (b), the term "income-producing asset" means (i) an asset of a type that generates ordinary income, or, (ii) a market discount bond issued before July 19, 1984. Accordingly, an income producing asset includes, but is not limited to, a business, a certificate of deposit, a savings account, stock (whether or not dividends are paid), bonds and rental property.

* * *

Proposed § 1.7872–9 (LR–165–84, Aug. 20, 1985) De minimis exception for compensation related or corporation-shareholder loans. [*Omitted. Ed.*]

Proposed § 1.7872–10 (LR–165–84, Aug. 20, 1985) Other definitions. [*Omitted. Ed.*]

Proposed § 1.7872–11 (LR–165–84, Aug. 20, 1985) Special Rules. [*Omitted. Ed.*]

Proposed § 1.7872–12 (LR–165–84, Aug. 20, 1985) Computational rules to determine sufficient stated interest for short periods. [*Omitted. Ed.*]

Proposed § 1.7872–13 (LR–165–84, Aug. 20, 1985) Computation of foregone interest. [*Omitted. Ed.*]

Proposed § 1.7872–14 (LR–165–84, Aug. 20, 1985) Determination of present value. [*Omitted. Ed.*]

§ 1.7872–15 Split-dollar loans. [*Omitted. Ed.*]

[T.D. 9092, 68 FR 54352, Sept. 17, 2003]

§ 1.7872–16 Loans to an exchange facilitator under § 1.468B–6. [*Omitted. Ed.*]

[T.D. 9092, 68 FR 54352, Sept. 17, 2003.]

APPENDIX. PRIORITY OF CLAIMS; PERSONAL LIABILITY OF EXECUTOR

31 U.S.C. § 3713 Priority of Government Claims*

(a)(1) A claim of the United States Government shall be paid first when—

* * *

(B) the estate of a deceased debtor, in the custody of the executor or administrator, is not enough to pay all debts of the debtor.

* * *

(b) A representative of a person or an estate (except a trustee acting under title 11) paying any part of a debt of the person or estate before paying a claim of the Government is liable to the extent of the payment for unpaid claims of the Government.

* Although not part of the Internal Revenue Code (IRC), this section, formerly 31 U.S.C. §§ 191, 192, is examined in Treas. Regs. §§ 20.2002–1 and 25.2502–2. The IRC sections dealing with the personal liability of fiduciaries for estate or gift taxes are §§ 2204, 6324, 6901 and 6905. See also § 6501. *Ed.*